musicHound

Lounge

musicHound Lounge

The Essential Album Guide to

MARTINI Music and Easy LISTENING

edited by Steve Knopper
foreword by Martin Denny

VISIBLE INK PRESS

DETROIT • NEW YORK • LONDON

musicHound™ *Lounge*
The
Essential
Album
Guide to
Martini Music and
Easy Listening

Copyright © 1998 Visible Ink Press®

A Cunning Canine Production®

Published by Visible Ink Press
a division of Gale Research
835 Penobscot Building
Detroit, MI 48226-4094

Visible Ink Press, MusicHound, the MusicHound logo, and A Cunning Canine Production are trademarks of Gale Research.

Most Visible Ink Press books are available at special quantity discounts when purchased in bulk by corporations, organizations, or groups. Customized printings, special imprints, messages, and excerpts can be produced to meet your needs. For more information, contact Special Markets Manager, Gale Research, 835 Penobscot Bldg., Detroit, MI 48226. Or call 1-800-776-6265.

Cover photo of Frank Sinatra © UPI/Corbis-Bettmann

Library of Congress Cataloging-in-Publication Data

MusicHound Lounge : the essential album guide to martini music and
    easy listening / edited by Steve Knopper.
        p.   cm.
    Limited to currently available compact discs available in the
U.S.; each entry includes biographical information.
    Includes bibliographical references and indexes.
    ISBN 1-57859-048-5 (alk. paper)
    1. Popular music—Discography. I. Knopper, Steve, 1969– .
ML156.4.P6M894 1998
016.78164'0266—dc21   98-19584
                                 CIP
                                 MN

ISBN 1-57859-048-5
Printed in the United States of America
All rights reserved

10 9 8 7 6 5 4 3 2 1

musicHound *Contents*

musicHound *Cocktail Classics*

Across the map of America, from Honolulu to New York City, from Chicago to New Orleans, countless cocktail lounges, like oases in the desert, cater to the thirst and amusement of millions. The martini crowd flocks to its favorite watering hole to be entertained. Lounges have become an indispensable part of our culture.

In such places, Bobby Troup, composer of "Route 66," could hold an audience and keep the bartenders busy concocting drinks all night for the hep crowds. Nat "King" Cole and his Trio, consisting of piano, bass, and guitar, could pack the clubs with his great jazz stylings and "unforgettable" voice.

Just what is lounge music? It may be a piano player who vocalizes, a trio, or a female singer. But it has to be distinctive.

In the '50s, you could recognize pianist George Shearing's chord clusters no matter how packed the lounge he was playing. Or Erroll Garner, or Art Tatum. Or the voice of Ella Fitzgerald. You couldn't miss. I started out playing piano in the same kinds of places.

Cocktail lounges were called saloons long before Prohibition was repealed in 1932, and they featured legendary performers: Eddie Cantor, Jimmy Durante, Al Jolson, Georgie Jessel, Ruth Etting. At that time, I was touring with a band in South America and recorded my first Victor record in Buenos Aires. When I returned again to the States in 1935, "saloons" and "speakeasies" were out and "cocktail lounges" were in. It sounded more respectable to order martinis.

Las Vegas has always abounded with lounges, each competing with one another, showcasing entertainers that appealed to different tastes. You could hear country-western, jazz, Dixieland, and the big bands. The array of entertainers to suit every palate was fabulous.

In the early '50s, I recall hearing Shearing alternating with the Mary Kaye Trio at the Thunderbird in Las Vegas. If you made the rounds, you could tour the Strip and hear the big bands of Woody Herman, Count Basie, Stan Kenton, Artie Shaw, Xavier Cugat, Del Courtney, and other greats.

Every entertainer worth his calling has played the lounges. That includes Shearing, Peter Nero, Andre Previn, Bobby Darin, and Dave Brubeck. I still feel honored to have been included among such big names. I never dreamed it could happen to me.

I started out playing piano in bars, ranging from a lounge in Eureka, California, to the Surf Room of the Royal Hawaiian Hotel in Honolulu. In 1957, I performed with my group at Las Vegas' Flamingo Hotel, on an elevated circular stage that revolved like a merry-go-round. On a lower level, surrounding the stage, was a bar. Any time was martini time. In the background, you could hear the clinking of glasses and the noise of bartenders blending drinks.

The bartenders would pass notes to me from the pit bosses in the casino to "knock off the bird calls"—they distracted the attention of the gamblers, who were curious to know where the sounds were coming from.

I didn't invent lounge music; it had long existed in hotel bars and smoky dives. I was the anti-rocker. My contemporaries were Jackie Gleason, Les Baxter, Dean Martin, and Esquivel.

I introduced my exotic arrangements with my first Liberty Records LP, *Exotica*, which was #1 on the national *Billboard* charts. Les Baxter, composer of the song "Quiet Village," had recorded it with a large orchestra. I recorded it with a five-piece group, adding bird calls and jungle effects. It followed *Exotica* as a single, and Liberty presented me with a gold record. The album became a tonic to an older generation turned off by rock 'n' roll.

Today, artists such as Tony Bennett, Esquivel, and myself are enjoying a renewed popularity, now that they have been discovered by the children of the baby-boom generation and younger bands such as Love Jones and Combustible Edison. A few years ago, V. Vale, writer and publisher of the books *Incredibly Strange Music, Vol. 1* and *Vol. 2,* wrote about me in a 10-page profile replete with photos and biography. Subsequently, many other publications, including *Seconds* and *Cool and Strange Music,* have interviewed me. The Internet, too, gives me extensive coverage.

It has been exciting to be part of this resurgence.

MusicHound Lounge: The Essential Album Guide to Martini Music and Easy Listening contains bios and rates albums of artists who have survived their lounge beginnings and are superstars today. *MusicHound Lounge* identifies lounge music as easy listening, ultra-lounge, or space-age bachelor pad, and uses more general terms like "wild" and "swinging." This guide is the most comprehensive I've seen, a must for music buffs and collectors as an authentic source of reference.

I'm pleased to know that after four decades of performing, I shared a part in the revival of lounge music. If you stick around long enough, "what goes around comes around."

Martin Denny's 1959 album, Exotica, *hit #1 on the charts and remains one of the landmark recordings in easy-listening music. His groups produced several hit singles, including a classic version of Les Baxter's composition "Quiet Village," and he hit on his trademark bird and frog noises by accident. A one-time child prodigy who studied piano at the Los Angeles Conservatory of Music, Denny has recorded 37 albums, which have sold more than four million copies around the world, featuring instruments as diverse as the 200-pound New Guinea talking drum and the Moog synthesizer. Denny, who lives in Honolulu, Hawaii, has in recent years led the "space-age bachelor pad music" revival, along with Esquivel, Les Baxter, and his old sideman Arthur Lyman. Dubbed the "King of Exotica" by* Rolling Stone *magazine, he's retired, but occasionally performs concerts in Japan and Los Angeles.*

George Clooney, the heartthrob of *ER* and *Batman and Robin*, recently summed up the music-industry tragedy at the heart of *MusicHound Lounge*. Of his aunt, the great Rosemary Clooney, he said: "Rosemary was a very successful singer, but by 1955, when rock 'n' roll came in, she was suddenly not successful. And she didn't become less of a singer. In fact, she got to be a better singer."

He's right. Nothing against Elvis Presley, who appears in this book, but his success, and the enduring popularity of rock 'n' roll, transformed many of the 20th century's greatest performers into instant has-beens. That's an extraordinary shift; in the mid-'50s, once-sure-thing million-sellers like Clooney, Jo Stafford, and even the great Bing Crosby suddenly became media misfits. Cole Porter standards had given way to Bob Dylan folk songs. The rock revolution had counted its first casualties of war.

For a while, antidote-to-rock performers—such as the Hollyridge Strings, who reproduced the Beatles' melodies but undermined their rebellious attitude and youthful enthusiasm, and Ray Conniff, whose light orchestras were in every pre–baby boomer's LP collection—kept the pop charts safe for non-rockers. But in the early '80s, as rock fans began to get a little older, radio programmers replaced even these easy-listening juggernauts with lite-contemporary stars such as Joe Cocker, Rod Stewart, Billy Joel, and, later, Mariah Carey and Celine Dion.

Many of the artists in this book have sold millions and millions of records but, with notable exceptions like Frank Sinatra and Tony Bennett, have not (at least until lately) enjoyed the benefits of the CD revolution. Many of their albums are out of print

and, save for a network of U.S. radio stations catering to a cadre of swinging senior citizens, receive little airplay. We've almost completely forgotten that Guy Lombardo's version of "Auld Lang Syne" was as much a New Year's Eve tradition as the dropping of the ball in Times Square.

Fortunately, the revivalists recognized why these people were so popular in the first place. After years of non-exposure, old-fashioned easy listening and lounge music climbed out of history's dustbins.

Lounge music, with its accompanying swizzle sticks, martinis, and buxom young album-cover women, returned in the early '90s. Tony Bennett, without changing his good old crooning style a bit, charmed the hearts of alternative-rock fans much younger than his usual audience. Tom Jones, using collaborations with hip rock bands and a cameo on *The Simpsons*, seduced even the children of his longtime fans. The great instrumentalists Juan Garcia Esquivel and Martin Denny started to receive phone calls from record companies, collaborators (including the neo-lounge bands Love Jones and Combustible Edison), and writers (like the ones who put out *Incredibly Strange Music*). New swing bands, such as the Squirrel Nut Zippers and Big Bad Voodoo Daddy, hit the pop charts. The hipster film *Swingers*, with its climactic jitterbug scene, became an out-of-nowhere smash. CD compilations, from Capitol's massive *Ultra-Lounge* series to Rhino's *Cocktail Classics* set, arrived to document the trend.

And the music keeps coming. Just before press time, a techno band called the Propellerheads invited R&B singer Shirley Bassey, perhaps best known for her *Goldfinger* theme song, to sing James Bond music on its debut album. Pinup model Bettie Page's swanky albums, lovingly repackaged on CD, have shown up in record stores. Rhino Records' easy-listening CD of original music from the *Titanic* voyage has become a minor hit.

Into this surreal world, where Elvis Costello collaborates with Burt Bacharach, Stereolab plays Muzak, k.d. lang sings Andre Previn, and Tony Bennett appears on *MTV Unplugged,* steps *MusicHound Lounge.* Though historical books such as Joseph Lanza's *Elevator Music* have laid the groundwork, this guide is the first encyclopedia to document "lounge culture." It's certainly the first to recommend which albums to buy and which to avoid.

"Lounge" is a broad term. It refers to a place, where people gather to hear music and drink martinis, not a style, such as country or blues. The best answer to the question "What is lounge?," as one of our editors theorized, may be "whatever sounds good when you're drinking a martini." So we've included a smattering of surf, a little bit of soul, rockers with a twist, classic pop songwriters, music from movies, actors who have made dangerous detours into the music industry, and some surprises.

But overall, this book defines "lounge music" according to the following three categories:

- Crooners. Before rock 'n' roll, the world's most popular performers—Crosby, Dick Haymes, Sinatra, Stafford, Clooney, Bennett, Wayne Newton—sang in lounges. They all but built Las Vegas, even if the lounges there have recently become gigantic corporate showrooms. These artists' recent "comebacks," from the resurgence in Rat Pack culture to Liza Minnelli's appearance on a Pet Shop Boys rock record, have been testaments to their enduring talent.

- Space-age bachelor pad music. Were Juan Garcia Esquivel's zum-zum-zums, Martin Denny's croaking bullfrogs, and Perrey and Kingsley's strange Moog synthesizers part of easy listening? Yes, but they were weirder than that, which is why early '90s revivalists applied catch-all labels like "exotica" and "incredibly strange music." Futuristic at the time—a good Les Baxter song recalls *The Jetsons* as much as it does big-band swing—these albums sound at least as quaint and fresh as the Jefferson Airplane's *Surrealistic Pillow.*

- Elevator music. Schmaltz. Beginning with Paul Weston's 1945 album *Music for Dreaming* and continuing until radio companies finally dislodged "beautiful music" from the airwaves in the early '80s, Ray Conniff, Percy Faith, Mantovani, the 101 Strings, and the Living Strings were faceless pop superstars. Carpoolers in the '70s may never have known the French composer Francis Lai was behind the tinkly melodies of "Un Homme et une Femme," or that Antonio Carlos Jobim was responsible for "The Girl from Ipanema," but they most definitely knew the tunes.

Admittedly, in this guide, we've split a few hairs. You won't find much of today's "adult-contemporary" music, although Lite FM stations serve roughly the same purpose as beautiful-music stations did 20 years ago. That's because Celine Dion, Mariah Carey, and their peers are more popular among rocking concertgoers than among lounge-loving pipe smokers. Maybe in 30 years, when they retire to Vegas, we'll get to them. Also, there's very little New Age music here, because that's in the works for a future *MusicHound* guide.

In the end, *MusicHound Lounge* is simply a book of good stories. Crooner Russ Columbo, for example, was a handsome young ladies' man who competed with Rudy Vallee and Bing Crosby in the early '30s before he died in a bizarre pistol accident. Songwriter Eden Ahbez, a homeless Los Angeles streetwalker, was America's first hippie; Nat "King" Cole somehow discovered his song "Nature Boy," turned it into a smash in 1948, and supplied Ahbez with massive royalty payments the rest of his life. Denny McLain, once a heroic pitcher who led the Detroit Tigers to a World Series title, put out some goofily gratifying late '60s albums of Hammond organ instrumentals before landing in prison on racketeering charges.

Many of the artists herein have made serious music—we've included the 19th-century composer Erik Satie and the pioneering swing musicians Benny Goodman and Duke Ellington, whose artistic contributions can't be reduced to a martini glass and an olive. But it's impossible to read entries on Robert Mitchum (a calypso star, didn't you know?) and William Shatner without smirking. So have fun. Enjoy the entries—and the sidebars, which guide you toward timeless pop standards: an excellent version (18-Karat) and a dud (Bombsville!). And don't forget the cocktail onions.

So how do you use *MusicHound Lounge*? Here's what you'll find in the entries, and what we intend to accomplish with each point:

• An introductory paragraph, which will give you not only biographical information but also a sense of the artist's or group's sound and its stature in the lounge/easy listening—and overall music—pantheon.

• **what to buy:** The album or albums that we feel are essential purchases for consuming this act. It may be a greatest hits set, or it may be a particular album that captures the essence of the artist in question. In any event, this is where you should start—and don't think it wasn't hard to make these choices when eyeballing the catalogs of Frank Sinatra, Tony Bennett, Nat "King" Cole, Mel Tormé, and some of the other lounge titans. Note that for acts with a limited catalog, **what's available** may take the place of **what to buy** and the other sections.

• **what to buy next:** In other words, once you're hooked, these will be the most rewarding next purchases.

• **what to avoid:** Seems clear enough. This is Hound poop.

• **the rest:** Everything else that's available for this act, rated with the Hound's trusty bone scale (see below for more on this). Note that for some artists with sizeable catalogs, we've condensed this section down to **best of the rest.**

• **worth searching for:** An out-of-print gem. A bootleg. A guest appearance on another artist's album or a film soundtrack. Something that may require some looking but will reward you for the effort.

• ◀◀: The crucial influences on this act's music.

• ▶▶: The acts that have been influenced by this artist or group. Used only where applicable; it's a little early for Erykah Badu or the Friends of Dean Martinez to have influenced anybody.

We should also remind you that *MusicHound Lounge* is a *buyer's* guide. Therefore, for the most part we only discuss CDs that are currently in print and available in the United States.

Now, you ask, what's with those bones? (Down, boy! Sheesh....) It's not hard to figure out—𝄞𝄞𝄞𝄞𝄞 is nirvana (not Nirvana), a **woof!** is dog food. Keep in mind that the bone ratings don't pertain just to the act's own catalog, but to its worth in the whole music realm. Therefore a lesser act's **what to buy** choice might rate no more than 𝄞𝄞𝄞; some even rate 𝄞𝄞𝄞, a not-so-subtle sign that you might want to think twice about that act. Note that for recent releases that were not available to be reviewed before press time, N/A will appear instead of a rating.

As with any opinions, all of what you're about to read is subjective and personal. MusicHound has a bit of junkyard dog in it, too; it likes to start fights. We hope it does, too. Ultimately, we think the Hound will point you in the right direction, and if you buy the 𝄞𝄞𝄞𝄞𝄞 and 𝄞𝄞𝄞𝄞 choices, you'll have an album collection to howl about. But if you've got a bone to pick, the Hound wants to hear about it—and promises not to bite (but maybe bark a little bit). If you think we're wagging our tails in the wrong direction or lifting our leg at something that doesn't deserve it, let us know. If you think an act has been capriciously excluded—or charitably included—tell us. Your comments and suggestions will serve the greater *MusicHound* audience and future projects, so don't be shy.

Editor

Steve Knopper has spent most of his journalistic career writing about rock 'n' roll music, but the content of *MusicHound Lounge* is in his blood. His mother had always said she would immediately leave his father if the tempting *Oklahoma!* star and classic pop singer Gordon MacRae were ever to come knocking. But MacRae died and Knopper's parents are still happily listening together to Neil Diamond, Frank Sinatra, Barbra Streisand, and other easy-listening CDs they get from their son in the mail. Knopper is a Chicago-based freelance writer whose stories have run in *Rolling Stone, George, Newsday, Chicago,* the *Chicago Tribune, Request, Billboard, Yahoo! Internet Life,* and many other publications. He also writes a regular column, "Blues," for the Knight-Ridder Newspapers wire service and has contributed hundreds of entries to all of the *MusicHound* books. He owns five official Juan Garcia Esquivel swizzle sticks and drives his wife, Melissa, crazy by insisting on playing *Merry Xmas from the Space-Age Bachelor Pad* every December 25 even though he's Jewish.

Supervising Editor

Gary Graff is an award-winning music journalist and supervising editor of the *MusicHound* album guide series. A native of Pittsburgh, Pennsylvania, his work is published regularly by Reuters, *Guitar World, ICE,* the *San Francisco Chronicle,* the Cleveland *Plain Dealer,* Michigan's *Oakland Press,* SW Radio Networks, *Country Song Roundup,* and other publications. A regular contributor to the Web sites Mr. Showbiz/Wall of Sound, Jam TV, and Electric Village, his weekly "Rock 'n' Roll Insider" report airs on Detroit rock station WRIF-FM (101.1). He also appears on public TV station WTVS' *Backstage Pass* program and is a board member of the North American Music Critics Association and co-producer of the annual Detroit Music Awards. He lives in the Detroit suburbs with his wife, daughter, and two stepsons.

Managing Editor

Dean Dauphinais is a senior editor at Visible Ink Press and a contributor to *MusicHound Rock* and *MusicHound R&B.* He digs a Gershwin tune (how 'bout you?) and regrets the fact that it took him 30 years to figure out that his dad's Frank Sinatra records were indeed cool. His favorite Sinatra album is *Songs for Swingin' Lovers!* and he'll even admit to carrying a Frank Sinatra MasterCard. The co-author of two books, *Astounding Averages!* and *Car Crazy,* Dauphinais lives in suburban Detroit with his wife, Kathy, and two sons, Sam and Josh.

Associate Managing Editor

Judy Galens is a swingin' senior editor at Visible Ink Press and the managing editor of *MusicHound Jazz* and *MusicHound Folk.* She confesses to preferring a tall, cool gin & tonic to a martini, but still feels she has lounge in her soul. She resides in the Detroit suburbs with her smoking-jacket-wearing husband and some pets.

Copy Editor

Brigham Narins is a freelance copy editor and a PhD aspirant who lives near Detroit with his lovely wife, Judy, their beautiful dog, Alice, and their two cats: the fair Cookie and the big, fat, criminal-minded dimwit Ernie. Brigham is very happy that the Friends of Dean Martinez are represented in this book.

Publisher
Martin Connors

MusicHound Staff
Michelle Banks, Christa Brelin, Jim Craddock, Kathy Dauphinais, Beth Fhaner, Jeff Hermann, Brad Morgan, Jim Olenski, Carol Schwartz, Devra Sladics, Christine Tomassini

Art Direction
Tracey Rowens, Michelle DiMercurio, Cindy Baldwin

Contributing Photographers
Jack Vartoogian grew up in late 1950s Detroit and heard, but did not get to see, some of the best performers in music. To compensate, he and his wife, Linda, have devoted themselves to photographing musicians (and dancers) from across the country and around the world. While their New York City home virtually guarantees that, eventually, most acts come to them, they continue to seek opportunities to discover new talent and new venues—the farther from home the better. Their images appear regularly in *The New York Times, Time, Newsweek, Living Blues,* and *JazzTimes,* among many others, as well as in innumerable books, including their own *Afropop!* (Chartwell Books, 1995) and *The Living World of Dance* (Smithmark, 1997), and *MusicHound Blues, MusicHound R&B, MusicHound Folk,* and *MusicHound Jazz.*

Ken Settle is a Detroit-area photographer who has specialized in music photography for over 16 years. His photos have been published worldwide in magazines such as *Rolling Stone, People, Guitar Player, Playboy, Audio,* Japan's *Player,* France's *Guitarist,* and Australia's *Who Weekly.* His work also appears in *MusicHound Country, MusicHound Blues, MusicHound R&B,* and *MusicHound Folk.*

Graphic Services
Randy Bassett, Pam Reed, Barbara Yarrow

Permissions
Maria Franklin, Michele Lonoconus

Production
Mary Beth Trimper, Dorothy Maki, Evi Seoud, Shanna Heilveil, Wendy Blurton

Technology Wizard
Jeffrey Muhr

Typesetting Virtuoso
Marco Di Vita of the Graphix Group

Marketing & Promotion
Marilou Carlin, Kim Marich, Betsy Rovegno, Nancy Hammond, Susan Stefani

MusicHound Development
Julia Furtaw

Contributors
Grant Alden lives in a white-trash artist's garrett in Nashville, Tennessee. He pays for these luxurious accommodations by co-editing *No Depression* magazine and scribbling for music magazines and Web sites.

John Bitter is a retired procedures analyst whose hobby since his early teens has been jazz record collecting, sparked by working six years as a full-time jazz buyer in a Lakewood, Ohio, record shop. For the last 20 years, he has been a photojournalist on the jazz party/festival scene. He is a contributing editor for *Mississippi Rag,* a traditional jazz publication.

Steve Braun is a Chicago-based national correspondent for the *Los Angeles Times.* He only listens to lounge music in lounges, but appreciates a well-mixed martini anywhere.

G. Brown has written about popular music for *The Denver Post* for the last 21 years (even longer than he spent in high school). He is also the popular host of several specialty programs on Denver-area radio stations and has served as a kids' show host on local television (Uncle G!).

Mike Brown is a DJ, a rave organizer, and a system administrator for Hyperreal, an Internet Web site that provides a home for alternative culture and expression.

Ken Burke is a singer-songwriter whose column, "The Continuing Saga of Dr. Iguana (The Story So Far)," has been running in small press publications since 1985. He lives in Arizona with the two best people he knows: his wife, Lorraine, and daughter, Emily.

Salvatore Caputo is a freelance writer living in Phoenix with his wife and three kids. The pop music columnist for *The Arizona Republic* from 1990 to 1997, he was a finalist in the 1996 Music Journalism Awards for his retrospective column on Dean Martin. Salud!

Norene Cashen writes for *Alternative Press,* Detroit's *Metro Times,* and *Etch.*

Jay Dedrick is entertainment editor of the *Daily Camera* newspaper in Boulder, Colorado. A photo taken backstage with Tony Bennett is among his prized possessions.

Eric Deggans is the television and pop culture critic for the St. Petersburg *Times* newspaper in Florida, where he's inspired by three children, a wife, and two cats. In that order.

Jim DeRogatis is the pop music critic at the *Chicago Sun-Times* and the author of *Kaleidoscope Eyes: Psychedelic Rock from the '60s to the '90s* and a forthcoming biography of the late rock critic Lester Bangs. He prefers a unique variation on the martini: two parts vodka, one part Cointreau, shaken not stirred.

Josh Freedom du Lac hates martinis and has never been spotted in public wearing a smoking jacket. He did, however, dine once at the original Trader Vic's, where he learned just about everything he never wanted to know about lounge culture. The co-editor of *MusicHound R&B*, du Lac has been the pop music critic for *The Sacramento Bee* since 1994.

Daniel Durchholz is co-editor of the forthcoming second edition of *MusicHound Rock* and a contributor to *MusicHound Country, MusicHound R&B, MusicHound Blues, MusicHound Folk,* and *MusicHound Jazz*. He was founding editor of the now-defunct *Replay* magazine, and is a former associate editor of *Request* magazine and St. Louis, Missouri's *Riverfront Times*. He writes for various magazines, newspapers, and Web sites from his home outside St. Louis. And if you're buying, make his a Rob Roy.

Geoff Edgers is a features and arts writer for the *News & Observer* in Raleigh, North Carolina. He was formerly a staff writer at the *Boston Phoenix* and has contributed to *Nickelodeon, Request, Salon,* and *Swoon* magazines. In his children's book, *The Midnight Hour,* he quotes the first verse of the Beach Boys' "Drive-In" on page 100. He's also a commentator for National Public Radio.

Christina Fuoco is a music journalist for the Livonia, Michigan–based *Observer & Eccentric* newspapers and has contributed to *MusicHound Rock, MusicHound Folk,* and *MusicHound R&B*. She lives in Berkley, Michigan, with her portly cat.

Lawrence Gabriel is a Detroit-based writer, poet, and musician who is also editor of Detroit's *Metro Times*.

Andrew Gilbert is a Bay Area–based writer who contributes regularly to *The San Diego Union-Tribune, Contra Costa Times, East Bay Express,* and the on-line magazine *Salon*. His writing on jazz has also appeared in the *Los Angeles Reader,* the *Los Angeles View,* the *San Jose Metro,* the *Santa Cruz County Sen-*

tinel, Musician, and *Jazziz*. He is working on a documentary on the singer Weslia Whitfield.

Anna Glen is the former managing editor of *Urb* magazine in Los Angeles. She is currently freelancing and working on her first novel.

Gary Pig Gold has been publisher of *The Pig Paper* fanzine since 1975. A proud contributor to *MusicHound Rock, MusicHound Country, MusicHound R&B,* and *MusicHound Folk,* the Hoboken, New Jersey–based songwriter-musician-producer is most pleased to discover his dad's old Jackie Gleason LPs are finally worth something.

Alex Gordon is an associate editor of *Inside Sports* magazine and the co-author of the book *College: The Best Five Years of Your Life,* published by Hysteria Press and available in finer bookstores. He still considers himself a hep cat even though he wrote the Kathie Lee Gifford entry.

Gary Graff is supervising editor of Visible Ink Press' *MusicHound* series.

Ben Greenman is a journalist whose work has appeared in *Rolling Stone, Wired,* the *Village Voice, TimeOut New York,* the *Miami New Times,* the *Chicago Reader, Yahoo! Internet Life,* and other publications. He is also the author or co-author of 10 books, including *NetMusic: Your Guide to the Music Scene in Cyberspace* (Michael Wolff and Company), and a contributor to *Alt.Culture: An A-to-Z Guide to the '90s* (HarperCollins). He has recently attempted, without much success, to open his heart to Zamfir.

Teresa Gubbins is a staff writer for *The Dallas Morning News*.

Alex Henderson is a Philadelphia-based journalist, public relations writer, and technology enthusiast whose work has appeared in *Billboard, Spin, Pulse!, Jazziz,* and many other national publications. He has been writing professionally since the age of 15 and has contributed news-features to *The Los Angeles News Globe,* promotional material to Priority Records, a column to *JazzTimes,* and liner notes to Rhino, Concord Jazz, Del-Fi, and many other record labels.

Jack Jackson was never proud to say—until now—that the first album he ever bought was *Kenny Rogers' Greatest Hits*. A freelance journalist now living in Denmark, he misses the oldies programs on American AM radio. His articles have appeared in the New Orleans *Times-Picayune, Offbeat,* Denver's *Westword,* and *The Miami Herald*.

Michael Kosser is a Nashville-based freelance author and songwriter who has had 10 books published—six nonfiction books on popular music and four historical novels about Native Americans—and has heard his songs recorded by numerous pop and country artists.

George W. Krieger (a.k.a. "The Rock 'n' Roll Dentist") is a general dentist in Elizabeth, Colorado, and has written articles for *Goldmine, Colorado Heritage,* the *Pueblo Chieftain,* the *Roundup of the Denver Westerners,* and the *Journal of the Colorado Dental Association.*

Jim Lester is a retired psychologist, moonlighting musician, and author of *Too Marvelous for Words: The Life and Genius of Art Tatum* (Oxford University Press, 1994).

Robert Levine is the music editor at *Details* magazine. He has written about music and media (both multi- and the old-fashioned kind) for *Rolling Stone,* the *Village Voice,* and *Wired.*

Garaud MacTaggart is a Buffalo, New York–based freelance writer with 20 years of experience in music retailing (management/buyer). His work has appeared in newspapers such as the Buffalo *News,* Royal Oak, Michigan's *Daily Tribune,* Detroit's *Metro Times,* the *Orlando Weekly,* the *Columbus Guardian,* and Chicago's *In These Times.*

Brian Mansfield is a Nashville-based journalist and critic who has co-edited *MusicHound Country* and *MusicHound Folk.* His work appears at CountryNow.com and in *USA Today, New Country,* and *ICE* magazine, and his favorite drink is Coke and grapefruit juice.

Lynne Margolis is a pop music critic and entertainment writer at the Pittsburgh *Tribune-Review* who believes lounge is a word that goes with chaise—however you spell it—and margaritas, but thinks martinis are fine, too, though the glasses are too hard to drink out of without spilling.

Sandy Masuo has written about a bewildering variety of music for a wide range of publications, including the *Boston Phoenix,* the *Los Angeles Times, Musician, Rolling Stone, RayGun,* and several on-line publications, including *All-star, MTV Online,* and *Launch.* She is the associate editor at *Request* magazine and lives in Los Angeles with her anti-social cat, Spot.

Roger Matuz is the Michigan-based founder of Manitou Wordworks, Inc., which develops book and electronic projects in the areas of sports, the outdoors, the arts, and history, with free-

lance writers and editors (and chanteuses singing in the background).

Jim McFarlin is an award-winning critic and columnist on music, pop culture, and the media whose work has appeared in *People, Life, Hit Parader, Entertainment Weekly, USA Today, Electronic Media, USA Weekend, The Detroit News, The Detroit Sunday Journal,* the NAACP's *Crisis,* and *The Rock Yearbook* (St. Martin's Press U.K.). Featured as a pop culture expert on *Entertainment Tonight* and other national TV programs, McFarlin is also co-editor of *MusicHound R&B.*

Adam McGovern has covered everything from comic books to truck-mounted street theater for outlets as diverse as *Smug* magazine and *MusicHound Rock,* though he was raised on show tunes and all-around entertainers. Since therapy has been no use, he's trying *MusicHound Lounge.*

David Menconi is the music critic at the *News & Observer* in Raleigh, North Carolina, and has written for *Spin, Billboard, Request, No Depression, MusicHound Rock, MusicHound Country, MusicHound R&B, and MusicHound Folk.*

David Okamoto is the music editor for *The Dallas Morning News* and a contributing editor to *ICE* magazine. His work has also appeared in *Jazziz, Rolling Stone,* and *CD Review,* but he still doesn't know where Ipanema is.

Allan Orski has written for *Rolling Stone Online, Replay, Requestline, Black Book,* and SW Radio Networks, as well as for *MusicHound Rock, MusicHound R&B,* and *MusicHound Country.* He lives in a loft under the Manhattan Bridge, where he alienates his peers by singing along with Sam Cooke records.

James Person is a senior editor at Gale Research and a musician who has written songs for small gatherings.

Bryan Powell is a musician and freelance writer-editor based in Lawrenceville, Georgia. He is a regular contributor to *Blues Access* and *Acoustic Guitar* magazines and has also written for *MusicHound Blues* and *MusicHound Folk.*

Barry M. Prickett is a Sacramento-based freelance writer, editor, and musician who only lacks an opinion when asleep. He has been known to mix a mean martini, but prefers a good tequila.

Domenic Priore has had his work featured in *Rolling Stone, Billboard,* and *Pulse!* He is the author of *Look! Listen! Vibrate! SMILE!* (Last Gasp), a comprehensive study of the Beach Boys' legendary *Smile* sessions. He has produced television programs on rock 'n' roll and has just published his second book, *Riot on Sunset Strip* (Chronicle).

Jim Prohaska is a Lakewood, Ohio, resident and an avid collector and enthusiast of vintage jazz and blues of the 1920s and 1930s. He owns more than 20,000 jazz and blues 78 rpm records and 10,000 LPs, and has written liner notes and supplied recordings from his collection for the Document record label's blues reissue series and other CD projects. His articles on jazz have run in the *IAJRC Journal* and other publications.

Carl Quintanilla is a Chicago-based staff reporter for *The Wall Street Journal.*

Jay Reeg of Newton Centre, Massachusetts, is the founder of the 1968 Museum, collects copies of old *Vogue* magazines, and thinks Nico's *Marble Index* is the greatest album ever made in the universe.

John K. Richmond has produced jazz history radio programs, written about jazz for the *Cleveland Press* and the Cleveland *Plain Dealer,* and frequently gives lectures and film programs on jazz. He is executive director of the Northeast Ohio Jazz Society (a 1,000-member jazz support organization), a jazz history instructor at Cleveland State University, and a working jazz musician.

Leland Rucker is managing editor of *Blues Access,* a quarterly journal of blues music. He edited *MusicHound Blues* and has contributed to each *MusicHound* volume. Under pressure, he admits to trimming his holiday tree to Robert Mitchum's *Calypso—Is Like So . . . .*

Christopher Scapelliti is an associate editor of *Guitar* magazine and a contributor to *MusicHound Rock* and *MusicHound Country.*

Bruce Schoenfeld writes from his Colorado home on topics ranging from wine to bullfighting for *The New York Times Magazine, Outside, Travel & Leisure,* and other national publications. While writing, he often listens to the new wave and power pop albums of the late '70s and early '80s that helped transform him from an unsteady youth to a sober, sophisticated adult—as well as Puccini, Dean Martin, and Blue Rodeo. It gives his work a certain edge.

Joel Selvin has covered pop music for the *San Francisco Chronicle* since 1970 and has contributed to *MusicHound Rock, MusicHound R&B,* and *MusicHound Country.* His seventh book,

Sly and the Family Stone: On the Record, will be published in 1998.

Stuart Shea is managing editor of *Total Baseball Daily,* a full-service daily Internet baseball newsmagazine published by Total Sports. He has been a full-time baseball professional since 1991, contributing to several different books and publications, and served as associate editor of *The Scouting Report: 1995* and *The Scouting Report: 1996* for HarperCollins. He has also written for *Reactor* magazine and *Home Office Computing.*

Jim Sheeler is a staff writer for the *Boulder Planet* in Colorado, where he makes most excellent mix tapes.

David Simons is a freelance writer who fronts a rock band, the Raymies, in New England.

Chuck Taylor is radio editor for *Billboard* magazine and terms himself a connoisseur of pop music. His first influences were the Carpenters and the Partridge Family. So what'd you expect?

Tom Terrell is a freelance music journalist based in New York who claims to know everything about pop music since 1955— and remembers it all despite a longtime backstage association with George Clinton and Funkadelic.

Chris Tower is a freelance writer and college radio broadcaster who lives in Richland, Michigan, with his ghost cat, Bumba-Head. His work has appeared in *MusicHound R&B, Cyber-Hound's Web Guide, The Kalamazoo* (Michigan) *Gazette,* and a variety of national and international magazines.

Brandon Trenz is a technical editor at Gale Research as well as a freelance writer and film critic.

Aidin Vaziri is a freelance journalist in California whose work has been published in the *San Francisco Chronicle, Guitar Player,* and *Vibe.*

Marc Weingarten does not own a kelly green, crushed velvet smoking jacket—but he's still looking. The former editor of *Request* magazine, Weingarten's work has also appeared in the *Los Angeles Times, Mojo,* and *Entertainment Weekly.*

Ben Wener is the pop music critic for *The Orange County Register.* He is currently at work on his first novel and a collection of critical essays on forgotten albums. He doesn't mind a strong martini now and then, but he prefers vodka. Ice cold and straight. And with a Bacharach chaser.

Sam Wick is editor-in-chief of *Lounge* magazine. "Back when we created *Lounge* in the early '90s, Frank Sinatra was just about the only person living the high life," he says. "My, how the world has changed." *Lounge* is credited with spurring the sputnik ascension of the so-called "cocktail nation." In addition

to penning books, Wick is a frequent contributor to *Drink*, *Grammy*, and just about every bartender's pension plan.

Stephen Williams is the pop music editor at *Newsday*.

In many ways, this guide is new territory. Surprisingly, books and CDs on widely popular, influential artists such as Perry Como—not to mention Korla Pandit and Dakota Staton—are hard to find these days in stores. So the writers of *MusicHound Lounge* had to be especially resourceful. First and foremost, thanks to the contributors for persevering and digging up much more information than they initially planned. It was a pleasure working with you all, whether I know what you look like or recognize your name solely from an e-mail address.

Melissa Knopper, an incredibly patient and brilliant woman, supported me enthusiastically on this project, though it occasionally involved waking involuntarily to the Mystic Moods Orchestra at 7 a.m. on weekdays. She even agreed to marry me a month before the final manuscript deadline, and her insistence that I not discuss or worry about *MusicHound Lounge* during our honeymoon was exactly what we both needed. My parents, Morton and Dorothy Knopper, undoubtedly glad I was writing about music they'd actually heard of, supplied the occasional Gordon MacRae or Neil Diamond CD for key research. Melissa's parents, Don and Peggy Ramsdell, had a deep affinity for this material from the start—I knew the book was on the right track one night at a Chicago Chinese restaurant, when Don listed the artists of his childhood, rapid-fire, and they had already been covered in the book.

The people at Visible Ink Press, especially Marty Connors, Dean Dauphinais, and Judy Galens, have a refreshing tendency to reward hard work. Dean seems to hold these *MusicHound* books together with his bare hands, and his suggestions, gentle nudging, confidence, and mass e-mails frequently kept me afloat. Gary Graff, who recommended me for the project, pa-

tiently answered numerous questions and has been an invaluable friend, resource, booster, and inspirational fellow freelance writer. Leland Rucker, who was just finishing the superb *MusicHound Blues* as I was beginning *MusicHound Lounge,* has book editing and life in general all figured out; he always drops everything to listen to me complain, then nicely says I should get over it. He also writes a mean Robert Mitchum entry. As for contributors, Ken Burke was immediately enthusiastic, then kicked into overdrive just when I needed him most. Without his suggestions for crucial new entries, and tireless churning of clean, well-written copy—in addition to his unwavering good humor and Detroit Tigers anecdotes—this book would have been a nightmare. Martin Denny, in Honolulu, was a quintessential gentleman who seemed genuinely impressed by the manuscript and even made occasional corrections. He offered great historical perspective, and our charming telephone conversations were some of the more pleasant fringe benefits of the book. Thorough and easy-to-work-with copy editor Brigham Narins rescued me from embarrassment on several occasions and fixed all the serial commas. And thanks to Brian McCafferty at EMI-Capitol for helping us land the cool *Ultra-Lounge* CD sampler.

There's no definitive Encylopedia of Lounge to set the standard, so I alternated among several references for key background information. Invaluable were Roy Hemming and David Hajdu's *Discovering Great Singers of Classic Pop* (Newmarket Press, 1992); Dylan Jones's *Ultra Lounge: The Lexicon of Easy Listening* (Universe Publishing, 1997); Joseph Lanza's *Elevator Music* (Picador, 1994); Peter Gammond's *The Oxford Companion to Popular Music* (Oxford University Press, 1991); Joel Whitburn's

Pop Memories, 1890–1954 (Record Research, 1986); and *Incredibly Strange Music, Vol. 1* (RE/Search, 1993) and *Incredibly Strange Music, Vol. 2* (Juno Books, 1994). Our contributors, myself included, visited many Web sites, including the consistently informative Space Age Pop Music Standards Page (http://home.earthlink.net/~spaceagepop/index.htm), plus the CD-selling sites CDnow (http://www.cdnow.com), CD Universe (http://www.cduniverse.com), and @Tower (http://www.tower records.com). Producers Irwin Chusid and Brad Benedict provided information on certain artists, and Otto von Stroheim of *Tiki News* recommended excellent contributors.

The following publicists, musicians, and other music-industry types gave key advice and provided music and background for contributors: Dan Cohen and Ashley Warren at Scamp and Caroline Records; Darcy Mayers at Rykodisc; Claudia Draeger at Capitol, provider of the *Ultra-Lounge* CDs; Tom Muzquiz at Rhino; Michael Omansky and Todd Schenkenberger at RCA; Marc Fenton at Razor & Tie; Steve Weed with Madacy Entertainment Group, who helped make sense of the massive 101 Strings catalog; Jeffrey Kaye at Third Floor Media; Robbie Baldock, who runs *Spaced Out,* the excellent Enoch Light Web page (http://easyweb.easynet.co.uk/~rcb/light/); Dr. Wax Records on Clark Street in Chicago, whose easy-listening racks contain gems like Regis Philbin's album and *Billy May's Greatest Hits*; Jessica Sowin at Sony/Legacy; Buddy Greco; Stu Phillips, formerly of the Hollyridge Strings; Jack Costanzo; Peter Torza at Harlow's; Nancy Carballo with Barbara Shelley Public Relations, who sent a dozen of the Right Stuff's Mystic Moods Orchestra CDs and a half-dozen Yma Sumac CDs on a few days' notice; Cary E. Mansfield of Varese Sarabande; Sarah Geist, who works with the Mighty Blue Kings; WDUQ-FM in Pittsburgh; Susan Darnell at Setanta; and Debbie Metcalf at BIA Publications, who provided the radio station list. And praise be to liner notes.

Thanks also to my non-*MusicHound* editors, who were nice enough to understand that with editing a book and planning a wedding, it was difficult to write the usual number of freelance stories. Some of these brave people contributed to *Music-Hound Lounge*: the aforementioned Leland Rucker of *Blues Access*; Stephen Williams at *Newsday*; Chuck Taylor at *Billboard*; Sandy Masuo at *Request*; Rob Levine at *Rolling Stone Online* and now *Details*; Alex Gordon, formerly of the late, lamented *Internet Underground*; and Ben Greenman, who coordinates the annual music issue for *Yahoo! Internet Life.* For general advice, friendship, counsel, and just plain entertaining phone conversations, I'm indebted to David Menconi, Bruce Schoenfeld, Jim DeRogatis, Josh Freedom du Lac, Gil Asakawa, and Daniel Durchholz. Finally, thanks to my brothers, Mark and Doug Knopper—for teaching me everything I know—and anybody else I may have missed.

Steve Knopper

ABBA

Formed 1973, in Stockholm, Sweden. Disbanded 1983.

Anni-Frid "Frida" Lyngstad, vocals; Benny Andersson, keyboards, vocals; Bjorn Ulvaeus, guitar, vocals; Agnetha "Anna" Faltskog, vocals.

Simply put, ABBA is the Swedish Beatles. Starting with its win of the Eurovision Song Contest in 1973 with "Waterloo," ABBA grew into a global pop phenomenon in the 1970s, earning a string of shimmering hits. Built by the studied European songcraft of producers-writers Andersson and Ulvaeus, and buoyed by the golden harmonies of Lyngstad and Faltskog, ABBA's music celebrated impossibly pretty melody. American listeners may have been the least impressed during ABBA's tenure on the scene, but a revival spurred by techno-popsters Erasure and an uncanny Australian tribute band, Björn Again, won new converts starting in 1992. Since then, new compilations of hits have flourished, and ABBA songs have provided some of the most talked-about moments in recent films, including *The Adventures of Priscilla, Queen of the Desert* and *Muriel's Wedding*. The ladies' kitschy kittycat costumes have not aged well. The party-ready songs have.

what to buy: Supplanting earlier out-of-print hits collections, *Gold: Greatest Hits* ♫♫♫♫♫ (Polydor, 1993, prod. Benny Andersson, Bjorn Ulvaeus) gathers 19 tuneful triumphs on one disc. From the glistening disco of "Dancing Queen" to the quaint Euro-balladry of "Chiquitita" and "Fernando," all the best singles by one of pop's best singles groups are here. *More ABBA*

Gold: More ABBA Hits ♫♫♫♫ (Polydor, 1993, prod. Benny Andersson, Bjorn Ulvaeus) rounds up the remaining singles and the best album tracks, including "Ring, Ring" and "When I Kissed the Teacher." Diehard ABBA fanatics might want to skip these two compilations in favor of the four-disc *Thank You for the Music* ♫♫♫♫ (Polydor, 1995, prod. Benny Andersson, Bjorn Ulvaeus), which digs deeper than the casual fan may desire.

what to buy next: Consistency isn't a trademark of most ABBA albums. The group peaked relatively late on the fine *Super Trouper* ♫♫♫♫ (Atlantic, 1980, prod. Benny Andersson, Bjorn Ulvaeus), which includes the dreamy ballad "Our Last Summer" and the spunky "On & On & On." Listen to "Happy New Year" and "The Way Old Friends Do" and see if you can resist playing one or the other at your next mixer.

what to avoid: A disarmingly dull afterthought, *ABBA Live* ♫ (Atlantic, 1986) doesn't add much to the ABBA mythos. You're better off waiting for Björn Again to play your town. The title track of *Ring Ring* ♫♫ (Polar, 1973, prod. Benny Andersson, Bjorn Ulvaeus) is fun, but otherwise it's a shrill start to the quartet's album career.

the rest:
Waterloo ♫♫♫ (Atlantic, 1974)
ABBA ♫♫♫ (Atlantic, 1975)
Arrival ♫♫♫♫ (Atlantic, 1977)
The Album ♫♫♫♫ (Atlantic, 1978)
Voulez-Vous ♫♫ (Atlantic, 1979)
The Visitors ♫♫♫ (Atlantic, 1981)

worth searching for: Completists might want *Oro* ♫♫♫ (Polydor, 1994, prod. Benny Andersson, Bjorn Ulvaeus), a Spanish language version of *Gold*. There's also an import combo pack of

the *Gold* and *More Gold* albums that adds a disc with a handful of tracks not included on the two core discs.

solo outings:
Anni-Frid "Frida" Lyngstad:
I Know There's Something Going On 🎵🎵🎵 (Polydor, 1993)

Agnetha "Anna" Faltskog:
Wrap Your Arms Around Me 🎵🎵 (Polydor, 1993)

Benny Andersson and Bjorn Ulvaeus:
(With Tim Rice) *Chess* 🎵🎵🎵 (Polydor, 1984)

influences:
⏪ The Beach Boys, the Beatles, Stevie Wonder, the Bee Gees, Elton John

⏩ Ace of Base, Lisa Stansfield, Erasure, Madonna, Roxette, the Cardigans, U2, Josefin Nilsson

see also: *Björn Again*

Jay Dedrick

Barry Adamson

Born June 1, 1958, in Manchester, England.

Barry Adamson's relationship to lounge music has more to do with attitude than anything else; he's an archivist with the soul of a post-modernist. A former bassist for Nick Cave's Bad Seeds and the proto–new wave band Magazine, Adamson has a fondness for all things sleazy, slinky, and subversive, subsuming his love of vintage movie soundtracks, film noir, and modern jazz into sprawling, wide-screen sonic scenarios that have the sweep and epic grandeur of movie shorts shot in Cinemascope. Shortly after leaving Cave in 1990, Adamson cut three EPs in succession, the titles of which—*The Man with the Golden Arm*, *Moss Side Story*, and *The Taming of the Shrewd*—should give you a good idea of what's contained therein. The plot thickens on *Soul Murder*, as Adamson serves up some startling juxtapositions: voice-overs about rape and death and audio-verite samples compete with swelling string sections and snappy cocktail jazz.

what to buy: All of Adamson's albums are worth investigating, but *Soul Murder* 🎵🎵🎵 (Mute, 1992, prod. Barry Adamson) is perhaps the best primer for the neophyte, as it provides the most focused crystallization of his aesthetic.

ABBA (AP/Wide World Photos)

what to buy next: *The Negro Inside Me* 🎵🎵🎵 (Mute, 1993, prod. Barry Adamson) finds Adamson exploring dance-music textures in greater depth than he had previously hinted. Great album cover, too.

the rest:
The Man with the Golden Arm 🎵🎵🎵 (UK Mute, 1988)
Moss Side Story 🎵🎵🎵 (Mute/Restless, 1989)
The Taming of the Shrewd 🎵🎵🎵 (UK Mute, 1989)
Delusion 🎵🎵 (Mute, 1991)
Cinema Is King 🎵🎵🎵 (UK Mute, 1992)
Oedipus Schmoedipus 🎵🎵🎵 (Mute, 1996)

influences:
⏪ Nick Cave, Magazine, Serge Gainsbourg, Scott Walker

⏩ Sisters of Mercy, PJ Harvey

Marc Weingarten

Cannonball Adderley

Born Julian Edwin Adderley, September 15, 1928, in Tampa, FL. Died August 8, 1975, in Gary, IN.

One of the premier alto saxophonists of the 1960s, Adderley spawned a generation of alto players who tried to copy his warm, lush sound. Adderley, whose brother Nat still plays trumpet on the jazz circuit, was blessed with an engaging tone that brought out the best in the alto's bright upper register. He was known for spirited solos, but as his lounge music demonstrates, it was his ability to milk a ballad that gave his music long-lasting stature. Adderley's career started slow. He played in an Army band and small-time gigs in Florida, where he and his brother were raised. But then came Miles Davis, who put the young horn player in his quintet in 1957 to replace Sonny Rollins. The result: Adderley played on Davis's classic album *Kind of Blue* and later signed his own record deal, assembling a quintet of his own with an eclectic group of musicians ranging from Joe Zawinul to Yusef Lateef. Eventually, he became a star in his own right—even playing a musician in Clint Eastwood's 1971 film *Play Misty for Me*. His girth (he was so big that an alto sax looked like a toy in his hands) made him popular with mass audiences.

what to buy: It's tough to beat Cannonball's sound when it's paired with the Bill Evans's vibrant piano on *Know What I Mean?* 🎵🎵🎵 (Riverside, 1961/1996, prod. Orrin Keepnews). Percy Heath and Connie Kay, two big sidemen of the decade, also sit in on this New York session. *Dizzy's Business* 🎵🎵🎵 (Milestone, 1993), a re-release of nine songs originally recorded in 1963, pays tribute to Dizzy Gillespie, from whom

Adderley took much of his knowledge of bebop and Latin music. This one includes accompaniment from brother Nat, bassist Sam Jones, and drummer Louis Hayes.

what to buy next: *Somethin' Else* ♫♫♫ (Blue Note, 1958, prod. Alfred Lion), the first of Adderley's truly great recording sessions, features the saxophonist at an early age—accompanied by a more musically mature Miles Davis. Cannonball's rendition of "Autumn Leaves" is reason enough to buy this album. *Mercy, Mercy, Mercy! Live at "The Club"* ♫♫♫ (EMI, 1966/1995, prod. David Axelrod) is a terrific live album with Adderley's constant companion from his later years, Joe Zawinul. It was recorded at the Club in Chicago, with Cannonball's brother Nat on cornet.

what to avoid: Other albums from later years, like *Country Preacher* ♫♫ (Capitol, 1969/1994), won't deliver the laid-back sounds listeners may anticipate.

best of the rest:
Sophisticated Swing ♫♫♫♪ (EmArcy, 1957)
Portrait of Cannonball ♫♫♫ (Riverside, 1958)
Cannonball Adderley Quintet in San Francisco ♫♫♫ (Original Jazz Classics, 1959)
What Is This Thing Called Soul? ♫♫♫ (Pablo, 1960)
Nippon Soul ♫♫ (Riverside 1963)

worth searching for: Unfortunately, Adderley's canon hasn't been well cataloged on CD—unlike the alto's brighter star, Charlie Parker, whom Adderley idolized as a youngster. But some out-of-print albums, like *Lush Side of Cannonball* ♫♫♫♫ (Mercury, 1962), are worth finding if only for their rich lounge sound.

influences:
◄◄ Charlie Parker, Dizzy Gillespie, Miles Davis
►► Phil Woods, Richie Cole

Carl Quintanilla

Helen Folasade Adu

See: Sade

Eden Ahbez

Born Alexander Aberle, April 15, 1908, in Brooklyn, NY. Died March 4, 1995, in Desert Hot Springs, CA.

Once upon a time in Los Angeles, a paradise impossible to realize in the here and now, there was a man who carved wood flutes of various shapes and sizes and wrote songs whose lyrics gave people inclinations to shed their clothing and run around naked and free. He accomplished this in the era of the grey-flannel suit with a #1 record, and he did it more succinctly than any hippie or Woodstock attendee ever could. Ahbez might be considered a jazz/pop artist if only for the diversity of recording stars who covered his tunes. His first composition, "Nature Boy," was Nat King Cole's first crossover #1 hit in 1948. During the Depression, his large family had suffered from hunger, and he and his twin sister were placed in an orphanage. They were adopted by the McGrews, of Lawrence, Kansas, but left home to live in California in about 1943. He and his family lived outdoors, their only possessions being a sleeping bag, a bicycle, and a juice squeezer. He also wrote songs, including a four-part piece titled "Nature Boy Suite," and showed up at a theater, dressed as usual in rags, sandals, and a long beard, to drop off the sheet music to Nat King Cole. The song became a hit, and Capitol Records officials, armed with a $30,000 royalty check, put out word through Hollywood to find Ahbez, who had a street reputation as "the Hermit" or "the Yogi." When they finally found him, he was living beneath the first "L" in the "Hollywood" sign, spending nights in a sleeping bag and living off fruits, nuts, and berries. All this had little effect on Ahbez's sensibilities; he continued to live on three dollars a week for vegetables, fruits, and nuts, without working, for years. "Nature Boy" was later covered by Frank Sinatra, Sarah Vaughan, John Coltrane, Dick Haymes, Grace Slick, and, most ethereally, Don Reed and Loreli. In 1955, Ahbez saw his complete version recorded by jazz artist Herb Jeffries on the Olympic LP *The Singing Prophet*. When Martin Denny, Arthur Lyman, Les Baxter, and others ushered in the "exotica" craze in the mid-'50s, bebop flutist Bob Romeo recorded three Ahbez tunes on his seductive *Aphro-Disia* LP, featuring guitarist Laurindo Almeida and pianist Eddie Cano. (The sleeve showed model Anita Ekberg removing one of seven veils, and a warning notice on the cover concerning the sexual dangers of the LP.) The Ahbez tunes were standouts, and soon the composer released an entire exotica album. Mickey McGowan, in the RE/search book *Incredibly Strange Music, Vol. 1*, said of Ahbez's music: "It's as if Jack Kerouac had got on a boat with Martin Denny and not become a beatnik." Ahbez died at age 86 after suffering injuries in a California auto accident.

what's available: The only in-print evidence of Ahbez's recording career is *Eden's Island* ♫♫♫♫ (Del Fi, 1960/1995, prod. Bob Keane); based on "Gospel of Nature," a long poem Ahbez had written on the back of another album, it's a masterpiece of the exotica genre. Much easier to find is Nat King Cole's smooth hit interpretation of "Nature Boy," on, to name just one of many

Cole greatest-hits collections, *The Unforgettable Nat King Cole* ♫♫♫♫♫ (Capitol, 1992, prod. various).

worth searching for: Herb Jeffries's out-of-print *The Singing Prophet* ♫♫♫♫ (Olympic, 1955) is based on Ahbez's poetry. It's a weird opera album, but invaluable for being the only place you can hear "Nature Boy" as it was originally intended—in a four-part suite. For hardcore collectors, there are always Ahbez's original pseudonymous singles (some in 78 rpm form), such as "California" b/w "End of Desire," by "Nature Boy and Orchestra"; "Surfer John" b/w "John John," by "Nature Boy and Friends"; "The Old Boat" b/w "Tobago," by "Nature Boy"; and "Divine Melody," by "Ahbe Casabe."

influences:

◀◀ Mahatma Gandhi, Martin Denny, Arthur Lyman

▶▶ Nat "King" Cole, Bob Romeo, Herb Jeffries, John Coltrane, Jefferson Airplane

Domenic Priore

Ronnie Aldrich

Born Ronald Aldrich, February 15, 1916, in Erith, Kent, England.

This British pianist's recent instrumentals have had the same tinkly, sleepy feeling of most piped-in supermarket music from the 1960s and 1970s. He's more notable for his swinging past: during World War II he performed in the Royal Air Force dance orchestra, which became known as the Squadronaires. Despite the squaresville military association, the band showcased real talent, including George Chisholm and Jimmy Miller (and for a time, according to interviews, the father of Who rock guitarist Pete Townshend), and became one of the country's most recognizable swing bands. After the war, Aldrich took over the group's leadership, building on its wartime popularity throughout the '50s. He then went freelance, conducting, arranging, and performing music with radio orchestras and his own bands.

what to buy: *Twin Piano Magic* ♫♫ (Rebound, 1994/1996) is modern-day beautiful music, with versions of pop standards— "Ebb Tide," "Smoke Gets in Your Eyes," "Love Letters"—so bland they're almost humorous. As a piano player, Aldrich sure likes those Liberace-style trills.

what to buy next: Aldrich teams with the London Festival Orchestra for *Great Themes to Remember* ♫♫ (PolyGram Special Markets, 1996), and takes the totally unsurprising career step

Cocktail Classics

Ac-cent-tchu-ate the Positive

18-Karat Bing Crosby & the Andrews Sisters *Their Complete Recordings Together* (MCA/Decca)

Bombsville! Clint Eastwood *Midnight in the Garden of Good and Evil (Soundtrack)* (Malpaso/Warner Bros.)

of recording holiday music on *Christmas with Ronnie Aldrich* ♫♫ (PolyGram Special Markets, 1997).

worth searching for: Yes, the Squadronaires actually recorded swing albums, and yes, it's possible to find them if you look hard enough and happen to be in England. *There's Something in the Air* ♫♫♫ (Hep, 1994) is a surprisingly strong collection of big-band music, although novices are advised to plunder Glenn Miller, Benny Goodman, and Duke Ellington CDs first.

influences:

◀◀ Benny Goodman, Glenn Miller, Francis Lai

▶▶ Pete Townshend, Liberace

Steve Knopper

Alessi

Formed 1952, in Long Island, NY.

Bill Alessi, keyboards; Bobby Alessi, guitar.

The Alessi brothers had a built-in gimmick—Billy and Bobby were identical twins from Long Island, New York's bastion of suburbanism. They started their career in jingles work, then won roles in the hit Broadway musical *Hair* and became half of Barnaby Bye (a Beatle-esque group that recorded two albums on Atlantic). A move to A&M resulted in four Alessi albums from 1976 to 1979, mixtures of spritely rockers, white-boy R&B, and dreamy romantic ballads. Alessi's songs were also covered by the likes of Frankie Valli, Olivia Newton-John, and Richie Havens. But the brothers never scored a big breakthrough in the U.S. Their greatest drawing power was among teen listeners—as special guests on Andy Gibb's tour, their clean-cut exuberance and fey power-pop drove thousands of screaming schoolgirls into pubescent frenzy.

worth searching for: None of Alessi's albums are in print. The debut, *Alessi* &&& (A&M, 1976), contained the pair's one substantial international hit, "Oh, Lori." A look through used vinyl bins may yield *Long Time Friends* && (Quest/Warner Bros., 1982), a project co-produced by Christopher Cross and overseen by Quincy Jones—the resulting hard-soft sound was compelling at the time.

influences:

◀◀ The Everly Brothers, the Beach Boys

▶▶ Hanson, Kristy and Jimmy McNichol

G. Brown

Peter Allen

Born 1944, in Australia. Died June 18, 1992, in San Diego, CA.

Though his obituaries prominently mentioned his brief marriage to singer Liza Minnelli (they divorced in 1970), Allen's behind-the-scenes accomplishments in the music industry were substantial, making his young death that much more tragic. He wrote Olivia Newton-John's hit "I Honestly Love You," turned "Quiet Please (There's a Lady on Stage)" into his on-stage showstopper, and won an Oscar for his theme to the movie *Arthur*. The Australian-born singer began his career by scrounging around clubs in his hometown, Tenterfield, then gained enough name recognition to earn engagements in other countries. He had been singing in Hong Kong in 1964 when singer Judy Garland discovered him; the connection led to much larger gigs, including a role in the 1970 Broadway show *Soon*, with Nell Carter and Richard Gere. (His marriage to Garland's daughter, Minnelli, lasted from 1967 to '70.) Allen, who had a bunch of solo hits in the late '70s, died of AIDS-related causes.

what's available: Allen's only in-print collection, which focuses on his solo material from 1974 to 1980, is *At His Best* &&& (A&M, 1993/1994). This includes his takes on "One Step Over the Borderline," "Don't Cry Out Loud," and "I Go to Rio." Beyond that, it's all Australian imports.

influences:

◀◀ Judy Garland, Perry Como, Al Jolson

▶▶ Liza Minnelli, Olivia Newton-John, Christopher Cross

Steve Knopper

Steve Allen

Born Stephen Valentine Patrick William Allen, December 21, 1921, in New York City, NY.

Allen was the first host of *The Tonight Show*, which later turned Johnny Carson into an entertainment legend and changed the entire television industry. Since then, much more quietly, he has written 6,000-plus songs (mostly of the jazz-lounge variety, such as "This Could Be the Start of Something Big" and "Impossible"), 48 books, and recorded more than 50 albums. He created, hosted, and wrote an Emmy-winning PBS television series called *Meeting of Minds*, which was a serious-minded panel discussion in which actors played noted philosophers and thinkers from history. More prolific than talented—as a musician, anyhow—the comedian wrote parts of songs eventually recorded by Louis Armstrong and Bing Crosby. He plays piano and organ, sometimes in a soft, tinkly, space-age bachelor-pad mode and sometimes in a serious, improvisational swing-jazz mode. He continues to perform, both on television and in music halls.

what to buy: Don't bother trying to find all 50 of Allen's original studio albums, unless you're a hardcore collector or masochist. *Steve Allen Plays Hi-Fi Music for Influentials* &&& (Varese Sarabande, 1996) pretty much sums it up: it includes easy-listening (and occasionally bossa-nova) versions of jazz standards like "Stormy Weather," plus songs by Cole Porter and Irving Berlin.

Peter Allen (© Jack Vartoogian)

what to buy next: As a comedian, of course, Allen doesn't take his music too seriously. So *On the Air! The Classic Comedy of Steve Allen* 🎵🎵 (Varese Sarabande, 1996, prod. Steve Allen) is a refreshing companion piece to *Plays Hi-Fi Music*. It includes the funny Tony Bennett spoof "I Left My Nose in San Diego."

what to avoid: Allen is a decent pianist, but his mostly instrumental versions of "Body and Soul," "A Sinner Kissed an Angel," and even "Gone with the Wind" on *Steve Allen Plays Jazz Tonight* 🎵🎵 (Concord Jazz, 1993) should have been left to heavyweight players.

the rest:
Steve Allen Plays Cool, Quiet Bossa Nova 🎵🎵 (Laserlight, 1993)

influences:

⏪ Louis Armstrong, Eddie Fisher, Hoagy Carmichael, Eddie Cantor, Bing Crosby, Nat "King" Cole, Mose Allison

⏩ Johnny Carson, Jay Leno, William Shatner, Dudley Moore

Steve Knopper

Mose Allison

Born Mose John Allison Jr., November 11, 1927, in Tippo, MS.

Though Allison's light, improvisational piano style has more in common with jazz than blues, he built his early reputation by personalizing Sonny Boy Williamson's "Eyesight to the Blind," Willie Dixon's "Seventh Son," and Muddy Waters's "Rollin' Stone." Interpreting blues standards in his lazy and smart-alecky—but always warm—voice, he also influenced rockers Pete Townshend, Van Morrison, the Clash, and the Yardbirds. Townshend in particular, who liked the blues but didn't want the Who to become another blues-reviving Yardbirds or Rolling Stones, found inspiration in "Eyesight to the Blind" and Allison's most enduring anthem, "Young Man's Blues." But all the rock influence has distorted Allison's legend. He has been recording albums and touring nightclubs (where he refuses to let anybody smoke) for 40 years, and his devastating sense of humor led to such wonderful jazz songs as "Your Mind Is on Vacation" and "If You're Going to the City." His piano style, reminiscent of longtime Waters sideman Otis Spann, is fast and playful but never so busy it clutters up the lyrics. Not much has changed over the past several decades for Allison, though he collaborated on *Tell Me Something* with Van Morrison (who once covered his "If You Only Knew") and occasionally does joint interviews with his country-rocking daughter, the talented Parlor James singer Amy Allison.

what to buy: *Allison Wonderland: The Mose Allison Anthology* 🎵🎵🎵🎵 (Rhino, 1994, prod. Joel Dorn, James Austin) shows why Allison was such an important link between mid-century Chicago blues and early-1960s British rock 'n' roll. The compilation displaced *The Best of Mose Allison* 🎵🎵🎵 (Atlantic, 1988, prod. Bob Porter) and *Greatest Hits* 🎵🎵🎵 (Prestige, 1959/1988, prod. Bob Weinstock) as the essential places to find "The Seventh Son," "Eyesight to the Blind," "Young Man's Blues," and "Your Mind Is on Vacation."

what to buy next: His original studio albums are hard to find, but *Back Country Suite* 🎵🎵🎵 (Prestige, 1957, engineer Rudy Van Gelder), *Local Color* 🎵🎵🎵 (Prestige, 1958, prod. Bob Weinstock), and *Ramblin' with Mose Allison* 🎵🎵🎵 (Prestige, 1961) are among the best of a prolific recording career. His 1980s Elektra period, which produced *Middle Class White Boy* 🎵🎵🎵 (Elektra, 1982, prod. Esmond Edwards) and *Lesson in Living* 🎵🎵🎵 (Elektra, 1983, prod. Philippe Rault), allowed him to revitalize his style with a more soulful touch. *Tell Me Something* 🎵🎵🎵 (Verve, 1996, prod. Van Morrison, Ben Sidran, Georgie Fame), a collaboration with Morrison and Fame, is a nice tribute and return to form after years of nondescript studio albums.

what to avoid: Allison has been churning out records with incredible regularity for four decades, and sometimes he releases a rushed batch of stuff: *Mose Alive!* 🎵🎵 (Atlantic, 1966), *Western Man* 🎵🎵 (Atlantic, 1971), and *Mose in Your Ear* 🎵🎵 (Atlantic, 1972) are examples of this lack of inspiration.

the rest:
Parchman Farm 🎵🎵🎵 (Original Jazz Classics)
Creek Bank 🎵🎵🎵 (Prestige, 1958)
Ol' Devil Mose 🎵🎵🎵 (Prestige, 1958)
Young Man Mose 🎵🎵🎵 (Prestige, 1958)
Autumn Song 🎵🎵🎵 (Prestige, 1959)
Mose Allison Plays for Lovers 🎵🎵🎵 (Prestige, 1959)
Transfiguration of Hiram Brown 🎵🎵🎵 (Columbia, 1960)
I Love the Life I Live 🎵🎵 (Columbia, 1961)
V-8 Ford Blues 🎵🎵 (Epic/Legacy, 1961)
Mose Allison Takes to the Hills 🎵🎵🎵 (Epic/Legacy, 1962)
Mose Allison Sings 🎵🎵🎵 (Prestige, 1963)
Swingin' Machine 🎵🎵 (Atlantic, 1963)
The Word from Mose Allison 🎵🎵🎵 (Atlantic, 1964)
Wild Man on the Lane 🎵🎵 (Atlantic, 1966)
I Been Doin' Some Thinkin' 🎵🎵 (Atlantic, 1968)
Mose Goes 🎵🎵 (Columbia, 1968)
Hello There Universe 🎵🎵 (Atlantic, 1970)
Retrospective 🎵🎵🎵 (Columbia, 1971)
Mose Allison 🎵🎵🎵 (Prestige, 1972)
The Seventh Son 🎵🎵🎵 (Prestige, 1973)

Your Mind Is on Vacation 🎵🎵 (Atlantic, 1976)
Ever Since the World Ended 🎵🎵 (Blue Note, 1988)
My Backyard 🎵🎵 (Blue Note, 1990)
Mose Allison Sings and Plays 🎵🎵🎵 (Prestige, 1991)
I Don't Worry about a Thing 🎵🎵🎵 (Rhino, 1993)
The Earth Wants You 🎵🎵 (Blue Note, 1994)
High Jinks! The Mose Allison Trilogy 🎵🎵🎵🎵 (Columbia, 1994)

influences:

◀◀ Muddy Waters, Willie Dixon, Art Tatum, Ray Charles, Charles Brown, Sonny Boy Williamson II (Rice Miller), Otis Spann

▶▶ Pete Townshend, Bonnie Raitt, Van Morrison, Elvis Costello, Ray Davies

Steve Knopper

Laurindo Almeida /Laurindo Almeida & the Bossa Nova All-Stars

Born September 2, 1917, in San Paolo, Brazil. Died July 26, 1995, in Los Angeles, CA.

Almeida, an incredible guitarist with a superb sense of melody, singlehandedly brought Brazil's light, romantic guitar style to American jazz—working with Stan Getz, Stan Kenton, Charlie Byrd, and many other big names in the process. More significantly, and for the purposes of this book, he was one of the first and most successful practioners of catchy bossa nova music. After developing a reputation as one of Brazil's most talented session guitarists, Almeida moved to Los Angeles and immediately hooked up with Kenton's popular orchestra in the late 1940s. Though Almeida dabbled in classical, swing, and pop instrumental music, he was best known for creating the blueprint for bossa nova—a distinctive, percussive Latin beat with horns and guitars trading melodic solos—while collaborating with jazzman Bud Shank in 1953. Ten years later, Almeida's solo band, the Bossa Nova All-Stars, discovered a hitmaking formula: they set pop standards, such as "I Left My Heart in San Francisco" and "Hava Nagila," to a swinging bossa nova beat. A craze was born, giving Almeida enough star power to make successful jazz recordings, including a series of albums with American guitarist Charlie Byrd, for the rest of his career.

what to buy: Some jazz fans might steer new listeners to Almeida's more serious duets with Byrd, or his later trio sessions with bassist Bob Magnusson, but none of that is as fun

as *Best of Laurindo Almeida and the Bossa Nova All-Stars* 🎵🎵🎵🎵 (Curb, 1996, prod. various). The CD collects most of Almeida's early-'60s bossa nova hits, from the pure-Latin "Lisbon Antiqua" to the Brazilianized versions of American standards "Satin Doll," "Misirlou," and "I Left My Heart in San Francisco." Much cornier (but with just as much campy fun) is a later session of instrumentals, *Virtuoso Guitar* 🎵🎵🎵 (Laserlight, 1991, prod. various), that includes the Barry Manilow signatures "I Write the Songs" and "Copacabana."

what to buy next: Almeida made several albums of excellent soft jazz: his duets with guitarist Charlie Byrd peaked on *Brazilian Soul* 🎵🎵🎵 (Concord Picante, 1981/1987, prod. Carl E. Jefferson), with a nice Brazilian-tinged version of "Don't Cry For Me Argentina," which puts the later Sinéad O'Connor and Madonna versions to shame. His early-'50s work with saxophonist and flutist Bud Shank nicely mix still-fresh Brazilian guitar sounds with then-new bop and swing sounds: two compilations, *Brazilliance, Vol. 1* 🎵🎵🎵 (Blue Note, 1991) and *Brazilliance, Vol. 2* 🎵🎵🎵🎵 (Blue Note, 1991, prod. Richard Bock), are reasonably thorough documents of the historic sessions.

what to avoid: Almeida's classical material lacks both his bossa nova playfulness and his jazzy sensuality: *First Concerto for Guitar and Orchestra* 🎵🎵 (Concord Concerts, 1980/1987) could use a few Barry Manilow melodies to lighten things up.

the rest:
(With Charlie Byrd) *Tango* 🎵🎵🎵 (Concord Picante, 1987)
(With Carlos Barbosa-Lima) *Music of the Brazilian Masters* 🎵🎵🎵 (Concord Picante, 1989)
(With Charlie Byrd) *Latin Odyssey* 🎵🎵🎵 (Concord Picante, 1990)
Duets with Spanish Guitar 🎵🎵 (EMI Classics, 1990)
Chamber Jazz 🎵🎵🎵 (Concord Jazz, 1991)
Artistry in Rhythm 🎵🎵🎵 (Concord Jazz, 1994)

influences:

◀◀ Tito Puente, Tito Rodriguez, Cal Tjader, Stan Kenton, Stan Getz

▶▶ Perez Prado, Elvis Presley, Ann-Margret, Louis Prima

Steve Knopper

Herb Alpert

Born March 31, 1935, in Los Angeles, CA.

It is hard today to remember the impact Herb Alpert and his Tijuana Brass had on pop music in the mid-1960s: the band's shrewdly styled south-of-the-border arrangements of show-

Herb Alpert (l) with some of his Tijuana Brass **(AP/Wide World Photos)**

tunes, rock, and most everything in between was as much a soundtrack of that era as anything John Lennon and Paul Mc-Cartney created. In fact, in May 1966, the Brass placed an unprecedented four albums in the *Billboard* Top 10 simultaneously, a feat that stands unduplicated to this day.

Playing trumpet since the age of eight, Alpert was initiated into the music business in 1958 when, teamed with an insurance salesman named Lou Adler, he took a $42-a-week staff-writing job at Keen Publishing. While there, the duo wrote several hits with Sam Cooke, as well as "Baby Talk" for the surf duo Jan and Dean, which became Alpert's first Top Ten success. He soon began recording as a vocalist for RCA (under the name Dore Alpert) and even landed bit parts in such Hollywood epics as *The Ten Commandments*. But in 1962, upon forming a partnership with his RCA producer Jerry Moss, the real breakthrough began: from Alpert's garage, they launched A&M Records with a $1,000 loan, $65 of which was spent recording a rearrangement of Sol Lake's "Twinkle Star." Re-

leased under the title "The Lonely Bull," and despite warnings from industry pals that a trumpet instrumental would never succeed on the U.S. charts, the record hit #6 by year's end, establishing both Alpert and A&M as commercial forces on the burgeoning West Coast music scene. Several quickly produced albums, utilizing the best Los Angeles session players, soon helped ingratiate Alpert's Mexicali-lite, "Ameriachi" sound so heavily onto the international consciousness that by mid-decade the Tijuana Brass could be heard performing not only at Carnegie Hall, the London Hammersmith Odeon, *and* the White House, but on television (where "Spanish Flea" later became the theme for *The Dating Game*) and the big screen (the Brass's version of Burt Bacharach's "Casino Royale" was the hit theme of 1967's James Bond movie). A year later, with 45 million albums sold, Alpert proclaimed the trumpet "my enemy," disbanded the Tijuana Brass, and announced his retirement from live performing.

He spent most of the 1970s signing new talent, such as the Carpenters, to his A&M label while recording himself only occasionally (a 1974 collaboration with Hugh Masekela was particularly inspired). By decade's end, he returned with "Rise," which knocked no less than Michael Jackson from the top of the charts; later, he collaborated the pop-reggae band UB40, Janet Jackson producers Jimmy Jam and Terry Lewis, and, most recently, ex-Nirvana bassist Krist Novoselic. Although A&M Records was sold to PolyGram in 1989 for a whopping $460 million—not a bad return on that original $1,000 investment!—Alpert and Moss remain active, seeking talent for their new label, Almo Sounds, and the trumpeter himself enjoys painting and philanthropic work when not continuing to record and perform.

what to buy: From the abundance of greatest-hits packages available, *Foursider* 𝄞𝄞𝄞𝄞 (A&M, 1973, prod. Herb Alpert, Jerry Moss) and *Classics, Vol. 20* 𝄞𝄞𝄞 (A&M, 1987, prod. various) together provide a suitable overview of Alpert's work, both with the Brass and beyond.

what to buy next: The classic original, *Whipped Cream and Other Delights* 𝄞𝄞𝄞 (A&M, 1965, prod. Herb Alpert, Jerry Moss), is the quintessential Alpert. From its crossover wallop of covers ("Lemon Tree," the monster hit "A Taste of Honey," and even the R&B classic "Love Potion #9") to its cover photograph (of a cream-drenched, finger-licking young bride), this album was no less than the *Sgt. Pepper* of the middle-of-the-road set.

best of the rest:
Rise 𝄞𝄞𝄞 (A&M, 1979)
Keep Your Eye on Me 𝄞𝄞𝄞 (A&M, 1987)
North on South Street 𝄞𝄞 (A&M, 1991)
Midnight Sun 𝄞𝄞𝄞 (A&M, 1992)
Second Wind 𝄞𝄞 (Geffen, 1996)
Passion Dance 𝄞𝄞𝄞 (Almo Sounds, 1997)

worth searching for: One of the most bizarre Yuletide offerings ever, *Christmas Album* 𝄞𝄞𝄞𝄞 (A&M, 1968) contains salsa-soaked renditions of "Winter Wonderland," "Let It Snow! Let It Snow! Let It Snow!," and Mel Tormé's "Christmas Song," which absolutely must be heard to be believed.

influences:

◀◀ Miles Davis, Louis Prima, Carlos Arruza, Dizzy Gillespie, Tito Puente

▶▶ Sergio Mendes, Chuck Mangione

see also: *The Baja Marimba Band*

Gary Pig Gold

Cocktail Classics

Alexander's Ragtime Band

18-Karat **Ella Fitzgerald** *The Irving Berlin Songbook* (Verve)

Bombsville! **Liza Minnelli** *At Carnegie Hall* (Telarc)

Joey Altruda with the Cocktail Crew /Jump with Joey

Formed 1989, in Los Angeles, CA.

Joe Altruda, upright bass; Dave Ralicke, trombone; Bill Ungerman, saxophone; Mike Boito, keyboards; Jason Goodman, guitar; Willie McNeil, drums; Elliott Caine, trumpet.

Technically a ska band, Jump with Joey mixes in enough swing and mambo rhythms to make even its most reggae-heavy albums sound like lounge music. Altruda's band, which originally released most of its albums in Japan and once recorded with the pioneering reggae producer Clement "Sir Coxsone" Dodd, finally succumbed to the inevitable. The upright bassist created the alternate identity Joey Altruda with the Cocktail Crew, and recorded such Perez Prado–inspired songs as "Cha Cha #69"— which landed on his solo album and the lounge-revival *Swingers* soundtrack. Altruda is terrific at stitching together several different, seemingly disparate styles of music, and like all good soundtrack artists, he knows how to shift a mood. The only problem is, few of his songs leap out at you in a particularly distinctive way.

what to buy: *Cocktails with Joey* ♫♫♫ (Will, 1995) showcases the 18-piece Mambo Noir Orchestra, and relies on sprightly bongos, Hammond organs, vibraphones, and horns; some of this stuff may seem familiar, because "A Martini for Mancini" was in the comedy *Spy Hard* and "Mucci's Jag MK II" wound up in *Swingers*.

what to buy next: Despite album titles such as *Ska-Ba*, Jump with Joey's music has just as much lounge as ska; an excellent sampler of the Japanese releases is *Come . . .* ♫♫♫ (Rykodisc, 1997, prod. various), which includes five songs produced by the veteran reggae studio whiz Dodd.

what to avoid: *Ska-Ba* ♫♫ (Rykodisc, 1997, prod. Joe Altruda) isn't sure whether it wants to be ska, lounge, or mambo, and good songs like "Ton Tok" and "Whitey Palmer" never quite hit their potential.

the rest:
Strictly for You, Vol. 2 ♫♫♫ (Rykodisc, 1997)
Generations United ♫♫♥ (Rykodisc, 1997)

worth searching for: *The Winner Original Soundtrack* ♫♫♥ (Rykodisc, 1997, prod. Carol Sue Baker) is less punchy, despite the presence of "Cha Cha #69," because the moods of the Rebecca DeMornay–Vincent D'Onofrio movie score were so downbeat.

influences:
◀◀ The Specials, Madness, Juan Garcia Esquivel, Tito Puente, Perez Prado, Dizzy Gillespie, Martin Denny, Bob Marley

▶▶ Combustible Edison, Squirrel Nut Zippers, Royal Crown Revue, Mighty Mighty Bosstones, No Doubt

Steve Knopper

The Ames Brothers /Ed Ames

Formed 1948, in Malden, MA. Disbanded 1960.

Joe Ames (born Joe Urick, May 3, 1924, in Malden, MA), vocals; Gene Ames (born Gene Urick, February 13, 1925, in Malden, MA), vocals; Vic Ames (born Vic Urick, May 20, 1926, in Malden, MA; died January 23, 1978, in Nashville, TN), vocals; Ed Ames (born Ed Urick, July 9, 1927, in Malden, MA), vocals.

The Ames Brothers were, hands down, the most popular vocal group of the late '40s through the mid-'50s. Their uncluttered harmonies and playful stage antics entertained millions and prepped mainstream audiences for the doo-wop sounds of later rock 'n' roll. Whether singing in close baritone harmony on slow romantic numbers or letting all the stops out, college-style, on bouncy novelties, the Ames Brothers mixed interpretive poise with irresistible enthusiasm. Other acts, such as the Four Freshmen, may have blended their harmonies with more technical skill, but they weren't half as crowd-pleasing or successful as the Ames Brothers.

Singing together since the late '30s, the Urick Brothers changed their name to Ames and turned pro after winning several amateur contests in the Boston area. Commercial success came quickly for the group. Their first single on Signature Records, "A Tree in the Meadow," hit the Top 20 and led to a more lucrative contract with Coral. After several lesser chart entries, the brothers hit #1 with two of their best-remembered songs, "Ragmop" and "Sentimental Me." Their vigorous stage style and brother Vic's incessant clowning made them a natural for early TV, and appearances on the Jackie Gleason, Milton Berle, Ed Sullivan, and Perry Como shows eventually led to their own network variety series. With RCA in 1953, the Ameses released their two biggest-selling discs, "You, You, You" and "The Naughty Lady of Shady Lane." The former inspired Sid Caesar (along with Carl Reiner and Howard Morris) to parody their exuberant style with his classic send-up, the Three Haircuts. By the time they retired the act in 1960, the brothers had racked up more than 50 chart singles.

On his own, Ed Ames set out to be an interpreter of serious music. His expressive baritone brought unusual sincerity to the hits "My Cup Runneth Over," "Who Will Answer" (the first protest song to make middle-of-the-road radio playlists), and "Try to Remember." Though he recorded a dozen chart LPs for RCA, Ed Ames is best remembered as "Mingo" in the *Daniel Boone* TV series, and for the hilarity surrounding his famous hatchet throw (into the crotch of a male chalk outline) on Johnny Carson's *Tonight Show*. The youngest of his famous family, Ed Ames is still performing to enthusiastic worldwide audiences.

what's available: The group's biggest hits are on *The Best of the Ames Brothers* ♫♫♫♫ (Varese Vintage, 1995, compilation prod. Cary E. Mansfield), which contains a detailed, informative booklet. Almost as good, *Sentimental Me: The Best of the Ames Brothers* ♫♫♫ (Pair, 1988, prod. various) has fewer tracks and is harder to find.

solo outings:
Ed Ames:
My Cup Runneth Over ♫♫♫ (RCA, 1967/1994)
Who Will Answer/My Cup Runneth Over ♫♫♫ (Collectables, 1997)

influences:
◀◀ The Mills Brothers, the Ink Spots

▶▶ The Four Lads, the Four Preps, the Four Freshmen, the Three Haircuts, the Kirby Stone Four

Ken Burke

Leroy Anderson
Born June 29, 1908, in Cambridge, MA. Died May 18, 1975, in Woodbury, CT.

For a man with such a serious resume—he could speak nine languages, including Icelandic, fluently, and he earned a music degree at Harvard University—Anderson sure made playful music. His catchy, light songs were unmistakably classical, with strings, flutes, orchestras, and crescendos, but they approximated the sound of typewriters clacking, alarm clocks ringing, and cats waltzing. His relentlessly upbeat 1938 composition, "Jazz Pizzicato," was a staple of his friend Arthur Fiedler's Boston Pops Orchestra; "Blue Tango" became an inescapable hit in 1952. Originally a trombonist (because his father wanted him to have good seats at football games), Anderson studied music at Harvard and played at dances and churches. After waffling between music and language careers for several years, earning prominent academic degrees in both fields, he finally graduated from Harvard Band arranger to the Boston Symphony. Fiedler heard him from there and enthusiastically started a partnership, which lasted well into the 1950s. During that decade, Anderson led a 55-musician orchestra, recording short, simple tunes that captured straightforward emotions impeccably—and using simple gimmicks, such as a real typewriter behind 1953's "The Typewriter." His philosophy, too, was simple: "I just did what I wanted to do," he said in 1997 liner notes, "and it turned out that people like it."

what's available: Anderson recorded many singles and albums, but most of them were out of print until *The Best of Leroy Anderson: Sleigh Ride* ♫♫♫ (MCA, 1997, prod. Israel Horowitz)—a 20-song set of soft, playful music, including the snappy hit "Blue Tango," the melancholy "Summer Skies," the ticking-and-ringing "The Syncopated Clock," and, of course, the well-titled "Plink, Plank, Plunk!" There are other collections, such as *Fiddle Faddle* ♫♫ (Analogue Productions) and *Greatest Hits: Blue Tango* ♫♫♫ (Pro Arte Maxiplay), but they cover the same ground with inferior packaging and are harder to find.

influences:
◀◀ Nelson Riddle, Billy May

▶▶ Mantovani, Ray Conniff, Gordon Jenkins

see also: *Arthur Fiedler*

Steve Knopper

Julie Andrews
Born Julia Elizabeth Wells, October 1, 1935, in Walton-on-Thames, England.

Andrews is the spoonful of sugar that has helped several generations down the medicine of good, wholesome family entertainment. Whether playing a novice in *The Sound of Music* or the ultimate nanny in *Mary Poppins,* Andrews's innocent image always fit her crystalline soprano voice, which could scale four and a half octaves. A child star on the British music-hall stage, Andrews became a Broadway phenom at age 19, and conquered the silver screen several years later. Musicals were her forte, and her career dipped in the '70s as the form became less popular, and she was unable to convert her stage and screen success into a solo recording career. She made a comeback after her marriage to director Blake Edwards, though, playing against type in his films *10, S.O.B.* (where she bared her breasts), and *Victor/Victoria,* where she played the challenging gender-bending role of a woman playing a man playing a woman. Through it all, Andrews's voice has remained magnificent; it is one of the definitive instruments of the Broadway stage and movie musicals.

what to buy: *The Best of Julie Andrews* ♫♫♫ (Rhino, 1996, prod. various) compiles tracks from the original cast recordings of *Camelot* and *My Fair Lady* and the soundtracks of *Mary Poppins, The Sound of Music,* and *Thoroughly Modern Millie,* and it's laid end-to-end with classics like "I Could Have Danced All Night," "Wouldn't It Be Lovely," "Super-cali-fragil-istic-expi-alidocious," "The Sound of Music," and "My Favorite Things."

what to buy next: A beautiful tribute to one of the stage's great lyricists, *Broadway: Here I'll Stay—The Words of Alan Jay Lerner* ♫♫♫ (Philips, 1996, prod. Jay David Saks) finds Andrews singing new renditions of selections from *Camelot, My Fair Lady, On a Clear Day You Can See Forever,* and other classics. The Grammy-nominated *Broadway* ♫♫♫ (Philips, 1994) offers still more show tunes, including "Oh, What a Beautiful Morning" and "Eidelweiss."

the rest:
A Little Bit of Broadway ♫♫♫ (Columbia, 1988)
A Christmas Treasure ♫♫♫♫ (RCA, 1990)
(With Bob Florence) *Love, Julie* ♫♫♫ (USA, 1993)

worth searching for: Diehard Andrews fans will want to seek out most of Andrews's cast recordings and soundtracks. The recently rereleased soundtrack from *Mary Poppins* ♫♫♫♫ (Disney, 1997) includes previously unreleased demos and archival material.

influences:

◀◀ Mary Martin, Fanny Brice, Ethel Merman, Judy Garland

▶▶ Barbra Streisand, Linda Eder

see also: *Carol Channing, Richard Rodgers*

Daniel Durchholz

The Andrews Sisters

Formed 1930s, in New York City, NY.

Laverne Andrews (born July 6, 1915, in Minneapolis, MN), vocals; Maxine Andrews (born January 3, 1918, in Minneapolis, MN), vocals; Patti Andrews (born February 16, 1920, in Minneapolis, MN), vocals.

With their close harmonies and all-American looks, the Andrews Sisters were so popular in the 1940s their sound came to define World War II Americana. Shortly after starting their careers with a small orchestra in New York, they made it big with their first hit, "Bei Mir Bish Du Shoen," in 1937 and later achieved virtual immortality with "Boogie Woogie Bugle Boy" in 1941. For the next decade, they toured the country and appeared in films—playing themselves—with actors such as Bing Crosby, in films like 1947's *The Road to Rio.* Although some listeners are bound to dismiss the Andrews Sisters as 1940s malt-shop Muzak, a closer listen shows their harmonies are surprisingly complex. And no one can deny the girls have a gift for swing. With the possible exception of the Manhattan Transfer, there hasn't been a vocal group like it in the 40 years since the Sisters were at the top of the charts. While a little Andrews Sisters can go a long way, the group demonstrates that even wartime nostalgia can be endearing.

what to buy: *50th Anniversary Collection, Vols. 1 & 2* ♫♫♫♫ (MCA, 1987) is the best retrospective of the Andrews Sisters' career, complete with the standards that made them famous, as well as some rarer renditions of "Tuxedo Junction" and "Sing, Sing, Sing." *Their All-Time Greatest Hits* ♫♫♫♫ (Decca MCA, 1994), a comprehensive two-disc set, is a good buy for listeners who are already devoted fans of the group.

what to buy next: *The Andrews Sisters* ♫♫♫ (ASV, 1992) features annoyingly short recordings, but also offers a good overview of the trio's work. It's a good purchase for listeners just being introduced to the group.

best of the rest:
Andrews Sisters Greatest Hits: The 60th Anniversary Collection ♫♫♫♫ (MCA, 1998)

worth searching for: *Rum & Coca-Cola* ♫♫♫ (Golden Stars, 1996) is a collection of the Andrews Sisters' best-known work. Not exactly inventive in its inclusion of music, but features good recordings of "Pennsylvania Polka" and "Shortenin' Bread."

influences:
◀◀ Ella Fitzgerald, Bing Crosby

▶▶ Lambert, Hendricks & Ross, the Manhattan Transfer, Mel Tormé and the Mel-Tones

Carl Quintanilla

Maya Angelou

Born Marguerite Johnson, April 4, 1928, in St. Louis, MO.

Decades before she read poetry at President Clinton's Inauguration, Angelou made a pretty fair living as a calypso singer. Her gospel-trained voice, cute songs, and dramatic presentation made a powerful impact on the cabaret circuit. Working an extended gig at the Purple Onion in San Francisco, Angelou drew rave reviews and steady crowds of college kids who viewed calypso as the ultimate rhythmic folk music. Her success in clubs led to a featured role in the off-Broadway musical *Calypso Heat Wave* as well as in its 1957 film version. However, not many artists—outside of Harry Belafonte—were able to use calypso as a springboard to lasting fame. When the fad dissipated, Angelou began her career as a historian, screenwriter, poet, and character actress. She didn't abandon music,

The Andrews Sisters (AP/Wide World Photos)

though. Angelou wrote songs for Sidney Poitier's *For the Love of Ivy*, as well as tunes for soul singer Roberta Flack. A Pulitzer Prize–nominated author, Angelou has found time to win an Emmy nomination for her performance in the TV mini-series *Roots*; earn a Tony nomination for *Look Away*; and make well-received appearances in films such as *How to Make an American Quilt* and *Poetic Justice*.

what to buy: Angelou wrote nearly half the songs on *Miss Calypso* ♫♫♫ (Liberty, 1956/Scamp, 1996, reissue prod. Ashley Warren), a fine reproduction of her lone musical LP. The bongo-and-conga patterns perfectly accent Tommy Tedesco's guitar work, and Angelou's vocals are first-rate.

the rest:
Black Pearls: The Poetry of Maya Angelou N/A (Rhino WordBeat, 1998)

worth searching for: Angelou contributes solid vocals to Herbie Mann's excellent jazz disc *Evolution of Mann* ♫♫♫ (Atlantic, 1960/Rhino, 1992, prod. Herbie Mann, Frank Socolow, Pat Rebilot). Most people know Angelou as a distinguished best-selling writer, whose books include the compelling autobiographies *I Know Why the Caged Bird Sings* ♫♫♫ (Random House Audio Books, 1996) and *Wouldn't Take Nothing for My Journey Now* ♫♫♫ (Random House Audio Books, 1993), as well as the poem she read at Clinton's inauguration, *On the Pulse of the Morning* ♫♫♫ (Random House Audio Books, 1993).

influences:

◀◀ Harry Belafonte, Mahalia Jackson

▶▶ Cicely Tyson, Rita Dove, Roberta Flack

Ken Burke

Paul Anka

Born July 30, 1941, in Ottawa, Ontario, Canada.

If for nothing else, Anka deserves credit for being one of the few late-1950s teen idols who actually wrote his own material, and as a result he maintained a healthy career (and bank balance) long after all the other Frankies and Bobbys had faded into *Bandstand* oblivion. Nevertheless, after having composed more than 400 songs, racked up 53 hit singles, and sold more than 100 million records worldwide, Anka has never really been able to raise his artistic standing above that of old pals like Fabian.

Since his first public appearances as a child, impersonating Johnnie Ray at local talent contests, Anka seems to have been driven by an ambition to succeed in show business at all costs,

whatever the price. Writing songs and leading vocal groups while still in high school, spending summers with an uncle in Los Angeles, collecting enough Campbell's soup can labels to win a trip to New York City, he was eventually signed at age 16 to ABC Paramount Records on the strength of a song he'd written about the family babysitter he was sweet on. "I'm so young and you're so old," the voice gulped, and within a year "Diana" had become one of the biggest and fastest-selling records of the era. This was quickly followed by another international hit, "You Are My Destiny," an appearance alongside Mamie Van Doren and Mel Tormé in the B-movie "Girls Town," and a highly publicized fling with fellow teen sensation Annette Funicello.

As the 1960s dawned, Anka wisely began to diversify into more "adult" markets, appearing in and scoring the World War II epic "The Longest Day," signing a new million-dollar contract with RCA Records, and becoming the youngest performer ever to headline at New York's Copacabana nightclub. As with most of his ilk, however, the Beatles soon put an end to Anka's days in the Top Ten, yet he remained active with selected club and film work while his theme for Johnny Carson's *The Tonight Show* kept the cash flowing. In 1969, he threw English lyrics atop a Claude Francois ballad, Frank Sinatra agreed to record it, and "My Way" became yet another feather in Anka's cap. (Also highly recommended are versions by Elvis Presley and the Sex Pistols' Sid Vicious.) Two years later, he recorded one of his greatest-ever slices of classic schmaltz: "(You're) Having My Baby" gave Anka his first #1 hit in more than a decade, despite howls of protest from the National Organization of Women, which awarded him its Keep Her In Her Place citation for 1974. (Duly chastised, he revised the lyrics to "You're Having *Our* Baby" on stage.) Anka has since skipped from label to label, worked with such MOR icons as Peter Cetera, Kenny G, and David Foster, become a U.S. citizen and NHL franchise team owner, played an ex-con on *Perry Mason,* and continues to tour the world when not appearing in his adopted hometown of, naturally, Lake Tahoe, Nevada.

what to buy: Anka has released more than 70 albums—but even the most discriminating listener really only needs the ably assembled *30th Anniversary Collection* ♫♫♫ (Rhino, 1989, prod. various). Every hit and miss, from "Diana" to "My Way," is included for your dining and dancing pleasure.

what to buy next: True aficionados of the Anka oeuvre may also be tempted toward *The Best of the United Artists Years, 1973–1977* ♫♫ (EMI America, 1996, prod. Ron Furmanek); better still is the (unintentionally) hilarious *Amigos* ♫♫♫ (Sony International /Globo Records, 1996, prod. various), wherein Anka croons his hits in pigeon-toed Spanish alongside such notable amigos as Julio Iglesias, Barry Gibb, and Ofra Haza. Similarly, *Paul Anka in Vegas* 🎵🎵 (Laserlight/Delta, 1995) is a hoot and a half, with its opening decimation of "This Land Is Your Land" followed by an ill-advised Stevie Wonder/Ray Charles medley.

what to avoid: Besides the many skimpy best-of collections issued recently by Curb Records, the still widely available *21 Golden Hits* **woof!** (RCA, 1963, prod. Joe Sherman) is a wholly redundant set of re-recordings of ABC material, possibly whipped out in a single afternoon to butter up Anka's new RCA bosses.

the rest:
Live 🎵🎵 (GNP Crescendo, 1975)
Remember Diana 🎵 (RCA, 1975)
Diana and Other Hits 🎵 (RCA, 1976)

worth searching for: In the throes of Disney-sanctioned puppy love, Anka composed all of the material on the utterly charming *Annette Sings Anka* 🎵🎵🎵 (Buena Vista, 1960, prod. Tutti Camarata), which rightfully became the Mouseketeer's highest-ever charting album. Also, the Canadian documentary film *Lonely Boy* is utterly fascinating, surprisingly candid, and was supposedly an influence on Richard Lester's *A Hard Day's Night*; it's available on a White Star budget video called *Paul Anka '62*.

influences:
◀◀ Bobby Darin, Frank Sinatra

▶▶ Neil Diamond, Barry Manilow, Bobby Bittman

Gary Pig Gold

Ann-Margret

Born Ann-Margaret Olsson, April 28, 1941, in Valsjobyn, Jamtland, Sweden.

Despite her singing and acting accomplishments, Ann-Margret is still badgered by interviewers more interested in this one-time sex kitten's trysts with Elvis Presley. Her irresistible fuzzy sweaters, burning red hair, and provocative rear-wiggling with Presley in the 1964 movie *Viva Las Vegas*—kept alive by endless Nick at Nite reruns—remain her most enduring pop-culture image. But she also earned five Golden Globe awards for her movie work, and was Oscar-nominated for her memorable sexy-older-woman portrayal of stewardess Bobbie Templeton in the 1971 classic *Carnal Knowledge*. After fronting a jazz trio called the Suttletones, the 19-year-old singer wound up performing on *The Jack Benny Show,* where comedian George

Cocktail Classics

Autumn Leaves

18-Karat **Cannonball Adderley**
Mercy, Mercy, Mercy!
Live at "The Club"
(EMI)

Bombsville! **Ferrante & Teicher**
Autumn Leaves
(Sony)

Burns spotted her, asked her to perform with him in Las Vegas, and advised her to dump the mousy stage outfits for tights and sweaters. Movie scouts took over from there, and, after landing many movie and singing gigs, she became a major American pinup girl. (Some Vietnam veterans still slobber over the memory of her "Suzie Q" performance during an overseas Bob Hope visit.) She had a nice singing voice, which landed several hits—including 1962's "Thirteen Men," a finger-snapping number about nuclear holocaust. An onstage fall in the late 1960s required plastic surgery; then she disappeared, only to return as the horrific mother in Ken Russell's 1975 film version of the Who's rock opera *Tommy*. Her most memorable work since then has come in TV movies, a bestselling biogra-

phy (*Ann-Margret: My Story*), and her Ann-Margrock role in *The Flintstones*.

what's available: Saving listeners the trouble of tracking down all the out-of-print 1960s LPs, *Let Me Entertain You* ♫♫♫ (RCA, 1996, prod. various) collects most of the singer's sprightly pop hits. As a singer, Ann-Margret's primary strength is sex, which she uses to great effect on come-hither numbers like "Let Me Entertain You" and "Lovin' Spree." It's obvious on rock songs (such as Presley's "Heartbreak Hotel") and soul songs (Otis Blackwell's "Slowly") that her singing talent was limited. But with the right material, such as the snappy "Thirteen Men," she actually sings with power and style. And guys won't want to miss the generous helping of vintage pictures.

worth searching for: The singer's leering pinups—a clear antecedent to the famous Farrah Fawcett 1970s poster and the Spice Girls' entire career—are the main reason for buying her original 1960s albums. "Thirteen Men" shows up on *The Vivacious One* ♫♫ (RCA Victor, 1962, prod. Dick Peirce), but unless you're a hardcore collector, we recommend finding the same song on *Cocktail Mix, Vol. 2: Martini Madness* ♫♫♫♫ (Rhino, 1996, prod. various), where you also get Perez Prado, Les Elgart, and Sergio Mendes.

influences:

◀◀ Elvis Presley, Rosemary Clooney, Doris Day, George Burns, Nancy Wilson

▶▶ The Spice Girls, Madonna, Farrah Fawcett, Mariah Carey

Steve Knopper

Ray Anthony

Born Raymond Antonini, January 20, 1922, in Bentleyville, PA.

Anthony is one of the most vital living links to the big-band era. A young trumpet player in the Al Donahue, Glenn Miller, and Jimmy Dorsey orchestras, Anthony formed his own band after World War II and was able to keep it alive and flourishing well into rock 'n' roll's heyday. Besides blowing a cool Harry James–inspired trumpet, when his band's regular singers, the Skyliners and Tommy Mercer, went on break, Anthony sang with warmth and humor. Recording for Capitol, Anthony's orchestra scored its first hits in 1950 with "Sentimental Me," "Count Every Star," and "Harbor Lights," but really hit it big

when "The Bunny Hop" inspired a national dance craze. Anthony himself achieved a bit of pop-culture immortality when he co-wrote the hit theme for Jack Webb's classic TV cop show *Dragnet* in 1953. Anthony's band was able to play both the reed-oriented Glenn Miller–era standards and pick up on the brassier new pop sounds of the burgeoning rock 'n' roll scene. His popularity spread to Hollywood, where he wrote a paean to the reigning movie goddess Marilyn Monroe and appeared in movies such as 1955's *Daddy Long Legs* (with Fred Astaire) and 1956's *The Girl Can't Help It*. This won the handsome Anthony even more fans, including his soon-to-be-wife, B-movie Monroe-wannabe Mamie Van Doren. Anthony appeared in 15 films and even got a chance to portray his old boss Jimmy Dorsey in the 1959 Red Nichols biopic *The Five Pennies*. Anthony's orchestra had a few more hits in the late '50s with "Skokiaan" and Henry Mancini's "Peter Gunn Theme," but was unable to keep a large orchestra going into the '60s. He continued recording with a sextet until his departure from Capitol (where he recorded nearly 100 albums) in 1968. These days, besides re-releasing his classic masters on his new record label and cutting fresh tracks, the never-idle Anthony vigilantly promotes the resurgence of big-band sounds on the radio.

what to buy: The best introduction to Anthony's work is provided by *Ray Anthony: Capitol Collector's Series* ♫♫♫ (Gold Rush 1991/1996, compilation prod. Bob Furmanek, Ron Furmanek), a 22-track disc with his hits "(The Theme from) Dragnet," "Theme from Peter Gunn," "The Bunny Hop," and many more.

what to buy next: Short on hit power but long on first-rate music, *Swing Back to the '40s* ♫♫♫ (Aero Space Records, 1991, reissue prod. Ray Anthony) and *Young Man with a Horn, 1952–54* ♫♫♫ (Hindsight, 1988/1993, compilation prod. Thomas Gramuglia) contain the swinging cream of Anthony's crop.

what to avoid: Anthony has the pedigree, but lacks inspiration on *I Remember Glenn Miller* ♫♫ (Aero Space Records, 1953/1993, reissue prod. Ray Anthony), a by-the-numbers tribute LP. And there's just no excuse for *Macarena Dance Party* ♫♫ (Aero Space Records, 1996, prod. Ray Anthony).

the rest:
Jam Session at the Tower ♫♫♫ (Aero Space Records, 1953/1990)
Sweet & Swingin' 1943–53 ♫♫ (Circle 1953/1991)
Hits of Ray Anthony ♫♫♫ (Capitol/EMI, 1989)
1988 & All That Jazz ♫♫ (Aero Space Records, 1990)
Dancing in the Dark ♫♫ (Aero Space Record, 1990/1997)
Hooked on Big Bands ♫♫ (Aero Space Records, 1990/1995)
Dance Party ♫♫ (Aero Space Records, 1990/1995)
In the Miller Mood ♫♫ (Aero Space Records, 1992)

Ann-Margret **(AP/Wide World Photos)**

Dancing & Dreaming 🎵🎵 (Pair, 1992)
In the Miller Mood, Vol. 2 🎵🎵 (Aero Space Records, 1993)
Dream Dancing 2 🎵🎵🎵 (Aero Space Records, 1994)
Touch Dancing 🎵🎵 (Aero Space Records, 1995)
Swing's the Thing 🎵🎵🎵 (Aero Space Records, 1995)
Dancing Alone Together/Dream Dancing Around the World 🎵🎵🎵 (Aero Space Records, 1995)
Dream Dancing Christmas 🎵🎵🎵 (Aero Space Records, 1995)
Tenderly 🎵🎵 (Aero Space, 1995)
Boogie Blues & Ballads 🎵🎵🎵 (Aero Space Records, 1997)
Dream Dancing in Hawaii 🎵🎵🎵 (Aero Space Records, 1997)
Trip through 50 Years of Music 🎵🎵🎵🎵 (Aero Space Records, 1997)
Dirty Trumpet for a Swinging Party 🎵🎵🎵🎵 (Aero Space Records, 1997)

worth searching for: Anthony aficionados who own a VCR will probably dig *Club Anthony* 🎵🎵🎵 (Aero Space Video, 1995, prod. Ray Anthony), a nice video showcase featuring Red Norvo, Vikki Carr, and an all-star big band.

influences:

◀◀ Glenn Miller, Harry James, Billy May

▶▶ Al Hirt, Mamie Van Doren, Doc Severinsen

Ken Burke

Harold Arlen

Born Hyman Arluck, February 15, 1905, in Buffalo, NY. Died April 23, 1986, in New York City, NY.

Pop-music history is full of stories about singers and songwriters absorbing the gospel music they heard in church; well, Arlen learned how to perform from his father, a cantor at a Buffalo synagogue. Though his parents encouraged him to get a respectable job as a music teacher, Arlen instead wrote (with other lyricists, most notably Ted Koehler) some of this century's most familiar standards: "Over the Rainbow," "Stormy Weather," "Let's Fall in Love," "Ac-cent-tchu-ate the Positive," and "Get Happy." Like Cole Porter and other more heralded songwriters, Arlen did most of his work for Broadway musicals and, later, movies. He and Koehler penned *I've Got the World on a String*, to name one of many shows, while scoring Cotton Club revues. Later, Arlen and lyricist E.Y. Harburg earned an Oscar for *The Wizard of Oz*, which launched Judy Garland's acting and singing career as well as the dreamiest song of the 1930s. His flops were sensational—though he co-wrote excellent scores for *St. Louis Woman* and *House of Flowers* with Johnny Mercer and author Truman Capote, respectively, both shows took box-office dives. But his successes were even better—his music helped *Jamaica* become a Broadway smash late

in the 1950s, and he earned Oscar nominations through the mid-1950s.

what to buy: You won't find many albums with Arlen performing his own songs, but maybe you'd settle for Ella Fitzgerald or Rosemary Clooney. Fitzgerald recorded several volumes of Arlen's work, including "Let's Fall in Love" and "Over the Rainbow," of course, in the early 1960s—the best CD reissue is *Harold Arlen Songbook* 🎵🎵🎵🎵 (Verve, 1961/1990, prod. Norman Granz). *Rosemary Clooney Sings the Music of Harold Arlen* 🎵🎵🎵 (Concord Jazz, 1983, prod. Carl E. Jefferson) is more straightforward but less shimmering than Fitzgerald's work.

what to avoid: Much more corny is pianist Andre Previn's *Come Rain or Come Shine: The Harold Arlen Songbook* 🎵🎵 (Philips Classics), a pop-classical tribute album featuring soprano singer Sylvia McNair.

best of the rest:
Dick Hyman: *Harold Arlen Songs: Blues in the Night* 🎵🎵🎵 (Musicmasters, 1990)

worth searching for: *Harold Sings Arlen (With Friend)* 🎵🎵🎵 (Vox Cum Laude, 1966) is difficult to find, but it's nice to hear Arlen's own voice (and, oh yes, it includes collaborations with Duke Ellington and Barbra Streisand).

influences:

◀◀ Cole Porter, Irving Berlin, Hoagy Carmichael, Scott Joplin, Art Tatum

▶▶ Ella Fitzgerald, Johnny Mercer, Barbra Streisand, Rosemary Clooney, Neil Diamond

Steve Knopper

Louis Armstrong

Born August 4, 1901, in New Orleans, LA. Died July 6, 1971, in New York, NY.

Despite his groundbreaking career and his serious reputation as one of the giants of 20th-century music, Armstrong had a warm, exuberant sense of humor. As a result, for every "What a Wonderful World"—the moving R&B hit that took on new life after its inclusion in the film *Good Morning, Vietnam*—he pulled off a comedic vamp like the playful Dixieland-in-a-stripjoint "Heebie Jeebies." Or he transformed the Kurt Weill showtune "Mack the Knife" into a humor anthem simply by shouting, exuberantly, "Take it, Satch!" before a trumpet solo. (Neither Bobby Darin nor Frank Sinatra ever wrenched as much fun out of it.) Armstrong's gruff, personable voice had immeasurable soul, of course, but his trademark bulging eyes and gigantic smile gave his music a vaudevillian, crowd-pleasing charm. And, like many early jazzmen, he focused on pop standards, like those written by Hoagy Carmichael and other major American songwriters. Born and raised in New Orleans as the jazz age was taking off, Armstrong was the first improviser to blend disparate riffs and accents into extended solos that hung together as unified musical statements. This was obvious during his early days with the King Oliver and Clarence Williams groups, but his recordings with his own bands—Hot Five and Hot Seven—are some of the most important works of any music. These were just studio bands, but their musical treatments took New Orleans jazz out of the collective improvisation mode into that of the featured solo improviser. Pieces such as "Potato Head Blues," "Hotter Than That," and "Cornet Chop Suey" set standards for improvisation and composition. Armstrong's unequaled technical mastery so overshadowed his contemporaries that he was held as a model for all to follow.

what to buy: Armstrong's early recordings are historic, and many of them are included on the four-CD set *Portrait of the Artist as a Young Man, 1923–1934* 🎵🎵🎵🎵🎵 (Columbia/Legacy, 1994, compilation prod. Nedra Olds-Neal). This is an essential Armstrong collection, with recordings from his Oliver and Williams days in addition to seminal collaborations with Bessie Smith ("St. Louis Blues"), Lonnie Johnson, Jimmie Rogers (yes, the country-western guy), and others. The Hot Five/Seven stuff is here, along with some of his early big band work. *The Complete Studio Recordings of Louis Armstrong and the All Stars* 🎵🎵🎵🎵🎵 (Mosaic, 1993, compilation prod. Michael Cuscuna) completes the picture with a six-CD set of Armstrong recordings spanning 1950–58. This is a great collection showing the band in top form with the likes of Earl Hines, Jack Teagarden, and Gene Krupa on board. Many of the standards ("Muskrat Ramble," "Struttin' with Some Barbecue," "Body and Soul," "Lazy River") are here, captured fresh without the burden of an audience to entertain. "Baby, Your Slip Is Showing" provides a taste of how Armstrong could still capture the old feeling. Both sets include excellent booklet essays and photos.

what to buy next: *Hot Fives and Hot Sevens—Vol. 2* 🎵🎵🎵🎵🎵 (CBS, 1926/Columbia, 1988, prod. various) shows Armstrong's first flush of maturity and defining of the art of jazz.

what to avoid: *What a Wonderful World* **woof!** (Decca, 1970, prod. Bob Thiele) contains little of what made Armstrong great, pandering to the rock generation with electric bass and guitar on covers that include "Give Peace a Chance" and "Everybody's Talking."

Cocktail Classics

Begin the Beguine

18-Karat **Les Paul**
The Complete Decca Trios—Plus (1936–47)
(Decca/MCA)

Bombsville! **Lawrence Welk**
Musical Anthology
(Ranwood)

the rest:
Louis Armstrong and Earl Hines 🎵🎵🎵🎵 (CBS, 1927/Columbia Jazz Masterpieces, 1989)
Disney Songs the Satchmo Way 🎵🎵🎵🎵 (Disneyland, 1968/Walt Disney Records, 1996)
The Essential Louis Armstrong 🎵🎵🎵🎵 (Vanguard, 1987)
Stardust 🎵🎵🎵🎵 (CBS, 1988)
Laughin' Louie 🎵🎵🎵 (RCA, 1989)
The Sullivan Years 🎵🎵 (TVT, 1990)
Mack the Knife 🎵🎵🎵🎵 (Pablo, 1990)
Rhythm Saved the World 🎵🎵🎵🎵 (Decca, 1991)
In Concert with Europe 1 🎵🎵🎵🎵 (RTE, 1992)
Blueberry Hill 🎵🎵🎵 (Milan, 1992)
The California Concerts 🎵🎵 (MCA, 1992)

Sings the Blues 🎵🎵🎵 (BMG, 1993)

Young Louis Armstrong (1930–1933) 🎵🎵 (BMG, 1993)

Louis Armstrong and His Friends (Pasadena Civic Auditorium, 1951) 🎵🎵 (GNP, 1993)

Happy Birthday Louis 🎵🎵🎵 (Omega, 1994)

Swing that Music 🎵🎵🎵 (Drive, 1994)

Pocketful of Dreams, Vol. III 🎵🎵🎵 (Decca, 1995)

Satchmo at Symphony Hall 🎵🎵🎵 (MCA, 1996)

worth searching for: *Ella Fitzgerald and Louis Armstrong* 🎵🎵🎵🎵 (Verve, 1957, prod. Norman Granz) offers a double treat with two of the world's greatest classic jazz singers swinging together. A great cast of Oscar Peterson, Herb Ellis, Ray Brown, and Buddy Rich back them up.

influences:

◀◀ Joe "King" Oliver, Buddy Bolden, Kid Rena

▶▶ Bix Beiderbecke, Dizzy Gillespie, Wynton Marsalis, Louis Prima, Victoria Williams, Buster Poindexter, Chicago, Blood, Sweat & Tears

Lawrence Gabriel

Desi Arnaz

Born Desiderio Alberto Arnaz y de Acha III, March 2, 1917, in Santiago, Cuba. Died December 2, 1986, in Del Mar, CA.

Best known as hot-headed Ricky Ricardo, the Latin bandleader with the wiseacre wife Lucy on the beloved sitcom *I Love Lucy,* Arnaz's frequent musical numbers on television were largely responsible for introducing the blazing sounds of conga and mambo to Middle America. Before his days as a sitcom star and studio mogul—he and his real-life wife, Lucille Ball, headed up Desilu Productions—Arnaz was an accomplished musician and bandleader. His first break came in 1938, when well-known Latin-jazz bandleader Xavier Cugat caught the Cuban emigre's act in Miami and asked him to join his band as a vocalist. A year later, Arnaz struck out on his own, heading the Desi Arnaz Orchestra. Audiences adored his band's infectious, if somewhat goofy, numbers, and Arnaz's charisma led to a role in the Broadway musical and movie *Too Many Girls,* where he met Ball. The two married in 1940. After a stint in the army for World War II, Arnaz resumed his musical career, recording most of his signature songs for Victor in the late 1940s before turning his attention full-time to *Lucy.* After 20 somewhat acrimonious, but profitable, years of "'splaining," Arnaz and Ball divorced in 1960. Arnaz, however, had left music permanently behind and lived in semi-retirement until his death from lung cancer in 1986.

what to buy: *The Best of Desi Arnaz: The Mambo King* 🎵🎵🎵🎵 (RCA, 1992, prod. Eli Oberstein, Russ Case, Walt Heebner, Herman Diaz Jr.) is a rollicking good time, including the raucous call-and-response "El Cumbanchero" and the melodic smash hit "Babalu."

what to buy next: Focusing on songs from 1946 to 1949, *Babalu (We Love Desi)* 🎵🎵🎵🎵 (RCA, 1996, prod. Paul Williams) covers the hits and includes some rarer tracks.

the rest:

Big Bands of Hollywood 🎵🎵 (Laserlight, 1992)

worth searching for: *Lucy* aficionado "Weird" Al Yankovic, who paid homage to Arnaz with his early-1980s parody hit "Hey Rickey," produced a collection of songs culled from *I Love Lucy* and Arnaz's 1951 radio show "Your Tropical Trip." *Babalu Music: I Love Lucy's Greatest Hits* 🎵🎵🎵 (Columbia, 1991, prod. "Weird" Al Yankovic) is fun, but overall the collection is weighed down by novelties like a duet with Bob Hope on "Nobody Loves the Ump" and a cast version of "Jingle Bells" dominated by Ball's signature shrill.

influences:

◀◀ Machito, Tito Puente, Xavier Cugat, Perez Prado, Les Elgart, Juan Garcia Esquivel

▶▶ Buster Poindexter, Gloria Estefan, "Weird Al" Yankovic

Alex Gordon

The Art of Noise

Formed 1983, in London, England. Disbanded 1990.

Anne Dudley, keyboards, string arrangements; J.J. Jeczalik, Fairlight, keyboards; Gary Langan, engineer (1983–86).

Hailed by hip-hop and techno musicians for its pioneering use of samplers as song construction tools rather than random noise boxes, the Art of Noise was formed in 1983 as a side project of studio wizards Jeczalik, Langan, and Dudley, who had been brought together by Trevor Horn for the production of Yes's *90125* album and Frankie Goes to Hollywood's *Welcome to the Pleasuredome* sessions. The band's sleepy, hypnotic electronic songs were some of the first stirrings of "ambient," a catch-all term for slow techno music; Dudley, who occasionally created environmental sounds for the Muzak company, was a

Desi Arnaz **(Archive Photos)**

link between old-school easy-listening music and the early-'90s rave-party scene. The group's first experiments, captured on *Into Battle* and *Who's Afraid?*, were catchy, arty instrumentals assembled almost entirely from pre-recorded sound snippets via Horn's newly purchased Fairlight sampling keyboard—one of the first such devices ever made. After scoring dance club and chart success with "Beat Box" and its drastically remixed counterpart, "Close (to the Edit)," the Art of Noise split from the ZTT camp in 1985 over creative differences. Its subsequent releases through China Records, although generally well received, included dodgy novelty collaborations (a dance track featuring manufactured media personality Max Headroom, a cover of Prince's "Kiss" featuring Tom Jones, and the Grammy-winning "Peter Gunn" remake with twang legend Duane Eddy), syrupy orchestral arrangements, and an uninteresting trough of remixes, compilations, and repeated reissues of the same material. An amicable parting in 1990 allowed Dudley and Jeczalik to pursue solo projects; Dudley continued her orchestral work for film soundtracks, while Jeczalik collaborated with Ten Years After's Alvin Lee before entering the techno scene in 1995–96 with the Art of Silence.

what to buy: An electronic music classic, the concept album *Who's Afraid Of? (The Art of Noise!)* 🎵🎵🎵🎵 (ZTT/Island, 1984, prod. Trevor Horn, Paul Morley, the Art of Noise) has itself been sampled by scores of musicians in tribute. *In Visible Silence* 🎵🎵🎵🎵 (China/Chrysalis/Off Beat, 1986, prod. the Art of Noise) is more accessible and equally competent, although it is markedly different from—in fact, almost a parody of—the band's ZTT-era sound. Although bombastic at times, *In No Sense? Nonsense!* 🎵🎵🎵 (China/Chrysalis, 1987, prod. Anne Dudley, J.J. Jeczalik) is an engaging, stereophonic tour de force, seamlessly gliding from string interludes to boys choirs to dance tracks and beyond; worlds away from "Beat Box," it is the cream of the post-ZTT Art of Noise.

what to buy next: Dismissed as "pretentious" by some critics, *Below the Waste* 🎵🎵 (China/Polydor, 1989, prod. Anne Dudley, J.J. Jeczalik) is the least experimental of the band's output but makes a good follow up to *In No Sense? Nonsense!* The African-influenced tracks—"Dan Dare," "Chain Gang," and "Yebo!"—are well worth the price.

what to avoid: All the post-ZTT cash-in compilations—*The Best of the Art of Noise* 🎵🎵 (China/Polydor, 1988/1997, prod. the Art of Noise), *The Ambient Collection* 🎵🎵 (China/Polydor, 1990/1997, prod. the Art of Noise), *The FON Mixes* 🎵🎵 (China, 1991/1997, prod. the Art of Noise), and *The Drum and Bass Col-*

lection 🎵 (China, 1997, prod. the Art of Noise)—are inferior representatives of the band's pioneering ideas. *The Ambient Collection*, however, interestingly bridges the gap between the old beautiful-music sounds of Ray Conniff and Percy Faith and the hip "electronica" styles of the Orb and some Moby and Aphex Twin albums.

the rest:
Into Battle with the Art of Noise 🎵🎵🎵 (ZTT/Island, 1983)
Re-Works of Art of Noise 🎵 (China/Chrysalis, 1986)
The Best of the Art of Noise 🎵🎵 (China, 1992)

worth searching for: The import-only compilation *Daft* 🎵🎵🎵🎵 (ZTT/Warner, 1986, prod. the Art of Noise) contains all of *Who's Afraid* . . . plus remixes of "Moments in Love" and a long version of "Snapshot."

solo outings:
Anne Dudley:
(With Jaz Coleman) *Songs from the Victorious City* 🎵🎵🎵 (China/Polydor/TVT, 1991)
(With Jaz Coleman) *Alice In Wonderland: Symphonic Variations* 🎵🎵🎵 (Sound Stage, 1994)
(With Jaz Coleman) *Ancient and Modern* 🎵🎵🎵 (The Echo Label, 1995)

J.J. Jeczalik:
The Art of Sampling 🎵🎵🎵 (AMG, 1994)
(With Art of Silence) *artofsilence.co.uk* 🎵🎵🎵🎵 (Permanent, 1996)

influences:
◄◄ Kraftwerk, Tangerine Dream, Mike Oldfield, John Cage, environmental noise recordings

►► Future Sound of London, the Orb, 808 State, William Orbit, Yello, Shinjuku Thief, Global Communication, Severed Heads

Mike Brown

The Association

Formed 1965, in Los Angeles, CA.

Terry Kirkman, vocals, keyboards; Gary "Jules" Alexander, vocals, guitar; Jim Yester, vocals, guitar; Russ Giguere, vocals, guitar; Brian Cole, vocals, bass; Ted Bluechel Jr., vocals, drums; Larry Ramos Jr., vocals, guitar, harmonica.

Despite its unquestionable vocal prowess and occasionally brilliant recordings, the Association is remembered today as little more than the voices behind some of the best Muzak ever produced. Hardly as hip as the Mamas and the Papas or as zany as the Turtles, the Association's biggest hits, all lushly crafted, soft-swinging ballads, epitomized all that felt plastic about the Southern California music scene in the mid-1960s. The group rose out of the legendary Monday night after-hour jams at the Troubadour club, where local scenesters Kirkman and Alexander formed a loose-knit affiliation with Bluechel and Cole called the Inner Tubes. (Giguere and Yester joined in mid-1965, and the band formally called itself the Association.) Their first hit, 1966's "Along Comes Mary," was a bizarre, rambling Tandyn Almer composition which hit the Top Ten—despite falling victim to the marijuana witchhunt then all the rage amongst balding non-Top 40 DJ's and bored Washington housewives. Kirkman's lovely "Cherish" topped the charts later that year, only to be followed by Alexander's wild semi-psychedelic romp "Pandora's Golden Heebie Jeebies," which the group considered a chart failure. Nevertheless, "Windy" put them back at #1 the next summer, quickly followed by one of the most-played songs in history, "Never My Love." Despite opening the legendary Monterey Pop Festival that June and making several overt stabs at social relevance on record (such as the anti-Vietnam War "Requiem for the Masses"), these two 1967 hits forever typecast the group as pop lightweights. Battles with producer Bones Howe, coupled with the band's fervent desire to become "heavy" and "progressive," forever doomed the group commercially. After a failed 1972 comeback album and Cole's heroin overdose, the band all but collapsed. In 1981, following a successful HBO television special, the original group reunited with Howe (and Ric Ulsky replacing Cole) to record for Elektra and duly head onto the golden moldies circuit.

what to buy: Still in print, and still selling respectfully year after year, *The Association's Greatest Hits!* 𝄞𝄞𝄞 (Warner Bros., 1968, prod. various) contains the only 13 songs one really requires.

what to avoid: A great argument in support of the maxim that reunited stars of yesteryear should restrict their activities to supper clubs and stay far from the recording studio, *Association 95: A Little Bit More* **woof!** (On Track, 1995, prod. Stan Vincent, John Allen) features mediocre versions of "Walk Away Renee" and the Nat King Cole hit "Nature Boy" (written by Eden Ahbez).

worth searching for: For a taste of the wacky yet intriguing "other side" of the band, *The Association's Golden Heebie Jeebies* 𝄞𝄞𝄞 (Edsel, 1987, prod. various) is a wonderful British compilation focusing on the kind of musical and lyrical tomfoolery that was unfortunately nipped in the bud thanks to "Never My Love" and so forth.

influences:
◀◀ The Hi-Lo's, Brian Wilson, Simon & Garfunkel

▶▶ The Carpenters, Bread, the Brady Kids

Gary Pig Gold

Fred Astaire

Born Franz Austerlitz, May 10, 1899, in Omaha, NB. Died June 22, 1987, in Los Angeles, CA.

Hard as it is to picture Astaire doing anything but lifting the gossamer Ginger Rogers through the air, the truth is that the "song" side of his "song-and-dance man" title is well worthy of rediscovery through his few CDs in release. Astaire began his professional career at age 5, starring in vaudeville with his sister, Adele. They performed in marginal shows on Broadway until composer George Gershwin wrote *Lady Be Good* for them in 1924, a show that skyrocketed Astaire's career. He appeared in the original versions of Gershwin's *Funny Face* and Cole Porter's *The Gay Divorcee*. And, of course, Hollywood eventually nabbed him. (One Tinseltown legend has it that casting directors, after his first screen test, wrote: "Can't act. Slightly bald. Also dances.") The Astaire music that has been collected is largely his film and stage soundtracks. Historians sometimes overlook his treatments of Gershwin's "Fascinating Rhythm" or Porter's "Night and Day"—both extremely skillful in their delivery. He manages a confident vocal presence even when surrounded by musicians of a much higher caliber. Moreover, there's something about that quaint, Midwestern accent that cloaks a very real sophistication in jazz singing. Astaire may never be noted among the great vocalists of his time, but he proves repeatedly he's more than a footnote.

what to buy: *Fred Astaire at MGM* 𝄞𝄞𝄞𝄞 (Rhino, 1997, prod. George Feltenstein, Bradley Flanagan), a two-disc set, has tons of rare and previously unreleased performances, including a good mix of familiar and obscure tunes. It's a good purchase for the solid Astaire fan. *Let's Sing and Dance with Fred Astaire* 𝄞𝄞𝄞𝄞 (Promo Sound, 1997) is a good original mix of Astaire tunes, including songs from *Top Hat* and *Swing Time*—two films for which Astaire is arguably most famous.

what to buy next: *Top Hat: Hits from Hollywood* 𝄞𝄞𝄞 (Columbia, 1994, compilation prod. Didier C. Deutsch) offers traditional Astaire tunes, but sounds better than many other albums that have repackaged the dancer-singer's career.

what to avoid: *Crazy Feet* 𝄞𝄞 (ASV, 1986) is an unremarkable collection of Astaire tunes—and short ones, at that. It's nothing you can't get from a more creative compilation.

best of the rest:

Puttin' on the Ritz 🎵🎵🎵 (Golden Stars, 1996)

worth searching for: The outstanding but hard-to-find collection *The Astaire Story* 🎵🎵🎵🎵 (Verve, 1988) has Astaire alongside bassist Ray Brown and pianist Oscar Peterson singing Gershwin and Porter tunes. Besides the fine digital remastering job, it features Astaire's personal liner notes. The import *The Incomparable Fred Astaire: Love of My Life* 🎵🎵🎵 (Halcyon, 1994, prod. John Wadley) is a respectable collection of tunes highlighting Astaire's flair for ballads. Finally, also difficult to dig up is *Nice Work: Fred Astaire Sings Gershwin* 🎵🎵🎵 (Conifer, 1989), with renditions of Fred singing with his sister, Adele, on some truly unknown Gershwin songs.

influences:

◀◀ Bill "Bojangles" Robinson

▶▶ Bing Crosby, Mel Tormé, Gene Kelly, Bobby Short

Carl Quintanilla

Gene Austin

Born Eugene Lucas, June 24, 1900, in Gainsville, TX. Died January 24, 1972, in Palm Springs, CA.

When popular music historians revisit the 1920s, they usually focus on blues, jazz, and other influential anthems of the downtrodden. Inexplicably forgotten are early-century crooners such as the tragic Russ Columbo and the massively successful Austin, best known for the smash "My Blue Heaven" and for selling more than 86 million singles between 1924 and 1942. Austin, known as "The Voice of the Southland," ran away from home as a teenager and joined the circus, which explains his unashamed vaudeville style—his Muppet-ish but wonderfully smooth voice, on recordings, is surrounded with playful swing horns and strummed guitars. When Bing Crosby came along in the early 1930s, Austin's musical profile dimmed and he downshifted into film. Austin wrote music for Mae West and several other actors, and he appeared in 1935's *Klondike Annie* and *Going Places*. Though his career died down up until his last appearance in 1971, his influence as one of the first (if not the first) crooners and his enduring songs, such as "The Lonesome Road," continue to be felt in mainstream pop music.

what's available: You can find most of Austin's classics, including "My Blue Heaven," "Carolina Moon," and "Girl of My

Dreams," on the 25-song *Voice of the Southland* 🎵🎵🎵 (Living Era, 1997, prod. various), which is really his only in-print career document. The excellent collection *Art Deco: The Crooners* 🎵🎵🎵🎵 (Columbia, Legacy, 1993, prod. various) includes Crosby, Columbo, Jack Teagarden, and a young Frank Sinatra, and pithy liner notes link all the artists together in historical context.

influences:

◀◀ Al Jolson

▶▶ Russ Columbo, Bing Crosby, Frank Sinatra, Rosemary Clooney, Mae West, Vic Damone, Rudy Vallee, Jack Jones

Steve Knopper

Fred Astaire (AP/Wide World Photos)

Patti Austin

Born August 10, 1948, in New York, NY.

Austin has one of the purest, most familiar voices in all of pop music—and she has paradoxically enjoyed even more success as the Unknown Voice in countless advertising jingles. A protege of both Dinah Washington and Sammy Davis Jr., Austin has been a pro since the age of five. In 1969, United Artists released her debut single "Family Tree," which was a hit in the Northeastern corridor. For Austin, however, "Family Tree" was aural Fool's Gold, as her career didn't quite take off. Instead she plunged into the profitable yet anonymous world of demos, jingles, and backup sessions, which are still her bread-and-butter gigs to this day. In 1976, Austin released her solo debut, *End of a Rainbow*, on CTI Records to the favor of the burgeoning progressive urban audience. The next year's followup, *Havana Candy*, made her an overgrown cult favorite. During this period, Austin sang on albums by Quincy Jones (*Sounds & Stuff*), George Benson (*Give Me the Night*), and Paul Simon (*One Trick Pony*). Austin's career took a quantum leap in 1981 when "Razzamatazz," from Jones's *The Dude*, went gold. Signed to Jones's Qwest label the following year, Austin enjoyed her only platinum success with the James Ingram duet "Baby Come to Me"; *Every Home Should Have One*, the corresponding LP, was also very successful. She recorded three more records for Qwest, but she never again reached those previous heights. Austin moved to GRP in 1990, and although she's still a radio favorite, her glory days with the general public seem to be over.

what to buy: *Every Home Should Have One* 𝄞𝄞𝄞𝄞 (Qwest, 1981, prod. Rod Temperton, Quincy Jones) is the crown jewel of Austin's career, a pop confection equal to Michael Jackson's epochal *Off the Wall* LP. *Live at the Bottom Line* 𝄞𝄞𝄞 (CTI, 1979, prod. Creed Taylor) is loose (epitomized by her wry country-western take on Randy Newman's "Rider in the Rain") and endearing, capturing Austin in a rare concert setting.

what to buy next: *The Ultimate Collection* 𝄞𝄞𝄞 (GRP, 1995, prod. various) is a good display of Austin in her most current incarnation.

the rest:
Havana Candy 𝄞𝄞𝄞 (CTI, 1977/Sony, 1997)
The Real Me 𝄞𝄞𝄞 (Qwest, 1988)
Love Is Gonna Getcha 𝄞𝄞𝄞 (GRP, 1990)
That Secret Place 𝄞𝄞𝄞 (GRP, 1994)
The Best of Patti Austin 𝄞𝄞𝄞 (Epic, 1994)

worth searching for: Austin has been a guest on plenty of albums, including the soundtrack to *The Blues Brothers* 𝄞𝄞𝄞 (Atlantic, 1980/1995).

influences:
◀◀ Dinah Washington, Dakota Staton, Barbara Lewis
▶▶ Phyllis Hyman, Luther Vandross, Siedah Garrett, Dianne Reeves

Tom Terrell and Gary Graff

Charles Aznavour

Born Varenagh Aznavourian, May 22, 1924, in Paris, France.

Armenian by decent, Parisian by birth, Aznavour typifies the European lounge singer, the guy whose hard drinking and chain smoking conceals a tender underbelly. Azvanour began to forge his tough-but-tender persona as a singer in the 1950s, drawing on French vocalists and American stars like Frank Sinatra, and he cemented the corresponding visuals—the cigarette, the melancholy visage—in such films as Truffaut's *Shoot the Piano Player*. His suave sentimentality has influenced a wide range of American performers, ranging from Tom Waits to Leonard Cohen; Azvanour was even mentioned in "11 Outlined Epitaphs," the liner notes to Bob Dylan's 1964 *Times They Are A-Changin'* LP. In addition to writing two books, *Aznavour by Aznavour* and *Yesterday When I Was Young*, Aznavour has continued to record and act regularly—one of his most winning performances came in the 1985 television show *Children's Songs & Stories with the Muppets*, which found the veteran performer playing alongside Jim Henson's popular felt creatures.

what to buy: Aznavour's catalog is filled with greatest hits sets and "golden years" compilations, along with reissues and the occasional new LP. A set of excellent originals elevate *Il Faut Savior* 𝄞𝄞𝄞𝄞 (Angel, 1995), including the title track, "Lucie," and "Alleluia."

what to buy next: *Je M'Voyais Deja* 𝄞𝄞𝄞𝄞 (Angel, 1995) features Gallicized versions of George Gershwin's "I've Got Plenty of Nuttin'" and "It Ain't Necessarily So," along with the usual complement of Aznavour's sophisticated lounge singing. And *You and Me* 𝄞𝄞𝄞 (Angel, 1995) is an English translation of *Toi et moi* 𝄞𝄞𝄞 (Angel, 1994), which includes such Aznavour originals as "Times We've Known" ("Les Bons Moments") and "Haunted House" ("La Maison hantée").

what to avoid: *Exitos Inolvidables* 𝄞𝄞 (International Music, 1997) collects Aznavour's Spanish songs, which represent the weakest part of his catalog.

Charles Aznavour (AP/Wide World Photos)

the rest:
65 ♫♫♫♪ (Angel, 1995)

worth searching for: Aznavour has always had a bit of Sinatra in him, and he appeared alongside Ol' Blue Eyes on Frank's *Duets* ♫♫♪ (Capitol, 1993, prod. Phil Ramone), an album more noteworthy for its gimmicky pairs than for the quality of its music. Aznavour's contribution? A playful duet on "You Make Me Feel So Young."

influences:
◀◀ Frank Sinatra
▶▶ Tom Waits, Leonard Cohen, Bob Dylan

Ben Greenman

Burt Bacharach

Born May 12, 1928, in Kansas City, MO.

Nearly three decades after the golden era of his work, and years after his last significant chart hit, Bacharach has become a cultural signifier of the mostly lost art of pop songwriting. And no wonder: his hits, many of which were written with lyricist Hal David, are complex mini-dramas, filled with odd time signatures, unconventional orchestrations, and innovative melodies. The pair wrote dozens of timeless tracks for a wide array of performers, including Marty Robbins, "The Story of My Life"; Gene Pitney, "24 Hours from Tulsa"; Tom Jones, "What's New Pussycat?"; Dusty Springfield, "The Look of Love"; Jerry Butler, "Make It Easy on Yourself"; the Carpenters, "(They Long to Be) Close to You"; and B.J. Thomas, "Raindrops Keep Fallin' on My Head," among others. Then there was Dionne Warwick, in whom the duo's muse came to full flower: "You'll Never Get to Heaven (If You Break My Heart)," "Alfie," "A House Is Not a Home," "Do You Know the Way to San Jose?," "Don't Make Me Over," "I Just Don't Know What to Do with Myself," "This Girl's in Love with You," and "I Say a Little Prayer," are some of the many hits they wrote for her. Bacharach and David split in the early '70s after their score for *Lost Horizon* sank like the embarrassing film it accompanied. Bacharach hit only sparsely after that, writing "On My Own" for Patti LaBelle with his third wife, Carole Bayer Sager, and "Arthur's Theme (The Best That You Can Do)" with Sager, Peter Allen, and Christopher Cross,

who sang it. Bacharach and Sager also wrote "That's What Friends Are For," which was originally sung by Rod Stewart over the credits of the film *Night Shift*, but was resurrected several years later by Dionne and Friends to benefit the American Foundation for AIDS Research. Inexplicably, a decade later, Bacharach is suddenly everywhere. He's on the soundtracks of *Austin Powers* (he made a campy cameo in the movie), *My Best Friend's Wedding,* and *Grace of My Heart* (he sang a duet with strange bedfellow Elvis Costello, and a longer-term collaboration is in the works); on the turntables of "bachelor-pad music" aficionados; and once again in the minds of record executives—Rhino is preparing what promises to be a definitive box set for release in 1998. Few pop resurrections have been so long in coming or so well deserved.

what to buy: It's reportedly only the first wave of a flood of Bacharach reissues, but *Burt Bacharach Plays His Hits* ♫♫♫ (MCA, 1997, compilation prod. Jim Pierson) is an interesting place to start your reassessment of his work. Many of the famous Bacharach/David hits are here, but mostly in instrumental versions augmented by the occasional lead vocal and a female chorus. The effect is kind of cheesy, but Bacharach's orchestrations are especially lively, making for some enjoyable listening. *Plays His Hits* is a newer and lengthier version of an album released in the '60s under the same title, which, as a mark of added kitsch value, was featured in the movie *Austin Powers* as the album in the secret agent's possession when he was cryogenically frozen.

what to buy next: Though one of the great pop composers, Bacharach is not much of a singer, and it's best to seek out his songs in versions by other artists. Still, *Greatest Hits* ♫♫♫ (A&M, 1973) offers just that. It's a prime selection of easy-listening classics. *Classics, Vol. 23* ♫♫♫♪ (A&M, 1991) fulfills the same function with a greater song selection.

what to avoid: The sappy Bacharach/David score to *Lost Horizon* **woof!** (Bell, 1973/Razor & Tie, 1997) was so dispiriting it caused one of pop's most successful duos to acrimoniously split.

the rest:
Reach Out ♫♫♫ (A&M, 1967/Rebound, 1995)

worth searching for: Proof positive of Bacharach's resurgent popularity and influence can be found on *Great Jewish Music:*

Burt Bacharach ♫♫♫ (Tzadik, 1997, prod. various), a two-disc set of Bacharach compositions deconstructed by avant-gardist executive producer John Zorn and a number of today's more adventurous musicians, including Marc Ribot, Robin Holcolm, Wayne Horvitz, Fred Frith, Bill Frisell, Kramer, and Elliott Sharp. Some of the tracks are pointlessly vexing—easy-listening made difficult, if you will—but the set definitely achieves its goal of revealing Bacharach's genius in completely unexpected ways. McCoy Tyner's *What the World Needs Now: The Music of Burt Bacharach* ♫♫♫ (Impulse!, 1997, prod. Tommy LiPuma) offers straight-jazz versions of Bacharach's hits with symphony accompaniment.

influences:

◀◀ Irving Berlin, George Gershwin, Johnny Mercer

▶▶ Elvis Costello, Noel Gallagher, John Zorn, Pizzicato Five

Daniel Durchholz

Angelo Badalamenti

Born 1938, in Brooklyn, NY.

Although he'll probably always be best known for penning the haunting theme to David Lynch's television series and movie *Twin Peaks,* Badalamenti has had a diverse musical career. He was born to an Italian father and an American mother, and he grew up listening to opera and classical music. He studied at the Eastman School of Music and the Manhattan School of Music, and got his big break in 1986 when Lynch hired him as a singing coach for Isabella Rosselini in the film *Blue Velvet.* He wound up scoring the movie, and he has worked with Lynch ever since (as well as scoring many other films, not all of them memorable—his music didn't help *National Lampoon's Christmas Vacation*). Badalamenti worked with Lynch and singer Julee Cruise on the haunting lounge-in-hell music for *Twin Peaks* as well as on Cruise's two albums, which are only slightly less spooky. He continues to keep busy scoring films and TV shows, with and without Lynch, as well as collaborating with pop musicians such as Tim Booth of James and the great Marianne Faithfull.

what to buy: *Floating into the Night* ♫♫♫♫ (Warner Bros., 1989, prod. Angelo Badalamenti, David Lynch) is Julee Cruise's stellar debut and a stunning testament to Badalamenti's abilities to create a mood with his evocative music. The followup, *The Voice of Love* ♫♫♫♫ (Warner Bros., 1993, prod. Angelo Badalamenti, David Lynch), is nearly as good, although there are few variations on the original formula. Dark and atmospheric, *Twin Peaks: Original TV Soundtrack* ♫♫♫♫ (Warner Bros., 1990, prod. David Lynch, Angelo Badalamenti) perfectly fits the bill for Lynch's request for music that is "a little bit dark, a little bit off-center, and tragically beautiful."

what to buy next: Like the film, *Twin Peaks: Fire Walk with Me, Original Soundtrack* ♫♫♫ (Warner Bros., 1992, prod. David Lynch, Angelo Badalamenti) simply isn't as good as the TV show. With the exception of his creepy "Dark Lolita," Badalamenti doesn't make much of an impact on *Wild At Heart, Original Soundtrack* ♫♫♫ (Polydor, 1990, prod. David Lynch). Made in collaboration with Tim Booth of James and his hero Brian Eno, *Booth & the Bad Angel* ♫♫♫ (PolyGram, 1990) is less than the sum of its parts. Slightly more inspired is Badalamenti's pairing with Marianne Faithfull, *Secret Life* ♫♫♫ (PolyGram, 1996, prod. Angelo Badalamenti).

worth searching for: Badalamenti's soundtrack for Lynch's classic 1986 film *Blue Velvet* ♫♫♫ (Varese Sarabande, 1986, executive prod. Tom Null, Richard Kraft) goes in and out of print with regularity.

influences:

◀◀ Brian Eno, Philip Glass, Nino Rota

▶▶ Marilyn Manson, Trent Reznor, Smashing Pumpkins

see also: *Julee Cruise, Marianne Faithfull*

Jim DeRogatis

Erykah Badu

Born Erica Wright, February 26, 1971, in Dallas, TX.

Few divas have arrived on the scene as full-formed as Erykah Badu. Dressed like a proud African queen—"strapped and wrapped," as she calls it—and with a voice that recalls Billie Holiday, the singer espouses "Baduizm," a self-made philosophy of Afrocentrism and spirituality. Her name, she says, is a sound you make scat singing, and it means "manifest truth" in Arabic. Whatever. Ultimately, it's Badu's honeyed vocals, sensual grooves, and seemingly bottomless well of self-confidence that wins the day. Classy and sassy, the singer is part of the current crop of young R&B artists (D'Angelo, Maxwell, Me'Shell Ndegeocello) that is reviving the form by looking to elders such as Stevie Wonder, Marvin Gaye, and Chaka Khan—for their smooth grooves, yes, but also for their hard-won wisdom. Already it seems certain Badu and Co. will take the music to the next level.

what to buy: On her debut, *Baduizm* ♫♫♫♫ (Kedar Entertainment/Universal, 1997, prod. various), the accompaniment is minimal, the vibe is retro, but the lyrics are conscious and the beats prove Badu knows from hip-hop production. "On & On," the song that drove *Baduizm* to the upper reaches of the charts, is a spare anthem about perseverance in the face of hard times; the shimmering "Next Lifetime" chronicles the formation of a love triangle; and "Drama" deals with a host of social ills. Badu is not without a sense of humor, though. The free-form skit "Afro" throws out some wicked lines as Badu delivers a bluesy *a cappella* vocal. Finally, there's a nice cover of the Atlantic Starr chestnut "4 Leaf Clover." All in all, it's amazing how together this debut album is.

what to buy next: A cynic would suggest that putting out a live album the same year as her first hit is merely a way for Badu to jam the marketplace with product while she's still a hot commodity. And they'd be right. Most of *Live* ✍✍✍ (Kedar Entertainment/Universal, 1997, prod. Erykah Badu, Kenny "Keys" Hurt) reprises tunes too recently heard on *Baduizm*. But the set reveals the capable and assured live performer that Badu is, and includes some choice covers, such as a medley of Heat Wave's "Boogie Nights" and the Mary Jane Girls' "All Night," plus the assertive original "Tyrone."

influences:

◀◀ Billie Holiday, Stevie Wonder, Chaka Khan

Daniel Durchholz

Pearl Bailey

Born March 29, 1918, in Newport News, VA. Died August 17, 1990, in Philadelphia, PA.

A legendary cabaret performer, Tony Award–winning actress, best-selling author, movie star, and the U.S. Goodwill Ambassador to the United Nations under three presidents, Bailey brought a touch of droll humor and class to everything she did. Her supple alto vocals embraced both the blues and Broadway pop, and her trademark comic asides created the persona of a performer willing to tell it like it is.

Bailey began singing and dancing in her father's Pentecostal revivals at age three. After picking up a few steps from her brother (dancer Bill Bailey), she was good enough at age 15 to sing and dance for Noble Sissle's Band. She also sang with bands fronted by Edgar Hayes, Cootie Williams, and Count Basie before making her 1944 solo debut at the Village Vanguard, where Greenwich Village bohemians and the cream of cafe society alike dug her off-the-cuff remarks almost as much as her singing. Bailey replaced Sister Rosetta Tharpe in Cab Calloway's band until she was cast in the Broadway production

of *St. Louis Woman,* for which she won a Donaldson award. Soon she was alternating starring theater roles such as *Arms and the Girl* and *House of Flowers* with scene-stealing film appearances in *Variety Girl* and *Porgy & Bess.* Recording prolifically for several different record labels, Bailey didn't have many hit singles; songs such as "Tired" (which prefigured rap), "It Takes Two to Tango," and "Baby It's Cold Outside" became associated with her sexy, slurred delivery. Her reputation as a risque sophisticate also caused her *For Adults Only* LP to be banned from radio play—which, of course, only helped it sell more copies. Bailey's career peaked in 1967 with her Tony Award–winning performance in the all-black cast version of

Hello, Dolly! In 1970, President Nixon named her America's "Ambassador of Love" and she became a special delegate to the U.N. under the Ford, Carter, and Bush administrations. However, Bailey never ceased working as an entertainer. She hosted her own TV show, wrote the first of many books about her life and times, and played all the top nightspots until ill health forced her to slow down. For her work with the United Nations and many charitable endeavors, President Reagan awarded her the Medal of Freedom in 1988.

what to buy: Several of Bailey's greatest performances (c. 1945–50), including "St. Louis Blues," "Baby It's Cold Outside," "Saturday Night Fish Fry," "A Woman's Prerogative," and "Legalize My Name," are on *16 Most Requested Songs* ♫♫♫♫ (Legacy, 1991, compilation prod. Michael Brooks). It's an essential introduction to the talents and style of this one-of-a-kind personality.

what to buy next: Bailey's Tony Award–winning performance is preserved on *Hello, Dolly!* ♫♫♫ (RCA, 1967/1991, prod. George R. Marek, Andy Wiswell); its superior cast includes Clifton Davis, Cab Calloway, Joe Williams, and Mabel King in supporting roles.

the rest:
Won't You Come Home, Pearl Bailey ♫♫♫ (Compose, 1995)
It's a Great Feeling ♫♫♫ (Sony Music Special, 1995)
Some of the Best ♫♫♫ (Laserlight, 1996)
More of the Best ♫♫♫ (Laserlight, 1996)

worth searching for: Bailey's best moments from her many so-called "adults-only" LPs for Roulette are compiled on *Best of Pearl Bailey—The Roulette Years* ♫♫♫♫ (Roulette, 1991, prod. various). Her provocative charm still resonates through "It Takes Two to Tango" and many others.

influences:
◀◀ Ethel Waters, Billie Holiday, Sister Rosetta Tharpe
▶▶ Abbe Lane, Freda Payne, Sylvia

Ken Burke

The Baja Marimba Band

Formed 1964, in Los Angeles, CA.

Julius Wechter, vibes, arrangements, bandleading; Lee Katzman, trumpet; Frank DeCaro, rhythm guitar; Dave Wells, trombone; Curry Tjader, bass marimba; Mel Pollan, bass; Frank DeVito, drums; Bernie Fleischer, flute; Bud Coleman, lead guitar; Charlie Chiarenza, lead guitar.

A spinoff of Herb Alpert's Tijuana Brass in the 1960s, the Baja Marimba Band began as a similar-sounding mariachi-and-pop instrumental band and evolved to play jazz fusion, Dixieland, rock, and novelty music. Wechter, who grew up in Hollywood, had been a session player on the Beach Boys' *Pet Sounds* and with lesser-known surf bands such as the Astronauts; recorded a few solo albums, including 1959's *Linear Sketches*; and replaced Arthur Lyman as the vibes player in Martin Denny's influential Hawaiian "exotica" band. Upon moving back to Hollywood and joining Alpert, he formed the Baja Marimba Band—mostly with rotating session musicians as the band's "members," although entirely different live touring musicians were usually listed on the LP covers—and rode the Tijuana Brass's coattails with hits like "Comin' in the Back Door" and even "Spanish Flea." Wechter, though, had an even more lighthearted sense of humor than Alpert, his longtime boss and collaborator. The covers of the Marimba Band's 10-plus LPs were filled with photos of men in sombreros and fake moustaches. Long after slipping off Alpert's A&M Records roster, the group released *Naturally* in 1982; on the cover, the band members stand buck naked behind a giant marimba, and the album includes "Theme from *Deep Throat*." Like most of the original BMB LPs, it's out of print and highly collectible. In an era where the Frito Bandito was pushing corn chips, the band's floppy sombreros, monster stogies, and droopy moustaches were considered humorous caricature. It is up to today's listener to determine if a bunch of white dudes playing "Pancho Villa" was stereotypically racist or simply harmless fun.

what's available: Unbelievably, there's almost no proof in any mainstream CD store that the once-mega-selling band even existed. Scrounge around and you'll find a handful of individual tracks on compilations, such as the upbeat, Latin-spiced version of "Georgy Girl" on *Bachelor Pad Pleasures* ♫♫♫ (PolyGram/Chronicles, 1996, compilation prod. Howard Smiley, Nancy Lombardo) and "Cast Your Fate to the Wind," on the more cohesive *Lounge Music Goes Latin* ♫♫♫♫ (PolyGram/Chronicles, 1996, compilation prod. Howard Smiley, Nancy Lombardo), which also includes Juan Garcia Esquivel, Perez Prado, and other good people.

worth searching for: Sadly, all the dozen-or-so Baja Marimba Band LPs have yet to be reissued on CD, so you'll have to scour the used bins to find the old smash "Comin' in the Back Door." *Foursider* ♫♫♫♫ (A&M, 1973, prod. various), an old-fashioned greatest-hits collection, contains that hit plus BMB takes on "Spanish Flea" and the melancholy showtune "Sunrise, Sunset." The band's debut, *Baja Marimba Band* ♫♫♫ (A&M, 1964, prod. Julius Wechter, Herb Alpert), contains "Acapulco" and

"Baja Nights" and was one of Alpert's first non–Tijuana Brass releases. (Alpert, former head of A&M Records with Jerry Moss, went on to break Joni Mitchell, Cat Stevens, the Carpenters, Joe Jackson, the Police, and Janet Jackson.) The mail-order set *More Instrumental Gems of the '60s* ♫♫♫♫ (Collector's Choice Music, 1995, compilation prod. Bob Hyde) contains the song "Riders in the Sky" from perhaps the band's best (out-of-print) LP, *Watch Out* ♫♫♫ (A&M, 1966).

influences:

◀◀ Herb Alpert and the Tijuana Brass, Tito Puente, Perez Prado, Les Elgart, Cal Tjader, Juan Garcia Esquivel

▶▶ Living Marimbas, Acapulco Marimbas

Steve Knopper and George W. Krieger

Chet Baker

Born December 23, 1929, in Yale, OK. Died May 13, 1988, in Amsterdam, Netherlands.

Underneath the messiness of his life and the fog of myth surrounding Baker is the undeniable fact that he was one of jazz's great lyric trumpeters, a natural musician with a gift for melodic invention. Strongly influenced by Miles Davis, Baker developed a singular ballad style and was fully capable of playing effective bop-derived lines. The vulnerability and fragility he communicated with his voice made him a compelling, charismatic singer, though late in his career it became impossible to separate the pathos of his life from his art.

After leaving the Army, Baker played with Charlie Parker on the West Coast in 1952. He joined Gerry Mulligan's ground-breaking pianoless quartet at the Haig in Los Angeles and it soon became one of the hottest groups in jazz. Baker struck out on his own in the mid-'50s, but drug addiction and his undisciplined life style soon began taking a toll on his career. A 1960 drug bust in Italy marked the start of precipitous decline, and Baker lost much of the '60s to addiction, though he did manage to make a few recordings worthy of his talent. At his nadir in 1968, Baker had his teeth knocked out in a drug-related incident, though a few years later he began an amazing comeback. He spent much of the latter part of his life in Europe, returning occasionally to the United States and recording much too frequently for a variety of labels. Though his voice was little but a whisper in his last decade, he remained a fine trumpeter right up until his death, when he either fell or was pushed out of a hotel window. A beautiful man who could have been a model or a movie star, Baker by the end of his life looked like Dorian Grey's portrait, with a lifetime of hard living etched in his face.

what to buy: Since his death, Baker's great 1950s Pacific Jazz recordings have been reissued in many different forms, from "best of" anthologies to completist multi-disc collections. *The Best of the Gerry Mulligan Quartet with Chet Baker* ♫♫♫♫ (Pacific Jazz, 1991, prod. Dick Bock) is an anthology of the classic 1952–53 sessions by one of the great small groups in modern jazz. Baker was at the peak of his popularity when *Quartet: Russ Freeman and Chet Baker* ♫♫♫♫ (Pacific Jazz, 1956, prod. Richard Bock) was released. Freeman, a brilliant writer and improvisor, composed all the material except for the opening "Love Nest" and a gorgeous, early version of Billy Strayhorn's "Lush Life." The rapport between Freeman and Baker makes this one of the trumpeter's strongest sessions, a long-hard-to-find gem that bears repeated listening. *The Route* ♫♫♫♫ (Pacific Jazz, 1956, prod. Richard Bock) unites Baker and alto saxophonist Art Pepper, two of jazz's most chaotic figures. Baker's breathy trumpet sound blends well with Pepper's hot and lustrous alto. Baker's finest vocal album, *It Could Happen to You* ♫♫♫♫ (Riverside, 1958, prod. Bill Grauer) was recorded when his voice was still fresh and sweet but already marked by the terrible knowledge of self-destruction. Baker croons a dozen standards, including his classic version of "Everything Happens to Me." Other standout tracks include "Old Devil Moon" and the irony-tinged "I'm Old Fashioned."

what to buy next: Though the sound quality isn't great, *Witch Doctor* ♫♫♫ (Contemporary, 1985, prod. Lester Koenig) is a fascinating slice of history, recorded live at the Lighthouse in the summer of 1953 during one of the legendary Sunday jam sessions. Baker, who had recently left Gerry Mulligan's popular quartet, is in top form battling with trumpeter Rolf Ericson. This session was released for the first time in 1985. *Songs for Lovers* ♫♫♫ (Pacific Jazz, 1997, prod. Richard Bock) is a compilation of a dozen standards Baker recorded in the mid-'50s for Pacific Jazz. Baker's voice is an acquired taste, but he was at his best singing world-weary romantic ballads, including affecting versions of "My Old Flame," "Darn that Dream," and especially "Lush Life." *Chet Baker in New York* ♫♫♫ (Riverside, 1958, prod. Orrin Keepnews) is a strong session that shows Baker wasn't afraid of being compared to Miles Davis by playing a number of tunes associated with him ("Solar" and "When Lights Are Low"). One of Baker's last quality sessions, *The Legacy, Vol. 1* ♫♫♫ (Enja, 1995, prod. Matthias Winckelmann) was recorded live in 1987 in Hamburg, Germany, with the NDR Big Band directed by Dieter Glawischnig. The program is mostly mid-tempo standards and ballads, but his playing on Herbie Hancock's "Dolphin Dance" and Hal Galper's "Mister B" show that Baker kept his ears open until the end.

what to avoid: Baker lovers might want this one, but with the plodding orchestra charts and unchanging tempos, *Chet Baker with 50 Italian Strings* ✍✍ (Riverside, 1960, prod. Orrin Keepnews) is a snooze.

best of the rest:

Pacific Jazz Years ✍✍✍ (Pacific Jazz, 1952–57)

Complete Pacific Jazz Studio Recordings of the Chet Baker Quartet with Russ Freeman ✍✍✍✍ (Mosaic, 1953–56)

Complete Pacific Jazz Live Recordings ✍✍✍ (Mosaic, 1954)

Chet in Paris, Vols. 1–4 ✍✍✍ (EmArcy, 1955–56)

Playboys ✍✍✍ (Pacific Jazz, 1957)

Embraceable You ✍✍✍ (Pacific Jazz, 1958)

Plays the Best of Lerner and Lowe ✍✍✍ (Riverside, 1959)

Chet ✍✍✍ (Riverside, 1960)

Lonely Star ✍✍✍ (Prestige, 1965)

On a Misty Night ✍✍✍ (Prestige, 1965)

Blues for a Reason ✍✍✍♥ (Criss Cross, 1985)

My Favorite Songs ✍✍✍ (Enja, 1988)

Chet Baker in Tokyo ✍✍✍♥ (Evidence, 1993)

worth searching for: Chet was often at his best with spare accompaniment, and *Chet's Choice* ✍✍✍♥ (Criss Cross, 1985, prod. Gerry Teekens) finds him in a trio context with guitarist Philip Catherine and bassist Jean-Louis Rassinfosse. His gift for melodicism is intact, and this is one of his best later sessions.

influences:

◀◀ Bix Beiderbecke, Miles Davis, Kenny Dorham

▶▶ Rick Braun

Andrew Gilbert

Josephine Baker
/Josephine Carson

Born Freda J. McDonald, June 3, 1906, in St. Louis, MO. Died April 12, 1975, in Paris, France.

Josephine Baker was the Madonna of the jazz age. Her provocative, openly sexual performances caused a sensation throughout Europe, but in later years she reinvented herself as the ultimate high-fashion diva. Baker danced professionally at the age of 13 on the T.O.B.A. circuit (the acronym stood for Theater Owners Booking Association, but performers felt it meant "Tough on Black Asses"). She was good enough by 1921 to be featured in Noble Sissle and Eubie Blake's stage show *Shuffle Along* and their later productions of *Chocolate Dandies*. During the lengthy runs of these shows, Baker acquired a reputation as a scene-stealing eccentric dancer, whose comic mugging and energetic style amused even the toughest audiences. In 1925, while working at the Cotton Club in Harlem, Baker and seven others were hired by a talent scout from the Folies-Bergere for *La Revue Negre*, an all-black musical. Baker, bare-breasted and wearing a bikini made of feathers and bananas, took Paris by storm when she danced the Charleston, and sang "I Want to Yodel." She capitalized on her success by opening her own club (which she walked to every day with a leopard on a leash), and starring in shows built around her exotic looks and increasingly flamboyant lifestyle. She also recorded the song that would become her theme: "J'ai Deux Amours," or "I Have Two Loves (My Home and Paris)." Initially, Baker learned the French lyrics phonetically, but in a few years she became fluent in the new language. Baker's voice, a trilling soprano, was pure and sweet for the many torch songs she liked to sing, though she was perfectly capable of scatting out some nasty jazz when the occasion called for it. Baker eventually recorded 230 songs in English, French, Portuguese, German, and Italian, a groundbreaking early attempt at developing a world market. Baker's image as an exotic primitive followed her into the French cinema for such films as *Les Sirene des Tropiques, Zou Zou,* and *Princess Tam-Tam*. A perennial star of the Folies-Bergere and cabarets, Baker eventually toned down the nudity in her act, yet she remained a master of milking titillation and controversy for all its inherent publicity value. Attempting to translate her European success to the American stage, Baker took part in the *Ziegfield Follies of 1936,* which also starred Bob Hope and Fanny Brice. Theater critics bashed her unmercifully with thinly veiled racial taunts, yet her concurrent nightclub act was reviewed in glowing terms. During World War II, Baker's travels offered her the perfect opportunity to be a courier for the French Resistance, for which she was awarded the Croix de Guerre, the Rosette de la Resistance, and the Legion d'Honneur. In the post-war era, Baker transformed into a diva sophisticate, and she toured the world demanding to play before desegregated audiences, especially in America where she was a vigorous supporter of civil rights. She retired in 1956, but with 12 adopted children of different nationalities to support ("The Rainbow Tribe"), she was forced to make a comeback in the early '60s. When a heart attack kept her from working and she was illegally evicted from her home, Princess Grace gave her a villa in Monaco while she recuperated and tried to rebuild her career. Struggling at the end, Baker's life and career closed in dramatic show-biz fashion, with a revival show honoring her 50 years in France. After fourteen smash performances, Baker suffered a massive stroke, and died five days later. Baker's life was por-

Josephine Baker **(AP/Wide World Photos)**

trayed fairly accurately in the 1992 HBO film *The Josephine Baker Story* (starring Lynn Whitfield), but it didn't contain half the drama or personal charisma of the real Josephine Baker.

what to buy: You don't really need much else once you own *Josephine Baker* ♪♪♪♪ (Sandstone, 1994, compilation prod. Steve Hoffman), a two-disc, 50-song set recorded for the most part in France between the years 1926 and 1936. Disc one features Baker's spirited performances of such jazzy standards as "Bye Bye Blackbird," "Blue Skies," and "Dinah" in English. Disc two contains all her best known French language recordings, including her personal theme, "J'ai Deux Amours." An instant slice of history and some pretty good music once you get used to the old-timey sound of the 78 rpm discs from which these sides were remastered.

what to buy next: Great sound and a seldom-reissued track selection make *The Fabulous Josephine Baker* ♪♪♪ (RCA 1962/1995, supervisor Nate Johnson) worth having. For this

collection of tunes she did from her 1950s world tour, Baker mixes some risqué sass with the French torch songs.

the rest:
13 Songs ♪♪ (Socadisc, 1995)
Exotique ♪♪♪ (Flapper, 1995)
Breezin' Along ♪♪♪ (Columbia/Legacy, 1995)
Original Recordings ♪♪♪ (Les Eternals, 1996)
Upbeat Stepper ♪♪ (Bob, 1996)
J'ai Deux Amours ♪♪♪♪ (Golden Stars, 1996)
Banana Girl ♪♪♪ (PMF Music Factory, 1996)
J'ai Deux Amours ♪♪♪ (Eclipse Records, 1996)
Jazz After Dark: Great Songs ♪♪♪ (Public Music, 1996)
The Star of Folies Bergere ♪♪♪ (EPM Musique, 1997)
J'ai Deux Amours ♪♪♪ (Arkadia Chanson, 1997)
Star of Les Folies-Bergers ♪♪♪ (ASV, 1998)

influences:

◀◀ Clara Smith, Florence Mills, Maude Russell

▶▶ Lena Horne, Dorothy Dandridge, Pearl Bailey

Ken Burke

Charlie Barnet

Born October 26, 1913, in New York City, NY. Died September 4, 1991.

Barnet could afford to be a liberal dilettante (he was born into a wealthy family), but it is a tribute to his basic instincts that he became a solid musician and a deceptively casual social do-gooder. Even though Barnet was a big fan of the Fletcher Henderson and Duke Ellington big bands, his outfits of the early 1930s were more like the white society bands of Paul Whiteman with a jazzier edge. By the mid-1930s Barnet's band had more of a swinging jazz flavor, and he cut some records with Red Norvo that included Artie Shaw and Teddy Wilson backing up Barnet's Coleman Hawkins–inspired tenor playing. After 1939, the year of "Cherokee," the Ray Noble barnburner that became Barnet's theme and one of the most frequently played of all jazz standards, Barnet was at his peak. He was also playing a lot of Ellington during this period and Duke remarked (in his autobiography *Music Is My Mistress)* that "he constantly bolstered my ego by playing a book almost full of our compositions." Barnet was so enamored of Ellington that he would sometimes hire Duke's band for his own private parties. Barnet also led the first white band to play the Apollo Theater and his colorblind hiring practices prevented him from playing a lot of venues during this period. The roll call of major musicians that spent time in his band is remarkable—singers Lena Horne and Kay Starr, trumpeters Clark Terry and Doc Severinsen, and arrangers Benny Carter and Eddie Sauter, to name a few. When Barnet gave up his big band he would still go out with an occasional sextet/septet or, in the case of his 1958 studio dates, work with an amazing big band, but most of his time was spent in comfortable retirement.

what to buy: *An Introduction to Charlie Barnet: His Best Recordings, 1935–1944* 🎵🎵🎵🎵 (Best of Jazz, 1996) is a well-conceived overview of Barnet's most popular and important recordings for Bluebird and Decca. If there is a weakness to the set it is the under-representation of Barnet's hottest band of the mid-1940s, with only three of the Decca sides included. For that, get *Drop Me Off in Harlem* 🎵🎵🎵🎵 (Decca Jazz, 1992)—Barnet's band of the early to mid-1940s included a fair number of proto-boppers and swing practitioners playing together in harmony, and artistically they may be more rewarding than earlier bands, although this shouldn't be taken as a knock against some of their predecessors. This album contains Barnet's biggest hit from the post-Bluebird years, "Skyliner."

the rest:
Clap Hands, Here Comes Charlie 🎵🎵🎵 (Bluebird, 1987)

Cherokee 🎵🎵🎵🎵 (Bluebird, 1992)
Charlie Barnet and His Orchestra: 1941 🎵🎵🎵 (Circle, 1992)
Charlie Barnet and His Orchestra: 1942 🎵🎵🎵 (Circle, 1992)
Cherokee 🎵🎵🎵🎵 (Evidence, 1993)
More 🎵🎵🎵 (Evidence, 1995)

worth searching for: Back in the days of vinyl Bluebird had an awesome six-volume set of "twofers," *Complete Charlie Barnet, Vols. 1–6* 🎵🎵🎵🎵🎵 (Bluebird, 1935–42, prod. various), which, if it were in print today, would go right to the top of the list.

influences:
◀◀ Coleman Hawkins, Johnny Hodges, Duke Ellington

▶▶ Pete Christlieb

Garaud MacTaggart

John Barry

Born November 3, 1933, in York, England.

The spooky, orchestral spy music that follows 007 around in *Goldfinger* and *Dr. No,* among other famous James Bond flicks, usually came from Barry's lively and dramatic imagination. He's amazing at arranging horns to give a scene the right kind of personality, be it playful or frightening. While he earned an Oscar nomination for his *Chaplin* soundtrack and did famous scores for *Body Heat* and *Out of Africa,* most moviegoers know his music as another Bond prop, as crucial to the mythology as the shaken, not stirred, martini or the ubiquitous Miss Moneypenny.

Barry, son of a classical pianist and a movie theater owner, developed a love for both symphonies and film as a teen-ager. After a stint in the U.S. Army, he formed a rock 'n' roll band—John Barry and the Seven—then signed an EMI record deal for tinkly instrumental music. (The Seven frequently backed British pre-rock singing star Adam Faith.) His spare, playful first score, for the 1959 movie *Beat Girl,* barely sounds like the big orchestral sound that made him famous. But that led to several other movies, in addition to pop singles, until his career-defining break, *Dr. No,* in 1962. Since then, he has remained incredibly prolific, but the shadow of Bond continues to hang over his career.

what to buy: Both *Moviola* 🎵🎵🎵 (Sony, 1992, prod. John Barry) and *Moviola II: Action and Adventure* 🎵🎵🎵🎵 (Sony, 1995, prod. John Barry) make for excellent samplings of Barry's soundtrack history, including the familiar suites from *Body Heat, Chaplin, Out of Africa, Dances with Wolves,* and *Born Free.* The second volume packs the most punch, however, opening with eight straight Bond songs, including the Jaws-jumping-out-of-the-plane "007." Most are performed by the Royal Philharmonic Orchestra, with liner notes by Barry himself.

what to buy next: *John Barry: The EMI Years, Vol. 3: 1962–64* ♪♪♪ (Scamp, 1996, prod. various) is a funny glimpse of the composer's pop and rock oriented side. His versions of Fats Domino's "Blueberry Hill" and Perez Prado's signature mambo, "Cherry Pink and Apple Blossom White," are tinkly and bouncy, unintentionally fitting the space-age bachelor pad feel pioneered by Enoch Light and Juan Garcia Esquivel. The soundtrack *Octopussy* ♪♪♪ (1983/Rykodisc, 1997, prod. John Barry) had been so out of print that collectors were known to pay $250 for the original album; Rykodisc recently reissued it, as well as soundtracks by Frank Zappa, Quincy Jones, and Elmer Bernstein.

what to avoid: *Film Music of John Barry* ♪♪♪ (Sony, 1988, prod. various) essentially collects the same handful of James Bond themes you can find on the better packages, like *Moviola II* or even the various-artist *The Best of James Bond: 30th Anniversary Collection* ♪♪♪♪ (EMI, 1992, comp. prod. Ron Furmanek), which also includes familiar Bond themes (many written by Barry) from Paul McCartney, Tom Jones, Dionne Warwick, Duran Duran, and Shirley Bassey.

best of the rest:
Until September/Car Crash ♪♪♪ (Silva Screen, 1992)
Chaplin ♪♪♪♪ (Epic Soundtrax, 1992)
Film Scores ♪♪♪ (Silva America, 1994)
Across the Sea of Time ♪♪ (Epic Soundtrax, 1995)
John Barry: The EMI Years, Vol. 1 ♪♪♪ (Scamp, 1996)
John Barry: The EMI Years, Vol. 2 ♪♪♪♪ (Scamp, 1996)

worth searching for: Barry's original soundtracks, especially the older material, are tough to find—despite the glut of excellent packages and reissues on the market. In fact, Barry's original LPs, not to mention out-of-print James Bond soundtracks in general, are frequently high-priced collectors' items. *Beat Girl* ♪♪ (Columbia, 1959) is his first soundtrack, and while it sounds nothing like the Bond spy-drama to come, it's an interesting transitional piece between Barry's early pop product and his more substantial soundtracks.

influences:

◀◀ Ennio Morricone, Benny Goodman, Glenn Miller, Louis Armstrong, Duke Ellington, Rodgers & Hammerstein

▶▶ Lalo Schifrin, Phil Spector, Phil Ramone, Bruce Springsteen

Steve Knopper

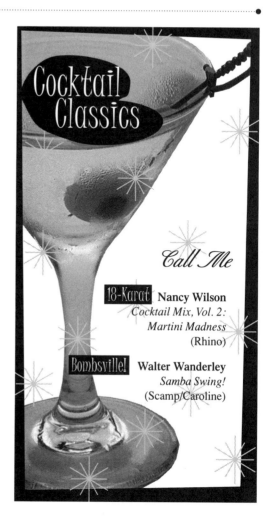

Basia

Basia Trzetrzelewska, September 30, 1956, in Jaworzno, Poland.

If there is such a thing as a truly international sound, it should be found somewhere in the music of Basia Trzetrzelewska. She began her performing career in her native country, with the female trio Alibabki, then toured the Soviet Union. She later lived in Chicago, where she soaked up American R&B and blues, and London, where she joined the band Matt Bianco, whose album *Whose Side Are You On?* (now out of print) was a hit in England and Europe. She went solo in 1985, continuing to collaborate with Matt Bianco keyboardist Danny White. On her own albums, Basia surveys an intriguing mix of pop-jazz, favoring Latin styles such as samba and bossa nova.

what to buy: Recorded during a 1994 stint at New York City's Neil Simon Theater, *Basia on Broadway* ♫♫♫♫ (Epic, 1995, prod. Danny White, Basia) is a de-facto greatest-hits package, featuring Basia's best-known numbers, "Copernicus," "Cruising for Bruising," "Baby You're Mine," "New Day for You," "Time and Tide," and several new songs. Spyro Gyra saxophonist Jay Beckenstein sits in on "Yearning."

what to buy next: *London Warsaw New York* ♫♫♫♫ (Epic, 1989, prod. Basia, Danny White) is the album on which Basia's sound truly came of age, kicking off with the pop-jazz "Cruising for Bruising," which is so slick that the song's bittersweet kiss-off lyric goes down smoothly. "Best Friends" apes ebullient Gloria Estefan–style pop, but the soaring self-actualization "Brave New Hope," the Aretha Franklin cover "Until You Come Back to Me," and the rhythmic hands-across-the-water number, "Copernicus," make this a fine effort. *The Sweetest Illusion* ♫♫♫♫ (Epic, 1994, prod. Danny White, Basia) is nearly that album's equal, thanks to "Third Time Lucky" and the elegant "Yearning."

the rest:
Time and Tide ♫♫♫ (Epic, 1987)
Brave New Hope ♫♫♫ EP (Epic, 1991)

worth searching for: Matt Bianco's out-of-print *Whose Side Are You On?* ♫♫♫ (Atlantic, 1984, prod. Mark Reilly) is the Polish diva's impressive recording debut.

influences:
◀◀ Astrud Gilberto, Gloria Estefan, Sade
▶▶ Swing out Sister, Lisa Stansfield

Daniel Durchholz

Sid Bass

Born January 22, 1913, in New York City, NY. Died June 19, 1993, in Putney, VT.

Bass studied music at New York University, then broke into the music business by landing a job at the Muzak company, where he learned how to produce preprocessed musical cheese from the masters. He then moved to RCA, where he was hired as a staff composer, primarily for the pre-stereo, hi-fi demonstration records that the label produced as a cross-promotional tool to sell their audio components. It was at RCA that Bass secured his place in the lounge music pantheon, as original LPs like

With Bells On and *From Another World* feature wacky crossfades, over-the-top orchestral arrangements, and all manner of loopy sound effects.

worth searching for: None of Bass's half-dozen or so original LPs, mostly recorded for RCA's budget label, Vik Records, are in print. If you can track them down, *With Bells On* ♫♫♫♫ (RCA Camden, 1959) and *From Another World* ♫♫♫♫ (Vik) are classic space-age bachelor pop albums, full of strange noises and tinkly melodies.

influences:
◀◀ Juan Garcia Esquivel, Martin Denny, Raymond Scott
▶▶ Combustible Edison

Marc Weingarten

Shirley Bassey

Born Shirley Veronica Bassey, January 8, 1937, in Cardiff, Wales.

Known to some as the James Bond soundtrack star, Shirley Bassey's career shows that she is indeed much more. Long before she applied her flamboyant vocal treatment to 007 anthems in *Goldfinger* (1964) and *Diamonds Are Forever* (1972), making the songs worldwide hits, Bassey was a blossoming cabaret star. She was signed to Philips in 1957 and recorded a cover version of Harry Belafonte's "Banana Boat Song" that hit #1 on the charts that year. Her songs "Kiss Me Honey Kiss Me" and "As I Love You" both entered the Top 10 in 1959. Bassey emerged full-force as a vocal stylist and dazzling live performer after signing to Columbia during the early 1960s, the peak of her career. Enchanting interpretations of "Climb Ev'ry Mountain" (1961) from *The Sound of Music* and "What Kind of Fool Am I?" (1963) from *Stop the World I Want to Get Off* showed Bassey's flair for showtunes. Her successful recording of "Goldfinger," her only major hit in America, led to a contract deal with United Artists in 1967. She also sang the theme song for the less triumphant 1979 James Bond film *Moonraker*. While she may not have directly influenced many singers in her genre, Bassey's glitzy show-stoppers inspired the most unlikely of artists—including Detroit rocker Mitch Ryder, whose only solo hit was a cover of Bassey's "What Now My Love" (Dyna Voice, 1967), and English rockers Status Quo, who covered her "I Who Have Nothing" (Pye, 1966). Bassey lives in Switzerland but travels to the U.S. occasionally to record and perform.

what to buy: *Goldsinger: The Best of Shirley Bassey* ♫♫♫♫ (EMI, 1995, prod. various) offers a little of everything, from her film and show tune interpretations to her innovative approaches to pop.

the rest:

Sassy Bassey 🎵🎵🎵 (Pair, 1991)

Shirley Bassey Sings the Songs of Andrew Lloyd Weber 🎵🎵🎵 (EMI, 1995)

worth searching for: Bassey made a guest-appearance on the Swiss synth-pop duo Yello's album *One Second* 🎵🎵🎵 (Mercury, 1987). *The Best of James Bond* 🎵🎵🎵 (EMI, 1992) features Bassey's Bond contributions, plus some outtakes, in the illuminating context of the rest of the film franchise's musical *oeuvre*.

influences:

◀◀ Josephine Baker, Harry Belafonte, Lena Horne, Dinah Washington, Nina Simone

▶▶ Phyllis Hyman, Anita Baker, Vanessa Williams

Norene Cashen

Mario Bauza

Born April 28, 1911, in Havana, Cuba. Died July 11, 1993, in New York City, NY.

Bauza was involved in two of the major jazz and Latin trends of the 1930s and 1940s. He was responsible for introducing Dizzy Gillespie to conga legend Chano Pozo and for bringing the standard Cuban rhythm section into line with the big-band sound of Cab Calloway and Chick Webb. The meeting of Gillespie and Pozo was influential in the development of a hybrid known as "Cubop," which included among its proponents Stan Getz and Charlie Parker. The blending of big band arrangements with Cuban rhythms made Bauza's brother-in-law, Machito (Frank Grillo), the leader of what was arguably the most influential Latin-flavored band in the first half of this century. His innovations also built the foundation for the bossa nova, mambo, cha-cha-cha, and other Latin-dance crazes of the '50s and '60s.

Bauza's first instruments were the clarinet and the bass clarinet, which he played in the Havana Philharmonic. In 1930, shortly after arriving in the United States, Bauza got a job with Cuarteto Machin playing trumpet, an instrument he learned to play in the two weeks preceding his first job with the band. His first major jazz gig was with Chick Webb in 1933 and from there Bauza worked briefly with bands led by Don Redman and Fletcher Henderson before joining Cab Calloway's outfit in 1939. In 1940 Bauza made the move to Machito's newly formed band as the musical director, and there he stayed until 1976,

when Bauza left the band. During the late 1970s and early 1980s Bauza and Graciela (his sister-in-law and former vocalist with Machito) recorded a couple albums for small labels which have since turned into prized collector's items. It was in 1992 that he made a recording featuring Chico O'Farrill's arrangement of "Tanga," a tune originally written by Bauza back in 1943, and this led to a resurgence in his career.

what to buy: *Tanga* 🎵🎵🎵🎵 (Messidor, 1992, prod. Mario Bauza) is by a truly big band, something like 24 pieces not counting vocalists and special guest Paquito D'Rivera. Things could get messy when arrangers work with an ensemble this big, but everyone involved in this project is top notch. Special honors go to Chico O'Farrill, whose transformation of Bauza's "Tanga" into the subtitled "Afro-Cuban Jazz Suite in Five Movements" is a masterpiece. There is not a weak moment in the whole album. The end result is not only a paean to the spirit of Latin jazz but a celebration of one of its cardinal figures, Mario Bauza. *My Time Is Now* 🎵🎵🎵🎵 (Messidor, 1993, prod. Mario Bauza) is another splendid album from one of the most important musicians in Latin jazz history. The band romps through Cuban classics by Arsenio Rodriguez and others, in addition to re-arranging Kurt Weill's "Moritat" into a Latin version of "Jack the Knife" (no, that's not a typo). Many of the players from *Tanga* show up on this album, including major participants vocalist Rudy Calzado, drummer Bobby Sanabria, and conga legend Carlos "Patato" Valdez.

what to buy next: Two months before he died, Bauza was actively involved in recording what would be his swan song. On *944 Columbus* 🎵🎵🎵 (Messidor, 1994, prod. Mario Bauza), the writing, arranging, and playing are still at a remarkably high level from all the participants, but that spark of genius that informed the other two efforts on Messidor was starting to fade along with the leader. There are crucial performances on this disc, however, and it is almost too easy to read some sort of subliminal clue into the titles chosen for inclusion on this album. One of the Bauza-composed works is entitled "Lourdes' Lullaby" and there is a version of Dizzy Gillespie's "Night in Tunisia" to go with "Chano" by Cascaser and Joe Santiago.

worth searching for: One of the albums Bauza recorded with Graciela after Machito's death in 1984 was *Afro-Cuban Jazz* 🎵🎵🎵🎵 (Caiman, 1984).

influences:

◀◀ Antonio Machin, Don Apiazo, Cab Calloway

▶▶ Dizzy Gillespie, Tito Puente, Perez Prado, Xavier Cugat

Garaud MacTaggart

Les Baxter

Born March 14, 1922, in Mexia, TX. Died January 22, 1996, in Newport Beach, CA.

One of the most renowned names in lounge music, Baxter originally wanted to be a concert pianist. He studied at the Detroit Conservatory of Music, then attended Pepperdine College in Los Angeles. At 23, he accepted an offer to work as a singer, joining Mel Tormé's Meltones and the Artie Shaw Band. This led to work as an arranger for radio shows such as Bob Hope's and Abbott and Costello's, and eventually for TV (including _Lassie_ and _The Flintstones_) and film (his 250 credits include _The Pit and the Pendulum_ and _Fall of the House of Usher_ by Roger Corman, _The Man With the X-Ray Eyes, How to Stuff a Wild Bikini,_ and, of course, _Dr. Goldfoot and the Bikini Machine_). In the 1940s, Baxter became a regular conductor and arranger for Capitol, working with artists ranging from Nat King Cole to Yma Sumac. Finally, in 1950, he developed his own laid-back but exotic big-band style, following it through a long list of releases under his own name. Mixing various ethnic instruments with those of the traditional orchestra, Baxter became known as the godfather of "exotica." He last performed in public at the Century Club in Century City in November 1995 before dying of a heart attack at age 73.

what's available: _Les Baxter's Best_ ♫♫♫ (Capitol/EMI, 1996, prod. various) is the place to start for the Baxter initiate; it includes classics such as "Never on Sunday," "I Love Paris," and his signature tune, "Quiet Village." _The Exotic Moods of Les Baxter_ (Capitol/EMI, 1996, prod. various) is a more extensive overview of Baxter's exotica. Winter got you down? _Colors of Brazil African Blue_ ♫♫♫ (GNP/Crescendo, 1991, prod. Les Baxter) and _Que Mango_ ♫♫♫ (Scamp, 1996, prod. Les Baxter) are almost as good as a tropical vacation. Finally, there's _The Lost Episode_ ♫♫♫ (Dionysus/Bacchus Archives, 1996, prod. Les Baxter), a live recording from 1961, and _Les Baxter by Popular Request_ ♫♫♫ (Dionysus/Bacchus Archives, 1996), yet another best-of collection.

worth searching for: While a wealth of Baxter's best has been reissued in recent years, there's still plenty that is languishing in the used bins of old record stores. Keep an eye out for _Music Out of the Moon_ ♫♫♫ (Capitol, 1950), one of the first albums to try to evoke the ethereal sound and feel of outer space with a theremin. Also, Baxter left his mark all over Yma Sumac's _Voice of the Xtabay_ ♫♫♫ (The Right Stuff, 1996, prod. Les Baxter).

influences:
◀◀ Tommy Jones, Maurice Ravel

▶▶ Combustible Edison, Love Jones, Stereolab, Martin Denny, Juan Garcia Esquivel, Arthur Lyman, Yma Sumac

Jim DeRogatis

The Beach Boys

Formed 1962, in Hawthorne, CA.

Brian Wilson (born June 20, 1942, in Inglewood, CA), piano, guitar, bass, vocals; Carl Wilson (born December 21, 1946, in Hawthorne, CA; died February 6, 1998, in Los Angeles, CA), guitar, vocals; Dennis Wilson (born December 4, 1983, in Hawthorne, CA; died December 28, 1983, in Marina Del Rey, CA), drums, vocals; Mike Love (born March 15, 1941, in Los Angeles, CA), vocals; Alan Jardine (born September 3, 1942, in Lima, OH), guitar, vocals; Bruce Johnston (born June 24, 1944, in Chicago, IL), keyboards, vocals (1965–98); Blondie Chaplin, guitar, vocals (1971–74); Ricky Fataar, drums, vocals (1972–74).

The Beach Boys were the first major and longest-running American rock 'n' roll band/soap opera, led by the reclusive, unstable prodigy Brian Wilson. Rising from the sun-and-convertible culture of post-war Southern California and careening off Chuck Berry's small-combo rock 'n' roll, the choir-like harmonies of the Four Freshmen, and the surf craze of the early '60s, the Beach Boys' early hits, "Surfin' U.S.A.," "Be True to Your School," "Fun, Fun, Fun," "Help Me, Rhonda," "I Get Around," "California Girls," remain pithy aural descriptions of teen-age life circa 1962. Brian Wilson was an auteur, the heart and soul of the group, a sensitive, intelligent kid whose fun-and-sun themes were a smokescreen for a darker side (in the person of Murry Wilson, a violent, abusive musician wannabe particularly jealous of his eldest son's gifts, and who eventually recorded his own terrible lounge songs) exposed dramatically in songs like "In My Room." The Boys' inclusion here comes mostly in the form of _Pet Sounds_, although eliminate the Chuck Berry, and most BB material belongs here. A rhapsodic ode to teen-age love, _Pet Sounds_ has been praised as a rock classic but is an easy-listening icon as well. The pressures of producing a sequel, the never-officially-released _Smile_, left Wilson in a state of mental illness from which he seems still to be recuperating. As a live act, the Boys have persevered long after they became Beach Men, with little to show the last 25 years but internal squabbles and litigation over their piggy banks.

what to buy: _Pet Sounds_ ♫♫♫♫ (Capitol, 1966/1990, prod. Brian Wilson), recorded in full-blown monaural sound, is frozen in time, forever young and fresh and, even 32 years later, irresistibly romantic. Program out "Sloop John B" (a dumb cover

Al Jardine (l), Dennis Wilson, Brian Wilson, and Mike Love of the Beach Boys (© Jack Vartoogian)

added as an afterthought) and *Pet Sounds* is as close to perfect as it gets. Whether the endless possibilities of "Wouldn't It Be Nice?," the earnest resolution of "You Still Believe in Me," or the coming-of-age epiphany in "I Know There's an Answer" (originally sung and better titled "Hang on to Your Ego"), *Pet Sounds* is 36 minutes of what it feels like to be 19. *Smiley Smile/Wild Honey* ✺✺✺✺ (Capitol, 1967/1990, prod. Brian Wilson) includes some of the bright parts of the original *Smile* (hence *Smiley Smile*) and the ragged soul of *Wild Honey*, both among the Boys' best recorded moments. *Surf's Up* ✺✺✺✺ (Caribou/Epic, 1971, prod. the Beach Boys) is a group effort that includes two of Brian's all-time best tunes, "Until I Die" and "Surf's Up," both written with Van Dyke Parks and originally slated for *Smile*. Wilson's duet disc with Parks, *Orange Crate Art* ✺✺✺ (Warner Bros., 1996, prod. Brian Wilson, Van Dyke Parks) is wallpaper music at its very finest.

what to buy next: Many aficionados prefer the two rather lushly produced albums leading up to *Pet Sounds*, *The Beach Boys Today/Summer Days and Summer Nights* ✺✺✺✺ (Capitol, 1965, 1990, prod. Brian Wilson), to their more-hyped sequel. *Beach Boys Love You* ✺✺✺✺ (Caribou/Epic, 1977, prod. Brian Wilson) is a whimsical, low-key, congenial, partial return to earth from Wilson in 1977. "Solar System" and "Johnny Carson" alone make it worthwhile. If you've got all those, the next logical step would be *Good Vibrations* ✺✺✺✺✺ (Capitol, 1993, prod. Brian Wilson), a cluttered, eccentric box set that's a blast for BB fans, with a fascinating collage of hits, remixes, studio talk, interviews, and other fun, arcane stuff, beginning with a young Brian pounding out "Surfin' U.S.A." and including a "version" of *Smile* on disc two.

what to avoid: Take your pick. Stay away from the woefully mistitled *15 Big Ones* ✹ (Caribou/Epic, 1976, prod. the Beach Boys), *M.I.U.* **woof!** (Caribou/Epic, 1978, prod. the Beach Boys), or *L.A. (Light Album)* **woof!** (Caribou/Epic, 1979, prod. the Beach Boys), in which the group is heavy in the grip of Mike Love's meditation obsession.

best of the rest:
Surfer Girl/Shut Down, Vol. 2 ♪♪♪ (Capitol, 1963)
Friends/20/20 ♪♪♪ (Capitol, 1968/1990)
Holland ♪♪♪ (Caribou/Epic, 1973)
Endless Summer ♪♪♪♪ (Capitol, 1974)
Rarities ♪♪♪♪ (Capitol, 1983)

worth searching for: Besides the original remastered mono album, there are stacks of outtakes, noodling, studio chatter, Wilson's directions to musicians, even a "stereo" remix on *The Pet Sounds Sessions* ♪♪♪ (Capitol, 1997). For the record, the mono version is still better, and only hardcore fanatics will need (or want) this one.

solo outings:
Brian Wilson:
Brian Wilson ♪♪♪♪ (Sire, 1988)

Dennis Wilson:
Pacific Ocean Blue ♪♪♪ (Caribou, 1977)

influences:
◀◀ The Four Freshmen, Chuck Berry, the Lettermen, the Everly Brothers, Phil Spector

▶▶ The Beatles, the Byrds, Jan & Dean, the Eagles, Elvis Costello

Leland Rucker

The Beau Hunks

Formed 1991, in Holland.

Menno Daams, trumpet; Jos Driessen, trumpet; Jilt Jansma, trombone; Robert Veen, alto and soprano sax, clarinet; Ronald Jansen Heijtmajer, alto sax, baritone sax, clarinet; Leo van Oostrom, tenor sax, clarinet, bass clarinet; Ilona De Groot, violin; Tineke de Jong, violin, viola; Eelco Beinema, cello; Jan Robijns, piano; Ton Van Bergeijk, banjo, guitar; Louis Debij, percussion; Peter Stove, tuba; Gert-Jan Blom, bass.

While most of us giggled at Bugs Bunny, a bunch of guys from Holland were watching more than the wabbit. While we giggled at the Little Rascals, a number of Dutch musicians were taking notes. Literally. With painstaking precision, Amsterdam's Beau Hunks have recreated the sounds of some of America's best-known, yet unrecognized, composers. The 14-piece band—which can expand to 30 pieces or shrink to a sextet—began with the works of Leroy Shield, who scored *Little Rascals* and Laurel and Hardy films. To recreate Shield's music, the Beau Hunks worked from Library of Congress films, meticulously cataloguing and transcribing notes from each frame to compile a

database of more than 2,000 sound cues. To recreate the true feel of the music, the takes were recorded with the band huddled around one pair of overhead microphones. The results—two CDs and more than 100 tracks of Shields's works—are staggering both in quantity and quality. While the original music of Raymond Scott has been recently rediscovered and released (on Columbia's *Reckless Nights and Turkish Twilights* and other compilations), the Beau Hunks continue to dig, unearthing even more of the unearthly sounds of Scott, whose music is known to anyone familiar with Warner Bros. cartoons or the more recent sloppy animated heroes Ren and Stimpy. There's something strange about hearing the music clearly and cleanly on CD without either the scratchy, warbling sound-tracks that usually accompanied "Our Gang" shorts, or without the familiar cartoon characters that accompanied Scott's music. Somehow, because of the new technology—or perhaps despite it—the Beau Hunks stay true to the tunes, bringing the background to the forefront.

what to buy: Beginning with "Good Old Days," the opening theme of *The Beau Hunks Play the Original Little Rascals Music* ♪♪♪♪ (Koch Screen, 1994, prod. Gert-Jan Blom), it's difficult not to imagine the pictures that accompanied this music in the classic 1930s Hal Roach comedies. Thanks to the extensive liner notes, the pictures are provided, detailing the uses of each song in each film. Contrary to most jazz albums, the Beau Hunks play the cues in mostly less than a minute, but the 50 tracks segue together surprisingly well. *On to the Show: The Beau Hunks Play More Little Rascals Music* ♪♪♪♪ (Koch Screen, 1995, prod. Gert-Jan Blom, Piet Schreuders) begins with the trademark roar of the MGM lion, with the sound quality perfectly reflecting the era, boasting that it is "newly recorded in authentic Lo-Fi." There's even CD art by Shield fan R. Crumb.

what to buy next: On *The Beau Hunks Sextette Manhattan Minuet* ♪♪♪ (Koch Screen, 1996, prod. Gert-Jan Blom), from the raggedy trumpets to the frenetic clarinets, the sextet captures the sounds of Scott so precisely it's difficult not to join in with mouth-made sound effects and cartoon noises. The CD includes accolades (though not appearances) from Elvis Costello and Irwin Chusid, and even provides an excerpt from a bad review of the band in *Rhythm* magazine titled "You Can Keep Raymond Scott." *The Beau Hunks Sextette Celebration on the Planet Mars: A Tribute to Raymond Scott* ♪♪♪ (Koch Screen, 1995, prod. Gert-Jan Blom) has the distinction of including the Scott tune with the longest name, "Dedicatory Piece to the Crew and Passengers of the First Experimental Rocket Express to the Moon." Though that's exactly what the tune sounds like, there's still plenty left to the imagination. Liner notes are, as usual, detailed and wonderful. Noticing the song "Ectoplasm" is one of Scott's more somber tunes, a Beau Hunk called it "music to bury your mother-in-law by."

worth searching for: Collectors may want the tidy double CD combining *Original Little Rascals* and *On to the Show*, although novice Beau Hunks (and *Little Rascals*) fans are advised to stick to the individual albums.

influences:

◀◀ Raymond Scott, Leroy Shield, *Little Rascals,* Carl Stalling, Danny Elfman

▶▶ Don Byron

Jim Sheeler

The Beautiful South

Formed 1989, in Hull, England.

Paul Heaton, vocals; Dave Rotheray, guitar; Dave Hemingway, vocals; Brianna Corrigan, vocals (1989–92); Sean Welch, bass; Dave Stead, drums; Jacqueline Abbott, vocals (1993–present).

Combining cynical messages about sex, politics, and society with lush, booze-drenched melodies, England's Beautiful South formed in 1989 out of the ashes of the Housemartins, a purer pop-rock band with a strong political bent. With the band's jazz stylings and succulent melodies standing in stark contrast to the serious subject matter of the lyrics, Beautiful South's debut album was an immediate hit in the U.K. The band has continued to be hugely successful on the other side of the Atlantic—a 1994 greatest hits package was the third-fastest-selling of all time in Great Britain—while never making much of an impact stateside.

what to buy: A quintuple platinum CD in the band's native land in 1994, *Carry on Up the Charts: The Best of the Beautiful South* ♫♫♫♫ (PolyGram, 1995, prod. various) was released a year later in the U.S. with a few less tracks. Nonetheless, it's a great introduction to the band's lush harmonic sounds and world weary views. The band is in top form on *0898* ♫♫♫♫ (Elektra, 1992, prod. Jon Kelly); its instantly catchy songs on weighty topics like pornography ("36D") and alcoholism ("Old Red Eyes Is Back") hold up to repeat listenings.

what to buy next: For a debut album, *Welcome to the Beautiful South* ♫♫♫ (Elektra, 1989, prod. Mike Hedges, John Rowley) is a polished effort, but the slow arrangements—perhaps an effort to distance the band from the peppier Housemartins—begin to drag after a while.

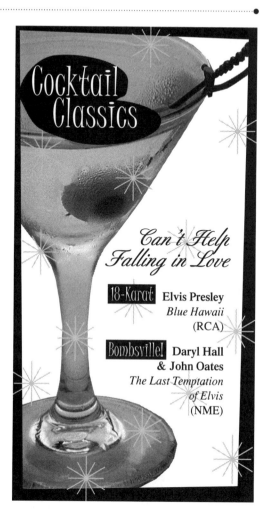

Cocktail Classics

Can't Help Falling in Love

18-Karat Elvis Presley
Blue Hawaii
(RCA)

Bombsville! Daryl Hall & John Oates
The Last Temptation of Elvis
(NME)

what to avoid: The band's second effort, *Choke* ♫♫ (Elektra, 1989), lives up to its name.

the rest:

Miaow ♫♫♫ (Go! Discs, 1994)

worth searching for: Dropped from Elektra after *0898*, the group's most recent album, *Blue Is the Colour* ♫♫♫ (Go! Discs, 1996), is a solid work that's available only as an import.

influences:

◀◀ The Style Council, Elvis Costello, the Housemartins, the Smiths, Burt Bacharach

Alex Gordon

Jaymz Bee

Born James Doyle, April 13, 1963, in North Bay, Ontario, Canada.

Ruthless self-promoter or the Great White North's guru of all things "swellegant"? Jaymz Bee's wild and cuckoo trip from the Ontario backwoods to his reign as Canada's undisputed King of Cocktail is more a testament to his unapologetic drive and chutzpah than to his actual musical prowess, but most of his growing legion of worldwide fans are too busy dancing and dressing up in second-hand leisure suits to really give such matters much thought. It was his self-described "epiphany" at visiting Las Vegas as a child that possibly led to the young Jamie being booted from high school one momentous day for showing up in full, showgirl drag. Wisely leaving North Bay soon afterwards for the comparatively hipper burg of Toronto, he waited tables and even auditioned (unsuccessfully, unfortunately) for a role on *Fraggle Rock* before forming his first band alongside the son of folk legends Ian and Sylvia. Next, the ever-restless Bee answered an ad in a local paper for a Swiss band in need of a lead singer, figuring it'd be an easy way to score a trip to Europe. This was followed by a season as musical director on the Canadian TV talk show *Friday Night*, where Jaymz was decidedly more Doc Severinsen than Paul Shaffer, and a spell throwing parties in Toronto for such visiting luminaries as Jim Carrey, Timothy Leary, and Wes Craven. These shindigs found Bee spinning a potent mix of Vegas nuggets, classic exotica, and even big-band swing on his turntables, naturally leading in 1993 to the formation of his own 12-piece nouveau-lounge combo, the Royal Jelly Orchestra. Today, when not on the road with the Smirnoff Vodka–sponsored RJO (who routinely perform in front of "cockpits" full of mamboing conga-liners), he heads his own record label, Leisure Lab; produces music videos for Queensryche and the Jim Rose Circus Sideshow; stars in the Rhombus Films documentary *Cocktail through the Ages*; helps write books like *Cocktail Parties for Dummies* and *20th-Century Cocktail*; and is developing his own late-night talk show, *The Happy Hour*.

what's available: The Jaymz-supervised *Cocktail: Shakin' and Stirred* 𝄞𝄞𝄞 (Milan/BMG, 1996, prod. Jono Grant, Walter Zwiefel) is a surprisingly intricate and at times even semi-reverent series of swanked-up takes on classics by Bachman-Turner Overdrive, Alanis Morissette, and other Canadian rock icons. Similarly, *A Christmas Cocktail* 𝄞𝄞 (Milan/BMG, 1997, prod. Jono Grant) really only serves to provide Yuletide yuks with the Herb Alpert-meets-*Shaft* version of "Sleigh Ride."

influences:

◀◀ Martin Denny, Juan Garcia Esquivel, Combustible Edison, Burl Ives

▶▶ Mike Flowers, *Austin Powers: International Man of Mystery*

Gary Pig Gold

Harry Belafonte

Born Harold George Belafonte, March 1, 1927, in New York City, NY.

Whether you consider him primarily a singer, an actor, or a humanitarian, there's no disputing that Belafonte is one of the most beloved entertainers of the 20th century. A native New Yorker, he spent his formative years in Jamaica, where he was exposed to the West Indian folk music he later made hugely popular across the globe. While Belafonte is forever identified by his signature tune, "Day-O (The Banana Boat Song)," several other of his songs ("Matilda," "Jamaica Farewell") have also become standards in the easy-listening canon. Belafonte first came to singing via acting. After serving in the U.S. Navy in World War II, he studied theater and landed singing roles in various productions. His voice caught the attention of a club owner, and soon Belafonte was touring the nation as a nightclub singer with a pop repertoire. In the early 1950s, Belafonte lent his diverse talents to a number of projects, while further embracing folk standards. He won a Tony in 1953, but it wasn't until the incredible success of his 1956 albums *Belafonte* and *Calypso* that Belafonte became a national sensation. In fact, *Calypso*, a collection of songs from the West Indies, was lodged at the top of the *Billboard* album charts for 31 weeks—on its way to becoming the first one-million seller by a single artist. Belafonte refused to be typecast as a calypso singer, releasing pure calypso albums only at five-year intervals, in 1961, 1966, and 1971. In the intervening years, Belafonte explored a mind-boggling number of musical styles, tackling blues, chain-gang hymns, Gershwin standards, Christmas carols, cowboy ballads, and Hebrew love songs. In between albums and tours, he continued acting, becoming the first African American to win an Emmy in 1960 and appearing in numerous films. Though his output and commercial appeal slowed somewhat by the late 1960s (his last Top 40 album was in 1964), he continued to be an influential performer as well as a tireless humanitarian and activist. Belafonte was one of the primary organizers of the USA for Africa recording session that led to 1986's inescapable "We Are the World" single. An appearance on the Marlo Thomas–organized *Free to Be You and Me* album and movie in 1972 (a 1970s elementary school staple), and Winona Ryder's

Harry Belafonte **(AP/Wide World Photos)**

lip synching to "Jump in Line (Shake, Shake Senora)" in 1989's *Beetlejuice* have further introduced him to new audiences.

what to buy: The album that made Belafonte's name synonymous with calypso, *Calypso* ♫♫♫♫ (RCA, 1956, prod. Herman Diaz Jr., Henri Rene, Joe Reisman, E.O. Welker) is an unadulterated joy, from the fun drumbeat of "Day-O" to the poignant pennywhistle of "Jamaica Farewell" to the surprisingly feminist sentiment of "Man Smart (Woman Smarter)." *All-Time Greatest Hits, Vols. 1–3* ♫♫♫♫ (RCA, 1987, prod. various) is a more definitive package of more than 50 Belafonte classics, highlighting his ability to seamlessly and successfully cross genres. *Belafonte at Carnegie Hall* ♫♫♫♫♫ (RCA, 1959, prod. Bob Bollard) captures the artist in legendary form on what was the first commercially successful live album.

what to buy next: *Belafonte Returns to Carnegie Hall* ♫♫♫♫ (Mobile Fidelity, 1960) marks the singer's triumphant return to the venerable concert hall for what was scheduled to be its last

event. On his second all-calypso album, *Jump Up Calypso* ♫♫♫♫ (RCA, 1961, prod. Bob Bollard), Belafonte proves that his earlier foray into the music of the islands was no fluke. His most recent album of original material, *Paradise in Gazankulu* ♫♫♫♫ (EMI America, 1988, prod. Hilton Rosenthal) finds Belafonte newly recharged, recording anti-apartheid music in Johannesburg with South African musicians.

what to avoid: As charming as he is, Belafonte's *To Wish You a Merry Christmas* ♫♫ (RCA, 1962), a compilation of 19 holiday classics, grates on the nerves.

best of the rest:
Three for Tonight (O.S.T.) ♫♫♫ (RCA, 1955)
Evening with Belafonte/Mouskouri ♫♫♫ (RCA Victor, 1966)
Island in the Sun ♫♫♫♫ (Pair, 1990)
An Evening with Harry Belafonte ♫♫♫ (PolyGram, 1997)

worth searching for: An out-of-print collection of folk standards, *Midnight Special* ♫♫♫ (RCA, 1962) is notable for being the first album to feature a harmonica player named Bob Dylan, then 20, who played on the title track, then quit after clashing with Belafonte.

influences:

◀◀ Leadbelly, Woody Guthrie

▶▶ The Kingston Trio, Peter, Paul & Mary, the Chad Mitchell Trio, Bob Dylan, Bob Marley

Alex Gordon

Tony Bennett

Born Anthony Dominick Benedetto, August 3, 1926, in New York, NY.

There is no stronger candidate for the "Greatest Interpreter of American Song" award during the past half-century than Bennett. Frank Sinatra and Bing Crosby singled him out as the best singer in the business, and who's to argue? His impeccable tone, which has only grown deeper and stronger over the years, and swinging phrasing are the archetypal traits that lounge singers have aspired to for the past four decades. His greatest commercial success came in the early 1960s, but triumphant returns in the mid-1980s and early 1990s cemented his stature as a musical icon. By 1994's *MTV Unplugged* appearance, even the cynical grunge-loving crowd had championed the optimistic smoothie as an ironic hero.

Growing up in Queens, Bennett spent his teens as a singing waiter. After a stint in the military during World War II, he studied singing at the American Theatre Wing School. Bob Hope and Pearl Bailey discovered him and dished out advice, and Bennett signed with Columbia Records and earned his first hit, "Boulevard of Broken Dreams," in 1950. Through 1964 he notched two dozen Top 40 hits, including "Because of You," "Cold, Cold Heart," "Rags to Riches," "Stranger in Paradise," and his signature number, "I Left My Heart in San Francisco." His emphasis shifted from singles to albums in the mid-1960s, but he continued to draw on material from what he called the "Great American Songbook," filled with George and Ira Gershwin, Irving Berlin, and Johnny Mercer. He also nurtured strong ties to jazz, working with Count Basie, Dizzy Gillespie, Duke Ellington, and George Benson. He recorded infrequently in the 1970s and 1980s—partly because he resisted pressure from Columbia to record more mainstream pop—and instead concentrated on touring and his other talent, painting. The first high-profile beneficiary of the lounge revival in the early 1990s, Bennett found new popularity—showing up on late-night talk shows and *The Simpsons*, starring on and releasing an album

from *MTV Unplugged,* touring, and recording several well-executed concept albums paying tribute to Sinatra, Fred Astaire, Billie Holiday, and others. His voice today has a smokier edge than the impossibly smooth tone of his younger days, but it also has grown richer.

what to buy: If you can afford it, by all means go for *Forty Years: The Artistry of Tony Bennett* 𝄢𝄢𝄢𝄢 (Columbia, 1991, prod. Didier Deutsch), a chronologically arranged 87-song anthology and one of the best box sets of the box-set era. The four-disc collection was re-released in 1997 in an unabridged but smaller, more affordable package. The Grammy-winning *MTV Unplugged* 𝄢𝄢𝄢𝄢 (Columbia, 1994, prod. David Kahne) took the momentum built by the box set and launched a full-fledged comeback; Bennett gives a confident, commanding performance of career highlights—plus, Elvis Costello and k.d. lang make cameos. *The Art of Excellence* 𝄢𝄢𝄢𝄢 (Columbia, 1986/1997, prod. Ettore Stratta, Danny Bennett) marked Bennett's return to Columbia and significant sales. It mixes standards with great new finds like "How Do You Keep the Music Playing."

what to buy next: *I Left My Heart in San Francisco* 𝄢𝄢𝄢𝄢 (Columbia, 1962/1997 prod. Ernest Altschuler) is Bennett's first great studio album, containing "Smile," "The Best Is Yet to Come," and the unforgettable title track, which won two Grammys. *At Carnegie Hall: The Complete Concert* 𝄢𝄢𝄢𝄢 (Columbia, 1962/1997, prod. Ernest Altschuler, Robin McBride) is an expanded version of the original live album.

what to avoid: *Tony Sings the Great Hits of Today* 𝄢𝄢 (Columbia, 1969, prod. Wally Gold) is the type of corporate collection that Bennett loathed and that led to his retreat from the business. "MacArthur Park," "My Cherie Amour," and three Beatles tunes represent one ill-fitting choice after another.

best of the rest:

The Beat of My Heart 𝄢𝄢𝄢𝄢 (Columbia, 1957/1997)
In Person! with the Count Basie Orchestra 𝄢𝄢𝄢𝄢 (Columbia, 1959/1994)
Tony Sings for Two 𝄢𝄢 (Columbia, 1960/1996)
I Wanna Be Around 𝄢𝄢𝄢𝄢 (Columbia, 1963/1995)
Who Can I Turn To? 𝄢𝄢𝄢𝄢 (Columbia, 1964/1995)
If I Ruled the World: Songs for the Jet Set 𝄢𝄢 (Columbia, 1965/1997)
The Movie Song Album 𝄢𝄢𝄢 (Columbia, 1966/1988)
Snowfall: The Christmas Album 𝄢𝄢𝄢𝄢 (Columbia, 1968/1997)
Something 𝄢𝄢𝄢 (Columbia, 1970/1995)

Tony Bennett (© Ken Settle)

All-Time Hall of Fame Hits 𝄞𝄞𝄞 (Columbia, 1970/1987)
The Very Thought of You 𝄞𝄞𝄞 (Columbia, 1971/1995)
All-Time Greatest Hits 𝄞𝄞𝄞𝄞 (Columbia, 1972/1987)
Rodgers and Hart Songbook 𝄞𝄞𝄞 (DRG, 1973/WMO, 1997)
Jazz 𝄞𝄞𝄞𝄞 (Columbia, 1987)
Bennett/Berlin 𝄞𝄞𝄞 (Columbia, 1987)
Astoria: Portrait of the Artist 𝄞𝄞𝄞𝄞 (Columbia, 1989/1997)
Perfectly Frank 𝄞𝄞𝄞𝄞 (Columbia, 1992)
Steppin' Out 𝄞𝄞𝄞𝄞 (Columbia, 1993)
Here's to the Ladies 𝄞𝄞𝄞𝄞 (Columbia, 1995)
On Holiday 𝄞𝄞𝄞 (Columbia, 1997)

worth searching for: Never released commercially, *Selections from the Box Set 40 Years: The Artistry of Tony Bennett* 𝄞𝄞𝄞𝄞 (Columbia, 1991, prod. various) is just what the title indicates: a sampler of 12 tracks from the exceptional anthology. Also, the out-of-print *Tony's Greatest Hits, Vol. III* 𝄞𝄞𝄞𝄞 (Columbia, 1965, prod. various) is a snapshot of his peak impact era, anchored by "I Left My Heart in San Francisco," "I Wanna Be Around," and "When Joanna Loved Me."

influences:

◀◀ Art Tatum, Mildred Bailey, Frank Sinatra, Mel Tormé

▶▶ Sammy Davis Jr., Barbra Streisand, Jack Jones, Steve Lawrence, Anthony Newley, Robert Goulet, Engelbert Humperdinck, Wayne Newton, k.d. lang, Elvis Costello, Harry Connick Jr.

Jay Dedrick

Bent Fabric

See: Fabric, Bent

Bunny Berigan

Born Roland Bernard Berigan, November 2, 1908, in Hilbert, WI. Died June 2, 1942, in New York, NY.

Berigan's fiery trumpet tone and unmistakable growl provides excitement for even the casual jazz listener. No ordinary big-band sideman or leader, Berigan's sheer force and inventive attack could spark any variety of musical settings. Berigan's musical career began at age eight on violin. By age 13 he had started to play trumpet, and by the next year he played well enough to join some local bands. Soon, he quit school and became a professional musician. His travels ultimately took him to New York City, where he joined Hal Kemp's Orchestra and made his first recordings in 1930. After quitting Kemp, Berigan freelanced around New York extensively, spending brief periods with the bands of Paul Whiteman, Fred Rich, and others. He was continually in recording studios because of his quick read-ing skills and improvisational expertise. Thus, hundreds of exciting examples exist of Berigan's playing in various large and small groups in the years 1931 to 1936. Berigan was a regular fixture on 52nd Street, and his presence on many small-group swing records of this period are gems of 1930s jazz. After a short stint with Benny Goodman's Orchestra in 1935 and Tommy Dorsey's Orchestra in 1937, Berigan formed his own big band and recorded for RCA Victor from mid-1937 until the band went bankrupt in 1940.

Berigan was a stellar trumpet player and a workaholic. Unfortunately, he was not a good businessman, and he was a heavy drinker. Collectively, these factors ultimately brought on his untimely death at age 33 in 1942.

what to buy: Some of Berigan's best recordings from the early to mid-1930s can be found on *Portrait of Bunny Berigan* 𝄞𝄞𝄞𝄞 (ASV Living Era, 1992) and *Swingin' High* 𝄞𝄞𝄞𝄞 (Topaz, 1993). On these, Berigan is featured with the Dorsey Brothers, Frankie Trumbauer, Glenn Miller ("Solo Hop" is a Berigan tour de force), and others. *Bunny Berigan and His Boys: 1935–36* 𝄞𝄞𝄞𝄞 (Classics, 1993, prod. Gilles Petard), *Bunny Berigan: 1936–37* 𝄞𝄞𝄞𝄞 (Classics, 1993, prod. Gilles Petard), *Bunny Berigan: 1937* 𝄞𝄞𝄞𝄞 (Classics, 1994, prod. Gilles Petard), *Bunny Berigan: 1937–38* 𝄞𝄞𝄞𝄞 (Classics, 1994, prod. Gilles Petard), and *Bunny Berigan: 1938* 𝄞𝄞𝄞𝄞 (Classics, 1995, prod. Gilles Petard) cover possibly the best period of Berigan's career.

what to buy next: To get a taste of Berigan's prowess, *Bunny Berigan: Pied Piper* 𝄞𝄞𝄞𝄞 (Bluebird, 1995, prod. Steve Backer) offers a nice cross-section of Berigan's Victor recordings. Berigan's entire output on radio transcription recordings have been released on the two-CD set *Bunny Berigan and the Rhythm Makers* 𝄞𝄞𝄞 (Jazz Classics, 1996). These have good fidelity, plus a lot of titles that were never commercially recorded. Although many titles are pop tunes, Berigan's solos add quite a bit of spark to these performances. "Shanghai Shuffle," "Sing You Sinners," and other titles make this acquisition most worthwhile.

best of the rest:
The Complete Bunny Berigan, Vol. III 𝄞𝄞 (Bluebird, 1993)
Bunny Berigan: 1938–1942 𝄞𝄞 (Classics, 1996)

worth searching for: Berigan was always at his best in a small group setting. The 1935 and 1936 recordings with Red McKenzie's group, the *Mound City Blues Blowers* 𝄞𝄞𝄞𝄞 (Timeless, 1994, prod. Chris Barber, Wim Wigt), feature Berigan extensively. Titles such as "What's the Reason," "Indiana," and "I'm Gonna Sit Right Down and Write Myself a Letter" should leave the listener in awe as Berigan rips through his solos, teases with muted accompaniment, then pounces once again, exuding a fire to which few other trumpet players could come even close. For listeners interested in recordings before Berigan's Victor recording period, the trumpeter can be appreciated to great advantage on *Harlem Lullaby* ♪♪♪♪ (Hep, 1992, prod. Alastair Robertson, John R.T. Davies) or *Best of the Big Bands: Dorsey Brothers* ♪♪♪♪ (Columbia, 1992, prod. Michael Brooks). His awe-inspiring solos on "She's Funny That Way," "Shim Sham Shimmy," and "She Reminds Me of You" (which might well be one of Berigan's best-ever offerings) are added bonuses to overall fine recordings by the Dorsey Brothers' band.

influences:

◀◀ Louis Armstrong, Bix Beiderbecke, Bob Mayhew

▶▶ Manny Klein, Pee Wee Irwin, Roy Eldridge, Johnny Best, Billy Butterfield, Charlie Spivak

Jim Prohaska

Irving Berlin

Born Israel Baline, May 11, 1888, in Temun, Siberia, Russia. Died September 22, 1989, in New York City, NY.

Though he never learned to formally read music, and played the piano using only the black notes, Berlin wrote "White Christmas," "God Bless America," "Puttin' on the Ritz," "Always," "There's No Business Like Show Business," and other classics that have defined America for much of the 20th Century. Plagiarism charges (never founded) dogged him since his first hit, 1911's "Alexander's Ragtime Band," but publishing royalties made him a multimillionaire, and he lived a long life as a reclusive New York City tycoon.

Berlin's life story was a collection of rich, dramatic anecdotes. His father died soon after the family immigrated from Russia. Berlin was very young at the time, and he started singing on New York sidewalks to make money. He learned that writing music would lead to even bigger money, and he started contributing novelty songs and production one-offs to various shows through World War II. After he fell in love with his second wife, Ellin Mackay, a contributing journalist to the *New Yorker*, her wealthy father—who disdained Berlin's poverty, his commitment to show-business, and his Jewish heritage—sent her on a trip around the world; Berlin wrote one of his best-known songs, "Always," while she was away. They married when she returned. Late in his life, he effectively retired to his New York City home, where he lived in almost total anonymity. His wife died in 1988. After he died at age 101, people gathered outside his residence to sing "God Bless America."

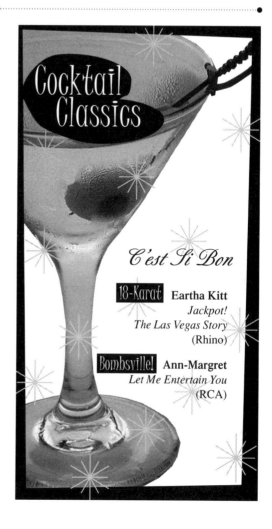

what to buy: Countless star singers, from Rosemary Clooney to Frank Sinatra, have loaded up their albums with Berlin songs, so when searching for a representative Berlin album, it's best to rely on your favorite performers. Among the best are *Irving Berlin: A Hundred Years* ♪♪♪♪ (Columbia, 1988, prod. various), including Bing Crosby (who put out the best-known version of "White Christmas"), Eddie Cantor, and Tony Bennett; and *Great American Songwriters—Irving Berlin* ♪♪♪♪ (Delta, 1994), featuring Clooney and Fred Astaire.

what to buy next: *Cheek to Cheek: The Irving Berlin Songbook* ♪♪♪♪ (Verve, 1997, prod. various) has excellent performances by Billie Holiday and Sarah Vaughan, among others, showing Berlin's wide reach into jazz.

worth searching for: A more easy-listening collection of Berlin standards, *Showcase* ♪♪♪ (Pearl Flapper, 1991, prod. various), is light on jazz and pop performers, but includes soft-spoken stuff by Rudy Vallee and Mantovani.

influences:

◄◄ Cole Porter

►► Frank Sinatra, Billie Holiday, Ella Fitzgerald, Rosemary Clooney, Bing Crosby, Paul McCartney

Steve Knopper

Elmer Bernstein

Born April 4, 1922, New York City, NY.

A Hollywood legend, Bernstein was one of the first movie composers to rely heavily on jazz idioms for his scores, thereby influencing the master of the swinging soundtrack, Henry Mancini, and every other composer who came of age in the '50s and early '60s. He studied music at Juilliard and worked for a brief time as a pianist. During World War II he worked as an arranger for Glenn Miller's Army Air Force Band as well as Armed Forces Radio. He eventually migrated to Hollywood, where he continues to work steadily as a film composer, writing music for more than 100 films. He also contributed the "Peter Gunn"–like title song for the '50s crime show *Staccato*. Bernstein's swaggering, jazz-tinged scores for films like *The Man with the Golden Arm* and *The Sweet Smell of Success* played an integral role in setting a mood of moral dissipation and urban grit for those seminal films.

what to buy: Though almost of all of Bernstein's original albums, including his soundtracks, are out of print, he shows up repeatedly on volumes of Capitol's excellent *Ultra-Lounge* series. You can find the theme to *Stacatto* as well as "Thinking of Batty" on *Ultra-Lounge, Vol. 7: Crime Scene* ♪♪♪♪ (Capitol, 1996, compilation prod. Brad Benedict).

the rest:

The Great Escape ♪♪♪ (Original Soundtrack) (MGM, 1963/Rykodisc, 1998)

The Return of the Magnificent Seven ♪♪♪♪ (Original Soundtrack) (MGM, 1966/Rykodisc, 1998)

influences:

◄◄ Glenn Miller, Benny Goodman

►► Henry Mancini, John Barry, Lalo Schifrin

Marc Weingarten

Big Bad Voodoo Daddy

Formed 1992, in Los Angeles, CA.

Scotty Morris, vocals, guitar; Josh Levy, piano; Andy Rowley, saxophone; Karl Hunter, saxophone; Glenn Marhevka, trumpet; Jeff Harris, trombone; Dirk Shumaker, bass; Kurt Sodergren, drums.

It's an absolute rarity: a low-budget independent film gets a huge buzz, finds a cult audience, and along the way catapults its featured musical act to limited but significant national attention. As capable and catchy as its jumping jive may be, Big Bad Voodoo Daddy owes what little fame it has received thus far to Doug Liman's hip 1996 art-house favorite *Swingers*, in which the octet's then-mushrooming weekly appearance at Hollywood's famed Derby nightclub was played up for sharply effective cinematic energy. The band had been toiling away at its own brand of Cab Calloway/Louis Jordan swing and city-blues since 1992, releasing a pair of now-out-of-print homemade albums that earned it a well-regarded reputation among the hep-set of L.A.'s burgeoning lounge revival. After *Swingers* struck gold (and its accompanying soundtrack started selling in moderate numbers), BBVD's local gigs were soon teeming with cool cats and hot chicks decked out in the snazziest vintage clothing. Still, the band has yet to truly capitalize on its sudden notoriety, taking more than a year to issue its major-label debut. Whether it can crack into the modern-rock camp, like its Dixie-laden colleagues, the Squirrel Nut Zippers, remains uncertain.

what to buy: There are dozens of reasons to own the soundtrack to *Swingers* ♪♪♪ (Hollywood, 1996, prod. various), from classics by old standbys such as Dean Martin, Tony Bennett, and Bobby Darin, to cheeky tunes by fresh upstarts such as Love Jones and Joey Altruda to out-of-character entries from Roger Miller and George Jones. Still, BBVD's three cuts—the Brian Setzer-ish "Go Daddy-O," a splendid cover of the Disney samba classic "I Wan'na Be Like You," and the group's signature number, "You & Me & the Bottle Makes 3 Tonight (Baby)"—are knockouts that give you a strong sense of what future releases will hold. It's an unlocked, can't-miss-it doorway into the Cocktail Nation.

what to buy next: Digging this '90s version of Cab? Then keep swingin' to *Big Bad Voodoo Daddy* ♪♪♪ (Coolsville/EMI/Capitol, 1998, prod. various), the band's major-label debut. If your jump-blues brain is still a fairly clean slate, it will likely be a revelation—a blast of high-spirited fun amid a world of whiny noise and aimless thunder. If you've heard Calloway, Louis Jordan, and the best of the big bands, however, you'll probably find it all a bit sterile. As with Squirrel Nut Zippers, there's a spark and vitality that's lacking, despite the band's proficiency. And unlike, say, Boston's Slackers, BBVD hasn't made an attempt to suffuse the exuberance of a bygone era with a dose of cutting '90s irony. (To think of what could have been done with Cab's "Minnie the Moocher"! It's rotely covered here.) Instead, BBVD merely mimics what it can never match.

worth searching for: BBVD's earlier home-grown works—*Big Bad Voodoo Daddy* ♫♫♫ (Hep Cat, 1993, prod. Big Bad Voodoo Daddy) and *Whatchu' Want for Christmas?* ♫♫♫ (Hep Cat, 1995, prod. Big Bad Voodoo Daddy)—are both fine, if not expertly produced, efforts.

influences:

◀◀ Cab Calloway, Louis Jordan, Louis Prima, Bill Haley

▶▶ Squirrel Nut Zippers, the Wonderful World of Joey, the Slackers, Big Sandy and His Fly-Rite Boys

Ben Wener

Björk

Born Björk Gudmundsdottir, November 21, 1965, in Reykjavik, Iceland.

Sure, the pixieish Icelandic singer makes some of the most mysteriously compelling and forward-looking pop music of the '90s. But Björk's greatest achievement may be that she managed to get MTV to play a video in 1995 for an old silver-screen Betty Hutton showtune, "It's Oh So Quiet." The whimsical, Spike Jonze–directed clip seemed charmingly out of place alongside brash videos by the heavy-metal band White Zombie and gangsta rapper 2Pac, partially because of its golden-era-Hollywood look and feel, but more significantly because of the dynamic cover's breathy vocals, "zing-boom!" theatrics, Frank Sinatra–like pizzazz, and crisp, brassy sound. The song seemed out of place on MTV, but it actually makes perfect sense in the ex-Sugarcubes singer's catalog, a wildly eclectic assemblage in which anything seems to go—murky trip-hop, throbbing dance-pop, a curious jazz standard, a baffling nursery rhyme, or, of course, a revived showtune.

what to buy: The Grammy-nominated *Post* ♫♫♫♫ (Elektra, 1995, prod. Nellee Hooper, Tricky, Howie Bernstein, Björk, Graham Massey) is full of sonic twists and turns, many of which actually come from Björk herself, as the singer charges with joyful abandon through a world apparently full of vocal possibilities, playing a seductive jazz crooner or octave-jumping, chopped-English pop singer one moment, and then a warbling little girl or psychotic screamer the next. Loaded with odd, challenging arrangements, the dance-oriented album features varied instru-

Cocktail Classics

Cherry Pink and Apple Blossom White

18-Karat **Perez Prado** *Mondo Mambo! The Best Of* (Rhino)

Bombsville! **John Barry** *The EMI Years, Vol. 3* (Scamp/Caroline)

mentation, too, with jazzy horns, hammered dulcimers, orchestral strings, growling guitars, and booming electronic beats. The openers "Army of Me" and "Hyper-ballad" make for an arresting one-two dance-floor punch, and "It's Oh So Quiet" is an essential listen; but the slower and softer songs (the murky "Enjoy," the ambient "Headphones") are the most interesting.

what to buy next: Björk set the unusual tone of her post-Sugarcubes career with *Debut* ♫♫♫ (Elektra, 1993, prod. Nellee Hooper, Björk), an album of somewhat exotic instrumentation (a timpani! a harp! a tabla!), bold dance music ("Human Behavior," "Big Time Sensuality"), electronic torch songs ("Venus As a Boy"), and even an old chestnut ("Like Someone in Love").

the rest:
Homogenic 🎵🎵🎵🎵 (Elektra, 1997)
Telegram 🎵🎵🎵 (Elektra, 1997)

worth searching for: Temporarily moving away from the usual dance-world producers, Björk collaborated with avant-gardist Hector Zazou on the brooding, icy "Visur Vatnsenda-Rosu," off Zazou's *Songs from the Cold Seas* 🎵🎵🎵🎵 (Columbia, 1995). Meanwhile, back in said dance world, Tricky put Björk's voice through a processor for the spooky "Keep Your Mouth Shut," the best track from his side-project album *Nearly God* 🎵🎵🎵 (Island, 1996).

influences:

◄◄ Soul II Soul, Frank Sinatra, Cocteau Twins, Dead Can Dance, Joy Division, Siouxsie and the Banshees, Betty Hutton

►► Ruby, Garbage, Tricky, Pizzicato Five, Shelleyan Orphan

Josh Freedom du Lac

Björn Again

Formed 1988, in Melbourne, Australia.

Benny Anderwear, keyboards, vocals; Frida Longstokin, vocals; Agnetha Falstart, vocals; Bjorn Volvo-us, guitar, vocals; Rutger Sonofagunn, bass; Ola Drumkitt, drums.

Officially, this ABBA tribute band likes to say it formed when a collision between a helicopter (a reference to ABBA's *Arrival* album cover) and a giant platform shoe from outer space left the four performers stranded on a deserted island. Amnesia allegedly robbed them of all non-ABBA thoughts. Actually, the tribute band was the brainchild of Australian bassist Rod Leissle (the group's "Rutger Sonofagunn"), who has recruited various anonymous performers over the years to portray the ABBA-esque characters. The group was on the cutting edge of the ABBA revival of the early '90s, answering Erasure's EP of ABBA covers with a Björn Again single of Erasure covers ("A Little Respect" and "Stop"). The band has recorded a pair of albums and several singles, but its stage work is its most outstanding. In its first decade, the group has donned platform boots and satin robes in more than 1,300 shows in 30 countries. Björn Again does an amazingly accurate job of recreating ABBA's pop magic, adding guitar-heavy arrangements and

Björk (Archive Photos)

laugh-inducing camp and kitsch, and has won praise from unlikely fans (Metallica, Nirvana) as well as the original members of ABBA.

worth searching for: Both Björn Again albums are available paired as an import-only two-CD set. *Live Album* 🎵🎵🎵🎵 (M&G, 1994, prod. Rod Leissle) captures the Björn Again experience, with glistening renditions of "Waterloo," "Ring Ring," "Dancing Queen," and 11 other ABBA hits. The group's token non-ABBA rocker represented here is Nirvana's "Smells Like Teen Spirit." *Flashback* 🎵🎵🎵 (M&G, 1993, prod. Rod Leissle) is a collection of 16 non-ABBA pop gems done in the Swedish style. "When Will I See You Again" and "Cecilia" are treats.

influences:

◄◄ Um, well . . . that would be ABBA

Jay Dedrick

Black Velvet Flag

Formed in New York City, NY.

Fred Stesney, vocals; Jason Zasky, guitar; Jeff Musser, bass, maracas; Juditta Musette, background vocals.

As one-joke bands go, Black Velvet Flag are a notch below the reggae-and-Elvis flukes Dread Zeppelin—they're a foursome whose entire act consists of nothing more than lounge-style covers of punk rock classics like Fear's "I Don't Care About You" and Suicidal Tendencies' "Institutionalized." Like the joke in theory? Then you'll like it in practice. Hate it in theory? Don't bother.

what's available: *Come Recline with Black Velvet Flag* 🎵🎵🎵 (Go-Kart, 1994, prod. Joe Lambert) is the only Black Velvet Flag record in existence, and it will hit the spot if you've spent weeks combing record stores for cocktail-hour covers of "Media Blitz," "Wasted," and "I Shot JFK."

influences:

◄◄ Coolies, Bonzo Dog Band, Dread Zeppelin, Mojo Nixon, Dr. Demento, Love Jones, Combustible Edison

Ben Greenman

Pat Boone

Born Charles Eugene Boone, June 1, 1934, in Jacksonville, FL.

Though he's now known best for his gospel albums and support for Republican politicians, there was a scary period in the late 1950s and early 1960s when Boone, whose specialty was ready-for-Las Vegas rock music long before U2 and the Grateful Dead played the Emerald City, was once nearly crowned the king of rock 'n' roll. He had more pop hits in his peak than any artist save Elvis Presley. Raised in rural Tennessee, Boone parlayed an appearance on the *Ted Mack Amateur Hour* television show into a year-long stint on Arthur Godfrey's amateur show and a recording contract. Boone enjoyed a few pop hits with such songs as "Two Hearts, Two Kisses" in 1955, but it wasn't until he began recording sanitized, de-ethnicized versions of R&B and rock hits—including Little Richard's "Tutti Frutti" and "Long Tall Sally"—that Boone's place in history was assured. With his crewcut and white buckskin shoes, Boone was the perfect bridge between early rock 'n' roll "race records" and the white pop mainstream, covering tunes by Fats Domino, Ivory Joe Hunter, and others. Beatlemania eventually made his efforts irrelevant, but not before Boone had moved on to his own television show and movie soundtrack work. In all, Boone enjoyed 38 chart-topping pop hits. In 1996, however, he made an album of heavy-metal covers: his vamping in leather, chains, and a fake tattoo got him in hot water with his core Christian audience, but his Buddy Greco–like takes on Metallica's "Enter Sandman," Judas Priest's "You've Got Another Thing Comin'," and Deep Purple's "Smoke on the Water" are essential, classic kitsch.

what to buy: Most of what's available are retrospectives, holiday collections, and Christian recordings. Many—though not all—of the hits are on *Pat Boone's Greatest Hits* ♫♫♫ (MCA, 1993, prod. various).

what to buy next: Boone actually has quite a wit, which he displays on *In a Metal Mood: No More Mr. Nice Guy* ♫♫♫ (MCA, 1997, prod. Michael Lloyd, Jeffrey Weber), a collection of heavy-metal cover tunes by the likes of Ozzy Osbourne, Metallica, and, of course, Alice Cooper. It works on two levels: Boone thinks it's a tremendous joke (which it is); he also plays it straight, with complex, if kind of goofy, big-band charts.

the rest:
Best of ♫♫♫ (MCA)
Greatest Hits ♫♫♫ (Curb, 1990)
A Date with Pat Boone ♫♫ (Pair, 1992)
Pat's Greatest Hits ♫♫ (Curb, 1994)
The Inspirational Collection N/A (Varese Vintage, 1998)

worth searching for: There's also a video anthology of his chart successes, *40 Years of Hits* ♫♫♫ (Rhino, 1995); or you can dig for the German import *Jivin' Pat* ♫♫♫♫ (Bear Family, 1986), a sardonic collection of his rock covers.

influences:

◄◄ Elvis Presley, Metallica, Alice Cooper, Deep Purple, Little Richard, Al Jolson

►► Johnny Tillotson, Debby Boone, Chris Isaak

Eric Deggans and Brian Mansfield

Victor Borge

Born January 3, 1909, in Copenhagen, Denmark.

Victor Borge is one of the funniest, most durable classical-music attractions in the world. Whether he's heckling audience requests, mischievously reinventing trite public domain ditties in the style of the great composers, or parodying grand opera, he is always charming, witty, and thoroughly entertaining. On top of that, he is a talented classical pianist with masterful technique.

Borge began his career as a concert pianist in Denmark when he was 13, and played with many of the top symphony orchestras in Europe. Bit by bit, he surreptitiously added physical comedy to the classical musical programs, until he developed a greater reputation as a comic than as a musician. In addition to concert work, Borge composed, directed, and conducted popular musical comedies. By the late 1930s, he was a star on Danish radio and in movies, and his satirical anti-Nazi remarks provoked the ire of the Third Reich. From Finland, his home after Denmark fell to Germany, he sought sanctuary in the U.S. in 1940. Initially, he found work doing pre-show audience warm-ups for Rudy Vallee's radio show, but his big break came when he did his classic routine, "Phonetic Punctuation," on Bing Crosby's *Kraft Music Hall* program. An instant hit, Borge became a regular on Crosby's show until he was offered his own five-minute daily spot on NBC, which led to a feature part in the the 1944 film *Higher and Higher*. Borge's throw-away classical brilliance and gift for visual shtick made him a major television star during the '50s. Though offered his own network variety show, Borge, wary of quick burnout and overexposure, limited his TV appearances to guest shots and specials. In 1953, he created his critically acclaimed one-man show, and he has toured the world with variants of that program ever since. A series of best-selling videos has introduced the comedy and music of Victor Borge to modern audiences, and his popularity has never been greater.

Victor Borge **(AP/Wide World Photos)**

what to buy: Borge's finest, funniest bits and routines are on *Live* 🎵🎵🎵🎵 (Sony Broadway, 1953/1992, compilation prod. George Avakian), which features his classic "Phonetic Punctuation."

what to buy next: *Comedy in Music* 🎵🎵🎵 (Tri-Star Music, 1996, prod. various) contains much of the same material with some spontaneous additions. Worthwhile if you can't find *Live*.

worth searching for: Borge's wonderfully skewed sense of humor and considerable knowledge of classical music are vividly on display in two books he wrote with Robert Sherman, *My Favorite Intermissions* 🎵🎵🎵🎵 (Doubleday, 1971) and *My Favorite Comedies in Music* 🎵🎵🎵 (Franklin Watts, 1980).

influences:

◀◀ Danny Kaye, Oscar Levant

▶▶ Liberace, Peter Schickele

Ken Burke

Boston Pops Orchestra

See: Arthur Fiedler

The Boswell Sisters

Formed 1924. Disbanded 1936.

Connee Boswell (born December 3, 1907, in New Orleans, LA; died October 11, 1976, in New York, NY), vocals; Martha Boswell (born 1905; died July 2, 1958, in Peekskill, NY), vocals; Helvetia Boswell (born 1909; died November 12, 1988), vocals.

The Boswell Sisters were the first female vocal group to bring the feeling of Southern blues and jazz to pop music. Their rich, close harmonies and jazzy scatting and phrasing gave their music a unique feeling of excitement and spontaneity. They were all skilled musicians: Martha played piano, Helvetia played the banjo, guitar, and violin, and Connee could wail on the saxophone, trombone, cello, and piano. Though Connee Boswell had been stricken with polio as a child and was confined to a wheelchair, she had tons of ambition and drive. She was a preteen when she cut her first record (a blues written by sister Martha). Encouraged by Connee's success, the sisters teamed up for a series of amateur contests, eventually becoming popular vaudeville attractions. Their first recordings as a group featured their vocal imitations of various musical instruments, à la the Mills Brothers. After winning a radio contest, the Boswells moved to California for regular work on radio, where their elaborate yet vivacious harmony style (arranged by Connee) made them stars. They cut dozens of fine discs with the most accomplished jazz musicians of their era (including the Dorsey Brothers, Bunny Berrigan, and Manny Klein). Their ability to swing a chorus and switch into overdrive with changes in vocal key and pitch amazed their peers and fans. Success on records and radio led to appearances in such feature films as *Rambling 'Round Radio Row, Close Harmony,* and *Transatlantic Merry-Go-Round,* in which the Boswells became the first white group to sing about the glories of "rock 'n' roll" (although in this case it was about the motion of a ship, not a euphemism for sex). The Boswells were at their commercial and artistic peak when they disbanded. All three had married and only Connee wanted to continue performing.

As a solo performer, Connee Boswell's style blended perfectly with Bing Crosby's on a series of duet smashes, and she registered solo hits with versions of "Stormy Weather" and "Sand in My Shoes." She appeared in several films and as a regular on TV's *Pete Kelly's Blues.* Though her career never fulfilled its potential, she remained a favorite of other singers (such as Ella Fitzgerald) until she retired in the late '60s.

what to buy: The Tommy Dorsey Orchestra backs the Boswells on *That's How Rhythm Was Born* 🎵🎵🎵🎵 (Legacy, 1995, prod. Didier C. Deutsch), an invigorating collection of the Sisters' hottest jazz-drenched sides, including "Rock and Roll," "Between the Devil and the Deep Blue Sea," and "The Object of My Affection." Recorded in the '30s, these tracks really swing, and the Boswells bring warmth and verve to every song.

the rest:

Everybody Loves My Baby 🎵🎵🎵 (Pro Arte/Pro Jazz, 1991)
It's the Girls 🎵🎵 (ASV, 1992)
Syncopating Harmonists from New Orleans 🎵🎵🎵 (Take Two, 1992)
It's You 🎵🎵🎵 (Flapper, 1996)
Airshots & Rarities: 1930–35 🎵🎵🎵 (Challenge, 1997)

worth searching for: Some import services carry *Okay America! Alternate Takes & Rarities* 🎵🎵 (Jass Records, 1992/Vintage Jazz, 1997), which contains Connee's guest appearance with Red Nichols and the Casa Loma Orchestra as well as alternate takes of records by the Boswell Sisters. Also, you can see the sisters singing "Rock and Roll" in the video version of *Transatlantic Merry-Go-Round* 🎵🎵🎵 (Video Late Show, 1986), a 1934 feature film starring Jack Benny and Nancy Carroll.

solo outings:

Connee Boswell:

Deep in a Dream 🎵🎵🎵 (Harlequin, 1996)
Heart & Soul 🎵🎵🎵 (ASV, 1997)
Sings Irving Berlin 🎵🎵 (Simitar, 1997)

influences:

◀◀ Emmett Hardy, Bessie Smith, Ethel Waters, Bing Crosby

▶▶ The Andrews Sisters, the MacGuire Sisters, Ella Fitzgerald, Billie Holiday

Ken Burke

Brave Combo

Formed 1979, in Denton, TX.

Carl Finch, vocals, accordion, guitar; Bubba Hernandez, bass, vocals; Jeffrey Barnes, saxophone, clarinet, percussion.

A self-described "nuclear polka" band, Brave Combo is often shortchanged as a novelty act since its frenetic live shows zigzag from stampede-inducing romps through "Who Stole the Kishka" and "The Happy Wanderer" to a surf version of "Oh, What a Beautiful Morning" and a swinging take on Wayne Newton's "Danke Schoen." But over the years, the Combo—a revolving six-piece band built around the nucleus of Finch, Hernandez, and Barnes—has evolved into a versatile outfit capable of being both faithful and funky as they parade through polkas, rancheras, sambas, cumbias, and anything else you can dance to. Once a band to simply get wrecked to, Brave Combo is now a group to be reckoned with.

what to buy: *No, No, No, Cha Cha Cha* ꝏꝏꝏꝏ (Rounder, 1993, prod. Brave Combo) focuses on the group's Latin influences and boasts a seamless medley of the Rolling Stones' "Satisfaction" and Ringo Starr's "No No Song," a festive salsa version of Cher's "The Way of Love," and a boss bossa-nova rendition of "Fly Me to the Moon." *Polkas for a Gloomy World* ꝏꝏꝏꝏ (Rounder, 1995, prod. Brave Combo) is their Grammy-nominated return to straight-ahead polka, mixing infectious originals like "Flying Saucer" with traditional Mexican, Russian, and German polkas. *It's Christmas, Man!* ꝏꝏꝏ½ (Rounder, 1992, prod. Brave Combo) is an irreverent antidote to all those Mannheim Steamroller holiday albums thanks to the delightful title track, a ska version of "The Christmas Song," and an inspired reading of "Must Be Santa," once recorded by Lorne Greene.

what to buy next: *Girl* ꝏꝏꝏ (Rounder, 1996, prod. Brave Combo, Bucks Burnett), a surprisingly listenable collaboration with Tiny Tim, demonstrates the depth of Brave Combo's musical vocabulary and its astounding ability to make anyone sound good. Check out the hepcat-jazz version of "Stairway to Heaven" and the "Wooly Bully"–like reworking of "Bye Bye Blackbird."

what to avoid: Although hardly horrid, *Musical Varieties* ꝏꝏ (Rounder, 1988, prod. Brave Combo), a compilation of pre-Rounder tracks from the early '80s, leans toward predictable gimmickry ("People Are Strange" and "Sixteen Tons" as polkas), sideswiping genres the band would eventually tackle head-on.

the rest:

Polkatharsis ꝏꝏꝏ (Rounder, 1987)
Humansville ꝏꝏꝏ (Rounder, 1989)
A Night on Earth ꝏꝏꝏ½ (Rounder, 1990)

worth searching for: *The Hokey Pokey* ꝏꝏꝏ (denTone, 1994, prod. Brave Combo) is a self-released EP of wacky concert favorites like "The Hava Nagila Twist," "The Jeopardy Schottis-che," and a Devo-like demolition of the title track.

influences:

◀◀ You name it, from Xavier Cugat to Astor Piazzolla

▶▶ New Orleans Klezmer All Stars

David Okamoto

Teresa Brewer

Born Theresa Breuer, May 7, 1931, in Toledo, OH.

Briefly, Brewer was America's singing sweetheart. A teenager blessed with good looks, a perky disposition, and a sassy-but-sweet vocal style, she charmed adults and amazed her peers. Her run of big '50s hits not only estab-lished her as a powerhouse entertainer, but set the stage for the boom in teen-oriented music that would come later in that decade.

Brewer began her career at age two, singing "Take Me Out to the Ballgame" on *Uncle August's Kiddie Show* over WSPD radio in Toledo, Ohio. By age 5 her singing and tap-dancing were regular features of the *Major Bowes Amateur Hour*. In 1949, Brewer signed with London Records and recorded her classic "Music! Music! Music!," which sold more than a mil-lion copies despite a pressing-plant strike. She quickly fol-lowed with "Choo'n Gum," "Molasses," and "Longing for You," and, beginning in 1951, a string of hits for Coral Records (including her infamous tribute to Mickey Mantle, "I Love Mickey"). She also dabbled in country sounds with "A Tear Fell" and "Bo Weevil Song," and R&B with cover ver-sions of Ivory Joe Hunter's "Empty Arms" and Sam Cooke's "You Send Me." Despite her willingness to expand her style, Brewer's youthful image was so successful her label refused to let her grow up. For every hit adult ballad she recorded, such as "Pledging My Love," Coral saddled her with juvenilia like "The Hula Hoop Song" or "Pickle Up a Doodle." By 1961, she had left the label, and with producer-husband Bob Thiele, set out to record more serious grown-up sounds. Throughout the '60s, she mined the country and jazz mar-kets, though her cute-as-a-button, perfect-pitch vocal tech-nique never changed.

Brewer semi-retired in the late '60s, cutting occasional singles, but Thiele brought her back in a big way in the '70s, teaming her with jazz greats Count Basie, Dizzy Gillespie, Wynton Marsalis, and many others for a string of jazz and big-band LPs. Her '80s highlight, an LP recorded in London with Chas and

Dave, Peter Frampton, and Albert Lee, featured Brewer's in-spired rock remake of her first hit, "Music! Music! Music!" These days, ever youthful and cheery, Brewer still performs be-fore capacity crowds.

what to buy: The best of Brewer's hits from her early years at London and Coral Records are on *Music! Music! Music! The Best of Teresa Brewer* ♫♫♫♫ (Varese Vintage, 1995, compilation prod. Cary E. Mansfield, Marty Wesker).

what to buy next: Brewer's later years as an unfailingly chipper pop and jazz singer are best exemplified on *16 Most Requested Songs* ♫♫♫ (Legacy, 1991, compilation prod. Michael Brooks) and includes material recorded with Albert Lee and Peter Frampton.

what to avoid: The cobbling of classic tunes of the '40s into endless medleys makes *I Dig Big Band Singers* **woof!** (Signa-ture/CBS Special Products, 1983/1989, prod. Bob Thiele) a par-ticularly tedious experience.

the rest:

Live at Carnegie Hall & Montreaux, Switzerland ♫♫♫ (Signature/CBS Special Products, 1974 and 1983/1991)
Best of Teresa Brewer ♫♫ (RCA, 1975/1993)
Midnight Cafe (A Few More for the Road) ♫♫♫ (Sony Special Music, 1982/1995)
Teresa Brewer/Mercer Ellington ♫♫♫♫ (Signature/CBS Special Prod-ucts, 1985/1991)
Best of Teresa Brewer ♫♫♫♫ (MCA Jazz, 1989)
What a Wonderful World ♫♫♫ (Signature/CBS Special Products, 1989)
American Music Box—Vol.2: The Songs of Harry Warren ♫♫ (Red Baron, 1993)
Teenage Dance Party ♫♫♫ (Bear Family, 1994)
Good News: The World's Greatest Jazz Band of Yank Lawson & Bob Haggart ♫♫ (Sony Special Music Products, 1995)
Good Ship Lollipop ♫♫ (Sony Special Products, 1995)
It Don't Mean a Thing If It Ain't Got that Swing ♫♫♫ (Sony, 1995)

worth searching for: Brewer's tribute to Louis Armstrong, *Teresa Brewer & Friends: Memories of Louis Armstrong* ♫♫♫ (Red Baron, 1991, prod. Bob Thiele), features guest stars Wyn-ton Marsalis, Freddy Hubbard, and Dizzy Gillespie on a rather fun compilation of tunes associated with the great Satchmo.

influences:

◀◀ Jo Stafford, Kay Starr

▶▶ Connie Francis, Brenda Lee, Donna Fargo

Ken Burke

Hadda Brooks

Born Hadda Hopgood, October 29, 1916, in Los Angeles, CA.

This classically trained boogie-woogie pianist's time came and went quickly, but not before her mid-1940s singles were successful enough to establish jukebox operator Jules Bihari as a credible record-company owner. (Later Bihari Records artists included B.B. King, Charles Brown, Elmore James, and Etta James.) Brooks, known as "Queen of the Boogie," played with a pristine, jazzy style—like a torch singer—and became famous for "boogie-izing" pop standards like "I Hadn't Anyone Till You." She began singing when a Los Angeles bandleader told her to "fake it" on her first vocal hit, "You Won't Let Me Go." Brooks's sleek, friendly charisma led to several movie roles, including one where she sings to Humphrey Bogart in *In a Lonely Place*. But as with so many 1940s boogie experts, Brooks's career slowed down when first dirtier R&B, then explicitly sexy rock 'n' roll, made her music a pop anachronism. She retired in 1971, but a chapter in a "Whatever Became of . . . ?" book gave her a second career performing in Los Angeles clubs (such as Johnny Depp's swanky Viper Room) and recording new albums (including a single on *The Crossing Guard* soundtrack).

what to buy: Her Modern tracks—"Out of the Blue" and "Anytime, Anyplace, Anywhere," among many others—return on *That's My Desire* ♫♫♫♫ (Virgin, 1994, prod. various), a collection of styles ranging from pure boogie to slick jazz.

what to buy next: Brooks's comeback album, *Time Was When* ♫♫♫♪ (Pointblank/Virgin, 1996, prod. John Wooler), travels in the Charles Brown zone between slick cocktail jazz and raunchy blues. In fact, Brooks's recent recordings make nice supplements to Brown's newer material in any piano/blues collection.

the rest:
Anytime, Anyplace, Anywhere ♫♫♫ (DRG, 1994)
Jump Back Honey: The Complete OKeh Sessions ♫♫♫♫ (Columbia, 1997)

worth searching for: The album *Femme Fatale* ♫♫♫ (Crown, prod. Jules Bihari) was a nice change of pace from Brooks's singles-dominated career, but it came out at the wrong time—just as Elvis Presley and Bill Haley were taking over the charts—and sunk commercially.

influences:
◀◀ Art Tatum, Victoria Spivey, Sippie Wallace, Bessie Smith, Billie Holiday, Nat "King" Cole

▶▶ Charles Brown, Dr. John, Rosemary Clooney, Etta James, Deanna Bogart

Steve Knopper

Charles Brown

Born 1920, in Texas City, TX.

Ever wonder how pop piano music changed just after World War II from slick Gershwin tunes to hot, fast R&B? Blame Charles Brown. The blues pianist's first band, Johnny Moore's Three Blazers, modeled themselves after the slick hitmaker Nat King Cole and his trio. The band's primary talent, of course, was Brown; he penned the smooth 1945 hit "Driftin' Blues" and became a minor blues celebrity. Then Ray Charles, paying close attention to Brown's style and songwriting, copied the Three Blazers for his early bands. In "Driftin' Blues"—like Brown's later standards, "Merry Christmas, Baby" and "Trouble Blues"—you can hear both the cocktail-party-ready feeling of Cole's pop and the rocking-house-party feeling of Charles's R&B. Around 1956, not so coincidentally when Elvis Presley was pushing rock 'n' roll onto the radio, Brown's stardom started to dry up. He continued to record and tour throughout the 1960s and 1970s, making a decent living, but he retired in the early 1980s. Then Bonnie Raitt, using her newfound star power to share fame with her blues influences, brought Brown on tour and recorded several duets. Since then, the revitalized singer-pianist has become prolific and multi-dimensional. His straightforward 1992 piano blues comeback, *Someone to Love*, is almost as excellent as his confident 1996 jazz release, *Honey Dripper*.

what to buy: *Driftin' Blues: The Best of Charles Brown* ♫♫♫♫♪ (EMI, 1992, prod. Adam Block) does a great job of collecting the early Three Blazers hits (including, of course, the title track) and Brown's later work, such as "Merry Christmas, Baby." His 1992 collaboration with Raitt, *Someone to Love* ♫♫♫ (Bullseye Blues/Rounder, 1992, prod. Ron Levy), is the sound of an old musician tickled to have such high-profile fans. Much more confident is *Honey Dripper* ♫♫♫♫ (Verve, 1996, prod. John Snyder), which stacks the goofy New Orleans novelty hit "Gee" against beautiful romantic ballads like "When Did You Leave Heaven" and "There Is No Greater Love."

what to buy next: Brown's pre-Raitt-tour comeback, *All My Life* ♫♫♫ (Bullseye Blues/Rounder, 1990, prod. Ron Levy), is a solid piano blues album, but he hadn't yet hit his second recording career's stride. His post-Raitt material—*Just a Lucky So and So*

♫♫♫ (Bullseye Blues/Rounder, 1994, prod. Ron Levy) and *These Blues ♫♫♫* (Verve, 1994, prod. John Snyder)—is much more versatile and finds Brown stretching out vocally.

what to avoid: Brown's best periods were the 1940s and 1990s, and his singles in between, documented on *Southern Blues 1957–63 ♫♫* (Paula, 1994, prod. Willie Dixon), are uneven at best.

the rest:
Blues 'n' Brown ♫♫♫ (Jewel, 1971)
One More for the Road ♫♫♫ (Blueside, 1986/Alligator, 1989)
Driftin' Blues ♫♫♫ (Mainstream, 1989)
Blues and Other Love Songs ♫♫ (Muse, 1994)
Cool Christmas Blues ♫♫♫ (Bullseye Blues/Rounder, 1994)

worth searching for: *The Complete Aladdin Recordings of Charles Brown ♫♫♫♫♫* (Mosaic, 1994, prod. Michael Cuscuna), a limited-edition box set, gathers more than one hundred sides, every single that Brown and the Three Blazers recorded for Philo and Aladdin between 1945 and 1956, on five compact discs, with serious information about each one. For extreme fans and historians, it's the early Brown motherlode.

influences:
◀◀ Nat "King" Cole, T-Bone Walker, Art Tatum, Scott Joplin
▶▶ Ray Charles, Bonnie Raitt, Otis Spann, Floyd Dixon

Steve Knopper

Clifford Brown

Born October 30, 1930, in Wilmington, DE. Died June 16, 1956, in PA.

The doomed Brown packed a lot of experimenting into his abbreviated career—and he rarely botched the job. Even his requisite strings album showed few of the cliches that plague most orchestral jazz albums. Not only were Brown's solos achingly tender and romantic, but Neil Hefti's arrangements were perfectly subdued—he had learned a lot since his first strings efforts with Charlie Parker. The result was the meekly titled *Clifford Brown with Strings*, a 1955 classic of the genre. This was fireplace romance music at its finest. Unlike Miles Davis's acerbic skitterings, Brown's tone was brassy and silverine, floating along as the strings webbed around him. Brown may have been so sure-footed because of the crack rhythm section beneath the frills, including the protean Max Roach on

Charles Brown (© Ken Settle)

drums and George Morrow on bass. Whatever the reason, this is a mellow masterpiece that is as much art as it is confection.

what to buy: The remastered classic *Clifford Brown with Strings ♫♫♫♫♫* (Emarcy, 1997, prod. Neil Hefti) is just one example of why Brown's voice is still so missed more than 40 years after his fatal car crash on the Pennsylvania Turnpike. The album sounds as lush as any 1950s mood music release—a perfect complement to the excellence of the musicianship. Even the songs are pefectly chosen. A lovely version of "Yesterdays" and the ethereal "Memories of You" are only two of the 12 sides that are sure to sink you deep into your naugahyde Eames chair.

best of the rest:
Study in Brown ♫♫♫♫♫ (Emarcy, 1955)
At Basin Street ♫♫♫♫♫ (Emarcy, 1956)
More Study in Brown ♫♫♫♫ (Emarcy, 1956)
Clifford Brown Memorial Album ♫♫♫♫ (Blue Note, 1989)

influences:
◀◀ Roy Eldridge, Dizzy Gillespie, Fats Navarro
▶▶ Sonny Rollins, Lee Morgan, Freddie Hubbard

Steve Braun

Les Brown

Born Lester Raymond Brown, March 14, 1912, in Reinerton, PA.

Best known as the house band on *The Dean Martin Show* and countless Bob Hope TV specials, Les Brown and His Band of Renown was arguably the most versatile orchestra of the big-band era. Brown's outfit could blow sweet and reedy like Isham Jones or Sammy Kaye, update the classics Freddy Martin– and Frankie Carle–style, and wail hot and brassy à la Glenn Miller or Stan Kenton. And you could always dance to it.

A clarinetist, Brown led his first band at Duke University (the Duke Blue Devils), and worked as a professional arranger for orchestras led by Ruby Newman, Isham Jones, Jimmy Dorsey, Larry Clinton, and Red Nichols before going out on his own. Immediately, his sense of organization and professionalism won him the respect of bookers and top vocalists alike, and he scored some fair-sized hits with "'Tis Autumn," "Bizet Has His Day," and "Mexican Hat Dance." The turning point in Brown's career came when he hired Doris Day away from Bob Crosby's band. Their collaboration on such hits as "Sentimental Journey," "You Won't Be Satisfied Until You Break My Heart," and "My Dreams Keep Getting Better All the Time" made them both household names. After Day's departure, Brown's orchestra continued to thrive with records like "I've Got My Love to Keep Me Warm" and their jumpin' theme "Leap Year." Never lacking for fine warblers, at one time or another Brown's orchestra employed Miriam Shaw, Betty Bonney, Ray Kellog, Lucy Polk, and novelty singer-saxophonist Butch Stone. During the '50s, while competing bands were retiring or being forced out of the business by rock 'n' roll, Brown's orchestra was busier than ever and won *Down Beat* magazine's Best Dance Band Poll five years in a row. By 1962, Brown had tired of the road and settled his orchestra into a staff job at NBC, recording occasionally. His band's work behind Dean Martin, the Golddiggers, and Bob Hope was the best of any prime-time orchestra, and led in no small part to a big-band resurgence in the late '70s. These days, the retired Brown has handed the baton to his son, Les Brown Jr.

what to buy: The best-known numbers by Brown and His Band of Renown are on *Les Brown: Best of the Big Bands* 𝄞𝄞𝄞𝄞 (Legacy, 1990, compilation prod. Michael Brooks), including "Leap Frog," "Sentimental Journey," "My Dreams Are Getting Better All the Time," "Bizet Has His Day," and "Mexican Hat Dance." It's an excellent sampler and starting point for listners new to this versatile band.

what to buy next: The best numbers sung with Brown's best singers (including Doris Day) are on *Best of the Big Bands: His Great Vocalists* 𝄞𝄞𝄞 (Legacy, 1995, prod. Didier C. Deutsch). There's romance a-plenty in "I Guess I'll Have to Dream the Rest," "I Got It Bad and That Ain't Good," and the flirty "Rock Me to Sleep." Equally fine is *The Essence of Les Brown* 𝄞𝄞𝄞𝄞 (Legacy, 1994, compilation prod. Michael Brooks), which contains some similar tracks, plus the good-humored jive of "Joltin' Joe DiMaggio" and many others.

what to avoid: The song selection is good but the sound quality is awfully thin on *Giants of the Big Band Era* 𝄞 (Pilz, 1994).

the rest:
The Uncollected Les Brown & His Orchestra 1944–46 𝄞𝄞𝄞 (Hindsight, 1977/1994)
The Uncollected Les Brown & His Orchestra, Vol. 2 𝄞𝄞𝄞 (Hindsight, 1978/1994)
Digital Swing 𝄞𝄞𝄞 (Fantasy, 1986)
22 Original Big Band Recordings 𝄞𝄞𝄞 (Hindsight, 1987/1992)
Jazz Collector Edition 𝄞𝄞 (Laserlight, 1992)
1944–1946 𝄞𝄞𝄞 (Circle, 1992)
Greatest Hits 𝄞𝄞𝄞 (Curb, 1993)
Live at Elitch Gardens 1959 𝄞𝄞𝄞 (Status, 1994)
Live at Elitch Gardens 1959, Part 2 𝄞𝄞 (Status, 1994)
Sentimental Journey 𝄞𝄞𝄞 (Columbia Special Products, 1994)

Anything Goes 𝄞𝄞𝄞 (USA, 1994)
America Swings—The Great Les Brown 𝄞𝄞𝄞 (Hindsight, 1995)
Lullaby in Rhythm 𝄞𝄞𝄞 (Drive Archive, 1995)
At the Hollywood Palladium 𝄞𝄞𝄞 (Starline, 1995)
Sentimental Journey 𝄞𝄞𝄞 (MCA Special Products, 1995)

worth searching for: Featured vocalists Margaret Whiting, Johnny Mercer, and Jimmy Wakely bring extra zest to the swinging *The Les Brown Show from Hollywood 1953* 𝄞𝄞𝄞 (Magic, 1994, prod. various), which you might find in the import racks. Also, during the big prom scene of *The Nutty Professor* 𝄞𝄞𝄞𝄞 (Paramount, 1963, director Jerry Lewis), Professor Julius Kelp can't keep still while Les Brown and His Band of Renown play their hit theme "Leap Frog." Neither will you.

influences:
◀◀ Isham Jones, Jimmy Dorsey, Red Nichols, Glenn Miller
▶▶ Si Zentner, Randy Brooks, Les Brown Jr.

Ken Burke

Dave Brubeck
Born December 6, 1920, in Concord, CA.

It would be difficult to overstate Dave Brubeck's role as a jazz pioneer. In the wake of the post–World War II demise of the big bands, Brubeck was a principal architect of the modern jazz combo, augmenting the piano trio with saxophone as a featured solo instrument. Then, throughout the 1950s and early 1960s, the Dave Brubeck Quartet redefined the jazz boundaries of counterpoint, harmony, and—most significantly—musical time. The group transcended the 4/4, 2/4, and occasional 3/4 rhythms that had characterized the genre, creating masterworks in time signatures such as 9/8 ("Blue Rondo à la Turk") and 5/4 ("Take Five") that, while not uncommon now, were groundbreaking innovations in their day. Along the way, the quartet crossed over from the traditional jazz audience to the then-untapped college market and to mainstream popularity, as evidenced by Brubeck's appearance on the cover of *Time* magazine in 1954. In the wake of his remarkable commercial success, jazz purists attacked his credibility, criticizing his work as too intellectual and less than authentic. Fellow artists had no such concerns: Brubeck recorded and performed with Louis Armstrong, Carmen McRae, Charles Mingus, Jimmy Rushing, and others.

The quartet's work is quintessential lounge listening, featuring a relentless capacity for swing. Alto saxophonist Paul Desmond, who died in 1977, created the definitive alto sax tone for jazz, which he described as a "dry martini" sound. The most famous edition of the quartet (including, beginning in 1958, Brubeck, Desmond, bassist Eugene Wright, and drummer Joe Morello) disbanded in 1967 after touring the world almost continuously for a decade. Brubeck turned a portion of his energies to composing, creating successful works, both religious and secular, for orchestra and chorus. He continued to work in a jazz quartet setting, however, often with baritone saxophonist Gerry Mulligan. A 1970s version of the group, first dubbed Two Generations of Brubeck and later the New Dave Brubeck Quartet, featured Brubeck's sons, Darius, Chris, and Danny, on electric keyboards, bass (and bass trombone), and drums, respectively. A 1980s edition included clarinetist Bill Smith, with whom Brubeck recorded in 1961. As he approaches age 80, Brubeck continues to perform and create vital recordings.

what to buy: There are two ways to go about adding Brubeck to your collection. For an intense introduction to his life in music, *Time Signatures: A Career Retrospective* ♪♪♪♪ (Columbia/Legacy, 1992, executive prod. Dave Brubeck, compilation prod. Russell Gloyd, Amy Herot) is a luscious four-disc box set, including 59 cuts (in chronological order) recorded between 1946 to 1991. Also included is a 76-page book, printed on heavy stock, recapping Brubeck's life and career and detailing the recordings included in the set. Otherwise, begin with *Time Out* ♪♪♪♪ (Columbia/Legacy, 1959/1997, prod. Teo Macero), Brubeck's landmark exploration of unorthodox time signatures that includes "Blue Rondo à la Turk" and Desmond's classic, "Take Five." Complement *Time Out* with its "blues suite" follow-up, *Time Further Out* ♪♪♪♪ (Columbia/Legacy, 1961/1996, prod. Teo Macero), and you'll be hooked. Then, add a pair of live releases that offer a superb entree to the quartet's improvisational genius. The first, *The Dave Brubeck Quartet featuring Paul Desmond* ♪♪♪♪ (Fantasy, 1986), repackages almost all of the material from *Jazz at Oberlin* ♪♪♪♪ (Fantasy, 1953/1987) and *Jazz at the College of the Pacific* ♪♪♪♪ (Fantasy, 1954/1987). It's a great look at the early years with Desmond and includes a scintillating version of "Perdido." The second live set to purchase is *The Great Concerts* ♪♪♪♪♪ (Columbia, 1988, prod. Teo Macero, Cal Lampley), which collects 74 minutes of cuts from live shows in Amsterdam and at Carnegie Hall in New York (both 1963) and Copenhagen (1958). Included is a vigorous 12-minute romp through "Blue Rondo" from the Carnegie Hall set.

what to buy next: *Dave Brubeck/Paul Desmond* ♪♪♪♪♪ (Fantasy, 1982) offers more of the quartet's early work (1952–54). *Brubeck à la Mode* ♪♪♪♪ (Fantasy, 1960/1990) is a fine example

of Brubeck's quartet work with Smith on clarinet. *We're All Together Again for the First Time* ♪♪♪♪ (Atlantic/Rhino, 1973, prod. Dave Brubeck, Siegfried Loch) is a live set recorded on a fall 1972 European tour, featuring both Desmond and Mulligan. Look out for 16 riveting minutes of "Take Five"; as with all of Brubeck's best live material, it's pure improvisation that remains true to the song's structure and character. Brubeck's 1990s releases on Telarc are consistently gorgeous. *Night Shift: Live at the Blue Note* ♪♪♪♪ (Telarc, 1995, prod. Russell Gloyd, John Snyder) showcases Brubeck's gift for blues piano.

what to avoid: If you follow either of the purchasing paths described above, you won't need the two-CD *Jazz Collection* ♪♪♪♪

Dave Brubeck **(© Jack Vartoogian)**

(Columbia/Legacy, 1995, executive prod. Dave Brubeck). It's a fine set, but it's redundant if you have the Columbia/Legacy releases listed above. It does provide another introductory route to Brubeck, however.

best of the rest:

Last Set at Newport ♪♪♪♫ (Rhino/Atlantic, 1972)
All the Things We Are ♪♪♪♫ (Rhino/Atlantic, 1976)
Back Home ♪♪♪ (Concord, 1979)
Tritonis ♪♪♪♫ (Concord, 1980)
Concord on a Summer Night ♪♪♪ (Concord, 1982)
The Dave Brubeck Trio: 24 Classic Original Recordings ♪♪♪ (Fantasy, 1982)
Stardust ♪♪♪♫ (Fantasy, 1983)
Dave Brubeck Octet ♪♪♪ (Fantasy, 1984)
Music from "West Side Story" ♪♪♫ (Columbia, 1987)
25th Anniversary Reunion ♪♪♫ (A&M, 1988)
Moscow Night ♪♪♪♫ (Concord, 1988)
Jazz Goes to College ♪♪♪♫ (Columbia, 1989)
The Dave Brubeck Quartet with the Montreal International Jazz Festival Orchestra: New Wine ♪♪♪ (MusicMasters, 1990)

Jazz Impressions of New York ♪♪♪♫ (Columbia, 1990)
Quiet as the Moon ♪♪♪♫ (MusicMasters, 1991)
Interchanges '54 ♪♪♪ (Columbia/Legacy, 1991)
Jazz Impressions of Eurasia ♪♪♪♫ (Columbia, 1992)
Once When I Was Very Young ♪♪♪♫ (MusicMasters, 1992)
Dave Brubeck Plays and Plays and Plays ♪♪♪ (Fantasy, 1992)
Trio Brubeck ♪♪♪ (MusicMasters, 1993)
Just You, Just Me ♪♪♪ (Telarc, 1994)
Late Night Brubeck: Live from the Blue Note ♪♪♪♫ (Telarc, 1994)
Near-Myth/Brubeck-Smith ♪♪♪♫ (Fantasy, 1995)
Dave Brubeck Trio & Gerry Mulligan: Live at the Berlin Philharmonie ♪♪♪♫ (Columbia/Legacy, 1995)
A Dave Brubeck Christmas ♪♪♪♫ (Telarc, 1996)
In Their Own Sweet Way ♪♪♪ (Telarc, 1997)

worth searching for: *Marian McPartland's Piano Jazz with Guest Dave Brubeck* ♪♪♪♫ (The Jazz Alliance, 1993, prod. Dick Phipps) was taken from a National Public Radio program. It's an entertaining hour-long set that features Brubeck performing solo and in duets with McPartland. Approximately half of the recording is conversation and interview. Contact Jazz Alliance at P.O. Box 515, Concord, CA 94522. The aforementioned 1963 Carnegie Hall show, complete in one package, is available in the two-CD Japanese import, *Brubeck Quartet at Carnegie Hall* ♪♪♪♪ (Columbia, 1997), but be prepared to pay more than $40.

influences:

◀◀ Art Tatum, Cleo Brown, Fats Waller, Billy Kyle, Darius Milhaud, Duke Ellington, Erroll Garner

▶▶ Bill Evans, Vince Guaraldi, Ramsey Lewis, Jeff Lorber Fusion

Bryan Powell

Harold Budd

Born May 24, 1936, in Los Angeles, CA.

Budd's ambient, minimalistic, almost classical compositions are lounge in a literal sense—they're dreamy, pensive songs made for lounging around and doing nothing. A late bloomer, Budd was 48 when his first album was released on EG Records, the label founded by ambient master Brian Eno, with whom Budd also collaborated. Their joint efforts comprise some of his best work. He also teamed up with Robin Guthrie of the Cocteau Twins.

what to buy: As Eno records go, *Ambient 2: The Plateaux of Mirrors* ♪♪♪♪ (EG, 1980, prod. Brian Eno) and *The Pearl* ♪♪♪♪ (EG, 1984, prod. Brian Eno) rank as simply two more fine releases—but for Budd, they're a zenith. *Pavillion of Dreams* ♪♪♪♪ (EG, 1978, prod. Brian Eno) is Budd's debut; it's a lovely record that stands as a point of reference to establish Before and After Eno.

what to buy next: *The White Arcades* ♪♪♪ (Opal, 1988, prod. Harold Budd) includes one gorgeous Eno/Budd composition ("Totems of the Red-Sleeved Warrior") and the contributions of Cocteau Twin Robin Guthrie.

what to avoid: There's nothing wrong with *Music for 3 Pianos* ♪♪♪ (Gyroscope, 1993, prod. Harold Budd, Michael Hoenig), with Ruben Garcia and Daniel Lentz, and *Luxa* ♪♪♪ (Gyroscope, 1996)—as long as you really, really like piano.

the rest:
Lovely Thunder ♪♪♪ (E.G., 1986)
By the Dawn's Early Light ♪♪♪ (Opal, 1991)
She Is a Phantom ♪♪♪ (New Albion, 1994)

worth searching for: *Angels in Architecture* ♪♪♪♪ (EG, 1987) is out of print but can occasionally be spotted in used-CD bins;

it's a compilation of Eno and his friends, including his brother, Roger, and Robert Fripp. Budd appears on the first two tracks.

influences:

◀◀ Brian Eno, Roger Eno, Robert Fripp, Scott Walker

▶▶ Orb, Aphex Twin, Spiritualized, Nick Cave & the Bad Seeds

Teresa Gubbins

Sam Butera

Born August 17, 1927, in New Orleans, LA.

Butera made his name as the bandleader and tenor sax player for Louis Prima's band during the height of the trumpeter-singer's Las Vegas fame. He then went on to record and tour under his own name, something he continues to do to this day. A native of New Orleans, Butera apprenticed under some of that city's greatest first-generation jazzmen; he claims to have even learned a few licks from Louis Armstrong. Butera's first professional gig came right out of high school with bandleader Ray McKinley; that job eventually led to his short tenures with the Tommy Dorsey and Joe Reichman big bands. Butera formed his own group in 1950, and began a four-year engagement at the 500 Club in New Orleans, which was owned by Louis Prima's brother. An appearance with Woody Herman's band led to a recording contract with RCA in 1953. Butera's early recordings feature his raucous, untamed fusion of roadhouse R&B and hard-swinging bop, but he never really caught fire on a national level. Prima first hooked up with Butera for a live date on the way to his first Vegas gig; upon arriving in Vegas, he hired Butera to lead his new backing band, which he called the Witnesses. Their act, which also featured vocalist Dorothy "Keely" Smith, was an immediate smash, and featured Prima's unique blend of risque jazz and Italiano-pop. Butera recorded seven albums with Prima over the next five years, and even appeared in a film with him called *Hey Boy! Hey Girl!* After Prima died in 1978, Butera forged ahead on his own, keeping the Prima legacy alive with interpretations of his ex-boss's most famous songs, jazz standards, and original compositions, all steeped in the loose-limbed Prima style.

what to buy: *The Wildest* ♪♪♪♪ (Capitol, 1956) captures Prima and Butera at their finger-snapping, shucking-and-jiving peak.

what to buy next: *A Tribute to Louis Prima, Vols. 1 and 2* ♪♪♪ (Jasmine, 1994) is a spirited run-though of some of Prima's most popular songs.

the rest:
The Whole World Loves Italians 𝄞𝄞𝄞 (USA, 1997)

worth searching for: The import *By Request* 𝄞𝄞𝄞 (Jasmine, 1986) is a fine document of Butera's current stage act.

influences:

◀◀ Louis Armstrong, Louis Jordan, Tito Puente, Benny Goodman, Glenn Miller

▶▶ Cal Tjader, Perez Prado, Buddy Greco

see also: *Louis Prima & Keely Smith*

Marc Weingarten

Don Byron

Born November 8, 1958, in New York City, NY.

You know a jazz artist is interesting—or at least taps into the spirit of cartoon-soundtrack bandleader Raymond Scott—when he names a serious album after an episode of *The Flintstones*. Byron, a young clarinetist, bandleader, and occasional singer, lovingly preserves the memories of a diversity of great composers, including Scott (whose classic instrumental "Powerhouse" he nails in a short, punchy 1995 version), Duke Ellington, Mickey Katz, Ornette Coleman, Tchiakovsky, and a 1927 silent film called *Scar of Shame*. His orchestra music is both playful (with bursts of tinkly percussion dropping in at the goofiest possible moments) and reverential (with impeccable horns swinging carefully so as not to mess up the original Ellington music). Though some jazz critics have ripped him for indulging his overly nostalgic pop-culture visions of the past, Byron says, quite reasonably, that he's just interested in Katz's klezmer music, Ernie Kovacs's television shows, and plain old stuff he experienced as a kid. He's perhaps the only artist in this book who belongs to the Black Rock Coalition, a terrific New York union formed in the early '90s by Living Colour guitarist Vernon Reid. "All the producers of the film are dead," Byron told the *Chicago Tribune* about his *Scar of Shame* music, "so they don't have that much to say about how loud I am or how weird my music might be."

what to buy: *Bug Music* 𝄞𝄞𝄞𝄞 (Nonesuch/Warner Bros., 1996, prod. Don Byron), inspired by an episode of *The Flintstones* in which "Bug Music" (a subtle depiction of the Beatles) frightens many Bedrock residents, is a bizarre mashing of many diverse

styles. Usually in three minutes or less, Byron's tightly conducted orchestra captures the heavy spirit of an easily recognizable classical piece but adds a certain goofy element, as in the Tchiakovsky-derived "Bounce of the Sugar Plum Fairies" and Ellington's "The Dicty Glide." Thus the tinkering Raymond Scott, whose music dominates the album, is the perfect hero.

what to buy next: Continuing his exploration of unconventional musical sources, Byron salutes the comic klezmer musician Mickey Katz (the clarinetist for Spike Jones's parody bands) on *Don Byron Plays the Music of Mickey Katz* 𝄞𝄞𝄞𝄞 (Nonesuch, 1993, prod. Hans Wendl).

what to avoid: Byron's experiments come across more loose and hard to follow without the restraint imposed by working in a studio; thus *Live* 𝄞𝄞𝄞 (Knitting Factory, 1996, prod. Don Byron, Hope Carr) proves to be less than you would hope for.

the rest:
Tuskegee Experiments 𝄞𝄞𝄞 (Nonesuch, 1992)
Music for Six Musicians 𝄞𝄞𝄞 (Nonesuch, 1995)

influences:

◀◀ Raymond Scott, Mickey Katz, Tchaikovsky, *The Flintstones*, Duke Ellington, the Ramones, Living Colour, Scott Joplin

Steve Knopper

Sammy Cahn

Born June 18, 1913, in New York City, NY.

Some of Frank Sinatra's most playful standards—"My Kind of Town," "Love and Marriage," "Come Dance with Me"—came from the pen of lyricist Sammy Cahn (and, frequently, his songwriting partner Jimmy Van Heusen). But while Cahn never quite reached the stature of Irving Berlin or Cole Porter, a wide variety of pop stars—first the Andrews Sisters and eventually Dinah Washington, Sarah Vaughan, and Dean Martin—personalized his buoyant material. In short, you know you're an important writer when one of your goofiest songs, "Let It Snow, Let It Snow, Let It Snow," airs ad nauseum every Christmas for 50 years and counting. One of Cahn's first songs, "Rhythm Is Our Business," co-written with his dance-band partner Saul Chaplin, became a minor hit for bandleader Jimmie Lunceford in the late '30s. The success led Cahn to Hollywood, where he

Harold Budd (© Jack Vartoogian)

Ann Hampton Callaway (© Jack Vartoogian)

began a series of lucrative songwriting partnerships, beginning with Jule Styne and peaking with pianist Van Heusen. Success came quickly: he was writing songs for films by 1942, and won Academy and Emmy awards by the mid-'50s. Eventually he developed his own performing career, appearing on radio and television and spinning off entire Broadway and London musicals devoted to his music, like 1974's *The Sammy Cahn Songbook*. His son, jazz-fusion guitarist Steve Khan, performs around the world.

what to buy: Though it's much easier, and ultimately more rewarding, to find great singers' versions of Cahn's songs, his own *An Evening with Sammy Cahn* &&& (DRG, 1992, prod. Maurice Levine) has a certain unthreatening vanilla charm. It's one of the few in-print documents of Cahn singing "Call Me Irresponsible," "Come Fly with Me," "High Hopes," and "My Kind of Town."

what to buy next: There are more comprehensive Sinatra sets, of course, but for inarguable evidence of Cahn's lyrical greatness, both *Frank Sinatra Sings the Songs of Sammy Cahn* &&&&

(Vintage Jazz Classics, 1991, prod. Doug Pomeroy) and *Frank Sinatra Sings the Select Sammy Cahn* &&& (Capitol/EMI, 1996, prod. various) are excellent CD compilations.

what to avoid: Despite the presence of saxophonist Gerry Mulligan, the Ralph Sharon Trio's instrumental *Swings the Sammy Cahn Songbook* && (DRG, 1995) is a real sleeper, good for lazy background music and not much else.

worth searching for: The greats—Nat King Cole singing "Teach Me Tonight," Lena Horne doing "All the Way," plus Dean Martin, Dinah Washington, and Keely Smith—show up on the excellent *It's Magic: Capitol Sings Sammy Cahn, Vol. 14* &&&& (Gold Rush, 1995/1996, prod. Brad Benedict).

influences:

◄◄ Irving Berlin, Cole Porter, Hoagy Carmichael, Saul Chaplin, Jimmy Van Heusen

►► Frank Sinatra, the Andrews Sisters, Paul McCartney

Steve Knopper

Al Caiola

Born September 7, 1920, in Jersey City, NJ.

Although he is just as talented as his guitar-playing peers Dick Dale and Duane Eddy, Caiola avoided rock 'n' roll, using his thin, melodic solos for big-sounding swing instrumentals like "Underwater Chase" and "Midnight Swim." Like Enoch Light's influential behind-the-scenes player Tony Mottola—with whom Caiola backed Johnny Mathis on 1958's *Open Fire, Two Guitars* album—Caiola was an important session man at various record labels in the 1950s and 1960s. He played behind easy-listening stars Percy Faith, Andre Kostelanetz, and Hugo Winterhalter, but also recorded several bouncy, fun albums under his own name. His versions of the themes from *Bonanza* and *The Magnificent Seven* were hits in the early '60s, and his cult fame endures among the legions of guitar fanatics who are interested in pop-music history beyond rock, blues, and country.

what to buy: Caiola plays mostly standards on *Soft Picks* 🎵🎵🎵 (Bainbridge, 1990)—which includes "'S Wonderful," "Try a Little Tenderness," and "Stella by Starlight"—and *Guitar of Plenty* 🎵🎵🎵 (Bainbridge, 1997), with "Gone with the Wind," "The Sound of Music," and "Cherokee."

what to buy next: More rewarding, even though it's just a few tracks, are the mid-'60s Caiola documents on *Ultra-Lounge, Vol. 8: Cocktail Capers* 🎵🎵🎵🎵 (Capitol, 1996, compilation prod. Brad Benedict)—which also includes Les Baxter, Nelson Riddle, and April Stevens—and *Ultra-Lounge, Vol. 18: Bottoms Up!* 🎵🎵🎵🎵 (Capitol, 1997, compilation prod. Brad Benedict), which sets his "Big Noise from Winnetka/Midnight Swim" medley between Martin Denny's "Fandango" and Leroy Holmes's hilarious "Mah-Na, Mah-Na."

the rest:
Music of Gershwin/Heritage of Broadway 🎵🎵🎵 (Eclipse, 1997)
Soft Guitars 🎵🎵🎵 (Bainbridge, 1997)

worth searching for: Caiola's classic guitar album, which in some circles is just as influential as Dick Dale's early surf singles or even Jimi Hendrix's classic-rock material, is the out-of-print *Tuff Guitar* 🎵🎵🎵 (Capitol, 1964), which prompted the less-interesting spinoffs *Tuff Guitar English Style* and *Tuff Guitar Tijuana Style*.

influences:
◄◄ Tony Mottola, Enoch Light, Les Paul, Chet Atkins, Merle Travis, Charlie Christian

►► Dick Dale, Duane Eddy, Stanley Clarke

Steve Knopper

Ann Hampton Callaway

Born May 30, 1959, in Chicago, IL.

One of New York City's most popular nightclub singers, Callaway stretches the legacies of such classic pop singers as Ella Fitzgerald and (on her jazzier material) Billie Holiday. Because it's hard to become a smash national success as a lounge singer, her commercial achievements have been subtle—she wrote and performed the theme to the television sitcom *The Nanny*, and Barbra Streisand oversung Callaway's 10-year-old song, "At the Same Time," on her big-selling 1997 album. In an age when the top divas squeeze every conceivable vibration out of every note, the scat-singing Callaway sounds like she just graduated from the old school, smoothly hitting the high notes and, just as easily, nailing the low ones. Though Callaway has been slowly moving in a serious jazz direction, collaborating with pianist Kenny Barron and trumpeter Randy Brecker on the standards-dominated *After Hours*, she's certainly not above rehashing Christmas classics like Bing Crosby, Rosemary Clooney, Nat King Cole, or any of the other great pure entertainers.

what to buy: Callaway's most mature album, *After Hours* ♪♪♪♪ (Denon, 1997, prod. Danny Weiss), was actually recorded in 1994; in addition to classic romantic showtunes like Rodgers and Hart's "It Never Entered My Mind" and "My Funny Valentine," and a Miles Davis remake, "All Blues," Callaway adds Cyndi Lauper's "Time after Time" to her blue canon. The album is slow, soft, smoky, with the tight jazz combo allowing the singer to throb without clutter.

what to buy next: *Bring Back Romance* ♪♪♪ (DRG, 1994) barely touches on the jazz-heavy material to come in Callaway's career, but it's a nice document of one of the great underrecognized lounge singers.

what to avoid: If you really, really need another Christmas album, *This Christmas* ♪♪ (Angel, 1997) is worth buying only after you get the ones by Bing Crosby, Nat King Cole, Johnny Mathis, Neil Diamond, and, well, you get the idea.

the rest:
To Ella with Love ♪♪♪ (Touchward, 1996)
(With Liz Callaway) *Sibling Revelry* ♪♪♪ (DRG, 1996)

influences:

◀◀ Billie Holiday, Ella Fitzgerald, Dinah Washington, Blossom Dearie, Jo Stafford, Sarah Vaughan

▶▶ Roseanna Vitro

Steve Knopper

Cab Calloway

Born Cabel Calloway III, December 25, 1907, in Rochester, NY. Died November 18, 1994, in Greenburgh, NY.

While you rarely see his name mentioned alongside the likes of Duke Ellington or Louis Armstrong, Cab Calloway was nevertheless one of the giants of 20th-century popular music. Purists frequently dismiss him as a novelty act, which is about as relevant as criticizing James Brown for being singleminded and repetitive. If more people were as purely entertaining as Calloway, the world would be a much better (not to mention hipper) place. Calloway was a key transitional figure during the

1930s and 1940s, when the big band era was giving way to R&B. He was there to goose it along every step of the way with acrobatic performances that predated Jackie Wilson and James Brown by decades. A consummate showman, he also more or less invented rap as a combination of jazz scat and minstrel-era "dozens" jive talk. And his popularity cut across racial lines in the South as well as the North, when that was not a safe thing for a black man to do. Calloway always employed first-class bands, numbering Dizzy Gillespie, Lena Horne, Milt Hinton, Pearl Bailey, and Doc Cheatham among the notable players who passed through his orchestra. But where Calloway really made his mark was in the realm of style, contributing riffs, routines, and jive to the pop-culture lexicon that linger into the present day. His influence continues to pop up where you'd least expect it. Jim Carrey's cartoonish star turn in the 1994 movie *The Mask,* for example, was little more than an extended Cab Calloway homage, right down to the jive talk ("Smmmmokin'!") and the yellow zoot suit.

what to buy: The essential package is *Are You Hep to the Jive?* ♪♪♪♪ (Columbia/Legacy, 1994, prod. Bob Irwin), a 22-track collection drawn from Calloway's 1939–47 prime. Here is the Professor of Jive in all his hilarious glory, including "Everybody Eats When They Come to My House," "The Calloway Boogie," and the well-worn signature "Minnie the Moocher." The jokes are great and the music is absolutely killer.

what to buy next: The 16-track *Cab Calloway: Best of the Big Bands* ♪♪♪♪ (Columbia, 1990, prod. Michael Brooks) broadens the picture a bit, filling in some of the gaps left by *Hep to the Jive* with a fabulous cover of Ellington's "Take the 'A' Train" showing just how solid the Calloway Orchestra was on a purely musical level. Put this together with *Hep* and you've got a near-perfect two-disc Calloway sampler.

worth searching for: *Hi De Ho Man: Classics* ♪♪♪ (CBS, 1974, prod. Teo Macero), an out-of-print two-record compilation, has lots of overlap with the two sets above. It's worth seeking out primarily for the gatefold packaging, which includes period photos of the heart-stoppingly handsome Calloway lookin' sharp in his canary yellow zoot suit from the 1943 movie *Stormy Weather.*

influences:

◀◀ Duke Ellington, Count Basie, Louis Armstrong

Cab Calloway **(AP/Wide World Photos)**

▶▶ Louis Jordan, Little Richard, the Time, Joe Jackson, Phil Alvin, Squirrel Nut Zippers

David Menconi

Glen Campbell

Born April 22, 1936, just outside Billstown, AR.

Although unjustly remembered as a somewhat ingratiating, over-the-top cornball (his hugely successful CBS Television series *The Glen Campbell Goodtime Hour* can still strike terror into the faint of heart), Campbell's long and successful career as an entertainer is testament to the obvious drive and abundant talent behind the rhinestones.

First leaving home as a teen to tour with his Uncle Dick Bills's Western swing combo, the Dick Bills Band, Campbell landed in Los Angeles in 1960 at the perfect time to make use of his growing prowess on the guitar. Over the next five years, he was one of the city's most sought-after studio musicians, performing behind everyone from Phil Spector to Frank Sinatra. (He was even a bona fide Beach Boy for a while!) He also worked with his friend Jimmy Bowen for an L.A. music publisher, and performed in an early incarnation of Merle Haggard's Strangers alongside James Burton and Glen D. Hardin. After signing to Capitol Records in 1962, he quickly scored a Top 20 country hit with "Kentucky Means Paradise." He first appeared in the Top 50 three years later with a version of Donovan's "Universal Soldier," and in 1967 his signature tune, John Hartford's "Gentle on My Mind," placed respectably on both the country and pop charts. But it wasn't until he began recording the brilliant songs of Jimmy Webb that he became a regular visitor to the Top Ten ("By the Time I Get to Phoenix," "Wichita Lineman," and "Galveston" remain classics of their genre). After several years spent entertaining on both the small and big screens, he returned to the top of the charts in 1975 ("Rhinestone Cowboy") and 1977 ("Southern Nights") before hitting the scandal sheets with Tanya Tucker and letting years of pharmaceutical dabbling get the better of him. The following decade was spent bouncing somewhat aimlessly from label to label and from style to style (including successful reunions on MCA with Jimmys Bowen and Webb), culminating with a self-confessed "work-horse" stint in the lounges of Branson, Missouri. The 1990s found him both physically and spiritually cleansed and refreshed, and he remains a popular performer—and red-hot guitarist—to this day.

what to buy: *Essential Glen Campbell* 🎵🎵🎵🎵 (Capitol Nashville, 1995, prod. various) gathers, in three gorgeous-sounding volumes, all the hits as well as just enough rarities, instrumentals, and live recordings to demonstrate both the depth and scope of this decidedly all-round entertainer. *The Glen Campbell Collection (1962–1989)* 🎵🎵🎵 (Razor and Tie, 1997, prod. various) provides a more compact and concise overview.

what to buy next: Capitol has begun a long-overdue reissue of Campbell's earliest albums, starting with his very first from 1962, *Big Bluegrass Special* 🎵🎵🎵 (Capitol Nashville, 1996, prod. Nick Venet), originally released by the Green River Boys. Also newly available are his three fine breakthrough LPs from 1967 and 1968: *Gentle on My Mind* 🎵🎵🎵 (Capitol Nashville, 1996, prod. Al DeLory), *By the Time I Get to Phoenix* 🎵🎵🎵🎵 (Capitol Nashville, 1996, prod. Al DeLory, Nick Venet), and *Wichita Lineman* 🎵🎵🎵🎵 (Capitol Nashville, 1996, prod. Al DeLory).

what to avoid: Beware the myriad greatest-hits and in-concert recordings, all of which have been rendered superfluous by the *Essential* series.

the rest:
Favorite Hymns 🎵🎵🎵 (Word/Epic, 1992)
Christmas with Glen Campbell 🎵🎵 (Laserlight, 1995)
Wings of Victory 🎵🎵🎵 (Intersound International, 1996)
Jesus and Me: The Collection 🎵🎵🎵 (New Haven, 1997)

worth searching for: Campbell's oft-overlooked gift as an instrumentalist is readily apparent on any of the budget reissues of his early Folkswingers recordings, particularly the *12-String Guitar* albums on World Pacific; also fascinating is his just-before-fame work with the baroque Beach Boy band Sagittarius alongside Gary Usher, Terry Melcher, Bruce Johnston, and Curt Boettcher.

influences:
◀◀ Django Reinhardt, Barney Kessel, Roger Miller, Jimmy Dickens

▶▶ Jim Stafford, Ricky Skaggs, Garth Brooks

Gary Pig Gold

Eddie Cantor

Born Isidore Israel Itzkowitz, January 31, 1892, in New York City, NY. Died October 10, 1964, in Hollywood, CA.

Cantor sang, wrote books, appeared in movies, entertained troops in World War II, and hosted a major television show, but more than anything else, the bug-eyed comedian was a radio star. He had perfect timing for the medium, rambling in a nice, insecure, pre–Woody Allen way, spontaneously bursting into funny little songs like "If You Knew Susie (Like I Knew Susie)" or, affecting an exaggerated German accent, "Baby Face." He was a major talent—when Franklin D. Roosevelt seized the airwaves in 1940 because of the war, an undeterred Cantor ad-libbed an entire show anyhow. It never reached the public until years later, when CD technology gave longtime fans a peek at gems like "Oh Suzanna, Dust Off That Old Piana." Behind all the laughs, there was sadness. Both of Cantor's parents died when he was three, leaving his grandmother to take care of him in her poor neighborhood on New York's Lower East Side. His natural charisma drew crowds whenever he sang or juggled on the streets, and before long he was winning talent contests and getting big breaks in vaudeville shows like *Midnight Frolic* and *Ziegfeld Follies*. He became a major star—and very rich, although he lost it in the Depression, then earned it back with book sales—and landed on the radio in 1931. There, for two decades, he built a massive audience, appearing in the films *Palmy Days* and *The Kid from Spain* before switching to NBC's popular *Colgate Comedy Hour*. His later years were painful: Cantor suffered two heart attacks, then endured the deaths of his daughter and wife before he died in 1964.

what to buy: Two excellent CD collections capture Cantor's fast-talking, nervous humor and surprisingly solid comedic songs: *A Centennial Celebration: Best of Eddie Cantor* 🎵🎵🎵 (RCA, 1992, prod. Brian Gari) has "Yes Sir, That's My Baby" and a hilarious "Baby Face," in which Cantor instructs, "When you make love in the hall, stay away from the wall"; and *The Columbia Years: 1922–1940* 🎵🎵🎵 (Sony/Legacy, 1994, prod. Brian Gari), which includes the still-funny "I've Got the Yes! We Have No Bananas Blues."

what to buy next: Though it's overlong and not as consistent as the best-of stuff, *The Show That Never Aired* 🎵🎵🎵 (Original Cast, 1993, prod. Brian Gari) is a fascinating cultural document and an entertaining record of one of the country's top comedic talents broadcasting under bizarre wartime circumstances—it also includes several songs by longtime straightwoman singer Dinah Shore.

what to avoid: By and large, entire radio-show transcripts rarely translate well to today's listeners; *Radio Shows 1942–43* 🎵🎵 (Original Cast, 1994, prod. Brian Gari) has a few precious moments, but it gets tedious where the best-of sets frequently change the pace.

the rest:
The Carnegie Hall Concert 🎵🎵🎵 (Original Cast, 1992)
Cantor Loves Lucy 🎵🎵🎵 (Original Cast, 1996)

worth searching for: The *Art Deco* CD series does an excellent job of capturing an important era of U.S. entertainment—in ad-

dition to Cantor's classic 1939 recording of "If You Knew Susie (Like I Know Susie)," *Charming Gents of Stage & Screen* 🎵🎵🎵🎵 (Columbia/Legacy, 1994, prod. Didier C. Deutsch) also includes tracks by Louis Prima, Fred Astaire, Russ Columbo, and Bing Crosby.

influences:

◀◀ Al Jolson, Bing Crosby, Fred Astaire, Louis Armstrong

▶▶ Eddie Fisher, Lenny Bruce, Billy Crystal, Dinah Shore, Johnny Carson, Adam Sandler

Steve Knopper

The Captain & Tennille

Formed 1973, in Los Angeles, CA.

Toni Tennille (born May 8, 1943, in Montgomery, AL), vocals; Daryl Dragon (born August 27, 1942, in Los Angeles, CA), piano.

Like the Carpenters, adult-contemporary superstar duo Captain & Tennille offered a tonic to the darker realities of 1970s culture with optimistic dashes of sugar. Their loving spoonfuls gave the pair nine Top 40 hits from 1975 through 1979. Captain (a former keyboardist for the Beach Boys, so named for his nautical headgear by Mike Love) and Tennille's debut single, "Love Will Keep Us Together," immediately established the couple, hitting #1 on the *Billboard* Hot 100, selling a million, becoming the #1 record of the year, and catapulting their debut album, *Love Will Keep Us Together*, to #2. It's also the year the two entered into the marriage that endures to this day. Network executives at ABC, meanwhile, were enchanted by the couple's charm and panache, and signed them to their own TV variety show. Audiences were less intrigued—the program endured only one season, 1976–77. The duo's last hit turned out to be its second-biggest, "Do That to Me One More Time," which hit #1 and sold more than 500,000 copies. In all, the Captain & Tennille earned four gold albums, six gold singles, and one platinum album. In 1984, Tennille launched a solo career, capitalizing on her luscious, smoky cabaret vocal stylings. She released two albums in the 1980s.

what to buy: *Love Will Keep Us Together* 𝄞𝄞𝄞 (A&M, 1975, prod. Daryl Dragon, Toni Tennille) earned the pair a Grammy for Best Song of 1975 and, in addition to "Love Will Keep Us Together," spawned a second Top Five hit, "The Way That I Want to Touch You."

what to buy next: Captain & Tennille's second effort, *Song of Joy* 𝄞𝄞𝄞𝄞 (A&M, 1976, prod. Daryl Dragon, Toni Tennille), was the duo's most successful, selling platinum and spawning three Top Five hits: "Lonely Night (Angel Face)," "Shop Around," and its mushiest, albeit most memorable, single, "Muskrat Love." Each of these first five singles reached #1 on *Billboard*'s adult contemporary chart, establishing the two as one of the most popular duos in history. The gold-selling *Come in from the Rain* 𝄞𝄞𝄞𝄞 (A&M, 1977, prod. Daryl Dragon, Toni Tennille) featured only one hit, "Can't Stop Dancin'," which peaked at #13 on the pop chart. Next came the guilty pleasure, *Captain & Tennille's Greatest Hits* 𝄞𝄞𝄞𝄞 (A&M, 1977, prod. Daryl Dragon, Toni Tennille).

what to avoid: *Keeping Our Love Warm* 𝄞𝄞 (Casablanca, 1980) is unfailing in Tennille's vocals. However, it's scant on hooks.

the rest:
Dream 𝄞𝄞 (A&M, 1978)
Make Your Move 𝄞𝄞 (Casablanca, 1979)

worth searching for: *Twenty Years of Romance* 𝄞𝄞𝄞 (Nouveau, 1995) is soft, squishy pillow talk with the advantage of Tennille's elegant vocal prowess.

solo outings:
Toni Tennille:
Moonglow 𝄞𝄞𝄞𝄞 (Mirage, 1984)
All of Me 𝄞𝄞𝄞 (Gaia, 1987)
Toni Tennille Sings Big Band 𝄞𝄞𝄞 (Honest, 1998)

influences:
◀◀ Tony Orlando & Dawn, Sonny & Cher, Dionne Warwick, Roberta Flack

▶▶ Donny & Marie Osmond, *The Love Boat*

Chuck Taylor

The Cardigans

Formed 1992, in Jonkoping, Sweden.

Bengt Lagerberg, drums and flutes; Lasse Johansson, guitar and keyboards; Magnus Sveningsson, bass; Nina Persson, vocals; Peter Svensson, guitar.

If nothing else, the Cardigans are one of the most stylistically restless bands in, well, Scandinavian pop. In the span of just three albums, the quintet already has undergone two major overhauls, moving first from the jazzy-cool, Smiths- and Sundays-inspired pop of the introverted debut, *Emmerdale*, to the thoroughly giddy easy-listening feel of *Life*—and, most recently, to the sprightly pop-rock of the less-infectious U.S. breakthrough, *First Band on the Moon*. The band itself takes its latest effort most seriously and even considers the sweet, '60s-lounge flashback *Life* to be (and we quote) "a joke." But the latter recording will live the longest in space-age bachelor padville, with its lush, cocktail-jazz arrangements and instrumentation and, of course, Persson's dreamy vocals.

what to buy: *Life* 𝄞𝄞𝄞𝄞 (Minty Fresh, 1996, prod. Tore Johansson) is a kitschy but loveable compilation of the group's first two European albums. Loaded with '60s motifs, the almost cinematic recording goes heavy on the vibraphones, woodwinds, synthesizers, strings, finger snaps, and even awkward guitar licks. The band has a knack for crafting delectable pop hooks

Nina Persson of the Cardigans (© Ken Settle)

("Daddy's Car," "Rise & Shine"), but it can also go the ambient route, as evidenced by the trip-hop of "Our Space." And you'll never be able to look Ozzy Osbourne straight in the eyes again after hearing the cooing cover of Black Sabbath's heavy-metal classic, "Sabbath Bloody Sabbath."

what to buy next: *First Band on the Moon* ♫♫♫ (Mercury, 1996, prod. Tore Johansson) features the band's infectious U.S. breakthrough, "Lovefool," and is highlighted by a perversely sweet cover of yet another erstwhile heavy metal classic, Black Sabbath's "Iron Man." But the band takes the rock thing a bit far, including too many power-pop chords for its own good.

worth searching for: Much of the material from the group's uneven debut, *Emmerdale* ♫♫ (Trampolene, 1994, prod. Tore Johansson), is duplicated on the U.S. version of *Life*, but it shows just how much more serious the band was when it first arrived.

influences:

◄◄ Peggy Lee, Burt Bacharach, Ennio Morricone, Astrud Gilberto, Francoise Hardy, Abba, Black Sabbath, Nick Drake, the Sundays, Pizzicato Five, St. Etienne, Stereolab, the Smiths

►► The Rentals, Dubstar

Josh Freedom du Lac

Hoagy Carmichael

Born Howard Hoagland Carmichael, November 22, 1899, in Bloomington, IN. Died December 28, 1981, in Palm Springs, CA.

Cole Porter and Irving Berlin, two of America's most beloved song writers, wrote their standards purely for pop purposes, often for the movies and Broadway shows. Hoagy Carmichael, their contemporary, was a different kind of American character—he was a jazz cat who loved Dixieland music in general, cornetist Bix Beiderbecke in particular, and really knew how to swing. In that spirit, he penned "Georgia on My Mind," "Rockin' Chair," "Heart and Soul," and dozens of others. Countless singers, from Frank Sinatra to Willie Nelson, took on his 1927 composition "Stardust," and Ray Charles made "Georgia on My Mind" a signature ballad.

Carmichael was born into a poor family, and his mother encouraged his piano-playing talent at an early age. Though he briefly considered a law career, he couldn't get jazz out of his head, and took ragtime lessons and led several Indiana University bands. In 1922 he met Beiderbecke, who recorded his first song, "Riverboat Shuffle"; he gave up law

for good when he heard a Red Nichols version of his "Washboard Blues" and determined he could make more money doing something fun. Unlike Porter and Berlin, Carmichael was a prolific (if nasal-voiced) performer of his own songs. He became enough of a personality to land roles (as a pianist and singer, surprisingly enough) in *To Have and Have Not, Johnny Angel, The Best Years of Our Lives,* and a dozen other films. In the 1960s, rock eliminated the need for Carmichael's jazz-pop-standard songwriting style—although it was eventually taken up in Nashville—but the composer didn't let it bother him. He retired to Palm Springs in the 1970s, where he played golf and lived the easy life until his death in 1981.

what to buy: The consummate Carmichael collection is *The Classic Hoagy Carmichael* ♫♫♫♫♫ (Smithsonian, 1994, prod. John Hasse), which, in addition to 10 solo performances, includes interpretations by Louis Armstrong, Mel Tormé, Billie Holiday, Wynton Marsalis, and many, many others. The three-disc set includes an excellent 64-page biography, and the six versions of "Stardust" demonstrate the diverse reach good songwriting can have.

what to buy next: Though *The Classic Hoagy Carmichael* overlaps with and frequently trumps smaller collections, *Stardust & Much More* ♫♫♫♫ (RCA Bluebird, 1989, prod. Orrin Keepnews) is noteworthy for its original Carmichael performances. There's a 1933 version of "Stardust," for example, and a 1929 "Rockin' Chair."

what to avoid: *The Stardust Road* ♫♫♥ (MCA, 1982, prod. various) is a run-of-the-mill greatest-hits collection, rendered irrelevant by more recent CD packages.

the rest:
Hoagy Sings Carmichael ♫♫♫ (Blue Note, 1995)

worth searching for: *Song Is Hoagy Carmichael* ♫♫♥ (Living Era, 1992, prod. various) features Louis Armstrong and the Mills Brothers, and the more-fun *Mr. Music Master* ♫♫♥ (Pearl, 1993) has Bob Hope and Bing Crosby.

influences:

◄◄ Cole Porter, Irving Berlin, Bix Beiderbecke, Duke Ellington, Louis Armstrong, Benny Goodman, Tommy Dorsey, Glenn Miller

►► Ray Charles, Harlan Howard, Willie Nelson, Frank Sinatra, Jerry Leiber & Mike Stoller, Carole King

Steve Knopper

The Carpenters

Formed 1969, in Downey, CA.

Richard Carpenter (born October 15, 1946, in New Haven, CT), piano, vocals; Karen Carpenter (born March 2, 1950, in New Haven, CT; died February 4, 1983), drums, vocals.

A brother-and-sister duo whose music is the very definition of easy-listening, the Carpenters were on top of the pop world in the '70s. Between 1970 and 1981, the Carpenters' brand of soft California pop, intermittently sunny and melancholy, translated to a dozen Top 10 singles and 17 platinum-selling albums. The siblings were bitten by the musical bug in their early teens in New Haven, and after their family moved to California in the mid-'60s, Karen and Richard, both individually and together, had a number of false starts as they tried to break into the recording industry. Their big break came when a demo tape landed in the hands of trumpeter and executive Herb Alpert, who immediately signed the group to his record label, the risk-taking A&M. Their first minor hit was a cover version of the Beatles' "Ticket to Ride" in 1969, but it wasn't until 1970 that the duo forever forged their place in pop kitsch history by an-swering the ornithological question, "Why do birds suddenly appear every time you are near?" That magical reworking of the Burt Bacharach–penned tune, "Close to You," led to a Best New Artist Grammy and was the first in a string of lushly or-chestrated Top 10 hits that included such '70s wedding and bar-mitzvah standards as "We've Only Just Begun," "Rainy Days and Mondays," and "Top of the World." The band's stay at that precipice, however, was short-lived, and by the mid-'70s the Carpenters' ultra-saccharine style had fallen out of favor. It was also at this time that Karen began her battle with anorexia, a fight that would ultimately lead to her death in 1983 of heart failure. Her tragic death cast the Carpenters' song catalog in a new light, and in recent years, the oft-derided group has gained punk-rock credibility—a trend that culminated with a tribute album, 1994's *If I Were a Carpenter*, featuring covers by a number of ultrahip alternative-rock stars.

what to buy: The Carpenters were best known for their mini pop masterpieces, so the perfect place to start is *The Singles, 1969–1973* ♪♪♪♪ (A&M, 1973, prod. Richard Carpenter, Karen Carpenter, Jack Daugherty), which contains most of their clas-sic hits and avoids the numerous missteps that clutter their studio albums.

what to buy next: It has more Carpenters than a clearance sale at Home Depot, but in case a dozen or so singles isn't enough, check out the four-CD box set *From the Top* ♪♪♪ (A&M, 1991,

prod. various). Yes, they're sweeter than a sticky candy cane, but the classics on *Christmas Portrait* ♪♪♪ (A&M, 1978, prod. Richard Carpenter) are perfect for those already over-sentimen-talized holiday moments.

what to avoid: Not only does it contain the intolerable single "Sing," but *Now & Then* ♪ (A&M, 1973, prod. Richard Carpenter) is heavy with cover versions of early rock hits like "One Fine Day" and "Johnny Angel," done up with the Carpenters' signa-ture lush orchestration. There's probably a reason Karen's only solo album, *Karen Carpenter* ♪ (A&M, 1996, prod. Phil Ramone), didn't come out when it was first completed. It stinks. Only 16 years later, now that the Carpenters are kitschy easy-listening heroes, was their record company brave enough to release it.

the rest:
Close to You ♪♪ (A&M, 1970)
Carpenters ♪♪♪ (A&M, 1971)
A Song for You (A&M, 1972)
Horizon ♪♪ (A&M, 1975)
Kind of Hush ♪♪ (A&M, 1976)
Passage ♪♪♪ (A&M, 1977)
Love Songs N/A (A&M, 1998)

worth searching for: For a tribute album, *If I Were a Carpenter* ♪♪♪♪ (A&M, 1994, prod. various) is particularly reverential and revealing, especially the haunting cover of "Superstar" by Sonic Youth and Shonen Knife's jubilant "Top of the World."

solo outings:
Richard Carpenter:
Pianist-Arranger-Composer-Conductor ♪♪ (A&M, 1998)

Karen Carpenter:
Karen Carpenter ♪ (A&M, 1996)

influences:
◀◀ The Beatles, the Beach Boys, the Bee Gees, Burt Bacharach

▶▶ Sonic Youth, countless wedding bands

Alex Gordon

Vikki Carr

Born Florencia Bisenta De Castilla Martinez Cordona, July 19, 1941, in El Paso, TX.

Carr's warm tone and dramatic flair made her one of the reign-ing queens of '60s middle-of-the-road music. At the same time she opened the door for the Latin-pop explosion of the '80s and '90s. Carr was barely out of high school when she began singing professionally under the name "Carlita" with Pepe "The

Irish Mexican" Callahan's band. In Las Vegas she hooked up with the Chuck Leonard Quartet before signing with Liberty Records and going solo. Trivia buffs know that Carr cut the first version of "He's a Rebel," and it was a hit in Australia, though the Crystals' disc outsold it everywhere else (and rightly so). Aided by numerous network TV appearances, Carr placed several LPs on the charts before she scored her first big hit with "It Must Be Him" (the song Vincent Gardenia's character drove his family nuts with in *Moonstruck*). While follow-up hits "With Pen in Hand," "There I Go," "The Lesson," and "Eternity" firmly established her mainstream pop style, Carr made overtures to the world market with several songs sung in Spanish. By the time she signed with Columbia Records in 1971, Carr was recording in Spanish almost as much as in English. Eventually, Carr's easy-listening style went out of favor, and her label dropped her after seven LPs, though she never stopped working. She resumed recording in 1980 with the Mexican division of CBS Records just as the Latin-pop movement, which she helped create, began gathering momentum. A three-time Grammy winner and a major concert attraction for more than 30 years, Vikki Carr still possesses one of the finest voices singing today.

what to buy: If you're just looking for the hits "It Must Be Him" and "With Pen in Hand," *Greatest Hits* 🍸🍸🍸🍸 (Curb, 1994) is a decent sounding budget disc, though it's a bit skimpy with info and tracks. A better starting point is *The Unforgettable Vikki Carr* 🍸🍸🍸🍸 (Capitol/EMI, 1997, prod. various) or the import *Best of the Liberty Years* 🍸🍸🍸🍸 (Musicrama, 1997, prod. various), both of which feature all her early hits and some fine LP tracks.

what to buy next: Many of Carr's best mid-career Latin-pop recordings are compiled on *Mis 30 Mejors Cancione* 🍸🍸🍸🍸 (Sony Latin, 1997, prod. various). Or you could opt for a reissue of her 1980 Grammy-winning LP, *Cosas Del Amor* 🍸🍸🍸🍸 (Sony Latin, 1980/1992, prod. various). Is it necessary to speak Spanish to enjoy them? Absolutamente no!

what to avoid: Carr sings only two songs on *Merry Christmas from Pat Boone, Vikki Carr, Tony Orlando, Debbie Reynolds* 🍸🍸 (Laserlight, 1995)—even at this budget price you can find more complete solo discs on any one of these artists.

the rest:
Canta En Español 🍸🍸🍸🍸 (Columbia, 1972)
Simplemente Mujer 🍸🍸🍸🍸 (Sony, 1976)

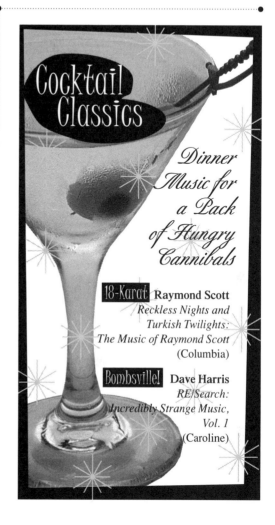

Cocktail Classics

Dinner Music for a Pack of Hungry Cannibals

18-Karat Raymond Scott
Reckless Nights and Turkish Twilights: The Music of Raymond Scott
(Columbia)

Bombsville! Dave Harris
RE/Search: Incredibly Strange Music, Vol. 1
(Caroline)

Todos 🍸🍸🍸 (Sony, 1984/1995)
Brino a la Vida, al Bolero, a Ti 🍸🍸🍸 (Sony Latin, 1993)
Recuerdo a Javier Solis 🍸🍸🍸 (Globo Records, 1994)
Vikki Carr 🍸🍸 (Sony, 1994)
16 Exitos Originales 🍸🍸🍸🍸 (Sony, 1995)
20 De Collecion 🍸🍸🍸 (Sony International, 1996)
Emociones 🍸🍸🍸 (Rodven Records, 1996)
Sus 15 Grande Exitos 🍸🍸🍸🍸 (Sony, 1996)
Personalidad 🍸🍸🍸 (Sony Discos, 1996)
Leyendas 🍸🍸🍸 (Sony Latin, 1996)
Ques Sea El: Vikki Carr Sings in Spanish and English 🍸🍸🍸🍸 (EMI America, 1996)
Vikki Carr 1947–97: 50 Años Sony Music Mexico 🍸🍸🍸 (Sony International, 1996)

Cara a Cara 🎵🎵🎵 (Sony International, 1997)

worth searching for: Carr never sounded better than on *Live at the Greek Theater* 🎵🎵🎵🎵 (Columbia, 1973), a solid set of hits and middle-of-the-road standards performed before an adoring crowd.

influences:

⏪ Carol Lawrence, Eydie Gorme

⏩ Linda Ronstadt, Gloria Estefan

Ken Burke

Josephine Carson

See: Josephine Baker

Nick Cave & the Bad Seeds

Formed 1984, in London, England.

Nick Cave (born Nicholas Edward Cave, September 22, 1957, in War-racknabeal, Australia), vocals, piano, organ; Mick Harvey, drums, keyboards, guitar; Blixa Bargeld, guitar, vocals; Barry Adamson, guitar, piano (1984–86); Hugo Race, guitar (1984–86); Tracy Pew, bass (1984–86); Thomas Wydler, drums (1986–present); Kid Congo Powers, guitar (1986–90); Martyn P. Casey, bass (1992–present); Conway Savage, piano (1992–present).

Following his tenure fronting clangorous post-punk rockers the Birthday Party, Cave embarked on a solo career that brilliantly combines edgy avant-noise and a stirring Gothic gloom with a rich and complex obsession with the dark undercurrents of blues and Americana. Cave boldly takes this highly evocative formula to always inventive and often enthralling heights. Unlike so many post-modern hipsters, Cave doesn't feel compelled to slather his musical obsessions (with Elvis Presley, country-western, and blues) in irony, and his dramatic experiments with these idioms are genuinely moving. For this reason the music evokes the kind of intimate emotional power that so many neo-lounge-lizard kings can only summon with a sarcastic nudge and a wink.

what to buy: *From Her to Eternity* 🎵🎵🎵🎵 (Mute, 1983, prod. Nick Cave & the Bad Seeds) is essential Cave. This features the piquant, dramatic title track (which the band performed in Wim Wenders's enchanting film, *Wings of Desire*) as well as a stirring rendition of "In the Ghetto," popularized by Elvis Presley. *The Firstborn Is Dead* 🎵🎵🎵🎵 (Mute, 1985, prod. the Bad Seeds, Flood) is every bit as powerful an album as *Eternity*, though it focuses more strictly on blues themes and the production gives the Bad Seeds' spare sound a lush finish. With a veritable

smorgasbord of musical Americana (covers of the Velvet Underground's "All Tomorrow's Parties," "By the Time I Get to Phoenix," plus material by Leadbelly, John Lee Hooker, Johnny Cash, and a couple traditional spirituals), *Kicking Against the Pricks* 🎵🎵🎵🎵 (Mute, 1986, prod. Nick Cave & the Bad Seeds) finds Cave and company in top form. Cave was destined to make *Murder Ballads* 🎵🎵🎵🎵 (Mute/Reprise, 1996, prod. Nick Cave & the Bad Seeds, Tony Cohen, Victor Van Vugt), and it's a brilliantly brooding showcase for Cave and the genre. After exploring the dark and deadly side of love with *Murder Ballads*, the next album, *The Boatman's Call* 🎵🎵🎵🎵 (Mute/Reprise, 1997, prod. Nick Cave & the Bad Seeds, Flood), is a dark celebration of love—simple arrangements that support elegantly lyrical sentiments, whether they glow with warm affection or bittersweet passion. Awash with strings and chorales, *The Good Son* 🎵🎵🎵🎵 (Mute/Elektra, 1990, prod. the Bad Seeds) is an opulent collection of elegantly melancholy songs tinged with artful melodrama and gospel undercurrents that mesh beautifully with the Bad Seeds' usual moody edge.

what to buy next: Creepy organ and positively cavernous production enhance the gloomy romanticism and uber-noir ambience of the *Let Love In* 🎵🎵🎵🎵 (Mute/Elektra, 1994, prod. Tony Cohen, the Bad Seeds) tracks, including the deliciously horrific "Red Right Hand" (which *The X-Files* fanatics will recall provided a luridly apropos accompaniment to Agent Scully's abduction). *Your Funeral, My Trial* 🎵🎵🎵🎵 (Mute, 1986, prod. Nick Cave & the Bad Seeds, Flood, Tony Cohen) is less concerned with blues, focusing instead on narrative songs that twist and turn on deliciously dark themes. *Tender Prey* 🎵🎵🎵🎵 (Mute/Elektra, 1988, prod. Nick Cave & the Bad Seeds) finds Cave's usual alluring gloom spiced up with heftier arrangements that feature wailing harmonica, xylophone, extra guitars, and percussion. The uncharacteristically spry "Deanna," which bops along on undertones of '60s pop somewhere between "Gloria" and "I'm a Believer," is charged with particularly driving rock energy. *Live Seeds* 🎵🎵🎵 (Mute/Elektra, 1993) was recorded in Europe and Australia between 1992 and 1993 and features a hearty range of songs spanning the Bad Seeds' career.

what to avoid: *Henry's Dream* 🎵🎵🎵 (Mute/Elektra, 1992, prod. David Briggs, Mick Harvey, Nick Cave) doesn't break from character, though it doesn't feature quite as many memorable moments as other Cave interludes.

Nick Cave (© Ken Settle)

worth searching for: Mick Harvey, who has worked with Cave off and on over the years since the Birthday Party, recorded two albums of Serge Gainsbourg songs—*Intoxicated Man* ♫♫♫♪ (Mute, 1995, prod. Mick Harvey, Victor Van Vugt, Tony Cohen) and *Pink Elephants* ♫♫♫♪ (Mute, 1997, prod. Mick Harvey, Victor Van Vugt, Tony Cohen). Translated from French into English and delivered with a suave and savvy grit, Gainsbourg's wry and rakish etudes fit Harvey like a glove.

influences:

◀◀ Robert Johnson, Elvis Presley, Leonard Cohen, Screamin' Jay Hawkins, Johnny Cash, Edgar Allan Poe, the Old Testament

▶▶ Jesus & Mary Chain, Metallica, Danzig, Mark Eitzel

Sandy Masuo

Al Cernik

See: Guy Mitchell

Carol Channing

Born January 31, 1921, in Seattle, WA.

With her wide, makeup-shimmering face and rich, deep singing voice, Channing was a star singer in popular musicals in the '40s and has endured as something of a camp icon. She sang "Diamonds Are a Girl's Best Friend" in 1949's *Gentlemen Prefer Blondes,* which amounted to her big breakthrough, and continued to act in movies (such as 1954's *Wonderful Town* and 1974's *Lorelei*) and sing in nightclubs. She has won a Tony and an Emmy, earned an Oscar nomination, and her most memorable performance came in 1964's hit *Hello, Dolly.* In a strange Broadway phenomenon in the mid-'90s, the biggest musical stars were stage actresses of 30 years ago—Julie Andrews, Carol Burnett, and Channing. "I do find audiences react differently today than when we first opened back in 1964," Channing told the *Chicago Tribune,* refering to her hit Broadway return to *Hello, Dolly.* "We get the same laughs in the same places— nothing was changed from the original. But now they cheer for Dolly when she's working—women relate to that more now than they did then."

what's available: The Broadway retread of Channing's best-known musical led to a hit original-cast soundtrack, *Hello, Dolly* ♫♫♫ (Varese Sarabande, 1994), which earned a Grammy nomination for Best Musical Show Album. What year is this, anyhow? Otherwise, it's hard to find evidence of Channing's musical talent on CD.

influences:

◀◀ Judy Garland, Ethel Merman

▶▶ Liza Minnelli

Steve Knopper

Ray Charles

Born Ray Charles Robinson, September 23, 1930, in Albany, GA.

Not for nothing is he known as the Genius. In a career almost unparalleled in American popular music, Charles has done more than almost any other artist to obliterate the lines that once existed between R&B, gospel, country, pop, jazz, and rock. And his tunes, such as "Georgia on My Mind" and "One Mint Julep," have become standards as beloved as anything sung by Frank Sinatra or written by Cole Porter. Beginning as an imitator of the urbane vocal stylings of Nat King Cole and the uptown blues of Charles Brown, Charles eventually forged his own style, combining gospel music and harmonies and the country music of his youth with decidedly earthier lyrics reflecting love, lust, heartbreak, and hard times.

Though Charles's increase in popularity occured simultanously with the rise of rock 'n' roll, he correctly commented in his autobiography that his work has little to do with the nascent genre—it contained too much despair to compete on the charts with the up-tempo ravings of Little Richard, Jerry Lee Lewis, and Elvis Presley. Yet Charles remains a seminal influence on rock, and he was rightfully inducted into the Rock 'n' Roll Hall of Fame in 1986. In R&B, Charles is revered both for his voice, which reveals a seemingly depthless capacity for heartache, and for his deftly intuitive ideas, which find him mining influences as varied as Count Basie and Hank Williams, and turning the result into works of staggering originality. A man of Herculean determination, few opponents from the world of music—or from life in general, for that matter—have faced him down. Not all of his decisions have been right ones, but he stands behind them all. And why not? He is one of the most recognizable figures in all of music, thanks to such timeless hits as "I Got a Woman," "What'd I Say," "The Night Time Is the Right Time," "Hit the Road Jack," "Unchain My Heart," "You Don't Know Me," "Busted," and countless others, to say nothing of his famous "Uh-huh" Diet Pepsi commercials. There is no one else like him.

what to buy: Charles's illustrious career has been documented with several excellent box sets, but *Genius & Soul: The 50th Anniversary Collection* ♫♫♫♫ (Rhino, 1997, prod. various) stands above them all, if only for pulling together for the first time material from all facets of Charles's career and from all of the labels he's recorded for. At five discs, it's a hefty investment in time and money, but it's an absolute treasure. Starting with an early single from his Seattle days, the set moves through his "genius" phase at Atlantic, to the even more unbridled innovation of his ABC days—recording soulful country & western classics and covering the Beatles—to the quiet classics (such as his recent reading of Leon Russell's "A Song for You") that he records to this day. *Genius & Soul* is one of the best box sets ever assembled. For those unwilling or unable to treat themselves, start with both *Anthology* ♪♪♪♪ (Rhino, 1988, prod. Sid Feller, Joe Adams) and *The Best of Ray Charles: The Atlantic Years* ♪♪♪♪ (Rhino, 1994, prod. Jerry Wexler, Zenas Sears, Nesuhi Ertegun, Ahmet Ertegun). The 20-track *Anthology* contains the ABC material, including "Georgia on My Mind," "Let's Go Get Stoned," "Eleanor Rigby," "Hit the Road Jack," and "Unchain My Heart." *The Atlantic Years*, which also contains 20 tracks, features "I Got a Woman," "What'd I Say," "The Night Time Is the Right Time," and "Drown in My Own Tears." Both are the best single-disc representations of those periods of Charles's music currently available.

what to buy next: They're advertised as country & western, but there are few recordings as soulful as Charles's takes on Eddy Arnold's "You Don't Know Me," Hank Williams's "You Win Again," and Frankie Laine's "That Lucky Old Sun." On *Modern Sounds in Country and Western Music* ♪♪♪♪ (ABC, 1963, prod. Sid Feller, Joe Adams), those songs and others stand as monuments to Charles's innovation and sheer audacity. During the heightened racial tensions of the early 1960s, what other black man could have pulled this off? *Live* ♪♪♪♪ (Atlantic, 1987/Rhino 1990, prod. Nesuhi Ertegun, Zenas Sears) combines a pair of essential late 1950s live recordings, *Ray Charles at Newport* and *Ray Charles in Person*. The set reveals Charles's intensity and charisma as a concert performer and includes explosive versions of "The Right Time," "What'd I Say," and "Drown in My Own Tears."

what to avoid: Some of Charles's albums are ill-conceived or carried out, but none are truly wretched. The things to beware, however, are the numerous cheap repackagings of his hits. If it's not on Atlantic, ABC, Rhino, or DCC, proceed with caution.

the rest:
The Great Ray Charles/The Genius After Hours ♪♪♪ (Atlantic, 1958 and 1961/Rhino, 1987)
(With Milt Hinton) *Soul Brothers/Soul Meeting* ♪♪♪ (Atlantic, 1958 and 1962/Rhino, 1989)

The Genius of Ray Charles ♪♪♪♪ (Atlantic, 1959/Rhino, 1990)
The Genius Hits the Road ♪♪♪ (ABC, 1960/Rhino, 1997)
The Best of Ray Charles ♪♪♪ (Atlantic, 1970/Rhino, 1988)
Would You Believe? ♪♪ (Warner Bros., 1990)
The Birth of Soul: The Complete Atlantic Rhythm & Blues Recordings, 1952–1959 ♪♪♪♪ (Rhino, 1991)
My World ♪♪♪ (Warner Bros., 1993)
Ain't That Fine ♪♪♪ (Drive Archive, 1994)
Blues + Jazz ♪♪♪♪ (Rhino, 1994)
The Early Years ♪♪♪♪ (Tomato, 1994)
Strong Love Affair ♪♪♪ (Qwest, 1996)
Berlin, 1962 ♪♪♪♪ (Pablo, 1996)
Sings Standards ♪♪♪♪ (Rhino, 1998)
(With Betty Carter) *Dedicated to You* ♪♪♪♪ (Rhino, 1998)

worth searching for: At press time, Rhino Records was in the midst of an extensive program of reissuing Charles's ABC sides. One worth waiting for is *A Message from the People* ♪♪♪♪ (ABC, 1972), which includes "Abraham, Martin, and John," "There'll Be No Peace without All Men As One," and Charles's brilliant renderings of "Look What They Done to My Song, Ma" and "America the Beautiful." It's a protest album of sorts, from a man whose politics before this album, and since, have seldom been on display.

influences:
◀◀ Nat "King" Cole, Charles Brown, Count Basie, the Grand Ole Opry, Louis Jordan, Claude Jeter

▶▶ Van Morrison, Joe Cocker, Billy Joel

Daniel Durchholz

The Ray Charles Singers

Formed late 1950s, in Philadelphia, PA.

Ray Charles (born in Chicago, IL), director; rotating group of female singers.

Charles, who couldn't possibly be less related to the man who invented soul music (i.e., Ray "What'd I Say" Charles), had a vision of soft, whispering romantic instrumentals that, along with the Ray Conniff, 101 Strings, Living Strings, and George Melachrino juggernauts, proved incredibly lucrative in the '50s and '60s. Charles, who had been a singer and choral director for both *The Perry Como Show* and *Hit Parade,* taught his choirs to never, ever yell and to always sing as if they were murmuring to lovers standing less than a few feet away. The formula led to many big-selling albums, such as *Quiet Moments for Young Lovers*, plus jingle-singing work for Lucky Strike cigarettes and Lipton Tea.

what's available: The Ray Charles Singers recorded for several different record labels, including Enoch Light's Command Records, but almost all of those once-huge LPs have yet to meet the CD era. In print, however, is *Love Me with All Your Heart* ✶✶✶✶ (Varese Sarabande, 1995, prod. Enoch Light), which includes several "la-la-la" versions of showtunes and standards, such as "One of Those Songs," "People," and "Hello, Dolly!" Light's stable of excellent session musicians, including organist Dick Hyman and guitarist Tommy Mottola, provide the backbone for the Singers' out-of-print *Something Wonderful* ✶✶✶ (Command, 1961), featuring "Misty" and "Embraceable You."

influences:

◀◀ Paul Weston, George Melachrino, 101 Strings, Enoch Light

▶▶ Ray Conniff, Percy Faith, Living Strings, Hollyridge Strings

Steve Knopper

Cher
See: Sonny & Cher

Don Cherry
Born November 18, 1936, in Oklahoma City, OK. Died October 19, 1995, in Malaga, Spain.

"Out there" is about the best way to describe pocket trumpet player Don Cherry's esoteric, free-jazz musical leanings. Considered a great, fluid, though technically imperfect improviser, Cherry has been described by jazz writer Doug Ramsey as having an "unorthodox approach to improvisation." Cherry also was called a leader of the iconoclastic avant-garde jazz movement.

After moving to Los Angeles at age four, Cherry grew up in Watts, dancing at parties for money with the early lounge lizards his father knew from tending bar. He got his first trumpet in 1950 and, in high school, met drummer Billy Higgins. During the '50s they hung out with alto saxophonist George Newman, performing tunes by Charlie Parker, Thelonious Monk, Bud Powell, Miles Davis, and Sonny Rollins. In 1955, Cherry and tenor sax player John Clay fronted a group they called the Jazz Messiahs, playing intermissions at the Chase Hotel in Santa Monica, California. That's how they met Davis, Coltrane, and Cannonball Adderley. Clay and Higgens went to work for bassist Red Mitchell in 1957 and fell under the spell of alto saxophonist Ornette Coleman. That influence changed Cherry's musical direction permanently. Classical bebop was out; free jazz was in. Cherry worked with Coleman through 1959 and appeared with

him at the Five Spot in New York on December 21, 1960. The show was recorded by Atlantic Records, and the resulting disc, *Free Jazz (A Collective Improvisation)*, is considered to be the catalyst of a controversy about free jazz that still hasn't abated. Cherry also worked with Rollins and Coltrane (recording *The Avant-Garde* with the latter), then joined the New York Contemporary Five in the '60s. He also played with Pharaoh Sanders, then traveled the world, meeting Gato Barbieri and luring him back to America. Cherry's world travels also sparked an interest in exploration of world beats, styles, and instruments, which he studied intently. (His daughter, Neneh Cherry, shares her stepfather's interest, recording with Senegalese vocalist Youssou N'-Dour.) Among his other achievements, Cherry taught at Dartmouth College, worked with Velvet Underground rocker Lou Reed in the late '70s and early '80s, and played in the Leaders (1984–86). Though he also would use a full-sized cornet at times (along with many other instruments), the half-sized instrument is the one with which he is most closely identified.

what to buy: Cherry's music might be considered an acquired taste—which could explain why most of it is out of print. For a representative sampling, try *Art Deco* ✶✶✶ (A&M, 1989, prod. John Snyder), Cherry's first recording in years with his old buddy John Clay, Billy Higgins, and bassist Charlie Haden (and the first time Higgins, Cherry, and Clay played together since 1954). It's notable for its outstanding rendition of "Body and Soul," with Clay's melodic, moody tenor sax. But you know how those bass things go, and there's an obtuse Haden composition ("Folk Medley") that is, mercifully, only two minutes and 42 seconds long.

the rest:
Symphony for Improvisers ✶✶✶✶ (Blue Note, 1966)
Old and New Dreams (PolyGram, 1978)

worth searching for: The out-of-print LPs *Don Cherry* ✶✶✶✶✶ (BYG, 1971), *Avant-Garde* ✶✶✶✶✶ (Atlantic, 1961), and *Don Cherry* ✶✶✶✶ (Horizon, 1977) stand out as the strongest examples of Cherry's eclectic style.

influences:

◀◀ Fats Navarro, Clifford Brown, Miles Davis, Harry Edison, Ornette Coleman, John Coltrane

▶▶ Sun Ra, Lou Reed

Lynne Margolis

Don Cherry (© Jack Vartoogian)

Cherry Poppin' Daddies

Formed 1989, in Eugene, OR.

Steve Perry, vocals, guitars; Dan Schmid, bass; Jason Moss, guitar; Dana Heitman, trumpet; Sean Flannery, alto saxophone; Ian Early, alto and baritone saxophones; Dustin Lanker, keyboards.

Either too far ahead or too far behind the times, the Cherry Poppin' Daddies were among the first to realize the horns in early '60s ska and late '40s swing could be easily merged into modern hipster dance music. They predated both the *Swingers* movie and Squirrel Nut Zippers radio phenomenon, touring the country throughout the '90s with original songs set to styles lifted from earlier eras. It's unclear why the Daddies, even when successors such as Big Bad Voodoo Daddy and the Royal Crown Revue get major-label recording contracts, continue to remain relatively unknown despite nonstop touring. But maybe the band's punk irreverence—like the Beastie Boys, they rolled giant phalluses on stage for a few years, plus the name is a little strange—isn't a perfect fit with swing-loving audiences.

what to buy: For a band with only three studio albums and no "hits" to speak of, *Zoot Suit Riot: The Swingin' Hits of the Cherry Poppin' Daddies* 🎵🎵🎵🎵 (Universal, 1997, prod. Steve Perry) is a bit premature. But the swing music is terrific, all horns and Perry's declarative high pitch on the title track and the playful "Ding Dong Daddy of the D Car Line."

what to buy next: *Rapid City Muscle Car* 🎵🎵🎵 (Space Age Bachelor Pad, 1994) plays up the ska and (slightly) plays down the big-band sound, but maintains the goofiness— "Sockable Face Club" and "Hazel, South Dakota" have the sprightliest jump.

what to avoid: *Ferociously Stoned* 🎵🎵 (Space Age Bachelor Pad, 1994) has its funny bits—such as "Flovilla Thatch vs. the Garbage Man" and "Teenage Brain Surgeon"—but the sound quality is poor and it's unclear whether the Daddies want to play ska, swing, or noodling rock.

the rest:
Kids on the Street 🎵🎵🎵 (Space Age Bachelor Pad, 1996)

influences:
◀◀ Cab Calloway, Glenn Miller, David Rose, the Specials, Madness, Louis Jordan, Mighty Mighty Bosstones

▶▶ Squirrel Nut Zippers, Royal Crown Revue, the Senders, Big Bad Voodoo Daddy

Steve Knopper

Alex Chilton

Born December 28, 1950, in Memphis, TN.

If it weren't for former Pink Floyd trendsetter Syd Barrett, Chilton could be formally recognized as rock's most mysterious underachiever. Actually, since Barrett is clinically insane and Chilton is merely nuts, our man gets the crown. As a teenager, Chilton led the Box Tops to #1 with "The Letter." In Big Star, he laid out the blueprint for all that would become power-pop. And then, short of his 25th birthday, Alex Chilton appeared to be washed up. So he drank a lot, stopped recording, and on those rare occasions when he did re-enter the studio, the results were sloppy and embarrassing. A sober Chilton reappeared in the mid-1980s proving he could record and play perfectly servicable rock—minus the dark, sonic brilliance that marked Big Star's final days. Of course, any underachiever worth his salt wants to keep his dwindling fan base aggravated. Hence *Clichés*, released in 1994, features Chilton doing his favorite big-band standards—only without a band. If this had come out in 1975, on the heels of the pop craftmanship that distinguished Big Star, well, maybe. But as it stands, *Clichés* is a cruel joke at the expense of those who stuck it out through the lean years. Which, even then, would be excusable had Chilton not showed he could craft splendid cheese in his version of "Volare" on 1987's *High Priest*. But that was just one song in the middle of his strongest collection in a decade. *Clichés* features Chilton singing 12 standards—from Cole Porter to Mel Tormé—accompanied only by his acoustic guitar. When he stumbles, and he does, you wonder whether the singer actually practiced these tunes.

what to buy: *19 Years: A Collection* 🎵🎵🎵🎵 (Rhino, 1991, prod. various) features a handful of songs from the third and final Big Star album, and a smattering of Chilton's solo output leading up to *High Priest*. It's a great survey, from the twang of "Free Again" to the white-boy soul of "Make a Little Love." But beware. If you don't like *19 Years*, stop here. *Bach's Bottom* 🎵🎵🎵 (Razor & Tie, 1993, prod. Jon Tiven, Alex Chilton) was supposed to be Chilton's post–Big Star solo debut. The most recent version includes some extra singles and B-sides, including a crunching cover of the Seeds' "Can't Seem to Make You Mine."

what to buy next: After a virtually silent decade, Chilton came back in the mid-1980s with *Feudalist Tarts/No Sex* 🎵🎵🎵 (Razor & Tie, 1994, prod. Alex Chilton) and *High Priest/Black List* 🎵🎵🎵🎵 (Razor & Tie, 1994, prod. Alex Chilton). Both include lots of covers (including a full-band "Volare") and are driven by Chilton's new bar-band ethos. *1970* 🎵🎵🎵 (Ardent, 1996, prod. Terry Manning) was recorded in, you guessed it, 1970, after the Box Tops and before Big Star.

what to avoid: *Clichés* 🎵 (Ardent, 1994, prod. Alex Chilton, Keith Keller) begs the question: does Chilton really like this album or is he simply mocking the thankless many who would approve if he came onstage with a bottle of Cheerwine and proceeded to practice belching?

the rest:
Live in London 🎵🎵🎵 (Fuel, 1981)
Like Flies on Sherbert 🎵🎵 (Line, 1987)
A Man Called Destruction 🎵🎵🎵 (Ardent, 1995)
Cubist Blues w/Alan Vega and Ben Vaughn 🎵🎵🎵 (2.13.61, 1996)

worth searching for: Unlike most tribute albums, *Not the Singer but the Songs* 🎵🎵🎵 (Munster Records, 1991, prod. various) features nobody famous. Instead of the usual suspects—Eric Clapton, Jon Bon Jovi, Michael Stipe—we get Mitch Easter, the now-defunct Popes (from Chapel Hill, N.C., not Ireland), and the Dambuilders.

solo outings:
Big Star:
#1 Record/Radio City 🎵🎵🎵🎵 (Stax, 1992)
Third/Sister Lovers 🎵🎵🎵🎵 (Rykodisc, 1992)
Big Star Live 🎵🎵🎵🎵 (Rykodisc, 1992)
Columbia: Live at Missouri University 4/25/93 🎵🎵🎵 (Zoo, 1993)

influences:
◀◀ The Beatles, the Beach Boys, the Kinks, Johnnie Taylor
▶▶ The db's, the Replacements, the Posies, Teenage Fanclub

Geoff Edgers

June Christy
Born November 20, 1925, in Springfield, IL. Died June 21, 1990, in Sherman Oaks, CA.

Emerging from Stan Kenton's blustery big band of the 1940s, Christy reached the peak of her popularity in the '50s as a slick purveyor of torch songs and saloon balladry. Christy, who went by the stage name of Shirley Luster early in her career, worked in various big bands around Springfield and Chicago before she replaced Anita O'Day as the singer in Kenton's band. During her five-year tenure with Kenton, Christy met and married the band's arranger, Bob Cooper; the two would collaborate closely on many of Christy's greatest solo recordings. Her 1953 debut, *Something Cool*, which began her 20-year association with Capitol Records, is considered by many to be her greatest recording, an intimate showcase for her dusky soprano. Subse-

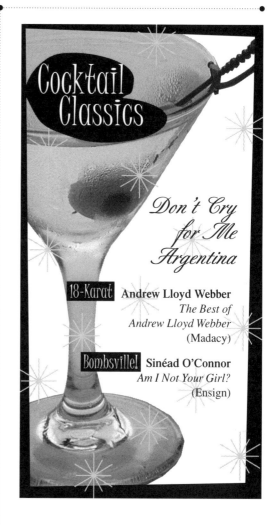

Cocktail Classics

Don't Cry for Me Argentina

18-Karat Andrew Lloyd Webber *The Best of Andrew Lloyd Webber* (Madacy)

Bombsville! Sinéad O'Connor *Am I Not Your Girl?* (Ensign)

quent albums found the singer ably tackling everything from Broadway show tunes to straight-up jazz and children's songs. She continued recording and touring up until her death in 1990.

what to buy: If you're going to buy one Christy album, *Something Cool* 🎵🎵🎵🎵 (Capitol/EMI, 1953) is it. Her debut is a perfect marriage of great songs, inventive arrangements, and the singer's burnished voice.

what to buy next: *Go for Duet* 🎵🎵🎵🎵 (Capitol/EMI, 1955), her spare and stunning reunion with Kenton, features Christy accompanied only by the maestro's piano.

the rest:

The Misty Miss Christy 🎵🎵🎵 (Capitol, 1956)
June Christy and the Kentones 🎵🎵🎵🎵 (Hindsight, 1993)
The Uncollected June Christy 🎵🎵🎵 (Hindsight, 1994)
Daydream 🎵🎵🎵 (Capitol, 1995)
Spotlight on June Christy 🎵🎵🎵 (Gold Rush, 1996)
The Jazz Sessions 🎵🎵🎵🎵 (Blue Note, 1996)
The Song Is June 🎵🎵🎵 (Capitol, 1997)

influences:

⏪ Stan Kenton, Anita O'Day, Edith Piaf, Billie Holiday

⏩ Sinéad O'Connor, Patsy Cline

Marc Weingarten

Alfred Cini

See: Al Martino

Buddy Clark

Born Samuel Goldberg, July 26, 1912, in Dorchester, MA. Died October 1, 1949, in Los Angeles, CA.

Big-band crooner Clark was on the verge of solo stardom at the time of his death. He began his career as a singer with Nat Brandwynne's orchestra in 1932 and was a regular singer on Benny Goodman's radio series, *Let's Dance*, a few years later. His recurrent spots on radio's *Hit Parade* led to work with the Ben Bernie and Wayne "The Waltz King" King orchestras. Clark's individual star began to rise in the '40s when he hosted his own radio show, *Here's to Romance*, and appeared in such films as *Seven Days Leave, I Wonder Who's Kissing Her Now,* and *Melody Time*. After he joined Freddy Martin's Orchestra he scored big hits dueting with Doris Day ("I Confess," "Love Somebody," "My Darling, My Darling") and Dinah Shore ("Baby, It's Cold Outside"). His own recordings, which highlighted his folksy charm and smooth command of melody, were just beginning to make significant chart impact when he died in a plane crash.

what to buy: Clark's all-too-short recording career is chronicled on *16 Most Requested Songs* 🎵🎵🎵🎵 (Legacy, 1992, compilation prod. Didier C. Deutsch), which includes duets with Doris Day, Dinah Shore, and the Girlfriends, as well as standout solo work on such tracks as "Now Is the Hour," "You're Breaking My Heart," and "I'll Get By As Long As I Have You." The Harry Zimmerman, Xavier Cugat, and Ray Noble Orchestras add considerable musical diversity, but the charismatic Clark is unquestionably the star. Also, *Buddy Clark Collection* 🎵🎵🎵🎵 (Collector's Series, 1993) has a similar track lineup with four more tunes.

the rest:

Big Band Vocals from the Thirties 🎵🎵🎵 (Take Two, 1991)

worth searching for: A fine alternate take of Clark's duet with Doris Day on "My Darling, My Darling" can be found on *Doris Day: 16 Most Requested Songs, Encore!* 🎵🎵🎵🎵 (Legacy, compilation prod. Didier C. Deutsch), which contains liner notes speculating that Clark was on his way to becoming as popular as Frank Sinatra and Perry Como before he died.

influences:

⏪ Gene Vaughn, Perry Como, Frank Sinatra

⏩ Merv Griffin, Guy Mitchell

Ken Burke

Doug Clark & the Hot Nuts

Formed 1955, in Chapel Hill, NC.

Doug Clark, drums; John Clark Jr., vocals, manager; Tommy Goldston, keyboard, vocals; Monty Clark, drums, sound; Delaney McQuaig, vocals, guitar; Billy Payne, saxophone; A.J. Griffith, bass.

Nine presidents have resided in the White House since Doug Clark and the Hot Nuts hit the road in 1955 with a mix of straightforward R&B and raunchy, double-entendre humor. It is the latter, the "Hot Nuts Show," for which the group became famous in frat houses, convention halls, and barrooms up and down the East Coast and across the South. The material—dirty jokes and limericks, off-color, sexually explicit, but good-natured—is perfectly crafted for drunken reverie, and can strike fond, nostalgic chords of memory decades later. (Remember "Bang Bang LuLu," "Barnacle Bill the Sailor," "Two Old Maids," or "The Gay Cabelero"?) Not surprisingly, the band's first recording was banned or sold under-the-counter in the '60s. The post office deemed it obscene, so promoters sent the recordings to stores in unmarked boxes by Greyhound bus. Brothers Doug and John Clark, founders of the group, have survived the British Invasion, the racial unrest of the '60s (striking their own blow for integration, they were among the first blacks to desegregate Atlanta hotels), the '70s gas crisis, the onslaught of disco and grunge, and still play roughly 200 nights a year. The show, virtually unchanged since the '50s despite more than 70 personnel changes, was filmed for the Playboy channel in 1990, but an ideal audio document of the band's unique show has never been produced.

what to buy: The band's self-produced debut LP, *Nuts to You* 🎵🎵🎵 (Gross, 1961), was pressed by Jubilee Records, which noted the band's substantial sales success and signed them to the label. The band recorded eight LPs for Jubilee between 1963 and 1969, with four reaching the Top 10 on the *Billboard* college and comedy charts. Jubilee declared bankruptcy in 1969 and the band has not recorded again. These releases are out of print; however, all nine recordings are available on cassette directly from the band; contact John Clark Jr., P.O. Box 725, Chapel Hill, NC 27514, (919)544-2035, (919)942-1422, or (919)929-2754. Be prepared for minimal packaging: the cassettes have no "J-card," song listings, or other information. *On Campus* ♫♫♫ (Jubilee, 1963), the band's first release on Jubilee, is more of the same, but features better sound quality than *Nuts to You*. Both recordings include two versions of their classic "Hot Nuts" theme, and all four versions are distinctive. If you're choosing between the two, take *On Campus*.

the rest:

Homecoming ♫♫♫ (Jubilee, 1963)
Rush Week ♫♫♫ (Jubilee, 1964)
Panty Raid ♫♫♫ (Jubilee, 1965)
Summer ♫♫♫ (Jubilee, 1966)
Hell Night ♫♫♫ (Jubilee, 1967)
Freak Out ♫♫♫ (Jubilee, 1968)
With a Hat On ♫♫♫ (Jubilee, 1969)

worth searching for: All of the original LP releases of the recordings above are worth finding, if only for the packaging. The band also released three singles in the '60s, "Baby Let Me Bang Your Box," "Go Doug Go," and "Milk the Cow."

influences:

◀◀ The Platters, Little Richard

▶▶ Chuck Berry's "My Ding-a-Ling," Otis Day & the Knights (from the film *Animal House,* the producers of which auditioned the Hot Nuts but didn't select them), Wilson Pickett, Otis Redding

Bryan Powell

Petula Clark

Born November 15, 1932, in Epson, England.

While "Listening to Prozac" may be the '90s cure for depression, in the '60s the cure for the blues was listening to "the music of the traffic in the city," or at least listening to Petula Clark's pollyannaish signature song, "Downtown." In addition to extolling the virtues of concrete canyons and bossa nova music, Clark has enjoyed a fruitful career spanning six decades, in which she has entertained British troops during World War II and headlined Broadway musicals in the '90s.

Already a singing and acting superstar in Europe, Clark found her first U.S. hit with the aforementioned "Downtown" off the album of the same name, which reached #1 in 1964 and earned a Grammy. Penned and arranged by her frequent collaborator Tony Hatch and buoyed, no doubt, by the British Invasion, "Downtown" was the first in a series of buoyant mid-'60s Clark hits, including "I Know a Place" and "My Love." Armed with boundless cheer and lucid vocals, she would chart several more times, most notably with "Don't Sleep in the Subway" and "Kiss Me Goodbye." As her commercial appeal began to wane in the late '60s, she returned to acting, with roles in *Finian's Rainbow* and *Goodbye, Mr. Chips.* Occasional studio albums since the early '70s have had little impact, but Clark has remained a popular entertainer, starring in a number of stage musicals, including her Broadway debut in 1993's *Blood Brothers* opposite David Cassidy. Despite her many successes, Clark has never quite escaped the legacy of her signature tune; "Downtown" reached the British Top Ten as a disco record (1976) and an acid-house dance single (1988).

what to buy: Sorting through the morass of Clark collections can be daunting, but for a general overall collection of her brightest moments, *Greatest Hits* ♫♫♫♫ (GNP, 1986, prod. various) satisfies with consistently lively and sparkling arrangements of favorites like "Downtown" and "My Love."

what to buy next: Clark puts forth a stellar effort with her requisite holiday album, *Merry Christmas/Joyeux Noel* ♫♫♫ (Sequel, 1997). Her takes on the classics "My Favorite Things" and "Away in the Manger" refresh like a sunny December morning.

what to avoid: Despite its grandiose title, *Treasures, Vol. 1* ♫ (Scotti Bros., 1992, prod. Catherine Farley) is a mishmash of Clark classics and ill-advised covers like Hank Williams's "Your Cheatin' Heart" and Gordon Lightfoot's "The Gypsy."

the rest:

Downtown ♫♫ (Collectables, 1964)
I Know a Place ♫♫ (Collectables, 1965)
My Love ♫♫ (Sequel, 1966)
Live at the Copacabana ♫♫♫ (Sequel, 1994)
Blue Lady ♫♫ (Varese Sarabonde, 1995)
In Memphis ♫♫♫ (Sequel, 1996)
Pye Years, Vol. 1/Don't Sleep in the Subway ♫♫♫ (RPM, 1996)
Pye Years, Vol. 2/Winds of Change ♫♫♫ (RPM, 1996)

worth searching for: Most rock fans associate bands like the Beatles, the Kinks, and the Yardbirds with the British Invasion, but as *The British Invasion: The History of British Rock* ♫♫♫♫ (Rhino, 1991, prod. various) shows, some-hit wonders like Tom

Jones, Lulu, the Honeycombs, and Chad & Jeremy were part of the conquering force and endure surprisingly well. Clark's three songs on this nine-disc set, "I Know a Place," "My Love," and, of course, "Downtown," are nice companion pieces to Deep Purple's pre-metal classic, "Hush," and Pocol Harum's hippie signature, "A Whiter Shade of Pale."

influences:

◀◀ Julie Andrews

▶▶ Lulu, the Carpenters

Alex Gordon

Richard Clayderman

Born Phillipe Pages, December 28, 1953, in Paris, France.

If "beautiful music" died out in the '80s, the millions upon millions of worldwide listeners who have given this instrumental pianist more than 200 gold records haven't heard the news. What he does is hardly revolutionary. Clayderman plays soothing romantic songs, usually written by past stars such as the Carpenters, Andrew Lloyd Webber, and ABBA, and fills up the empty space with lush orchestral arrangements—booming tympani drums, reassuring strings, the works. Worldwide fans can't get enough; in 1987, he performed for the first time in China, and 800 million Asian viewers tuned in to watch the concert on television. Nancy Reagan called him "The Prince of Romance" and, while he's no Percy Faith or Mantovani, his shoulder-length blonde hair, starched smile, and pink and white jackets give him the perfect vanilla look for easy-listening superstardom.

Like Mantovani, Clayderman was a piano-playing child prodigy who won all sorts of honors (first prize in a prominent Paris Conservatoire of Music piano competition, for example) before, unexpectedly, turning away from classical and towards the more lucrative pop industry. He played in bad rock bands, working odd jobs to make a living until his father (a piano player himself) died, forcing Clayderman to support himself by accompanying prominent classical musicians. Soon producers Olivier Toussaint and Paul de Senneville heard his work, signed him up to their Delphine record label, and a recording career began. Taking on his Swedish grandmother's name, he started selling and never stopped. Muzak itself may have grown beyond its stereotypical days as a tinkly elevator-music provider,

Petula Clark **(Archive Photos)**

but Clayderman fills the void as a one-man Muzak machine. He has blunted ABBA's "Dancing Queen," Andrew Lloyd Webber's "Phantom of the Opera," Percy Sledge's "When a Man Loves a Woman," Bruce Springsteen's "Streets of Philadelphia," and countless others, and made big bucks in the process. Most of the old Hollyridge Strings and 101 Strings Orchestra LPs may be out of print, but Clayderman's similar-sounding CDs, which could fill up entire record stores, more than make up for it.

what to buy: For sheer Clayderman-music girth, begin with the older-oriented *For Happy Hour Lovers* ♪♪♪ (Rodven, 1997, prod. various), which contains standards like "As Time Goes By," "Besame Mucho," and "My Way." The next volume of the same series is more interesting and modern, with schmaltzy (and funny in an ironic sort of way) versions of the Dolly Parton–penned Whitney Houston smash "I Will Always Love You" and, most unusually, Bruce Springsteen's Oscar-winning movie song, "Streets of Philadelphia." Beyond that, it's impossible to envision anybody needing more Clayderman music than the three-CD set *World of Romance* ♪♪♪ (Warlock, 1996, prod. various).

what to buy next: Clayderman's soft style meshes nicely with the material on *Love Songs of Andrew Lloyd Webber* ♪♪♪ (Quality, 1991, prod. Paul de Senneville); he has good instincts, knowing when to soften his playing during the orchestra's crescendos, and when to dominate the album with solo flourishes. He's also up on modern production techniques, using snappy drum machines and a dance-floor style to prove he's not just rehashing "Theme from *A Summer Place*" his whole career. For hipsters who own the alternative-rock-heavy Carpenters tribute CD, *If I Were a Carpenter*, Clayderman's totally earnest *Carpenters Collection* ♪♪♪ (Quality, 1996), with versions of "We've Only Just Begun" and "Superstar," makes for a nice antidote.

what to avoid: Beware of bland French romanticists trying to make sense of Latin culture: instead of bothering with *My Bossa Nova Favorites* ♪♪ (Quality Latino, 1997), seek out the real thing and track down Laurindo Almeida LPs. Similarly, *Tango Passion* ♪ (Quality Latino, 1997), while occasionally upbeat, just won't kick-start most dance floors.

best of the rest:

(With the Royal Philharmonic Orchestra) *Concerto* ♪♪♪ (Sony, 1989)
My Classic Collection ♪♪♪ (Quality, 1991)
Remembering the Movies ♪♪♪ (Quality, 1992)
Amour and More ♪♪♪ (Quality, 1992)
When Love Songs Were Love Songs ♪♪♪ (Quality, 1992)

Desperado 🎵🎵 (Quality, 1993)
Little Romance 🎵🎵 (Quality, 1994)
Classical Passion 🎵🎵🎵 (Quality, 1994)
Romance of Richard Clayderman 🎵🎵🎵 (Sony Special Products, 1995)
Unchained Melody 🎵🎵🎵 (Sony Special Products, 1995)
Love American Style 🎵🎵 (Quality, 1996)
Love French Style 🎵🎵🎵 (Quality, 1996)
Love Italian Style 🎵🎵 (Quality, 1996)
Christmas 🎵🎵🎵 (Quality, 1997)

worth searching for: It's hard to find the American disc, *ABBA Collection* 🎵🎵🎵 (Warlock, 1993), in record stores, but a nice alternative is the Holland import *Plays ABBA Hits* 🎵🎵🎵🎵 (BR Music, 1996), which is even more hilarious than the ABBA tribute band, Björn Again, because Clayderman isn't trying to be funny. At least, that's one way of looking at it. You could probably hold hands and whisper sweet nothings, too, to Clayderman's piano takes on "Dancing Queen," "One of Us," and "Waterloo."

influences:

⏪ Mantovani, Percy Faith, Paul Weston, Andre Previn, George Shearing, Laurindo Almeida, Julio Iglesias, João Gilberto, Ray Conniff, Living Strings, Hollyridge Strings, ABBA, the Carpenters

Steve Knopper

Rosemary Clooney

Born May 23, 1928, in Maysville, KY.

Because she was a straightforward pop singer instead of a rock 'n' roll belter or a jazz chanteuse, Clooney's incredible hitmaking career is frequently dismissed by critics and historians with their noses upturned. Yes, she sang many novelty tunes, including the surprisingly forceful and sexy "Mambo Italiano," which unashamedly piggybacked on the 1954 mambo fad. And yes, her backup musicians sang in an exaggerated deep-country twang, played harpsichords, or mimicked player-piano solos from old Western movies. But, while she doesn't communicate with quite the expression of Billie Holiday, Clooney's clear, perfect voice is a marvel—she makes "tra la la la la" sound sexy and subversive, communicates a fierce romanticism in "Invitation," and has a perfect understanding of a song's rhythm.

As teenagers, Clooney and her sister, Betty, began singing for a Cincinnati radio station; bandleader Tony Pastor heard their songs and quickly signed them up to sing for his touring orchestra. In the early 1950s, Clooney signed with the influential pop label Columbia, then recorded 1951's "Come On-A My House," a bouncy, sensual number with "hit" stamped all over it. The song went to #1 and kicked off a prolific recording career, including several million-selling records and a detour into films. She starred with Bob Hope in 1953's *Here Comes the Girls,* and began a life-long friendship with Bing Crosby on the set of *White Christmas.* But rock 'n' roll, especially in the 1960s, was a lousy era for both jazz and mainstream pop singers. The Beatles, among others, usurped Clooney's brand of standard-singing from the charts. Perfectly good albums, such as 1963's *Love*—delayed from release for two years because RCA was concentrating on rock, then tanking when it finally came out—were no longer what young people wanted to hear. Clooney, frustrated, went into semiretirement. She came back, gradually, beginning in the late '70s, recording a number of jazz-based albums and eventually singing at President Clinton's White House jazz concert. Her nephew, *ER* and movie heart-throb George Clooney, has told interviewers that his aunt's experience is an enduring lesson about the public's fickle taste.

what to buy: Because Clooney has recorded for so many different record labels, and because she has had hits in so many different decades, there are lots of greatest-hits collections available. Aim for the songs you like: "Mambo Italiano" shows up on *The Essence of Rosemary Clooney* 🎵🎵🎵 (Legacy, 1993, prod. various), and "Look to the Rainbow" and "Come On-A My House" are on *Greatest Songs* 🎵🎵🎵 (Curb/MCA, 1996, prod. various). For great old stuff, there's *The Uncollected Rosemary Clooney, 1951–1952* 🎵🎵🎵 (Hindsight, 1986/Rounder, 1994, prod. Dave Dexter Jr.) and *Everything's Rosie 1952/1963* 🎵🎵🎵 (Hindsight/Rounder, 1994, prod. various).

what to buy next: In her post-retirement years, recording for the receptive Concord Jazz label, Clooney dedicated herself to paying tribute to big-band heroes and classic pop songwriters. Highlights include *Rosemary Clooney Sings the Music of Irving Berlin* 🎵🎵🎵 (Concord Jazz, 1984, prod. Carl E. Jefferson), *Rosemary Clooney Sings the Music of Cole Porter* 🎵🎵 (Concord Jazz, 1982, prod. Carl E. Jefferson), and the tremendous *Here's to My Lady—Tribute to Billie Holiday* 🎵🎵🎵 (Concord Jazz, 1979, prod. Carl E. Jefferson). One of her most interesting solo albums, though it occasionally devolves into string-heavy schmaltz, is the underrecognized *Love* 🎵🎵🎵 (Reprise, 1963/Warner Archives, 1995, prod. Dick Peirce), which includes solemn romantic anthems like "Black Coffee" and "If I Forget You."

what to avoid: Clooney's orchestral Christmas album, *White Christmas* 🎵🎵 (Concord Jazz, 1996, prod. Peter Matz), is just like any other Christmas album. If you have Bing Crosby and everybody else, there's no reason to get this new album of old Christmas standards.

the rest:

Blue Rose 🎵🎵🎵 (Columbia, 1956)

Everything's Coming Up Rosie 🎵🎵 (Concord Jazz, 1977)

Rosie Sings Bing 🎵🎵🎵 (Concord Jazz, 1978)

My Buddy 🎵🎵🎵 (Concord Jazz, 1983)

Rosemary Clooney Sings the Music of Harold Arlen 🎵🎵🎵 (Concord Jazz, 1983)

Rosemary Clooney Sings Ballads 🎵🎵 (Concord Jazz, 1985)

Rosemary Clooney Sings the Music of Jimmy Van Heusen 🎵🎵🎵 (Concord Jazz, 1986)

Rosemary Clooney Sings the Lyrics of Johnny Mercer 🎵🎵🎵 (Concord Jazz, 1987)

Show Tunes 🎵🎵 (Concord Jazz, 1989)

With Love 🎵🎵 (Concord Jazz, 1989)

The Music of Rodgers, Hart & Hammerstein 🎵🎵🎵 (Concord Jazz, 1990)

Rosemary Clooney Sings the Lyrics of Ira Gershwin 🎵🎵 (Concord Jazz, 1990)

For the Duration 🎵🎵🎵 (Concord Jazz, 1991)

Girl Singer 🎵🎵🎵 (Concord Jazz, 1992)

Tenderly 🎵🎵🎵 (Columbia Special Products, 1992)

Do You Miss New York? 🎵🎵🎵 (Concord Jazz, 1993)

Still on the Road 🎵🎵 (Concord Jazz, 1994)

Demi-Centennial 🎵🎵 (Concord Jazz, 1995)

Dedicated to Nelson 🎵🎵🎵 (Concord Jazz, 1996)

The Best of Rosemary Clooney 🎵🎵🎵 (Tri Star, 1996)

Mothers & Daughters 🎵🎵🎵 (Concord Jazz, 1997)

influences:

◀◀ Bing Crosby, Billie Holiday, Ira Gershwin, Cole Porter, Duke Ellington, Doris Day

▶▶ Sinéad O'Connor, Ann-Margret, Barbra Streisand, Bette Midler, George Clooney

Steve Knopper

Holly Cole

Born in Canada.

One of the most exciting lounge singers to come along in the past 10 years, Holly Cole is inventive, seductive, and fearless. She hit it big in 1993 with *Don't Smoke in Bed*—a collection of jazz standards performed with her drummer-less trio. Aaron Davis, her pianist, is a gentle, impressionistic player who never gets in the way of Cole's big vocals. Acoustic bassist David Piltch provides the foundation for the music—plucking strings and slapping the hell out of the instrument for percussion. In her more recent works, the creatively restless Cole has strayed from her lounge/jazz roots—taking time out to do an album of

Tom Waits lyrics, and taking on a more avant-garde sound. With a big, physical presence, her stage shows continue to be riveting no matter what type of music is striking her fancy.

what to buy: *Don't Smoke in Bed* 🎵🎵🎵🎵 (Manhattan/Capitol, 1993, prod. David Was), her can't-miss breakthrough album, contains a selection of cheesy showtunes turned cool: "Tennessee Waltz," "Que Sera Sera," and "I Can See Clearly Now."

what to buy next: *Temptation* 🎵🎵🎵 (Capitol, 1995, prod. Craig Street) and *Dark Dear Heart* 🎵🎵🎵 (Warner Bros., 1997, prod. Larry Klein), two of Cole's later, darker albums, are effective avenues for her considerable pipes, but not exactly relaxing. For devoted Cole fans. *It Happened One Night* ♫♫♫ (Metro Blue, 1996) is a collection of Cole's greatest hits—plus a very nice offering of interviews and music videos via a CD-ROM included in the set. It takes advantage of Cole's admitted fascination with on-line technology.

influences:

◀◀ Peggy Lee, Marlene Dietrich, Doris Day, Billie Holiday

Carl Quintanilla

Nat "King" Cole

Born Nathaniel Adams Coles, March 17, 1917, in Montgomery, AL. Died February 15, 1965, in Santa Monica, CA.

He was known as the "King," and during his incredible, too-brief reign he actually ruled over two domains. Nathaniel Adams Cole was one of the finest jazz swing pianists in history, and his classic smooth-voiced ballads, "Unforgettable," "Our Love Is Here to Stay," and the jaunty "Route 66," remain standbys at any wedding reception, ballroom-dancing class, or, yes, cocktail lounge.

Cole became one of the single most successful pop ballad singers of the 20th century, with a voice so warm, rich, and unmistakable that it seems nearly impossible to believe he spent the early years of his career trying to make it as a piano player. After his family moved to Chicago from the Deep South, Cole began taking keyboard lessons while playing the organ and singing in church. After working in bands with his brothers, he struggled to find his place in the music world, finally organizing the King Cole Trio, and began performing on radio. The combo became popular when it recorded Cole's "Sweet Lorraine" in 1940, and other musicians (notably Art Tatum and Oscar Peterson) formed their own trios, inspired by his sound. The trio rose to prominence during that decade, recording exciting jazz music, mostly for Capitol, and performing in the movies *Here Comes Elmer* and *Pistol Packin' Mama,* and the first-ever Jazz at the Philharmonic concert. Along the way, Cole grew more confident in his vocal ability and became increasingly more popular as a singer. When a string of now-classic recordings, including "The Christmas Song," "I Love You for Sentimental Reasons," and "Nature Boy," culminated in a #1 hit with "Mona Lisa" in 1950, Cole became a full-time pop singer. He landed his own NBC-TV series from 1956–57, an almost unheard-of accomplishment for a black man of that era. Despite being accompanied by the Nelson Riddle Orchestra and hosting many of the biggest stars of the day (Tony Bennett, Sammy Davis Jr., Peggy Lee), the show ultimately died due to lack of sponsorship and

the refusal of some stations to carry it. Cole continued to be a major attraction, appearing in many movies (including *Cat Ballou* and *The Nat King Cole Story*) and becoming a musical holiday tradition at Christmas. One of the trademarks of the "King" was a lit cigarette held regally in a cigarette holder; when he died of lung cancer at the age of 47, the world mourned the loss of one of the most beloved voices of all time.

what to buy: Why it took the success of Natalie Cole's *Unforgettable* tribute to her father to prompt the release of a hit singles collection for Cole is inconceivable, but *The Greatest Hits* ♫♫♫♫ (Capitol/EMI, 1994, prod. various) is such a package. Covering the King's work from 1944 through 1963 in 62 minutes and 22 tracks, the collection skips some of his famous Christmas songs but does focus on his best pop productions, such as "Mona Lisa" and "Sentimental Reasons." The cuts are arranged by style and quality rather than chronology, which gives an imperfect sense of history but a better sense of the music. *Jazz Encounters* ♫♫♫♫ (Blue Note, 1992, prod. Michael Cuscuna) combines the great work of jazz masters like Coleman Hawkins, Benny Carter, and Dizzy Gillespie with Cole's piano and vocal stylings. Here you'll find Cole's non-trio performances and some of his best collaborations with Woody Herman and Johnny Mercer.

what to buy next: If you're looking for big box sets, start with *Nat King Cole* ♫♫♫♫ (Capitol/EMI, 1992, prod. Lee Gillette), which boasts four discs and a 60-page booklet covering 20 years in 100 different tracks. As a side dish, you'll find the previously unreleased novelty "Mr. Cole Won't Rock & Roll" as well as Leonard Feather liner notes, complete track annotations, rare photographs, and some of the King's most inspiring jazz sets. Starting with records like *Lush Life* ♫♫♫♫ (Capitol/EMI, 1993) with the Pete Rugolo Orchestra, Cole was phasing out of trio work and trying to establish a vocal career over his keyboard fare.

what to avoid: Some musicians just could do no wrong—you didn't think they called him "King" simply because his last name was Cole, did you? His only albums worth avoiding are ones with weak or offbeat selections, such as *Greatest Country Hits* ♫♫ (Curb, 1990).

the rest:
Big Band Cole ♫♫♫♫ (EMI/Capitol, 1950)

Nat "King" Cole **(AP/Wide World Photos)**

The Billy May Sessions ♫♫♫ (EMI/Capitol, 1951)

Nat King Cole Live ♫♫♫ (A Touch of Magic)

Early American ♫♫ (A Touch of Magic)

(With the Nat King Cole Trio) *Hit That Jive, Jack: The Earliest Recordings (1940–41)* ♫♫♫♫ (Decca/MCA Jazz, 1990)

The Very Thought of You ♫♫♫♫♫ (Capitol/EMI, 1991)

The Jazz Collector Edition ♫♫♫♫ (Laserlight, 1991)

(With the Nat King Cole Trio) *The Trio Recordings* ♫♫♫ (Laserlight, 1991)

(With the Nat King Cole Trio) *The Complete Capitol Recordings of the Nat King Cole Trio* ♫♫♫♫♫ (Capitol/EMI, 1991)

(With the Nat King Cole Trio) *The Trio Recordings, Vol.2* ♫♫♫♫ (Laserlight, 1991)

(With the Nat King Cole Trio) *The Trio Recordings, Vol. 3* ♫♫♫ (Laserlight, 1991)

(With the Nat King Cole Trio) *The Trio Recordings, Vol. 4* ♫♫♫ (Laserlight, 1991)

The Unforgettable Nat King Cole ♫♫♫♫♫ (Capitol/EMI, 1992)

(With the Nat King Cole Trio) *The Best of the Nat King Cole Trio: Instrumental Classics* ♫♫♫♫ (Capitol/EMI, 1992)

The Piano Style of Nat "King" Cole ♫♫♫♫ (Capitol/EMI, 1993)

(With the Nat King Cole Trio) *Early Years of Nat King Cole Trio* ♫♫♫ (Sound Hills, 1993)

(With the Nat King Cole Trio) *Nat King Cole & the King Cole Trio: Straighten Up & Fly Right (Radio Broadcasts 1942)* ♫♫♫ (VJC, 1993)

(With the Nat King Cole Trio) *The Nat King Cole Trio: World War II Transcriptions* ♫♫♫♫ (Music & Arts Programs of America, 1994)

Spotlight on Nat King Cole ♫♫♫ (Capitol/EMI, 1995)

The Jazzman ♫♫♫♫ (Topaz Jazz, 1995)

To Whom It May Concern ♫♫♫♫ (Capitol/EMI, 1995)

Swinging Easy Down Memory Lane ♫♫♫ (Skylark Jazz, 1995)

The Complete After Midnight Sessions ♫♫♫♫♫ (Capitol/EMI, 1996)

Sweet Lorraine (1938–1941 Transcriptions) ♫♫♫♫ (Jazz Classics, 1996)

The Vocal Classics ♫♫♫♫ (Capitol/EMI, 1996)

The Nat King Cole TV Show ♫♫♫♫ (Sandy Hook, 1996)

The McGregor Years (1941–1945) ♫♫♫♫ (Music & Arts Programs of America, 1996)

Love Is the Thing (Gold Disc) ♫♫♫♫♫ (DCC, 1997)

worth searching for: For a fascinating insight into the performing medium and the painstaking polishing of brilliance, Cole's *Anatomy of a Jam Session* ♫♫♫♫ (Black Lion, 1945) with drummer Buddy Rich is especially choice. Cole attacks the keys only, no vocals, and his dynamic jams with Charlie Shavers, Herbie Hayner, John Simmons, and Rich are superb. Famous for his rendering of "The Christmas Song" and "Frosty the Snowman," Cole became the unofficial herald angel of Christmas. If you take the time to hunt down the reissues of *The Christmas Song* ♫♫♫ (Capitol, 1990, prod. Lee Gillette) and *Cole, Christmas and Kids* ♫♫♫♫ (Capitol, 1990, prod. Ron Furmanek), you won't be sorry.

influences:

◀◀ Billy Kyle, Louis Armstrong, Louis Jordan, Duke Ellington, Teddy Wilson, Earl "Fatha" Hines

▶▶ Johnny Mathis, Frank Sinatra, Johnny Hartman, Oscar Peterson, Al Jarreau, Bing Crosby, Mel Tormé, Billy Eckstine

Chris Tower

Natalie Cole

Born February 6, 1950, in Los Angeles, CA.

The second of Nat "King" Cole's five children, Natalie Cole almost destroyed her career and her life under the weight of her father's enormous image, then rebounded to phenomenal heights because of it. Growing up in the Hancock Park section of Hollywood, Natalie thrived in the musical and entertainment environment and worshipped her father, making her singing debut with him at the age of 11. Tragically, the great "King" of pop vocalists died of lung cancer four years later. Natalie attended the University of Massachusetts at Amherst, earned a degree in child psychology, and began singing in local clubs with a group called Black Magic. However, the 1970s were difficult for Cole: arrested for possession of heroin in 1973, she struggled with alcohol and drug abuse through the 1980s. Despite those woes, her voice quickly earned commercial success and critical praise. During an appearance in Chicago, Cole was approached by record producers Marvin Yancy (whom she would later marry) and Chuck Jackson about making an album. That debut LP, *Inseparable*, produced two major hits, went gold, and won her two Grammy Awards. She was hailed as the next Aretha Franklin because of her powerfully soulful style. In the 1980s, she divorced Yancy and married Andre Fischer of Chaka Khan's R&B group Rufus, but her continued drug and alcohol abuse plunged Cole into a career freefall from which she did not emerge until 1987. But in the 1990s, Natalie Cole rocketed to superstardom, sweeping the Grammy Awards and securing a platinum album with 1991's *Unforgettable*. The LP was her own tribute to her father after years of squirming beneath his massive shadow, and was inspired by the song she contributed to a Johnny Mathis tribute album in 1983. The title cut was a duet between Cole and the late Nat—his voice added through feats of engineering wizardry—and was named Song of the Year. In recent years, Cole has branched out into acting (appearing on the TV show *I'll Fly*

Natalie Cole (with Wynton Marsalis conducting)
(© Jack Vartoogian)

Away, among others) and continues to release superior albums in a contemporary jazz-pop vein.

what to buy: Five million album buyers cannot be wrong, and *Unforgettable* &&&& (WEA/Elektra, 1991, prod. Andre Fischer, Tommy LiPuma, David Foster) shows that an album packaged to be a commercial gimmick can also be what the title suggests. Showcasing Cole as a principal diva in the pop music world through its variety of Nat "King" Cole classics, the LP rises not only on the strength of its sentimentality but on its genuine beauty. Some sincerely argue that *Unforgettable* is one of the best albums ever recorded.

what to buy next: After *Unforgettable,* continue the exploration of Natalie's own musical repertoire with *The Natalie Cole Collection* &&&& (Capitol/EMI, 1988, prod. Chuck Jackson). A collection of Cole's 1975–1981 recordings on Capitol, almost all of which are out of print (including her excellent debut LP, *Inseparable*), the disc displays her stylings as a soul artist heavily influenced by Aretha Franklin. Songs like "Inseparable" and "This Will Be" highlight some of Cole's strongest vocal work. While *Take a Look* &&&& (WEA/Elektra, 1993, prod. Andre Fischer, Tommy LiPuma) was not as big a commercial success as *Unforgettable,* it was an equal critical achievement, with 18 gleaming jazz-seasoned tracks earning her a Grammy for Best Jazz Vocalist.

what to avoid: Cole parted ways with Capitol after recording *Don't Look Back* && (One Way Records, 1980, prod. various); arguably, she left one album too late. Unquestionably her weakest work, with vocals lacking any trace of intensity or passion, this LP might have better been titled *Don't Look Here.*

the rest:
Natalie &&&& (One Way, 1976)
Thankful &&& (One Way, 1977)
Natalie . . . Live &&&& (One Way, 1978)
I Love You So && (One Way, 1979)
(With Peabo Bryson) *We're the Best of Friends* &&&& (One Way, 1979)
Happy Love && (One Way, 1981)
Dangerous &&&& (Modern, 1985)
Everlasting &&&& (WEA/Elektra, 1987)
Good to Be Back &&&& (WEA/Elektra, 1989)
Unforgettable with Love: Special Edition w/video &&&& (WEA/Elektra, 1991)
Holly & Ivy &&& (WEA/Elektra, 1994)
Stardust &&& (WEA/Elektra, 1996)
This Will Be: Natalie Cole's Everlasting Love &&&& (EMI America, 1997)

worth searching for: Most critics agree that Cole's debut, *Inseparable* &&&& (Capitol, 1975), is a bravura, breakthrough

performance. Though no longer in print, the album revealed that Cole is an amazing talent, a budding superstar in the same league as her father. It's worth the time investment to start beating down the used record bins. On the other end of the spectrum, Natalie pits her latter-day vocal prowess against the spectacular power of world-class tenors Jose Carreras and Placido Domingo on the holiday LP *A Celebration of Christmas* &&&& (Erato, 1996) and more than holds her own.

influences:
◀◀ Nat "King" Cole, Aretha Franklin, Diana Ross, Sarah Vaughan, Ella Fitzgerald, Billie Holiday, Roberta Flack, Patti LaBelle, Carmen McRae

▶▶ Anita Baker, Whitney Houston, Mariah Carey, Taylor Dayne, Toni Braxton

Chris Tower

Cy Coleman

Born Seymour Kaufman, June 14, 1929, in New York, NY.

A gifted, often underrated pianist and composer who was giving piano recitals by the time he was six, Coleman went on to pen some of jazz's most enduring tunes—mostly notably, "Witchcraft," which Frank Sinatra immortalized in 1957, and "The Best Is Yet to Come" in 1959. Coleman started out his career in television, writing music for shows called *Date in Manhattan* and *John Murray Anderson's Almanac.* He even became musical director for Kate Smith's television show in 1955. But after meeting lyricist Carolyn Leigh in 1957, he settled into writing music for the stage and screen—a move culminating in *Sweet Charity,* the 1966 musical that launched Shirley MacLaine's career and still finds revivals on Broadway today. Coleman is known less as a pianist than as a songwriter, but listeners are likely to be rewarded with his extremely dry and gentle touch on the keyboard.

what's available: Aside from Sinatra's easy-to-find versions of "Witchcraft"—on, for example, *The Very Best of Frank Sinatra* &&&&& (Reprise, 1997, prod. various)—it's tough to find recorded evidence of Coleman's work. His excellent musical, *The Life* &&&& (RCA Victor, 1996), has him performing solo on just a few tracks, including "The Oldest Profession" and "Was That a Smile?" It's about Times Square—back when Times Square was full of drugs and hookers. What a pick-me-up. It's also notable for an actual George Burns singing turn, "Easy Money," plus the presence of Liza Minnelli, Jack Jones, Bobby Short, and a veritable Lounge Music Hall of Fame.

influences:

◀◀ George Gershwin, Cole Porter, Rodgers & Hart

▶▶ Frank Sinatra, Stephen Sondheim, John Kander & Fred Ebb, Jerry Herman

Carl Quintanilla and Steve Knopper

Edwyn Collins /Orange Juice

Born August 23, 1959, in Edinburgh, Scotland.

Always interested in mixing genres, Collins and his early '80s Scottish punk band, Orange Juice, made frequent forays away from simple song structure into what later was called "world music," as well as dub reggae, lounge music, ballads, Velvet Underground–like noise, and even country. After one British hit single, 1983's melodic and funky "Rip It Up," follow-ups failed and Orange Juice unpeeled for good. Collins continued to record and tour as a solo artist for several years before reemerging in 1995 with the hit single "A Girl Like You," which combined a slinky '60s-soundtrack feel with a classic guitar line. The hit, and the CD that followed, brought Collins attention he hadn't seen in nearly two decades of music making. Already an influence to alternative pop groups for his work with Orange Juice, Collins cemented his place in lounge history with "The Magic Piper (of Love)," the opening track of the Burt Bacharach–reviving soundtrack for *Austin Powers,* and a wicked version of "Witchcraft" on the 1996 rock-and-lounge CD *Lounge-A-Palooza.* Tongue tucked firmly in cheek, Collins remains a frustrating figure to follow, an erratic talent with a perverse instinct who has never reached his potential.

what to buy: Collins's storm to stardom began with 1994's *Gorgeous George* 🍸🍸🍸 (Setanta, 1994, prod. Edwyn Collins), which included not only "A Girl Like You" but also Collins classics like "Low Expectations" and "If You Could Love Me." His follow-up to *Gorgeous George, I'm Not Following You* 🍸🍸 (Setanta, 1996, prod. Edwyn Collins) contained some of Collins's best songs, including "Country Rock," "Adidas World," "Seventies Night," and "I'm Not Following You." However, despite the presence of good melodic and instrumental material, Collins's constant genre-jumping feels a little forced and almost petulant, with a refusal to commit to anything.

what to buy next: Collins's first two solo albums were more in the singer-songwriter mold and began to show more clearly the pre-rock influences in his songwriting. *Hope and Despair* 🍸🍸🍸 (Demon, 1989) is most notable for its dark, smoky mood, cap-

tured in the title track, "50 Shades of Blue," and "Ghost of a Chance." The next project, the equally ambivalently titled *Hellbent on Compromise* 🍸🍸🍸 (Demon, 1990), boasted "Means to an End" and "It Might As Well Be You," but once again could not crack the market.

what to avoid: *The Orange Juice* 🍸🍸 (Polydor, 1986, prod. Dennis Bovell) stands as an overly cynical stab at the pop of the time, including very little of value for either musical or historical purposes. The cover shot of an overly prettified Collins in dark sunglasses reflected the album's offputting tone, and the inclusion of several previously issued tracks meant for short listening. It has never been in print in America.

the rest:

Ostrich Churchyard ♫♫♫ (Postcard, 1992)

The Esteemed Orange Juice ♫♫♫ (Polydor, 1992)

worth searching for: The first Orange Juice LP, *You Can't Hide Your Love Forever* ♫♫♫♫ (Polydor, 1982, prod. Adam Kidron), sat in the can for six months before being released and lost much of its contemporary cachet. However, the 14-song collection remains Collins's best work, featuring a great cover of Al Green's "L-O-V-E (Love)" and 13 original gems ranging from sweet balladry to punky pop. It has never been in print in America. Neither has *Rip It Up* ♫♫♫ (Holden Caulfield Universal, 1983, prod. Martin Hayles), which featured Tanzanian drummer Zeke Manyika, who contributed two songs rich with African rhythms. However, Collins's songwriting was not its best, though the smooth "Flesh of My Flesh" and the delicate ballad "Tenterhook" stood out. The out-of-print EP *Texas Fever* ♫♫♫ (Polydor, 1985, prod. Dennis Bovell) was Orange Juice's last important work, containing the song "The Day I Went Down to Texas."

influences:

◀◀ The Buzzcocks, the Velvet Underground, Al Green, the Byrds, Chic, Motown, Broadway musicals, country music, '70s soundtracks

▶▶ Weezer, Supergrass, Cast

Stuart Shea

Judy Collins

Born May 1, 1939, in Seattle, WA.

What? You aren't hip to the fact that the great earth mother of folk music and art-song chanteuse may be the only person aside from Bobby Darin to pioneer folk-lounge fusion? She didn't start out that way. Collins grew up in Denver and studied classical piano with the pianist and conductor Antonia Brico. At age 13 Collins gave her debut piano performance with the Denver Businessmen's Symphony. Three years later, though, she gave up classical for folk music. Collins became a part of the Greenwich Village scene and was signed by Elektra Records to sing in her shimmering alto and play acoustic guitar. When she included songs from the stage production of *Marat/Sade* on her 1966 album *In My Life*, critics began to classify some of her repertoire as "art songs." From a 1997 vantage point, these "art songs" stand in the same league as the classic pop that Frank Sinatra and Ella Fitzgerald performed. What was arty about Collins's choice of material—Jacques Brel, Kurt Weill and Bertolt Brecht, Stephen Sondheim—may have been the intellectual air of the writers or just her classically trained attention

to detail. Her love for Leonard Cohen, whose "Bird on the Wire" embodies the same sense of loss as the classic showtune "One for My Baby," also fits in with the lounge thing in a sad, Euro-cabaret kind of way. Despite her classical sense of taste and restraint, Collins had three major hit singles—the #5 "Both Sides Now" in 1968, #15 "Amazing Grace" in 1971, and #19 "Send in the Clowns" in 1977. Even without hit singles, her albums usually charted and often went gold in the '60s and '70s. This put her in a good position to do other projects, such as co-directing the Oscar-nominated documentary film *Antonia: Portrait of a Woman,* about her piano teacher. After she left Elektra in 1984, her visibility wound down a bit. MTV hurt her commercial cachet, and her son, Clark Taylor, committed suicide in 1992. Still, she continued her blend of genres on albums for various big small record labels. Time, however, has taken a small toll on her voice.

what to buy: From a lounge point of view, the pickings in Collins's catalog are slim, just a few cuts on each album. The suite from *Marat/Sade* on *In My Life* ♫♫♫♫ (Elektra, 1966, prod. Jac Holzman, Mark Abramson) is her showtune, art-song starting point. Better yet is *Wildflowers* ♫♫♫♫ (Elektra, 1967, prod. Mark Abramson): besides a bona fide hit in "Both Sides Now," it's all orchestral. And while "La Chanson Des Vieux Amants" may not swing, it has that one-for-the-road saloon mood down pat. The album that best showcases the lounge-Collins link is *Judith* ♫♫♫♫ (Elektra, 1975, prod. Arif Mardin), which features "Send in the Clowns" and such old-time pop as "Brother, Can You Spare a Dime" and "I'll Be Seeing You."

what to buy next: *Wind Beneath My Wings* ♫♫♫ (Laserlight, 1992, prod. various) features Collins's interpretations of pop hits. Besides the title tune, it includes "When You Wish upon a Star," "From a Distance," "Cat's in the Cradle," and "The Rose." Collins has two Christmas flavors, the lounge-heavy *Come Rejoice! A Judy Collins Christmas* ♫♫♫♫ (Mesa/Bluemoon, 1994, prod. Judy Collins, Alan Silverman) and the more contemporary *Christmas at the Biltmore Estate* ♫♫♫ (Elektra, 1997).

what to avoid: The cheesy, arch *Hard Times for Lovers* ♫ (Elektra, 1979, prod. Gary Klein) reeks of the smug "El Lay" atmosphere, Collins isn't singing well, and the collection seems phoned in.

the rest:

Fifth Album ♫♫♫♫ (Elektra, 1965)

Who Knows Where the Time Goes ♫♫♫♫ (Elektra, 1968)

Recollections ♫♫♫♫ (Elektra, 1969)

Whales & Nightingales ♫♫♫♫ (Elektra, 1970)

Living 🎵🎵🎵 (Elektra, 1971)
Colors of the Day: The Best of Judy Collins 🎵🎵🎵🎵 (Elektra, 1972)
True Stories and Other Dreams 🎵🎵🎵 (Elektra, 1973)
Times of Our Lives 🎵🎵🎵 (Elektra, 1982)
Home Again 🎵🎵🎵 (Elektra, 1984)
Sanity and Grace 🎵🎵🎵 (Delta, 1989)
Fires of Eden 🎵🎵🎵🎵 (Columbia, 1990)
Shameless 🎵🎵🎵 (Mesa/Bluemoon, 1994)
Live at Newport 🎵🎵🎵🎵 (Vanguard, 1995)
Forever . . . The Judy Collins Anthology 🎵🎵🎵🎵 (Elektra, 1997)

worth searching for: *Maid of Constant Sorrow* 🎵🎵🎵🎵 (Elektra, 1961, prod. Jac Holzman), *Golden Apples of the Sun* 🎵🎵🎵🎵 (Elektra, 1962, prod. Jac Holzman), and *Judy Collins #3* 🎵🎵🎵🎵 (Elektra, 1963, prod. Jac Holzman, Mark Abramson) are out of print and available only on vinyl.

influences:

◀◀ Jacques Brel, Marlene Dietrich

▶▶ Joni Mitchell, Shawn Colvin

Salvatore Caputo

Anita Belle Colton

See: Anita O'Day

Russ Columbo

Born Ruggerio de Rodolfo Columbo, January 14, 1908, in either San Francisco, CA, or Camden, NJ. Died September 2, 1934, in Hollywood, CA.

The circumstances of Columbo's bizarre death made him larger than life, like James Dean, in the 1930s—although his name, since then, has hardly endured as a household word. Columbo, a handsome crooner with lots of personality and emotion in his low-pitched voice, was once Bing Crosby's key rival. But he died after a shooting accident. Details remain sketchy, but Columbo was visiting a photographer friend, who allegedly lit a match on one of his souvenir antique Civil War pistols. That set off an unknown bullet, which bounced off a table and hit Columbo's head. The singer died later in a hospital.

Columbo, nicknamed "the Romeo of the Airwaves," was the son of an Italian musician and, as a young performer, worked on silent-movie sets to help actors "get in the mood" for love scenes. This work led to connections that helped Columbo score a violinist's job at a hotel and, finally, a recording contract and occasional cameo appearances in films. Unlike the more straightforward Crosby, Columbo frequently improvised with his excellent voice, stretching out the emotion in every romantic sentiment of "Prisoner of Love" and "When You're in Love."

what's available: While records by bluesman Robert Johnson, another performer of that era who died young in mysterious and violent circumstances, have resurfaced and become easily available on compact disc, Columbo's songs are comparatively hard to track down. His recorded work is still mostly out on LP, including *Russ Columbo—A Legendary Performer* 🎵🎵🎵🎵 (RCA, 1976, prod. various), which includes many of his big love-themed hits, and *Russ Columbo—Prisoner of Love* 🎵🎵🎵 (Pelican, 1975), which documents his last-ever recording session in 1934.

influences:

◀◀ Bing Crosby, Al Jolson, Fred Astaire

▶▶ Tony Bennett, Frank Sinatra, Eddie Fisher, Gordon MacRae, Judy Garland, Vic Damone

Steve Knopper

Combustible Edison

Formed 1991, in Boston, MA.

Michael "The Millionaire" Cudahy, guitars; Liz "Miss Lily Banquette" Cox, drums and vocals; Peter Dixon, organ; Aaron Oppenheimer, vibes.

Think of it as the Buddy Love of lounge music, a twisted but ultra-suave Frankenstein born out of a nerdy past. When an un-noticed underground group called Christmas got its first dose of stereophonic wizard Juan Garcia Esquivel's groovy tunes, that band's jangle-pop proliferators Michael Cudahy and Liz Cox became, respectively, The Millionaire and Miss Lily Banquette, while the ailing Christmas picked up some Moog keyboards, a theremin, and a harpsichord, some exotic instrumentation like marimba and gamales . . . and a new name, Combustible Edison.

In 1991, Cudahy wrote and premiered a two-hour performance-art piece called *The Tiki Wonder Hour* that featured a 14-piece outfit called the Combustible Edison Heliotropic Oriental Mambo and Foxtrot Orchestra. A few more shows, a demo, and a record label later and the group was pitted as the Sherpas of Snazzy, the heads of honorable hip, the chiefs of the Cocktail Nation—to the point that equally "now" movie directors such as Quentin Tarantino and Robert Rodriguez hit the band up to score their episodic film *Four Rooms*. (Which, despite some choice Edison cuts, was an artistic disaster for all involved.) A better application of Edison's influence has come via an at-tempted resuscitation of Esquivel's career, though the pioneer is now 80 and fairly infirm. Still, Combustible Edison is the deserved keeper of his flame, keeping one foot steeped firmly in an experimental (though melodic) tradition, the other skipping lightly along a camp surface.

what to buy: The band's debut, *I, Swinger* ♫♫♫ (Sub Pop, 1994, prod. Carl Plaster), was partly responsible for the lounge revival that swept through major cities in the mid-'90s and sent hordes of easy-listening collectors to trample through used-record stores before new fans devoured every last Three Suns and Enoch Light platter they could find. As devoted to its sources as to further progression—though equally in love with the culture as much as the sound (the cover sports a highball on the rocks)—it's no surprise that after a few years *I, Swinger* holds up remarkably well, ironically because it already sounds aged; songs such as "The Millionaire's Holiday" and "Breakfast at Denny's" seem stolen from another era.

what to buy next: Though not as successful a project as the debut, *Schizophonic! The Progressive Sound of Combustible Edison* ♫♫♫ (Sub Pop, 1996, prod. Combustible Edison, Brian Capouch) is still worth hearing. The mood is decidedly darker, which isn't always beneficial, but it's a sign that Edison is taking its sound seriously enough to expand it beyond kitsch boundaries. (Though that could also lead to its downfall; fun with a laidback twist, after all, is the point.) And though the soundtrack to *Four Rooms* ♫♫♫ (Elektra, 1995, prod. various) is long on atmospheric fluff, it does contain the irresistible "Vertigogo," a sassy, nonsensical gem that deserved to be a modern-rock hit when it was released, as well as some classic Esquivel moments and the theme from *Bewitched*.

worth searching for: The CD-single version of *Blue Light* ♫♫♫ (Domino, 1993, prod. various) features early tracks "Satan Says" and "Intermission"; *Spy S.O.U.N.D.S.* ♫♫♫ (Mai Tai Records, 1995, prod. various) is a collection of spy and crime-noir tunes with Henry Mancini's "A Shot in the Dark"; *Short Double Latte* ♫♫♫ (Bungalo Records, 1996, prod. various) is a Europe-only single release with "Hellraiser"; and *Get Easy! Vol. 2: The Future Collection* ♫♫♫ (Motor Music, 1996, prod. various) is one-half of a two-volume German set of past and present easy-listening favorites, including "Intermission."

influences:

◀◀ Juan Garcia Esquivel, Martin Denny, Enoch Light, the Three Suns, Les Baxter

▶▶ Love Jones, Friends of Dean Martin, the Lounge Lizards

Ben Wener

Perry Como

Born Pierino Como, May 18, 1912, in Canonsburg, PA.

One of the most popular and enduring stars of this century, Como almost traded a career in entertainment for standing behind a barber's chair. Back in 1933, he was making more cutting hair than he would have as a singer for Freddie Carlone's band, and he would have passed on the opportunity to sing if it weren't for his father's encouragement. Even after his success with Ted Weems's big band, Como kept up his membership in the barbers' union, just in case. That proved unnecessary, however, because by the mid-'40s, his appearances in New York and on radio had turned him into a teen idol, much like his contemporary, Frank Sinatra. Unwilling to tour, Como performed in a few movies, then landed a television variety show that became one of the top-rated shows of the '50s. At first a romantic balladeer in the mold of Bing Crosby, Como's TV fame pushed him into more novelty-oriented material, such as "Hoop Dee-Doo," "Papa Loves Mambo," and "Hot Diggity (Dog Ziggity Boom)." But he also recorded the country-flavored "Don't Let the Stars Get in Your Eyes" and the lovely "Catch a Falling Star." Como's image was that of everyone's favorite neighbor—personable, sweet, and utterly uncontroversial. The '60s saw his career flag in the face of rock 'n' roll, but he re-emerged in the '70s with the Top 10 hit "It's Impossible," making him a torchbearer for middle-of-the-road entertainers everywhere.

what to buy: A box set that couldn't hope to amass all of Como's hits, but does a terrific job trying, *Yesterday & Today: A Celebration in Song* ♫♫♫♫ (RCA, 1993, compilation prod. Paul Williams) traces his progression from crooner to superstar to wizened elder statesman across three CDs. Because most of Como's prodigious output is long out of print, the set is especially valuable, preserving more than 50 years of hits, many of them available for the first time on CD. The sound is marvelous, as well, having been compiled using only original master recordings. It's a nearly perfect compilation.

what to buy next: Those without deep enough pockets for the *Yesterday & Today* set should start with *Pure Gold* ♫♫♫ (RCA, 1984), which has the most essential hits. Its only disadvantage is its brevity. *All-Time Greatest Hits, Vol. 1* ♫♫♫ (RCA, 1988) is another fine compilation.

what to avoid: There's enough good material available on Como without having to resort to the budget releases, of which

Perry Como **(AP/Wide World Photos)**

there are plenty, including *You Are Never Far Away* ♪ (RCA Camden Classics, 1996) and *Sings Just for You* ♪ (RCA Special Products, 1996).

the rest:

Season's Greetings from Perry Como ♪♪♪ (RCA, 1959)
And I Love You So ♪♪ (RCA, 1973)
I Wish It Could Be Christmas Forever ♪♪♪ (RCA, 1982)
Today ♪♪♪ (RCA, 1987)
A Legendary Performer ♪♪♪ (RCA, 1992)
Como's Golden Records ♪♪♪♪ (RCA, 1992)

influences:

◄◄ Bing Crosby, Russ Columbo

►► Andy Williams, Engelbert Humperdinck, Julio Iglesias, Harry Connick Jr.

Daniel Durchholz

Harry Connick Jr.

Born September 11, 1967, in New Orleans, LA.

A child piano prodigy who grew up in a house and a city infused with the jazz tradition, Connick has made a career mimicking the voice, swagger, and good looks of a young Sinatra—with the musical skills of the jazz masters. The result is an anachronistic sound that's often beguiling for someone his age.

After studying music intently through his teens, Connick left the Crescent City for New York to follow in the footsteps of his friend Wynton Marsalis and sign a recording contract. Recording for Columbia, his second adult album, *20*, marking his age, brought his brand of throwback jazz to the attention of critics, but it wasn't until two years later, with the soundtrack to the immensely popular film *When Harry Met Sally*, that Connick became a sensation and an early pioneer in the mid-'90s lounge-music resurgence. With undeniable charisma, Connick soon began a successful detour into acting, most memorably as a cocky pilot fighting the alien masses alongside Will Smith in the blockbuster *Independence Day*. With his mind occupied by the silver screen, his albums in the '90s have been uneven and somewhat tiresome. *To See You*, a collection of newly penned romantic songs, finds Connick showcasing a surprising new maturity in his arrangements and songwriting.

what to buy: Buoyed by the hit film of the same name, *When Harry Met Sally* ♪♪♪♪ (Columbia, 1989, prod. Mark Shaiman, Harry Connick Jr.) showcases Connick at the height of his crooning abilities as his voice soars thorough standards like "It Had to Be You" and "Let's Call the Whole Thing Off."

what to buy next: At the tender age of 20, Connick released his third album, *20* ♪♪♪♪ (Columbia, 1987, prod. Kevin Blanq), which displays an already talented pianist clearly in his element. The best tracks find Connick joined by jazz greats like Dr. John and Carmen McRae. A return to form, *To See You* ♪♪♪ (Columbia, 1997, prod. Tracey Freeman) is Connick's endeavor to make a romantic album. With 10 original songs and a somewhat stripped-down sound, this CD could be a Valentine's Day staple for years to come.

what to avoid: Talent plus hype often leads to indulgence, and such is the case with *Blue Light, Red Light* ♪♪ (Columbia, 1991, prod. Tracey Freeman), which includes his laborious 10-minute-plus ode to his then-girlfriend (and current wife), former underwear model Jill Goodacre.

the rest:

11 ♪♪ (Columbia, 1978)
Harry Connick Jr. ♪♪♪ (Columbia, 1987)
We Are in Love ♪♪♪ (Columbia, 1990)
Lofty's Roach Soufflé ♪♪ (Columbia, 1990)
25 ♪♪ (Columbia, 1992)
When My Heart Finds Christmas ♪♪ (Columbia, 1993)
She ♪♪ (Columbia, 1994)
Whisper Your Name ♪♪ (Columbia, 1995)
Star Turtle ♪♪♪ (Columbia, 1995)

worth searching for: Having established himself with the soundtrack to *When Harry Met Sally*, Connick shows up on *Sleepless in Seattle* ♪♪♪♪ (Sony, 1993, various prods.), another soundtrack for a romantic comedy starring Meg Ryan. Connick's contribution, "A Wink and a Smile," sparkles among this mix of timeless classics performed by luminaries like Louis Armstrong and Jimmy Durante, and contemporary artists like Joe Cocker and Rickie Lee Jones.

influences:

◄◄ Frank Sinatra, Tony Bennett, Mel Tormé, Thelonious Monk, Eubie Blake, James Booker, Buster Poindexter

►► Squirrel Nut Zippers, G. Love & Special Sauce, Royal Crown Revue

Alex Gordon

Ray Conniff

Born November 6, 1916, in Attleboro, MA.

Some artists scoff at "commercial success." Since his early years as a big-band trombonist, Conniff has embraced, studied, and mastered the concept. He has released more than 90 albums, all with the same up-tempo rhythms, supermarket-ready melodies, and the Ray Conniff Singers contributing the browbeatingly gentle "la la las." Along with Percy Faith and Mantovani, Conniff's lush big-band arrangements have dominated elevators, easy-listening radio stations, and parental Christmastime hi-fis for decades. Whether you recognize his name or not, odds are excellent that you've heard Conniff's ubiquitous music many, many times. And on the slim chance that you haven't, it's distinctively overdramatic, with the Singers spewing their syrup in every direction, and bouncy guitars and rhythms robbing already overblown hits like "Winchester Cathedral" and "Georgy Girl" of whatever subtlety they originally had. "Ray Conniff wants you to accept THIS IS MY SONG as *your* album," read typically understated liner notes. "It's an opportunity not to be missed. Take it."

Conniff started his career organizing dance orchestras in high school. After nailing a post-graduation job as a musician and truck driver for the Boston-based Musical Skippers, big-dreaming Conniff moved to New York City and quickly found work in swing bands (including Artie Shaw's). During World War II he joined the U.S. Army and arranged songs for Armed Forces Radio; later, he did the same for Harry James, but bebop jazz cut the swing era short and Conniff was adrift. So he became obsessed with what sells, listening to Glenn Miller's most popular hits and radio jingles and conducting a thorough study of public musical tastes. Armed with this data, he set out to conquer the music world—and succeeded. In the mid-1950s, Columbia Records' Mitch Miller hired Conniff as an arranger, which began a reputable career of working with jazz trumpeter Don Cherry, pop balladeer Johnny Mathis, country singer Marty Robbins, and "Rawhide" singer Frankie Laine. His first album, *'S Wonderful*, with the Conniff formula of high-pitched female singers, fastidiously arranged trumpet and sax bits, and low-pitched male singers, was a smash. It began an overwhelmingly prolific anti-rock career. Conniff's very picture, a beaming white-bearded man in a white leisure suit holding a trombone, is the essence of easy-listening.

what to buy: Because Conniff has been a reliable Columbia hitmaker for four decades, most of his 90-plus albums are still in print and easy to locate on CD. They're mostly interchangeable; we're not about to vehemently recommend any studio album over another, so begin with either *16 Most Requested Songs* 🎵🎵🎵 (Sony, 1987, prod. various), which includes such instrumental smashes as "Somewhere, My Love" and "Love Is a Many Splendored Thing," or *The Essence of Ray Conniff* 🎵🎵🎵 (Sony, 1993, prod. various), which focuses on slightly more ob-

Cocktail Classics

Enter Sandman

18-Karat **Metallica**
Metallica
(Elektra)

Bombsville! **Pat Boone**
*In a Metal Mood:
No More Mr. Nice Guy*
(MCA)

scure material. One of the best original sets is *Somewhere My Love* 🎵🎵🎵 (Columbia, 1966/Sony, 1987, prod. Ernie Altschuler), which includes the *Dr. Zhivago* theme.

what to buy next: You'll need, of course, one Conniff Christmas album, although come holiday time he winds up all over the radio. *Christmas with Conniff* 🎵🎵🎵 (Columbia, 1959) is the classic, but either *Christmas Album* 🎵🎵🎵 (Sony, 1996, prod. Ernie Altschuler) or *Christmas Caroling* 🎵🎵🎵 (Sony, 1995) make for reliable eggnog-drinking soundtracks. For trivia's sake, Conniff's debut, *'S Wonderful* 🎵🎵🎵 (Columbia, 1956/Sony, 1988), is an excellent easy-listening set for any hipster lounge cat's collection.

what to avoid: Conniff was a master at repeating a formula ad nauseum. Many of the other "S" albums, such as *'S Awful Nice* ♪♪ (Columbia, 1958/Sony, 1988), *'S Continental* ♪ (Columbia, 1961/Sony, 1988, prod. Rann Productions), *'S Marvelous* ♪♪ (Columbia, 1957/Sony, 1987), and *'S Always Conniff* ♪ (Sony, 1992, prod. Ray Conniff), have little purpose once you've already bought the greatest hits and historical documents.

best of the rest:
Broadway in Rhythm ♪♪ (Columbia, 1958/Sony, 1988)
You Make Me Feel So Young ♪♪ (Columbia, 1960/Sony, 1993)
(With Billy Butterfield) *Just Kiddin' Around* ♪♪♪ (Sony, 1993)
Latinisimo ♪♪ (Sony, 1994)
Friendly Persuasion ♪♪ (Sony, 1994)
Music from "Mary Poppins" ♪♪ (Sony, 1995)
Mi Historia ♪♪♪ (PolyGram Latino, 1997)

worth searching for: Without having to worry about which Columbia records to resell, the *Ray Conniff* ♪♪♪ (Time Life, prod. various) volume captures just the best stuff. Also interesting is *Homenaje A* ♪♪♪ (Sony/Orfeon, 1995), a various-artists tribute album.

influences:
◀◀ Glenn Miller, Harry James, Artie Shaw, Benny Goodman, Mantovani, Enoch Light

▶▶ Percy Faith, Ferrante & Teicher, Herb Alpert

Steve Knopper

Barbara Cook

Born October 25, 1927, in Atlanta, GA.

The premier Broadway ingenue of the '50s and early '60s, Cook introduced several standards to the musical stage with her pretty, expressive soprano. She started at the top, working such chic supper clubs as the Blue Angel in New York, and bowling over critics with her versions of tunes penned by George Gershwin, Jerome Kern, and Rodgers and Hart. After earning good reviews in the short-lived Broadway musicals *Flahooley* and a revival of *Carousel,* she was cast in a bona fide hit, *Plain and Fancy,* where she scored heavily with the tune "Young and Foolish." She followed up with Leonard Bernstein's ambitious *Candide,* which was considered a failure by critics though many noted Cook's stand-out dramatic and vocal performance. Cook's Tony-winning turn as Marian the librarian in 1957's *The Music Man* made her a star, and provided her with such song classics as "Goodnight My Someone" and "Till There Was You." After appearing in 1,300 Broadway performances of *Music Man,* Cook was devastated to learn Shirley Jones had

been cast in the movie version. Cook rebounded in 1964's *She Loves Me,* singing the effervescent "Will He Like Me?" and "Dear Friend." Though her career declined along with Broadway musicals in general, a voice as dramatically polished as Cook's couldn't be silenced for long, and she made her concert debut at Carnegie Hall in 1975. Her overwhelming success there opened the door to a whole new career as a live performer. With the passing years she has lost a little of her range, but Cook is still the standard by which all live musical theater performers are measured.

what to buy: Culled from original cast LPs of such hit shows as *Flahooley, The Music Man, The Gay Life,* and *Show Boat, The Broadway Years* ♪♪♪♪ (Koch International, 1995, reissue prod. James Gavin) features Cook's best solo numbers and classic duets with Robert Preston, John Raitt, and James Courtland.

what to buy next: Cook put the world on notice that she was a great solo star with *Live at Carnegie Hall* ♪♪♪♪ (Sony Classical, 1975/1996, prod, Thomas Frost), perhaps her greatest concert performance. Also, there is no better match of talents and material than on *The Disney Album* ♪♪♪♪ (MCA, 1988, prod. Thomas Z. Shepard), a beautifully done theme LP that Walt himself would have loved.

the rest:
Candide ♪♪♪♪ (Original Cast Recording) (Sony Broadway, 1956/1991)
She Loves Me ♪♪♪ (Original Cast Recording) (Polydor, 1963/1988)
Carousel: 1987 Studio Cast ♪♪♪♪ (MCA, 1987)
Close as Pages in a Book ♪♪♪ (DRG, 1993)
She Loves Me ♪♪♪♪ (Varese Sarabande, 1993)
Live from London ♪♪♪♪ (DRG, 1994)
Oscar Winners: The Lyrics of Oscar Hammerstein II ♪♪♪♪ (DRG, 1997)
Sings from the Heart ♪♪♪ (Drive Archive, 1997)

worth searching for: Cook's triumphant 1980 return to Carnegie Hall is captured on *It's Better with a Band* ♪♪♪ (Moss Music Group, 1986), which contains contemporary tunes as well as the satirical "The Ingenue." Also, two of Cook's better duets with John Raitt, "Make Believe" and "You Are Love," can be found on *The Best of John Raitt* ♪♪♪ (Ranwood, 1995, prod. Bonnie Pritchard). And Cook's version of "Look to the Rainbow" with Barry Manilow on his LP *Showstoppers* ♪♪♪ (Arista, 1991, prod. Barry Manilow, Eddie Arkin) lends a genuine touch of class to the proceedings.

influences:
◀◀ Maria Callas, Kitty Carlisle

▶▶ Florence Henderson, Shirley Jones, Julie Andrews

Ken Burke

Florencia Bisenta De Castilla Martinez Cordona
See: Vikki Carr

Don Cornell
See: Sammy Kaye

Jack Costanzo
Born in Chicago, IL.

Costanzo introduced bongos in American music with the Stan Kenton Orchestra during 1947 and 1948. He bent an ear to Nico's bongo playing with Xavier Cugat, then colored Kenton's "progressive" big-band sound with various forms of Latin percussion. When the Kenton group disbanded in 1948, Costanzo hooked up with the King Cole Trio for some recordings and live performances between 1949 and 1953. He became Hollywood's first-call session percussionist, playing on soundtracks and appearing in a handful of major films. By 1955, the jazz community began to recognize his talent. Norman Granz (soon to be head of Verve Records) put together the great all-star LP called *Afro-Cuban Jazz North of the Border*, featuring Costanzo prominently alongside Art Pepper, Benny Carter, and several others. His reputation grew and he played a major role in albums by Buddy Cole, Fred Katz, Howard Rumsey, Francis Faye, and Pete Rugulo. The mid- to late-'50s saw Costanzo doing regular gigs with Peggy Lee as well. These successes led to a solo deal for Liberty Records and, working with production wizards such as Si Waronker, Felix Slatkin, and Ray Stanley, Costanzo cut six albums, including *Latin Fever*. The music thankfully lacked the overambitious nature of many of Kenton's later recordings. Costanzo concentrated on jazzed-up versions of Latin standards, and also added this flavor to popular American tunes. If the indelible cartoon image of the bongo-beatin' beatnik is in our minds, you can be sure that character (and his real-life manifestation) bent an ear to these LPs by "Mr. Bongo."

what's available: Costanzo's only CD, *Mr. Bongo Cha Cha Cha* ♪♪♪♪ (Paladium, 1956, prod. Geordie Hormel), has been licensed six times and reissued under several different names. It's especially entertaining, as the original record company marketed Costanzo in a multi-colored calypso costume, bashing a hot-blooded beat for a flamenco chick. The music inside (originally cut for Zephyr) matches the intensity of the cover again. Though most of Costanzo's original albums are difficult to find, 15 of his cuts have landed on Capi-

tol Records' multivolume *Ultra-Lounge* series, including "The Inch Worm," on the appropriately titled *Ultra-Lounge, Vol. 17: Bongoland* ♪♪♪♪ (Capitol, 1997, compilation prod. Brad Benedict).

worth searching for: If a vote were ever taken, the out-of-print LP *Latin Fever* ♪♪♪♪ (Liberty, 1958, prod. Ray Stanley)—with its image of a young siren in a jungle bikini with her head thrown back, beating on a zebra drum in front of a red background—would have a shot at being voted "best LP cover of all time." Costanzo can best be viewed on the *Person to Person* ♪♪♪♪ (1995) volume of the Edward R. Murrow videotape series. The segment features Mr. Bongo hanging out and performing a percussive duet in the home basement of a young Marlon Brando (on congas).

influences:

◀◀ Stan Kenton, Nat "King" Cole, Tito Puente, Xavier Cugat

▶▶ Joe Lala

Domenic Priore

Elvis Costello
Born Declan Patrick McManus, August 25, 1954, in London, England.

Like fellow new-waver David Johansen, Costello has always been drawn to lounge singing—as an establishment form to be tweaked, but also as a way to pay homage to previous generations of solo performers. But while Johansen ultimately disengaged from rock 'n' roll to reinvent himself as Buster Poindexter, the ultimate lounge lizard, Costello has limited himself to periodic forays into the genre. His 1981 album *Almost Blue*, mostly covers of U.S. country songs, shows Costello's range as a crooner. But he is never as effective there as in his cover of Rodgers and Hart's "My Funny Valentine," released as the B-side of an import single of "Oliver's Army" and then paired with "(What's So Funny 'Bout) Peace, Love and Understanding" for concert giveaways, radio contests, and other promotional uses. Though he was still the lean, hungry Elvis of his early career, prone to an anarchic worldview deftly packaged in wonderfully approachable, commercially viable pop tunes, he doesn't so much deflate the old romantic standard as elevate it. It was always hard to determine how much of Costello's vaunted emotion was real and how much he fabricated for effect—which is even a better reason to classify him as a lounge singer—but in the brief rendition of "My Funny Valentine" (running time 1:28), he reveals an emotional depth other artists need entire CDs to unearth. (The same can be said for his col-

laboration with lounge-pop songwriter Burt Bacharach on 1995's *Grace of My Heart* soundtrack.)

what to buy: Of course, Costello is most notably a pop song-writer—albeit a particularly lyrical one, with influences ranging from Motown to ska to the British Invasion—and his pure tune-fulness is shown off to best effect on *This Year's Model* 𝄢𝄢𝄢𝄢 (Columbia, 1978, prod. Nick Lowe) and *Get Happy!!* 𝄢𝄢𝄢𝄢 (Columbia, 1980, prod. Nick Lowe).

what to buy next: You almost can't go wrong with early Elvis, particularly *My Aim Is True* 𝄢𝄢𝄢𝄢 (Columbia, 1977, prod. Nick Lowe), *Armed Forces* 𝄢𝄢𝄢𝄢 (Columbia, 1979, prod. Nick Lowe), *Imperial Bedroom* 𝄢𝄢𝄢𝄢 (Columbia, 1982, prod. Geoff Emerick), and *Blood and Chocolate* 𝄢𝄢𝄢𝄢 (Columbia, 1986, prod. Nick Lowe, Colin Fairley).

what to avoid: *Kojak Variety* (Warner Bros., 1995, prod. Elvis Costello, Kevin Killen), an album of obscure cover songs, is redundant.

worth searching for: The Rykodisc CD re-release of *Armed Forces* 𝄢𝄢𝄢𝄢 adds eight tracks to the original version, including several live versions of popular Costello songs and the easiest access to Costello's "My Funny Valentine" cover. And several of the original 13 tracks—including "Oliver's Army," "Accidents Will Happen," and Nick Lowe's "(What's So Funny 'Bout) Peace, Love and Understanding"—will stand with any of Costello's work, though don't expect much crooning. Rykodisc has repackaged almost all of Costello's Columbia albums with excellent artist-penned liner notes and several bonus tracks each. They're generally superior to the original Columbia CDs. The four-disc box set *2 1/2 Years* 𝄢𝄢𝄢𝄢 (Rykodisc, 1993, prod. various) includes *My Aim Is True*, *This Year's Model*, and *Armed Forces*, plus the excellent, hungry, previously unissued 1978 concert document *Live at El Mocambo*.

influences:

◀◀ Little Richard, the Sex Pistols, the Clash, the Buzzcocks, Elvis Presley, Nick Lowe, Screamin' Jay Hawkins, Burt Bacharach

▶▶ John Wesley Harding, the Smithereens, Joe Jackson, Todd Snider, the Jags, the Records, Squeeze, the Replacements, Nirvana

Bruce Schoenfeld

Elvis Costello (© **Jack Vartoogian**)

Floyd Cramer

Born October 27, 1933, in Samti, LA. Died December 31, 1997, in Nashville, TN.

The primary pianist on the Chet Atkins–produced RCA recordings of the 1950s and 1960s, Cramer contributed one of the most distinctive components of the "Nashville Sound"—the "slip note" piano style. Inspired by the note-bending qualities of the steel guitar, Cramer would add a whole-tone grace note to his piano melodies, creating a sound that contained both a country melancholy and a diatonic pleasantness suitable for Atkins's crossover vision.

Cramer, born near Shreveport, Louisiana, but raised primarily in Arkansas, returned to his home state and joined *The Lousiana Hayride* radio show in 1951 and backed the likes of Elvis Presley, Webb Pierce, and Faron Young before moving to Nashville during the mid-1950s and becoming one of the town's top session players. He cut his first sides for Lousiana's Abbott Records during 1953–54, but began recording for RCA in 1959. His "Last Date" became a pop and country hit in 1960. He recorded dozens of albums, many of them long out of print, including a *Class of . . .* series from 1965–1974, in which he reprised each year's top hits. Like Atkins and saxophonist Boots Randolph, Cramer provided an urbane, instrumental version of country music, though his solo recordings ranged to pop and light classical—all approached with the same distinctive, but conservative, style.

what to buy: Cramer is better known for the records on which he played than the ones he made. *The Essential Series: Floyd Cramer* 𝄢𝄢𝄢 (RCA, 1995, prod. Chet Atkins, comp. prod. Paul Williams) contains his two most significant chart hits: 1960's "Last Date" (#2 pop, #11 country) and his 1961 rendition of "San Antonio Rose" (#8 pop and country), as well as 18 more tunes cut for RCA between 1958 and 1966.

what to buy next: *The Best of Floyd Cramer* 𝄢𝄢𝄢 (Pair, 1988, prod. Chet Atkins) frequently overlaps with *Essential*, but it's the best of a number of Pair reissues of Cramer's RCA recordings.

the rest:
Country Classics 𝄢𝄢 (Pair, 1986)
Country Gold 𝄢𝄢 (Step One, 1988)
Special Songs of Love 𝄢𝄢 (Step One, 1988)
Just Me and My Piano! 𝄢𝄢 (Step One, 1988)
Collector's Series 𝄢𝄢 (RCA, 1988)
The Magic Touch of Floyd Cramer 𝄢𝄢 (Pair, 1989)
Forever Floyd Cramer 𝄢𝄢 (Step One, 1989)
Gospel Classics 𝄢𝄢 (Step One, 1990)

Piano Masterpieces 1900–1975 ♫♫♫ (RCA, 1990)
Easy Listening Favorites ♫♫ (Pair, 1991)
Originals ♫♫ (Step One, 1991)
The Best of Floyd Cramer ♫♫♫ (RCA, 1994)
Great Country Hits ♫♫♫ (RCA, 1994)
Never Ending Love ♫♫ (Pair, 1994)
The Piano Magic of Floyd Cramer ♫♫ (Ranwood, 1994)
We Wish You a Merry Christmas ♫♫ (Step One, 1994)
Favorite Country Hits ♫♫ (Ranwood, 1995)
The Piano Magic of Floyd Cramer, Vol. 2 ♫♫ (Ranwood, 1996)
Super Hits: Floyd Cramer ♫♫♫ (RCA, 1996)
Blue Skies ♫♫ (Ranwood, 1997)
Forever in Love ♫♫ (BMG/RCA Special Products, 1997)
Favorite Country Hits, Vol. 2 ♫♫ (Ranwood, 1997)

worth searching for: As its title suggests, the 16-track German import *Hello Blues* ♫♫♫ (RCA, 1996, prod. Chet Atkins) features more blues-oriented material ("Blues Stay Away from Me," "Trouble in Mind," "The Swingin' Shepherd Blues") than the typical Cramer collection.

influences:

◀◀ Del Wood, Moon Mullican, Chet Atkins, Maybelle Carter

▶▶ Boots Randolph, Hargus "Pig" Robbins

Brian Mansfield

Jim Croce

Born January 10, 1943, in Philadelphia, PA. Died September 20, 1973, in Natchitoches, LA.

Croce may not have sipped martinis (nor did the rugged characters in his unforgettable story songs), but he did smoke cigars. And his sense of humor and knack for storytelling—within songs and during concerts—set him apart from the oh-so-serious folkie crowd. The singer-songwriter got his start playing the coffeehouse circuit and landed several Top 40 hits, which were recorded in the brief 1971–73 period. Many of his songs became posthumous hits after his death in a plane crash.

what to buy: *Photographs & Memories: His Greatest Hits* ♫♫♫♫ (Atlantic, 1974, prod. Terry Cashman, Tommy West) is the essential Croce hits collection, including the chart-topping "Bad, Bad Leroy Brown" and "Time in a Bottle."

what to buy next: *You Don't Mess Around with Jim* ♫♫♫ (ABC, 1972, prod. Terry Cashman, Tommy West) offers the sage wisdom of the title track, along with "Operator (That's Not the Way It Feels)."

what to avoid: *Faces I've Been* ♫♫ (Lifesong, 1975, prod. Jim Croce) comprises material from Croce's pre-major-label signing.

He has yet to find his niche, and sounds too similar to those serious folkies.

the rest:
I Got a Name ♫♫♫ (ABC, 1973)
Time in a Bottle: Greatest Love Songs ♫♫♫ (Atlantic, 1976)
Live: Final Tour ♫♫♫ (Saja, 1980)
50th Anniversary Collection ♫♫♫♫ (Atlantic, 1992)
Gold in a Bottle ♫♫♫♫ (DGC Gold, 1994)

influences:

◀◀ Paul Simon, Gordon Lightfoot, Cat Stevens, James Taylor

▶▶ Dan Fogelberg, Suzanne Vega, Lyle Lovett

Jay Dedrick

Bing Crosby

Born Harry Lillis Crosby, May 3, 1903, in Tacoma, WA. Died October 14, 1977, in Madrid, Spain.

No less an authority than Dean Martin once proclaimed, "Bing's the daddy of us all. We all learned how to sing from listening to his records." And Crosby taught them all plenty. His 50-year recording career spawned more than 200 hit records, and was the launching pad for equally successful forays into radio, motion pictures, and television. His ability to effortlessly interpret jazz, swing, cowboy, Hawaiian, boogie-woogie, polkas, and religious material allowed him a now-unheard-of longevity in the face of changing musical trends.

Crosby began his career in 1925 singing and playing drums for Al Rinker's orchestra the Musicladers. The following year, Rinker and Crosby recorded their first Columbia single, "I've Got the Girl," as a duet, just before joining bandleader Paul Whiteman's orchestra. Whiteman teamed them with Harry Barris and dubbed his new trio the Rhythm Boys, and recorded dozens of hits with them, including "Side by Side," "I'm Coming Virginia," and "My Blue Heaven." The Rhythm Boys left Whiteman in 1930 to establish themselves as a solo act and constant chart presence. Crosby's increasingly popular solo spots, combined with union problems (concerning missed bookings), broke up the act, and he signed with Brunswick in 1931. Under the direction of Jack Kapp, Crosby's recording career exploded. His jazz-influenced phrasing and casual, erudite manner led to major hits, such as "Just One More Chance," "I Surrender Dear," and "Where the Blue of the Night" (where he whistles and scats the immortal phrase "boo-boo-boo-boo"), and established him as a household name. Crosby's concurrent rise as a radio and motion picture star dovetailed into a publicity bonanza, and he became King of the Crooners, the biggest star of the Depression Era. However, his enormously busy schedule was not without consequences: after severely straining his vocal chords, Crosby had to lower his pitch and be coached on proper breathing technique. The result was the warmer, more intimate style most people associate with Bing Crosby.

When Kapp left Brunswick for Decca Records in 1934, Crosby went with him and continued his dominance of the charts with such classics as "Pennies from Heaven," "Sweet Leilani," "I'm an Old Cowhand," and dozens of others. Kapp was instrumental in expanding Crosby's style to other genres, and paired him with stars the Mills Brothers, Connee Boswell, Louis Armstrong, Judy Garland, and the Andrews Sisters for a series of amazingly popular discs. And if Crosby was hot in the '30s, he supernovaed in the '40s. He became Hollywood's leading box office draw (with and without his *Road Picture* partner, Bob Hope), had one of the highest rated radio shows in the country, and recorded the biggest-selling single of all time, "White Christmas" (from the 1942 movie *Holiday Inn*). A seasonal Top 10 record for the next several years, Decca pressed so many copies of "White Christmas," that the company damaged the master recording and had to rerecord the tune in 1947. Perhaps Crosby's absolute peak as a multi-media star was in 1944, when he won a best actor Oscar for *Going My Way,* as well as scoring seven #1 hit records ("Swinging on a Star," "Don't Fence Me In," and "I'll Be Seeing You" among them). Crosby also weathered the rise of a new crooner who threatened his popularity—Frank Sinatra, of whom he said, "A voice like that comes along once in a generation. Why did it have to be mine?" Despite Sinatra's sudden fame, Crosby sold more records.

Crosby's enormous popularity extended well past the war years into television's golden age, but his amazing string of hit records dried up after 1951. His final Top 10 hit, "True Love" (a duet with Grace Kelly from the film *High Society*), came in 1956. In the 1950s, as a freelance artist, Crosby returned to his jazz roots, cut some swing and standards songs, and released movie soundtracks and remakes; throughout the '60s, he generally attempted to update his pop style for Sinatra's Reprise Records and other labels. By the '70s, a "semi-retired" Crosby hosted occasional TV specials and golf tournaments, made commercials, took feature parts in movies, recorded two LPs for United Artists (one with Count Basie), and profited handsomely from his many entertainment business interests. During his last Christmas TV special, Crosby shared a stage with David Bowie, and thoroughly outperformed the outlandish (and out-of-his-element) rocker.

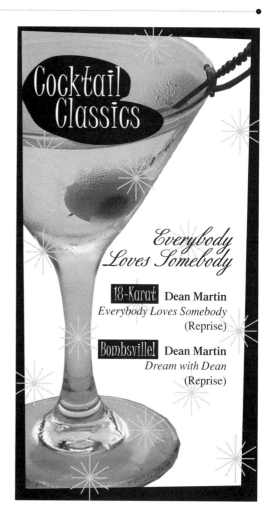

what to buy: As a starting point, *Best of Bing* ♫♫♫♫ (MCA, 1987, prod. various) and *Greatest Hits* ♫♫♫♫ (MCA, 1995, prod. various) are inexpensive 12-song collections featuring similar hits, such as "Too-Ra-Loo-Ra-Loo-Ral," "Ac-cent-tchu-ate the Positive," "White Christmas," and "Don't Fence Me In." However, *Bing's Gold Records* ♫♫♫♫ (Decca, 1997, compilation prod. Andy McKaie) has 21 songs and encompasses the best of those two releases.

what to buy next: The epiphany of true Bing-ness can be achieved by purchasing *Bing Crosby: His Legendary Years, 1931–1957* ♫♫♫♫ (MCA, 1993, compilation prod. Steve Lasker, Andy McKaie), a four-CD, 101-track box set culled from his great

years with Decca that includes Crosby's hit collaborations with the Andrews Sisters, Judy Garland, Louis Armstrong, Louis Jordan, and his son, Gary, as well as a comprehensive 68-page booklet.

what to avoid: They're OK for completists, but don't be misled, *Christmas through the Years* ♪♪ (Laserlight, 1995) and *White Christmas* ♪♪ (Laserlight, 1993) do not feature Crosby's original Decca renditions of his famous seasonal offerings. Also, Crosby himself considered *Hey Jude/Hey Bing!* ♪ (Amos, 1969, prod. Jimmy Bowen) the worst LP of his career.

the rest:
Blue Skies ♪♪♪ (Sandy Hook, 1946/1996)
Bing's Buddies ♪♪♪ (Magic, 1951/1994)
Best of Bing Crosby & Fred Astaire: A Couple of Song & Dance Men ♪♪♪ (Curb 1975/1993)
Bing Crosby's Christmas Classic ♪♪♪ (Capitol/EMI, 1977/1997)
Bing Crosby Sings Again ♪♪♪♪ (MCA, 1986)
Radio Years–20 Songs ♪♪♪♪ (GNP/Crescendo, 1987)
Radio Years–25 Songs ♪♪♪ (GNP/Crescendo, 1988)
Pocketful of Dreams ♪♪♪♪ (Pro Arte, 1989)
Pennies from Heaven ♪♪♪♪ (Pro Arte, 1989)
Remembering 1927–34 ♪♪♪♪ (Happy Days 123, 1989)
The Radio Years, Vol. 1 ♪♪♪ (GNP/Crescendo, 1990)
The Radio Years, Vol. 2 ♪♪♪ (GNP/Crescendo, 1990)
The Radio Years, Vol. 3 ♪♪♪ (GNP/Crescendo, 1990)
The Radio Years, Vol. 4 ♪♪♪♪ (GNP/Crescendo, 1990)
All-Time Best of Bing Crosby ♪♪♪ (Curb Records, 1990)
That's Jazz ♪♪♪ (Pearl, 1991)
Bing Crosby & Some Jazz Friends ♪♪♪♪ (Decca Jazz, 1991)
The Movie Hits ♪♪♪♪ (Pearl, 1992)
On the Sentimental Side ♪♪♪ (ASV, 1992)
Here Lies Love ♪♪♪♪ (ASV, 1992)
16 Most Requested Songs ♪♪♪♪ (Columbia/Legacy, 1992)
The Jazzin' Bing Crosby 1927–40 ♪♪♪♪ (Affinity, 1992)
Original Soundtrack Sessions: "Holiday Inn" & "Blue Skies" ♪♪♪♪ (Vintage Jazz Classics, 1993)
Merry Christmas ♪♪♪♪ (MCA, 1993)
The Great Years ♪♪♪♪ (Pearl, 1993)
That Christmas Feeling ♪♪♪ (MCA Special Products, 1993)
On Treasure Island ♪♪♪♪ (JSP, 1993)
Sings Christmas Songs ♪♪♪♪ (MCA Special Products, 1993)
Classic Bing Crosby 1931–1938 ♪♪♪ (DRG/ABC, 1994)
World War II Radio ♪♪♪ (Laserlight, 1994)
Bing Crosby 1927–34 ♪♪♪♪ (Mobile Fidelity Lab, 1995)
Swingin' on a Star ♪♪♪ (Flapper, 1995)

I'm an Old Cow Hand ♪♪♪ (Living Era, 1995)
Bing Crosby with Paul Whiteman ♪♪♪ (Chanson's Cinema, 1995)
Bing Crosby & Friends ♪♪♪ (Living Era, 1995)
Greatest Hits on the Radio, Vol.1 ♪♪♪ (Enterprise/Radio Years, 1995)
Bing Crosby in Hollywood 1930–1933 ♪♪♪ (Chansen's Cinema, 1995)
Bing Crosby in Hollywood, Vol. 3 ♪♪♪ (Chansen's Cinema, 1995)
Duets 1947–1949 ♪♪♪ (Viper's Nest, 1996)
Bing Crosby/Andrews Sisters: Their Complete Recordings ♪♪♪♪♪ (MCA, 1996)
Top O' the Morning: His Irish Collection ♪♪♪♪ (MCA, 1996)
Bing Sings Whilst Bregman Swings ♪♪♪♪ (Mobile Fidelity, 1996)
My Favorite Cowboy Songs ♪♪♪♪ (MCA, 1996)
On the Radio in the Thirties ♪♪♪ (Enterprise/Radio Years, 1996)
A Little Bit of Irish ♪♪♪ (Atlantic, 1996)
Love Songs ♪♪♪ (MCA Special Products, 1997)
My Favorite Hymms ♪♪♪ (MCA Special Products, 1997)
American Legends # 7 ♪♪♪ (Laserlight, 1997)
My Favorite Hawaiian Songs ♪♪♪♪ (MCA Special Products, 1997)
That Christmas Feeling: Bing Crosby & Frank Sinatra ♪♪♪ (Unison, 1997)
The EP Collection ♪♪♪ (See For Miles, 1997)
WWII Christmas Shows ♪♪ (Laserlight, 1997)
WWII Radio: Special Christmas Show ♪♪♪ (Laserlight, 1997)
My Favorite Irish Songs ♪♪♪ (MCA Special Products, 1998)

worth searching for: Crosby's early years as a young sensation with a high, hard vocal technique are on *The Crooner: The Columbia Years 1928–1934* ♪♪♪♪ (Columbia, 1988, prod. various), which has 67 tracks, including his work as part of the Rhythm Boys, with Paul Whiteman, and his first solo efforts. Also, *Two Fantastic Stories* ♪♪♪♪ (MCA, 1957/1962/1993, prod. various) features Crosby's eloquent readings of *The Small One* and *The Happy Prince* (with Orson Welles). For a first-rate example of how Der Bingle got better as he aged, dig through the $1.99 vinyl racks for *Bing Crosby: A Legendary Performer* ♪♪♪♪ (RCA, 1977, compilation prod. Ethel Gabriel). Side one features early hits "Just One More Chance," "Just a Gigolo," and others recorded with the Paul Whiteman, Duke Ellington, and Gus Arnheim orchestras in the late 1920s and early 1930s. Side two has six cool and jazzy tracks recorded in 1957 with Bob Scobey's Frisco Jazz Band.

influences:

◀◀ Rudy Vallee, Mildred Bailey, Al Jolson, Louis Armstrong, Ethel Waters

▶▶ Russ Columbo, Dick Haymes, Frank Sinatra, Dean Martin, Frankie Laine, Carl "Alfalfa" Switzer, Perry Como

Bing Crosby **(Archive Photos)**

Ken Burke

Bob Crosby

Born George Robert Crosby, August 25, 1913, in Spokane, WA. Died March 9, 1993, in La Jolla, CA.

He lived his entire life in the shadow of brother Bing, but Bob Crosby's big bands in the '30s and '40s flung horns in every swinging direction and racked up a long list of hits—some with the most famous singers of the era, from Connee Boswell to, yes, Bing Crosby. Crosby, a skilled bandleader with a natural feel for swing music, was never much of a singer, so he suffered from harsh critical comparisons to his brother his whole career. But in retrospect, the Dixieland-influenced songs he left behind—"South Rampart Street Parade" and "Wolverine Blues," among many—hold up as fun, jittery, horn-rich standards. At age 18, orchestra leader Anson Weeks invited Crosby to join his orchestra, and another opportunity quickly opened up. Several musicians in Ben Pollack's popular band got tired of arguing with their fiesty bandleader, so they declared a mutiny and labored briefly under skilled businessman but not-so-personable Gil Rodin until Crosby, with his love of Dixieland and family connections, won the job. With these players—saxophonist Eddie Miller and trumpeter Yank Lawson among them—Crosby's big band and its smaller, tighter incarnation, the Bobcats, went on to huge commercial success; the fame led to singing engagements for Crosby, plus small roles in films such as *Two Tickets to Broadway* and *Let's Make Music*. The band's popularity waned as rock 'n' roll took over the music industry, but despite the bandleader's death in 1993 and legal hassles with the name, Crosby's late-career saxophonist, Bobby Levine, continues to lead the Bob Crosby Orchestra on tours of the country.

what to buy: The most comprehensive Crosby CDs, unfortunately, are only available on British import, but some domestic record companies have released his material in dribs and drabs. *The Bobcats Play 22 Original Big Band Records* ♫♫♫♫ (Hindsight, 1987/1994) captures many of Crosby's popular early '50s recordings with his small Dixieland revival combo, including "March of the Bobcats," "March of the Mustangs," "Jazz Me Blues," and "In a Sentimental Mood." *Uncollected* ♫♫♫♫ (Hindsight, 1992) reissues the orchestra's early 1940s hits, and *Uncollected, Vol. 1* ♫♫♫♫ (Hindsight, 1992) continues into the early 1950s.

what to buy next: *South Rampart Street Parade* ♫♫♫ (Decca, 1989) is a jazzier sampling of Crosby's prolific days with Decca Records; it includes "Dixieland Shuffle," "Air Mail Stomp," "Wolverine Blues," and several others in which the horns jump around like characters in a cartoon. With singing guests June Christy and Polly Bergen, *The Bob Crosby Orchestra with Guests* ♫♫♫ (Hindsight, 1990, prod. Tom Gramuglia) features snappy, slightly exotic, songs like "Ostrich Walk," "Song of the Islands," and the crooning standard, "Willow Weep for Me."

best of the rest:
The Bob Crosby Orchestra and the Bobcats ♫♫♫ (Living Era, 1992)
1939–42 Broadcasts ♫♫♫ (Jazz Hour, 1995)
Eye Opener ♫♫♫ (Topaz Jazz, 1996)

worth searching for: The best way to delve into Crosby's overshadowed career is via English import: several available, the most thorough being *Complete Discography 1939–1940* ♫♫♫♫ (Halcyon, 1997, prod. various). For more context, Crosby's hits show up on several big-band compilation boxes, including the excellent *Swing Time! The Fabulous Big Band Era, 1925–1955* ♫♫♫♫ (Columbia/Legacy, 1993, prod. various), which contains Crosby's hit "South Rampart Street Parade" among tracks by Claude Thornhill, Bunny Berigan, Benny Goodman, Duke Ellington, Cab Calloway, and many others.

influences:

◄◄ Bing Crosby, Duke Ellington, Louis Armstrong, Dixieland jazz

►► Fats Domino, the Boswell Sisters, Guy Lombardo, Buddy Greco

Steve Knopper

Christopher Cross

Born Christopher Geppert, May 3, 1951, in San Antonio, TX.

Few artists have burst upon the music scene with as much radio-ready appeal as Cross. His high tenor vocals and romantic, metaphor-laden songwriting brought modern soft-rock clearly into the lounge category. Initially a singer and guitarist with the hard-rock band Flash (which opened for Led Zeppelin and Deep Purple during the early '70s), Cross quit the group to study medicine and work on his pop ballad style. In 1978, Cross's polished songs and performance resulted in a lucrative contract with Warner Bros., which allowed him to control his publishing (rare for a new artist). Enlisting the aid of such luminaries as Don Henley, Nicolette Larson, J.D. Souther, and Michael McDonald as back-up vocalists, Cross's first LP was a hell of a calling card. Besides spending more than two years on the charts and spawning the mega-hits "Ride Like the Wind" and "Sailing," *Christopher Cross* earned its creator Grammy awards in five different categories. While working up his next LP, Cross recorded the romantic title track for the Dudley Moore comedy *Arthur*, which hit #1 on the charts for three weeks. It seemed Cross could do no wrong, but great success breeds great criticism, and detractors viciously assailed his second LP. Despite carping reviews, *Another Page* (with backup vocals from Art Garfunkel, Karla Bonoff, and Carl Wilson) was a fair seller, mostly on the strength of "Think of Laura," a clever single incorporating a popular character from the daytime TV drama *General Hospital.* After that, Cross's career seemed to freefall. Promising singles such as "A Chance for Heaven" and "Charm the Snake" (a pretty fair rocker) stalled at the lower region of the charts, and LPs fared no better. Soon Cross was passe and his plight had many speculating about the curse of being a Grammy winner. He kept at it, though, recording for the reactivated Reprise label, and contributing the song "Loving Strangers" to the Tom Hanks movie *Nothing in Common,* though little clicked chartwise. During the '90s, Cross supplied music to the 1991 documentary *Whales and Dolphins* and put out a new LP on the Rhythm Safari Label, where he updated the technological side of his sound while continuing to explore the many facets of mellow pop.

what to buy: Cross's first LP, *Christopher Cross* ♫♫♫♪ (Warner Bros., 1980, prod. Michael Omartian), remains his definitive work. His first two LPs have been combined on one disc, *Christopher Cross/Another Page* ♫♫♫♪ (Warner Bros., prod. Michael Omartian), so you can get "Think of Laura" and "Arthur's Theme (Best That You Can Do)" in the same package as "Ride Like the Wind," "Never Be the Same," "Sailing," and "Say You'll Be Mine." Nice deal.

the rest:
Window ♫♫ (Rhythm Safari, 1995)

worth searching for: Cross makes guest appearances on discs by virtuoso guitarist Eric Johnson, *Venus Isle* ♫♫♫ (Capitol/EMI, 1996, prod. Eric Johnson, Richard Mullen); Alan Parsons, *On Air* ♫♫♫ (River North, 1996, prod. Alan Parsons); America, *View from the Ground* ♫♫♫ (One Way Records, 1996, prod. Russ Ballard); and David Lee Roth, *The Best of David Lee Roth* ♫♫♫♪ (Rhino Records, 1997).

influences:
◀◀ Michael McDonald, Eric Johnson, Brian Wilson

▶▶ Richard Marx, Peter Cetera

Ken Burke

Julee Cruise
Born December 1, 1956, in Creston, IA.

Cruise's singing could be compared to floating weightless in space—or, for those of us more grounded to earth, soaking in a hot tub in darkness. Her velvety voice, frequently coupled with Angelo Badalamenti's ethereally rich orchestra and deep guitar notes, instantly relaxes you, while simultaneously giving a feeling that something dangerous lurks around the corner. Maybe it's the fact that her voice became known on the score to David Lynch's eerie 1986 film, *Blue Velvet.* (She began working with Lynch after studying the French horn at Drake University, working with the Chicago Symphony, acting in various theater productions, and singing in advertisements.) Maybe it's the fact that her lush singing became ingrained in a million viewers' minds during the showing (and reruns) of Lynch's Badalamenti-scored cult TV series *Twin Peaks.* Or maybe it's just the way her voice seems to pass through you, lifting you slowly, and then vanishing and leaving you wondering what hit you.

what to buy: *Floating into the Night* ♫♫♫♪ (Warner Bros., 1990, prod. David Lynch, Angelo Badalamenti) floats indeed, taking you deep within its dreamlike atmosphere. The tunes will be recognizable to fans of Lynch's work, and they seem to fill a "trip-lounge" void between traditional and nontraditional genres.

what to buy next: *The Voice of Love* ♫♫♫ (Warner Bros., 1993, prod. David Lynch, Angelo Badalamenti) hovers in the same air space as her debut, offering such gems as the quietly smoldering "Up in Flames." The groovy "Kool Kat Walk" doesn't fade into the moonlight when it should—it keeps walking and walking and walking.

influences:
◀◀ Billie Holiday, David Lynch, Angelo Badalamenti, Enya, Roxy Music, Kate Bush, Nick Cave

▶▶ Chris Isaak, Portishead, Jane Siberry, Björk

see also: *Angelo Badalamenti*

Jack Jackson

Xavier Cugat
Born Francisco de Asis Javier Cugat Mingall de Bru y Deulofeo, January 1, 1900, Gerona, Spain. Died October 27, 1990, Barcelona, Spain.

Latin music has always been malleable enough to fit a wide range of American pop tastes, and few made rumbas and cha-cha-chas easier to stomach than Cugat and his orchestra. He's still best known, perhaps, as the swarthy Cuban womanizer who made the beautiful singer Abbe Lane his third wife. But if not for Cugat, the 1960s easy-listening crowd wouldn't have been fully prepared to embrace Herb Alpert's Tijuana Brass or Sergio Mendes's Brasil '66.

Originally a child-prodigy classical violinist, Cugat lived with his family in Cuba before moving to New York City around 1918. To get by during the Depression, he became a well-known cartoonist with the King Features Syndicate, his work running in newspapers around the country. He immediately established connections in the Latin community, befriending actor Rudolph Valentino, who encouraged him to start a tango band. Cugat also wound up in such movies as *In Gay Madrid* and *Bathing Beauty*—he was the playboy in many MGM musicals who spoke while cradling a chihuahua. But his passion was music, and the more popular, the better. He and Perez Prado were among the first performers to add Latin touches to American popular music, and Cugat sired a young Desi Arnaz in his orchestra. (Eventual celebrity Charo, then a folk guitarist, was one of many Latinos who first got a break from Cugat.) He adapted easily to all the Latin crazes, first the rumba, then the samba, the mambo, the cha cha cha, and the tango. His light, easy orchestra featured prominent tinkly percussion and strong, loud horns, with the occasional electric guitar or organ to spice up a verse, but it never became even as heavy as Alpert's later smash "The Lonely Bull." Rock 'n' roll and younger, more marketable artists like Alpert forced Cugat to change his approach. He spent most of the 1960s and 1970s re-recording movie music, from "Chim, Chim Cher-ee" (from *Mary Poppins*) to *Thunderball*. He appeared on several hip cocktail compilations during the early-1990s lounge-music comeback.

what to buy: To fully experience Cugat's tinkly, roly-poly brand of easy-listening music, you'll need a sampling of his earlier sambas and cha cha chas and his film music of the '60s. *Cugie A-Go-Go* 🎵🎵🎵 (MCA, 1966/1997, prod. Harry Meyerson) reprints the space-villain femme fatale, complete with raygun and dark blue glasses, on the cover, and includes such swinging horn music as "Judith"; John Barry's James Bond anthem, "Goldfinger"; and the Disney standard "Zip-a-Dee-Doo-Dah."

what to avoid: Though MCA has reissued several of Cugat's '60s albums on CD, there's no real point to adding anything beyond *Cugie a-Go-Go* to your library. So don't bother with *Xavier Cugat Today!* 🎵🎵 (Decca, 1967).

best of the rest:
Feeling Good! 🎵🎵🎵 (Decca, 1965)
Bang Bang 🎵🎵🎵 (Decca, 1966)
De Colleccion 🎵🎵🎵 (PolyGram Latino, 1994)
Say Si! Si! 🎵🎵 (Pair, 1994)

worth searching for: *Waltzes—But by Cugat!* 🎵🎵🎵 (Columbia) and *Cugat Caricatures* 🎵🎵🎵 (Mercury) are excellent finds, and a

decent representation of the bandleader's Columbia and Mercury years. And, while the pairing isn't exactly Frank Sinatra and Nelson Riddle, the Cugat–Dinah Shore collaborative CD *1939–1945* 🎵🎵 (Harlequin import) will look hilarious and sound decent in any respectable record collection.

influences:

◀◀ Dizzy Gillespie, Duke Ellington, Benny Goodman, Glenn Miller

▶▶ Perez Prado, Tito Puente, Charo, Desi Arnaz, Juan Garcia Esquivel, Abbe Lane, Herb Alpert, Sergio Mendes

Steve Knopper

Tim Curry

Born April 19, 1946, in Cheshire, England.

Although Curry will probably be remembered longest for his role as Dr. Frank N. Furter in *The Rocky Horror Picture Show,* one of the greatest cult films ever made, he's actually had a stellar and varied (if not always highly visible) acting career on stage and screen: from Bertolt Brecht to Tom Stoppard, *Roseanne* to the original stage production of Peter Shaffer's *Amadeus.* Curry's fine baritone voice proved ideal for such nefarious characters as Mack the Knife (in Brecht's *The Three Penny Opera*), Satan (in the film *Legend*), Bill Sikes (from a television production of Charles Dickens's *Oliver Twist*), and, of course, Frank N. Furter; and he has recorded four albums in addition to stage work. The main problem with his pop singing is that of most theatrically rooted singers—technique and style often overwhelm or overshoot the material. For example, when Screamin' Jay Hawkins sang "I Put a Spell on You," there was no doubt that the voice you heard belonged to an eccentric voodoo doctor doing some heavy magic; when Curry sings it on his 1981 album *Simplicity*, you hear a well-trained voice but no specific character. He did, however, record some pop efforts that pack almost as much appeal as his theatrical work.

what to buy: Curry's campy, looming presence as Frank N. Furter may have cast a permanent shadow on his acting career, but it was the fact that he is such a fine actor that made Frank so memorable. For all the luridly kitschy visual appeal of the *Rocky Horror* fable, the soundtracks to both the stage production, *The Rocky Horror Show Original Roxy Cast Recording* 🎵🎵🎵🎵 (Ode Records, 1974, prod. Lou Adler), and the film, *The Rocky Horror Picture Show Original Soundtrack* 🎵🎵🎵🎵 (Ode Records, 1975, prod. Richard Hartley), are excellent.

the rest:

Read My Lips 🎵🎵🎵 (A&M, 1978)

Simplicity 🎵🎵🎵 (A&M, 1981)

worth searching for: All of Curry's pop albums are currently out of print, including a handy collection, *The Best of Tim Curry* 🎵🎵🎵🎵 (A&M, 1989, prod. various); but *Fearless* 🎵🎵🎵 (A&M, 1979, prod. Dick Wagner, Michael Kamen) is a superb find. It features the wry uber-paean to name-droppers everywhere, "I Do the Rock," as well as "Paradise Garage," in which Curry struts along the same swervy line between disco, lounge, and rock that Debbie Harry did in Blondie's "Rapture."

influences:

 Screamin' Jay Hawkins, Mick Jagger, Barry White, David Johansen, David Bowie

▶▶ David Lee Roth, Marilyn Manson

Sandy Masuo

D

Vic Damone

Born Vito Rocco Farinoli, June 12, 1928, in Brooklyn, NY.

This sad-voiced romantic crooner has always been a favorite among great singers—including Frank Sinatra, who famously said he has "the best pipes in the business"—but never earned quite the superstar level he deserves. His talent is astounding; where Sinatra had a better knack for phrasing and certainly more charisma, few compare with Damone in terms of out-and-out vocal ability. But Damone, despite some good fortune in his first few performing years, continues to labor (compared to Sinatra, anyway) in obscurity.

Growing up in New York City, Vito Farinoli sang Italian pop songs with his family and worked as a Paramount Theater usher. Though he planned to be an electrician, he tied for first place after a spontaneous entry in Arthur Godfrey's *Talent Scouts* show. Milton Berle, who happened to have been backstage, helped him snag a key nightclub gig, and before long Damone was singing Sinatra's old flop "I Have But One Heart" and hitting the Top Ten. After hooking up with overly schmaltzy producer Mitch Miller, Damone continued a string of hits into the early 1950s. But Damone couldn't duplicate the success of his predecessor, Sinatra, because he just didn't have the per-

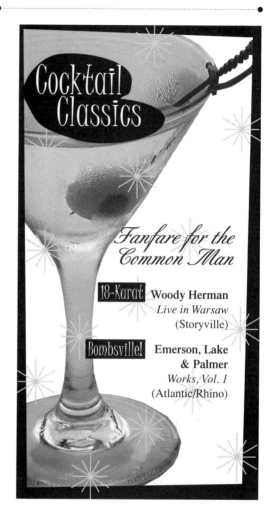

Cocktail Classics

Fanfare for the Common Man

18-Karat **Woody Herman** *Live in Warsaw* (Storyville)

Bombsville! **Emerson, Lake & Palmer** *Works, Vol. 1* (Atlantic/Rhino)

sonality or presence. He also lost career opportunities due to major tax, gambling, and—many say—Mafia problems. (Interestingly, Johnny Fontane, the singer character in *The Godfather* who sings "I Have But One Heart" at the wedding of Don Corleone's daughter, is widely believed to have been based on the careers of Damone and Sinatra.) More recently, thanks to a spiritual center he found years ago in the Baha'i faith, Damone has been singing impeccably at nightclubs around the country.

what to buy: Damone recorded for several record labels, and each one has put out a greatest-hits sampler. If you can, try all of them, starting with *The Best of Vic Damone: The Mercury Years* 🎵🎵🎵🎵 (Chronicles/PolyGram, 1996, prod. various), which

includes slightly more obscure hits such as "Again" and the downtrodden "Vagabond Shoes."

what to buy next: *16 Most Requested Songs* ♫♫♫♪ (Columbia/Legacy, 1992, prod. Didier Deutsch) is how most fans remember Damone's immense talent, leaning on love-heavy hits like "On the Street Where You Live" and "My Romance." Finally, *The Glory of Love* ♫♫♫ (RCA, 1992, prod. various) collects Damone's less-consistent but still interesting material recorded between 1966 and 1968.

what to avoid: Some of the many Damone greatest-hits collections are redundant; *16 Most Requested Songs* is a better bet than either *Best of Vic Damone* ♫♫♪ (Curb, 1991, prod. various) or *Best of Vic Damone Live* ♫♫ (Ranwood, 1988, prod. various).

best of the rest:
Let's Face the Music and Sing ♫♫♫ (Pair, 1991)

worth searching for: *Spotlight on Vic Damone* ♫♫♫ (Gold Rush, 1995/1996, prod. various) has Damone covering other people's hits, including "Ebb Tide," "Laura," and "Shangri-La."

influences:
◀◀ Frank Sinatra

▶▶ Tony Bennett, Dean Martin, Michael Bolton, Vince Gill

Steve Knopper

Johnny Dankworth
See: Cleo Laine

Bobby Darin
Born Walden Robert Cossoto, May 14, 1936, in Bronx, NY. Died December 20, 1973, in Los Angeles, CA.

Darin assumed many identities in his career: Brill Building songwriter, '50s teen idol, Frank Sinatra heir apparent, hipster, actor, folkie, political activist, and all-round Vegas-style entertainer. He was successful at nearly every phase of his career, but had he narrowed his scope he might have been much bigger than he was. Several childhood bouts with rheumatic fever left Darin with damaged heart valves and the painful knowledge that his life would be short. So he attempted to cram as much into his career as possible. A versatile musician (piano, drums, guitar, and vibes) and a prolific composer, Darin got his start writing commercial jingles and pitching songs with future pop mogul Don

Kirschner. In 1956, he signed with Decca Records and released a series of high-profile bombs that would've destroyed the career of a less determined artist. Finally, in 1958, he and disc jockey Murray the K cobbled together the quintessential rock 'n' roll novelty, "Splish Splash." His second label, Atlantic, forced Darin to re-record the single "Early in the Morning" under the name the Rinky Dinks, and it hit #24. Upon cementing his Top 10 status with "Queen of the Hop" and the teen masterpiece "Dream Lover," Darin switched directions, and (against the advice of Dick Clark) recorded a Sinatraesque version of "Mack the Knife," a lounge classic and his biggest hit ever. In the mid-60s, despite Darin's successful sidestep into films, the combination of the British Invasion and a string of lame films rendered his singing career irrelevant. Darin tried to rebound by raising his social consciousness, eschewing his toupee and tuxedo, dressing in denim, and in 1966, returning to Atlantic to record folk music. His version of Tim Hardin's "If I Were a Carpenter" is definitive and was a solid Top 10 hit, but despite worthy follow-ups, the public could not reconcile its image of the finger-snapping Sinatra wannabe with his new identity, ultra-serious folk singer "Bob" Darin. Robert Kennedy's death in 1968 totally unhinged his personality. He abandoned show business, moved into a trailer in the Big Sur, and spent his fortune writing, producing, directing, and starring in an unreleasable film about a heroic folk singer. Darin's career seemed over until his old protégé, Wayne Newton, got him to come back and perform live in Las Vegas. A magnificent stage performer, he blended elements of his folk career into his supper-club act, and kept his principles while recapturing his old fans. Darin's comeback was highlighted by a hit summer variety series on NBC, where he proved to be as deft a comedian as he was a singer. Darin recorded his final chart entry, "Happy (Lady Sings the Blues Love Theme)," for Motown before dying, at 37, during heart-valve replacement surgery.

what to buy: Darin's fertile hit years at Atco/Atlantic are well represented on some fine solo discs. *Splish Splash: The Best of Bobby Darin, Vol. 1* ♫♫♫♪ (Atco, 1991, compilation prod. Greg Geller) highlights the best of his teen material. *Mack the Knife: The Best of Bobby Darin, Vol. 2* ♫♫♫♪ (Atco, 1991, compilation prod. Greg Geller) contains 21 tracks from his Sinatra period. *Bobby Darin Story* ♫♫♫♫ (Atlantic, 1989, prod. Ahmet Ertegun) and *The Ultimate Bobby Darin* ♫♫♫♫ (Warner Bros. Special Products, 1986, prod. Ahmet Ertegun) are nice varied compilations as well. However, if your budget can stand the strain, the four-disc set, *As Long as I'm Singin'* ♫♫♫♫ (Rhino, 1995, prod. Ahmet Ertegun), features every decent note Darin recorded for Atco, as well as 11 previously unreleased songs and alternate takes.

what to buy next: Darin unsuccessfully fought the British Invasion at Capitol Records, where he alternated retro-Sinatra sounds with some smart country pop. *Bobby Darin: Capitol Collector's Series* 𝄞𝄞𝄞 (Capitol/EMI, 1996, compilation prod. Ron Furmanek) features hits such as "You're the Reason I'm Livin'," "18 Yellow Roses" (which Darin wrote for his wife, Sandra Dee), and standards such as "Hello, Dolly." Darin made his move from Teen Idol to All-Round Adult Entertainer on *Darin at the Copa* 𝄞𝄞𝄞 (Atlantic, 1994, prod. Ahmet Ertegun), a 17-track reissue of the 1960 LP recorded live at Frank Sinatra's old stomping grounds, the Copacabana.

what to avoid: Darin's post–Bobby Kennedy assassination depression asserts itself most gloomily on *Born: Walden Robert Cosotto* 𝄞𝄞 (Direction, 1968, prod. Bobby Darin), a folk protest LP that Darin believed in so strongly he refused to wear his toupee while recording it.

the rest:
Darin 𝄞𝄞 (Motown, 1989)
This Is Darin 𝄞𝄞𝄞 (Atlantic, 1994)
That's All 𝄞𝄞𝄞𝄞 (Atlantic, 1994)
Bobby Darin 𝄞𝄞𝄞𝄞 (Atlantic, 1994)
Two of a Kind: Bobby Darin & Johnny Mercer 𝄞𝄞𝄞 (Atlantic, 1994)
Spotlight on Bobby Darin 𝄞𝄞𝄞 (Capitol/EMI, 1995)
Say Willie 𝄞𝄞 (MCA Special Products, 1996)
Bobby Darin 𝄞𝄞𝄞 (A Touch of Class, 1997)

worth searching for: Darin's cocky vocal style is oddly appealing on *25th of December* 𝄞𝄞𝄞 (Atco, 1991, prod. Ahmet Ertegun), a true lounge lizard's idea of how to make holiday fare really swing.

influences:

◀◀ Frank Sinatra, Ray Charles, Tim Hardin

▶▶ Bobby Rydell, Wayne Newton, Harry Connick Jr.

Ken Burke

Hal David
See: Burt Bacharach

Richard Davies
Born March 9, 1964, in Sydney, Australia.

Artists like Brian Wilson may have invented orchestral pop, but Australian multi-talent Richard Davies helped make it relevant in—if not always commercially safe for—the post-

grunge rock era. First with the Moles, then with Cardinal, and then on his own, Davies marched bravely into pop music's past to the jazzy beat of his own drummer, crafting catchy, complex pop at a time when the zeitgeist smelled more like teen spirit. The Moles' first record, *Untune the Sky*, made enough of a critical splash in England that Davies and the Moles moved to London from their home city of Sydney, Australia, in 1992. Unfortunately, commercial success eluded the Moles, and the quartet broke up the following year. After moving to Boston and recording an album with another edition of the Moles, Davies met the transplanted Oregonian Eric Matthews, who shared his interest in making pop that combined the studio sophistication of late-period Beatles with the orchestral instrumentation of Burt Bacharach. After Davies and Matthews decided they were both solo acts at heart, Davies lightened up his arrangements and made more personal-sounding albums.

what to buy: *There's Never Been a Crowd Like This* 𝄞𝄞𝄞𝄞 (Flydaddy, 1996, prod. Richard Davies) is complex but also haunting and emotional, and remains Davies's strongest work to date; even moving in a more singer-songwriterly direction, Davies still represents an intriguing alternative to the directness of most '90s rock and pop.

what to buy next: With Davies handling the lion's share of the singing and songwriting and Matthews adding elaborate arrangements, *Cardinal* 𝄞𝄞𝄞𝄞 (Flydaddy, 1994, prod. Cardinal, Thee Slayer Hippy, Tony Lash) is strikingly grand and extraordinarily nuanced at the same time.

what to avoid: His first record with the Moles, *Untune the Sky* 𝄞𝄞𝄞 (Waterfront/Seaside, 1992, prod. the Moles), only hints at the grandeur of his later work.

worth searching for: After Davies moved to Boston, he recorded a more layered and evocative Moles album, *Instinct* 𝄞𝄞𝄞 (Flydaddy, 1994, prod. Richard Davies, Greg Talenfeld), with another group of musicians.

influences:

◀◀ The Beatles, Brian Wilson, Nick Drake

see also: *Eric Matthews*

Robert Levine

Billy Davis Jr.
See: The Fifth Dimension

Mac Davis

Born January 21, 1942, in Lubbock, TX.

Like rocker Eddie Rabbitt, country-pop guitarist-songwriter Davis got a big lift by scoring a hit with Elvis Presley, the insightful "In the Ghetto," then quickly followed that success with yet another Presley smash, "Don't Cry Daddy." During that time, Davis also concocted another fine tune for Kenny Rogers and the First Edition, "Something's Burning." Those songs shed enough light on the former record company rep to help him parlay his good looks and songwriting smarts into a successful solo career, one that has included a TV variety show and some big roles in major movies, most notably *North Dallas Forty*. But his one enduring hit, "Baby Don't Get Hooked on Me," was followed by a torrent of easy-listening schlock ("One Hell of a Woman," "It's Hard to Be Humble").

what's available: *Greatest Hits* ♪♪♪ (Sony, 1979, prod. various) sums it up in succinct fashion; it includes Davis's own rendering of "Something's Burning" and all the major hits, but you have to wade through some real tripe as well (including "Watchin' Scotty Grow," a cloying hit for Bobby Goldsboro). *Very Best and More* ♪♪ (Mercury Nashville, 1984, prod. various) contains mostly Davis's latter-day country fare, including a reading of Rodney Crowell's "Shame on the Moon."

influences:

◄◄ Elvis Presley, Neil Diamond

►► Dan Seals, Eddie Rabbitt

David Simons

Miles Davis

Born May 25, 1926, in Alton, IL. Died September 25, 1991, in Santa Monica, CA.

For all his outlaw image, his disdain for live audiences, and his seemingly frosty indifference to how the public might perceive his sybaritic lifestyle, Miles Davis was practically a poster boy for the lounge movement in the late 1950s and early 1960s. Consciously or unconsciously, Miles was the jazz world's version of Frank Sinatra, down to his studied surliness, the streamlined sports cars he favored, his sleek-tailored suits, and the models and actresses who strode arm-in-arm with him in public and graced his album covers. Even Miles's jazz experiments with Gil Evans's laconic band charts appeared to be subtly aimed at the lounge market—as stunning and detailed as the music was, it rode the crest of the record-buying public's fascination with Gershwin and Latin exotica. Davis had shown a willingness to play with large-scale band music since 1948, when he, Evans, baritone saxman Gerry Mulligan, and pianist John Lewis formed the *Birth of the Cool* nonet, the celebrated New York–based band whose brief lifespan begat the cool jazz era. Like Charlie Parker, Dizzy Gillespie, and most of bebop's heroes, Davis had come up through the big-band movement, clocking time with orchestras led by Benny Carter, Billy Eckstine, and Gillespie. But as Miles was wont to do, he quickly left the 1948 experiment behind him, sinking into drug addiction and a series of desultory recordings in the early 1950s. He returned in 1954 with a sharp set at the Newport Jazz Festival and soon was leading a tight combo that eventually made the careers of such illustrious sidemen as John Coltrane, Cannonball Adderley, and Bill Evans. The Davis group's acidic modal forays on the classic *Kind of Blue* in 1958 made jazz listeners hold their breath—and the record still maintains its power 40 years on. Davis showed his willingness to experiment just months earlier with the release of *Miles Ahead*, his first of the late 1950s collaborations with Evans. The album sold well enough to embolden Miles for more experimentation, and he returned in 1958 with his version of *Porgy and Bess,* a favorite among lounge-oriented jazz types like Louis Armstrong, Ella Fitzgerald, and Cab Calloway. With his crack small band about to lose Coltrane, its most edgy stylist, in 1960, Miles again turned to Evans and produced perhaps his greatest mood classic, *Sketches of Spain*, a flamenco-influenced suite that is modern jazz's equivalent of *Sgt. Pepper*. A fourth go with Evans came in 1962 after the two tried out several live orchestra experiments, but that year's *Quiet Nights* seemed both tame and shrunken compared with the three earlier masterpieces. He made one last sortie into lounge territory with 1969's *In a Silent Way*, an eerie, edited tone poem with electronic backing that presaged his more chaotic carom into full-fledged rock and fusion for the next two decades.

what to buy: *Sketches of Spain* ♪♪♪♪ (Columbia, 1960, prod. Teo Macero) is an elegaic, mysterious suite of flamenco-influenced compositions that somehow welds the passion of Spanish dance music to the elliptical innovation of jazz. And as bracing and strange as Miles's trumpet is leading the maracas and airy flutes, it is as romantic as all get out. For *Porgy and Bess* ♪♪♪♪ (Columbia, 1958, prod. Cal Lampley), Davis and Evans had to graft their sensibilities onto George Gershwin's music, but of all the shmaltzy versions of this Gershwin classic that became the rage in the late 1950s (seek out Bob Crosby and the Bobcats for the unadulterated cheesiest version), this one remains the freshest 30 years later. Columbia had to be using

Miles Davis (© Jack Vartoogian)

Miles Ahead 🎵🎵🎵🎵 (Columbia, 1957, prod. George Avakian) to troll for young suburban turks who had just bought their first AR speakers and tube amplifiers. The cover shows a healthy looking group of romantics out on the briny in a wave-flecked sailboat. The label would get blunter in this approach over the next few years, featuring a bevy of Miles's girlfriends (including a young Cicely Tyson) on his covers. If a gurgling brook could contain a symphony, *In a Silent Way* 🎵🎵🎵🎵 (Columbia, 1969, prod. Teo Macero, Ray Moore) would be it. Sometimes monotonous, the music still contains enough hypnotic detail to carry the listener onward until the serene end.

what to buy next: As fruitful as the jazz world was in the late 1950s—Thelonious Monk, John Coltrane, Sonny Rollins, Ornette Coleman, Cecil Taylor, Sun Ra, Art Blakey, and Max Roach all produced seminal music in that period—nothing matters like *Kind of Blue* 🎵🎵🎵🎵 (Columbia, 1959, reissue prod. Teo Macero). Its impact has been compared to Louis Armstrong's Hot Five recordings and not many jazz fanatics would argue the point.

what to avoid: There are people who say if you're going to buy one Miles, you might as well buy them all. *Quiet Nights* 🎵🎵 (Columbia, 1962, prod. Teo Macero) was not exactly a stiff, but compared to the duo's earlier collaborations, the charts are wheezy and Miles sounds like his thoughts are elsewhere.

best of the rest:
Birth of the Cool 🎵🎵🎵🎵 (Capitol, 1950)
Walkin' 🎵🎵🎵🎵 (Prestige, 1954)
Workin' 🎵🎵🎵🎵🎵 (Prestige, 1954)
Miles Smiles 🎵🎵🎵🎵 (Columbia, 1966)
Bitches Brew 🎵🎵🎵🎵 (Columbia, 1968)

worth searching for: There is plenty of great live Miles on record, ranging from a tight 1958 set at the Newport Jazz Festival with Coltrane and Cannonball to the volumnious eight-CD set of 1965 performances at the Plugged Nickel nightclub in Chicago featuring Shorter, Hancock, Carter, and Williams. But the two-disc *Live in Stockholm, 1960* 🎵🎵🎵🎵 (DIW, 1994), now found as a bootleg on this Japanese label and scheduled to be eventually released by Columbia, comes from a tape of a monumental set featuring Coltrane just before he left to go out on his own. The sound, from a radio broadcast, is nearly impeccable for the period.

influences:

◀◀ Dizzy Gillespie, Charlie Parker, Billy Eckstine, Clark Terry, Gil Evans

▶▶ John Coltrane, Cannonball Adderly, Bill Evans, Herbie Hancock, Wayne Shorter, Chick Corea, Wynton Marsalis

Steve Braun

Sammy Davis Jr.

Born December 8, 1925, in New York, NY. Died May 16, 1990, in Los Angeles, CA.

Davis was a key member of the Rat Pack, that gang of entertainers that included Frank Sinatra, Dean Martin, Peter Lawford, and Joey Bishop. The group defined the lounge ethos with their swaggering, cocktail-in-hand, doll-on-each-arm, hipperthan-thou attitude; see the films *Ocean's Eleven* and *Robin and the Seven Hoods* to witness this species of lizard in its natural habitat.

Davis was the ultimate cabaret performer. Onstage he was intensely dramatic, comic, physically expressive, and a peerless dancer, but recordings seldom conveyed the full depth of his abilities. After leaving the Will Mastin Trio, Davis began recording with Decca Records in 1954 and established a pattern of reinterpreting Broadway show tunes and movie hits, and jazzing up standards, à la Billy Daniels and Frank Sinatra. In the mid-1950s, he scored hits with "Hey There" (also a hit for Johnnie Ray), "Something's Gotta Give," "Love Me or Leave Me," "That Old Black Magic," "I'll Know," "Earthbound," and "New York Is My Home." Rock 'n' roll's popularity knocked Davis's efforts off the charts, though he continued to record prolifically for Decca. After signing with Sinatra's Reprise Records in 1961, he was able to exert much more creative control over his musical output, though his recording career would continue to take a back seat to his fabulously successful work in Broadway musicals, films, TV shows, and nightclubs. Davis's first million-selling record, "What Kind of Fool Am I?" (from the musical *Stop the World I Want to Get Off*), crystallized his persona as an artist who sang less about romance than about being a heartbroken man facing impossible odds. "As Long as She Needs Me" and "The Shelter of Your Arms" were sung with similar dramatic intensity and were sizable hits, but once again musical tastes changed, this time towards the British Invasion, and

Davis's chart momentum stalled. Davis recorded several highly regarded jazz, pop, and musical variety LPs throughout the 1960s, but he didn't have another big hit single until 1968's "I've Gotta Be Me" (from the musical *Golden Rainbow*). With "I've Gotta Be Me," Davis was doing what he always had done—but this time the burgeoning baby-boomer culture, grappling with changing identities, responded positively and adopted the record as a pop anthem. This began Davis's let's-get-down-and-be-groovy-love-children phase, where he dressed in psychedelic clothes, spouted peace-and-love rhetoric, and began experimenting with drugs. Musically, however, little changed, and soon his hippie garb and "peace, love, and brotherhood" raps became fodder for comedians and impressionists. Davis's only #1 hit, 1972's frivolous smash "Candy Man" (inspired by the film *Willy Wonka and the Chocolate Factory*), briefly re-energized his career, but his follow-up, "People Tree," let him down. Afterwards, Davis recorded sporadically for Motown, EMI, and Columbia, without much success or enthusiasm. However, even in his last sickly years, during any given concert, he could still lay claim to the title "World's Greatest Entertainer."

what to buy: Davis personally culled his best-selling singles and most memorable cuts for *His Greatest Hits, Vols. 1 & 2* 🎵🎵🎵🎵 (DCC, 1990, reissue prod. Sammy Davis Jr.), brilliantly chronicling his years with Decca, Reprise, and MGM.

what to buy next: The singer cut his most consistent material for Frank Sinatra's Reprise label, and *I've Gotta Be Me: The Best of Sammy Davis Jr. on Reprise* 🎵🎵🎵 (Reprise Archives, 1996, compilation prod. Greg Geller) features the cream of his work there. Also, Davis is obviously having a ball jamming live with legendary drummer Buddy Rich on *The Sounds of '66: Sammy Davis Jr./Buddy Rich* 🎵🎵🎵 (DCC Jazz, 1966/1996 prod. Jimmy Bowen), and the digitally remastered sound is gorgeous.

what to avoid: Davis is really out of his depth on *From Nashville with Love* 🎵 (EMI/Capitol Special Products, 1994, prod. various), a belated stab at high-gloss country crossover music that seldom sounds convincing.

the rest:

Sammy Davis Jr. Sings, Laurindo Almeida Plays 🎵🎵🎵 (DCC Jazz, 1966/1997)
The Great Sammy Davis Jr. 🎵🎵 (Columbia, 1989)
Capitol Collector's Series 🎵🎵🎵 (Capitol/EMI, 1990)
Sammy Davis Jr. 🎵🎵 (MCA Special Products, 1990)
Greatest Songs 🎵🎵🎵 (Curb, 1990)
The Decca Years 1954–1960 🎵🎵🎵 (MCA, 1990)
What Kind of Fool Am I? 🎵🎵🎵 (Pair, 1993)

Sammy Davis Jr. **(AP/Wide World Photos)**

The Wham of Sam: Sammy Davis Jr. ✍✍✍✍ (Warner Archives, 1994)
That Old Black Magic ✍✍✍ (MCA Special Products, 1995)

worth searching for: One of the best recorded examples of Davis performing live in a nightclub can be found on *Sammy Davis Jr. at the Coconut Grove* ✍✍✍ (Reprise, 1961, prod. various), a freewheeling set featuring Broadway medleys, 1950s rock and country segues, some hits, and 17 of his best celebrity impersonations.

influences:

◄◄ Frank Sinatra, Billy Daniels, Frankie Laine, George Kirby

►► Gregory Hines, Ben Vereen, Billy Crystal

Ken Burke

Doris Day

Born Doris Mary Anne von Kappelhoff, April 3, 1924, in Evanston, OH.

Before becoming a perennial top box-office draw in major motion pictures, Day was one of the finest big-band singers of the

'40s. Her sultry style and clean phrasing brought shades of complex emotion and sensuality to a wide variety of jazz- and pop-oriented songs. She was only 15 years old, and still known as Doris Kappelhoff, when she began appearing with Barney Rapp's band on Cincinnati radio. One of the songs she sang, "Day after Day," proved so popular that she became known as "the Day after Day Girl," then finally just Doris Day. A short stint with Bob Crosby's band attracted the attention of orchestra leader Les Brown. With him, Day developed her intimate approach to a song, singing as if to one person, not a mass audience. "My Dreams Keep Getting Better All the Time" and the classic "Sentimental Journey" were major hits from this period, as were her duets with Buddy Clark, "Love Somebody" and "Confess." Day almost quit the business after a failed marriage, but an opportunity to replace the pregnant Betty Hutton in the film *Romance on the High Seas* opened up a new career avenue and supplied the million-seller "It's Magic." Bringing the same tender persona to the big screen that made her recordings so special, Day turned in some top-quality dramatic performances before appearing in the Rock Hudson bedroom farces that unjustly tarred her cinematic reputation. The movies also supplied two classic songs that most people identify with Doris Day: "Secret Love" and "Que Sera Sera (Whatever Will Be Will Be)." At Columbia, Day's work fell under the supervision of the aesthetically challenged Mitch Miller, who had her record such cutesy stuff as "I Said My Pajamas (and Put on My Prayers)," "Hoop De Doo," "A Guy Is a Guy," and "A Bushel and a Peck." The fact that these records were hits and still listenable is a testament to Day's remarkable charm, interpretive skills, and star power. Day also recorded hit duets with such other top Columbia acts as the Four Lads, Frankie Laine, and Johnnie Ray, which helped further their respective careers. Despite the rock 'n' roll siege of the '50s, Day continually charted with movie themes and Miller-produced novelties well into the '60s. Her son, Terry Melcher (who would later work with the Byrds), co-wrote and produced her last big hit, "Move Over Darling." After the death of her husband, Martin Melcher, Day learned her finances had been mismanaged to the tune of $20 million, and she had been signed to star in a sitcom she hadn't even been consulted about. She regained the money in a damage suit against her husband's former lawyer, but ended up starring in a CBS sitcom that constantly changed its cast and her character's circumstances for three seasons. Appropriately, the show's theme song was "Que Sera Sera." During the '80s, she hosted a pets-oriented cable TV show, *Doris Day & Friends*. (The highlight was this exchange between her and former co-star Rock Hudson: "Rock, what was your favorite movie we did together?" "*Ice Station Zebra*." Day wasn't in that movie.) Though retired, Day recently released *The Love Album*, an LP of previously unreleased material from her last recording session in 1968.

what to buy: You could quench your thirst for such standards as "Que Sera Sera," "It's Magic," and "Secret Love" with *Greatest Hits* ♪♪♪♪ (Columbia, 1987, prod. various), but the skillful mixing of Day's big-band work with her movie hits on *16 Most Requested Songs* ♪♪♪♪♪ (Legacy, 1992, compilation prod. Didier C. Deutsch) and *16 Most Requested Songs: Encore!* ♪♪♪♪♪ (Columbia, 1996, compilation prod. Didier C. Deutsch) are much more exhilarating.

what to buy next: Day is unusually jivey on *Best of the Big Bands* ♪♪♪♪ (Legacy, 1990, prod. various), with 16 tracks recorded with Les Brown and His Band of Renown. It's worthwhile to hear Day bounce through the inspired sass of "Tain't Me" and the sensual "Dig It."

Cocktail Classics

Frosty the Snowman

18-Karat **Jimmy Durante**
Santamental Journey:
Pop Vocal Christmas Classics
(Rhino)

Bombsville! **Juan Garcia Esquivel**
Merry Xmas from the
Space-Age Bachelor Pad
(Bar/None)

what to avoid: As tempting as it may be to get the two queens of nice on one budget disc with *Merry Christmas from Doris Day & Dinah Shore* ♪♪ (Laserlight, 1992), you could get fuller, more satisfying solo collections by either artist for the same price.

the rest:
Hooray for Hollywood, Vol. 1 ♪♪♪ (Columbia, 1959/1988)
(With Andre Previn) *Duet* ♪♪♪♪ (Columbia Special Products, 1962/1992)
Doris Day Christmas Album ♪♪♪ (Columbia, 1964/1989)
A Day at the Movies ♪♪♪ (Columbia, 1988)
Sings 22 Original Big Band Hits ♪♪ (Hindsight, 1992)
The Essence of Doris Day ♪♪♪ (Legacy, 1993)

Love Me or Leave Me 🎵🎵🎵 (Legacy, 1993)
Personal Christmas Collection 🎵🎵🎵 (Legacy, 1994)
Sentimental Journey 🎵🎵🎵 (Hindsight, 1994)
Live It Up 🎵🎵🎵 (Sony Special Music, 1995)
Magic of Doris Day 🎵🎵🎵 (Sony Special Music, 1995)
Uncollected Doris Day, Vol. 1: 1953 🎵🎵🎵 (Hindsight, 1995)
(With the Page Cavanaugh Trio) *Uncollected Doris Day, Vol. 2: 'S Wonderful* 🎵🎵🎵 (Hindsight, 1995)
Golden Hits 🎵🎵🎵 (ITC Masters, 1996)
Pillow Talk 🎵🎵🎵 (Bear Family, 1996)
16 Very Special Songs 🎵🎵🎵 (Prism, 1997)
Blues Skies 🎵🎵 (MSI, 1997)
Day by Day/Day by Night 🎵🎵🎵 (MusicRama, 1997)
Love Album 🎵🎵🎵 (Vision Music, 1997)
Cuttin' Capers/Bright & Shiny 🎵🎵🎵 (Columbia, 1997)
Sentimental Journey 🎵🎵🎵 (Musketeer, 1997)
Complete Doris Day with Les Brown 🎵🎵🎵🎵 (Collector's Choice, 1997)

worth searching for: In the event you want everything Doris Day cut from the '40s to the '60s, some import shops and catalog services carry *It's Magic* 🎵🎵🎵🎵 (Bear Family, 1993, prod. Richard Weize), a six-disc set covering 1947 to 1951 with a 91-page booklet; *Secret Love* 🎵🎵🎵🎵 (Bear Family, 1995, prod. Richard Weize), a five-disc set of her work from 1952 to 1955; *Que Sera Sera* 🎵🎵🎵 (Bear Family, prod. Richard Weize), a five-disc set from 1956 to 1959; and *Move Over Darling* 🎵🎵🎵 (Bear Family, 1997, prod. Richard Weize), which extensively covers her work well into the next decade. An instant comprehensive library all for the price of a few car payments.

influences:

◀◀ Ella Fitzgerald, Jo Stafford, Betty Hutton

▶▶ Debbie Reynolds, Rosemary Clooney, Tracey Ullman

Ken Burke

Blossom Dearie

Born April 28, 1926, in East Durham, NY.

Even in her 60s, Dearie's high, borderline squeaky, pitch still makes her sound like a teenager—only with lots more soul. She's a cabaret singer today, a mainstay at the New York City lounge Danny's Skylight Room after years at the Ballroom supper club in Chelsea. Most post-baby boomers are more likely to recognize her voice from another source, however. She sang "Unpack Your Adjectives," among other educational jingles, on the Saturday-morning commercial series *Schoolhouse Rock!* and was a longtime collaborator with the show's creator, jazzman Bob Dorough.

Dearie, who supposedly earned her unconventional name because a neighbor brought peach blossoms to her mother after her birth, formed a singing group and toured as a member of the Blue Flames, a vocal group that toured with Woody Herman's orchestra in the '40s. After performing briefly with Alvino Rey's Blue Reys, she landed in Paris, hitting the charts with a French version of "Lullaby in Birdland." (Her Blue bands formed the basis of the Swingle Singers and the Double Six Quartet of Paris, both popular in the mid-'50s.) In 1956, she recorded a few albums for the influential Verve label, with a respected jazz combo featuring drummer Jo Jones, and wound up collaborating with Stan Getz and marrying bebop saxophonist Bobby Jaspar (who died in 1963). But she never quite launched herself to the level of stardom reached by her contemporaries like Carmen McRae. Instead, she formed her own record label, Daffodil, and did odd projects like *Schoolhouse Rock!* Few singers capture the same mix of playfulness and soul in a single song; when Dearie sings the *Oklahoma!* classic "Surrey with the Fringe on the Top," it sounds less like a country hick singing about the corn than a lonely girl wondering why she's trapped on the farm.

what to buy: *Once Upon a Summertime* 🎵🎵🎵🎵 (Verve, 1958/1992, prod. Norman Granz) is one of a few reissued Dearie albums from the '50s—the singer takes on extremely familiar material, such as "Tea for Two," "Surrey with the Fringe on the Top," "Our Love Is Here to Stay," and "Amazes Me." But, with her voice perfectly complementing the upbeat moodiness of the piano, it all comes out with Dearie's mesmerizing mixture of loneliness and playfulness.

what to buy next: A more thorough collection of Dearie's late 1950s material, although not as cohesive as *Once Upon a Summertime*, is *Verve Jazz Masters 51* 🎵🎵🎵🎵 (Verve, 1996, prod. Norman Granz), which, in addition to including respected jazz players such as drummer Jo Jones, showcases Dearie's rich and expressive voice. "Tea for Two" and "Surrey" show up again, along with the goofier "Give Him the Ooh-La-La," "Manhattan," and her funny signature song, "I Won't Dance."

best of the rest:
Blossom Dearie 🎵🎵🎵🎵 (Verve, 1989)
Christmas Spice So Very Nice 🎵🎵🎵 (Daffodil, 1996)

worth searching for: The box set *Schoolhouse Rock!* 🎵🎵🎵🎵🎵 (Kid Rhino, 1996, prod. George Newall, Radford Stone), in addi-

Doris Day **(Archive Photos)**

tion to being a really fun nostalgia trip for cartoon-watching kids from the early '70s, showcases Dearie's most playful side. She sings lead on "Figure Eight," "Unpack Your Adjectives," and several other songs that stand up surprisingly well for '70s kids' commercials. Cindy Crawford, Drew Barrymore, and the Lemonheads lend their, um, expertise to liner notes and performances.

influences:

◀◀ Billie Holiday, Stan Getz, Bobby Jaspar, Judy Garland

▶▶ Bob Dorough, Carmen McRae, Peggy Lee, Rosemary Clooney, Squirrel Nut Zippers

Steve Knopper

Lenny Dee

Born Leonard G. DeStoppelaire, January 5, 1923, in Chicago, IL.

With his only hit, 1955's Top 20 "Plantation Boogie," this suave cornball helped introduce the Hammond organ into pop music. Countless hitmakers, from Dee's lounge successors Sir Julian and Walter Wanderley to soul men Booker T. and the MG's, took the organ-playing baton from there. He was a child accordion prodigy and an accomplished musician, having studied organ at the Conservatory of Chicago after a brief stint in the U.S. Navy. Country singer Red Foley discovered him in the early '50s and had him back singer Ethel Smith, which led to a Decca recording contract. But throughout his prolific career—Dee put out more than 50 albums, most of which began with "Dee," such as *Dee-Lightful*, *Dee-Lirious*, *Dee-Licious*, and *Dee-Most!*—he rarely convinced anybody to take him too seriously. Though he continued his easy-listening career well into the '70s, even putting out country albums and instrumental versions of Leo Sayer dance hits, Dee was last seen running a restaurant in St. Petersburg, Florida.

what's available: Used record stores, especially those with substantial easy-listening sections, are the places to go for *Dee-Lightful*, *Hi-Dee-Fi*, *Mellow-Dee*, and other Dee-pun-titled Decca and MCA studio albums. *Dee-Most! Hi-Fi Organ Solos with a Beat!* ♪♪♪ (Decca, 1956) is a good grail for collectors. Otherwise, you may wind up confusing him with the hardcore/techno DJ Lenny Dee and, believe us, that would be a mistake. His snappy little organ instrumental, "China Boy (Go Sleep)," winds up among Jack Costanzo, Rolley Polley, Henri Rene, and other forgotten lounge characters on the excellent *Cocktail Mix, Vol. 1: Bachelor's Guide to the Galaxy* ♪♪♪♪ (Rhino, 1995, compilation prod. Irwin Chusid).

influences:

◀◀ Red Foley, Leroy Anderson, Stan Getz, Art Tatum

▶▶ Walter Wanderley, Denny McLain, Booker T. & the MG's, Sir Julian

Steve Knopper

Martin Denny

Born April 10, 1911, in New York City, NY.

In a sense, Denny owes everything to a frog. A bullfrog, to be exact. That was the "added instrument," you might say, that cropped up one night at the Shell Bar at the island club known as the Hawaiian Village where Martin Denny and his band were playing. The croaking amphibian inspired Denny's band to let out a few key bird calls. And when a few patrons returned the next night eager to hear a replication of it, "exotica" was on its way toward being born. Soon after the incident, Denny, born on the mainland but a Hawaiian resident since 1954, became almost obsessed with conjuring up the sounds of the South Pacific. Jungle Jazz, some called it. "An exotic fruit salad," Denny once dubbed it, as it employed everything from standard jazz combo figures to Hawaiian slack-key guitar, ukuleles, vibraphones, and marimba to more bizarre and unusual instrumentation such as gamelans, gongs, koto, and Burmese temple bells. And virtually out of nowhere it became a national (though short-lived) craze. Driven by a post-war fascination with far-flung locales; sensuous romantic fantasies like the movies *South Pacific*, *The King and I*, and *World of Suzy Wong*; the enticement of Disneyland rides like the Jungle Cruise and Robinson Crusoe's Desert Island Hideaway; and a longing for the seemingly constant at-ease lifestyle of Hawaii, listeners helped exotica records leap out of stores in the late '50s and early '60s. Denny, the progenitor of the style and the inspiration behind the careers of Les Baxter and Denny protégé Arthur Lyman, hit the charts in a big way. His tiki-tinged version of Baxter's "Quiet Village" went to #2 on the Top 40 in 1959, and its accompanying album, *Exotica*, topped the album charts the same year. Denny followed that success with a series of efforts that now sound like one long Pacific Rim soundtrack. But what's overlooked in Denny's work is his accomplished playing and arranging. A classically trained pianist (Denny studied the instrument at the Los Angeles Conservatory of Music), his supple hands trip gently across the keys in a way that evokes both

Martin Denny **(Courtesy of Martin Denny)**

jazz and classical foundations. And under his tutelage came not only Lyman but Julius Wechter, Lyman's replacement in Denny's combo who later formed the mildly successful Baja Marimba Band. Denny, retired, still lives in Honolulu.

what to buy: Though many of his albums are quite good, the definitive statement on Denny's music comes from *The Exotic Sounds of Martin Denny* 𝅘𝅥𝅘𝅥𝅘𝅥𝅘𝅥 (Capitol, 1997, compilation prod. Brad Benedict), a lavish and extensive two-disc set that tells you everything you'll ever need know of the tiki master. It spans Denny's entire spectrum of interest—not just Hawaiian but Polynesian and Indonesian sounds as well—and is transferred in 20-bit sound to capture every last little chirp and whistle. It also has rare tracks that are unavailable elsewhere (including a version of "Hava Nagila!"), unreleased alternate takes, and R.J. Smith's thorough liner notes that put the exotica phenomenon in proper perspective. For the beginners, though, *Exotica! The Best of Martin Denny* 𝅘𝅥𝅘𝅥𝅘𝅥𝅘𝅥 (Rhino, 1990, compilation prod. Bill Inglot) is a fine primer with a clear sense of overview.

what to buy next: Much like the Esquivel reissues, you can find excellent, reasonably-priced two-for-one wonders. There's little variation between any of them, so take your pick of the sexiest cover and dig in. *Exotica/Exotica II* 𝅘𝅥𝅘𝅥𝅘𝅥𝅘𝅥 (1957/Scamp, 1996, prod. Si Waronker) catches the mania on the rise and the birdcalls in full bloom (plus extensive liner notes by Denny himself). *Hypnotique/Exotica III* 𝅘𝅥𝅘𝅥𝅘𝅥𝅘𝅥 (1959/Scamp, 1997, prod. Si Waronker) carries on the tradition with little change. *Quiet Village/The Enchanted Sea* 𝅘𝅥𝅘𝅥𝅘𝅥𝅘𝅥 (1959,1960/Scamp, 1997, prod. Si Waronker) finds Denny reprising his early hit and similar sounds on the former and ably tackling some heavyweight standards ("Stardust," "Sentimental Journey," "Baubles, Bangles and Beads") on the latter. And *Forbidden Island/Primitiva* 𝅘𝅥𝅘𝅥𝅘𝅥𝅘𝅥 (1960/Scamp, 1996, prod. Si Waronker) finds the style moving into more hybridization but beginning to tread water. Also, the spicy *Afro-Desia* 𝅘𝅥𝅘𝅥𝅘𝅥 (1959/Scamp, 1995, prod. Si Waronker) is worth picking up, if only to hear the work of the zingy Randy Van Horne Singers, known for their work with Esquivel and their themes to *The Flintstones* and *The Jetsons*.

what to avoid: Any anthology of Denny's work will do, but why waste good money on 10 tracks when you can get double the amount elsewhere? Logically, *Greatest Hits* 𝅘𝅥𝅘𝅥 (Curb, 1994, prod. Si Waronker) and *Bachelor in Paradise: The Best of Martin Denny* 𝅘𝅥𝅘𝅥 (Pair, 1996, compilation prod. Allan Steckler) are simply superfluous when compared to the superior Capitol and Scamp sets.

worth searching for: *Exotic Sounds Visit Broadway* 𝅘𝅥𝅘𝅥𝅘𝅥 (Liberty, 1960, prod. Si Waronker); *Exotic Sounds from the Silver Screen*

𝅘𝅥𝅘𝅥𝅘𝅥 (Liberty, 1960, prod. Si Waronker); *Exotica Suite* 𝅘𝅥𝅘𝅥𝅘𝅥 (Liberty, 1963), featuring Les Baxter and Si Zentner; *Exotic Percussion* 𝅘𝅥𝅘𝅥𝅘𝅥 (Liberty, 1961); and *A Taste of India* 𝅘𝅥𝅘𝅥𝅘𝅥 (Liberty, 1968) are worth the trip to used-record stores for their cheap thrills.

influences:

◀◀ Juan Garcia Esquivel, Les Baxter

▶▶ Arthur Lyman, Combustible Edison, Devo, Love Jones

Ben Wener

John Denver

Born Henry John Deutschendorf, December 31, 1943, in Roswell, NM. Died October 12, 1997, in Monterey Bay, CA.

Rock 'n' roll hipsters always had a football-field day making fun of John Denver for writing sunny, heartfelt songs about his unconditional love for trees, flowers, mountains, and his wife. We can even remember tuning into a Chicago Top 40 station in 1974 and hearing "Annie's Song" playing while the DJ imitated the sounds of a cow mooing in the background. While it's true that his early albums veered toward cheesy, middle-of-the-road ballads that made him come across as a hunting-lodge lounge singer, Denver also built a sturdy career out of three impressive country-folk albums—1971's *Poems, Prayers and Promises* (which featured his career-making hit, "Take Me Home, Country Roads"), 1972's *Rocky Mountain High*, and 1974's *Back Home Again*—that exuded more passion and conviction than most of what comes out of Nashville today. He also possessed an unwavering commitment to humanitarian causes, standing up for what he believed in, no matter how "far out" or square it might make him look. In 1985, he bravely stood beside Frank Zappa and Dee Snider of Twisted Sister at a Senate hearing to argue against mandatory labeling of sexually explicit rock albums. Still active in the Windstar Foundation, an environmental education and research center that he co-founded, and a reforestation project called Plant-It 2000, Denver was even regaining some of his artistic stature at the time of his death (the single-engine airplane he was piloting crashed). The enjoyable *Wildlife Concert*, a two-CD set benefitting the Wildlife Conservation Society, marked one of the rare perfect marriages of his social consciousness and his art; and a 1997 one-disc distillation called *The Best of John Denver Live* put his name back on the country charts for the first time in a decade.

what to buy: Of his early works still in print, *Rocky Mountain High* 𝅘𝅥𝅘𝅥𝅘𝅥 (RCA, 1972, prod. Milton Okun) sounds the least dated, with fine musicianship, genuinely gorgeous ballads in "For Baby (for Bobbie)" and "Goodbye Again," and cool John

Prine and Beatles covers ("Paradise" and "Mother Nature's Son," respectively). *An Evening with John Denver* 🎵🎵🎵 (RCA, 1975, prod. Milton Okun) captures him at the height of his fame, when all he had to do was utter "far out" to get applause. The between-song patter and notorious cover of New Christy Minstrels leader Randy Sparks's "Saturday Night in Toledo, Ohio" complement the faithful renderings of the hits. If you're not one of the 10 million who already own 1973's *Greatest Hits*, then the two-disc *Rocky Mountain Collection* 🎵🎵🎵 (RCA, 1996, prod. various) is the best primer, with 39 tracks spanning his career and his three greatest-hits collections.

what to buy next: The songs are familiar, but the rustic feel, acoustic band instrumentation, and laid-back, Western-flavored arrangements on *The Wildlife Concert* 🎵🎵🎵 (Sony/Legacy, 1995, prod. Bob Irwin) lend an infectious vitality to this two-disc set. We could do without the flutes, but former Elvis Presley guitarist James Burton adds some tasteful fuel to "Wild Montana Skies," "Back Home Again," and an Appalachian-style "Take Me Home, Country Roads."

what to avoid: In a weak attempt at a concept album about the environment, *Earth Songs* **woof!** (Windstar, 1990, prod. Lee Holdridge) gathers lackluster re-recordings of such 1970s favorites as "Rocky Mountain Suite," "Rocky Mountain High," "Sunshine on My Shoulders," "Eagle and the Hawk," and "Calypso" around new compositions like "Earth Day, Every Day."

the rest:
Poems, Prayers, and Promises 🎵🎵🎵 (RCA, 1971)
Farewell Andromeda 🎵🎵 (RCA, 1973)
Greatest Hits 🎵🎵🎵 (RCA, 1973)
Back Home Again 🎵🎵🎵 (RCA, 1974)
Rocky Mountain Christmas 🎵🎵 (RCA, 1975)
Spirit 🎵🎵🎵 (RCA, 1976)
Windsong 🎵🎵 (RCA, 1976)
I Want to Live 🎵🎵 (RCA, 1977)
Greatest Hits, Vol. 2 🎵🎵🎵 (RCA, 1977)
Some Days Are Diamonds 🎵🎵 (RCA, 1981)
Seasons of the Heart 🎵🎵 (RCA, 1982)
Greatest Hits, Vol. 3 🎵🎵 (RCA, 1984)
Dreamland Express 🎵🎵 (RCA, 1985)
One World 🎵🎵 (RCA, 1986)
The Flower That Shattered the Stone 🎵🎵 (Windstar, 1990)
Different Directions 🎵🎵 (Windstar, 1991)
Higher Ground 🎵🎵 (Windstar, 1991)
Country Hits N/A (RCA, 1998)

worth searching for: *Minneapolis Does Denver* 🎵🎵🎵 (October, 1995, prod. John Strawberry Fields) features such Minneapolis

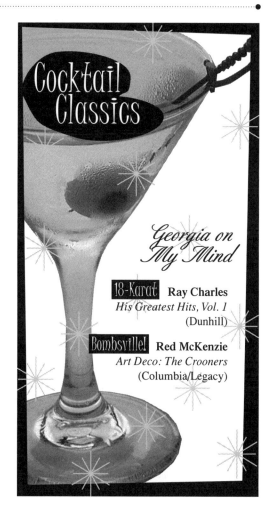

rock acts as the Honeydogs, Steeplejack, Tina and the B-Side Movement, and the Delilahs paying surprisingly faithful tribute to Denver's 1970s material. If there's any doubt that he always knew how to write a memorable melody, check out Marlee McLeod and Kristin Mooney's duet on a jangly, uptempo rendition of "Follow Me."

influences:

◀◀ The New Christy Minstrels, Tom Paxton, James Taylor, Bread

▶▶ Dan Fogelberg

David Okamoto

Paul Desmond

See: Dave Brubeck

Devo

Formed 1972, in Akron, OH.

Mark Mothersbaugh, vocals, guitar, keyboards; Gerald V. Casale, vocals, bass, keyboards; Bob Mothersbaugh, guitar, vocals; Bob Casale, keyboards, guitar; Alan Myers, drums (1972–88); David Kendrick, drums (1988–present).

Possibly the most unlikely success story in pop, Devo's music, wardrobe, stage show, interviews, and mini-movies all preached a vague philosophy of "de-evolution," the dehumanization of mankind by technology, industry, and apathy—an idea Devo alternately praised and derided. (It's unclear whether the band's sole stab at beautiful music, *E-Z Listening Album*, played into this philosophy or not.) Formed on the campus of Kent State University (shortly after the shooting of four students by the National Guard), Devo gained underground popularity during the mid-1970s due to its bizarre stage shows, in which the musicians would dress in identical yellow jumpsuits, plastic masks, and fake hair, sometimes accompanied by the helmeted "General Boy" (actually Mark and Bob's father). Playing an early form of synth-pop, the group won a contract with Warner Bros. in 1978, bowing before a quizzical public with *Q: Are We Not Men? A: We Are Devo* and its kinetic cover of the Rolling Stones' "(I Can't Get No) Satisfaction." Devo was a curiosity until it won over the masses with its 1980 single, "Whip It," but the spotlight faded fast. Though it never officially disbanded—Devo performed at the 1996 Sundance Film Festival—the musicians have since 1990 concentrated on film, TV, and multi-media projects, including the animated children's series *Rugrats*.

what to buy: Nowhere is Devo more Devo than on its first album, *Q: Are We Not Men? A: We Are Devo* 🎵🎵🎵🎵 (Warner Bros., 1978, prod. Brian Eno). Containing songs both curious—"Mongoloid," "Space Junk," "(I Can't Get No) Satisfaction"—and perverse—"Uncontrollable Urge," "Sloppy (I Saw My Baby Gettin')"—it is a much better rebellion against the stagnant music of the '70s than many of the most celebrated punk albums.

what to buy next: *Oh, No! It's Devo* 🎵🎵🎵🎵 (Warner Bros., 1983, prod. Roy Thomas Baker) displays the band's ability to create catchy tunes without watering down its trademark philosophy.

what to avoid: *Total Devo* 🎵🎵 (Virgin, 1988, prod. Devo) while featuring some strong songs, is burdened by poor production that renders the songs flat and lifeless.

the rest:
Duty Now for the Future 🎵🎵 (Warner Bros., 1979)
Freedom of Choice 🎵🎵🎵 (Warner Bros., 1980)
Live 🎵🎵🎵 EP (Warner Bros., 1981)
New Traditionalists 🎵🎵🎵🎵 (Warner Bros., 1981)
Shout 🎵🎵 (Warner Bros., 1984)
Now It Can Be Told 🎵🎵🎵🎵 (Enigma, 1989)
Smooth Noodle Maps 🎵🎵🎵🎵 (Enigma, 1990)
Hardcore Devo, Vol. 1, 1974–1977 🎵🎵🎵 (Rykodisc, 1990)
Devo's Greatest Hits 🎵🎵🎵🎵 (Warner Bros., 1990)
Devo's Greatest Misses 🎵🎵🎵 (Warner Bros., 1990)
Hardcore Devo, Vol. 2, 1974–1977 🎵🎵🎵 (Rykodisc, 1991)
Devo Live: The Mongoloid Years 🎵🎵 (Rykodisc, 1992)

worth searching for: The satiric *Devo E-Z Listening Disk* 🎵🎵🎵🎵 (Rykodisc, 1987, prod. Devo) features the band performing elevator music versions of its songs, muzaking its own work before Muzak can get it.

influences:
◀◀ Kraftwerk, Can, Brian Eno, Robert Fripp, the Rolling Stones
▶▶ They Might Be Giants, the Residents, Toni Basil, Nirvana, Foo Fighters

Brandon Trenz

Neil Diamond

Born January 24, 1941, in Brooklyn, NY.

Though he's at times bombastic, melodramatic, and overreaching, there's no denying that Diamond is still a magical performer. Despite his foibles, he is able to whip crowds of middle-aged women into ecstasy and inspire fans of all ages to dance in their seats.

Diamond began his career as a songwriter in the Brill Building tradition, penning classic pop songs like "I'm a Believer," a #1 hit for the Monkees in 1966. Yearning to perform his own material, Diamond signed with Bang Records in 1965. He had five straight Top 20 singles, showcasing his wide range of influences and styles, including the delightful "Cherry, Cherry" and the despairing "Girl, You'll Be a Woman Soon." Looking to expand as an artist, Diamond left Bang for Uni Records and the West Coast, where he continued to crank out the hits like "Sweet Caroline," "Cracklin' Rosie," and "Holly Holy." His appetite for overindulgence began to blossom in this era with the gospel-tinged "Brother Love's Traveling Salvation Show" and the pompous "I Am I Said." By 1973, Diamond was a one-man tour de force, selling out concerts all over the globe. He signed a then-lucrative $5 million deal with Columbia, and the first album for his new label, the soundtrack to the quintessential '70s film *Jonathan Livingston Seagull*, actually out-earned the movie and earned Diamond a Grammy and an Oscar nomination. The strain of performing live began to wear on Diamond during this time and the consummate showman took 40 months off to recharge his batteries. In 1976, he emerged re-energized and released a concept album, *Beautiful Noise*, produced by the Band's Robbie Robertson, which helps explain, but doesn't really excuse, Diamond's presence during the Band's legendary *Last Waltz* that same year. In the late '70s, Diamond starred in two TV specials that further strengthened his grip on the middle-of-the-road audience, while continuing to crank out hits like "You Don't Bring Me Flowers," a duet with Barbra Streisand—originally conceived by Louisville DJ Gary Gutrie, who mixed together the two singers' solo versions of the song. A benign tumor on his spinal cord slowed Diamond at the end of the decade, but he rebounded quickly. Never a favorite of critics for his music, Diamond's acting took it on the nose, too, with his starring role in the 1980 remake of *The Jazz Singer*. Though the film was a flop, the music from the soundtrack, including "Love on the Rocks," "Hello Again," and the declamatory "America," would prove to be Diamond's last significant commercial output. In 1982, he scored his last pop hit with the insipid *E.T.*-inspired "Turn on Your Heartlight." Throughout the '80s and '90s, Diamond has continued to release tepid albums, while touring the country to sold-out arenas. In concert, his legions of fans willingly forgive his many trespasses—like not one but two Christmas albums from this non-Christian performer—to watch the energetic boy from Brooklyn strut his stuff forever in blue jeans.

what to buy: The best collection of Diamond's gems is *The Greatest Hits 1966–1992* ♫♫♫♫ (Columbia, 1992, prod. various), which follows the singer's career over two CDs from his early mono rockers like "Cherry, Cherry" to the height of his schmaltz like "Love on the Rocks." Depending on your taste, the collection is either enhanced or marred by the inclusion of several live versions of "Sweet Caroline" and "Cracklin' Rosie." To love Diamond is to have seen Diamond live, but if you've never had the opportunity, *Hot August Night* ♫♫♫♫ (MCA, 1972, prod. Tom Catalano) is a worthy showcase spread over two CDs of Diamond at the top of his passionate game.

what to buy next: Real loyalists should invest in the three-CD box set *In My Lifetime* ♫♫♫ (Columbia, 1997, prod. various). Of course, all the hits you most likely already own are included, but scattered among them are some treasures for true fans—

like 16 demos, an alternate take of the rollicking "Cherry, Cherry," and Diamond's performance of "Dry Your Eyes" from *The Last Waltz*. But that's not all: the set comes with a 72-page booklet featuring rare photos, a complete discography, and extensive liner notes. Order before midnight tonight and receive this handsome *Jonathan Livingston Seagull* collector's plate absolutely free. Sorry, no CODs. Though his acting ability is questionable, his singing was still in fine form on the soundtrack for *The Jazz Singer* ♫♫♫ (Capitol, 1980, prod. Bob Gaudio). Overblown, overwrought, and undeniably catchy, songs like "America" and "Hello Again" still delight today as this continues to be Diamond's biggest-selling album.

what to avoid: There's really no excuse for either *Christmas Album* ♫ (Columbia, 1992, prod. Peter Asher) or *Christmas Album, Vol. 2* ♫ (Columbia, 1994, prod. Peter Asher). Hey, how about a Chanukah album? Equally frightening is Diamond's foray in country music, *Tennessee Moon* ♫ (Columbia, 1996, prod. Richard Landis). Someone please persuade Neil to keep coasting on his hits and stop genre exploring.

the rest:
Touching You, Touching Me ♫♫♫ (MCA, 1969)
Sweet Caroline ♫♫♫ (MCA, 1969)
Jonathan Livingston Seagull ♫♫♫ (Columbia, 1973)
Beautiful Noise ♫♫♫ (Columbia, 1976)
Love at the Greek ♫♫♫ (Columbia, 1977)
You Don't Bring Me Flowers ♫♫ (Columbia, 1978)
September Morn ♫♫♫ (Columbia, 1979)
Heartlight ♫♫ (Columbia, 1982)
Hot August Night ♫♫♫♫ (Columbia, 1987)
Up on the Roof: Songs from the Brill Building ♫♫♫ (Columbia, 1993)

worth searching for: Rock luminaries Bob Dylan, Eric Clapton, Van Morrison, and Neil Young were on hand to play during the Band's legendary farewell performance at San Francisco's Winterland in 1976. The all-star event was captured both on vinyl and celluloid (by Martin Scorsese) as *The Last Waltz* ♫♫♫♫♫ (Warner Bros., 1978, prod. Robbie Robertson, John Simon, Rob Froboni). Others lending a hand at the show included Ringo Starr, Ron Wood, Joni Mitchell, Dr. John, Paul Butterfield, Emmylou Harris, the Staple Singers, Muddy Waters, and, oh yeah, a certain singer-songwriter from Brooklyn performing a blistering version of "Dry Your Eyes."

influences:
◀◀ Bob Dylan, Paul Simon, the Beatles, Elvis Presley
▶▶ Barry Manilow

Alex Gordon

Marlene Dietrich

Born Maria Magdalene Dietrich, December 27, 1901, in Berlin, Germany. Died May 6, 1992, in Paris, France.

Long before Madonna strutted her stuff and Marilyn Monroe discovered the power of platinum hair dye, Marlene Dietrich had vamped and titillated her way across silver screens and theater stages everywhere. Though she had starred in a number of silent films, her first big splash was in Josef von Sternberg's 1929 movie *Der Blaue Engel (The Blue Angel),* in which she portrayed Luisa "Lola" Froelich, a worldly and world-weary cabaret singer who seduces, uses, and discards a schoolmaster in the throes of a mid-life crisis. The part captured the epitome of cabaret. Dietrich went on to star in countless films, often playing variations on the Lola character. As for singing, however, her vocals were limited in range. Husky, deep, and not particularly flexible, Dietrich's voice was nonetheless an ideal instrument for her sultry style and sentiments. (Neither Monroe nor Madonna packed particularly remarkable pipes either—the impact they made, as with Dietrich, was in their delivery.) Before Hollywood instituted censors in the '30s, Dietrich turned in some surprisingly provocative performances in cabaret films like *Morocco*, in which she dressed in men's clothing.

what's available: *The Cosmopolitan Marlene Dietrich* ♫♫♫♩ (Legacy/ Columbia, 1993, prod. Mitch Miller, compilation prod. Michael Brooks) is an 18-song collection that features standards, show tunes, and Dietrich's signature song, "Lili Marlene," in both German and English. Also included is her rendering of "La Vie en Rose," popularized by Edith Piaf, and a truly goofy German version of the old *Oklahoma!* classic "Surrey with the Fringe on the Top." The European compilation *Lili Marlene* ♫♫♫ (Sarabandas, 1996) includes several songs from films. The remaining Dietrich catalog is scattered among some eight different record labels—most rather obscure or based far from the U.S.

influences:

⏪ Claere Waldoff

⏩ Madonna, Marilyn Monroe, Nico, Marianne Faithfull, Ute Lemper

Sandy Masuo

Dimitri from Paris

Born October 27, 1963, in Istanbul, Turkey.

Dimitri from Paris (not be confused with DJ Dmitry from the colorful disco-funk band Deee-Lite) describes his style as "anything that fits." His groundbreaking debut release, *Sacre-bleu!* fits snugly between the crossroads of lounge and dance, creating a sound he called "Cocktail Club." Dimitri spent most of the '80s as a disco/acid house DJ. It wasn't until he hooked up with Yellow Productions' Chris the French Kiss that he discovered the virtues of the easy-listening life. Together they created the basis of the "yellow sound": a mix of trip-hop and easy-listening records, plus obscure French music blurred into a danceable flare of late-night beats. Along with Pizzicato Five and Easy Tunes, Dimitri is one of the rising stars of modern lounge culture.

what's available: *Sacre-bleu!* ♫♫♫♫ (East/West, 1996) is a concept record (although you'd have trouble figuring that out by listening to it) that traces the journey of a long-absent American soldier returning to Paris. *Sacre-bleu!* is frequently cited as the most egregious case of sampling in lounge culture; if you feel the need to play "spot the sample," make it a drinking game.

influences:

⏪ Henry Mancini, Pizzicato Five, Yellow Productions, United Future Organization, Deee-Lite

⏩ Tipsy, David Holmes

Sam Wick

Divine Comedy

Formed 1991, in Ireland.

Neil Hannon, vocals, piano.

Divine Comedy is Neil Hannon. That's it. There was a band on the early releases, but on the masterpieces *Cassanova* and *A Short Album about Love*, it's just one man. One man who thinks he's great. Just ask him, he'll tell you. Lucky for him he truly is great, a maestro of the kind of over-orchestrated, over-emotional, and over-dramatic poetry that went out of style when Scott Walker went off the deep end in the mid-'70s. Hannon, a bishop's son, lived a shy, waifish, and almost friendless childhood. Thank God he had a grand piano that his father never tired of listening to him hammer on. Divine Comedy's early efforts featured a tantilizing mix of electropop, new wave, and overly abundant literary references. Hannon came to England's attention when he shed his bandmates in 1996 and released *Cassanova*. The track "Something for the Weekend" became a minor hit, but Hannon himself, using words like "genuinely inspired" to describe his own work, became a star.

what to buy: On *A Short Album about Love* ♫♫♫♫ (Setanta, 1997, prod. Jon Jacobs, Neil Hannon), especially the chain-smoking, lovelorn masterpieces "Everyone Knows (I Love You)" and "If," Hannon's tendency for simpy, syrupy arrangements and poetic lyrical indulgences peaks with his commandeering of a 32-piece orchestra.

what to buy next: *Cassanova* 𝄞𝄞𝄞𝄞 (Setanta, 1996, prod. Darren Allison, Neil Hannon), despite even more musicians than *A Short Album about Love*, is less orchestral and atmospheric. Highlights include the minor hit "Something for the Weekend," the unintentional Burt Bacharach tribute "Becoming More Like Alfie," and "The Frog Princess."

what to avoid: *Fanfare for the Comic Muse* (Setanta, 1990) is an unfocused, jangly mess.

the rest:
Liberation 𝄞𝄞 (Setanta, 1993)
Promenade 𝄞𝄞𝄞 (Setanta, 1994)

influences:
◀◀ Burt Bacharach, Scott Walker, Neil Diamond
▶▶ Tindersticks

Sam Wick

Lonnie Donegan

Born Anthony James Donegan, April 29, 1931, in Glasgow, Scotland.

Lonnie Donegan is the undisputed King of Skiffle—a jazz-tinged hybrid of American folk and blues that set the stage for the British rock 'n' roll movement in the early 1960s. Performed with acoustic guitars, banjos, a tea-chest bass, and a washboard for scrubbing out the backbeat, skiffle was a crude, spirited music played at rent parties and working men's pubs. Donegan brought skiffle to mass audiences during his years with Ken Colyer's and Chris Barber's jazz bands. Initially just a pleasant intermission distraction, Donegan's "skiffle breaks" soon became the most popular aspect of their live shows, leading to a featured spot on Barber's first LP. Donegan reworked an old Leadbelly tune, "Rock Island Line," into a Top 10 hit in both the U.K. and America. Because he was paid a flat fee for the session, Donegan didn't receive any royalty payments for his most popular and influential song, but his newfound popularity allowed him to strike out as a solo act. Beginning in the mid-'50s, Donegan enjoyed a string of 34 British hits, such as "Puttin' on the Style," "Cumberland Gap," and "Does Your Chewing Gum Lose Its Flavor (On the Bedpost Overnight)." Donegan's energy, humor, and showmanship inspired untold scores of British teens to hunt down cheap guitars, banjos, and washboards so they could start their own skiffle units. Many of these aspiring Donegan-wannabes, such as Cliff Richard and John Lennon, dis-

Cocktail Classics

The Girl from Ipanema

18-Karat **Astrud Gilberto** *Getz/Gilberto* (Verve)

Bombsville! **Denny McLain** *Ultra-Lounge, Vol. 11: Organs in Orbit* (Capitol)

covered that their skiffle skills perfectly prepared them to play amplified blues-based American rock 'n' roll. Donegan himself detested rock 'n' roll, though its emergence didn't really impede his career until the early '60s. In addition to being a perennial favorite in British clubs and television, Donegan is an astute businessman with lucrative music publishing interests, including the repackaging of his own work.

what's available: You'll have to hit the import racks or catalog services if you want prime material by this great, highly underrated artist, but it's worth it to dig up *Puttin' on the Style* 𝄞𝄞𝄞 (Sequel , 1993, prod. various), a three-disc set with most of Donegan's ground-breaking hits (sadly, it doesn't have his original version of "Rock Island Line"). If you've got the bucks, the German import *More Than Pie in the Sky* 🎵🎵🎵🎵 (Bear Family, 1994, compilation prod. Richard Weize) is an eight-disc box set with all of his originals hits, live material, and many previously unreleased songs and alternate takes. If you have this, you don't need anything else, including the earlier collection *Lonnie Donegan* 🎵🎵🎵 (Laserlight, 1991).

influences:

◀◀ Leadbelly, Big Bill Broonzy, Chris Barber

▶▶ Cliff Richard, the Beatles, Gerry and the Pacemakers

Ken Burke

Bob Dorough

Born December 12, 1923, in Cherry Hill, AK.

Vocalist and pianist Dorough began his lengthy career playing in jazz clubs and accompanying dance lessons in a local studio. He toiled in the business for 20-some years (even working with Miles Davis once) until he was asked to work on a project for ABC Television in 1970. But for all those serious credentials, he's best known for his work as the musical director for the *Schoolhouse Rock!* series of animated shorts. Whether it was "Multiplication Rock," "Grammar Rock," "America Rock," "Money Rock," or even "Science Rock," Dorough had his hand in it—singing "Three Is a Magic Number" and "My Hero, Zero," and writing "Conjunction Junction." From 1973 to 1985, these brief weekend morning cartoons taught us sentence structure, math, history, and science without the painful realization we were learning. The collection is misnamed, however, because this former scat-cat's arrangements have more in common with jazz than actual rock music. While Dorough has continued to record other material, he recently toured the U.S. with a few of his original collaborators performing songs from *Schoolhouse Rock!*

what to buy: *Schoolhouse Rock!* 🎵🎵🎵🎵 (Kid Rhino, 1996, prod. George Newall, Radford Stone) is an essential four-disc collection packaged in a denim three-ring binder that still grooves (check out Ben Tucker's very funky basslines). This set might have been the most important reissue of 1996 because the original LPs were long out of print. Finally available again are the classics, like "I'm Just a Bill," "Lolly, Lolly, Lolly, Get Your Adverbs Here," and "Three Is a Magic Number" (brilliantly sampled, yet un-credited by the rap trio De La Soul on the track "The Magic Number" from *Three Feet High and Rising*), among many others. Also included are the vocals and/or writing of Blossom Dearie, Jack Sheldon, Essra Mohawk, Lynn Ahrens,

David Frishberg, and others. Dorough's recordings away from this effort are pleasant, but lines like "Apple, peaches, pumpkin pie, who's not ready holler aye!" are pretty much as good as it gets. Cole Porter was talented, but he was no Bob Dorough.

what to buy next: *Devil May Care* 🎵🎵🎵 (Bethlehem, 1957/1996) is an interesting precursor to Dorough's future success; it's a worthy collection of jazz covers (including tracks written by Charlie Parker, Dizzy Gillespie, and Duke Ellington) and originals. He was a fairly hip guy back then, so this set is a neat foreshadowing of his later, more famous work. Also available is his recent recording, *Right on My Way Home* 🎵🎵🎵 (Blue Note, 1997, prod. Bill Goodwin), where he is joined by *Schoolhouse Rock!* drummer-singer Grady Tate on half the tracks. It's pretty cool to hear Dorough wrap his distinctive pipes around "Moon River," the first song on the disc. Extra credit for the photos showing this 73-year-old with a ponytail.

what to avoid: *Schoolhouse Rock! Rocks* 🎵🎵 (Lava, 1996, prod. Janet Billig, Andrew Leary) contains covers of the originals by "alternative-rock" artists such as Blind Melon and the Lemonheads (also included on the Kid Rhino box set) and others. It's sacrilege, pure sacrilege.

the rest:
Just About Everything 🎵🎵🎵 (Evidence, 1967/1994)

worth searching for: Dorough's side work appeared on many other artists' releases, but his collaboration with bassist Bill Takas on the import-only *Memorial Charlie Parker* 🎵🎵🎵 (Philogy) would appear the most interesting.

influences:

◀◀ *Sesame Street*, *Electric Company*

▶▶ Barney the dinosaur

Barry M. Prickett

Arnold George "Gerry" Dorsey

See: Engelbert Humperdinck

Jimmy Dorsey

Born February 29, 1904, in Shenandoah, PA. Died June 12, 1957, in New York, NY.

Of the two swinging Dorsey brothers, Jimmy was more committed to jazz. A lover of fast tempos and blaring brass, his high technical skill on both the clarinet and alto saxophone is still admired by musicians today. Dorsey was only 17 years old when he turned pro with the Scranton Sirens. As in most of his early band affiliations, Dorsey would join and then later persuade the other members to include younger brother Tommy on trombone. Popular session musicians for the likes of Red Nichols, the Boswell Sisters, and Ben Pollack, the Dorseys were also part-time recording stars until 1934 when they formed the Dorsey Brothers Orchestra. After the brothers went their separate ways, Jimmy Dorsey was not immediately successful, even though his band featured some of the finest talent of his era (Ray McKinley, Dave Matthews, Freddie Slack, Charlie Teagarden, and so on). It wasn't until the '40s that Dorsey's Orchestra became popular on the strength of big hits sung by Helen O'Connell ("Green Eyes," "Tangerine") and Bob Eberle ("Amapola"). At its peak, the Jimmy Dorsey Orchestra appeared in such films as *I Dood It, Four Jills in a Jeep,* and *Hollywood Canteen.* Success often breeds forgiveness, and the Dorsey Brothers patched up their differences long enough to make the 1947 turkey *The Fabulous Dorseys,* in which the brothers ineptly played themselves. (At least the music was good.) During the post-war years, Jimmy Dorsey added Maynard Ferguson to his group and began embracing modern bop, but the stylistic adaptation wasn't enough to reduce his declining fortunes. Jimmy reteamed with his brother Tommy and his band in 1953, billed as the Tommy Dorsey Orchestra featuring co-leader Jimmy Dorsey. The brothers' comeback bid was given a big boost when they signed to do *Jackie Gleason's Stage Show*—at the time, the only bandstand series on TV. After Tommy died in 1956, Jimmy carried on with his brother's band. Their 1957 recording of "So Rare" became the last hit from a major big band, just as Jimmy Dorsey was dying of cancer.

what to buy: Some big hits and hot instrumental moments reside on *Best of Jimmy Dorsey & His Orchestra* ✍✍✍ (Curb, 1992, compilation prod. Don Ovens), which has Helen O'Connell's "Tangerine" and "Green Eyes," Bob Eberle's "Amapola," and Dorsey's swan song, "So Rare." As budget discs go, this is a great one.

what to buy next: The largely instrumental LP *Contrasts* ✍✍✍ (Decca Jazz, 1993, prod. Dave Grusin, Larry Rosen, Orrin Keepnews) features Jimmy Dorsey's strongest orchestra lineup with Ray McKinley and piano-boogie legend Freddy Slack on a mix of cool jams and jazz jumpers.

what to avoid: The sound quality leaves a lot to be desired on *Jazz Collector's Edition* ✍ (Laserlight, 1991), an easy-to-find budget disc with few engaging performances. Worse still is *Giants of the Big Band Era: Jimmy Dorsey* ✍ (Pilz, 1992), which skimps on tracks as well. Others worth skipping are *Plays His Greatest Hits* ✍ (Hollywood/Rounder, 1987) and *Best of the Big Band* ✍ (Hollywood, 1994)—cheapies for completists only.

the rest:
Dorsey, Then & Now—Fabulous New Jimmy Dorsey ✍✍ (Rhino, 1988)
Pennies from Heaven ✍✍ (ASV, 1992)
1939–1940 ✍✍ (Hindsight, 1993)
1940 ✍✍ (Circle, 1993)
1939–1940 ✍✍✍ (Circle, 1993)
Uncollected Jimmy Dorsey ✍✍✍ (Hindsight, 1993)
22 Original Recordings ✍✍ (Hindsight, 1994)
Perfidia ✍✍ (Laserlight, 1994)
At the 400 Restaurant 1946 ✍✍✍ (Hep, 1994)
Don't Be That Way ✍✍✍ (Aerospace, 1995)
Jimmy Dorsey ✍✍✍ (Empire, 1995)
Tangerine ✍✍ (MCA Special Products, 1995)
America Swings—The Great Jimmy Dorsey ✍✍ (Hindsight, 1996)
Mood Hollywood ✍✍✍ (Hep, 1996)
So Rare: Jimmy Dorsey's Boogie Woogie ✍✍✍ (Richmond, 1996)

worth searching for: Among the many live radio transcriptions available, the import *Frolic Club, Miami 7/16/44* ✍✍✍ (Canby, 1995) stands out as especially atmospheric and musically complete.

influences:
◀◀ Red Nichols, Paul Whiteman, Ben Pollack
▶▶ Ray McKinley, Freddy Slack, Maynard Ferguson

see also: *Tommy Dorsey*

Ken Burke

Tommy Dorsey
/The Dorsey Brothers

Born November 19, 1905, in Manahoy City, PA. Died November 26, 1956, in Greenwich, CT.

Whether teamed with brother Jimmy as part of the Dorsey Brothers, or leading his own band, Tommy Dorsey was one of the most successful and important figures of the big-band era. (His orchestra was also the first to truly develop the young Frank Sinatra as a vocalist.) A trombone player possessing an amazing command of tone, Dorsey could let out all the stops on hot swing or play sweet and cozy on sentimental ballads. During the early '20s, Dorsey and older brother Jimmy co-led such groups as Dorsey's Novelty Six and Dorsey's Wild Canaries before hiring on with Jean Goldkette's orchestra and then with Paul Whiteman. Billed as featured soloists with Whiteman, the brothers began cutting popular swing records as the Dorsey Brothers in 1928, but didn't form their own outfit until 1934. Packed with talent (Bunny Berigan played trumpet, Glenn Miller wrote arrangements and played in the horn sec-

Tommy Dorsey **(Archive Photos)**

tion), the Dorsey Brothers Orchestra was wildly popular with swing fans and musicians alike. However, the intense sibling rivalry between the Dorseys (hot-headed Tommy and perfectionist Jimmy) resulted in creative disputes, constant quarrels, and even fistfights. Their 1935 split was inevitable. Jimmy kept their established band, and Tommy took over an excellent orchestra from retiring bandleader Joe Haymes. (He also appropriated their joint hit "In a Sentimental Mood" as his theme song.) The Tommy Dorsey Orchestra employed several top jazz musicians through the years (Alex Stordahl, Buddy Rich, Yank Lawson, Charlie Shavers, and Bud Freeman among them), but it's best known for its famous vocalists. Sy Oliver, Jack Leonard, Jo Stafford, and Connie Haines all cut hits with Dorsey, but with young Frank Sinatra at the mike, his orchestra truly hit the big time. Sinatra had already hit with the Harry James Orchestra, but it was with Dorsey's outfit that he developed his unique breathing technique—which led to the sensual interpretive style that drove bobbysoxers wild. With a

string of monster hits, Sinatra and Dorsey established each other as major stars. When Sinatra left in 1942, Dorsey replaced him with Dick Haymes, causing fans to argue over which was the greater vocalist. (It's a moot point today.) During the war years, Dorsey expanded his orchestra to include string sections and vocal choirs for his increasingly ballad-heavy style. In his spare time, he cut solid jazz with a changing core of musicians called Tommy Dorsey and the Clambake Seven. Dorsey's popularity continued into the post-war years, but during the early '50s, the big-band decline began affecting him, too. In a stroke of publicity genius, he reunited with brother Jimmy (whose own band had folded in 1953) to play nostalgic dance-band music. Their reunion earned much publicity and resulted in their hosting *Jackie Gleason's Stage Show*, where they introduced the nation to yet another singer destined to become a pop icon, Elvis Presley. After Tommy Dorsey died in 1956, brother Jimmy followed seven months later. Subsequent editions of the band, billed as The Tommy

Dorsey Orchestra under the Direction of Sam Donahue, toured with another familiar name, Frank Sinatra Jr.

what to buy: The Dorsey Brothers are joined by Bunny Berigan and Glenn Miller on *The Dorsey Brothers: Best of the Big Bands* 𝄞𝄞𝄞𝄞 (Legacy, 1992, compilation prod. Michael Brooks), a strong set of their early recordings featuring vocals by Mildred Bailey and Johnny Mercer. As an introduction to Tommy as a solo artist, *Best of Tommy Dorsey* 𝄞𝄞𝄞𝄞 (RCA, 1992, compilation prod. John Snyder) or *Greatest Hits* 𝄞𝄞𝄞𝄞 (RCA, 1996, compilation prod. Hank Hoffman) are pretty solid, mid-priced hits compilations featuring vocalists Jack Leonard, Charlie Shavers, and the Pied Pipers. Or, you can get a full disc of Dorsey and that skinny kid from Hoboken with *Tommy Dorsey/Frank Sinatra: Greatest Hits* 𝄞𝄞𝄞𝄞 (RCA, 1996, reissue prod. Chick Crumpacker), a 15-song collection with Ol' Blue Eyes crooning "Night and Day," "Once in Awhile," and his theme, "Polka Dots and Moonbeams."

what to buy next: The five-disc, 120-track *This Song Is for You* 𝄞𝄞𝄞𝄞 (RCA, 1994, compilation prod. Paul Williams) contains every note of Dorsey and Sinatra's work together on one set. The analytical booklet, gorgeous sound quality, and six previously unreleased performances make this a must-have for serious collectors of both artists.

what to avoid: The poorly assembled *Golden Hits* 𝄞 (ITC Masters, 1997) won't improve your collection one iota. Also, even at budget prices, for the money you spend on a split disc such as *Tommy Dorsey Orchestra & David Rose String Orchestra* 𝄞𝄞 (Laserlight, 1994), you could get a full disc by either artist (although Rose's CDs are largely out of print). There's nothing new here. And both the Dorseys had been dead for several years by the time *Live 1962 at Villa Venice Chicago* 𝄞 (Jazz Hour, 1994) was recorded, so don't even bother with this Sam Donahue–led curio.

the rest:
(With the Clambake Seven) *Having a Wonderful Time* 𝄞𝄞𝄞 (RCA, 1958/1995)
One and Only 𝄞𝄞𝄞 (RCA Camden, 1988)
Best of the Big Bands 𝄞𝄞𝄞𝄞 (Columbia, 1988)
(With Frank Sinatra) *All-Time Greatest Hits, Vol. 1* 𝄞𝄞𝄞𝄞 (RCA Bluebird, 1988)
(With Frank Sinatra) *All-Time Greatest Hits, Vol. 2* 𝄞𝄞𝄞 (RCA Bluebird, 1988)
(With Frank Sinatra) *All-Time Greatest Hits, Vol. 3* 𝄞𝄞𝄞 (RCA Bluebird, 1989)
Well Get It! The TD CD 𝄞𝄞𝄞 (Jass Records, 1989)
Best of Tommy Dorsey 𝄞𝄞 (MCA, 1989)

Sentimental 𝄞𝄞 (MCA Jazz, 1989)
The 17 Number Ones 𝄞𝄞𝄞 (RCA Bluebird, 1990)
(With Frank Sinatra) *Oh! Look at Me Now & Other Big Band Hits* 𝄞𝄞𝄞 (RCA Bluebird, 1990)
The Great Tommy Dorsey 𝄞𝄞 (Pearl, 1991)
Jazz Collector's Edition, Vol. 1 𝄞𝄞 (Laserlight, 1991)
Jazz Collector's Edition, Vol. 2 𝄞𝄞 (Laserlight, 1991)
Best of Tommy Dorsey & His Orchestra 𝄞𝄞𝄞 (Curb, 1991)
1942 War Bond Broadcasts 𝄞𝄞𝄞 (Jazz Hour, 1992)
Boogie Woogie 𝄞𝄞𝄞 (Pro Arte, 1992)
Radio Days 𝄞𝄞𝄞 (Star Line, 1992)
Live in Hi-Fi at Casino Gardens 𝄞𝄞 (Jazz Hour, 1992)
(With Frank Sinatra) *Stardust* 𝄞𝄞𝄞 (RCA Bluebird, 1992)
The Post War Era 𝄞𝄞𝄞 (RCA Bluebird, 1993)
Stop, Look & Listen 𝄞𝄞𝄞 (Living Era, 1993)
New York Jazz in the Roaring Twenties 𝄞𝄞𝄞 (Biograph, 1994)
Tommy Dorsey and His Greatest Band 𝄞𝄞𝄞𝄞 (Jasmine, 1994)
At the Fat Man's 1946–48 𝄞𝄞𝄞 (Hep, 1994)
The Carnegie Hall V-Disc Session—April 1944 𝄞𝄞𝄞 (Hep, 1994)
All Time Hit Parade Rehearsals 1944 𝄞𝄞𝄞 (Hep, 1994)
1936–1938 𝄞𝄞𝄞 (Jazz Archives, 1994)
(With Frank Sinatra) *I'll Be Seeing You* 𝄞𝄞𝄞𝄞 (RCA, 1994)
(With the Clambake Seven) *Panic Is On* 𝄞𝄞 (Viper's Nest, 1994)
24 Gems 𝄞𝄞𝄞 (Skylark, 1994)
Sheik of Swing 𝄞𝄞𝄞 (Drive Archive, 1995)
1935–1936 𝄞𝄞𝄞 (Jazz Chronological Classics, 1995)
His Best Recordings 1928–1942 𝄞𝄞𝄞 (Best of Jazz, 1996)
1936 𝄞𝄞 (Jazz Chronological Classics, 1996)
Irish American Trombone 𝄞𝄞𝄞 (Avid, 1996)
Dance with Dorsey 𝄞𝄞𝄞 (Parade/Koch International, 1996)
The Sentimental Gentleman of Swing 𝄞𝄞𝄞 (Music Memories, 1996)
Tommy Dorsey 𝄞𝄞 (Eclipse, 1997)
Tommy Dorsey: Members Edition 𝄞𝄞 (United Audio, 1997)
1936–1937 𝄞𝄞 (Jazz Chronological Classics, 1997)
(With the Clambake Seven) *Best of Tommy Dorsey & the Clambake Seven 1936–38* 𝄞𝄞𝄞 (Challenge, 1997)
1937 𝄞𝄞 (Jazz Chronological Classics, 1997)
1936–41 Broadcasts 𝄞𝄞𝄞 (Jazz Hour, 1997)
1938–1939 in Hi-Fi Broadcasts 𝄞𝄞𝄞 (Jazz Hour, 1997)

worth searching for: Dorsey and his orchestra were at their popular peak on *One Night Stand with Tommy Dorsey* 𝄞𝄞𝄞 (Radiola, 1992), which is reflected in this spirited, live radio performance. Also, *Yes, Indeed!* 𝄞𝄞𝄞𝄞 (RCA Bluebird, 1991) focuses more on hot jazz (c. 1939–1942) than sentimental pop, and is well worth tracking down.

solo outings:
The Dorsey Brothers:
I'm Getting Sentimental Over You 𝄞𝄞 (Pro Arte, 1990)
Harlem Lullaby 𝄞𝄞𝄞 (Hep, 1994)

Live in the Big Apple 🎵🎵 (Magic, 1994)
NBC Bandstand 8/2/56 🎵🎵 (Canby, 1995)
Live in the Meadowbrook 🎵🎵 (Jazz Hour, 1995)
Mood Hollywood 🎵🎵🎵 (Hep, 1996)
Opus No. 1 🎵🎵🎵 (K-Tel, 1996)
Dorsey-itis 🎵🎵🎵🎵 (Drive Archive, 1996)
Stage Show 🎵🎵🎵 (Jazz Band, 1996)
Dorsey Brothers, Vol. 1—New York 1928 🎵🎵🎵🎵 (Jazz Oracle, 1997)
Dorsey Brothers, Vol. 2—New York 1929–1930 🎵🎵🎵 (Jazz Oracle, 1997)
1954–1956 🎵🎵🎵 (Pmf Music Factory, 1997)

influences:

⏪ Paul Whiteman, Joe Haymes, Jean Goldkette

⏩ Glenn Miller, Ziggy Elman, Sam Donahue

see also: *Jimmy Dorsey, Frank Sinatra*

Ken Burke

Mike Douglas

Born Michael Delaney Dowd Jr., August 11, 1925, in Chicago, IL.

Mike Douglas is best known as the singing host of the syndicated Cleveland (later Philadelphia) talk show that ran from the early 1960s to late 1970s. Of his contemporaries, he was a better singer than Merv Griffin or Steve Allen, a more open personality than Johnny Carson, and had a knack for getting guests to speak more honestly than Les Crane or Dick Cavett.

As a vocalist, his career began in the big-band era, and he sang under his given name for Bill Carlsen and His Band of a Million Thrills and later on Ginny Simms's radio show. After his discharge from the U.S. Navy, Dowd was discovered by bandleader Kay Kyser, who changed his name to Douglas and made him a regular on the radio program *Kay Kyser's Kollege of Musical Knowledge*. After Kyser retired in 1950, Douglas became just another show-biz foot-soldier, cutting commercial jingles, getting booked in small-time clubs, hosting a local TV show in Oklahoma City, and singing Prince Charming's part in the 1959 Disney classic *Sleeping Beauty*. Douglas began his syndicated afternoon talk/variety program in 1961, and as its popularity grew, so did interest in his singing career. In 1965, he signed with Columbia Records and began cutting nostalgic ballads, including his sole Top 10 hit, "The Men in My Little Girl's Life," rife with unashamed sentiment. After the expiration of his record contract and the cancellation of his show (good ratings, bad demographics), Douglas took some feature parts in movies, briefly hosted a show on CNN, and retired. Talk-show host Rosie O'Donnell has revived his nice-guy interviewing style,

and a highlight of her early episodes was a rare guest appearance by one of her childhood favorites: Mike Douglas.

what to buy: Douglas's career as a family-man crooner is perfectly encapsulated on *The Men in My Little Girl's Life* 🎵🎵🎵🎵 (Cleveland Int'l, 1997, prod. various), which features the title track as well "Father of the Bride," "Parents of the Kids in Love," "Is There a Baby in the House," and several other sentimental favorites purposely designed to make grown men cry.

what to buy next: Douglas sounds like he's really having fun on *You Don't Have to Be Irish* 🎵🎵🎵 (Legacy/Epic, 1995, prod. various), a nice budget disc with plenty of standards ("Danny Boy," "When Irish Eyes Are Smiling," "Those Endearing Young Charms"). Corny stuff, but would you really want it any other way?

the rest:
Men in My Little Girl's Life 🎵🎵🎵 (Collectables, 1995)

worth searching for: For an example of Douglas's big-band work, check out *Kay Kyser: Best of the Big Band* 🎵🎵🎵🎵 (Legacy, 1995, prod. various), which not only features "Ole Buttermilk Sky" and "The Old Lamplighter," but tracks by the Glee Club, the Campus Kids, and Sully Mason. Also, Douglas's trademark hit is featured on *Donna Reed's Dinner Party* 🎵🎵🎵 (Sony, 1995, prod. various), a defiantly bland compilation of hits by such easy-listening icons as Doris Day, Johnny Mathis, Percy Faith, and Andy Williams.

influences:

⏪ Bing Crosby, Dennis Day

⏩ Jack Jones, Rosie O'Donnell

Ken Burke

Robert Drasnin

Born November 17, 1927, in Charleston, WV.

Until recently, Drasnin was nothing more than a footnote in the tropical world of exotica. His lone exotic release, 1959's *Voodoo*, would become a lost masterpiece, much talked about, yet difficult to find. Drasnin's true calling was jazz. Raised in Los Angeles, he started his musical career as an alto sax player, working with the big bands of Tommy Dorsey, Les Brown, and many others. Switching to flute in the '50s, he migrated to small combo work. With the release of *Voodoo*, at the insistence of A&R chief David Pell, Drasnin flirted with exotica. His follow-up project was to arrange *Latin Village*, by the big kahuna of exotica, Martin Denny. Drasnin soon found himself music director for CBS Television, where he composed the scores to *The Hot Angel* and *The Kremlin Letter*. Today he's enjoying a revival thanks to Dionysus' CD reissue of *Voodoo*.

what's available: *Voodoo* 🎵🎵🎵 (Dionysus, 1996), while a gem, is truly an exoitc oddity. Serious jazz musicians like Robert Drasnin just didn't make exotica records, and it was considered popular kitsch. Today, though, *Voodoo* is recognized as one of the greatest exotica albums of all time.

influences:

◀◀ Martin Denny, Les Baxter, Arthur Lyman

▶▶ Combustible Edison, Don Tiki

Sam Wick

Jimmy Durante

Born February 10, 1893, in New York City, NY. Died January 29, 1980, in Santa Monica, CA.

An original in every sense of the word, Durante was a consummate showman with a huge nose, an undeniable style, and a gravelly voice, who charmed audiences to no end. He began his show-business career playing piano in Jimmy Durante's Original Jazz Novelty Band. Struggling to make a buck, Durante and some partners opened their own speakeasy, the Club Durant, where along with Lou Clayton and Eddie Jackson, he developed his comedic chops in one of the prohibition era's most popular acts. Hollywood beckoned, and Durante went West, where his trademark "shnozzola" became an icon. Among his many memorable films was 1934's *Palooka*, which marked the first time he sang his trademark tune, "Inka Dinka Doo." Durante, however, would find his biggest success in the '50s on his self-titled TV variety show, where, after an hour of slapstick and singing, he ended each night with the melancholy line, "Goodnight Mrs. Calabash, wherever you are." Durante continued to thrill TV and nightclub audiences throughout the '60s and he even had a Top 40 album of standards with 1963's "September Song." A stroke in 1970 kept Durante confined to a wheelchair until he passed away 12 days short of his 87th birthday in 1980.

what to buy: Twelve of Durante's classics are collected on *As Time Goes By: The Best of Jimmy Durante* 🎵🎵🎵🎵 (Warner Bros., 1993, prod. various), including his indelible take on the CD's title song and "September Song." No Durante collection should be without a version of his signature song "Inka Dinka Doo," which is just one of the many highlights found on *Inka Dinka Doo* 🎵🎵🎵🎵 (MCA, 1995, prod. various). Among the other

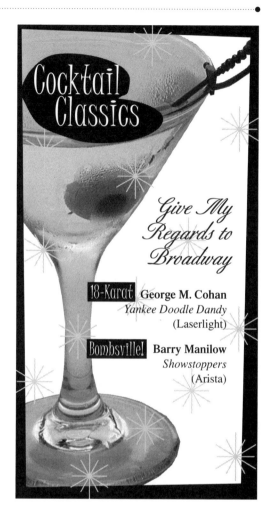

treasures is a version of "Black Strap Molasses" with Groucho Marx, Danny Kaye, and Jane Wyman.

the rest:
Club Durante 🎵🎵🎵 (Decca, 1959)
September Song 🎵🎵🎵🎵 (Warner Bros., 1963)
Patron of the Arts 🎵🎵🎵 (Vipers Nest Go, 1994)
Start Off Each Day with a Song 🎵🎵🎵 (JSP, 1994)

worth searching for: Durante's classic version of "Frosty the Snowman" (perhaps the second-best version of the song next to Leon Redbone's) shows up on *Santamental Journey: Pop Vocal Christmas Classics* 🎵🎵🎵🎵 (Rhino, 1997, prod. various)

along with required holiday fare like Bing Crosby's "White Christmas" and Jack Jones's "Jingle Bells."

influences:

◀◀ Eddie Cantor, Bing Crosby, Al Jolson

▶▶ Harry Connick Jr., Buster Poindexter

Alex Gordon

Sheena Easton

Born Sheena Shirley Orr, April 27, 1959, in Belshill, Scotland.

Like Olivia Newton-John before her, Scottish songbird Easton (who garnered the named Easton from her first marriage in 1979) has demonstrated a penchant for reinvention since her launch in 1981 with the confectionery "Morning Train (9 to 5)." That #1 song from her debut, *Sheena Easton*, was followed by the credibility-enhancing James Bond theme, "For Your Eyes Only," a Top Five hit, the spark for her 1982 Best New Artist Grammy, and still her signature track. As the decade—and popular musical tastes—evolved, so did Easton, working her way through adult-contemporary, top 40, dance, R&B, country, a funky, sexually charged stint with Prince, and even Latin dance music. As a result of such versatility (some critics termed it a lack of focus), Easton has ranked for a decade as the only artist in *Billboard* history to score Top Five hits on the magazine's five major singles charts. In all, between 1981 and 1991, she scored seven Top 10 hits and 14 Top 40 hits. Since, she has appeared alongside a new class of contemporaries in PBS television showcases and has toured nationally with the likes of Peabo Bryson, Patti Austin, and James Ingram in an ongoing adult contemporary–flavored Christmas concert. She has also played a hand in acting, with a five-episode appearance as Sonny Crocket's wife on TV's *Miami Vice* in 1987; and on Broadway with starring roles in *Man of La Mancha* alongside the late Raul Julia, and in *Grease* as Rizzo. In addition, Easton is involved in animated voiceover work and appears often in Las Vegas and Atlantic City, but has slowed considerably since the adoption of

Jimmy Durante (AP/Wide World Photos)

two children, Jake in 1994 and Skylar in 1996, and a third marriage in the summer of 1997.

what to buy: Along with her six gold or platinum pop albums, Easton's considerable vocal mettle gave her a second wind on an album of standards recorded live in a single take with a full band and orchestra, *No Strings* 𝅘𝅥𝅮𝅘𝅥𝅮𝅘𝅥𝅮𝅘𝅥𝅮 (MCA, 1993, prod. Patrice Rushen). The project, which she refers to as "a little album," includes standards like "The Nearness of You," "Someone to Watch Over Me," and "How Deep Is the Ocean."

what to buy next: For a solid review of her pop career, you can't beat *The World of Sheena Easton, The Singles Collection* 𝅘𝅥𝅮𝅘𝅥𝅮𝅘𝅥𝅮𝅘𝅥𝅮 (EMI America, 1993, prod. various), a loving and beautifully adorned package. Others showcasing particularly inspired tracks are *The Lover in Me* 𝅘𝅥𝅮𝅘𝅥𝅮𝅘𝅥𝅮𝅘𝅥𝅮 (MCA, 1989, prod. various), *Best Kept Secret* 𝅘𝅥𝅮𝅘𝅥𝅮𝅘𝅥𝅮𝅘𝅥𝅮 (EMI America, 1983, prod. Christopher Neil), *A Private Heaven* 𝅘𝅥𝅮𝅘𝅥𝅮𝅘𝅥𝅮𝅘𝅥𝅮 (EMI America, 1984, prod. Greg Mathieson), and *Madness, Money & Music* 𝅘𝅥𝅮𝅘𝅥𝅮𝅘𝅥𝅮 (EMI America, 1982, prod. Christopher Neil).

what to avoid: The outdated, overproduced *Freedom* 𝅘𝅥𝅮 (MCA Japan, 1997, prod. various) is (fortunately) available only in Japan or on Easton's Web site, www.sheenaeaston.com.

the rest:

Sheena Easton 𝅘𝅥𝅮𝅘𝅥𝅮𝅘𝅥𝅮 (EMI America, 1981)
You Could Have Been with Me 𝅘𝅥𝅮𝅘𝅥𝅮𝅘𝅥𝅮 (EMI America, 1982)
Do You 𝅘𝅥𝅮𝅘𝅥𝅮𝅘𝅥𝅮 (EMI America, 1985)
No Sound but a Heart 𝅘𝅥𝅮𝅘𝅥𝅮 (EMI America, 1987)
The Best of Sheena Easton 𝅘𝅥𝅮𝅘𝅥𝅮𝅘𝅥𝅮𝅘𝅥𝅮 (EMI America, 1989)

worth searching for: Easton visited the Latin charts in 1984 in a Grammy-winning duet with Luis Miguel, from her hard-to-find album *Todo Me Recuerda a Ti* 𝅘𝅥𝅮𝅘𝅥𝅮𝅘𝅥𝅮 (Capitol/EMI Latin, 1984, prod. Greg Mathieson, Juan Carlos Calderon, Christopher Neil). Her other out-of-print LPs include *What Comes Naturally* 𝅘𝅥𝅮𝅘𝅥𝅮 (MCA, 1991, prod. various) and *My Cherie* 𝅘𝅥𝅮𝅘𝅥𝅮𝅘𝅥𝅮 (MCA, 1995, prod. various).

influences:

◀◀ Barbra Streisand, Prince, Babyface

▶▶ Celia Cruz, Gloria Estefan

Chuck Taylor

Clint Eastwood

Born May 31, 1930, in San Francisco, CA.

As a vocalist, the Oscar-winning actor is only slightly less tone-deaf than, say, Burt Reynolds, but his contributions as a pro-

ducer outweigh his shortcomings before the microphone. In 1963, Eastwood made his singing debut with an LP of cowboy songs meant to cash in on his fame as Rowdy Yates on the TV series *Rawhide.* His slightly off-kilter light baritone sounded heavily tutored but showed little in the way of expressive ability. Six years later, Eastwood listlessly warbled "I Talk to the Trees" in the Hollywood musical mega-flop *Paint Your Wagon,* and showed little improvement. Once he established his production company, Malpaso, Eastwood took greater control over the music in his films, one of which, *Any Which Way You Can,* provided him with "Barroom Buddies," a hit duet with country legend Merle Haggard. Hag was clearly carrying Eastwood, whose presence gave the record some novelty value. Though he was a longtime jazz buff, country music seemed to fit Eastwood's image best, and he eventually recorded some mildly popular duets with T.G. Sheppard and Randy Travis (who weren't as shy about outsinging the screen star as Haggard had been). The film *Honkytonk Man* provided Eastwood his best chance to gain acceptance as a vocalist, but his clenched Dirty Harry–style crooning made it hard for audiences to believe they were seeing a film about a man who actually made his living as a singer. As a producer, Eastwood has expressed his longtime love of music with much more style and taste. The soundtrack LPs he has issued for such films as *Bird,* the Johnny Hartman–dominated *Bridges of Madison County,* and *Midnight in the Garden of Good and Evil* are consistently diverting and have generally garnered better reviews than their respective films.

what to buy: Eastwood lines up some great tunes and talent for the soundtrack to *Midnight in the Garden of Good and Evil* 𝄞𝄞𝄞𝄞 (Malpaso Records, 1997, prod. Clint Eastwood, Matt Pierson). Tracks by such artists as Tony Bennett, k.d. lang, Alison Krauss, and Rosemary Clooney are effectively mixed in with those by cast member Kevin Spacey and Cassandra Wilson. Eastwood himself takes a not unpleasant turn on "Ac-cent-tchu-ate the Positive."

what to buy next: Eastwood did a fine job anthologizing jazz old and new on *Bird* 𝄞𝄞𝄞 (CBC, 1990, prod. Clint Eastwood, Lennie Niehaus), the soundtrack to the Charlie Parker biopic he directed. Parker's scorching alto sax never sounded better, and anything that introduces "Ko Ko" to new audiences merits a listen.

what to avoid: Don't be misled. Eastwood doesn't contribute anything (except inspiration) to Derek Wadsworth & the City of

Prague Philharmonic's *Music from the Films of Clint Eastwood* 𝄞𝄞𝄞 (Silva America, 1994) or *Western Movie Themes from Clint Eastwood Movies* 𝄞𝄞 (K-Tel, 1995). They're just cashing in on his name.

the rest:
The Bridges of Madison County 𝄞𝄞𝄞 (Malpaso Records, 1996)
Remembering Madison County 𝄞𝄞 (Malpaso Records, 1996)

worth searching for: If for whatever reason you absolutely must own a disc of Clint Eastwood singing (to ward off bugs or convince people to recalibrate their stereo equipment), Eastwood actually turns in a decent vocal performance on the soundtrack of his movie *Honkytonk Man* 𝄞𝄞𝄞 (Malpaso Records, 1982, prod. Clint Eastwood), the story of a 1930s country singer wracked with tuberculosis. Also, Eastwood sings "Make My Day" with country star T.G. Sheppard on *Best of T.G. Sheppard* 𝄞𝄞𝄞 (Curb, 1992, prod. various), and "Smokin' the Hive" with Randy Travis on *Heroes & Friends* 𝄞𝄞𝄞 (Warner Bros., 1990, prod. Kyle Lehning).

influences:

◀◀ John Wayne, Lee Marvin

▶▶ Nick Nolte, Burt Reynolds

Ken Burke

Easy Tunes

Formed 1996, in Amsterdam, Holland.

Richard Cameron, samplers, programmers; Gerry Arling, samplers, programmers.

With the slogan "introducing the sound of now," Easy Tunes—and its numerous pseudonymous groups, including Easy Sisters, Easy Alohas, Ca Va, Constellation 69, and Gay Fantasy Express—have quickly become Holland's finest export in lounge music and culture. A collective stable fronted by two people, the band created several terms—such as "popcorn," which means a bouncy, danceable branch of lounge music—that have caught on in its home country. Since founding Easy Tunes, Cameron has collaborated with Pizzicato Five (on 1997's *Happy End of the World*) and earned his stripes as one of the globe's most popular cocktail DJs (along with the Karminskys, Stereo de Luxe, and Lucien Samaha).

what to buy: *Best of Easy Tunes* 𝄞𝄞𝄞𝄞 (Outland, 1996, prod. Richard Cameron, Gerry Arling) is essential listening if you want see where lounge culture is heading. Moving from '70s blaxploitation-movie cheese (Gay Fantasy Express's "Beachboy") to

Sheena Easton (© Ken Settle)

bossa-nova beats (Horst Jansen's "Happy Bossa") to disco exotica (Easy Alohas' "Aloha!"), the fun never stops.

what to buy next: As *All-In* ♫♫♫ (Readymade, 1997, prod. Richard Cameron, Gerry Arling) proves, nothing says "jet-set" like international voiceovers, and the songs here are in German ("Ein Abend in Wein"), Japanese ("Here We Go"), and French ("Voulez-Vouz").

the rest:
Easy Tune, Vol. 1 ♫♫♫♫ EP (Outland, 1996)
Easy Tune, Vol. 3 ♫♫♫ EP (Outland, 1996)
Easy Tune, Vol. 4 ♫♫♫ EP (Outland, 1996)
Popcorn ♫♫♥ (Outland, 1996)

influences:
◀◀ Pizzicato Five

▶▶ Fantastic Plastic Machine, Stereo Total, Dimitri from Paris

Sam Wick

Billy Eckstine

Born William Clarence Eckstine, July 8, 1914, in Pittsburgh, PA. Died March 8, 1993, in Pittsburgh, PA.

Often considered a groundbreaker for black vocalists, Eckstine cut a racial swath through America even before Nat "King" Cole came to the scene. He was one of the very first African American matinee idols, singing first for Earl Hines's orchestra, then veering off with his own band in 1943. Besides making a name for himself, he helped launch the careers of Charlie Parker, Sarah Vaughan, and Dizzy Gillespie by recommending that Hines hire them for the band. Eckstine's deep baritone is immediately arresting, and he was also known for his ability to play trumpet, guitar, and trombone—which he often did on his many tours of Europe and Australia. Between 1949 and 1952, he had a dozen tunes hit the charts—some of them in the top 10—and soon thereafter secured a lucrative contract with MGM. In the meantime, he became well known for being a keen scout of young talent; he gave jobs to a young Miles Davis, Art Blakey, Dexter Gordon, and Lena Horne, among others, paving the way for a generation of bop performers to surface. Eckstine's mass appeal wore off in the mid-1950s, although he continued his career overseas, doing all-star jazz gigs and club acts.

what to buy: *At Basin Street East* ♫♫♫♫♫ (Mercury, 1962/1990) is a terrific re-release of some original sessions with Eckstine and a young Quincy Jones. If for nothing else, buy it for the superb recordings of "Caravan" and "Sophisticated Lady." Ecks-

tine resurfaced in the 1980s with *Billy Eckstine Sings with Benny Carter* ♫♫♫♫ (Verve, 1986, prod. Kiyoshi Koyama), a surprisingly energetic album that took jazz observers by surprise and even snagged a Grammy nomination. Eckstine is likely to appeal to lovers of robust swing ballads—in the mode of Johnny Hartman—and is unlikely to disappoint.

what to buy next: *Mister B and the Band* ♫♫♫♫ (Denon, 1947/1995, prod. Herb Abramson) puts Eckstine alongside Miles Davis and Dexter Gordon, just as the two bop players were hitting their stride—a can't-miss purchase. *No Cover, No Minimum* ♫♫♫♫ (Blue Note, 1992), a nice collection of jazz standards, like "Lush Life" and "Till There Was You," makes a perfect introduction into Eckstine's world. With Bobby Tucker on piano.

best of the rest:
Billy and Sarah ♫♫♫♫ (Lion, 1959)
Basie and Eckstine, Inc. ♫♫♫♫ (Roulette, 1959)

worth searching for: The British import *Boppin with B* ♫♫♫ (Indigo, 1997) isn't a bad album by any means, but it's not on a par with other available Eckstine albums. It features a more obscure mix of songs.

influences:
◀◀ Louis Armstrong

▶▶ Nat "King" Cole, Sarah Vaughan, Frank Sinatra, Joe Williams, Johnny Hartman

Carl Quintanilla

Nelson Eddy

Born June 29, 1901, in Providence, RI. Died March 6, 1967, in Miami Beach, FL.

Though he's been dead more than 30 years, Eddy remains an important figure in American music; along with Jeanette MacDonald, he created the Hollywood model of the onscreen singing team. Baritone Eddy, whose training was mostly in light opera and stage singing, was first paired with ex–chorus girl MacDonald for the 1935 MGM film version of the operetta *Naughty Marietta*. The partnership proved hugely successful, and the two "Singing Sweethearts" (who in fact did not get along offscreen) made eight films together and produced such hits as "Indian Love Call" and "Rose Marie." In 1942, the pair broke up, and without his more appealing half, Eddy's career never fully recovered. A midlevel radio, television, and stage performer for the next 25 years, he died onstage of a stroke at a Miami Beach hotel.

what to buy: *The Artistry of Nelson Eddy: Popular Songs Adapted from Classical Music* ♫♫♫♫ (Sony, 1992) has an interesting concept—it takes songs like "Tonight We Love," "Lamp Is Low," and "Stranger in Paradise," and it matches them with their classical precursors. Eddy's deep voice anchors the project.

what to buy next: *Rose Marie* ♫♫♫♈ (Pro Arte, 1989) is unapologetically nostalgic, like everything else about Eddy's career. But if you want to hear "Song of the Volga Boatmen," "Ah! Sweet Mystery of Life," or "By the Waters of Minnetonka" sung in the old musical theater style, look no further.

what to avoid: *In the Still of the Night* ♫♫♈ (Laserlight, 1995) is a cheap repackaging of Eddy standards, including "Rosalie," "It Ain't Necessarily So," and "That Great Come and Get It Day."

the rest:
Greatest Hits ♫♫♫♈ (Sony, 1992)

influences:

◀◀ Fred Astaire, Ginger Rogers

▶▶ Robert Goulet, Richard Harris

Ben Greenman

Jonathan & Darlene Edwards
See: Jo Stafford, Paul Weston

Tommy Edwards
Born February 17, 1922, in Richmond, VA. Died October 22, 1969, in Henrico County, VA.

Edwards was a singer-pianist with a velvety smooth vocal style in the Nat King Cole/Ivory Joe Hunter mode. He started entertaining around Richmond at age nine, and eventually played piano and sang on his own radio program. After writing Louis Jordan's hit "That Chick's Too Young to Fry," Edwards moved to New York City in 1949, where he worked performing demos of other writers' songs and cut his first unsuccessful sides for the Top label. His move to MGM in 1950 yielded his first R&B chart entries, "All Over Again" and "The Morning Side of the Mountain." Seven years passed without a hit, but then Edwards added a pop-rock arrangement to a song he had first recorded in 1951, "It's All in the Game." Besides being the only #1 hit ever co-written by a former U.S. Vice President (Charles Dawes, who served under Calvin Coolidge), the 1958 easy-listening single "It's All in the Game" was one of the few records of the rock 'n' roll era that both kids and parents could agree on. Edwards followed up with a series of lesser hits such as "Please Love Me

Forever" (which Bobby Vinton later covered), "Love Is All We Need," "Please Mr. Sun," and "New in the Ways of Love." Then he turned to country: 1960's "I Really Don't Want to Know," "Don't Fence Me In," and "It's Not the End of Everything" were as smooth and affecting as anything he had ever done, but subsequent releases faltered. Experimental LPs, featuring Hawaiian and string-oriented sounds, did nothing to reverse his downward career spiral.

what to buy: All of Edwards's best known MGM sides are on *It's All in the Game: The Complete Hits of Tommy Edwards* ♫♫♫♈ (Eric Collections, 1995, prod. various), a nice 20-track helping of romantic pleading.

what to buy next: Cheaper and easier to get is *It's All in the Game* ♫♫♫ (PolyGram Special Products, 1996, prod. various), which features the title track, "Love Is All We Need."

worth searching for: Edwards sings his #1 hit, "It's All in the Game," live on *The Sullivan Years: Rock 'n' Roll Pioneers* ♫♫♫ (TVT, 1993, prod. Steve Gottleib, Oscar A. Young), a 17-track sampling of '50s rockers, such as Jerry Lee Lewis and Buddy Holly, who appeared on Ed Sullivan's TV variety hour. Drawn mostly from kinescopes, the sound quality on these tracks is a little thin, but their historical value is immense. Fun, too.

influences:

◄◄ Louis Jordan, Nat "King" Cole, Ivory Joe Hunter

►► Jesse Belvin, Carl Dobkins Jr., Bobby Vinton

Ken Burke

Danny Elfman

Born May 19, 1953, in Los Angeles, CA.

Like all great movie music, the spooky-and-playful instrumentals written by Danny Elfman have become almost as distinctive as the vivid characters they surround. The former Oingo Boingo rock singer—best known for his whining, Cure-like vocals on the hit "Dead Man's Party," which still gets plenty of jukebox time every Halloween—went solo in the mid-'80s and immediately established himself as an important soundtrack artist. Borrowing ideas from the quirky, experimental orchestras of '40s big bandleader Raymond Scott, Elfman created instantly memorable scores. When Pee-wee Herman knocks on the evil Francis's door in *Pee-wee's Big Adventure* to find his stolen bike, Elfman's staccato bursts fall in behind him. When Bart Simpson leaps out of nowhere on a skateboard at the beginning of *The Simpsons* credits every week, Elfman's merry-go-round arrangements swirl around him. His darker material, in *Nightmare before Christmas, Batman Returns,* and *Edward Scissorhands,* similarly fits those films' surreal moods. In an age when most movie music either follows a generic formula or simply stitches together a handful of already-familiar rock songs, Elfman's style and inventiveness refreshingly recall John Barry and Ennio Morricone in their prime.

what to buy: It's too bad film soundtracks, because of consumer whims and the realities of the movie business, go out of print with such regularity. As a result, it's frequently difficult to scare up a decent copy of the original *Pee-wee's Big Adventure* soundtrack, which is terrific party music. Fortunately, the best snippets of that score—minus the repetition, which is a good

thing—appear on Elfman's *Music for a Darkened Theatre: Film and Television Music, Vol. 1* ♫♫♫♫ (MCA, 1990, prod. Richard Kraft, Bob Badami), along with *The Simpsons, Dick Tracy,* and *Batman* themes. Much darker and almost as good is the follow-up, *Music for a Darkened Theatre: Film and Television Music, Vol. 2* ♫♫♫♫ (MCA, 1996, prod. Ellen Segal, Danny Elfman), which has familiar music from *Edward Scissorhands, Nightmare before Christmas,* and the late, lamented children's television show, *Pee-wee's Playhouse.*

what to buy next: Until Oingo Boingo's career ended with the thudding sound of 1994's terrible album, *Boingo,* Elfman was more memorable as leader of a Los Angeles rock band than as a wacko film composer. The compilation *Best O'Boingo* ♫♫♫ (A&M, 1991, prod. various) contains "Dead Man's Party," of course, along with the band's other spooky and danceable hits.

what to avoid: *Boingo* ♫♫ (Giant, 1994, prod. John Avila, Steve Bartek, Danny Elfman) was a totally unmemorable attempt to regenerate buzz for a pooped-out '80s band. Though some of Elfman's twisted experimentation is interesting to hear—once—there's really nothing salvageable here.

the rest:

So Lo ♫♫♫ (MCA, 1984)

worth searching for: *Pee-wee's Big Adventure/Back to School* ♫♫♫ (Varese Sarabande, 1985, prod. various) packages Elfman's finest movie soundtrack with average music for an average Rodney Dangerfield movie whose only distinction is the prominent use of Oingo Boingo's "Dead Man's Party."

influences:

◄◄ Raymond Scott, Carl Stalling, Frank Zappa, Camper Van Beethoven, the Cure, John Barry

►► Morrissey, Pee-wee Herman, Presidents of the United States of America

Steve Knopper

Larry Elgart

See: Les Elgart

Les Elgart

Born August 3, 1918, in New Haven, CT.

In the context of big bands, Elgart was a talented role player, a lead trumpeter with personality who also knew exactly how to plug into a swinging horn section. But after playing in the early 1940s with such bandleaders as Harry James and Woody Herman, he formed his own band and really developed a style. El-gart and his saxophonist brother, Larry, played swing music rooted in pop-jazz tradition but playfully willing to adapt to popular dance fads, most notably the twist. The Les Elgart Band, formed in 1953 and intensely popular on college campuses, produced lounge-ready, finger-tapping music like "Frenesi-Twist" well into the 1960s.

what to buy: Though Elgart's many studio albums haven't quite seen the reissue renaissance of his better-known forebears, such as Benny Goodman and Harry James, *Best of the Big Bands: Sophisticated Swing* ✍✍✍✍ (Sony, 1992, prod. George Avakian) is an excellent recollection of the bandleader's 1953 and 1954 New York City sessions. (Among the twisty gems: "The Weasel Pops Off," "Sophisticated Lady," and "Senior Hop.")

the rest:

Elgart Touch/For Dancers Also ✍✍✍ (Collectors Choice, 1996)

worth searching for: The 18-song collection *Cocktail Mix, Vol. 2: Martini Madness* ✍✍✍✍ (Rhino, 1996, prod. Janet Grey) unites big-band, mambo, cha-cha-cha, classic pop, and R&B within the "martini music" context; Elgart's lightheaded "Frenesi-Twist" fits snugly among Perez Prado's bouncy Latin jazz and Connie Francis's sophisticated bossa nova.

influences:

◀◀ Duke Ellington, Benny Goodman, Glenn Miller, Nelson Riddle, Chubby Checker

▶▶ Ray Conniff, Perez Prado, Enoch Light, Steve Allen

Steve Knopper

Duke Ellington

Born Edward Kennedy Ellington, April 29, 1899, in Washington, DC. Died May 24, 1974, in New York, NY.

If you haven't heard of Duke Ellington, you were obviously placed in suspended animation in the 19th century and were unfrozen yesterday. Even people who listen to Muzak all day long and never know the names of the composers who penned the pasteurized tunes know who Duke Ellington is. Ellington is quite possibly the greatest musician and composer of the 20th century—certainly one of the top five. As a composer, he wrote thousands of songs and arranged and rearranged those and others his whole life. He wrote his songs for the individual musicians in his orchestra and not for "sections." As a bandleader, he performed nearly constantly for most of his career. As a musician, he was a giant, considered one of the best pianists of his era. And unlike most of his contemporaries, he was able to

update his work, modernizing it to blend into the sound of the decade in which he was creating. Ellington's orchestra was his main vehicle, and he worked with "his" orchestra—though it changed constantly—throughout his career, recording more than 200 albums, currently available, with more collections and newly reissued work coming out annually, as if he hadn't died in 1974.

He started studying the piano at age seven, adopting the nickname "Duke" around the same time. Every one of his family friends knew he was destined to be great. Drawn by the ragtime music of the time, he became a musician. Ellington joined the music world in 1917 with the biggest ad in the telephone Yellow Pages and a desire to be a bandleader despite his then-limited repertoire. The ad worked, and he was soon heading up several Washington, D.C.–area bands. He worked on his technique by analyzing fingering from slowed-down piano rolls. In 1923, he ventured to New York and soon formed the Washingtonians with friends. He landed the band a job at the Hollywood Club, where they began to play regularly and where Bubber Miley helped Ellington create the "jungle sound" that made his group distinct. After some struggles to find the right sound or breakthrough music, Duke Ellington and His Orchestra was born around 1926 with hot numbers like "East St. Louis Toodleoo" and "Birmingham Breakdown." The very next year, the group scored its break, earning a permanent spot at the Cotton Club on the strength of numbers such as "Black and Tan Fantasy" and "Creole Love Call." From there Ellington and crew began radio broadcasts and became famous throughout the country. By the time the Great Depression struck, Ellington had found the road to success so that hardship did not really affect him. He never again lacked work or suffered through hard times. He was a celebrity and one of the greatest performers in the world. During the 1930s, he built his band up with eight soloists—most bands didn't even have three—and left the Cotton Club in 1931 for greener pastures. The Ellington Orchestra hit the road and became a big act throughout the country and soon throughout the world, touring Europe and Sweden in 1933 and 1939. By 1940, Duke Ellington's Orchestra was the greatest in the world, featuring newly acquired musicians like Ben Webster on tenor sax, Jimmy Blanton on bass, and Billy Strayhorn as an arranger and composer—all of whom, like many of the musicians who worked with Ellington, would go on to become some of the greatest names in jazz music. His 1940–42 band was one of his best, and Ellington added many songs to his repertoire during those years that would become lifelong standards—"Take the 'A' Train," "Perdido," and "The 'C' Jam Blues," among others. Ellington gave his first performance at Carnegie Hall in 1943, debuting "Black, Brown, and Beige." As the 1940s killed the big bands and bebop rose to prominence, Ellington continued to perform, tour, and record with his orchestra. The 1950s is considered his "slump" decade, even though his artistic output was never stronger, and it was simply the illusion of waning commercial success. In 1956, Duke soared back into the spotlight at the Newport Jazz Festival. During the 1960s, Duke dabbled in religious music and collaborated with jazz greats who had not started under his wing, including Charles Mingus, Max Roach, Count Basie, John Coltrane, and Louis Armstrong. Ellington continued to tour and record extensively throughout the 1960s despite his age and received the recognition he so richly deserved. He outlasted many of his closest working partners, including Billy Strayhorn and Johnny Hodges, and he continued making music despite the deaths of his associates and friends, updating the orchestra and persevering until 1974 when, stricken with cancer, he died a month after his 75th birthday. With Duke Ellington's passing, one of the greatest musicians of the 20th century was lost to the world. Ironically, though he is one of the most widely known artists, there is still much that is unknown about the man personally. He was reticent to speak about his life, and he is conspicuously absent as a character in his own autobiography, *Music Is My Mistress*. Ellington was an even-tempered man, some said almost saintly in demeanor. Even in the face of obvious prejudice—for example, when the Pulitzer Prize committee of 1965 denied him a special lifetime achievement award, overruling its own official judges—Ellington was unphased, saying, "Fate doesn't want me to be famous too young." He was 66 years old when he said that.

what to buy: Ellington and his orchestra performed all over the world, thousands of times. And though each performance couldn't be the greatest ever, there were nights when the crew reached a unique level of inspiration and craft. *All Star Road Band, Vol. 2* 🎵🎵🎵🎵 (Signature, 1957/CBS Special Products, 1990) is one such occasion. At a dance one evening in Chicago in 1964, Ellington and his orchestra rocked the hall and tried out some new arrangements of the standards. He got superb solo work from trumpeters Cootie Williams and Cat Anderson, trombonists Lawrence Brown and Buster Cooper, and the entire saxophone section. Ellington revitalized his career with *Ellington at Newport* 🎵🎵🎵🎵 (Columbia, 1956/1987, prod. George Avakian), a big commercial comeback for the musician. "Diminuendo and Crescendo in Blue" was one of the concert's most intense tunes, and the 27-chorus blues marathon solo by Paul Gonsalves drove the audience wild, so much so that there was

nearly a riot. Ellington made worldwide news as a result and was back on top of the music world.

what to buy next: *All Star Road Band* 🎵🎵🎵🎵 (Signature, 1964/1989) is not as wild as Vol. 2, but it's enjoyable and fun and includes Ellington's best standards, such as "Take the 'A' Train," "Mood Indigo," and "Sophisticated Lady." Then, if you're looking for a good sampler of the Duke's works, try *Compact Jazz: And Friends* 🎵🎵🎵🎵 (Verve, 1987, prod. Norman Granz), a hot collection with a variety of the best of jazz and blues musicians working with Ellington, including Ella Fitzgerald, Ben Webster, Johnny Hodges, Oscar Peterson, and Dizzy Gillespie. *The 1952 Seattle Concert* 🎵🎵🎵🎵 (RCA, 1954/1995, prod. Jack Lewis) is another fine live recording, with great backup and impressive versions of "Skin Deep," "Sultry Serenade," "Sophisticated Lady," and "Perdido," not to mention a sublime rendering of "Harlem Suite."

what to avoid: There's really no bad Ellington. But when it comes to collections, there are some that are clearly not the best places to start. *16 Most Requested Songs* 🎵🎵🎵 (Columbia/Legacy, 1994, prod. various) is just too incomplete to serve as an introduction to his career.

best of the rest:

Duke Ellington Presents . . . 🎵🎵🎵🎵 (Bethlehem, 1956/1995)

Ellington Jazz Party 🎵🎵🎵🎵 (Columbia, 1959)

Paris Blues 🎵🎵🎵 (Original Soundtrack) (MGM, 1961/Rykodisc, 1998)

The Great Paris Concert 🎵🎵🎵🎵 (Atlantic, 1963/1989)

(With Ray Brown) *This One's for Blanton—Duets* 🎵🎵🎵🎵 (Original Jazz Classics, 1972/1994)

Duke's Big Four 🎵🎵🎵🎵 (Pablo, 1973/1988)

Duke Ellington: The Blanton-Webster Band, 1939–1942 🎵🎵🎵🎵 (Bluebird, 1986)

(With Coleman Hawkins) *Duke Ellington Meets Coleman Hawkins* 🎵🎵🎵🎵 (MCA, 1986)

(With Johnny Hodges) *Side by Side* 🎵🎵🎵🎵 (Verve, 1986)

Money Jungle—1962 🎵🎵🎵🎵 (Blue Note, 1986)

(With Count Basie) *First Time: The Count Meets the Duke–1961* 🎵🎵🎵🎵 (Columbia, 1987)

Uptown—Early 1950s 🎵🎵🎵🎵 (Columbia, 1987)

The Duke Ellington Orchestra: Digital Duke 🎵🎵🎵🎵 (GRP, 1987)

Walkman Jazz/Compact Jazz 🎵🎵🎵🎵 (Verve, 1988)

Black, Brown & Beige 1944–46 🎵🎵🎵🎵 (Bluebird, 1988)

Blues in Orbit—1960 🎵🎵🎵🎵 (Columbia, 1988)

Duke Ellington & John Coltrane 🎵🎵🎵🎵 (MCA/Impulse!, 1988)

The Piano Album 🎵🎵🎵🎵 (Capitol, 1989)

Braggin' in Brass: The Immortal 1938 Year 🎵🎵🎵🎵 (Portrait Masters, 1989)

Ellington Indigos: Sept.–Oct. 1957 🎵🎵🎵🎵 (Columbia, 1989)

The Private Collection, Vols. 1–4 🎵🎵🎵🎵 (Saja, 1989)

Duke Ellington **(Archive Photos)**

The Private Collection, Vol. 5: "The Suites" 1968 🎵🎵🎵🎵 (Saja, 1989)

The Private Collection, Vols. 6-10: Dance Dates, California, 1958 🎵🎵🎵🎵 (Saja, 1989)

The Best of Duke Ellington 🎵🎵🎵🎵 (Signature, 1989)

New Mood Indigo 🎵🎵🎵🎵 (Signature, 1989)

Solos, Duets & Trios 🎵🎵🎵🎵 (Bluebird, 1990)

The Jungle Band: The Brunswick Era, Vol. 2 (1929–1931) 🎵🎵🎵🎵 (Decca Jazz, 1990)

The Intimacy of the Blues 1967 & 1970 🎵🎵🎵🎵 (Fantasy, 1991)

1924–1927 🎵🎵🎵🎵 (Classics, 1991)

Up in Duke's Workshop—1969–1972 🎵🎵🎵🎵 (Fantasy, 1991)

The Essence of Duke Ellington: I Like Jazz 🎵🎵🎵🎵 (Columbia, 1991)

Duke Ellington's My People 🎵🎵🎵🎵 (Red Baron, 1992)

Sophisticated Lady: Masters of the Big Bands 🎵🎵🎵🎵 (Bluebird, 1992)

Duke Ellington & His Orchestra: Jazz Cocktail: 1928–1931 🎵🎵🎵🎵 (ASV Living Era, 1992)

Live at the Blue Note—1952 🎵🎵🎵🎵 (Bandstand, 1992)

Duke Ellington, Vol. 4: 1928 🎵🎵🎵🎵 (MA Recordings, 1992)

The Pianist 1966, 1970 🎵🎵🎵🎵 (Fantasy, 1992)

1937 w/Chick Webb 🎵🎵🎵🎵 (Classics, 1993)

Original Hits, Vol. 1: 1927–31 🎵🎵🎵🎵 (King Jazz, 1993)

Original Hits, Vol. 2: 1931–38 🎵🎵🎵🎵 (King Jazz, 1993)

The Great London Concerts—1964 🎵🎵🎵🎵 (MusicMasters, 1993)

Duke Ellington and His Orchestra—1938, Vol. 2 🎵🎵🎵🎵 (Classics, 1993)

Duke Ellington and His Orchestra—1938, Vol. 3 🎵🎵🎵🎵 (Classics, 1993)

In the Twenties—Jazz Archives No. 63 🎵🎵🎵🎵 (EPM, 1993)

Things Ain't What They Used to Be 🎵🎵🎵🎵 (LRC, 1993)

Things Ain't What They Used to Be/S.R.O. 🎵🎵🎵🎵 (LRC, 1993)

Live at the Rainbow Grill 🎵🎵🎵🎵 (Moon/FTC, 1993)

Mood Indigo 🎵🎵🎵🎵 (EPM Musique, 1994)

Live at the Blue Note 🎵🎵🎵🎵 (Roulette Jazz, 1994)

Black, Brown & Beige—Mastersound Series 🎵🎵🎵🎵 (Columbia, 1994)

Duke Ellington, 1938–1939 🎵🎵🎵🎵 (Classics, 1994)

Duke Ellington, Vol. 2: Swing 1930–1938 🎵🎵🎵🎵 (ABC Music, 1994)

Duke Ellington & His Orchestra Live at Newport—1958 🎵🎵🎵🎵 (Columbia/Legacy, 1994)

Uptown Downbeat w/His Orchestra: Cotton Club, Jungle Band—1927–1940 🎵🎵🎵🎵 (Empire/Avid, 1995)

Satin Doll, 1958–1959 🎵🎵🎵🎵 (Jazz Time, 1995)

Duke Ellington, 1924–1930—Box Set 🎵🎵🎵🎵 (Classics 6, 1995)

From the Blue Note—Chicago 1952 ✍✍✍✍ (Musicdisc, 1995)

In a Mellotone—1940–1944 ✍✍✍✍ (RCA, 1995)

70th Birthday Concert—Nov. 1969 ✍✍✍✍ (Blue Note, 1995)

Live at the Whitney: April 10, 1972 ✍✍✍✍ (MCA/Impulse!, 1995)

The Cornell University Concert—December 1948 ✍✍✍✍ (MusicMasters, 1995)

New York Concert: In Performance at Columbia University—1964 ✍✍✍✍ (MusicMasters, 1995)

Duke Ellington & His Great Vocalists ✍✍✍✍ (Legacy, 1995)

The Best of Duke Ellington ✍✍✍✍ (Blue Note, 1995)

Duke Ellington & John Coltrane with Jimmy Garrison, Aaron Bell, etc., Recorded September 1962 ✍✍✍✍ (MCA/Impulse!, 1995)

Duke Ellington: Greatest Hits ✍✍✍✍ (RCA, 1996)

Ellingtonia ✍✍✍✍ (Fat Boy, 1996)

This Is Jazz ✍✍✍✍ (Columbia, 1996)

Vol. 4: The Mooche, 1928 ✍✍✍✍ (EPM Musique, 1996)

Vol. 5: Harlemania, 1928–1929 ✍✍✍✍ (EPM Musique, 1996)

Vol. 6: Cotton Club Stomp ✍✍✍✍ (EPM Musique, 1996)

Vol. 9: Mood Indigo—1930 ✍✍✍✍ (EPM Musique, 1996)

Vol. 10: Rockin' in Rhythm, 1930–31 ✍✍✍✍ (EPM, 1996)

Sophisticated Lady—1941–1949 ✍✍✍✍ (Vocal Jazz, 1996)

Ellington at Basin Street East: The Complete Concert of 14 January 1964 ✍✍✍✍ (Music & Arts, 1996)

Rockin' In Rhythm, 1958–1959 ✍✍✍✍ (Jazz Hour, 1996)

Duke Ellington at the Cotton Club—1938, Band Remotes from Harlem ✍✍✍✍ (Sandy Hook)

1941: The Jimmy Blanton/Ben Webster Transcriptions ✍✍✍✍ (VJC)

Duke Ellington & His Famous Orchestra: Fargo, North Dakota, Nov. 7, 1940 ✍✍✍✍ (VJC)

Duke Ellington & His Famous Orchestra: Hollywood, CA—Jan.–Dec. 1941 ✍✍✍✍ (VJC)

The Complete Capitol Recordings of Duke Ellington, 1953–1955 ✍✍✍✍ (Mosaic)

Second Sacred Concert—1968 ✍✍✍✍ (Prestige)

New Orleans Suite—1970 ✍✍✍✍ (Atlantic)

Lullaby of Birdland ✍✍✍✍ (Intermedia)

(With Billy Strayhorn) Great Times ✍✍✍✍ (Fantasy)

worth searching for: Ellington didn't do very much work with the movies, but his out-of-print soundtrack for *Anatomy of a Murder* ✍✍✍✍ (Anadisq, 1959/Rykodisc, 1987) fit the story and movie perfectly and is one of the very best soundtracks of the era, as well as a good stand-alone album. Dave Grusin's *Homage to Duke* ✍✍✍✍ (GRP, 1993) is a great collection of different interpretations of Ellington tunes by one of the masters of contemporary light jazz.

influences:

◀◀ Fats Waller, James P. Johnson, Sidney Bechet, Willie "The Lion" Smith

▶▶ Thelonious Monk, Cecil Taylor, Count Basie, Quincy Jones, Gil Evans, Fletcher Henderson, Sun Ra, Maurice White

Chris Tower

Cass Elliot

Born Ellen Naomi Cohen, November 29, 1941, in Halifax, Nova Scotia, Canada. Died July 29, 1974, in London, England.

At the time of her death, Cass Elliot was in the process of changing her professional persona from that of a '60s flower child/earth mother to an all-round entertainer and cabaret stylist. Early on, her voice could be heard soaring above the mix in such erstwhile folk groups as the Big Three and the Mugwumps. As part of the Mamas & the Papas, Elliot was able to establish herself as both a potent aspect of the group's rich harmony sound ("I Saw Her Again Last Night," "Go Where You Wanna Go," "I Call Your Name") and as a romantic lead voice ("Words of Love," "Dream a Little Dream of Me"). Moreover, her ability to convincingly interpret a mix of old-time Tin Pan Alley and idealistic folk/pop tunes allowed her to build a fan base as an individual, something that eluded other group members (in particular, one of the finest voices of the '60s, "Papa" Denny Doherty). Elliot's solo hits ("Make Your Own Kind of Music," "It's Getting Better") featured her old group's production style and were credited to "Mama" Cass, an identity she found distasteful, but held on to for publicity purposes. When folk-pop went out of vogue, Elliot sought to rock harder, cutting a pretty fair LP with Traffic's Dave Mason, and several never released tracks with Electric Flag. Sales fell off, and the early '70s found Elliot nearly broke and without career direction. Taking a cue from her friend Cher, she began tailoring her recordings for hipper middle-of-the-road audiences and glitzing up her stage persona. Fans loved her new glamorous image because they sensed Elliot's honest personality and humor underneath. (When referring to her garish stage attire, the overweight Elliot often quipped, "If you can't hide it—decorate it!") Though she ceased scoring with hit singles, Elliot's kiss-off of her famous nickname ("Don't Call Me Mama Anymore") effectively established her new solo identity as she became a major draw in Las Vegas and Atlantic City. After a prestige-building gig at the London Palladium, ironically highlighting her uplifting personal anthem "I'm Coming to the Best Part of My Life," Elliot died. She was only 33 years old.

what to buy: Material from nearly all phases of Elliot's career (except the Mugwumps) is neatly compiled on *Dream a Little Dream of Me: The Cass Elliot Collection* ✍✍✍✍ (MCA, 1997, compilation prod. Owen Elliot-Kugel, Andy McKaie). From her bluesy take on "Wild Women" with the Big Three, through her solo hits "Make Your Own Kind of Music" and the title track, to a live version of "Don't Call Me Mama Anymore," Elliot repeatedly crosses the line from folk/pop idealist to cabaret chanteuse and back again. Great stuff.

the rest:
(With the Mamas and the Papas) *If You Can Believe Your Eyes and Ears* ♫♫♫ (MCA, 1966/1998)
(With the Mamas and the Papas) *Greatest Hits* ♫♫♫ (MCA, 1998)

worth searching for: Elliot's early days in the Weavers-inspired folk and blues group the Big Three are chronicled in *The Big Three featuring "Mama" Cass Elliot* ♫♫♫ (Sequel, 1995, prod. various) and is available in some catalogs and import services. If you just want Elliot's hits with the Mamas & the Papas, *16 of Their Biggest Hits* ♫♫♫ (MCA, 1986, compilation prod. Steve Hoffman) is an easy-to-find budget disc. However, the two-disc, 40-song box set, *Creeque Alley: The History of the Mamas & the Papas* ♫♫♫♫ (MCA, 1991, prod. various) is a far more satisfying experience, containing all that group's work, as well as selected tracks from the Big Three and the Mugwumps.

influences:
◄◄ Sophie Tucker, Ronnie Gilbert, Judy Garland
►► Bette Midler, Belinda Carlisle, Kathy Najimy

Ken Burke

Norma Delores Engstrom
See: Peggy Lee

Brian Eno
Born Brian Peter George St. John le Baptiste de la Salle Eno, May 15, 1948, in Woodbridge, Suffolk, England.

Through a long and varied career spanning three decades of popular and avant-garde music, Brian Eno has played many different roles: he has been the flamboyant synthesizer player in Roxy Music; the groundbreaking solo artist and "non-musician" behind a series of influential rock albums; the inspired producer of artists such as David Bowie, Talking Heads, U2, and James, and the artistic instigator behind genres as diverse as no wave and ambient house. For the purposes of us lounge lizards, though, Eno the ambient musician is the relevant concern. While much of the man's output in this vein may be a bit too, um, static for partying purposes, its influence can't be denied, and much of it serves as primo soundtrack music for the space-age bachelor pad. Eno wrote that he started thinking about am-

bient music when he was laid up with an immobilizing leg injury; he left the stereo set at a volume that was barely audible, but he couldn't get up to fix it, so he had to deal with this new way of listening. He began contemplating music that "rewards close attention but does not demand it," and he decided to use his rudimentary keyboard skills to record non-vocal compositions that would enhance the tasks of everyday life without necessarily being in the foreground—"perhaps in the spirit of Satie, who wanted to make music that could mingle with the sound of the knives and forks at dinner." In the process, he helped define a new genre—though "New Age" is a term that makes both him and many others gag—and he created an impressive body of work that continues to grow in the '90s.

what to buy: *Thursday Afternoon* ♫♫♫♫ (EG, 1985, prod. Brian Eno) is the very best of Eno's ambient efforts, with a title track that is the perfect quiet soundtrack for rainy afternoon introspection. Every bit as lulling and quietly intoxicating is *Discreet Music* ♫♫♫♫ (EG, 1975, prod. Brian Eno), which features a beautiful 30-minute title track, plus three variations of the "Canon in D Major" by Johann Pachelbel. *On Land* ♫♫♫♫ (EG, 1982, prod. Brian Eno) paints vivid sonic landscapes such as "Lizard Point" and "Lantern Marsh" by reworking sounds that were originally recorded for other albums. Finally, *Wrong Way Up* ♫♫♫♫ (Warner Bros., 1990, prod. Brian Eno, John Cale) is Eno's groovy pop-ambient collaboration with former Velvet Underground viola player John Cale. Various world beats, electronic dance grooves, and layered harmonies merge to form slinky, sexy tunes such as "Lay My Love," "One Word," and "Spinning Away." (Eno has been in a bit of a rut of late, and this is the only album he made in the '90s that approaches the brilliance of his earlier work.)

what to buy next: *Music for Films* ♫♫♫♫ (EG, 1978, prod. Brian Eno) is a compilation of fragments and out-takes from Eno's rock work, salvaged and retooled to serve as the soundtracks for scenes from imaginary films. Eno was thrilled when *Music for Airports* ♫♫♫♫ (EG, 1978, prod. Brian Eno) was actually piped into New York's LaGuardia Airport, though the quiet melody never seemed particularly aerobatic. Eno and David Byrne of Talking Heads joined forces for *My Life in the Bush of Ghosts* ♫♫♫ (Sire, 1981, prod. Brian Eno, David Byrne), a globe-trotting album that was among the first to "sample" found sounds from many different cultures. Eno also made several worthwhile albums in collaboration with Dieter Moebius and Hans-Joachim Roedelius of the German synthesizer duo Cluster; these include *Cluster & Eno* ♫♫♫ (Caroline, 1977, prod. Brian Eno, Dieter Moebius, Hans-Joachim Roedelius, Conrad Plank) and *After the*

Heat ♫♫♫ (Caroline, 1978, prod. Brian Eno, Dieter Moebius, Hans-Joachim Roedelius, Conrad Plank), which are sometimes pleasantly tranquil, and sometimes just plain boring. Last and probably least, Eno originally collaborated with King Crimson guitarist Robert Fripp in 1973 on *No Pussyfooting* and in 1975 on *Evening Star*; those tracks and similar ambient efforts are compiled on *The Essential Fripp and Eno* ♫♫♫ (Caroline/Gyroscope, 1994, prod. Brian Eno, Robert Fripp).

the rest:

Here Come the Warm Jets ♫♫♫♫ (EG, 1973)
Taking Tiger Mountain (By Strategy) ♫♫♫ (EG, 1974)
Before and After Science ♫♫♫ (EG, 1977)
Possible Musics ♫♫♫ (EG, 1980)
The Plateaux of Mirror ♫♫♫ (EG, 1980)
Apollo Atmospheres & Soundtracks ♫♫♫ (EG, 1983)
Music for Films, Vol. 2 ♫♫♫ (EG, 1983)
The Pearl ♫♫♫ (EG, 1984)
Music for Films III ♫♫♫ (Warner Bros., 1988)
The Shutov Assembly ♫♫♫ (Warner Bros., 1992)
Nerve Net ♫♫♫ (Warner Bros., 1992)
Neroli: Thinking Music Part IV ♫♫♫ (Gyroscope, 1993)
Spinner ♫♫ (Gyroscope, 1995)
The Drop ♫♫ (Thirsty Ear, 1997)

worth searching for: If you're looking for one handy compilation of Eno's lounge-leaning ambient music, *Brian Eno I: Instrumental* ♫♫♫ (Virgin, 1994) is a well-produced three-CD box set that rounds up much of his best work, though it doesn't replace any of the must-owns. It also includes some of the tracks from his four rock albums that foreshadowed his later ambient work, among them the extraordinary *Another Green World* ♫♫♫♫ (EG, 1975).

influences:

◄◄ John Cage, Miles Davis, Eric Satie, Karlheinz Stockhausen, LaMonte Young

►► David Bowie, David Byrne, Richard James (Aphex Twin), Alex Patterson (the Orb)

Jim DeRogatis

Erasure

Formed 1985, in England.

Andrew Bell, vocals; Vincent Clarke, synthesizer.

As one of the most enduring synth-pop groups in the world, Erasure has flavored musical tastes on both sides of the Atlantic for more than a decade. The duo of Andy Bell and Vince Clarke has rolled out a dozen albums and, in its native U.K.,

some 20 Top 40 hits. In the U.S., the pair has scored only three Top 40 hits, though they have maintained favorable cult status with or without radio's nod. The band formed when Clarke, a graduate of Depeche Mode, Yaz, and the short-lived Assembly, placed an ad for a vocalist in the British music newspaper *Melody Maker;* Bell was his 43rd audition. Clarke customarily arranges instrumentation and the music, while Bell handles lyrics and all vocals. From the start, the duo crafted strong pop hooks with dance leanings, but it wasn't until 1988 that the outfit crossed over to the U.S. with the #12 summer smash "Chains of Love." Two #1 hits followed in the U.K., and Erasure relentlessly toured to support each album, establishing its reputation for highly theatrical staging to accompany the flamboyant Bell, one of the first openly gay public performers in the music industry. Despite a high-camp EP, *Abba-Esque,* and a solid follow-up, Erasure's recent material has failed to hit the charts. Even so, Erasure's fans are relentlessly faithful to the group, as evidenced by consistently sold-out worldwide shows and dozens of Internet web sites offering a staggering amount of minutia on the band's performances, albums, and lives— such as translations of lyrics into other languages and the pair's blood types (both Bell and Clarke are Type E, thank you).

what to buy: *Erasure Pop! The First 20 Hits* ♫♫♫ (Sire, 1992, prod. various) offers a plump, cohesive hit catalog, including "Chains of Love," "Oh L'Amour," and "The Circus." The radiant *Circus* ♫♫♫♫ (Sire, 1987, prod. Flood) contained the band's irresistible first single "Sometimes." The platinum-selling *The Innocents* ♫♫♫♫ (Sire, 1988, prod. Stephen Hague) became Erasure's first #1 album in the U.K., and featured the international hit "A Little Respect."

what to buy next: The duo's 10th album, *I Say I Say I Say* ♫♫♫ (Mute/Elektra, 1994, prod. Martyn Ware) spurred the Top 20 hit "Always" and arbitrarily became Erasure's high-ranking album in the U.S., peaking at #18. *Cowboy* ♫♫♫ (Maverick, 1997, prod. Gareth Jones, Neil McLellan) once again showed the pair's penchant for potion-like melodies and lyrics—though, for the first time, it failed to set the U.S. or U.K. charts ablaze.

what to avoid: Erasure's first album, *Wonderland* ♫♫ (Sire, 1986, prod. Flood), was well received by neither the public nor critics.

the rest:

Two Ring Circus ♫♫ (Sire, 1987)
Crackers International ♫♫ (Sire, 1989)
Wild! ♫♫ (Sire, 1989)
Chorus ♫♫♫ (Sire, 1991)
Erasure ♫ (Elektra, 1995)

worth searching for: The high-camp EP *Abba-Esque* ♫♫♫♫ (Mute, 1992, prod. David Bascome) paid loving respects to four songs by the Swedish supergroup ABBA; it was accompanied by hilarious videos, one featuring Bell and Clarke in drag, imitating ABBA.

influences:

◀◀ Pet Shop Boys, ABBA, Cole Porter, Kraftwerk, Yaz, New Order

▶▶ Ministry, Pansy Division, the Chemical Brothers, the Cure

Chuck Taylor

Juan Garcia Esquivel

Born January 20, 1918, in Tampico, Tamaulipas, Mexico.

He's the genius of space-age pop, a mad-scientist of an arranger hellbent on sending big-band sounds swirling into orbit through controlled zaniness. He's a misunderstood master whose prodigious skills at composing, transposing, and performing predates the rush to electronic instrumentation while mirroring America's mounting interest in space travel and alien abduction. Above all, he (and the many reissue CDs of his '50s and '60s music) has become one of the preeminent icons of the current lounge craze.

Esquivel was a born bandleader, having composed and arranged for a 22-piece outfit by age 18 and having amassed a 54-piece orchestra for his use by the early '50s. Not content to merely mimic the sounds of the previous decade, Esquivel widened his palette with underappreciated sounds (slide guitar, harpsichord, Jew's harp) and then-unheard-of shadings, including Chinese bells, spooky-sounding theremin, Ondioline, and a variety of Latin flavors such as mariachi and bongos. Thrown together into his now-26-member band, and spotlighting the Randy Van Horne Singers—who were given charts of "pows" and "zu-zu-zus" to chant rather than traditional lyrics—Esquivel rode the sensational wave away from mono (or hi-fi) albums and toward stereophonic recordings where individual quirks could zip and zag from speaker to speaker like comets. (He called it "Sonorama," after the word panorama; others called it "Living Stereo.") His albums, many of which have long been out of print but the bulk of which have been restored, were far-reaching, forward-thinking wonders; still easy on the ears and unchallenging enough to serve as cocktail-party fodder, but also exuberantly crafted so a listener can study an arrangement's every twist and turn. After moving from Mexico City to Los Angeles for a 20-year stay, Esquivel began

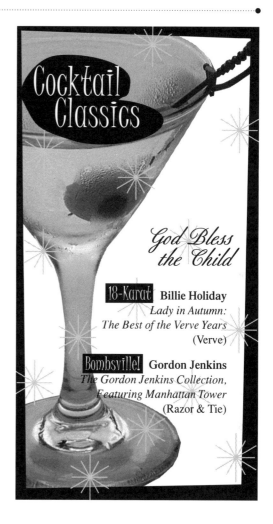

Cocktail Classics

God Bless the Child

18-Karat **Billie Holiday**
Lady in Autumn: The Best of the Verve Years
(Verve)

Bombsville! **Gordon Jenkins**
The Gordon Jenkins Collection, Featuring Manhattan Tower
(Razor & Tie)

his most fruitful recording period from 1957 to 1962 for RCA, for which he served up platefuls of distorted standards (his "Sentimental Journey," "Cherokee" and "Begin the Beguine" are standouts) and kooky originals ("Whatchamacallit," "Mucha Muchacha"). The album titles tell the story: *Experiments in Stereo*, *Infinity in Sound*, *Strings Aflame*—all delivered so as to be easily digested but leave a strange aftertaste.

But while his stage show (*The Sights and Sounds of Esquivel*) was a popular Las Vegas attraction, and Esquivel later ventured successfully into TV and film work, it has only been in this decade that he has found due acclaim—thanks in part to word-of-mouth through groups like Combustible Edison (whose erstwhile helper Brother Cleve is among Esquivel's biggest revivalists) and Stereolab, but mostly because of the attention paid the reissued 1994 CD compilation *Space-Age Bachelor Pad Music*. Esquivel's stubborn unconventionality set him apart from the prevailing tastes of the times and led him further into Vegas obscurity. His last great album, *The Genius of Esquivel*, came out in 1967. Since then, he has only done work for a few Mexican television programs. Esquivel currently lives with his brother Sergio in Cuernavaca, Mexico, where he is confined to bed after a debilitating hip injury. At press time, some newspapers had just published reports about a possible movie of Esquivel's life, starring John Leguizamo.

what to buy: *Space-Age Bachelor Pad Music* 𝄞𝄞𝄞𝄞 (Bar None/BMG, 1994, compilation prod. Irwin Chusid) has become for lounge what *Sgt. Pepper* is for rock—the Holy Grail of production mesmerism and an indispensible introduction into a peculiar artistry. Mind you, it's a compilation; most any of Esquivel's individual albums can give you the same thrill. But this one started the revival. Matching it in breadth is *Music from a Sparkling Planet* 𝄞𝄞𝄞𝄞 (Bar None/BMG, 1995, compilation prod. Irwin Chusid), a second volume culled from the RCA vaults, this time focusing on more Latin numbers and a few later gems such as "Flower Girl of Bordeaux."

what to buy next: If you get into it—and you will, it's that infectious—the next stop is a series of two-for-one reissues that nearly tell the rest of the story. *Other Worlds, Other Sounds/Four Corners of the World* 𝄞𝄞𝄞𝄞 (1958/Bar None/BMG, 1997, prod. Johnnie Camacho) puts Esquivel's richly detailed first stereo release, *Other Worlds*, against the rushed and imperfect *Four Corners*. The latter is mostly a showcase for the artist's strong piano skills. *Exploring New Sounds in Stereo/Strings Aflame* 𝄞𝄞𝄞𝄞𝄞 (1959/Bar None/BMG, 1997, prod. Johnnie Camacho) is probably the most accessible double-stuffed presentation; the former title swings mightily through classics such as "My Blue Heaven" and "Boulevard of Broken Dreams," while also displaying Esquivel's darker side on cuts such as "Spellbound" and "Bella Mora"; the latter album expands upon that moodiness, veering closer to Martin Denny's brand of exotica. And *Infinity in Sound, Vol. 1/Infinity in Sound, Vol. 2* 𝄞𝄞𝄞𝄞 (1960/Bar None/BMG, 1997, prod. Neely Plumb) is just what its title implies—spacious, inventive, quirky arrangements with marble-smooth vocals that punctuate the air like an Ali jab. *Latin-Esque/See It in Sound* 𝄞𝄞𝄞𝄞𝄞 (1962/Bar None/BMG, 1997, prod. Neely Plumb) pairs Esquivel's most daring work with a more by-the-numbers follow-up. And *The Genius of Esquivel/Esquivel!!* 𝄞𝄞𝄞𝄞 (1967/Bar

None/BMG, 1997, prod. various) is notable for the former release, one of the artist's last great moments.

what to avoid: Tossed off quickly, *More of Other Worlds, Other Sounds* 𝄞𝄞𝄞 (1962/Warner Reprise Archives, 1996, prod. Juan Garcia Esquivel) is less demanding and, thus, less exciting. After the rapid heyday of stereophonic recordings, Esquivel seemed to be turning toward more studied arranging, something others had already done to greater success. Oddity suits him; normalcy does not. And the two-fer *To Love Again/Early Mexican Recordings* 𝄞𝄞𝄞 (1957/Bar None/BMG, 1997, prod. various) is only for the extremely curious.

the rest:
Cabaret Mañana 𝄞𝄞𝄞𝄞 (Bar None/BMG, 1995)

worth searching for: You'll probably only be able to find it during the holiday season, but *Merry Xmas from the Space-Age Bachelor Pad* 𝄞𝄞𝄞𝄞 (Bar None/BMG, 1996, prod. various) is a delight. Consisting of an assortment of previously released seasonal tracks and all of 1959's lively *The Merriest of Christmas Pops* (plus a newly recorded introduction by the maestro himself), it's the perfect swizzle stick in your audio eggnog.

influences:

◄◄ Martin Denny, Les Baxter, Randy Van Horne Singers, Perez Prado

►► Combustible Edison, Love Jones, Stereolab

Ben Wener

Everything but the Girl

Formed 1982, in London, England.

Tracey Thorn, vocals; Ben Watt, guitar, piano, vocals.

Forerunners in the early '80s lite jazz-pop-lounge movement that emerged in post-punk Britian, Thorn and Watt were signed independently to record deals before collaborating for the first time as Everything but the Girl in 1982 on a samba interpretation of Cole Porter's "Night and Day." (The duo's unique name comes from a sign in a furniture store.) The two would work again separately before recording their second single, a cover of the Jam's "English Rose," which led to an impressed Paul Weller having them contribute on the Style Council's genre-defining 1984 debut album, *Café Bleu*. Later that year, EBTG released their own stunning jazzy debut, *Eden*. The combination of Thorn's beguling and seductive vocals and Watt's well-honed instrumental skills continued to entrance select listeners over subsequent CDs throughout the late '80s and early '90s, most notably 1988's torchlight

Ben Watt (l) and Tracey Thorn of Everything but the Girl (© Jack Vartoogian)

masterpiece *Idlewild*. In 1993, Watt was striken with a rare auto-immune disease and hovered near death. Following his recovery, the duo received their biggest mainstream success when their single "Missing" was remixed by DJ Todd Terry. It went to #2 in the United States and its success inspired the group to move more toward an electronica sound on 1996's *Walking Wounded*. Despite dabbling in other genres, Thorn's distinctive voice has remained consistently pleasurable.

what to buy: Delicious and resonant from start to finish, *Idlewild* ♪♪♪♪ (Blanco y Negro, 1988, prod. Ben Watt) showcases Thorn's melancholy yearning and Watt's lean production on songs like "Apron Strings" and "Shadow on a Harvest Moon."

what to buy next: Inspired by a series on unplugged concerts, *Acoustic* ♪♪♪♪ (Atlantic, 1992, prod. Everything but the Girl) is an intriguing studio and live mix of stripped-down versions of EBTG classics and eclectic covers, such as Elvis Costello's "Allison" and Tom Waits's "Downtown Train."

what to avoid: Following *Idlewild*, *Language of Life* ♪♪ (Atlantic, 1990) comes off sounding forced and, surprisingly, emotionally hollow.

the rest:
Everything but the Girl ♪♪♪ (Blanco y Negro, 1984)
Love Not Money ♪♪♪ (Blanco y Negro, 1985)
Baby the Stars Shine Bright ♪♪♪ (Blanco y Negro, 1986)
Worldwide ♪♪♪ (Atlantic, 1991)
Amplified Heart ♪♪♪♪ (Atlantic, 1994)
Walking Wounded ♪♪♪♪ (Atlantic, 1996)

worth searching for: For a more varied look at the duo's career, pick up the import *Best of Everything but the Girl* ♪♪♪♪ (Blanco y Negro, 1996, prod. various). Before he was known for insipid child-beats-up-hoodlum movies, John Hughes was known for smart young adult comedies augmented by cutting-edge soundtracks. EBTG contributed a hauntingly sparse version of "Apron Strings" for the soundtrack to *She's Having a Baby* ♪♪♪♪ (Atlantic, 1988, prod. various).

influences:

◀◀ The Style Council, Spandau Ballet, Sade

▶▶ The Beautiful South, Swing out Sister

Alex Gordon

Fabian

Born Fabiano Forte, February 6, 1943, in Philadelphia, PA.

He wasn't even close to being a major artist, but he was fun. Legend has it Fabian Forte was discovered on his doorstep, but actually he was introduced to producer Bob Marcucci by Frankie Avalon. Marcucci figured he could make a lot of money from a doe-eyed kid who looked like a cross between Elvis Presley and Ricky Nelson. Of course there existed the problem of talent: Fabian couldn't dance and could barely croon. Marathon coaching sessions, electronic enhancement, and backing by top musicians didn't help either—Fabian's first releases flopped. Marcucci remained undeterred for he had two important factors in his favor: focus groups comprised of teenaged girls raved about Fabian's good looks, and Marcucci had strong business ties with Dick Clark of *American Bandstand*. Marcucci did finally manage to squeeze some half-decent pop-rock out of Fabian, including "I'm a Man," "Hound Dog Man," and "Tiger." These proto-Presley performances capitalized more on the singer's enthusiasm than his vocal gifts, but Fabian did seem capable of aping Elvis's feel for the blues. Fabian scored nine Top 40 hits between 1958 and 1960, but his recording career ground to a halt when he was called before a Congressional investigating committee as a prime example of a star "manufactured" for the purposes of payola. With disarming candor, Fabian explained at length how his voice had been electronically enhanced and his image packaged and sold. He never had another record on the charts, but Fabian appeared as an actor in several major motion pictures (most notably *North to Alaska* and *Ten Little Indians*) as well as low-budget beach party and race-car flicks throughout the '60s. Though his career faded, Fabian never entirely went away. In the late '80s and early '90s, he began packaging and promoting his own nostalgia concerts under the banner *Fabian's Good Time Rock 'n' Roll Show*. The highlight of every program featured the still handsome performer racing through his hits while old fans screamed for him.

what to buy: For good or ill you can find all of Fabian's hits on *The Best of Fabian* ♪♪♪ (Varese Vintage, 1995, compilation prod. Cary E. Mansfield), a fine 10-song compilation with an extremely informative booklet. If you're a major fan or glutton for punishment, *This Is Fabian* ♪♪♪ (Ace, 1991, prod. Bob Marcucci) has several extra tracks and a great cover.

what to avoid: Unless you like skimpy portions of two different brands of Philadelphia Cream Cheese on one disc, bypass *Greatest Hits of Fabian & Frankie Avalon* ♪♪♪ (MCA, 1997, compilation prod. Andy McKaie), which offers just five hits apiece from the boys. Even at this budget price, you can get more fulfilling single discs on either performer.

worth searching for: As an actor, Fabian was never better than in the Samuel Z. Arkoff cheapie *Fireball 500* ♪♪♪ (American International, 1966), starring teen idols Fabian and Frankie Avalon beating the living hell out of each other.

influences:

◀◀ Elvis Presley, Ricky Nelson, Frankie Avalon

▶▶ Bobby Rydell, Bobby Sherman, Milli Vanilli

Ken Burke

Bent Fabric

Born Bent Fabricius-Bjerre, December 7, 1924, in Copenhagen, Denmark.

Fabric's music isn't about instrumental pyrotechnics, just the qualities of a catchy tune. Starting as a jazz pianist, Fabric switched to pop and, with stripped-down and deceptively simple arrangements, had his greatest success. Most of Fabric's songs use thick electric bass, rhythmic electric guitar, and tasteful drumkit brushes, but the heavily reverbed piano is most distinctive. Fabric had a popular Danish TV program, *Blue Hour*, on Saturday nights, and he composed music for films. Though he didn't write it, the huge international hit and 1962 Grammy winner "Alley Cat" originated as the theme song to a Danish TV show for which Fabric conducted the music. Starting in 1950, he headed up the Danish division of the Swedish record label Metronome, which happened to represent Atlantic Records for Scandinavia. The most memorable characteristic of Fabric's albums was his use of colorful animal photos on the LP covers (except, curiously, on *Relax*). The most important characteristic, though, was the instantly hummable melodies, which maddeningly drill into your brain, only to emerge hours, weeks, or even years later during mundane tasks—such as ironing bent fabrics.

what to buy: *The Very Best of Bent Fabric* ♪♪♪♪ (Taragon, 1997, compilation prod. Eliot Goshman) is a great 17-song distillation of Fabric's seven Atco solo LPs (plus two non-LP 45s). The goofy vocal version of Fabric's biggest hit, "Alley Cat," retitled "Alley Cat Dance" with the Alley Kittens, immediately makes the disc worth the price.

what to buy next: An excellent alternative—including "Alley Cat," of course—is the 40-track, two-CD set of other artists' takes on Fabric's music, *Instrumental Gems of the '60s* ♫♫♫♫ (Collector's Choice Music, 1995, compilation prod. Bob Hyde); it is available only through mail-order, call 1-800-923-1122. This set is a great introduction to artists as diverse as Lawrence Welk, Jimmy Smith, the T-Bones, and Billy Strange.

worth searching for: Far and away the best of Fabric's out-of-print vinyl material is *Operation Lovebirds* ♫♫♫♫ (Atco, 1966), which breaks from the formulaic arrangements of the other LPs; it has horns à la Herb Alpert's Tijuana Brass, lowstring guitar à la Al Caiola, and even banjo and accordion. The other LPs are as follows: *Alley Cat* ♫♫♫ (Atco, 1962); *The Happy Puppy* ♫♫♫ (Atco, 1962); *Organ Grinder's Swing* ♫♫♫ (Atco, 1964); *The Drunken Penguin* ♫♫♫ (Atco, 1964); *Never Tease Tigers* ♫♫♫♫ (Atco, 1966); and *Relax* ♫♫♫ (Atco, 1968).

influences:

◀◀ Teddy Wilson, Duke Ellington, Art Tatum, Benny Goodman

▶▶ Harry Connick Jr., Ben Folds Five

George W. Krieger

Eleanora Fagan

See: Billie Holiday

Donald Fagen

Born January 10, 1948, in Passaic, NJ.

Once half of the popular '70s rock duo known as Steely Dan, the reclusive Fagen has made two solo albums since the Dan broke up in 1980, both jazz-tinged concept records that sparkle with the same levels of wit, sophistication, and polish of the best of his former band. Fagen's pronounced, edgy, nasal tenor voice, careful lyrics and arrangements, and funky keyboards are as classy and clean as his live appearances are rare (though the Dan has toured in recent years as a greatest-hits ensemble). Fagen wrote music for a few films, was a columnist for *Premiere* magazine in its early days (where he once memorably defended Henry Mancini), and toured briefly in the early '90s with a group that included his wife, Libby Titus, called the New York Rock & Soul Revue.

what to buy: *The Nightfly* ♫♫♫♫ (Warner Bros., 1982, prod. Gary Katz), Fagen's bittersweet memoir of a childhood rooted in the early Cold War, is as close as it gets to a perfect jazz/rock synthesis. Fagen's '50s adolescence is set to a soundtrack of Henry Mancini, Dave Brubeck, and all-night, cool, independent-station jazz disc jockeys (the title character spins the turntables in lazy Baton Rouge, Louisiana); Chuck Berry and Buddy Holly are not in the mix here—even his version of Dion's "Ruby Baby" swings rather than rocks. As an evocation of the period, it expresses the optimism of the emerging baby boomers and the exuberance of John F. Kennedy's election ("I.G.Y.," "New Frontier") without forgetting the growing American cynicism ("The Goodbye Look") that Steely Dan would capitalize on a decade later.

what to buy next: A futuristic fantasy based around a trip in an unconventional automobile-of-the-future, *Kamakiriad* ♫♫♫♫ (Reprise, 1993, prod. Walter Becker), though not as successful as *The Nightfly*, is nearly as good.

the rest:

Live at the Beacon ♫♫♫ (Warner Bros., 1991)

worth searching for: It could be argued that every Steely Dan album qualifies as lounge, but none is cooler than *Pretzel Logic* ♫♫♫♫ (MCA, 1974, prod. Gary Katz), with the Dan's Duke Ellington remake, "East St. Louis Toodle-Oo," the bitterly sarcastic anti-Moonie diatribe, "Barrytown," and the satiric Bird tribute, "Parker's Band."

influences:

◀◀ Dave Brubeck, Steely Dan, Henry Mancini, Stan Getz, Gerry Mulligan, Miles Davis, Charlie Parker, Sonny Rollins, Chet Baker

▶▶ Hall & Oates, Dire Straits

Leland Rucker

Percy Faith

Born April 7, 1908, in Toronto, Ontario, Canada. Died February 9, 1976, in Encino, CA.

Both celebrated and maligned as a pioneer of middle-of-the-road easy-listening music, Faith was astonishingly prolific throughout the '50s and '60s, recording more than 80 albums with compositions that ranged from the sublime (he had three #1 hits, most notably 1960's "Theme from *A Summer Place*") to the ridiculous (Santana's "Black Magic Woman"). A piano prodigy, Faith moved to composing and arranging after injuring his hands in a fire at age 18. He was a fixture on Canadian radio

in the '30s before moving to the United States, where he became a citizen in 1945 while working in New York City for NBC radio. Throughout the '50s, recording for Columbia Records, Faith kept busy with his own material, film scores, and Broadway hits, weaving the varied facets of his orchestra together with his own distinctive light touch. He also arranged hits for a multitude of artists, including Doris Day, Tony Bennett, and Johnny Mathis. As "beautiful music" became relegated to elevators and dentist's office in the '60s, Faith struggled to remain relevant, rearranging contemporary hits into schmaltzy orchestrations, but to the end he remained a consummate craftsman true to his craft—regardless of its relevance.

what to buy: Proving his worth as an excellent composer, *16 Most Requested Songs* ♪♪♪♪ (Columbia, 1978, prod. Michael Brooks) showcases Faith's signature tunes, including "Theme from *A Summer Place*," "Romeo and Juliet," and "The Girl from Ipanema."

what to buy next: With its lilting melodies, *Music of Christmas* ♪♪♪ (CBS, 1966) is the perfect CD to send the kids off to bed on Christmas Eve.

what to avoid: One Beatles cover is amusing, but *The Beatles Album* ♪ (Columbia, 1970, prod. Irving Townsend), an entire album of Faith's bastardizations of Lennon and McCartney classics like "Norwegian Wood," "Lucy in the Sky with Diamonds," and "Let It Be," is just plain annoying. Luckily the album is out of print, making it that much easier to avoid.

best of the rest:
Latin Rythms ♪♪♪ (Ranwood, 1995)
Plays Richard Rodgers ♪♪♪ (Sony, 1995)
Columbia Album of George Gershwin ♪♪♪ (Sony, 1997)
Great Movie Themes ♪♪♪ (Ranwood, 1997)
Tara's Theme/Jealousy ♪♪♪ (Collectables, 1997)

worth searching for: Most of Faith's more bizarre interpretations—his stab at remaining relevant as rock 'n' roll gained prominence—are out of print, but on *Spy Magazine Presents, Vol. 3: Soft, Safe & Sanitized* ♪♪♪♪ (Rhino, 1996), you not only get Faith making the Beatles' "The Ballad of John & Yoko" into his trademark beautiful music, but also Bing Crosby's take on "Hey Jude" and the Lettermen harmonizing the Doors' "Touch Me."

Marianne Faithfull (© Jack Vartoogian)

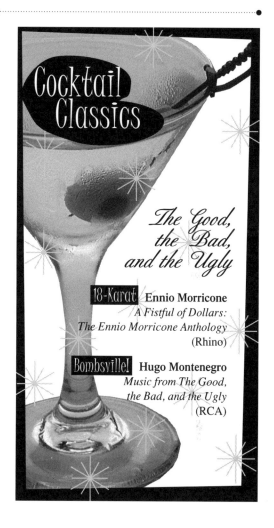

influences:

◀◀ Ray Conniff, Mantovani, Paul Weston, Glenn Miller, Benny Goodman

▶▶ 101 Strings, Henry Mancini

Alex Gordon

Marianne Faithfull

Born December 29, 1946, in London, England.

The singing career of Marianne Faithfull, the onetime model and girlfriend of Mick Jagger, includes two distinct voices: her early unbridled innocence tinted with sophistication, and her later Marlene Dietrich–inspired, world-weary vamp. Faithfull's fractured torch-singing album, 1979's *Broken English*, earned high marks from rock critics enamored of raw punk; in the late '90s, her concert tour was a serious showcase of tunes written about Germany's Weimar Republic era. But we shouldn't dismiss her unique sound in the 1960s, before her frail and soulful voice fell beyond the edge it had always seemed to be teetering near.

In the mid-'60s her music provided a plaintive pause to see the trees in the confusing dash of social revolution. As such, she had hit singles such as Jackie DeShannon's "Come and Stay with Me," John D. Loudermilk's "This Little Bird," and the Jagger–Keith Richards ballad "As Tears Go By." Back then, Faithfull was a hero and role model for young girls aspiring to the "English look" of swinging London, and the boys were stung pretty hard. She became involved with Jagger and was led willfully down the path of late '60s rock decadence—Faithfull was the "naked woman in the rug" during the Stones' infamous career-damaging 1967 drug bust. Although she starred in her own biker flick, *Girl on a Motorcycle*, the bust began a personal descent, culminating in a near overdose in Australia. In 1994, having recovered cleanly from her '80s drug-addiction years, she wrote an autobiography; a year later, she released a collaboration album, *A Secret Life*, with spooky film-music master Angelo Badalamenti.

what to buy: *Faithfull: A Collection of Her Best Recordings* ♫♫♫♫ (Island, 1994, prod. various) is a surprisingly cohesive 11-song collection that draws from the various and varied aspects of Faithfull's 32-year recording career. Selections include the first innocent blush of "As Tears Go By"; the bitterly vulgar "Why'd Ya Do It" (from *Broken English*); the moody "Trouble in Mind"; torch numbers from the Hal Willner–produced album *Strange Weather*; and a track from *A Secret Life*. Faithfull indulges her German cabaret obsession on *20th-Century Blues* ♫♫♫ (RCA Victor, 1997, prod. Marianne Faithfull), in which she delivers a "Mack the Knife" that's far more punk Patti Smith and gloomy Marlene Dietrich than peppy Bobby Darin; backed with a small jazz combo, including the expressive pianist Paul Trueblood, her voice is so haggard it's impossible to believe this was the same plaintive model who sang "This Little Bird."

what to buy next: *Broken English* ♫♫♫ (Island, 1979, prod. Mark Miller Mundy) couldn't possibly have the dramatic impact today that it did when it was released 17 years ago. There was no way then to be prepared for the stark deterioration of Faithfull's formerly breathy voice, now a withered but powerfully

emotive tool ravaged by drugs and a beautiful life turned hard. Producer Mundy and guitarist Barry Reynolds showcased that torch-singing voice without obstructing it.

what to avoid: Faithfull's collaboration with *Twin Peaks* and *Blue Velvet* composer Angelo Badalamenti, *A Secret Life* ♫♫ (Island, 1995, prod. Angelo Badalamenti), is an interesting idea that doesn't work. Both make haunting music on their own, but this is just too dull.

the rest:
Marianne Faithfull's Greatest Hits ♫ (Abkco, 1969)
Dangerous Acquaintances ♫♫♫ (Island, 1981)
A Child's Adventure ♫♫♫ (Island, 1983)
Strange Weather ♫♫ (Island, 1987)
Blazing Away ♫♫♫ (Island, 1990)

worth searching for: Real collectors might have a tough time hunting down three rarities: the import-only *Faithless* ♫♫♫ (Sony, 1978), which broke an 11-year recording gap, and the original material from her days as an innocent, rock-star-cavorting pop singer—the long out-of-print albums *Come My Way* ♫♫♫ (Decca, 1965) and *Faithfull Forever* ♫♫ (London, 1966).

influences:

◀◀ Joan Baez, Buddy Holly, the Everly Brothers, Charlie Parker, Billie Holiday, Marlene Dietrich

▶▶ Ann-Margret, Björk, Rickie Lee Jones, Madonna

Domenic Priore and Doug Pullen

Georgie Fame

Born Clive Powell, June 26, 1943, in Leigh, Lancashire, England.

Undisputedly one of the greatest talents ever to climb behind a Hammond organ, Fame squandered what many believed to be a great career in R&B and jazz in a vain quest for British fun-for-the-family wholesomeness. However, having finally abandoned his dreaded All-Round Entertainer aspirations, Fame has happily returned to his more rugged, bluesier roots.

While vacationing in Wales one summer, the young Powell found himself filling in for an ill keyboardist with a local rock combo, whose leader quickly recognized the 16-year-old's ability and invited him to give up his job at the cotton mill and join the band on a full-time basis. The group disbanded, but he quickly found work entertaining in an East End pub, where singer Lionel Bart heard him and suggested he audition for Larry Parnes, at the time Britain's top rock 'n' roll impresario. Parnes renamed his newest discovery Georgie Fame, and added him to his powerful stable of young stars. In 1961, he was invited to join the Blue Flames, the permanent backing group behind Parnes's biggest star, Billy Fury. By year's end, Fury fired the Flames, but Fame quickly commandeered them and secured a residency at London's famed Flamingo Club. Two years later, Fame and the Flames signed to EMI Columbia Records, cut their classic first LP live at the Flamingo, and had a U.K. chart-topper with the infectious Afro-Cuban number "Yeh Yeh." The Blue Flames, along with John Mayall's Bluesbreakers, soon became the training ground of choice for Britain's aspiring young musicians, including future Jimi Hendrix drummer Mitch Mitchell. In 1966 Fame inexplicably disbanded the Blue Flames in order to pursue a more "flexible" career. Sure enough, despite the occasional class move (such as a Royal Albert Hall gig accompanied by the Count Basie Orchestra), Fame spent the next two decades puttering around on English television and cabaret stages, recording such fluff as "The Ballad of Bonnie and Clyde," and eventually producing jingles for Esso Oil. Thankfully, the 1990s found Fame's profile, to say nothing of his musical credibility, retained as he began touring and recording with singer Van Morrison, doing occasional soundtrack work, and proudly sitting once again behind his trusty B3, weaving the same bluesy, jazzy mix that rightfully gave his name Fame in the first place.

what's available: Other than his work with Morrison—the most highly recommended of which is *How Long Has This Been Going On* ♫♫♫ (Verve, 1996, prod. Van Morrison, Georgie Fame)—all that is readily available on Fame in this country is *Cool Cat Blues* ♫♫♫ (Bean Bag Entertainment, 1996, prod. Ben Sidran) and *The Blues and Me* ♫♫♫ (Bean Bag Entertainment, 1996, prod. Ben Sidran), two pleasing if unspectacular returns-to-form for the former Blue Flame guiding light. He also appears on *The Go Jazz All-Stars* ♫♫♫ (Bean Bag Entertainment, 1996, prod. Ben Sidran).

worth searching for: Lounge lizards take note: *Georgie Fame Does His Own Thing with Strings* ♫ (CBS, 1970) represents the absolute nadir of his immediate post–"Bonnie & Clyde" work. This is not for the musically faint of heart; Georgie and his deplorable Strings maul "And I Love Her," "In the Wee Small Hours" and—is *nothing* sacred?—"This Guy's in Love with You." Just for fun, why not send a copy backstage at your next Van Morrison concert for an autograph? Also, the best of several (unfortunately import-only) career retrospectives is the wonderful *20 Beat Classics* ♫♫♫ (Polydor U.K., 1997, prod. various), which contains just enough hits and key album tracks to demonstrate what a remarkably trail-blazing and trend-setting outfit the Blue Flames were in their mid-1960s, pre–"Bonnie &

Clyde" heyday. And if you can find it, don't let the legendary debut LP, *Rhythm and Blues at the Flamingo* ♫♫♫♫ (EMI Columbia, 1963, prod. Ian Samwell), slip through your fingers.

influences:

◄◄ Hoagy Carmichael, Mose Allison, Fats Domino, Ray Charles, Booker T. & the MG's

►► The Animals, Brian Auger, the Specials

Gary Pig Gold

Michael Feinstein

Born September 7, 1956, in Columbus, OH.

Not only does Michael Feinstein's obsession with classic American composers provide him with a unique career identity, it ensures he won't run out of great material. Feinstein's sensitive phrasing and flawless piano playing enables him to transform nearly forgotten archival material into compelling vehicles for personal expression. He learned to play show tunes by ear when he was only five years old, and assimilated a style from his increasingly massive record collection. After discovering and returning some rare acetate recordings to the widow of pianist/wit Oscar Levant (a renowned interpreter of George Gershwin in his day), Feinstein was put in touch with legendary songwriters Ira Gershwin and Harry Warren. Working as personal assistant and archivist, Feinstein was able to quiz his bosses and their friends (such as Irving Berlin) about the minutiae of performance, songwriting, and musical history. After Gershwin's goddaughter, Liza Minnelli, hired Feinstein as accompanist for a *Tonight Show* appearance, he played behind such other artists as Rosemary Clooney and Jessie Matthews. His image as the non-threatening, romantic cabaret singer jelled when his ghostly tuxedoed image sang "But Not for Me" during his 1987 appearance on *thirtysomething*. Besides recording full theme LPs of his heroes' work, he often brings the creative legends themselves into the studio to sing, play an instrument, or supervise the proceedings. Serving as his own A&R man, Feinstein likes nothing better than to dig up lost songs by famous writers, or restore forgotten lyrics to songs that have become standards. This approach gives his work a resonant edge undetected in similar lounge revivalists. Feinstein's Broadway debut in *Michael Feinstein in Concert* was a smash, and he has since toured the world doing all he can to foster the resurgence of the great American composers of a bygone era.

what to buy: Feinstein is alone at the piano for *Pure Gershwin* ♫♫♫♫ (Elektra, 1985, prod. Herb Eiseman), which allows him to

directly communicate every cozy nuance and sensual undercurrent inherent in the material. It's perfect for late-night supper dates, romantic wool-gathering, or dancing in the dark.

what to buy next: For his belated all-Gershwin follow-up, *Nice Work if You Can Get It: Songs by the Gershwins* ♫♫♫ (Atlantic, 1996, prod. Hank Cialo), Feinstein brings in the strings, brass, conductors, and lost never-before-recorded songs. The fact that Feinstein can make it all sound so intimate is a tribute to his artistry.

what to avoid: Feinstein goes to the well one time too often for *Sings the Burton Lane Songbook, Vol. 2* ♫♫ (Nonesuch, 1992, prod. Herb Eiseman), a collaborative sequel with the great songwriter that never quite satisfies.

the rest:
Live at the Algonquin ♫♫♫ (Elektra, 1987)
Remember: Michael Feinstein Sings Irving Berlin ♫♫♫ (Elektra, 1987)
The MGM Album ♫♫♫ (Elektra, 1989)
Isn't It Romantic ♫♫♫♫ (Elektra, 1988)
Sings the Burton Lane Songbook, Vol. 1 ♫♫♫♫ (Nonesuch, 1990)
Sings the Jules Styne Songbook ♫♫♫ (Nonesuch, 1991)
Pure Imagination ♫♫♫♫ (Elektra, 1992)
Sings the Jerry Herman Songbook ♫♫ (Nonesuch, 1993)
Forever ♫♫♫ (Elektra, 1993)
Such Sweet Sorrow ♫♫♫♫ (Atlantic, 1995)
Sings the Hugh Martin Songbook ♫♫♫ (Nonesuch, 1995)

worth searching for: Feinstein teams with Rosemary Clooney and the Duke Ellington Orchestra for the enjoyable *Michael Feinstein & Friends* ♫♫♫ (Kulture Video, 1991), a 50-minute video featuring such tunes as "I Can't Give You Anything but Love" and "It Don't Mean a Thing if It Ain't Got That Swing."

influences:
◀◀ Oscar Levant, Bobby Short, Mel Tormé
▶▶ Harry Connick Jr.

Ken Burke

Jose Feliciano
Born September 10, 1945, in Lares, Puerto Rico.

Blind at birth from congenital glaucoma, Feliciano became a pop sensation in the late 1960s. Moving easily between flamenco, soul, jazz, and softer pop, between English-language

Michael Feinstein **(AP/Wide World Photos)**

and Spanish-language recording, Feliciano has been a notable performer for more than three decades now.

Feliciano moved with his family to Spanish Harlem in the early '50s. A musical prodigy from a young age on the accordion and guitar, he spent his teenage years busking on the same Greenwich Village coffeehouse scene that produced Bob Dylan. After an appearance at the Newport Jazz Festival, he released a pair of albums that showcased his supple vocals and flamenco-influenced fretwork—*The Voice and Guitar of Jose Feliciano* and *The Fantastic Feliciano*—and then a set of Spanish-language LPs. But Feliciano's big break came in 1968, when he recorded a cover of the Doors' "Light My Fire" and performed the National Anthem at the World Series. The following year, his "Light My Fire" seemed to be everywhere, and Feliciano was everywhere else, releasing three new albums, charting with a cover of Tommy Tucker's "Hi Heeled Sneakers," and netting a Grammy for Best New Artist. Quieter in the '70s and '80s, Feliciano still released records regularly, recorded the holiday standard "Feliz Navidad," hit the charts occasionally (most notably with the theme song to the Freddie Prinze sitcom *Chico and the Man*), and guested on records by performers as diverse as Michael Nesmith, Joni Mitchell, Minnie Riperton, and John Lennon. Named the head of Motown's Latin division in 1980, he continues to tour and record.

what to buy: *Feliciano!* ♫♫♫♫ (RCA, 1968, prod. Rick Jarrard) is the album that took the nation by storm, proving that Feliciano's Latin-jazz take on pop standards (including "Light My Fire," "California Dreaming," "Don't Let the Sun Catch You Crying," and a pair of Beatles songs) had mass-market appeal.

what to buy next: *Souled* ♫♫♫♫ (RCA, 1969) is almost the equal of its illustrious predecessor, with a smash cover of Tommy Tucker's "Hi Heel Sneakers" (which Feliciano had originally recorded on his 1964 debut) and a jaunty take on Bob Dylan's "I'll Be Your Baby Tonight." *On Second Thought* ♫♫♫ (Thirty-Two Records, 1996) is a greatest-hits collection with a twist—rather than simply collect Feliciano's biggest and best, it includes rerecordings of 25 of his best-known songs.

what to avoid: *Escenas De Amor* ♫♫ (Motown, 1982) is typical of Feliciano's lesser '80s work—it's soft Latin pop, overtly romantic, with none of the strength and power of his best albums.

worth searching for: Joni Mitchell's *Court and Spark* ♫♫♫♫♫ (Asylum, 1974, prod. Joni Mitchell) is one of the folk singer's finest albums, and her best-selling effort. It also has a raft of

Arthur Ferrante (l) and Louis Teicher (AP/Wide World Photos)

guest stars, including Robbie Robertson, David Crosby, Joe Sample, and Felicano, who contributes electric guitar.

influences:

◀◀ Carlos Puebla, the Beatles, Bob Dylan, Tito Puente, João Gilberto, Laurindo Almeida

▶▶ War

Ben Greenman

Ferrante & Teicher

Formed 1940s, in Boston, MA.

Arthur Ferrante (born September 7, 1921, in New York, NY), piano; Louis Teicher (born August 24, 1924, in Wilkes-Barre, PA), piano.

This duo bested Liberace (musically if not theatrically) by squaring him: they were pioneers of piano pyrotechnics for four hands. True, some of the appeal lay in the sheer novelty of their arrangements, but there was also a spark of genuine inventive-

ness behind them. Arthur Ferrante and Louis Teicher first crossed paths at the renowned Julliard School in the '40s. After discovering that they could double their pleasure, double their fun, by doubling the concert piano attack, they performed the requisite classics backed by orchestras for years before they really started expanding their horizons to include pop hits. Adding percussion and dabbling with outlandishly whimsical treatments of classics like "I Got Rhythm," "Chopsticks," and "Ain't Misbehavin'," as well as lively interpretations of show tunes and film music, they established themselves as fine purveyors of camp.

what to buy: Fans of "space-age" lounge music will be intrigued by *Blast Off!* 🎵🎵🎵 (Varese Sarabande, 1959/MCA, 1997, reissue prod. Cary E. Mansfield), a collection of old favorites and a few originals rendered in interstellar style, complete with futuristic and other amusing noises.

what to buy next: *Broadway to Hollywood* 🎵🎵🎵 (Columbia, 1987) includes "I Love Paris," "The Continental," and "Wonderful Copenhagen." *Broadway Shows Remembered* ♫♫♫ (MCA Special Products, 1995) features "Everything's Coming Up Roses," "Till There Was You," and "The Sound of Music." *Autumn Leaves* ♫♫♫ (Sony Music, 1995) contains live renderings of a variety of tunes, including "St. Louis Blues," "Slaughter on Tenth Avenue," and "Chariots of Fire."

worth searching for: *A Few of Our Favorites on Stage* ♫♫♫ (Bainbridge, 1995) and *All Time Favorite Hits* ♫♫♫ (CEMA Special Products, 1992) feature themes from *The Godfather, Midnight Cowboy,* and *Exodus. All Time Great Movie Themes* ♫♫♫ (Alliance, 1997) contains everything from *Elvira Madigan* to *Lawrence of Arabia. Easy Listening Favorites* ♫♫♫ (MCA Special Products, 1995) is actually sort of a vague concept album that revolves around lyrical images of the sun, the moon, and the stars.

influences:

◀◀ Liberace

▶▶ Ben Folds Five, Combustible Edison, Love Jones

Sandy Masuo

Bryan Ferry

Born September 26, 1945, in Washington, England.

The erstwhile leader of the pioneering glam rock band Roxy Music, Ferry has carved a substantial solo career as a suave pop sophisticate who's as comfortable reworking standards and rock hits with his smoky style as he is performing his own sultry material. The son of a coal miner, Ferry was (what else?) an art student before turning to music. In 1971, he and Graham Simpson formed Roxy Music, and a year after the band's self-titled debut album, Ferry released his solo debut, *These Foolish Things.* With a diverse array of covers (everyone from Bob Dylan and the Beatles to the Brill Building writers), the album stood in stark contrast to Roxy's more ornate sound. As Ferry continued to record both with the band and as a solo artist, the line between the two eventually blurred, as witnessed by the intimate and sensual sound of both Roxy's final CD, 1982's *Avalon,* and Ferry's first solo effort afterwards, 1985's *Boys and Girls.* On subsequent efforts Ferry has continued his obsession with the possibilities and disappointments of romance while further slipping into the role of charming crooner; thankfully his fine voice and profound musical talents have kept him from slipping into self-parody.

what to buy: With 20 hits culled from both his solo and Roxy material, *Street Life* ♫♫♫♫ (Reprise, 1986, prod. various) is amazingly coherent as it glides effortlessly from soulful covers

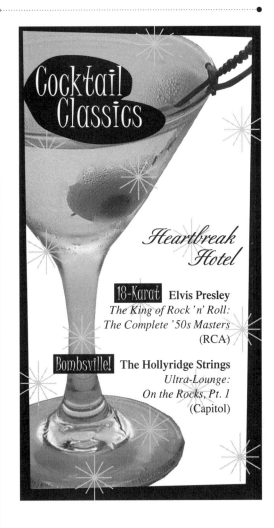

Cocktail Classics

Heartbreak Hotel

18-Karat Elvis Presley
The King of Rock 'n' Roll: The Complete '50s Masters (RCA)

Bombsville! The Hollyridge Strings
Ultra-Lounge: On the Rocks, Pt. 1 (Capitol)

like "These Foolish Things" and "Smoke Gets in Your Eyes" to mid-'80s makeout classics like "More Than This," "Angel Eyes," and "Slave to Love."

what to buy next: A good cover version of a song will both pay homage and reinterpret the original, and *These Foolish Things* ♫♫♫♫ (Reprise, 1973, prod. John Punter, Bryan Ferry) finds Ferry deftly achieving that goal on Bob Dylan's "A Hard Rain's A-Gonna Fall," the Rolling Stones' "Sympathy for the Devil," "It's My Party," and the beguiling cover track. Ferry is at his sensual, sultry, and seductive best on *Boys and Girls* ♫♫♫♫ (Reprise, 1985, prod. Rhett Davis, Bryan Ferry), especially with the track "Slave to Love" epitomizing his tortured romantic persona.

what to avoid: Ferry revisits the cover concept on *Taxi* 🎵🎵 (Reprise, 1993), but the results this time seem tired, perhaps because of the bland song selection.

the rest:

Another Time, Another Place 🎵🎵🎵 (Reprise, 1974)
Let's Stick Together 🎵🎵🎵🎵 (Reprise, 1976)
In Your Mind 🎵🎵🎵 (Reprise, 1977)
The Bride Stripped Bare 🎵🎵🎵🎵 (Reprise, 1978)
Bete Noire 🎵🎵🎵 (Reprise, 1987)
Mamouna 🎵🎵🎵 (Reprise, 1994)

worth searching for: Ferry's interpretive abilities and atmospheric vocals have led to his appearance on a number of soundtracks. He does an enthusiastic turn on Van Morrison's "Crazy Love" for *She's Having a Baby* 🎵🎵🎵🎵 (Atlantic, 1988, prod. various) and his best Elvis impersonation on "Are You Lonesome Tonight" for *Honeymoon in Vegas* 🎵🎵🎵 (Epic, 1992, prod. Peter Afterman, Glen Brunman).

influences:

◀◀ Billie Holiday, Frank Sinatra, Smokey Robinson, Bob Dylan, Lou Reed, Otis Redding, Humphrey Bogart

▶▶ David Bowie, Duran Duran, Midge Ure, George Michael

Alex Gordon

Arthur Fiedler
/The Boston Pops Orchestra

Born December 17, 1894, in Boston, MA. Died July 10, 1979, in Brookline, MA.

Light classical music is by definition a hybrid, denigrated by serious classical listeners as a frivolous form and ignored by aficionados of film and Broadway show music who prefer to go directly to the "original" cast or soundtrack source. Both extremes had dismissed "light classical" as music for people who don't listen to music—until Arthur Fiedler.

A proper (and occasionally improper) Bostonian for all of his life, the Boston Pops impresario symbolized for a half-century a bold, bright, colorful approach to pop; it was commercially successful music played to the pops of champagne corks in venerable Symphony Hall in the Back Bay, and just as effervescent. Of course, one expects a pops orchestra to play the accessible, easy-to-swallow melodies of Copland and Gershwin and Cole Porter as well as forays into "Bolero" and Strauss waltzes. But Fiedler's band played "The Music from Peter Gunn" and the "Theme from the Man from U.N.C.L.E." alongside Offenbach and John Philip Sousa. Fiedler, with his silvery hair, his mous-

tache, and his—dare we use the word?—funky approach, conducted with such flair and imagination that he made the Pops an archetype that today is still very much valid. In his heyday, Fiedler led the Pops every spring for 10 weeks, made dozens of guest appearances around the world each year, and recorded voluminously for the RCA label. Fiedler's father, Emanuel, who moved to New England from Vienna, played in the first violin section of the Boston Symphony. Fiedler—German for "fiddler"—himself studied violin overseas and later played with the Boston Symphony, but his calling was conducting. In 1926, an unexpected resignation gave Fiedler the chance to conduct the Boston Pops in performance; he took over the orchestra full-time four years later. Fiedler's festive approach to the classics and popular music endeared him immediately to audiences that had previously abandoned the too-staid Pops, which had become mired in Italian operatic overtures. Fiedler had a far less snobbish attitude. "I often feel like a chef planning a meal," he wrote in *Atlantic Monthly.* "There should be hors d'oeuvres, a light course, a substantial entree, and so on. . . . Variety is the spice we want." Sure, there was Wagner and Chopin and "Moonlight Sonata." But Fiedler stretched: when the Pops played symphonic arrangements of "I Want to Hold Your Hand" and "She Loves You," the string section harmonized "Yeah, yeah, yeah!" as the coda. Worldwide, audiences were exposed to Fiedler's exuberance via radio and television concerts as well as through the organization's RCA catalog. *Evening at Pops,* which began in the early '70s on National Educational Television, became a staple of PBS. The Pops also had their share of hit albums under the maestro; more than 50 million albums of music conducted by Fiedler have been sold— including *Saturday Night Fiedler*, with a *Saturday Night Fever* medley. Fiedler, who loved auto racing and was obsessed by the art of firefighting—he collected firemen's uniforms and hats and was an honorary fireman in more than 350 cities— died in 1979. His baton was eventually given over to John Williams, who had a long run with the orchestra but was, personality-wise, a bit too distant for Pops fans. He had a tough act to follow.

what to buy: Fiedler tried so many different types of music, and his Boston Pops Orchestra was so prolific, that it's nearly impossible to build the definitive home recording collection. In keeping with his spirit of diversity, we recommend sampling several of his specialties. For showtunes and movie music, there's *Motion Picture Classics, Vol. 1* 🎵🎵🎵🎵 (RCA Victor, 1990), with the familiar themes from *Ben-Hur* and *Laura*, *Motion Picture Classics, Vol. 2* 🎵🎵🎵 (RCA Victor, 1990), and *Broadway's*

Greatest Hits 𝄢𝄢𝄢 (RCA Victor, 1993), which, while it only contains a skimpy five tracks, includes the Kurt Weill classic "Mack the Knife," "The Sound of Music," and "Guys and Dolls." For pop and rock hits that have since become standards—which, to Fiedler's credit, he recognized early on while his classical contemporaries were sneering at the Beatles—there's *Greatest Hits of the '6os* 𝄢𝄢𝄢 (RCA Victor, 1988). It doesn't stretch quite into Jimi Hendrix or Cream, but symphonic covers of "I Want to Hold Your Hand," "Hey Jude," and even "Aquarius" were pretty radical for audiences in their day. For kids, long a Fiedler specialty, there's *Fiedler's Favorites for Children* 𝄢𝄢𝄢 (BMG Classics, 1987), with segments of *The Nutcracker,* the *Snow White and the Seven Dwarfs* anthem, "Whistle While You Work," and something called "Jamaican Rhumba." For sheer volume, *100 Fiedler Favorites* 𝄢𝄢𝄢𝄢 (RCA Victor, 1994) is about as definitive as you can get.

what to buy next: Every December, when you get inundated with new holiday standards and reissued albums of singers who never should have tackled Christmas in the first place, remember the names Bing Crosby and Arthur Fiedler. *Pops Christmas Party* 𝄢𝄢𝄢𝄢 (RCA Victor, 1997, prod. Richard Mohr, John Pfeiffer), a collection of 1959 and 1964 recordings, contains all the classics: "Joy to the World," "Deck the Halls," the best bits from *The Nutcracker* suite, and so forth.

what to avoid: Several greatest-hits collections, including *Peace, Love, and Pops—Greatest Hits* 𝄢𝄢 (Philips, 1995), *Greatest Hits* 𝄢𝄢 (RCA Victor, 1991), and *Collection* 𝄢𝄢 (RCA Victor, 1994), have been eclipsed by *100 Fiedler Favorites.*

best of the rest:
Greatest Hits of the '5os, Vol. 2 𝄢𝄢𝄢 (RCA Victor, 1974/1987)
Concert in the Park 𝄢𝄢𝄢 (RCA Victor, 1987)
Overtures 𝄢𝄢𝄢 (RCA Victor, 1987)
More Favorites for Children 𝄢𝄢𝄢 (BMG Classics, 1987)
Pops Concert 𝄢𝄢𝄢 (RCA Victor, 1987)
American Salute 𝄢𝄢𝄢 (RCA Victor, 1988)
Classics for Children 𝄢𝄢𝄢 (RCA Victor, 1988)
Favorite Marches 𝄢𝄢𝄢 (RCA Victor, 1990)
Fiedler's Favorites 𝄢𝄢 (Pro Arte Maxiplay, 1990)
Fiedler on the Roof 𝄢𝄢𝄢 (RCA Victor, 1990)
Conducts Tchiakovsky 𝄢𝄢 (Laserlight, 1991)
Irish Night at the Pops 𝄢𝄢𝄢𝄢 (RCA Victor, 1991)
Lullaby 𝄢𝄢 (RCA Victor, 1992)
Hi-Fi Fiedler 𝄢𝄢𝄢 (RCA Victor, 1993)
Pops Around the World 𝄢𝄢𝄢 (RCA Victor, 1993)
Offenbach in America 𝄢𝄢𝄢 (RCA Victor, 1993)
Marches in Hi-Fi 𝄢𝄢𝄢 (RCA Victor, 1993)
Stars & Stripes 𝄢𝄢 (RCA Victor, 1993)

Favorites and Friends 𝄢𝄢𝄢 (RCA Victor, 1994)
Pops Caviar 𝄢𝄢 (RCA Victor, 1995)
Fiedler Sinfonietta 𝄢𝄢 (RCA Victor, 1995)
Fiedler at the Ballet 𝄢𝄢𝄢 (RCA Victor, 1995)
Christmas at the Pops 𝄢𝄢 (RCA Victor, 1995)
Christmas Festival 𝄢𝄢 (RCA Victor, 1997)
Boston Tea Party 𝄢𝄢𝄢 (RCA Victor, 1997)
Rhapsody in Blue 𝄢𝄢𝄢 (RCA Victor, 1997)

worth searching for: John Williams, who took over the Boston Pops Orchestra shortly after Fiedler's death and ran it until 1993, made a lucrative connection with Steven Spielberg in the mid-'70s. He wound up conducting the distinctive scores to films like *Jaws* and *Raiders of the Lost Ark*—and while soundtrack albums go in and out of print with regularity, *Jaws* 𝄢𝄢𝄢𝄢 (MCA, 1975/1992) is a nice item for movie buffs. It contains, of course, the menacing theme that warns you a giant shark is coming.

influences:

◀◀ Leroy Anderson, Paul Weston, Andre Kostelanetz, Mantovani, Tchaikovsky, Rodgers & Hammerstein, the Beatles, Bing Crosby, Nelson Riddle, Billy May

▶▶ John Williams, Keith Lockhart

Stephen Williams and Steve Knopper

The Fifth Dimension

Formed 1966, in Los Angeles, CA.

Marilyn McCoo, vocals; Billy Davis Jr., vocals; Lamonte McLemore, vocals; Ron Towson, vocals; Florence LaRue, vocals.

As an all-black group accused of "singing white" (they once played at the Nixon White House), the Fifth Dimension exposed middle America to their unique and safe brand of colorblind harmony with palatable top 10 hits like "Up, Up and Away," "Stoned Soul Picnic," "Wedding Bell Blues," and others penned by hitmakers Jimmy Webb, Laura Nyro, and others. Originally formed as the Versatiles, the band scored its biggest hit in 1969 with its rousing, Grammy-winning rendition of "Aquarius/Let the Sun Shine In" from the musical *Hair.* The band slowly faded from relevancy in the early '70s as its sound further softened. The founding members, husband and wife Marilyn McCoo and Billy Davis Jr., left the band to perform as a duo in 1975 and scored a #1 single in 1976 with "You Don't Have to Be a Star." They even hosted their own variety series on CBS in the summer of 1977. McCoo and Davis split in 1980, with McCoo going on to host the syndicated TV show *Solid Gold.* As for the band, with various new members, the Fifth Dimension continued to tour through the mid-'80s on the Vegas and club circuits—it recorded an awful comeback album in 1995.

what to buy: As soulful bubble gum, there's no denying the guilty pleasures like "Wedding Bell Blues," "Never My Love," and, of course, "Aquarius/Let the Sun Shine In"—all found on *Greatest Hits on Earth* &&&& (Arista, 1972, prod. Bones Howe).

what to buy next: For an even more complete look at the band, *Up, Up & Away: The Definitive Collection* &&& (Arista, 1997) includes a staggering 60 songs.

what to avoid: A scary studio comeback, *In the House* **woof!** (Click/Columbia, 1995, prod. Ollie E. Brown) finds the band struggling for relevancy in the '90s while covering the Bee Gees and Neil Sedaka.

worth searching for: Marilyn McCoo and Billy Davis Jr.'s first effort after leaving the Fifth Dimension, *I Hope We Get to Love in Time* &&& (Razor & Tie, 1996, prod. Don Davis), features the band's #1 hit, "You Don't Have to Be a Star," and other sunny "soul" songs that will take you back to the days of pet rocks, mood rings, and *Battle of the Network Stars*.

influences:

◀◀ Johnny Rivers, Ray Charles, Neil Sedaka

▶▶ Lionel Richie, the Carpenters, Earth, Wind & Fire, Peaches & Herb

Alex Gordon

First Edition

See: Kenny Rogers

Eddie Fisher

Born Edwin Jack Fisher, August 10, 1928, in Philadelphia, PA.

Decades after Fisher's million-selling records—including "Any Time" and "O! My Papa!"—slipped off the charts, this singer has been more famous as a personality than a performer. He was married to Connie Stevens, Elizabeth Taylor, and Debbie Reynolds, and fathered actress-author Carrie Fisher and *Ellen* sitcom co-star Joely Fisher. His delivery was silky smooth, usually with big bands in the background and occasionally in imitation of Al Jolson, although he tried to rock with 1955's missing-the-point hit "Dungaree Doll." Fisher got his start singing on his mentor Eddie Cantor's 1940s radio show—and was a frequent guest on Cantor's later television shows—before embarking on his own hit career. He still sings.

what to buy: The funny, playful "O! My Papa!" is the highlight of *The Very Best of Eddie Fisher* &&& (MCA, 1987, prod. various), which does an excellent job of documenting Fisher's string of hits, beginning in 1950 and lasting until rock 'n' roll knocked him off the charts after "Dungaree Doll" lost its novelty power.

what to buy next: Fisher's original label, RCA Victor, supplements the MCA collection with *All-Time Greatest Hits, Vol. 1* &&& (RCA, 1989, prod. Chick Crumpacker), and includes his very first hit, 1950's "Thinking of You."

influences:

◀◀ Eddie Cantor, Frank Sinatra, Perry Como, Doris Day, Fred Astaire, Dean Martin, Bing Crosby

▶▶ Johnny Mathis, Julio Iglesias, Jon Secada, Michael Bolton, Carrie Fisher

Steve Knopper

Ella Fitzgerald

Born April 25, 1917, in Newport News, VA. Died June 14, 1996, in Beverly Hills, CA.

Many critics consider Ella Fitzgerald "The First Lady of Song," the best female jazz singer ever, though in her customary modesty Fitzgerald hailed Sarah Vaughan as the finest vocalist of all time. Regardless, there can be no debate that Ella—the first name is all that's required—belongs in that select pantheon of incomparable voices (Vaughan, Billie Holiday) that could transform the weakest material into a masterpiece, making any song uniquely her own. She could swing with the best of them, is credited with creating the free-form singing style known as "scat," and interpreted every number with spectacularly clear diction and a powerful, versatile voice.

The perpetually cheerful lilt in that voice made her records, in addition to all her other accomplishments, a perfect fit alongside pop crooners and easy-listening instrumentalists on upscale nightclub jukeboxes. Her voice's high spirits also stood in sharp contrast to an early life spent in abysmal poverty; she was a homeless 16-year-old in 1933, but turned her fortunes around the following year. Fitzgerald showed up at an amateur talent contest at Harlem's Apollo Theater and won the $25 first prize by singing an impromptu version of "Judy" in the style of her main influence, Connee Boswell. Jazz great Benny Carter was in the audience and soon landed Fitzgerald a spot singing with Chick Webb's orchestra; by 1937, she was the featured attraction. Webb died in 1939, and Fitzgerald took over as leader of

Ella Fitzgerald (**UPI/Corbis-Bettmann**)

his orchestra until 1941 when she broke up the band to go solo. In the '40s, Ella collaborated with acts like the Ink Spots and the Delta Rhythm Boys, eventually finding a home with Norman Granz's Jazz at the Philharmonic. She began performing more jazz and bop numbers, teaming with Dizzy Gillespie and doing raucous, scat-filled numbers in her sets. She hit the charts with "Lady Be Good" and "Flying Home," married bassist Ray Brown in 1948 (a union that would last only four years), appeared in the films *St. Louis Blues* and Jack Webb's *Pete Kelly's Blues,* and made many TV appearances starting in the '50s and continuing throughout her career. All these events were concurrent with Ella's signing to Granz's Verve label and beginning her project of making her seminal and very popular "songbook" recordings. She achieved the pinnacle of her career in 1960 with her European concert tour, notably the Berlin show featuring her scat-heavy spoof of "Mack the Knife." Fitzgerald's radiance lost some luster in the late '60s as she tried to cash in on the popular music of the day, but she rebounded with live recordings in the '70s. In the 1980s, however, Ella began to fade. Her health de-

clined and she lacked the "verve" she had displayed so effortlessly in her younger years. Heart and eye trouble prevented her from performing or recording for long stretches. By 1994, she had completely retired. Ella Fitzgerald died in the spring of 1996, though her legacy lives on in more than 100 available recordings and a reputation that has made her name synonymous with great singing, great jazz, and scat coolness.

what to buy: In 1956, Fitzgerald signed with Verve Records and undertook a massive project: a series of "songbooks" featuring the works of the greatest composers of the 20th century. Though not her finest jazz performances, the best of these albums is *The Cole Porter Songbook* ♫♫♫♫ (Verve, 1956/DCC, 1995, prod. Norman Granz), and it serves as a wonderful introduction to Ella if you prefer not to drop a quarter of a grand for *The Complete Ella Fitzgerald Song Books* ♫♫♫♫♫ (Verve, 1993, prod. Norman Granz). A solid companion piece to the Porter disc is Fitzgerald's *The Complete Duke Ellington Songbook* ♫♫♫♫ (Verve, 1956, prod. Norman Granz), though this Verve offering is a two-volume box set and priced accordingly. If the Porter set is Fitzgerald at her popular song best, the Ellington sessions find Ella at her jazz singing best, backed by jazz music's best: Dizzy Gillespie, Johnny Hodges, Oscar Peterson, Billy Strayhorn, and, of course, Sir Duke. Predictably, a flood of new recordings and reshuffled compilations have hit the market since Ella's death. The wide-ranging collection *The Best of the Songbooks* 𝄪𝄪𝄪𝄪 (Verve, 1996) is certainly worthy, but has the disadvantage of moving the songs far away from their original context.

what to buy next: By 1960, Fitzgerald had reached the pinnacle of her dazzling career. She carried the experience 30 years of singing brings, along with the energy and intensity she had when she began. *Mack the Knife: The Complete Ella in Berlin Concert* 𝄪𝄪𝄪𝄪𝄪 (Verve, 1993, prod. Phil Schaap) is an example of Ella at her best. Her hilarious and legendary take on "Mack the Knife" made this concert perhaps her most memorable. This disc combines the concert tracks with several rare and previously unreleased recordings, as Ella sparkles on her rendition of Sarah Vaughan's "Misty," her own scat-filled "How High the Moon," and standards like "The Lady Is a Tramp" and "Too Darn Hot." For all-around collections, there are none better than *75th Birthday Celebration* 𝄪𝄪𝄪𝄪 (Decca, 1993, compilation prod. Orrin Keepnews). It's a two-CD set that charts 39 songs from the first half of her career.

what to avoid: There's nothing inherently wrong with K-Tel except that their TV ads are annoying. But *Ella Fitzgerald* 𝄪 (K-Tel, 1996, prod. various) is just a weak assortment compared to all the others competing with it. Should you get the urge to order by phone at 3 a.m., strap yourself in bed until you can get to the CD store the next day and purchase a truly good compilation.

the rest:
Swingin' NBC Radio 1940 Big Band Remotes 𝄪𝄪𝄪𝄪 (Sandy Hook, 1940)
Gershwin Songbook 𝄪𝄪𝄪𝄪 (Verve, 1950)
Ella & Louis 𝄪𝄪𝄪𝄪 (Laserlight, 1956)
Ella Fitzgerald & Jazz at the Philharmonic 𝄪𝄪𝄪𝄪 (Tax, 1957)
Ella Fitzgerald Sings the George & Ira Gershwin Songbook 𝄪𝄪𝄪𝄪𝄪 (Verve, 1959)
Ella & Basie 𝄪𝄪𝄪𝄪 (Verve, 1963)
The Johnny Mercer Songbook 𝄪𝄪𝄪 (Verve, 1964)
Ella & Louis 𝄪𝄪𝄪𝄪 (Verve, 1972)
Ella in London 𝄪𝄪𝄪𝄪 (Pablo, 1974)
Dream Dancing 𝄪𝄪 (Pablo, 1978)
Ella Fitzgerald/Count Basie/Joe Pass: Digital III at Montreux 𝄪𝄪𝄪𝄪𝄪 (Pablo, 1979)
Ella Fitzgerald & Joe Pass: Speak Love 𝄪𝄪𝄪𝄪 (Pablo, 1983)
Silver Collection: The Songbooks 𝄪𝄪𝄪𝄪 (Verve, 1984)

The Jerome Kern Songbook 𝄪𝄪𝄪𝄪 (Verve, 1985)
These Are the Blues 𝄪𝄪𝄪𝄪𝄪 (Verve, 1986)
Ella Fitzgerald at the Opera House 𝄪𝄪𝄪 (Verve, 1986)
The Irving Berlin Songbook Vols. 1 & 2 𝄪𝄪𝄪𝄪 (Verve, 1986)
Fine and Mellow 𝄪𝄪𝄪 (Pablo, 1987)
Ella Fitzgerald & Louis Armstrong, "Compact Jazz" series 𝄪𝄪𝄪𝄪 (Verve, 1988)
The Harold Arlen Songbook, Vol. 1 𝄪𝄪𝄪 (Verve, 1988)
The Harold Arlen Songbook, Vol. 2 𝄪𝄪𝄪 (Verve, 1988)
Fitzgerald and Pass . . . Again 𝄪𝄪𝄪𝄪 (Pablo, 1988)
Ella Fitzgerald & Count Basie: A Classy Pair 𝄪𝄪𝄪𝄪 (Pablo, 1989)
Ella Fitzgerald & Joe Pass: Easy Living 𝄪𝄪𝄪𝄪 (Pablo, 1989)
Ella Fitzgerald & Count Basie: A Perfect Match 𝄪𝄪𝄪𝄪 (Pablo, 1989)
Ella Fitzgerald/Tommy Flanagan, Montreux 1977 𝄪𝄪𝄪𝄪 (Original Jazz Classics, 1989)
Ella Fitzgerald & Duke Ellington: The Stockholm Concert—Feb. 7, 1966 𝄪𝄪𝄪𝄪𝄪 (Pablo, 1989)
Clap Hands, Here Comes Charlie 𝄪𝄪𝄪𝄪𝄪 (Verve, 1989)
Ella: Things Aren't What They Used to Be: And You Better Believe It 𝄪𝄪𝄪𝄪 (Reprise, 1989)
The Best of Ella Fitzgerald 𝄪𝄪𝄪𝄪 (Pablo, 1989)
The Intimate Ella 𝄪𝄪𝄪𝄪𝄪 (Verve, 1990)
Ella and Louis Again 𝄪𝄪𝄪𝄪𝄪 (Verve, 1990)
Ella à Nice 𝄪𝄪𝄪𝄪 (Original Jazz Classics, 1990)
Ella Live! 𝄪𝄪 (Verve)
Ella Fitzgerald/Count Basie/Benny Goodman Jazz Collector Edition, Vol. 2 𝄪𝄪𝄪𝄪 (Laserlight, 1991)
Ella Fitzgerald & Joe Pass: Take Love Easy 𝄪𝄪𝄪𝄪 (Pablo, 1991)
Returns to Berlin 𝄪𝄪𝄪 (Verve, 1991)
Like Someone in Love 𝄪𝄪𝄪𝄪 (Verve, 1991)
Ella Fitzgerald & Oscar Peterson: Ella and Oscar 𝄪𝄪𝄪𝄪 (Pablo, 1991)
Ella Swings Lightly 𝄪𝄪𝄪 (Verve, 1992)
The Essential Ella Fitzgerald: The Great Songs 𝄪𝄪𝄪 (Verve, 1992)
Ella Swings Gently with Nelson 𝄪𝄪𝄪𝄪 (Verve, 1993)
Ella Swings Brightly with Nelson 𝄪𝄪𝄪𝄪𝄪 (Verve, 1993)
At the Montreux Jazz Festival, 1975 𝄪𝄪𝄪𝄪 (Original Jazz Classics, 1993)
First Lady of Song 𝄪𝄪𝄪𝄪 (Verve, 1993)
Compact Jazz—Ella & Duke 𝄪𝄪𝄪 (Verve, 1993)
The Best of Ella Fitzgerald 𝄪𝄪𝄪𝄪 (Curb, 1993)
The Best of Ella Fitzgerald: First Lady of Song 𝄪𝄪𝄪𝄪𝄪 (Verve, 1994)
The Best of the Songbooks: The Ballads 𝄪𝄪𝄪𝄪 (Verve, 1994)
Jazz 'Round Midnight 𝄪𝄪𝄪𝄪 (Verve, 1994)
Jazz 'Round Midnight Again 𝄪𝄪𝄪𝄪 (Verve, 1994)
The War Years 𝄪𝄪𝄪𝄪 (Decca Jazz, 1994)
Pure Ella 𝄪𝄪𝄪 (Decca Jazz, 1994)
The Concert Years 𝄪𝄪𝄪𝄪𝄪 (Pablo, 1994)
Verve Jazz Masters 6 𝄪𝄪𝄪𝄪 (Verve, 1994)
Verve Jazz Masters 24 𝄪𝄪𝄪 (Verve, 1994)
The Jazz Sides: Verve Jazz Masters 46 𝄪𝄪𝄪𝄪 (Verve, 1995)
Ella: The Legendary Decca Recordings 𝄪𝄪𝄪𝄪𝄪 (Decca Jazz, 1995)

Live from the Roseland Ballroom—New York 1940 ♫♫♫♫ (Musicdisc, 1995)

Newport Jazz Festival/Live at Carnegie Hall ♫♫♫♫ (Classics, 1995)

Ella Fitzgerald/Billie Holiday/Dinah Washington, Jazz 'Round Midnight: Three Divas ♫♫♫♫ (Verve, 1995)

The Early Years Parts 1 & 2 ♫♫♫♫ (Decca Jazz, 1995)

Let No Man Write My Epitaph ♫♫♫♫♫ (Classic, 1995)

Lady Time ♫♫♫♫ (Pablo, 1995)

Dreams Come True ♫♫♫ (Drive Archive, 1995)

Daydream: The Best of the Duke Ellington Songbook ♫♫♫♫ (Verve, 1995)

Love Songs: Best of the Verve Songbooks ♫♫♫♫♫ (Verve, 1996)

The Best of Ella Fitzgerald w/Chick Webb and his Orchestra ♫♫♫♫ (Decca Jazz, 1996)

Oh, Lady Be Good! Best of the Gershwin Songbook ♫♫♫♫ (Verve, 1996)

Ella & Friends ♫♫♫ (Decca Jazz, 1996)

Sunshine of Your Love ♫♫ (Verve, 1996)

Ella Fitzgerald ♫♫ (Dove Audio, 1996)

Bluella: Ella Fitzgerald Sings the Blues ♫♫♫ (Pablo, 1996)

You'll Have to Swing It ♫♫♫ (Eclipse, 1996)

Rock It for Me ♫♫♫ (Eclipse, 1996)

The Best Is Yet to Come ♫♫♫ (Pablo, 1996)

Sings the Rodgers & Hart Songbook ♫♫♫♫♫ (Verve, 1997)

Rhythm & Romance ♫♫♫ (Living Era, 1997)

A-Tisket, A-Tasket ♫♫♫ (ITC Masters, 1997)

The Best of Ella Fitzgerald & Louis Armstrong on Verve ♫♫♫♫♫ (Verve, 1997)

The Complete Ella Fitzgerald & Louis Armstrong on Verve ♫♫♫♫♫ (Verve, 1997)

Ella Fitzgerald/Sarah Vaughan/Carmen McRae: Ladies of Jazz ♫♫♫♫ (Laserlight, 1997)

Ella Fitzgerald with the Tommy Flanagan Trio ♫♫♫ (Laserlight, 1997)

Priceless Jazz Collection ♫♫♫♫ (GRP, 1997)

worth searching for: Christmas albums are not always easy to find since they're usually only big in the bins during the season to be jolly. But Fitzgerald's Christmas offerings, *Ella Fitzgerald's Christmas* ♫♫♫♫ (Capitol/EMI, 1996, prod. Ron Furmanek, Bob Furmanek) and *Wishes You a Swinging Christmas* ♫♫♫♫ (Verve, 1993, prod. Norman Granz), are worth tracking down. Once you get in the spirit, you'll be jolly to have Ella's swinging versions of timeless Christmas standbys.

influences:

◀◀ Maxine Sullivan, Connee Boswell, Billie Holiday, Bessie Smith

▶▶ Sarah Vaughan, Lena Horne, Betty Carter, Mel Tormé, Carmen McRae, Joe Williams, Shirley Horn, Diana Ross, Whitney Houston, Gladys Knight, Bette Midler, Barbra Streisand

Chris Tower

Fred Flange

See: Matt Monro

The Fleetwoods

Formed 1958, in Olympia, WA. Disbanded 1966.

Barbara Ellis, vocals; Gretchen Christopher; vocals, Gary Troxel, vocal, guitar.

It's as corny as a made-for-television movie and it's true. Christopher and Ellis were born days apart, wound up in the same maternity ward, and grew up together. In high school they formed their own vocal duo, the Saturns, then ran into another student, Troxel, and created an appealing, tripartite, white doo-wop vocal group whose first recording, "Come Softly to Me," went straight to #1 on the charts. Like their fairy-tale-ish formation, however, their string of hits—"Mr. Blue," "Tragedy," "(He's) the Great Imposter"—belied the actual work and craft involved. Every song contained intricate vocals, exquisite arrangements, and professional musicianship (among the regulars were studio aces Glen Campbell and Leon Russell and jazz bassist Red Callendar). "Come Softly to Me" demonstrated all the elements of one of pop's most unusual vocal groups. Troxel's casual, hummable "dum dum dum do dum a doobie do" pattern is joined by the girls' delicate "come softly darling" for two measures before Troxel's voice takes over the lead and the girls' voices wind oohs and aahs all around him. It ends as it began, with Troxel's easy "dum dum dum do dum a doobie do." Interestingly enough, it doesn't include the words of the title. "Tragedy" expresses teen angst (being jilted as catastrophe) with the Doomsday harmonies and most economical pop lyrics until the Ramones' "Blitzkreig Bop." They knew good material: "(He's) the Great Imposter" is an early Jackie DeShannon tune, and they were the first to record a song by a fledgling Randy Newman. But the fairy tale ran its course by 1963, when the group ran out of ideas as it found itself in the new rock market, where their genteel, low-key image and precise harmonies couldn't compete. The group broke up after *Folk Rock*, a desperate attempt to appear relevant, fell on deaf ears.

what's available: All of the above hits and the others are included on *The Best of the Fleetwoods* ♫♫♫ (Rhino, 1990, compilation prod. Bill Inglot), with some interesting non-hits, including a version of "A Lover's Concerto" from the ill-fated *Folk Rock*. *Come Softly to Me: The Very Best of the Fleetwoods* ♫♫♫ (Alliance, 1997) includes out-takes not included on the Rhino set, including the *a cappella* versions of "Mr. Blue" and "Come Softly to Me" and a radio commercial. *Greatest Hits* ♫♫♫ (Capitol Special Products, 1994) is just the basics, a cut below either of the above.

influences:

◀◀ The Penguins, the Dell-Vikings, the Capris, the Flamingos, the Clovers, the Marcels, the Impalas, the Crests, the Platters

▶▶ The Mamas & the Papas

Leland Rucker

Myron Floren

Born November 5, 1919, near Webster, SD.

With his bright, toothy smile and fast-moving fingers across his huge accordion keys, Floren became the biggest star of the Lawrence Welk Orchestra in its prime, and he continues to keep the Welk family tradition alive under his own name. A musical prodigy—he could play the family pump organ at age seven—Floren was already on the radio pumping the keys at age 19. He moved to St. Louis in 1946 to join the Buckeye Four, and it was there that he was hired on the spot after delighting the Welk band with a career-making solo during an audition at the Casa Loma Ballroom. It was the perfect arrangement for both: Welk no longer had to rely on his accordion skills, and Floren, a natural showman and consummate professional, got the center stage he deserved. Floren worked with Welk for 32 years and still performs regularly with the Stars of the Lawrence Welk Show, where his self-deprecating humor and easy-going style have made him a kind of Bruce Springsteen for the geriatric set.

what to buy: You can always find Floren's latest work for sale after his concerts, in both cassette and compact discs, and you can get your picture taken with the entire cast, too. If you're not so lucky, *The Polka King* 🎵🎵🎵 (Ranwood, 1993) is the premiere collection of this accomplished polka master.

best of the rest:

22 of the Greatest Polkas 🎵🎵🎵 (Ranwood, 1988)
22 Great Accordion Classics 🎵🎵🎵 (Ranwood, 1993)
22 Dance Party Favorites 🎵🎵🎵 (Ranwood, 1993)
Inspirational Songs 🎵🎵 (Ranwood, 1993)
22 Great Polka Hits, Vol. 2 🎵🎵🎵 (Ranwood, 1993)
Dance Little Bird 🎵🎵🎵 (Ross, 1997)

influences:

◀◀ Lawrence Welk

▶▶ "Weird Al" Jankovic

see also: *Lawrence Welk*

Leland Rucker

Frank Fontaine

Born April 19, 1920, in Cambridge, MA. Died August, 1978.

Fontaine was a singer-comedian who had a decent run in the movies as a character actor and bit player. Brief glimpses of his work can still be seen in *Here Comes the Groom* (1951) and the Dean Martin–Jerry Lewis vehicle *Scared Stiff* (1953). However, Fontaine's main claim to baby-boomer fame was his recurring role as Crazy Guggenheim on Jackie Gleason's CBS variety hour in the '60s. In the days when chronic alcoholism and reduced mental capacity were still considered wholesome prime-time entertainment, Fontaine would stagger into Gleason's "Joe the Bartender" sketches with the brim of his hat turned up, his face a mask of rubbery glee, ready to spout comic nonsense for the benefit of Joe and the ever-present (though unseen and un-heard) Mr. Donehy. The sketches went something like this:

Joe: You want Craze, Mr. Donehy? I'll call for him. Oh Cra-aze!

(Fontaine enters to tumultuous applause.)

Crazy: Hiya, Joe! Hiya, Mr. Donehy. Hee-yee-yee-yee-yee-yee-yee!

Joe: What have you been up to lately, Craze?

Crazy: Oh, you know. I ain't been doin' nuthin'. Jus' hangin' aroun', doin' nuthin'. Nuthin' at all, Joe. You know me Joe, just hangin' aroun', doin' nuthin'. Alla time, jus' doin' nuthin'. Jus' hangin' aroun', doin' nuthin' . . .

Joe: All right, already!

(Major applause and cheering.)

At that point, Fontaine would utilize his pure, nearly operatic Irish tenor to sincerely interpret a heartfelt ballad from the '20s or '30s, and cause Joe to wipe a tear from his eye. Fontaine's stint on the Gleason show was immensely popular, and re-sulted in three strong-selling LPs of nostalgic song material for the Paramount label. Afflicted with chronic heart disease, Fontaine was never able to fully capitalize on his success as Crazy Guggenheim, but he paved the way for another talk-in-one-voice-sing-in-another performer, Jim Nabors.

what's available: Crazy Guggenheim is nowhere to be found on *Let Me Call You Sweetheart* 🎵🎵🎵 (MCA Special Products, 1989, prod. various), but this eight-song compilation features Fontaine's affecting versions of songs from yesteryear such as "Heart of My Heart" and "Have You Ever Been Lonely." Fontaine's original nostalgia LPs are long out of print.

influences:

◀◀ Dennis Day

⏩ Jim Nabors, Foster Brooks

see also: *Jackie Gleason*

Ken Burke

Mary Ford
See: Les Paul

Helen Forrest
Born April 12, 1918 in Atlantic City, NJ.

Though largely forgotten today, Forrest was one of the finest vocalists of the big-band era. Her ability on lush romantic numbers as well as hot swing earned her the respect of the top orchestra leaders of the '30s and '40s. She was the star vocalist in Artie Shaw's band during its greatest years—beginning in 1938, when she replaced Billie Holiday. Attractive and sensual, Forrest's renditions of "I Don't Want to Walk without You Baby," "What's New," and others added an intimate dimension Shaw's band had previously been lacking. When the mercurial Shaw suddenly disbanded his outfit (he was never at ease with public life), Forrest signed on briefly with Benny Goodman. She didn't really get along with the King of Swing, but cut fine sides such as "I'm Nobody's Baby" and "It Never Entered My Mind" before departing. Brief stints with Nat King Cole's trio and Lionel Hampton led to her big hits with Harry James and His Orchestra, "I Had the Craziest Dream" and "I've Heard That Song Before" among them. All that high-profile band work led to feature film appearances in *Springtime in the Rockies, Bathing Beauty,* and *You Came Along.* After leaving James's orchestra, Forrest teamed up with singer Dick Haymes for a series of solid hit singles and radio appearances. After disappearing in the '50s, she resurfaced for a tour with Tommy Dorsey's Orchestra during 1961–62, and again in 1983 when she recorded an LP for Stash Records. Two years later, she reunited on film with one of her old bosses in *Artie Shaw: Time Is All You've Got* and followed up with a solid appearance in another documentary, *Symphony of Swing.* She has dropped from public view since then.

what to buy: Some of Forrest's better moments with the Artie Shaw, Benny Goodman, and Harry James Orchestras are on *Voice of the Big Bands* 𝄫𝄫𝄫𝄫 (Jasmine, 1997, prod. various), a fine introduction to this underrated vocalist, with the hits "I Had the Craziest Dream," "I've Heard That Song Before," and "The Devil Sat Down and Cried," with Dick Haymes.

what to buy next: From late in the big-band era (1949–50), *I Wanna Be Loved* 𝄫𝄫𝄫 (Hindsight, 1993, prod. Thomas Gra-

muglia) offers excellent performances with the Harry James Orchestra, including "Bill," "Too Marvelous for Words," "I Hadn't Anyone Till You," and the hit title track.

the rest:
On the Sunny Side of the Street 𝄫𝄫𝄫 (Audiophile, 1994)
Embraceable You 𝄫𝄫𝄫 (Hindsight, 1995)
Sentimental Swing 𝄫𝄫𝄫 (Sony Music Special, 1996)
Them There Eyes 𝄫𝄫𝄫 (Mr. Music, 1996)
Now and Forever: The 1983 Studio Sessions 𝄫𝄫𝄫 (Viper's Nest, 1996)
The Cream of Helen Forrest 𝄫𝄫𝄫 (Flapper, 1996)

worth searching for: You can find more work by Forrest scattered over discs by the famous bandleaders for whom she sang. On Benny Goodman's *Benny & the Singers* 🎵🎵🎵 (Memoir Classics, 1996), Forrest sings "It Never Entered My Mind," "Oh Look at Me Now," and "When the Sun Comes Out," on a disc featuring tracks by Peggy Lee, Louise Tobin, Martha Tilton, and Helen Ward. Artie Shaw's *Best of the Big Bands* 🎵🎵🎵🎵 (Legacy, 1990, compilation prod. Michael Brooks) features Forrest singing "I Don't Want to Walk without You Baby," and "I've Heard That Song Before." Forrest also guests on *Artie Shaw— 22 Original Big Band Recordings* 🎵🎵🎵 (Hindsight, 1993), *Harry James & His Orchestra: Jump Sauce* 🎵🎵🎵 (Viper's Nest, 1995), *Harry James—Yes Indeed!* 🎵🎵🎵🎵 (ASV, 1993), and *Harry James & His Orchestra 1943–46* 🎵🎵🎵 (Hindsight, 1994).

influences:

◀◀ Billie Holiday, Mildred Bailey, Ella Fitzgerald, Kitty Kallen

▶▶ Peggy Lee, Martha Tilton, Anita O'Day, Helen Ward

see also: *Les Paul*

Ken Burke

The Four Dukes
See: The Four Lads

The Four Freshmen
Formed 1947, in Chicago, IL.

Don Barbour (1947–60); Ross Barbour (1947–77); Hal Kratzsch (1947–53); Marvin Pruitt (1947–48); Bob Flanigan (1948–92); Ken Errair (1953–56); Ken Albers (1956–82); Bill Comstock (1960–73); Ray Brown (1973–77); Dennis Grillo (1977–82); Autie Goodman (1982–87, 1990–92); Rod Henley (1982–86); Gary Lee Rosenberg (1986–91); Mike Beisner (1982–90, 1991–92); Greg Stegeman (1989–present); Kevin Stout (1992–present); Bob Ferreira (1992–present); Alan Mac-Intosh (1994–96); Brian Eichenberger (1996–present), all vocals.

From the start, the Four Freshmen proudly positioned themselves a step or two behind everyone else. In the 1940s, when Sinatra was crooning Sammy Cahn songs, the boys from Indiana formed a barbershop quartet to sing tunes from the turn of the century. By the mid-1950s, as rock 'n' roll hit, they had updated their setlist. They sang Sammy Cahn. Stan Kenton discovered the Freshmen in 1950 at the Esquire Lounge in Dayton, Ohio. He helped them get a deal at Capitol, where they released, on average, two LPs a year between 1954 and 1965. The big hits came in 1956 with the top-20 single, "Graduation Day," and the first of a pair of Top 10 albums. Respect was more elusive. Years later, on stage, they would even joke about it, calling themselves "the Osmonds of the Stone Age."

(Even so, the Freshmen must have been surprised by the attention they received in Don Was's 1995 Brian Wilson documentary, *I Just Wasn't Made for These Times*. The four-part harmonies and the driving falsetto in the 1956 classic "Angel Eyes," off the *5 Trombones* album, are what young Wilson spent hours breaking down at his hi-fi and building up a few years later in the studio.) But back in the 1950s, the Freshmen emerged as heroes of the anti-hip, every dad's answer to Elvis Presley, Chuck Berry, and the other rock 'n' roll rabble-rousers. The Freshmen are still around today, sort of. The 15th to 20th incarnation, depending on who's counting, bounces from Ramada Inn to Red Lion with none of the original members on stage. In other words, stay away.

what to buy: The Capitol long-plays never made it to CD, but a lone twofer reissue, *5 Trombones & 5 Trumpets* 🎵🎵🎵 (EMI-Capitol, 1996, prod. Voyle Gilmore), features the band at its commercial peak. The backing is superb, with drummer Shelly Manne, a Sonny Rollins sideman, along on *5 Trombones*. There's a sort of stand-around-the-Christmas tree vibe as the Freshmen turn the previously smooth and sensual "Somebody Loves Me" into something downright goofy. And the boys swing through one of the silliest chorus in the history of recorded music: "Venus de Milo was noted for her charms/Strictly between us, you're cuter than Venus, and what's more you've got arms." There are surprisingly few greatest-hits collections out there, but go for *Spotlight on . . . The Four Freshmen* 🎵🎵🎵 (Capitol, 1995, prod. Brad Benedict), which spans their best years, from 1954 to 1961.

what to buy next: *Live at Butler University with Stan Kenton and His Orchestra* 🎵🎵🎵 (GNP Crescendo, 1972, arrangers Willie Maiden, Ken Albers) is a reissue of a solid concert that would only have been better if it had been recorded in 1962 instead of 1972. The G-rated stage banter is priceless, and the band is live at a point when it still includes three-quarters of the glory day members.

what to avoid: If Debby Boone and Walter Cronkite had produced a love child, he would probably sound a lot like the singers on *Fresh!* 🎵 (Ranwood, 1986, prod. Rod L. Henley), an irritating attempt by the latter-day Freshmen to take on "modern" pop. They cover Donald Fagan, Stevie Wonder, and Christopher Cross—actually making you long for the latter's rollicking version of "Sailing."

The Four Freshmen **(Archive Photos)**

the rest:

Collectors Series 🎵🎵🎵 (Capitol, 1991)
Freshmas! 🎵🎵 (Ranwood, 1992)
Graduation Day 🎵🎵 (Laserlight, 1992)
Greatest Hits 🎵🎵 (Curb, 1993)
Voices in Standards 🎵 (Hindsight, 1994)
Day by Day 🎵🎵🎵 (Hindsight, 1995)
Angel Eyes 🎵🎵🎵🎵 (Viper's Nest, 1995)
It's a Blue World 🎵🎵🎵🎵 (Viper's Nest, 1995)
22 Legendary Hits 🎵🎵🎵 (CEMA Special Markets, 1995)

influences:

◀◀ Jack Teagarden, the Andrews Sisters

▶▶ The Beach Boys, the Lettermen, the Manhattan Transfer

Geoff Edgers

The Four Lads

Formed 1950, as the Four Dukes, in Toronto, Canada. Renamed the Four Lads in 1951.

Bernie Toorish, second tenor; Jimmie Arnold, first tenor; Frank Busseri, baritone; Connie Codarini, bass.

The Four Lads were so well regarded by Columbia Records they were actually given their choice of acts with whom they wanted to record. The Lads developed their smooth blend of harmonies at the St. Michaels' Cathedral Choir School, and when they weren't studying, they sang at various Toronto hotels. One night, the leader of the Golden Gates Quartet was so impressed with the new group's imitation of the Gates style that he held the phone up to the stage so his manager could hear them. Instantly signed to a management contract, the Four Lads were booked into lengthy engagements at New York nightspots and began appearing on early TV's top variety shows. In 1951, Columbia's Mitch Miller hired them as both session singers and as a solo act. The first artist they chose to accompany was the then unknown Johnnie Ray. The group's tender background crooning provided perfect counterpoint to Ray's passionate R&B wailing, and soon "Cry" b/w "The Little White Cloud That Cried" became the biggest-selling record in the country. The Lads backed Ray for other hits, such as "Please, Mr. Sun," "Here I Am Brokenhearted," and "What's the Use?" The Lads brought bouncy exotic rhythms to the Top 10 hits "Skokiaan" and "Istanbul (Not Constantinople)," but their stock in trade was the lush romantic balladry of "There's Only One of You," "No Not Much," and "Moments to Remember." Even after dozens of hit records, the group continued backing other artists in the studio, cutting hits with Frankie Laine and Doris Day, among others. Their solo career peaked

in 1956 with "Standing on the Corner (Watching All the Girls Go By)," from the Broadway musical *The Most Happy Fella*. Though subsequent singles made the charts, the forces of rock 'n' roll eventually rendered irrelevant their clean-cut style and straight-laced musical tastes. The group splintered off in 1961, with Arnold and Busseri fronting new lineups of the Four Lads and Bernard Toorish singing with the Vince Maestro Quartet. However, their hits from the '50s are perpetual staples of nostalgia anthologies, and in 1990, eclectic rockers They Might Be Giants recorded a surprisingly faithful version of "Istanbul," which became a popular video on *Tiny Toons Adventures.*

what to buy: "Moments to Remember," "Istanbul (Not Constantinople)," "No Not Much," "Standing on the Corner," and many other hits, both romantic and rhythmic, are on *16 Most Requested Songs* 🎵🎵🎵🎵 (Sony, 1991, compilation prod. Michael Brooks), one of Sony's most worthwhile "Nice Price" collections.

the rest:

That Great Gettin' Up Morning 🎵🎵🎵 (Sony Music Special, 1995)
Love Songs 🎵🎵🎵 (Ranwood, 1997)

worth searching for: The perfect marriage of talent and material, *The Four Lads Sing Frank Loesser* 🎵🎵🎵🎵 (Columbia, 1957, prod. Mitch Miller) contains exquisitely sung medleys of Loesser songs culled from *Hans Christian Andersen, Guys and Dolls,* and *Where's Charley?*

influences:

◀◀ The Ames Brothers, the Golden Gate Quartet

▶▶ The Four Freshmen, the Four Preps, the Four Coins, the Four Voices, They Might Be Giants

Ken Burke

The Four Preps

Formed 1956, in Los Angeles, CA. Disbanded 1968.

Bruce Belland, lead tenor; Ed Cobb, bass (1956–66); David Sommerville, bass (1966–68); Marvin Inabnett, high tenor; Don Clark, high tenor; Glen Larson, baritone.

Capitol signed this vocal group to a long-term contract while the members were 16 and still in high school, and they paid off with several huge hits over the next few years. They honed a carefully rehearsed, low-key stage act founded on their choirboy harmonies and fine-tuned around the light topical humor favored by contemporaries the Kingston Trio, Peter, Paul and

Mary, and the Limeliters. Belland and Larson wrote the group's best-known songs—"26 Miles (Santa Catalina)," "Big Man," "Down by the Station," "More Money for You and Me (Medley)"—and the Preps appeared in films (*Gidget*) and on television (*Ozzie and Harriet, The Ed Sullivan Show, American Bandstand,* and *The Lawrence Welk Show*). "More Money for You and Me," a parody of their contemporaries recorded live in 1961, is a snapshot of them at their best. And though their 1964 "Letter to the Beatles" gently parodies the growing commercialism of what would become known as "rock," they couldn't compete with the update. An attempt to use "Phil Och's Draft Dodger Rag" as a comedy song shows how far out of touch they had gotten by the end. Meanwhile, Cobb produced and wrote "Dirty Water" and "Sometimes Good Guys Don't Wear White" for the Standells and "Tainted Love" for Gloria Jones (it was later a worldwide hit for the electronic dance band Soft Cell in 1982). Recently, Cobb, Belland, David Sommerville (he was lead singer on the Diamonds' "Little Darlin" before joining the original Preps), and former Association member Jim Yester somehow find time to perform as the New Four Preps.

what's available: *The Four Preps* ✍✍✍ (Capitol, 1989, prod. Ron Furmanek) is about all you really need to capture the Preps' essence, with all the irresistible, syrupy early hits and late misfires, with added B-sides and outtakes. *The Best of the Four Preps* (WEA Special Products, 1993) contains four tracks not included in the Capitol Collector's Series disc, but do you really need their version of "Moon River"?

worth searching for: Their straight version of "Smoke Gets in Your Eyes" (not the parody on "More Money for You and Me") is on the hard-to-find *Capitol Sings Jerome Kern* ✍✍ (Capitol, 1992) alongside tracks by Judy Garland, Peggy Lee, and Nat King Cole. *When AM Was King* ✍✍ (Capitol, 1992) includes "26 Miles (Santa Catalina)" with other Capitol hitmakers of the '60s, including Tennessee Ernie Ford, Bobby Darin, and Grand Funk Railroad.

influences:

◀◀ The Limeliters, the Kingston Trio, the Four Freshmen

▶▶ The Ames Brothers, the Four Lads, the Four Aces, the Lettermen, the Association, Peter, Paul & Mary

Leland Rucker

The Four Seasons

See: Frankie Valli

Cocktail Classics

Hey Jude

18-Karat The Beatles *1967–1970* (Apple)

Bombsville! Bing Crosby *Hey Jude/Hey Bing!* (Amos)

Connie Francis

Born Concetta Rosa Maria Franconero, December 12, 1938, in Newark, NJ.

Along with Brenda Lee, Connie Francis was the most popular female rock singer between the rise of Elvis Presley and the arrival of the Beatles. She had 35 Top 40 hits between 1958 and 1964, including three Number Ones: "Everybody's Somebody's Fool," "My Heart Has a Mind of Its Own," and "Don't Break the Heart That Loves You." But Francis more closely resembled a pop singer of the classic mold than she did a rock 'n' roller. An Italian-American from New Jersey, young Connie showed her musical precociousness at age three when she learned to play accor-

dion; by age 10 she was performing on local telvision. When she began recording, Francis's popularity crossed from pop into country, R&B, and film markets as well. Francis's material ranged from new songs from the likes of Jeff Barry, Ellie Greenwich, and John Loudermilk to the tunes of such classic pop writers as Sammy Cahn, Jule Styne, and Jimmy Van Heusen, making her popular with both teens and their parents. She starred in four films: *Where the Boys Are* (which included one of her biggest hits), *Follow the Boys, Looking for Love,* and *When the Boys Meet the Girls*. She frequently recording new vocal tracks for her hit singles in Italian, Spanish, and other languages; by the time her hits stopped coming in the mid-1960s, Francis had developed a substantial international market.

Francis's status as a teen idol decreased dramatically as rock grew more rebellious in the late '60s, and medical problems and a traumatic rape and robbery kept her from performing for much of the '70s and '80s. But lately, nostalgic listeners have grown to appreciate the talent that made her the best-selling female singer of her time.

what to buy: *The Very Best of Connie Francis* 🎵🎵🎵🎵 (Polydor, 1986, compilation prod. Tim Rogers) contains most of Francis's biggest pop singles, including the chart-topping "My Heart Has a Mind of Its Own" and "Don't Break the Heart That Loves You." Also, "Everybody's Somebody's Fool," from 1962, was a cross-format smash, and "Second-Hand Love" is a Phil Spector tune recorded in Nashville.

what to buy next: *Souvenirs* 🎵🎵🎵 (Polydor, 1996, comp. prod. Don Charles, Bill Levenson, Patrick Niglio) provides a wide-ranging overview of Francis's recordings during her heyday, from her first single, 1958's "Who's Sorry Now," to 1969's "Zingara (Gypsy)," her final single for MGM. In between, there are all her major hits; pop, country, and R&B songs; plus tunes in Italian, Spanish, and Hebrew.

what to avoid: Too many of Francis's original recordings remain in print to settle for the remakes on *Greatest Hits* 🎵🎵 (Dominion, 1994).

the rest:
Greatest Hits 🎵🎵🎵 (Polydor)
Greatest Italian Hits 🎵🎵🎵 (Polydor)
The Very Best of Connie Francis, Vol. II 🎵🎵 (Polydor, 1988)
Where the Hits Are 🎵🎵 (Malaco, 1990)

Connie Francis **(Archive Photos)**

Hits Of 🎵🎵 (Sound Choice, 1992)
Best of Connie Francis 🎵🎵🎵 (PolyGram Special Markets, 1996)
Christmas in My Heart 🎵🎵🎵 (Polydor, 1996)
The Return Concert: Live at Trump's Castle 🎵🎵 (Sony, 1996)
Swinging Connie Francis 🎵🎵🎵 (Audiophile, 1996)
Where the Boys Are: Connie Francis in Hollywood 🎵🎵🎵 (Rhino, 1997)
On Guard 🎵🎵🎵 (Jazz Band, 1997)
Christmas Cheer 🎵🎵 (PolyGram Special Markets, 1997)
Italian Collection, Vol. 1 🎵🎵🎵 (PGD, 1997)
Italian Collection, Vol. 2 🎵🎵🎵 (PGD, 1997)

worth searching for: The German label Bear Family has issued the duets Francis recorded in 1964 with Hank Williams Jr. on *Sing Great Country Favourites* 🎵🎵🎵 (Bear Family), which are worth hearing mainly for the sheer strangeness of the concept. Bear Family has also released two five-CD box sets of Francis's recordings: *White Sox, Pink Lipstick . . . and Stupid Cupid* 🎵🎵🎵 (Bear Family, 1994) and *Kissin' Twistin' Goin' Where the Boys Are* 🎵🎵🎵 (Bear Family, 1996). *De Colección* 🎵🎵🎵 (Polydor, 1995) is a collection of Spanish-language tunes including "Besame Mucho" and "Vaya Con Dios."

influences:

⏮ Kay Starr, Jo Stafford, Patti Page

⏭ Brenda Lee, Petula Clark

Brian Mansfield

Michael Franks

Born September 18, 1944, in La Jolla, CA.

A charter member of Warner Bros.' "jazz and progressive" roster in the early 1970s, Michael Franks has always been harder to market than then-labelmates George Benson and Al Jarreau. Too smooth for jazz, too sophisticated for pop, and too clever for his own commercial good, Franks is an offbeat lyricist who delights in expressing gooey, romantic sentiments with a warped sense of humor and a straight face. He namedrops everyone from Cole Porter to Marc Chagall and rhymes words like "pulchritude" and "raison d'etre." But just when lines like "We touched like watercolor fawns/in landscapes painted by Cezanne" start painting him as an intellectual hot dog, he turns around and writes such stingingly economical comebacks as "You gave me that sweet look/ . . . I swallowed your meat hook" and "I hear from my ex/on the back of my checks." If lounge fans don't appreciate his tongue-in-cheek humor, they certainly will be smitten by his seductive singing voice—a breathy tenor that swings and lopes with the hepcat ease of a beachcombing Mose Allison. His recent albums lean more toward keyboard-dominated contemporary pop-jazz with such collaborators as Jeff Lorber and the Yellowjackets, but his 1970s albums are a finger-popping, Brazilian-flavored mother-lode just waiting to be rediscovered.

what to buy: His major-label debut, *The Art of Tea* 𝄞𝄞𝄞𝄞 (Reprise, 1975, prod. Tommy LiPuma), is his most playful and jazziest effort, thanks to backing by Joe Sample, Larry Carlton, and Wilton Felder and upbeat love songs that push the metaphorical envelope: his inspiration ranges from movies in "Nightmoves" to food in "Eggplant" to geography in his lone Top 40 hit, "Popsicle Toes" ("You've got the nicest North America this sailor ever saw/I like to feel your warm Brazil and touch your Panama"). Equally suave and silly is *Burchfield Nines* 𝄞𝄞𝄞𝄞 (Warner Bros., 1978, prod. Tommy LiPuma), highlighted by the bluesy "Wrestle a Live Nude Girl" and the boy-meets-hair quest "In Search of the Perfect Shampoo" ("Gonna suds away all our troubles/in a million low-pH bubbles").

what to buy next: The four Jeff Lorber–produced tracks tread dangerously close to suburban R&B, but most of *Dragonfly Summer* 𝄞𝄞𝄞 (Reprise, 1993, prod. Jeff Lorber, the Yellowjackets, Gil Goldstein, Ben Sidran) proves Franks hasn't lost his tender touch. Lovely duets with Dan Hicks ("Keeping My Eye on You") and Peggy Lee ("You Were Meant for Me") are upstaged by the nostalgic "Monk's New Tune" and a dreamy vocal version of the theme from *I Love Lucy*.

what to avoid: Robotic drum and keyboard programs dominate *The Camera Never Lies* **woof!** (Warner Bros., 1987, prod. Rob Mounsey) and drown out any semblance of Franks's charm.

the rest:
Sleeping Gypsy 𝄞𝄞𝄞 (Warner Bros., 1977)
Tiger in the Rain 𝄞𝄞𝄞 (Warner Bros., 1979)
One Bad Habit 𝄞𝄞 (Warner Bros., 1980)
Object of Desire 𝄞𝄞𝄞 (Warner Bros., 1982)
Passionfruit 𝄞𝄞 (Warner Bros., 1983)
Skin Dive 𝄞 (Warner Bros., 1985)
Blue Pacific 𝄞𝄞𝄞 (Reprise, 1990)
Abandoned Garden 𝄞𝄞𝄞 (Reprise, 1995)

worth searching for: "I Bought You a Plastic Star for Your Aluminum Christmas Tree," Franks's humorous contribution to *Warner Bros. Jazz Christmas Party* 𝄞𝄞𝄞 (Warner Bros., 1997, prod. Matt Pierson), indeed is the life of the party.

influences:
◀◀ Mose Allison, Antonio Carlos Jobim, Bob Dorough

▶▶ Ben Sidran, Dan Hicks, Al Jarreau

David Okamoto

Stan Freberg
Born Stanley Victor Freberg, August 7, 1926, in Los Angeles, CA.

Freberg's comedy recordings opened the door for the "sick" humor movement of the late '50s. More importantly, he viciously (and brilliantly) parodied many of the artists discussed in this guide. Freberg was good enough at age 18 to do voice-overs for classic Warner Bros. cartoons alongside the legendary Mel Blanc, and as a character actor on the popular Jack Benny and Henry Morgan radio shows. A decent guitarist and singer, he also toured with Red Fox and His Musical Hounds, where he developed the material for his first comedy hit, "John & Marsha." In this classic soap opera parody, the only dialogue heard are the words "John" and "Marsha," repeated with varying degrees of dramatic shading and intensity by Freberg, who plays both roles. It is a masterpiece of voice-acting. Aided by voice-over superstars Daws Butler, Paul Frees, and June Foray, Freberg also scored hit records with comedy sketches based on Jack Webb's *Dragnet*, "St. George & the Dragonet," and "Little Blue Riding Hood" (which hit #1 for four weeks). Yet it is as a musical parodist that Freberg made his greatest impact. His string of hit records targeted Johnnie Ray's sobbing ("Try"), Mitch Miller's vapid mainstream pop ("Yellow Rose of Texas"), Harry Belafonte's calypso ("Banana Boat Song"), Lonnie Donegan's skiffle ("Rock Island Line"), Les Paul and Mary Ford's technical wizardry ("Waiting for the Sunrise"), and Eartha Kitt's French affectations ("C'est Si Bon"), among others. Freberg reserved his most acerbic comedic bile for such stars of early rock as the Crew Cuts ("Sh-Boom"), the Platters ("The Great Pretender"), and Elvis Presley ("Heartbreak Hotel"). For most of these parodies, Freberg employed the same dramatic device: "What if we could hear what went on at the latest hitmaker's recording session?" The resultant satire painted a resonant picture of an industry rife with gimmick-addled clods and hipster sell-outs, an idea as true today as it was then. What distinguishes Freberg's parodies, as much as the humor content, is how hard he tried to capture the flavor and spirit of the original recordings. He hired top musicians for his sessions and consulted with producers on how certain effects were achieved. More of a comedic method actor than an impressionist, Freberg could deliver a first-rate performance à la Elvis Presley or Joe Friday because he seemed to know what it actually felt like to be those characters. Freberg's fame on records led to his caustically funny radio series on CBS. It was there he fashioned his greatest, darkest satire, covering the A-bomb, TV Westerns, political correctness, and censorship in a fashion that is still fresh and funny today. However, by 1957 network radio had succumbed to the forces of television, and Freberg's show lasted a scant 12 episodes. Too hostile and ironic for commercial TV, Freberg tried his hand at longer forms of comedy, but his appeal waned just as the golden age of comedy LPs got underway. He eventually gravitated to Madison Avenue, where his hip, irreverent humor racked up 21 CLIO Awards for creatively pitching such products as Jeno's Pizza Rolls and Sunsweet Prunes. In recent times, Freberg has run daily two-minute commentaries on National Public Radio, written his autobiography, and released his first new LP in decades, *Stan Freberg Presents the United States of America, Vol. 2: The Middle Years*. Once you have heard a Stan Freberg parody, you'll never be able to listen to the original version in quite the same way again.

what to buy: There have been several Freberg repackages through the years, and most are similar to *Greatest Hits* 𝄞𝄞𝄞𝄞 (Curb, 1993, prod. Stan Freberg), which includes his best-charting parodies, such as "Yellow Rose of Texas," "Sh-Boom," "Heartbreak Hotel," and "John & Marsha," mixed with lesser-known comic bits. The best disc ever issued on Freberg is *Capitol Collector's Series* 𝄞𝄞𝄞𝄞 (Capitol, 1990, compilation prod. Ron Furmanek), which contains the big hits and includes all three of his *Dragnet* parodies, and the wonderfully cynical "Green Christmas." Some stores and catalogs still have this one, and it's more than worth the effort to find.

what to buy next: The first two shows of Freberg's 1957 CBS radio series are on *Stan Freberg Show* 𝄞𝄞𝄞𝄞 (Radiola, 1993) and are sterling examples of the type of satire that kept him from really making it on TV. A hilarious introduction to a radio comic who was at his peak but too far ahead of his time. After this, by all means, seek out the Radio Spirits compilations.

what to avoid: Not so much a bad disc as a lesser work, *Presents the United States of America, Vols. 1 & 2* 𝄞𝄞𝄞 (Rhino, 1996, prod. Stan Freberg) is Freberg's attempt to transform events in U.S. history into a satiric musical. Volume one was originally released in 1961, and its companion volume was recorded (with special guest John Goodman) in 1996. On both, the overlong musical numbers too often get in the way, and dilute what should've been a great comedy outing.

the rest:
First 7 Episodes 𝄞𝄞𝄞𝄞 (Radio Spirits/Original Cast, 1997)
Final 5 Episodes 𝄞𝄞𝄞𝄟 (Radio Spirits/Original Cast, 1997)

worth searching for: Freberg attempted to revive radio comedy with *Freberg Underground! Show #1* (a.k.a. *Pay Radio*) 𝄞𝄞𝄞𝄞 (Capitol, 1964, prod. Stan Freberg), wherein the comic hilariously demonstrates the advantages of radio special effects over those of television. Also, Freberg's autobiography, *It Only Hurts When I Laugh* 𝄞𝄞𝄞 (Times Books/Random House, 1989), reveals quite a lot about the comic's life, creative method, and pet peeves.

influences:

◀◀ Mel Blanc, Fred Allen, Jack Benny, Henry Morgan, Spike Jones

▶▶ Allan Sherman, Ray Stevens, Firesign Theatre, Duck's Breath Mystery Theater, "Weird Al" Yankovic, *Saturday Night Live*, SCTV

Ken Burke

Friends of Dean Martinez

Formed 1995, in Tucson, AZ.

Bill Elm, guitar; John Convertin, vibes; Van Christian, drums; Tom Larkins, percussion; Joey Burns, guitar.

Though this band makes albums for Sub Pop Records, the same label that brought us Nirvana and Soundgarden, its sophisticated blend of 1960s kitsch music references with authentic American idioms is anything but grungey. Originally called the Friends of Dean Martin, the band is actually a side project, with two members each from the rock bands Giant Sand and Naked Prey. A kind of mutant morphing of Ennio Morricone, Santo and Johnny, and the house band at Trader Vic's, the quintet creates sun-kissed lounge-rock with a heavy melancholy undertow by fusing precise slide guitar work with twinkly vibes and leisurely, frequently samba-tinged, tempos.

what's available: The band's two albums, *The Shadow of Your Smile* 𝄞𝄞𝄞𝄞 (Sub Pop, 1995, prod. Craig Schumacher, Friends of Dean Martinez) and *Retrograde* 𝄞𝄞𝄞𝄞𝄞 (Sub Pop, 1997, prod. Craig Schumacher, Bill Elm), mix original compositions with sundry jazz and lounge standards, and both are worth owning. There is a grandeur to *Retrograde*, and a subtle sense of loneliness, that is not quite as well articulated on *The Shadow of Your Smile*.

influences:

◀◀ Santo & Johnny, Dean Martin, Giant Sand, Naked Prey, Ennio Morricone

Marc Weingarten

Ethel Gabriel

See: The Living Strings, George Melachrino

Slim Gaillard

Born Bulee Gaillard, around 1915, in Detroit, MI. Died February 26, 1991, in London, England.

One of jazz music's most inventive humorists, "Slim" Gaillard was truly sui generis, a pianist, guitar player, and drummer who fashioned positively surreal musical concoctions using his own twisted syntax and mongrel vernacular; nonwords like "voit," "voutee," and "reenie" frequently cropped up in his work. Gaillard grew up in Detroit and began his musical career as a guitar-playing, tap-dancing novelty act. In 1937, Gaillard hooked up with bassist Slam Stewart to form the duo Slim and Slam, whose biggest hit was "Flat Fleet Floogie" (as in "the flat fleet floogie with a floy joy"). After a brief stint in the army, Gaillard moved to California in 1944, where he found steady work on various radio shows and attracted the attention of Charlie Parker and Dizzy Gillespie, who toured with him in 1945. Gaillard continued to tour the jazz circuit until the mid-'50s, but his career lost momentum by the end of the decade. He made a reunion album with Stewart in 1958, and appeared in the film *Absolute Beginners* in 1985.

what to buy: *Laughing in Rhythm: The Verve Years* ☟☟☟☟ (Verve, 1994) is all the Slim you'll ever really need. Sample tracks: "Boip! Boip!," "Mashugana Mambo," "Chicken Rhythm" . . . you get the idea.

the rest:
Anytime, Anyplace ☟☟☟ (Hep, 1994)
Frankie's Jump ☟☟☟ (Affinity, 1994)
Slim's Jam ☟☟☟ (Drive Archive, 1996)
Slim Gaillard at Birdland 1951 ☟☟☟☟ (Hep, 1996)
Trio, Quartet, and Orchestra ☟☟☟ (Jazz Anthology, 1996)
Slim and Slam ☟☟☟☟ (Columbia/Legacy, 1996)

influences:
◀◀ Charlie Parker, Dizzy Gillespie, Al Jolson, Louis Armstrong

▶▶ Stan Freberg, Mickey Katz, Eddie Fisher

Marc Weingarten

Serge Gainsbourg

Born 1928, in Paris, France. Died March 2, 1991, in Paris, France.

The son of Russian Jewish immigrants, Gainsbourg was an outsider for much of his life in France. But on the strength of sheer personality, he emerged as one of that country's most beloved and controversial cultural icons. Gainsbourg was a legendary raconteur, pioneering rapper, and all-around rogue who brought a distinctive sneer and a lecherous wink to a variety of styles that have made him the toast of the post-modern lounge scene in the '90s.

He originally dabbled as a painter and pianist in the mid-'50s while sipping Pernod in the seedy nightclubs and cafes of Pigalle. He didn't find his true calling until 1958 when, at age 30, he launched his recording career by delivering romantic and risqué monologues about the Bohemian arts scene with a distinctive voice best described as a mix of Lou Reed and Maurice Chevalier. Early on he intoned his monologues over relatively straightforward jazz backings, like a Beat poet reciting his lines over improvised jams. By the early '60s the music was incorporating different ethnic rhythms and poppier arrangements (Serge was particularly fond of the cha-cha). Then Gainsbourg went rock 'n' roll. From 1966 to 1969, he played the bad boy to the hilt and scored a series of hit singles, one more outlandish than the next. His non-musical "specialty" was corrupting young starlets, innocent nubiles like Brigitte Bardot and Jane Birkin (who became his wife). He recorded a series of memorable duets, including the immortal "Bonnie and Clyde" with Bardot and his most infamous tune, "Je T'Aime . . . Moi Non Plus," a lustful musical seduction of Birkin replete with orgasmic gasps years before Donna Summer's "Love to Love You." Gainsbourg died of a heart attack in 1991, not long after he made headlines one more time by voicing his explicit carnal desire for Whitney Houston on live TV. Irrepressible to the end, he was truly a lounge lizard of considerable style.

what's available: Gainsbourg's original albums are expensive and hard to find, but thankfully Mercury Records recently issued a series of compilations that include most of his best work. *Du Jazz dans le Ravin* ☟☟☟☟ (Mercury, 1996) collects the relatively straight jazz tracks he released between 1958 and 1964. *Coleur Cafe* ☟☟☟☟ (Mercury, 1996) chronicles the same period, but focuses on Gainsbourg's attempts to introduce France to various "ethnic musics," including Latin American rhythms and what today would be called Afro-pop. Best of all is *Comic Strip* ☟☟☟☟ (Mercury, 1996), which includes lounge-rock classics such as "Bonnie and Clyde," "Je T'Aime . . . Moi Non Plus," "Docteur Jekyll et Monsieur Hyde," and "Ford Mustang."

influences:

⏪ Chet Baker, Maurice Chevalier, Leonard Cohen, Miles Davis, Dizzy Gillespie, Thelonious Monk

⏩ The Bad Seeds, Beck, Luna, Luscious Jackson, Stereolab, Steve Wynn

Jim DeRogatis

The Galaxy Trio

Formed 1993, in Portland OR.

Jim Crabbe, guitar; Bryson Cater, bass; Elmo, drums; Scott Galpher, drums.

Started in Portland and guided by Criswell (the noted single-named prophet, author, and pal of movie director Ed Wood), this band has recorded some of the best surf-style music since the Ventures started drawing Social Security. Their recorded output is small—two singles, two 10" records, and tracks on Dick Dale and Link Wray tribute albums. Not as kitschy as Man or Astro-Man? nor as dreamy as the Mermen, these guys nevertheless excel within the limited expanses (to some) of surf music. Sadly, they don't tour much, but the live feel of their records is enough to make you pour sand on the living room floor and break out the tiki torches.

what to buy: *In the Harem* ♫♫♫♫ (Estrus, 1995, prod. Criswell) is a groovy collection that includes a ripping version of "Fur Elise" (you'll recognize it) and the clever "Surfcide." Though it's less than 20 minutes long, it's right for any mood, and especially recommended for wakes, christenings, Bar Mitzvahs, and Sunday worship. It's also essential for the amusing cover art, which includes turbans, leering looks, bad facial hair, a hookah, harem girls, and liner notes by Criswell.

what to buy next: *Saucers over Vegas* ♫♫♫ (Estrus, 1995, prod. Conrad Uno, Richard Head) is not quite as fully realized as *In the Harem*, and the cover art isn't as clever, but it's not bad. With song titles like "Jack Lord's Hair," "Log Jam," and "Saddle Sore," it deserves a spot on your shelf.

influences:

⏪ The Ventures, Man or Astro-Man?, the Phantom Surfers, Shadowy Men on a Shadowy Planet, the Raybeats, Los Straitjackets, Laika & the Cosmonauts, Jon & the Nightriders

⏩ The Volcanos, Huevos Rancheros

Barry M. Prickett

Cocktail Classics

How High the Moon

18-Karat — **Les Paul & Mary Ford**
Best of the Capitol Masters
(Capitol)

Bombsville! — **Ferrante & Teicher**
Autumn Leaves
(Sony)

James Galway

Born December 8, 1939, in Belfast, Ireland.

Galway's accomplishments in the classical milieu are many and varied. Unfortunately, the world of classical music has a rather limited commercial appeal, and those musicians who rise to the top in it often feel compelled to reach out to pop audiences. But the refined style of such artists and their tendency to prefer well-groomed popular music usually means they have more resonance in the lounge sector than anywhere else. Galway's efforts outside the classical arena are interesting when they afford him the opportunity to display his playing prowess. Alas, not all of his pop efforts really do him justice and he often seems to sacrifice musical integrity for soothing pleasantries. His work with traditional Irish musicians such as the Chieftains shows off the down-to-earth side of his talent in the beautiful lyrical quality of the sad songs and the joyous spirit of more upbeat dance numbers. When Galway tackles film music, increasingly popular in his pop repertoire, he often generates new nuances and fresh interpretations (as on the excellent *In the Pink* album, which paired Galway with Henry Mancini). But in recent years he has demonstrated an unfortunate tendency to veer into the schlocky showtune world of Andrew Lloyd Webber and straight-up adult-contemporary pop, and the general lack of character in these milieus doesn't provide him with the substantive material that pushes his playing into top form, and his flute ends up sounding like a fluttering garnish atop the cloying, cloddish quasi-rock arrangements.

what to buy: Galway interprets Henry Mancini beautifully on *In the Pink* ♫♫♫♫ (RCA, 1984, prod. Ralph Mace), which is as whimsical, poignant, distinctive, and colorful as the characters they complemented. Among the stand-outs: "The Pink Panther" and "Baby Elephant Walk," amusingly rendered by Galway on the petite pennywhistle. On *In Ireland* ♫♫♫♫ (RCA, 1987, prod. Ralph Mace, Paddy Maloney), a collaboration with Ireland's celebrated traditionalists, the Chieftains, Galway gracefully delivers such classics as "Danny Boy" and "When You and I Were Young, Maggie." The album was apparently recorded live with dancers participating, and the spirit of the dance is apparent. It's a pity there aren't more complete liner notes detailing the origins of these songs. *Over the Sea to Skye* ♫♫♫♫ (RCA Victor, 1990, prod. Ralph Mace, Paddy Maloney), a second collaboration with the Chieftains, is fiery and dreamy by turns; it's a vibrant musical history lesson, with a few links to Scotland—and one to China.

what to buy next: *Beauty and the Beast: Galway at the Movies* ♫♫♫♫ (RCA Victor, 1993, prod. Ralph Mace) includes a variety of film music old and new—from the instrumentalized version of the Beatles' "In My Life," from *For the Boys,* to "Never on a Sunday," from *Zorba the Greek,* and Mancini's classic "Moon River," from *Breakfast at Tiffany's. The Lark in the Clear Air* ♫♫♫♫ (RCA Victor, 1994, prod. Ralph Mace) finds Galway reunited with Japanese synthesizer-meister Hiro Fujikake, who generally restrains the New-Agey tendencies that proved such an annoyance on Galway's previous collaborations with him. Primarily classical selections, these tracks offer simple, uncluttered vehicles for Galway—a reminder of his prowess as a classical player. *Greatest Hits, Vol. 2* ♫♫♫♫ (RCA Victor, 1992, prod. Jeff Berger, Karl Hereim) features newly recorded material, in-

cluding the theme from "Beauty and the Beast," "Blue Eyes," "Nadia's Theme," "Unforgettable," "Something for the Leprechaun," and the "Viewer Mail Theme" from *Late Night with David Letterman. Greatest Hits* ♫♫♫♫ (RCA Victor, 1988, prod. various) is a convenient 20-track collection that neatly covers the range of Galway's pop repertoire, from film themes to traditional tunes, plus Rimsky-Korsakov's "Flight of the Bumblebee" and the Bee Gees' "I Started a Joke."

what to avoid: On *The Wind Beneath My Wings* ♫♫ (RCA Victor, 1991, prod. Ralph Mace) Galway does the show tune routine. The saccharine sentimentality quotient is a bit high—"Send in the Clowns," "Memory," and "The Windmills of Your Mind" all on one album—and all the "nice" vibes make for a pleasant mood but don't really challenge him. The "nice" music continues on *Wind of Change* ♫♫ (RCA Victor, 1994, prod. Ralph Mace), and as admirable as the tremendous range of this collection is (every thing from Mariah Carey's "Dreamlover" to the Scorpions' "Wind of Change"), it feels like Galway is slumming in pop-land, cruising on the easy-to-digest updraft of adult rock. *The Enchanted Forest—Melodies of Japan* ♫♫ (RCA Victor, 1990, prod. Ralph Mace), the follow-up to *Songs of the Seashore,* is a fanciful excursion that once again combines contemporary airs with traditional Japanese melodies. Unfortunately, the arrangements (heavy on synthesizers) lack the earthy feel of traditional instrumentation and often lapse into a kind of spacey New Age blandness.

the rest:
The Celtic Minstrel ♫♫♫ (RCA Victor, 1996)
Seasons ♫♫♫ (RCA Victor)
Greatest Hits, Vol. 3 ♫♫♫ (RCA Victor, 1998)

worth searching for: *The Wayward Wind* ♫♫♫ (RCA, 1982, prod. Tom Collins), Galway's country album, is a hit-and-miss affair. While his take on "Duelin' Banjos" is sly and full of vim, most of this album tends toward a kind of flaccid mellowness.

influences:
◀◀ Jean-Pierre Rampal, the Pied Piper of Hamlin
▶▶ Ian Anderson

Sandy Masuo

Judy Garland

Born Frances Ethel Gumm, June 10, 1922, in Grand Rapids, MN. Died June 22, 1969, in London, England.

Although for many people she will always be the naïve 17-year-old explorer named Dorothy from *The Wizard of Oz,* Garland maintained a substantial second career outside the movies as a singer. First as a teen member of the Gumm Sisters and later as a clear-voiced crooner, she had big hits with movie tunes (especially "Over the Rainbow") and pop standards. She sang classics like "Skip to My Lou" and "Embraceable You" with such syrupy smooth sincerity that she has become a pop-culture icon for fans of camp everywhere. To millions of World War II servicemen, especially, Garland's image symbolized a clean, safe place and a nice girl any man would want to marry. E.Y. Harburg, who wrote "Over the Rainbow," compared Garland to songwriter George Gershwin: "They both brought a quality and a vitality that was typically and uniquely American," he said in 1996 liner notes. Despite (or perhaps because of) so much success at such an early age, Garland lived a tormented life. She had five husbands (in other words, four divorces) and tried to commit suicide in 1950. (Some say she overdosed on pills, which she began taking in the late 1940s to live up to the body image Hollywood expected of her.) She died of liver fibrosis, leaving her talented daughter, Liza Minnelli, to follow in her cabaret-singing footsteps.

what to buy: Though it has since been displaced by various box sets, Garland's most prominent career sampler remains *Greatest Hits* 𝄞𝄞𝄞𝄞 (Curb, 1990, prod. various), which includes "Over the Rainbow," of course, plus fun minutiae like "Zing! Went the Strings of My Heart." Obsessive types may opt instead for *50 Hit Songs from the Immortal* 𝄞𝄞𝄞𝄞 (Laserlight, 1995, prod. various) or the companion collections, *Best of the Decca Years, Vol. 1* 𝄞𝄞𝄞 (MCA, 1990, prod. various) and *Changing My Tune: Best of the Decca Years, Vol. 2* 𝄞𝄞𝄞 (MCA, 1992, prod. various), both of which focus on Garland's material from the 1940s.

what to buy next: Most Americans are more familiar with Garland's movie work—in addition to *The Wizard of Oz* she starred in *A Star Is Born, Meet Me in St. Louis,* and *Everybody Sing*—so it makes sense to buy a movie-oriented Garland CD. *Judy Garland: The Complete Decca Original Cast Recordings* 𝄞𝄞𝄞 (MCA, 1996, prod. various) organizes her mid-1940s material according to movies, including *Girl Crazy* (with Mickey Rooney duets) and *The Harvey Girls.*

what to avoid: There are at least three Garland collections titled *Over the Rainbow,* creatively enough, and the one not to get is *Over the Rainbow* 𝄞𝄞 (MCA, 1997), which heavily overlaps with previous and more superior MCA sets.

best of the rest:
Dear Mr. Gable 𝄞𝄞𝄞 (MCA Special Products, 1989)
Best of the Capitol Masters 𝄞𝄞𝄞 (Alliance, 1992/1996)

1936–1943: All the Things You Are 𝄞𝄞𝄞 (Vintage Jazz Classics, 1993)
Judy 𝄞𝄞𝄞𝄞 (MCA, 1994)
In Paris 𝄞𝄞𝄞 (RTE, 1994)
Over the Rainbow 𝄞𝄞𝄞 (Laserlight, 1995)
25th Anniversary Retrospective 𝄞𝄞𝄞 (Capitol/EMI, 1995)
Collectors' Gems from the MGM Films 𝄞𝄞𝄞 (Rhino, 1996)
Judy! That's Entertainment 𝄞𝄞 (Capitol, 1996)
Original Cast Recordings 𝄞𝄞 (MCA, 1996)

worth searching for: Garland's classic album, *Judy Garland at Carnegie Hall* 𝄞𝄞𝄞 (Capitol, 1961/1989), earned five Grammy Awards and was her most triumphant recording achievement. With all the box sets and greatest-hits collections confusing consumers, though, it's hard to find in CD bins.

influences:

◀◀ George Gershwin, Hoagy Carmichael, Mickey Rooney, Bing Crosby, Harold Arlen

▶▶ Gordon MacRae, Liza Minnelli, Doris Day, Rosemary Clooney, Marilyn Monroe, Ann-Margret

Steve Knopper

Erroll Garner

Born Erroll Louis Garner, June 15, 1921, in Pittsburgh, PA. Died January 2, 1977, in Los Angeles, CA.

Garner is arguably famous for three things: 1) being one of the most technically skilled jazz pianists to record since Art Tatum; 2) writing "Misty," a jazz standard that has been covered to the hilt; and 3) never having learned to read music. Either way, Garner cannot be dismissed as a serious contributor to jazz piano. His playing style was totally unique—perhaps because he wasn't bounded by notes on the page—and the results are in his astonishingly textured performances. Garner was a locally famous musician in Pittsburgh in the 1940s when he moved to New York and began playing clubs. Then, in 1946, an *Esquire* poll picked him as the year's New Star, propelling him into the recording studio with the likes of Charlie Parker. He made numerous television appearances in the 1950s. And by decade's end, Garner was one of the best-selling jazz pianists in the world—touring regularly overseas and toting with him his signature tune, "Misty," which has become not only a standard but an iconic American song (evidence of which is its central place in Clint Eastwood's 1971 film, *Play Misty for Me*).

what to buy: Thankfully, Garner's work has been steadily reissued on CD, so listeners are likely to find what they're looking for the first time out. But one record should be kept in mind: *Concert by the Sea* 𝄞𝄞𝄞𝄞 (Columbia, 1970/1987), perhaps his

single finest recording and an album that captures the complex technique of his synchopated piano voicings. Any other album in which he plays "Misty," such as *Erroll Garner Plays Misty* ♫♫♫♪ (EmArcy, 1954/Verve, 1987), is also highly recommended.

what to buy next: *Long Ago and Far Away* ♫♫♪ (Columbia, 1951) is a great recording of Garner in his prime—however, without the sound quality to back it up. *Plays Gershwin & Kern* ♫♫♪ (EmArcy, 1968) is a reissue of recordings from the mid-1960s, conveniently packaged from a variety of old record labels; it's also available as a package with *Magician* as the CD *Magician & Gershwin & Kern* ♫♫♪ (Telarc, prod. Martha Glazer).

best of the rest:
Greatest Garner ♫♫♫ (Atlantic)
Complete Savoy Sessions, Vol. 1 ♫♫♫ (Savoy, 1945)
Yesterdays ♫♫♫ (Savoy, 1949)
Gone-Garner-Gonest ♫♫♫ (Columbia, 1953)
Original Misty ♫♫♫♫ (Mercury, 1954)
Dancing on the Ceiling ♫♫♫♫ (EmArcy, 1989)
Body and Soul ♫♫♫♫ (Columbia, 1991)

worth searching for: *Afternoon of an Elf* ♫♫ (Mercury, 1955) is a strange album of solo piano works in which Garner disassembles jazz standards and puts them back together with his own tempo and pace. It's interesting, but not for the mainstream Garner fan.

influences:
◄◄ Fats Waller, Art Tatum, George Gershwin
►► Bill Evans, Kenny Barron, George Shearing

Carl Quintanilla

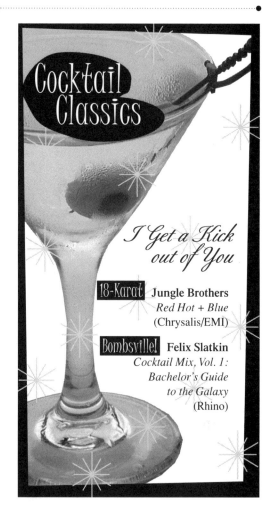

Cocktail Classics

I Get a Kick out of You

18-Karat **Jungle Brothers** *Red Hot + Blue* (Chrysalis/EMI)

Bombsville! **Felix Slatkin** *Cocktail Mix, Vol. 1: Bachelor's Guide to the Galaxy* (Rhino)

John Gary

Born in Watertown, NY. Died January 4, 1998, in Dallas, TX.

From the time his voice changed onstage—in the middle of "When Irish Eyes Are Smiling"—Gary aimed his smooth crooning voice at older audiences. The bearded, acoustic-guitar-toting singer's career was filled with sporadic big hits, including the million-selling early-1960s single "More," but Gary never quite leaped to the household-name level of Rudy Vallee, Vic Damone, or Jack Jones. He started singing at age

nine, earning a three-year scholarship at the New York City–based Cathedral of St. John the Divine; after the voice-losing incident, he gave up performing and enlisted in the U.S. Marines. (Later he shifted gears, briefly, using his penchant for underwater endurance to form an underwater-salvage company in New Orleans; he also sculpted, painted, and wrote a book called *A Fragment of Time.*) In 1962, he resumed his career and became popular enough to host his own syndicated television program, *The John Gary Show,* and become a frequent guest of Carol Burnett, Ed Sullivan, and Johnny Carson. But, possibly because of his career detours, or maybe because he refused to do shows in his home state of Texas, Gary is still thought of as a second-tier standards singer. He

Judy Garland **(Archive Photos)**

performed at nightclubs and suburban theaters around the U.S. before dying of cancer.

what's available: Though Gary recorded more than two dozen albums, there's thin evidence of him in contemporary CD stores: *The Very Best of John Gary* ♫♫♫ (RCA, 1997, prod. various) is all you really need. It includes his version of "Unchained Melody" (which Elvis Presley, Gary once told interviewers, knew so well he sang it back to him with the same phrasing), "Ebb Tide," and "My Foolish Heart."

influences:

◄◄ Frank Sinatra, the Righteous Brothers, Bing Crosby, Elvis Presley, Dinah Shore, Eddie Fisher

►► Elvis Presley, Jack Jones, Mike Douglas, Jackie Gleason

Steve Knopper

Edith Giovanna Gassion

See: Edith Piaf

Marvin Gaye

Born Marvin Pentz Gay Jr., April 2, 1939, in Washington, DC. Died April 1, 1984, in Los Angeles, CA.

A moody, mercurial soul who always seemed to be searching for some elusive happiness but reveled in—and sometimes seemed to invent—his own personal miseries, Gaye was Motown's most ambivalent pop star. His real desire, so he said, was to be a crooner along the lines of Frank Sinatra and Nat King Cole. But if the lush, orchestral *Vulnerable* album, one of Gaye's few stabs at easy-listening music, is any indication, he made the right career choice in walking away from Sinatra and towards Ray Charles. His fame—and, indeed, his best music—came from his early pop hits and his socially conscious spiritual journeys, culminating in the 1971 masterpiece *What's Going On*.

Gaye came to Motown via the Marquees (a group that enjoyed the patronage of Bo Diddley) and the Moonglows; it was during one of the latter's performances in Detroit that Berry Gordy Jr. heard Gaye and signed him to his burgeoning label. Starting as a session drummer and marrying Gordy's sister Anna (their breakup would be the focus of his harrowing 1978 album *Here, My Dear*), Gaye began his string of hits in 1962 with "Stubborn Kind of Fellow," a run that would last into the mid-1970s. Gaye also established himself as a generous duet partner, scoring hits with Mary Wells, Kim Weston, Tammi Terell, and Diana Ross. Gaye's biggest solo hit, "I Heard It through the Grapevine" in 1968, signaled a shift into deeper material—and

darker subject matter; he fought hard to get Motown to release *What's Going On*, an epic song cycle over which Gaye took total creative control, weaving his observations about inner city youth, the ecology, and race relations. He followed that with *Let's Get It On*, an immersion in eroticism that remained a focus through his last big hit, 1982's "Sexual Healing." Addled by drugs and depression, Gaye was in the midst of a career comeback when his father fatally shot him after an argument. His has been one of the most lamented of the Motown passings, commemorated every year in Detroit with a special ceremony or concert.

what to buy: You have to ask? *What's Going On* ♫♫♫♫ (Motown, 1971/1998, prod. Marvin Gaye) is not just a great Gaye album but is one of the great pop albums of all time. (Splurge and get the deluxe edition.) *The Master, 1961–1984* ♫♫♫♫ (Motown, 1995, prod. various) is one of those rare box sets that sustains its quality over the course of four discs. *Superhits* ♫♫♫♫ (Motown, 1970/1991, prod. various) isn't the most comprehensive of Gaye's collections, but it was *the* Gaye album to own at the time and is still worth having for its cheesy superhero caricature on the cover.

what to buy next: *Let's Get It On* ♫♫♫♫ (Motown, 1973/1998, prod. Marvin Gaye) offers the visceral desire of a man in serious heat. *Midnight Love* ♫♫♫♫ (Columbia, 1992, prod. Marvin Gaye) is much the same, though it's a little softer and just a touch more subtle. *Marvin Gaye & His Girls* ♫♫♫♫ (Motown, 1969/1990, prod. various) is a nice collection of his duets with Wells, Weston, and Terrell, missing only Diana Ross to make it a complete overview.

what to avoid: *Vulnerable* ♫♫ (Motown, 1997, prod. Amy Herot, Art Stewart) is the major document of Gaye's work as a standards crooner. Arranger Bobby Scott props the soul man in front of a lush orchestra, and he proceeds to adapt his falsetto to love ballads like "The Shadow of Your Smile" and "She Needs Me." It doesn't work. *Dream of a Lifetime* ♫ (Columbia, 1985, prod. Marvin Gaye, Gordon Banks, Harvey Fuqua), a posthumous release of material Gaye was working on at the time of his death, is as bald a violation of his artistry as the releases that came out after Jimi Hendrix's death.

the rest:
Together with Mary Wells ♫♫♫ (Motown, 1964/1991)
When I'm Alone I Cry ♫♫ (Motown, 1964/1994)
A Tribute to the Great Nat King Cole ♫♫♫ (Motown, 1965/1989)
The Soulful Moods of Marvin Gaye ♫♫♫ (Motown, 1966/1994)
I Heard It through the Grapevine ♫♫♫ (Motown, 1968/1989)

Trouble Man ♫♫♫ (Original Soundtrack) (Motown, 1972/1989/1998)
Live ♫♫♫ (Motown, 1974/1998)
I Want You ♫♫♫ (Motown, 1976/1998)
Greatest Hits ♫♫♫ (Motown, 1976/1989)
Live at the London Palladium ♫♫♫ (Motown, 1977)
Here, My Dear ♫♫♫ (Motown, 1978/1994)
In Our Lifetime: The Final Motown Sessions ♫♫ (Motown, 1981/1994)
Every Great Motown Hit ♫♫♫ (Motown, 1983)
Great Songs & Performances That Inspired Motown 25 ♫♫♫ (Motown, 1983)
Romantically Yours ♫♫ (Columbia, 1985/1989)
A Musical Testament ♫♫♫ (Motown, 1988)
The Marvin Gaye Collection ♫♫♫♫ (Motown, 1990)
The Last Concert Tour ♫♫♫ (Giant, 1991)
Adults ♫♫ (Hollywood/Rounder, 1992)
Seek and You Shall Find: More of the Best ♫♫♫ (Rhino, 1993)
The Norman Whitfield Sessions ♫♫♫♫ (Motown, 1994)
Motown Legends ♫♫♫♫ (ESX, 1994)
Classics Collection ♫♫♫♫ (Motown, 1994)
Anthology ♫♫♫♫ (Motown, 1995)

worth searching for: In 1986, Motown put both *What's Going On* and *Let's Get It On* on a single CD. The fidelity isn't quite up to the standards of later CD releases, but it's still a wonderful trip to slap it on and hear two of Gaye's finest albums flow back to back.

influences:

◀◀ Nat "King" Cole, Frank Sinatra, Billie Holiday, Ray Charles, Clyde McPhatter, Little Willie John, Rudy West, the Orioles, the Capris

▶▶ Stevie Wonder, Frankie Beverly, Rick James, Terence Trent D'Arby, Barry White, Al B. Sure!, Keith Sweat, El DeBarge

Gary Graff

The Gentle People

Formed 1995, in London, England.

Dougie Dimensional; Honeymick; Laurie Lemans; Valentine Cornelian, all DJs.

Claiming to have come from the outer reaches of the galaxy, the ever fashionable Gentle People landed in London when the intermingling of lounge and dance cultures was still to come. With an emphasis on style, naugahyde, and their "love bubble," they created an updated, chilled-out version of lounge music. It's what Mantovani or Mauriat would record if synthesizers and MIDI had existed 30 years ago, and it was good enough to land them a contract with the influential Rephlex Records. The Gentle People do not play live (unless you con-sider singing over backing tapes live); like the majority of the nouveau European loungers, they are DJs.

what's available: Most current lounge music is either a pallid recreation of the masters or has fallen so far from the family tree that it's a stretch to even call it "lounge." *Soundtracks for Living* ♫♫♫♫ (Rephlex 1997, prod. the Gentle People) is a mixture of ambient music, ba-boping Johnny Mann Singers, and shuffling late-'60s rhythms, proving that you didn't have to be born before World War II to create easy-listening music.

influences:

◀◀ Serge Gainsbourg, John Barry, the Karminsky Brothers, Pizzicato Five

▶▶ Easy Tunes, Tipsy, Dimitri from Paris, Count Indigo, Stereo Total

Sam Wick

Christopher Geppert

See: Christopher Cross

George & Ira Gershwin

George Gershwin born Jacob Gershwine, September 28, 1898, in Brooklyn, NY. Died July 11, 1937, in Beverly Hills, CA. Ira Gershwin born Israel Gershwine, December 6, 1896, in New York, NY. Died August 17, 1983, in Hollywood, CA.

It would be an exaggeration to say that this book could not exist without the contributions of the Gershwins . . . but it wouldn't be much of an exaggeration. Although he lived just 39 years, George Gershwin elevated American popular music from the simple ditties of Tin Pan Alley to an art form. True, this eventually led to the Rock Opera, Paul McCartney's recording with an orchestra, and other unseemly mutations, but it also helped create much of the memorable English-language music of the 20th century.

George was the genius in the family, Ira his talented collaborator. At 16, George left school to write songs for a music publisher. At 18, working with lyricist Murray Roth, he sold "When You Want 'Em, You Can't Get 'Em, When You've Got 'Em, You Don't Want 'Em," his first published work. By 1919, he was contributing regularly to jazz revues and stage musicals. His "Swanee," as recorded by Al Jolson, became a hit in 1920, when he was 22. For the next 17 years, working with Ira and alone, he wrote piano concertos, songs for the stage and screen, jazz works, and various combinations of those genres, including the opera *Porgy and Bess*, the score for *Of*

Thee I Sing (the first musical to win the Pulitzer Prize), and, over a couple of weeks, "Rhapsody in Blue" (Ira came up with the title, which was inspired by the title of James Mc-Neill Whistler's famous painting, *A Study in Black and White,* also known as "Whistler's Mother"). George and Ira's songs—including "Fascinating Rhythm," "Summertime," "They All Laughed," "Someone to Watch over Me," "Shall We Dance," "They Can't Take That Away from Me," and "Embraceable You"—have been covered by artists ranging from Fred Astaire to Leslie Uggams, Judy Garland to Liza Minnelli, Chet Baker to Linda Ronstadt. After George's sudden death from a cerebral hemmorage in 1937, Ira collaborated with Jerome Kern, Harold Arlen (on the movie musical *A Star Is Born*), and others.

what to buy: To fully appreciate the range of the Gershwins' music, it's best to buy one of the several anthologies that have been released (or re-released on CD) in recent years. *The Great American Composers—George and Ira Gershwin* 𝄞𝄞𝄞𝄞 (Columbia, 1989, prod. various) isn't the most exhaustive, but it might be the most enjoyable. All the best-known songs are there, interpreted by the likes of Sarah Vaughan, Billie Holiday, Fred Astaire, and Johnny Mathis and spread over two CDs. There's hardly a weak cut among them, and there are even a few surprises, such as Aretha Franklin's cover of "It Ain't Necessarily So" from *Porgy and Bess.*

what to buy next: The most impressive part of the Smithsonian Institution's four-CD set *I Got Rhythm* 𝄞𝄞𝄞𝄞 (BMG Music, 1995, prod. various) might well be the 64 pages of liner notes. Subtitled "The Music of George Gershwin," it organizes his career into four parts, "Gershwin and the Popular Song," "Gershwin on Stage and Screen," "Gershwin in the Concert Hall," and "Gershwin and Jazz," and devotes a full CD to each—which may be too much for the casual listener. Though Ira's contributions are only passingly acknowledged, information about each cut is detailed. (Did you know, for example, that "How Long Has This Been Going On?," written in 1937 for the Broadway musical *Funny Face,* was never performed for that show and reached a mass audience only with Audrey Hepburn's rendition in the almost unrelated movie of the same name 30 years later?) Musical highlights include Georges Guetary singing "I'll Build a Stairway to Paradise," from *An American in Paris* (instead of the Joel Grey version in

the Columbia compilation), Louis Armstrong and Ella Fitzgerald standing in for Fred Astaire on "They All Laughed," and an "Embraceable You" from Tommy Dorsey that far outdistances Columbia's Andy Williams rendition. As for "Summertime" and "The Man I Love," done here by Billie Holiday and on the Columbia collection by Sarah Vaughan . . . well, that's just a matter of taste.

worth searching for: For a quirkier (and much cheaper) single-CD anthology of the Gershwin's work, find *Fascinatin' Rhythm* 𝄞𝄞𝄞𝄞 (Capitol, 1992, prod. various). Subtitled "Capitol Sings George Gershwin," it offers the Liza Minnelli version of "I'll Build a Stairway to Paradise" and Peggy Lee singing "They Can't Take That Away from Me," as well as cuts by Vic Damone, Anna Maria Alberghetti, June Christy, and Gordon MacRae singing "Summertime."

influences:

◀◀ Mozart, Jerome Kern, Irving Berlin

▶▶ Billie Holiday, Frank Sinatra, Paul McCartney, Ray Davies, Paul Simon, Andrew Lloyd Webber, Elvis Costello, Richard Thompson, Michael Feinstein

Bruce Schoenfeld

Stan Getz

Born Stanley Gayetzsky, February 2, 1927, in Philadelphia, PA. Died June 6, 1991, in Los Angeles, CA.

By many standards a nonpareil on the tenor saxophone, Getz is remembered not only for his mastery of the unruly instrument but for the huge body of first-rate work he left behind. From the 1940s to his death in 1991, Getz produced few albums that wouldn't rate among the classics of bossa nova or cool jazz—his true musical home. Suffice it to say that any collection of lounge music ought to pay healthy tribute to "Stan the Man."

Getz began playing professionally at age 15, working in the bands of Jack Teagarden, Stan Kenton, and Benny Goodman. His real breakthrough, however, came in 1948 as one of the "Four Brothers"—the horn section of Woody Herman's big band, along with Zoot Sims, Serge Chaloff, and Herbie Steward. Getz's reputation as a brilliant tenor player was solidified on one single recording of "Early Autumn," after which he began producing solo albums with Verve's powerful producer, Norman Granz, and touring in his favorite countries of Europe and Scandanavia. Getz is often remembered for his huge success in bringing bossa nova to the U.S. in 1962–64, when he, João

---

George (l) and Ira Gershwin **(AP/Wide World Photos)**

Gilberto, and Astrud Gilberto hit #5 on the charts with "The Girl from Ipanema." The *Getz/Gilberto* albums brought him Grammys in 1962 and 1964 and not only made a sensation of Getz but paved the way for the Brazilian influence on American jazz, which can still be heard today. But Getz was arguably at his finest in 1989, shortly before he succumbed to lung cancer.

what to buy: *Stan the Man*, later repackaged as *The Artistry of Stan Getz: The Best of the Verve Years, Vol. 1* 🎵🎵🎵🎵 (Verve, 1991, prod. Creed Taylor, Norman Granz), is probably the best album from which to derive an introduction to Getz's work.

what to buy next: His three late-career albums with pianist Kenny Barron—*Anniversary* 🎵🎵🎵🎵 (Verve, 1989, prod. Stan Getz), *Serenity* 🎵🎵🎵🎵 (Verve, 1991, prod. Stan Getz), and *People Time* 🎵🎵🎵🎵🎵 (Verve, 1992, prod. Jean-Philippe Allard)—are by far his best work and shouldn't be overlooked.

what to avoid: *Stan Getz at Storyville, Vols. 1 and 2* 🎵🎵 (Roulette, 1951/Blue Note, 1990) offers a harsher, less lyrical Getz than we're used to hearing; it doesn't do the saxophonist's chops justice. Besides a less-than-ideal recording, the album strays far from Getz's strengths in ballads or Latin music.

best of the rest:
Stan Getz and the Oscar Peterson Trio 🎵🎵🎵🎵 (Verve, 1957)
Bossa Nova Years 🎵🎵🎵🎵 (Verve, 1962–64)
Getz/Gilberto 🎵🎵🎵🎵 (Verve, 1963/1987)
Getz Au Go Go 🎵🎵🎵🎵 (Verve, 1964)
Sweet Rain 🎵🎵🎵🎵 (Verve, 1967)

worth searching for: It's sometimes difficult finding Getz's collaborative albums with other jazz artists. Best among these is *Diz & Getz* 🎵🎵🎵🎵 (Verve, 1953), which offers a rare treat: Getz with Dizzy Gillespie, two of the most witty jazz musicians to grace the latter half of the 20th century. It also features pianists John Lewis and Oscar Peterson on various tracks. Others like *Stan Meets Chet* 🎵🎵🎵🎵 (Verve, 1958, prod. Norman Granz) and *Stan Getz and Bill Evans* 🎵🎵🎵🎵 (Verve, 1973, prod. Creed Taylor) are sure to be next in line.

influences:
◀◀ Lester Young, Coleman Hawkins, Charlie Parker

▶▶ Scott Hamilton, Tom Scott, Wayne Shorter, Teddy Riley

Carl Quintanilla

Stan Getz **(AP/Wide World Photos)**

Kathie Lee Gifford

Born Kathie Epstein, August 16, 1953, in Paris, France.

Forgetting for a moment her nearly insufferable public persona, Gifford is a serviceable singer, a talent that comes through more in her live nightclub performances than on recordings. A born entertainer, Gifford got her first big singing breaks as a performer on *Name That Tune* and as a cast member on *Hee Haw Honeys* in the late 1970s. Admittedly, it's hard to forget her gratingly perky personality, her ubiquitous cruise boat commercials, the sweatshop scandals, and her philandering husband (NFL broadcaster Frank Gifford), but there's no denying her popularity—her nightclub act with Regis Philbin (not to mention their morbidly perky morning show *Regis and Kathie Lee*) continues to thrill audiences in Atlantic City and Las Vegas. Her recent output on vinyl has been limited to holiday or children's fare, but here's hoping she puts out an album soon of classic done-me-wrong ballads like "Who's Sorry Now" (which is already in her nightclub act), "Your Cheatin' Heart," and "Stand By Your Man."

what to buy: If you really want the social stigmatism that comes with having a Gifford disc in your CD collection, pick up *Sentimental* 🎵🎵🎵 (Warner Bros., 1993, prod. Jim Ed Norman, Danny Kee) for 33 whole minutes of simply arranged pop standards like "Over the Rainbow" and "It Had to Be You."

what to buy next: Giffophiles will treasure *It's Christmas Time* 🎵🎵🎵 (Warner Bros., 1993, prod. Jim Ed Norman, Danny Kee, Edd Kalehoff), a predictable collection of holiday standards that's notable for a duet with the excitable Philbin on "Silver Bells." In case you're planning an extra long Christmas party, there's *Christmas Carols* 🎵🎵🎵 (Warner Bros., 1993) and *Rock N Tots Cafe: Christmas Giff Song Album* 🎵🎵 (Time Warner Kids, 1995).

what to avoid: In some communities, parents who subject their helpless kids to *Dreamship: Lullabies for Little Ones* 🎵 (Time Warner Kids, 1995) can be brought up on abuse charges.

worth searching for: Giff does disco? Sure, on *Finders Keepers* 🎵🎵🎵 (Petra Studio, 1978). Amazingly, the CD has merits beyond its obvious novelty factor.

influences:
◀◀ Doris Day, Barbra Streisand, Sandi Patti

▶▶ Nirvana, Nine Inch Nails, Pearl Jam, Marilyn Manson

Alex Gordon

Astrud Gilberto

Born March 30, 1940, in Bahia, Brazil.

Gilberto is lounge music's Lana Turner, the accidental star. Married to the Brazilian bossa-nova singer and guitarist João Gilberto, she was serving as an unofficial interpreter during a studio session for the legendary 1963 jazz album *Getz/Gilberto* when a chorus of English was needed on Antonio Carlos Jobim's "The Girl from Ipanema." Her wistful evocation of Norman Gimbel's lyric supplanted her husband's Portuguese vocals on the 1964 single release—and made her an international sensation. At her best, she doesn't sound like a trained vocalist so much as a dreamy amateur, artless yet seductive. She had the same kind of sensual, South American appeal that mid-1960s National Airlines commercials were able to tap into, and is equally evocative of that era. She's most effective singing in her native Portuguese, especially the handful of songs—including "Corcovado" and "Vivo Sonhando"—written for her by Jobim and Gene Lees. In her later work much of that innocence is lost, and so is much of her allure. Her adaptations of show tunes and pop standards such as Tony Hatch's "Call Me" are to be avoided.

what to buy: Of her solo work, *Verve Jazz Masters 9* ✍✍✍✍ (PolyGram/Verve, 1994, prod. Creed Taylor) artfully combines studio sessions and live performances from 1964 and 1965, mostly off the mid-'60s LPs *A Certain Smile a Certain Sadness*, *Look to the Rainbow*, and *The Astrud Gilberto Album with Antonio Carlos Jobim*. It includes the haunting Carnegie Hall performance of "Ipanema" from October 9, 1964, an appealingly spare studio version of "Take Me to Aruanda" with Don Sebesky's orchestra, and an ethereal adaptation of Sammy Cahn's "Day by Day." *Getz/Gilberto (20-Bit Master)* ✍✍✍✍ (Verve, 1963/1987, prod. Creed Taylor) is the master session of the largest-selling jazz album ever recorded, a collaboration between jazzman Stan Getz and Gilberto's husband João, though Astrud's presence is limited. The sequel, *Getz/Gilberto, Vol. 2* ✍✍✍ (Verve, 1964/1993, prod. Creed Taylor), was recorded at the 1964 Carnegie Hall concert.

what to buy next: *Compact Jazz: Astrud Gilberto* ✍✍✍✍ (PolyGram/Verve, 1987, prod. Creed Taylor) duplicates *Jazz Masters 9*'s versions of many of Gilberto's better-known songs. It omits the lilting "Frevo," though, replacing it with "Summer Samba (So Nice)" from her Englewood Cliffs 1966 session with organist Walter Wanderley and others. The album also provides studio versions of "Ipanema" and "Corcovado" in place of the Carnegie Hall concert.

what to avoid: *Beach Samba* ✍✍ (PolyGram/Verve, 1993) has some cuts of interest, but it's not worth braving Gilberto as the Brazilian Vikki Carr, singing "It's a Lovely Day Today," "You Didn't Have to Be So Nice" (with her six-year-old son), and "Misty Roses."

best of the rest:

Plus James Last Orchestra ✍✍ (Verve, 1969)
Look to the Rainbow ✍✍ (Verve, 1987)
The Silver Collection: The Astrud Gilberto Album ✍✍✍✍ (Verve, 1987)
Astrud Gilberto with Stanley Turrentine ✍✍ (CBS, 1988)
Jazz 'Round Midnight: Astrud Gilberto ✍✍✍ (Verve, 1996)

worth searching for: *The Girl from Ipanema: The Antonio Carlos Jobim Songbook* ✍✍✍✍ (PolyGram/Verve, 1995, prod. Creed Taylor, Quincy Jones, Richard Seidel, Norman Granz, Hans Georg Brunner-Schwer, Aloysio de Oliviera) includes the talents of Sarah Vaughan, Billy Eckstine, Ella Fitzgerald, Oscar Peterson, and Dizzy Gillespie, among others. Gilberto's contributions—the original album release of "Ipanema" and the standard version of "Dindi" and "Agua de Beber"—hold their own among offerings by such luminaries.

influences:

◀◀ Antonio Carlos Jobim, Walter Wanderley, Rosemary Clooney

▶▶ Sade, Suzanne Vega, Ann-Margret

see also: *João Gilberto, Stan Getz*

Bruce Schoenfeld

João Gilberto

Born June 10, 1931, in Bahia, Brazil.

With a murmuring romantic voice and an impossibly smooth guitar style, Gilberto revolutionized Brazilian guitar, became an influential star in his home country, and practically invented bossa nova. Unlike easy-listening stars Ray Conniff and Mantovani, who created elaborate orchestras and leaned on catchy, syrupy melodies, Gilberto had a natural touch for love music. His late '50s Brazilian hits, most notably Antonio Carlos Jobim's "Chega de Saudade," made countless Latin American women weak in the knees. Later, collaborating with hitmaking saxophonist Stan Getz—on the pioneering *Getz/Gilberto* bossa-nova album—he brought his feathery touch to the U.S. His

Astrud Gilberto (© Jack Vartoogian)

then-wife, Astrud Gilberto, sang the words to Jobim's standard "The Girl from Ipanema," which became a massive hit. The singer-guitarist moved gradually towards a light-jazz style after that, and recorded a number of excellent jazz-heavy albums throughout the '70s, '80s, and '90s. He reaches emotional heights with a few easygoing syllables and guitar notes what Kenny G and his overcrowded mood music have never been able to accomplish.

what to buy: Not only is *Getz/Gilberto (20-Bit Master)* 𝄞𝄞𝄞𝄞 (Verve, 1963/1987, prod. Creed Taylor) a superbly remastered CD document of one of the great international jazz collaborations, it was the first true bossa-nova album, kicking off a lucrative North American craze. It includes Astrud Gilberto's definitive version of "The Girl from Ipanema," and lots of melodic, romantic jazz. The most comprehensive collection of Gilberto's solo work remains *The Legendary João Gilberto: The Original Bossa Nova Recordings (1958–1961)* 𝄞𝄞𝄞𝄞 (World Pacific, 1990, prod. various), which, with airy murmurs like "Chega de Saudade," "O Amor," and the "O Nosso Amor/A Felicidade" medley, changed Brazilian music forever.

what to buy next: Heavy on the Jobim standards, the two-in-one CD set *Amoroso/Brasil* 𝄞𝄞𝄞 (Warner Bros., 1993, prod. Tommy LiPuma, Helen Keane, João Gilberto) proves Gilberto hadn't lost his touch long after his hits had faded from the charts. Younger Brazilian singers Gilberto Gil and Maria Bethania show up to honor, but not overwhelm, their elder, and there's a nice overall mix of "Brazilianized" American standards (such as "All of Me" and a weird-sounding "'S Wonderful") and more straightforward Brazilian music ("Zingara," "Besame Mucho").

what to avoid: Though it's certainly not awful, Gilberto released his first album in several years, *João* 𝄞𝄞 (Verve, 1991, prod. Mayrton Bahia, Carmela Forsin), and his fingers sounded just a little clunkier and his voice a little rustier than they were at his peak. He doesn't quite click with the material, such as the corny "I Really Samba" and "A Woman," as well as he once did with Gershwin and Jobim standards.

best of the rest:

Getz/Gilberto, Vol. 2 𝄞𝄞𝄞 (Verve, 1964/1993)
Ela E' Carioca 𝄞𝄞 (Orfeon, 1995)
Eu Sei Que Vou Te Amar: Ao Vivo 𝄞𝄞𝄞 (Sony Discos, 1995)
Mi Historia 𝄞𝄞𝄞 (PolyGram Latino, 1997)

worth searching for: Like many non-rock artists of the '50s and '60s, Gilberto recorded tons of original LPs, then watched as they slowly went out of print. One of his best, *Boss of the Bossa Nova* 𝄞𝄞𝄞 (Atlantic, 1962), is an unfortunately forgotten gem.

influences:

◀◀ Tito Puente, Stan Kenton

▶▶ Laurindo Almeida, Michael Hedges, Ottmar Leibert

see also: *Stan Getz, Astrud Gilberto, Antonio Carlos Jobim*

Steve Knopper

Dizzy Gillespie

Born John Birks Gillespie, October 21, 1917, in Cheraw, SC. Died January 7, 1993, in Englewood, NJ.

Hive-cheeked jazz revolutionary Dizzy Gillespie was a decade past his musical insurrection in the late 1950s, but he wasn't beyond experimenting with new forms—even if they ventured into mellow territory. Norman Granz, the impresario of Clef and Verve records, had a reputation for pushing his artists toward the mainstream and had even convinced Diz's fellow brigand and occasional sparring partner, Charlie Parker, that playing against a background of syrupy strings could produce a sweet-and-sour hybrid. Gillespie did not need much pushing. In the late 1940s, while most of his bop stablemates toughed it out in small combos, Gillespie daringly went on tour with a huge band playing at breakneck tempos. The bands succumbed to economic pressures, leaving the trumpeter to scrounge for a while on his own before joining Granz's company in the early 1950s. Gillespie and the rhythm section from his big band played on four aborted cuts in 1946 with a string and oboe section. But it wasn't until 1961 that he went all the way. Perhaps eyeing Miles Davis's success with Gil Evans, Gillespie teamed up with bop trombonist and composer J.J. Johnson and conductor and author Gunther Schuller. Rounding up a conglomeration of jazzmen and orchestra session players, they released "Perceptions," a suite composed by Johnson. The resulting album veered from Gillespie's signature keening horn solos to trumpet fanfares and airy harp solos. Gillespie returned to lounge forms several years later, but despite their moodiness they rarely approached his collaboration with Johnson for artistic worth. Both 1963 efforts, a weird joust with a Parisian vocal ensemble and a woozy rendering of early '60s film themes, were best forgotten.

what to buy: *Perceptions* 𝄞𝄞𝄞 (Verve, 1961, prod. Creed Taylor) was the best of Gillespie's orchestral flings and one of the best of Verve's many strings-and-jazz attempts. What gives the album its extra brio is J.J. Johnson's score. Like Gil Evans did with Miles Davis, Johnson made sure Gillespie had more behind him than a bunch of violinists sawing away at hackneyed love songs. Even if the suite occasionally jars, Gillespie is always present, blasting away like Gabriel.

what to buy next: *Dizzy's Diamonds* 🎵🎵🎵🎵 (Verve, 1992, prod. various), a three-disc tribute to Gillespie's classic Verve years, came out just weeks before his death. Inside is a bountiful menu of his 1950s and early-1960s efforts—from tight combos to his Latin forays to the crackerjack big band he took on world tour for the State Department. *Complete RCA Victor Recordings* 🎵🎵🎵🎵 (BMG, 1995, prod. various), a top-notch two-CD set, doesn't include the dozen or so of Gillespie's earliest big band classics (no "Emananon" or "One Bass Hit," for example). But all of the band's later fireballs are here. There are the Cuban-influenced voodoo numbers like "Manteca," bop express trains like "Cool Breeze," and giddy scat diddlings like "Hey, Pete, Le's Eat Mo' Meat."

what to avoid: *Dizzy Gillespie and the Double Six of Paris* 🎵 (Verve, 1963) conjures visions of Diz mockingly shaking his rump behind this wall-of-chirps organization. Bop legend Bud Powell was apparently on hand, too, and what he heard might have driven him right back into the asylum. Like everyone else in the early '60s, Gillespie made a soundtrack album, *Dizzy Gillespie Goes Hollywood* 🎵🎵 (Verve, 1963). Why not? If soul singer Jerry Butler managed to find something to salvage in "Moon River," Diz deserved a turn, too. But on his own time and his own dime.

best of the rest:
Shaw 'Nuff 🎵🎵🎵🎵 (Musicraft, 1989)
Roy and Diz 🎵🎵🎵🎵 (Verve, 1995)
Birks Works 🎵🎵🎵🎵 (Verve, 1995)
Duets 🎵🎵🎵🎵 (Verve, 1997)

influences:

◄◄ Louis Armstrong, Roy Eldridge, Teddy Hill, Benny Carter, Charlie Parker

►► Fats Navarro, Kenny Dorham, Miles Davis, the Modern Jazz Quartet, John Coltrane, John Faddis, Tito Puente, Perez Prado, Les Elgart

Steve Braun

Jackie Gleason

Born February 26, 1916, in Brooklyn, NY. Died June 24, 1987, in New York City, NY.

The Great One was at his greatest on the small screen, in *The Life of Riley, Calvalcade of Stars,* and *The Honeymooners,* but Gleason was also a popular vocalist, with a series of string-laden romantic records in the '50s. *Music for Lovers Only*, the first record, was released in 1953, and Gleason continued to

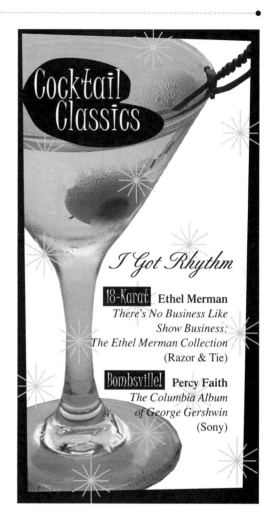

Cocktail Classics

I Got Rhythm

18-Karat Ethel Merman
There's No Business Like Show Business: The Ethel Merman Collection
(Razor & Tie)

Bombsville! Percy Faith
The Columbia Album of George Gershwin
(Sony)

chart with his music until the late '50s. Though they're considered novelty records today, at the time they helped kick off a mood-music craze that peaked with hugely popular albums by Ray Conniff, Percy Faith, Mantovani, and the 101 Strings. Gleason, who never read a note of music and was proudly untrained, composed credibly beautiful instrumentals like "Melancholy Serenade" and once conducted trumpeter Bobby Hackett in an orchestra with 40 mandolins. The large, Dixieland-inspired comedian started his show-business career with circuses and carnivals, then used his roly-poly charisma to earn roles in shows, including *Keep Off the Grass,* and films, including *Navy Blues,* in the early 1940s. Over time, he developed a wide variety of funny alter-egos, from Joe the Bartender to Reggie "My Hobby Is

Jackie Gleason **(Archive Photos)**

Booze" Van Gleason III, all with different personalities and goofy hats. He was nominated for an Academy Award for his performance as pool shark Minnesota Fats in Robert Rossen's 1961 film noir masterpiece *The Hustler*, in which he played opposite Paul Newman's Fast Eddie Felson. One of his last movies, *Nothing to Lose*, co-starred a pre-Oscar-winning Tom Hanks.

what to buy: *The Romantic Moods of Jackie Gleason* ♫♫♫♫ (Gema/Capitol, 1996, prod. Brad Benedict) is a comprehensive collection of Gleason's mood music, with 46 easy-listening gems that include "Moon River," "Moonglow," "The Girl from Ipanema," "Laura," and "You and the Night and the Music."

what to buy next: *How Sweet It Is! The Jackie Gleason Velvet Brass Collection* ♫♫♫ (Razor & Tie, 1996) gives you "Cherokee," "The Man I Love," and the novelty song "One of These Days (Pow!)."

the rest:
Merry Christmas ♫♫♫ (Razor & Tie, 1997)

worth searching for: *And Awaaay We Go!* ♫♫♫ (Scamp, 1996, reissue prod. Ashley Warren) combines easy-listening pop and out-of-context comedy routines.

influences:
◄◄ Paul Weston, Mitch Miller

►► Dick Van Dyke, Joey Bishop, Eddie Murphy, Frank Fontaine

Ben Greenman

Samuel Goldberg
See: Buddy Clark

Benny Goodman
Born May 30, 1909, in Chicago, IL. Died June 13, 1986, New York, NY.

Benny Goodman, the first great clarinetist in the history of jazz, perfected a style of playing that is still the dominant influence on the instrument. It is a style based on clearly articulated, hard-swinging melodic lines, played with a very centered, clear, clarinet tone. It was the incredible excitement and clarity of his playing that made it great, rather than any profound harmonic or rhythmic invention. There was no gratuitous musical posturing in his work, and his remarkable avoidance of cliches actually added effectivness and poignance to the few familiar phrases he did use. Although Goodman became fantastically popular, and performed a good deal of classical music, he remained first and foremost a jazzman throughout his career. His classic "Sing, Sing, Sing" still packs wedding dance floors all around the world.

Perhaps because of Goodman's enigmatic personality—he tended to be interested in music above all else, tending to forget even basic social civility—his role as a jazz explorer has been underappreciated. In the mid-1930s it was Goodman who first brought the music of the Harlem jazz bands to the general public through his purchase and presentation of the compositions and arrangements of Fletcher Henderson and others. Unlike many other white musicians at the time, he didn't try to steal anyone's music and he freely credited his sources, though sometimes he added his own name. He simply wanted the best charts he could get his hands on. Goodman was also a pioneer in the presentation of racially mixed ensembles; African American pianist Teddy Wilson and vibraphonist Lionel Hampton were stars in his trio and quartet. While Goodman himself was never an effective bop soloist, he made sure his bands of the 1940s included, at various times, boppers Fats Navarro, Wardell Grey, and others. After that, he never again jumped head first into bop, but he often returned to bop principles, especially with the 10-piece band he led in 1959 and 1960. Goodman's groups were great incubators of talent, giving the first prominent exposure—either in concert or on records—to Billie Holiday, Harry James, Gene Krupa, Teddy Wilson, Lionel Hampton, Charlie Christian, Peggy Lee, Stan Getz, Roland Hanna, Zoot Sims, and many others.

what to buy: There are hundreds of Goodman studio performances and live dates from his peak years (1937 through 1939) on CD. The Victor studio sessions reveal well-rehearsed, precise ensembles, and were well recorded, although they have not always been well-remastered for reissue. The best of the live dates are a little muddier, but still sound fine, and reveal a much more exciting band, mistakes and all. The live sessions have the edge. Duplicating the 1950s LPs titled *Jazz Concert No. 2*, the two-CD set *On the Air, 1937–1938* 🎵🎵🎵🎵 (Columbia, 1993, reissue prod. Michael Brooks) offers a fine set of 14 remastered tracks. Most are up-tempo, but Fletcher Henderson's sensuous arrangement of "Sometimes I'm Happy" makes a wonderful

change of pace. The apogee of Goodman's career was his 1938 Carnegie Hall concert. The triumphant energy of the Goodmanites conquering the august Carnegie in 1938 comes through on the two CDs of *Benny Goodman Carnegie Hall Jazz Concert* 🎵🎵🎵🎵 (Columbia, 1987). "Sing, Sing, Sing" was the concert's high point, with a solo by pianist Jess Stacy and a crowd-pleasing tom-tom solo by Krupa. The fine three-CD set *Benny Goodman/The Birth of Swing* 🎵🎵🎵🎵 (Victor-Bluebird 78s/Bluebird, 1991, prod. Orrin Keepnews) documents the start of the swing era, and includes the sides Bunny Berigan cut as a Goodmanite, as well as a session with a very young Ella Fitzgerald. Delights are found in superior versions of pop songs of the day, as well as in the "killer-dillers." The Goodman trio and quartet of the 1930s was important for social as well as musical reasons (it was the first high-profile racially integrated jazz ensemble). The entire Victor studio output of these small Goodman groups, including previously unissued alternate takes, was recently released on a three-CD set, *The Complete RCA Victor Small Group Recordings* 🎵🎵🎵🎵 (RCA, 1997, reissue prod. Orrin Keepnews). This set incorporates the following LPs: *The Original Trio & Quartet Sessions, Vol. 1* (Victor/Bluebird 78 rpm recordings/Bluebird, 1987) and *Avalon: The Small Bands, Vol. 2* (Victor/Bluebird 78 rpm recordings/Bluebird, 1990).

what to buy next: In 1939, Goodman added Charlie Christian—the first significant electric guitarist in jazz—to his entourage. The resulting recordings, many of which are found on *Featuring Charlie Christian* 🎵🎵🎵🎵 (Columbia 78s, various LP compilations/Columbia, 1989), provided much inspiration for the beboppers coming just around the corner. Columbia has not reissued their wonderful early 1940s Goodman catalog, but until they do, *Featuring Peggy Lee* 🎵🎵🎵🎵 (Columbia, Okeh 78s/Columbia, 1993, prod. Michael Brooks) provides great insight into the "let's play beautiful music without getting cutesy or worrying about the jitterbuggers" side of Goodman. Lee, brand new on the scene, sings very well, and the Eddie Sauter and Mel Powell arrangements can be equated to early, very good Gil Evans. On the limited edition four-CD set *Benny Goodman: Complete Capitol Small Group Recordings* 🎵🎵🎵🎵 (Mosaic, 1993, prod. Michael Cuscuna), Goodman displays incredible clarinet technique and seems bound by few stylistic limitations. Among the many highlights are the angular "Hi 'Ya Sophia" (from 1947) and a slashing "Air Mail Special" (from 1954). Goodman's 10-piece band of 1959–60 has been largely forgotten. Too bad—it was one of his loosest, most swinging bands. This fresh group, featuring such inventive sidemen as saxophonists Jerry Dodgion and Flip Phillips, trumpeter Jack

Sheldon, and bop-leaning veteran Red Norvo, didn't rely on any of the old swing charts. Several recent CDs have rectified the inadequacy of the band's two commercial recordings (one on MGM and one on Columbia), which didn't capture it at its best. A concert from Basel, Switzerland, is documented on the single-CD *Legendary Concert* ♫♫♫♫ (TCB, 1993, prod. Gino Ferlin), as well as on the four-CD set *B.G. World-Wide* ♫♫♫♫ (TCB, 1993, prod. Gino Ferlin).

what to avoid: Even Goodman's most commercial recordings display admirable musicianship, so the real Goodman collector will find little to avoid on CDs currently in print. A number of out-of-print LPs (which may eventually be released on CD), such as *Hello Benny* ♫♫ (Capitol, 1964, prod. Dave Cavanaugh), *Made in Japan* ♫♫ (Capitol, 1964, prod. Dave Cavanaugh), and *Let's Dance Again* ♫♫♫ (Mega, 1969, prod. John Franz), should interest completists.

best of the rest:
B.G. in Hi-Fi ♫♫♫ (Capitol, 1954/1989)
Together Again ♫♫♫♫ (RCA Victor, 1964/Bluebird, 1996)
Let's Dance ♫♫♫ (Music Masters, 1986)
Benny Goodman's 1934 Bill Dodge All-Star Recordings Complete ♫♫♫♫ (Original broadcast transcriptions/Melodeon LP/Circle, 1987)
Air Play ♫♫♫♫ (Signature, 1989)
Best of the Big Bands ♫♫♫♫ (Columbia and Okeh 78s, various dates /Columbia, 1990)
Solo Flight ♫♫♫♫ (VJC, 1991)
B.G. & Big Tea in NYC ♫♫♫♫ (Brunswick 78s/Decca, 1992)
The Harry James Years, Vol. 1 ♫♫♫♫♫ (Victor/Bluebird 78s/Bluebird, 1993)
Swing, Swing, Swing ♫♫♫♫ (Music Masters, 1993)
The Alternative Goodman ♫♫♫♫ (Phontastic, 8 double CDs, 1993–1994)
Swing Sessions ♫♫♫♫ (Hindsight, 1994)
Wrappin' It Up, The Harry James Years, Part 2 ♫♫♫♫ (Victor and Bluebird 78s/Bluebird, 1995)
Undercurrent Blues ♫♫♫♫ (Capitol, various dates/1995)
Benny Goodman Plays Eddie Sauter ♫♫♫♫♫ (Columbia and Okeh 78s/Hep, 1996)
The King of Swing ♫♫♫♫ (Music Masters, 1996)

worth searching for: If you still have a turntable, the three-LP box set (also issued as single LPs) *Treasure Chest Series* ♫♫♫♫ (MGM, c. 1959) is about as good as the previously noted *On the Air, 1937–1938* recordings. These peak-era big band and combo air-checks find Goodman, Harry James, Gene Krupa, and the rest of the Goodman firmament exhibiting the spontaneity that

Benny Goodman (l) and Gene Krupa **(UPI/Corbis-Bettmann)**

is the essence of jazz. The best concert by Goodman's 1959–60 10-piece band is on the separate LPs *Session* ♫♫♫♫ (Swing House, 1981, prod. Christopher A. Pirie) and *Jam* ♫♫♫♫ (Swing House, 1983, prod. Christopher A. Pirie). Vocalist Anita O'Day was still with the band for this Berlin concert. Goodman fired her shortly thereafter.

influences:

◄◄ Fletcher Henderson, Chick Webb, Casa Loma, Tommy Dorsey, Jimmy Dorsey

►► Frank Sinatra, Billy May, Nelson Riddle, Louis Prima, Buddy Greco, Jo Stafford, Paul Weston, Jack Maheu, Buddy DeFranco, Eddie Daniels, Ken Peplowski

John K. Richmond

Ron Goodwin
Born February 17, 1925, in Plymouth, England.

This lighthearted Brit brought his jolly orchestrations to the U.S. shores (and shopping-mall Muzak) via the Capitol label. His style was very lush and Percy Faith-like, but it was the strength of the songs that made his work in the '50s and '60s memorable. Goodwin began his career by working in an insurance office, then scored a job with music publishers Campbell, Connelly & Co. After going to music school, he became arranger for Ted Heath and Stanley Black, among others, and worked behind such British hitmakers as Petula Clark. It was as a composer of film music that many still know him best. Such movie themes as "Where Eagles Dare," "Those Magnificent Men in Their Flying Machines," and "Of Human Bondage" are among his best known, but if he had only written and recorded the awesome harpsichord romp "Miss Marple's Theme," he would still be remembered. This song graced all the great Margaret Rutherford Miss Marple movies and is also known as "Theme from 'Murder at the Gallop,'" released on a long-out-of-print MGM 45.

what's available: Sadly, there are no domestic, non-import CDs of Goodwin's music currently available, and his sole CD, the out-of-print *Adventure and Excitement* ♫♫ (EMI), isn't the greatest-hits album his output cries for. Old vinyl is tough to come by, but his best LP may have been *Swinging Sweethearts* ♫♫♫♫ (Capitol, 1957). The best Goodwin release ever was on the double cassette *The Ron Goodwin Collection* ♫♫♫♫ (EMI Australasia, 1987, prod. various), which in 28 songs still managed to miss some of his great Capitol 45s, including "Swedish Polka" and "Red Cloak."

influences:

◀◀ Percy Faith, Dick Jacobs

▶▶ Ray Conniff, Michael Kamen, Hans Zimmer

George W. Krieger

Dexter Gordon

Born February 27, 1923, in Los Angeles, CA. Died April 26, 1990, in Philadelphia, PA.

I once watched Dexter Gordon lean over a bar in a punk rock club in Baltimore and nonchalantly knock back a row of five shot glasses filled with whiskey, ignoring the vacant-eyed green-haired women and slack-jawed heathens in safety pins who stared at him as if HE were from another planet. As imposingly tall and tough (even in his later years) as he often looked, Long Tall Dexter glided through life just as he did in *Round Midnight,* the movie in which he starred. For an entire career, he alternated harsh, booting sax blasts with lush, dreamy ballads. Most of his impeccably crafted love songs were recorded with jazz quartets. But like many of his contemporaries, Gordon had a sax-and-strings album in him. He let it out in 1975, teaming up with Swedish conductor Palle Mikkelborg on *More Than You Know*, a tour-de-force with a 20-piece orchestra. Citing Charlie Parker, Billie Holiday, and Clifford Brown as artists who had ached to play with strings, Gordon wrote in his liner notes that "I'm certainly no exception to such a dream." The resulting album was pretty much a success, but Gordon never tried it again before his untimely death from cancer in 1990.

what to buy: *More Than You Know* 𝄞𝄞𝄞 (Steeplechase, 1975, prod. Nils Winther) came after Gordon spent much of the 1950s trying to wean himself from heroin; he exiled himself to Europe, finding a haven in Sweden and France. Much of his finest work came in the smoky clubs of Copenhagen and Paris, but this bracing collusion with Palle Mikkelborg's jazz orchestra was on a par with his best. Starting off with a dignified reading of John Coltrane's "Naima," the record rarely flags, only stumbling on the alien Swedish vocals (pre-ABBA?) of "Good Morning Sun." And check Gordon's own cool warbling on "This Happy Madness."

what to buy next: *Dexter Gordon Plays* 𝄞𝄞𝄞 (Fresh Sound, 1955), 12 cuts for the Bethlehem label, was Gordon's return from a California prison stint for heroin possession. As romantic as a fall day in New York, these two 1955 sessions let the world know that a long-neglected jazzman was back on track. *Dexter Calling* 𝄞𝄞𝄞 (Blue Note, 1961) was as basic as Dexter got in those days, heading a steaming quartet on eight tunes—divided between flag-wavers and torch songs.

best of the rest:

Go 𝄞𝄞𝄞 (Blue Note, 1987)
Swiss Nights 𝄞𝄞𝄞 (Steeplechase, 1987)
Homecoming 𝄞𝄞𝄞 (Columbia, 1990)
Rides Again 𝄞𝄞𝄞 (Savoy, 1992)
The Chase 𝄞𝄞𝄞𝄞 (Stash, 1995)

worth searching for: *Body and Soul* 𝄞𝄞𝄞 (Black Lion, 1967) was one of several dozen recordings for Swedish, French, and British record labels. Almost everything he touched was first rate, but Gordon seemed most focused on a series of albums made in 1967 at the Montmarte Jazzhus in Copenhagen. If exile produced music as timeless as this, there would hardly be any jazz players left in the U.S.

influences:

◀◀ Lester Young, Coleman Hawkins, Charlie Parker, Lionel Hampton, Billy Eckstine

▶▶ John Coltrane, Booker Ervin

Steve Braun

Lesley Gore

Born May 2, 1946, in New York City, NY.

Aided by the deft production of Quincy Jones, Lesley Gore exploded onto the Phil Spector-dominated girl-group scene in the early '60s with smash hits like "It's My Party," "Judy's Turn to Cry," and the proto-feminist "You Don't Own Me." While continuing to espouse teen romance with her golden, throaty style through the mid-'60s, shifting public musical tastes rendered Gore largely irrelevant at age 21 (her last charting single was a laughable cover of "Eve of Destruction"). Gore turned to acting, appearing most notably as Catwoman's assistant on the *Batman* TV series. In the '70s she attempted two comeback albums, but even a reunion with Jones on "Love Me by Name" failed to ignite her early career's spark. While occasionally touring with cabarets and oldies shows, Gore even took up songwriting, penning a tune for the soundtrack of the 1980 film *Fame*, a subject she knew for all too short a time.

what to buy: All the hits and then some can be found on the 26 tracks of *Anthology* 𝄞𝄞𝄞 (Rhino, 1986, prod. various). The combination of Gore's sure voice and Jones's skillfull tweaks remains fresh and amazingly relevant.

what to buy next: For diehard fans, *It's My Party: Mercury Anthology* 𝄞𝄞𝄞 (Mercury, 1996, prod. various) contains 52 tracks of hits, misses, and interesting rarities, like "Look of Love" and "Wedding Bell Blues."

what to avoid: There are several other—by comparison, weak—greatest-hits collections, such as *Golden Hits of Lesley Gore* ♫♫♫ (Mercury, 1965) and *Greatest Hits* ♫♫♫ (DJ Specialist, 1996), in print, covering the same material as the aforementioned superior anthologies.

worth searching for: Fans intrigued by Gore's early hit-making years might want to give *Love Me by Name* ♫♫♫ (A&M, 1978, prod. Quincy Jones) a try. Fifteen years after they collaborated on "It's My Party," Jones is still able to coax a little magic, especially with the title song. Notably, Gore and lyricist Ellen Weston penned all the album's songs.

influences:

◄◄ The Shangri-La's, the Four Seasons, Brenda Lee, Phil Spector

►► Alanis Morissette, the Go-Go's, Blondie, the Bangles

Alex Gordon

Eydie Gorme

See: Steve Lawrence & Eydie Gorme

Morton Gould

Born December 10, 1913, in Richmond Hill, NY. Died February 21, 1996, in Orlando, FL.

In addition to being a major easy-listening star, who along with Percy Faith and Ray Conniff virtually invented Muzak and beautiful-music radio stations, Gould was a major music-industry player for several decades. He was president of the American Society of Composers, Authors, and Publishers for eight years, earned the Pulitzer Prize, and led orchestras all over the world.

As one of the top names in easy-listening music in the '60s, Gould admirably tried to stay in touch with popular trends, incorporating rock and pop melodies into his symphonic sounds. (In *Elevator Music,* author Joseph Lanza quotes a critic hailing Gould's "infectious contemporary pulse," but Rolling Stones fans at the time would have begged to differ.) Those high-profile recording years, though, were just one phase of an influential career that leaned heavily towards Arthur Fiedler's style of orchestral, melodic pop. After publishing his first composition at age six, teen prodigy Gould studied at what became the prestigious Julliard School. During the Depression, he worked at movie theaters before signing on as Radio City Music Hall's staff pianist—which led to all sorts of opportunities, broadcasting on WOR Mutual Radio and side-stepping into shows and film. He created the soundtrack music for *Billion Dollar Baby* on Broadway, *Holocaust* on tele-

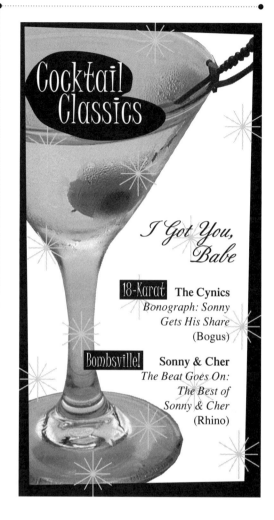

vision, and *Windjammer* on film. Prestigious groups all over the world, including the New York Ballet and the Van Cliburn International Piano Competition, commissioned his work, and for his trouble he won a Grammy, a Pulitzer, and the prestigious ASCAP post. In 1996, just before a symphony show in Orlando, Gould suddenly took ill and was advised not to perform; he died shortly thereafter.

what to buy: Gould's *Jungle Drums* ♫♫♫ (RCA Victor, 1996) was among five of his well-known albums reissued shortly after his death. It's more quirky and bizarre than the more straightforward pop-classical work that characterized Gould's recording career.

what to buy next: The best of the other available Gould CDs, *Blues in the Night* ♫♫♫ (RCA Victor, 1996, prod. John Pfeiffer) and *Kern/Porter Favorites* ♫♫♫ (RCA Victor, 1996, prod. John Pfeiffer) focus on mainstream blues and pop standards, respectively. They're recommended for fans of Arthur Fiedler and Ray Conniff, who appreciate the uneasy allliance between rock and classical music. Exotica fans are steered instead back to *Jungle Drums*.

the rest:
Brass & Percussion ♫♫♫ (RCA Victor, 1993)
Carmen for Orchestra ♫♫ (RCA Victor, 1996)
Moon, Wind and Stars ♫♫ (RCA Victor, 1996)

worth searching for: *Morton Gould Makes the Scene* ♫♫ (RCA Victor) is worth owning just for the title; Gould, like many easy-listening composers from Squaresville, decided to make love, not war, with the hippies in the 1960s. In retrospect, though, his album is more fun than anything by Joan Baez or Crosby, Stills, and Nash, simply because Gould simply didn't take himself that seriously.

influences:
◀◀ Arthur Fiedler, Mantovani, Andre Kostelanetz
▶▶ Percy Faith, Ray Conniff

Steve Knopper

Robert Goulet
Born November 26, 1933, in Lawrence, MA.

In the late '50s Goulet played Sir Lancelot in *Camelot,* the Lerner & Loewe musical that captivated a generation and provided the mythic frame for the Kennedy Administration. Goulet staked his reputation on that performance, and used it to launch a career as a popular singer in 1962. Though he has charted a few singles, including "What Kind of Fool Am I?" and "My Love, Forgive Me (Amore, Scusami)," Goulet recorded regularly until the early '70s, when he shifted his efforts into concert and television appearances.

what to buy: The vast majority of Goulet's in-print albums are greatest-hits collections or Christmas albums. Recommended among albums of more or less equal merit is *Greatest Hits* ♫♫♫ (Columbia, 1969), which includes his smooth performances of "The Impossible Dream," "If Ever I Should Leave You," "Summer Sounds," and "Autumn Leaves."

what to buy next: *Personal Christmas Collection* ♫♫♫ (Sony, 1993) finds Goulet performing holiday favorites new and old,

including "O Holy Night," "Let It Snow! Let It Snow! Let It Snow!," and "Have Yourself a Merry Little Christmas."

what to avoid: *Golden Classics Edition* ♫♫♫ (Collectables, 1997) duplicates material that can be found elsewhere.

worth searching for: *The Sullivan Years: Best of Broadway* ♫♫♫♫ (TVT, 1992) lets you hear the glory days of the Great White Way, including Pearl Bailey, Cab Calloway, and John Raitt. Goulet is represented, of course, by "Camelot."

influences:
◀◀ Nelson Eddy, Gordon MacRae, John Raitt
▶▶ Richard Harris

Ben Greenman

Buddy Greco
Born August 14, 1926, in Philadelphia, PA.

Buddy Greco's name looks funny in small print—it's much more at home in giant capital letters on the late, lamented Sands or the modern Caesar's Palace marquees in Las Vegas. Along with Steve and Eydie, Tom Jones, Jack Jones, and a few of the other surviving showroom singers, Greco has come to epitomize Vegas showmanship and culture. The singer-pianist's biggest hit, the finger-snapping 1960 lounge classic "The Lady Is a Tramp," hipsterized from Frank Sinatra's well-known version of a few years earlier, solidified his commercial cachet in the Emerald City. But he didn't start out as a crooner in a smoking jacket and a big white-toothed smile: a superb pianist, Greco began playing at age 4 and was already making public appearances at age 16, when Benny Goodman spotted him. The swing hero hired Greco to tour the world with his band; the collaboration lasted four years, then Greco went solo and embarked on a long hitmaking career. Though he's not nearly as talented a singer as Sinatra or Dean Martin, Greco has impeccable swing credentials, having revered Nat King Cole as a child and having direct experience in Goodman's band. Recently, he and his fourth wife, singer Lezlie Anders, have been selling out concerts in Vegas and beyond, and Greco continues to add to his list of 65-plus recorded albums.

what to buy: Wouldn't you know it? Most of Greco's dozens of albums are out of print, but he's popular enough to merit a few excellent greatest-hits CD sets. Start with *16 Most Requested*

Buddy Greco **(Archive Photos)**

Songs ♫♫♫ (Sony, 1993, compilation prod. Didier C. Deutsch), which of course has "The Lady Is a Tramp," but also swing-pop standards such as "My Kind of Girl."

what to buy next: Greco indulges his lifelong Nat King Cole fascination with *Route 66: A Personal Tribute to Nat King Cole* ♫♫♫ (Candid, 1995), which doesn't quite match Cole's masterful phrasing or pure soul, but, as a more-fun alternative to the inescapable Natalie Cole tribute, includes impeccably played renditions of "Smile" and "Unforgettable."

what to avoid: Like Jack Jones and Andy Williams, Greco can also embody the schmaltzy, almost unlistenable side of lounge culture: *MacArthur Park* ♫♫ (Candid, 1996) has its charms, including a romantic "My Funny Valentine," but it gets old real fast.

the rest:
Walk a Little Faster ♫♫ (USA Music Group, 1996)
Movin' On ♫♫♫ (USA Music Group)

worth searching for: *Jackpot! The Las Vegas Story* ♫♫♫♫ (Rhino, 1996, compilation prod. James Austin, Richard Foos, Will Friedwald, Tony Natelli), in addition to including Greco's "The Lady Is a Tramp," is the ultimate Vegas-music collection. Liberace's "Cherry Hill Park/MacArthur Park/Echo Park" suite is not to be missed, and Dean Martin, Sammy Davis Jr., Vic Damone, and Miss Ann-Margret show up to swingify the standards.

influences:

◀◀ Benny Goodman, Frank Sinatra, Dean Martin, Sammy Davis Jr., Russ Columbo, Bing Crosby, Nat "King" Cole

▶▶ Jack Jones, Liza Minnelli, Tom Jones, Ann-Margret, Jerry Vale, Liberace

Steve Knopper

Dave Grusin

Born June 26, 1934, in Denver, CO.

Grusin is one of those prolific, seemingly ubiquitous musicians whose piano, keyboard, and composing work might pop up on anything from a television or film soundtrack to discs on his own Grusin-Rosen Productions (GRP Records) label, from orchestral recordings to Henry Mancini cover albums. A printed list of recordings on which he appears in some capacity, including producer or executive producer, covers eight pages—an extraordinary output. Yet there was a time in his life when he planned to be sticking needles into animals as a veterinarian rather than tickling ivories or building suspense into movies. He's not considered a great player, but Grusin gives great back-

ground music, as his resume shows. He scored that lounge-o-rama love story, *The Fabulous Baker Boys,* along with *The Goodbye Girl, Three Days of the Condor, And Justice for All . . . , Reds, Tequila Sunrise, Selena,* and the HBO film *In the Gloaming.* He received Academy Award nominations for *Heaven Can Wait, The Champ, On Golden Pond, Tootsie* (he co-wrote that gooey confection, "It Might Be You," with Stephen Bishop), *The Firm,* and *Havana.* He won in 1988 for *The Milagro Beanfield War.* His first film, for which he left *The Andy Williams Show,* was that swinging '60s Norman Lear creation, *Divorce American Style.* TV scores included *Good Times, Maude, Baretta,* and *St. Elsewhere.* Grusin studied classical piano at the University of Colorado, but got caught up in a jazz groove and worked during that time with Terry Gibbs and Johnny Smith. He headed to the Manhattan School of Music in New York in 1959, intending on a career as a professor. But then he hooked up with Andy Williams, with whom he worked until 1964. He then started composing for TV and film. While working with Williams, Grusin recorded in 1960 with Benny Goodman's quintet, led a hard bop trio with Milt Hinton and Don Lamond from 1961–62, and performed in 1964 in a quintet with Thad Jones and Frank Foster. Artists for which Grusin has done arrangements include Peggy Lee, Sarah Vaughan, Billy Joel, Quincy Jones, Sergio Mendes, Paul Simon, Carmen McRae, and Grover Washington Jr. In the last couple of decades, Grusin has gotten into several idioms, from pop to fusion to symphonies, and the GRP big band. His hits include *Night-Lines* (1984), *Harlequin* (1985, with Lee Ritenour) and the double Grammy-winner *The Fabulous Baker Boys* (1989). At last count, he held 10 Grammys. Grusin holds honorary doctorates from Berklee College of Music and his alma mater, and he is co-founder with Rosen of the National Foundation for Jazz Education. Oh, and he raises cattle on his Montana ranch—in his spare time, of course. All this from a guy who's not even considered a virtuoso.

what to buy: It's hard to screw up the Duke, and on *Homage to Duke* ♫♫♫ (GRP, 1993, prod. Dave Grusin), a collection of common Ellington classics ("Take the 'A' Train," "Satin Doll," "Mood Indigo," "Sophisticated Lady"), Grusin doesn't. With sidemen Tom Scott, Harvey Mason, Clark Terry, and others, he scores on this very loungey outing. Dave and his younger brother, Don, duet nicely on *Sticks and Stones* ♫♫♫ (GRP, 1988, prod. Dave Grusin). *The Gershwin Connection* ♫♫♫ (GRP, 1991, prod. Dave Grusin), considered one of Grusin's more creative efforts, includes a bit of strangely inserted funk ("I've Got Plenty o' Nuthin'"), but comes off pretty well, with some good improvisational moments.

what to buy next: As they listen to *The Fabulous Baker Boys* 𝄞𝄞𝄞 (GRP, 1989, prod. Dave Grusin, Joel Sill), lounge hounds will have no trouble envisioning Michelle Pfeiffer rolling around atop that polished piano, and the actress acquits herself amazingly well on her two singing tracks. Until this film, no one knew she could.

what to avoid: *The Orchestral Album* 𝄞𝄞 (GRP, 1994, prod. Dave Grusin) proves a lot of great players does not a great album make, particularly if one tries to combine a cowboy medley with "Porgy and Bess." As for *Cinemagic* 𝄞𝄞 (GRP, 1987, prod. Dave Grusin), let's just say the name overstates the case.

best of the rest:

One of a Kind 𝄞𝄞𝄞 (GRP, 1978/1984)
Out of the Shadows 𝄞𝄞𝄞 (GRP, 1982)
Night-Lines 𝄞𝄞𝄞 (GRP, 1985)
(With Lee Ritenour) *Harlequin* 𝄞𝄞𝄞𝄞 (GRP, 1985)
Collection 𝄞𝄞𝄞𝄞 (GRP, 1989)
Two for the Road: The Music of Henry Mancini 𝄞𝄞𝄞 (GRP, 1997)
Dave Grusin Presents: "West Side Story" 𝄞𝄞𝄞 (N2K Encoded Music, 1997)

influences:

◀◀ Benny Goodman, Duke Ellington, Quincy Jones, Vince Guaraldi

▶▶ Chick Corea, Lee Ritenour, the Rippingtons

Lynne Margolis

Vince Guaraldi

Born Vincent Anthony Guaraldi, July 17, 1928, in San Francisco, CA.

Guaraldi will probably be most affectionately remembered as the man behind the vibrant music that accompanied all those beloved *Peanuts* television specials. But the Bay Area pianist had a fruitful career in jazz long before he gave Charles M. Schulz's characters their musical souls. Before graduating from San Francisco State College, Guaraldi had already been making the rounds playing cool jazz at beatnik hang-outs like the Cellar and the hungry i. Though he sat in with other combos (those of Conte Candoli, Frank Rosolino, Cal Tjader, and Woody Herman), he made a name for himself leading his own outfits—from his original trio (with guitarist Eddie Duran and bassist Dean Reilly) to a sextet complete with timbales and congas. Unlike more avant garde schools of jazz, such as bop, which ruffled many feathers in its quest to stretch the boundaries of jazz, the Guaraldi Trio lounged comfortably within the mellow improvisational parameters of West Coast cool jazz.

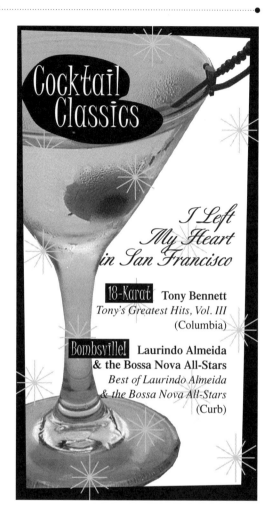

what to buy: *A Charlie Brown Christmas* 𝄞𝄞𝄞𝄞 (Fantasy, 1988) is certainly some of Guaraldi's best work, and possibly the coolest Christmas album ever. On *In Person* 𝄞𝄞𝄞𝄞 (Fantasy, 1963), the trio expands to a quintet—Guaraldi, Duran back on guitar, Fred Marshall on bass, drummer Colin Bailey, and Benny Velarde on the scratcher. This actually has a Brazilian flair, with Guaraldi delving into some more exotic melodies. *The Latin Side of Vince Guaraldi* 𝄞𝄞𝄞 (Fantasy, 1964) has the combo bolstered to a sextet (Guaraldi, Duran, Marshall, and Velarde, plus Bill Fitch on congas and drummer Jerry Granelli). It's a super bossa nova-fied collection of familiar tunes (such as Nat Adderley's "Work Song" and Henry Mancini's "Mr. Lucky") and Guaraldi originals. Between *Oh Good Grief* 𝄞𝄞𝄞 (Warner Bros./Seven Arts) and *A Boy*

Named Charlie Brown 𝄞𝄞𝄞 (Fantasy, 1989), it's possible to collect all of Guaraldi's great *Peanuts* tunes.

what to buy next: In 1963 Guaraldi was commissioned by the Rev. Charles Gompertz at San Francisco's Grace Cathedral to compose a contemporary musical setting for the choral Eucharist, and *The Grace Cathedral Concert* 𝄞𝄞𝄞 (Fantasy, 1965) is the result. The juxtaposition of the priest's antiphon and the gentle jazzy interludes is less jarring than you might expect, and oddly reminiscent of the choral moments in Guaraldi's *Peanuts* work; "Holy Communion Blues" especially stands out. *The Vince Guaraldi Trio* 𝄞𝄞𝄞 (Fantasy, 1956) is calm, with an almost classical elegance in places as the trio wends its way through full-bodied melodies (both original and standards like "Three Coins in the Fountain" and "It's De-lovely") with poise and intensity. *A Flower Is a Lovesome Thing* 𝄞𝄞𝄞 (Fantasy, 1957) is delicate and pensive, but the trio also swings (albeit sedately) on a couple tracks. *Jazz Impressions of Black Orpheus* 𝄞𝄞𝄞 (Fantasy, 1962) collects Guaraldi's interpretations of several songs from the 1959 film *Black Orpheus*. The Brazilian feel isn't terribly pronounced, but the trio (with a new lineup: Guaraldi, bassist Monty Budwig, and drummer Colin Bailey) does simmer more than usual. Non-*Orpheus* material includes Henry Mancini's "Moon River." *Live at El Matador* 𝄞𝄞𝄞 (Fantasy, 1987) is a cassette-only concert recording of Guaraldi and Brazil's Bola Sete. An earlier collaboration, *Vince Guaraldi, Bola Sete and Friends* is now out of print, so *Live* and *Greatest Hits* 𝄞𝄞𝄞 (Fantasy, 1989) are important in that they contain some of the only recordings of Guaraldi's work with the Brazilian guitarist. The latter also provides a concise overview of Guaraldi's repertoire.

best of the rest:
Jazz Impressions 𝄞𝄞𝄞 (Fantasy, 1964)

influences:
◀◀ Oscar Peterson, Tal Farlow

Sandy Masuo

Frances Gumm
See: Judy Garland

Oscar Hammerstein II
See: Richard Rodgers

Herbie Hancock
Born Herbert Jeffrey Hancock, April 12, 1940, in Chicago, IL.

Hancock started his music career as a child prodigy, performing a Mozart piano concerto movement with the Chicago Symphony Orchestra at 11. Little could he know, back then, that he was on the way to becoming not only one of the coolest cats in jazz, but in rock and funk, too. He was even doing techno before techno was cool—on his hit, "Rockit," Hancock not only brought scratching and hip-hop beats to the world at large, he also used robotics in a totally new way for his accompanying video. Even before that 1983 hit, Hancock was considered one of the major pioneers of jazz fusion and is listed alongside cool kings Miles Davis, Charlie Mingus, and John Coltrane as one of the giants of new jazz. During his career, Hancock has gone in a zillion directions, including 'froing his hair and doing disco ("Chameleon" kept those platforms scuffing up those lighted dance floors for ages). Though his high-minded jazz fans might shudder at the thought, Hancock's lounge credentials were cemented the day he took off with his first solo disc, 1962's *Takin' Off*, which contained his first hit, "Watermelon Man" (it became a hit after Mongo Santamaria covered it). Hancock later became a member of Davis's group, then discovered funk and fused it with jazz, creating a new subgenre. He's still experimenting, jumping back to his jazz roots now and then with the V.S.O.P. Quintet, and forward with computerization and sampling. Regardless of what jazz purists have to say about his moves, he continues to do what he wants—including hosting a former Showtime cable television music series, *Coast to Coast*.

what to buy: *Maiden Voyage* 𝄞𝄞𝄞𝄞 (Blue Note, 1965, prod. Alfred Lion) is one of Hancock's masterpieces, with bassist Ron Carter and drummer Tony Williams, his Miles Davis bandmates. It's a concept album, with each song thematically related to the sea. *Empyrean Isles* 𝄞𝄞𝄞𝄞 (Blue Note, 1964/1985, prod. Alfred Lion) reunites Hubbard, Carter, and Williams, an unbeatable combo that dominated jazz-funk both together and individually for years. *Headhunters* 𝄞𝄞𝄞𝄞 (Columbia, 1973/1992, prod. David Rubinson, Herbie Hancock), Hancock's attempt to find more funk, worked like a charm (make that a gold medallion, shining from a hairy, semi-exposed chest). His disco-flavored "Chameleon" helped give this disc platinum sales. But Hancock has a softer side, displayed on the delicate "Vein Melter." Until Kenny G started his reign of smooth jazz, this album was the biggest-selling album in jazz chart history.

what to buy next: The soaring wine-drinking soundtrack *Takin' Off* 𝄞𝄞𝄞𝄞 (Blue Note, 1962/1987, prod. Alfred Lion) features the oh-so-smooth trumpet of Freddie Hubbard, along with sax-man Dexter Gordon, bassist Butch Warren, and drummer Billy Higgins—and Hancock's impeccable piano, which he used to play once upon a time before he went electronic. *Sound System* 𝄢𝄢𝄢 (Columbia, 1984/1985, prod. Bill Laswell/Material, Herbie Hancock) is full of heavily layered, catchy funk that utilizes scratching, Fairlight programming, and other then-innovative electronic instruments and techniques. Wig out your ultra-hip friends with a little dose of Hancock's *Dis Is da Drum* 𝄢𝄢𝄢 (Mercury, 1994, prod. Herbie Hancock, Bill Summers), a jazz-funk-techno-whatever album of jungle-boogie, with Dr. Synth himself funking up the fake ivories. Looping African rhythms and everything else he can all over the place, Hancock even throws down with his bad rap self on "The Melody (On the Deuce by 44)," getting just a little carried away. But he's just taking a cue from Big Daddy Q—Quincy Jones, that is—and still finds time to deliver the lush pop-jazz-funk piece here and there ("Butterfly," "Hump," "Bo Ba Be Da"). On *The New Standard* 𝄢𝄢𝄢 (Verve, 1996, prod. Herbie Hancock, Guy Eckstine), Hancock takes pop songs and renders them nearly unrecognizable, but that's not necessarily a bad thing because he still makes them listenable—they're just nothing like you'd expect to hear. On "Norwegian Wood (This Bird Has Flown)," he doesn't hit the familiar opening notes until a minute and 20 into the song. With four songs clocking in at more than eight minutes and two more nearing that, you'd better be lounging around while listening. The shortest tune? Kurt Cobain's "All Apologies"—at five minutes and four seconds. Aside from the Artist Formerly Known as Prince's "Thieves in the Temple," the songs on this album are it—if you're looking for schmaltz, instrumental-style.

what to avoid: *Monster* 𝄢𝄢 (Columbia, 1980/1994, prod. David Rubinson & Friends Inc., Herbie Hancock) is plodding, formulaic funk; when all else fails, Hancock relies on repetition. In between, the disc is filled with soulless lite-FM ballads. Other than the seminal dance-floor funk of "Rockit," *Future Shock* 𝄢𝄢𝄢 (Columbia, 1983, prod. Material, Herbie Hancock) doesn't offer much, despite contributions by Bill Laswell, Bernard Fowler, and Sly Dunbar.

best of the rest:
The Best of Herbie Hancock: The Blue Note Years 𝄢𝄢𝄢𝄢 (Blue Note, 1962/1988)
My Point of View 𝄢𝄢𝄢𝄢 (Blue Note, 1963/1996)
Inventions and Dimensions (now called *Succotash*) 𝄢𝄢𝄢 (Blue Note, 1963/Pausa)
Speak Like a Child 𝄢𝄢𝄢𝄢 (Blue Note, 1968/1988)

The Prisoner 𝄢𝄢𝄢𝄢 (Blue Note, 1969/1996)
Thrust 𝄢𝄢𝄢𝄢 (Columbia, 1974)
Jazz Africa 𝄢𝄢𝄢𝄢 (Verve, 1990)

worth searching for: The *Blow-Up* 𝄢𝄢𝄢 soundtrack (MGM, 1966/Sony Special Products, 1992, prod. Pete Spargo), a bizarre jazz-and-funk instrumental gem from the psychedelic '60s, includes "Bring Down the Birds," which is at least as swinging as Quincy Jones's earlier "Soul Bossa Nova"; the early-'90s dance-funk band Deee-Lite sampled its central hook almost completely. The Yardbirds, with guitarists Jeff Beck and future Led Zeppelin founder Jimmy Page, show up for "Stroll On." Very weird stuff.

influences:

◀◀ Miles Davis, Bill Evans, Horace Silver, Ahmad Jamal, James Brown, Stevie Wonder, Sly & the Family Stone, John Coltrane

▶▶ Chick Corea, Joe Zawinul, Earth, Wind & Fire, Ray Parker Jr., Quincy Jones, Us3, Parliament/Funkadelic

Lynne Margolis

Francoise Hardy

Born January 17, 1944, in Paris, France.

Francoise Hardy emerged from France's pop music scene in the mid-'60s singing lovesick ballads and baroque pop songs in a voice that was as inscrutably waifish and delicate as her movie-star good looks. As a Parisian teen, Hardy was weaned on American rock 'n' roll and the sultry stylings of the immensely popular French singer Sylvie Vartan. By the time she was 15, Hardy had already taught herself how to play guitar and write her own songs. At 17, she was singing professionally in local clubs, which eventually led to her signing a recording contract with French label Vogue Records in 1961. Her recording of the song "Tous les Garcons et les Filles" became a massive hit throughout Europe in 1962; two years later, it reached the U.K. Top 40. Hardy, who wrote most of her own material, recorded steadily throughout the decade, tackling everything from over-the-top pop to the blues and cabaret music. Hardy also made appearances in films as diverse as Jean-Luc Godard's *Masculin-Feminin* and *What's New Pussycat?*, both of which were released in 1966. In recent years, Hardy's coolly detached style has been discovered by a new generation of artists—she has appeared on recent recordings by the British pop band Blur and dance-music impresario Malcolm McClaren.

what's available: The mediocre *Danger* ♫♫♫ (Virgin, 1996) is Hardy's only domestic release available on CD. But *Ma Jeunesse Fout le Camp* ♫♫♫ (Virgin, 1967) best captures Hardy's florid pop style. Her writing and singing had matured considerably by the time she recorded *Le Question* ♫♫♫♫ (Virgin, 1971), an all-acoustic album of smoldering, moody torch-pop songs. *Francoise Hardy en Anglais* ♫♫ (Sonopress, 1969) finds Hardy attempting to capture the English-speaking market, but her vocals come off sounding stilted and stiff.

influences:

◀◀ Sylvie Vartan, Elvis Presley, Ann-Margret

▶▶ Blur, Madeleine Peyroux

Marc Weingarten

Phil Harris

Born January 16, 1904, in Linton, IN. Died August 11, 1995, in Rancho Mirage, CA.

Modern audiences know Phil Harris best as the voice of Baloo the Bear in Walt Disney's animated 1966 classic *The Jungle Book*, but he was also a top bandleader in the 1930s and 1940s, as well as a beloved radio comedian. Harris began his career as a drummer for Francis Craig's band in the early 1920s, then co-founded the Lofner-Harris Orchestra with Carol Lofner in 1928. Four years later, the singer formed his own band and broadcast live shows from the Coconut Grove over NBC radio. His stints there led to a popular short subject film about him, which in turn earned his orchestra the house band slot on *The Jack Benny Program* in 1936. On radio, Harris developed his wisecracking, soused band-rat character years before Dean Martin came up with the same idea, and he routinely garnered big laughs and applause with his zoot-suit greetings of Jack Benny and Mary Livingstone. ("Hiya Jackson!" he shouted. "Hello Livvy . . . you doll, you!") When he and his band weren't backing Dennis Day or some special guest star, Harris sang such ditties as "That's What I Like About the South," "G.I Jive," and "Smoke! Smoke! Smoke! That Cigarette," all of which became substantial hits. Harris wasn't a great vocalist, but as his recordings attest, his phrasing was hep-cat cool and his style was instantly identifiable. In 1946, Harris and his wife, Alice Faye, started their own sitcom on CBS radio, which lasted eight years. Tired of touring, he eventually disbanded his orchestra; Harris's early-'50s youth-oriented hits "The Thing" (a purposefully vague novelty which still gets airplay on Dr. Demento's radio show) and "I Know an Old Lady" were his last chart entries. He remained in demand as a nightclub entertainer, TV

guest, supporting player in movies, and voice for feature-length cartoons. His last major voiceover role, in 1992's *Rock-a-Doodle*, featured an 88-year-old Harris singing "Life Is Just Like Tying Your Shoes" with the philosophic verve of a lifelong southern-fried hipster.

what to buy: Harris's late-1940s/early-1950s jaunty novelties are collected on *The Thing About Phil Harris* ♫♫♫♫ (Living Era, 1996, prod. various), featuring the wonderfully vague hit "The Thing."

what to buy next: His first blush of fame, with his own band, is neatly documented on *Echoes from the Coconut Grove* ♫♫♫♫ (Take Two Records, 1996, prod. various), with radio transcriptions from 1932–33.

the rest:
The Jungle Book ♫♫♫♫ (Original Soundtrack) (Disney, 1967/1997)
1933–Phil Harris & His Orchestra ♫♫♫ (Hindsight, 1992)

worth searching for: Some catalogs carry *That's What I Like About the South* ♫♫♫♫ (Good Music, 1997, prod. various), which contains 24 tracks of fun-loving jive such as "Smoke! Smoke! Smoke! That Cigarette," "Ain't Nobody Here But Us Chickens," and "Preacher and the Bear." Also, some old-time radio catalogs have *The Phil Harris–Alice Faye Show* ♫♫♫♫ (Adventures in Cassettes, 1997, prod. various) and *Phil Harris–Alice Faye Show "What's a Rexall?"* ♫♫♫♫ (Adventures in Cassettes, 1996, prod. various), both six tape compilations from radio's golden age.

influences:

◀◀ Francis Craig, Carol Lofner, Bert Williams

▶▶ Kay Kyser, Tex Beneke, Dean Martin

Ken Burke

Richard Harris

Born October 1, 1930, in Limerick, Ireland.

Harris was part of a triumvirate of British actors (including Peter O'Toole and Richard Burton) who stormed the stage in the 1960s. He has appeared in dozens of films and countless stage productions, most memorably as King Arthur in *Camelot* on stage and screen. Like many successful actors, he was offered the opportunity to record pop albums, and like many successful actors, he was a failure as a pop star despite his most vigorous and (melo-)dramatic efforts. Harris's 1968 album, *A Tramp Shining*, was entirely written and produced by turbo songwriter Jimmy Webb, who penned hits for Glen

Richard Harris **(Archive Photos)**

Campbell and the Fifth Dimension, among others. The album, a billowy blend of showtune orchestration and florid pop gestures, nonetheless yielded a #2 hit for Harris in "MacArthur Park." The song would subsequently be covered by many artists, most notably disco diva Donna Summer, whose #1 1978 version would secure *A Tramp Shining* cult status for years to come. Indeed, it is the only Harris album still in print, other than a 1974 collection of gooey, dramatic, semi-orchestrated readings of works by the poet/philosopher/New Age guru Kahlil Gibran and an obscure collection titled *The Webb Sessions*, which may or may not be studio outtakes from the *Tramp Shining* sessions.

what to buy: *A Tramp Shining* 🎝🎝🎝 (MCA, 1968, prod. Jimmy Webb) features "MacArthur Park" and a smattering of other equally overdone but less memorable pop tunes. The lurid appeal of the album is the gusto with which Harris lets the schmaltz fly.

the rest:
The Prophet Kahlil Gibran 🎝 (Atlantic, 1974)

influences:

◀◀ Tom Jones, Anthony Newley, Roy Orbison, Engelbert Humperdinck, Rod McKuen

▶▶ Donna Summer, the Carpenters, Dave Barry

Sandy Masuo

Lorenz Hart
See: Richard Rodgers

Johnny Hartman
Born John Maurice Hartman, July 3, 1923, in Chicago, IL. Died September 15, 1983, in New York, NY.

Perhaps the most underrated jazz singer of his generation, Hartman has been resurrected in recent years as the supreme vocal stylist his colleagues knew him to be. Hartman—with a pure, honey-rich sound that lent itself to a wide array of standards—was virtually forgotten by mass audiences until director Clint Eastwood used a few of his tracks in *The Bridges of Madison County*. Since then, jazz labels have been quick to reissue many of his albums—particularly after the *Bridges* soundtrack went on to huge sales. Hartman is perhaps the best of all the so-called "mellow" jazz singers. He got his start singing in high school and was set to embark on a career when he was drafted into the military. After his discharge, he worked with Erroll Garner and Dizzy Gillespie before setting out on a solo career. RCA Victor, in original press releases introducing him, called him "the next Billy Eckstine" and, with his slender build, said he had "Sinatra type appeal . . . for the gals."

what to buy: Hartman recorded largely forgettable albums in the 1950s until *John Coltrane and Johnny Hartman* 𝄢𝄢𝄢𝄢 (Impulse!, 1963, prod. Bob Thiele) lit the jazz world on fire. Its evocative melodies fit Hartman's style perfectly. And Coltrane, showing miraculous restraint on his horn, serves as the ideal foil for Hartman's baritone. It's a crucial element of any lounge music collection, although listeners may also find *Unforgettable* 𝄢𝄢𝄢𝄢 (Impulse!, 1966, prod. Bob Thiele) a valuable addition.

what to buy next: *The Voice That Is* 𝄢𝄢𝄢 (Impulse!, 1964/1994, prod. Michael Cuscuna, Bob Thiele), a nice reissue of Hartman's prime vocal years, features a selection of complex tunes that were ideal for Hartman's interpretation, including "The More I See You" and "These Foolish Things." *For Trane* 𝄢𝄢𝄢 (Blue Note, 1995, reissue prod. Michael Cuscuna), Hartman's tribute to his saxophonist/soulmate John Coltrane, is a terrific collection of Trane's signature tunes: "Summertime," "My Favorite Things," and others.

best of the rest:
I Just Dropped by to Say Hello 𝄢𝄢𝄢 (MCA, 1963)
The Voice That Is 𝄢𝄢𝄢 (Impulse!, 1964)
Once in Every Life 𝄢𝄢𝄢 (Bee Hive, 1980)

worth searching for: The soundtrack album for Clint Eastwood's movie *The Bridges of Madison County* 𝄢𝄢𝄢 (Malpaso/Warner Bros., 1995, prod. Clint Eastwood) singlehandedly renewed popular interest in Hartman's career. His songs "I See Your Face Before Me," "It Was Almost Like a Song," and "For All We Know" stand up nicely among tracks by Dinah Washington and Barbara Lewis.

influences:
◀◀ Billy Eckstine, Nat "King" Cole, Joe Williams, Mel Tormé, John Coltrane

▶▶ Lou Rawls, George Benson

Carl Quintanilla

Mick Harvey
See: Nick Cave & the Bad Seeds

Tony Hatch & Jackie Trent
Formed 1964, in England.

Tony Hatch (born June, 1939, in Pinner, Middlesex, England), songwriting; Jackie Trent (born September, 1940, in Newcastle-under-Lyme, England), vocals.

The far-less-famous British equivalent of Sonny & Cher, Hatch and Trent hooked up in the mid-1960s after careers as (respectively) a grizzled television host and a moderately-well-known cabaret singer. Though Hatch had written a few hit songs, including Petula Clark's "Downtown" and the Searchers' "Sugar and Spice," his main jobs had been insulting the poor contestants of the televised talent show *New Faces* and composing soap-opera theme music. (He also had a respectable career as a publisher, composer, pianist, and arranger, having his own hit with 1960's "Look for a Star" before signing on as producer at Clark's label, Pye Records.) After meeting Trent, though, he found the perfect outlet for his cheesy romantic pop songs, setting her up with "Call Me," "My Love," "Don't Sleep in the Subway," and her #1 hit and trademark song, 1965's "Where Are You Now?" When the British Invasion ended, they shifted in the 1970s to musicals, including *Nell,* starring Trent and musically directed by Hatch.

worth searching for: The only place to find Trent's kitschy love song "Where Are You Now?" is, unfortunately, in used-record stores' bargain bins; she doesn't even show up, like her one-time contemporaries Petula Clark and Sandie Shaw, on British Invasion retrospective collections. Until that stuff comes out, you'll have to settle for an English import of Hatch's more serious work, *The Best of Tony Hatch and His Orchestra* 𝄢𝄢𝄢 (Sequel, 1997, prod. various).

influences:
◀◀ Phil Spector, Ike Turner, Brian Epstein, George Martin

▶▶ Sonny & Cher, Petula Clark, the Searchers, Ann-Margret

Steve Knopper

Coleman Hawkins
Born November 21, 1904, in St. Joseph, MO. Died May 19, 1969, in New York, NY.

The first giant of the tenor saxophone, Coleman Hawkins redefined the art of the jazz ballad with his superhuman 1939 performance of "Body and Soul." But curiously, his collaborations with string sections in the 1950s rarely approached that beatific level. Perhaps it was the mundane arrangements. Or maybe Hawk never found a way to overcome the sugary grip of the violins. But where his old rival, Ben Webster, bullied the orchestral session men into submission with his authoritative tone, Hawkins often sidled along with the strings, rarely taking what was rightly his. Hawkins found other ways of keeping his flame alive in the 1950s, pioneering the first wholly realized unaccompanied sax solos on record. But his string sessions too often lapsed into the lounge music that his labels at the time clearly hoped would sell big with pipe-smoking hi-fi enthusiasts.

what to buy: *At the Opera House* 𝄞𝄞𝄞𝄞 (Verve, 1994) is Hawkins at his most eloquent. No strings here. Instead, he stretches out with his frequent sparring partner, trumpeter Roy Eldridge, and the Modern Jazz Quartet minus vibraphonist Milt Jackson. Some of these live cuts are alternate takes but the fiery and tender solos are varied enough to make you forget you're hearing the same song over again.

what to buy next: *The Indispensable Coleman Hawkins* 𝄞𝄞𝄞 (BMG, 1992) does contain a bit of disposable Hawkins, but most of the music, which spans from 1927 to 1956, is enjoyable stuff. The two-disc set includes the immortal 1939 "Body and Soul" and even has three nice with-strings cuts from 1956. Too bad Hawk didn't expand on those. Mais oui, there's a comely femme in a tight skirt sitting at a cafe table on the cover of *The Hawk in Paris* 𝄞𝄞𝄞 (RCA/Bluebird, 1993, prod. John Snyder). (Why she's clutching a deadly hawk makes as much sense as any other 1950s lounge album cover.) But she's not in Paris and neither was Hawkins. Maybe he should have been. This skimpy 12-track album surpasses most jazz-and-strings tries, but rarely lifts away from cliche.

what to avoid: Hawkins tried once more with strings in the 1963 session *Hawk Talk* 𝄞𝄞 (Fresh Sound, 1990), but despite featuring some of Hawkins's own bright tunes, too many of the cuts were obscure. Hawk gave it a game try, but the orchestra sawed away as if its members couldn't wait for payday.

best of the rest:
Complete Keynote Recordings 𝄞𝄞𝄞𝄞 (Mercury, 1987)
Hollywood Stampede 𝄞𝄞𝄞𝄞 (Capitol, 1989)
Rainbow Mist 𝄞𝄞𝄞𝄞 (Delmark, 1992)
Coleman Hawkins Encounters Ben Webster 𝄞𝄞𝄞𝄞 (Verve, 1997)

influences:
◀◀ Fletcher Henderson, Louis Armstrong

Cocktail Classics

If I Had a Hammer

18-Karat **Trini Lopez**
From the Original Master Tapes
(Reprise import)

Bombsville! **Leonard Nimoy**
Golden Throats 1: The Great Celebrity Sing-Off
(Rhino)

▶▶ Lester Young, Don Byas, Ben Webster, Charlie Parker, Sonny Rollins, Chu Berry, Wardell Gray

Steve Braun

Isaac Hayes

Born August 6, 1938, in Covington, TN.

Was there a cooler brother in the universe than Isaac Hayes in the 1970s? Though he was one of the pre-eminent and most successful songwriters at Stax Records, churning out '60s hits with his writing partner David Porter for Sam & Dave, Johnnie Taylor, Carla Thomas, and Mable John, Hayes truly

made his mark with his own recordings and, of course, his image as the sexually charged Black Moses. Bald, sweaty, and shirtless, and always sporting sunglasses and fur, the basso profundo oozed sexuality and defined '70s black cool with his sweaty, epic musical productions, which featured extended sides of influential soul orchestration—often in the form of re-worked compositions by the likes of the Beatles, Jimmy Webb, and, yes, Burt Bacharach—and ushered R&B into the concept-album era. Hayes's work on the Oscar- and Grammy-winning *Shaft* soundtrack even paved the way for similar blaxploitation artists such as Curtis Mayfield and Marvin Gaye. Meanwhile his groundbreaking half-sung, half-spoken pillow-talk monologues became standard practice for 1970s soul recordings. Quickly, though, Hayes seemed to run out of creative gas, as the quality of his albums began to decrease at an astonishing rate. Hayes also ran out of luck: in 1976 he declared bankruptcy. By the 1980s, he had become seemingly more interested in Hollywood than Memphis, his acting credits (*Escape from New York, I'm Gonna Git You Sucka, Robin Hood: Men in Tights, It Could Happen to You*) accumulating more rapidly than his album sales. Hayes, who currently voices a character on the acclaimed but controversial animated series *South Park*, also became active in the Church of Scientology. In 1995 he attempted a comeback with two albums, one of which included his first songwriting collaboration with Porter since the pair split during the late 1960s. Unfortunately for the former Cool Brother No. 1, the public did not react warmly to either album.

what to buy: The seminal Hayes concept album, *Hot Buttered Soul* ✍✍✍✍ (Enterprise, 1969/Stax, 1987, prod. Al Bell, Marvell Thomas, Allen Jones) contains just four songs, including the sprawling, nearly 19-minute interpretation of Jimmy Webb's "By the Time I Get to Phoenix," a loping, 12-minute cover of Burt Bacharach's "Walk on By," and the essential high-hat groove, "Hyperbolicsyllabicsesquedalymistic." For a slightly more traditional album, the soundtrack album *Shaft* ✍✍✍✍ (Enterprise, 1971, prod. Isaac Hayes) features several shorter cuts, including the classic title track and a series of instrumentals. Yet it, too, contains a lengthy workout, the nearly 20-minute vocal ramble, "Do Your Thing." While the soundtrack does not address social concerns, à la Curtis Mayfield's *Superfly*, it still grooves hard. Both *Hot Buttered Soul* and *Shaft* feature a crack rhythm section, the Bar-Kays.

what to buy next: *The Isaac Hayes Movement* ✍✍✍ (Enterprise/Stax, 1970, prod. Isaac Hayes) features more orchestral, string-heavy soul, including a tremendous reading of Jerry Butler's "I Stand Accused" and a 12-minute cover of the Beatles' "Something." *Double Feature* ✍✍✍ (Enterprise, 1974/Stax, 1993, prod. Isaac Hayes) combines the underheard soundtracks from *Truck Turner* and *Tough Guys*.

what to avoid: Hayes's work is best digested whole; taking songs out of context can lessen their impact, particularly when they've been trimmed for radio purposes. As such, *Best of Isaac Hayes, Vol. 1* ✍✍ (Stax, 1986, prod. various), *Best of Isaac Hayes, Vol. 2* ✍✍ (Stax, 1986, prod. various), and *Greatest Hit Singles* ✍✍ (Stax, 1991, prod. various) should be avoided, as seminal songs are edited down and sequenced haphazardly, making for a poor introduction to Hayes's work.

the rest:
Presenting Isaac Hayes ✍✍✍ (Enterprise/Stax, 1967)
To Be Continued ✍✍✍ (Enterprise/Stax, 1970)
Black Moses ✍✍ (Enterprise, 1971)
Live at the Sahara Tahoe ✍ (Enterprise/Stax, 1973)
Joy ✍✍ (Enterprise, 1973)
Hotbed ✍ (Stax, 1978)
Don't Let Go ✍✍ (PolyGram Special Products, 1979)
Enterprise: His Greatest Hits ✍✍ (Stax, 1980)
Love Attack ✍✍ (Columbia, 1988)
Branded ✍✍ (Pointblank, 1995)
Wonderful ✍✍✍ (Stax, 1995)
Movement: Raw and Refined ✍✍ (Pointblank, 1995)
Soul Essentials: The Best of the Polydor Years ✍✍✍ (Polydor/Chronicles, 1996)

worth searching for: *Branded/Raw & Refined Sampler* ✍✍✍ (Pointblank, 1995) is a one-disc distillation of Hayes's two 1995 albums—which creates, in effect, the single-disc set these works should have been in the first place.

influences:

◀◀ Henry Mancini, Nat "King" Cole, Burt Bacharach, Brook Benton, Rufus Thomas, Wilson Pickett, Percy Sledge, Motown

▶▶ Gamble & Huff, Barry White, Teddy Pendergrass, Marvin Gaye, Al Green, Lenny Kravitz, Terence Trent D'Arby

Josh Freedom du Lac

Dick Haymes

Born Richard Benjamin Haymes, September 13, 1916, in Buenos Aires, Argentina. Died March 28, 1980, in Los Angeles, CA.

Though Haymes was a terrific crooner and a suave, long-faced

Coleman Hawkins **(Archive Photos)**

hunk in a bow tie, he's most frequently remembered as the guy who replaced Frank Sinatra in Harry James's swing band. In his time, though, Haymes was far more than an answer to a pop-music trivia question: his trademark songs, such as "My Silent Love," "For You, For Me, Forevermore," and "It Might as Well Be Spring" were big hits, and he briefly rivaled Sinatra and Bing Crosby in the 1940s. Born to an Englishman and an Irishwoman, Haymes emulated his concert-singing mother in his teens, catching on with the Johnny Johnson band in age 16 and becoming a Hollywood songwriter and movie extra throughout the 1930s. James was receptive to Haymes's song-selling pitches, and hired him as a singer in 1940; that led to higher-profile gigs with the Benny Goodman and Tommy Dorsey bands. His smooth, smooth voice was perfect for ro-mantic balladeering, but he wasn't suited for the faster num-bers (which gave the more versatile Sinatra a competitive edge). By 1941, Haymes was a bona fide solo star, and he suc-cessfully transferred his charisma to film, from 1943's *Dubarry Was a Lady* to 1948's *Up in Central Park*. Haymes, who was born in Argentina, managed to avoid the WWII draft by regis-tering as a "resident alien." When he returned to the U.S. from a trip abroad with Rita Hayworth (one of his seven wives), the government tried to deport him as an "undesirable alien." The deportation papers were later revoked. He survived that, plus two later declarations of bankruptcy, and became a reason-ably popular touring singer in England, the U.S., Ireland, and Spain through the 1970s.

what to buy: Though the two volumes of the thorough compila-tion *The Very Best of Dick Haymes, Vols. 1 and 2* 🎵🎵🎵 (Taragon, 1997, prod. various) have recently outpaced it, *The Best of Dick Haymes* 🎵🎵🎵 (Curb, 1991, prod. various) has long been the consummate Haymes set. It shows off his vibrato-less voice as he croons like Nat "King" Cole on "Our Love Is Here to Stay," "Where or When," and "Love Walked In."

best of the rest:

Ballad Singer 🎵🎵 (Jasmine, 1994)
For You, For Me, Forevermore 🎵🎵🎵 (Audiophile, 1994)
Serenading with the Big Bands 🎵🎵🎵 (Sony Special Products, 1995)
Star Eyes 🎵🎵 (Jazz Classics, 1996)
Soft Lights and Sweet Music 🎵🎵🎵 (Hindsight, 1997)
You'll Never Know 🎵🎵🎵 (ASV, 1997)

worth searching for: Haymes was already a mature, confi-dent singer when he joined James's big band in the early 1940s, and two British import sets, *Dick Haymes with Harry James: How High the Moon* 🎵🎵🎵 (Memoir Classics, 1994, prod. Gordon Gray) and *Dick Haymes with Harry James: It*

Had to Be You 🎵🎵🎵 (Memoir Classics, 1995, prod. Gordon Gray), prove that. The latter includes "Fools Rush In" and "All or Nothing at All."

influences:

◀◀ Frank Sinatra, Harry James, Russ Columbo, Bing Crosby, Al Jolson, Louis Armstrong

▶▶ Vic Damone, Jack Jones, Rudy Vallee, Buddy Greco

Steve Knopper

Neal Hefti

Born October 29, 1922, in Hastings, NE.

Although he's best known as a composer of film and televi-sion music—specifically, and deservedly, for the theme to the *Batman* TV series—Hefti was a polished and highly-re-garded big-band arranger long before he hit the big time in Hollywood. Hefti was barely out of his teens when he was writing charts for the likes of Earl Hines, Charlie Barnett, Woody Herman, Count Basie, and Frank Sinatra. Some critics suggest that Hefti was the force behind Basie's sound in the mid-'50s. Even after he was drafted into the ranks of com-posers, Hefti continued to convene musicians for concert and record sessions. Beyond *Batman,* a tedious instrumental once you've heard it, Hefti will be remembered for the pre-cise hooks of his theme for *The Odd Couple.* Underrecog-nized were *The April Fools* (with the title track by Burt Bacharach) and *Duel at Diablo,* which was a breakthrough of sorts as it was a gritty, no-nonsense Western with back-ground music that smacked of jazz.

what's available: New to the market is the CD reissue of *Bat-man Theme and 19 Hefti Bat Songs* 🎵🎵 (RCA, 1966/Razor & Tie, 1997, prod. Neely Plumb), which captures the cartoonish camp of Hefti's most lasting musical legacy.

worth searching for: Serious devotees should find an old vinyl copy of *Duel at Diablo* 🎵🎵🎵🎵 (United Artists); with tongue oc-casionally planted in cheek, Hefti constructed a lounge-esque score around a meaty Western starring James Garner and Sid-ney Poitier.

influences:

◀◀ Lalo Schifrin, John Barry, Nino Rota, Ennio Morricone

▶▶ Michael Kamen, Maurice Jarre, the Who, Danny Elfman

Stephen Williams

Mel Henke

Born August 4, 1915, in Chicago, IL. Died March 31, 1979, in Canoga Park, CA.

What would the P.C. police think of Henke if he were making records today? A former jingle composer and boogie-woogie piano player, Henke put out a series of albums in the '50s with prominent sexual double-entendres, cooing female voices, and fill-in-the-blanks sound effects, as well as his trademark brazen big-band arrangements. A high-school drop-out, Henke gigged around Illinois as both a pianist and drummer in various local bands before moving to New York, where he worked as a sideman for the NBC orchestra and Paul Whiteman's popular big band. Henke moved to Los Angeles in the mid-'50s and tried to make it as a jazz bandleader. After working on various L.A. radio shows, Henke was hired by Disney to compose the music for the Disneyland television show. In the early '60s, Henke, like so many of the era's composers-for-hire, was commissioned to produce albums that would showcase the newfangled stereo technology. *Dynamic Adventures in Sound* and *La Dolce Henke* are both kitsch masterworks, replete with otherworldly sound effects, celebrity cameos from actor Herschel Bernardi and the king of cartoon voices, Mel Blanc, and nudge-wink titles like "Old McDonald Had a Girl" and "Let's Put Out the Lights." Henke died of a stroke in 1979.

what's available: The reissue of *La Dolce Henke* ♪♪♪♪ (Scamp, 1997, prod. Mel Henke) features a handful of selections from 1962's *Dynamic Adventures in Sound*, so look no further. Besides, it's the only Henke record currently in print.

influences:

◄◄ Paul Whiteman, Raymond Scott, Carl Stalling, Mel Blanc, Spike Jones, Jackie Gleason

►► "Weird Al" Yankovic, Mike Judge, Mel Brooks

Marc Weingarten

Woody Herman

Born Woodrow Charles Thomas Hermann, May 16, 1913, in Milwaukee, WI. Died October 29, 1987, in West Los Angeles, CA.

Herman was the consummate orchestra leader, a "road father" to many of his musicians, and a durable jazzman whose lengthy, difficult career as leader spanned more than 50 years. A versatile reedman, he recorded as clarinetist and alto/soprano saxophonist, and was an above average band vocalist. Like his famous contemporary, Duke Ellington, whose first love was his band, Herman's instrumental skills often took a back

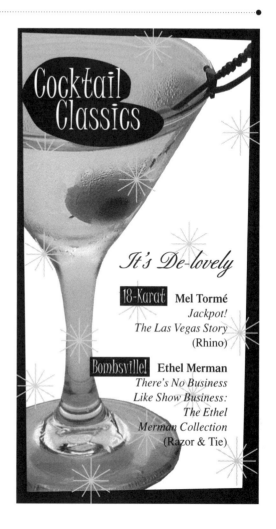

seat to keeping his top-flight musical aggregations on the road and one step ahead of the competition. The "Woodchopper" was responsible for unleashing some of the best sidemen and arrangers in the dance band business. He had a knack for setting the right tempos, discovering fresh, young talent, and keeping abreast of an ever-changing jazz scene. With all the financial and health problems that confronted him near the end of his life, Herman was able to fall back on what he called "the great escape," his love of jazz music.

Herman did some vaudeville song-and-dance routines at an early age and worked the old Orpheum circuit as the "Boy Wonder of the Saxophone." At age 16, still in high school, he played as sideman in Joey Lichter's band at Eagles Million Dollar Ballroom in Milwaukee. In February 1931, Herman entered Brunswick recording studio in Chicago to cut his first records with bandleader Tom Gerun, and in 1932, waxed his first vocals. Leaving Gerun in 1934, Herman returned to Milwaukee, joined Harry Sosnik's band, and later, while touring with Gus Arnheim, met his next employer, famous composer-bandleader Isham Jones. Herman remained with Jones until September 1936 when Jones sought retirement. A hot contingent from the defunct Jones organization formed the nucleus of the band billed as Woody Herman and the Band That Plays the Blues. Originally a cooperative unit, the band employed a quasi-Dixieland style, struggling at the outset but eventually landing a Decca recording contract. Herman had the support of his new wife, Charlotte, and after scuffling for almost three years, had a big hit single with "Woodchopper's Ball." After that, the band landed in several movies, started playing major locations, and adopted a new theme song, "Blue Flame."

Tremendous personnel changes occurred in the Herman bigband ranks during the early World War II years—singer Anita O'Day, arrangers Dizzy Gillespie and Neal Hefti, saxophonist Ben Webster, and vibesman Red Norvo were among the stellar names to perform with Herman's outfit. The sound of this magnificent band was heard coast to coast via ABC Radio, and those broadcasts are still fondly remembered by aging swingsters. Due to Herman family problems, the First Herd disbanded at the height of its popularity, after having won numerous prestigious "best band" awards. In mid-1947, Herman reemerged with the Second Herd, also known as the Four Brothers Band, with saxophonists Stan Getz and Zoot Sims, among others. The Third Herd emerged in the 1950s, with Kai Winding, Nat Pierce, Dick Collins, and others. By the summer of 1955, it was becoming increasingly grueling to maintain a big band, and Woody opted for taking an octet into the Las Vegas gig at the Riviera Hotel. The Herd that formed going into 1956 was a different group in personnel and conception, and by mid-1959 had been identified in an album title as the Fourth Herd. This gang made a U.S. State Department tour of South America, Central America, and the Caribbean in 1958, and upon return went into the recording studios with Tito Puente and a group of his Latin percussionists. The next year, jobs were erratic as Herman was experiencing difficulties booking the big band and was often forced to work with various smaller groups. The early 1960s saw the birth of the Swingin' Herd, and a resurgence of interest in the Woody Herman Band. In the late 1960s and early 1970s, the Herd of the moment experimented with electric piano and bass, and entered into the era of fusion which lasted for approximately a decade. Pianist/composer/ arranger Alan Broadbent joined the band of September 1969, and became a major influence on the band book of the early 1970s. Tenor saxophonist Frank Tiberi joined a month later and remained for years, as acting leader during Herman's illnesses. By the 1970s, Herman's health was in a downward spiral, and his personal problems mounted—with pressure from the IRS relating to management problems over the years, and the death of his wife (Charlotte) of more than 46 years. Like his characteristic Herdsmen, Herman was still full of thunder and enthusiasm, appearing cheerful with his public, and celebrated his 50th anniversary as a bandleader in 1986. Herman was in and out of hospitals until his death in October 1987, his remarkable longevity taking him through most all of the eras of jazz.

what to buy: The roar and bite of the First Herd is captured in *The Thundering Herds, 1945–1947* 𝄞𝄞𝄞𝄞 (Columbia, 1988, prod. Michael Brooks), which allocates 14 tracks to the explosive 1945–46 band, and two tracks to the Second Herd. Titles include Herman classics "Apple Honey," "Northwest Passage," "Wildroot," and "Your Father's Mustache," which, 50 years later, remain the ultimate in swinging big-band fare. The bluestinged "Goosey Gander" and Neal Hefti's well-constructed "The Good Earth" are welcome additions to the mix. *The First Herd* 𝄞𝄞𝄞𝄞 (Le Jazz, 1996) is a generous set offering 17 tunes by the full Woody Herman orchestra of 1945–46 Columbia Masters, and adds six exciting Woodchopper-like Keynote sides with Bill Harris, Flip Phillips, and Chubby Jackson at their best. There is some overlap with the Columbia set, but this one includes some obscure minor classics like "Let It Snow" and "Put That Ring on My Finger." For the many Herman fans who can't get enough of the First Herd, seek out *Woody Herman: The V-Disc Years, Vols. 1 & 2, 1944–46* 𝄞𝄞𝄞𝄞 (Hep, 1994, prod. various). This collection offers extended versions of many of the 1944 to 1946 Herman delights ("Apple Honey," "Wildroot," and "Blowin' Up a Storm"), plus others that were never recorded commercially ("Red Top" and "Jones Beachhead"). The 19 tunes on *Keeper of the Flame: Complete Capitol Recordings of the Four Brothers Band* 𝄞𝄞𝄞𝄞 (Capitol, 1992, prod. Pete Welding, Michael Cuscuna) contain some of the best tracks by Herman's Second Herd, which had a decided bop flavor and an impressive lineup of soloists, such as Al Cohn, Stan Getz, and Zoot Sims. The lovely "Early Autumn" and "Tenderly" are here amidst the wacky "Lemon Drop," and swingers like "The Great Lie," "More Moon," and "Not Really the Blues."

what to buy next: A newly discovered treasure for Herman fans, *Jantzen Beach Oregon 1954* 𝄞𝄞𝄞𝄞 (Status, 1996, prod.

Dave Kay) offers previously unissued material recorded live by Wally Heider, and brings the Third Herd to the forefront in a 15-tune collection for a dance date. Considering the source, it is remarkable that the band got away with a virtually all-jazz program. This band, more than preceding Herds, was cast in a Count Basie mold, due in part to the presence of Nat Pierce in both the piano and arranger chairs. "Moten Swing" is handled neatly under the guise of "Moten Stomp," and "Prez Conference," "Mulligantawny," and "Cohn's Alley" swing in a very relaxed groove as they pay tribute to legendary jazz performers. *Verve Jazz Masters 54: Woody Herman* 🎜🎜🎜🎜 (Verve, 1996, prod. Jack Tracy) is a compilation of 13 driving examples by the 1960s band known as the Swingin' Herd, favored by many Herman fans for its swinging sound. Herman's alto sax generates some exceptional moments on "Body and Soul" and "Deep Purple," and the entire band has a funky approach on "Sister Sadie," "Camel Walk," and "Better Git It in Your Soul." This album is definitely not for the faint-hearted. Another rousing session, recorded live at Basin Street West in San Francisco, *Woody's Winners* 🎜🎜🎜🎜 (Columbia, 1965, prod. Teo Macero) highlights a slightly later edition of the band; tearing it up are regulars Sal Nistico, Bill Chase, and Nat Pierce, as well as trumpeters Don Rader and Dusko Goykovich, and tenor saxist Gary Klein.

best of the rest:

The Fourth Herd/New World of Woody Herman 🎜🎜🎜 (Ultradisc, 1959–1962/Mobile Fidelity, 1995)
The Raven Speaks 🎜🎜🎜ᵛ (Original Jazz Classics, 1972)
Giant Steps 🎜🎜🎜ᵛ (Original Jazz Classics, 1973/1996)
The Thundering Herd 🎜🎜🎜ᵛ (Original Jazz Classics, 1974/1995)
Woody Herman Presents, Vol. 1, A Concord Jam 🎜🎜🎜🎜 (Concord, 1981/1990)
Woody and Friends 🎜🎜🎜🎜 (Concord, 1981/1992)
Woody Herman Big Band Featuring Stan Getz Live at the Concord Jazz Festival 🎜🎜🎜🎜 (Concord, 1981/1997)
Woody Herman Presents, Vol. 3, A Great American Evening 🎜🎜🎜🎜 (Concord, 1983)
World Class 🎜🎜🎜🎜 (Concord, 1984/1987)
(With Woody Herman and His Big Band) *50th Anniversary Tour* 🎜🎜🎜🎜 (Concord, 1986)
(With Woody Herman and His Big Band) *Woody's Gold Star* 🎜🎜🎜🎜 (Concord, 1987/1989)
The Sound of Jazz 🎜🎜🎜🎜 (Cleopatra, 1988/1996)
Best of the Big Bands: Woody Herman 🎜🎜🎜🎜 (Sony/Columbia, 1990)
The Best of Woody Herman and His Orchestra 🎜🎜🎜🎜 (Curb/Capitol, 1990)
Blues on Parade 🎜🎜🎜🎜 (Decca/GRP, 1991)
Northwest Passage, Vol. 2 🎜🎜🎜ᵛ (Jass, 1991)

The Herd Rides Again 🎜🎜🎜🎜 (Evidence, 1992)
Herman's Heat and Puente's Beat 🎜🎜🎜🎜 (Evidence, 1992)
(With Woody Herman and His Thundering Herd) *Crown Royal* 🎜🎜🎜🎜 (Laserlight, 1992)
(With Stan Getz) *Early Autumn* 🎜🎜🎜🎜 (RCA/Bluebird, 1992)
Blowing Up a Storm 🎜🎜🎜🎜 (Drive, 1994)
The Essence of Woody Herman 🎜🎜🎜🎜🎜 (Columbia/Legacy, 1994)
Live in Stereo at Marion, June 8, 1957 🎜🎜🎜🎜 (Jazz Hour, 1994)
Live at Peacock Lane, Hollywood 1958 🎜🎜🎜🎜 (Jazz Hour, 1994)
(With Tito Puente) *Blue Gardenia* 🎜🎜🎜🎜 (Laserlight, 1994)
At the Woodchopper's Ball 🎜🎜🎜🎜 (ASA/AJA, 1995)
Woody Herman and the Band That Plays the Blues 🎜🎜🎜🎜 (Circle, 1995)
At Lake Compounce 1959/Jantzen Beach '54 🎜🎜🎜🎜🎜 (Status, 1995)
Blues and the First Herd, Vol. 1 🎜🎜🎜🎜 (Jazz Archives, 1996)
Amen 1937–1942 🎜🎜🎜🎜 (Aero Space, 1997)
Blues on Parade, 1938–1941 🎜🎜🎜🎜 (Aero Space, 1997)
This Is Jazz 24: Woody Herman 🎜🎜🎜🎜🎜 (Sony/Columbia, 1997)
The Second Herd 🎜🎜🎜🎜 (Storyville, 1997)
Feelin' So Blue 🎜🎜🎜ᵛ (Original Jazz Classics, 1997)

worth searching for: *The 1940s—The Small Groups: New Directions* 🎜🎜🎜🎜🎜 (Columbia, 1988, prod. Michael Brooks) is an anthology containing selections from the Gene Krupa Trio, a Harry James Octet, and 10 tracks (all jewels) from Woody Herman and the Woodchoppers, a small unit drawn from the First Herd. These sides kick and swing, reminiscent of Norvo groups past, and hint at Shorty Rogers units to come. *Woody Herman Presents, Vol. 2—Four Others* 🎜🎜🎜🎜 (Concord, 1982, prod. Carl E. Jefferson) features four of Woody Herman's stellar tenor sax players from separate, distinctive band periods forming a section and offering individual solos. Al Cohn, Sal Nistico, Bill Perkins, and Flip Phillips sally forth into eight extended pieces from the Herman repertoire. Woody himself was on hand to set the tempos and approve the final takes, adding his sonorous alto to "Tenderly." Singer Rosemary Clooney headlines with the Woody Herman big band on *My Buddy* 🎜🎜🎜🎜 (Concord, 1983, prod. Carl E. Jefferson), working well with the band and Woody on an eight-tune set. There is some exceptional arranging by pianist John Oddo, who left the band to join forces with Clooney shortly after this attractive session.

influences:

◀◀ Johnny Hodges, Benny Goodman, Barney Bigard, Duke Ellington

▶▶ Rosemary Clooney, Stan Getz, Dizzy Gillespie

John T. Bitter

The Hi-Lo's

Formed 1953, in Los Angeles, CA. Disbanded 1964. Re-formed 1977.

Eugene Thomas Puerling; Robert Morse (1953–58); Don Shelton, (1958–present); Clark Burroughs; Robert Strasen, all vocals.

The Hi-Lo's were far more influential than their limited chart success would suggest. Their innovative mix of swinging harmonies and ability to hit swooping high notes in unison earned them the unqualified admiration of many other vocal groups. They developed their close harmony sound and unique tonal blends while sharing a house and working menial jobs until they were discovered by orchestra leader Jerry Fielding. While waiting for their own recording contract, the group worked as back-up vocalists for actress Anna Maria Albergetti, which led to lucrative session work with many other artists. After receiving critical raves as an opening act for Judy Garland, the group was hired to replace the departing Four Esquires on *The Red Skelton Show*. This abundance of exposure helped make "My Baby Just Cares for Me" a hit in 1954, but the jazzy Hi-Lo's were unable to establish themselves as a singles act in the age of rock 'n' roll. Their work with Marty Paich Dekette and Rosemary Clooney on "Ring Around Rosie" charted well in 1957, but subsequently the Hi-Lo's became album-only artists who covered a wide variety of styles from barbershop and musical theater to folk and bossa nova. Though they recorded 27 LPs and guest starred on numerous TV variety shows, the Hi-Lo's are probably best remembered for their early '60s Hertz Rent-a-Car jingles ("Let Hertz put Yeeeoooooou! In the driver's seat . . . "). Their sound provided the formula for hit singles by the Four Freshmen, and later the Beach Boys, yet their own career stalled. They disbanded in 1964, and Puerling and Shelton formed the *a cappella* group Singers Unlimited. The Hi-Lo's reunited at the Monterey Jazz Festival in 1977, and resumed recording, eventually earning three Grammy nominations. These days, their appearances at various nostalgia venues reinforces their reputation as a vocal group's vocal group.

what to buy: The group's original lineup and finest early sides (1953–56) are on *The Best of the Hi-Lo's: Nice Work If You Can Get It* 𝄐𝄐𝄐𝄐 (Varese Vintage, 1996, compilation prod. Cary E. Mansfield, Elliot Kendall) and features their lone hit, "My Baby Just Cares for Me."

what to buy next: Classy late '50s stylings fill *Best of the Columbia Years* 𝄐𝄐𝄐𝄐 (Koch International, 1996, prod. various), a 16-track compilation of such wonderfully reworked standards as "Life Is Just a Bowl of Cherries," "How Are Things in Glocca Morra," and the dazzling "Swing Low, Sweet Chariot."

the rest:
And All That Jazz 𝄐𝄐𝄐 (Sony Special Products, 1991)
Cherries & Other Delights 𝄐𝄐𝄐 (Hindsight, 1993)
Together Wherever We Go 𝄐𝄐𝄐 (Sony Special Products, 1996)

worth searching for: The Hi-Lo's can be seen singing their famous commercial for Hertz Rent-a-Cars in *Good Neighbor Sam* 𝄐𝄐𝄐 (Columbia Pictures, 1964, director David Swift), a film spoof on advertising starring Jack Lemmon. The Hi-Lo's are an integral part of the film's most successful running gag.

solo outings:
Singers Unlimited:
Christmas 𝄐𝄐𝄐𝄐 (PolyGram, 1972/Verve, 1990)
A Capella 𝄐𝄐𝄐𝄐 (Verve, 1985/1990)

influences:
◀◀ The Encores, the Modernaires, the Mel-Tones
▶▶ The Four Freshmen, the Beach Boys, the Manhattan Transfer

Ken Burke

Al Hibbler

Born August 16, 1915, in Tyro, MS.

Blind since birth, singer Hibbler has succeeded as both a sideman and a solo artist. His resonant, smoky baritone was featured prominently in Duke Ellington's band from 1943 to 1951; the Hibbler showcase "Do Nothing 'Til You Hear from Me" was one of the biggest Ellington hits of the '50s. Hibbler then left Ellington to stake out a successful solo career, one that endured in fits and starts for more than 30 years.

Reared in Mississippi, Hibbler learned to sing while attending the Arkansas School for the Blind. After leaving school, he tried his luck on the southern roadhouse circuit, only to discover that gut bucket blues was not his calling; he really aspired to croon in a big band. Hibbler botched his first big break when he showed up drunk for an audition with Duke Ellington, and wound up fronting Jay McShann's band, instead. After an 18-month tenure with McShann, Hibbler got a second chance with Ellington and landed the singing gig in his band. Hibbler's suavely urbane manner and silky smooth delivery was a fixture of Ellington's band for eight years, until a salary dispute ended his relationship with the jazz legend. As a solo artist, Hibbler was the first performer to have a big hit with the song "Unchained Melody" in 1955. Hibbler continued to record steadily well into the '60s, and even became a vocal civil rights advocate, but his output diminished considerably by the early '70s. In recent years, Hibbler has been active again, and made two strong albums, *Solitude* and *Al Hibbler*, with the Roland Hanna Trio, in 1997.

what to buy: Two Hibbler albums from the mid-'50s, *Starring Al Hibbler* ✻✻✻✻ (1956/Jasmine, 1996) and *Here's Hibbler* ✻✻✻✻ (1957/Jasmine, 1996), have been reissued on a single import CD, which is a mixed blessing. *Here's Hibbler* is hindered on some tracks by maudlin backing vocals. Nonetheless, it's a good introduction to one of jazz's classiest vocal stylists.

the rest:
After the Lights Go Down Low ✻✻✻✻ (Atlantic, 1956)
The Best of Al Hibbler ✻✻✻ (MCA, 1958)
Christmas with Al Hibbler ✻✻✻ (Black Label, 1992)
Solitude ✻✻✻ (Simitar, 1997)

influences:
◀◀ Duke Ellington, Jay McShann, Fletcher Henderson, Bing Crosby, Glenn Miller

▶▶ Big Joe Turner, Jimmy Rushing

Marc Weingarten

The High Llamas

Formed 1992, in London, England.

Sean O'Hagan, vocals, guitar, keyboards; Marcus Holdaway, keyboards, vocals; John Fell, bass; Rob Allum, drums; John Bennett, guitars.

Dedicating oneself to recreating the sound of the Beach Boys is one thing, but painstakingly recreating the sound of Brian Wilson's unfinished demos represents another order of obsessiveness altogether. That is the course Sean O'Hagan has taken since his former group, Microdisney, disbanded in the late 1980s. There is an oddly liturgical feel to the High Llamas, in both the mood and stately pacing of their music (their tempos are the most deliberate this side of the Cowboy Junkies). While *Pet Sounds* and *Smile* are the Beach Boys albums most frequently cited as reference points for the High Llamas, a more precise one is *Stack-O-Tracks*—the 1968 karaoke collection of Beach Boys backing tracks, without vocals.

what to buy: *Gideon Gaye* ✻✻✻✻ (Alpaca Park/Epic, 1995, prod. Sean O'Hagan, Charlie Francis) is a high point O'Hagan is unlikely to surpass anytime soon. The album has beautifully tuneful and detailed arrangements, copping from the Beatles as well as the Beach Boys. After this album's 1994 European release, O'Hagan and the Llamas toured as backup band for former Love singer/guitarist Arthur Lee, the 1960s psychedelic pop equivalent of Bob Dylan's 1986 tour with Tom Petty's Heartbreakers.

what to buy next: The followup, *Hawaii* ✻✻✻ (Alpaca Park/V2, 1997, prod. Sean O'Hagan, Charlie Francis), is not unlike Utopia's 1980 Beatles parody/tribute, *Deface the Music*. Most of the 29 tracks sound more like sketches than complete songs, evoking Brian Wilson's mid-'60s California dreams. As O'Hagan himself put it in the oft-quoted manifesto "The Hot Revivalist," "Let's rebuild the past/'Cause the future won't last." Undeniably pleasant, but pointless. Note that the U.S. version of *Hawaii* includes a six-song bonus disc with a lovely cover of Nick Drake's "Chime of a City Clock." Though hardly any less derivative than *Hawaii*, *Cold and Bouncy* ✻✻✻✻ (Alpaca Park/V2, 1998, prod. Sean O'Hagan) nevertheless shows encouraging forward movement, transposing more overt electronic flourishes onto the Beach Boys formula. Somehow both spacier and better-focused than its predecessor, *Cold and Bouncy* sounds like the record *Hawaii* should've been—and also like the best Stereolab record of recent years. Before the High Llamas became a formal group, O'Hagan made an extremely whimsical solo album titled *High Llamas* ✻✻✻ (Demon, 1990, prod. Sean O'Hagan). Less fussy than his subsequent work, *High Llamas* could almost pass for the Steely Dan-influenced lounge-pop of China Crisis.

the rest:
Santa Barbara ✻✻✻ (Alpaca Park 1992/V2 1997)

worth searching for: O'Hagan has also been an unofficial recent member of Stereolab, contributing invaluable studio and arranging smarts. He and Stereolab's Tim Gane and Andy Ramsay make up yet another sideband, Turn On. Their album *Turn On* ✻✻✻ (Drag City, 1997, prod. Sean O'Hagan) is an intriguing midpoint between the High Llamas' ornate pop and Stereolab's space-age fuzak.

influences:
◀◀ The Beach Boys, the Beatles, Love
▶▶ Eric Matthews

David Menconi

Al Hirt

Born Alois Maxwell Hirt, November 7, 1922, in New Orleans, LA.

Though this trumpet player is an enormously gifted musician, his detractors complain he would rather play Dixieland or popular tunes than stretch the boundaries of his talents on more challenging material. They obviously miss the point. Hirt is no supercilious bebopper too proud to take the bandstand with musicians of a lesser genre. He's an entertainer! His music was meant to accompany good times in rec rooms, rib joints, at pool parties, or during Mardis Gras. Perhaps he makes it seem too easy; in a blindfold test, Miles Davis once lavishly praised Hirt's technique, but that only increased the ire of his critics.

A classically trained musician, Hirt divided the early part of his career between playing in symphony orchestras and working in the trumpet sections of the Tommy Dorsey, Jimmy Dorsey, Horace Heidt, and Ray McKinley bands. An eight-year stint as the leader of the house band at a New Orleans radio station led to Hirt's first recordings; he subsequently teamed with legendary clarinetist Pete Fountain. After Fountain left the combo in the late '50s to become a regular on *The Lawrence Welk Show*, Hirt signed with RCA. Under the guidance of Steve Sholes (who tamed Elvis Presley's sound for the mass market), Hirt released a series of top-selling singles, including "Java," "Cotton Candy," and "Fancy Pants," which drew their inspiration from country-pop and gospel as much as Dixieland. Using his own Crescent City club as a base, Hirt's sound and bearded visage became synonymous with New Orleans. Throughout his peak years in the '60s, Hirt recorded extensively both as a solo act and in pairings with such singing celebrities as Brenda Lee and Ann-Margret, with more than three dozen of his LPs hitting the charts. Hirt's many TV appearances and high-profile concerts with major pops and symphony orchestras showcased his spectacular technique and won him new fans well into the '70s. In recent times, Hirt's weight-related health problems have kept his name in the news more frequently than his trumpet playing, though his best-selling singles still receive airplay on jazz and adult-contemporary radio stations worldwide.

what to buy: An outstanding introduction, *The Al Hirt Collection: Featuring Beauty and the Beard with Ann-Margret* 🎵🎵🎵🎵 (Razor & Tie, 1997, compilation prod. Mike Ragogna) has both Hirt's instrumental hits "Java," "Cotton Candy," and "Sugar Lips," and a complete reissue of his 1964 duet LP with Ann-Margret. Hirt's gruff-and-easy vocals perfectly accent the Hollywood sex-kitten's purring on such tracks as "Tain't What You Do," "Mutual Admiration Society," and "Personality," creating an irresistible chemistry.

what to buy next: If you want Al Hirt and nothing but Al Hirt, check out *That's a Plenty* 🎵🎵🎵🎵 (Pro Jazz Records, 1988/1996, compilation prod. Steve Vining) and *Al Hirt's Greatest Hits* 🎵🎵🎵🎵 (Pro Arte, 1990, compilation prod. Steve Vining), with all his adult-contemporary hits and finest instrumental moments from the early to late 1960s.

what to avoid: It's bad karma to knock a Christmas LP, but despite the generous 22-track lineup, *The Sound of Christmas* 🎵 (RCA, 1992, prod. Steve Sholes) is an unusually weak seasonal LP, featuring bloated, sugary arrangements, and a by-the-numbers approach from Hirt. Muzak from hell.

the rest:
Al Hirt/Pete Fountain: Super Jazz 🎵🎵🎵🎵 (Columbia, 1988)
Jazzin' at the Pops 🎵🎵 (Pro Arte, 1989)
All-Time Great Hits 🎵🎵🎵🎵 (RCA, 1989)
Cotton Candy 🎵🎵🎵 (Pro Jazz Records, 1989/1993)
Al Hirt & the Alliance Hall Band: Dixieland's Greatest Hits 🎵🎵🎵 (Pro Arte, 1991)
Raw Sugar, Sweet Sauce, & Banana Pudd'n' 🎵🎵 (Monument Records, 1991)
The Golden Trumpet of Hirt 🎵🎵🎵 (Spectacular Sound, 1995)
Brassman's Holiday 🎵🎵🎵 (Hindsight, 1996)

worth searching for: A little corny, a little slick, and occasionally brilliant, the out-of-print *Our Man in New Orleans* 🎵🎵🎵🎵 (RCA, 1962, prod. Steve Sholes) is the quintessential Al Hirt LP. With the Anita Kerr singers providing occasional lyrical interludes, Hirt's trumpet embraces moods sassy and sensitive, wacky and warm. Many fans received their introduction to Hirt via this LP.

influences:

◀◀ Harry James, Roy Eldridge

▶▶ Herb Alpert, Doc Severinsen, the Baja Marimba Band

Ken Burke

Don Ho

Born August 13, 1930, in Oahu, HI.

If Don Ho didn't exist, the Hawaiian Tourism Council surely would have invented him. Few entertainers have achieved such international renown as a must-see regional attraction, and he is as positive a promotional asset to Hawaii as Graceland is to Memphis. In essence, Ho is the ultimate lounge performer who just happens to be Hawaiian. Six nights a week he sits behind the Hammond organ, cracking jokes and crooning a heady mix of Island standards, pop hits, and a little supper-club rock 'n' roll.

Ho got his start at a Kaneohe cocktail lounge named for his mother, Honey's. Cowed by his own inexperience, he sang extra soft, which resulted in an intimate, almost sleepy style that mesmerized audiences. Ho credits 1962 as the year that things really started rolling for him. He and his band, Aliis, began playing Duke's in Waikiki, which led to prestige-building appearances at the Coconut Grove, the Palmer House, and the Sands Hotel. Recording for Reprise Records, Ho scored his only real hit with "Tiny Bubbles," which peaked at #57 but stayed on the charts for 17 weeks. Constant exposure as a guest on *The Tonight Show, The Joey Bishop Show, Batman,* and *I Dream of Jeannie,* among others, led to Ho's own network program, which in turn helped him sell a lot of LPs in lieu of hit singles. Though his national star power diminished in the late '70s, Ho saw interest in his career revived by an appearance in the 1996 film *Joe's Apartment.* These days, Ho records for his own label, Honey Records, and when he's not touring, appears nightly at his own Hawaiian nightspot—now get this—the Ho House.

what to buy: Get out your flowered shirt , mix up a mai-tai, and dig into Ho's *Greatest Hits* 🎵🎵🎵 (Reprise, 1989, prod. Sonny Burke), a compilation of his best work, including "Tiny Bubbles," "Pearly Shells," "Beach Party Song," and the rocking "Ain't No Big Thing."

the rest:
With All My Love (Me Ke Aloha Pumehana) 🎵🎵 (Honey Records, 1990/1995)
Hawaiian Favorites 🎵🎵🎵 (Spectacular, 1994)
I Think About You 🎵🎵 (Honey Records, 1995)

worth searching for: Luau-maniacs who want to see Ho live (and can't afford a trip to Hawaii) should scout around for the video *A Night with Don Ho* 🎵🎵🎵 (Honey Records, 1990). Don't forget to pop the poi.

influences:
◀◀ Bing Crosby, Robin Luke, Trini Lopez
▶▶ Taran Erikson, Hoku Ho

Ken Burke

Billie Holiday

Born Eleanora Fagan, April 7, 1915, in Baltimore, MD. Died July 17, 1959, in New York City, NY.

Despite a tragic career that took her from the spotlight too soon, Holiday ranks with Ella Fitzgerald as the greatest female vocalist in the history of jazz. Her unmistakable sound—a thin, airy voice and an ability to stretch lyrics into a completely unique style—made her the popular sensation of her day. Drugs, abusive relationships, and financial strains finally took their toll, but not before Holiday influenced entire generations of female vocalists—both in and out of the jazz world.

Not much is known about Holiday's childhood, despite decades of investigation by jazz historians. We know she was aban-

doned by her father at an early age, and that he resurfaced only after she had become famous. Her mother moved to New York early on and left Holiday with relatives, whom Holiday later said abused her. Holiday began singing in Harlem nightclubs as a teenager, and was discovered in the 1930s by pioneering Columbia scout John Hammond, who set up recording dates for her with Benny Goodman. She also recorded with Teddy Wilson, establishing herself as a serious vocalist and eventually sealing a long-lasting partnership with Lester Young, the saxophonist who gave her the nickname "Lady Day." (Because, he said, her mother must have been a duchess.) Holiday and Young were a huge sensation in the late 1930s. Soon thereafter, she began singing for Count Basie and

Artie Shaw, becoming one of the first black vocalists to sing for a white band. In 1939, she recorded her first rendition of "Strange Fruit," Lewis Allen's haunting song about a black lynching, and her career hit a fever pitch: She became known for specializing in sad ballads about hurtful relationships and love gone awry.

But that's when Holiday was introduced to opium and heroin by her first husband, James Monroe. She tried to beat the habit but eventually was jailed in 1947. Worse, her cabaret card—the license that allowed her to perform—was revoked, leaving her at the mercy of club owners who continued to book her but shortchanged her salary. Addicted to heroin, she continued to perform through the early 1950s, going on disasterous tours with Red Norvo and Charles Mingus. Finally, after her voice had deteriorated to the point where bad reviews were flowing in, Holiday went into isolation in the spring of 1959. After attending Lester Young's funeral in March, she went into a coma. Laid up in the hospital with liver and heart trouble, she finally suffered one last indignity: being fingerprinted and arrested—in bed, while dying—for drug possession. She died weeks later. Holiday's biography, while tragic, doesn't illustrate the impact she had on jazz vocalists, however. The unabashed emotional attachment she had with her lyrics, no matter what the song, hasn't been recreated in the 40 years since her death.

what to buy: Holiday's catalog is simply massive, with nine-CD boxes and smaller live sets taking up rows and rows of record stores. Start with *First Issue: The Great American Songbook* ♪♪♪♪♪ (Verve, 1994, prod. Norman Granz), a remarkably comprehensive, two-disc set of Billie's finest recordings made possible by the most powerful jazz producer at the time. Holiday's voice is in fine shape, and her interpretation has never been better. *Complete Decca Recordings* ♪♪♪♪ (Decca Jazz, 1991, prod. Milt Gabler) is a terrific two-disc set with a more popular feel than her Verve recordings. The sound quality is excellent.

what to buy next: *Lady in Satin* ♪♪♪♪ (Columbia, 1958/1997, prod. Michael Brooks), one of Holiday's most unforgettable recordings, was made (it's obvious) toward the end of her career. Her voice is raspy, even difficult to listen to. But her emotional power is unwavering. It's aurally arresting.

what to avoid: *Embraceable You* ♪♪♪ (Verve, 1957) isn't a poor retrospective, but it has been improved upon since its release.

Billie Holiday **(Archive Photos)**

Verve anthologies are more likely to satisfy the impassioned Holiday fan.

best of the rest:
Billie's Blues ♪♪♪♪ (Blue Note, 1987)
The Quintessential Billie Holiday ♪♪♪♪♪ (Columbia, 1991)
Lady in Autumn: The Best of the Verve Years ♪♪♪♪ (Verve, 1991)
Essential Billie Holiday ♪♪♪♪ (Verve, 1992)
Complete Billie Holiday on Verve ♪♪♪♪ (Verve, 1993)

worth searching for: On the French import version of *Lady Sings the Blues* ♪♪♪♪ (1956/Accord, 1995), an ensemble of top-notch performers join Holiday in recordings from 1954 and 1956—shortly before her unfortunate decline.

influences:
◀◀ Louis Armstrong, Bessie Smith

▶▶ Carmen McRae, Lena Horne, Diane Schuur, Dinah Washington, Betty Carter, Carol Sloane

Carl Quintanilla

The Hollyridge Strings

Formed around 1961, in Los Angeles, CA.

Stu Phillips, arrangements, production.

In January 1964—just to remind those of you who weren't on this planet at the time—the Beatles swept through the U.S. musical landscape like a firestorm (or a plague, depending on your perspective back then). Everyone wanted to sound like, look like, or in some way be associated with those lovable moptops—and that included the world of easy-listening artists. The feeling was, stripped of their teen-oriented veneers, the Beatles' songs actually held up quite well as melodies and could be made palatable to the "legit" music crowd if recorded with pops orchestras. Capitol Records (who just happened to release Beatle records in the U.S.) brought in arranger and producer Stu Phillips to create the resulting vocal combo, the Hollyridge Strings. (Phillips had scored TV shows like *Gidget* and *The Donna Reed Show*, movies like *Ride the Wild Surf*, and produced great rock hits for Shelley Fabares, Paul Petersen, and the Marcels. His arrangements give the illusion of rock, and use lots of echo and staccato strings, and the violin sound heavily recalls Percy Faith's hugely popular 1963 LP *Themes for Young Lovers*. The resulting LP, *The Beatles Songbook*, was immensely successful and led naturally to a similar treatment for Capitol's other big stars, the Beach Boys. After that, Phillips recorded under his own name with a similar style—unfortunately adding Swingle Singers-like choruses to the mix for the *Feels Like Lovin'* album. With Phillips on his own, Perry Botkin Jr. and, later, Mort Garson, took over the Hollyridge Strings franchise. Phillips later returned, for the next decade, though a jazzy chorus singing John Lennon's "Imagine" has to be some sort of nadir on the awful LP, *Hits of the 70's.* Still, Phillips's wonderful sound on the first six or so Hollyridge Strings LPs, as far as orchestral interpretations of rock songs are concerned, can't be topped.

what's available: *The Best of the Beatles Song Book* &⅄&⅄ (Varese Sarabande, 1996, compilation prod. Cary E. Mansfield) is an 18-song set that relies too heavily on the later Hollyridge Strings LPs. Capitol's *Ultra-Lounge* series, including the installments *On the Rocks, Part One* &⅄&⅄ (Capitol, 1997, compilation prod. Brad Benedict) and *On the Rocks, Part Two* &⅄&⅄ (Capitol, 1997, compilation prod. Brad Benedict), collects Muzaky versions of rock songs. The former includes Phillips's "Tired of Waiting" (originally by the Kinks), the Hollyridge Strings' "Theme from *Shaft*" (originally by Isaac Hayes), and the Elvis Presley medley "Heartbreak Hotel/Don't Be Cruel." *Part Two* includes the Beach Boys' "I Get Around/California Girls" and the Beatles' "Can't Buy Me Love/Sgt. Pepper's Lonely Hearts Club Band."

worth searching for: While a search may prove futile, a great three-CD set with 40 songs was available for a time at warehouse clubs such as Sam's and Costco: *The Beatles Songbook—Their Greatest Hits* &⅄&⅄&⅄ (CEMA Special Markets, 1992). The Japanese import CD *Memories of the Beach Boys/The Four Seasons* &⅄&⅄&⅄ (Jasrac, 1993) is now out of print, but collects two excellent LPs, including the the haunting "Candy Girl." Scourers of the used-record bins should keep an eye out for the superior *The Beatles Songbook* &⅄&⅄&⅄ (Capitol, 1964) above either *Feels Like Lovin'* &⅄ (Capitol, 1965) or *Hits of the 70's* &⅄ (Capitol, 1972).

influences:

◀◀ Percy Faith, David Rose

▶▶ Robert Stigwood Orchestra

George W. Krieger

Rupert Holmes

Born February 24, 1947, in Northwich, Cheshire, England.

Holmes is most famous (or infamous) for "Escape (The Piña Colada Song)," the smarmy novelty single that nonetheless bears the distinction of being the last hit of the '70s and first of the '80s, having occupied the *Billboard* chart's #1 spot on

New Year's Eve 1979. This catchy tale of on-the-rocks lovers who reconcile after answering each other's anonymous personal ad hints at Holmes's way with economical storytelling and memorable hooks. In fact, Holmes exemplified—and abandoned—the Cole Porter-ish tradition of pithy and craftsmanlike cabaret songwriting long before it became hip again. Prior to hitting it big (and somewhat losing his way) with "Escape" from *Partners in Crime*, Holmes released four very personal and listenable albums, in addition to some notable production work for Barbra Streisand. Meanwhile, high-profile covers by the likes of Barry Manilow ("Studio Musician") and Engelbert Humperdinck ("Last of the Romantics") made Holmes's music more well known than he was. Evident ambivalence over "Escape"'s successful bid for stardom left him hovering between sincere art and cautious commercialism for his final three albums. He left solo recording after *Full Circle* in 1981, resurfaced as a songwriting presence with the mid-'80s Broadway musical *The Mystery of Edwin Drood* and the Jets' late-'80s hit "All Over Him," and then indefinitely left music altogether to become a successful scriptwriter for stage and TV (including the AMC cable channel's current series *Remember WENN*). Though his past life's work is all out of print, it would well reward rediscovery.

what to buy: Not the hits collection its title implies, *Singles* &⅄&⅄ (Epic, 1977, prod. Jeffrey Lesser) was a reflective album penned by a then-unknown Holmes in rebellious response to a label exec's demand for the title commodity. *Pursuit of Happiness* &⅄&⅄ (Private Stock, 1978, prod. Rupert Holmes) was Holmes's most lush and mature work, equally tuneful and ambitious.

what to buy next: Each of Holmes's first two albums, *Widescreen* &⅄& (Epic, 1974, prod. Jeffrey Lesser) and *Rupert Holmes* &⅄& (Epic, 1975, prod. Jeffrey Lesser), has almost as many gems as the two which followed.

what to avoid: *Partners in Crime* &⅄ (Infinity, 1979, prod. Rupert Holmes, Jim Boyer), *Adventure* &⅄ (MCA, 1980, prod. Rupert Holmes), and *Full Circle* &⅄ (Elektra, 1981, prod. Rupert Holmes) mark Holmes's long epilogue. Die-hards may want to check out the *Partners* title track, a strange bit of gangsta lounge unequaled in Holmes's or anyone else's oeuvre, and "The People That You Never Get to Love," to which King Crimson's popular "Matte Kudasai" bears a suspicious resemblance. After Holmes's vocal retirement came the overwrought music-hall gothic of *The Mystery of Edwin Drood* &⅄ (Polydor/PolyGram, 1986, prod. Rupert Holmes).

the rest:
Daybreak Lover ♪ (Klatt, 1980)
Rainy Night in Georgia ♪ (Excelsior, 1980)
She Lets Her Hair Down ♪ (Excelsior, 1981)

worth searching for: Holmes lent fine songs and a downright ambient production sound to Barbra Streisand's *Lazy Afternoon* ♪♪♪♪ (Columbia, 1975, prod. Rupert Holmes), making it the all-time best of her pop albums. Your local library may have a copy of *The Forties* (Consolidated Music Publishing, 1975, Ed. Jeffrey Weiss), a book on the music of that decade co-authored by Holmes and Martha Saxton.

influences:

◀◀ Cole Porter, Glenn Miller, Benny Goodman, Stephen Sondheim

▶▶ Barbra Streisand, Hanson, Combustible Edison

Adam McGovern

Telma Louise Hopkins
See: Tony Orlando

Lena Horne
Born June 30, 1917, in Brooklyn, NY.

Though frequently lumped into the pantheon of jazz singers, non-improviser Horne is more correctly relegated to the world of pop vocalists/song stylists—which is not to say she lacks talent; on the contrary, she's got a wonderful voice and presence, both on and offstage. She's even been tapped for Gap commercials—at the ripe old age of . . . 80! (OK, so maybe she's had a few facelifts, but what's money for?) Horne started performing at age six and appeared as a dancer in the chorus line at Harlem's famed Cotton Club in 1934. Though she wanted to be a teacher, her destiny turned out to be in music and film. After fronting a variety of bands and recording with Artie Shaw, she hit the big screen in such films as *Boogie Woogie Dream, Cabin in the Sky, Words and Music,* and *Stormy Weather,* then as a poster girl for the NAACP, which used her to help push aside stereotypical on-screen images of African Americans. She used that fame to become one of the world's greatest lounge singers, full of sophistication and elegance, as well as a staunch civil-rights advocate. At the time of its 1957 release, *Lena Horne at the Waldorf-Astoria* became the largest seller by a female in the history of the RCA/Victor label. Horne left the limelight for a while in the '70s following the deaths, in an 18-month span, of her father, son, and husband. A decade later, she came back with a bang, returning to the Broadway stage with *The Lady and Her Music,* the sound-

track of which earned her a 1982 Grammy (she also earned a Grammy for Lifetime Achievement in 1989). She's been the subject of countless profiles, including a PBS "American Masters" segment titled *Lena Horne: In Her Own Voice,* in which actor Ossie Davis declares, "Anybody who is not madly in love with Lena Horne should report to his undertaker immediately."

what to buy: *Lena Horne at MGM* ♪♪♪♪ (1942/Rhino, 1996, prod. Marilee Bradford) is where it all began. On *An Evening with Lena Horne (Live at the Supper Club)* ♪♪♪♪ (Capitol, 1995, prod. Michael Cuscuna, Sherman Sneed), this jazz crooner extraordinaire plays her voice like the bass being plucked beside her on a mood indigo stage. Though she *is* in a lounge for this

album, only the last few tunes take on the lounge singer effect, overcoming the earlier jazz motif.

what to buy next: *Lena Goes Latin/Lena Sings Your Requests* 𝄢𝄢𝄢 (RCA, 1963/Charter, 1963/1990, prod. various), a CD reissue of two earlier LPs, is quite the lounge collection, complete with horn section. It's kitsch incarnate as Horne delivers "More" with a Latin beat. *We'll Be Together Again* 𝄢𝄢𝄢 (Blue Note, 1994, prod. Sherman Sneed) is a lovely tribute to Horne's soulmate, Billy Strayhorn, and her pal Duke Ellington, as well as a promise to all those who entered the pearly gates before her: they will be together again.

what to avoid: *Some of the Best* 𝄢𝄢 (Delta, 1997) isn't. *More of the Best* 𝄢𝄢 (Delta, 1997) isn't either.

the rest:
Live on Broadway (Lena Horne: The Lady and her Music) 𝄢𝄢𝄢 (Qwest, 1981)
Stormy Weather: The Legendary Lena (1941–58) 𝄢𝄢𝄢 (Bluebird, 1992)

influences:

⏪ Sarah Vaughan, Billie Holiday, Billy Strayhorn, Duke Ellington, Josephine Baker, Ethel Waters

⏩ Nancy Wilson, Dionne Warwick, Diana Ross

Lynne Margolis

Eddy Howard

Born September 12, 1914, in Woodland, CA. Died May 23, 1963, in Palm Springs, CA.

If you're over the age of 35 (and have been in a few bars), you've probably heard the music of Eddy Howard, whose hit versions of "Happy Birthday" and "The Anniversary Waltz" were oft-played jukebox staples. Far from being a one-hit wonder, the multi-talented Howard sang, composed hit songs, and led one of the most popular "sweet" bands of the '40s and early '50s. At the start of his career, Howard gained valuable experience singing and playing guitar for bands fronted by George Olsen, Tom Gerun, and Ben Bernie. In 1934, bandleader Dick Jurgens hired him as a trombonist, though at the time he didn't know Howard couldn't read music and had memorized his audition tunes. Impressed with the young singer's nerve, Jurgens created a spot for Howard in his band as a vocalist and rhythm guitar player. Howard scored several hits with Jurgens's

Lena Horne (© Jack Vartoogian)

band, including two songs he co-wrote: "My Last Goodbye" and his theme, "Careless." After forming his own orchestra in 1941, Howard became a consistent hitmaker with such tunes as "My Adobe Hacienda," "Be Anything, But Be Mine," "Auf Wiedersehn Sweetheart," "Now Is the Hour," and "Room Full of Roses." At his peak in 1946, Howard's orchestra was voted band of the year on the strength of big-sellers like "To Each His Own" and "I Love You (For Sentimental Reasons)," which led to appearances in short subject films. In the early '50s, Howard's single of "Happy Birthday" b/w "The Anniversary Waltz" was enormously popular, and he hit number one with "Sin (It's No Sin)," but his chart clout diminished dramatically in the rock 'n' roll era. After failing to attract new audiences with "The Teenager's Waltz," Howard settled into a career as a nostalgia act, and he played resorts and casinos until his death. Country singer Mickey Gilley successfully revived Howard's "Room Full of Roses" in 1974, and on a jukebox somewhere, someone has punched up his version of "Happy Birthday."

what to buy: Howard's biggest mainstream hits reside on *The Best of Eddy Howard: The Mercury Years* 𝄢𝄢𝄢 (Chronicles, 1996, compilation prod. Ron Furmanek, Joseph F. Laredo), a 25-song compilation that includes "Careless," "Sin (It's No Sin)," "Room Full of Roses," "The Anniversary Waltz," and of course, "Happy Birthday."

what to buy next: Derived from previously unissued radio broadcasts, *The Uncollected Eddy Howard and His Orchestra (1946–1951)* 𝄢𝄢𝄢 (Hindsight, 1993, prod. Wally Heider) is a sterling example of Howard's work during his salad days, and includes live versions of his hits "Careless," "Sin (It's No Sin)," and many popular tunes of the day.

the rest:
Eddy Howard and His Orchestra: 1949–1953 𝄢𝄢𝄢 (Circle, 1993)
Eddy Howard and His Orchestra Play 22 Song Hits 𝄢𝄢𝄢 (Hindsight, 1995)
America Swings—The Great Eddy Howard 𝄢𝄢 (Hindsight, 1995)

worth searching for: To hear what Eddy Howard sounded like as a singer-for-hire, check out *The Uncollected Dick Jurgens and His Orchestra: Vol. 1 (1937–1939)* 𝄢𝄢𝄢 (Hindsight, 1993, prod. Wally Heider), an 18-track compilation of previously unissued live radio tracks. Howard shares vocals with Stan Noonan and Ronnie Kemper.

influences:

⏪ Ben Bernie, Dick Jurgens, Isham Jones

⏩ Mitch Miller, Sammy Kaye

Ken Burke

Engelbert Humperdinck

Born Arnold George Dorsey, May 2, 1936, in Madras, India.

What a difference a name makes: as "Gerry" Dorsey, this English crooner could barely get stopped for speeding but as Engelbert Humperdinck, he became a chart-dwelling hitmaker and an old-fashioned sex symbol with incredible staying power. Humperdinck will probably always be linked with singer Tom Jones. Both emerged in the '6os with the same manager, a big set of pipes, and a fondness for wearing suits. But while Jones always seems to be hiding a smirk behind the song, Humperdinck plays it without irony, straight from the heart. He's a dreamboat balladeer, downright gentlemanly next to Jones's bawdy, hepcat persona. That said, Humperdinck nonetheless possesses an unattainable remoteness—one that was carefully plotted from the start, by having him vanish after every show—which epitomizes the no-strings-attached lounge ethic. But there's nothing like that voice. Smooth and powerful, it has the ability to transform a country tune like "Release Me"—the song that made him a star in 1967—into something rich and grand. Of course, like any worthy lounge act, Humperdink knows his way around Vegas, and performs there regularly.

what to buy: While many of Humperdinck's original releases have fallen out of print, there's no shortage of latter-day compilations; the man may be single-handedly responsible for half of the discs sold on late-night TV. He's also a regular best-seller in countries such as Germany and Holland. *Greatest Songs* 𝄢𝄢𝄢 (Curb, 1995) includes non-Engelbert hits like "Killing Me Softly with Her Song" and "My Cherie Amour." *16 Most Requested Songs* 𝄢𝄢𝄢 (Epic, 1996) is a hodgepodge of songs recorded between 1980 and 1989.

what to buy next: Like almost every performer in this book, Humperdinck has stamped his personal touch on old-fashioned Christmas standards—*A Merry Christmas* 𝄢𝄢𝄢𝄢 (Epic, 1980) is one of many such collections.

what to avoid: *All of Me* 𝄢𝄢 (Epic, 1988) is a live album of the you-had-to-be-there variety.

the rest:
Live at the Riviera—Las Vegas 𝄢𝄢 (1972/Varese Vintage, 1998)
Don't You Love Me Anymore 𝄢𝄢 (Epic, 1981)
You & Your Lover 𝄢𝄢 (Epic, 1983)
Love Is the Reason 𝄢𝄢 (Critique, 1991)
After Dark 𝄢𝄢 (Macola, 1996)

worth searching for: There are many import collections of Humperdinck's better-known songs (some of which are available through his Web site), including *Greatest Hits* 𝄢𝄢𝄢 (Polydor, 1974) and *Feelings* 𝄢𝄢𝄢 (Special Music Co., 1996, prod. Leslie Mandoki, Dieter Bohley), the latter of which includes "Spanish Eyes" and the title track. On *You Are So Beautiful* 𝄢𝄢𝄢 (Pair, 1995, prod. Leslie Mandoki), Humperdinck covers likable tunes such as "Let's Fall in Love" and "Tell It Like It Is."

influences:

◄◄ Neil Diamond, Tom Jones, Rudy Vallee, Vic Damone, Frank Sinatra, Dean Martin, Sammy Davis Jr., Jack Jones

►► Wayne Newton, Andy Williams, Michael Bolton

Teresa Gubbins

Betty Hutton

Born Elizabeth June Thornburg, February 26, 1921, in Battle Creek, MI.

With the ability to convincingly condense a four-hour Shakespearean epic into less than three minutes, the gall to hock up a spit-glob in mid-song, and the balance to turn around and croon a straight standard, Hutton's allure came as much from her honesty and versatility as it did her voice. Known primarily as a silver-screen blonde bombshell for her roles in films such as 1950's *Annie Get Your Gun* and 1952's *The Greatest Show on Earth,* the bulk of Hutton's hits in the '4os and '5os came from her movies. Though some were dismissed at the time as novelties, she refused to treat them as throwaways. Owing to Hutton's full-bore interpretations, the songs on both available CD compilations still stand strong. With a Rosie the Riveter-meets-Lucille Ball candidness, Hutton had the capacity to transform herself from sultry to silly, all the while remaining undeniably sexy. Considering Hutton got her start singing for the customers of her mother's Speakeasy (her father left the family when she was two years old), her blue-collar, street-smart attitude almost always rings true. Still, she could pull off an edgy vulnerability. Hutton regained a modicum of fame with a new generation in the '9os when Björk covered the Hanslang/Reisfeld number "It's Oh So Quiet," with the lyrics: "You blow a fuse/zing boom/the devil cuts loose/zing boom/so what's the use/wow bam/of falling in love?" In her version on 1995's *Post,* Björk remains faithful to Hutton's famous take, right down to the bordering-on-psychotic screams that accompany Hutton's inevitable charm. Hutton's life would hardly follow her rendition of Irving Berlin's uplifting "Blue Skies"—she lost all her millions, ran into

Engelbert Humperdinck (Archive Photos)

problems with alcohol, and watched as her marriages failed. Recently, she has bounced back, cleaning up physically and mentally, even earning an acting degree. In the words of a certain rebel: "I Wake Up in the Morning Feeling Fine."

what to buy: *Betty Hutton: Best of the RCA Years* 𝄞𝄞𝄞𝄞 (One Way Records, 1996, compilation prod. Terry Wachsmuth), released after Björk's version of "It's Oh So Quiet" returned the song to radio, begins with the "Shhh" that becomes more than a warning for Hutton's original whisper-to-a-screech. *RCA Years* includes some of Hutton's early work with bandleader Vincent Lopez. Unfortunately, the album's design is bare-bones, offering nowhere near the elaborate liner notes of the Columbia collection (it doesn't even list songwriters). The songs, however, fill in Hutton's story well, from the self-imposed stuttering on the ragtime-like "Who Kicked the Light Plug (Out of the Socket)" to the growls of "Murder, He Says" and the squeaks that punctuate "On the Other End of a Kiss." The collection does a fine job of highlighting Hutton's usually smart, always expansive, range.

what to buy next: *Spotlight on Great Ladies of Song—Betty Hutton* 𝄞𝄞𝄞𝄞 (Capitol, 1994, compilation prod. Brad Benedict), with the song "A Square in the Social Circle," has Hutton singing "Take your blue blood and stick it in your fountain pen/She'll not only tell you she's got a muscle of steel/she'll go on to shout, anyone here wanna feel?" Nearly half of the songs are penned by Frank Loesser, including "Hamlet," a stripped-down, just-the-basics version of the Bard's classic. In contrast to the RCA collection, *Spotlight* contains detailed liner notes on each song, including take numbers.

influences:

◀◀ Jo Stafford, Billie Holiday, Bessie Smith, Frank Sinatra, Perry Como, Bing Crosby

▶▶ Björk, Rosemary Clooney

Jim Sheeler

Dick Hyman

Born Richard Roven Hyman, March 8, 1927, in New York, NY.

An impressively hard-working pianist and arranger, Hyman is mostly known for his solo piano work and for scoring many Woody Allen films, including *The Purple Rose of Cairo* and *Radio Days*. Hyman studied classical music as a child and, while a student at Columbia University, won a set of music lessons with pianist Teddy Wilson through a radio station contest. Besides playing with Charlie Parker, Dizzy Gillespie, and

Benny Goodman, Hyman served for years as a studio musician during the 1950s—and even did time as NBC's staff pianist from 1952 to 1957. While technically brilliant, Hyman arguably brings little to lounge music that listeners couldn't get from another, more innovative musician. Still, his CDs serve as wonderful retrospectives of *other* pianists, from Duke Ellington to Jelly Roll Morton. It's in this role as jazz historian that Hyman has really made his name in the jazz world.

what to buy: Hyman, with his trademark attention to detail, painstakingly recreates the music of Duke on *Plays Duke Ellington* 𝄞𝄞𝄞𝄞 (Reference, 1993, prod. J. Tamblyn Henderson Jr.). It's more of an homage than a true jazz album, but Hyman still knows his subject. "Prelude to a Kiss" is the highlight. On *Plays Fats Waller* 𝄞𝄞𝄞𝄞 (Reference, 1990), another fine tribute to a grandfather of the piano, Hyman pays respects to Waller—with songs like "Ain't Misbehavin'" and "Honeysuckle Rose"—while also making his own voice heard.

what to buy next: On *Music of Jelly Roll Morton* 𝄞𝄞𝄞 (Smithsonian, 1978), Hyman explores the artistry of maybe his greatest musical influence.

what to avoid: *Themes and Variations on "A Child Is Born"* 𝄞 (Chiaroscuro, 1977) is a strange and unfortunate album in which Hyman takes "A Child Is Born" and plays it in the style of 11 other pianists—from Jelly Roll Morton to George Shearing. Not worth buying unless you're a serious jazz historian/pianist, yourself.

the rest:

Manhattan Jazz 𝄞𝄞 (Music Masters, 1985)

worth searching for: *Stride Piano Summit* 𝄞𝄞𝄞 (Milestone, 1991) is a fun look at the style of stride piano, in which the left hand bounces up and down the keyboard, creating a bassy, swing feel. Hyman gets to show off a few technical skills in the process.

influences:

◀◀ Scott Joplin, Jelly Roll Morton, James Johnson, Fats Waller, Duke Ellington, Teddy Wilson

▶▶ Marcus Roberts, Ralph Sharon, John Campbell

Carl Quintanilla

Phyllis Hyman

Born July 6, 1950, in Pittsburgh, PA. Died June 30, 1995, in New York, NY.

Every chanteuse, whether she works in a saloon or a disco, conveys equal parts sadness and sexuality. A few, such as Judy Garland and Hyman, spend their careers singing preludes to their inevitable heartbreak and demise. Hyman's particular style was the disco/soul derivative "quiet storm," but her sultry alto and breathy resonance conveyed a sense of bruised sensuality that reached across several musical barriers.

Hyman began her career in the early '70s with the groups New Direction, the Hondo Beat, and the P/H Factor before Norman Connors featured her vocals on his *You Are My Starship* LP. Their hit duet on the Stylistics' "Betcha By Golly, Wow," paved the way for her minor hits on the Buddah label, "Loving You, Losing You" and "I Don't Want to Lose You." By 1978, Hyman had moved to Arista Records where they successfully marketed her version of Exile's "Kiss You All Over" and "You Know How to Love Me" to dance clubs (the latter becoming something of an anthem in gay discos). Her Tony-nominated role in the Broadway tribute to Duke Ellington, *Sophisticated Ladies,* and hit duet with Michael Henderson on "Can't We Fall in Love Again" allowed Hyman to break through to larger audiences and cultivate a distinct persona. A statuesque beauty, Hyman's remarkable face and figure were featured on a series of provocative LPs, which helped create her image as "The Goddess of Love." Hyman felt lost in the shuffle at Arista, and her departure sparked a four-year legal battle, limiting her recording output to guest appearances on discs by Barry Manilow, the Whispers, the Four Tops, and Chuck Mangione. Hyman also appeared in Spike Lee's *School Daze* and co-starred with Fred Williamson in *The Kill Reflex.* At Gamble and Huff's Philadelphia International soul-music subsidiary, Manhattan, Hyman's sound finally came together, leading to her only #1 R&B hit, "Don't Wanna Change the World." Hyman's troubles with finances, romance, family deaths, and alcohol exacerbated her bouts of manic-depression, eventually driving her to commit suicide in 1995. She left behind a final LP with her most personal work to date, *I Refuse to Be Lonely.*

what to buy: A fine introduction to this artist, *Under Her Spell: Phyllis Hyman's Greatest Hits* 𝄞𝄞𝄞𝄞 (Arista, 1989, prod. Larry Alexander) features her big solo hits "You Don't Know How to Love Me," "Somewhere in My Lifetime," and duets with Norman Connors on "Betcha By Golly, Wow" and Michael Henderson on "Can't We Fall in Love Again."

what to buy next: *The Legacy of Phyllis Hyman* 𝄞𝄞𝄞𝄞𝄞 (Arista, 1996, compilation prod. Leo Sacks), a two-disc, 28-track collection of all the high points in Hyman's career, boasts guest appearances by Herbie Hancock, Paul Shaffer, and Barry Manilow. On *I Refuse to Be Lonely* 𝄞𝄞𝄞𝄞 (Zoo/Volcano, 1995, prod. Kenneth Gamble, Nick Martinelli, Jud Friedman, Steven Ford, Dex-

ter Wansell, Dave "Jam" Hall, Barry J. Eastman, Phyllis Hyman), the LP she was working on at the time of her death, Hyman asserts an ethereal tone with "Waiting for the Last Tear to Fall," "It's Not About You (It's About Me)," and "Give Me One Good Reason to Stay."

the rest:
Phyllis Hyman 𝄞𝄞𝄞 (Buddah, 1977/The Right Stuff, 1997)
Sing a Song 𝄞𝄞𝄞 (Buddah, 1979/Unidisc, 1995)
Prime of My Life 𝄞𝄞𝄞 (Zoo/Volcano, 1991)
Loving You, Losing You: The Classic Balladry of Phyllis Hyman 𝄞𝄞𝄞𝄞 (RCA, 1996)
Living All Alone 𝄞𝄞𝄞 (Gold Rush, 1996)
Best of Phyllis Hyman 𝄞𝄞𝄞𝄞 (Musicrama, 1997)
One on One N/A (Hip-O, 1998)

worth searching for: Hit the import racks and catalog services for *The Best of Phyllis Hyman: The Buddah Years* 𝄞𝄞𝄞𝄞 (Sequel, 1995), a strong anthology of Hyman's early work.

influences:
◀◀ Nancy Wilson, Sarah Vaughan, Norman Connors

▶▶ Toni Braxton, Whitney Houston, Pharoah Sanders

Ken Burke

Julio Iglesias

Born September 23, 1943, in Madrid, Spain.

The undisputed voice of romance during the '80s, Iglesias brought poetic sensuality and Latin charm back to mainstream pop music. Whether he sings in Spanish, Portuguese, Italian, French, or English, Iglesias is a master of the confessional tone: a vocal style which implies "I am singing to you alone, my dear."

Iglesias, a Cambridge-educated lawyer-in-training and soccer player, turned to singing and songwriting while recuperating from a car accident. His performance of "La Vida Sique Igual" won him first prize at the 1968 Spanish Song Festival, resulting in a recording contract. Over the next several years, Iglesias racked up such multilingual international hits as "Hey," "Manuela," and "Begin the Beguine." His American debut LP, *Julio,* sold more than a million copies without the benefit of a hit single, but Juliomania didn't really ignite until the release of his duet with then-hot Willie Nelson on "To All the Girls I've Loved Before." Iglesias charmed U.S. audiences when he sang the massive hit on the *Tonight Show* with Johnny Carson (who imitated Nelson's voice in the adenoidal goat register). Iglesias also scored big hit singles in tandem with Diana Ross ("All of You") and Stevie Wonder ("My Love"), but for the most part, his appeal in America is as an LP artist and concert attraction. During the '90s, with the Salsa revolution in full swing, and his own son making inroads on the world market, Iglesias no longer feels the need to record in English.

what to buy: If you need the added incentive of big-name guest stars, *1100 Bel Air Place* 🎵🎵🎵 (Columbia, 1984/1996, prod. Ramon Arcusa, Richard Perry) features Iglesias's hit duets with Willie Nelson on "To All the Girls I've Loved Before" and "All of You" with Diana Ross. The Beach Boys add some much appreciated backup vocals, but Iglesias's charisma brings the whole thing together.

what to buy next: Iglesias plays the romance card in many different languages on *Julio* 🎵🎵🎵 (Columbia, 1987, prod. Ramon Arcusa), a smooth collection with sensual versions of "Amor," "Begin the Beguine," and "Wrap Your Arms Around Me."

what to avoid: You'll probably want to steer clear of anything you find in the import racks with the tag-line "Sung in German." Even Julio Iglesias can't make this language sound sexy.

the rest:
America 🎵🎵🎵 (Sony Latin, 1976)
Emociones 🎵🎵🎵 (Sony Latin, 1979)
De Nina a Mujer 🎵🎵🎵🎵 (Sony Latin, 1982)
Moments 🎵🎵🎵🎵 (Columbia, 1982)
In Concert 🎵🎵🎵 (Columbia, 1983)
Libra 🎵🎵🎵 (Columbia, 1987)
From a Child to a Woman 🎵🎵🎵 (Columbia, 1987)
Non-Stop 🎵🎵🎵 (Columbia, 1988)
Hey 🎵🎵🎶 (Columbia, 1988)
Raices 🎵🎵 (Sony Latin, 1989)
Starry Night 🎵🎵🎵 (Columbia, 1990)
Crazy 🎵🎵🎵🎵 (Columbia, 1994)
24 Greatest Songs 🎵🎵🎵🎶 (Sony, 1995)
La Carretera 🎵🎵 (Sony Latin, 1995)
Tango 🎵🎵🎵 (Columbia, 1996)

worth searching for: Iglesias sounds just as sexy singing in French on *Amer la Vie* 🎵🎵🎵 (Sony, 1996) as he does in Spanish and English. Also, Iglesias sings "Torero" with Jose Luis Rodriguez on the latter's *Piel De Hombre* 🎵🎵🎵 (Sony Latin, 1992).

influences:

◀◀ Charles Aznavour, Al Martino, Frank Sinatra

▶▶ Enrique Iglesias, Jose Luis Rodriguez

Ken Burke

The Ink Spots

Formed 1931, in Indianapolis, IN.

Original members: Deek Watson, tenor (1931–45); Jerry Daniels, tenor (1931–36); Bill Kenny, tenor (1936–52); Billy Bowen, tenor (1945–53); Charlie Fuqua, baritone; Orville "Hoppy" Jones, bass; Herb Kenny, bass (1945–53).

Though their styles could not have been more different, the two great, seminal vocal groups in all of recorded music were the Mills Brothers and the Ink Spots. Whereas the Mills Brothers were distinguished by their flawless four-part harmonies, the Ink Spots cast the spotlight on their soloists—quivering tenor Bill Kenny and bass singer Hoppy Jones, who was best known for his mid-song recitations—in laying the foundation for the doo-wop phenomenon of the 1950s. The group started out in 1930s Indianapolis with Deek Watson, Charlie Fuqua (the uncle of Moonglows lead singer Harvey Fuqua), and Jerry Daniels, performing first as the Swingin' Gate Brothers, then as King, Jack and Jester. That name had to go, too, because there was already a group singing with bandleader Paul Whiteman called the King's Jesters, so the group's new manager, Moe Gale, came up with "Ink Spots." By the mid-1930s the group had acquired Jones, and in January 1935 they cut their first record, "Swingin' on Strings" b/w "Your Feet's Too Big." Trademark tenor Kenny replaced Daniels in 1936, and the Ink Spots did plenty of touring, both in the U.S. and abroad, while putting out 10 records on the Decca label. Yet the business continued to be a struggle for them until the 1939 release of "If I Didn't Care": that satiny, melodramatic romantic ballad introduced the world to the distinctive Ink Spots sound—the low background "oohs" and "aahs" behind Kenny's soaring solos and Jones's rumbling bass—and reached #2 on the *Billboard* charts, selling more than a million copies. Throughout World War II, the group released one Top 10 hit after another, including the standards-to-be "Maybe," "My Prayer," "When the Swallows Come Back to Capistrano," "I Don't Want to Set the World on Fire," and "Don't Get Around Much Anymore." But nothing this good lasts forever: in 1944, Watson left and tried to form his own Ink Spots, but the courts wouldn't let him (he called his group the Brown Dots instead); that same year, Jones died. Yet the group continued to record throughout the 1940s, drawing huge crowds wherever they appeared. In the early 1950s, however, the Ink Spots did split up. Amazingly, the name had become so popular that instead of disappearing, Ink Spots groups began to proliferate (notwithstanding periodic lawsuits). Even into the 1990s, there were dozens of acts calling themselves the Ink Spots performing across the country.

what to buy: The number of Ink Spots compilations is almost as vast as the number of counterfeit Ink Spots groups still at work. (There is, for example, a 1994 cassette release on the Bainbridge label called *I'll Still Be Loving You* on which the group that disbanded in the 1950s performs its versions of "Three Times a Lady" and "Purple Rain"!) The original is almost always the best, and *Greatest Hits: The Original Recordings 1939–1946* ♫♫♫ (MCA, 1989, prod. various) captures the group in its peak form from the 1939 breakthrough of "If I Didn't Care" through the departures of Watson and Jones. Included are "I'll Never Smile Again," "We Three (My Echo, My Shadow and Me)," "I Don't Want to Set the World on Fire," and "Someone's Rocking My Dreamboat."

what to buy next: While many of the obligatory "best of" cuts are also included, the tracks are generally more diversified on *Whispering Grass* ♫♫♫ (Pearl, 1991, prod. various), adding the humorous "That Cat Is High," "Stompin' at the Savoy," "Don't Let Old Age Creep up on You," and the original single, "Your Feet's Too Big."

what to avoid: The collection *Truck Stop Country* ♫♫ (Jewel, 1996)—you have to ask?

the rest:
I'll Never Smile Again ♫♫ (Orfeon)
Ink Spots ♫♫ (K-Tel, 1956)
Best of the Ink Spots ♫♫♫♫ (MCA, 1980)
On the Air ♫♫♫ (Sandy Hook, 1986)
Java Jive ♫♫♫ (Laserlight, 1992)
Encore of Golden Hits ♫♫♫ (Juke Box Treasures, 1994)
18 Hits ♫♫♫ (King, 1996)
Swing High, Swing Low ♫♫♫♫ (Eclipse, 1996)
Golden Memories ♫♫♫ (ITC Masters, 1997)

worth searching for: Both of pop music's greatest vocal ensembles are available for comparison and contrast on the Ella Fitzgerald album *Ella & Friends* ♫♫♫ (Decca Jazz, 1996, prod. various) as both the Ink Spots and the Mills Brothers share guest-artist honors with the First Lady of Song. Add in duet appearances by Louis Jordan and Louis Armstrong, and you get a

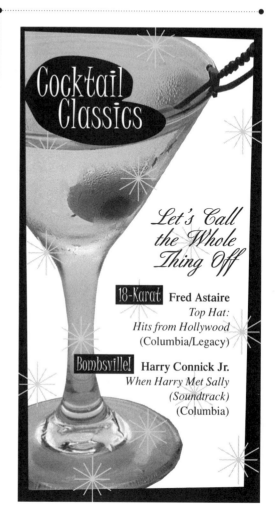

complete crash course in black music for the first half of the 20th century.

influences:

◄◄ Cab Calloway, the Harmonizing Four, the Delta Rhythm Boys

►► Louis Jordan, the Platters, the Five Royales, the Clovers, the Coasters, the Temptations, Boyz II Men, BLACKstreet

Michael Kosser

Isidore Israel Itzkowitz

See: Eddie Cantor

J

Joe Jackson

Born August 11, 1954, in Burton-on-Trent, England.

Few artists have had a more wrongheaded assessment of their own relative strengths and weaknesses than this modestly talented journeyman pianist. In hindsight, Jackson's first four albums sound like preliminary sketches for his fifth album, 1982's brilliant *Night and Day*. Tying together the jittery new wave of *Look Sharp!* and *I'm the Man* with *Beat Crazy*'s third world rhythms and the old-school jump blues of *Jumpin' Jive*, *Night and Day* plays as a seamless whole. It remains Jackson's commercial as well as aesthetic high point. Unfortunately, Jackson's stubbornness began to get the better of him shortly afterward. While he contented himself with flaky gimmicks like applause-free, three-sided live albums (1986's *Big World*), his indulgences remained at least intermittently entertaining. But then he started hiring orchestras, succumbing to his own worst tendencies with a series of pointless and ill-conceived stabs at classical music. Though admirable in a to-thine-own-self-be-true kind of way, Jackson's adamant refusal to be pigeonholed would count for more if better music came out of it.

what to buy: *Night and Day* ✶✶✶✶ (A&M, 1982, prod. David Kershenbaum, Joe Jackson) is a marvelous record. With salsa and jazz flavorings added to Jackson's warmest-ever set of songs, the album's after-hours cocktail lounge vibe wears well. Equally warm is *Jumpin' Jive* ✶✶✶✶ (A&M, 1981, prod. Joe Jackson), an all-covers homage to Louis Jordan and Cab Calloway. At the time of its release, *Jumpin' Jive* seemed like a one-off lark. But it foreshadowed the magnum opus to come with *Night and Day*.

what to buy next: Though not terribly loungey, Jackson's first three rock 'n' roll albums are all worthwhile, especially the debut *Look Sharp!* ✶✶✶✶ (A&M, 1979, prod. David Kershenbaum). There's not a weak cut anywhere, and for pure adrenaline rushes it's tough to beat the two "time" bookends (the opening "One More Time" and the closing "Got the Time"). Though its reception was mixed at the time of its release, *Body and Soul* ✶✶✶✶ (A&M, 1984, prod. David Kershenbaum, Joe Jackson) has held up well. It reprises much of what made *Night and Day* so outstanding, just with material that isn't quite as strong.

what to avoid: Jackson's first major misstep was the all-instrumental *Will Power* ✶✶ (A&M, 1987, prod. Joe Jackson). Given an orchestra to work with, all he comes up with is stupefying sub-Stravinsky noodling. *Night Music* ✶✶ (Virgin, 1994, prod. Joe Jackson, Ed Roynesdal) is similarly dull, with chamber pop boring enough to induce narcolepsy. But the absolute low point is *Heaven & Hell* ✶ (Sony Classical, 1997, prod. Joe Jackson, Ed Roynesdal), an excruciatingly pretentious song cycle about the Seven Deadly Sins. Listening to Jackson hold forth on the subject of "pride"—on "Song of Daedalus," which concludes with him bellowing, "Call me God!"—may be the silliest listening experience this side of Spinal Tap's "Stonehenge."

the rest:
I'm the Man ✶✶✶✶ (A&M, 1979)
Beat Crazy ✶✶✶✶ (A&M, 1980)
Mike's Murder ✶✶✶ (A&M, 1983)
Big World ✶✶✶ (A&M, 1986)
Live 1980/86 ✶✶✶✶ (A&M, 1987)
Tucker: The Man and His Dream ✶✶✶ (Original Soundtrack) (A&M, 1988)
Blaze of Glory ✶✶✶ (A&M, 1989)
Laughter & Lust ✶✶✶ (Virgin, 1991)
Greatest Hits ✶✶✶✶ (A&M, 1996)

worth searching for: The import collection *This Is It: The A&M Years, 1979–1989* ✶✶✶✶ (A&M UK, 1997, prod. David Kershenbaum, Joe Jackson) is a pricey yet well-chosen two-disc sampler, much more complete than the 1996 U.S. single-disc, *Greatest Hits*. Jackson also does a fine job covering "'Round Midnight" on *That's the Way I Feel Now: A Tribute to Thelonious Monk* ✶✶✶✶ (A&M, 1984, prod. Hal Willner).

influences:
◄◄ Cole Porter, Cab Calloway, Louis Jordan, Randy Newman, Elvis Costello

►► Ben Folds Five

David Menconi

Harry James

Born March 15, 1916, in Albany, GA. Died July 5, 1983, in Las Vegas, NV.

Considering how we've deified Count Basie, Duke Ellington, and even Benny Goodman, it might come as some surprise that the top big-band leader between 1942 and 1946 was none

Joe Jackson (© Ken Settle)

other than Harry James. It was a glamorous time for the trumpet player, who was only 19 when he made his recording debut with Ben Pollack's big band, and just 21 when he joined Goodman's band. In 1939, James took his own group on the road. For a stretch, he was romantically involved with his sensuous vocalist, Helen Forrest. Then he met Betty Grable, appeared in several films, and eventually married the Hollywood pin-up. The bebop era, which killed off most swing musicians' livelihoods, didn't end James's career. He simply cut his string section and continued to tour, as the greatest white big band trumpeter of his time. His final recording, done in 1979 for the specialty label Sheffield Labs, included one of the strangest big-band covers ever, the theme to *Sanford and Son.*

what to buy: To truly get a taste of James you need to hear both his instrumentals and his work with vocalists like Dick Haymes and Helen Forrest. The three-disc *Bandstand Memories* 𝄢𝄢𝄢𝄢 (Hindsight, 1994, prod. Pete Kline) is the best place to start. If you're interested in less, try *Best of the Big Bands* 𝄢𝄢𝄢𝄢 (Columbia, 1990, prod. Michael Brooks). The only difference between this and *Great Vocalists* 𝄢𝄢𝄢𝄢 (Columbia/Legacy, 1995) is more instrumentals.

what to buy next: Listening to *Jump Sauce* 𝄢𝄢𝄢𝄢 (Viper's Nest, 1994) and *Always* 𝄢𝄢𝄢 (Viper's Nest, 1994) is like stepping back in time. These radio shows were recorded in 1943, when James was at the peak of his popularity but couldn't put out a single 78, because shellac was needed for World War II. Thankfully, these acetates were recorded.

the rest:
Trumpet Blues 𝄢𝄢𝄢 (Drive Archive, 1955)
Mr. Trumpet 𝄢𝄢 (Hindsight, 1972)
The King James Version 𝄢𝄢𝄢 (Sheffield Lab, 1976)
Comin' from a Good Place 𝄢𝄢𝄢 (Sheffield Lab, 1976)
Still Harry After All These Years 𝄢𝄢𝄢 (Sheffield Lab, 1979)
Live in London 𝄢𝄢𝄢 (Jasmine Records, 1981)
Best of the Big Bands: Harry James and His Great Vocalists 𝄢𝄢𝄢𝄢 (Columbia/Legacy, 1995)
Featuring Frank Sinatra 𝄢𝄢𝄢 (Columbia/Legacy, 1995)

worth searching for: *The Small Groups: New Directions* 𝄢𝄢𝄢𝄢 (Columbia, 1988, prod. Michael Brooks) only features James on two of the compilation's 17 songs, but it's worth getting if only to hear how the big band era's stars—Woody Herman, Gene Krupa, and James—reacted to the new wave of bebop jazzmen. James's sextet swings so hard it almost bops.

influences:
◀◀ Louis Armstrong, Joe "King" Oliver

▶▶ Louis Belson, Buddy Rich, Harry Connick Jr.

Geoff Edgers

Horst Jankowski
Born January 30, 1936, in Berlin, Germany.

Today, Jankowski is remembered as a one-hit wonder for his extremely catchy "Eine Schwarzwaldfahrt." (In case you don't hail from the Land of Oom-Pa-Pa, the title translates as "A Walk in the Black Forest.") The sound is piano octaves for the leads, with creamy Bavarian strings dancing around the melody; while the guitar is mostly used as a percussive instrument, at times it takes the lead with staccato firmness. In the '50s, Jankowski studied piano, tenor sax, trumpet, and tuba at the Berlin Music Conservatory. After that, he worked with the German orchestra leader Erwin Lehn and as an accompanist for singer Caterina Valente and jazz pioneers Miles Davis, Benny Goodman, Ella Fitzgerald, Michel Legrand, and Oscar Peterson. Because Jankowski also loved choruses (leading the Jankowski choir since 1960), several of the songs (though, gratefully, not the hit) included a heavenly "ah" sung over the melody. Every LP after his debut, *The Genius of Jankowski*, was an attempt to recreate the hit, but Jankowski's subsequent songs could never seem to tickle the U.S. audience as well as "Eine Schwarzwaldfahrt."

what's available: The song "A Walk in the Black Forest" is on the excellent two-CD mail-order compilation *Instrumental Gems of the '60s* 𝄢𝄢𝄢𝄢 (Collector's Choice Music, 1995, compilation prod. Bob Hyde); call (800) 923-1122. Another two-CD mail-order collection, *'60s Instrumentals* 𝄢𝄢𝄢𝄢 (Time-Life Music), also contains the song; call (800) 382-2348.

worth searching for: Every other Jankowski release is out of print, but probably available in used-vinyl stores. His second U.S. LP, *More Genius of Jankowski* 𝄢𝄢𝄢𝄢 (Mercury, 1965), is the strongest, with a much fuller sound and better material (generally) than the debut, *The Genius of Jankowski* 𝄢𝄢𝄢 (Mercury, 1965). The next LP showed a lack of imagination in the title—*Still More Genius of Jankowski* 𝄢𝄢𝄢𝄢 (Mercury, 1966)—but thankfully cut back on use of the choir. At least he broke out of the title rut with his next LP, *So What's New* 𝄢𝄢𝄢 (Mercury, 1966), but the sound was again boxier, like his first LP.

influences:
◀◀ Bert Kaempfert, Ferrante & Teicher
▶▶ Frank Mills

George W. Krieger

Maurice Jarre

Born September 13, 1924, in Lyons, France.

Jarre is one of those gifted film composers who can create music that hovers subtly in the background then surges to the foreground when needed, like a nimble Greek chorus. He often incorporates exotic elements into his scores when a film's content suggests them (such as gamelan music in *The Year of Living Dangerously*, which was set in Indonesia, and the balalaika flourishes in *Doctor Zhivago*); he never treats these elements as novelties or decorative garnishes, however.

Prior to his career in film, Jarre studied composition at the Paris Conservatory of Music, worked with renowned French composer Pierre Boulez, and served as musical director for the French National Theater, during which time he worked with such esteemed writers as Harold Pinter, Jean Cocteau, and Albert Camus. It is the depth of his understanding of the stories he scores that makes his compositions such a striking complement to the narratives. As a result of his prudent choices in selecting projects to work on (collaborating with such eminent directors as David Lean, Peter Wier, and John Huston), many of the films he has scored have become classics for which the soundtracks are always available. With most of these scores, it is possible to appreciate Jarre's artistry with the ears alone, but for the full impact of his talents as a composer, it's best to take in the film itself—and in many cases the videos will actually be less expensive than the CDs.

what to buy: The haunting music that courses through *The Year of Living Dangerously* 🍸🍸🍸🍸 (Original Soundtrack) (Varese Sarabande, 1983, prod. Maurice Jarre), a reverberant, intoxicating blend of electronics and Indonesian percussion, pushes the envelope of soundtrack recordings, verging on some of the ambient music created by musicians like Brian Eno. With *Witness* 🍸🍸🍸🍸 (Original Soundtrack) (Varese Sarabande, 1985, prod. Maurice Jarre), Australian film director Peter Wier managed to make the American heartland seem as exotic and otherworldly as an extraterrestrial landscape. Jarre's soundtrack underscores perfectly the journey that the hardened city cop in the story takes into that alien world. *Dr. Zhivago* 🍸🍸🍸🍸 (Original Soundtrack) (Rhino, 1995, prod. Marilee Bradford, Bradley Flanagan), Jarre's 1965 masterpiece, was reissued in a deluxe 30th anniversary edition, complete with thorough liner notes and a foreword by Jarre himself. But even without all the useful information and the three different versions of "Lara's Theme" tacked onto the end, this soundtrack is an astonishing work, a rich and diverse musical tapestry that draws on folk and orchestral traditions as well as

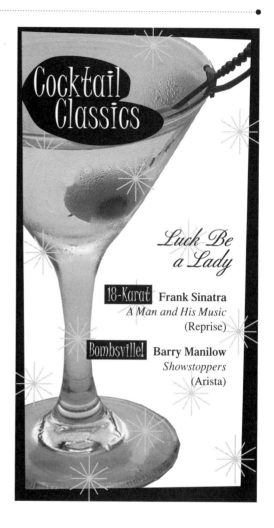

Jarre's own inventive musicality. *Lawrence of Arabia* 🍸🍸🍸🍸 (Original Soundtrack) (Silva Screen Records, 1962/1989/1992, prod. Geoffrey Alexander), the reissue of Jarre's 1962 Oscar-winning score, features music not previously included in the soundtrack, including some stirring action sequences.

what to buy next: On *A Walk in the Clouds* 🍸🍸🍸 (Original Soundtrack) (Milan/BMG, 1995, prod. Maurice Jarre), Jarre artfully incorporates undercurrents of Mexican music from classical guitar to festive folk music into this Golden Globe-winning score. On *Gorillas in the Mist* 🍸🍸🍸🍸 (Original Soundtrack) (MCA, 1988, prod. Maurice Jarre), Jarre weaves together epic orchestral elements with traditional African music to capture the essence of wonderment and foreboding. *Jacob's Ladder* ♫♫♫ (Original Soundtrack) (Varese Sarabande/MCA, 1990, prod. Maurice Jarre) is Jarre's creepiest effort, threaded with haunting chorales, the breathy shakuhachi flute, and what sounds like troubled spirits wafting in the mix. It includes a semi-comic denouement: Al Jolson's "Sonny Boy." *A Maurice Jarre Trilogy* ♫♫♫ (DRG, 1995, prod. Maurice Jarre) compiles the original soundtracks to three Italian films—*The Damned, A Season in Hell,* and *For Those I Loved*—that explored controversial and intense subject matter.

the rest:

The Mosquito Coast ♫♫♫ (Original Soundtrack) (Fantasy, 1986)
Jarre by Jarre ♫♫♫ (CBS Masterworks, 1987)
Only the Lonely ♫♫♫ (Original Soundtrack) (Varese Sarabande, 1991)
Seville Film Concerts ♫♫♫ (Varese Sarabande/MCA, 1991)
Maurice Jarre at Abbey Road ♫♫♫ (Milan/BMG, 1992)

worth searching for: *Lean by Jarre* ♫♫♫ (Milan/BMG, 1992, prod. Maurice Jarre), a tribute to director David Lean, features Jarre conducting the Royal Philharmonic Orchestra through suites culled from Lean's films, including *Ryan's Daughter, A Passage to India, Doctor Zhivago,* and *Lawrence of Arabia.*

influences:

◄◄ Pierre Boullez, Maurice Ravel

►► Trent Reznor

Sandy Masuo

Al Jarreau

Born March 12, 1940, in Milwaukee, WI.

Jarreau can turn the most complicated jazz songs into singable fodder, chewing the notes, digesting them, and spitting them out in surprising new ways. He has been a mainstay of easy-listening radio stations since his first album, 1975's *We Got By,* but the exposure has also made him an enemy of rock critics: J.D. Considine once compared his vocal sound to "the twanging of rubber bands." A San Francisco social worker who heard the Beatles, quit his job, and roamed the country before nailing a record deal, Jarreau borrowed his trademark style of "vocalese" (previously instrumental jazz music that has been arranged for singing) from the clicks of African song and jazz scat-singing. While his defiantly unobtrusive music compares with the Manhattan Transfer (both artists have been heavily influenced by vocalese master Jon Hendricks), Jarreau adds more of an R&B feel to his work. His commercial hits have been more straightforward pop numbers, leaving the sophisticated scatting to the cuts in between.

what to buy: *Breakin' Away* ♫♫♫ (Warner Bros., 1981, prod. Jay Graydon) provides the most accessible look into Jarreau's anachronistic styles with a cover of Dave Brubeck's "Blue Rondo à la Turk," a jazz standard that would seem to be otherwise impossible to sing. Alongside evergreens like "We're in This Love Together" and the title song, this record showcases some of Jarreau's best work.

what to buy next: *Best of Al Jarreau* ♫♫♫ (Warner Bros., 1996, prod. various) is a solid retrospective of Jarreau's biggest hits, which have successfully made the transition from the easy-listening '70s to the smooth-jazz and adult-contemporary '90s. Songs include "Never Givin' Up," "Heaven and Earth," and "Agua de Beber."

what to avoid: A horribly neutered cover of Otis Redding's soul classic "(Sittin' On) the Dock of the Bay" is just one blandness on the trying-too-hard *All Fly Home* ♫ (Warner Bros., 1978, prod. Al Schmitt), which barely hints at the interesting stuff that started Jarreau's career.

best of the rest:

We Got By ♫♫♫ (Warner Bros., 1975)
Glow ♫♫♫ (1976)
Look to the Rainbow: Live in Europe ♫♫ (Warner Bros., 1977)
This Time ♫♫♫ (Warner Bros., 1980)
Jarreau ♫♫♫ (Warner Bros., 1983)
High Crime ♫♫♫ (Warner Bros., 1984)
Al Jarreau Live in London ♫♫ (Warner Bros., 1985)
Lean on Me ♫♫♫ (Masters, 1986)
L Is for Lover ♫♫ (Warner Bros., 1986)
Heart's Horizon ♫♫ (Warner Bros., 1988)
Heaven & Earth ♫♫♫ (Warner Bros., 1992)
Tenderness ♫♫♫ (Warner Bros., 1994)

influences:

◄◄ Jon Hendricks, Louis Armstrong, Ella Fitzgerald, Dave Brubeck, Astrud Gilberto, John Coltrane

►► The Manhattan Transfer, Bobby McFerrin

Jack Jackson and Steve Knopper

Gordon Jenkins

Born May 12, 1910, in Webster Groves, MO. Died May 1, 1984, in Malibu, CA.

One of the finest composers and arrangers of the big-band era,

Al Jarreau (© Jack Vartoogian)

Jenkins brought semi-classical sounds to mainstream pop in the '50s. His expressionistic use of strings brought high drama to his own works and those by such top vocalists as Judy Garland, Frank Sinatra, Nat King Cole, Eartha Kitt, and Peggy Lee. During the '30s, Jenkins's multi-instrumental ability gave him a special edge as an arranger, and the charts he supplied to bandleaders Isham Jones, Woody Herman, Vincent Lopez, and Benny Goodman heightened their respective sounds. A respected songwriter as well, Jenkins wrote or co-wrote such big hits as "Blue Prelude," "You Have Taken My Heart," "Homesick, That's All," "San Fernando Valley," and several others. Jenkins conducted on Broadway and was the musical director of radio's *Dick Haymes Show* before he became a staff conductor at Decca Records in 1943. With his own orchestra, he recorded the hits "My Foolish Heart," "Bewitched," "Don't Cry Joe," and "I Don't See Me in Your Eyes Anymore," among others. Jenkins's greatest achievement as a composer/conductor was his symphonic ode to New York City, *Manhattan Tower,* an extended work released in a set of four 78 rpm records. At Decca, Jenkins was the first to recognize the potential of the Weavers. Many folk purists believe he diluted their sound, but without Jenkins, the Weavers never would have scored their massive hit versions of "Goodnight Irene" and "So Long, It's Been Good to Know Ya" (which opened the door for many other folk groups later in the decade). After Jenkins left Decca for Capitol, his output as a solo artist and conductor slowed, although he continued arranging for the biggest names in the business. His relationship with Frank Sinatra was especially enduring. Not only did Jenkins arrange and conduct for two of Sinatra's most devastatingly moody LPs at Capitol (*No One Cares* and *All Alone*), but his best LPs at Reprise as well. When Sinatra starred in his final film (*The First Deadly Sin*), he would let no one else but Jenkins compose the musical score.

what to buy: Jenkins's original 1946 four-part series, *Manhattan Tower,* and "The Nightmare" from his *Seven Dreams* LP, are on *Collection* ✍✍✍✍ (Razor & Tie, 1997, prod. various), a definitive compilation of his most influential work as a composer, arranger, and hit producer. Also included are Jenkins's solo hits "I'm Forever Blowing Bubbles," "Bewitched," and "I Don't See Me in Your Eyes Anymore," as well as hit singles featuring the Weavers ("Tzena Tzena Tzena," "So Long, It's Been Good to Know Ya"), Billie Holiday ("God Bless the Child"), and Judy Garland with Dick Haymes ("For You, For Me, For Evermore"), among others.

the rest:
Gordon Jenkins' France ✍✍✍ (Bainbridge, 1991)
Soul of a People ✍✍✍ (Bainbridge, 1991/1994)

worth searching for: Jenkins won a Grammy award for his work on Frank Sinatra's *September of My Years* ✍✍✍✍ (Capitol, 1965). His sensitive string arrangements encase Sinatra's melancholy with sweeping poignancy. Also, Jenkins's later expanded version of his best conceptual piece is on *Gordon Jenkins' Complete Manhattan Tower* ✍✍✍ (Capitol, 1955), and is well worth owning for its superior fidelity.

influences:
◀◀ Isham Jones, George Gershwin, Andre Kostelanetz
▶▶ David Rose, 101 Strings, Living Strings

Ken Burke

Antonio Carlos Jobim

Born Antonio Carlos Brasileiro de Almeida Jobim, January 25, 1927, in Rio de Janerio, Brazil. Died December 8, 1994, in New York, NY.

Brazilian pianist and guitarist Jobim is best known for making bossa nova a household word and for penning the quintessential lounge tune, "The Girl from Ipanema." Yet Jobim had intended to become an architect, and even registered for architecture school, though he found himself unable to escape the pull of his musical muse.

Starting his recording career in 1954, he first found fame in 1956 by working on the score of a play called *Orfeo da Conceicao* (which was made into the award-winning film *Black Orpheus*). When his songs were covered by the Brazilian singer-guitarist João Gilberto, bossa nova was born. Jobim has described bossa nova's meaning as "a proturberance, a bump," as in "the bossa (hunchback) of Notre Dame." Since the human brain has bumps, if someone has a bossa for something, it means a bump in the brain—a talent. It came to mean a flair for something, and bossa nova came to mean "a new flair." When Stan Getz and Charlie Byrd recorded Jobim's "Desafinado" in 1962, Jobim—and bossa nova—became internationally known. Jobim didn't consider himself a jazz musician, however. He called himself a samba player. After discovering the piano in the '30s, he began hanging out with the samba people—fans and musicians who followed the Sambistas (samba composers) in bohemian-style bar crawls and jam sessions. From them, he learned guitar, playing in a lyrical style known for its sensual beauty. It's been said that, as Brian Wilson's songs made images of California so clear to those who had never been there, Jobim's songs evoked the beauty of the Brazilian ocean and rainforests even for those who'd never left middle America. He once said of the island paradise where he spent his boyhood, "I believe I learned my songs from the birds of the Brazilian forest." In the liner notes to

Antonio Carlos Jobim (r) performs with Frank Sinatra **(Archive Photos)**

Jobim's *Songbook* album, writer Zeca Ligiero describes bossa nova songs as being "characterized by their softness, with lyrics that speak directly to the heart about life's simple things." Because his songs were so accessible, they became among the most recorded of all time. Just about every great jazz artist, from Ella Fitzgerald to Dizzy Gillespie, Wes Montgomery, Oscar Peterson, and Sarah Vaughan, have recorded Jobim's songs. He's reportedly the only one to whose work Frank Sinatra has devoted two entire albums. In 1967, his compositions were recorded so often he was bested by only one entity: the Beatles. The names Lennon and McCartney come up often in writings about Jobim; his composing skills and song output are often compared to those titans of popular music. In 1964, "The Girl from Ipanema," a #1 hit, challenged the Beatles for chart dominance. Remarkably, Astrud Gilberto, João's wife, had to be coaxed into singing the song. Among other popular Jobim compositions are "Wave," "Corcovado," "Aguas de Marco," "Felicidade," "Once I Loved," "One Note Samba," and "Triste."

what to buy: The tribute concert album, *Antonio Carlos Jobim and Friends* ♪♪♪♪ (Verve, 1993, prod. Oscar Castro-Neves, Richard Seidel), featuring "The Boy from Ipanema" (with Shirley Horn on vocals) and "The Girl from Ipanema," includes a variety of American artists who were influenced by Jobim's innovative playing. It was recorded September 27, 1993, at the Free Jazz Festival in Sao Paulo, Brazil. *Wave* ♪♪♪♪ (A&M, 1967) features a lineup that, even then, constituted a supergroup: Herbie Hancock, Ron Carter, Harvey Mason, and Alex Acuna, with Paulo Jobim, Antonio's son, and Oscar Castro-Neves. *The Girl from Ipanema: The Antonio Carlos Jobim Songbook* ♪♪♪♪ (Verve, 1995, compilation prod. various) contains schmaltz galore (such as Billy Eckstine's work on the string-drenched "Felicidade"), but there's beauty as well, particularly in the smooth, cool voice of Astrud Gilberto with Jobim on "Agua de Beber." *The Man from Ipanema* ♪♪♪♪ (Verve, 1995, compilation prod. Oscar Castro-Neves) is as comprehensive as you can get on Jobim, with a healthy sampling of his romantic Latin music

("Amor Em Paz," "Lamento") and—count them—four versions of "The Girl from Ipanema." With a 64-page booklet and three CDs, it's actually intimidating.

what to buy next: *Antonio Carlos Jobim: Composer* ♫♫♫♪ (Warner Archives, 1995, prod. various) offers Jobim singing Jobim, in a soft, sweetly romantic way. Nelson Riddle's rich strings are heard throughout these songs (among them "Wonderful World" and "A Certain Mr. Jobim"), but it's on a track produced by Ray Gilbert and Louis Oliveira, "Hurry Up and Love Me," that it almost sounds as if Doris Day and Rock Hudson will come romping to life. It's easy to understand from these songs what Sinatra found so attractive; on some, such as "Don't Ever Go Away/Por Causa De Voce," Jobim almost sounds like the chairman.

best of the rest:
Stone Flower ♫♫♫♫ (Epic/CTI, 1970)
Elis and Tom ♫♫♫♫ (Verve, 1974)
Urubu ♫♫♫♫ (Warner Archive, 1976)
Passarim ♫♫♫♫ (Verve, 1987)
Verve Jazz Masters 13 ♫♫♫♫ (Verve, 1994)

worth searching for: *Francis Albert Sinatra & Antonio Carlos Jobim* ♫♫♫♪ (Reprise, 1967/1988, prod. Sonny Burke) pairs Jobim with the Chairman of the Board. It's a divine album, falling short of perfection only because it clocks in at a measly 28:33.

influences:

◀◀ Cole Porter, Gerry Mulligan, Chet Baker, Barney Kessel, Claude Debussy

▶▶ Frank Sinatra, Weather Report, Tom Ze

see also: *Stan Getz, Astrud Gilberto, João Gilberto*

Lynne Margolis

Billy Joel

Born May 9, 1949, in the Bronx, NY.

Joel has described himself as "a melody freak," and it's that love of a hummable tune that has made him one of pop music's most enduring, and endearing, stars. Though his superstardom has come mostly from straightforward rock and pop songs, he initially derived his public identity from the 1973 hit "Piano Man," about a sympathetic lounge-bar performer who listens carefully to his customers' tales of woe. From his early days playing in Long Island rock bands to his storytelling piano-man stretch to a logical merger of both roles, Joel has consistently penned memorable melodies. He studied classical piano before rocking through the '60s with the Hassles and Attila, then worked briefly as a solo pianist in California. Joel enjoyed moderate success with several albums, but when he teamed up with noted producer Phil Ramone, the result was his 1977 pop-rock masterpiece, *The Stranger*. Joel stretched his lyrical sights to include topical issues ranging from unemployment to the plight of Vietnam veterans. Meanwhile, he has filed several multimillion-dollar lawsuits against his former management over songwriting revenues and endured two failed marriages, including one to model Christie Brinkley. But the former amateur boxer always manages to bounce back; 1993's *River of Dreams* was the first of his career to debut at #1 on the *Billboard* chart.

what to buy: With such a long record of chart success, the two-disc *Greatest Hits, Vol. I & II* ♫♫♫♫ (Columbia, 1985, prod. Phil Ramone) covers the highlights from 1973–85 in fine fashion, with 25 of Joel's most memorable songs. *River of Dreams* ♫♫♫♪ (Columbia, 1993, prod. Dan Kortchmar) matches soul-baring lyrics to masterful melodies, from the minor-key blues of "Shades of Grey" to the exotic rhythms of the title track to Beatlesque rock and metaphorical angst of "Great Wall of China." There's more to *The Stranger* ♫♫♫♫ (Columbia, 1977, prod. Phil Ramone) than its four hit singles—the suite "Scenes from an Italian Restaurant," for one, is a Joel classic. *Piano Man* ♫♫♪ (Columbia, 1973, prod. Michael Stewart), obviously, documents his early lounge-pianist phase, including the title track and the anti-cocaine anthem "Captain Jack."

what to buy next: *The Nylon Curtain* ♫♫♫♫ (Columbia, 1982, prod. Phil Ramone) is one of Joel's most ambitious and satisfying efforts, combining lyrical depth with radio-friendly tunes such as "Allentown" and "Goodnight Saigon." The rhythmic snare of "We Didn't Start the Fire" and the confessional bravado of "Shameless," covered later by Garth Brooks, highlight *Storm Front* ♫♫♫♫ (Columbia, 1989, prod. Billy Joel, Mick Jones).

what to avoid: Joel sounds pretty green on his first album, *Cold Spring Harbor* **woof!** (Columbia, 1972, prod. Artie Ripp), which also suffers from recording problems. *Kohuept (In Concert)* ♫ (Columbia, 1987, prod. Jim Boyer, Brian Ruggles) was recorded live during a tour of the Soviet Union but was released against Joel's objections.

Billy Joel (© Ken Settle)

the rest:
Streetlife Serenade ♫♫ (Columbia, 1974)
Turnstiles ♫♫♫ (Columbia, 1976)
52nd Street ♫♫♫ (Columbia, 1978)
Glass Houses ♫♫♫ (Columbia, 1980)
Songs in the Attic ♫♫ (Columbia, 1981)
An Innocent Man ♫♫♫♫ (Columbia, 1983)
The Bridge ♫♫ (Columbia, 1986)
Greatest Hits, Vol. III ♫♫♫ (Columbia, 1997)
The Complete Hits Collection, 1973–1997 ♫♫♫ (Columbia, 1997)

worth searching for: *Live at the Bottom Line* ♫♫♫♫ (Mistral, 1993), one of many bootlegs of Joel's live radio show on June 10, 1976—a show nearly as crucial to his career as Bruce Springsteen's radio broadcast from the same venue was a year earlier.

influences:

◀◀ The Beatles, the Rolling Stones, Ray Charles, Bob Dylan, the Four Seasons, Dion and the Belmonts, George and Ira Gershwin, Elton John

▶▶ Amy Grant, Garth Brooks, Barry Manilow, Richard Marx

David Yonke

David Johansen

See: Buster Poindexter

Al Jolson

Born Asa Yoelson, on or about May 26, 1886, in Seredzius, Lithuania. Died October 23, 1950, in San Francisco, CA.

The Shubert Theater Organization billed Al Jolson as "The World's Greatest Entertainer." Today, listening to his affected, leathery "Mammy" voice overwhelming the mechanical recording horn, we might laugh at our ancestors' naivete. Then again, how will future listeners who never had a chance to see performances by Elvis Presley, Michael Jackson, or Bruce Springsteen rate them based on recordings and videos?

Jolson's audiences loved him, and the word from commentators who saw him live is that none of the recordings or movies he made captured the magic of his performances. He was born into a world where movies, radio, and recording did not yet exist, and he developed a love-hate relationship with those media. Only on stage could Jolson tear down barriers between performer and audience. The humor of his ad-libs and asides rested on being able to step out of the "performance" into the world where the audience lived while still being part of the performance on stage. His dancing and humor also had a sexual brashness that was Elvis-like in scope but rarely comes across

in the artifacts he left behind. Jolson's exuberant personality carried many a thin script and tune. He set up the world in which pop singers, by dint of their personality, could be stars. Still, when listening to Jolson it's important to remember that he wasn't a pop-music star but a musical-theater star. In fact, he was thought of mostly as a comedian until he began making movies. He sang to the back of the house and never learned how to be intimate with microphones and movie cameras. That task would be left to the next generation of singers, such as Bing Crosby and Judy Garland, whom Jolson influenced mightily.

E.L. Doctorow, in his novel *Ragtime*, called Jolson "the last of the great shameless mother lovers," and psychoanalysts could have a field day analyzing the way Jolson substituted the audience for his departed mother. Insecure and driven, Asa Yoelson was about eight when he saw his mother screaming in the childbirth that killed her. An egotist who publicly was the brashest man on earth (when he had to follow Enrico Caruso on stage, he delighted the audience with his trademark, "You ain't heard nothin' yet!"), Jolson sought constant reassurance. Yoelson became Jolson when he and his brother Harry were working in vaudeville in the early 1900s. That's also when he donned blackface (today an embarrassing reminder of America's racial troubles), which helped him overcome stage jitters and unleashed his overpoweringly sexy alter-ego. Jolie, as he called himself, recorded successively for the Victor, Columbia, Brunswick, American, and Decca record labels, starting in 1911 with two tunes from his stage vehicle, *Vera Violetta*. Jolson's hold on audiences is clear, because despite unsympathetic orchestral backing, virtually everything he put out for Columbia was a hit in the years 1913–23. He was similarly successful at Brunswick from 1924–30. However, a dispute with a Brunswick executive led Jolson to stay out of the recording studio, except for five songs he cut for American in 1932, until 1945. Shortly before he began recording again, Jolson had a major part of his left lung removed—but you'd never know it from his full-voiced, powerful recordings. Listen through the leather, and you'll hear that Jolson could carry a tune beautifully and that he possessed a richly shaded voice and a fresh, spontaneous sense of phrasing. His return to recording can't be separated from the 1946 movie *The Jolson Story*, the best film of his career. Jolson, 60, played himself in only one long-shot scene, but he sang all the songs and did a remarkable job of coaching star Larry Parks to mimic his performances. It's one of the best jobs of lip-synching ever, and the mesmerizing tandem gives some clue to Jolson's on-stage power and appeal. (It's out there on videocassette and may well be a better buy than any Jolson album!) After the movie, Jolson shook off a career decline, staying in the forefront of the show-business world until his death in 1950, a heart attack brought on by a typically hard-driving schedule. He had only recently returned from performing 42 shows in seven days for U.S. troops in Korea.

what to buy: *The Best of the Decca Years* ♪♪♪♪ (MCA, 1992, compilation prod. Tony Natelli) is a thoroughly satisfying collection of songs associated with every phase of Jolson's career, including remakes of "Swanee," "April Showers," "Rock-a-Bye Your Baby with a Dixie Melody," "Anniversary Song," and a lively duet with Crosby on the hoary "Alexander's Ragtime Band." Best of all, you don't have to listen "through" the recording process to really hear him; his voice comes bounding out of the speakers with all the salacious zest (if not all of the bottom) that he had in live performance. To top it off, orchestras by the post-War era had learned to play pop songs with a much more sympathetic and lively feel that perfectly supports Jolson's singing. This will do until a box set comes along containing all 71 titles he recorded for Decca. The most complete collection of Decca recordings is on cassette but not CD: *The Best of Al Jolson* ♪♪♪♪ (MCA, 1962).

what to buy next: *Let Me Sing and I'm Happy: Al Jolson at Warner Bros., 1926–1936* ♪♪♪♪ (Turner Classic Movies/Rhino, 1996, prod. Ian Whitcomb) fills in Jolson's big recording gap by culling songs from eight of his Warner Bros. movies, including *The Jazz Singer*, which was hailed then and is known today as "the first talkie" and the film that ended the silent movie age (it wasn't really). The performances, especially the up-tempo numbers such as "I'm Sitting on Top of the World" and "There's a Rainbow Round My Shoulder," are winning, in stark contrast to Jolson's hammy "acting" in these flicks. A special treat is Jolson's interplay with Cab Calloway, who gives no hint of being uncomfortable with the former blackface performer on "I Love to Sing-A." *You Ain't Heard Nothin' Yet: Jolie's Finest Columbia Recordings* ♪♪♪ (Columbia/Legacy, 1994, prod. Didier C. Deutsch) is more of historical interest than musical interest. The modern ears of all but the most extreme Jolson fanatics will need a special dose of imagination to hear the real Jolie in the relatively staid readings of such jumpers as "Swanee." Still, there's a thrill in hearing the original recordings, especially "naughty" novelties such as "O-Hi-O (O My! O!)," in which he opines "a country girl, you know, is just like a Ford/they're not so stylish/but the service, oh Lord!" This disk opens a window on musical scenes nearly 90 years gone.

the rest:
You Ain't Heard Nothin' Yet ♪♪♪ (ASV/Living Era, 1992)
Volume 1: Stage Highlights, 1911–1925 ♪♪♪ (Pearl Flapper, 1993)

Volume 2: The Salesman of Song 1911–1923 ♪♪♪ (Pearl Flapper, 1993)
The First Recordings, 1911–1916: You Made Me Love You ♪♪♪ (Stash, 1993)
The Jolson Story: Rock-a-Bye Your Baby ♪♪♪♪ (MCA, 1995)
Rainbow 'Round My Shoulder ♪♪♪♪ (MCA, 1995)
Live ♪♪♪ (Laserlight, 1995)
American Legends, Vol. 11 ♪♪♪ (Laserlight, 1996)
Legends of Big Band: Al Jolson ♪♪♪ (Intersound, 1996)
I Love to Sing ♪♪♪ (Jasmine, 1996)
Volume 3: The Twenties—From Broadway to Hollywood ♪♪♪ (Pearl Flapper, 1996)
Al Jolson on Broadway ♪♪♪ (Intersound, 1997)
Very Best of Al Jolson ♪♪♪ (Prism, 1997)
Golden Collection ♪♪♪ (IMG, 1997)
Great ♪♪♪ (Goldies, 1997)
Hits ♪♪♪ (Public Music, 1997)

influences:

◀◀ Bert Williams, Eddie Leonard

▶▶ Bing Crosby, Judy Garland, Jerry Lee Lewis

Salvatore Caputo

Etta Jones

Born November 25, 1928, in Aiken, SC.

Possessing a rare combination of vocal power and interpretive poise, Jones invests emotion in every note she sings. Her ability to transform pop standards into vehicles for inspired jazz and R&B results in unique, poignant performances that have been the envy of her peers for more than 40 years. Jones hit the road early, touring at age 16 with Buddy Johnson's band and recording Dinah Washington-style R&B with Benny Bigard. Work with bands led by Pete Johnson, J.C. Heard, and Earl "Fatha" Hines helped her develop a large enough following to become a solo act. Her big 1960 hit, "Don't Go to Strangers," mixed rich blues feeling with jazzy phrasing and led to several more LPs on the Prestige label. Because of soul music's '60s dominance, she was off record for several years until she teamed with her husband, tenor saxophonist Houston Person, for a series of highly regarded discs from the '70s to the '90s. Still reinterpreting middle-of-the-road classics into emotive vocal jazz, Jones continues to play critically acclaimed gigs all around the world.

what to buy: Jones's breakthrough LP, *Don't Go to Strangers* ♪♪♪♪ (Prestige, 1961/Original Jazz Classics, 1991, compilation prod. Phil De Lancie), repeatedly crosses the lines between R&B and jazz, making for an exhilarating introduction to this undeservedly obscure artist. Jones brings something fresh to

the oldies "Bye Bye Blackbird," "Yes Sir, That's My Baby," "All the Way," and, of course, the hit title track.

what to buy next: Recorded during her later vocal peak, *My Mother's Eyes* ♪♪♪♪ (Muse, 1977/32 Records, 1997, prod. Houston Person), features Jones giving exceptionally expressive treatment to a potent mix of jazz and pop standards, such as "The Way You Look Tonight," "This Girl's in Love with You," and "You Do Something to Me." Also, *Something Nice* ♪♪♪♪ (Prestige, 1961/Original Jazz Classics, 1994, compilation prod. Phil De Lancie) brilliantly showcases Jones's interpretive chops on such melodic warhorses as "Till There Was You," "Almost Like Being in Love," and "Fools Rush In."

the rest:
Lonely and Blue ♪♪♪ (Prestige 1962/Original Jazz Classics, 1992)
Love Shout ♪♪ (Prestige, 1963/Original Jazz Classics, 1997)
So Warm ♪♪♪ (Original Jazz Classics, 1996)
The Melody Lingers On ♪♪♪ (Highnote Records, 1997)

worth searching for: The out-of-print *Christmas with Etta Jones* ♪♪♪♪ (Muse, 1990/1994), a stylistic tour de force of jazz and soul, has Jones subtly imposing her style on "White Christmas," "Have Yourself a Merry Little Christmas," and "Santa Claus Is Coming to Town."

influences:

◀◀ Billie Holiday, Dinah Washington, Thelma Carpenter

▶▶ Della Reese, Sylvia Sims

Ken Burke

Jack Jones

Born January 14, 1938, in Los Angeles, CA.

Others claim to sing love songs, but few can jump inside romantic lyrics like "this is the one you've been waiting for" as enthusiastically and dramatically as Jones. While most of his peers were grooving to rock 'n' roll or railing against the Vietnam War, Jones was emulating the popular crooning of the previous generation. His voice contains neither the edge of Frank Sinatra nor the warm friendliness of Tony Bennett, but he can sing even the most hackneyed love lyric (his hits include "You're My Girl," "Alfie," and the Henry Mancini co-penned "Dear Heart") and make it sound like a Hallmark card from heaven. (Evidence: he sang the unavoidably catchy theme song

for television's *The Love Boat* from 1977 until 1985, when Dionne Warwick took it over.)

Jones began his career by roughly imitating his father, Allan Jones, a movie star and occasional hitmaking singer; before long, despite rock's dominance in the 1960s, Jones's star was on the rise. (At the time, Frank Sinatra said he was "the next major singing star of show business.") His biggest hits, 1961's "Lollipops and Roses" and a vanilla take on the Beatles' croon "And I Love Her," were almost as effective as Johnny Mathis for inspiring backseat teen lovers. Today, despite a bizarre sarcastic streak, which has occasionally resulted in weirdly mean-spirited versions of his old hits, Jones continues to be a major lounge and showroom draw.

what to buy: The best of many best-of collections is clearly *Greatest Hits* ♪♪♪ (MCA, 1995, compilation prod. Andy McKaie), which includes liner notes by author Will Friedwald and 18 tunes, including "Lady," "Lollipops and Roses," "Alfie," and "And I Love Her."

what to buy next: It's tough to find a contemporary singer worthy of Gershwin these days, but Jones does a nice job with "Embraceable You," "'S Wonderful," and other classics on *The Gershwin Album* ♪♪♪ (Sony, 1992, prod. Mike Berniker).

what to avoid: In picking the right hits collection, look for MCA's same-titled set rather than the much-skimpier *Greatest Hits* ♪♪ (Curb, 1990, prod. various), although it includes "The Impossible Dream" and "Wives and Lovers."

best of the rest:
Sings Michel Legrand ♪♪ (Laserlight, 1993)
Live at the Sands ♪♪♪ (Laserlight, 1993/1994)
I Am a Singer ♪♪♪ (USA/Rounder, 1994)

worth searching for: Of course, Jones has a cornball side, and his squaresville impression of the Police's rock hit "Every Breath You Take" is a highlight of *New Jack Swing* ♪♪♪ (Honest, 1997, prod. Jim Long, Jack Jones). (The title is also hilarious, a reference to the hip 1980s R&B pioneered by young singers Bobby Brown and Keith Sweat.)

influences:

◀◀ Allan Jones, Frank Sinatra, Vic Damone, Russ Columbo, Bing Crosby, Tony Bennett

▶▶ Frank Sinatra Jr., Tina Martin, Paul McCartney

Steve Knopper

Etta Jones (© Jack Vartoogian)

Quincy Jones

Born March 14, 1933, in Chicago, IL.

Despite Quincy "Q" Jones's numerous contributions to jazz, he's probably still best known as the man who gave Michael Jackson his *Thriller* and the only man respected enough by his peers to have pulled off the "We Are the World" studio session. (The kitschy *Austin Powers: International Man of Mystery* soundtrack further trivialized Jones's accomplishments: because of its appearance there, "Soul Bossa Nova," his funky 1962 merging of big-band jazz and soul music, recently emerged as a cocktail-culture anthem.) His loungiest period was the early '60s, when he won Grammys for the LPs *Walking in Space* and *Smackwater Jack*, and composed such memorable TV themes as *Ironside* and *Sanford and Son*. He was also married (briefly) to Peggy Lipton of TV's *The Mod Squad*.

Jones started his career as a jazz trumpeter, forming a band with Ray Charles at age 14 and playing with Lionel Hampton before he was old enough to drive. After winning a scholarship in his teens and attending Boston's Berklee School Music, he was invited to write arrangements for Oscar Pettiford and began hobnobbing with the likes of Miles Davis, Charlie Parker, Dizzy Gillespie, and Thelonious Monk. Returning to New York in 1961, he became one of the first African Americans to become a music industry executive, as a vice president for Mercury Records (for whom he recorded "Soul Bossa Nova" with Lalo Schifrin and experimental jazzman Rahsaan Roland Kirk). He began producing and playing on other people's sessions and continued to arrange, winning Grammy Awards for his 1963 arrangement of the Count Basie Orchestra's "I Can't Stop Loving You" and Frank Sinatra's "Fly Me to the Moon." He cemented his producing preeminence in the '70s with his work for Aretha Franklin, the *Roots* mini-series soundtrack, and Michael Jackson's monster hits *Off the Wall* and *Thriller*. Jones was at the center of some of the most important projects of the '80s, producing "We Are the World" as well as Steven Spielberg's film *The Color Purple*. In the 1990s, Jones was honored with a Grammy Legend Award; saw the release of his film biography, *Listen Up: The Lives of Quincy Jones*; produced the hit TV sitcom *Fresh Prince of Bel-Air*; launched the hip-hop music magazine *Vibe* and a spinoff television version; and released *Miles and Quincy Live at Montreux*, a document of Miles Davis's final recording. On an astounding variety of fronts, "Q" continues to prove he is one of the essential cogs of the entertainment industry machine.

what to buy: Of Jones's several greatest-hits packages, *The Best of Quincy Jones* ♫♫♫ (A&M, 1981, prod. Quincy Jones) is

the standout, combining his best efforts for A&M ("Killer Joe," "Smackwater Jack") with key tracks off his blistering pop albums, like 1974's *Body Heat*. *The Best, Vol. 2* ♫♫♫ (Rebound, 1988) celebrates "Q's" TV themes, like the streetwise *Sanford and Son* music and the kooky "Hikky-Burr" scat from *The Bill Cosby Show*.

what to buy next: The best feature of *Back on the Block* ♫♫♫♫ (Qwest, 1989), like many projects from Quincy the Great, is a guest list that reads like a Who's Who of the music world: Sarah Vaughan, Dionne Warwick, George Benson, Ray Charles, Miles Davis, Ella Fitzgerald, Dizzy Gillespie, Luther Vandross, Ice T, Sheila E, Take 6, Chaka Khan, James Moody, and Kool Moe Dee. Some nitpicky music critics with horns for brains complain that "Q" steers clear of jazz and instead puts together a buffet of run-of-the-mill urban pop. What do they know? The LP was still a huge Grammy-winning hit and features some the best work Jones has ever done. *Pawnbroker/Deadly Affair* ♫♫♫ (Verve, 1996, prod. Quincy Jones) is a recently re-released double dip soundtrack that features some scintillating Quincy Jones compositions, particularly "Main Theme to the Pawnbroker."

what to avoid: Too much of a good thing can sometimes be a bad thing, and *Q's Jook Joint* ♫♫ (Qwest, 1995) proves that adage true. Sure, at the drop of a hat Jones can assemble a bevy of musicians that any hip pleasure-monger would love to have as guests at his party. But this dispassionate rehashing of old formulas shows that "Q" must constantly guard against letting that power spin out of control. There are brief cameos by literally hundreds of superstar performers, but all that's not enough to keep *Jook* from being a gyp.

the rest:

This Is How I Feel about Jazz ♫♫♫ (UNI/Impulse!, 1957/1992)
Live at the Alhambra, 1960 ♫♫♫ (Jazz Music Yesterday)
Vol.1—Swiss Radio Days Jazz Series ♫♫♫ (TCB Music, 1960)
In the Heat of the Night/They Call Me Mister Tibbs! ♫♫♫♫ (Original Soundtracks) (MGM, 1967, 1970/Rykodisc, 1998)
Body Heat ♫♫♫ (A&M, 1974)
Roots ♫♫♫♫ (A&M, 1977/1997)
Sounds . . . and Stuff Like That! ♫♫♫ (A&M, 1978)
The Dude ♫♫♫ (A&M, 1981)
The Quintessence ♫♫♫ (MCA Jazz/Impulse!, 1986)
Quincy Jones: Compact Jazz Series ♫♫ (Verve, 1989)
Sarah Vaughan/Quincy Jones, "Misty" ♫♫♫ (Mercury, 1990)
Miles Davis & Quincy Jones Live at Montreux ♫♫♫♫ (Warner Bros., 1993)
Pure Delight: The Essence of Quincy Jones and His Orchestra, 1953–1964 ♫♫♫ (Razor & Tie, 1995)
Q Live in Paris Circa 1960 ♫♫♫♫ (Qwest, 1996)

Greatest Hits ✹✹✹ (A&M, 1996)
Jazz 'Round Midnight ✹✹✹ (Verve, 1997)

worth searching for: With Jones at his artistic and career peak, the out-of-print *Walking in Space* ✹✹✹✹ (A&M, 1969) is a return to the big-band styles with contemporary flair that resurrected "Q"'s rep as a bandleader and artist after a long spell of hacking for Hollywood. Mindful of the modern era, Jones merges old styles with new, blending in electric instruments and pop music while making a sizzling version of "Hair" (from the hit Broadway show) the album's hallmark. At the same time, he gathered some of the best jazz musicians of his age— Freddie Hubbard, Roland Kirk, Hubert Laws, J.J. Johnson, Jimmy Cleveland—to add their expertise.

influences:

◀◀ Clark Terry, Dizzy Gillespie, Ray Charles, Lionel Hampton

▶▶ Thad Jones, Gil Evans, Benny Carter, Mel Lewis, the Brothers Johnson, George Benson, Michael Jackson, James Ingram, Patti Austin, Patrice Rushen, Luther Vandross, Prince, Maxwell

Chris Tower

Spike Jones

Born Lindley Armstrong Jones, December 14, 1911, in Long Beach, CA. Died May 1, 1965, in Bel Air, CA.

Among Spike Jones's many musical accomplishments over his 30-plus-year career, perhaps his biggest was introducing such instruments as the latriophone (a toilet seat strung with wire) and the burpaphone (self-explanatory) to the lexicon of American popular music. Much more than a novelty act, Jones was a musical visionary. "I'm the dandruff in longhair music," Jones has said about his comical presence in the world of more serious bandleaders in the '50s and '60s.

He began his career as a studio musician drummer, most notably playing on Bing Crosby's monster hit "White Christmas." Bored by conventional music, Jones began to add unusual instruments to his drum set and set out to form a band to fulfill his zany vision. In the early '40s, he formed the City Slickers and Jones set out to turn the world of pop music on its ear with crazy parodies and bizarre musical collages. The band's unlikely first hit was 1942's Hitler spoof "Der Fuehrer's Face," on the basis of which the band successfully toured the country. By the late '40s Jones had expanded the band's live shows to include midgets, jugglers, and other loony acts, while scoring on the charts with song interpretations like "Cocktails for Two"—

replete with a hiccuping chorus. Jones and the band appeared in several films and brought their brand of musical folly to TV in the '50s and early '60s with four versions of *The Spike Jones Show.* Jones died of emphysema in 1965, but not before establishing himself as one of the true musical pioneers of the 20th century, and easily the most hilarious.

what to buy: Among the numerous greatest-hits packages is an inspired sampling of Jones's lunacy on *Musical Depreciation Revue: The Spike Jones Revue* ✹✹✹✹ (Rhino, 1994, prod. various), which features 40 classics, including the funniest song ever written about Hitler, "Der Fuehrer's Face," and his famous gargling rendition of "William Tell's Overture." The title says it all on *Dinner Music for People Who Aren't Very Hungry* ♪♪♪♪ (Rhino, 1957). The "interpretations" of polite music make it the perfect CD for an intimate date with someone with a sense of humor.

what to buy next: You'll have trouble listening to straight renditions of classic carols after hearing *Let's Sing a Song for Christmas* ♪♪♪♪ (MGM, 1978, prod. various).

the rest:
Riot Squad ♪♪♪ (Harlequin, 1989)
Louder & Funnier ♪♪♪ (Harlequin, 1994)
Corn's a-Poppin' ♪♪♪ (Harlequin, 1995)
Cocktails for Two ♪♪♪ (Pro Arte, 1997)

worth searching for: With a cover by cartoonist Art Spiegelman, liner notes by author Thomas Pynchon, and some previously unreleased tracks, *Spiked!* ♪♪♪♪ (Catalyst, 1994, prod. Paul Williams) is a fantastic alternative overview of Jones's career.

influences:
◄◄ Al Jolson, Harmonica Frank, Emmett Miller

►► "Weird Al" Yankovic, Allan Sherman, Phillip Glass, the Beatles, Jerry Lewis, Frank Zappa

Alex Gordon

Tom Jones

Born Thomas Jones Woodward, June 7, 1940, in Pontypridd, Wales.

Jones was the best white R&B shouter of the 1960s and one of the British Invasion's most underrated performers. A former English "Teddy Boy," he modeled his sexually provocative style on the rock dynamics of Elvis Presley, the gospel intensity of Little Richard, and the country soul of Jerry Lee Lewis. His first recordings were produced by the legendary Joe Meek while he was still performing under the name Tommy Scott. His new manager, Gordon Mills, got him signed to Decca, and wrote the aggressive Welsh singer's first great hit, 1965's "It's Not Unusual." Initially, BBC Radio banned the record for being too overtly sexual, and U.S. soul stations assumed the singer was African American, controversies which Jones accepted as the ultimate validation of his style. His international hit followup, "What's New Pussycat?" (from the flop motion picture of the same name), played up his image as a preening loverboy. His concerts attracted so many screaming, sex-crazed female fans that his manager began to rope off the stage like a boxing ring. Anxious fans then began throwing their panties at him. Jones's droll quips, in response, drove them to an even greater frenzy.

Though Jones was known as an up-tempo pop singer, he turned in one of his career's most soulful performances with a remake of Billy Eckstine's "With These Hands." In 1969, Jones began a two-year stint on the television variety show *This Is Tom Jones*, which showcased him an an all-round entertainer and helped catapult "I'll Never Fall in Love Again," "She's a Lady," and several others into the Top 10. Save 1977's countryish "Say You'll Stay Until Tomorrow," Jones's chart power flickered out afterwards. In an attempt to resurrect his career, à la Jerry Lee Lewis, Jones signed with Mercury to record country music in 1981. "Touch Me (I'll Be Your Fool Once More)" and "I've Been Rained on Too" were solid hits, but after Mills's death in 1986, the singer returned to England to tinker with his career.

Jones's work on the *Matador* musical cast LP brought good reviews and "A Boy from Nowhere," his first U.K. hit in 15 years. But good, unpredictable ideas truly fueled his comeback and solidified his appeal with a new generation; in 1989, the electronic pop group Art of Noise produced his version of Prince's sexy "Kiss." Nearing age 60, Jones still gives shake-'em-out, sweaty performances in Las Vegas and elsewhere, and still makes the ladies scream and throw their undergarments. As his tongue-in-cheek cameo on *The Simpsons* and version of the hip British band EMF's early-1990s hit "Unbelieveable" proved, Jones continues to revel in his dual status as pop icon and camp classic.

what to buy: All of Jones's biggest hits, from his days as a pop sex god to his country music period to his Art of Noise-produced comeback, are represented on the impeccable introductory set *The Complete Tom Jones* ♪♪♪♪ (Deram, 1993, prod. various).

what to buy next: Country music has never been sung with more Welsh soul than on *Things That Matter Most to Me* ♪♪♪ (Mercury 1988/1993, prod. Steve Popovich, Bill Justis, Gordon Mills), a top-notch collection of Jones's best-selling and most interesting sides for Mercury. Jones revived his career with *Move Closer* ♪♪♪ (Jive Records, 1989, prod. various), which features the hit version of Prince's "Kiss."

what to avoid: For the price of a split disc such as *Back to Back: Tom Jones/Engelbert Humperdinck* ♪♪♪♪ (Rebound Records, 1994, compilation prod. Howard Smiley, Bill Crowley), you could get fuller more satisfying compilations on either artist.

Tom Jones (© Ken Settle)

the rest:

Green Green Grass of Home 🎷🎷🎷 (London 1967/1989)
Live at Caesars Palace 🎷🎷🎷 (1971/Varese Vintage, 1998)
Darlin' 🎷🎷🎷 (Mercury 1981/1993)
Tom Jones Country 🎷🎷🎷 (Mercury 1982/1993)
Don't Let Our Dreams Die Young 🎷🎷🎷 (Polydor, 1983/1993)
Love Is on the Radio 🎷🎷 (Mercury, 1984/1993)
Tender Loving Care 🎷🎷 (Mercury 1985/1993)
Country Memories 🎷🎷🎷 (Rebound Records, 1994)
The Lead and How to Swing It 🎷🎷🎷 (Interscope Records, 1994)
By Request 🎷🎷 (Special Music Company, 1995)
Tom Jones Live! 🎷 (BMG Special Products, 1997)
Tom Jones & Friends Live! 🎷🎷 (BMG Special Products, 1997)
Great Performances N/A (32 Pop, 1998)

worth searching for: As a live performer, Jones is at the peak of his powers on *Live in Las Vegas* 🎷🎷🎷 (Parrot, 1969, prod. various), a two-disc set on which Jones belts out his biggest hits to date.

influences:

◄◄ Elvis Presley, Jerry Lee Lewis, Little Richard

►► Engelbert Humperdinck, Michael Bolton, Prince

Ken Burke

Al Jordan

See: Matt Monro

Louis Jordan

Born July 8, 1908, in Brinkley, AK. Died February 4, 1975, in Los Angeles, CA.

Yes, Louis Jordan's jumping novelty music bridged the gap from old-school R&B and big-band music to Little Richard and Chuck Berry's fast-paced rock 'n' roll. But more importantly, today his songs still swing—maybe that's why the musical *Five Guys Named Moe*, loosely based on Jordan's life and music, has had so much staying power around the world. Among Jordan's classics, which are both party-happy and aware of poverty, racism, and other social problems, are: "Caldonia," "Let the Good Times Roll," "Beans and Corn Bread," and "What's the Use of Getting Sober (When You're Gonna Get Drunk Again)."

Son of an Arkansas bandleader, Jordan left town in his 20s to play in Philadelphia with Charlie Gaines and in Harlem with drummer-bandleader Chick Webb and then-unknown singer Ella Fitzgerald. Soon, after Webb's sudden death, the alto sax player built on his musical talent and fun-loving sense of humor to create a more popular, accessible version of Louis Armstrong and Duke Ellington's jazz. "What makes your big

head so hard?" he wondered of "Caldonia," the subject of which also had "great big feet." On "Beans and Corn Bread," a subtly disguised social commentary about racial conflict, the beans fight at a party with the corn bread. Countless artists, from Ray Charles to B.B. King, heard Jordan's records on the radio and tried to copy his style. Years after Jordan's peak, Chuck Berry stepped up the old blues beat, added humorous lyrics about dances and teenagers and sounded uncannily like Jordan's famed seven-member Tympani Five—only with guitar solos where the sax bits used to be. In 1981, British rocker Joe Jackson's *Jumpin' Jive* paid further homage.

what to buy: *The Best of Louis Jordan* 🎷🎷🎷🎷🎷 (MCA, 1975, prod. Milt Gabler) has all his 1940s hits, including "Choo Choo Ch'-Boogie," "Caldonia," and "School Days (When We Were Kids)," and it remains the most thorough Jordan retrospective.

what to buy next: Slowly, the rest of Jordan's material has seeped into other sets: though they're not essential, fans will find different, jazzier perspectives on *I Believe in Music* 🎷🎷🎷 (Evidence, 1973/Classic Jazz, 1980, prod. various) and *Just Say Moe! Mo' of the Best of Louis Jordan* 🎷🎷🎷 (Rhino, 1992, prod. Milt Gabler). *Rock 'N' Roll* 🎷🎷🎷 (Mercury, 1989, prod. various), with re-recorded 1956–57 versions of older hits, features conductor-arranger Quincy Jones.

what to avoid: *No Moe! Decca Recordings* 🎷🎷 (MCA, 1992, prod. various) is deceptively advertised; despite a few original Jordan tracks, the bulk of it is actors' versions of songs from *Five Guys Named Moe*. *Rock 'n' Roll Call* 🎷🎷🎷 (RCA Bluebird, 1993, prod. John Snyder) reissues Jordan's 1950s recordings even though they sound just as good on earlier collections.

the rest:

One Guy Named Louis 🎷🎷🎷 (Blue Note, 1954)
No Moe! Louis Jordan's Greatest Hits 🎷🎷🎷 (Verve, 1992)

worth searching for: *At the Cat's Ball—the Early Years* 🎷🎷🎷 (JSP, 1991, prod. various), an import, is a nice historical look into the big-band swing sound that led up to Jordan's seminal 1940s recordings.

influences:

◄◄ Louis Armstrong, Duke Ellington, Bessie Smith, Charlie Christian, Cab Calloway

►► Elmore James, Chuck Berry, B.B. King, Ray Charles, Robert Jr. Lockwood, Joe Jackson, Royal Crown Revue, Squirrel Nut Zippers

Steve Knopper

Jump with Joey

See: Joey Altruda with the Cocktail Crew

K

Bert Kaempfert

Born October 16, 1923, in Hamburg, Germany. Died June 21, 1980, in Majorca, Spain.

Yeah, yeah, he was the first man to produce the Beatles, reluctantly, after they backed singer Tony Sheridan in their early years playing Hamburg clubs. He's a rock 'n' roll footnote for that. Much more importantly, he wrote "Strangers in the Night"! And "Danke Schoen"!

Just before World War II he studied at the Hamburg School of Music, mastering accordion, piano, clarinet, and other instruments, then became a musical arranger for the popular *Radio Danzig*. When the war ended, he started a long career as an A&R man for the international record label Polydor, which led to his reluctant siring of the Beatles. A music publishing executive who had seen the Beatles/Sheridan act dragged Kaempfert to one of their Hamburg shows, and he wound up producing the joint "My Bonnie Lies Over the Ocean" single, plus "Ain't She Sweet" and "Cry for a Shadow"—which gave them exposure enough to catch eventual manager Brian Epstein's attention. But Kaempfert haphazardly referred to the group as "The Beat Brothers" and quickly moved on to other things. In 1961, his orchestra recorded his "Wonderland by Night," which hit #1 in the U.S. He penned several hits after that, most notably a song for the 1966 Frank Sinatra career-reviving spy movie *A Man Could Get Killed*. The song, "Strangers in the Night," is perhaps Sinatra's best-known signature after "My Way," and it has become a pop culture icon (e.g., the throwaway bit in Chevy Chase's movie *Fletch* where he sings "Strangers in the night . . . exchanging clothing" and the recent Nissan commercial in which the song accompanies a scene of cars mating at a supermarket). Kampfert's long string of solo albums, most of which contained original compositions, have been high-profile staples of supermarkets, elevators, and easy-listening radio stations for the past three decades.

what to buy: Kaempfert's easy-listening albums are gradually starting to come back in print: *The Very Best of Bert Kaempfert* ♫♫♫♫ (Taragon, 1996, prod. various) is filled with big-band

background music, including Kaempfert's version of "Strangers in the Night," plus "Tenderly" and the extremely happy "Magic Trumpet (Happy Trumpeter)."

what to buy next: Just in time for Halloween 1997, two of Kaempfert's Christmas albums, *Christmas Wonderland* ♫♫ (Decca/Taragon, 1997) and *That Happy Feeling* ♫♫ (Decca/Taragon, 1997), reappeared to compete with the 9 million other holiday-music collections for consumer stocking space.

worth searching for: Aside from used-record stores, which tend to carry more out-of-print Kaempfert LPs than they'd like to admit, the only place to find the orchestra leader's original

albums is on German import: *Easy Loungin'* 🎵🎵 (Polydor, 1997) is as good a place to start as any. Oh, and the much easier to find Beatles set, *Anthology 1* 🎵🎵🎵🎵 (Capitol, 1995, prod. George Martin) reproduces three famous songs from the Sheridan-Kaempfert Hamburg sessions, including "My Bonnie Lies Over the Ocean." But that's not really the primary reason for buying *Anthology*.

influences:

◀◀ Ray Conniff, Percy Faith, Mantovani, Cole Porter, Irving Berlin

▶▶ The Beatles, Al Martino, Frank Sinatra

Steve Knopper

Michael Kamen

Born 1948, in New York City, NY.

There's very little Kamen hasn't done in his expansive, largely behind-the-scenes, three-decade career. After attending New York's High School for the Performing Arts as well as Julliard, he went on in the '60s to distinguish himself as the lead singer and oboist for the New York Rock and Roll Ensemble. He has won numerous awards and honors, composed works for the opera and ballet as well as film and television, penned songs for everyone from Eric Clapton to the Eurhythmics, and worked out arrangements for rock behemoths like Pink Floyd and Aerosmith. But it's his instrumental works in the world of film scoring that admits him into the moody world of lounge—from the dreamy romanticism of *Don Juan De Marco* to the wacked out shenanigans of *The Adventures of Baron Munchausen* and the chilling future depicted in Terry Gilliam's *Brazil*. Unfortunately, the success of soundtrack recordings is inextricably tied to the success of the films that initiate them, and many of Kamen's scores are no longer in print.

what to buy: For Gilliam's bleakly whimsical vision of the future, *Brazil* 🎵🎵🎵🎵 (Original Soundtrack) (Milan/BMG, 1985, prod. Michael Kamen, Ian P. Hierons), Kamen combines the dreamy and the dark. The wry contrast between the relentlessly upbeat Brazilian samba motifs, light-hearted retro-pop, and tongue-in-cheek surrealism with the black satire of the film is ingenious, further driving home Gilliam's biting commentaries. For *Don Juan De Marco* 🎵🎵🎵🎵 (Original Soundtrack) (A&M, 1995, prod. Michael Kamen, Stephen McLaughlin,

Christopher Brooks), incredibly, rock singer Bryan Adams pulls off a demi-Latin twist on the single that opens the soundtrack, "Have You Ever Really Loved a Woman?"—though it has more to do with the sweetly shuffling rhythms and Paco de Lucia's guitar work. *Highlander: The Original Scores* 🎵🎵🎵🎵 (Edeltone, 1985, prod. Michael Kamen) combines the first and best of the *Highlander* films with scores from the two subsequent movies. In addition to Kamen's suitably dramatic compositions, this includes "Who Wants to Live Forever," a surprisingly poignant writing collaboration between Kamen and the British rock group Queen. *The Dead Zone* 🎵🎵🎵🎵 (Original Soundtrack) (Milan/BMG, 1983, prod. Michael Kamen) was Kamen's first big venture in scoring film after much success writing and arranging for big rock outfits. He was in fact working with Pink Floyd when this project came up—which might explain why the bleak brooding came so naturally. As compared with some of his subsequent work, and considering the movie is based on a Stephen King novel, the music is surprisingly understated.

what to buy next: For *The Three Musketeers* 🎵🎵🎵🎵 (Original Soundtrack) (Hollywood, 1993, prod. Michael Kamen, Stephen McLaughlin, Christopher Brooks), Bryan Adams, Sting, and Rod Stewart join forces for the big rock ballad opener, "All for Love," then the score settles into a big sweeping quasi-medieval orchestral affair that's alternately brooding and triumphant. *Jack* 🎵🎵🎵🎵 (Original Soundtrack) (Hollywood, 1996, prod. Michael Kamen, Stephen McLaughlin), opening with a saucy conga excursion, manages to capture all the ups and downs of childhood—from whimsical interludes to manic outbursts and delicate melancholy.

the rest:

Die Hard with a Vengeance 🎵🎵🎵 (Original Soundtrack) (RCA Victor, 1995)

Circle of Friends 🎵🎵🎵 (Original Soundtrack) (Warner Bros., 1995)

worth searching for: *Die Hard 2: Die Harder* 🎵🎵🎵 (Original Soundtrack) (Varese Sarabande/MCA, 1990, prod. Michael Kamen, Stephen P. McLaughlin, Christopher Brooks) seethes with anxious energy, ominous dissonance, and panicky outbursts. Rather than opening with a Big Rock Number, it closes with an excerpt of Sibelius's "Finlandia."

influences:

◀◀ Maurice Jarre, Ennio Morricone, Hugo Montenegro, Lalo Schifrin

▶▶ Danny Elfman

Bert Kaempfert (Archive Photos)

Sandy Masuo

Doris Kappelhoff

See: Doris Day

Mickey Katz

Born 1910. Died April 30, 1985, in Los Angeles, CA.

There was a time not too long ago when Katz was probably best known as the father of actor Joel Grey. But all that changed in 1993, when jazz clarinetist Don Byron recorded a whole album of his Yiddish musical parodies to great critical acclaim. Now, hipsters and blue-haired Catskills dwellers alike regard Katz as one of the great ethno-musical pranksters. Katz apprenticed as a clarinetist for the beloved parodist Spike Jones's band, the City Slickers, before branching out on his own in 1947. For Katz, nothing was sacred or off limits: he assayed everything from bossa-nova to straight-up jazz, wedding music, and classical standards, singing everything in a mutant Yiddish patois spiked with humorous wordplay. Like Jones, Katz was fond of nutty sound effects: Haim Afen Range ("Home on the Range") features horse whinnies, pig snorts, and other amusing noise-making. He was a big hit on the borscht-belt circuit for much of the '50s, then faded into obscurity until Byron resurrected him with his album, *Don Byron Plays the Music of Mickey Katz*.

what's available: Unfortunately, the Byron record and *Simcha Time: Mickey Katz Plays Music for Weddings, Bar Mitzvahs, and Brisses* ♪♪♪♪ (World Pacific/Capitol, 1994) are all that's currently in print at the moment. *Don Byron Plays the Music of Mickey Katz* ♪♪♪♪ (Elektra/Nonesuch, 1993, prod. Hans Wendl) is a wonderful, and surprisingly faithful, tribute to the master.

influences:

◄◄ Eddie Fisher, Al Jolson, Spike Jones

►► Jerry Lewis, Don Byron, Joel Grey, "Weird Al" Yankovic, Bob Rivers, Eddie Cantor

Marc Weingarten

Sammy Kaye

Born March 13, 1910, in Rocky River, OH. Died June 2, 1987, in Ridgeway, NJ.

"Swing and sway with Sammy Kaye" was this bandleader's famous tag-line, and while he didn't swing particularly hard, his popular "sweet" band racked up nearly 100 chart records between 1937 and 1953. In addition to writing and arranging tunes for his own band, Kaye was a respected songwriter who penned hits for Perry Como ("A—You're Adorable") and Nat King Cole ("My Sugar Is So Refined," "Too Young"), among oth-

ers. Unique among bandleaders, Kaye didn't serve an apprenticeship with any other band—he made a name for himself leading an orchestra at Ohio University, and simply turned pro after graduation. After successful stints on Cincinnati and Pittsburgh radio, Kay and his orchestra hit the big time with a series of network radio programs such as *The Old Gold Cigarette Program*, *The Chesterfield Supper Club*, and *So You Want to Lead a Band*. For the latter, Kaye offered fans the opportunity to come on stage, lead his band, and win a band baton, an immensely successful gimmick. This potent exposure resulted in such major hit records as "Until Tomorrow," "Remember Pearl Harbor," "Wanderin'," "Rosalie," and many others. Among Kaye's many vocalists, Tommy Ryan and Don Cornell were able to establish an especially large fan base, and their mellow crooning was responsible for a large portion of Kaye's success. Most of the big bands died out in the '50s, yet Kaye was able to keep his orchestra's sweet, reed-heavy style popular throughout the decade via his TV version of *So You Want to Lead a Band* and his later show, *The Manhattan Shirt Program*. The 1964 instrumental "Charade" was Kaye's final Top 40 hit. Afterwards, Kaye cut an LP of brassy Dixieland, which drew positive reviews but few sales, and he began slowly phasing himself out of the business. In 1986, he handed the baton over to Roger Thorpe, who toured with a new lineup of the Sammy Kaye Orchestra, though Kaye maintained creative and quality control until his death.

what's available: Kaye's run of hits at Columbia is compiled on *Sammy Kaye: Best of the Big Bands* ♪♪♪♪ (Columbia, 1990, compilation prod. Nedra Neal) and features the #1 hits "Daddy," "Tennessee Waltz," and "Harbor Lights." Also, taken from live radio transcriptions, *Sammy Kaye & His Orchestra: 22 Original Big Band Recordings, 1941–44* ♪♪ (Hindsight, 1987/1993, prod. Wally Heider) has thin sound but is a nice piece of history.

worth searching for: The out-of-print *Sammy Kaye* ♪♪♪♪ (RCA Special Products, 1993) and *Best of Sammy Kaye* ♪♪♪♪ (MCA Jazz, 1974) cover Kaye's big hits and finest moments from his era with those respective labels.

influences:

◄◄ Isham Jones, Guy Lombardo, Kay Kyser

►► Eddy Howard, Roger Thorpe, Ralph Flanagan

Ken Burke

Gene Kelly

Born Eugene Curran Kelly, August 23, 1912, in Pittsburgh, PA. Died February 12, 1996.

Kelly is justly regarded as an innovative choreographer and remarkably athletic dancer in classic Hollywood musicals, but he was no slouch as a singer either. His warm, foggy tone and mastery of phrasing (dig the barely suppressed glee in the last line of "Singin' in the Rain") brought a unique personal interpretation to material written by Rodgers and Hart, Jerome Kern, and George and Ira Gershwin, among others. Unlike Fred Astaire (who cut a few jazz LPs outside of his movie soundtracks), Kelly reserved his singing exclusively for the silver screen. As a result, he doesn't have much of a discography, but what exists is choice stuff indeed.

Kelly ran a dance studio and was a gymnastics instructor before he became a star in such Broadway musicals as *Pal Joey* and *Best Foot Forward*. In the course of his early Hollywood career, Kelly dueted with Judy Garland in *For Me & My Gal,* romanced Rita Hayworth in *Cover Girl,* danced with both a cartoon mouse and Frank Sinatra (with whom he more than held his own vocally) in *Anchors Aweigh,* and feuded comically with Astaire in *Ziegfeld Follies.* For his later movies, Kelly pushed for greater artistic vision and control and achieved spectacular results. His directorial debut (with Stanley Donen) in *On the Town* made for big box-office results, and Kelly's work in Vincent Minelli's *An American in Paris* earned him a special Academy Award for his work as a choreographer, actor, and singer. Kelly co-directed his best-loved film, 1952's *Singing in the Rain,* wherein he transforms a throwaway tune from a Mickey Rooney/Judy Garland B-picture into the most memorable song and dance routine in cinematic history. Kelly directed, choreographed, produced, and starred in several more pictures until the public's interest in big-budget musicals waned, and he began to carve out a career as a respected character actor. Eventually he turned to directing, taking on such projects as the Broadway musical *Flower Drum Song* and the screen version of *Hello Dolly,* which made Barbra Streisand a star. After the nostalgic clip-fests of the *That's Entertainment* movies reignited interest in his career, Kelly appeared in his final film, the awful *Xanadu,* where his effortless grace and charm routinely overshadowed star Olivia Newton-John.

what's available: "Singin' in the Rain," "I Got Rhythm," "For Me and My Gal," "You Wonderful You," and Gershwin's "'S Wonderful" are all on *Gene Kelly at MGM: 'S Wonderful* 𝄞𝄞𝄞𝄞 (Turner Classic Movies Music, 1996, compilation prod. George Feltenstein, Bradley Flanagan), an 18-song compilation with star power to burn. Judy Garland, Debbie Reynolds, Donald O'Connor, Mitzi Gaynor, and Fred Astaire duet with Kelly on a string of amazing and memorable melodies. The only thing missing is the dance steps.

influences:

◀◀ Fred Astaire, George Murphy

▶▶ Donald O'Connor, Mel Tormé, Michael Crawford

Ken Burke

Stan Kenton

Born Stanley Newcomb Kenton, December 15, 1911, in Wichita, KS. Died August 25, 1979, in Los Angeles, CA.

Kenton, a master arranger who never seemed satisfied with the status quo of big-band jazz music, turned more heads in the 1940s and 1950s with his self-proclaimed "progressive" approach to big bands. Armed with huge orchestras—he sometimes had 50 or more musicians in the studio—he set about creating new, more symphonic approaches to jazz standards, experimenting with multiple voicings and complex harmonies. Kenton started out playing piano and writing arrangements for dance bands in the 1930s, including Benny Goodman's. In 1941 he formed the Artistry in Rhythm Orchestra (he was already into congratulatory band names) and eventually employed some serious soloists such as Stan Getz, Conte Candoli, Maynard Ferguson, and Anita O'Day. In 1949, he toured with a group called the Innovations in Modern Music Orchestra.

what to buy: One album, *The Ballad Style of Stan Kenton* 𝄞𝄞𝄞𝄞 (Capitol, 1958, prod. Lee Gillette), is perhaps a good start for lounge-music fans looking to dip their toes into Kenton's strange world. But *The Kenton Era* 𝄞𝄞𝄞𝄞 (Creative World, 1941–1955) is a four-record collection that is also likely to satisfy newcomers to Kenton's music. Remember that, for some, Kenton is an acquired taste. And even those intrigued by his lush, symphonic sounds are likely to find him bordering on easy listening.

what to buy next: *Artistry in Bossa Nova* 𝄞𝄞𝄞 (Creative World, 1963) isn't quite as successful as Stan Getz in bringing the Brazilian music to the surface, but somehow the rhythms seem to fit Kenton's style naturally. It's worth a listen, especially for those who are already familiar with Kenton's more mainstream big-band orchestrations.

what to avoid: On *Kenton/Wagner* 𝄞𝄞 (Creative World, 1964), Kenton offers his take on classical composer Richard Wagner, recording some of Wagner's well-known compositions. Don't bother getting near this one. *Stan Kenton and His Innovations Orchestra* 𝄞𝄞 (Laserlight, 1992) is one of Kenton's most daring recordings in which he plays liberally with time signatures, rhythms, and harmonies. The process results in an interesting sound, but probably nothing you want to listen to for long.

best of the rest:
Jazz Compositions of Stan Kenton ♪♪♪ (Creative World, 1956/1973)
Retrospective ♪♪♪ (Blue Note, 1992)

worth searching for: *Kenton Showcase* ♪♪♪ (Creative World, 1953) demonstrates Kenton's ability to develop talent, even if his orchestrations were too strange for some listeners. Trumpeters Conte Candoli (a regular from Johnny Carson's *Tonight Show* band) and Maynard Ferguson sit in the horn section.

influences:
◀◀ Duke Ellington, Woody Herman, Count Basie
▶▶ Marty Paich, Buddy Rich, Doc Severinsen

Carl Quintanilla

Jerome Kern

Born January 27, 1885, in New York, NY. Died November 11, 1945, in New York, NY.

Put simply, the modern American musical wouldn't exist without Kern, who helped the form evolve away from its European roots and introduced more contemporary sounds onto the New York stage. Kern's first efforts came in 1914, when he helped write songs for an American staging of the British musical *The Girl from Utah*. After collaborating with author P.G. Wodehouse on a series of theatricals, Kern came into his own with *Show Boat* (1927), which marked the beginning of the modern musical. Songs from that show include "Ol' Man River," which was a hit for Paul Robeson the following year. Kern went on to write many of the most famous songs in Broadway history, and died during the writing of *Annie Get Your Gun* in 1945. His career is synonymous with the development of Broadway.

what to buy: *The Complete Jerome Kern Songbooks* ♪♪♪♪ (PolyGram, 1997) isn't really complete—Kern contributed to almost 40 shows, and there are only four dozen songs on this three-CD set. Still, there are classic performances of "Smoke Gets in Your Eyes" (by Billy Eckstine), "I Won't Dance" (Blossom Dearie), "All the Things You Are" (Ella Fitzgerald), "The Way You Look Tonight" (Roy Eldridge), "Pick Yourself Up" (Anita O'Day), and "The Song Is You" (Bing Crosby), and that's only the beginning.

what to buy next: *American Legends: Vol. 15* ♪♪♪ (Laserlight, 1996) suffers from some poor-quality selections, but still gives a good overview of Kern's career.

Stan Kenton **(Archive Photos)**

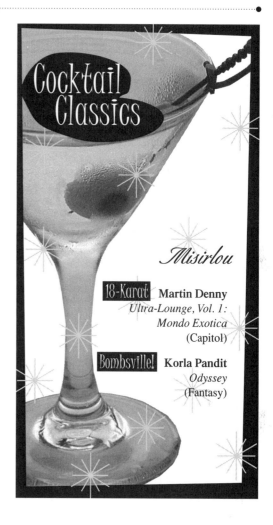

Cocktail Classics

Misirlou

18-Karat **Martin Denny**
*Ultra-Lounge, Vol. 1:
Mondo Exotica*
(Capitol)

Bombsville! **Korla Pandit**
Odyssey
(Fantasy)

worth searching for: Jazz vocalists like Paul Jouard, J. Lawrence Cook, and Dick Watson play Kern on *Classic Movie and Broadway Shows* ♪♪♪ (Biograph, 1996, prod. Arnold S. Caplin).

influences:
◀◀ Gilbert and Sullivan, Irving Berlin
▶▶ Johnny Mercer, Frank Sinatra, Bing Crosby

Ben Greenman

Gershon Kingsley

See: Perrey & Kingsley

Eartha Kitt

Born January 26, 1928, in Columbia, SC.

A controversial figure through the late '60s and early '70s because of her outspoken opposition to the Vietnam war, Kitt was also an extremely sensual performer with a distinctive singing style best described as a monotone growl. In other words, she accomplished a lot more than playing Catwoman on *Batman*. When she was eight, her family gave up farming and moved to Harlem, and Kitt went on to study dance at New York's High School for the Performing Arts. Next, she performed with Katherine Dunham's dance troupe, and she discovered her love for singing when she was touring Europe. She stayed in Paris in 1950 and launched a career as a cabaret chanteuse, eventually moving into acting as well. She remains an active (and sultry) force even in her 70s.

what to buy: Compared to the five-disc import *Eartha Quake*, a more sane, available, and reasonably priced collection is *Miss Kitt, to You* 🎵🎵🎵 (RCA, 1992, prod. various), which rounds up signature tracks such as "Je Cherche un Homme," "Just an Old Fashioned Girl," "C'est Si Bon," and "Monotonous." (It's anything but.) There's also *Best of Eartha Kitt* 🎵🎵🎵 (MCA, 1983, prod. various) for a quick career overview.

what to buy next: For a taste of live Eartha, try *In Person at the Plaza—Eartha Kitt* 🎵🎵🎵 (GNP/Crescendo, 1986, prod. Wally Heider). And to sample Kitt of a more recent vintage, there's *Back to Business* 🎵🎵🎵 (DRG, 1994, prod. Hugh Fordin).

what to avoid: *Thinking Jazz* 🎵🎵 (ITM, 1990) finds Kitt doing exactly that. It wasn't her best genre.

worth searching for: The holy grail for Kitt fanatics is the import *Eartha Quake* 🎵🎵🎵🎵 (Bear Family, 1993, prod. various), a five-CD box set compiling her RCA and KAPP recordings from 1950 to 1960. It comes with a 40-page booklet of notes and photos.

influences:

◀◀ Josephine Baker, Billie Holiday

▶▶ Dionne Farris, Me'Shell Ndegeocello, Salt-N-Pepa

Jim DeRogatis

Gladys Knight & the Pips

Formed 1952, in Atlanta, GA.

Gladys Knight (born May 28, 1944, in Atlanta, GA), lead vocals; Merald "Bubba" Knight, vocals; William Guest, vocals; Brenda Knight, vocals (1952–59); Eleanor Guest, vocals (1952–59); Langston George, vocals (1959–62); Edward Patten, vocals (1959–present).

Unlike other soul singers of her generation, such as Marvin Gaye and Aretha Franklin, Knight and her Pips were quick to embrace polished easy-listening pop music and aim for the middle-of-the-road radio audience. Knight began her performing career as a child when she, her brother Merald, and two cousins formed a youth gospel quartet that would become the standard bearer for modern R&B; she and the Pips inspired many of the singing groups that became popular in the 1950s, 1960s, and 1970s, yet they never reached the full superstardom they deserved. At age seven, Gladys won the grand prize on *Ted Mack's Original Amateur Hour*, and many other television appearances followed. Her solo success sparked the formation of Gladys Knight & the Pips in 1957; their first gig was at a birthday party for Merald, after which they began to tour and record. They finally scored their first Top 20 hit in 1961 with the Johnny Otis tune "Every Beat of My Heart," but the group faded in the 1960s when Gladys had a child. Signing with Motown Records later in the decade jump-started their career with a string of hits, but Motown never fully appreciated the act's potential. Gladys Knight and the Pips proved their star value as soon as they left Motown and signed with Buddah, where they landed their biggest hit in 1973, "Midnight Train to Georgia." They followed that success with many others, as Motown continued to release albums under their name without paying them royalties. Subsequent lawsuits kept Gladys from recording for three years, though the group continued to perform live. But the entanglements stalled their momentum and caused the group's popularity to decline. During this period, Gladys recorded a solo album and appeared in a movie and on television. She and the Pips reunited in 1980 and made a resurgence with many more hits, earning a Grammy for "Love Overboard" in 1988. The group officially "suspended" after Gladys released a solo LP in 1991; she went on to record many best-selling singles on her own, such as "It's Gonna Take All Our Love," "License to Kill," (from the James Bond film), and "Men." In 1986, she won a Grammy with Elton John, Dionne Warwick, and Stevie Wonder for the AIDS-benefit record "That's What Friends Are For."

what to buy: Though they had been performing together for more than a decade when they signed with Motown, *All the*

Eartha Kitt **(AP/Wide World Photos)**

Great Hits ♫♫♫♫ (PGD/Motown, 1974, prod. various) affirms that Gladys Knight and the Pips really came into their own when they began to work with the label. Aided by producer Norman Whitfield, the group created classics in the distinctive Detroit/Motown groove, including "Everybody Needs Love," "I Heard It through the Grapevine," "Friendship Train," and, later, "If I Were Your Woman" and "Neither One of Us (Wants to Be the First to Say Goodbye)."

what to buy next: The first album they recorded after leaving Motown, *Imagination* ♫♫♫♫ (Buddah, 1974/The Right Stuff, 1997) captures a group rejuvenated by its newfound status as a label's showcase attraction. Even though they rushed this LP to the streets, Knight sounds exhilarated and celebratory, singing with depth and emotion. Many say this is the group's finest album.

what to avoid: Though more musicians, singers, and engineers worked on this album than on a Hollywood movie soundtrack, *All Our Love* ♫♫ (MCA Special Products, 1988) is a random collection of trendy, vacuous saccharine. Knight's voice displays her chameleon-like versatility, but there is no passion, no intensity here.

the rest:
That Special Time of Year ♫♫♫ (Sony, 1971)
Best of: Columbia Years ♫♫♫ (Sony, 1974)
I Feel a Song ♫♫♫♫ (Buddah, 1975/The Right Stuff, 1997)
The One & Only/Miss Gladys Knight ♫♫♫ (Sequel, 1978/1994)
Touch ♫♫♫♫ (Sony, 1981/1993)
Christmas Album ♫♫♫ (Special Music, 1989)
Soul Survivors: The Best of Gladys Knight & the Pips, 1973–1983 ♫♫♫♫ (Rhino, 1990)
Greatest Hits ♫♫♫♫ (Curb/Warner Bros., 1990)
Room in Your Heart ♫♫ (Drive Archive, 1994)
The Best of Gladys Knight & the Pips: Anthology ♫♫♫♫ (Motown, 1995)
Blue Lights in the Basement ♫♫♫ (RCA, 1996)
The Lost Live Album ♫♫♫♫ (Buddah, 1996)
The Ultimate Collection ♫♫♫♫ (Motown, 1997)

worth searching for: Rereleased under an obscure label made specially for those preoccupied by the past, *Letter Full of Tears/Golden Classics* ♫♫♫ (Collectables, 1961) is an album of unique perspective. It's a collection of Gladys and Pips pre-Motown material recorded in the early 1960s for the Fury label. And, though currently out of print, *Neither One of Us* ♫♫♫♫ (Motown, 1973) is the last of the Motown recordings for Gladys Knight and the Pips, at the peak of their skills as recording artists. The LP is a testament to the reason the act left Motown: the Pips were never properly promoted by the company, and proved as much to the world as soon as they left.

solo outings:
Gladys Knight:
Good Woman ♫♫♫♫ (MCA, 1991)
Just for You ♫♫♫ (MCA, 1994)

influences:

◄◄ The Platters, the Flamingos, Dinah Washington, Mary Wells, Sam Cooke, Jackie Wilson, Van McCoy

►► Dionne Warwick, Betty Wright, Anita Baker, Deniece Williams, Toni Braxton, Cornelius Brothers & Sister Rose, Brand New Heavies

Chris Tower

Andre Kostelanetz

Born December 23, 1901, in St. Petersburg, Russia. Died January 13, 1980, in Port-au-Prince, Haiti.

Just as radio was emerging as a powerful medium that could touch millions of people, this transplanted Russian conductor and pianist was building huge orchestras and teaching them to play catchy, light versions of classical pieces. Like Victor Herbert before him and Mantovani afterwards, Kostelanetz made this formula a major commercial success, transforming Tchaikovsky's Fifth Symphony into a melodramatic 1939 singalong called "Moon Love" and, later, converting classic opera pieces into easy-listening instrumentals.

Early in life, in his Russian homeland, the young pianist studied at the St. Petersburg Academy of Music and quickly became the Petrograd Grand Opera's assistant conductor. In 1922, his family emigrated to America, where Kostelanetz found opportunity at New York City's Metropolitan Opera and, later, as an orchestra conductor on CBS radio. His "light music" didn't take long to catch on with mass radio audiences—"Moon Love" was everywhere, well into the 1930s, and the similar-sounding "On the Isle of May" helped him sell more than 52 million records overall. Kostelanetz, who guest-conducted the New York Philharmonic for years, also provided backup music for crooner Perry Como and opera singer Lily Pons (whom Kostelanetz married and later divorced). Though he wasn't a particularly prolific composer, Kostelanetz was an easy-listening superstar long before Ray Conniff, Percy Faith, and Mantovani parlayed the style into an established radio format. When he died, according to Joseph Lanza's book, *Elevator Music,* President Jimmy Carter eulogized his style as a "great music hall with the roof lifted off."

what to buy: Perhaps because he was established so long before rock 'n' roll rebelled against symphonic easy-listening songs,

Diana Krall **(© Jack Vartoogian)**

Kostelanetz's impossibly smooth, catchy music escaped significant backlash. But despite his talent, it's tough not to fall asleep—or perhaps that's the point—while his most comprehensive CD collection, *16 Most Requested Songs* ♫♫ (Sony, 1972/1986, compilation prod. Mike Berniker), is playing. This was instant Muzak, stuff you'd hear in 1970s elevators and supermarkets before Bryan Adams and Rod Stewart started their adult-contemporary dominance, and even a version of the Beatles' "Yesterday" can't spread Fab Four liveliness to "My Favourite Things," "Theme from *Love Story*," or "You Do Something to Me."

what to buy next: Kostelanetz had a soft spot for show tunes, and he does a decent job paying homage to the great musical writer on *Columbia Album of Richard Rodgers* ♫♫ (Sony Special Products, 1991), which contains "Oklahoma!" and "Some Enchanted Evening."

what to avoid: We recommend closer attention to Kostelanetz's earlier pop-classical hit material than his various "without words"

takes on operatic standards, such as *Carmen without Words* ♫♫ (Sony, 1991) and *Opera without Words* ♫♫ (Sony, 1989).

best of the rest:
Stars & Stripes Forever ♫♫ (Sony, 1989)
Moon River ♫♫ (Sony Special Products, 1996)
Beloved Classics ♫♫ (Sony Special Products, 1996)

influences:
◄◄ Tchaikovsky, Victor Herbert

►► Mantovani, Morton Gould, Percy Faith, Ray Conniff, Arthur Fiedler, Leroy Anderson

Steve Knopper

Diana Krall

Born November 16, 1964, in Nanaimo, British Columbia, Canada.

Unlike her Candian contemporary Holly Cole, Krall stems from a rich tradition of female pianist-singers. Her heroes include

Shirley Horn, Dinah Washington, and Carmen McCrae, and through four albums she's positioned herself as something of a pure heir to that long-missing artistry. Her work reveals none of the pretentious precociousness and muddled ambition that a Harry Connick Jr. promotes as evidence of his august influences.

Krall was a student at Boston's prestigious Berklee College of Music and a pupil of noted pianist Jimmy Rowles, and her adept, if not virtuosic, playing is as integral to her sound as her smoky, often sultry voice. Playing in a trio format (and, like her idol, Nat King Cole, without drums), Krall most often uses standards like "All or Nothing at All," "They Can't Take That Away from Me," and "Is You Is or Is You Ain't My Baby," as well as more obscure numbers like "Frim Fram Sauce," to open up and explore the interplay between the four instruments—her voice and piano, guitar, and bass. Krall, a Grammy nominee and rising club favorite, is skilled at nuanced delivery.

what to buy: Krall's most recent efforts, *Love Scenes* ⅊⅊⅊⅊ (Impulse!/GRP, 1997, prod. Tommy LiPuma) and *All for You: A Dedication to the Nat King Cole Trio* ⅊⅊⅊⅊ (Impulse!/GRP, 1996, prod. Tommy LiPuma), show the young performer at the top of her game, with her phrasing equaling her spirited, though conservative, arrangements. Throw in some expert work from guitarist Russell Malone and bassist supreme Christian McBride, and the result is remarkably cool.

what to buy next: On Krall's first two releases, *Stepping Out* ⅊⅊⅊ (Justin Time, 1993/Impulse!, 1998, prod. Jim West) and *Only Trust Your Heart* ⅊⅊⅊ (GRP, 1995, prod. Tommy LiPuma), she hasn't quite found her footing on either of her instruments, and some of the flourishes (fiddle, for instance, on a version of "Do Nothin' Till You Hear from Me") don't always make much sense. But anyone fool enough to attempt "I've Got the World on a String" on her sophomore effort has the right amount of chutzpah to make at least half the tracks cook.

influences:

◀◀ Carmen McRae, Nat "King" Cole, Shirley Horn, Dinah Washington

▶▶ Holly Cole, Harry Connick Jr., Diane Schuur

Ben Wener

Gene Krupa

Born January 15, 1909, in Chicago, IL. Died October 16, 1973, in Yonkers, NY.

Gene Krupa transformed the drums from a mere time-keeping device into a full-fledged solo instrument. Whether he played jivey and fast with wire brushes or pounded the toms with heavy hands and sticks, Krupa was the most exciting and energetic drummer of his day.

At age 16 Krupa helped establish the Chicago style of jazz with the Frivolians and Eddie Condon's Austin High School Gang. With the McKenzie/Condon Chicagoans in 1927, Krupa became the first musician to use a full drum kit in a recording studio. A popular session man, Krupa also played in bands fronted by Russ Columbo, Buddy Rogers, and Red Nichols, before joining Benny Goodman's orchestra in 1934. The King of Swing made the most of Krupa's extroverted, highly visual style, and before long Goodman's orchestra was not only perceived as the best, but the most popular as well. Krupa's pneumatic drum solo on the classic "Sing, Sing, Sing" created a popular sensation, and his spotlight-stealing performance at Goodman's 1938 Carnegie Hall concert made him a household name. Krupa split with Goodman and formed his own band in 1938. Hits like "Wire Brush Stomp," "Drummin' Man," and "Drum Boogie" propelled the handsome drummer's individual popularity to even greater heights, and led to appearances in more than a dozen Hollywood movies. Krupa's band (featuring Roy Eldridge and Anita O'Day, among others) peaked in the early '40s with hits such as "Bolero at the Savoy," "Let Me Off Uptown," "After You've Gone," "Rockin' Chair," and "Thanks for the Boogie Ride," but it all came crashing down in 1943. After a drug bust and the resultant waves of bad publicity, Krupa disbanded his orchestra. Once cleared of the charges, he publicly rehabilitated himself in stints with Goodman and Tommy Dorsey. Krupa started another band in 1944, one which allowed the bebop arrangements of Gerry Mulligan to permeate swing-band aesthetics (an artistic and commercial risk at the time). Krupa backed a few more hit records and kept various lineups of his orchestra going until 1951. By then, the big bands were dying, and Buddy Rich's superior technical skill eclipsed Krupa's in the minds of fans. Always a workhorse, Krupa continued recording LPs with trios and quartets throughout the '50s, and was a featured star of Norman Granz's "Jazz at the Philharmonic" tours. Interest in his career was revived by the 1959 film *The Gene Krupa Story,* a largely inaccurate biopic and a vehicle for Sal Mineo with Krupa's work on the soundtrack. Krupa recorded with small jazz groups and in big-band reunion settings throughout the '60s and early '70s until his death.

what to buy: Krupa's best orchestra lineup (1941–42) and biggest hits can be found on *Drum Boogie* ⅊⅊⅊⅊ (Legacy, 1993, compilation prod. Michael Brooks). It's an essential introductory collection, with "Drum Boogie," "No Name Jive," "How About That Mess," and "Rum Boogie."

what to buy next: There's more prime Krupa on *Drummer* ♫♫♫ (Pearl 1993, compilation prod. Colin Brown, Tony Watts), a 22-track disc culled from his 1935–41 output and featuring the amazing "Wire Brush Stomp." Also, a good mix of hits and percussion pyrotechnics can be found on *Drummin' Man* ♫♫♫ (Charly, 1989, prod. various), an import collection with "Bolero at the Savoy," "Leave Us Leap," "After You've Gone," and lots more jumpin' jive.

what to avoid: The sound quality is poor on the budget rack perennial *Giants of the Big Band Era* ♫♫ (Pilz, 1992). For a few extra bucks you can get the same tracks with better fidelity elsewhere.

the rest:
Krupa & Rich ♫♫♫ (Verve, 1955/1994)
Drummer Man ♫♫♫ (Verve, 1956/1996)
Compact Jazz ♫♫♫ (Verve 1988/1992)
Compact Jazz ♫♫♫♫ (Verve, 1993)
1946 Live! ♫♫♫ (Jazz Hour, 1994)
Gene Krupa 1935–38 ♫♫♫♫ (Classics, 1994)
Gene Krupa—1938 ♫♫♫♫ (Classics, 1994)
Gene Krupa—1939 ♫♫♫♫ (Classics, 1995)
What's This? 1946, Vol. 1 ♫♫ (Hep, 1995)
Radio Years; 1940 ♫♫♫♫ (Jazz Unlimited, 1995)
Gene Krupa & His Orchestra ♫♫♫♫ (Jazz Hour, 1995)
The Radio Years ♫♫♫♫ (Jazz Hour, 1995)
It's Up to You; 1946, Vol. 2 ♫♫♫ (Hep, 1995)
The Legendary Big Bands ♫♫♫ (Sony Music Special Products, 1995)
Gene Krupa 1939–40 ♫♫♫ (Classics, 1995)
Hollywood Palladium 1/18/45 ♫♫♫♫ (Canby Records, 1995)
Vol. 13—Masterpieces ♫♫ (EPM Musique, 1996)
1940, Vol. 2 ♫♫♫♫ (Classics, 1996)
Volume 3: Hop, Skip, & Jump ♫♫♫ (Hep, 1996)
Leave Us Leap ♫♫♫ (Vintage Jazz Classics, 1996)
Swings with Strings ♫♫ (Vintage Jazz Classics, 1996)
1940 ♫♫♫ (Classics, 1997)

worth searching for: Krupa's sextet delivers some effective hard bop on *Leave Me Off Uptown* ♫♫♫ (Drive Archive, 1996), recorded at three live performances around 1949. Also, for an example of Krupa, Hollywood-style, check out the Gary Cooper-Barbara Stanwyck comedy *Ball of Fire* ♫♫♫♫ (Goldwyn Productions, 1941, director Howard Hawks). Krupa's version of "Drum Boogie" on a matchbox is still a killer-diller.

influences:
◀◀ Roy C. Knapp, Edward B. Straight, Chick Webb
▶▶ Big Sid Catlett, Buddy Rich, Louis Belson, Keith Moon

see also: *Tommy Dorsey, Benny Goodman*

Ken Burke

Cocktail Classics

Mission: Impossible

18-Karat Lalo Schifrin *Music from Mission: Impossible* (Hip-O/MCA)

Bombsville! Billy May *Ultra-Lounge, Vol. 7: The Crime Scene* (Capitol)

Kay Kyser

Born James King Kern Kyser, June 18, 1906, in Rocky Mount, NC. Died July 23, 1985, in Chapel Hill, NC.

Dressed in professorial attire and addressing his faithful listeners as "students," Kyser's use of southern-fried hep-talk and singing song titles helped him stand out in an era of colorful musical figures. Kyser, who could neither write nor read music, formed his first band in the mid-'20s, shifting to jazz later in the decade. Sensing a shift in popular music, Kyser adopted the "sweet" band style, and began prominently featuring a series of vocal groups and singers on a variety of catchy (sometimes gimmicky) pop tunes. His career really took off when NBC Radio hired him to fill a hole in its Monday night lineup. In an attempt to fit as much music as possible into his 15-minute time slot, Kyser developed the technique of having his vocalists sing a song title, with his orchestra vamping while he introduced them. Kyser's radio popularity expanded further when he added a quiz-show format, with audience participation, to his college-themed program, *Kay Kyser's Kampus Klass,* later retitled *Kay Kyser's Kollege of Musical Knowledge.* Recording for Columbia, Kyser and his band notched 20 Top 10 hits, including "(I Got Spurs) That Jingle Jangle Jingle," "Ole Buttermilk Sky," "The Old Lamplighter," "Woody Woodpecker," and their classic "Slow Boat to China." Among the many singers featured in Kyser's band were Hollywood star-in-training Jane Russell, future talk-show host Mike Douglas, and Kyser's wife, Georgia Carroll. Kyser's popularity led to appearances in 10 feature films, with 1939's *That's Right, You're Wrong* based on one of his many catch-phrases. The war years were Kyser's peak, and despite recording bans and shellac shortages, his orchestra sold millions of records. Soldiers especially appreciated his band's playful sound, and Kyser returned the compliment by tirelessly raising money for the war effort and playing free shows for the troops. (During this time, his band hit with "Praise the Lord and Pass the Ammunition.") Despite the post-war big-band decline, Kyser was still popular and had successfully transformed his radio show into an early TV hit, when chronic arthritis forced him to retire.

what to buy: Kyser's biggest hits, "Slow Boat to China," "(I Got Spurs) That Jingle Jangle Jingle," "There Goes That Song Again," "Woody Woodpecker," the perennial sabre-rattler "Praise the Lord and Pass the Ammunition," and many more are on *Kay Kyser: Best of the Big Bands* &&&& (Legacy, 1990, prod. Michael Brooks), an easy-to-find budget disc. Ginny Simms, Georgia Carroll, the Glee Club, the Campus Kids, Gloria Wood, and Mike Douglas do the singing.

what to buy next: There's a generous selection of songs on *Songs of World War II, Vol. 2: I'll Be Seeing You* &&&* (Vintage Jazz Classics, 1993, prod. various), a fine representation of Kyser's radio years featuring guest stars the King Sisters, the Town Criers, and fellow big-bandleader Phil Harris.

what to avoid: Kyser doesn't appear at all on *Kay Kyser's Greatest Hits* &* (Capitol, 1962/1989), which features his original band (fronted by Billy May) rerecording its best-known songs with comedian Stan Freberg imitating the voice of Kyser. It's out of print, but some CDs may still be in stores.

the rest:
Sentimental Favorites &&& (Columbia, 1988)
Kay Kyser's Kollege of Musical Knowledge &&& (Jazz Hour, 1996)
Music Maestro Please &&& (Empire, 1998)

influences:
◀◀ Hal Kemp, Isham Jones, Phil Harris
▶▶ Sammy Kaye, Eddy Howard, Sully Mason, George Duning

Ken Burke

The L.A. Four
See: Laurindo Almeida

Francis Lai
Born 1932, in Nice, France.

No song, with the possible exception of "The Girl from Ipanema," captures the heart and soul of the entire easy-listening genre as effectively as Lai's title tune for Claude Lelouch's 1966 romance *Un Homme et une Femme (A Man and a Woman).* It's hard to describe in writing, but if you listened to the radio in the 1970s, chances are you've heard the tune's maddeningly spacey la-la melody. Its upbeat Brazilian beat gave it staying power: the song has landed in countless movies, television shows (including *The Monkees*), commercials, and the ubiquitous 1970s beautiful-music radio stations. Lai, a versatile keyboardist, started out as a backing pianist for Edith Piaf and a songwriter for Yves Montand; after hooking up with Lelouch for *Un Homme,* his commercial cachet rose considerably. He had several other instrumental hits, including "Today It's You," and a prolific soundtrack-music career in France, England, and the U.S. Among his credits are the even-more-maddening music in *Love Story* and a collaboration with director David Hamilton for *Bilitis.*

what's available: Most of Lai's soundtrack music is compiled on French reissue CDs, but you can find some of them in U.S. record stores: *30 Ans de Musiques de Films 1966–1996* &&&& (Positiva, 1997, prod. various) is a two-disc set with just about everything, and *The Very Best of Francis Lai* &&& (Skyline) collects "Bilitis," "Happy New Year," "Love in the Rain," and other instrumentals guaranteed not to make any listener aggressive. His irresistible classic, "A Man and a Woman (Un Homme et une

Femme)," opens a fun set of cornball instrumental music on *Cocktail Mix, Vol. 4: Soundtracks with a Twist!* ♪♪♪♪ (Rhino, 1996, compilation prod. Janet Grey); the set also includes Herbie Hancock's "Bring Down the Birds" and Quincy Jones's "Happy Feet."

influences:

◀◀ Edith Piaf, Yves Montand, Claude Lelouch, John Barry, Paul Weston, Ennio Morricone, Henry Mancini

▶▶ Michel Legrand, Combustible Edison, Michael Kamen

Steve Knopper

Cleo Laine

Born Clementina Dinah Campbell, October 27, 1928, in Southall, Middlesex, England.

An excellent singer who takes cues from Dinah Washington and Ella Fitzgerald, but smoothes out many of the bluesy edges of their styles, Laine has racked up several huge-selling albums and major Broadway concerts and musicals. She and her husband, longtime producer and collaborator Johnny Dankworth, make music that's technically "pop"—standards, as defined by Frank Sinatra and the Gershwins earlier in this century—but aspires to be much higher than that. Laine frequently performs with philharmonic orchestras, appears at jazz festivals, and occasionally sets Shakespeare sonnets to music. In the early '50s she sang at small British clubs; a musician friend recommended her show to then-bandleader Dankworth, and he fell for both the music and its maker. She joined his band in 1952, married him six years later, and has used him as her producer and creative collaborator ever since. In the late '50s her acting career took off, with roles in *Valmouth,* the Kurt Weill-Bertold Brecht musical *Seven Deadly Sins,* and a London production of the popular *Show Boat.* After several solo singing tours, in 1973 she began a long-term series of concerts (and subsequent hit live recordings) at New York City's Carnegie Hall. She won a 1983 Grammy, earned an honorary doctoral degree from Boston's prestigious Berklee College of Music, and continues to perform and teach with her husband.

what to buy: *A Beautiful Thing* ♪♪♪♪ (RCA Victor, 1994, prod. Mike Berniker, Kurt Gebauer, John Dankworth), recorded in 1974 (and partially in 1993) features flutist James Galway and focuses almost exclusively on standards, such as "Send in the Clowns" and "All in Love Is Fair"; the jazzier *Blue & Sentimental* ♪♪♪♪ (RCA Victor, 1994, prod. Kurt Gebauer, John Dankworth) features saxophonist Gerry Mulligan (a longtime Laine friend

and collaborator) and pianist George Shearing, and snappier numbers such as "Afterglow" and "I've Got a Crush on You."

what to buy next: *The Very Best of Cleo Laine* ♪♪♪ (RCA Victor, 1997, prod. various) collects her biggest hits, including old showtunes like "I Loves You Porgy," big-band classics like Duke Ellington's "Solitude," and interesting but slightly bizarre uptempo numbers like "Creole Love Call." It's an interesting representation of her long career, but not as valuable as her better solo albums.

what to avoid: "Solitude," with a snippet of Ellington's actual piano-playing from 1941 spliced into the new recording, is the centerpiece of Laine's uneven Ellington tribute, *Solitude* ♪♪ (RCA Victor, 1995, prod. Steve Vining), in which she fronts the Duke Ellington Band on his old standards, including "I'm Beginning to See the Light," "Sophisticated Lady," and a Laine bastardization titled "Cleo's 'A' Train."

best of the rest:

I Am a Song ♪♪♪ (RCA Victor, 1973/1994)
Cleo at Carnegie Hall: 10th Anniversary ♪♪♪ (RCA Victor, 1983/1993)
That Old Feeling ♪♪♪ (Sony, 1984)
Cleo Laine Sings Sondheim ♪♪♪ (RCA, 1988)
Woman to Woman ♪♪♪ (RCA, 1989)
Jazz ♪♪♪♪ (RCA Victor, 1991)
Cleo's Choice ♪♪♪ (GNP/Crescendo, 1993)
Live at Carnegie Hall ♪♪♪♪ (RCA Victor, 1993)

worth searching for: Some of Laine's original LPs have been reissued on CD, but her earliest material, on which you can hear her hunger and freshness, are sadly long gone from the market. Among the best is *All About Me* ♪♪♪ (Fontana, 1962).

influences:

◀◀ Johnny Dankworth, Ella Fitzgerald, Dinah Washington, Margaret Whiting, Rosemary Clooney, Carmen McRae

▶▶ Mariah Carey, Celine Dion, Whitney Houston

Steve Knopper

Frankie Laine

Born Francesco Paul LoVecchio, March 30, 1913, in Chicago, IL.

Laine, best known for his definitive whip-cracking version of the *Rawhide* television-show theme, was also one of the most phenomenally successful recording artists of the late 1940s through the mid-1950s. With his soaring baritone, Laine mixed jazz phrasing, gospel-flavored sentiments, show-biz standards, blues and folk rhythms, and Western themes with utter joy and abandon.

He began his career as a marathon dancer (he and Ruthie Smith set a world's record of 3,501 hours) and part-time singer in the 1930s. Although he did chorus work for movies such as *The Harvey Girls* and *The Kid from Brooklyn,* Laine scuffled in clubs for most of his early career; during World War II he made more money working in a defense plant than as a singer and emcee. Laine's early imitation of Nat King Cole, "Maureen," was a big seller on the East Coast, but his small record label couldn't build on its success. A novelty B-side earned radio attention, which led to a Mercury Records contract. Soon a goosed-up version of "That's My Desire" was the record sensation of 1947, and "Shine," among several others, quickly followed it onto the charts. Laine, who prided himself on his 1,000-song repertoire, soon delegated song-selection duties to the label's new A&R man, Mitch Miller. Noting the "universality" in the singer's voice, the famously schmaltzy producer found powerful hit ballads for Laine, such as "Lucky Old Sun." When Miller left Mercury for Columbia in 1951, Laine brought his hitmaking power with him. Though rock 'n' roll diminished his profile considerably, he recorded one last chart smash, 1956's "Moonlight Gambler," and remained a popular LP artist throughout the decade. In 1959, Laine's boisterous version of the *Rawhide* television theme exposed the singer's voice to a large audience every week. Laine left Columbia in 1964 for Capitol, but after two frustrating years with no hits, he departed for ABC. Benefiting from the late-1960s nostalgia movement, Laine began hitting the easy-listening charts with reworked oldies such as "I'll Take Care of Your Cares" and "Making Memories." He left ABC in 1969, recording sporadically for many small labels; in 1987, his collaboration with the Cincinnati Pops orchestra Round-Up, made it to #4 on the classical-album charts. Despite heart problems, Laine still manages to perform one or two special event concerts every month.

what to buy: Laine's first great jazz-tinged pop hits ("That's My Desire," "Shine") and his early Western and folk classics ("Mule Train," "The Cry of the Wild Goose") are packaged neatly on *The Frankie Laine Collection: The Mercury Years* ♫♫♫♫ (Mercury, 1991, compilation prod. Ron Furmanek). The hits keep coming with *16 Most Requested Songs* ♫♫♫♫ (Columbia/Legacy, 1989, compilation prod. Michael Brooks), an inexpensive collection of some of his best-known Columbia sides.

what to buy next: Laine's last volley of hits for ABC makes up *The Very Best of Frankie Laine* ♫♫♫ (Tarragon, 1996, prod. Jimmy Bowen, Bob Thiele, Eliot Goshman), which features tracks such as "Laura, What's He Got That I Ain't Got," "You Gave Me a Mountain," and the cult classic "Dammit Isn't God's Last Name."

what to avoid: Late in his career Laine rerecorded his big hits and mixed them with unlikely modern selections, such as Creedence Clearwater Revival's "Proud Mary" and Bill Anderson's "Po' Folks," on *16 Greatest Hits* ♫♫ (Trip, 1978, prod. various). Stick with the original hit versions.

the rest:
Memories ♫♫♫ (Columbia Special Products, 1985)
Mule Train ♫♫♫♫ (PolyGram Special Products, 1989)
You Gave Me a Mountain ♫♫♥ (MCA Special Products, 1990)
High Noon ♫♫♥ (Charly, 1992)
Best of Frankie Laine ♫♫♥ (Curb, 1993)
The Essence of Frankie Laine ♫♫♫ (Columbia/Legacy, 1993)
The Uncollected Frankie Laine—1947 ♫♫ (Hindsight, 1994)
Duets: Frankie Laine/Jo Stafford ♫♫♫♫ (Bear Family, 1994)
Return of Mr. Rhythm: 1945–1948 ♫♫♥ (Hindsight, 1995)
Greatest Hits ♫♫♥ (Columbia, 1995)
Dynamic ♫♫♥ (ITC Masters, 1996)
Portrait of a Legend ♫♫♥ (After 9, 1997)

worth searching for: Laine's robust vocal style was never put to better use than on *On the Trail* ♫♫♫♫ (Bear Family, 1990, compilation prod. Richard Weize) and *On the Trail Again* ♫♫♫♫ (Bear Family, 1992, compilation prod. Richard Weize), which contain all his great whip-cracking, cowboy-flavored classics, including "High Noon," "Moonlight Gambler," and "Rawhide." Also, one of the undisputed highlights of Laine's career was his wonderfully straight rendition of the title song to Mel Brooks's raunchy Western parody *Blazing Saddles* (1974), which is included on *High Anxiety* ♫♫♫♫ (Asylum, 1978, prod. various), a collection of songs from Brooks's best comedy features. Finally, *Round-Up, with Eric Kunzel and the Cincinnati Pops Orchestra* ♫♫♫♫ (Telarc, 1987, prod. various) is filled with lushly orchestrated Western themes.

influences:
◄◄ Bing Crosby, Louis Armstrong, Al Jolson, Carlo Buti, Nat "King" Cole

►► Anita O'Day, Johnnie Ray, Marty Robbins

Ken Burke

Nancy LaMott

Born December 30, 1951, in Midland, MI. Died December 13, 1995, in New York City, NY.

An excellent singer who died way too young, LaMott bridged the gap between the old generation of smooth-voiced standards crooners and the new generation of vibrato-happy adult-contemporary pop stars. During her short public career, which began in San Francisco and New York nightclubs in the late '70s, and ended with a string of six solid CDs, she sang for President Clinton at the White House twice. An Ella Fitzgerald devotee, LaMott emulated her heroines and usually selected material by the classic pop songwriters—her 1992 album, *Come Rain or Come Shine*, is exclusively made of Johnny Mercer covers. LaMott's voice, unlike more rich contemporaries such as Ann Hampton Callaway, had more of a pop sheen, so she could slip easily into the background of a treacly Kathie Lee Gifford album in the mid-'90s. But overall, she was versatile enough to inject the pain into slow numbers like "The Secret O' Life" and the zip into big-band revival songs like "Have You Got Any Castles, Baby?" LaMott, who suffered from health problems her whole life, succumbed to uterine cancer.

what to buy: Margaret Whiting wasn't the only woman maintaining Johnny Mercer's songs in the late 20th century; LaMott's *Come Rain or Come Shine* 🎵🎵🎵 (Midder Records, 1992, prod. David Friedman) nicely recalls the great songwriter's "That Old Black Magic"; his famous Henry Mancini collaboration, "Moon River"; and the always-relevant "Accentuate the Positive."

what to buy next: *Listen to My Heart* 🎵🎵🎵 (Midder Records, 1995, prod. David Friedman, Peter Matz) stretches LaMott into adult-contemporary music, and she trembles her voice almost to Whitney Houston's extreme. She has much more class, though, telling a nice story in "The Lady Down the Hall" and matching the horns' enthusiasm on the big-band arrangement "Have You Got Any Castles, Baby?"

what to avoid: LaMott hasn't quite found her style on *Beautiful Baby* 🎵🎵 (Midder Records, 1991, prod. David Friedman), with "The Surrey with the Fringe on the Top," "Skylark," "Blue Skies," and other standards. There's really no point to picking this album over one by Ella Fitzgerald.

the rest:
Just in Time for Christmas 🎵🎵🎵 (Midder Records, 1994)
What's Good About Goodbye? 🎵🎵🎵 (Midder Records, 1996)

worth searching for: The only interesting thing about Kathie Lee Gifford's shiny *Dreamship Time* 🎵🎵 (Time Warner Kids, 1995) is listening for LaMott's better-than-the-star background vocals on the children's song "Goodnight, Moon."

influences:
◀◀ Johnny Mercer, Ella Fitzgerald, Rosemary Clooney, Cleo Laine

Cocktail Classics

Moon River

18-Karat Henry Mancini
*Breakfast at Tiffany's
(Soundtrack)*
(RCA)

Bombsville! The Mystic Moods Orchestra
Nighttide
(The Right Stuff)

▶▶ Whitney Houston, Celine Dion, Mariah Carey, Ann Hampton Callaway

Steve Knopper

k.d. lang

Born Kathryn Dawn Lang, November 2, 1961, in Consort, Alberta, Canada.

Can a vegetarian lesbian from north of the border make it in Music City? If lang had stopped to consider the ignorance and intolerance that's out there she might not have left the Great White North. Thankfully, she did leave. lang, who in campy garb

Nancy LaMott (© Jack Vartoogian)

and rhinestone spectacles initially approached crooning countrypolitan tunes as performance art, and who for a time even claimed to be the reincarnation of Patsy Cline (thus, the name of her band, the Reclines), is a singer-songwriter of rare talent and determination who eventually won the war, even if she lost the opening battle.

After her U.S. debut mistakenly cast lang as a Canadian cow-punk, she brought legendary Cline producer Owen Bradley out of retirement for *Shadowland*, a triumphant album that proved lang could take Nashville on its own terms and succeed. After her next album took lang's torch-and-twang sound to its logical conclusion, she progressed to a more expansive pop sound, a move that coincided with lang declaring her lesbianism in *The Advocate* during 1992. (She has had some fun, though, with the notoriety this brought, declaring at some concerts that she is a "L . . . L . . . L . . . Lawrence Welk fan" and cranking up the bubble machine.) Her continuing interest in other types of performance led her to a bold starring role in Percy Aldon's 1991

film *Salmonberries,* and she co-composed and performed the soundtrack to Gus Van Sant's 1993 film *Even Cowgirls Get the Blues.* Her political and social views, notably her 1990 "meat stinks" ads for People for the Ethical Treatment of Animals, often draw more attention than her music, but they're part and parcel of her outspoken personality. And besides, her music continues to speak for itself.

what to buy: On *Absolute Torch and Twang* ♪♪♪♪ (Sire, 1989, prod. Greg Penny, Ben Mink, k.d. lang) lang not only invented the perfect tag for her particular brand of music, she made her best album by internalizing her influences enough to come up with a sound all her own. "Three Days," "Wallflower Waltz," and especially the transcendent "Pullin' Back the Reins" reveal how much she'd learned from her sophisticated crooning on *Shadowland*. Speaking of which, *Shadowland* ♪♪♪♪ (Sire, 1988, prod. Owen Bradley) is the album on which lang realized the full range of her powerful voice, but also how to sing with restraint and nuance. Bradley's careful production returns countrypolitan to its former luster, and the material is first rate, particularly the aching "Western Skies" and the weary, after-hours "Black Coffee." The "Honky Tonk Angel" medley is something of an event, matching lang with three of Bradley's former charges, Loretta Lynn, Kitty Wells, and Brenda Lee.

what to buy next: lang jokingly called *Ingenue* 🎵🎵🎵🎵 (Sire, 1992, prod. Greg Penny, Ben Mink, k.d. lang) her "stalker" album, for it is full of songs about desire and obsession. Despite such onerous implications, the album is a charmer, thanks to her sincerity and passion and the (sorry) lang-orous arrangements of songs such as "Constant Craving," "The Mind of Love," and even the campy "Miss Chatelaine." Switching genres is no small thing. On *Ingenue*, lang moves from country to adult-contemporary pop with admirable elan. *Drag* 🎵🎵🎵🎵 (Warner Bros., 1997, prod. Craig Street, k.d. lang) extends her campy torch-singing identity, with songs exclusively about smoking cigarettes, including Willard Robison's "Don't Smoke in Bed" and Jane Siberry's "Hain't it Funny?"

what to avoid: There's nothing really wrong with lang's U.S. debut, *Angel with a Lariat* 🎵🎵 (Sire, 1987, prod. Dave Edmunds). It's just that lang never really clicks with producer Edmunds, and with the exception of the opening track, "Turn Me Round," nothing ever really takes off. And who needs a remake of Lynn Anderson's hit "Rose Garden?"

the rest:
Music from the Motion Picture Soundtrack: Even Cowgirls Get the Blues 🎵🎵🎵 (Sire/Warner Bros., 1994)
All You Can Eat 🎵🎵🎵 (Warner Bros., 1995)

worth searching for: lang's Canadian debut *a truly western experience* 🎵🎵 (Bumstead, 1984, prod. Jamie Kidd, k.d. lang, Gary Delorme) is an interesting look at lang before she truly hit her stride. The high-stepping "Bopalena" and "Hanky Panky" are standouts.

influences:
◀◀ Patsy Cline, Marshall Chapman, Roy Orbison, Gertrude Stein

▶▶ Shelby Lynne, the Murmurs, Mrs. Fun

Daniel Durchholz

Lester Lanin

Born August 26, 1911, probably in Philadelphia, PA.

Lanin's name is synonymous with "society music"—by his own recollection, he had his orchestras booked at more than 10,000 weddings, 3,000 debutante parties, and 1,500 proms. He followed in the footsteps of his father and grandfather as a bandleader—the youngest of 10 boys, he originally studied to be a criminal attorney, but his father took ill and he assumed one of his commitments. His father told him to be as individual as he could, so Lanin sang the phrasing he wanted to the men in the band. His career ended up spanning four decades, and he eventually performed for the high society element in every major American city—the DuPonts, the Rockefellers, the Fords, the Whitneys, the Vanderbilts, and the Chryslers, as well as members of international royalty. He was most proud of having played at seven presidential inaugural balls; he had 13 White House performances all told.

what to buy: Where other big-bandleaders played by the books, never varying from their routine, Lanin always adapted to the times, adding Dixieland, Latin, and rock music. He didn't even have sheet music up on the bandstand—his orchestras had memorized thousands of songs, and they were always learning new standards. *This Is Society Dance Music* 🎵🎵 (Columbia/Legacy, 1956/1993), a reissue, is a live mono recording made during the Monte Carlo Ball in New York circa 1956.

the rest:
Best of the Big Bands 🎵🎵 (Sony, 1990)
1960–62 🎵🎵 (Hindsight, 1992)

worth searching for: Lanin and his orchestra contributed the song "Christmas Night in Harlem" to the compilation *Big Band Christmas* 🎵🎵 (Sony, 1987), which also features Artie Shaw, Red Norvo, and Les Brown.

influences:
◀◀ Glenn Miller, Tommy Dorsey

▶▶ Frank Sinatra Jr.

G. Brown

James Last

Born Hans Last, April, 17, 1929, in Bremen, Germany.

When Last updated the big-band sound with brass and bass-heavy arrangements of modern popular tunes in the '60s, he revolutionized pop music and paved the way for the disco and dance-mix eras. Last played bass in Hans-Guenther Oesterreich's Radio Bremen Dance Orchestra and led the Becker-Last Ensemble before taking a job as a staff arranger for Polydor Records. After several years or arranging music for radio and German films, Last hit upon the idea of combining big-band arrangements with modern hit songs into edited full-length

party discs and, in 1965, released *Non-Stop Dancing*, an international smash. Dozens of discs with variations on his hit format followed. Last's work is mainly popular in Europe; his sole American hit was 1980's "The Seduction" from the the the film *American Gigolo*. But wherever you hear non-stop bass-heavy music showcasing brief versions of hit tunes with abrupt segues into other hit tunes, you'll recognize Last's influence.

what to buy: Domestically, not much of Last is in print these days, but thankfully his most cohesive and enduring work, *Romantic Dreams* ♫♫♫ (Polydor, 1987, prod. James Last), is still in stores. Last's unique interpretations of "Scarborough Fair," "Amazing Grace," "Yosaku," and many other eclectic selections are included.

the rest:
Classics Up to Date, Vol. 1 ♫♫♫ (Verve, 1973/1987)
Tango ♫♫ (Verve, 1986)
Viva España ♫♫ (PolyGram, 1994)
Andrew Lloyd Webber ♫♫♫ (Polydor, 1997)

worth searching for: Some import shops and catalogs carry *Very Best of James Last* ♫♫♫♫ (Polydor, 1996), a first-rate sampler of the revolutionary party style he championed in his groundbreaking early period. Also, the original *Non-Stop Dancing* ♫♫♫♫ (Polydor, 1965) is a must-have item for fans of this genre and can be found in some used vinyl outlets. For completists, much of Last's influence is felt on *Astrud Gilberto Plus the James Last Orchestra* ♫♫♫ (Verve, 1969), which is still in print.

influences:
◄◄ Glenn Miller, Hans-Gunther Oesterreich

►► Helmut Zacharias, Stars on 45, Hooked on Classics

Ken Burke

Steve Lawrence & Eydie Gorme /Steve & Eydie

Formed c. 1957.

Steve Lawrence (born Sidney Leibowitz, July 8, 1935, in Brooklyn, NY), vocals; Eydie Gorme (born Edith Gormezano, August 16, 1931, in New York, NY), vocals.

As independent artists, Steve & Eydie qualify handily for the Lounge Music Hall of Fame. Together, they are king and queen. Gorme established her membership decisively with her first hit, the jaunty "Blame It on the Bossa Nova," which both captured and galvanized the passion of the day (1963) for the zesty Latin dance (not unlike the '90s song-dance phenomenon "The Macarena"). Lawrence had already scored his own lounge-breaking coup with his first hit, a cerebral little number from 1957 called "The Banana Boat Song." The pair met on *The Tonight Show* with Steve Allen (himself a god of lounge); subsequently, they performed as a couple. Over the years, they've had success both together, with recorded duets and a variety show on TV in 1959, and individually, with Lawrence charting pop hits like "Go Away Little Girl" and "Pretty Blue Eyes," and Gorme later releasing a number of Spanish-language discs with the trio Los Panchos. But the crowning achievement came when they bagged the plum job in the world of entertainment: a long-standing gig as Frank Sinatra's opening act. Nightclubs, Vegas, the strip—it didn't get any better than this. Despite occasional public humiliation—*Saturday Night Live* unveiled a dead-on, almost venomous parody a few years back—the duo continues to be one of Las Vegas's most reliable acts. And they're not above laughing at their own reputation: on *Lounge-A-Palooza*, a strange 1997 Hollywood Records CD of alternative-rock bands paired with old-school lounge singers or songs, Steve & Eydie actually croon Soundgarden's grunge hit "Black Hole Sun."

what to buy: For some reason, Steve & Eydie have reissued very little of their early, out-of-print material; only a few compilations have surfaced. *Best of Steve & Eydie* ♫♫♫♫ (Curb, 1977) is the definitive one, with old-timey songs such as "I'll Be Seeing You in Apple Blossom Time," "Besame Mucho," and "This Could Be the Start of Something New."

what to avoid: Eydie's Spanish-language discs, such as *Canta en Español* ♫♫ (Sony, 1989), are an acquired taste.

worth searching for: *We Got Us/Eydie & Steve Sing Golden Hits* ♫♫♫♫ (Jasmine, 1996), an import available at most chains, combines two out-of-print albums, including 1960's *Golden Hits* (which has also been reissued by MCA Special Products).

solo outings:
Steve Lawrence:
Songs by Steve Lawrence ♫♫♫ (Taragon, 1995)
Very Best of Steve Lawrence ♫♫♫ (Taragon, 1995)

Eydie Gorme:
Eydie Swings the Blues ♫♫♫ (1957/Taragon, 1996)

k.d. lang (© Ken Settle)

Best of Eydie Gorme ♫♫♫ (Curb, 1991)

Eydie Gorme ♫♫♫♫ (ABC/Paramount/Taragon, 1996)

influences:

◀◀ Frank Sinatra, Jonathan and Darlene Edwards, Tony Bennett, Engelbert Humperdinck, Wayne Newton, Soundgarden, Barbra Streisand, Johnny Mathis, Steve Allen

▶▶ Sonny & Cher, Donny & Marie Osmond

Teresa Gubbins

Bernadette Lazzaro

See: Bernadette Peters

Brenda Lee

Born Brenda Mae Tarpley, December 11, 1944, in Lithonia, GA.

Lee was the teen-age queen of pre-Beatles rock 'n' roll. Her expressive vocal style allowed her to joyously rave rockabilly one moment, then croon country heartache the next. In 1956, after creating a sensation on the Red Foley, Perry Como, and Ed Sullivan television shows, the 11-year-old Lee signed with Decca Records. Her first discs, including "Jambalaya" and "Dynamite" (which earned her the nickname "Little Miss Dynamite"), were kick-ass performances but minor chart successes. Lee's career didn't really pick up until she toured Europe, where her manager instigated major waves of publicity by starting a rumor that the diminutive teen was actually a 32-year-old midget. After playing packed houses all over the world, Lee returned to the U.S. and began to assault the pop charts with a vengeance in 1960. Adults marveled at her womanly vibrato and emotional command, while teens dug her for being one of them. Lee was a remarkable vocalist and stage performer, and her ordinary looks and plain dress style inspired more loyalty than jealousy among her female fans. As a result, when the British Invasion groups began to dominate the charts, Lee remained a force on Top 40 radio long after many of her American contemporaries had been relegated to obscurity. Though most of her mid-to-late-'60s output was country-pop in nature, Lee showed some of her old rock verve on "Is It True" (with Jimmy Page on guitar), and the remarkable "Coming on Strong," her final Top 15 hit. After her 1969 single "Johnny One-Time" received more air play on country than pop stations, Lee switched to that genre exclusively. Since the '70s, Lee has maintained a moderately successful solo

Cocktail Classics

My Favorite Things

18-Karat Julie Andrews
The Best of Julie Andrews
(Rhino)

Bombsville! Tennessee Ernie Ford
Capitol Sings Rodgers & Hammerstein
(Capitol)

career, particularly in Europe, where she is rightly acknowledged as one of pop music's greatest all-time performers.

what to buy: All phases of Brenda Lee's career as a hit vocalist, from 1956's "Bigelow 6-2000" to 1974's "Big Four Poster Bed," are included on *Anthology, Volumes 1 & 2* ♫♫♫♫ (MCA, 1991, compilation prod. Andy McKaie), a two-disc, 44-song set. *The Brenda Lee Story* ♫♫♫ (MCA, 1974/1991, prod. Owen Bradley) is a more concise offering with only her biggest hits.

what to buy next: Lee's Christmas perennial "Rockin' Around the Christmas Tree" is on *Jingle Bell Rock* ♫♫♫ (MCA Special Products, 1993, prod. various) along with nine other seasonal

Steve Lawrence and Eydie Gorme **(AP/Wide World Photos)**

favorites. Buy it before you're driven nuts by its constant play on department store easy-listening speakers. Also, there's a good variety of hit tunes and LP tracks on *The EP Collection* 𝄢𝄢 (See For Miles Records, 1995, prod. various), a reasonably priced 25-track disc.

what to avoid: Unless you're proficient in German, French, and Spanish and dig Lee's phonetic rendering of her hit songs in those languages, *Weidersehn Ist Wunderschon* 𝄢𝄢 (Bear Family, 1992, compilation prod. Richard Weize) will leave you shaking your head, or laughing uncontrollably.

the rest:
Brenda Lee 𝄢𝄢 (MCA Special Products, 1990)
Brenda Lee 𝄢𝄢𝄢 (Warner Bros., 1991)
A Brenda Lee Christmas 𝄢𝄢𝄢 (Warner Bros., 1991)
Greatest Hits Live 𝄢𝄢 (K-Tel, 1992)
Greatest Country Hits 𝄢𝄢𝄢 (MCA Special Products, 1993)

worth searching for: *Little Miss Dynamite* 𝄢𝄢𝄢𝄢 (Bear Family, 1995, compilation prod. Richard Weize) contains everything Lee recorded for Decca Records between 1956 and 1962 in a 122-song box set.

influences:

⏪ Ray Charles, Mahalia Jackson, Teresa Brewer

⏩ Lesley Gore, Tanya Tucker, LeAnn Rimes

Ken Burke

Peggy Lee

Born Norma Delores Engstrom, May 26, 1920, in Jamestown, ND.

Lee's renaissance talents as singer, composer, arranger, and lyricist made her one of the biggest stars from the 1940s through the 1960s. A consummate jazz/R&B stylist with a husky, sexy voice and smoky onstage demeanor, Lee starred in and scored musicals and films and recorded more than 60 albums of jazz, blues, swing, Latin, and rock. Though never considered a great vocalist, Lee's quiet delivery—she made singing sound so *easy*—and chartbusting singles ("Fever," "Big Spender," "Mañana," and "Is That All There Is?" among them) made her an enormous crossover star. It wasn't always easy. Lee left Capitol for Decca Records over "Lover," a Rodgers and Hart tune that she jump-started with an innovative mambo rhythm arrangement to became one of her biggest hits in 1952. The next year, her moody, intensely bluesy montage, *Black Coffee*, was an example of a "concept" album long before *Sgt. Pepper's Lonely Hearts Club Band*. Then she wrote some of her biggest hits, including "Fever," "Mañana," and "Is That All There Is?"

She left North Dakota for Hollywood after graduating from high school, but wound up in Minneapolis, where she toured with the Will Osborne Band. Her first break came when Benny Goodman picked her to replace Helen Forrest in 1941, which produced her first hit, "Why Don't You Do Right?" Lee starred in several films and was nominated for an Academy Award for her work in *Pete Kelly's Blues,* and her songs and voice are all over Disney's *Lady and the Tramp.* In recent years Lee has produced books of verse, worked in painting and design, and written her autobiography, *Miss Peggy Lee* (Donald J. Fine, 1989). She continues to perform occasionally and does benefit work for Women's International Center and the Peggy Lee Music Scholarship.

what to buy: Until a career box set comes out, you'll need at least a couple of discs to gather the good stuff (because she recorded for several different labels). Start with any one of the following three and work your way through the others. The arrangements often steal the show on *Best of the Decca Years* 𝄢𝄢𝄢𝄢 (MCA, 1997, compilation prod. Andy McKaie), which includes orchestra work with Bing Crosby recorded between 1952 and 1956 and representative songs from *Black Coffee* and *Lady Is a Tramp.* Don't miss "Lover." *Best of Peggy Lee* 𝄢𝄢𝄢𝄢 (Capitol Jazz/Blue Note, 1997) gathers a selection of recordings with Benny Goodman, Quincy Jones, Benny Carter, Billy May, and George Shearing. *Capitol Collector's Series: Vol. 1, the Early Years* 𝄢𝄢𝄢𝄢 (Capitol, 1990/Gold Rush, 1996, compilation prod. Ron Furmanek) is a generous 26 tunes from one of her most productive periods.

what to buy next: *Black Coffee & Other Delights: The Decca Anthology* 𝄢𝄢𝄢𝄢 (Decca, 1994, prod. Tony Natelli) is a two-disc, 46-song extension of *Best of the Decca Years*. A quiet, small-combo, 1961 session recorded in a New York club became *Basin Street East Proudly Presents* 𝄢𝄢𝄢𝄢 (Blue Note, 1995). *Peggy Lee Sings with Benny Goodman* 𝄢𝄢𝄢𝄢 (Sony Special Products, 1994) captures the raw appeal of her earliest recordings.

what to avoid: Watch out for the many budget discs that offer one hit (usually "Fever") amid a short list of mediocre material; *If I Could Be with You* 𝄢𝄢 (Jasmine, 1992) or *Fever & Other Great Hits* 𝄢𝄢 (Capitol Special Products, 1994) are examples and offer little bang for the buck.

Peggy Lee **(UPI/Corbis-Bettmann)**

best of the rest:

Christmas Carousel 𝄪𝄪𝄪𝄪 (Capitol, 1960)

Close Enough for Love 𝄪𝄪𝄪 (DRG, 1989)

(With George Shearing) *Beauty and the Beat* 𝄪𝄪𝄪𝄪 (Cema/Capitol, 1990)

Sings the Blues 𝄪𝄪𝄪𝄪 (Musicmasters, 1990)

Jazz Collector Edition 𝄪𝄪𝄪 (Laserlight, 1991)

Moments Like This 𝄪𝄪𝄪𝄪 (Chesky Jazz, 1992)

Live—1947 & 1952 𝄪𝄪𝄪 (Jazz Band, 1993)

The Uncollected Peggy Lee with the David Barbour and Billy May Bands 1948 𝄪𝄪𝄪𝄪 (Hindsight, 1994)

Some of the Best 𝄪𝄪𝄪𝄪 (Laserlight, 1996)

More of the Best 𝄪𝄪𝄪 (Laserlight, 1996)

Peggy Lee, Vol. 1, The Early Hits 𝄪𝄪𝄪𝄪 (Alliance, 1997)

Miss Peggy Lee N/A (Capitol, 1998)

worth searching for: *The Quintessential Peggy Lee* is a video of a New Jersey concert that reprises 90 minutes of her classic repertoire.

influences:

◄◄ Jo Stafford, Billie Holiday, Sarah Vaughan, Mildred Bailey, Benny Goodman, Doris Day, Frank Sinatra, Dick Haymes

►► k.d. lang, Dakota Staton, Elvis Costello, Madonna

Leland Rucker

Raymond Lefevre

Birthdate and birthplace unknown.

When listening to Lefevre, one can't help but be transported to a sidewalk cafe on the Champs-Elysées, eating baguettes and cheese with a strong French wine poured by a girl named Babette in a slit skirt . . . aah. But we digress. His first U.S. hit was "The Rains Came," a pleasant 1958 orchestrated ditty, but the true Lefevre sound comes through on his other hit, the transcendent "Ame Caline (Soul Coaxin')," from 1968. The sound is of lush strings and an angelic choir over a basic rock beat driven home by drums, piano, and a strong electrified bass. This sound never quite coalesced on any of his other Kapp or Buddah records, but when "on," he could transport the listener to a softcore world of earthly delights via songs like "Emmanuelle" and "Je T'Aime Moi Non Plus."

worth searching for: With at least 23 CDs available in several foreign markets, it's tough to know where to start. The sad fact is that the best releases of Lefevre's music are on expensive Japanese imports. Probably the best way to obtain his music is on the five volumes of *Les Plus Grandes Succes*, with the best volume being the first: *Les Plus Grandes Succes de Raymond*

Lefevre 𝄪𝄪𝄪𝄪 (Victor Japan, 1987), which contains "Ame Caline." Old vinyl yields such goodies as *La La La La (He Give Me Love)* 𝄪𝄪 (4 Corners of the World/Kapp, 1968), *Soul Coaxin'* 𝄪𝄪𝄪 (4 Corners of the World/Kapp, 1968), *Raymond Lefevre & His Orchestra* 𝄪𝄪𝄪 (Buddah, 1971), and *Oh Happy Day* 𝄪 (Buddah, 1972).

influences:

◄◄ Nino Rota

►► Paul Mauriat, Michel Legrand

George W. Krieger

Michel Legrand

Born February 24, 1932, in Paris, France.

Though Legrand's classical-music background defined his career—his father was Raymond Legrand, another "light music" pioneer who accompanied Edith Piaf and Maurice Chevalier—the pianist indulged his jazz fascination, and wound up working with some of the greatest names in bebop. Despite his collaborations with Sarah Vaughan, Miles Davis, John Coltrane, and others, Legrand's best-known work remains his film scores. From 1968's *Ice Station Zebra* to 1983's *Yentl*, he was a soundtrack pioneer, developing a successful formula of classical orchestra technique, jumpy mood music, and jazz soloing and phrasing. Legrand first recorded with an orchestra at age 23, and quickly proved an impeccable arranger and conductor; his love for American jazz took him to Hollywood, where he recorded in the idiom for several years. After scoring works for Jacques Demy and Orson Welles (*F for Fake*, 1973), and winning an Academy Award for his *Yentl* score, Legrand finally tried film directing, with 1988's *Cinq Jours en Juin*.

what to buy: Soundtracks go in and out of print with regularity, so, as with John Barry and Ennio Morricone, many of Legrand's original soundtrack albums are quite collectible. Much of his jazz work remains easily available on CD, however: *Legrand Jazz* 𝄪𝄪𝄪𝄪 (Verve, 1958) is an album of Legrand-conducted classics (such as "Round Midnight," "Rosetta," and "A Night in Tunesia") with players you may have heard of—Gerry Mulligan, John Coltrane, Donald Byrd, and Ben Webster. (It's more notable for Legrand's impeccable arranging and conducting than his unimaginative piano playing, which pales next to the fire-filled solos by those other guys.) The gimmick of *I Love Paris* 𝄪𝄪𝄪 (Sony, 1954/1994) is that all the songs have something to do with the city of lights—you know, "Paris Je T'Aime," "A

Paris," and "Paris in the Spring." Of course, it's no novelty: Miles Davis is the soloist.

what to buy next: Less of an important historical document than *Legrand Jazz*, the cleverly titled *Le Jazz Grand* ♫♫♫♫ (DCC, 1978/1990, prod. Norman Schwartz) has wonderful collaborators (including saxophonist Mulligan and bassist Ron Carter) on good songs like "Baguette" and "Southern Routes."

what to avoid: Showing that he's always up on the latest jazz whiz kids, Legrand went lighter, working with Latin saxophonist Arturo Sanvodal on *Michel Plays Legrand* ♫♫ (Laserlight, 1994), which has syrupy instrumentals such as "How Do You Keep the Music Playing?" and "Brian's Song."

the rest:
Michel Legrand at Shelly's Manne-Hole ♫♫♫ (Verve, 1968/1989)
After the Rain ♫♫♫ (Fantasy/Original Jazz Classics, 1982/1994)
Columbia Album of Cole Porter ♫♫♫ (Sony Special Products, 1991)
The Warm Shade of Memory ♫♫♫ (Evidence, 1996)
Paris Was Made for Lovers ♫♫ (Laserlight, 1997)

worth searching for: Collectors have been eyeing the soundtrack to *The Thomas Crown Affair* ♫♫♫♫ (United Artists, 1968) for years, but the rest of us humans will have to settle for one bouncy, fun track—"The Boston Wrangler"—on the much-easier-to-find *Cocktail Mix, Vol. 4: Soundtracks with a Twist!* ♫♫♫♫ (Rhino, 1996, compilation prod. Janet Grey). The video *In Concert* ♫♫♫ (Music Video Distributors) shows off Legrand's classical-jazz solo side, as he tinkles through "Windmills of Your Mind," "Summer of '42," and "What Are You Doing the Rest of Your Life?"

influences:
◀◀ John Barry, Raymond Legrand, John Coltrane, Miles Davis, Art Tatum, Francis Lai, Ennio Morricone, Nino Rota

▶▶ Michael Kamen, Hans Zimmer, Lalo Schifrin

Steve Knopper

Tom Lehrer

Born Thomas Andrew Lehrer, April 9, 1928, in New York, NY.

Musical satirist Lehrer released only a few LPs in his career, but they have been continually repackaged, and his status as a cult comic grows with each new generation. A product of the '50s "sick" comedy movement, Lehrer's politically incorrect humor is brilliantly supported by his versatile piano playing, and offset by a chipper vocal style reminiscent of a '30s song-plugger.

A Harvard-educated mathematician, Lehrer began performing his satires during intermissions at campus dances and small clubs. Under the guise of refurbishing popular song styles, Lehrer cheerfully vocalized the romantic viewpoints of psychopaths ("I Hold Your Hand in Mine"), pushers ("The Old Dope Peddler"), bigots ("I Wanna Go Back to Dixie"), and fey collegians ("Fight Fiercely, Harvard"), among others. It was wildly shocking material for its time, but college students dug Lehrer's droll commentary, muffled rage, and ironic point-of-view. Their enthusiastic response encouraged him to record a 10" LP on his own label, which word of mouth transformed into the underground sensation of 1954. After a two-year hitch in the army (where he allegedly co-invented the vodka Jell-O shot), Lehrer returned to recording on his own label, adding to his satiric targets kinky sex ("Masochism Tango"), positive thinking ("We Will All Go Together When We Go"), animal abuse ("Poisoning Pigeons in the Park"), and the armed services ("It Makes a Fellow Proud to Be a Soldier"). During the late '50s Lehrer's following grew steadily and led to successful tours in England, Australia, and New Zealand, but at the peak of his early success he quit show business to teach mathematics. He resurfaced in 1964 to contribute songs to *That Was the Week That Was,* a short-lived, Americanized version of a British satirical sketch show (and a precursor to *Laugh-In*)—which won an Emmy and led to a Top 20 LP. Since then, save for a few songs he wrote for the PBS children's series *The Electric Company,* Lehrer has been a full-time academic, teaching mathematics and musical theater. In 1980, his work was the basis of a British musical revue, *Tomfoolery,* but only Lehrer can do his songs comedic justice.

what to buy: Lehrer is especially funny on *That Was the Year That Was* ♫♫♫♫ (Reprise, 1965/1990, prod. Jimmy Hilliard), a polished set of satirical songs. Taped before a live audience at the Hungry I in San Francisco, Lehrer's live versions have a gleeful "sick" quality that was missing from the TV show. The powerful issues brought up by such songs as "Pollution," "Smut," "National Brotherhood Week," and "The Vatican Rag" are just as valid today as they were back then. So is the humor.

what to buy next: Lehrer's early songs recorded for his own label (1953–59), collected on *Songs & More Songs by Tom Lehrer* ♫♫♫♫ (Rhino, 1997, compilation prod. Tom Lehrer, David McLees, Bill Inglot, Barry "Dr. Demento" Hansen), are wonderful excursions into the world of singing sick humor, and feature a nod to Danny Kaye on "Lobachevsky." Several previously unavailable tracks, including the ultra-rare orchestrated versions of "Poisoning Pigeons in the Park," "The Masochism Tango," "We Will All Go Together When We Go," and the relatively new "I

Ute Lemper (© Jack Vartoogian)

Got It from Agnes," make this a set even longtime fans will want. Equally fine, *Tom Lehrer Revisited* 🎵🎵🎵 (Reprise, 1990) contains the tracks Lehrer rerecorded for Reprise in 1965, plus two previously unreleased songs, the instructional travesties "L-Y" and "Silent E." Also, recorded in 1959 before a live college audience, *An Evening Wasted with Tom Lehrer* 🎵🎵🎵 (Reprise, 1990) has an edgier kind of energy, and some of the most intelligent in-between song patter you'll ever hear. Lehrer's "Bright College Days," "The Elements," and "The Christmas Song" veer away from the deliberate grotesquerie of his earlier songs.

worth searching for: A vinyl sampling of the TV show that commissioned Lehrer's best work, *That Was the Week That Was* 🎵🎵🎵 (Radiola, 1981, compilation prod. Michael Rophone) is a "best of" collection showcasing the comedic talents of David Frost, Henry Morgan, Allan Sherman, Mort Sahl, Woody Allen, and Buck Henry. The show's regular vocalist, Nancy Ames, sings slightly altered versions of Lehrer's "The Old Dope Peddler," "So Long, Mom," "Who's Next," and "We Will All Go Together When We Go."

influences:

◀◀ Gilbert and Sullivan, Victor Borge, Danny Kaye, Stan Freberg

▶▶ Allan Sherman, Mark Russell, "Weird Al" Yankovic, Bonzo Dog Doo-Dah Band

Ken Burke

Ute Lemper

Born July 4, 1963, in Munster, Germany.

A young German cabaret singer, Lemper has recorded the songs of Kurt Weill, Edith Piaf, and Marlene Dietrich, and she has also branched out into film, with roles in Robert Altman's *Pret-a-Porter* and Peter Greenaway's *Prospero's Books*.

what to buy: *Ute Lemper Sings Kurt Weill* 🎵🎵🎵 (BMG, 1991, prod. Michael Haas) is a perfect showcase for Lemper's Teutonic pipes. This collection was followed by a second volume.

what to buy next: *Illusions: Songs of Dietrich and Piaf* ♫♫♫ (London, 1993) finds Lemper paying tribute to two chanteuses of times past.

the rest:
Ute Lemper Sings Kurt Weill, Vol. 2 ♫♫♫ (London, 1993)

worth searching for: Lemper contributed vocals to *The Wall in Berlin* ♫♫♫ (Mercury, 1990, prod. Roger Waters), former Pink Floyd leader Roger Waters's political restaging of his totalitarian-themed concept album.

influences:
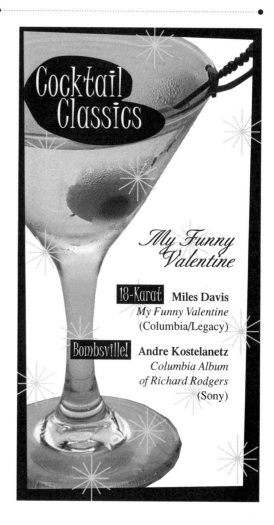 Marlene Dietrich, Edith Piaf, Lotte Lenya, Dagmar Krause, Teresa Stratas

Ben Greenman

The Lennon Sisters

Formed 1955, in Venice, CA.

Dianne Lennon; Janet Lennon; Peggy Lennon; Kathy Lennon, all vocals.

If you remember watching Lawrence Welk in the '60s, then you probably remember Dianne, Janet, Peggy, and Kathy, whose squeaky-clean appearances appealed to young and old alike, and whose soft harmonies decorated such hits as "Tonight You Belong to Me" and "Sad Movies (Make Me Cry)." The Lennons also recorded inspirational and religious music, as well as covering folk-rock compositions like the Mamas and the Papas' "California Dreamin.'" Their departure from the Welk show in 1967 effectively ended their career.

what to buy: The two-CD set *Yesterday & Today* ♫♫♫ (Ranwood, 1994) collects most of the noteworthy music from the Lennons's career, including "Tonight You Belong to Me," "Sad Movies," covers of "The Banana Boat Song," "Jamaica Farewell," and solo material from all four sisters. Especially interesting are the covers of edgier pop songs like "Hit the Road Jack," in which the sisters sound just as ingenuous and insulated as ever.

what to buy next: *22 Songs of Faith and Inspiration* ♫♫♫ (Ranwood, 1983, prod. John Bahler) highlights the Lennons's gospel talents, with an elegant "Ave Maria," an original composition by Andrae Crouch, and chestnuts like "The Battle Hymn of the Republic" and "Amazing Grace."

the rest:
Among Our Souvenirs ♫♫♫ (Ranwood, 1994)
Christmas with the Lennon Sisters ♫♫♫ (Ranwood, 1994)

worth searching for: The Lawrence Welk compilation *Lawrence Welk Presents His Favorite Hymns* ♫♫♫ (Ranwood, 1995, prod.

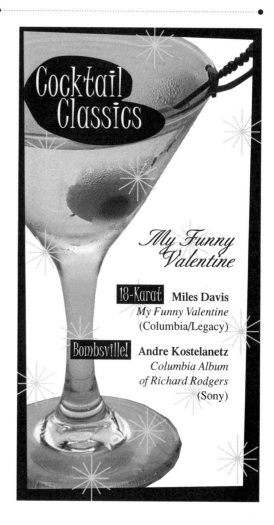

Cocktail Classics

My Funny Valentine

18-Karat **Miles Davis**
My Funny Valentine
(Columbia/Legacy)

Bombsville! **Andre Kostelanetz**
*Columbia Album
of Richard Rodgers*
(Sony)

Bonnie Pritchard) puts the Lennon sisters alongside Norma Zimmer, Guy and Ralna, and Welk himself.

influences:
◀◀ The Pied Pipers, Lawrence Welk
▶▶ The Roches

Ben Greenman

Annie Lennox

Born December 25, 1954, in Aberdeen, Scotland.

Regarded as one of the more regal singer-songwriters in the pop-rock camp, the former Eurythmics frontwoman has forged a near-limitless arena for her lounge-cum-lawless vocal prowess. She launched her musical career in the English new-wave scene in the late 1970s, teaming with Dave Stewart. Lennox joined his new band, the Tourists, which scored a Top Five hit in the U.K. with a cover of Dusty Springfield's "I Only Wanna Be with You," but by 1980, mounting tensions in the band prompted the two—by this point lovers—to form their own outfit, the Eurythmics. The synth-pop duo was a leading force through the 1980s with 10 Top 40 hits, including such staples as their debut #1 U.S. single "Sweet Dreams (Are Made of This)," "Would I Lie to You," "Missionary Man," "Who's That Girl," and "Here Comes the Rain Again." But in 1990, as their chart success waned, Lennox announced she was taking a couple years off to have a baby. In 1992, as the band decided to dissolve itself, Lennox came out with her first solo album, *Diva*. More recently, she has participated alongside other popular vocalists, such as Whitney Houston on "Step by Step," a song she wrote on the soundtrack to *The Preacher's Wife*. Another memorable side project included "Love Song for a Vampire" in 1992, from *Bram Stoker's Dracula*. But according to the artist, her most memorable project these days is being a mother.

what to buy: *Diva* ♫♫♫ (Arista, 1992, prod. Stephen Lipson), an elegant collection of adult-fused brunch music, including the timeless international hits "Why" and "Walking on Broken Glass." The disc was nominated for three Grammys, including Album of the Year. Always a potent presence on video, Lennox's visual interpretations of songs on *Diva* won a Grammy for long-form music video. In all, she sold 2 million copies of the LP in the U.S., and garnered an MTV award for Best Female Video for "Why."

what to buy next: *Medusa* ♫♫♫ (Arista, 1995, prod. Stephen Lipson) was a record of covers, including the little-known "No More 'I Love You's,'" which peaked at #11, helping push the album to platinum status. The project also included the memorable cuts "Waiting in Vain" and "A Whiter Shade of Pale."

worth searching for: Though *Greatest Hits* ♫♫♫ (RCA, 1991, prod. various) collects all the Eurythmics' familiar songs, from "Missionary Man" to "Sweet Dreams (Are Made of This)," the band excelled at original studio albums. Best of these are the urgent, hard-rocking *Revenge* ♫♫♫ (RCA, 1986, prod. David A. Stewart) and the more danceable breakthrough album *Sweet Dreams (Are Made of This)* ♫♫♫ (RCA, 1983, prod. Dave Stewart).

influences:

◀◀ The Sex Pistols, X, Marianne Faithfull, Aretha Franklin, Etta James, Rosemary Clooney

▶▶ k.d. lang, Alanis Morissette, Ani DiFranco

Chuck Taylor

Lotte Lenya
See: Kurt Weill

Sonny Lester
Birthdate and birthplace unknown.

This mysterious character did the heavy lifting for a then-sexist but now-camp LP series titled *How to Strip for Your Husband*. Though those two albums, with wonderful drawings of an unzipped '50s woman posing seductively for her pleased, leering husband, have long been collectors' treasures, the bulk of the music within has been reissued on a funny Rhino CD. In liner notes for the reissue, New York DJ Eddie Gorodetsky offers this biography: "To be honest, I don't know who Sonny Lester is. He could have been a journeyman horn player who hung around Birdland. . . . Or perhaps he was a fictious creation given a name melded from two great sax players—Sonny Stitt (or perhaps Rollins) and Lester Young. On a number of cuts Sonny Lester's alto sax seems influenced by Lester Young's tenor." Either way, as Rhino's *Take It Off! Striptease Classics* proves, Lester's curvy, horny big-band music is the perfect complement for David Rose's classic "The Stripper" in any of your town's most unsavory establishments.

what to buy: *Take It Off! Striptease Classics* ♫♫♫ (Rhino, 1997, compilation prod. Andrea Kinloch, Jill Ruzich, James Austin) compiles 18 tracks by Lester, all with the same va-va-voom big-band arrangements, and all operating on both campy and quality-music levels (this stuff is really, really cheesy—it's also really, really well performed). Standouts include a version of Irving Berlin's "A Pretty Girl Is Like a Melody" and Bill Grundy's more-salacious "Lonely Little G-String." The liner notes, holographic cover photo, and seductive pictures of ladies stripping are not to be missed.

worth searching for: As the Rhino collection explains, the original LPs—*Ann Corio Presents: How to Strip for Your Husband/Music to Make Marriage Merrier* ♫♫♫♫ (Roulette, 1962, prod. Sonny Lester) and *Ann Corio Presents: More How to Strip for Your Husband, Vol. 2/Music to Make Marriage Merrier* ♫♫♫♫ (Roulette, 1963, prod. Sonny Lester)—are long out

of print. If you happen upon them in a record store or a collectors' convention, don't hestitate to buy.

influences:

◀◀ David Rose, Raymond Scott, Duke Ellington

▶▶ Every strip joint in America, Combustible Edison, Love Jones

Steve Knopper

The Lettermen

Formed 1958, in Los Angeles, CA.

Tony Butala; Bob Engemann (1958–67); Gary Pike (1967–present); Jim Pike, all vocals.

The Lettermen are the last of the great collegiate-style vocal groups. Their clean harmonies and emphasis on romantic material updated the Four Freshmen's sound for the twist, Beatles, and psychedelic rock eras.

As a solo artist, singer Butala was something of a show-biz veteran. He had appeared in movies as part of the Mitchell's Boys Choir, provided the singing voice for Tommy Rettig on *Lassie*, and recorded unsuccessfully with the group Foremost. Butala managed to get his new group, the Lettermen, a contract with Warner Bros. in 1959, but their two singles flopped. The Lettermen then auditioned for Capitol Records, who told them they had too many vocals groups already. However, producer Nick Venet was impressed enough to sneak them into the tail end of a Four Preps session, where they cut their first regional hit, "That's My Desire." With Venet behind the glass, the Lettermen reworked the standards "The Way You Look Tonight," "When I Fall in Love," "Where or When," and "I Only Have Eyes for You" into hit records that appealed to both teens and their parents. During the British Invasion years, the group continued to score with dreamy smashes such as "Theme from *A Summer Place*," but on LP they began to embrace a brassier, more vigorous style. Their 1967 medley, "Goin' Out of My Head/Can't Take My Eyes Off of You," had all the trappings of a show-stopping Las Vegas lounge number, and it became a solid Top 10 hit. The revitalized Lettermen continued hitting the charts through the '70s with reworked oldies, including "Put Your Head on My Shoulder" and "It Hurt So Bad," contemporary tunes such as "She Cried," and the medley "Traces/Memories." By the time they left Capitol, the group had recorded 20 pop and middle-of-the-road hits and nearly three dozen LPs. Since then, Butala and various new lineups of the Lettermen have continued to record for his Alpha Omega record label into the '90s. As popular as ever, the Lettermen are booked up solid with tour dates all over the world.

what to buy: If you're just looking for the Lettermen's best-sellers, *All-Time Greatest Hits* ♫♫♫♫ (Capitol/EMI, 1974/1996, prod. David Cavanaugh) has 13 of their biggest hits and is a solid choice. However, if you want real insights into the diversity of their sound, buy *Capitol Collector's Series* ♫♫♫♫ (Gold Rush, 1996, compilation prod. Ron Furmanek), a 25-track compilation with an informative booklet.

what to avoid: It won't matter to their devout fans, but *Today* ♫♫ (Dominion, 1997, prod. Jack Jackson, Tony Butala) contains rerecordings of the Lettermen's hits, with Butala the only remaining original member. Stick with the originals on Capitol; they're true classics.

the rest:

For Christmas This Year ♫♫♫♫ (Capitol, 1966/1996)
Greatest Hits ♫♫♫ (CEMA Special Products, 1992)
When I Fall in Love ♫♫♫ (CEMA Special Products, 1992)
Close to You ♫♫♥ (CEMA Special Products, 1992)
Best of the Lettermen ♫♫♫ (Curb, 1993)
Christmas with the Lettermen ♫♫♥ (Unison, 1997)

worth searching for: The original lineup of the Lettermen never sounded better than on *College Standards* ♫♫♫♫ (Capitol, 1963, prod. Nick Venet), a unique theme LP with some absolutely gorgeous harmonies.

influences:

◀◀ The Four Freshmen, the Four Preps, the Four Lads

▶▶ The Association, the Vogues, the Sandpipers

Ken Burke

Jerry Lewis

Born Jerome Levitch, March 16, 1926, in Newark, NJ.

Music has always been an important facet of this beloved big-faced comedian's career. While Dean Martin, his straightman partner beginning in 1946, held the stage like a traditional show-biz singer, Lewis would scramble around, plot jokes, heckle his partner, dive-bomb the audience, and make Martin chase him through the orchestra pit. If the wild physical shtick and zany banter failed, they would pad their act with songs. Martin and Lewis were, of course, one of the most fabulously successful comedy duos this country has ever seen, but their appeal was largely visual. So when Capitol issued the duo's first single ("That Certain Party") in 1948, it sold even worse than Martin's solo outings. Subsequently, Capitol recorded both artists separately. Keenly competitive with his suave, good-looking partner, Lewis eventually insisted upon singing as many songs as Martin did in their movies and TV shows. This, along with Lewis's Charlie Chaplinesque dominance of the team's creative direction, were important factors in the dissolution of their highly successful act (as well as their friendship) in 1956.

Lewis's recording career was reborn after he performed his first solo comedy stint in Las Vegas. Subbing for an ailing Judy Garland, Lewis brought the house down and was looking for a way to get off stage. Informed that Garland's closing number was the Al Jolson oldie "Rock-a-Bye Your Baby," Lewis commanded the orchestra to play it; the audience, stunned by hearing him sing in a straight voice, erupted into a standing ovation. Thrilled, Lewis paid for a "Rock-a-Bye" recording session. His old label, Capitol, wanted nothing to do with it, but Decca Records saw the commercial potential and had him record a full serious-music LP. In 1956, the song was a million-selling hit, and the LP, *Jerry Lewis Just Sings*, hit #3. Follow-up albums sold poorly, but Lewis never completely abandoned his musical aspirations. His hit record became a staple of his live shows, and he wrote, sang, and arranged songs for his own movies. Some people interpreted Buddy Love, Lewis's arrogant, preening, greasy character in the classic 1963 film *The Nutty Professor*, as a pot-shot at Martin, or maybe Frank Sinatra or Bobby Darin. But Shawn Levy's 1996 biography, *The King of Comedy*, proves Love was merely a pale version of the private Jerry Lewis. Either way, the movie was an excuse to sing "That Old Black Magic." You can't miss Lewis every year on his celebrated Muscular Distrophy telethon.

what to buy: The cream of Lewis's work as a straight, sometimes swinging vocalist for Decca is on *Just Sings* ♫♫♫ (1956/ Razor & Tie, 1995, reissue prod. Mike Ragogna). It includes the smash hit "Rock-a-Bye Your Baby," the lesser chart record "It All Depends on You," and several standards. Lewis imitates Al Jolson on some tracks, but mostly sounds fresh and enthusiastic, without the cynical and condescending tone he adopted in the 1960s.

what to buy next: Lewis recorded several musical comedy pieces without partner Dean Martin, which appear on *Jerry Lewis: Capitol Collector's Series* ♫♫♫ (Capitol, 1990, prod. Bob Furmanek). Tracks such as "I Like It, I Like It" and "Sunday Driving" chronicle the catch-phrases and mannerisms of the hottest comic of the 1950s, and are the neglected gems of his career.

worth searching for: Let's face it: Jerry was at his best with Dean. Though the duo was never as big on radio as they were

on TV and in the movies, *Dean Martin & Jerry Lewis: On Radio* ♫♫♫ (Radiola, 1979, prod. Michael Raphone) showcases their early (circa 1948) chemistry perfectly. Also, *Dean Martin: Capitol Collector's Series* ♫♫♫ (Capitol, 1989, prod. Lee Gillette) features Martin and Lewis on their first recording together, "That Certain Party." Lewis does a pretty funny prank phone call on *On the Air! The Classic Comedy of Steve Allen* ♫♫♫ (Varese Sarabande, 1996, prod. Steve Allen), culled from Steve Allen's 1960s talk show.

influences:

◀◀ Danny Lewis, Al Jolson

▶▶ Gary Lewis, Martin Short, Jim Carrey

see also: *Dean Martin*

Ken Burke

Liberace

Born Wladziu Valentino Liberace, May 16, 1919, in Milwaukee, WI. Died February 4, 1987, in Palm Springs, CA.

One of this writer's fondest memories of his days as a music journalist revolves around a newspaper story he'd done in the mid-'80s. It began like this: "The view from the plush apartment on one of the highest floors of the Trump Tower in midtown Manhattan is fabulous: Liberace sitting on his sofa." Lee, as he was affectionately known even to his loving mass audience, was very sick at the time—he passed on shortly after the visit, from what was presumed to be an AIDS-related disease. Yet he was welcoming to a stranger, and cheerful about the prospects for an upcoming sell-out concert at Radio City Music Hall—a venue where he'd always been wildly successful.

While some may say he was a product of clever marketing—initially, at least—Liberace's endearing way, his outrageous costumes and props, and his over-the-top shtick made him a mythical figure in American popular culture. Musically, he was no slouch, either. He helped bring classical music to the masses. Although his eclectic repertoire included boogie-woogie, showtunes, and cocktail jazz, Chopin, Mozart, and Paganini were high on his musical dance card. "I'm an entertainer and a concert pianist, although certain music critics have disagreed with the latter," he quipped. Yet Liberace parleyed his own blend of epic vulgarity into vast wealth through his record sales and the popularity of his nationally broadcast television show.

The son of Salvatore, who played in John Philip Sousa's band, and brother of George, who later became Lee's manager and eventually wound up a curator of the fabled Liberace Museum

Liberace (Archive Photos)

in Las Vegas (where Liberace, fittingly, lived), young Walter played music by ear. He won a seat at the Wisconsin College of Music when he was seven. He served—and entertained—during World War II. When his career began, Liberace played at the Persian Room in New York City—where his trademark lighted candelabra sat upon his oversized Bluthner grand piano. When his parents divorced, he moved to Los Angeles with his mother and brother. He broke into TV, and cleverly marketed films of his show to outlets around the country. By 1953, he was a national craze. In September of that year he played to a capacity crowd at Carnegie Hall. Howard Taubman of the *New York Times* later dissected the Candelabra Casanova this way: "Liberace is not much more than a parlor pianist who ought to be kept in someone else's parlor." By the next year, he was drawing crowds of 16,000 fans—mostly women—and selling records by the ton. "Ave Maria" was a hit for him; "Clair de Lune" and "September Song" had sold well. Not to mention his "*Readers' Digest* condensed" version of Beethoven's "Moon-

light Sonata" and his interpretation of "Mairsy Doats," done in the various styles of Mozart, Chopin, Bach, and Strauss. In the U.K., where his cover of "I Don't Care" was a fixture on the charts, Liberace gave three Royal Command Performances in the mid-'50s.

Liberace consistently pulled in big box-office takes. His Easter 1965 engagement at Radio City—21 performances—became the stuff of legend. He arrived on opening night in a Rolls Royce with mink carpeting, and made his entrance on stage by emerging from a giant Faberge egg, wearing a 100-pound cape comprised of pink-dyed turkey feathers. Liberace had withstood some notorious times—including a sizzling affair with a blond lover named Scott Thorson that ended in the mid-'80s with Thorson filing a palimony suit against Liberace (the warring parties settled with Liberace making a cash payment to Thorson in 1986). Throughout the good and bad times, though, Liberace was true to his glitzy image. In a priceless vignette in Bob

Thomas's biography, *Liberace,* Thomas describes a scene where Lee, giving a series of telephone interviews during the Thorson business to promote a tour, turns white when he's asked a question by a woman reporter. "I have said that he was a disgruntled employee, and that's what he was," Liberace said firmly. He listened again, and the brown eyes turned to a shade of black. "If you continue with this shit, I'm going to hang up on you," he muttered. Pause. The color returned to his face, and he continued, "Yes, I'll be wearing the rings. . . ."

what to buy: While Liberace didn't qualify as superstar when it came to records, he had a fairly consistent stream of hits. As his generation of fans passes on, there isn't a lot of momentum among the current generation to rekindle his star. Which means we shouldn't expect digitally remastered compilations of his musical output in the near future. That said, a couple of CDs reprise his career and would make fine gifts for Granny: *The Best of Liberace* ♫♫♫ (MCA, 1972, prod. various) is a compilation of 24 tracks, including "September Song," "Theme from *A Summer Place,*" "Tammy" (a real tear-jerker), "More" (the theme from *Mondo Cane*), and Liberace's ultimate coda, "I'll Be Seeing You." Complementing this best-of package is the live *Liberace: The Golden Age of Television, Vol. 1* ♫♫♫ (Atlantic/Curb, 1991, prod. various). Lee will have his fans up and dancing with renditions of "Flight of the Bumble Bee Boogie," "Me and My Shadow," and "Unchained Melody."

what to avoid: *Here's Liberace* ♫♫ (MCA, 1987) has the pianist in a French mode. Among the selections are "Under Paris Skies," "Last Time I Saw Paris," and "Poor People of Paris." *Love Letters* ♫♫ (MCA Special Products, 1994) features Lee crooning still more standards, including "Around the World in 80 Days" and "Fascination."

influences:

◄◄ Chopin, Mozart, nursery rhymes, Bing Crosby

►► Elton John, Queen, Gary Glitter, Kiss

Stephen Williams

Enoch Light

Born August 18, 1905, in Canton, OH. Died July 13, 1978, in West Redding, CT.

Along with Juan Garcia Esquivel and Martin Denny, this classically trained violinist used hi-fi technology—plus bizarre experiments with bongo drums, horns, and xylophones—to create the quirky, easy-on-the-ears swing known as "space-age bachelor pad music." He was originally a classical musician looking

to catch on with a prominent orchestra, but World War II and an almost-fatal car wreck made him change directions. He formed a big band, the Light Brigade (and later the Enoch Light Orchestra, which had nothing to do with the rock band ELO), to play "sweet music" and other swinging songs for hipsters who weren't sold on rock 'n' roll or even jazz.

But Light did most of his best-known musical work while moonlighting as the head of several record labels. After working for Waldorf Music Hall Records, among others, he formed Command in 1959—and, a year later, put out his groundbreaking album, *Persuasive Percussion*. With almost no AM radio play, the album built on massive retail exposure to become one of the top 25 hits in recording history. Light experimented relentlessly with emerging stereo recording techniques, channeling horns and drums to come out in separate speakers on home hi-fi systems. (An obsessive tinkerer, he made a minor innovation by recording with 35mm film instead of the less-pristine magnetic tape.) Though his session musicians were rarely stars, some, such as trumpeter Doc Severinsen and keyboardist Dick Hyman, went on to prominent solo careers. From the mid-1960s to the late 1970s—the heyday of "beautiful music" radio and old-school Muzak—Light's orchestras were among the most popular musicians in the world. Listeners, though, rarely knew who he was.

what to buy: *Persuasive Percussion* ♫♫♫ (Command, 1960/MCA, 1995, prod. Enoch Light) and *Provocative Percussion* ♫♫♫ (Command, 1960/MCA, 1995, prod. Enoch Light) were once anathema to rock fans, their bongoes and harpsichords soothing listeners instead of riling them up. But, in retrospect, they were incredibly innovative: Light and his musicians took old pop and jazz standards, such as George Gershwins' "'S Wonderful" and Duke Ellington's "Mood Indigo" and restructured them into spacey instrumental music, complete with trombones, tango arrangements, and Chinese bell trees. Though Light recorded dozens of albums on the Command label, these two CDs—which include tracks from the out-of-print *Persuasive Percussion, Vol. 2* and *Provocative Percussion, Vol. 2,* respectively—are the only ones in print.

what to buy next: The Light Brigade's early big-band music, created before the bandleader went to work for the record company and switched to easy-listening experimenting, is competent and fun: *Big Band Hits of the Thirties* ♫♫♫ (Project 3, 1997), of all the many big-band albums Light recorded, is the only one in print.

worth searching for: Light put out more than 30 hi-fi albums, many of which are out of print: to go beyond *Persuasive Per-*

cussion, try *Great Themes from Hit Films* ♪♪♪ (Command, 1962), *Moments to Remember, Vol. II: Melody of Love* ♪♪♪ (Waldorf Music Hall, 1957), *I Want to Be Happy Cha Chas* ♪♪♪ (Command, 1959), or *Stereo 35/mm* ♪♪♪ (Command, 1961).

influences:

◀◀ Duke Ellington, George Gershwin, Glenn Miller, Benny Goodman

▶▶ Juan Garcia Esquivel, Doc Severinsen, Martin Denny, Arthur Lyman, Dick Hyman

Steve Knopper

Gordon Lightfoot

Born November 17, 1938, in Orillia, Ontario, Canada.

Lightfoot is one of the few singer-songwriters who emerged during the folk music revival of the early '60s to achieve and retain recognition as a distinctive, enduring talent. Strongly influenced by Bob Dylan, Lightfoot specializes in simple yet compelling melodies and evocative lyrics about bittersweet love, the history and natural splendor of rural Canada, maritime adventures (and disasters), wanderlust, and memories of happier times—all sung in Lightfoot's rich baritone voice and accompanied by expert guitar arrangements. As a songwriter, his work has been recorded by Marty Robbins ("Ribbon of Darkness"), Ian and Sylvia Tyson ("Early Morning Rain"), and Peter, Paul, and Mary ("For Lovin' Me"). His own hit list includes 1970's "If You Could Read My Mind" (since covered by more than five dozen other artists), 1974's "Sundown," and the epic ballad of "The Wreck of the Edmund Fitzgerald."

what to buy: *Gord's Gold* ♪♪♪♪ (Warner/Reprise, 1975, prod. various) is a terrific collection for which Lightfoot even re-recorded some of his pre-1970 material to good effect.

what to buy next: *Don Quixote* ♪♪♪♪ (Warner/Reprise, 1972, prod. Lenny Waronker) showcases Lightfoot at the height of his musical powers, from the show-stopping country stomper "Alberta Bound" (featuring superb bottleneck guitar licks by Ry Cooder) to the spare, energetic title cut and such mellow pieces as "Beautiful" and "Christian Island (Georgian Bay)." *Summertime Dream* ♪♪♪♪ (Warner/Reprise, 1976, prod. Lenny Waronker, Gordon Lightfoot) has "The Wreck of the Edmund Fitzgerald" and a wide variety of song styles. *If You Could Read My Mind* ♪♪♪♪ (Warner/Reprise, 1970, prod. Joseph Wissert, Lenny Waronker) is Lightfoot's breakthrough album, marked mostly by its gentle, celestial melodies.

what to avoid: On *Endless Wire* ♪♪ (Reprise, 1978, prod. Lenny Waronker, Gordon Lightfoot), Lightfoot's images are muddy, while the songs lack the strength of his earlier work.

the rest:
Lightfoot! ♪♪♪ (United Artists, 1965)
The Way I Feel ♪♪♪ (United Artists, 1967)
Did She Mention My Name ♪♪♪ (United Artists, 1968)
Back Here on Earth ♪♪♪ (United Artists, 1968)
Sunday Concert ♪♪♪ (United Artists, 1969)
Sundown ♪♪♪♪ (Warner/Reprise, 1974)
Cold on the Shoulder ♪♪♪ (Warner/Reprise, 1975)
East of Midnight ♪♪♪ (Warner/Reprise, 1986)
Gord's Gold II ♪♪♪♪ (Warner/Reprise, 1988)
Best of Gordon Lightfoot ♪♪♪ (Curb, 1991)
Waiting for You ♪♪♪ (Warner/Reprise, 1993)
Gordon Lightfoot: The United Artists Collection ♪♪♪♪ (EMI, 1993)
Summer Side of Life ♪♪♪ (Warner Bros., 1994)
Early Morning Rain ♪♪♪ (Capitol Special Products, 1994)
Live ♪♪♪ (Capitol, 1996)

worth searching for: The bootleg *If You Could Read My Mind: Live in Montreaux 1977* ♪♪♪♪ (Trade Service, 1977) includes "Edmund Fitzgerald" and others purported to be from the Montreux '77 concert. Others worth scouring used record stores for include the four albums not re-released on CD and deserving of at least ♪♪♪ apiece—*Old Dan's Records* (Warner/Reprise, 1972), *Dream Street Rose* (Warner/Reprise, 1980), *Shadows* (Warner/Reprise, 1982), and *Salute* (Warner/Reprise). A new CD is scheduled for release in 1998.

influences:

◀◀ Woody Guthrie

▶▶ Nanci Griffith, James Taylor, Harry Chapin, Tracy Chapman, Janis Ian

James Person

The Limeliters

Formed 1959, in Hollywood, CA. Disbanded 1963.

Lou Gottlieb, bass, vocals; Alex Hassilev, guitar, banjo, vocals; Glenn Yarbrough, vocals, guitar.

This literate musical/comedy folk trio was in business two months after meeting in 1959 in a Hollywood coffeehouse. Lou Gottlieb had come down from San Francisco to write arrangements for the Kingston Trio. With an irrepressible wit and sophistication (he had a doctorate in music from the University of California—Berkeley), and his huge acoustic bass as a prop, Gottlieb was the perfect frontman. His voice found harmonic sympathy with Hassilev's baritone and Yarbrough's smooth tenor (whose whistle was as slick as his voice). The group's biggest hit was 1961's "A Dollar Down," and they remained very popular through the early '60s, especially after signing with RCA, for whom they recorded a series of albums before going their separate ways: Gottlieb founded Morning Star, a commune near San Francisco; Hassilev became a writer and producer; Yarbrough pursued a solo career. He worked with Rod McKuen, and from 1963 to 1965 recorded 14 albums for RCA, with the biggest hit of his career coming with "Baby the Rain Must Fall" in 1965. The Limeliters reunited in the 1970s and again in the 1980s, with Red Grammer, and later, Rick Dougherty in Yarbrough's spot. Yarbrough continues to perform and record as a solo, while Hassilev occasionally performs with some other musicians as the Limeliters.

what to buy: Recorded at Hollywood's Ash Grove, *Tonight: In Person* ♪♪♪♪ (RCA, 1961, BMG/RCA, 1989, prod. Neely Plumb) is the best showcase of the trio's individual talents, including Gottlieb's outrageous seduction song, "Madeira, M'Dear," and the lovely closer, "Proschai."

what to buy next: *Two Classic Albums from the Limeliters* ♪♪♪♪ (Collector's Choice, 1996, prod. Neely Plumb) is the best way to still hear the group's topical, if dated, humor, and nice examples of their delicate harmonies. It packages *The Slightly Fabulous Limeliters* from 1961, a live recording with plenty of the wise-cracking Gottlieb's between-song patter, and *Sing Out!*, another nifty balance of over-the-top humor and harmony. Gottlieb's "Vikki Dougan," about a woman "whose dress was cut so low in the back—that it revealed a new cleavage," sounds pretty tame in the Paula Jones vs. Bill Clinton era, but it's still funny, while "Harry Pollitt" pokes gentle fun at communist fears of the early '60s.

the rest:
Folk Matinee ♪♪♪♡ (RCA, 1962)
Makin' a Joyful Noise ♪♪♪♪ (RCA, 1963)
Alive in Concert ♪♪♪♡ (GNP/Crescendo, 1985)
Alive, Vol. II ♪♪♪ (GNP/Crescendo, 1986)
Singin' for the Fun ♪♪♪ (GNP/Crescendo, 1992)
Joy Across the Land ♪♪♪♡ (GNP/Crescendo, 1993)
Through Children's Eyes ♪♪♪♪ (RCA, 1962/Folk Era, 1995)

worth searching for: The Limeliters find their place alongside their peers on *Troubadors of the Folk Era, Vol. 3* ♪♪♪♪ (Rhino, 1992, prod. Bill Inglot). Though it might not seem the label for the Limes, *Reunion, Vol. 1* ♪♪♪♪ (Stax, 1976), recorded during their first extended reunion, includes "Acres of Limeliters,"

their own, often very funny tale of their on-again-off-again career, recorded with a small band.

solo outings:
Glenn Yarbrough:
Baby the Rain Must Fall ♪♪♪♪ (RCA, 1965/Folk Era, 1997)
Glenn Yarbrough Sings Rod McKuen/I Think of You ♪♪♪ (Laserlight, 1994)
(With Holly Yarbrough) *Family Portrait* ♪♪♪ (Folk Era, 1994)
Divine Love ♪♪♡ (Folk Era, 1995)
Live at the Troubadour ♪♪♪ (Folk Era, 1995)
I Could Have Been a Sailor ♪♪♪ (Folk Era, 1995)
All-Time Favorites ♪♪♪♡ (Folk Era, 1997)

influences:

◀◀ The Kingston Trio, the Weavers, the Brothers Four

▶▶ Peter, Paul & Mary, Rod McKuen

Leland Rucker

Living Strings
/Living Brass
/Living Marimbas
/Living Voices

Formed late 1950s, in Los Angeles, CA.

Ethel Gabriel, producer; dozens of rotating symphony musicians.

Far more subversive than Elvis Presley, the Strings seeped quietly into millions of braincells via elevators and easy-listening radio stations for almost four decades, until radio programmers began injecting "soft rock" into their background-music mix in the early 1980s. The faceless group, which grew from an idea by George Melachrino's "Moods in Music" producer Ethel Gabriel, became massively popular. Though rock 'n' roll earned all the industry and media attention at the time, the Living Strings—and their spinoffs, Living Voices, Living Organ, Living Brass, and Living Marimbas, usually fronted anonymously by big easy-listening names like the Anita Kerr Singers and Al Caiola—became one of RCA's most popular live and recorded acts throughout the late '50s, '60s, and '70s. Recording for RCA's budget label, Camden Records, Gabriel initially hired the Oslo Symphony to make classical music; quickly, she capitalized on previously successful ideas by Mantovani and Paul Weston and shifted to a more symphonic pop sound. That clicked, and in addition to selling buckets of records all over the U.S., the Strings' music started showing up in American Airlines cabins. "Between the Living Strings and Melachrino," Gabriel told *Elevator Music* author Joseph Lanza, "I controlled at least 95 percent of easy-listening music on the radio."

worth searching for: Unlike the group's longtime rival, the 101 Strings Orchestra, whose 200-album catalog has been painstakingly preserved on CD, it's almost impossible to find any Living Strings album in, say, Tower Records or Sam Goody. Bring a few dollar bills to almost any used record shop, however, and you'll come away with an armful: for example, Living Brass' *What Now My Love and Other Favorites* ♫♫♫ (RCA Camden, 1966, prod. Ethel Gabriel), with arranger-conductor Ray Martin's takes on "Strangers in the Night" and the Tijuana Brass' "Spanish Flea"; Living Voices' *The Impossible Dream*

♫♫♫ (RCA Camden, 1969, prod. Ethel Gabriel), feeding off the folk movement with "Kumbaya" and Ed Ames's hit "Who Will Answer"; and Living Brass' *Plays Moods of Mancini* ♫♫♫ (RCA Camden, 1967, prod. Ethel Gabriel), a tribute to one of the cocktail kings.

influences:

◀◀ Mantovani, Paul Weston, George Melachrino

▶▶ 101 Strings, Mystic Moods Orchestra, Hollyridge Strings, Ray Conniff

Steve Knopper

Andrew Lloyd Webber

Born March 22, 1948, in London, England.

It's nearly impossible to accurately describe Lloyd Webber's impact on the world of popular music. The composer's groundbreaking and oft-derided 1981 musical, *Cats*, is the longest running musical in both London's West End and Broadway history. The show's signature song, "Memory," has been recorded by a staggering 180 artists. Worldwide, *Cats* has earned $2.2 billion with more than 50 million people having seen those singing felines. What's staggering is that Lloyd Webber also composed the brand-name stage hits *Joseph and the Amazing Technicolor Dreamcoat, Jesus Christ Superstar, Evita,* and *Phantom of the Opera*. Add to that body of work a handful of lesser-known musicals and you have some idea of the sweep and scope of his collected compositions.

The son of the director of the London College of Music, Lloyd Webber took to the family business early—his first composition, "The Toy Theatre Suite," was published when he was nine. In college, Lloyd Webber met an equally ambitious lyricist, Tim Rice, and together the duo unwittingly set out to revolutionize musical theater. Their first collaboration, *The Likes of Us*, has still never been produced, but the two struck pay dirt on their second work, *Joseph*. Based on the Biblical story of the dream interpreter and his 12 brothers, the score borrows from a number of different styles, including rock, country, calypso, and cabaret. Debuting in 1968 as a 15-minute show, the musical has undergone numerous revisions leading up to an enormously successful and buoyant two-hour plus production that has toured the United States in the '90s with Donny Osmond, among others, in the title role. The enterprising duo went back to the Bible for their next work, a rock opera chronicling the last week in the life of Jesus. Unable to persuade anyone to fund a stage version of *Jesus Christ Superstar*, the pair made a cast recording that went on to sell three million copies in the United States. Broadway took notice and the highly anticipated show was credited with helping legitimizing the use of rock music in a theatrical context. A movie version followed in 1973, earning Lloyd Webber an Oscar. After a brief split, the pair reunited for what would be their final collaboration, *Evita.* This time they purposely released it as an album first to whet theatergoers' appetites. The story of Eva Peron, the wife of Argentine dictator Juan Peron, opened on Broadway in 1979 and became an immediate hit, netting seven Tony awards. The elaborate show ran for almost four years and after many years of starts and stops, hit big screens in 1996 with Madonna in the lead role.

Rice and Lloyd Webber split for good after *Evita,* and Lloyd Webber turned his attention to making a little-known collection of T.S. Eliot poems into the Tony-winning *Cats.* That musical, for better or worse, ushered in an entire new era on Broadway where long-running, and some would say low-brow, spectacles dominated the box office primarily by attracting scores of tourists. Lloyd Webber struck gold again in 1986 with his musical adaptation of *The Phantom of the Opera.* By the time the show hit Broadway in 1988, it had racked up an amazing $16 million in advance ticket sales. From the amazing effects, including a chandelier that crashes to the floor, to the soaring operatic score, which many critics call Lloyd Webber's best, the show is perhaps the most popular musical of all time. In early 1997, *Phantom* was still going strong in both London and New York, while also playing in Japan, Toronto, Hong Kong, Hamburg, Switzerland, Australia, and Holland. In addition, there were three touring companies in the United States, one in Canada and one in the United Kingdom producing the musical. Lloyd Webber's record since *Phantom* is somewhat mixed, with the highly anticipated *Aspects of Love* and *Sunset Boulevard* ultimately proving to be critical and financial disappointments. His most recent musical, *Whistle Down the Wind,* debuted in 1996 in Washington, D.C., but has yet to reach Broadway. Still, an animated film version of *Cats* is set to be released in 1998 and a *Phantom* film is also in the works. Meanwhile, many of his songs and melodies have become ubiquitous—when was the last time you didn't hear one of his compositions at a wedding?

what to buy: There are dozens of collections of Lloyd Webber's work available. They are of varying quality, but one of the best "greatest hits" compilations is *The Premiere Collection* &&&&& (MCA, 1988, prod. various), with all the well-known hits performed by the original artists. Highlights include Yvonne Elliman's stirring "I Don't Know How to Love Him," Michael Craw-

ford's robust "The Music of the Night," and Julie Covington's touching "Don't Cry for Me Argentina." It's his most beloved musical, and the original soundtrack to *Phantom of the Opera* &&&& (PolyGram, 1987) shows just why it deserves that status. With Sarah Brightman as the heroine and Michael Crawford as the phantom, you'll be transfixed even if you're one of the seventeen people who haven't seen the show in person. The best rendition of *Joseph and the Amazing Technicolor Dreamcoat* &&&&& (PolyGram, 1994), of the dozen or so versions out there, is the 1994 Canadian cast recording featuring the luminous Donny Osmond sounding like he was born to play *Joseph.* The show isn't nearly as melodramatic as the composer's later fare, making it a joyous diversion.

what to buy next: For more highlights, go with the *Premiere Collection Encore* &&&& (PolyGram, 1993, prod. Andrew Lloyd Webber, Mike Batt, Mike Moran, Nigel Wright). The CD digs a little deeper into the composer's catalog for gems like "Love Changes Everything" from *Aspects of Love,* and "Everything's Alright" from *Joseph.* Featuring Madonna, Jonathan Pryce, and Antonio Banderas, the soundtrack for the film version of *Evita* &&&& (Warner Bros., 1996, prod. Nigel Wright, Alan Parker, Andrew Lloyd Webber, David Caddick) is one of the best recordings of a Lloyd Webber work. The double CD also features Madonna's touching rendition of "You Must Love Me," a song written exclusively for the film. Finally, for each of Lloyd Webber's shows, from megahits like *Cats* to second-tier shows like *Starlight Express,* there are numerous cast recordings available, but a good rule of thumb is to go with the original Broadway or London cast versions. Likewise, a perusal of the Lloyd Webber bin at the CD store will reveal a mind-numbing selection of "Best of —," "Essential —," "Very Best of —," "Music of —," and "Greatest Songs of —." Your best bet is to go with reputable labels, well-known artists, or original recordings. Buyer beware.

what to avoid: Among all the second-rate and schlocky collections available, stay clear of *Great Songs of Andrew Lloyd Webber—Pan Pipes Album* **woof!** (Music Club, 1997). You just can't convey the majesty of a Lloyd Webber composition on the pan pipe.

worth searching for: Avid Lloyd Webber fans can have a field day collecting all the permutations and different cast recordings. For instance, *Highlights from Jesus Christ Superstar* &&&& (PolyGram, 1997, prod. Andrew Lloyd Webber, Nigel Wright, Tim Rice) features the unlikely casting of Alice Cooper in the role of King Herod. Lloyd Webber composed music for two films in the early '70s, one of which is *The Odessa File* &&& (MCA, 1974), a

1974 spy thriller starring Jon Voight and featuring the pipes of Perry Como. One of the more interesting recordings of Lloyd Webber's work is *Jesus Christ Superstar—A Resurrection* 🎵🎵🎵 (Daemon, 1994, prod. Michael Lorant), on which folk rockers the Indigo Girls and a bunch of their friends pay homage to the rock opera with southern flare; Indigo Girl Amy Ray herself takes on the role of (gasp!) Jesus.

influences:

⏪ Richard Rodgers, George Gershwin, Cole Porter, the Beatles

⏩ Practically every singer and band performing popular standards today

Alex Gordon

Carol Lo Tempio

See: April Stevens

Guy Lombardo

Born Gaetano Lombardo, June 19, 1902, in London, Ontario, Canada. Died November 5, 1977, in Houston, TX.

"Enjoy Yourself," the name of Lombardo's trademark 1949 hit, was also the durable bandleader's musical philosophy. He could sing dramatic, swing-heavy pop like Frank Sinatra, but his best-known songs tended to come out like Sinatra's goofy, playful "High Hopes." His singing brother, Carmen, dribbled such phrases as "cuckoo like a cuckoo in a clock" as if to insist that listeners not take themselves so seriously. Lombardo's longtime radio show turned the band's version of "Auld Lang Syne" into a New Year's Eve ritual, like today's Dick Clark TV broadcasts and Times Square ball-dropping. Even when the big bands died out, Lombardo's "sweet music" perservered, and he continued performing until his death.

Lombardo's Italian-born father, a closet musician, advised his son at an early age to "don't forget the melody and choose songs people can sing, hum, or whistle," according to 1996 liner notes. He and his two brothers, singer-songwriter Carmen and squawky, lyrical trumpeter Lebert, formed a swing band and built their sound so straightforwardly that they refused to change keys during a song. In 1927, after naming themselves the Royal Canadians, they landed an influential Chicago radio gig, then converted that into a longtime broadcast at New York City's Roosevelt Grill. Thanks to the radio exposure—plus recurring movie roles for both Guy and Carmen—the Lombardo band began an impressive string of hits that lasted through the

mid-1950s. A speedboat racer who won a late-1940s national championship, Lombardo wound up selling more than 200 million records. Most of his 1940s singles, including "Boo Hoo," "Coquette," "What's the Reason (I'm Not Pleasin' You)," were big hits; the string let up only when a different type of up-tempo music, rock 'n' roll, began to dominate the pop charts. Late in his life, Lombardo organized revues at his Marine Theatre in New York—but the essence of "The Sweetest Music This Side of Heaven" really died when Carmen Lombardo succumbed to cancer in 1971. Guy Lombardo suffered a fatal heart attack six years later.

what to buy: The most impressively organized Lombardo package, *Enjoy Yourself: The Hits of Guy Lombardo* 🎵🎵🎵🎵 (Decca/MCA, 1996, prod. Marty Wekser), has excellent liner notes and a ready-for-New-Year's version of "Auld Lang Syne." Plus, the opening songs "Enjoy Yourself (It's Later Than You Think)" and "It's Love-Love-Love" are refreshing lessons on how to live life to the fullest. But the collection lacks some of Lombardo's biggest hits, including "Boo Hoo," which shows up instead on the Royal Canadians' *The Best of Guy Lombardo* 🎵🎵🎵 (Curb/Capitol, 1990, prod. various) and on *16 Most Requested Songs* 🎵🎵🎵 (Sony/Legacy, 1989, prod. various).

what to buy next: Though it doesn't show off the great strengths of either band, the Lombardo-Mills Brothers collaboration *Christmas* 🎵🎵🎵 (MCA, 1993) is a high-class holiday collection, lacking the corny nature of most pop artists' dutiful, moneymaking showings of spirit.

what to avoid: Because Lombardo recorded for several different record labels, it's easy to pick up redundant greatest-hits packages. We recommend the aforementioned instead of *Sweetest Music This Side of Heaven* 🎵🎵 (Living Era, 1995), although it does include a few collaborative cameos by Bing Crosby.

the rest:
Auld Lang Syne 🎵🎵 (MCA, 1990)

worth searching for: Lombardo's band takes on several blues songs, including "Frankie and Johnny" and "St. Louis Blues," on the hard-to-find *The Best of Guy Lombardo* 🎵🎵🎵 (MCA, 1977, prod. various).

influences:

⏪ Louis Armstrong, Duke Ellington, Frank Sinatra, Isham Jones

⏩ Tony Bennett, Dean Martin, Gordon MacRae, Paul McCartney, Rosemary Clooney

Steve Knopper

Julie London

Born Julie Peck, September 26, 1926, Santa Rosa, CA.

In the end, one of the last great torch singers may be better known to the television generation for her stint as nurse Dixie McCall on *Emergency* (1972–78) than for her quintessential version of "Cry Me a River." On screen (1944–71) and on vinyl (1956–67), London carried herself with quiet, elegant self-possession. Not gifted with exceptional range, London had wonderful phrasing that pushed along a gentle, breathy West Coast jazz swing, and an unmistakably smoky tone. Best known for her debut single "Cry Me a River," composed by high school classmate Arthur Hamilton and her sole Top 40 entry, London proved an exceptional and durable interpreter of standards (and songs which would become standards) for 30-odd LPs. She was married first to Jack (*Dragnet*) Webb, with whom she shared a passion for jazz, and then to singer-songwriter Bobby ("Route 66") Troup, who also went on to star in *Emergency*.

what to buy: Digital London choices are still limited, so begin with *The Best of Julie London* 𝄪𝄪𝄪𝄪 (Rhino, 1991, prod. various), a fair if occasionally frustrating 18-track summation that runs from the bass-and-drums early days to the lush orchestration of the late '60s.

what to buy next: Three two-LPs-in-one CDs are intermittently available: *Julie Is Her Name* 𝄪𝄪𝄪𝄪 (Alliance, 1956/1997, prod. Bobby Troup) is paired with *Julie Is Her Name, Vol. 2* 𝄪𝄪𝄪𝄪 (Alliance, 1958/1997); *Julie . . . At Home* 𝄪𝄪𝄪 (Capitol/EMI, 1960/1997, prod. Si Waronker) and *Around Midnight* 𝄪𝄪𝄪 (Capitol/EMI, 1960/1997, prod. Si Waronker); and *The End of the World* (Liberty, 1963, prod. "Snuff" Garrett) and *Nice Girls Don't Stay for Breakfast* 𝄪𝄪𝄪 (Liberty, 1967, prod. Calvin Carter).

worth searching for: Virtually any vinyl you can find in good condition is worth getting, if only for the elegance of the cover artwork. The vinyl-only *In Person at the Americana* 𝄪𝄪𝄪 (Liberty, 1964) is the only live recording of her oeuvre, and it seems to have enjoyed a limited release.

influences:

◄◄ Peggy Lee, Eartha Kitt, Rosemary Clooney, Doris Day

►► Combustible Edison, Madonna, April March

Grant Alden

Claudine Longet

Born January 29, 1942, in Paris, France.

Most people remember Longet (if they remember her at all) for

Cocktail Classics

Nature Boy

18-Karat Nat King Cole
The Unforgettable Nat King Cole
(Capitol)

Bombsville! The Association
Association 95: A Little Bit More
(On Track)

the notorious accidental shooting in 1976 of her then-boyfriend, professional skier Spider Sabich. Until this point her main accomplishments were a failed marriage to crooner Andy Williams and a forgettable career as a B-level cooer in the Brigitte Bardot/Astrud Gilberto mode. History, though, has a kinder view of Longet. In retrospect, her "sex behind the gauze" foreplay and breathy renditions of songs like "The Look of Love" and "Love Is Blue" reflect an artist who capitalized on a limited vocal range and profited from an indulgent, free-love, Hugh Hefner era. Today, Longet lives rather sedately in Aspen, Colorado, with her husband and defense lawyer in the Sabich case, Ron Austin.

worth searching for: Longet's original albums (all of them) are available only on Japanese imports. On *Love Is Blue* ♫♫♫ (A&M, 1968, prod. Tommy LiPuma), her third album, producer Tommy Lipuma helps Longet shake some of the morning haze that had limited her earlier productions. She sounds spacious and surprisingly punchy (for someone with such a limited vocal range) as she whispers her way through an assembledge of classics, like "Falling in Love Again" and "Love Is Blue." On *We've Only Just Begun* ♫♫♫ (A&M, 1971, prod. Nick DeCaro), Longet is a little bit country, and a little bit funky; she attempts a Francofied version of "Ain't No Mountain High Enough." And no one, not even the Beatles, is safe from Longet's sexy, morning-dew cover songs on her early albums *Claudine* ♫♫♫ (A&M, 1967, prod. Tommy LiPuma) and *Look of Love* ♫♫♫ (A&M, 1967).

influences:

◀◀ Astrud Gilberto, Brigitte Bardot

▶▶ The Cardigans, Ivy, Dubstar, St. Etienne

Sam Wick

Trini Lopez

Born May 15, 1937, in Dallas, TX.

A friend and colleague of Buddy Holly, a headliner at a Paris show opened by the Beatles, a protege to Frank Sinatra, an artist who recorded 42 albums in 25 years and had a single (Pete Seeger's "If I Had a Hammer") that—reportedly—reached #1 in 23 countries simultaneously, Lopez was also a successful interpreter of numerous lounge standards. After establishing himself as a Tex-Mex rock 'n' roller in his hometown, he moved to Los Angeles and landed a prominent nightclub gig at PJ's in Los Angeles. Frank Sinatra heard him there and immediately signed Lopez to his Reprise Records. From 1963 to 1968, Lopez had 13 hit singles. Though his fame died down after that, he never stopped performing in lounges, and he continues to play the Las Vegas showrooms.

what's available: Little of what makes Lopez interesting can be gleaned from his only CD in print, a best-of selection of pop standards that have either been re-recorded at what sounds like someone's New Year's Eve party or remixed beyond recognition. (They are, however, billed as the "Original Classics.") Buy *The Best of Trini Lopez* ♫ (Crescendo, 1993, prod. Don

Julie London **(Archive Photos)**

Costa, Snuff Garrett) only if you're willing to sit through Lopez's unique Tex-Mex take on "This Land Is Your Land," "Bye Bye Love," and Stephen Sondheim's "America" in order to get pallid versions of his lounge hits.

worth searching for: A much better collection exists that is available only, unfortunately, on a hard-to-find Japanese import, *From the Original Master Tapes* ♫♫♫ (Reprise, prod. various), which includes his lilting rendition of Will Holt's sentimental "Lemon Tree," plus "Kansas City," "Comin' Home, Cindy," and Lopez's other prominent '60s hits.

influences:

◀◀ Ritchie Valens, Buddy Holly, Joan Baez

▶▶ Freddy Fender, Neil Diamond

Bruce Schoenfeld

The Lounge Lizards

See: John Lurie

Love Jones

Formed 1990, in Los Angeles, CA.

Ben Daughtry, vocals and percussion; Chris Hawpe, vocals and guitars; Stuart Johnson, drums; Jonathan Palmer, vocals; Barry Thomas, bass and vocals.

Had Love Jones been featured as the house band in the cult film *Swingers,* instead of appearing only on the film's soundtrack, the kitschy group might have risen to slight but national prominence. (Big Bad Voodoo Daddy got the honor instead.) As it is, the five-piece combo that, along with Combustible Edison and Squirrel Nut Zippers, helped launch the cheeky lounge revival of the early '90s, has all but disappeared from sight, mostly due to apparent bitterness over being pigeonholed as retro.

Spearheaded by vocalists Ben Daughtrey and Jonathan Palmer, the Jones gang first attracted attention as a hilarious and highly proficient near-cabaret act at various Los Angeles clubs. Possessing not only Rat Pack–era crooning but also wicked bossa-nova with Stax/Volt and Motown soul shadings, plus smoothly harmonized oooh-aaah vocals and an inscrutable panache for placing even the most extreme sounds (mid-'80s punk, for instance) into proper cheesy perspective, as well, Love Jones was always too clever for its own good, and the band's ardent and cliquish following left many potential listeners cold. Currently, after the closing of Zoo Records, the band is without a label. They recently filed a lawsuit

Trini Lopez **(AP/Wide World Photos)**

against the makers of the film *Love Jones* over the use of its name.

what to buy: Sharply crafted and winkingly hip, *Here's to the Losers* ♫♫♫ (Zoo/BMG, 1993, prod. Rod O'Brien, Love Jones) is a breezy tour of easy-listening styles, though without much lushness. Martini madness is the goal here, and the album's sense of humor is what's vital, mostly in sex romps like "Custom Van" or "I Like Young Girls." Still, its assured musicality, though meant to seem hammy, is omnipresent and hard to ignore.

what to avoid: Pegged a novelty act, Love Jones played up its serious pop side on *Powerful Pain Relief* ♫♫ (Zoo/BMG, 1995, prod. Paul duGre). Bad move. Along with much of the lounge elements of before went most of the good-natured campiness. It's still competent, but the sound is more faux-R&B mixed with Tommy James ("World of Summer" sounds like "Crystal Blue Persuasion") and isn't nearly as enticing. Also, though the soundtrack to *Swingers* ♫♫♫ (PGD/Hollywood, 1996, prod.

various) is a fine introduction to the neo-hip movement, including tracks from Big Bad Voodoo Daddy and the Jazz Jury, don't get it for the Love Jones track, "Paid for Loving"; it's better heard on *Here's to the Losers*.

worth searching for: One of the better compilations documenting the lounge resurgence, *Livin' Lounge: The Fabulous Sounds of Now!* ♫♫♫ (Continuum Records, 1995, prod. various) sports one of the best cuts Love Jones has done—"Whiskey, the Moon, and Me," a snaky samba that quotes the *Star Trek* theme in its bridge. The set also features excellent work from the Wonderful World of Joey, Wall of Voodoo's Andy Prieboy, Useless Playboys, the Zimmermans, Everlounge, and Buster Poindexter.

influences:

◀◀ Tony Bennett, Frank Sinatra, Juan Garcia Esquivel, Motown

▶▶ Combustible Edison, Squirrel Nut Zippers, Big Bad Voodoo Daddy

Ben Wener

Norman Luboff Choir

Formed 1963, in Hollywood, CA.

Norman Luboff (born 1917, in Chicago, IL; died September 22, 1987, in Bynum, NC), director; rotating series of choirs for albums and tours.

"I hate snobbishness in music," Luboff once told *The News and Observer* of Raleigh, North Carolina, and he sure lived up to that philosophy, catering to the easiest, lightest possible portion of the public's collective taste. The composer and conductor led his choirs on musical journeys to many soothing fantasy versions of worldwide locales, such as the wild west, the Caribbean, and, with special emphasis, Scandinavia. He wrote a ton of hits, including "Yellow Bird" and "How Come," and worked with such notable crooners as Jo Stafford and, much later, future Mannheim Steamroller singer-founder Chip Davis. Luboff, who started his career as a singer and arranger for Chicago radio shows, moved to Hollywood in 1948 to write movie scores for Warner Bros. After building the choir, it took over his life, and he earned royalties off the group's hits and took varying incarnations of it on worldwide tours up until the time of his death, after a long battle with cancer. Though he lived in the small town of Bynum, Luboff was buried in Sweden, where he conducted choral orchestras for radio stations in his later years.

what's available: Surprisingly, despite the Choir's massive sales during the peak of "beautiful music" and old-school Muzak, few of the band's original LPs are in print. *Forever Frank* 🎵🎵🎵 (Simitar, 1997) and *Time for Us* 🎵🎵🎵 (Simitar, 1997), the latter of which is a collaboration with George Melachrino's vaunted easy-listening Strings, are the only ones Choir fans can find anywhere. One German import, *You're My Girl* 🎵🎵🎵 (RCA, 1961/1996), includes love songs like "Maria Elena," "You're My Girl," and "Warm."

influences:

◀◀ Paul Weston, George Melachrino, 101 Strings, Living Strings

▶▶ Jim Nabors, Mannheim Steamroller, Peter Allen

Steve Knopper

John Lurie /The Lounge Lizards

Born July 9, 1952, in Long Island, NY.

In 1981, at least a decade before people again started calling each other "swingers" and touting the merits of a fine cigar, the Lounge Lizards were already wearing '40s-era shirts and ties and

Cocktail Classics

A Night in Tunisia

18-Karat **Charlie Parker** *The Legendary Dial Masters, Vol. 1* (Stash)

Bombsville! **June Christy** *Capitol Sings around the World* (Capitol)

covering Thelonious Monk tunes. From the name of the band to its cool smugness to its retro aesthetic, the Lounge Lizards were a boilerplate for the '90s lounge revival. The band was formed by John Lurie, a smarty-pants New Yorker and sax player with connections to the city's underground art-rock scene, including a friendship with film director Jim Jarmusch that paid off for both. (The original Lizards' lineup included Lurie's pianist brother Evan; guitarist Arto Lindsay; bassist Steve Piccolo; and Anton Fier, former drummer for the New Jersey band the Feelies.) Along with "no-wave" acts like James Chance and the Contortions and even the Bush Tetras, the Lounge Lizards provided an arty alternative to the ruling punk of that time. The quintet hung together long enough to tour Europe before Lindsay and Fier moved on to other projects, such as the Golden Palominos. Subsequent line-ups never captured the cachet of the original. Meanwhile, Lurie starred in two Jarmusch films, and wrote the music for three. In 1996, by the time the rest of the world was hip to this cat's vision, Lurie put out *Queen of All Ears*, another Lounge Lizards disc, this time on the label launched by former Talking Head and fellow New York arty-rock guy David Byrne.

what to buy: *The Lounge Lizards* 𝄞𝄞𝄞 (EG, 1982, prod. Teo Macero) is the first, the original, and the best, especially the covers, including Thelonious Monk's "Well You Needn't" and Earle Hagen's classic, "Harlem Nocturne." *Live '79–'81* 𝄞𝄞𝄞 (ROIR, 1985) documents a series of dates performed by the original lineup; liner notes are written by Jarmusch.

what to buy next: Of the three Jarmusch soundtracks Lurie wrote, *Down by Law* 𝄞𝄞𝄞 (Intuition-Capitol, 1988) is not only the most engaging, it's the most "classic," because it was recorded by Lurie and the Lounge Lizards. *Stranger Than Paradise* 𝄞𝄞 (Enigma, 1986) is only half-soundtrack; the other half is a weird jumpy-jazz composition Lurie tacked on. *Mystery Train* 𝄞𝄞 (RCA, 1989) is more compilation than soundtrack, with heard-'em-before tunes from Elvis Presley, Roy Orbison, and so on.

what to avoid: On *No Pain for Cakes* 𝄞 (Antilles, 1987, prod. John Lurie), for the first time, Lurie sings. Oh boy.

the rest:
Big Heart 𝄞𝄞 (Island, 1987)
Big Heart—Live in Tokyo 𝄞𝄞𝄞
Voice of Chunk 𝄞𝄞 (Agharta, 1988)
Live in Berlin, Vol. 2 𝄞𝄞𝄞 (Intuition, 1991)
Live in Berlin, Vol. 1 𝄞𝄞 (Intuition, 1992)

worth searching for: Lurie wrote the soulful, Grammy-nominated instrumental score for Elmore Leonard's crime-novel film *Get Shorty* 𝄞𝄞𝄞𝄞 (Verve, 1995, compilation prod. Eric Calvi), which also contains vintage tracks by the album's clear forebear, Booker T. & the MG's.

influences:
◀◀ Thelonious Monk
▶▶ Golden Palominos

Teresa Gubbins

Arthur Lyman

Born 1936, in Kauai, HI.

This multi-instrumentalist—marimba, guitar, and especially the four-mallet vibes—supplied the spacey, echoey mood as a member of Martin Denny's popular exotica group throughout the 1950s. (He was the 21-year-old desk manager at the Halekulani Hotel when Denny more than doubled his salary to join the band.) After leaving the group for a solo career in 1957—often competing with his former bandleader in the very clubs Denny used to play—Lyman put out several defiantly soothing smash albums, always built on persistent, high-treble, swinging percussion. Coloring the music with slack-key guitar, bird calls, and other sounds that recalled his home state (or at least the prevailing Hawaiian stereotype), Lyman helped set off a brief Hawaiian craze among U.S. record collectors. It helped, too, that he had worked with Dave Brubeck and other jazzmen, thus giving him solid swing credentials and his easy-listening music a tough, danceable feel. His band's first album, *Taboo*, hit #6 and stayed on the charts for 62 weeks; he later had a hit single, "Yellow Bird." Lyman's soft and soothing sounds have always contained a touch of weirdness, from the tinkly percussion to the soothing vibes melodies. That's partially why, along with the other late-'50s exotica exporters, Juan Garcia Esquivel and Denny, he was such a prominent figure in the mid-1990s retro-cocktail craze. He continues to perform at Honolulu's New Otani Beach Hotel.

what to buy: Though Rykodisc has put together some nice repackages of Lyman's early albums—he has recorded more than 30 overall—it's easier to opt for one-stop shopping. Even casual fans of exotica (the term, coined on an early Martin Denny album, means a mixture of jazz-lounge and Hawaiian music) need *The Best of the Arthur Lyman Group* 𝄞𝄞𝄞𝄞 (DCC, 1996, prod. George Nazar), which contains "Taboo" and is an excellent introduction to Lyman's weird-but-easy-listening world.

what to buy next: The liner notes to *Sonic Sixties* 𝄞𝄞𝄞 (1964/Tradition, 1996, reissue prod. Dave Greenberg) frame Lyman as a musical alchemist, applying exotica to rock hits of the day, the way David Byrne and Paul Simon merged rock with Brazilian and African sounds several decades later. That's a stretch, but hearing the traditional Hawaiian version of the *Hawaii Five-O* theme is a much more rewarding surprise than any surf-music fan would expect. Also, after being out of print for decades, the debut Lyman album, *Taboo* 𝄞𝄞𝄞 (1958/Rykodisc, 1996), still sounds weird and fresh today.

what to avoid: With so much of Lyman's primary hit material in print, it's tough to justify *More of the Best of the Arthur Lyman Group* 𝄞𝄞 (DCC, 1996, prod. George Nazar), although it includes his biggest hit, 1961's essential "Yellow Bird."

the rest:
Taboo 2 𝄞𝄞𝄞 (1958/Rykodisc, 1998)
Hawaiian Sunset 𝄞𝄞𝄞 (1959/Rykodisc, 1996)
Bevona A 𝄞𝄞𝄞 (1959/Rykodisc, 1996)
Leis of Jazz 𝄞𝄞𝄞 (1959/Rykodisc, 1998)
Pearly Shells 𝄞𝄞𝄞 (Crescendo, 1993)
The Exotic Sounds of Arthur Lyman featuring Yellow Bird and Taboo 𝄞𝄞𝄞 (Columbia/Legacy, 1995)

worth searching for: Christmas albums were always a mainstay for easy-listening performers; that's still true today, and Lyman's Christmas instrumental music package, *With a Christmas Vibe* 𝄞𝄞𝄞 (Rykodisc, 1996, prod. Richard Vaughn), is worth stacking up next to Juan Garcia Esquivel's more heralded 1996 reissue, *Merry Christmas from the Space-Age Bachelor Pad.* (The Lyman album's original title was *Mele Kalikimaka.*)

influences:
◀◀ Martin Denny, Juan Garcia Esquivel, Les Baxter, Enoch Light

▶▶ Combustible Edison, Herb Alpert, Love Jones, Black Velvet Flag

Steve Knopper

Jeanette MacDonald

See: Nelson Eddy

Gordon MacRae

Born March 12, 1921, in East Orange, NJ. Died January 24, 1986, in Lincoln, NB.

Though American moviegoers fell in love with heartthrob MacRae after his starring roles in the smash musicals *Oklahoma!* and *Carousel,* he also had a prolific showtune recording career. Upon hearing MacRae sing "Oh What a Beautiful Mornin'," millions of transfixed young women were induced to contemplate the height of an elephant's eye for the first time.

MacRae's father, also a singer but whose success came in the manufacturing industry, asked his son early on what he wanted to do for a living. "Show biz," MacRae responded, and his father said he'd help. Soon he had won a magazine-sponsored singing contest and earned an engagement with the Harry James and Les Brown big bands. The exposure led to radio shows and a Capitol Records contract. MacRae made several albums before signing with Warner Bros. for a string of movies; it wasn't until he left Warners, though, that he snagged his best-known roles in *Oklahoma!* and *Carousel.* The singer overcame a long line of personal problems, including a divorce in 1966 and persistent alcohol abuse (which had led to some embarrassing on-stage moments), then wound down his career as a nightclub singer and alcohol-addiction counselor. After a long bout with throat cancer, he died in 1986.

what to buy: It's hard to find MacRae's early soundtrack albums, but *The Broadway Album* 𝄞𝄞𝄞𝄞 (Pair, 1995, prod. various) collects his best-known croons from *Carousel* ("If I Loved You"), *South Pacific* ("Some Enchanted Evening"), and, of course, *Oklahoma!* ("Oh What a Beautiful Mornin'").

worth searching for: In addition to showtunes, MacRae maintained a prolific career recording standards and Christmas tunes—he shows up on the compilations *Capitol Sings Johnny Mercer* 𝄞𝄞𝄞 (Alliance, 1996, prod. various) and makes you weak in the knees with "A Wonderful Christmas (Here's To)," from *Cuddly Christmas Classics* 𝄞𝄞𝄞 (Alliance, 1996, prod. various).

influences:
◀◀ Frank Sinatra, Tony Bennett, Dean Martin, Bing Crosby, Perry Como, Rosemary Clooney

▶▶ Johnny Mathis, Paul McCartney, Bobby Darin, Pat Boone

Steve Knopper

Madonna

Born Madonna Louise Ciccone, August 16, 1958, in Bay City, MI.

Some 15 years into a Hall of Fame career, Madonna still attracts attention mostly for her flashy stuff—beats-per-minute dance-club hits, sexcapades, out-of-wedlock childbirth, and so forth. A pity, because she has also matured into a first-rate torch diva. As in all things related to Miss M, considerable canniness is at work here.

Madonna developing her balladeer side is akin to an aging basketball star belatedly developing an outside jumpshot, in that it involves less wear and tear, and is quite a bit more dignified (after all, she wasn't going to stay that perky sexbomb forever). One imagines her becoming a grand dame along the lines of Marianne Faithfull in future years, a macabre salon singer who wears her scars proudly.

Early on, there was little sign of just how important an empire Madonna was going to build. Her early hits were thoroughly un-

remarkable dance-pop fluff, with her voice at its squeakiest and most irritating. But then Madonna discovered her lower vocal range on a pair of spectacular movie themes—1985's "Crazy for You," which proved she could actually sing; and 1986's eerie "Live to Tell," which proved that she had something to say. Since then, some of Madonna's best and biggest singles have been ballads, including "This Used to Be My Playground," "Take a Bow," and "I'll Remember." She also hooked the title role in Alan Parker's 1996 musical *Evita,* performing credibly despite being saddled with a typically bathetic Andrew Lloyd Webber score. Whatever she chooses to do next will doubtless be fascinating. Like the Rolling Stones and Bob Dylan, Madonna is a figure whose cultural influence far outweighs her sales figures.

what to buy: Madonna's ballads can seem anomalous and out-of-context on her regular albums. But grouped together on the compilation *Something to Remember* ♪♪♪♪ (Maverick, 1995, prod. various), they build a case for her as one of the most underrated ballad vocalists of modern popular music. There's some overlap between *Something to Remember* and the greatest-hits set *The Immaculate Collection* ♪♪♪♪ (Sire, 1990, prod. various), but *Immaculate* is primarily centered on the up-tempo hits like "Into the Groove" and "Express Yourself."

what to buy next: *Like a Prayer* ♪♪♪♪ (Sire, 1989, prod. various) is Madonna's strongest and deepest album. It is also the one on which the balladry is best-integrated with the dance material. *Like a Prayer*'s theme of sexual-spiritual melding is at its creepiest on "Oh Father," a ghostly graveside confrontation that is chilling to listen to. Though "Oh Father" ranks among her greatest singles, it's hardly surprising that it was also one of her least successful. *Erotica* ♪♪♪♪ (Maverick, 1992, prod. Madonna, Shep Pettibone, Andre Betts) was almost completely overshadowed by the accompanying "Sex" booklet, and it's too bad because it's one of her farthest-reaching albums. Years before anybody was hyping ambient techno as the Next Big Thing, Madonna was already there.

what to avoid: Madonna does what she can on the soundtrack to *Evita* ♪♪ (Warner Bros., 1996, prod. various), but one can only polish a turd so much. At two discs and 108 minutes, this is pretty tough sledding for all but the most dedicated. For what it's worth, Madonna does a better job with "Don't Cry for Me Argentina" than Sinéad O'Connor. The soundtrack to *Who's That Girl* ♪♪ (Sire, 1987, prod. various) is scarcely better.

Madonna (© Ken Settle)

the rest:
Madonna ♪♪♪ (Sire, 1983)
Like a Virgin ♪♪♪ (Sire, 1984)
True Blue ♪♪♪♪ (Sire, 1986)
You Can Dance ♪♪♪ (Sire, 1987)
I'm Breathless ♪♪♪ (Sire, 1990)
Bedtime Stories ♪♪♪♪ (Sire, 1994)
Ray of Light ♪♪♪♪ (Maverick/Warner Bros., 1998)

worth searching for: Sonic Youth's bizarre and hilarious sendup of (mostly) Madonna tunes, *The Whitey Album* ♪♪♪♪ (Blast First, 1989, prod. Ciccone Youth), is credited to Ciccone Youth, a sly parody of Madonna's surname.

influences:

◄◄ Elvis Presley, Michael Jackson, Ronnie Spector, Marilyn Monroe, Marianne Faithull

►► Paula Abdul, TLC, the Spice Girls, Janet Jackson, Tori Amos, Alanis Morissette

David Menconi

Mama Cass

See: Cass Elliot

Man or Astro-Man?

Formed 1992, in Auburn, AL.

CoCo the Electronic Monkey Wizard, alternate universe bass; Birdstuff, traps; Star Crunch, guitar; Dr. Delecto & His Invisible Vaportron, bass; Captain Zeno, anti-rhythm guitar.

Pretending to be intergalactic travelers who have ventured back in time to present-day Earth to expose the population of the world slowly to the harmonic evolution, Man or Astro-Man? is actually a group of former Auburn University students prolifically producing some of the finest lounge/surf revival music of the decade. The still-underground band's live shows are already legendary, featuring futuristic costumes—in a fashion sense that recalls Juan Garcia Esquivel's '50s era of "space-age bachelor pad music"—and playing a repertoire of thematic instrumentals saluting everything from spies to drag racing.

what to buy: The band's debut album, *Is It Man or Astro-Man?* ♪♪♪♪ (Estrus, 1993), showcases the band's fine licks, sense of humor, and range (within this somewhat limited genre), with slick ditties like "Taxidermist Surf," "Sadie Hawkins Atom Bomb," and the bizarre sexual tribute to the former *CHiPs* television star, "Eric Estrotica."

what to buy next: *Project Infinity* ♫♫♫♪ (Estrus, 1995) features the engineering of indie-rock impresario Steve Albini. *Made from Technetium* ♫♫♫♪ (Touch & Go, 1997) features a couple of interesting vocal tracks and a harder sound for variety.

what to avoid: *Live Transmissions from Uranus* ♫♫♪ (Touch & Go, 1997) doesn't do justice to the band's otherworldly stage show.

the rest:
Destroy All Astromen!! ♫♫♫ (Estrus, 1994)
Intravenous Television Continuum ♫♫♫ (One Louder, 1995)
Experiment Zero ♫♫♫ (Touch & Go, 1996)
What Remains inside a Black Hole ♫♫♫ (Au-Go-Go, 1997)
Your Weight on the Moon ♫♫♫ (Touch & Go, 1997)

worth searching for: The band from the future goes back to the recent past with a cover of "Interplanet Janet" on *Schoolhouse Rock! Rocks* ♫♫♫ (Lava, 1996, prod. Andrew Leary, Janet Billig). Their tribute to the "galaxy gal" is one of the better tracks on a CD of '90s rockers covering the three-minute lessons that aired in between *Scooby Doo* and *Hong Kong Phooey* on ABC Saturday mornings. Overall, the CD is a great concept, but surprisingly the sometimes hollow execution (especially Blind Melon's supermellow "Three Is a Magic Number") leaves you realizing just how perfect the original *Schoolhouse Rock!* ditties, like "Conjunction Junction" and "I'm Just a Bill," were.

influences:
◀◀ Dick Dale, Devo, Frigin D'an & the Modal Nodes, the Ventures, the Sentinels, Juan Garcia Esquivel, the Tubes, GWAR

▶▶ Combustible Edison, Laika & the Cosmonauts, Southern Culture on the Skids

Alex Gordon

Henry Mancini

Born Enrico Nicola Mancini, April 16, 1924, in Cleveland, OH. Died June 14, 1994, in Los Angeles, CA.

When he crossed that Big Moon River—at the age of 71—Mancini left the rest of us a legacy of light popular music as mountainous as the riches he accrued scoring nearly 80 films, plus about two dozen television shows and series, and recording more than 80 albums. Mancini—he of the gentle smile, the mellow demeanor, one of those not corrupted by Hollywood—was a unique crossover in what is normally a fairly secular profession. John Barry turned out terrific themes, Jerry Goldsmith created musical cues that were at once dramatic and melodramatic, and European émigrés like Max Steiner and Erich Korn-

gold reinvented classical symphonic music for the movies. Mancini, throughout his long career, did all of these things, and consistently one-upped the competition by churning out wonderful, stylized melodies. Mancini didn't only fit music to images. You could dance to it ("Something for Cat" from *Breakfast at Tiffany's*), march to it ("What Did You Do in the War, Daddy?"), make love to it ("Dreamsville," "Charade"), weep to it ("Soldier in the Rain," "Days of Wine and Roses"), and get scared out of your wits by it ("Wait Until Dark," "Experiment in Terror").

Mancini grew up near Pittsburgh and studied with Max Adkins, who also trained Billy Strayhorn. Adkins played a key role in Mancini's development as a musician: he introduced him to Benny Goodman, who in turned encouraged Mancini to study at Juilliard. Mancini was accepted, but the year was 1942. After serving overseas, he moved to New York, went to work for Tex Beneke's band as arranger and pianist, and met the woman he would marry. Henry and Ginny, who was solid with the young crowd in Hollywood (including Mancini's partner-to-be, Blake Edwards), gravitated to California. At Universal, Mancini's work included writing bits of music for films like *The Creature from the Black Lagoon* and *Ma and Pa Kettle at Home*. His big break was his assignment to score Orson Welles's *Touch of Evil* in 1958. He broke the mold set by the Europeans: *Touch of Evil* was subtle, flavored with jazz brass, and distinctly American. He always considered it among his best film scores.

"Peter Gunn" and "Mr. Lucky" were enormously successful, as pop music as well as adjuncts to two ahead-of-their-time television series. But soon Edwards would take Mancini on a ride that seemed to go nowhere but up: *Breakfast at Tiffany's, Experiment in Terror, The Pink Panther, The Days of Wine and Roses, The Great Race,* and more. Mancini worked with many of the best session musicians in the world; augmented his earnings (he averaged three film scores a year) with live concert appearances; and won numerous awards, including four Oscars.

what to buy: Among the many compendiums of Mancini's hits (and some misses) is the three-disc *Days of Wine and Roses* ♫♫♫♫ (1995, prod. various), which captures the Mancini magic spanning several decades. It's a terrific Mancini 101 course, collecting enough of the composer's greatest hits (starting with "Peter Gunn") to satisfy most beginners. The hard-to-find "Soldier in the Rain" theme is included. Mancini buffs should seek out the reissued score to the classic Orson Welles film *Touch of Evil* ♫♫♫♫ (1958/Varese Sarabande, 1993, reissue prod. Robert Townson, Tom Null), which contains many cues of what was to come. It's dark, moody, typically Mancini, and sounds, like so much of his work, strikingly modern even 40 years after the fact.

what to buy next: *Breakfast at Tiffany's* ♪♪♪ (Original Soundtrack) (RCA, 1962/1988, prod. Dick Pierce) was among Mancini's most facile scores, and certainly among the easiest to lay on the turntable and let play over and over. Some of it is too familiar—"Moon River" is probably the "Stairway to Heaven" of pop instrumentals—but much of it is just so endearing. *Cinema Italiano* ♪♪♪ (RCA, 1991, prod. John McClure) is one of Mancini's rare excursions on record into other film composers' works. There are some lovely treatments here of Ennio Morricone's theme to *The Untouchables* and his lyrical suite for *Cinema Paradiso*. It's a rare chance to hear Nino Rota's chirpy music from Fellini's *Boccaccio 70* as well as a Mancinified version of Rota's haunting waltz from *The Godfather*.

what to avoid: *The Best of Mancini* ♪♪ (RCA, 1980/1987, prod. Simon Rady, Dick Peirce, Steve Sholes, Joe Reisman) is the condensed version of the superior *Days of Wine and Roses* collection. It has all the predictable hits in one place (including "Peter Gunn," "Moon River," and the title track), but really skims the surface of Mancini's output. Also, Mancini fills out *Music from the Films of Blake Edwards: The Film Composers Series, Vol. IV* ♪♪ (RCA, 1991, prod. Simon Rady, Dick Peirce, Steve Sholes, Joe Reisman) with some marginal cues from his many film collaborations with director Edwards. The usual suspects are in place—"Peter Gunn," "Pink Panther," "Victor/Victoria"—but do we really need bits from "The Party" and yet another "Moon River" track?

best of the rest:
Collection ♪♪♪ (Pair, 1987)
Legendary Performer ♪♪ (RCA, 1987)
Academy Award Collection ♪♪♪ (Pair, 1988)
All Time Greatest Hits ♪♪♪ (RCA, 1988)
Premier Pops ♪♪ (Denon, 1988)
Mancini Rocks the Pops ♪♪♪♪ (Denon, 1989)
"As Time Goes By" and Other Classic Movie Love Songs ♪♪♪ (RCA Victor, 1992)
"The Pink Panther," "Baby Elephant Walk," "Moon River" and Other Hits ♪♪♪ (RCA Victor, 1992)
Top Hat: Music from the Films of Astaire and Rogers ♪♪♪ (RCA Victor, 1992)
Love Story ♪♪ (Pair, 1992)
Mancini Country ♪♪♪ (RCA, 1992)
Theme from "The Godfather" ♪♪♪ (RCA Victor, 1993)
Martinis with Mancini ♪♪♪ (RCA, 1997)
Merry Mancini Christmas ♪♪♪ (RCA, 1997)

Cocktail Classics

Our Love Is Here to Stay

18-Karat Nat "King" Cole
The Unforgettable Nat "King" Cole
(Capitol)

Bombsville! Jackie Gleason
And Awaaay We Go!
(Scamp/Caroline)

worth searching for: The Grammy Awards debuted in 1958, and Mancini had the honor of receiving the first Album of the Year award for the now-out-of-print LP *The Music from "Peter Gunn"* ♪♪♪♪ (RCA Victor, 1958, prod. Simon Rady). Few would disagree that the classic status of "Peter Gunn" has only appreciated over the years, and it sounds as fresh today as it did 40 years ago. Another out-of-print collectors' treasure, *Hatari!* ♪♪♪♪ (RCA, 1962, prod. Dick Peirce), was one of the many superior Mancini scores that accompanied a rather mediocre picture. The opening cut, "Sounds of Hatari," with its ominous brass and stunning percussion, is a tour de force of rushing percussion. The scores to *Charade* ♪♪♪ (RCA, 1963, prod. Joe

Reisman) and *Arabesque* (RCA, 1966, prod. Joe Reisman) both have their moments, and *Charade* is an especially fine souvenir of the film.

influences:

◀◀ Shorty Rogers, Benny Goodman, Tex Beneke, Glenn Miller, Nino Rota

▶▶ John Barry, James Newton Howard, Sergio Mendes, Michael Kamen, Herb Alpert

Stephen Williams

Chuck Mangione

Born Charles Frank Mangione, November 29, 1940, in Rochester, NY.

Mangione brought a sense of New Age to melodic jazz. His style is soulful but light, cerebral yet accessible. A masterful technician on trumpet, electric piano, and fluglehorn, his best recordings virtually defined popular jazz in the '70s and early '80s. Besides that, he has a cool hat (which vaguely resembles the hubcap of a '59 Plymouth).

Mangione was inspired to play trumpet by the 1950 film *Young Man with a Horn* (a soapy biography of Bix Beiderbecke starring Kirk Douglas) and drew much encouragement and influence from family friend Dizzy Gillespie. In 1960, Mangione and his older brother, Gap, formed the Jazz Brothers, a hard bop combo, which recorded several low-selling LPs for the Jazzland label. After dissolving the band in 1965, Mangione played in the trumpet sections of the Woody Herman and Maynard Ferguson orchestras, before joining Art Blakey and the Jazz Messengers. A live recording of "Hill Where the Lord Hides" at his "Friends & Love Concert" led to a deal with Mercury Records. Mangione's stylistic change from hard bop to fluglehorn-enhanced melodic jazz was instantly successful with record buyers; he earned several Grammy nominations and a Golden Globe Award for his soundtrack LP for the 1978 film *Children of Sanchez*. Mangione's career peaked in the mid-'70s, when his classic "Feels So Good" became one of the most played singles of the decade and set the stage for the lounge and exotica revival of the early '90s. During the '80s, Mangione recorded several LPs for Columbia, but when the impact of his sound began to wane, he decided to take a sabbatical from show business. Mangione resurfaced three years later with several high profile concert events and a self-mocking animated cameo on the *The Simpsons*. The death of Dizzy Gillespie inspired Mangione to return to the trumpet full-time, and he has begun reissuing his back catalog as well as releasing fresh sounds on his own label, Feels So Good Records.

what to buy: Mangione's biggest hit, "Feels So Good," as well as his breakthrough, "Hill Where the Lord Hides," plus "The Cannonball Run Theme" and his award-winning movie theme "Children of Sanchez" are all included on *Greatest Hits* 𝄞𝄞𝄞𝄞𝄞 (A&M, 1996, prod. Chuck Mangione); also included are several other affecting soft jazz tracks from his stay at A&M.

what to buy next: To hear Mangione, his brother Gap, and their early hard bop style, get *Recuerdo* 𝄞𝄞𝄞𝄞 (Original Jazz Classics, 1991, prod. various), on which the flavor of exotic regions fuels reinterpretaions of "I Had the Craziest Dream Last Night," "If Ever I Would Leave You," and several originals.

what to avoid: Mangione's hot streak was clearly over with *Love Notes* 𝄞𝄞 (Columbia, 1982, prod. Chuck Mangione), a meandering, tedious collection.

the rest:
Land of Make Believe/Chuck Mangione Quartet 𝄞𝄞𝄞𝄞 (Mercury, 1973/1990)
Chase the Clouds Away 𝄞𝄞𝄞 (Rebound Records, 1975/1996, A&M, 1998)
Feels So Good 𝄞𝄞𝄞 (A&M Records, 1977)
Children of Sanchez (Original Soundtrack) 𝄞𝄞𝄞 (A&M, 1979, PID, 1998)
Fun & Games 𝄞𝄞 (Rebound Records, 1979/1994, A&M, 1998)
Journey to a Rainbow 𝄞𝄞 (Columbia, 1983/1990)
Save Tonight for Me 𝄞𝄞 (Columbia, 1986)
Eyes of the Veiled Temptress 𝄞𝄞 (Columbia, 1988)
Hey Baby 𝄞𝄞𝄞 (Original Jazz Classics, 1992)
Compact Jazz 𝄞𝄞 (Verve, 1992)
Greatest Hits 𝄞𝄞 (Intersound, 1993)

worth searching for: You can almost smell the smoke from wacky-tabacky on Mangione's best live recording to date, *Live at the Village Gate* 𝄞𝄞𝄞𝄞 (Feels So Good Records, 1987, prod. Chuck Mangione, Mallory Earl), a two-disc set with ambience a-plenty and well-received jams. Also, the Grammy-winning *Bellavia* 𝄞𝄞𝄞 (A&M, 1975, prod. Chuck Mangione), is worth tracking down to hear Mangione's ability to fuse light jazz with elements of exotica.

influences:

◀◀ Dizzy Gillespie, Miles Davis

▶▶ Steve Gadd, Esther Satterfield

Ken Burke

The Manhattan Transfer (© Jack Vartoogian)

The Manhattan Transfer

Formed 1969, in New York, NY.

Tim Hauser, vocals (1969–present); Laurel Masse, vocals (1972–79); Cheryl Bentyne, vocals (1979–present); Alan Paul, vocals (1972–present); Janis Siegel, vocals (1972–present).

Beginning as a down-home jug band, the original Manhattan Transfer disintegrated in 1972, with remaining member Tim Hauser putting together the vocal ensemble that quickly found a cult following on the New York cabaret circuit. The band's 1975 self-titled record charted on both sides of the Atlantic, starting what was to become a tradition in global appeal. Weaving their voices in and out of each other with exquisite precision, the Manhattan Transfer can nail harmonies so effortlessly it sounds like anyone could do it. But as any amateur choir who has tried one of their arrangements will tell you, there's talent in them there voices. Working from the scat-singing solo tradition Louis Armstrong and Ella Fitzgerald built, the group has covered pop, swing, gospel, and rock. The under-

lying current—which explains the band's Grammy-winning success at least as much as its musicianship—is nostalgia.

what to buy: *The Manhattan Transfer* 🐾🐾🐾🐾 (Atlantic, 1975/ 1987, prod. Tim Hauser, Ahmet Ertegun) offers "Java Jive," an easy-listening tribute to coffee, as well as the down-on-your-knees gospel number "Operator" and the swinging "Tuxedo Junction." This record captures the group in straightforward confidence before it became hugely popular and started experimenting with the entire musical spectrum. *Vocalese* 🐾🐾🐾🐾 (Atlantic, 1985, prod. Tim Hauser), the word for the style of music that sets lyrics to previously recorded jazz instrumentals, racked up 12 Grammy nominations and won two. On it, the group rocks up Ray Charles's soulful piano stomp "Ray's Rockhouse," along with the catchy "That's Killer Joe" and the intricately playful "Another Night in Tunisia," with man-of-10,000-sounds Bobby McFerrin joining the group. All the lyrics were penned by vocalese master Jon Hendricks. *Swing* 🐾🐾🐾🐾 (Atlantic, 1997, prod. Tim Hauser) sets the group loose on swing-

era orchestral numbers. "A-Tisket, a-Tasket," an arrangement inspired from a 1938 Chick Webb recording, morphs Ella Fitzgerald's talent with Webb's orchestra style into one of the best numbers the band has ever recorded.

what to buy next: *The Manhattan Transfer Anthology* 🎵🎵🎵 (Rhino, 1992, prod. various) offers the span of hits—from "Trickle Trickle" to "Baby Come Back to Me (The Morse Code of Love)"—in a two-CD package. It's a good introduction, given that some Transfer albums can be sketchy in between the gems, dabbling in the latest sound of the times. *Mecca for Moderns* 🎵🎵🎵 (Atlantic, 1981, prod. Jay Graydon) includes the pop number "Boy from New York City." Any jazz vocal group worth its weight in lung power is expected to sing "Route 66," and Manhattan Transfer offers its groovy take on it on *Bop Doo-Wopp* 🎵🎵🎵 (Atlantic, 1985, prod. Tim Hauser).

what to avoid: On *Tonin'* 🎵 (Atlantic, 1995, prod. Arif Mardin), an exercise in pop horror, the group attempts to "jazz up" pop standards, featuring guest vocalists like Frankie Valli and Phil Collins. Smokey Robinson probably didn't even keep his copy of the CD, on which he sang a flat remake of his classic "I Second That Emotion." "The Thrill Is Gone" (and it really is) when the group sings behind blues greats B.B. King and Ruth Brown.

the rest:
Jukin' 🎵🎵 (Capitol, 1971)
Coming Out 🎵🎵🎵 (Atlantic, 1976)
Pastiche 🎵🎵🎵 (Atlantic, 1978)
The Manhattan Transfer Live 🎵🎵🎵 (Atlantic, 1978)
Best of the Manhattan Transfer 🎵🎵🎵 (Atlantic, 1981)
Bodies and Souls 🎵🎵 (Atlantic, 1983)
Live in Tokyo 🎵🎵 (Atlantic, 1987)
Brazil 🎵🎵🎵 (Atlantic, 1987)
The Offbeat of Avenues 🎵🎵🎵 (Columbia, 1992)
The Christmas Album 🎵🎵🎵 (Columbia, 1992)
The Manhattan Transfer Meets Tubby the Tuba 🎵🎵 (Summit, 1994)
Man Tora! Live in Tokyo 🎵🎵🎵 (Rhino, 1996)

worth searching for: The jazz-fusion rendition of Weather Report's "Birdland" on *Extensions* 🎵🎵🎵 (Atlantic, 1979, prod. Jay Graydon) has become the group's trademark song, a modern classic that will leave you wanting to drop everything and sing for a living. (Although the disco–new wave "Twilight Zone/Twilight Tone" is more reminiscent of the werewolf howls in Michael Jackson's *Thriller* than a showcase of musicianship.)

Barry Manilow (UPI/Corbis-Bettmann)

solo outings:
Janis Siegel:
Experiment in White 🎵🎵 (Atlantic, 1982)
At Home 🎵🎵🎵 (Atlantic, 1987)

influences:

◀◀ Jon Hendricks, Louis Armstrong, Ella Fitzgerald, Judy Garland, Benny Goodman, Count Basie, the Supremes, Nat "King" Cole, Bette Midler, Weather Report

▶▶ Take 6, Al Jarreau, Bobby McFerrin, Juan Luis Guerra, Matt Bianco

Jack Jackson

Barry Manilow

Born June 17, 1946, in Brooklyn, NY.

To some, he's a living, breathing punchline. To others, he's the last of the pure pop showmen, a singer-songwriter maintaining crucial ties to the Tin Pan Alley songwriting tradition. Trained at Juilliard, Manilow began his songcraft in the 1960s, working on commercial jingles (which later inspired a medley during live shows). In the early 1970s, he worked as pianist and arranger for Bette Midler at her New York bathhouse gigs, and arranged and produced some of her early recordings. After landing his own record contract and flopping with his first album, Manilow released "Mandy," which would become his prototypical ballad and set a pattern for his career. (His quiet start/bombastic finish singles, in fact, were the precursor to the ubiquitous "power ballads" of the 1980s, which simply added loud guitars to the equation.) "Mandy" was the first in a string of 25 consecutive Top 40 hits, which helped him become one of the top adult contemporary artists of all time. In the mid-1980s he turned his attention from singles to jazz- and Broadway-inspired concept albums, and added to his reputation as a crowd-pleasing live performer. Manilow has written and recorded plenty of treacly, sappy songs, and in the past he has practically begged for critical knocks when appearing onstage in black leather—a feeble attempt at contradicting the "wimp rock" image. But he also has crafted some memorable, tear-jerking standards, and has maintained a loyal fan base that craves his most common lyrical theme: Your heart may be broken, you may be alone, but it'll be all right.

what to buy: *Greatest Hits, Vol. I* 🎵🎵🎵 (Arista, 1988, prod. Barry Manilow, Ron Dante) and *Greatest Hits, Vol. II* 🎵🎵🎵 (Arista, 1988, prod. Barry Manilow, Ron Dante) feature the biggest hits of Manilow's 1970s heyday, including "Mandy," "I

Write the Songs," "Weekend in New England," and the stunning "Could It Be Magic." Manilow teamed with the likes of Mel Tormé and Sarah Vaughan for *2:00 A.M. Paradise Cafe* 𝄞𝄞𝄞𝄞 (Arista, 1984, prod. Barry Manilow, Eddie Arkin), a standards-inspired collection of jazz pop that predated the lounge revival by about a decade. His sole holiday set, *Because It's Christmas* 𝄞𝄞𝄞𝄞 (Arista, 1990, prod. Eddie Arkin, Barry Manilow), is in a similar vein, linking swing- and jazz-tinged takes on expected classics with originals (some with unpublished Johnny Mercer lyrics)—perfect for crying in your eggnog.

what to buy next: *Greatest Hits, Vol. III* 𝄞𝄞𝄞 (Arista, 1989, prod. Barry Manilow, Ron Dante, Jim Steinman, Eddie Arkin) rounds up the rest of his radio hits from the late-1970s and early 1980s. *Barry Live* 𝄞𝄞𝄞 (Arista, 1977, prod. Barry Manilow, Ron Dante) documents his stage charm, while *Barry Manilow II* 𝄞𝄞𝄞 (Arista, 1974, prod. Barry Manilow, Ron Dante) and *Even Now* 𝄞𝄞𝄞 (Arista, 1978, prod. Ron Dante, Barry Manilow) represent his best studio work of the 1970s. A sort of upbeat sequel to *Paradise Cafe*, *Swing Street* 𝄞𝄞𝄞 (Arista, 1987, prod. Barry Manilow, Eddie Arkin) includes appearances by Phyllis Hyman and Kid Creole.

what to avoid: For the cover of *Barry Manilow* 𝄞 (Arista, 1989, prod. Michael Lloyd), he sports George Michael–style beard stubble. Consider it fair warning.

the rest:
Manilow I 𝄞𝄞𝄞 (Arista, 1973)
Tryin' to Get the Feeling 𝄞𝄞𝄞 (Arista, 1975)
This One's for You 𝄞𝄞𝄞 (Arista, 1976)
One Voice 𝄞𝄞𝄞 (Arista, 1979)
Barry 𝄞𝄞𝄞 (Arista, 1980)
If I Should Love Again 𝄞𝄞𝄞 (Arista, 1981)
Live in Britain 𝄞𝄞𝄞 (Arista, 1981)
Here Comes the Night 𝄞𝄞𝄞 (Arista, 1982)
Manilow 𝄞𝄞 (RCA, 1985)
Live on Broadway 𝄞𝄞𝄞 (Arista, 1990)
Showstoppers 𝄞𝄞𝄞 (Arista, 1991)
The Complete Collection . . . and Then Some 𝄞𝄞𝄞𝄞 (Arista, 1992)
Singin' with the Big Bands 𝄞𝄞𝄞 (Arista, 1994)
Summer of '78 𝄞𝄞𝄞 (Arista, 1996)

worth searching for: With almost as many tracks as the two 1988 hits packages, the out-of-print *Greatest Hits* 𝄞𝄞𝄞𝄞 (Arista, 1978, prod. Barry Manilow, Ron Dante) is the definitive single-disc set.

influences:
◀◀ Barbra Streisand, Bette Midler, Neil Sedaka, Bing Crosby, Engelbert Humperdinck, the Carpenters, Burt Bacharach

▶▶ Michael Bolton, Harry Connick Jr., Richard Marx, Whitney Houston

Jay Dedrick

Mannheim Steamroller

Formed 1974, in Omaha, NB.

Chip Davis, producer; varying singers.

When it comes to New Age music (that is to say, easy-listening for spiritually ambitious yuppies), there is no more successful enterprise than Mannheim Steamroller. Under the creative direction of producer Chip Davis, the varying members of the group skillfully augment classical sounds with techno-rock instrumentation, sound effects, and remarkably high production values. In his early professional life, Davis was a jingle writer. With advertising man Bill Fries, he created the fictional singing truck driver C.W. McCall for a series of Clio-award winning bread commercials. The ads proved so popular, Fries and Davis were able to parlay their McCall character into a series of hit country records, most notably the '70s C.B. radio anthem "Convoy." Davis's wildly successful collaborations with Fries provided the capital needed to create his own record label, American Gramaphone. Initially, Davis had trouble getting exposure for his self-proclaimed audiophile label. In a novel bit of promotion, he began distributing free copies of his disc to audio stores for demonstration purposes. Impressed customers would buy the stereo and then ask where they could find the music, and a multi-platinum phenomenon was born. In their impressively consistent body of work, Davis and Mannheim Steamroller offer classically oriented soundtracks to seasons, events, and nature. Mellow and melodic at times, atmospheric and intense during others, the best recordings of Mannheim Steamroller are as invigorating as a steaming cup of Red Zinger Tea.

what to buy: The best introduction to this genre is *Fresh Aire—Interludes* 𝄞𝄞𝄞𝄞 (American Gramaphone, 1981, prod. Chip Davis) which contains many fine samplings from the first five Fresh Aire discs. For full-length work, Davis and crew are at their creative peak on *Fresh Aire III* 𝄞𝄞𝄞𝄞 (American Gramaphone, 1979, prod. Chip Davis), an ode to summer with an actual cricket as part of the backup crew; included is "Tocatta," the favorite demonstration cut for audio salespeople everywhere. Equally fine, *Fresh Aire V* 𝄞𝄞𝄞𝄞 (American Gramaphone, 1983, prod. Chip Davis) is a musical tribute to winter, replete with crunching snow and a roaring fireplace.

what to buy next: Among the many fine seasonal offerings from Mannheim Steamroller, *A Fresh Aire Christmas* 🎵🎵🎵🎵 (American Gramaphone, 1988, prod. Chip Davis) stands out with its simply textured, New Age updating of such well-known pieces as "Little Drummer Boy," "Greensleeves," and "Hark! The Herald Angels Sing."

the rest:

Fresh Aire 🎵🎵🎵 (American Gramaphone, 1975)

Fresh Aire II 🎵🎵🎵 (American Gramaphone, 1977)

Christmas 🎵🎵🎵🎵 (American Gramaphone, 1984)

Fresh Aire IV 🎵🎵🎵 (American Gramaphone, 1986)

Fresh Aire VI 🎵🎵🎵 (American Gramaphone, 1986)

(With Mason Williams) *Classical Gas* 🎵🎵🎵 (American Gramaphone, 1987)

Yellowstone: The Music of Nature 🎵🎵🎵🎵 (American Gramaphone, 1989)

Fresh Aire VII 🎵🎵🎵🎵 (American Gramaphone, 1990)

To Russia with Love 🎵🎵🎵 (American Gramaphone, 1994)

Christmas in the Aire 🎵🎵🎵🎵 (American Gramaphone, 1995)

Christmas Live 🎵🎵🎵🎵 (American Gramaphone, 1997)

Mannheim Massage 🎵🎵🎵 (American Gramaphone, 1997)

worth searching for: Davis has produced similar-style discs under his own name, such as *Impressions* 🎵🎵🎵🎵 (American Gramaphone, 1994), *Holiday Musik, Vols. 1 & 2* 🎵🎵🎵 (American Gramaphone, 1997), and *Party 2: Music That Cooks* 🎵🎵🎵 (American Gramaphone, 1995). Davis has also produced the compilations *Day Parts: Dinner* 🎵🎵 (American Gramaphone, 1992), *Day Parts: Romance* 🎵🎵🎵 (American Gramaphone, 1992), and the best of the series, *Day Parts: Sunday Morning Coffee* 🎵🎵🎵🎵 (American Gramaphone, 1991).

influences:

⏪ Walter/Wendy Carlos, Mason Williams, the Electric Light Orchestra, Mike Post, Mystic Moods Orchestra

⏩ Yanni, John Tesh, Diodato, Shadowfax, Checkfield

Ken Burke

Mantovani

Born Annunzio Paolo Mantovani, November 15, 1905, in Venice, Italy. Died March 30, 1980, in Tunbridge Wells, England.

When you think of vintage Muzak, the defunct "beautiful music" radio stations, or elevator music in general—dozens of string instruments trying to play as softly and unobtrusively as possible—Mantovani's recorded sounds probably wind up in your head. He recorded dozens of albums, sometimes of instrumental Christmas songs, sometimes of traditional Italian music, sometimes inspired by Christopher Columbus, some-

times cover versions of rock or pop hits—all with the same lulling-you-to-sleep quality that characterizes most proud background music.

Before proceeding to the ratings, though, a defense: Joseph Lanza, author of the 1994 book *Elevator Music,* likens the composer's first hit, "Charmaine," to "a soft-focus descent of sequined angels wielding magic wands over dancers who float from the ballroom floor in a slow-motion version of waltz time turned dream time. Pastoral woodwinds offer a bit of earthly assurance, but the incessant violins lift us back into the melody unmoored." See? Schmaltz.

Inspired by more established fellow violinist Fritz Kreisler, who played unabashedly low-brow pop compositions, Mantovani embarked on a long career of merging classical styles with easy-listening melodies. He conducted several orchestras, including London's Hotel Metropole, and served as Noel Coward's musical director. In the early '50s he began his lush assault on American elevator passengers; using stereo technology, he began an incredibly prolific string of top-50 albums, all filled with waltzes and Christmas music, designed to make people forget their problems. Though many listeners turn up their noses today, they have to grudgingly admit how subversively influential his soft sounds were for almost three decades.

what to buy: Mantovani recorded more than 50 solo albums, and that was just during his sales peak—it doesn't count posthumous greatest-hits packages or box sets. Many of them are interchangeable, even offering slightly different versions of the same songs. *Love Songs* 🎵🎵 (Pair, 1991) captures the composer's uncanny ability to turn rock into syrup, with instrumental versions of Roberta Flack's "Killing Me Softly with His Song" and Stevie Wonder's "You Are the Sunshine of My Life." *Magical Moods of Mantovani* 🎵🎵 (Special Music Company) is three discs, and we can't imagine anybody, not even Yanni or John Tesh, needing more than this.

what to buy next: Every family that at least pretends to roast chestnuts and drink eggnog around a fire during the holidays needs one Mantovani Christmas album to help lighten the mood: good ones are *Christmas Favorites* 🎵🎵 (Polydor, 1988) and *Christmas with Mantovani* 🎵🎵 (Laserlight).

what to avoid: Even Mantovani's supporters admitted he had delusions of grandeur, and he frequently titled his works after major historical events. *Hello Columbus 1492–92: A Musical Voyage* **woof!** (Bainbridge, 1991, prod. Ray Few) has the audacity to link this totally insubstantial music to Columbus's discovery of America.

best of the rest:

best of the rest:

Moon River and Other Great Film Themes ♫♫ (Decca/London, 1963)
Incomparable Mantovani ♫♫ (PolyGram, 1964)
Mantovani's Golden Hits ♫♫ (London/PolyGram, 1967)
More Mantovani Greatest Hits ♫♫♫ (Decca, 1984)
Mantovani's Italia ♫♫ (Bainbridge, 1987)
Golden Instrumental Hits ♫♫ (Laserlight, 1990)
Latino Besame Mucho ♫♫ (Delta, 1994)
Latino Vaya Con Dios ♫♫ (Delta, 1994)
Mantovani Latino ♫♫ (Laserlight, 1994)

influences:

◀◀ Fritz Kreisler

▶▶ Andre Kostelanetz, John Tesh, Yanni, Peter Kater, Wind Machine, Ray Conniff, Percy Faith

Steve Knopper

Dean Martin

Born Dino Paul Crocetti, June 17, 1917, in Steubenville, OH. Died December 25, 1995, in Beverly Hills, CA.

Dean Martin's sly double-entendres and boozy persona make him one of the quintessential lounge stars. In addition, his influence on Elvis Presley's ballad singing should qualify him for the Rock and Roll Hall of Fame.

Martin sang well but never was as serious as his Rat Pack buddy, Frank Sinatra. That's probably why Martin recorded so many stinkers, but he did it with a wink. In fact, it seems as though Martin was never serious about anything. His school days established his pattern of doing only what came easily to him. Everything he ended up doing for a living—acting, comedy, singing—essentially was a con game. Fortunately for him, his voice was not a con. Singing is a staple among Italian families, and this son of Italian immigrants was about as Italian as an American can get. (Even so, the hardly Italian Bing Crosby influenced his singing.) Martin began working in Steubenville's underground gambling dens as a high schooler, had a short career as a boxer, and moved on to singing in nightclubs. With his good looks (aided by a nose job) and a devil-may-care sensuousness in his singing, Martin was first a hit with women. The con in his singing was that he could make the girls think he was crooning exclusively to them, even though he was not interested in anyone exclusively. Still, his career was at the third-tier level at best in 1946, when he and Jerry Lewis met up in Atlantic City. The team began tearing audiences apart with madcap comedy routines, becoming one of the biggest comedy phenomena of the late '40s and early '50s. They appeared in movies, radio, and TV series. Their egos ultimately crashed the partnership in 1956 after 16 flicks. Even though he was a natural at comedy, Martin focused more on singing, and his first real hit, "Memories Are Made of This," came as the partnership with Lewis was on its last legs. There was considerable speculation that Martin would fade away without Lewis, but the singer kept getting movie roles, even when his recording career stalled in the early '60s. When "Everybody Loves Somebody" knocked the Beatles' "A Hard Day's Night" out of *Billboard*'s #1 singles spot on August 15, 1964, he won a new audience. Martin charted more (11 times) than Sinatra did (eight times) in the subsequent three years. (Sinatra's own biggest hit of the period, "Strangers in the Night," relied on Martin's behind-the-scenes guys, producer Jimmy Bowen and arranger Ernie Freeman.) Martin's new hits were spurred at least in part by the popularity of his TV variety series on NBC from 1964–75. He also continued to play Vegas and make middle-of-the-road records.

From the end of his TV series until his death in 1995, Martin's story was one of slow dissolution. Never one to work too hard, he was more likely to be found wearing his jeans for a solitary dinner after work than decked out for a night on the town. Martin had been married three times and had seven kids. In 1987, Dean Jr., a captain in the Air National Guard, died when his jet fighter crashed. Martin, set to start a Rat Pack reunion tour in 1988 with Sinatra and Sammy Davis Jr., was devastated. While Sinatra and Davis basked in the glory of hitting the stage together one last time, to Martin it was nothing but ashes—and too much work. Citing health problems, he left the tour early. He was quickly back doing Vegas shows, reportedly soaked in Percodan, a loner until he died.

what to buy: *Dean Martin: Capitol Collector's Series* ♫♫♫♫ (Capitol, 1989, compilation prod. Ron Furmanek) is the best of the collections from Martin's Capitol years, 1948–61. It begins with his first recorded tune, "That Certain Party," a duet with Jerry Lewis. His first two hit singles—"Powder Your Face with Sunshine (Smile! Smile! Smile!)" and "I'll Always Love You (Day after Day)," reproduced here—came more than a year apart. Before "That's Amore," Martin sounded stiff, as if his tie were strangling him, but this cut loosened the tie. Originally, Martin didn't want to do the pidgin Italian tune, but it took off to #2. (Listen to the background singers mess up the pronunciation of the rolling Italian "r," while Martin glides through it liquidly.) The other big hits of his Capitol years—"Memories Are Made of This" and "Return to

Me"—are also included here. Martin's "Volare," while not as big a hit as these others, shows him at his best. The song is about the heady loss of control as infatuation hits, and Martin's "whoa-oh" captures the exact feeling of a heart taking off into the sky. Italian-American Martin understood and performed this song better than any Italian tenor of the time. The album wraps up with Martin's boozy "Ain't That a Kick in the Head," which didn't chart because it was banned by some radio stations as "too suggestive" (1960 was a different world). This perfect embodiment of the Rat Pack spirit came from *Ocean's 11*.

what to buy next: *The Capitol Years* 𝄞𝄞𝄞𝄞 (Capitol, 1996, compilation prod. Bob Furmanek) is a two-CD set that features nine of the 20 cuts from *Capitol Collector's Series*. *Capitol Years* tries to flesh out what rockers would call "the album cuts" side of Dino; the rarities, unreleased tracks, and extra songs don't add much. Still, it's pretty cool to hear him dueting with Nat King Cole on "Open Up the Dog House (Two Cats Are Coming In)." A team-up with Peggy Lee on "You Was" lets both play off their languorous sensuality. *That's Amore: The Best of Dean Martin* 𝄞𝄞𝄞𝄞 (Capitol, 1996, prod. various) covers much of the same ground, but this one is weighted toward the Italian songs. Such staples as "Volare" and "That's Amore" act as the iceberg tip for "Return to Sorrento," "Vieni Su," and "Arrivederci Roma." That last track is a must. Martin's "eat, drink and be merry" approach meshes perfectly with a tune from the *La Dolce Vita* era of Italy. *Sleep Warm* 𝄞𝄞𝄞 (Capitol, 1959, prod. Lee Gillette) is the only CD issue of an original Martin album left in print (the rest are compilations). A fairly average record for its time, *Sleep Warm*'s most notable feature is that Frank Sinatra conducted the orchestra. The Sinatra-like concept album featured songs about sleep and dreaming—from the title cut to the closing "Brahms' Lullaby."

the rest:
Best of Dean Martin 𝄞𝄞𝄞 (Capitol, 1990)
All-Time Greatest Hits 𝄞𝄞𝄞 (Curb, 1991)
Season's Greetings from Dean Martin 𝄞𝄞𝄞 (Capitol, 1992)
Collection 𝄞𝄞𝄟 (Castle, 1992)
Spotlight on Dean Martin 𝄞𝄞𝄞 (Capitol, 1995)
Solid Gold 𝄞𝄞𝄟 (Madacy, 1995)
Sings Italian Favorites 𝄞𝄞𝄞 (Capitol, 1995)
You're Nobody Till Somebody Loves You 𝄞𝄞𝄞 (Capitol, 1995)
I Wish You Love 𝄞𝄞𝄟 (Great Hits, 1996)
Love Songs by Dean Martin 𝄞𝄞𝄟 (Ranwood, 1997)

worth searching for: *The Best of Dean Martin 1962–1968* 𝄞𝄞𝄞𝄞𝄞 (Charly, 1996, prod. Jimmy Bowen) covers Martin's Reprise Records singles, none of which are available on CD in the United States. This import collection includes the zenith of his chart ca-

reer, "Everybody Loves Somebody." These songs dovetailed with Dino's weekly TV persona as a singing Hugh Hefner. The distinctive slurs, which, in his early career, added a casual bon vivant vibe to the proceedings, become the dominant element in his singing here, as if he were perpetually buzzed. Dino's in total control here, with all the brilliance that his lazy approach ever offered. *Memories Are Made of This* 𝄞𝄞𝄞 (Bear Family, 1997, prod. various) deserves a mention because it's an eight-CD collection of everything Martin recorded for Capitol.

influences:
◄◄ Bing Crosby, Al Jolson
►► Elvis Presley

Salvatore Caputo

Freddy Martin

Born December 9, 1906, in Cleveland, OH. Died September 30, 1983.

During the '30s, saxophonist-bandleader Freddy Martin led a run-of-the-mill society band, which played smooth music at such elite venues as the Waldorf Astoria. In 1941, along with pianist Jack Fina, he stumbled upon the gimmick of transforming classical music themes into sweet, sentimental pop. His big instrumental hits, "Tonight We Love" and "I Look at Heaven" (taken from Tchaikovsky's B-flat Piano Concerto and Grieg's Piano Concerto, respectively), virtually created the concept of commercial "beautiful music," and still receive airplay today. Martin also had a good ear for vocalists, employing the likes of Russ Morgan, Gene Vaughn, Buddy Clark, Helen Ward, and future talk-show host Merv Griffin (who scored a big hit with the bouncy novelty "I've Got a Lovely Bunch of Coconuts"). At their peak, Martin and his orchestra hosted their own network radio shows and appeared in the movie musicals *Stage Door Canteen, What's Buzzin', Cousin?* and *The Mayor of 44th Street*. A perennial guest on early '50s TV, Martin hosted his own network show for two years, plus several local ones on the West Coast. Never lacking for work, Martin and various incarnations of his band played top nightspots into the late '60s. After a bout with semi-retirement, Martin and fellow bandleaders Bob Crosby and Frankie Carle formed the *Big Band Cavalcade*, which toured with great success in the early '70s.

what to buy: The best of a skimpy lot, *Freddy Martin & His Orchestra: 1950–52* 𝄞𝄞𝄟 (Collector's Choice, 1996) showcases some nice selections, such as "Once in Love with Amy," "You Do Something to Me," "Please Mr. Sun," "Heaven Drops Her Curtains," and the hit "Early in the Morning."

the rest:
Uncollected Freddy Martin & His Orchestra, Vol. 2: 1944–1946 🎵🎵 (Hindsight, 1992)

Uncollected Freddy Martin & His Orchestra, Vol. 3: 1952 🎵🎵 (Hindsight, 1992)

Uncollected Freddy Martin & His Orchestra, Vol. 4: 1948–52 🎵🎵 (Hindsight, 1992)

worth searching for: It's worth the extra trouble to find *Hits of Freddy Martin* 🎵🎵🎵🎵 (Capitol/EMI, 1989), which features "Tonight We Love," "Bye Lo Bye Lullabye," and Merv Griffin's early claim to fame, "I've Got a Lovely Bunch of Coconuts." Though out of print, it's a much more powerful collection of hits than the Collector's Choice disc.

influences:

◄◄ Guy Lombardo, Arnold Johnson, Jack Albin

►► Frankie Carle, Mort Lindsey, Merv Griffin

Ken Burke

Tony Martin

Born Alvin Morris, December 22, 1912, in Oakland, CA.

This handsome, slick-haired crooner was a minor film star and major singing star in the 1950s, and he achieved enough notoriety on radio and television to maintain a long, lucrative nightclub singing career. Long before his biggest success, he captured the public's attention briefly in the mid-1930s, singing fluffy orchestral love songs like "Now It Can Be Told," from the film *Alexander's Ragtime Band.* His marriage to movie star Alice Faye amounted to a big break, even though the marriage lasted only four years: it led to movie work (occasionally with Faye) in *Sally, Irene, and Mary* and *Kentucky Moonshine,* among others. A dozen more movie roles and a singing role in Glenn Miller's U.S. Air Force band allowed Martin to gradually climb the stardom ladder, and he became one of MGM's leading singing personalities throughout the late 1940s and early 1950s. He performed frequently on radio and television and, with his singing second wife, Cyd Charisse, toured the nightclub circuit through the 1970s.

what's available: *The Best of Tony Martin: The Mercury Years* 🎵🎵🎵 (Chronicles/PolyGram, 1996, prod. various) collects some nice croons, including "As You Desire Me," "Guilty," and "Rumors Are Flying"; and *This May Be the Night* 🎵🎵🎵 (Living Era, 1993), featuring bandleader Ray Noble, documents his early crooning moments, from 1938 to 1941.

influences:

◄◄ Russ Columbo, Bing Crosby, Frank Sinatra, Ray Noble, Alice Faye

►► Jack Jones, Andy Williams, Vic Damone, Rudy Vallee, Wayne Newton

Steve Knopper

Al Martino

Born Alfred Cini, October 7, 1927, in Philadelphia, PA.

There aren't many of the old-guard Italian romantic singers left, but one of the best, Al Martino, is still going strong. Whether emoting heavy love ballads, swinging up-tempo showtunes, or crooning in Italian, Martino sells a tune with a unique mixture of operatic power and supper-club intimacy.

Martino was convinced by family friend Mario Lanza, the great opera singer, to become a professional singer, and his first records certainly show Lanza's influence. His 1952 version of "Here in My Heart" became the first record by an American artist to top both the British and U.S. charts. Switching to Capitol records the following year, Martino hit with "Rachel," "Take My Heart," and "When You're Mine." It's uncertain whether the public tired of his Lanzaesque recordings or his career suffered mismanagement by unscrupulous elements, but Martino suddenly stopped having hits. He moved to the U.K. for a time, where he recorded several records that hit their Top 20 but gained little notice in the States. Martino made a stunning comeback in the early '60s with hits such as "I Can't Get You Out of My Heart," "I Love You Because," "Painted Tainted Rose," and "I Love You More and More Every Day." His style had become warmer—less tonsils, more heart—and the response from a public starved for romance was overwhelming. Even after Beatlemania, Martino continued scoring big on the charts with "Spanish Eyes," "Mary in the Morning," "Can't Help Falling in Love," and others until 1970. His role as Johnny Fontaine in the 1972 Francis Ford Coppola classic, *The Godfather,* gave his career a mighty boost, and provided him with one last great U.S. pop hit, "Speak Softly Love." A consistently popular cabaret performer, he still packs the big rooms in Vegas and Atlantic City. In recent times, Martino's career has undergone a major revival in Europe, where TV advertised repackages of his greatest hits sell in the millions.

what to buy: Martino's biggest hits and most affecting performances, from "Here in My Heart" to "Speak Softly Love (Love Theme from *The Godfather*)," are brilliantly grouped together on the can't-miss *Al Martino: Capitol Collector's Series* 🎵🎵🎵🎵🎵 (Gold Rush, 1992/1996, compilation prod. Bob Furmanek, Ron Furmanek).

what to buy next: Martino's power as an interpreter of standards is clearly on display in *Spotlight on . . . Al Martino* 🎵🎵🎵🎵 (Gold Rush, 1996, prod. various), culled from his best years at Capitol.

the rest:
Spanish Eyes 🎵🎵🎵 (Capitol/EMI, 1966/1990)
The Best of Al Martino 🎵🎵🎵 (Collectables, 1968/1995)
Greatest Hits 🎵🎵🎵 (Curb, 1990)
Favorite Italian Love Songs 🎵🎵🎵 (Cema Special Products, 1992)

Here in My Heart 🎵🎵🎵 (Cema Special Products, 1992)
There Are Such Things 🎵🎵🎵 (Cema Special Products, 1992)
Merry Christmas 🎵🎵🎵🎵 (Capitol/EMI, 1993)
Volare 🎵🎵🎵 (Drive Entertainment, 1993)
Live in Concert 🎵🎵🎵 (Laserlight, 1993/1997)
Greatest Hits 🎵🎵🎵🎵 (Cema Special Products, 1994)
Al Martino 🎵🎵🎵🎵 (A Touch of Class, 1997)
Concert Collection 🎵🎵🎵 (Prism, 1997)

worth searching for: Bilingual romance never sounded better than on *The Exciting Voice of Al Martino* 🎵🎵🎵🎵 (Capitol/EMI, 1964/1991, prod. Voyle Gilmore, Andy Wiswell), 24 tracks of smoldering love themes in English and Italian.

influences:

◀◀ Mario Lanza, Frank Sinatra

▶▶ Vic Damone, Jerry Vale, Robert Goulet

Ken Burke

Johnny Mathis

Born John Royce Mathis, September 30, 1935, in San Francisco, CA.

People forget, sometimes, just how much Mathis's music was the polar opposite of rock 'n' roll. His ultrasmooth balladeering, from the 1957 smash "Chances Are" to his hit 1959 reading of "Misty," is all love and romance. There's no subversiveness whatsoever, not even the suggestion of sex, even though countless mid-century teenagers aired his music on car radios while they played doctor in the back seat. While Elvis Presley and the Beatles knocked his crooning predecessors Rosemary Clooney and Perry Como off the pop charts, Mathis hung on. Whether or not he was the first African American millionaire, as some have suggested, he was a talented, opera-trained singer with a savvy sense of niche marketing.

Mathis's career began with a choice—a music teacher encouraged him to sing in the opera, but he also tried out for the Olympic track team in Berkeley. Some accounts say Columbia Records executive George Avakian discovered him while he was singing the National Anthem at a track meet; others say it was during a performance at a San Francisco nightclub jam session. In 1956, entering the studio with easy-listening king Ray Conniff's orchestra, Mathis took Columbia A&R head Mitch Miller's advice and switched from jazz to smooth, orchestral pop music. The decision set off one of the biggest-selling ca-

reers in pop-music history: from his #14 debut, "Wonderful! Wonderful!," to his 490-week-charting album, *Johnny's Greatest Hits*, he owned the non-rock industries in the '50s and '60s. Tastes eventually changed, and Mathis surrendered his music-industry dominance beginning in the early 1970s. He did manage one 1978 hit, the Deniece Williams duet, "Too Much, Too Little, Too Late," and tried disco and rock with varying degrees of success throughout the 1980s. But his legacy remains the hitmaking period, and young lovers with a sense of history still crank up "The Twelfth of Never" when they're alone in the back seat. Only nowadays, they queue up CDs from the box set.

what to buy: The box set *The Music of Johnny Mathis: A Personal Collection* ♫♫♫ (Columbia/Legacy, 1993, compilation prod. Didier C. Deutsch) contains absolutely everything, all the #1 singles and even a new duet with Barbra Streisand, who has consistently cited Mathis's balladeering as a primary influence. *The Essence of Johnny Mathis* ♫♫♫ (Columbia/Legacy, 1994, prod. various) takes a different approach, focusing on his early years and including more spare songs, like "I'll Be Seeing You," instead of his trademark lush, orchestral ballads.

what to buy next: Mathis recorded more than 75 studio albums, so it's difficult to keep them straight, especially with so many different greatest-hits collections swirling around. *Open Fire, Two Guitars* ♫♫♫ (Columbia, 1958) is just the voice, two guitars, and a bass, so it frames Mathis's talent without relying on a bunch of expensive studio techniques; on CD it's packaged with *Warm* ♫♫♫ (Columbia, 1959). Other can't-go-wrong greatest-hits collections (if you're not quite a big enough Mathis fan for the box set) include *Encore! 16 Most Requested Songs* ♫♫♫ (Columbia, 1994, prod. various), *The Best of Johnny Mathis* ♫♫♫ (Columbia, 1980, prod. Jack Gold), *All-Time Greatest Hits* ♫♫♫ (Columbia, 1972, prod. various), and *The First 25 Years—The Silver Anniversary Album* ♫♫♫ (Columbia, 1981, prod. various).

what to avoid: Needless to say, all this lovey-dovey romance is bound to slip into cheese territory. Negligible are *Love Story* ♫♫ (Columbia, 1971), *Feelings* ♫ (Columbia, 1975), and *Friends in Love* ♫ (Columbia, 1982).

best of the rest:
Merry Christmas ♫♫♫ (Columbia, 1958)
Heavenly/Faithfully ♫♫♫ (Columbia, 1959/1975)
Johnny Mathis Sings the Music of Bacharach and Kaempfert ♫♫♫ (Columbia, 1970)
Johnny Mathis in Person ♫♫ (Columbia, 1972)
The First Time Ever I Saw Your Face ♫♫♫ (Columbia, 1972)
Killing Me Softly with Her Song ♫♫♫ (Columbia, 1973)

When Will I See You Again ♫♫ (Columbia, 1975)
Johnny Mathis & Deniece Williams: That's What Friends Are For ♫♫♫ (Columbia, 1978)
In the Still of the Night ♫♫♫ (Columbia, 1985)
In a Sentimental Mood: Mathis Sings Ellington ♫♫♫ (Columbia, 1990)
Better Together: The Duet Album ♫♫♫ (Columbia, 1991)
Ultimate Johnny Mathis N/A (Columbia/Legacy, 1998)

influences:

⏮ Frank Sinatra, Nelson Riddle, Ray Conniff, Percy Faith, Duke Ellington

⏭ Luther Vandross, R. Kelly, Whitney Houston, Jackie Wilson, Sam Cooke, Barbra Streisand

Steve Knopper

Eric Matthews

Born January 12, 1969, in Gresham, OR.

Although he's a native of the Northwest and signed to Seattle's Nirvana-breaking Sub Pop Records, Eric Matthews couldn't be less interested in grunge—an anecdote apparently irresistible to nearly every music scribe who has written about him. Still, it only begins to describe Matthews's aesthetic: first in Cardinal and especially on his own, the songwriter, arranger, and multi-instrumentalist makes orchestral pop that looks past such obvious antecedents as the Beatles and Beach Boys to a time of dinner jackets and casual sophistication. Matthews studied trumpet at the San Francisco Conservatory of Music, hardly an obvious career path for a Sub Pop signee, and eventually moved to Boston with ambitions of playing with the Boston Symphony Orchestra. There, he and Richard Davies, of the Australian pop group the Moles, formed the duo Cardinal. Davies sang and wrote most of the songs but Matthews handled the arrangements—and in 1994 released a self-titled album on the independent label Flydaddy. The group wasn't big enough for the duo's sweeping pop visions, and Matthews eventually returned to Oregon to record his first solo album. (He sang, conducted, and played recorder, harpsichord, and trumpet, while former Jellyfish member Jason Falkner played guitar.)

what to buy: Even further removed from the alternative-rock of the time than Cardinal's album, *It's Heavy in Here* ♫♫♫♫ (Sub Pop, 1995, prod. Eric Matthews) impresses with lush strings, evocative arrangements, and softly yearning vocals. Unfortunately, its title only begins to hint at the sheer weight of its lyrics.

what to buy next: Winning rave reviews and a decent amount of sales for such a challenging record, Matthews returned to the studio two years later to record *The Lateness of the Hour* ♪♪♪ (Sub Pop, 1997, prod. Eric Matthews). (The record also features Falkner and a number of other guests.) Slightly more accessible than his first solo outing, it's every bit as grand, sweeping, and dramatically beautiful.

influences:

◀◀ Brian Wilson, Burt Bacharach

see also: *Richard Davies*

Robert Levine

Billy May

Born William E. May, November 10, 1916, in Pittsburgh, PA.

May arranged one of the biggest big-band hits ever, Charlie Barnet's version of "Cherokee"—later a key inspiration for Charlie Parker, who styled his bebop classic "Koo-Koo" after it—then became an indispensable behind-the-scenes arranger and bandleader for many, many musicians and record labels. Beginning in the early '40s, May worked with Glenn Miller, Bing Crosby, Paul Weston, Nat King Cole, Yma Sumac, and Frank Sinatra. His squawking-horn music swung hard, but it never carried quite the trailblazing weight of past bandleaders such as Duke Ellington or Benny Goodman; May's style was much more playful, which explains his work on the Arthur Murray dance-instruction series and his enduring kid's song "I Tawt I Taw a Puddy Tat."

May, who always claimed to be self-taught, was a tuba player in high school, then turned out to be good at arranging. Never an astounding visionary, May's fast, workmanlike qualities impressed first Barnet, then Miller, who invited him to join his influential swing band. Later, as Capitol's musical director, his personal habits—such as knocking down vodka during sessions—only enhanced his reputation as a fun-loving, fast-working party animal. Naturally, Sinatra was drawn to him, and he employed May's orchestra on his classic *Come Fly with Me* album. In the '60s May scored several television series themes, including *The Mod Squad* and *Emergency;* though his intense lifestyle slowed him down, he continued working with Sinatra and on movie soundtracks through the '80s and '90s.

what to buy: Though May recorded his most influential music with other people, two volumes of his instrumental big-band work—*Best of Billy May, Vol. I* ♪♪♪ (Aerospace, 1990, prod. various) and *Best of Billy May, Vol. II* ♪♪♪ (Aerospace, 1990, prod. various)—are fast, playful, and almost intimidatingly brassy. On standards like "Little Brown Jug" and "Makin' Whoopee," both from *Volume II*, the "slurping saxophones" play melodies

Cocktail Classics

Pennies from Heaven

18-Karat **Bing Crosby**
Pennies from Heaven
(Pro Arte)

Bombsville! **Regis Philbin**
It's Time for Regis
(Mercury)

as thick as syrup, and the rhythm chugs along like a whistle-blowing train. *Volume I* is loaded with more familiar songs, such as "Charmaine," "Unforgettable," and "All of Me."

what to buy next: The two original LPs for the price of one CD, *Sorta May/Sorta Dixie* ♪♪ (Creative World, 1996) includes lesser-known May-slurped standards like "Deep Purple," "Soon," and "Thou Swell."

worth searching for: May, like Nelson Riddle before him, helped transform Sinatra from a stiff-shirted crooner to a hipster swing cat. The arranger also encouraged Sinatra to express his sense of humor and swaggering confidence; the result of these sessions, *Come Fly with Me* 🎵🎵🎵🎵 (Capitol, 1957, prod. Voyle Gilmore), included the classics "Blue Hawaii," "Isle of Capri," and the title track. Further evidence of May's style is on Nat King Cole's *Billy May Sessions* 🎵🎵🎵 (Capitol/EMI, 1993).

influences:

◀◀ Charlie Barnet, Nelson Riddle, Ray Noble

▶▶ Leroy Anderson, Mantovani, Charlie Parker, Frank Sinatra, Nat "King" Cole, Bing Crosby

Steve Knopper

Marilyn McCoo

See: The Fifth Dimension

Maureen McGovern

Born July 27, 1949, in Youngstown, OH.

McGovern's career has more in common with *The Poseidon Adventure* than she'd like to remember. Best known as the singer of the 1973 shipwreck epic's chart-topping theme, "The Morning After," McGovern followed that hit with the theme from *The Towering Inferno* and her reign as Queen of the Disaster Flick Soundtracks had begun. A slew of overproduced, underwhelming pop albums followed, but a chance meeting with the Manhattan Transfer, advice from Mel Tormé, and starring roles such musicals as *The Pirates of Penzance* and *Nine* reminded her of the difference between singing and merely applying her voice. In the mid-1980s, she went back to her lounge roots and began collaborating with pianist Mike Renzi in New York supper clubs and got signed to CBS Records. Reborn as a cabaret singer, McGovern has developed into an impressive interpreter of standards and torch songs, equally at home with jazz, pop, and theatrical styles.

what to buy: *Another Woman in Love* 🎵🎵🎵🎵 (CBS, 1987, prod. Maureen McGovern, Ron Barron) was her comeback and remains her most convincing showcase. Backed only by pianist Mike Renzi, she mixes such timeless tunes as "You're Getting to Be a Habit with Me" and Rodgers and Hart's "Why Can't I" with Peter Allen's "I Could Have Been a Sailor" and Stephen Sondheim's "I Remember" and demonstrates a startling command of her four-octave range.

what to buy next: *Naughty Baby* 🎵🎵🎵 (CBS, 1988, prod. Ron Barron) is a sassy live collection of George Gershwin compositions like "They Can't Take That Away from Me" and the recently unearthed "A Corner of Heaven with You," featuring a gently swinging quintet that includes bassist Jay Leonhart and drummer Grady Tate.

what to avoid: Yes, it includes "The Morning After" and "Can You Read My Mind?" from the *Superman* movie, but buying *Greatest Hits* 🎵 (Curb, 1990, prod. Michael Lloyd)—coincidentally assembled a couple of years after McGovern made her cabaret comeback—will only encourage major labels to pick the meat from the bones of the skeletons in any artist's closet. Just say no.

the rest:

State of the Heart 🎵🎵🎵 (CBS, 1988)
Christmas with Maureen McGovern 🎵🎵🎶 (CBS, 1990)
Baby I'm Yours 🎵🎵 (RCA, 1992)
Out of This World 🎵🎵🎵 (Sterling, 1996)
The Music Never Ends 🎵🎵🎵 (Sterling, 1997)

influences:

◀◀ Andrea Marcovicci, Lena Horne

▶▶ Diane Schuur, Mandy Patinkin

David Okamoto

Denny McLain

Born Dennis Dale McLain, March 29, 1944, in Chicago, IL.

Baseball and organists have always had a cozy relationship, but never as much as in 1968, when moonlighting musician McLain won 31 games and helped his Detroit Tigers to a World Series title. McLain, one of the most colorful figures in Detroit sports history, put out two instrumental albums of Hammond X-77 music in the late 1960s. Unfortunately, music wasn't his only extracurricular activity: he also had a thing for gamblers, which eventually got him banned from baseball altogether. He has floated in and out of prisons on gambling and racketeering charges ever since. The fact that he's the last pitcher to win 30 games in a single season is, depending on whom you ask, a source of great disgrace or great humor in Detroit. As for his organ albums, well, imagine the cheesiest possible sounds you can imagine coming from one of those late-1960s Hammonds many suburbanites kept in their living rooms. McLain's take on "The Girl from Ipanema" sounds like he's trying to graft the seventh-inning version of "Take Me Out to the Ball Game" onto a classic pop standard.

what to buy: Because McLain's original albums are far, far out of print, your best chance of finding him on CD comes from Capitol Records' *Ultra-Lounge* series, which sticks "The Girl from Ipanema," "Laura," and "Cute" on *Ultra-Lounge, Vol. 11: Organs in Orbit* 🎵🎵🎵🎵 (Capitol, 1996, prod. Brad Benedict) and

Ultra-Lounge, Vol. 18: Bottoms Up! ♫♫♫ (Capitol, 1997, prod. Brad Benedict).

worth searching for: Good luck on your quest for McLain's original album, *Denny McLain at the Organ* ♫♫ (Capitol, 1969, prod. Dave Dexter Jr.), a prized possession for Detroit Tigers fanatics everywhere. You'd have better luck contacting McLain in prison and asking him to perform over the phone on the warden's Hammond.

influences:

◀◀ Walter Wanderley, Sir Julian, Frank Sinatra, Booker T. & the MG's, Martin Denny, Cy Young

▶▶ Pete Rose, Mickey Lolich, Jack Morris, Greg Maddux, Steve Carlton

Steve Knopper

Declan Patrick McManus

See: Elvis Costello

Carmen McRae

Born April 8, 1922, in New York, NY. Died November 10, 1994, in Beverly Hills, CA.

In the pantheon of jazz singers, McRae doesn't rank with Ella Fitzgerald, Sarah Vaughan, or Billie Holiday, but she isn't too far beneath them. After working with Benny Carter, Count Basie, and Mercer Ellington through the '40s, McRae debuted as a leader in 1954 and quickly established her relaxed vocal style. Over the course of her long recording career, which lasted into the '90s despite emphysema, McRae recorded more than 50 albums, including numerous collections of standards, collaborations with Dave Brubeck and George Shearing, and a series of tributes to performers and composers such as Holiday, Vaughan, Nat King Cole, and Thelonious Monk.

what to buy: *The Great American Songbook* ♫♫♫♫ (Atlantic, 1992) is McRae's finest album, with standards like "Days of Wine and Roses," "I Only Have Eyes for You," "At Long Last Love," and a superb "It's Like Reaching for the Moon."

what to buy next: *Sings Great American Songwriters* ♫♫♫♫ (Decca, 1993, reissue prod. Orrin Keepnews) is another winning collection of standards, including "My Funny Valentine," "My Foolish Heart," "Basin Street Blues," "Love Come Back to Me," and "Ev'ry Time We Say Goodbye."

what to avoid: *Can't Hide Love* ♫♫ (PA. USA, 1976) manages to hide McRae's prodigious skill behind poor song selection and fussy arrangements.

best of the rest:

Here to Stay ♫♫♫♫ (Decca, 1959)
You're Looking at Me: A Collection of Nat King Cole Songs ♫♫♫♫ (Concord Jazz, 1984)
Sings Lover Man & Other Billie Holiday ♫♫♫♫ (Sony, 1997)

worth searching for: *Live in Robbie Scott's* ♫♫♫♫ (DRG, 1977, prod. Peter King) captures McRae live at the British jazz club, performing "If You Could See Me Now," "Evergreen," and "Weaver of Dreams," among others.

influences:

◀◀ Sarah Vaughan, Billie Holiday, Ella Fitzgerald

▶▶ Betty Carter, Dinah Washington, Nancy Wilson, Cassandra Wilson, Holly Cole

Ben Greenman

Joe Meek

Born Robert George Meek, April 5, 1929, in Newent, England. Died February 3, 1967, in London, England.

The first warning shot of the 1960s British Invasion was fired by Joe Meek. Though his chief innovations were in engineering, his 1962 production of the Tornados' instrumental "Telstar" was the first recording to top the pop charts in both the United States and Great Britain. Meek utilized elements of compression, reverb, delay, distortion, mike placement, and sound-on-sound to add ethereal aural halos to vocals, floor-stomping power to drums, and tart, eerie resonance to guitars.

Meek began his career as an engineer for IBC Studios in 1953, and worked behind the glass on several hits for Lonnie Donegan, Petula Clark, Shirley Bassey, and many others. By 1957, Meek had officially become the U.K.'s first producer/engineer, and he was writing songs for many of his artists as well. As rebellious as he was innovative, Meek despised big label, corporate mentality, and after being thrown out of every proper studio in London, he built his own facility (said to be the most technically advanced of that time) at 304 Holloway Road, and worked out distribution deals for his own labels. A fan of Buddy Holly and Eddie Cochran, Meek scored big hits with Mike Berry's "Tribute to Buddy Holly" and Heinz's "Just Like Eddie" (featuring future Deep Purple and Rainbow rocker Ritchie Blackmore on guitar), though for the most part he preferred light teen-pop of the Helen Shapiro variety to rock 'n' roll. His electronically-enhanced teen-pop hits such as Michael Cox's "Angela," John Leyton's "Johnny Remember Me," and "Green Jeans" by the Fabulous Flee-Rekkers gave him the financial freedom to explore his interest is "space music," celestial

themes played on a clavoline (an early version of the synthesizer) with subtle rock backing.

Meek produced more than 50 U.K. chart records, but his only other significant U.S. entry was "Have I the Right" by the Honeycombs, which hit #5 in 1964. Meek inspired great loyalty among his artists (most were signed to him personally rather than a record label), but he was not the best judge of talent or coming trends. He turned down the Beatles and Rod Stewart, and let sides by a young Tom Jones go unreleased, while continuing to enthusiastically record the likes of Houston Wells, Ian Gregory, and Glenda Collins. By 1967, Meek's string of hits had ended. He was broke, drug-addled, fighting lawsuits, paranoid that major labels were trying to steal his recording secrets, and began to "hear voices." While in a particularly agitated state, Meek murdered his landlady, reloaded his shotgun, and killed himself. Three decades later, Joe Meek's rediscovery by British fans is spreading worldwide, and scores of reissues and compilations attest to his productivity and his mad genius.

what to buy: Meek's biggest hits and some wonderfully weird failures are on *It's Hard to Believe It: The Amazing World of Joe Meek* ♪♪♪♪ (Razor & Tie, 1995, compilation prod. Rob Kemp), which includes the Tornados' "Telstar" and the Honeycombs' "Have I the Right."

what to buy next: *I Hear a New World: Joe Meek and the Blue Men* ♪♪♪ (RPM, 1991, prod. Joe Meek) is his quickly withdrawn, early-1960s space odyssey which clearly prefigured the New Age movement. *The Assassination of John F. Kennedy: Four Days That Shocked the World* ♪♪♪ (RPM, 1991, prod. Joe Meek) is Meek's masterful mix of snippets of news broadcasts with sound effects, and his own composition, "The Kennedy March."

what to avoid: *Let's Go! Joe Meek's Girls* ♪♪ (RPM, 1996, prod. Joe Meek) is a 29-track disc with many unfinished demos and production experiments.

the rest:
Joe Meek Story: Vol. 1 ♪♪♪ (Line, 1991)
Work in Progress: The Triumph Years ♪♪♪ (RPM, 1994)
Joe Meek Story: The Pye Years, Vol. 2 ♪♪ (Castle Records, 1994)
Joe Meek Story, Vol. 3: The Complete Houston Wells ♪♪♪ (Sequel, 1994)
Joe Meek Story, Vol. 4: The Best of Michael Cox ♪♪♪ (Sequel, 1994)
Joe Meek's Fabulous Flee-Rekkers ♪♪♪ (See for Mile, 1997)

Carmen McRae (Archive Photos)

worth searching for: Some import racks are carrying *Joe Meek Story: The Pye Years* ♪♪♪ (Sequel Records, 1991, prod. Joe Meek), a two-CD, 48-track compilation recorded from 1960 to 1968.

influences:

◀◀ Phil Spector, George Martin, Martin Denny, Les Baxter

▶▶ The Tornados, the Honeycombs, David Bowie

Ken Burke

George Melachrino /The Melachrino Strings

Born George Militiades Melachrino, May 1, 1909, in London, England. Died June 18, 1965, in London, England.

If you did *anything* in the 1950s and 1960s, Melachrino wanted to provide the soundtrack. Filling his orchestras with tiny strings, reeds, and percussion next to gigantic harp and piano, he created gentle background music, designed specifically to accompany listeners through each phase of certain everyday activities. His best-known album, *Music for Dining*, begins with tinkly little pieces for the appetizers, then explodes into a grandiose symphonic crescendo—"Warsaw Concerto"—for the entree. He geared other popular instrumental LPs, part of RCA Victor's growing "Living Stereo" series, similarly towards relaxation, romance, reading, sleep, and simply "faith and inner calm." Melachrino's smart and opportunistic producer, Ethel Gabriel, eventually shifted these ideas from his "Moods in Music" albums to an even more lucrative easy-listening juggernaut known as the Living Strings.

As a 14-year-old, the proficient reed-and-strings player studied at the Trinity College of Music, and began working at the BBC's prominent Savoy Hill studio four years later. World War II didn't kill his career; on the contrary, after he joined the British Army he directed dance bands and large military orchestras (including the prestigious "Orchestra in Khaki"), giving him crucial hands-on experience. The war ended and Melachrino formed two groups—the George Melachrino Orchestra and the Melachrino Strings—which he used interchangeably for his best-selling mood-music LPs on various record labels. Though he shifted successfully into film music, he died after a home accident in 1965. The Melachrino Strings, however, went on recording through the early 1980s.

worth searching for: When easy-listening music died, it really died. Though Melachrino's Strings and Orchestra recorded some of the best-selling LPs of the 1960s, record companies have never considered their unobtrusive mood music worthy of reissue in the Bryan Adams–Whitney Houston era of Lite FM radio stations. As usual, used record stores come to the rescue: you can still find *Music for Dining* ♫♫♫ (RCA Victor, 1958, prod. Ethel Gabriel), with its playful appetizer accompaniment and overdramatic main-course climaxes. Melachrino's groups recorded a great variety of mood music, from *Songs of Jerome Kern* to *Music to Help You Sleep* to *Rendezvous in Rome*, but they're difficult to find. Other good ones, at least for their titles, are *Music for Faith and Inner Calm* ♫♫♫ (RCA Victor, 1958, prod. Ethel Gabriel) and *More Music for Relaxation* ♫♫ (RCA Victor, 1961, prod. Ethel Gabriel).

influences:

◀◀ Mantovani, Paul Weston, Ray Noble, Charlie Barnet, Glenn Miller, Percy Faith, Ray Conniff

▶▶ Living Strings, 101 Strings, Mystic Moods Orchestra, Hugo Montenegro

Steve Knopper

Sergio Mendes

Born February 11, 1941, in Niteroi, Brazil.

Mendes might be considered one of the poster boys of loungedom, so involved was he with the "Blame It on the Bossa Nova" musical wave that swept through America in the early '60s. But one of his biggest hits was a 1968 easy-listening cover of a Beatles tune, "Fool on the Hill," recorded with his band Brasil '66 (originally named Brasil '65; the year would be updated occasionally).

Pianist Mendes first gained fame as the leader of the Bossa Nova Trio. He moved to the states in 1964 and began collaborating with fellow Brazilian Antonio Carlos Jobim and American Art Farmer before creating the band that became Brasil '66, with Jose Soares on vocals and percussion, Bob Matthews on vocals and bass, Jao Palma on drums, and Janis Hansen and Lani Hall on vocals. Hall was the wife of A&M Records co-founder Herb Alpert. The band's A&M debut release, *Sergio Mendes and Brasil '66*, contained the Top 10 hit, "Mais Que Nada." With an airy, Latin-laced jazz-pop sound and no pretensions toward making socially relevant or politically pointed music, Mendes and his band provided a bit of light escapism during a turbulent time. They released a series of albums filled with catchy originals and reworked covers, including Simon and Garfunkel's "Scarborough Fair," Otis Redding's "(Sittin' On) the Dock of the Bay," and even the Jimmy Webb tune that hit for Glen Campbell,

"Wichita Lineman." The band's first few A&M albums fared well; then the Brasil star began to sputter out. By 1975, Mendes released his first solo disc on Elektra; in 1977, he released *Sergio Mendes and the New Brasil '77*, to no one's interest. Mendes engineered a comeback with 1983's *Sergio Mendes* on A&M, reaching the Top 40 with "Never Gonna Let You Go," sung by Joe Pizzulo and Leza Miller. He dropped below the music world radar again after 1984's *Confetti*, but resurfaced with Brasil '99, another soon-to-be-outdated moniker.

what to buy: *Fool on the Hill* ♫♫♫♫ (A&M, 1968, prod. Sergio Mendes) is the quintessential post–"Girl from Ipanema" sound, using light bossa nova beats and laying lilting female vocals over big strings and Mendes's piano. *Greatest Hits of Brasil '66* ♫♫♫♫ (A&M, 1970, prod. Herb Alpert) showcases Mendes and Brasil '66 and what's been described as his "winningly sexy blend of American female voices, simplified bossa nova rhythms, and lavish Dave Grusin orchestrations." It contains versions of three Beatles compositions ("Day Tripper," "Fool on the Hill," and "With a Little Help from My Friends") alongside Cole Porter ("Night and Day") and Burt Bacharach/Hal David ("The Look of Love"). Also included are "Going Out of My Head," "Scarborough Fair," and other cuts destined for dentists' offices everywhere.

what to buy next: Much of Mendes's work is no longer in print, but you might try *Brasileiro* ♫♫♫ (Elektra, 1992, prod. Sergio Mendes), Mendes's percussion-drenched exploration of his own musical roots. "Magalenha" is quite catchy in its post–bossa nova way (he calls it samba-reggae). The disc really evokes the balmy breezes and intricate rhythms of Brazil, and "Kalimba" is quite funky. *Oceano* ♫♫♫ (Verve, 1996) puts Mendes firmly on Latin soil, musically speaking, with some very nice cuts. But for some reason, he felt the need to venture into rap territory with "Maracatudo," which proves that genre-jumping is not always a good thing.

best of the rest:
Four Sider ♫♫♫♫ (A&M, 1966)

worth searching for: Because many of Mendes's classic original albums, such as *Classics* ♫♫♫♫ (A&M, 1986) and *Crystal Illusions* ♫♫♫♫ (A&M, 1969), are either out of print or difficult to find, the best way to hear Brasil '66 in the CD era is on a variety of recent compilations. *Cocktail Mix, Vol. 2: Martini Madness* ♫♫♫♫ (Rhino, 1996, compilation prod. Janet Grey) stacks Mendes's "Mais Que Nada" in context with other Latin-style tinkly instrumentals, such as Perez Prado's "Why Wait" and Cal Tjader's "Soul Sauce (Guacha Guaro)." Also, "Mais Que Nada" shows up on the excellent, rock-heavy soundtrack *I Shot Andy Warhol* 🎵🎵🎵 (Tag/Atlantic, 1996, prod. Randall Poster).

influences:

 Antonio Carlos Jobim, Herb Alpert, Astrud Gilberto, Henry Mancini, the Beatles, Stan Getz, Charlie Byrd, João Gilberto

▶▶ Michael Sembello, Gilberto Gil, David Byrne, Paul Simon

Lynne Margolis

Johnny Mercer

Born John Herndon, November 18, 1909, in Savannah, GA. Died June 25, 1976, in Los Angeles, CA.

Primarily known as a songwriter, with more than 1,500 songs to his credit, Mercer is one of the giants of 20th-century popular music. Without him, we never would have had "Personality," "Come Rain or Come Shine," "Blues in the Night," "Jeepers Creepers," or hundreds of other standards. As a singer, Mercer was no titan, but he was an accomplished performer nonetheless, and his command of the rhythm of a lyric elevated his phrasing above that of many of his contemporaries. A sort of minor Frank Sinatra, his genius as a lyricist allowed him to recognize the abilities of others—over the course of his career, he recorded songs by Frank Loesser, Jimmy Van Heusen, and many others. Mercer's songs are covered by dozens of artists each year; most recently, the Clint Eastwood film *Midnight in the Garden of Good and Evil* paired his compositions with vocalists such as k.d. lang, Paula Cole, Diana Krall, and Tony Bennett. In addition, he was a major music-industry player, co-founding Capitol Records in 1942 and, after working with Benny Goodman on the radio, siring younger singers such as Margaret Whiting and collaborating with Henry Mancini on "Moon River" (from the consummate lounge film *Breakfast at Tiffany's*).

what to buy: Accompanied by the Pete Moore Orchestra during a London recording date in 1974, Mercer recorded 25 of his own compositions for *My Huckleberry Friend* 🎵🎵🎵 (DRG, 1996), including "Too Marvelous for Words," "Come Rain or Come Shine," "I Thought about You," "That Old Black Magic," and "Something's Gotta Give."

what to buy next: *Capitol Collector's Series* 🎵🎵🎵🎵 (Capitol, 1989, compilation prod. Ron Furmanek) assembles 20 of Mercer's hits, including songs he wrote—"Glow Worm," "On the Atchison, Topeka, and Santa Fe," and "One for My Baby (And One More for the Road)"—and songs he didn't—"Zip-a-Dee-Doo-Dah," "Gal in Calico," and "Baby It's Cold Outside." It's a treasury of American popular songs.

what to avoid: *Some of the Best* 🎵🎵 (Laserlight, 1997, prod. Rod McKuen) and *More of the Best* 🎵🎵 (Laserlight, 1997, prod. Rod McKuen) aren't just cheap—they're ultra-cheap, with recommended CD list prices of $5.49. But the performances are inferior and the annotation almost nonexistent.

best of the rest:

The Uncollected Johnny Mercer (1944) 🎵🎵🎵 (Hindsight, 1995)
Evening with Johnny Mercer 🎵🎵🎵 (DRG, 1992)

worth searching for: An old-fashioned soundtrack, *Midnight in the Garden of Good and Evil* 🎵🎵🎵🎵 (Warner Bros., 1997, prod. Matt Pierson, Clint Eastwood) pairs some of today's best voices—bluegrass singer Alison Krauss, jazz chanteuse Cassandra Wilson, country-torch heroine k.d. lang, and, less surprisingly, Rosemary Clooney and Tony Bennett—with Mercer classics such as "Days of Wine and Roses" and "This Time the Dream's on Me." For novelty value, actors Kevin Spacey and Clint Eastwood prove they have no business singing under any circumstances.

influences:

◄◄ Jimmy Durante, Bing Crosby, Hoagy Carmichael, Cole Porter

►► Bobby Darin, Jo Stafford, Perry Como, Mel Tormé, Tony Bennett, Frank Sinatra

Ben Greenman

Ethel Merman
Born Ethel Agnes Zimmerman, January 16, 1908 or 1912, in Astoria, NY. Died February 15, 1984, in New York City, NY.

Decades before rock singers like Janis Joplin and Michael Bolton earned notoriety for shrieking syllables at full blast, Merman broadcast formerly subtle romantic sentiments by George Gershwin and Irving Berlin. The naturally loud-voiced and highly talented Merman, though, knew the strength of her showmanship was in the personality, and she projected charisma and bombast in ways that her softly crooning contemporaries could never outshine.

A family connection earned Merman her first singing job at her organist father's Masonic Lodge in Queens; despite training for a secretarial career with the B.K. Vacuum Booster Brake Company, she wrangled tiny side jobs as a basement nightclub singer. Jimmy Durante eventually heard her and Merman wound up singing as part of his act. Soon she was belting her trademark overkill anthem, "I Got Rhythm," in the Gershwins' Broadway musical *Girl Crazy*, in 1929. Eventually the singer became one of America's most beloved stars, earning top roles in 15 Broadway shows, including *Annie Get Your Gun, Hello, Dolly,* and *Anything Goes.* She learned the hard way that the stage was the only place where she could shine, releasing several failed albums (including 1979's *Ethel Merman Disco Album*) and bombing on the radio. After what turned out to be a triumphant swan song, a 1982 orchestral show at Carnegie Hall, she underwent brain-tumor surgery and died in 1984.

what to buy: The CD age hasn't helped Merman's music find a huge new audience, but *The Ethel Merman Collection* ♪♪♪♪ (Razor & Tie, 1997, prod. Mike Ragogna, Will Friedwald) prevents you from having to track down all her old original-cast albums. It includes "I Got Rhythm," of course, and other Mer-

manized standards like Cole Porter's "I Get a Kick Out of You"; the set recalls that despite all her volume and bombast, Merman could sing with subtlety and restraint, making the highs so much more powerful.

best of the rest:
12 Songs from "Call Me Madam" ♪♪♪ (MCA, 1992)
Ethel Merman's Broadway ♪♪♪ (Varese Sarabonde, 1995)
I Get a Kick Out of You ♪♪♪ (Pearl Flapper, 1995)

influences:

◄◄ Al Jolson, Bessie Smith, Irving Berlin, Cole Porter

►► Judy Garland, Doris Day, Etta James, Whitney Houston, Janis Joplin, Michael Bolton

Steve Knopper

Bette Midler
Born December 1, 1945, in Patterson, NJ.

Sassy and brassy, witty and wily, Bette Midler is a pure entertainer. Among the divas who emerged in the past few decades, her voice doesn't rank near the top. Her taste in material, however, and her preservation of the most shameless vaudeville traditions, distinguishes her as one of the best all-around performers. Her crooning of "One for My Baby (And One More for the Road)" to Johnny Carson at his 1992 *The Tonight Show* farewell was one of the defining moments in the revival of cocktail chic.

Born in New Jersey and raised in Hawaii, Midler moved to New York in the 1960s. She soon won a Broadway role in *Fiddler on the Roof.* By the early 1970s, she had developed a nightclub act incorporating pop standards, choreography, and comedy; her creative partners included Barry Manilow and Melissa Manchester. After signing to Atlantic and making a nationwide splash with her brand of nostalgia, her career slowed somewhat. In 1979, she came back with her starring role and soundtrack for *The Rose,* a loose adaptation of Janis Joplin's life. She's the author of a book, *A View from a Broad,* and continues to please crowds with her films, recordings, and concerts.

what to buy: *The Divine Miss M* ♪♪♪♪ (Atlantic, 1972, prod. Barry Manilow, Ahmet Ertegun, Joel Dorn) is Midler's swinging debut, with the Top 40 hits "Friends," "Do You Want to Dance?" and the Andrews Sisters update "Boogie Woogie Bugle Boy." *Experience the Divine: Greatest Hits* ♪♪♪♪ (Atlantic, 1993, prod.

Ethel Merman **(AP/Wide World Photos)**

bette midler

Arif Mardin, Bette Midler) gathers those hits as well as her heartfelt if overexposed ballads "Wind Beneath My Wings" (winner of the 1989 Grammy for Record of the Year), "From a Distance," and her most-played hit, "The Rose."

what to buy next: *The Rose* 𝄞𝄞𝄞 (Atlantic, 1979, prod. Paul A. Rothchild) soundtrack includes the title track and Joplin-esque rockers. *Divine Madness* 𝄞𝄞𝄞 (Atlantic, 1989, prod. Dennis Kirk) is a fine document of one of her bawdy live shows.

what to avoid: Midler is a wonderful comedienne, but *Mud Will Be Flung Tonight!* 𝄞 (Atlantic, 1985, prod. Bette Midler), her only all-comedy album, is too much of a good thing.

the rest:
Bette Midler 𝄞𝄞𝄞 (Atlantic, 1973)
Songs for the New Depression 𝄞𝄞𝄞 (Atlantic, 1976)
Broken Blossom 𝄞𝄞𝄞 (Atlantic, 1977)
Live at Last 𝄞𝄞𝄞 (Atlantic, 1977)
Thighs and Whispers 𝄞𝄞𝄞 (Atlantic, 1979)
No Frills 𝄞𝄞𝄞 (Atlantic, 1983)
Beaches 𝄞𝄞𝄞 (Atlantic, 1988)
Some People's Lives 𝄞𝄞𝄞 (Atlantic, 1990)
For the Boys 𝄞𝄞𝄞 (Atlantic, 1991)
Gypsy 𝄞𝄞𝄞 (Atlantic, 1993)
Bette of Roses 𝄞𝄞 (Atlantic, 1995)

worth searching for: The Disney compilation *For Our Children* 𝄞𝄞𝄞 (Disney, 1991, prod. various) is a compilation of comfort songs, including Midler's "Blueberry Pie" (plus kids' songs by Bruce Springsteen, Brian Wilson, Meryl Streep, Barbra Streisand, Paul McCartney, and others).

influences:
◀◀ Barbra Streisand, Liza Minnelli, the Andrews Sisters, Ethel Merman, Judy Garland, Janis Joplin, Dionne Warwick

▶▶ Whitney Houston, Barry Manilow, Melissa Manchester, Linda Eder

Jay Dedrick

The Mighty Blue Kings
Formed August 1994, in Chicago, IL.

Ross Bon, vocals; Gareth Best, guitar; Jimmy Sutton, bass (1994–97); Jonathan Doyle, saxophone; Jerry DeVivo, saxophone; Samuel Burckhardt, tenor saxophone (1994–96); Jimmy Olson, drums; Bob Carter,

Bette Midler **(AP/Wide World Photos)**

drums (1994–97); Donny Nichilo, piano (1994–97); Clark Sommers, bass (1997–present); Simon Sweet, keyboards (1997).

After debuting at Chicago's famous Buddy Guy's Legends, opening for harpist Junior Wells, this contemporary swing band moved on to a weekly residency at the Green Mill jazz club a few miles north. Since then, the band has slowly amassed a huge local following and spread its effervescent "jump-jive" sound of the '40s and '50s to various clubs around the United States. The Kings' resume now includes dates opening for rocker Pete Townshend at Chicago's House of Blues, and for soul singer Tina Turner at a TV industry party Oprah Winfrey threw at her Harpo Studios. They also earned a song on the soundtrack to the David Schwimmer movie *Since You've Been Gone*; the exposure led to a 1997 deal with Sony Records' Work label.

what to buy: On their debut, *Meet Me in Uptown* 𝄞𝄞𝄞 (R-Jay Records, 1996, prod. Wally Hersom, Mighty Blue Kings), the Mighty Blue Kings pay tribute to their infancy with "Jumpin' at the Green Mill," and include blues-and-jazz covers by Percy Mayfield, Jimmy Lunceford, and Sonny Rollins. Buoyed by a tight, talented horn section, the Kings also refurbish "Cadillac Boogie" and "Pink Cadillac," and the nicely titled "Grinnin' Like a Cheesy Cat."

what to buy next: *Come One, Come All* 𝄞𝄞𝄞 (R-Jay Records, 1997, prod. Mighty Blue Kings), dedicated to Chicago blues harp master Wells, includes the bouncy "Go Tell the Preacher," which chides a woman who is mistreating her lover; on "Put Your Hand in Mine," Bon begs a woman to stay. Typically creative cover versions include "No Blow, No Show" by soul man Bobby "Blue" Bland, and "Green Grass Grows All Around" by jump-blues pioneer Louis Jordan.

influences:
◀◀ The Treniers, Wynonie Harris, Joe Williams, Count Basie, Jimmy Liggins, Louis Jordan, Squirrel Nut Zippers

▶▶ The Senders, Royal Crown Revue, Big Bad Voodoo Daddy

Christina Fuoco

Mrs. Elva Miller
Birthdate and birthplace unknown.

In the wacky world of mid-1960s Top 40 radio, where at any given moment Louis Armstrong could be found sharing the airwaves with Roger Miller and the Seeds, musical surprises were few and far between. That is, until Capitol Records, in a spectacular display of insight or insanity, decided to commit to tape

glenn miller

the sounds of a middle-aged-at-best housewife from Claremont, California, named Mrs. Elva Miller.

Little is really known of Miller's past, except she was reputed to have been quite the opera buff in her youth and actually attempted vocal lessons for seven years. Perhaps this is how she came to serve as executive secretary for the esteemed Foothill Drama and Choral Society during the 1950s. She is also said to have performed quite regularly at church and social functions throughout the Hollywood suburbs until, at the request of her family (and perhaps a goodly percentage of her audience) she stopped appearing on stage and restricted her musical performances to small local recording studios. Young organist-arranger Fred Bock heard several Mrs. Miller recordings and brought them to the attention of Capitol A&R man Lex de Azevedo. The label, at this time reaping untold millions in Beatle profits (and with their healthy sense of anything-goes humor apparently still intact), brought Elva into the Capitol Tower to warble in her own thankfully inimitable style on the very studio floor where Frank Sinatra and Gene Vincent once stood weaving their immortal magic. Capitol squeezed three albums out of the woman, and a small label called Amaret was blessed with still another, until the devil-may-care 1960s became the frightfully serious 1970s and Mrs. Miller was told she could no longer compete with the likes of Carole King, Linda Ronstadt, and Black Sabbath. After a brief stab at celluloid immortality via her bit part in Roddy McDowall's classic *The Cool Ones,* she once again retired to the Hollywood Hills, never to be heard from again.

what's available: Perhaps it's just as well that only one recorded sample of the Miller Sound currently remains available to the musically adventurous out there. Yes, her vibrato-wracked stomping of "These Boots Are Made for Walkin'" is a proud part of *Ultra-Lounge: On the Rocks, Part Two* 𝄞𝄞𝄞 (Capitol, 1997, prod. various).

worth searching for: Only a woman as seemingly confident in her craft as Elva would dare title her VERY FIRST RELEASE *Mrs. Miller's Greatest Hits* 𝄞𝄞𝄞𝄞 (Capitol, 1966, prod. Lex de Azevedo). Sometimes whistling, other times grumbling in a geriatric proto-rap, the renditions of "Let's Hang On," "Downtown," and especially "Chim Chim Cher-ee" herein absolutely defy description. *The Country Soul of Mrs. Miller* 𝄞𝄞𝄞𝄞 (Capitol, 1967) was "alternative country" three decades before the trend, and *Mrs. Miller Does Her Thing* 𝄞𝄞𝄞 (Amaret, 1969) demonstrates that even without the support of the Capitol Tower, a talent as rare as hers could not easily be stifled.

influences:

◀◀ Ethel Merman, Florence Foster Jenkins, Jonathan & Darlene Edwards

▶▶ Jo Anne Worley, Tiny Tim, Kathie Lee Gifford

Gary Pig Gold

Glenn Miller

Born Glenn Alton Miller, March 1, 1904, in Clarinda, IA. Reported missing, December 15, 1944, on a flight from England to France.

Miller's name is synonymous with the big-band swing era. While he was never more than a mediocre trombonist, as an arranger he developed perhaps the most distinctive of all the big-band sounds—and his band, some have said, provided the soundtrack for a generation.

Miller grew up poor, in Iowa, Nebraska, and Colorado. There were no musicians in his family and he connected with the trombone only when he found an old one in the basement of a butcher's shop where he was working as an errand boy. The butcher gave him his first lessons. By 1916 he was playing in the Grant City (Missouri) Town Band. After leaving high school he joined a now-unknown band in Laramie, Wyoming, and when it broke up after a year, Miller entered the University of Colorado, where he continued playing and took up arranging. After only two college years he joined the Ben Pollack Orchestra in California, then returned with Pollack to his base in New York and stayed with him until 1928 (Benny Goodman was a fellow band member). In September 1926, Pollack made the first known recordings using Miller's arrangements ("When I First Met Mary" and "'Deed I Do"). As a freelancer in New York he worked as an arranger, played on many studio recordings (including nearly 100 with the Dorsey Brothers Orchestra, for whom he provided at least half the arrangements), was in the pit for several Broadway shows, and studied arranging with Dr. Joseph Schillinger. In 1935 he helped organize and wrote arrangements for the first American band organized by Ray Noble, and wrote what later became his theme song, "Moonlight Serenade."

In January of 1937, Miller formed his own band, and in 1938, after a short hiatus, the reorganized band became increasingly popular. At its peak it was one of the highest-paid bands in the nation, with an instantly recognizable sound that sold millions

Glenn Miller **(AP/Wide World Photos)**

of recordings. The band had a wonderful way with finely arranged ballads, but his biggest hits were instrumental riff tunes such as "Little Brown Jug" (Miller's first swing hit), "In the Mood," "Tuxedo Junction," and "Pennsylvania 6-5000." The Miller arrangements (including many by Jerry Gray, Bill Finegan, and Billy May) were the basic strength of the band, but good soloists, such as Bobby Hackett and Tex Beneke, were not lacking. Miller and the band were featured in two major films, *Sun Valley Serenade* and *Orchestra Wives*. In mid-1942 Miller volunteered for service in the Army, where he put together an all-star service personnel band that first toured the U.S. on recruiting drives and, in 1944, was posted to England. On December 15, he was flying ahead of his band to a session in Paris when his small plane disappeared; a year later he was declared dead. Hollywood honored him with a posthumously released film, *The Glenn Miller Story,* in 1953. A Miller "ghost band," currently fronted by Jack O'Brien, is still on the road playing his arrangements, as are other bands around the world; there are recurrent Glenn Miller Festivals; music scholarships have been established in his name; his smiling face and horn grace the University of Colorado's Glenn Miller Ballroom; every wedding everywhere plays "In the Mood"; and Miller, though gone at age 40, is anything but forgotten.

what to buy: *Glenn Miller: A Memorial* 🎵🎵🎵🎵 (Bluebird, 1992, prod. Steve Backer) gives an excellent overview of the band's offerings between 1939 and 1942 (and includes one track by the Miller Army Air Force Band), with a good mixture of the band's sweet and swing styles. Almost all of the big hits are here, plus some lesser-known but equally engaging arrangements such as "Song of the Volga Boatmen," "Anvil Chorus," and "Kalamazoo." This CD is a re-release of a 1969 LP that sold more than a million copies. *The Spirit Is Willing (1939–42)* 🎵🎵🎵🎵 (Bluebird, 1995, prod. Orrin Keepnews) is a different and welcome take on the Miller band, focusing on "its substantial jazz content," limited to instrumentals, and avoiding the Miller favorites included everywhere else. Some of the early efforts are "King Porter Stomp," "Rug Cutter's Swing" (by Fletcher Henderson's brother Horace), and "Bugle Call Rag," while the band's later style is reflected in "I Dreamt I Dwelt in Harlem," "Boulder Buff," and "Caribbean Clipper." Billy May's conception of "Take the 'A' Train" as a ballad will surprise you.

what to buy next: For avid fans who want quantity as well as quality, there is *Glenn Miller: The Popular Recordings 1938–1942* 🎵🎵🎵🎵 (Bluebird, 1989), a three-disc set with all your favorite Miller recordings. Miller fans with a historical bent ought to consider *Glenn Miller: The Lost Recordings* 🎵🎵🎵🎵🎵

(RCA, 1995, prod. Alan Dell), which contains 45 tracks on two discs and consists of performances by Miller's Air Force band for broadcast to a German audience (to undermine their will to fight). This band maintained and in some ways surpassed the high standards of the civilian band (Miller's civilian band never had the likes of Mel Powell on piano, for example), and the sound quality is excellent (recorded in the famous Abbey Road studios in London).

what to avoid: *In the Digital Mood* 🎵🎵 (GRP, 1983, prod. Dave Grusin) presents fairly recent re-recordings of the most popular Miller arrangements by anonymous studio musicians. They are certainly competent, but unless you have a passion for the latest in digital recording technology you're better off with reissues of the original work.

best of the rest:
Pure Gold 🎵🎵🎵🎵 (Bluebird, 1988)
Classic Glenn Miller: Original Live Recordings 🎵🎵🎵 (Pair, 1989)
A Legendary Performer 🎵🎵🎵🎵 (Bluebird, 1991)
The Collector Edition: Glenn Miller 🎵🎵🎵🎵 (Laserlight, 1991)
Chattanooga Choo Choo: The No. 1 Hits 🎵🎵🎵 (Bluebird, 1991)
Best of the Big Bands: Evolution of a Band 🎵🎵🎵🎵 (Columbia/Legacy, 1992)

influences:

◀◀ Benny Goodman, Ray Noble, Duke Ellington, the Dorsey Brothers

▶▶ Nelson Riddle, Billy May, Frank Sinatra, Louis Armstrong, Louis Prima, Buddy Greco, Dean Martin, Tony Bennett, Charlie Parker, Miles Davis, Bob Wills, Raymond Scott

Jim Lester

Mitch Miller

Born July 4 , 1911, in Rochester, NY.

Miller has worn many hats during his decades in the record business—he was a jazz oboist who played with Charlie Parker; a producer who manned the boards for artists such as Rosemary Clooney, Doris Day, Frankie Laine, and Jo Stafford; and a bandleader in the jazz-pop tradition who patterned lush, easy-listening orchestras after his mentor, Andre Kostelanetz. Miller's trademark was singalong music, which was something like an early form of karaoke—his orchestra played the music while he encouraged listeners to belt out the lyrics. (His popular *Sing Along with Mitch* album series wasn't the only thing that made him a villain among Elvis Presley fans in the '50s. As the influential head of A&R at Columbia Records, he once said, according to the book *Rock of Ages: The Rolling Stone History* of Rock & Roll: "You can't call any music immoral. If anything is wrong with rock and roll, it is that it makes a virtue out of monotony." Still, the astute businessman did sign Buddy Holly to Columbia.) Miller hit #1 with "Yellow Rose of Texas" in 1956, and from 1961 to 1966 he hosted his own popular television show.

what to buy: *Sing Along with Mitch* 𝅘𝅥𝅘𝅥𝅘𝅥𝅘𝅥 (Columbia, 1958) is the album that put Miller on the charts and into America's heart. With easy-listening versions of standards like "That Old Gang of Mine," "Down by the Old Mill Stream," "You Are My Sunshine," "She Wore a Yellow Ribbon," and "Don't Fence Me In," it's the very definition of pleasant.

what to buy next: *Favorite Irish Sing-Alongs* 𝅘𝅥𝅘𝅥𝅘𝅥 (Sony , 1992) lets Miller get his Irish up, with a delightful collection of folk songs. *Christmas Sing-Along with Mitch Miller* 𝅘𝅥𝅘𝅥𝅘𝅥 (Columbia, 1958) shouldn't be confused with the later *Holiday Sing-Along with Mitch Miller* 𝅘𝅥𝅘𝅥𝅘𝅥 (Columbia, 1961), but both are pleasant collections of Yuletide music, with standards like "Deck the Halls," "Silent Night," and "Joy to the World" (Handel's version, not Three Dog Night's).

what to avoid: *Mitch's Greatest Hits* 𝅘𝅥𝅘𝅥𝅘𝅥 (Sony, 1988) isn't awful, but it's been rendered redundant by the many other Miller greatest hits collections.

worth searching for: If you're a diehard jazz fan, you may already have the 10-CD Charlie Parker box set *Bird: The Complete Charlie Parker on Verve* 𝅘𝅥𝅘𝅥𝅘𝅥𝅘𝅥 (Verve, 1988, prod. Phil Schaap). If not, borrow someone's, and listen for Miller's oboe and English horn.

influences:

◀◀ Andre Kostelanetz, Billy May, Nelson Riddle, Leroy Anderson, Arthur Fiedler, Charlie Parker

▶▶ Johnny Mathis, Ray Conniff, Percy Faith

Ben Greenman

Frank Mills

Born 1942, in Toronto, Ontario, Canada.

Just as the rock and pop genres have their one-hit wonders, so do the easy-listening and lounge genres. Canadian composer, orchestrator, and producer Mills is one of those wonders, an artist associated so closely with one hit song that his other chart placements—and in fact his whole career—pale by comparison. In Mills's case, that song is "Music Box Dancer," an instrumental that became a smash hit in 1979, rising all the way

Cocktail Classics

Puttin' on the Ritz

18-Karat Irving Berlin
The Complete Irving Berlin Songbooks (PolyGram)

Bombsville! Taco
Nipper's Greatest Hits: The 80's (RCA)

to #3 on the U.S. pop charts. With its tinkling piano and infectious melody, the song was ubiquitous on FM radio, not only breaking into regular playlists but appearing as background music. Mills had hit the charts before with "Love Me, Love Me Love" in 1972, and he would hit again, with "Prelude to Romance" in 1981. But he would never again attain the heights of "Music Box Dancer," which continues to pop up as a pop-culture artifact; the cartoon *The Simpsons* used it, albeit anachronistically, in a scene that dealt with Homer Simpson's high school gymnastics career.

what to buy: *Music Box Dancer* 𝅘𝅥𝅘𝅥𝅘𝅥 (Polydor, 1979) is the album that vaulted Mills into the spotlight, largely on the strength of the title track, a three-minute pop confection that apes the sound of a table-top music box. Other tracks include "Valse Classique" and "Poet and I."

what to buy next: Mills's gentle, orchestral approach is also in evidence on *A Traditional Christmas* 🎵🎵🎵 (Macola, 1994), which includes the Canadian Yuletide treat "Huron Carol," "Deck the Halls," and "Go Tell It on the Mountain." Also, *Best of Frank Mills* 🎵🎵🎵 (Macola, 1994) includes "Music Box Dancer," of course, and "Ski Fever," "Happy Song," and "Frank's Rag."

what to avoid: *Homeward* 🎵🎵 (Macola, 1994) finds Mills in a holding pattern.

worth searching for: Mills appeared as a vocalist on the smash title track of *USA for Africa: We Are the World* 🎵🎵 (Mercury, 1985, prod. Quincy Jones), an American hunger-relief effort that featured other Canadian luminaries like Joni Mitchell, Anne Murray, and Bryan Adams.

influences:

⏪ Scott Joplin, the Bells

⏩ Cliff Edwards

Ben Greenman

The Mills Brothers

Formed 1925, in Piqua, OH.

Herbert Mills (born April 2, 1912, in Piqua, OH, died April 12, 1989, in Las Vegas, NV), tenor; Donald Mills (born April 29, 1915, in Piqua, OH), tenor; Harry Mills (born August 19, 1913, in Piqua, OH, died June 28, 1982, in Los Angeles, CA), baritone; John Mills Jr. (born October 19, 1910, in Piqua, OH, died January 24, 1936 in Bellefontaine, OH), bass; John H. Mills Sr. (born February 11, 1882, in Bellefonte, PA, died December 8, 1967 in Bellefontaine, OH), bass (1936–67); John H. Mills II (born 1956 in Los Angeles, CA), vocals (1983–present).

Originally billing themselves as "Four Boys and a Kazoo," the Mills Brothers—Herb, Don, Harry, and John Jr.—toured the Midwest theater circuit and tent shows around their Ohio hometown as children with an act in which they imitated musical instruments with their voices. Their genetically matched voices, which created the kind of seamless pop-swing harmonies no instruments could equal, made for silky smooth music that's still perfect for wedding receptions and cocktail lounges.

By the 1930s, the group moved from Cincinnati's WLW Radio to New York City, becoming a top attraction on national radio broadcasts and recording their first major hit, "Glow Worm." They continued to release successful singles as one of the first African American vocal acts to achieve mainstream pop acceptance and were featured in several movie musicals, including *The Big Broadcast* of 1932, but suffered a severe blow when John Jr. died of tuberculosis in 1936. Their father, John Sr.—a concert vocalist and the man who taught the boys to sing—stepped in as a replacement and the quartet persevered. From the time of their signature recording, "Paper Doll," in 1942, the Mills Brothers became synonymous with buoyant, effortless harmonies that crossed generational lines of taste and popularity for more than a half-century. Since 1983, Donald, the last surviving brother, has toured in concert with his son, John H. II, keeping the Mills Brothers name alive; an octogenarian, Donald suffered a broken hip in a fall at LAX Airport in 1997, but John H. II says he and his father plan to resume performing.

what to buy: The epitome of class, style, and smooth sophistication, the Mills Brothers and their special musical aura are deliciously preserved in the 1995 box set *The Mills Brothers: The Anthology (1931–1968)* 🎵🎵🎵🎵 (MCA, 1995, prod. various), a digitally remastered life achievement award compiling 48 songs recorded over a three-decade span, from their first million-seller, "Tiger Rag," to their last Top 40 tune, "Cab Driver," and including their collaborations with Ella Fitzgerald, Bing Crosby, Louis Armstrong, Count Basie, and Al Jolson, among others.

what to buy next: There are so many Mills Brothers "greatest hits" LPs—approximately 17, at last count—basically covering the same material that the trick becomes finding discs that actually add songs to the collector's inventory. The British label JSP has reissued all of the brothers's earliest recordings from 1931–39 on six separate CDs titled *Chronological, Vol. 1* through *Chronological, Vol. 6* 🎵🎵🎵🎵 (JSP, 1996, prod. various); these fill in many of the sequential gaps most compilations leave blank. The same can be said of *Essential Mills Brothers: Four Boys and a Guitar* 🎵🎵🎵🎵 (MCA, 1995, prod. various). *50th Anniversary/Country Music's Greatest Hits* 🎵🎵🎵🎵 (Ranwood, 1972, prod. various), actually two old albums on one CD, finds the Millses crooning country in such rare and atypical tunes as "Red River Valley," "Tennessee Waltz," and "El Paso," and placing their distinctive stamp on barbershop standards like "My Gal Sal" and "Nevertheless (I'm in Love with You)."

what to avoid: *Best of the Mills Brothers and the Ink Spots* 🎵🎵 (Juke Box Treasures, 1994, prod. various) is a jumbled, directionless assortment that does little to celebrate either act, while the anthology *Mills Brothers* 🎵 (Pearl Flapper, 1994, prod. various) is simply an undersized waste of time.

Liza Minnelli (© Jack Vartoogian)

the rest:

Greatest Hits 🎵🎵🎵 (MCA, 1958)

Best of the Mills Brothers 🎵🎵🎵 (MCA, 1965)

16 Great Performances 🎵🎵 (UNI/MCA, 1972)

Lazy Bones 🎵 (Golden Stars)

22 Great Hits 🎵🎵🎵 (Ranwood, 1985)

Sweeter Than Sugar 🎵🎵 (ASV/Living Era, 1985)

Close Harmony 🎵🎵🎵 (Ranwood, 1990)

Louis Armstrong/Mills Brothers Greatest Hits 1932–1940 🎵🎵🎵🎵 (EPM/Jazz Archives)

Paper Doll 🎵🎵🎵 (MCA Special Products, 1995)

Essential 🎵🎵🎵 (Collector's Edition, 1996)

Country Music's Greatest Hits 🎵🎵🎵 (Ranwood, 1996)

Best of the Decca Years 🎵🎵🎵🎵 (UNI/MCA, 1996)

All Time Greatest Hits 🎵🎵🎵🎵 (UNI/MCA, 1997)

worth searching for: The video documentary *The Mills Brothers Story* 🎵🎵🎵🎵 (Kultur, 1993) is a 52-minute history that traces the four Mills offspring from their earliest moments caught on film to their innovative triumphs as movie and recording stars.

The video clips include renditions of "Paper Doll," "Glow Worm," and the foursome's other timeless hits.

influences:

◄◄ Duke Ellington, the Ink Spots, the Orioles, Bing Crosby, Billy Ward & the Dominoes

►► The Crows, Hank Ballard & the Midnighters, the Commodores, Harold Melvin & the Blue Notes, Boyz II Men

Jim McFarlin

Liza Minnelli

Born March 12, 1946, in Los Angeles, CA.

Without the most showstopping of pop voices, the daughter of actress-singer Judy Garland and director Vincente Minnelli compensates with adrenaline, energy, and charisma. In concert, she whirls through songs in a variety of colorfully sequined costumes, flailing her elbows and knees in every possible choreographed direction. Her most famous part remains the awed

Sally Bowles, from the Bob Fosse musical *Cabaret,* the movie version of which earned Minnelli a best actress Oscar in 1972.

Having grown up in a show-biz family—Ira Gershwin was her godfather—Minnelli tried her best to distance herself from her mother's image. In fact, she refused to sing any of the late Garland's trademark songs until recently, when she unveiled a 75th birthday tribute during a concert. The goal turned out to be easy: Minnelli's good looks developed much differently from her mother's all-American pinup-girl image, but she also had a more versatile face for comedy, theater, and energetic stage shows. Early in life, she had to deal with tending to her mother's debilitating emotional problems, plus resentment from fellow actresses who assumed she was coasting on connections. She shook all that off in the early 1960s when she started landing prominent Broadway musicals and adoring audiences; her biggest break, *Cabaret,* came in the early 1970s. Despite Valium and alcohol addiction problems, a series of divorces, and a growing public lack of interest in her specialty (musical varieties), Minnelli has remained a popular television and concert draw. She overcame most of her problems after checking into the Betty Ford Center in the late 1980s, and even wound up recording with the electronic rock band Pet Shop Boys.

what to buy: Minnelli's recorded work only hints at her showmanship, but *At Carnegie Hall* ♪♪♪ (1979/Telarc, 1987, prod. Larry Marks, Robert Woods) is a massive career document, spanning many of her shows and popular croons, including Nat King Cole's "Our Love Is Here to Stay" and, of course, the singer's trademark "Cabaret."

what to buy next: *Live from Radio City Music Hall* ♪♪♪ (Sony, 1992, prod. Phil Ramone) is a decent supplement to the Carnegie Hall collection, and it includes "Stepping Out" and "So What."

what to avoid: When Minnelli's popularity was peaking, especially after she won the Oscar for *Cabaret* in 1972, she shifted gears to television. Again, it was a nice showcase for her visual talents, but Minnelli's voice never was the best, so the recorded document *Liza with a "Z"* ♪♪ (Columbia, 1972, prod. Andrew Kazdin) falls flat in too many places.

the rest:
Highlights—Carnegie Hall Concerts ♪♪♪ (Telarc, 1989)
Gently ♪♪♪ (Angel, 1996)
Maybe This Time ♪♪ (Capitol, 1996)

worth searching for: *Results* ♪♪♪ (Sony, 1989) includes an electronic collaboration with the goofy rock band Pet Shop Boys on Stephen Sondheim's "Losing My Mind."

influences:
◀◀ Judy Garland, Vic Damone, Frank Sinatra, Billie Holiday, Ethel Merman

▶▶ Janet Jackson, Madonna, Mariah Carey

Steve Knopper

Carmen Miranda
Born Maria do Carmo Miranda Da Cunha, Februrary 9, 1909, in Lisbon, Portugal. Died August 5, 1955.

With considerable stage, screen, and radio exposure in Brazil, Miranda was already a popular South American entertainment personality when she came to the States in 1939 to appear in the Broadway musical review *The Streets of Paris.* A year later, she signed to 20th Century-Fox as a contract player. Miranda's timing was nearly perfect—during World War II, American films were not often shown in Europe, and South America dominated the foreign market. As a singer or a dancer, Miranda overpowered any shortcomings in technique with a nearly boundless charisma, not to mention a tolerance for absurd get-ups. In the 1943 musical *The Gang's All Here,* she performed "The Lady in the Tutti Frutti Hat" while wearing said hat, a cranially mounted fruit bowl that has become a Miranda signature. After the war, Miranda moved out of movies onto the nightclub circuit, and appeared on television regularly. A bad marriage and an exhausting schedule sapped her energy, and a dependence on energy-regulating drugs forced a short retirement in Brazil the early '50s. Miranda recovered, returned to the States, and continued as a popular performer until 1955, when she died of a heart attack only hours after an appearance on the *Jimmy Durante Show.* Four decades after her death, Miranda was the subject of an acclaimed 1994 documentary, *Carmen Miranda: Bananas Is My Business.*

what to buy: *Anthology* ♪♪♪♪ (One Way Records, 1994) collects 20 of the Brazilian Bombshell's most famous performances, including "Bambu-Bambu," "Rebola A Bola," "Chattanooga Choo-Choo," "Chica Chica Boom Chic," and "O Passo Do Kanguru (Brazilly Willy)."

what to buy next: Harlequin Records has released a pair of CDs, *The Brazilian Recordings* ♪♪♪ (Harlequin, 1994) and *Vol 2: Carmen Miranda 1930–1945* ♪♪♪ (Harlequin, 1994), which give a good overview of Miranda's entire recording career.

the rest:
South American Way ♪♪♪ (Jasmine, 1993)

worth searching for: *Maracas, Marimbas, and Mambos: Latin Classics at MGM* ♪♪♪♪ (WEA/Atlantic, 1997, prod. Will Friedwald, Bradley Flanagan) demonstrates the influence of Latin music on the movies during and just after World War II, with a collection of performances by Xavier Cugat and other bandleaders. Miranda is featured vocalist on three tracks: "Cuanto Le Gusta," "Caroom Pa Pa," and the immortal "Yipsee-I-O."

influences:

◀◀ Edith Piaf, Al Jolson, Cole Porter

▶▶ Patti LaBelle, Madonna

Ben Greenman

Guy Mitchell

Born Al Cernik, February 27, 1927, in Detroit, MI.

Mitchell's recordings were important factors in the mainstream commercial acceptance of country music, folk, and rockabilly. Robust and enthusiastic on all the styles decreed by producer Mitch Miller—Broadway ballads, heavy big-band pop, and German-accented novelties—Mitchell asserted his own musical identity in country music with a beat. As a result, he survived the onslaught of rock 'n' roll far better than most singers of his era.

Initially a child actor, Mitchell performed under his given name Al Cernik in bit parts for Warner Bros. Later he worked on ranches and in rodeos, absorbed cowboy culture, and sang regularly on Dude Martin's Western radio show. In 1950 he signed with Columbia Records, and Mitch Miller changed his name to Guy Mitchell. They immediately hit with "My Heart Cries for You," a big emotional pop ballad adapted by Percy Faith from a traditional French melody. Their follow-up, "The Roving Kind," had been previously recorded by the Weavers but it suited Mitchell's wide-open vocal style even better. With Miller supplying and orchestrating the material (a curse as well as a blessing), Mitchell had a string of folk-flavored pop hits in the early to mid-'50s, among them "Sparrow in the Treetop," "Unless," and the ridiculous "Feet Up (Pat Him on the Po-Po)," which would have killed the career of a lesser artist. He also recorded successful duets with Rosemary Clooney and Mindy Carson, and began appearing in movies again; his film work included 1953's *Those Redheads from Seattle* and the 1954 Western spoof *Red Garters*. Rock 'n' roll actually gave a boost to Mitchell's career as it freed him to sing in a more bluesy, honky-tonk manner. His cover version of Marty Robbins's "Singing the Blues" was a major smash in 1956, and he followed up with other country-flavored hits such as "Knee Deep in the Blues," "Sweet Stuff," and the deceptively titled "Rock-a-billy" (a bouncy country novelty). Mitchell hit #1 with his rendition of "Heartaches by the Number"

and he cemented his country image by appearing on several TV Westerns, but after 1960's "The Same Old Me" and "My Shoes Keep Walking Back to You," no more hits were forthcoming. Health problems slowed him down after that, but he's still a big favorite in Australia and the U.K., where he is revered as one of the men who opened the door for the roots music explosion of the '50s.

what to buy: Mitchell's best work and biggest hits are compiled on *16 Most Requested Songs* 𝄞𝄞𝄞𝄞 (Legacy Records, 1991, compilation prod. Michael Brooks).

the rest:
Singin' Up a Storm 𝄞𝄞𝄞 (Starday, 1969/1997)
Sings & Remembers 𝄞𝄞𝄞 (Sony Special Music Products, 1996)
Singin' the Blues—20 Greatest Hits 𝄞𝄞𝄞 (Remember, 1997)
Best of All—18 Greatest Hits 𝄞𝄞𝄞 (Prism, 1997)

worth searching for: Every important track Mitchell cut at Columbia is on *Heartaches by the Number* 𝄞𝄞𝄞𝄞 (Bear Family, 1970/1994, compilation prod. Richard Weize), including his duets with Mindy Carson and Rosemary Clooney.

influences:

◀◀ Frankie Laine, Bob Merrill

▶▶ Charlie Gracie, Marty Robbins

Ken Burke

Robert Mitchum

Born August 6, 1917, in Bridgeport, CT. Died July 1, 1997, in Los Angeles, CA.

Robert Mitchum is best known as one of his generation's leading actors, a young Hollywood tabloid bad boy (a marijuana bust in 1948 and a smoldering, cool demeanor that preceded both Marlon Brando and James Dean), and, more recently, as the deep voice that keeps reminding us that meat is "what's for dinner." But for one brief shining moment in 1957, Mitchum became quite the lounge stud. While filming *Fire in the Hole*, Mitchum spent 10 months immersed in the music of the region. When he came back he recorded *Calypso—Is Like So* . . . . Equal parts Dean Martin and Harry Belafonte (whose debut album had been released a year earlier), *Calypso—Is Like So* . . . wasn't a huge hit, but 40 years later it became the cornerstone release for lounge-oriented Scamp Records. Mitchum later put two singles in the Top 100: "The Ballad of Thunder Road" in 1958 (he starred in the film, and the song recharted in 1962), and "Little Old Wine Drinker Me," which snuck to #96 in August 1967, shortly before the music portion of his career ended.

what's available: *Calypso—Is Like So . . .* ♫♫♫♫ (Capitol, 1957/Scamp, 1995) is a camp masterpiece. Mitchum works hard on his below-the-border *patois* and cadence, but the general sweetening of the risque lyrics and schmaltzy L.A. recording techniques (i.e., trying to cash in on Belafonte's success) conspire to make a listener wonder whether to head out to the dance floor or laugh out loud: the perfect lounge record. The cover is the ultimate Mitchum wet dream: the swaggering bedroom smile, half-empty bottle of rum, and sultry island brunette at his side in a cleavage-revealing red dress. Inside, "Mama, Looka Boo Boo" had been popularized already by Belafonte. "I Learn a Merengue, Mama" precedes the worldwide dance craze by a few decades. "Not Me" makes fun of '50s notions of masculine superiority. "What Is This Generation Coming To?" is sympathetic to youthful infatuation with rock 'n' roll at a time when most adults were worried about Elvis Presley's mobile hips. Scamp's smart update conveniently adds the defiant faux rockabilly "The Ballad of Thunder Road" and its flipside, "My Honey's Lovin' Arms," a mock Presley ballad with a crazy rock 'n' roll guitar solo. If you can't live without more Mitchum, you'll have to seek a high-priced German import, *That Man* ♫♫♫ (Bear Family, 1990), which includes, besides the material on *Calypso*, another disc's worth of Mitchum in paradise.

influences:

◀◀ Harry Belafonte, Lord Melody, Mighty Sparrow, the Kingston Trio

▶▶ Clint Eastwood, William Shatner, Buster Poindexter, Combustible Edison

Leland Rucker

The Moles

See: Richard Davies, Eric Matthews

Matt Monro

Born Terry Parsons, December 1, 1932, in London, England. Died February 7, 1985, in London, England.

Monro was Britain's answer to Frank Sinatra. A talented soundalike, he brought his own warm, sentimental tone to a variety of standards and movie themes in the '60s. Under the name Al Jordan, he sang with Harry Leader's band in the mid-'50s. As Matt Monro his first taste of fame came as the singer of a Camay soap commercial, but he earned his real break when producer George Martin hired him to contribute to the Peter Sellers comedy LP *Songs for Swingin' Sellers*. Using the name Fred Flange, Monro's "You Keep Me Swingin'" was such a convincing imitation of Frank Sinatra, many fans believed they

were hearing Ol' Blue Eyes himself. Once signed to EMI/Parlophone, Monro became a constant chart presence in the U.K. with such hits as "Portrait of My Love," "Why Not Now/Can This Be Love," "Gonna Build a Mountain," and "When Love Comes Along." Once his records were distributed in the U.S., he actually scored a couple of Top 40 hits with the swinging "My Kind of Girl" and the over-the-top ballad "Walk Away." By this time, Sinatra had left Capitol Records, so his old label started importing Monro's discs in an effort to fill the void. The Beatles era, combined with Sinatra's own commercial resurrection on Reprise, blunted Monro's chart momentum, though his versions of "Yesterday" and "Softly As I Leave You" received some airplay. Monro moved to the U.S. full time in 1965 and recorded fine versions of such movie themes as "From Russia with Love," "Born Free," as well as contributing "Wednesday's Child" to the soundtrack of *The Quiller Memorandum*. On his later efforts, Monro tried to temper his Sinatra stylings with a more velvety, personal tone, but comparisons remained inevitable. (For the record, Monro thought he sounded more like Perry Como.) He remained a popular nightclub performer well into the '70s, and recorded some well-regarded (though lowselling) big-band jazz versions of contemporary tunes until ill health forced him to retire. He died of cancer in 1985, but his son Matt Monro Jr. carries on in his swinging tradition.

what to buy: The best available domestic collection of Monro's big Capitol/EMI hits, *Spotlight on Matt Monro* ♫♫♫ (Gold Rush, 1996, compilation prod. Brad Benedict) includes some choice LP tracks and Sinatraesque versions of Cole Porter and Hoagy Carmichael standards. The imports, *The Very Best of Matt Monro* ♫♫♫ (Musicrama, 1995) and *Born Free—His Greatest Hits* ♫♫♫ (Musicrama, 1997) are similar offerings with a greater emphasis on his British chart singles. They're both fine introductions to this nearly forgotten artist.

what to buy next: "Portrait of My Love" and the hit title track light up the romance-oriented *My Kind of Girl* ♫♫♫ (Warwick, 1961/Collectables, 1995, prod. George Martin), an exact reissue of Monro's first U.S. LP, which also features sterling versions of "Let's Face the Music and Dance" and "Cheek to Cheek."

the rest:

Softly As I Leave You ♫♫♫ (Musicrama, 1995)
Hollywood & Broadway ♫♫♫ (Musicrama, 1997)
Time for Love ♫♫♫ (Musicrama, 1997)
Matt Monro En Español ♫♫ (Disky, 1997)

worth searching for: Monro's best regarded LP and finest work is *Matt Monro Sings Hoagy Carmichael* ♫♫♫♫ (EMI, 1962, prod.

George Martin), a concept LP that showcases his warmest, most affecting vocals.

influences:

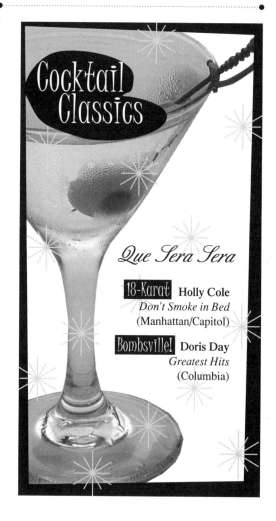 Frank Sinatra, Frankie Vaughn, Perry Como, Vic Damone

▶▶ Engelbert Humperdinck, Harry Connick Jr., Matt Monro Jr.

Ken Burke

Marilyn Monroe

Born Norma Jeane Mortensen, June 1, 1926, in Los Angeles, CA. Died August 5, 1962, in Los Angeles, CA.

The most famous screen goddess of her time, Monroe's life story has been meticulously documented in numerous books, movies, and television specials since her mysterious and untimely death. But Monroe was also a capable vocalist, singing both in films and on record. Her most famous song is probably "Diamonds Are a Girl's Best Friend."

Everybody knows the facts by now: Norma Jeane Baker (born Mortensen) was taken from her adopted home to live with her mentally unstable birth mother, and eventually wound up in various orphanages and foster homes. While working for a parachute factory during World War II, a photographer snapped her picture, and the exposure of her incredible good looks led to many modeling deals. By 1945, after changing her name and dying her dark hair blonde, she was the country's undisputed pin-up queen, gracing hundreds of magazine covers, acting in movies, and, in 1952, falling in love with baseball superstar Joe DiMaggio. Her career skyrocketed, with roles in smash movies such as *The Seven Year Itch* and *Gentlemen Prefer Blondes,* the occasional nude pictorial, and that immortal, iconic picture of a beaming Monroe trying to hold down her white dress above an upward blast of wind. She couldn't handle the fame, though, and she began relying on sleeping pills to get by; DiMaggio, furious with her sex-kitten image, provoked a divorce. Monroe later married playwright Arthur Miller, tried to become a serious actress instead of the ultimate dumb blonde, and hit it big again in the Tony Curtis–Jack Lemmon smash *Some Like It Hot.* Monroe's star began to decline after that—she divorced Miller, acted in flops, and allegedly had an affair with John F. Kennedy. Not long after her death, 20th Century-Fox Records put out an album, *Marilyn,* packed with songs Monroe sang in movies and other ephemera (occasionally filled with studio tinkering). Gradually, as the collectors market for Marilyn memorabilia has become so profitable, her recordings have slipped into public consumption. Today, several CDs exist of her work.

what to buy: *Essential Recordings* ♪♪♪♪ (Music Club, 1997) collects the best of Marilyn. There's some ephemera here, and some castaways, but most of the selections are quite strong, including "Kiss" (from *Niagara*), "A Fine Romance" (from an entertain-the-troops show in Korea), and "I Want to Be Loved By You" (from the movie *Some Like It Hot*). As an added bonus, the CD includes her legendary performance of "Happy Birthday, Mr. President," which she sang to John F. Kennedy in Madison Square Garden in 1962.

what to buy next: *Songs from the Movies* ♪♪♪ (Laserlight, 1992) brings the celluloid Marilyn onto CD, with "Diamonds Are a Girl's Best Friend," "I'm Gonna File My Claim," "When Love

Goes Wrong Nothing Goes Right," "Bye Bye Baby," and many more.

the rest:
Some Like It Hot ♫♫ (Original Soundtrack) (MGM, 1959/Rykodisc, 1998)
Marilyn Monroe ♫♫♫ (Hollywood Soundstage, 1964)
Marilyn Monroe ♫♫♥ (Galaxy, 1997)

influences:
◀◀ Judy Garland, Julie London, Peggy Lee
▶▶ Doris Day, Madonna

Ben Greenman

Vaughn Monroe

Born October 7, 1911, in Akron, OH. Died May 21, 1973, in Stuart, FL.

Monroe was one of the few singing big-band leaders whose work has enduring appeal. His clenched baritone (once described as "The Voice with Hair on Its Chest") brought an urgent, ethereal sense to pop and folk songs alike. Monroe began his career in 1932, playing trumpet and singing with Austin Wylie and His Golden Pheasant Orchestra, then with Larry Funk and His Band of a Thousand Melodies. A lucrative gig with a famous "society band," the Jack Marshad Orchestra, afforded him the opportunity to study at the New England Conservatory of Music. After he graduated in 1940, Monroe started his own society orchestra, but soon began playing a mix of hotter swing and more sentimental sounds, appealing to a larger audience. Aided by constant radio exposure, Monroe and His Orchestra scored a string of hits throughout the '40s, among them "There I Go," "The Trolley Song," "Racing with the Moon," and the singer's first #1 record, "Let It Snow! Let It Snow! Let It Snow!" Monroe's voice perfectly complemented the folk and Western craze of the late-'40s and early-'50s, leading to memorable chart smashes such as "Mule Train," "Cool Water," and Monroe's finest moment, the eerie "(Ghost) Riders in the Sky." Good looking and a credible cowboy-style vocalist, Monroe was cast in *Singing Guns, The Toughest Man in Arizona,* and other Hollywood Westerns. Though a bit stiff as an actor, crowds livened up when he opened his mouth to sing. The rock 'n' roll years slowed Monroe's hit streak considerably, but he demonstrated good humor and versatility by recording Top 40 versions of Leiber and Stoller's "Black Denim Trousers" and Johnny Horton's "The Battle of New Orleans." Monroe ended his career doing commercial voiceovers, network promos, and playing cruise ships, but the macho vocal style he pioneered still reverberates throughout pop-music history.

what to buy: Monroe's most memorable vocal hits can be found on *Best of Vaughn Monroe* ♫♫♫♫ (MCA, 1987, compilation prod. Steve Hoffman), a 12-track budget entry featuring "Racing with the Moon," "Red Roses for a Blue Lady," and the best-ever version of "(Ghost) Riders in the Sky."

the rest:
Red Roses for a Blue Lady ♫♫♫♥ (MCA Special Products, 1987)
Vaughn Monroe & His Orchestra: 1943 ♫♫ (Circle, 1996)
Vaughn Monroe & His Orchestra: 1943–44 ♫♫♥ (Circle, 1996)

worth searching for: *Camel Caravan Shows* ♫♫♫ (Collector's Choice, 1996), recorded live from the radio, is an entertaining collection of big-band sounds occasionally interrupted by some seemingly innocuous cigarette commercials during World War II.

influences:
◀◀ Jack Marshad, Bing Crosby, Perry Como
▶▶ Frankie Laine, Tennessee Ernie Ford, Johnny Cash, Bobby Vinton

Ken Burke

Hugo Montenegro

Born 1925, in New York City, NY. Died February 6, 1981, in Palm Springs, CA.

It's unfair to reduce Montenegro's wildly diverse career, which ranges from strangely percussive electronic music to tinkly instrumental versions of show tunes to his #2 version of Ennio Morricone's classic "The Good, the Bad and the Ugly." (Morricone himself has slammed Montenegro's slightly more rhythmic but mainly carbon-copy version of the song.) The arranger-composer deserves more retroactive respect than that: he was a key member of Andre Kostelanetz's lush easy-listening outfits, and he conducted Harry Belafonte's live shows for several years. While in the U.S. Navy, Montenegro was a military band arranger, then left to study music at Manhattan College. He scored a job as Kostelantez's staff manager, which led to the Belafonte gig and work with many other artists with Columbia and Time Records. His solo easy-listening career began in the mid-1950s and peaked commercially with the hit 1968 version of Morricone's distinctive Clint Eastwood movie soundtrack. Though he branched into bizarre lounge-music territory several times after that—releasing one album full of Moog synthesizer music and another called *The Dawn of Dylan*—soundtracks were his bread and butter. (He scored Frank Sinatra's *Tony Rome,* Dean Martin's *The Wrecking Crew,* and even Elvis Presley's *Charro!*) A struggle with emphysema forced Montenegro to retire shortly before his death in 1981.

what to buy: Though Morricone's versions are recommended, you can't go wrong with Montenegro's orchestral Western soundtrack music, and his Top 10 *Music from The Good, the Bad, and the Ugly* ♫♫♫ (RCA, 1968/1995, prod. Neely Plumb, Al Schmitt) includes good stuff from the soundtracks to *A Fistful of Dollars* and *For a Few Dollars More*.

what to buy next: In addition to his film music, Montenegro had a lifelong fascination with showtunes, and while four CDs is a bit much even for diehard fans, gems like "I Got Rhythm" and "Lucky in Love" are all over *Overture American Musical Theatre, Vol. 1: 1924–35* ♫♫♫ (Bainbridge, 1980/1992), *Overture American Musical Theatre, Vol. 2: 1935–45* ♫♫♫ (Bainbridge, 1980/1992), *Overture American Musical Theatre, Vol. 3: 1946–52* ♫♫♫ (Bainbridge, 1980/1992), and *Overture American Musical Theatre, Vol. 4: 1953–60* ♫♫ (Bainbridge, 1980/1992).

worth searching for: Montenegro was a prolific album artist, but he's woefully underrepresented on in-print CDs; among his more interesting recordings are the spacey easy-listening classic *Moog Power* ♫♫♫ (RCA Victor, 1972).

influences:

◀◀ Ennio Morricone, Lalo Schifrin, Cole Porter, Martin Denny, George & Ira Gershwin

▶▶ Danny Elfman

Steve Knopper

Chris Montez

Born Christopher Montañez, January 17, 1943, in Los Angeles, CA.

Montez had a schizophrenic little career, first as a rocker à la Ritchie Valens, then as a purveyor of light, romantic middle-of-the-road ballads. In 1961, Mongram label chief Jim Lee, who produced Montez's early work, had the 18-year-old Montez record his first single, "She's My Rockin' Baby," which became a strong West Coast seller. The following year, Lee and Montez added a vamping roller-rink organ to the pop-rocker "Let's Dance," which not only became an international Top 10 hit but inspired scores of teenaged boys to parody its opening line: "Hey, baby, won't you take a chance? Left my rubber in my other pants." Though Montez had plenty of other frisky, danceable numbers in his repertoire, only "Some Kinda Fun" received any chart action in the U.S. In 1966, he resurfaced on Herb Alpert's A&M label, and his records took on a more slickly

produced, lounge kinetic. "Call Me" and "The More I See You" were solid Top 40 hits. Montez faded from prominence when the '60s ended, but his first great hit, "Let's Dance," remains a staple of oldies radio, and the personification of eternal youth and vigor.

what's available: Montez's biggest, best early hit is on *Let's Dance: The Monogram Sides* ♫♫♫ (Ace Records, 1995, prod. Jim Lee), along with 19 other tracks aimed at the teenage dance market. *All-Time Greatest Hits* ♫♫♫ (Sandstone, 1992, prod. various) is equally good but contains fewer tracks.

worth searching for: Montez's biggest hits from his stint as a retooled MOR performer are on the long out-of-print *The More I See You* ♫♫♫ (A&M, 1966, prod. Herb Alpert), featuring the better-than-you'd-think hit "Call Me" and the title track.

influences:

◀◀ Ritchie Valens, Trini Lopez

▶▶ ? and the Mysterians, Joe "King" Carrasco

Ken Burke

The Moog Cookbook

Formed mid-1990s, in CA.

Uli Nomi (Roger Joseph Manning), Moog synthesizers; Meco Eno (Brian Kehew), Moog synthesizers.

The Moog Cookbook is joyfully derivative from a long line of forebears, including Kingsley & Perrey, Walter Murphy, Wendy Carlos, and Emerson, Lake, and Palmer. A listening suggestion is to play the band's records for non-initiated listeners and watch them squirm trying to name each tune. For the more sophisticated, you can spend countless hours guessing the origins of the appropriated riffs used to fill out the songs, like the Steve Miller Band's "Fly Like an Eagle" stuck in the middle of "Whole Lotta Love." Is it cheesy? Very much so. But is it fun? More so than a pair of rubber shorts full of tropical fish! Instead of listing who plays what instrument in the credits, these perpetrators of electronic farts, belches, whizzes, and whirs list what type of Moog or other device was used on each track. The prestigious Berkelee College of Music used the first CD as an example of how not to use a synthesizer, a tribute that the band enjoys.

what's available: Both CDs are fun, but it's doubtful every fan needs to own both. *The Moog Cookbook* ♫♫♫ (Restless, 1996, prod. Brian Kehew, Roger Manning) is a collection of mostly "alternative rock" songs played almost entirely on electronics

Morrissey (© Jack Vartoogian)

of various types and permutations (real drums and guitar sneak into a few songs). The highlights are a hilarious version of Offspring's "Come Out and Play"; an actually listenable Lenny Kravitz cover, "Are You Gonna Go My Way"; and an almost easy-listening rendition of Green Day's "Basket Case." *Plays the Classic Rock Hits* 𝄢𝄢𝄢 (Restless, 1997, prod. Brian Kehew, Roger Manning), subtitled "Ye Olde Space Band," is nearly as good, with a few missteps like the gets-old-even-during-the-first-listen multiple endings to Lynyrd Skynyrd's "Sweet Home, Alabama." But the great "Whole Lotta Love" (Led Zeppelin) and "25 or 6 to 4" (Chicago) easily overcome those small dalliances. Mark Mothersbaugh (Devo), Charlotte Caffey (Go Gos), Wayne Kramer (MC5), and Michael Penn make guest appearances on *Classic Rock Hits.*

influences:

◄◄ Dick Hyman, Meco, Walter Murphy, Rick Wakeman, Kraftwerk, Devo, 101 Strings, Perrey & Kingsley, Brian Eno, Sparks, Telex, Giorgio Moroder, Gary Numan, Walter/Wendy Carlos, Bob Moog, Klaus Nomi, Emerson, Lake & Palmer

Barry M. Prickett

Ennio Morricone

Born October 11, 1928, in Rome, Italy.

However hard you think you work, Ennio Morricone works harder. Nobody knows exactly how many movies he has scored (including Morricone himself), but the commonly accepted figure is approximately 400 since 1961—which, at the time of this writing, works out to the remarkable average of almost one per month. In the larger scheme of things, the key element of the Morricone catalog would be his Western scores, especially the spaghetti Westerns of fellow Italian director Sergio Leone. Morricone's operatic Western themes tend to be regarded as elegant cheese, but they're also quite sophisticated. A trumpet player by training, he pioneered the use of electric guitar and sound effects, reinventing the Western soundtrack as space-age surf music from Mars. It's actually surprising that Morricone's spaghetti Western scores have taken on such a life of their own apart from their original context, as they're so much of a piece with Leone's films (try watching *For a Few Dollars More* or *Once Upon a Time in the West* with the sound off sometime). But they've been little short of omnipresent since the mid-'6os, especially the main theme of *The Good, the Bad, and the Ugly*—maybe the most recognizable "Bad Guy" aural cue in American popular culture.

what to buy: How to do a representative sampler of 400 scores? That's an impossible task, but *The Ennio Morricone Anthology: A Fistful of Film Music* ♫♫♫♫ (Rhino/BMG, 1995, prod. David McLees) takes a gallant stab at it. The Western themes make up the heart of this two-disc collection, with tracks from other scores including 1991's *Bugsy* and 1987's *The Untouchables*. Honing in on just the Westerns, *The Legendary Italian Westerns* ♫♫♫♫ (RCA, 1990, prod. Didier C. Deutsch) includes music from the classics such as 1964's *A Fistful of Dollars* as well as more obscure Leone efforts like 1963's *Gunfight at Red Sands* (the latter's indescribably goofy "A Gringo Like Me" simply has to be heard to be believed).

what to buy next: Since *The Legendary Italian Westerns* doesn't have anything from it, *The Good, the Bad, and the Ugly* ♫♫♫♫ (Liberty, 1967, prod. Ennio Morricone) is a key supplemental purchase. Recent Morricone scores worth owning include the Oscar-nominated *The Mission* ♫♫♫♫ (Virgin, 1986, prod. Ennio Morricone), which is notable for its use of world music in a liturgical context, and the wistful *Cinema Paradiso* ♫♫♫♫ (DRG, 1989, prod. Ennio Morricone)—maybe the loveliest and most sentimental music he has ever composed. *Ennio Morricone: The Singles Collection* ♫♫♫♫ (DRG, 1997, prod. various) is the first compilation of the composer's long-out-of-print Italian singles; its 47 themes include *The Bird with the Crystal Plumage* and *The Last Days of Mussolini*.

best of the rest:

Once Upon a Time in the West ♫♫♫♫ (RCA, 1972)
Once Upon a Time in America ♫♫♫♫ (PolyGram, 1984)
Film Music, Vol. 1 ♫♫♫♫ (Virgin, 1987)
The Untouchables ♫♫♫ (A&M, 1987)
City of Joy ♫♫♫ (Epic, 1992)
In the Line of Fire ♫♫♫ (Epic, 1993)
Wolf ♫♫♫ (Epic, 1994)
Disclosure ♫♫♫ (Virgin, 1995)
U Turn ♫♫♫♫ (Epic, 1997)

Cocktail Classics

'*S Wonderful*

18-Karat Ella Fitzgerald
The Best of the Songbooks
(Verve)

Bombsville! Jack Jones
The Gershwin Album
(Columbia/Legacy)

influences:

◀◀ Alfred Newman, Dmitri Tiomkin, Duane Eddy, Nino Rota

▶▶ John Zorn, Herb Alpert, Stan Ridgway/Wall of Voodoo, Henry Mancini, Lalo Schifrin, Hugo Montenegro

David Menconi

Morrissey

Born Stephen Patrick Morrissey, May 22, 1959, in Manchester, England.

As lead singer of the Smiths, Morrissey became an icon for a legion of mournful followers. Blending angst with humor and homoerotic swagger with impenetrable attitude, Morrissey carried the Smiths out of the underground and into worldwide alternative music stardom. Though his gloomy, painfully introspective lyrics aren't exactly what Frank Sinatra and Perry Como used to sing, the singer's crooning delivery has always resembled the classic pop and lounge singers. He just hires terrific, jagged rock 'n' roll guitarists to make him sound more like a punker than he actually is. Releasing a small load of influential albums, the Smiths disintegrated in 1987 after only five years together, but the road had already been paved for Morrissey's solo career; he released his debut album, *Viva Hate*, the following year. Since the Smiths, many critics have suggested that he has turned into a caricature of his former self. Though he has scored an occasional hit single, his career has been on a steady decline—both artistically and commercially—in recent years.

what to buy: *Viva Hate* ♫♫♫ (Sire, 1988, prod. Stephen Street) doesn't drift far from the Smiths' well-established formula. While lacking the sonic finesse of guitarist Johnny Marr, it still contains some classic Morrissey intellect, particularly on standout tracks such as "Everyday Is Like Sunday" and "Suedehead."

what to buy next: *Bona Drag* ♫♫♫ (Sire, 1990, prod. Clive Langer, Stephen Street), a collection of singles, similarly showcased some of Morrissey's finest moments as a solo artist—including the indispensable "Interesting Drug" and "November Spawned a Monster."

what to avoid: Rather than pushing his work into new terrain, the solo Morrissey fell into a tired groove on insipid offerings such as *Kill Uncle* ♫ (Sire, 1991, prod. Clive Langer) and *Southpaw Grammar* ♫ (Sire, 1995, prod. Steve Lillywhite), both colorless takes on the former Morrissey sound.

the rest:
Your Arsenal ♫♫ (Sire, 1992)
Vauxhall & I ♫♫ (Sire, 1994)
World of Morrissey ♫♫ (Sire, 1995)
Maladjusted ♫♫♫ (PolyGram, 1997)

worth searching for: *Beethoven Was Deaf* ♫♫♫♫ (EMI, 1993) is a British live album recorded with one of his strongest bands cranking through 16 songs from throughout his solo career.

influences:
◀◀ David Bowie, Lou Reed, the Kinks, the Velvet Underground, the New York Dolls, Scott Walker, Nick Cave

▶▶ La's, the Sundays, James, Judybats, Smoking Popes

Aidin Vaziri

Ella Mae Morse

Born September 12, 1924, in Mansfield, TX.

Ella Mae Morse just may have been the first female rock 'n' roller. Her 1942 rendition of "Cow Cow Boogie" was Capitol Records' first million-selling single, and a stone rockin' gas besides. A white hepchick who flirtatiously belted a roadhouse mix of boogie, jazz, R&B, and country, Morse was only 14 years old when she joined Jimmy Dorsey's swing band in 1939. After Dorsey replaced her with Helen O'Connell three years later, piano legend Freddie Slack recruited her for his orchestra, and they produced some of the bawdiest jive of the pre-rock era: "Mister Five by Five," "Milkman Keep Those Bottles Quiet," "Patty Cake Man," and "The House of Blue Lights." At her peak in the '40s, Morse recorded dozens of great sides with the Nelson Riddle and Billy May orchestras, and was featured in motion pictures such as *Reveille with Beverly* (1943) and *South of Dixie* (1944). After a four-year hiatus from recording to start a family, Morse returned in 1951 and employed her lusty blues chops on the type of pop and country boogie material that made Tennessee Ernie Ford famous. She also covered R&B tunes such as "Money Honey" and "Lovey Dovey" with a credibility few singers of her era could match. She made her final vinyl appearance in 1957, just as the rock era was heating up. Even today, Morse's music seems startling in its boldness.

what to buy: A swinging overview of Morse's work with Freddie Slack, Nelson Riddle, and Billy May is on *Capitol Collector's Series* ♫♫♫♫ (Capitol, 1992, compilation prod. Ron Furmanek), 21 tracks of lusty rocking, years before it was fashionable. It's out of print, but some stores still have it.

what to buy next: Morse saucily belts several tunes live on *Radio Days* ♫♫♫ (Moon Records, 1995, prod. various), a compilation of radio appearances that also includes tracks by Louis Armstrong and Frank Sinatra, circa 1944.

worth searching for: Every blessed note the "Cow-Cow Boogie Girl" cut at Capitol records is on *Barrelhouse, Boogie, and Blues* ♫♫♫♫ (Bear Family, 1997, reissue prod. Richard Weize), a five-disc, 134-song box set that includes 20 previously unreleased tracks.

influences:
◀◀ Bessie Smith, Freddie Slack

▶▶ Rose Maddox, Kay Starr, Wanda Jackson

Ken Burke

Tony Mottola

Born April 18, 1918, in Kearney, NJ.

One of the great behind-the-scenes guitarists in pop-music history, Mottola was a key role player for tinkering bandleader Raymond Scott, space-age bachelor-pad pioneer Enoch Light, and, oh yes, crooners Perry Como and Frank Sinatra. A self-trained jazz player who worshiped the blues-and-swing guitarist Charlie Christian, Mottola played in several high school jazz combos before landing jobs with prominent orchestras, including the high-profile CBS radio studio band. On radio recordings, he wound up working with Scott, then backing a young, hungry Sinatra and his eventual replacement, Como. When Como went solo and landed a 1950s television variety show, Mottola joined as his primary arranger, and stayed with the singer for 16 years. (During that period, he also worked with *The King and I* actor Yul Brynner on his TV show, *Danger*.) In the 1960s, Light hired Mottola as a featured musician for his Command and Project 3 record labels; along with Dick Hyman and Doc Severinsen, Mottola became one of the architects of Light's influential easy-listening sound, and even recorded several guitar albums on his own. Sinatra, who tended not to forget a talented face, lured Mottola out of retirement in 1980 to play in his touring band, and the guitarist plays alongside George Benson, Lionel Hampton, and many others on the singer's 1984 *L.A. Is My Lady* album. He's not the same Mottola, by the way, as the Sony Records head who married and divorced singer Mariah Carey.

what's available: Unfortunately, few of the once-prominent Command and Project 3 instrumental recordings have yet surfaced on CD, so Mottola's two-dozen-album solo recording career is poorly documented. There's a short compilation, *The Romantic Guitar Collection* 𝄞𝄞𝄞 (Special Music Company, 1994), which includes standards like "Till There Was You" and "Send in the Clowns," and a few Christmas collections. It's worth digging through the used bins for his original stuff, such as *Tony & Strings* 𝄞𝄞 (Project 3, 1972) and *Mr. Big* 𝄞𝄞 (Command, 1959), which pioneered easy-listening guitar while Chuck Berry, Keith Richards, and Pete Townshend were pioneering rock guitar. Sinatra's *L.A. Is My Lady* 𝄞𝄞 (Qwest/Warner Bros., 1984, prod. Quincy Jones) lists Mottola as one of two orchestra guitarists.

influences:

◄◄ Enoch Light, Perry Como, Yul Brynner, Charlie Christian, Duke Ellington, Ray Noble, Dick Hyman, Frank Sinatra, Les Paul

►► George Benson, Pat Metheny, Stanley Jordan, Santo & Johnny

Steve Knopper

Nana Mouskouri

Born October 13, 1936, in Canea, Greece.

In her formative years, this Greek songstress (Europe's answer to Barbra Streisand) was heavily influenced by American music forms, from folk to jazz. Eventually she attended a classical music conservatory, but was summarily given the boot when she refused to relinquish her love of jazz. Undaunted, she continued to pursue music and eventually went on to become one of the world's most successful international pop singers. Ever since she began her recording career, she has covered a wide swath of musical terrain that ranges from classical "lieder" to bluegrass hoe-downs. An adept soprano, she certainly has the pipes to tackle it all, and her vast repertoire (almost exclusively covers of familiar material, whether pop, traditional, or classical) runs the gamut from the sublime to the schlocky. But whether the song of choice is by Mozart or John Denver, Mouskouri's delivery is always so unabashedly earnest that it's hard to criticize. Though she embraces a wider variety of music than other sirens like Marlene Dietrich, Edith Piaf, or even Liza Minnelli, and her *That Girl*-era Marlo Thomas-meets-Buddy Holly persona utterly eschews the tragic heroine/sultry chanteuse factor of such singers, Mouskouri remains true to the aesthetic of her forebears with a poised manner and coifed image.

what to buy: On *Vieilles Chansons de France* 𝄞𝄞𝄞𝄞 (Philips, 1978, prod. André Chapelle), the simple traditional French songs show off Mouskouri's voice beautifully. Many of the traditional and contemporary Spanish songs on *Nuestras Canciones, Vol. 1 & 2* 𝄞𝄞𝄞𝄞 (Philips, 1991, prod. André Chapelle) appeared again on subsequent two-disc collection titled *Recuerdos, Vol. 1 & 2.* This is a superior collection in that it features liner notes and omits the classical selections in favor of more thematically satisfying songs like "Vaya Con Dios" and a semi-traditional arrangement of "La Bamba." *Oh Happy Day* 𝄞𝄞𝄞𝄞 (Philips, 1990, prod. André Chapelle), Mouskouri's gospel album, is surprisingly convincing. Backed by a lush choir and tackling classics and traditional gospel pieces, she shows the depth and range of her voice. The cinematic selections on *Falling in Love Again—Great Songs from the Movies* 𝄞𝄞𝄞𝄞 (Philips, 1993, prod. Nana Mouskouri, André Chapelle) make more interesting vehicles for Mouskouri than her usual pop-rock, and most are tastefully done. It features a duet with Harry Belafonte on "How Do You Keep the Music Playing" from the film *Best Friends.*

what to buy next: Many of the pop ditties included on *Passport* 𝄞𝄞𝄞𝄞 (Philips, 1973, prod. André Chapelle) appear on other albums, although the following (at least) seem to have been newly recorded for this volume: "I Have a Dream," "The Loving Song," "Milisse Mou," "And I Love You So," and "If You Love Me" (an Edith Piaf song). The Greek songs ("Never on a Sunday," "Ta Pedia Tou Pirea," "Odos Oniron," "Milisse Mou," "Enas Mythos") are particularly engaging, as is Mouskouri's *a cappella* rendering of "Amazing Grace." *Concierto En Aranjuez* 🎵🎵🎵 (Philips, 1989, prod. André Chapelle) is a program of classical selections featuring songs and arias from operas by a variety of composers. Mouskouri sings in French, Greek, Italian, German, Spanish, English, and in wordless vocalizing. The title track of *Song for Liberty* 🎵🎵🎵 (Mercury, 1982, prod. André Chapelle) has appeared on several Mouskouri albums, but this seems to be the only version in English; several other tracks appear on subsequent collections ("The Rose," "Droom Droom"). *Nana* 🎵🎵🎵 (Philips/PolyGram, 1987, prod. Tony Visconti, Robin Smith) is another collection of lush pop covers of memorable tunes by Van Morrison, the Beatles, and Cole Porter. Her version of the Moody Blues' "Knights in White Satin" works especially well, remaining true to the drama of the original while updating it.

the rest:
Roses and Sunshine 🎵🎵🎵 (Philips, 1979)
Je Chante Avec Toi Liberte 🎵🎵🎵 (Philips, 1981)
La Dame de Coeur 🎵🎵🎵 (Philips, 1984)
Ma Verite 🎵🎵🎵 (Philips, 1984)
Alone 🎵🎵🎵 (Philips, 1985)
Tierra Viva 🎵🎵🎵 (Mercury, 1987)
Libertad 🎵🎵🎵 (Polydor, 1987)
The Magic of Nana Mouskouri 🎵🎵🎵 (Philips, 1988)
Only Love: The Very Best of Nana Mouskouri 🎵🎵🎵 (Philips, 1991)
Recuerdos, Vol. 1 & 2 🎵🎵🎵 (Mercury, 1995)
Nana Latina 🎵🎵🎵 (Mercury, 1996)
Return to Love 🎵🎵🎵 (Philips, 1997)

worth searching for: *Why Worry?* 🎵🎵🎵 (Philips, 1986, prod. André Chapelle, Robin Smith) is another well-mannered collection of pop-rock covers in English including material by Bob Dylan, Vangelis, Jim Croce, John Denver, and Elvis Presley ("Love Me Tender").

influences:
◄◄ Marlene Dietrich, Edith Piaf

►► Stereolab, Ivy

Sandy Masuo

Jerry Murad's Harmonicats

Formed 1944, in Chicago, IL.

Jerry Murad (born in Turkey; died May, 1996), lead harmonica; Al Fiore (died October 25, 1996), chord harmonica; Don Les (died August, 1994), bass harmonica.

Remarkably intricate and self-contained, the Harmonicats' music runs from cheek-to-cheek slow dances to raucous novelty jigs and rippling boogie-woogie. The formula became hugely successful: their haunting 1947 version of "Peg O' My Heart" spent 26 weeks at the top of the charts, and they hit the Top 20 several times after that.

Murad formed the group after breaking away from Borah Minevich's Harmonica Rascals. The Rascals were more of a novelty group, whereas the Harmonicats were serious musicians with a strong interest in jazz and the classics—which doesn't mean they weren't entertaining. They were a highly visual group featuring zany precision choreography and pinpoint comedic timing. As a recording outfit, the Harmonicats got their big break during the 1947 musician's strike. Because harmonicas weren't considered instruments by the union, Murad's group was allowed to record in spite of the recording ban; "Peg O' My Heart" came out through the loophole. Subsequently, the Harmonicats became the first harmonica players to be inducted into the American Federation of Musicians (which can either be seen as a profound honor or the union making sure such a thing never happened again). After hitting the Top 20 with "Hair of Gold" in 1948, the trio scored with a string of such lesser charts entries as "Malagueña," "The Harmonica Player," "Just One More Chance," and "Hora Stacatta." (Murad took a solo turn on the hit film theme "The Story of Three Loves" in 1953.) Their later-career lack of chart activity hardly bothered the Harmonicats. Frequent appearances on TV variety shows in the '50s (Milton Berle was an especially appreciative fan) helped Murad's group sell tons of LPs on the Mercury and Columbia labels. The group semi-retired in the '60s—Fiore and Les became popular session musicians and Murad published a series of influential harmonica-instruction booklets.

what's available: You'll believe you're listening to a full band on *Harmonicats: Original RKO/Unique Masters* 🎵🎵🎵 (Varese Vintage, 1997, compilation prod. Cary E. Mansfield). Outside of some occasional echo and a dab of electric guitar and upright bass on a few tracks, the Harmonicats play everything themselves, and their trio arrangements are so brilliantly executed you won't even notice missing instruments. Particularly awe-inspiring are their interpretations of "September Song," "Ritual

Fire Dance," and Chopin's "Fantasie Impromptu." Recorded in 1952, the sound is a bit muddy here and there, but the music comes across beautifully. The Harmonicats recorded dozens of LPs in the '50s. Let's hope this is the first of many reissues.

influences:

◀◀ Borah Minevich's Harmonica Rascals

▶▶ The Solidaires

Ken Burke

Anne Murray

Born Moma Anne Murray, June 20, 1945, in Springhill, Nova Scotia, Canada.

With her relaxed, yet warm and evocative singing style, Murray is the Perry Como of our era. A stylist of the old school, Murray's rich alto transforms everything she sings, be it gospel, pop, '50s torch songs, or country, into a smooth easy-listening experience.

Murray's early run of hits began in 1970 with the folk/pop smash "Snowbird," which led to a string of lesser chart entries with "Stranger in the House," "Talk It Over in the Morning," "Cotton Jenny," "Put Your Hand in the Hand," and "Danny's Song." When her grip on the pop charts began to slip during the mid-'70s, Murray peeled a few layers of technology off her voice and focused on the country market with spectacular results. "He Thinks I Still Care," "Son of a Rotten Gambler," "Shadows in the Moonlight," "Could I Have This Dance," "Walk Right Back," and "You Needed Me" were all major country hits that crossed over to the pop charts. Murray, able to convey romance and heartbreak without sounding sorry for herself, continued to score with such country hits as "Blessed Are the Believers," "Just Another Woman in Love," and "Now and Forever (You and Me)," deep into the '80s. Like many established country singers, Murray lost her spot on country playlists when Nashville began its massive youth movement, though she did manage to score a top ten hit with "Feed This Fire" in 1990. One of the greatest Canadian entertainers of all time, Murray has earned four Grammy Awards and three Juno Awards, and still sounds like she hardly breaks a sweat.

what to buy: Murray's abundant vocal warmth is showcased beautifully on *The Best . . . So Far* 𝄢𝄢𝄢𝄢 (EMI America, 1994, prod. Brian Ahern, David Foster, Jim Ed Norman, Tommy West), a collection of her 20 biggest hits, including "Snowbird," "Danny's Song," "You Needed Me," and "Could I Have This Dance."

what to buy next: Or, depending upon your interest level, you could go straight to the three-disc, 64-track set *Now & Forever* 𝄢𝄢𝄢𝄢 (SBK, 1994, compilation prod. Fraser Hill), which not only contains all of Murray's hits but several previously unreleased alternate takes, live cuts, and the Spanish rendition of "Broken Hearted Me." It's a fine career overview.

the rest:
New Kind of Feeling 𝄢𝄢𝄢 (Capitol, 1979/Green Line, 1994)
Love Songs 𝄢𝄢 (CEMA Special Products, 1992)
Croonin' 𝄢𝄢𝄢 (SBK, 1993)
Best of the Season 𝄢𝄢𝄢 (SBK, 1994)
Anne Murray 𝄢𝄢𝄢 (SBK, 1996)

My Christmas Favorites 🎵🎵 (CEMA Special Products, 1997)
Both Sides Now 🎵🎵 (Kingfisher, 1997)

worth searching for: Murray and Glen Campbell duet on "Show Me the Way" on his LP *Jesus and Me: The Collection* 🎵🎵 (New Haven, 1997); they again team up on the medley of "I Say a Little Prayer/By the Time I Get to Phoenix" on *The Essential Glen Campbell* 🎵🎵🎵🎵 (Liberty/Capitol Nashville, 1995, prod. various). Murray also croons "If I Ever Fall in Love" with Kenny Rogers on his LP *Something Inside So Strong* 🎵🎵 (Reprise, 1989).

influences:

◀◀ Karen Carpenter, Brenda Lee, Linda Ronstadt

▶▶ Mary Chapin Carpenter, k.d. lang, Kathy Mattea

Ken Burke

The Mystic Moods Orchestra

Formed 1965, in San Francisco, CA.

Leo Kulka, producer; Larry Fotine, arranger; Brad Miller, sound effects.

"Orchestra" wasn't the key word in this concept—although Kulka, a former Muzak employee, and his tinkering cronies hired adequate musicians to reproduce popular instrumentals and romantic non-rock ballads of the mid-'60s. The group's innovations were completely technical: the engineers methodically taped thunderstorms, wind chimes, freight trains, crashing waves, neighing horses, and various soothing percussive noises and spliced them in at key dramatic points in the music. The occasionally subversive result was throbbing background music, based on already-popular songs but transfigured just enough so listeners couldn't identify them. The Mystic Moods, which put out almost 20 albums, were a clear antecedent to the tinkly, spacey New Age music of the late '80s and early '90s. Even more importantly, though it took Kulka and his cronies a few years in the mid-'60s to sell the concept to Las Vegas showrooms and FM radio stations, the Orchestra became a fixture on beautiful-music radio stations throughout the '70s. The bottom line? Sex, of course. One original Moods album actually came with a romantic scented cloth.

what to buy: A fanatical company called the Right Stuff has repackaged and remastered most of the Mystic Moods Orchestra's original LPs with new art and better sound quality—just in time for the New Age. *Another Stormy Night*, which used to have a picture of a beautiful woman staring lovingly at a man in the shadows with a storm thundering outside the window, is now *The Best of Mystic Moods, Vol. 1* 🎵🎵🎵 (1966/The Right Stuff, 1995, prod. Brad Miller). It still opens with the soothing sounds of rain and contains such self-explanatory symphonic titles as "Far from the Madding Crowd," "A Dream," and "Love Theme from *Tristan and Isolde*." (It actually contains more tracks than the ones from *Another Stormy Night*.) For the definitive Mystic Moods, such as the version of "Theme from *A Summer Place*" you heard the most in '70s elevators, *Nighttide* 🎵🎵 (Mobile Fidelity, 1972/The Right Stuff, 1995) contains ultra-beautiful classics such as George Gershwin's "Summertime," Henry Mancini's "Days of Wine and Roses" and "Moon River," and the *Dr. Zhivago* song "Lara's Theme." Plus, there are hilarious liner notes trumpeting the sounds of crickets, a steam locomotive, thunder and rain, surf, horses, and a passenger train. It's very relaxing.

what to buy next: The Moods' most kitschy album, *Erogenous* 🎵🎵 (Mobile Fidelity, 1972/The Right Stuff, 1955, prod. Hal Winn, Bob Todd, Bob McGinnis, Brad Miller), tries to "borrow" the then-popular sounds of '70s soul, but aside from a few wah-wah guitars on the opening track and lighter-than-Ashford-and-Simpson vocals by a couple of singers, it's Muzak as usual. And guess what? It opens with the sound of a gentle thunderstorm. Anybody who listened to "beautiful music" radio stations in the '70s will immediately recognize "Love Is Blue," the opening track of *Stormy Weekend* 🎵🎵🎵 (Mobile Fidelity, 1972/The Right Stuff, 1995, reissue prod. Tom Cartwright), which is so soupy and unobtrusive it's likely to put you right to sleep. Which is a compliment.

the rest:
The Best of Mystic Moods, Vol. 2 🎵🎵🎵 (Mobile Fidelity, 1972/The Right Stuff, 1995)
(With Renee Hamaty) *Stormy Memories* 🎵🎵🎵 (Mobile Fidelity, 1972/The Right Stuff, 1995)
One Stormy Night 🎵🎵 (Mobile Fidelity, 1972/The Right Stuff, 1995)
Emotions 🎵🎵 (Mobile Fidelity, 1972/The Right Stuff, 1995)
Highway One 🎵🎵 (Mobile Fidelity, 1972/The Right Stuff, 1995)
More Than Music 🎵🎵🎵 (Mobile Fidelity, 1972/The Right Stuff, 1995)
Storm and Sea 🎵🎵 (Bainbridge, 1989)
Sounds of Hawaii 🎵🎵🎵 (Bainbridge, 1993)
Storm and Sea II 🎵🎵 (Bainbridge, 1993)
Extensions 🎵🎵🎵 (Capitol Special Products, 1994)
Mystic Moods Country 🎵🎵 (Capitol Special Products, 1994)

worth searching for: One of the Moods' most surreal original LPs, the out-of-print *Mexican Trip* 🎵🎵🎵 (Philips/Mercury, 1967), also titled *Mexico!*, applied the orchestra-and-effects formula to Mexican love ballads.

influences:

 101 Strings Orchestra, Paul Weston, Mantovani, Ray Conniff, Percy Faith

Vangelis, Yanni, Andreas Vollenweider, Mannheim Steamroller

Steve Knopper

Jim Nabors

Born James Thurston Nabors, June 12, 1933, in Sylacauga, AL.

Best known for his role as the genial lamebrain Gomer Pyle on *Andy of Mayberry* and *Gomer Pyle USMC*, Nabors went so far as to record in character ("Shazam," "Gomer Says Hey") before surprising the entire country with his serious semi-classical baritone on the *Danny Kaye Show*. So successful was his transformation from Gomer to pseudo-operatic vocalist and back again, many viewed Nabors as more of an idiot-savant than skilled character actor and balladeer. Nabors, a canny businessman and dedicated professional in real life, does little to dispel this notion, preferring to give his public exactly what it wants. Though Frank Fontaine had already done the talk-in-one-voice-sing-in-another bit with his drunken/mentally challenged character Crazy Guggenheim, Nabors's naive Gomer Pyle allowed audiences to laugh without feeling as if they were ridiculing someone less fortunate. (Andy Kaufman would later accomplish this same trick with his foreign guy/Elvis impersonator routine.)

Before entering show biz, Nabors typed letters and answered phones at the United Nations building in New York. An asthma sufferer, he moved to Los Angeles for his health, and took a day job as an NBC film and tape editor, and began singing and doing country comedy (à la Andy Griffith's early monologues) in small clubs. After an abrupt cancellation from Steve Allen's show, Andy Griffith hired Nabors to play the dim-witted grease-monkey, Gomer Pyle, which led to a recurring role on his series. In 1964, Griffith's company set Nabors up as the star of his own sitcom with the simple premise: Gomer Pyle becomes a Marine and everything goes wrong. While his character's catch-phrases "Gaa-aw-leeh," "Shazam," and "Surprise! Surprise! Surprise!" amused TV viewers, Nabors began to forge a career as a singer. With a voice well suited to

Broadway show tunes, Nabors scored a million-seller right out of the gate with his version of "The Impossible Dream" from *The Man of La Mancha*. As a pop stylist, Nabors was content to reinterpret standards and other people's hits for an incredibly responsive easy-listening crowd. Arguably, his finest work resides in his many gospel LPs, where he lightened up on his operatic style and crooned with palpable feeling and soul. Usually TV stars have a short shelf life in the music biz, but before his run at Columbia Records was over, Nabors had racked up 21 gold LPs. Nabors folded his sitcom at its peak and moved on to host his own network variety hour, which lasted two seasons. Since then, Nabors has toured extensively as a singer, keeping his hand in TV with voiceover work and guest shots, as well as taking supporting roles in three Burt Reynolds movies. During the early '90s, an infectious form of hepatitis nearly claimed his life, but after a well-publicized liver transplant, Nabors is back on the road, his vocal power undiminished.

what to buy: As budget discs go, *Best of Jim Nabors* 𝄞𝄞𝄞𝄞 (Sony Music Special, 1996, prod. various) is a pretty nice sampler, but *16 Most Requested Songs* 𝄞𝄞𝄞𝄞 (Legacy, 1989, compilation prod. Michael Brooks) is well worth tracking down. Besides containing such show-stopping standards as "Impossible Dream" and "You'll Never Walk Alone," this disc features Nabors's versions of Ed Ames's "My Cup Runneth Over," and Elvis Presley's "You Don't Have to Say You Love Me," which compete favorably with the original hits.

what to buy next: Nabors is a first-rate interpreter of religious material, and *Songs of Inspiration* 𝄞𝄞𝄞 (Legacy, 1997, compilation prod. Nedra Olds-Neal) is solid stuff, featuring sensitive versions of "Crying in the Chapel" and "In the Garden." But if you want value for your sacred song buck, look through the cassette racks for *Jim Nabors Sings the Lord's Prayer/How Great Thou Art* 𝄞𝄞𝄞𝄞 (Columbia, 1990, prod. various), two of Nabors's best religious LPs on one tape.

the rest:

Jim Nabors Christmas Album 𝄞𝄞𝄞 (Columbia, 1990)
Hymns & Country Favorites 𝄞𝄞𝄞 (Ranwood, 1993)
Favorite Hymms 𝄞𝄞𝄞 (Hamilton, 1994)
Home for the Holidays 𝄞𝄞𝄞 (Sony Music Special, 1995)
The Golden Voice of Jim Nabors 𝄞𝄞𝄞𝄞 (Sony Music Special, 1995)
A Personal Christmas Collection 𝄞𝄞𝄞 (Sony Music Special, 1995)

worth searching for: Nabors is surprisingly effective on the country selections included in *Sincerely/Town & Country* 𝄞𝄞𝄞𝄞 (Vanguard, 1980, prod. Snuff Garrett, Stephen Hartley Dorff), a two-LPs-on-one CD release. Nabors shines on "After the Lovin'," "Blues Eyes Cryin' in the Rain," and "Southern Nights." He also adds just the right amount of surreal operatic bombast to such staples of '70s pop as "Feelings," "I Write the Songs," and "Laughter in the Rain."

influences:

◀◀ Mario Lanza, Robert Merrill, Andy Griffith, Frank Fontaine

▶▶ George "Goober" Lindsey, Andy Kaufman

Ken Burke

Peter Nero

Born Bernard Nierow, 1934, in Brooklyn, NY.

Back when Peter Nero was Bernard Nierow, he was a piano prodigy, a classically trained ivory-tickler who had graduated to Beethoven and Haydn by the time he was in his early teens. But Nierow wasn't satisfied by classical music and moved on to jazz piano, after which he evolved a unique interpretive style that combined the rhythms of jazz with the formal elegance of classical composition. After playing unsuccesfully around New York, Nierow was discovered by RCA Records. The company encouraged him to change his name to Peter Nero, counseled the young pianist to spice up his act with pop standards, and then rewarded him with a recording contract. His first album, *Piano Forte*, helped him win the 1961 Grammy for Best New Artist, and Nero recorded and toured successfully throughout the decade, also working as the musical director of the Philadelphia Pops Orchestra. In recent years, he has returned to playing straight jazz.

what to buy: *Greatest Hits* ♫♫♫ (Sony, 1987) is Nero in all his gaudy, orchestral-pop glory, performing movie themes—*Love Story, The Godfather, Romeo and Juliet*—and contemporary standards such as "You Are the Sunshine of My Life," "You've Got a Friend," and "For Once in My Life."

what to buy next: *Plays the Music of Duke Ellington* ♫♫♫ (Concord Jazz, 1987) isn't particularly inspired in its song selection–it's basic Ellington like "Satin Doll," "Take the 'A' Train," and "Don't Get Around Much Anymore." But it's pleasant, and it showcases Nero's jazz roots. And *Love Songs for a Rainy Day* ♫♫♫ (Intersound, 1996) has orchestral versions of "Somewhere Out There" and "Stella by Starlight."

the rest:

Anything but Lonely ♫♫♫ (Pro Arte, 1990)
Great Songs from Movies ♫♫♫ (Sony, 1996)

influences:

◀◀ Leroy Anderson, Arthur Fiedler, Nino Rota

▶▶ Peter Allen, Michael Feinstein

Ben Greenman

Al Nevins
See: The Three Suns

Anthony Newley

Born 1931, in London, England.

Rock fans may know Anthony Newley best as one of Rich Little's favorite impersonations/parodies: the exaggerated vibrato technique and somewhat bizarre hand and facial gestures made him a rather easy target. But Newley does possess an impressive body of work. As a teen, he wanted to be a journalist, but he got a job as an office boy at a theater, and he was bitten by the acting bug. He won raves playing the Artful Dodger in David Lean's 1947 film *Oliver Twist;* a few years later, in 1950, he played a rocker who was drafted in *Idle on Parade.* He recorded a parody song, "Idle-Rock-a-Boogie," for the movie, and it became a surprise hit. His recording career was soon matching his acting achievements, and he collaborated with Leslie Bricusse on the unforgettable scores for *Willy Wonka and the Chocolate Factory* and *Goldfinger,* as well as contributing to *Doctor Doolittle.* Since the '70s, he has been much more active as an actor than as a singer. He was last seen in *Boris and Natasha: The Movie* in 1992, although he'd probably like to forget that one.

what to buy: *Once in a Lifetime . . .* ♫♫♫♫ (Razor & Tie, 1997, prod. various) includes most of your Newley faves, "What Kind of Fool Am I?" "The Candy Man," "Talk to the Animals," "Something in Your Smile," and "The People Tree" among them. *Anthony Newley's Greatest Hits* ♫♫♫ (GNP/Crescendo, 1995, prod. various) offers more of the same but isn't as much fun. Although it isn't strictly his album, *Willy Wonka and the Chocolate Factory: Special 25th Anniversary Edition Soundtrack* ♫♫♫♫ (Hip-O Records/MCA, 1996, prod. David L. Wolper) is probably the best collection of music that Newley has ever been associated with. (Come on, everybody now, sing: "Oompa loompa/Doomp-ity-do/I've got another lesson for you. . . . ")

influences:

◀◀ Ennio Morricone, John Barry

▶▶ Blur, David Bowie, Oasis, Lalo Schifrin, Danny Elfman

Jim DeRogatis

Wayne Newton performs with Count Basie (Archive Photos)

Wayne Newton

Born April 3, 1942, in Roanoke, VA.

Calling Wayne Newton a lounge singer would be an insult. He's been playing the big rooms nearly all his life. But these days—thanks, perhaps, to his severely dyed-black hair and the cheesy pencil-thin mustache he has worn for years—he's more associated with the concept of Vegas schmaltz than any other performer. Newton first wowed Vegas as a teenager in an act called the Newton Boys with his brother Jerry. He gained a national audience with appearances on Jackie Gleason's television show, and singer Bobby Darin took him under his wing, producing Newton's enduring hit "Danke Schoen." Aside from that chart hit and, much later, "Daddy Don't You Walk So Fast," Newton's records never really did much. Perhaps that's due to the fact that, in the '6os at least, his albums were filled with material for an older audience, while his singles pandered to younger tastes and aped the various styles of the day. But it's as a live performer that Newton has excelled, and he's held court for years

in Las Vegas as "the Midnight Idol," picking up where Elvis Presley left off with an energetic show filled with sweat, karate kicks, and a display of his multi-instrumental prowess. Newton's relationship with the media has been torturous over the years, and his finances shady—he had to declare bankruptcy in 1992—but he still plies his trade in Vegas and in Branson, Missouri, where he's thought of as "Mr. Excitement."

what to buy: A display of the talent that made him a teenage sensation, *Wayne Newton: Capitol Collector's Series* 𝄞𝄞𝄞 (Capitol, 1989/Gold Rush, 1996, compilation prod. Ron Furmanek) also reveals why Newton never matched his concert successes with record sales. Too many of the songs are in the style of other performers, leaving room for little of Newton's personality to shine through. Tunes mimic the Beach Boys, Neil Sedaka, Lesley Gore, and others. Even "Danke Schoen" is basically a Bobby Darin track. Still, Newton's voice is the draw here, and his performances of "They'll Never Know," "Red Roses for a Blue Lady," and yes, "Danke Schoen," are winning.

what to buy next: *The Best of Wayne Newton Now* 🎵🎵 (Curb, 1990) is a collection that contains versions of both his Top 40 hits, "Danke Schoen" and "Daddy Don't You Walk So Fast." If it's strictly Vegas cheese you want, though, opt for *Showstoppers* 🎵🎵 (CEMA Special Products, 1994), which focuses on grandiose numbers like "The Impossible Dream," "Born Free," and "More."

what to avoid: The two-drink minimum at his shows.

the rest:
Merry Christmas from Wayne Newton 🎵🎵 (Curb, 1990)
Coming Home 🎵🎵 (Curb, 1991)
Moods & Moments 🎵 (Curb, 1992)
Greatest Hits 🎵🎵🎵 (Curb, 1993)
The Ultimate Wayne Newton 🎵🎵 (Bransounds, 1994)

worth searching for: Newton contributes "Danke Schoen" to *Jackpot! The Las Vegas Story* 🎵🎵🎵🎵 (Rhino, 1996, prod. various), a release not only notable for its cheese quotient (other schmaltz classics include Al Martino's "Spanish Eyes," Tom Jones's "Delilah," and Jerry Vale's "Al Di La"), but for the cute little dice encased in some copies of the CD spine.

influences:
◀◀ Bobby Darin, Frank Sinatra, Elvis Presley
▶▶ Bono

Daniel Durchholz

Olivia Newton-John
Born September 26, 1948, in Cambridge, England.

Newton-John's massive early-1980s hits were a precursor for what the radio now calls "adult-contemporary pop." At the time, she looked hip and with-it, with good looks, a good voice, excellent taste in clothes, and perk to spare. But it's hard today to imagine anybody aerobicizing vigorously to Newton-John's "Let's Get Physical" or any of her other trademark hits; hearing them on a Las Vegas casino elevator seems much more appropriate.

When Newton-John was 16, she won a talent contest in Australia (where she was living at the time) and was sent to England to make her mark. Her first hit was a sweetened-up remake of Bob Dylan's "If Not for You," while in England she also scored with remakes of George Harrison's "What Is Life" and John Denver's "Take Me Home Country Roads." She even used her supple tones to mine the country market for a while, though she caused a stir when she was named the Country Music Association's Female Vocalist of the Year in 1974. Well, if

folks were going to get sassy with her, Newton-John could get sassy right back. Following her starring role in the film *Grease,* she put out two albums—*Totally Hot* and *Physical*—that let her body do the talking right around the time music videos were starting to take hold in the U.S. There were more films and more hits, though Newton-John did slow down after marrying actor Matt Lattanzi and giving birth to a daughter. During the early '90s, just after the release of a new greatest-hits collection, Newton-John was diagnosed with breast cancer, for which she was successfully treated.

what to buy: Singles are her stock in trade, so *Back to Basics: The Essential Collection 1971–1992* 🎵🎵🎵 (Geffen, 1992, prod. various) is a good place to start, though it would be much better if the brand-new songs were removed to make room for neglected hits such as "If Not for You."

what to buy next: It was a sales bust, but *The Rumour* 🎵🎵🎵 (MCA, 1988/1993, prod. Davitt Sigerson) was a daring, uncommercial twist for Newton-John, who worked with different textures as well as an inspired group of guests that included Elton John, Paulinho Da Costa, and rock troubadour David Baerwald.

what to avoid: *Physical* **woof!** (MCA, 1981, prod. John Farrar) was huge. But it stinks.

the rest:
Have You Ever Been Mellow 🎵🎵🎵 (Griffin, 1975/1995)
Come on Over 🎵🎵 (MCA, 1976)
Making a Good Thing Better 🎵🎵 (MCA, 1977/1990)
Greatest Hits, Vol. 2 🎵🎵🎵 (MCA, 1982)
(With John Travolta) *Two of a Kind* 🎵 (Original Soundtrack) (MCA, 1983/1997)
Soul Kiss 🎵 (MCA, 1985/1993)
Warm and Tender 🎵🎵🎵 (Geffen, 1989)

worth searching for: The out-of-print *Greatest Hits* 🎵🎵🎵 (MCA, 1977) has the crucial—and far more palatable—early hits.

influences:
◀◀ Sandra Dee, Lulu, Cilla Black, Julie London, Ann-Margret
▶▶ Debbie Gibson, Tiffany, Kylie Minogue

Gary Graff

Leonard Nimoy
Born March 26, 1931, in Boston, MA.

Before television executives discovered that infusing TV shows with hit songs by cool bands is a much better promotional strategy than coaxing actors from hit shows to sing popular tunes, a whole host of small-screen actors were offered record deals to augment their dramatic endeavors. Once upon a time, Paramount Pictures, the folks responsible for the epic interstellar television classic *Star Trek*, also ran a record label, Dot Records. Through the magic of contractual negotiation, Nimoy, the actor best known for his portrayal of Mr. Spock on the original series, wound up with a multi-album record deal despite his decidedly dubious pipes. (In fact, many of his songs are really deadpan spoken-word monologues with dramatic musical backdrops.) The results of this bold enterprise? A collection of some of the finest bad recordings in music history. *Leonard Nimoy Presents Mr. Spock's Music from Outer Space* is surely the musical equivalent of B-movie-meister Ed Wood's *Plan Nine from Outer Space*. He also released a string of mirthlessly bad albums with a few kitschy gems here and there. Fortunately, natural selection has ensured that only the best of the worst has survived.

what to buy: *Leonard Nimoy Presents Mr. Spock's Music from Outer Space* 🍸🍸🍸🍸 (Dot, 1967, prod. Charles R. Grean, Tom Mack) is the kind of poker-faced camp that today's postmodern hipsters can only dream about. The world we live in now is far too jaded for such perilously earnest stabs at pop by someone so colossally ill-suited for anything more musical than Shakespeare's blank verse. It's a classic—space-age bachelor-pad music with a *Star Trek* pedigree. Thankfully, MCA reissued this on CD in 1995 on its Varese Sarabande imprint, and the digital version includes six worthwhile tracks from *Two Sides of Leonard Nimoy*. *Golden Throats 1: The Great Celebrity Sing-Off!* 🍸🍸🍸🍸 (Rhino, 1988, prod. various) contains Nimoy's resonantly rigid renditions of "If I Had a Hammer" and "Proud Mary," plus equally groove-free tracks by his *Star Trek* compatriot William Shatner. Subsequent *Golden Throats* volumes feature Nimoy's interpretations of "Put a Little Love in Your Heart" and "I Walk the Line."

worth searching for: None of these albums are truly essential in a musical sense, but digging up any of the following as objets de curiosity might prove satisfying for a *Star Trek* aficionado or a reckless connoisseur of kitsch: *The Touch of Leonard Nimoy* 🍸🍸 (Dot); *Two Sides of Leonard Nimoy* 🍸🍸 (Dot, 1968); *The New World of Leonard Nimoy* 🍸🍸 (Dot, 1970); *Leonard Nimoy Space Oddyssey* 🍸🍸 (Dot); *Highly Illogical: Spock's Greatest Hits* 🍸🍸🍸 (Dot/Rev-ola/Creation, 1993); and *You Are Not Alone* 🍸🍸 (Dot).

influences:

◀◀ Rod McKuen, Jacques Brel

see also: *William Shatner*

Sandy Masuo

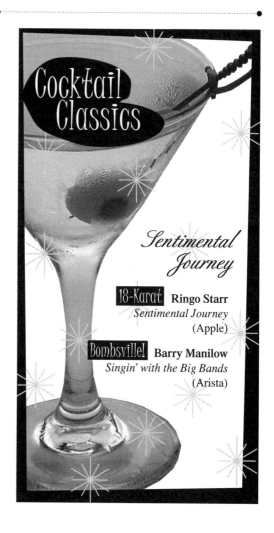

Cocktail Classics

Sentimental Journey

18-Karat **Ringo Starr**
Sentimental Journey
(Apple)

Bombsville! **Barry Manilow**
Singin' with the Big Bands
(Arista)

Ray Noble

Born November 17, 1903, in Brighton, England. Died April 3, 1978, in London, England.

Noble, who wrote the big-band standard "Cherokee," is best known for his 1930s work with singer Al Bowlly, but his orchestras were always smoother and more romantic than the jittery swing of Benny Goodman or Glenn Miller. "Goodnight, Sweetheart" was one of his first compositions in 1931, and in addition to becoming his trademark showstopper, it led to a lucrative career writing film music and collaborating with the lovey-dovey singer Alan Murray. At an early age, Noble won a dance-arrangement competition sponsored by *Melody Maker*, and that led to a high-level music director position at the record company His Master's Voice, and later EMI, where he led the house band. In 1935, his first U.S. tour was a fiasco; because of British union rules, he could only bring Bowlly with him, and the musicians Glenn Miller helpfully dug up were talented but totally undisciplined, and they got into all sorts of trouble. Abruptly, the impatient Noble disbanded the orchestra and shifted to a film career, where he took on many stereotypical roles as the goofy Englishman. Despite occasional returns to orchestra leading in the late 1930s and 1940s, he achieved his greatest U.S. prominence as a comedian on the George Burns–Gracie Allen and Edgar Bergen radio shows. Television crushed even that career, and Noble moved to a Mediterranean island where he lived for most of the rest of his life.

what's available: One of the few historical documents of Noble's highly respectable big-band career is the short *The Very Thought of You* ♫♫♫ (Living Era, 1993), which includes "Love Is the Sweetest Thing" and, of course, "Goodnight, Sweetheart." Some imports exist, including *1935–36 for Radio Only* ♫♫♫ (Jazz Band, 1994), released only in England.

influences:

◀◀ Duke Ellington, Benny Goodman, Glenn Miller, Tommy Dorsey, Coleman Hawkins

▶▶ Nelson Riddle, Les Elgart, Paul Weston, Ray Conniff, Mantovani, Frank Sinatra

Steve Knopper

Ken Nordine

Born April 13, 1920, in Des Moines, IA.

Nordine coined the phrase "word jazz" to describe his playful style of hipster free-association musing accompanied by bebop jazz. The transcendental moment in Nordine's career may have come when Fred Astaire danced to a word-jazz track on a '60s TV special. Nordine, who has paid the bills doing commercial and voice-over work his entire career, has enjoyed an artistic rebirth in the '90s, recording with members of the Grateful Dead, hosting a nationally syndicated radio show of his work and overseeing the reissue of his best album, 1967's *Colors*.

what to buy: Originally done as a series of 10 radio commercial ruminations for a paint company on its products' shades, *Colors* ♫♫♫♫ (Asphodel, 1995, prod. James Cunningham) is a fascinating trip through the spectrum from "Olive" to "Ecru" with

such insights as "amber believes in being neutral" and "orange, I said, the silly old color that lives next to red." When callers began requesting the commercials, Nordine headed into the studio and expanded the palette. The 1995 re-release features 10 previously unreleased tints.

what to buy next: *Best of Word Jazz, Vol. 1* ♫♫♫ (Rhino, 1990, prod. Tom Mack) combines the best tracks from Nordine's late '50s albums, including the epic "Confessions of 349-18-5171." It's worth picking up for the excellent liner notes by Tom Waits.

worth searching for: *Devout Catalyst* ♫♫♫ (Grateful Dead, 1992, prod. Dan Healy) was nominated for a Grammy and features Jerry Garcia and a cameo from Waits. The album convinced Nordine to perform some live shows, highlights of which were issued on *Upper Limbo* ♫♫♫ (Grateful Dead, 1994). Also, tapes of Nordine's fantastic syndicated "Word Jazz" radio show are available by mail order (Snail Records, Box 285-8c2, Florence, WI 54121).

influences:

◀◀ Jack Kerouac, Lenny Bruce

▶▶ Gil Scott-Heron, Last Poets, Tom Waits

Alex Gordon

Alex North

Born December 4, 1910, in Chester, PA. Died September 8, 1991, in Pacific Palisades, CA.

A classical composer-conductor who made his name with musical scores for major Hollywood epics, North was nominated for 15 Academy awards without ever actually winning. This is a shame because his melding of percussion instruments with symphonic, jazz, and folk sounds gave his work a uniquely expressive feel—perfect for the subtext of many classic films. He also penned "Unchained Melody," from the movie *Unchained,* which became a hit for Les Baxter, Al Hibbler, and the Righteous Brothers (twice).

North, a Julliard-trained pianist, won a scholarship to the Moscow Conservatory, eventually becoming the only American member of the Union of Soviet Composers. Before his arrival in Hollywood, North composed music for ballet troupes headed by Martha Graham and Agnes deMille, symphonic pieces for Benny Goodman and Leonard Bernstein, scores for government documentaries and training films, and themes for TV's *Your Show of Shows*. His incidental music for the Broadway production of *Death of a Salesman* so impressed Elia Kazan that North was asked to compose the score for the screen version of *A Streetcar Named Desire*. Critical acclaim and 55 more film assignments followed, including *Viva Zapata, The Rose Tattoo, Spartacus,* and many others. The one sour note in North's career was struck by director Stanley Kubrick, who commissioned him to write the score to his film *2001: A Space Odyssey*, only to discard his work in favor of pieces from "The Blue Danube Waltz" and "Thus Spake Zarathustra." As prolific as he was creative, North continued working on such high profile hit movies as *Good Morning, Vietnam* and *Prizzi's Honor* until his death. North was given an honorary Oscar in recognition of his vast body of work in 1986.

what to buy: *At the Movies* 𝄞𝄞𝄞𝄞 (X, 1993, reissue prod. John Steven Lasher) is a compilation of some of North's strong, moody work for such films as *Cheyenne, Dragonslayer,* and *South Seas Adventure.*

what to buy next: Practice Kirk Douglas's famous "I'm Spartacus" scene in time to the music on the original soundtrack recording of *Spartacus* 𝄞𝄞𝄞 (MCA, 1991).

what to avoid: It's not a bad disc by any means, but *Alex North's 2001* 𝄞𝄞 (Varese Sarabande, 1993, prod. Jerry Goldsmith, Robert Townson) doesn't live up to its hype as a great "lost" work. In hindsight, Kubrick made the right decision.

the rest:
South Seas Adventure 𝄞𝄞𝄞 (X, 1993)
North of Hollywood 𝄞𝄞 (Circumstantial, 1997)

worth searching for: North won a Golden Globe for Best Original Score for his work on *Shoes of the Fisherman* 𝄞𝄞𝄞 (MCA, 1969). Also, North contributes "Caesar's Assassination/Cleopatra's Entrance into Rome" to the very fine *Music from Hollywood* 𝄞𝄞𝄞𝄞 (Legacy, 1995, compilation prod. Didier C. Deutsch), a compilation with popular movie themes from Dimitri Tiomkin, Franz Waxman, Percy Faith, David Raskin, Alfred Newman, and others.

influences:

◄◄ Ernst Toch, Aaron Copland, Silverstre Revueltas

►► Andre Previn, Francis Lai, John Williams, Henry Mancini

Ken Burke

Red Norvo

Born Kenneth Norville, March 31, 1908, in Beardstown, IL.

Unlike the supercharged tones of the electric guitar, the brassy swagger of saxophone, or the imposing presence of a grand

Cocktail Classics

Smoke Gets in Your Eyes

18-Karat Eartha Kitt
Miss Kitt to You
(RCA)

Bombsville! Bryan Ferry
*Another Place,
Another Time*
(Reprise)

piano, there's something less than serious about the glowing tones of the vibraphone. The irrepressibly upbeat character of the instrument makes it a natural in the realm of lounge music, where nary an iota of angst exists in its raw form. But before "lounge" had evolved into a full-fledged genre, Norvo had channeled his warm vibes into jazz.

After starting out on the piano, the young Norvo was eventually inspired to pick up the mallets and tackle the xylophone. In the '30s he was the first musician to introduce the instrument to the jazz world. By the early '40s he had moved from xylophone to the vibraphone. Throughout the '40s and '50s he worked with some of the greatest names in jazz, playing in big bands led by Benny Goodman and Woody Herman, then assembling small combos that included Charlie Parker, Charles Mingus, and Dizzy Gillespie. Though he put together groups as large as seven, he preferred trios, and the Norvo catalog is dominated by various configurations of three. He was married for a time to jazz singer Mildred Bailey, and the couple (affectionately known as "Mr. and Mrs. Swing") recorded several albums together.

what to buy: Though *Red Norvo Septet featuring Charlie Parker and Dizzy Gillespie* 🎵🎵🎵🎵 (Stash, 1995, reissue prod. Tony Williams, Will Friedwald) isn't really an album proper (it's more like an EP of four tunes plus alternate takes) and the recording technology of the day (June 1945) make for rather flat sound fidelity, this interlude in jazz history nonetheless lives up to the title "Red Norvo's Fabulous Jam Session." It features Charlie Parker and Dizzy Gillespie as well as Flip Phillips, Teddy Wilson, and Slam Stewart. The sextet album *Music to Listen to Red Norvo By* 🎵🎵🎵🎵 (Original Jazz Classics, 1957) is a combination of shorter pieces plus clarinetist Bill Smith's 20-minute-plus "Divertimento." Though the group never loses its relaxed swinging demeanor, there are enough bop-ish spikes here and there to give it an edge. *The Red Norvo Trios with Jimmy Raney or Tal Farlow and Red Mitchell* 🎵🎵🎵🎵 (Prestige, 1995, digital prod. Phil De Lancie) compiles sessions recorded over a two-year period from September 1953 through October 1955 plus two albums, *The Red Norvo Trio* and *The Red Norvo Trios* (though one track from the former, "Puby La Keg," was deleted).

what to buy next: In order to make the original double album version of *The Red Norvo Trio with Tal Farlow and Charles Mingus* 🎵🎵🎵🎵 (Denon/Savoy, 1995, prod. Richard Bock) fit onto one CD, five tracks were omitted from this collection, so if you are a completist, your only option may be to track down the vinyl.

best of the rest:
Red Norvo and Mildred Bailey 🎵🎵🎵🎵 (Circle, 1938)
The Forward Look 🎵🎵🎵🎵 (Reference Recordings, 1991)
Live from the Blue Gardens 🎵🎵🎵🎵 (BMG/Musicmasters, 1992)
Red Norvo featuring Mildred Bailey 🎵🎵🎵🎵 (Legacy/Columbia, 1993)
#2 🎵🎵🎵🎵 (Vintage Jazz Classics)
1943–1944: Legendary V-Disc Masters 🎵🎵🎵🎵 (Vintage Jazz Classics)
The Complete Dial Sessions 🎵🎵🎵🎵 (Stash)
Rock It for Me 🎵🎵🎵🎵 (Hep, 1994)
Dance of the Octopus 🎵🎵🎵🎵 (Hep, 1995)
Wigwammin' 🎵🎵🎵🎵 (Hep, 1997)
Good Vibes 🎵🎵🎵🎵 (Drive Archive, 1997)
Red Norvo Quintet 🎵🎵🎵🎵 (Studio West, 1997)

worth searching for: Again, the prevalence of re-packaging in this CD age makes buying advice complicated. On occasion,

compilers omit a track or two to make two or three albums fit on a single CD, so tracking down *Move!* 🎵🎵🎵🎵 (Savoy/Denon, 1992, prod. Ozzie Cadena) depends on how much of a completist you are. All the tracks featured on this album were compiled onto *The Red Norvo Trio with Tal Farlow and Charles Mingus.* On the smooth and groovin' *Red Norvo Trio* 🎵🎵🎵🎵 (Original Jazz Classics, 1991, prod. Marvin Jacobs), Norvo's trio works through eight numbers—originals plus standards by Cole Porter, Duke Ellington, and others.

influences:
◀◀ Duke Ellington, Fletcher Henderson, Scott Joplin
▶▶ Lionel Hampton, Dave Brubeck

Sandy Masuo

The Nylons

Formed 1978, in Toronto, Canada.

Denis Simpson (1979); Paul Cooper (1979–89); Mark Connors (1979–91); Ralph Cole (1979–81); Claude Morrison; Arnold Robinson (1981–present); Micah Barnes (1989–94); Billy Newton-Davis (1992–94); Gavin Hope (1994–97); Garth Mosbaugh (1994–present); Mark Cassius (1997–present), all vocals.

Like the Manhattan Transfer, the Nylons practice smooth, jazz-tinged *a cappella* pop that's never less than tasteful, and often delightful. Despite many personnel changes—original members no longer with the group include Denis Simpson (who left early in the group's history), Paul Cooper (who left in 1989), and Mark Connors (the group's principal songwriter, he died in 1991)—the Canadian foursome has successfully mixed originals and covers since releasing a pair of albums in 1982. Despite recording several albums for two labels (Windham Hill until 1991, Scotti Bros. since), the Nylons have had only one major hit, a cover of Steam's "Kiss Him Goodbye (Na Na Hey Hey)" that charted in 1987.

what to buy: *Happy Together* 🎵🎵🎵🎵 (Windham Hill, 1987, prod. Val Garay) is the perfect starting place for any exploration of the Nylons' music. Blending the sound of a traditional vocal group with a smoother pop sound, the LP includes covers of the Turtles' "Happy Together" and Sam Cooke's "Chain Gang."

what to buy next: *Run for Cover* 🎵🎵🎵🎵 (Scotti Bros., 1996, prod. Peter Mann) serves up more of what Nylonions have come to expect—*a cappella* takes on Stevie Wonder's "My Cherie Amour," the Beatles' "Lady Madonna," the Beach Boys' "God Only Knows," and "Human Family," a song written by the late Connors. *The Best of the Nylons* 🎵🎵🎵🎵 (Windham Hill, 1993) collects the quartet's finest moments from its Windham Hill albums, including versions of rock and soul hits like "Poison Ivy," "Stepping Stone," "Chain Gang," "Up on the Roof," and "The Lion Sleeps Tonight." *Seamless* ♫♫♫ (Windham Hill, 1986) has "The Lion Sleeps Tonight," "Take Me to Your Heart," "Stars Are Ours," and more.

worth searching for: *Hits of the '60s: A Cappella Style* ♫♫♫ (Scotti Bros, 1997) seeks to repeat the forumla of the group's successful cover of "Kiss Him Goodbye (Na Na Hey Hey)," with versions of '60s hits like "One Fine Day," "Will You Still Love Me Tomorrow," and "A Change Is Gonna Come."

solo outings:
Billy Newton-Davis:
Spellbound ♫♫ (Columbia, 1989)

influences:
◀◀ Manhattan Transfer
▶▶ The Nields, Bobby McFerrin, Take 6

Ben Greenman

Sinéad O'Connor

Born December 8, 1966, in Dublin, Ireland.

To many, Sinéad O'Connor is the furthest thing from easy listening. With her frank lyrics and emotionally tormented vocals, as well as her arresting looks—which, when she first appeared on the music scene in 1987, featured the striking contrast of a model-esque face set off by a bald pate—O'Connor has made a controversial name for herself through audacious public displays, the introspective rock album *I Do Not Want What I Haven't Got*, politically charged statements to the press, and some of the most traumatized introspection in pop music since John Lennon. That said, O'Connor hasn't always been about doom and gloom and saving the world: in the midst of her most notorious period, the Irish singer turned to her childhood inspiration—the lush orchestration of the '50s and '60s—for her widely panned album *Am I Not Your Girl?* Since then, she has shifted further into quietude (albeit, a more Celtic form of it), grown her hair back, and stepped further out of the limelight to raise her son in London.

what to buy: *Am I Not Your Girl?* ♫♫♫ (Chrysalis/Ensign, 1992, prod. Phil Ramone, Sinéad O'Connor) is the reason Sinéad's in this book. Ask a dozen people who've heard it, though, and 11 of them will tell you it's awful. That's not exactly correct, however, and what you'll get out of it depends on how much you enjoy O'Connor's frail wispiness and off-kilter phrasing. True, she doesn't do right by Astrud Gilberto on "How Insensitive," and k.d. lang actually does a better "Black Coffee." Nor does O'Connor really have the emotion to pull off "Don't Cry for Me Argentina." But the whole is more effective than the work's negative reputation would suggest.

what to buy next: *I Do Not Want What I Haven't Got* ♫♫♫♫ (Chrysalis/Ensign, 1990, prod. Sinéad O'Connor) is her classic, centered on the hit version of Prince's "Nothing Compares 2 U" but also including the rockers "The Last Day of Our Acquaintance" and "The Emperor's New Clothes" and ending with the hymn "I Do Not Want What I Haven't Got." *The Lion and the Cobra* ♫♫♫ (Chrysalis/Ensign, 1987, prod. Sinéad O'Connor, Kevin Molloney) was O'Connor's breakthrough album, with the rocking single "Mandinka" and other personal and global political statements distilled into short pop songs.

the rest:
Universal Mother ♫♫♫ (Chrysalis/Ensign, 1994)
Gospel Oak EP ♫♫♫ (Chrysalis/EMI, 1997)
Best of . . . ♫♫♫ (Columbia, 1997)

worth searching for: *Red Hot + Blue: A Tribute to Cole Porter* ♫♫♫ (Chrysalis, 1990, prod. various) is an uneven but amusing collection of modern artists (including Annie Lennox, David Byrne, Tom Waits, and Lisa Stansfield) doing Porter classics. O'Connor pipes in with a warm reading of "You Do Something to Me" that's more beguiling than anything on *Am I Not Your Girl?*

influences:
◀◀ Astrud Gilberto, Julie London, Alison Moyet, Elaine Page, Enya, Prince
▶▶ Clanaad, Maire Brennan, Alanis Morissette, the Cranberries

Ben Wener

Anita O'Day

Born Anita Belle Colton, October 18, 1919, in Chicago, IL.

While she may not have invented the form, O'Day certainly perfected the art of scat-singing. Her crisp enunciation, rhythmic energy, and creative delivery heightened the bebop aspect of big-band jazz. O'Day got her start with the Erskine Tate Orches-

tra as a marathon dancer and part-time singer. One of her partners was Frankie Laine, whom she constantly quizzed about phrasing, pitch, and song selection. After failing auditions for Benny Goodman and Raymond Scott, O'Day was hired by drummer extraordinaire Gene Krupa for his band in 1941. She and trumpeter Roy Eldridge were key components in making Krupa's band one of the best of that era. O'Day's string of hits ("Let Me off Uptown," "Alreet," "Bolero at the Savoy") propelled Krupa's outfit to its popular peak just before a drug bust forced him to temporarily fold the band. After a brief stint with Woody Herman, O'Day recorded hits with Stan Kenton's band ("And Her Tears Flowed Like Wine," "The Lady in Red") before returning to Krupa's orchestra. O'Day went solo in 1946, recording with Signature and London, but didn't really find a sympathetic label until she signed with Norman Granz's Verve Records in 1952. At Verve, O'Day became a highly respected LP artist, collaborating on great sides with Ralph Burns, Billy May, Jimmy Giuffre, Barney Kessel, Cal Tjader, and Oscar Peterson. O'Day's filmed 1958 appearance at the Newport Jazz Festival, *Jazz on a Summer's Day* (where she scats up a storm on "Tea for Two"), is considered her career high-water mark. O'Day cut top-notch discs and toured worldwide well into the '60s, until her longstanding addiction to heroin nearly took her life. Drug-free, she rebounded in the '70s with a smash appearance at the Berlin Jazz Festival, and took complete charge of her recording career by leasing sides from her own label, Emily Records. In 1997, the National Endowment for the Arts presented O'Day with the American Jazz Masters Award.

what to buy: Backed by the Oscar Peterson Quartet, O'Day never sounded better than on *Anita Sings the Most* 𝄢𝄢𝄢𝄢 (Verve, 1957/1990, prod. Norman Granz), a rather remarkable collaboration featuring inspired versions of "Them There Eyes," "Bewitched, Bothered, and Bewildered," and "They Can't Take That away from Me." Equally fine, though less cohesive as an LP, *Verve Jazz Masters 49* 𝄢𝄢𝄢𝄢 (Verve, 1995, prod. Norman Granz) offers up such savory songs as "A Nightingale in Berkeley Square," "Angel Eyes," and "I Can't Get Started." Both are great starting points.

what to buy next: The Verve era was O'Day's hot period as a solo act, so you could just as easily be satisfied with *Compact Jazz* 𝄢𝄢𝄢𝄢 (Verve, 1993, prod. Norman Granz), with tracks recorded between 1952 and 1962 with the Gene Krupa, Buddy

Bregman, Billy May, and Marty Paich orchestras. Also, *Pick Yourself Up* 𝄢𝄢𝄢𝄢 (Verve, 1956/1992) and *This Is Anita* 𝄢𝄢𝄢𝄢 (Verve, 1956/1990) are great reissues of her original LPs, fattened up with previously unreleased alternate takes.

what to avoid: O'Day was well past her prime when she recorded *At Vine Street Live* 𝄢 (DRG, 1991, prod. Hugh Fordin) and *Rules of the Road* 𝄢 (Pablo, 1993, prod. Buddy Bregman), in which her voice sounds shot on new versions of her old classics.

the rest:
I Get a Kick Out of You 𝄢𝄢𝄢 (Evidence, 1975/1993)
Live in Person 𝄢𝄢𝄢 (Starline, 1976/1993)
In a Mellow Tone 𝄢𝄢𝄢𝄢 (DRG, 1989)
Sings the Winners 𝄢𝄢𝄢𝄢 (Verve, 1990)
(With Billy May) Swings Cole Porter 𝄢𝄢𝄢𝄢 (Verve, 1991)
I Told Ya I Love Ya, Now Get Out 𝄢𝄢𝄢 (Signature, 1991)
Mello Day 𝄢𝄢𝄢 (GNP/Crescendo, 1992)
Wave: Live at Ronnie Scott's 𝄢𝄢 (Castle, 1993)
Meets the Big Bands 𝄢𝄢𝄢 (Moon, 1994)
That's That 𝄢𝄢𝄢 (Moon, 1995)
Let Me off Uptown 𝄢𝄢𝄢 (Pearl, 1996)
Jazz 'Round Midnight 𝄢𝄢𝄢 (Verve, 1997)
Anita O'Day, Vol. 19: 1941–46 𝄢𝄢𝄢 (L'Art Vocal, 1997)

worth searching for: O'Day's early years swinging with Gene Krupa's big band are chronicled on *Sings with Gene Krupa* 𝄢𝄢𝄢𝄢 (Tristar, 1994, prod. various), which contains many of their biggest hits from the early '40s. *Drum Boogie* 𝄢𝄢𝄢𝄢 (Legacy, 1993, compilation prod. Michael Brooks) is another solid collection, with "Drum Boogie," "No Name Jive," "How about That Mess," "Rum Boogie," and more solid cuts with and without O'Day.

influences:
◀◀ Mildred Bailey, Billie Holiday, Connee Boswell, Frankie Laine
▶▶ June Christy, Chris Connor, Helen O'Connell

Ken Burke

Jane Olivor

Born 1947, in New York, NY.

A soulful Streisand-wannabe vocalist who appeared to be on her way to greatness during the late 1970s, Olivor stopped performing live and saw her career quickly snuffed out. Her voice—emotional and powerful—appealed to masses of women who found her unabashed romanticism addictive. With cover tunes like "Some Enchanted Evening" and "Vincent," she sang sweeping ballads about love and relationships. For the past 17 years, however, Olivor has recorded close to nothing and is reportedly

Anita O'Day (© Jack Vartoogian)

playing small clubs—a far cry from her peak performance at Carnegie Hall. In 1987, she told the *Chicago Tribune*: "Believe it or not, I suffered from great stage fright, and it never went away, never got better. If anything, it got worse. It was unbearable—it was always there. And I didn't do drugs and alchohol; I was completely a drug wimp. So I didn't have anything to ease the pain of the stage fright. Frankly, I don't know how people can go on stage loaded or whatever—it would put me to sleep." In any case, Olivor is clearly blessed with a voice that is reminiscent of Streisand's. Her gushy style is likely to appeal to a limited range of listeners, however. And her albums, already terribly dated, won't provide much of a draw.

what to buy: *First Night* 🎵🎵🎵 (Columbia, 1977, prod. Jason Darrow), without a doubt her best album, features a surprisingly strong collection of showtunes and obscure romantic pieces. "Carousel of Love" may be the finest single recording she has ever made.

what to buy next: *Stay the Night* 🎵🎵🎵 (Columbia, 1978), the last of Olivor's really strong albums, is a mish-mash of up-tempo and maudlin tunes. It's worth a listen, but not as a first purchase.

what to avoid: *Best Side of Goodbye* 🎵🎵 (Columbia, 1980, prod. Jason Darrow, Michael Masser, Louie Shelton), clearly the beginning of a career in decline, features only one memorable track: "The Greatest Love of All."

influences:

◀◀ Barbra Streisand

▶▶ Celine Dion, Whitney Houston

Carl Quintanilla

The 101 Strings

Formed early 1950s, in Hamburg, Germany.

Dick L. Miller, engineer; hundreds of rotating orchestra musicians, as many as 130 at a time.

Many other orchestras have hit on the 101 Strings' basic idea—hiring serious orchestral musicians to play pop music in a playful, overly dramatic, catchy way—but neither Mantovani, Ray Conniff, nor the Hollyridge Strings have been nearly as prolific as this massive international conglomerate. In the Strings' more than 200 albums, beginning in German concert halls but moving to London by 1957, engineer Dick L. Miller and his rotating orchestras have stamped their lush fingerprints onto pop, rock, Latin, Christmas, religious, folk, world-beat, big-band, jazz, country, soul, and classical songs. Miller's initial idea was to create lucrative easy-listening music without hiring an established star, such as Mantovani or Ray Conniff. He was right—and, surprisingly, the 101 Strings have, on extremely rare occasions, created music that's more interesting than any rock or experimental-sounds fan would have the right to expect. When the Beatles were big, the Strings capitalized with *The 101 Strings Play the Hits of the Beatles*; after men walked on the moon, the Strings put out the bizarre, spacey non-strings album *Astro Sounds from Beyond the Year 2000*; in the '70s, the Strings even pulled off softcore musical pornography, hiring panting singer Bebe Barton to simulate an impressively long orgasm during *The "Exotic" Sounds of Love*. The weird thing is, despite the inherent schmaltziness of the technique, some of the music worked in an eerie, almost rocking way. *Astro Sounds* captures a certain busy psychedelic sound that similarly serious predecessors Emerson, Lake, and Palmer and the Electric Light Orchestra rarely achieved.

what to buy: The 101 Strings catalog is massive and intimidating, but the good news is, thanks to Madacy Entertainment Group's 1995 purchase from Alshire's 101 Strings label, almost all the original albums have been reissued on CD. Most eclectic and interesting is *Astro Sounds from Beyond the Year 2000* 🎵🎵🎵 (101 Strings, 1969/Madacy/Scamp/Caroline, 1996, prod. Al Sherman): its "space music" is nothing more than successful psychedelic rock, especially on "A Disappointed Love with a Desensitized Robot," which apes the Spencer Davis Group's rock classic "Gimme Some Lovin'" while somehow escaping full songwriting credit. The buzzing synthesizers and overpowering string army mix oddly with the playful, catchy melodies, and the whole thing climaxes with the bonus tracks "Whiplash" and "Instant Nirvana," which sound literally like same-era porno movies.

what to buy next: Check the Strings' comprehensive Internet page—www.101strings.com—for a meticulously organized reissue list and pick a few from your favorite category: holiday music, such as *The Magic of Christmas* 🎵🎵🎵 (Alshire/Madacy, 1995); big-band swing, *Golden Age of Dance Bands* 🎵🎵 (Alshire/Madacy, 1995); gospel, *Praise the Lord and Other Sounds of Faith and Inspiration* 🎵🎵 (Alshire/Madacy, 1995); classical, *The Best of Johann Strauss Jr.* 🎵🎵🎵 (Alshire/Madacy, 1995); and country, *Take Me Home, Country Roads* 🎵🎵🎵 (Alshire/Madacy, 1995).

what to avoid: The Strings' "soul of" phase was international fakery at its finest, and despite the typical "serious" approach to the songs, the orchestras simply used flamenco guitar touches to simulate Mexico, accordions to approximate Hungarian "gypsies," and other hackneyed, stereotypical devices. *The Soul of Spain* 🎵🎵 (Alshire/Madacy, 1995), the orchestra's first bona fide hit album, is even more smoothed-over than the Tijuana Brass's decidedly non-Mexican take on mariachi music.

best of the rest:
The Great Musicals 🎵🎵 (Alshire/Madacy, 1995)
Gems of the Silver Screen 🎵🎵🎵 (Alshire/Madacy, 1995)
Treasury of Christmas Favorites 🎵🎵🎵 (Alshire/Madacy, 1995)
The Heart and Soul of Mexico 🎵🎵 (Alshire/Madacy, 1995)
The Soul of Greece 🎵🎵 (Alshire/Madacy, 1995)
101 Strings Play Million Seller Hits of Today Composed by Simon and Garfunkel 🎵🎵🎵 (Alshire/Madacy, 1995)
101 Strings Play Hits of the Beatles 🎵🎵🎵 (Alshire/Madacy, 1995)
A Big Band Polka Extravaganza 🎵🎵🎵 (Alshire/Madacy, 1995)

worth searching for: Though most baby-boomers' parents had at least one 101 Strings LP in their collections throughout the '60s and '70s, the LPs are awfully hard to find today: *The "Exotic" Sounds of Love* 🎵🎵🎵 (Alshire/Somerset, 1971), to name just one, contained an "Adults Only" warning long before L.L. Cool J, the 2 Live Crew, and Lil' Kim simulated the sounds of sex on their albums.

influences:
◀◀ Mantovani, Andre Kostelanetz, Morton Gould, Les Baxter, Bing Crosby, the Beatles, Simon & Garfunkel

▶▶ The Hollyridge Strings, the Mystic Moods Orchestra, Fats & the Chessmen, Sons of the Purple Sage, the Living Strings

Steve Knopper

Orange Juice
See: Edwyn Collins

Tony Orlando
Born Michael Anthony Orlando Cassavitis, April 3, 1944, in New York City, NY.

Every time there's a war or a hostage crisis, we have Orlando to thank for the spate of yellow ribbons tied around old oak trees. Orlando, along with two female back-up singers, Telma Louise Hopkins and Joyce Vincent-Wilson, known collectively as Dawn, had a #1 hit in 1973 with "Tie a Yellow Ribbon." Despite its actual subject of a paroled prisoner looking for romantic affirmation from his heartthrob, the song took on a symbolic meaning

Cocktail Classics

Sophisticated Lady

18-Karat Duke Ellington
Reminiscing in Tempo
(Columbia/Legacy)

Bombsville! Cleo Laine
Solitude
(RCA Victor)

during the waning years of the Vietnam War and has been used as a symbol of hope and remembrance ever since.

With the help of producer Don Kirshner and songwriter Carole King, Orlando first hit the charts as a teenager with three singles reaching the top 100 in 1961, most notably "Bless You" (#15). Orlando then went behind the scenes, working in music publishing until a friend asked him as a favor to sing lead vocals for a song by a Detroit female duo named Dawn. The song, "Candidia," hit #3 on the pop charts and led Orlando to quit his day job and team up with Dawn. The admittedly corny group enjoyed great success in the early '70s with two more #1 hits ("Knock Three Times" and "He Don't Love You (Like I Love

You)") and a popular CBS variety show. But in 1976, Orlando and Dawn went their separate ways. Orlando overcame a subsequent nervous breakdown and a drug problem to mount a minor late '70s comeback. He then appeared on Broadway in *Barnum* in 1981. Seven years later, he thankfully reunited with Dawn for a comeback tour and today visitors to Branson, Missouri, can hear the hirsute vocalist perform year-round in his own theater.

what to buy: All the big hits you remember blaring out of your AM radio are collected on *Best of Tony Orlando & Dawn* 🎜🎜🎜 (Rhino, 1994, prod. Gary Stewart), plus the cover photo is priceless.

what to buy next: Orlando's charmingly innocent teen hits and other early filler comprise *Bless You & 17 Other Great Hits* 🎜🎜🎜 (Collectables, 1997).

what to avoid: Orlando's late '70s comeback attempt is for some reason chronicled on *The Casablanca Years* 🎜 (PolyGram, 1996, prod. Hank Medress, Dave Appell). One listen and you'll be tempted to tie a yellow ribbon around your own neck.

worth searching for: Among the scores of classic tunes on the hard-to-find four-CD collection *The Brill Building Sound: Singers & Songwriters Who Rocked the '60s* 🎜🎜🎜🎜 (Era, 1994, prod. Steve Wilson) are Orlando's "Bless You" and "Halfway to Paradise."

influences:

◀◀ Neil Diamond, Sonny & Cher, the Carpenters, Carole King, Neil Sedaka, Paul Anka

▶▶ Buster Poindexter, the Captain & Tennille

Alex Gordon

The Out-Islanders

Formed 1960, in Hollywood, CA.

Marni Nixon, vocals; Loulie Jean Norman, vocals; Billy May, arranger; Charlie Barnet, bandleader.

The Out-Islanders' lone Capitol album is still one of the undiscovered gems of exotica. The abstract siren voices of Marni Nixon ("Return to Paradise") and Loulie Jean Norman ("Moon Mist," "Moon of Manakoora") are nearly unsurpassed in this style. The songs, especially "Return to Paradise," are especially wonderful, but the packaging is even better: ships crashing onto the rocks, and a naked native girl near a waterfall on the cover luring the listener into "an exotic musical mood adventure." The instrumentation is in good hands, with Billy May,

an arranger with Frank Sinatra and Nat King Cole during their Capitol years, and Charlie Barnet, whose stomping '30s and '40s big bands hit with "Cherokee" and "Red Skin Rhumba." Several big record labels released magnificent one-shots like this: Warner Bros. released Marty Wilson's *Jungala*, Columbia had Shel Magne's *Tropical Fantasy*, and Kapp put out Frank Hunter and His Orchestra's *White Goddess*.

what's available: "Moon Mist," possibly the only Out-Islanders' surviving in-print CD track, is full of sexy horns and uptempo Hawaiian rhythms; it appears among Martin Denny and Yma Sumac on *Ultra-Lounge: Mondo Exotica* 🎜🎜🎜🎜 (Capitol, 1996, compilation prod. Brad Benedict).

worth searching for: The band's original album is far out of print: hearing May's smooth woodwinds, bongos, dark electric bass, and vibes as background to Barnet's mature sax playing on *Polynesian Fantasy* 🎜🎜🎜🎜 (Capitol, 1961, prod. Dave Cavanaugh, Curly Walter) is a delicate thrill.

influences:

◀◀ Martin Denny, Les Baxter, Yma Sumac

▶▶ Southern Culture on the Skids

Domenic Priore

Patti Page

Born Clara Ann Fowler, November 8, 1927, in Muskogee, OK.

Patti Page was the best-selling female singer of the 1950s and the kind of pop singer from whom rock 'n' rollers liked to think they saved the world. But Page, who had grown up picking Oklahoma cotton with her 10 siblings, continued to appeal to more conservative audiences long after she quit having pop hits. Page's big-band recordings were occasionally marked by questionable material, like "(How Much Is) That Doggie in the Window?," though those songs were often quite successful. She helped pioneer the double-tracking technique of vocal recording, and her career was also aided by the advent of television. Her Okie background gave Page an affinity for Western swing, and she had many pop successes with country songs. Page's watershed record was her version of "Tennessee Waltz," a multi-million-selling crossover smash written by Western-swing bandleader Pee Wee King and singer Redd Stewart. Page learned the song from a version by R&B trumpeter Erskine Hawkins, which shows something of the tune's across-the-board appeal. The song topped the pop chart for 13 weeks and sold more than six million copies. Though Page's popularity diminished in the late 1950s, she continued having hits well into the rock 'n' roll era: her recording of the theme song from the film *Hush, Hush, Sweet Charlotte* reached #8 in 1965.

what to buy: *A Golden Celebration* 🎵🎵🎵 (Mercury Chronicles, 1997, prod. various) borders on overkill, with 80 songs on four CDs, but it includes "(How Much Is) That Doggie in the Window?" and showcases her versatile voice. Aside from that, the more cost-effective *Golden Hits* 🎵🎵🎵 (Mercury, 1960/1994) contains the best of Page's hits, many of them featuring the double-track vocal technique she helped pioneer on songs like "Tennessee Waltz."

what to buy next: *Golden Hits* is by far the best single collection of Page's hits, but if you want to go deeper into her music, *The Patti Page Collection, Mercury Years, Vol. 1* 🎵🎵🎵 (Mercury, 1991) and *The Patti Page Collection, Mercury Years, Vol. 2* 🎵🎵🎵 (Mercury, 1991) have 20 songs each. *Volume 2* also tacks on three radio promotional spots from the 1950s.

what to avoid: Page has often re-recorded her material, and none of those sessions were as good as the originals. Deceptive remake packages include *16 Best of Patti Page* 🎵 (Plantation, 1987, prod. Shelby S. Singleton); *16 Greatest Hits* 🎵 (Plantation, 1987, prod. Shelby S. Singleton); *Greatest Hits—Finest Performances* 🎵🎵 (Sun, 1995, prod. Shelby S. Singleton); and *Greatest Songs—Legendary Artist Series* 🎵🎵 (Curb, 1995). The Plantation packages each contain a charting country single or two recorded for that label during the early 1980s.

the rest:
Greatest Hits 🎵🎵 (Columbia, 1987)
16 Most Requested Songs 🎵🎵 (Columbia/Legacy, 1989)
The Uncollected Patti Page with Lou Stein's Music '49 🎵🎵🎵 (Hindsight, 1990)
Hits of—Volume 1 🎵🎵🎵 (Sound Choice, 1992)
A Touch of Country 🎵 (Laserlight, 1993)
Just a Closer Walk with Thee 🎵🎵 (Mercury, 1995)
Christmas with Patti Page 🎵🎵 (Mercury, 1996)
Dreaming 🎵🎵 (Sony Music Special Products, 1996)
Tennessee Waltz 🎵🎵 (Masters, 1996)
Golden Greats 🎵🎵🎵 (PolyGram Special Markets, 1996)
A Golden Celebration 🎵🎵🎵 (PGD, 1997)
Tennessee Waltz 🎵 (Sun, 1997)

worth searching for: The hour-long *Video Songbook* 🎵🎵🎵 (Image, 1997) features Page performing songs like "Tennessee Waltz," "(How Much Is) That Doggie in the Window?," and "I Went to Your Wedding" on 1950s television variety shows.

influences:

◀◀ Kay Starr, Jo Stafford, Dinah Shore

▶▶ Connie Francis, Anne Murray

Brian Mansfield

Paul Page

Born May 9, 1910, in North Vernon, IN. Died September 6, 1997, in Lake Montezuma, AZ.

Page's career would have been totally forgotten had he not self-produced his own independent LPs in the 1960s. They were made specifically for the audiences who saw him perform at Los Angeles–area tiki restaurants, and to capture the important little ideas constantly flowing from his ambitious mind.

Page, also a fine painter, newspaper editor, disc jockey, and male model, got his first break in Anchorage, Alaska, as a reporter with a radio show on the side. A chance meeting with Will Rogers provided him with the encouragement to return to the Midwest, where he landed a gig on *The Breakfast Club* radio show, broadcast out of Chicago, and played Hawaiian favorites. As Page's accompaniment grew from basic organ to a full Hawaiian big band, he secured a 10-year contract with NBC radio and quickly moved to Hollywood. With help from Hawaiian music legend Sol Hoopi, Page landed a full-time gig at the nautical-themed restaurant Seven Seas; during the '40s, crooner Kay Starr and her sisters were the vocal chorus, and Page's floor show featured a troupe of native hula dancers. When television began to show signs of life, his *Pages of Memory* radio show transferred to the small screen. All was going well until an automobile accident at the Los Angeles Airport sidelined him for several years. When he returned, due to television, the musical *South Pacific,* and the fading of the big bands, the entire scene had changed. Tiki lounges were everywhere, and Page found work on smaller stages throughout the greater Los Angeles area. Unlike typical Hawaiian artists of that era, Page sang like a sailor, and his songs came off like Polynesian sea chanties. Two songs from the classic *Pieces of Eight,* "Matey" and "My Fiji Island Queen," best display his tounge-in-cheek spirit: The former includes a line about "dancing the hornpipe" and in the latter, the queen "doesn't need a cent for her upkeep, for there's nothing that she needs, all she wears is a great big smile and a little string of beads."

worth searching for: Fans of Hawaiian and tiki music with an interest in Page should prepare, at least for the time being, for a serious quest. All of his albums are out of print and none of his songs even show up on the growing number of lounge-compilation CDs. Still, searches of used record stores can unearth these masterworks: *Hawaiian Honeymoon* ♪♪♪♪ (Paradise), a concept album drenched in off-time bird calls and jungle howls; and his tribute to prominent Hawaiian poet and *Vagabonds House* author Don Blanding, *I Remember Blanding* ♪♪♪♪ (Paradise).

influences:

◀◀ Martin Denny, Will Rogers, Sol Hoopi, Don Blanding, Walter Blaufus, Charles King

▶▶ Kay Starr

Domenic Priore

Korla Pandit

Born in New Delhi, India.

A strange character who played the pipe organ and wore a huge turban (with a big jewel, of course) on Los Angeles–area television commercials in the '50s, Pandit was said to have hypnotized housewives into falling in love with him. Whatever the case, though he never became hugely popular, he recorded several organ-rich albums and is one of the lesser-known proponents of the strange instrumental style known as exotica. He made a cameo in the 1952 movie *Something to Live For* and in Richard Pryor's 1977 comedy *Which Way Is Up?*, and, according to some reports, toured in the late '70s. He pops up every now and then in RE/Search's *Incredibly Strange Music* volumes, in which strange-music expert Brian King quotes Pandit thusly: "Music may not save your soul, but it will cause your soul to be worth saving." Pandit reportedly continues to do bizarre performances, such as an entire pipe-organ reading of the old movie soundtrack *Phantom of the Opera*.

what's available: Pandit put out several LPs for the jazz label Fantasy Records in the '50s, but none of those master recordings have survived the CD era—save *Odyssey* ♪♪♪♪ (Fantasy, 1996), recorded in Los Angeles in 1958 and 1959, and initially released as two LPs titled *Music of the Exotic East* and *Latin Holiday*. With bouncy instrumentals like "Tale of the Underwater Worshipers," "Kartikeya," and a non-surf arrangement of the Greek classic "Misirlou," it's considered a classic in the exotica genre, along with key albums by Les Baxter and Martin Denny. *Exotica 2000* ♪♪♪ (Sympathy for the Record Industry, 1996) is harder to find.

influences:

◀◀ Martin Denny, Les Baxter, Juan Garcia Esquivel

▶▶ Combustible Edison

Steve Knopper

Charlie Parker

Born April 29, 1920, in Kansas City, MO. Died March 12, 1955, in New York, NY.

The idea, at the time, should have been horrifying enough to send every beret-wearing, bongo-tapping bop freak screaming off into hipster hell. Consider this: a collaboration between Bird, the defiant architect of the bebop revolution, and Mitch Miller, the beaming, goateed master of bouncing-ball choral music and the man Frank Sinatra and rock critics by the hundreds still revile. And yet, Parker's dalliance with oboist Miller and a New York string section not only produced evanescent jazz, it paved the way for dozens of other jazz artists to swim upstream against brigades of syrupy violinists. More often than not, those experiments should have been kept in the lab. But Bird's example—the way his alto sax soared over, under, and around the charts—keeps the sax-and-strings tributes coming decades after his early 1950s classics were recorded. When Parker first took up with a lush orchestral unit in December, 1947—at New York's Carnegie Hall, no less—it was not the first time a jazz star combined with strings. Billie Holiday had been first to try it successfully in 1944 during sessions for Decca. Parker's first effort was "Repetition," a lilting Parker horn sortie paired with an eerie lunar arrangement by Neil Hefti. Verve producer Norman Granz brought Parker back into his New York studios in 1949 to record a box set of 78s. The decision was later hooted at by some jazz purists who blamed Granz for trying to popularize Parker's cultish pyrotechnics. But Parker himself insisted in at least one interview that he had dreamed of playing against a string section as early as 1941. Either way, the collaboration has stood the test of time. Among the first batch of 1949 winners—with Miller's oboe—were the swinging "Just Friends" and the dreamy "I Didn't Know What Time It Was." Bird returned for two more abbreviated sessions in 1950 and 1952 and a beatific live date at Carnegie Hall in 1952. There are also several bootleg tapes of other Parker and strings concerts from the early 1950s floating around in the jazz sections of record stores. But none have the lush clarity of the Verve experiments.

what to buy: All 24 of Parker's trend-setting Verve strings are on *Charlie Parker with Strings: The Master Takes* ♪♪♪♪♪

(Verve, 1995, prod. Norman Granz). From the romantic lilt of "April in Paris" to the splendor of "Autumn in New York," Bird's soaring alto turns every trite passage into magic. This album should be a cornerstone in any jazz collection, and it makes any other mood string collection seem a ghostly imitator. *The Cole Porter Songbook* 𝄞𝄞𝄞 (Verve, 1991, prod. Norman Granz), backed with a mix of string and combos, are mostly as good as late-period Parker gets. But there is a queasy Granz-inspired experiment with the Dave Lambert Singers on "In the Still of the Night" that almost sinks the entire disc.

what to buy next: Parker fanatics will argue until judgment day which label did the most right by Bird—the early Savoys, the late 1940s Dials, or the 1950s sunset fling with Verve—but the box set *The Complete Dial Sessions* 𝄞𝄞𝄞𝄞 (Stash, 1993, prod. Ross Russell) gives the fullest representation of Bird at his peak. There is nothing treacly about these 79 sides, but even the consumate lounge lizard will be swept away by the stratospheric gyrations of Parker's balladry.

best of the rest:
Savoy Recordings (Master Takes) 𝄞𝄞𝄞𝄞 (Savoy, 1988)
Bird: The Complete Charlie Parker on Verve 𝄞𝄞𝄞𝄞 (Verve, 1988)
Jazz at Massey Hall 𝄞𝄞𝄞𝄞 (Original Jazz Classics, 1990)
Birth of the Bebop 𝄞𝄞𝄞𝄞 (Stash, 1991)
Diz and Bird at Carnegie Hall 𝄞𝄞𝄞𝄞 (Blue Note, 1997)

worth searching for: There is only one Parker track on *The Jazz Scene* 𝄞𝄞𝄞𝄞 (Verve, 1994, prod. Norman Granz)—"Repetition"—and that can be found on the previous anthology. But this, like its 1949 counterpart, is a limited-edition two-CD set crammed with stunning photos and Granz's first jazz-and-strings tests of the late 1940s, featuring Parker sax rivals Lucky Thompson and Flip Phillips with violin sections and stunning mini-sets by such stalwarts as Ellington, Hawkins, Young, Billy Strayhorn, and Bud Powell.

influences:
◀◀ Budd Johnson, Earl Hines, Jay McShann, Lester Young, Coleman Hawkins

▶▶ Dizzy Gillespie, Miles Davis, Bud Powell, Max Roach, Sonny Rollins, Sonny Stitt, Dexter Gordon, Jackie McLean, J.J. Johnson

Steve Braun

Terry Parsons

See: Matt Monro

Mandy Patinkin

Born Novmber 30, 1952, in Chicago, IL.

These days he's best known as Dr. Jeffrey Geiger, the slightly unbalanced *Chicago Hope* surgeon most likely to break into song unannounced. But Patinkin has had a long and impressive stage and film career, and his work as a recording artist is no less distinguished. Patinkin won a Tony for his portrayal of Che in the Broadway production of *Evita,* his debut on the Great White Way. His performance in *Sunday in the Park with George* earned him another Tony nomination. His film work includes memorable turns in *The Princess Bride, Yentl, Dick Tracy,* and *Ragtime.* On television, his *Chicago Hope* role won him an Emmy. On disc, Patinkin eschews modern pop and rock styles for the popular music of another era and current material from the stage. His soaring tenor, which can dip into baritone range, is best surveying the work of Irving Berlin, Rodgers and Hammerstein, and Stephen Sondheim, among others. His concerts offer a kind of studied unpretentiousness—an empty stage, except for a piano and accompanist, and Patinkin himself, dressed in a black T-shirt, baggy pants, and track shoes. What's most interesting about his records, though, is how he interpolates material into medleys, mixing composers and eras in ways that give new voice to some old, and in some cases, well-worn material.

what to buy: All of Patinkin's albums to date are impressive, so it won't hurt to begin at the beginning. His debut disc, *Mandy Patinkin* 𝄞𝄞𝄞𝄞 (CBS, 1989, prod. Steve Epstein), opens with a stunning rendition of "Over the Rainbow" and moves on through classics such as "Brother, Can You Spare a Dime," "Rock-a-Bye Your Baby with a Dixie Melody," a dynamic grouping of vintage show tunes Patinkin calls "The Happy Medley." His explosive performances grip you by the lapels at the outset and don't let go for the duration of the album.

what to buy next: *Oscar & Steve* is an intriguing project that takes on the work of Oscar Hammerstein II and Stephen Sondheim, songs separated by, in some case, decades, but which combine to stand as a testament to the enduring brilliance of the musical theater. Patinkin's choices are instinctual, creating a medley of Hammerstein's "You've Got to Be Carefully Taught," from *South Pacific,* and Sondheim's "Children Will Listen," from *Into the Woods.* Fascinating stuff.

the rest:
Dress Casual 𝄞𝄞𝄞𝄞 (CBS, 1990)
Experiment 𝄞𝄞𝄞𝄞 (Nonesuch, 1994)
Mamaloshen 𝄞𝄞𝄞 (Nonesuch, 1998)

worth searching for: Available cast recordings of some of Patinkin's stage works include *Evita* 𝄢𝄢𝄢 (L.A. cast) (MCA, 1979, prod. Andrew Lloyd Weber, Tim Rice) and *Sunday in the Park with George* 𝄢𝄢𝄢 (RCA, 1984, prod. Thomas Z. Shepard).

influences:

◀◀ Al Jolson, Dennis Day

Daniel Durchholz

Les Paul

Born Lester William Polsfuss June 9, 1915, in Waukesha, WI.

Though his own musical tastes were perfect for post–World War II, pre–Elvis Presley America, guitarist and inventor Paul's serious contributions were in the development of the electric guitar and modern recording techniques.

He started performing at age 13, and his Les Paul Trio was a fixture on Fred Waring's NBC radio and television programs starting in the late '30s. After teaming with (and marrying) singer Mary Ford (born Colleen Summers, July 7, 1928; died September 30, 1977), the duo became one of the biggest acts in show business, with 37 Top 40 easy-listening hits from 1948–58 and a popular radio program that displayed Paul's guitar and studio innovations as much as his hits with Mary. Always a tinkerer, Paul began, around 1939, building a series of prototype solid-body electric guitars; these were instruments with steel strings and electro-magnetic pickups that could be connected to an amplifier (Paul's first experiments employed a household radio for this purpose) and thus produce a louder sound than was possible with an acoustic guitar. In 1941 Paul took his design—what has come to be known as "Les Paul's 'Log'" because the neck, body, and tailpiece (where the strings are anchored opposite the headstock) appeared to be a solid piece of wood—to the Gibson company. "They laughed at the idea," Paul remembers. Paul spent much of 1946–49 working on guitar designs at his garage studio in his Hollywood bungalow. He took the fruits of his further experimentation back to Gibson, and in 1952, responding to the popularity of the Fender company's electric guitar (the Broadcaster, forerunner of the classic Telecaster, was the first commercially available solid-body electric), Gibson released the first Les Paul model electric guitar. The historic rival of the Fender sound, the Les Paul has changed the way guitars sound and are played. His pioneering recording techniques, all

now basic, taken-for-granted parts of the studio process, include multiple tracks (which, in his case, made it sound like he was playing several guitars at once), delay, echo, phase shifting, flanging, and variable tape speeds. The hits dried up long ago, but Paul has remained active, still playing weekly at a New York club into the nineties. His guitars will live forever.

what to buy: *Best of the Capitol Masters* 𝄢𝄢𝄢𝄢 (Capitol, 1991, prod. Ron Furmanek) contains absolutely essential stuff for guitar lovers and fans of his fruitful partnership with Mary Ford, including "Vaya Con Dios," "Mockin' Bird Hill," "Tiger Rag," and "How High the Moon?" And if you're really interested, *Les Paul: The Legend and the Legacy* 𝄢𝄢𝄢𝄢 (Capitol, 1991, prod. Ron Furmanek) in-

Mandy Patinkin **(AP/Wide World Photos)**

cludes 100-plus tracks that allow you to hear Paul's guitar experiments chronologically, all the Les Paul/Mary Ford hits, and an entire disc of outtakes including three complete Les Paul/Mary Ford radio shows and commercials from the 1950s. A treasure trove of the period and of the history of the electric guitar.

what to buy next: Paul recorded extensively in many genres (jazz, big-band, blues, and country) and formats (small combos, solo, and with orchestras) for Decca *before* he met Mary Ford, and *Les Paul: The Complete Decca Trios–Plus (1936–47)* 🎜🎜🎜🎜 (Decca/MCA, 1997, compilation prod. Steven Lasker) gathers many of his best sides from that period. It's a decidedly mixed bag: Paul as Rhubarb Red playing hillbilly music with guitar and harmonica; arranging and backing singers as varied as Georgia White, Helen Forrest, Bing Crosby, the Andrews Sisters, and Dick Haymes; recordings with his own trio; even tracks from a Hawaiian album made to please Decca head Jack Kapp that belong in the lounge Hall of Fame. You'll find the very eclectic groundwork for Paul's later work with Ford on these 50 sides—this is the way he sounded before he started taking apart guitars and noodling with electronic effects.

the rest:
The Fabulous Les Paul and Mary Ford 🎜🎜 (Columbia, 1965)
Les Paul Now 🎜🎜🎜 (London, 1968)
(With Chet Atkins) *Chester and Lester* 🎜🎜🎜🎜 (RCA, 1976)

worth searching for: Paul is featured on any number of compilations, from a version of "Moten Swing" on *Jazz Club* 🎜🎜🎜🎜 (PGD/Verve, 1990) to "The World Is Waiting for the Sunset" alongside Chuck Berry, Duane Eddy, Link Wray, and Johnny Otis on *Guitar Player Presents Legends of Guitar: Rock: The '50s* 🎜🎜🎜🎜 (Rhino, 1990, prod. various). Or if you want to see the elderly Paul playing with those he influenced, seek out *He Changed the Music* 🎜🎜🎜🎜 (Video), which pairs him with, among others, Stanley Jordan, Rita Coolidge, David Gilmour, B.B. King, Steve Miller, and Eddie Van Halen.

influences:

◀◀ Deford Bailey, Sonny Terry, Gene Autry, Eddie Lang, Django Reinhardt

▶▶ Jeff Beck, George Benson, Michael Bloomfield, James Burton, Eric Clapton, Rick Derringer, Peter Frampton, Jerry Garcia, David Gilmour, Steve Howe, Stanley Jordan, B.B. King, Mark Knopfler, Steve Miller, Steve Morse, Jimmy Page, Joe Perry, Keith Richards, Brian Setzer, Slash, Bruce Springsteen, Billy Squier, Pete Townshend, Eddie Van Halen, Waddy Wachtel, Nancy Wilson, Link Wray, Frank Zappa

Leland Rucker

Minnie Pearl

Born Sarah Ophelia Colley, October 25, 1912, in Centerville, TN. Died February 25, 1996, in Nashville, TN.

Minnie Pearl's trademark "How-deee!" and the price tag hanging from her straw hat are among country music's most familiar sights and sounds—though Minnie only rarely sang as part of her act. A regular on Nashville's *Grand Ole Opry* radio show for more than four decades, the character Minnie was a man-crazy comedienne from Grinder's Switch, Tennessee, created by Sarah Colley, and she blazed trails for women in both country music and comedy.

Colley was a well-raised small-town girl, hardly the hillbilly queen her alter-ego appeared to be. She grew up with a knowledge of classics and theater, schooled at the Ward-Belmont College for Women in Nashville. She developed the Minnie Pearl character during a stint with a traveling theatrical troupe. Minnie joined the *Grand Ole Opry* in 1940 and for more than four decades her popularity on the radio show would be rivaled only by that of fiddler Roy Acuff. She was elected to the Country Music Hall of Fame in 1975, and was revered in Nashville: Amy Grant and Garth Brooks both named children after her.

what's available: Pearl's legacy comes more from her stage performances than from her sporadic recordings, and much of her appeal was visual. Two cut-out cassettes comprise the bulk of her available recordings. *Lookin' Fer a Feller* 🎜🎜🎜 (Country Road) contains some of her routines, performed in front of a small audience, as well as a couple of songs. Most of the stories are set in Pearl's fictitious hometown of Grinder's Switch. *The Best of Comedy* 🎜🎜🎜 (Starday, 1985) contains some of the same material with a few different tracks.

worth searching for: It's not easy to find, but at least *Queen of the Grand Ole Opry* 🎜🎜🎜 (Legacy International, 1993) is on CD. There's no information about the source of these live recordings, but they capture every bit of the charm and wit of Minnie's down-home comedy.

influences:

◀◀ Sarie & Sally, Boob & Rod Brasfield

▶▶ Jerry Clower, Archie Campbell, Speck Rhodes

Brian Mansfield

Dave Pell

Born February 26, 1925, in New York, NY.

Saxophonist Pell is, first and foremost, a pragmatist, someone who has always known how to make a living, whether it was working as a sideman in other bands, producing records, or leading his own combo, the Dave Pell Octet. Part of the early-'50s West Coast "cool" jazz scene—though not as well known as icons like Chet Baker—Pell always had a light, easygoing style reminiscent of legendary saxplayer Lester Young, his role model. His bread-and-butter job was playing with Les Brown, Bob Hope's musical director on radio and TV shows. In 1953, he spun off his own band, the Dave Pell Octet. Later, in the '70s, he formed a band honoring Young called the Prez Conference (named after Young's nickname).

what's available: Limited in number to begin with, most of Pell's releases are out of print. *Dave Pell's Prez Conference* ♪♪♪♪ (GNP, 1979, prod. Dave Pell) is a reissue starring vocalist Joe Williams, with Lester Young covers such as "Lester Leaps Again." Pell also contributes to and produces *Mel Tormé Collection* ♪♪♪ (Rhino, 1996, prod. Dave Pell). He also appears on a hokey compilation called *Ultra-Lounge, Vol. 4: Bachelor Pad Royale* ♪♪ (Capitol, 1996, compilation prod. Brad Benedict).

influences:

◄◄ Les Brown, Lester Young

►► David Sanborn

Teresa Gubbins

Jean-Jacques Perrey
See: Perrey & Kingsley

Perrey & Kingsley
Formed 1965.

Jean-Jacques Perrey (born January 20, 1929, in France), keyboards, synthesizers; Gershon Kingsley (born 1923, in Germany), synthesizers.

The world's strange technological advances of the '50s and '60s wreaked havoc not only on the minds of stoned and pilled-up teenagers and martini-quaffing suburbanites, but also on serious artists and scientists—such as Jean-Jacques Perrey and Gershon Kingsley, two musical tinkerers who became unheralded precursors of all electronic pop music. Perrey, a French musician with roots in medicine and mechanics, recorded with various groups of jazz and avant-garde musicians in his native France in the 1940s and 1950s—including one legendary, long-lost 45 ("Soul of a Poet") with singer Charles Trenet and gypsy guitarist Django Reinhardt. On coming to America in 1965, he was introduced to Kingsley, a classically trained arranger and composer who had branched out into Broadway musicals and

soundtrack arranging. The two found they had plenty in common—interest in the recording process, a love of all forms of song, and a desire to make electronic music not simply palatable but popular to the masses. Allowed to indulge their thoughts by Vanguard Records, the duo tried first with 1966's landmark LP *The In Sound from Way Out!*, a 12-song story of the history of music as it would have been told by an old IBM punchcard computer. The titles said it all: "Computer in Love," "Swan's Splashdown," "Girl from Venus," "Barnyard in Orbit," "Electronic Can-Can," "Jungle Blues from Jupiter." The inimitable P&K assembled the record—literally—out of found sounds and odd electronic sources that were slowed down, speeded up, run backwards, and chopped up into tiny bits of recording tape and then pieced together *by hand*. The LP sleeve estimated that 275 hours of work went into the recording of the album—an unprecedented timespan even in the low-tech days of 1966. The pair followed up somewhat later with *Kaleidoscopic Vibrations: Spotlight on the Moog*, which found them applying early versions of the Moog synthesizer to their cross-boundary music-making—bossa nova and other pop-Latin styles, such as "One Note Samba," "Spanish Flea," "Strangers in the Night," and "Mas Que Nada," as well as demented takes on "Winchester Cathedral" and "A Lover's Concerto." However, after these two LPs (both, happily, still in print), Perrey and Kingsley concentrated more on their own visions, mostly working with synthesizers in various genres.

Many modern groups and artists, such as Stereolab (which simply took its name from Vanguard's electronic-music series record label) and the Beastie Boys (who not only lifted an LP cover from *The In Sound* but also applied much of Perrey and Kingsley's music to their hip-hop base), owe the duo a great deal. It took nearly 20 years for their vision of electronic popular music to become a complete reality—techno, house, drum'n'bass, and all of the exotic "electronica" styles are indirect successors to the duo's experiments. But in their day, Perrey and Kingsley never lost sight of their aim—to make music for people to enjoy (such as "Popcorn," one of the biggest instrumental hits of all time, penned by Kingsley in 1972).

what to buy: Of course, *The In Sound from Way Out!* ♪♪♪♪♪ (Vanguard, 1966, prod. Jean-Jacques Perrey, Gershon Kingsley) is essential. Its timeless charms and still-remarkable sound collages—especially impressive considering the technology of the time—accomplish everything the liner notes say the prescient pair wanted to achieve: "Here are a dozen electronic pop tunes. They are the electrifying good-time music of the coming age, the switched-on dance music that will soon be *it*." The second LP, *Kaleidoscopic Vibrations: Spotlight on the Moog* 🎵🎵🎵 (Vanguard, 1969) is nearly as good in its own way, and still an early high point in Moog music. It's not in print on its own, but as part of the two-CD collection *The Essential Perrey and Kingsley* 🎵🎵🎵 (Vanguard, 1989), which also contains the original *The In Sound from Way Out!*

what to buy next: Two solo Perrey CDs are still in print on Vanguard: *The Amazing New Electronic Pop Sound of Jean-Jacques Perrey* 🎵🎵🎵 (Vanguard, 1968) and *Moog Indigo* 🎵🎵🎵 (Vanguard, 1970). The 1968 album is in some ways a continuation of the Perrey and Kingsley sound-collage theme of genre-mixing, containing songs like "The Minuet of the Robots" and "The Little Girl from Mars," as well as "Mister James Bond." By 1970, the Moog synthesizer was in its classic early period, and Perrey used it for songs like "Soul City" and "Country Rock Polka" as well as a wigged-out version of "Hello, Dolly!"

worth searching for: Gershon Kingsley recorded two solo Moog albums that are long out of print and prized by collectors: *First Moog Quartet* 🎵🎵🎵 (Audio Fidelity) and *Music to Moog By* 🎵🎵🎵 (Audio Fidelity). In the 1970s, Perrey put out many records in France, including *Moog Is Moog* (Montparnasse) and *Kartoonery* (Montparnasse). An overseas trip may well be needed to find them. The duo's 1966 hit, "Swan's Splashdown"—Smash Mouth's 1997 rock hit "Walkin' on the Sun" has a suspiciously similar bottom-line melody—appears on the excellently weird *RE/Search: Incredibly Strange Music, Vol. 1* 🎵🎵🎵 (Caroline, 1993, prod. Christopher Trela), which also includes tracks by Dave Harris, the Scramblers, Katie Lee, and the self-explanatory "A Cosmic Telephone Call," by Kali Bahlu. The companion book of the same name includes long separate interviews with both Perrey and Kingsley.

influences:

◀◀ Enoch Light, Dick Hyman, John Cage, Ray Bradbury, Edith Piaf, Walt Disney

▶▶ Stereolab, Negativland, the Beastie Boys, Kraftwerk, Brian Eno, Aphex Twin, Hot Butter, Spiritualized, Orbital, Smash Mouth

Stuart Shea

Pet Shop Boys

Formed 1983, in London, England.

Neil Tennant, vocals; Chris Lowe, instruments.

Ex–music journalist Tennant and former architecture student Lowe met and discovered they had a mutual love for Euro-

disco and pop—and that's "pop" in every sense of the word, even as defined by Judy Garland, Liza Minnelli, and the other great classic-standards singers. The Pet Shop Boys quickly found a successful formula for their music—sardonic lyrics with hypnotic synthesizer melodies and infectious beats, which led to a parade of hits in the U.K. (though somewhat fewer in the U.S.). The duo still reigns in an area where bands such as the Human League once reigned supreme. They maintain a low profile, seeming unemotional and scheming, with an intuitive sense for blending the artistically subversive and commercially populist. In a collaboration almost as bizarre as David Bowie's duet with Bing Crosby, Tennant and Lowe also lent their skills to diva Liza Minnelli's album, *Results*.

what to buy: *Discography: The Complete Singles Collection* 🎵🎵🎵🎵 (EMI, 1991, prod. various) provides ample evidence of the Pet Shop Boys' fine songwriting and musical sophistication. *Very* 🎵🎵🎵 (ERG, 1993, prod. Pet Shop Boys) achieves an effective balance between happiness and melancholy.

what to buy next: *Please* 🎵🎵🎵 (EMI, 1986, prod. Stephen Hague) contains the hit singles "West End Girls," "Opportunities (Let's Make Lots of Money)," "Love Comes Quickly," and "Suburbia." *Actually* 🎵🎵🎵 (Parlophone, 1987, prod. various) includes Tennant's duet with Dusty Springfield on "What Have I Done to Deserve This," "It's a Sin," and a cover of Elvis Presley's "Always on My Mind."

what to avoid: *Disco* 🎵🎵 (EMI, 1986, prod. various) and *Disco 2* 🎵🎵 (Capitol, 1994, prod. Pet Shop Boys, Harold Faltermeyer) are tedious remix albums.

the rest:
Introspective 🎵🎵🎵 (EMI America, 1988)
Behavior 🎵🎵🎵 (EMI America, 1990)
Alternative 🎵🎵🎵 (EMI, 1995)
Early: The Essential N/A (EPROP, 1998)

worth searching for: The special edition of *Very* comes in a textured, orange jewel box, which is a stylish way to own one of the essential titles.

influences:

◀◀ Human League, New Order, the Smiths, Kraftwerk

▶▶ Electronic

Anna Glen

Bernadette Peters

Born Bernadette Lazzaro, February 28, 1944, in Queens, NY.

Actress-comedienne Peters is a stylistic throwback as a singer. She can purr cute and campy like a boop-boop-a-doop flapper or cathartically belt out torch-songs Broadway-diva style. Though Peters has been singing professionally since childhood, she has been too busy being a multi-media star to devote much time to a recording career.

She made her professional debut at age four on TV's *Juvenile Jury* and had a regular role in the Broadway smash *The Most Happy Fella* at age 10. A true show-biz footsoldier, Peters toured in a series of shows before making a splash as a '30s style chorus girl in the 1968 off-Broadway hit *Dames at Sea*. In the years to follow, she became a full-fledged Broadway star in such shows as *George M, Mack and Mabel,* and *Sunday in the Park with George*. Winless after four previous Tony Award nominations, Peters finally won in 1986 for Andrew Lloyd Webber's *Song and Dance*. In the movies, though she has played a wide variety of roles, comedy seems to be what she does best. Peters won Golden Globe Awards for her work in Mel Brooks's *Silent Movie* and Steve Martin's *The Jerk* (in which she took a rather cool trumpet solo), and was the best aspect of the pretentious *Pennies from Heaven*. As a solo recording artist, Peters belatedly made her debut in 1980, touching all the stylistic bases that Bette Midler had a few years earlier, but with substantially less sales clout. Since then, besides appearing in movies, stage shows, and TV, Peters has also provided voices for the animated feature film *Anastasia* and TV's *Animaniacs,* where her Rita the Cat sings ironic show tune parodies with great skill. Not to be outdone by a cartoon cat, Peters reactivated her personal recording career in 1996 with the Grammy-nominated *I'll Be Your Baby Tonight*.

what to buy: Peters is surprisingly versatile on *Bernadette* ♫♫♫♫ (MCA, 1992, prod. various), a collection of tunes from the early '80s. Her takes on the standards of doo-wop ("Gee Whiz") and Tin Pan Alley ("I Don't Know Why I Just Do," "You'll Never Know," "If You Were the Only Boy") compare favorably with those of the great torch singers of another era.

what to buy next: Peters gives a tour de force concert on *Sondheim, Etc.: Live—At Carnegie Hall* ♫♫♫♫ (Angel, 1997, prod. Jay Landers), a compelling set of show tunes and heartbreakers put across with first-rate showmanship.

what to avoid: Peters doesn't get much to sing on *Disney's Beauty and the Beast: The Enchanted Christmas* ♫♫♪ (Original

Soundtrack) (Disney, 1997, prod. Robbie Buchanan, Paul Schwartz), an LP derived from one of Disney's lesser straight-to-video offerings.

the rest:
Sunday in the Park with George ♫♫♫♫ (Original Cast Soundtrack) (RCA, 1984)
I'll Be Your Baby Tonight ♫♫♪ (Angel, 1996)

worth searching for: Peters's Tony Award–winning performance is chronicled on *Andrew Lloyd Webber's Song and Dance* ♫♫♫♪ (Original Broadway Cast) (RCA, 1995), and is a must-have item for her fans. Also, Peters guests on Mandy Patinkin's *Dress Casual* ♫♫♫♫ (Columbia, 1990).

influences:

◀◀ Helen Kane, Ann-Margret, Mary Martin

▶▶ Bette Midler, Paige O'Hara

Ken Burke

Madeleine Peyroux

Born in Athens, GA.

Still in her early 20s, Peyroux has yet to develop an individual style, but her music has a definite sensibility. Either by design or by luck of the draw, Peyroux's vocal timbre and mannerisms are straight out of Billie Holiday, big and brassy, yet teasing and caressing the music from just behind the beat. Her selection of material indicates an assertive spirit, though, drawing as it does on the work of such strong female performers as Holiday, Patsy Cline, and Bessie Smith—singers who, after all, were the riot grrrls of their day. There's no agenda to Peyroux's music per se, but an abiding sense of feminist history informs her debut album *Dreamland*, and burbles to the surface in ways both melancholic (Edith Piaf's "La Vie En Rose") and giddy ("Was I?," a number drawn from the Zigfield Follies). A Georgia native who grew up in Southern California, New York, and Paris, where she busked with a blues and jazz band, Peyroux is a budding songwriter whose original material is less stylistically restrictive than her covers. Time will tell if those songs will eventually take her beyond the work of her sources.

what's available: Though it sounds fine coming out of modern stereo equipment, *Dreamland* ♫♫♫ (Atlantic, 1996, prod. Yves Beauvais, Greg Cohen) is an album that would be best appreciated if you heard it on a vintage cathedral-style radio. It sounds more like a product of the '20s and '30s than it does a contemporary release. And that's as it should be, for Peyroux fills her debut with material from the songbooks of such legendary performers as Edith Piaf, Patsy Cline, Fats Waller, and Bessie Smith, among others. Peyroux may be channeling Billie Holiday a little too much for some tastes, but she embodies these songs as well as any current performers, and the arrangements (by Tom Waits stalwart Greg Cohen) are imaginative and romantic, while the band—featuring first-stringers such as guitarists Marc Ribot and Vernon Reid, pianist Cyrus Chestnut, saxophonist James Carter, and drummer Leon Parker—is excellent. Her original material, especially the spindly blues "Hey Sweet Man" and the sweetly sentimental "Always a Use," suggest there's more to Peyroux than mere nostalgia.

influences:

◀◀ Billie Holiday, Patsy Cline, Bessie Smith

Daniel Durchholz

Regis Philbin

Born Regis Francis Xavier Philbin, August 25, 1930, in New York, NY.

Decades before his success as the popular co-host of *LIVE! with Regis & Kathie Lee,* Philbin was the transparently ambitious sidekick/announcer on ABC's ill-fated bid for late night supremacy, *The Joey Bishop Show.* He had hosted local and syndicated programs before being hired by ABC, yet he was unprepared to work with Bishop, one of the sharpest ad-lib comics in TV history. Instead of laughing off Bishop's one-liners and humorous inquisitions, Philbin openly flinched and sulked before the camera. (Gee, a talk show host using his on-air partner as a comedy foil. Who ever heard of such a thing?) Philbin eventually walked off the show, only to return amid much publicity after Bishop made both a public and private apology. Philbin tried to cash in on public sympathy by recording an LP of lounge music with the accent on nostalgia, titled *It's Time for Regis!* (The title came from his nightly introduction of Bishop, "It's time for JOEY!") Of his talk-show contemporaries, Philbin was a better vocalist than, say, Steve Allen or Arthur Godfrey, but not as stylistically evolved as Merv Griffin or Mike Douglas (who were professional singers before they started their chat shows). Joey Bishop bragged about his partner's LP, but despite his praise and nightly network exposure, it didn't sell. When Bishop couldn't dislodge Johnny Carson from his late night throne, cancellation rumors spread. Philbin tactlessly let it be known he would be glad to take over once ABC dumped Joey. It didn't happen. Bishop returned to the showrooms of Las Vegas and Philbin to various local and syndicated TV shows, where he became a mainstay. During the '80s, before teaming with Kathie Lee Gifford, he exhilarated viewers by rattling Cindy Garvey's cage in pretty much the same fashion that Bishop had rattled his. Now immune to insults and irony, Philbin's current ascent has been aided by David Letterman's constant use of him as a cameo/joke guest, and by Dana Carvey's over-the-top, wild-eyed impression of him on *Saturday Night Live.* (The scary part? Philbin has adopted a lot of the zany gestures and rant strategies that Carvey put into his impersonation to make it funny. Even scarier? Kathie Lee Gifford

Madeleine Peyroux (© Jack Vartoogian)

has started acting like Regis.) Though he doesn't sing much anymore, his status as a daytime superstar has prompted the rerelease of his lone musical outing.

what's available: The arrangements are corny and the song selection kitsch, but Philbin's vocal style is surprisingly light and smooth on *It's Time for Regis!* ♪♪♪ (Mercury 1968/1994, prod. Steve Douglas), 10 tracks of such retrofitted oldies as "Pennies from Heaven," "The Glory of Love," and Al Jolson standards from the '30s. Though the original LP sported a photo of young Regis in front of a marquee that read *The Joey Bishop Show,* this reissue features Bishop's original liner notes, but the cover photo is a cheesy painting sans marquee. (That Regis sure knows how to hold a grudge.)

worth searching for: Philbin duets briefly with his on-air partner Kathie Lee Gifford on *It's Christmas Time* ♪♪♪ (Warner Bros., 1993, prod. Jim Ed Norman, Danny Kee, Edd Kalehoff). Better is the audio version of Philbin's autobiography (co-written with Bill Zehme), *I'm Only One Man!* ♪♪♪ (Simon & Schuster Audio Works, 1995), wherein Philbin humorously rants and raves with far more authority and distinction than he ever showed as a singer.

influences:

◄◄ Joey Bishop, Jack Paar, Bing Crosby, Al Jolson

►► Dana Carvey, Kathie Lee Gifford, John Tesh, Danny Bonaduce

see also: *Kathie Lee Gifford*

Ken Burke

Stu Phillips /Stu Phillips Singers

See: The Hollyridge Strings

Edith Piaf

Born Edith Giovanna Gassion, December 19, 1915, in Paris, France. Died October 11, 1963, in Paris.

If Edith Piaf's life story weren't real, it would have to have been the product of a Hollywood made-for-TV movie. Born into poverty, raised in a house of ill repute, she began singing in the streets of Normandy as a child. "The Little Sparrow" followed her muse on a somewhat tumultuous life path that led her through substance abuse, true love, and a tragically cut-short marriage that was followed by a suicide attempt. Despite it all, or perhaps because of it all, Piaf clung tenaciously to the idea of love, and that bittersweet belief was integral to her music.

Piaf's vocals were strong and highly stylized, yet she also projected a certain frailty that gave the songs a poignant twist. Though she didn't write her own songs, she worked closely with her collaborators (most prominently Marguerite Monnot, Charles Dumont, and Francis Lai) to ensure they would generate the moods she sought, whether that was light-hearted and breezy or haunted and brimming with pathos.

what's available: As with many important performers whose long recording careers began before the modern record industry, there have been innumerable and varied Piaf recordings, many of which are imports. Piaf recorded her most famous song, "La Vie En Rose," in both French and English, and it is essential to any collection you choose. The best sets fall in two categories, comprehensive and concise. *30th Anniversaire Box* ♪♪♪♪ (Capitol, 1993, prod. various) is a handsome two-CD set that strikes a good balance between historical, career-spanning perspective and snappy pacing. The booklet features informative liner notes, both in English and French. *The Voice of the Sparrow: Very Best of Edith Piaf* ♪♪♪ (Capitol/EMI, 1991) is a no-frills collection of 18 of her best-known tracks. *L'Integrale (Complete Recordings) 1936–1945* ♪♪♪ (Philips/PolyGram) is indeed complete: four discs comprising some 80 tracks. Unfortunately, the accompanying booklet contains nothing beyond song lyrics—only given in French. *Master Serie: Edith Piaf* ♪♪♪ (Philips/PolyGram), a 16-track disc, features material from 1937–45.

influences:

◄◄ Charles Dumont

►► Madeleine Peyroux, Judy Garland, Liza Minnelli, Marlene Dietrich, Portishead, Ute Lemper, Nana Mouskouri

Sandy Masuo

The Pied Pipers

Formed 1938, in Hollywood, CA.

Chuck Lowry (1938–50s); Hal Hopper (1938, 1942–50s); Woody Newbury (1938–39); Whit Whittinghill (1938–39); Bud Hervey (1938–39); John Tait (1938–39); John Huddleston, (1938–42); Billy Wilson (1938–50s); Jo Stafford (1939–44); June Hutton (died 1973, in Encino, CA) (1944–50); Clark Yocum (1942–50s); Sue Allen (1950–50s), all vocals.

Most famous for exposing talented crooner Jo Stafford to the rest of the world, backing Tommy Dorsey's swing band in the early 1940s, and singing behind the young Frank Sinatra, the Pipers' various lineups were filled with vocal talent and playful personalities. Beginning as a septet, stretching to an octet, and finally condensing to four members, the versatile singing group bounced through the fun pop song "There's a Fella Waitin' in Poughkeepsie" and crooned Frankie Laine's barbershop-smooth love standard, "We'll Be Together Again," with equal swing spirit.

Vocal groups, such as the King Sisters and the Skylarks, were major commercial forces in the 1930s and 1940s; if they were good enough, they could catch swing bandleaders' attention and gain even greater stardom. After Stafford joined her husband, Huddleston, in the band around 1939, the Pipers gained a wide audience by singing with Dorsey on the prominent Raleigh-Kool radio show. (Stafford and Huddleton later divorced and she married the Pipers' longtime orchestra leader, Paul Weston, in 1952.) Because of the band's playful attitude, the Pipers tended to alienate the wrong people: a British sponsor, who had come to watch the radio show in person, was offended by their unusual arrangement of "Hold Tight (Want Some Sea Food Mama)" and kicked them off. After struggling briefly and shrinking to a quartet, Dorsey called for the Pipers to join him in Chicago. That lasted until the notoriously frosty Dorsey dumped a member (and, in solidarity, the rest of the band) at a train station in Portland, Oregon. But high-profile gigs quickly followed, including collaborations with Johnny Mercer and Bob Crosby, before Stafford went solo and was replaced by June Hutton. Many incarnations later, the Pipers continue to tour.

what's available: The definitive Pipers collection, *Capitol Collector's Series* ♫♫♫ (Capitol, 1992, compilation prod. Ron Furmanek, Bob Furmanek), is by and large a showcase for Stafford's considerable skills, but it also captures the band's sense of humor. Their take on the R&B hit "Open the Door, Richard" hilariously retells the story of breaking into a sleeping friend's room; "The Freedom Train" features guest stars Margaret Whiting, Benny Goodman, Peggy Lee, and Johnny Mercer, who shows up on several other tracks as well; and the croons, including "My Happiness" and "In the Middle of May," are classics. You can also find some decent Pipers interpretations of Dorsey standards, including *In a Tribute to Tommy Dorsey* ♫♫ (Simitar, 1997), but the essential in-print volume remains the Capitol set.

influences:

◀◀ Tommy Dorsey, Johnny Mercer, Judy Garland, Benny Goodman, Harold Arlen, Irving Berlin

▶▶ Rosemary Clooney, Kay Starr, the Four Freshmen, Frank Sinatra

see also: *Jo Stafford, Paul Weston*

Steve Knopper

Cocktail Classics

Strangers in the Night

18-Karat **Frank Sinatra**
The Capitol Years
(Capitol)

Bombsville! **Ray Conniff**
This Is My Song
(Columbia/Legacy)

Pizzicato Five

Formed 1984, in Tokyo, Japan.

Maki Nomiya, vocals; Yasuharu Konishi, keyboards, sound effects.

There probably isn't a piece of contemporary kitsch culture this Japanese group hasn't sampled, a TV theme song it hasn't covered, or a James Bond film it hasn't scrutinized for inspiration. Back in the late '80s, when Burt Bacharach was still for nerds only, Pizzicato Five was already paying the songwriter homage with tributes and sound clips. The band plays it tongue-in-cheek but with an innocence and carefree fun that's endearing, even when the piecemeal music and the Japanese

lyrics get in the way. Pizzicato—the nucleus consists of sonic playboy Yasuharu Konishi and singer Maki Nomiya—has been putting out records in Japan since 1987. But it wasn't until the band signed with hipster indie-label Matador in 1994 that it became known in the United States. Konishi and Nomiya strive for beautiful packaging, with bright colors and '60s-style graphics, and often releases EPs, as if the ideas and sound-bites are too dense to be comprehended in anything other than small doses.

what to buy: *Made in USA* 𝄞𝄞𝄞 (Triad/Matador/Atlantic, 1994), the band's first full-length U.S. disc, is a festive ride through familiar snippets, such as a Burt Bacharach song ("Another Night") and a segment from the *Hawaii Five-O* theme. *The Sound of Music by Pizzicato Five* 𝄞𝄞𝄞 (Triad/Matador/Atlantic, 1995) combines selections from two Japanese imports: *Overdose* and *Bossa Nova 2001*. The EP *Five by Five* 𝄞𝄞𝄞 (Triad/Matador/Atlantic, 1994, prod. Pizzicato Five) includes "Me, Japanese Boy," written by Bacharach and Hal David.

what to buy next: *Unzipped* 𝄞𝄞𝄞 (Triad/Matador/Atlantic, 1995), named after the documentary on clothing designer Isaac Mizrahi, has one of the band's favorite songs, "If I Were a Groupie," with English and Japanese lyrics.

what to avoid: *Sister Freedom Tapes* 𝄞𝄞 (Matador, 1995) consists of outtakes from *The Sound of Music*. With P5, that ends up sounding like outtakes of outtakes.

the rest:
Quickie One EP 𝄞𝄞 (Matador, 1995)
Quickie Two EP 𝄞𝄞 (Matador, 1995)
Combinaison Spaciale 𝄞𝄞𝄞 (Matador, 1997)
Happy End of the World 𝄞𝄞𝄞 (Capitol, 1997)

influences:
◀◀ Burt Bacharach, Julie Andrews, Deee-Lite, George Clinton, Shonen Knife, *Hawaii Five-O*, De La Soul

▶▶ Cibo Matto

Teresa Gubbins

Buster Poindexter

Born David Johansen, September 1, 1950, in Staten Island, NY.

Johansen, former lead singer of the pioneering early-'70s glam-punk band New York Dolls, revitalized his stagnant solo career

Maki Nomiya of Pizzicato Five (© Jack Vartoogian)

by adopting the persona of Buster Poindexter, Latin lounge Lothario, in 1987. Clad in a tuxedo, martini in hand, pompadour perfectly placed, Poindexter started playing New York clubs with his band, the Banshees of Blue, as a lark. But his outrageous and infectious live shows struck a chord, making Poindexter truly one of the pioneers in the early-'90s lounge music revival. Poindexter's 1987 self-titled solo album spawned the single "Hot, Hot, Hot," which is legally required to be played at weddings in 47 states. His successes led to Poindexter becoming a permanent persona for Johansen, leading to a dozen film roles and three more CDs.

what to buy: While not quite as fun as seeing him live, *Buster Poindexter* 𝄞𝄞𝄞 (RCA, 1987, prod. Hank Medress) is the next best thing. Besides the instant-classic version of "Hot, Hot, Hot," the CD features the future Mrs. Bruce Springsteen, Patti Scialfa, on background vocals.

what to buy next: *Buster's Spanish Rocket Ship* 𝄞𝄞𝄞 (Island, 1997, prod. Brian Koonin), a Caribbean buffet of rumbas, meringues, and cha-chas, proves a decade after Poindexter's "birth" that the singer is more than a novelty act. The Latin drinking album, *Buster's Happy Hour* 𝄞𝄞𝄞 (Rhino, 1994), won't find its way to the CD player at many Women's Temperance Union mixers.

worth searching for: Among the interesting renditions of Disney movie classics on *Stay Awake: Interpretations of Vintage Disney Films* 𝄞𝄞𝄞 (A&M, 1988) is Poindexter covering "Castile in Spain."

influences:
◀◀ Miami Sound Machine, Carmen Miranda, Dean Martin, Ruben Blades, Tony Orlando

▶▶ Combustible Edison

Alex Gordon

Cole Porter

Born June 9, 1891, in Peru, IN. Died October 15, 1964, in Santa Monica, CA.

In addition to writing "Night and Day," "I Get a Kick out of You," "I've Got You under My Skin"—to name just a few of his beloved American pop standards—Porter ushered in a significant change in the way people think about and buy music. Throughout his tortured life, Porter wrote songs mostly for musicals and theatrical shows, eventually writing entire productions like the classics *Kiss Me Kate* and *Jubilee*. But when recorded music started to take off, great singers such as Billie

Holiday and Frank Sinatra removed the songs from their show-tune context and reinterpreted them as stand-alone pop hits.

Porter started taking an interest in music and playing violin as a youngster, writing his first song around age 11; his avocation was encouraged by his mother but scorned by his grandfather. After studying both music and law at Harvard University, he entered the French army during World War I. He landed in Paris, which became the site of his most formative experiences. The roaring 1920s in "Gay Paree" were a time of great social change, with musicians and artists shedding the rigid social constraints of the early century. Though married, he began to acknowledge his homosexuality—which, when he returned to New York City during the Depression, created much social and personal turmoil. By then, his career had surged; Porter penned countless musicals, from the influential Broadway piece *The Gay Divorcee* to the films *Silk Stockings* and *High Society*. These shows included some of his most enduring standards, notably "Begin the Beguine" and "Night and Day." Though Porter's personal life took a tragic turn in 1937— a horse crushed his legs and he had to have one amputated—his songs were starting to reach massive audiences through popular pop and jazz singers. Rock 'n' roll, with its emphasis on southern blues, slowly shifted the pop marketplace away from Porter-style standards in the '50s and '60s. But the 1990 Porter tribute, *Red Hot + Blue*, an AIDS benefit disc featuring U2, Sinéad O'Connor, and the Jungle Brothers, proved his songs endure with enough flexibility to fit any context.

what to buy: Porter wrote songs specifically for other people to sing, so it's difficult to find evidence of him performing his own standards. An excellent starting compilation of other people's interpretations is *Great American Songwriters—Cole Porter* ♫♫♫♫ (Delta, 1994, prod. various), featuring Frank Sinatra and Rosemary Clooney. Two multidisc sets, *From This Moment On: The Songs of Cole Porter* ♫♫♫♫ (Smithsonian, 1993, prod. various) and *Complete Cole Porter Songbooks* ♫♫♫♫ (Verve, 1993, prod. various), are similarly great collections of classic singers. Oh, and an indispensable collection, for both Porter and Ella Fitzgerald fans, is the great scat singer's *The Cole Porter Songbook* ♫♫♫♫ (Verve, 1956/DCC, 1995, prod. Norman Granz), in which Porter and many other notables provide impeccable accompaniment.

what to buy next: After young rock-loving generations ignored Porter's work for decades, *Red Hot + Blue* ♫♫♫♫ (Chrysalis, 1990, prod. Leigh Blake, John Carlin) adapted his songs to world-beat music (David Byrne's "Don't Fence Me In"), Irish punk (Kirsty MacColl and the Pogues on "Miss Otis Regrets"), and hip-hop (Neneh Cherry's "I've Got You Under My Skin").

what to avoid: While interesting, *You're the Top: Cole Porter in the '30s* ♫♫♫ (Koch, 1993, prod. various) focuses on Porter's more obscure compositions, including the bizarre description of sexual longing, "Nymph Errant."

the rest:
Classic Movie and Broadway Show Tunes From . . . ♫♫♫ (Biograph, 1996)

worth searching for: It's rare to hear Porter's rough but charming singing voice, and jarring if you're accustomed to Sinatra or Ella Fitzgerald interpretations, but *Cole Sings Porter: Rare and Unreleased Songs from "Can-Can" and "Jubilee"* ♫♫♫ (Koch, 1994, prod. Steve Nelson) uses obscure work like "C'est Magnifique" and "I Do" to illuminate Porter's genius.

influences:
▶▶ Ella Fitzgerald, Frank Sinatra, Billie Holiday, Johnny Mathis, Irving Berlin, Harlan Howard, Paul McCartney, Carole King

Steve Knopper

Portishead

Formed 1991, in Bristol, England.

Geoff Barrow, programming, drums, keyboards; Beth Gibbons, vocals; Adrian Utley, musical director, guitar, bass, keyboards.

It's hard to believe now, with so many trip-hop copycats littering the pop landscape, but Portishead was a thoroughly original group when it first arrived in 1994. Created largely by Adrian Utley and prominent British studio worker Geoff Barrow, the reclusive band's debut, *Dummy*, blended spaghetti-Western guitars, cocktail keyboards, and eerie string arrangements with scratchy tape loops, languid hip-hop rhythms, and, of course, Beth Gibbons's melancholy torch vocals about longing and heartbreak. The alluring album was both artistically compelling and emotionally haunting—dark, atmospheric music that would not have sounded out of place in an abandoned cabaret. Three years passed between the debut and a self-titled follow-up, allowing expectations for the sophomore record to blossom, along with the careers of countless groups copying the Portishead sound and guy musician–girl singer setup. Even a dummy could have figured out that the elements were in place for a let-down, which is largely what the sophomore album, *Portishead*, was.

what to buy: It's hard to say what's most compelling about *Dummy* ♫♫♫♫ (Go! Discs/London, 1994, prod. Portishead). Is it Gibbons's detached, disturbed soprano? The dour lyrics in the surprising hit, "Sour Times (Nobody Loves Me)"? The icy, ambient soundscape Barrow and Utley created, using guitars, a Fender Rhodes keyboard, a drum machine, and samples of old records by Weather Report, Isaac Hayes, and Lalo Schifrin? Whatever, it makes for some of the most interesting and original dance music of the '90s.

what to buy next: *Portishead* ♫♫♫ (Go! Discs/London, 1997, prod. Portishead) employs just two traditional samples (from *The Pink Panther* and a Pharcyde record), but it still has the same sample-happy—if emotionally depressed—feel of *Dummy*. Several songs match up well with the first album's best, including "Leslie" and "Only You," but Portishead is already running in place.

worth searching for: The EP *Sour Times (Nobody Loves Me)* ♫♫♫ (Go! Discs/London, 1994, prod. Portishead) features a handful of tracks not included on *Dummy*, but the standout is a lengthy reworking of the title single.

influences:

◀◀ Ennio Morricone, Lalo Schifrin, Shirley Bassey, Edith Piaf, Massive Attack, Björk, Isaac Hayes

▶▶ Sneaker Pimps, Moloko, Lamb, Morcheeba, Hooverphonic, Tricky/Nearly God, Björk

Josh Freedom du Lac

Dick Powell

Born Richard Ewing Powell, November 14, 1904, in Mountain View, AR. Died January 3, 1963, in Hollywood, CA.

Dick Powell is best known as the coy song-and-dance man who appeared in the camp classic (sometimes surreal) Busby Berkely movie musicals of the 1930s. Powell, a musician and singing emcee with the Royal Peacock and Charlie Davis orchestras, recorded his first sides with the Vocalion label in 1928. He started crooning on film in 1932, where he was usually cast as the archetypal innocent American go-getter, ready to face any problem (personal or financial) with a song in his heart, a shine on his tap shoes, and about three inches of pancake makeup on his face. Depression Era audiences were eager for this brand of upbeat escapism, and the movies he made with and without Ruby Keeler were major smashes. Several songs from those films, including "I Only Have Eyes for You," "Lullabye of Broadway," "Honeymoon Hotel," and "Gold Dig-

ger's Song (We're in the Money)," were big hits as well, many of which have become pop standards. Powell's box-office clout declined when the musical craze of the 1930s gave way to the epic motion picture trend of the 1940s. He recharged his career (and proved his artistic mettle) with a dead-on accurate portrayal of Raymond Chandler's tough-talking, quip-a-minute private eye Phillip Marlowe in 1945's *Murder, My Sweet,* which led to a string of well-received serious roles. Powell sang in one last movie, *Susan Slept Here,* before shelving his on-camera career to concentrate full time on his successful, and occasionally innovative, production company: Four Star Television.

what's available: Powell's years as a top movie crooner are chronicled (with much repetition) on *In Hollywood (1933–1935)* ♫♫♫♫ (Legacy, 1995, prod. various) and *The Man from 42nd Street* ♫♫♫♫ (Flapper, 1996, prod. various), featuring such hits as "Honeymoon Hotel," "Gold Digger's Song (We're in the Money)," and the risqué-for-its-time "Pettin' in the Park."

worth searching for: Powell's stunning career comeback as Raymond Chandler's private eye Phillip Marlowe in 1945 is just as convincing on the LP *Lux Radio Theater: "Murder, My Sweet"* ♫♫♫♫ (Radiola, 1979, prod. Irving Pichel) as it is on screen. Powell gives Marlowe a wry gum-chewing snap that eluded portrayals by even Humphrey Bogart and Robert Mitchum. Chandler himself thought Powell was the best Marlowe on screen.

influences:

◀◀ Rudy Vallee, Bing Crosby, Fred Astaire

▶▶ Guy Marks, Barry Bostwick, Mandy Patinkin

Ken Burke

Perez Prado

Born Damaso Perez Prado, December 11, 1916, in Matanzas, Cuba. Died September 14, 1989, in Mexico City, Mexico.

Jazzman Tito Puente got his due in the 1992 film *The Mambo Kings,* but where was Perez Prado? Some say the native Cuban invented the mambo rhythm circa 1942, and his nickname throughout his career was "El Rey del Mambo," or "The Mambo King." Whether he was the pioneer or not, it's indisputible that when Prado moved from Cuba to Mexico in 1948, he set off the international mambo craze with his mixture of Afro-Cuban rhythms and American swing.

In Mexico City, Prado immediately set up shop at Club 1-2-3, earning the nickname "The Glenn Miller of Mexico," and using this notoriety to tour the U.S. and act in Mexican movies. His orchestra's mambo songs—built on a steady, tinny Latin rhythm and using an incredibly catchy, playful horn or whistle melody—became big hits in the late 1940s and led to an RCA Victor recording contract. His American tours, beginning in the early 1950s, gave him a massive audience, especially in such prominent New York City nightclubs as the Palladium. (Always a great showman, Prado's trademark cry was "Dilo!" which means "give it!") Though snooty jazz fans preferred Puente and Tito Rodriguez above Prado's unashamed hitmaking style, Prado's influence flowed in unexpected directions. Singer Rosemary Clooney, inspired by Prado and the 1954 mambo craze, recorded her wonderful "Mambo Italiano"; Perry Como, Dizzy Gillespie, and the Crows also adapted his style. Prado's first #1 American hit, 1955's "Cherry Pink and Apple Blossom White," cemented his long-term popularity. He recorded until the 1970s, then retired to live with his family in Mexico City. As with many musicians who thrive on whimsical public crazes, Prado's body of work is rarely taken seriously; but he was a major talent, and instrumentals like "Why Wait" still sound fresh and catchy.

what to buy: The hard part about navigating Prado's multi-album career is determining which Spanish imports overlap with the original studio albums, and which of those are out of print. *Mondo Mambo! The Best of . . .* ♫♫♫♫ (Rhino, 1995, prod. various) focuses on Prado's glory years—and, not coincidentally, the height of the mambo craze—and includes such classics as "Cherry Pink and Apple Blossom White" and "Patricia."

what to buy next: Prado's best-known studio album remains *Havana 3 A.M.* ♫♫♫ (BMG, 1956/1990), in which jazzman Maynard Ferguson contributes the lead trumpet parts and a big Latin swing band supplies the incredibly catchy pop melodies. Other noteworthy studio albums, handily reissued on CD, include the breakthrough *Prez* ♫♫♫♫ (RCA, 1958) and *Que Rico Mambo!* ♫♫♫ (BMG, 1982).

what to avoid: Like most pop musicians of his era, Prado was prolific, putting out a few albums every year during the height of his popularity; as a result, much of his stuff sounds like much of his other stuff, not to mention the other Latin-influenced easy-listening music of the same era. Among the examples of bland pop product are *The Mambo King* ♫♫ (RCA International, 1957) and the Spanish reissue, *Cuba, Grandes Idoles de Siempre* ♫♫ (Orfeon, 1997).

best of the rest:
King of Mambo ♫♫ (BMG, 1967/1989)
Concierto Para Bongo ♫♫♫ (PolyGram Latino, 1993)
Dance Date with . . . Perez Prado ♫♫♫ (Polydor, 1994)

Esta Si Viven ♫♫ (PolyGram Latino, 1996)
Sinfeonola Tropical, Vol. II ♫♫♫ (RCA, 1997)
15 Grandes Exito de Perez Prado, Vol. 2 ♫♫♫ (RCA, 1997)

worth searching for: Don't ignore the Latin import repackages, including *Go Go Mambo* ♫♫♫ (Tumbao, 1992) and *Perez Prado and Benny More: Mambos* ♫♫♫ (Saludos Amigos, 1994)—although novices are advised to stick with the Rhino compilation.

influences:

◄◄ Tito Puente, Arsenio Rodriguez, Orestes Lopez, Tito Rodriguez, Xavier Cugat

►► Rosemary Clooney, Herb Alpert, Sergio Mendes, Dizzy Gillespie

Steve Knopper

Elvis Presley

Born Elvis Aron Presley, January 8, 1935, in East Tupelo, MS. Died August 16, 1977, in Memphis, TN.

People sometimes forget that Elvis Presley—King of Rock 'n' Roll, movie star, tragic symbol of garish excess, paragon of moral decay, one of the best-selling pop artists of all time, even a pop-culture Jesus Christ figure—was actually talented. Whether or not he invented rock 'n' roll by linking, as myth recalls, white country music and black blues, he had an innate command of the stage and audience and was a terrific singer and interpreter.

Most critics say Presley, who began as a hillbilly who made it big, started his long, torturous descent into Las Vegas showrooms in the early 1960s, just after he returned from the Army and began making movies. In the decade of hippies, the Vietnam War, and baby-boom counterculture, Presley focused on lighthearted innocence, dancing with a sultry Ann-Margret (to name just one of his big-screen flames) in *Viva Las Vegas*. While songs like the tinkly, fad-hopping "Bossa Nova Baby" didn't have quite the same force as "Jailhouse Rock," they were still rock 'n' roll, and still fun. By the 1970s, Presley had created an isolationist world for himself—including the lavish Jungle Room, with its three television sets—and a close circle of family, friends, and hangers-on. Despite a triumphant television comeback in 1968, he spent the 1970s as a Vegas mainstay and became an almost total parody of himself, though some of his later hits—"In the Ghetto," "Suspicious Minds," "Burning

Love"—were underrated, explosive, and funky. Wracked with fear and insecurity and nearly broke despite his fame and success, Presley died alone in his Graceland bathroom at 42, leading to Colonel Tom Parker's famous statement that he "would go right on managing him." A fascinating and lucrative cottage industry has grown up around his image and Graceland in the two decades since his death.

what to buy: The recent five-disc box sets have been a godsend, because without them it was impossible to navigate the record store binfuls of studio albums and greatest-hits collections for the essential stuff. Start with *Elvis: The King of Rock 'n' Roll—The Complete '50s Masters* ♪♪♪♪♪ (RCA, 1992, reissue prod. Ernst Mikael Jorgensen, Roger Semon), and hear the young truck driver transform from raw talent in the early hits "Blue Moon of Kentucky" and "That's All Right" to accomplished showman in "Jailhouse Rock" and "Love Me Tender." Next stop: *From Nashville to Memphis: The Essential '60s Masters I* ♪♪♪♪♪ (RCA, 1994, reissue prod. Ernst Mikael Jorgensen, Roger Semon) proves that despite the Beatles and his late-1950s stint in the Army, Presley was still a vital performer; "Little Sister," "Suspicious Minds," "In the Ghetto," and "Fever" are among the transcendental tracks. You can hear Presley's lounge identity developing in *Walk a Mile in My Shoes: The Essential '70s Masters* ♪♪♪♪♪ (RCA, 1995, reissue prod. Ernst Mikael Jorgensen, Roger Semon) and *Command Performances: The Essential '60s Masters II* ♪♪♪♪ (RCA, 1995, reissue prod. Ernst Mikael Jorgensen, Roger Semon), the latter of which includes "Bossa Nova Baby," "Viva Las Vegas," "Charro!," and other rocking cornball anthems that came to define Presley's 1970s persona.

what to buy next: There's much, much more rock 'n' roll: *The Complete Sun Sessions* ♪♪♪♪♪ (RCA, 1987, original prod. Sam Phillips) is mostly revisited on the first box set, but it contains the fascinating sound of Elvis, guitarist Scotty Moore, bassist Bill Black, and producer Phillips inventing rock 'n' roll in the Sun Records studio; "Milkcow Blues Boogie" has Elvis stopping a slow blues song, announcing "that don't MOVE me" and proceeding to change it before our ears into something completely different.

what to avoid: Most of Presley's schlock, which became almost as famous as his great stuff, was in either the bad-live-performance or icky-movie-soundtrack categories. His bad live albums were most prominent in the 1970s, including *As Recorded at Madison Square Garden* ♪♪ (RCA, 1972, prod. Felton Jarvis), *Recorded Live on Stage in Memphis* ♪♪ (RCA, 1974, prod. Felton Jarvis), *Having Fun with Elvis on Stage* **woof!** (RCA,

1974) (just the King making bad jokes), *Elvis in Concert* **woof!** (RCA, 1977, digital prod. Don Wardell), and *Elvis on Stage* ♪ (RCA, 1977). His icky movie soundtracks were most prominent in the 1960s, with *Fun in Acapulco* ♪♪ (RCA, 1963, prod. Elvis Presley), *Live a Little, Love a Little/Charro!/The Trouble with Girls/Change of Habit* ♪♪ (RCA, 1995, reissue prod. Ernst Mikael Jorgensen, Roger Semon), and several others.

best of the rest:

Elvis ♪♪♪♪ (RCA, 1956)
Elvis Presley ♪♪♪♪ (RCA, 1956)
Elvis' Christmas Album ♪♪♪♪♪ (RCA, 1957)
Loving You ♪♪♪♪ (RCA, 1957)
King Creole ♪♪♪♪ (RCA, 1958)
Elvis' Golden Records, Vol. 1 ♪♪♪♪♪ (RCA, 1958)
A Date with Elvis ♪♪♪♪ (RCA, 1959)
For LP Fans Only ♪♪♪♪ (RCA, 1959)
Elvis Is Back! ♪♪♪♪ (RCA, 1960)
50,000,000 Elvis Fans Can't Be Wrong: Elvis' Golden Records, Vol. 2 ♪♪♪♪ (RCA, 1960)
Elvis' Golden Records, Vol. 3 ♪♪♪♪♪ (RCA, 1963)
Spinout ♪♪♪♪ (RCA, 1966)
How Great Thou Art ♪♪♪ (RCA, 1967)
Elvis NBC-TV Special ♪♪♪♪ (RCA, 1968)
Elvis' Golden Records, Vol. 4 ♪♪♪♪ (RCA, 1968)
From Elvis in Memphis ♪♪♪♪ (RCA, 1969)
Elvis Aron Presley ♪♪♪♪ (RCA, 1980/1998)
Elvis' Gold Records, Vol. 5 ♪♪♪ (RCA, 1984)
Kissin' Cousins/Clambake/Stay Away, Joe ♪♪♪♪ (RCA, 1994)

worth searching for: Check out these great songs about Elvis: "Elvis Is Dead," by Living Colour; "Elvis Is Everywhere," by Mojo Nixon; "My Boy Elvis," by Janis Martin; "Galway to Graceland," by Richard Thompson; "Elvis Ate America," by U2/Brian Eno as the Passengers; "Little Sister," by Dwight Yoakam; "Johnny Bye Bye," by Bruce Springsteen. Great versions of songs Elvis did: "Hound Dog," by Big Mama Thornton; "That's All Right (Mama)," by Arthur "Big Boy" Crudup; "Good Rockin' Tonight," by Roy Brown; "Burning Love," by Arthur Alexander; "Burning Love," by Grant Lee Buffalo; "Jailhouse Rock," by the Cramps; "Mystery Train," by Junior Parker's Blue Flames; and the entire soundtrack of *Honeymoon in Vegas* ♪♪ (Epic, 1992, prod. Peter Afterman, Glen Brunman), despite the lifeless carbon-copy Billy Joel versions of "All Shook Up" and "Heartbreak Hotel."

influences:

◀◀ Bill Monroe, Hank Snow, Arthur "Big Boy" Crudup, Little Richard, Chuck Berry, Lowell Fulson, Big Mama Thornton, Frank Sinatra, Hank Williams, Roy Brown, the Carter Family, Jimmie Rodgers, the Ink Spots, Eddy Arnold

▶▶ Buddy Holly, Carl Perkins, Roy Orbison, the Beatles, Johnny Cash, Bob Dylan, the Beach Boys, Janis Martin, Bruce Springsteen, Ann-Margret, Billy Joel, Mojo Nixon, Dwight Yoakam, the Band, the Blasters, Elvis Hitler, Elvis Costello, U2, the Stray Cats, Living Colour, Public Enemy

Steve Knopper

Andre Previn

Born Andre Prewin, April 6, 1929, in Berlin, Germany.

Previn is a renowned conductor of many prestigious symphony orchestras the world over. He has also won Academy Awards for his work on the musical scores of such motion picture classics as *Porgy and Bess, Gigi, My Fair Lady,* and *Irma la Douce.* Those are fabulous credentials, but many lounge-music fans know Previn best as a fine jazz piano cat. Whether he plays sweet and cool on romantic mood pieces, or swings bop-time on standards and showtunes, Previn showcases masterful artistry and the joy of performance.

He studied classical music as a child in Berlin and later in Paris when his family fled the Nazis. His move to Los Angeles in 1938 exposed him to the jazz stylings of Art Tatum, and he was hooked. Always a workhorse, when he wasn't studying Previn played piano for radio programs and on film scores, saving jazz for those moments when he needed to blow off some creative steam. Just a teenager when he made his first recordings, Previn initially dug swing music, but after World War II hard bop began to permeate his style. His trio's playful jazzing up of the score to *My Fair Lady* was a surprise hit, and led to a series of similar reworkings of Broadway themes, standards, and songwriter tributes. He also found time to cut an LP with then-wife Dory Previn (his collaborator on many film songs), and co-write *Coco* for the Broadway stage. While slowly moving away from both jazz and Hollywood, Previn cut his first all-classical LP in 1960, which led to a series of successful romantic mood music discs on Columbia. As always, his playing was fluid and showcased superb technique, but Previn could not deny his ambition to be a full-time conductor of classical music, and he ceased performing in the mid-'60s. After many celebrated years as a conductor, he returned to jazz part-time, releasing CDs on various record labels.

what to buy: Previn and his trio (featuring Red Mitchell and Frank Capp) reached a creative apex with *King Size* 𝄞𝄞𝄞𝄞 (Contemporary, 1960/Original Jazz Classics, 1992, prod. Lester Koenig), transforming six standards into swinging bop. Previn's

Cocktail Classics

Summertime

18-Karat **Billie Holiday**
I Got Rhythm
(Smithsonian/BMG)

Bombsville! **The Mystic Moods Orchestra**
Nighttide
(The Right Stuff)

piano work is especially freewheeling and cool on this fine reissue. For a taste of Previn's "beautiful music" style, *A Touch of Elegance* 𝄞𝄞𝄞𝄞 (Legacy, 1994, compilation prod. John Snyder, Irving Townsend) is a tribute to the music of Duke Ellington with his tasteful, yet moody takes on "What's New," "Mack the Knife," "Bye Bye Blackbird," the title track, and many others.

what to buy next: Previn is alone at the piano for *Plays Songs by Jerome Kern* 𝄞𝄞𝄞𝄞 (Contemporary, 1959/Original Jazz Classics, 1992, prod. Lester Koenig), with masterful interpretations of "Ol' Man River," "Long Ago and Far Away," and "All the Things You Are." Also, sports buffs who have a hard time getting into jazz ought to check out *Andre Previn/Russ Freeman:*

Double Play! 🎵🎵🎵 (Contemporary, 1957/Original Jazz Classics, 1992, prod. Lester Koenig), on which Previn gives the bop treatment to such baseball-oriented tunes as "Take Me out to the Ballgame," "Called on Account of Rain," "Batter Up," and "In the Cellar Blues."

what to avoid: They're cheap and easy to find, but the poor quality of *Some of the Best* 🎵🎵 (Laserlight, 1996, compilation prod. Rod McKuen) and *More of the Best* 🎵 (Laserlight, 1996, compilation prod. Rod McKuen) make them items for indiscriminate bargain-hunters and completists only.

the rest:

Pal Joey 🎵🎵🎵 (Contemporary, 1957/Original Jazz Classics, 1991)

Gigi 🎵🎵🎵 (Contemporary, 1958/Original Jazz Classics, 1990)

Plays Songs by Vernon Duke 🎵🎵🎵 (Contemporary, 1958/Original Jazz Classics, 1991)

West Side Story 🎵🎵🎵 (Contemporary, 1959/Original Jazz Classics, 1990)

Give My Regards to Broadway 🎵🎵 (Columbia Special Products, 1960/1993)

Plays Songs by Harold Arlen 🎵🎵🎵 (Contemporary, 1960/Original Jazz Classics, 1994)

After Hours 🎵🎵🎵 (Telarc, 1989)

The Piano Stylings of Andre Previn 🎵🎵 (RCA, 1990)

Uptown 🎵🎵🎵 (Telarc, 1990)

Plays a Classic American Songbook 🎵🎵🎵 (DRG, 1992)

Andre Previn/Mundell Lowe/Ray Brown: Old Friends 🎵🎵🎵 (Telarc, 1992)

What Headphones? 🎵🎵🎵 (Angel, 1993)

The Essence of Andre Previn 🎵🎵🎵🎵 (Legacy, 1994)

Andre Previn & His Friends Play Show Boat 🎵🎵🎵 (Deustche Grammophone, 1995)

Ballads—Solo Piano Standards 🎵🎵🎵 (Capitol, 1996)

Jazz at the Musikverein 🎵🎵🎵 (Verve, 1997)

Fats Waller Songbook 🎵🎵🎵 (Simitar, 1997)

worth searching for: Many of Previn's early studio recordings (c. 1945–46) can be found on *Previn at Sunset* 🎵🎵🎵 (Black Lion, 1993, reissue prod. Alan Bates) and strongly exhibit the influence of Oscar Peterson. Also, Previn contributes heavily to the success of *Shelly Mann & His Friends* 🎵🎵🎵 (Original Jazz Classics, 1996), originally recorded in 1944. Finally, lounge cats might dig Previn's versions of "I'm in the Mood for Love" and "Stella by Starlight" on *Instrumental Themes for Young Lovers* 🎵🎵🎵 (Legacy, 1997, compilation prod. Bruce Williamson), part of Sony's *Music for Gracious Living* series, which also features tracks by Andre Kostelanetz, Dave Grusin, Erroll Garner, and Percy Faith.

influences:

◀◀ Art Tatum, Oscar Peterson, Pierre Monteaux

▶▶ Roger Williams, Peter Nero, Francis Lai

Ken Burke

Louis Prima & Keely Smith

Formed late 1940s.

Louis Prima (born December 7, 1910, in New Orleans, LA; died August 24, 1978, in New Orleans, LA), trumpet, vocals; Keely Smith (born Dorothy Jacqueline Keely Smith, March 9, 1932), vocals.

Borrowing jolly enthusiasm and a horn-heavy jump-blues sound from a couple of other guys named Louis—Jordan and Armstrong—Prima held all-night swing court for years in Las Vegas lounges and showrooms. The trumpeter sang with a slurring boisterousness; led big bands all over the country; played hilariously off his longtime wife and duet partner, Keely Smith; wrote Benny Goodman's enduring swing classic "Sing, Sing, Sing"; sired saxman Sam Butera and his Witnesses; supplied King Louie the Orangutan's voice in the animated 1969 Walt Disney classic *The Jungle Book*; and, long after his death, dominated a movie (1995's *Big Night*) in which he never appeared.

Born just outside New Orleans's famed Storyville district, Prima spent his youth soaking up Dixieland jazz, specifically the horn-rich sounds of Joe "King" Oliver and Armstrong, then dropped out of high school to become a musician. He slowly advanced in the New Orleans nightclub pecking order, finally scoring a major break in 1934, when bandleader Guy Lombardo pushed him to move to New York City. He did, and things moved quickly: clubgoers loved him and his rollicking band, the New Orleans Gang, and he wound up in musicals with established singer Bing Crosby and young talent Martha Raye. In addition to writing his most enduring hit—Goodman's "Sing, Sing, Sing," still a must-play at weddings everywhere—he started recording humorous pop songs like "Robin Hood" and "Civilization." In the late '40s, Prima met 16-year-old Keely Smith, a crooner with a beautiful voice who was willing to play the straightwoman to Prima's rambunctious persona. They married in 1952 and, when big-band nightclub work eroded in New York, negotiated what turned out to be their most important gig, a two-week stint at Las Vegas's Sahara Hotel. They became a mainstay, hooking up with Butera and the Witnesses and amassing enough clout to record for Capitol Records. (The 1958 hit "That Old Black Magic," with Smith singing in her usual smooth, declarative voice and Prima exploding with clipped

Louis Prima **(AP/Wide World Photos)**

phrases like "look at the spin I'm in" and "put out the fire!" is one of the most hilarious and exuberant pop songs of all time.)

Prima and Smith recorded successful hits—solo and as a team—and played countless lucrative gigs in Las Vegas, eventually breaking up both the partnership and the marriage in 1961. Prima continued to make hits, including the 1967 Phil Harris duet "I Wanna Walk Like You," and perform with Butera in New Orleans. Though Smith and Butera continue to tour and perform, Prima had brain-tumor surgery in 1975 and spent the last three years of his life in a coma. In addition to his general influence on pop music, he was an icon in the Italian-American community—the acclaimed film *Big Night* is about two Italian brothers who emigrate to the U.S. and open a restaurant. They rely on a friend's connection with Louis Prima to save the business, but the anxiously awaited singer never shows up.

what to buy: Prima's recording career peaked in the '50s and '60s, when he recorded several albums for Capitol Records—

Capitol Collector's Series ♫♫♫♫ (Capitol, 1991, prod. Voyle Gilmore, compilation prod. Bob Furmanek), with 26 songs, captures Prima as a dominant and versatile performer. Though the great Smith shows up on just a few tracks, including "That Old Black Magic" and "Embraceable You," Prima careens between blues ("St. Louis Blues"), swing (his "Sing, Sing, Sing"), novelty ("Beep! Beep!"), and romantic ballads ("Lazy River").

what to buy next: *Wonderland by Night* ♫♫♫ (MCA Special Products, 1995, prod. various) recalls Prima's softer, smoother side, including ballads like "By the Light of the Silvery Moon" and "Moonlight in Vermont."

what to avoid: While Rhino Records compilations are almost always the definitive statement on a vintage performer, the Capitol collection immediately outpaced *Zooma Zooma: The Best of Louis Prima* ♫♫♫ (Rhino, 1990, prod. various), which overlaps many of the same songs and doesn't give quite as much quality for the price.

best of the rest:
Play Pretty for the People 𝄢𝄢 (Savoy, 1990)
Jazz Collectors Edition 𝄢𝄢𝄢 (Laserlight, 1991)
Very Best of Louis Prima 𝄢𝄢𝄢 (Pair, 1997)

worth searching for: The German eight-disc import *The Capitol Recordings* 𝄢𝄢𝄢𝄢 (Bear Family, 1994, prod. various) is overkill, but it's the logical next step beyond *Capitol Collector's Series*. Also, the import label Jasmine Records has nicely reissued several classic Prima and Smith albums, including the twisty two-LP combination *Twist with Keely Smith/Doin' the Twist with Louis Prima* 𝄢𝄢𝄢 (Jasmine, 1997, prod. various); Smith's *Cherokeely Swings* 𝄢𝄢𝄢 (Jasmine, 1994) and *Keely Christmas* 𝄢𝄢 (Jasmine, 1996); and Prima's *His Greatest Hits* 𝄢𝄢 (Jasmine, 1994), which is redundant given the superior Rhino and Capitol collections. For original Smith solo LPs and Smith-Prima duet LPs, Jasmine provides pretty much the only stuff available; still, if you're the type who enjoys rooting through used-record bins for original vinyl, *The Wildest!* 𝄢𝄢𝄢𝄢 (Capitol, 1956, prod. Voyle Gilmore), with "Buona Sera" and "Jump, Jive, and Wail," makes for an excellent holy grail.

influences:

◀◀ Louis Armstrong, Joe "King" Oliver, Al Jolson, Ethel Merman, Louis Jordan, Bob Wills, Jimmy Witherspoon, Charles Brown, Jelly Roll Morton

▶▶ Benny Goodman, Glenn Miller, Screamin' Jay Hawkins, Squirrel Nut Zippers, Royal Crown Revue

see also: *Sam Butera*

Steve Knopper

Tito Puente

Born Ernest Anthony Puente Jr., April 20, 1923, in New York, NY.

When the rock group Santana recorded "Oye Como Va," a classic Latin hit that Puente had written and recorded, the composer was slightly outraged that such a band would dare sully his music. As soon as the royalty check came (based on massive sales of Santana's first album), Puente discovered the upside of having other people perform his songs. The wonderful showman has prefaced the playing of "Oye Como Va" with that little story many times since then and come to realize that his music has done as much to promote Latin jazz for current audiences as Machito's did for an earlier generation. His playful and humorous side has trickled into numerous pop-music trends, including the mambo craze of the '50s; and pop culture finally caught up with him in the 1992 movie and soundtrack *The Mambo Kings,* in which he appears.

Puente's musical career began with Latin groups such as the Cuarteto Caney and Xavier Cugat. In the mid-1940s, after serving in the United States Navy during World War II, Puente came back to New York where Noro Morales and Machito gave the budding percussionist work. By the early 1950s he had formed his own ensemble, the Piccadilly Boys, and played the Palladium, New York's cultural Mecca for Latin bands. His band meanwhile had mutated into the Tito Puente Orchestra and, with lead vocalist Vincentico Valdes, proceeded to change the face of Latin music. Puente took the Cuban charanga form (with its flutes and violins) and arranged them in more of a jazz big band context, punching up the brass and reeds for a more powerful sound. He also started using a lot of non-Latin jazz artists like Doc Severinsen in his bands and playing arrangements of jazz standards with a Latin beat. During the 1960s and 1970s Puente recorded albums with large bands and small groups, continuing the heavy schedule of touring he had developed in the 1950s. By the 1980s Puente's popularity was even stronger than it was in the early 1950s due to a base of fans that included not only the hardcore Latin music lovers, but a fair number of jazz musicians and fans as well.

In 1983, the multi-talented Puente (timbales, drums, marimba, vibraphone, percussion, vocalist, arranger) won the first of his many Grammy Awards, for the album *Tito Puente and His Latin Ensemble on Broadway.* With more than 100 albums to his credit—fan Bill Cosby claims to love "his 82nd"—Puente has recorded with most of the major names in Latin music and become a major force in the Latinization of jazz during the last half of the 20th century.

what to buy: The three-CD compilation set, *50 Years of Swing* 𝄢𝄢𝄢𝄢𝄢 (RMM, 1997, prod. various), is a perfect starting place for anyone wanting a well-conceived, albeit abridged, introduction to Tito Puente's music. The 50 songs cover his stints with the major pop labels like MCA and RCA in addition to sampling material from Latin specialty companies. His big hits, "Para Los Rumberos" and "Oye Como Va," are included, along with distinguished covers of tunes made famous by Machito ("Tanga" and "Babarabatiri"), renditions of jazz classics like "Lullaby of Broadway" and "Moody's Mood for Love," and distinctly cheesy remakes of pop riffs ("Crystal Blue Persuasion"). The band on *The Best of Dance Mania* 𝄢𝄢𝄢𝄢𝄢 (BMG/International, 1994, prod. Fred Reynolds, Marty Gold) features his second

Tito Puente (© Jack Vartoogian)

great vocalist (after Vincentico Valdes), Santitos Colon, the remarkable bassist Bobby Rodriguez, and a host of stellar percussionists. This CD has 23 cuts, including some previously unreleased outtakes that showcase the care Puente took to craft the perfect performance of a song. *Mambo Beat, Vol. 1* 𝄞𝄞𝄞𝄞 (BMG/International, 1994, prod. various) is a well-put-together collection (compiled by Domingo Echevarria) with performances by Puente and his Afro-Cuban Jazz All Star Orchestras in jazz material with a Latin kick. Standards like "Yesterdays" by Jerome Kern and Oscar Pettiford's "Bohemia After Dark" (renamed "Birdland After Dark") share space with Puente's own wonderful "Night Ritual" and the percussion fest "Ti Mon Bo." On *Live at the Village Gate* 𝄞𝄞𝄞𝄞 (RMM, 1992, prod. Alfredo Cruz), Puente heads an all-star group through a well-chosen program of jazz favorites and a hip arrangement of "Oye Como Va." Especially noteworthy are Miles Davis's "Milestones" and Santamaria's "Afro Blue."

what to buy next: With the exception of a big band mini-suite entitled "Night Ritual," *Top Percussion* 𝄞𝄞𝄞𝄞 (BMG/International, 1957/1992) is one of the most subversive Latin albums (given the time it first appeared in the marketplace) ever released. Santeria practitioner Puente released this album of polyrhythmic percussion honoring the "voo-doo" ways decades before Milton Cardona's classic *Bembe*. Constructed mainly for people with a minimal budget who want to start exploring Puente's voluminous catalog, *El Rey Del Timbal: The Best of Tito Puente and His Orchestra* 𝄞𝄞𝄞𝄞 (Rhino, 1997, prod. various) is a good single-disc sampler of Puente's material covering the period from 1949 to 1987. *Special Delivery* 𝄞𝄞𝄞𝄞 (Concord Picante, 1996, prod. John Burk, Tito Puente) is a big band jazz album covering the bebop and post-bop composers that Puente is most comfortable with: Dizzy Gillespie, Thelonious Monk, and Horace Silver. In addition to playing timbales and other assorted percussion instruments, Puente is a gifted vibes player, and *Mambo of the Times* 𝄞𝄞𝄞𝄞 (Concord Picante, 1992, prod. John Burk, Allen Farnham, Tito Puente) contains some of his best work in that regard. His playing on Fats Waller's "Jitterbug Waltz" is firmly within the jazz camp even as his supporting cast flits about his melodic statement like Latin fireflies.

what to avoid: Puente contributes a skimpy two tracks to the soundtrack *The Mambo Kings* 𝄞𝄞 (Elektra, 1992, prod. Robert Kraft), which also includes a bland Celia Cruz version of "Guantanamera" and ill-advised singing performances by actor Antonio Banderas. Better you should see the film and buy Puente's solo albums.

best of the rest:

Goza Mi Timbal 𝄞𝄞𝄞𝄞 (Concord Picante, 1990)
Out of This World 𝄞𝄞𝄞𝄞 (Concord Picante, 1991)
In Session 𝄞𝄞𝄞𝄞 (RMM, 1994)
Tito's Idea 𝄞𝄞𝄞𝄞 (RMM, 1996)

worth searching for: *The Mambo King* 𝄞𝄞𝄞𝄞 (RMM, 1991, prod. Sergio George) is Puente's 100th album, marking a significant milestone in his career. More of a Latin recording than a straight jazz session, the album features Puente joined by major Latin vocal stars like Oscar D'Leon and Celia Cruz.

influences:

◀◀ Machito, Mario Bauza, Dizzy Gillespie, Gene Krupa, Xavier Cugat

▶▶ Guilherme Franco, Cal Tjader, Carlos Santana, Perez Prado

Garaud MacTaggart

John Raitt

Born January 19, 1917, in Santa Ana, CA.

Raitt's emotive baritone made him a Broadway star in the '40s and '50s. Onstage, his ability to temper the strains of light opera with folksy charm gave his heroic everyman roles added credibility, and his love ballads a sincere personal touch. Before making his mark in musical theater, Raitt appeared in such films as *Little Nelly Kelly, Flight Command, H.M. Pulham, Esq.,* and *Minstrel Man*. He didn't click in films, probably because there weren't many opportunities for him to sing. A successful run in the Chicago production of *Oklahoma* led to his breakthrough role in the Rodgers and Hammerstein classic, *Carousel,* in which he sang "Soliloquy" and "If I Loved You" to great acclaim. After a few less successful Broadway shows, Raitt hit the jackpot once again with 1954's *Pajama Game* (which he reprised later on film with Doris Day). In the show, Raitt sang "There Once Was a Man" and "Small Talk" with co-star Janis Paige, and introduced "Hey There," which went on to become an oft-covered standard. Preferring a live audience to the secluded grind of Hollywood, Raitt turned down further movie assignments to work concert halls, Broadway, and television—which he has done to this day. And, oh yeah . . . they say his daughter, Bonnie, is a pretty fair singer too.

what to buy: Raitt is superb on *Broadway Legend* 𝄢𝄢𝄢𝄢 (Angel, 1995, prod. Robbie Buchanan, Eddie Arkin, Jay Landers), the Grammy-nominated collection of showtunes from *Oklahoma, Carousel, Annie Get Your Gun, South Pacific,* and *The Pajama Game.* Bonnie Raitt makes a guest appearance.

what to buy next: Raitt does a fine job reinterpreting the Broadway songs he made famous on *Best of John Raitt* 𝄢𝄢𝄢 (Ranwood, 1995, compilation prod. Bonnie Pritchard), which features "Hey There," "Small Talk," and vocal contributions form Barbara Cook, Florence Henderson, Jan Clayton, and his *Pajama Game* co-star, Janis Paige.

the rest:
Pajama Game 𝄢𝄢𝄢𝄢 (Original Cast Soundtrack) (Columbia, 1954/1990)
Carousel 𝄢𝄢𝄢𝄢 (Original Cast Soundtrack) (MCA, 1993)

worth searching for: The sound is a little thin on *The Sullivan Years: Best of Broadway* 𝄢𝄢𝄢𝄢 (TVT, 1992, compilation prod. Steve Gottlieb), but Raitt, Pearl Bailey, Robert Goulet, Carol Lawrence, Florence Henderson, and Gertrude Lawrence all give peak-level performances of their big numbers from their respective hit Broadway musicals. Also, the video version of the 1957 film *The Pajama Game* 𝄢𝄢𝄢𝄢 (Warner Home Video, 1992) is well worth the price of a rental. Raitt and co-star Doris Day are marvelous together.

influences:

◄◄ Robert Merrill, Gordon MacRae, Howard Keel

►► Robert Goulet, Larry Kert

Ken Burke

Boots Randolph

Born Homer Louis Randolph III, June 3, 1927, in Paducah, KY.

Boots Randolph billed himself as the world's "only hillbilly saxophone player," but his music ranged much farther than that. He was one of Nashville's highest-profile musicians during the 1950s and 1960s, along with Chet Atkins and Floyd Cramer. Randolph's choice of instruments limited his session calls, though, and he was as close as many country fans got to jazz.

Randolph began playing as soon as he could learn an instrument, trying the ukelele and trombone before settling on the tenor saxophone in his high-school band. He played as a sideman and solo performer in the Midwest during the early 1950s. A demo tape of his "Yakety Sax," written by Randolph and friend James Rich, came to the attention of RCA Records executive Chet Atkins in Nashville. Atkins brought Randolph to Nashville for session work with the likes of Eddy Arnold, Elvis Presley, and Roy Orbison. He also recorded frequently with such pop and light-jazz musicians as Al Hirt, Perry Como, Burl Ives, and Pete Fountain. Randolph recorded for RCA, and later moved to Monument, where he had his lone pop hit with "Yakety Sax" in 1963. He built a solid fan base for his instrumental records, which usually consisted of conventional arrangements of popular country and pop songs. He ran a successful nightclub in Nashville's Printers Alley for many years.

what to buy: Boots Randolph never has had a charting country hit, and only 1963's "Yakety Sax" made the pop Top 40, so take the title of *The Greatest Hits of Boots Randolph* 𝄢𝄢𝄢 (Monument, 1976/1991) with a grain of salt. Still, these are the songs most associated with Randolph through his career, with plenty of his honking sax on tunes as dissimilar as "Charlie Brown" and "The Shadow of Your Smile."

what to buy next: Randolph played classic pop standards on *Sentimental Journey* 𝄢𝄢𝄢 (Monument, 1988, prod. Fred Foster), backed by an orchestra arranged by bandleader and saxophonist Bill Justis.

what to avoid: Yes, they're his well-known songs, but the recordings of "Yakety Sax," "King of the Road" and "Crazy" on *Best of Boots Randolph* 𝄢𝄢 (Curb, 1997) are recordings made for Sony/ATV Music Publishing during the mid-1990s, well after Randolph's commercial prime.

the rest:
Yakin' Sax Man 𝄢𝄢 (RCA Camden, 1964)
Boots & Stockings 𝄢𝄢 (Sony Music Special Products, 1969)
Country Boots 𝄢𝄢𝄢 (Monument, 1974/1988)
Homer Louis Randolph III 𝄢𝄢𝄢 (Monument, 1976/1991)
Sunday Sax 𝄢𝄢 (Monument, 1976/1991)
Yakety Sax! 𝄢𝄢𝄢 (Monument, 1988)
Live 𝄢𝄢 (Monument, 1992)
Christmas at Boots' Place 𝄢𝄢 (Laserlight, 1995)
Boots Randolph with the Knightsbridge Strings 𝄢𝄢 (Sony, 1996)

worth searching for: During the early '80s jazz saxophonist Richie Cole sought out Randolph and recorded an album of duets with him. *Yakety Madness* 𝄢𝄢𝄢 (Laserlight, 1992, prod. Richie Cole) was recorded in Nashville and California and offers a rare glimpse at Randolph's talents. The selections, which range from standards like "Walkin' with Mr. Lee" and "Body and Soul" to jumped-up hillbilly tunes like "Jambalaya" and "Wabash Cannonball," aren't that different from Randolph's usual fare, but trading licks with a bop player gave him the freedom to let loose more than on any other recording.

influences:

◀◀ King Curtis, Earl Bostic

▶▶ Ace Cannon, Jim Horn

Brian Mansfield

Lou Rawls

Born December 1, 1935, in Chicago, IL.

Lou Rawls's low-key croon, in all of its rich, smooth depth, has carried him through a career that has been both lackluster and captivating. His gospel background with the Pilgrim Travellers provided the vocal seasoning on Sam Cooke's "Bring It on Home to Me," which led to a contract with Capitol in 1962. However, his willingness to be buried under sprawling arrangements and cabaret shlock rob many of his recordings of any punch, reducing his timbre to a workmanlike trade tool. There are instances when Rawls catches fire, most notably the bruised lament of 1966's "Love Is a Hurtin' Thing," which exemplified his warm control and a perfectionist's sense of phrasing (not unlike Cooke's). The first of three Grammys came with 1967's "Dead End Street," a mix of spoken monologues and verse which became a staple of his live act. Although he had reached white audiences by this point, it wasn't until nearly a decade later that he enjoyed a true crossover smash with the disco-tinged ballad "You'll Never Find Another Love Like Mine." At the close of the 1980s, a relatively dormant period for him, he hooked up with the recently re-invigorated Blue Note label and returned to traditional blues with the music archivist Billy Vera in a promising return to form.

what to buy: The Philly soul team of Kenny Gamble and Leon Huff bring out the best in Rawls on *All Things in Time* 🎵🎵🎵🎵 (Philadelphia International, 1976/The Right Stuff, 1993, prod. various), which includes his enduring "You'll Never Find Another Love Like Mine" and the swinging "Groovy People." Clearly, when given the proper material and setting, Rawls will rise to the occasion. For a concise document of his more inspired performances, *The Legendary Lou Rawls* 🎵🎵🎵🎵 (Blue Note, 1992, prod. various) contains "Dead End Street," "Love Is a Hurtin' Thing," "Tobacco Road," and a pairing with sax great Cannonball Adderley.

what to buy next: *Portrait of the Blues* 🎵🎵🎵🎵 (Manhattan, 1993, prod. Billy Vera) is the strongest of his more recent fare. Guests such as Joe Williams, Phoebe Snow, and Buddy Guy up the ante for Rawls, resulting in an album with more oomph than he has made in ages.

what to avoid: Like most live albums, *Lou Rawls Live* 🎵🎵 (Philadelphia International, 1978/The Right Stuff, 1994, prod. Kenneth Gamble, Leon Huff) leaves you feeling like you're left holding a still-life. The abundance of overly long medleys doesn't exactly tip the scales in the right direction.

the rest:

Live at the Century Plaza 🎵🎵 (Rebound, 1973/1994)
When You Hear Lou, You've Heard It All 🎵🎵 (Philadelphia International, 1977/The Right Stuff, 1993)
Let Me Be Good to You 🎵🎵🎵 (Epic, 1983/The Right Stuff, 1993)
At Last 🎵🎵🎵 (Blue Note, 1989)
Stormy Monday 🎵🎵🎵 (Blue Note, 1990)
It's Supposed to Be Fun 🎵🎵🎵 (Blue Note, 1990)
Greatest Hits 🎵🎵 (Curb, 1991)
Christmas Is the Time 🎵🎵🎵 (EMI, 1993)
For You My Love 🎵🎵 (Capitol, 1994)
Love Songs 🎵🎵 (CEMA, 1994)
Spotlight on . . . Lou Rawls 🎵🎵 (Capitol, 1995)
Love Is a Hurtin' Thing: The Silky Soul of Lou Rawls 🎵🎵🎵 (EMI, 1997)

worth searching for: Rawls's late '60s work at Capitol broke him out of the Nat King Cole mold. His albums from that period, *Soulin'* 🎵🎵🎵🎵 (Capitol, 1966), *Too Much* 🎵🎵🎵🎵 (Capitol, 1967), and *That's Lou* 🎵🎵🎵🎵 (Capitol, 1967), are all worthy finds.

influences:

◀◀ Nat "King" Cole, Sam Cooke, Frank Sinatra, Joe Williams

▶▶ Billy Vera, Peabo Bryson, Luther Vandross

Allan Orski

Johnnie Ray

Born John Alvin Ray, January 10, 1927. Died February 25, 1990, in Los Angeles, CA.

In the years before rock 'n' roll, white pop singer Ray synthesized the post–World War II R&B sounds he heard in nightclubs into the most affecting, highly successful records of his time. He cut his first single, "Whiskey and Gin" (a top-notch supper-club blues), in Detroit and released it on Columbia's "race music" label OKeh, in 1951. After strong regional sales, Ray recorded his two-sided masterpiece "Cry" b/w "The Little White Cloud That Cried"—which became the first time two sides of a single hit both #1 and #2 on the charts. Onstage he was a frantic, nearly hysterical figure who threw himself to his knees, slid across the stage, pounded on his piano, and thrilled his fans with the most beautifully executed dramatic fits in pop music history. Bobbysoxers worshipped him, conventional singers sneered at his hearing aid, and the press had a field day inventing nicknames such as "The Cry Guy," "The Nabob of Sob," and "The Prince of Wails." Ray gave the "Cry" treatment to such hits as "Please, Mr. Sun," and "(Here I Am) Broken Hearted," before turning in a cool and jazzy performance on his sensational hit "Walkin My Baby Back Home." Then Mitch Miller, Columbia's notoriously schmaltzy and R&B-hating A&R man, took over Ray's song-selection duties. Many of his choices, unfortunately, were Tin Pan Alley dreck such as "Somebody Stole My Gal" and "Hernando's Hideaway." That, combined with bad publicity over an arrest early in his career on an alleged morals charge and a flop film, slowed his chart momentum. Still, his duets with crooners Frankie Laine and Doris Day were especially popular. The bluesiest of the pre-rock pop singers, Ray surprisingly didn't pursue rock audiences; as a result, he became irrelevant to '50s teens. Columbia sought to resurrect his career by recording him as a light-jazz singer, cowboy crooner, and all-around entertainer, but after 1959's "I'll Never Fall in Love Again," the hits stopped coming. A second arrest in 1961—he was loudly accused and quietly acquitted—prompted Columbia to drop Ray from its roster. Subsequent singles and LPs flopped, and Ray's recording career was over. But he continued to perform, as a major star in England and Australia.

what to buy: Ray's best known OKeh and Columbia sides are on *16 Most Requested Songs* ♪♪♪♪ (Legacy, 1991, prod. Michael Brooks), wherein his true pop classics, "Cry" and "Little White Cloud That Cried," still shudder with the eternal grief of perpetually lost love.

what to buy next: Bluesier by far is *High Drama: The Real Johnnie Ray* ♪♪♪♪ (Sony, 1997, compilation prod. Al Quaglieri), a smart compilation of hits mixed with lesser-known sides revealing Ray's love of R&B sounds, only slightly hampered by the vanilla wand-waving of Mitch Miller. It includes two previously unreleased tracks from his first session in Detroit: "Paths of Paradise" and "She Didn't Say Nothin' at All."

what to avoid: There's absolutely nothing wrong with *Back to Back: Frankie Laine/Johnnie Ray* ♪♪♪ (K-Tel, 1989, prod. various), but for the same price you can get much more of the Sultan of Sob on a solo disc.

the rest:
Best of Johnnie Ray ♪♪♪♪ (Columbia Special Products, 1989)
Greatest Hits ♪♪♪♪ (K-Tel, 1990)
Here and Now ♪♪♪ (Columbia Special Products, 1994)
Greatest Songs ♪♪♪ (Curb Records, 1995)

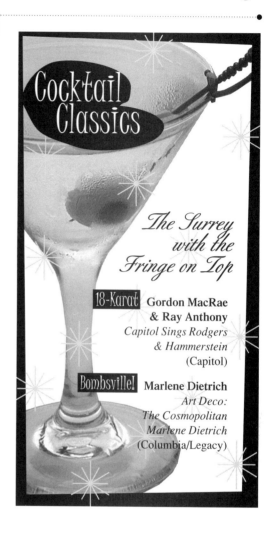

Cocktail Classics

The Surrey with the Fringe on Top

18-Karat **Gordon MacRae & Ray Anthony**
Capitol Sings Rodgers & Hammerstein
(Capitol)

Bombsville! **Marlene Dietrich**
Art Deco: The Cosmopolitan Marlene Dietrich
(Columbia/Legacy)

worth searching for: The German import *Cry* ♪♪♪♪ (Bear Family, 1990, prod. Richard Weize) features the largest selection of Ray's Okeh/Columbia sides to date and includes duets with Frankie Laine and Doris Day. Also, Ray is in peak form on *Live at the Paladium* ♪♪♪♪ (Bear Family, 1992, reissue prod. Richard Weize), a reissue of his original 1954 LP, recorded live in London, England.

influences:

◄◄ LaVern Baker, Dinah Washington, Al Hibbler, Frankie Laine, Jimmy Scott

►► Elvis Presley, Roy Orbison

Ken Burke

Helen Reddy

Born October 25, 1942, in Melbourne, Australia.

A childhood star from a show-biz family in her native Australia, Reddy enjoyed early success as a performer, including a stint on her own television series. By the late '70s, she'd crossed over into film stardom (*Pete's Dragon*). But she's best known for her '70s work as a pop vocalist: "I Am Woman" was one of the most discussed singles of the decade, with feminists (and humorists) still quoting its "hear me roar" message. Her tough, cavalier vocal style also was front-and-center on "Delta Dawn," the eerie "Angie Baby," and "That Ain't No Way to Treat a Lady."

what to buy: *Greatest Hits (And More)* 🎝🎝🎝🎝 (Capitol, 1975, prod. Kim Fowley, Frank Day, Earle Mankey, Larry Marks, Jay Senter, Joseph Wissert) is a 15-song summation of her best work. Everything's here, from the forceful "I Am Woman" to the sassy "Leave Me Alone (Ruby Red Dress)" and the melodramatic "You're My World."

what to buy next: *When I Dream: The Eighties Collection* 🎝🎝🎝 (Varese Vintage, 1996, prod. Cary E. Mansfield) gathers some of Reddy's overlooked, but outstanding, album tracks from the past.

what to avoid: With *Imagination* 🎝🎝 (MCA, 1983), Reddy must have imagined a comeback as a dance-floor diva. It didn't work.

the rest:
I Don't Know How to Love Him 🎝🎝🎝 (Capitol, 1971)
Helen Reddy 🎝🎝🎝 (Capitol, 1971)
I Am Woman 🎝🎝🎝 (Capitol, 1972)
Long Hard Climb 🎝🎝 (Capitol, 1973)
Love Song for Jeffrey 🎝🎝🎝 (Capitol, 1973)
Free and Easy 🎝🎝🎝 (Capitol, 1974)
No Way to Treat a Lady 🎝🎝🎝 (Capitol, 1975)
Music, Music 🎝🎝🎝 (Capitol, 1976)
Ear Candy 🎝🎝🎝 (Capitol, 1977)
Live in London 🎝🎝🎝 (Capitol, 1978)
Lust for Life 🎝🎝 (Pair, 1984)
All-Time Greatest Hits 🎝🎝🎝 (CEMA, 1992)
Ten Best All-Time Greatest Hits 🎝🎝🎝 (Capitol, 1997)

worth searching for: An out-of-print soundtrack, *All This and World War II* 🎝🎝🎝 (20th Century, 1976) boasted an all-Beatles track list performed by superstars of the bicentennial year, including Reddy.

influences:
◀◀ Carole King, the Beatles, Barbra Streisand

▶▶ Olivia Newton-John, Melissa Manchester, Maureen McGovern

Jay Dedrick

Della Reese

Born Dellaresse Taliaferro, July 6, 1932, in Detroit, MI.

Modern audiences know her best from her recurring role on TV's *Touched by an Angel* and for giving Eddie Murphy's character a first-class ass-whuppin' in the movie *Harlem Nights,* yet in the '50s and '60s, Reese was a soul chanteuse with a gorgeous face, eye-catching figure, and a string of hit records.

Reese began her professional career at age 14, singing gospel with Mahalia Jackson's troupe for four years before becoming one of the Clara Ward Singers; in 1953, she joined the Erskine Hawkins Orchestra. Her first recordings for were raw blends of pop, jazz, and gospel in the Sarah Vaughan and Dinah Washington styles. Her first hit, "And That Reminds Me," reached #12 on the pop charts, but she barely registered with her superior follow-up "Sermonette." Reese signed with RCA in 1959, where her sound became more supper-club chic, and she scored immediately with her biggest pop hit "Don't You Know," a torchy love ballad brimming with gospel intensity. Her appearance in the 1958 teen flick *Let's Rock!* (where she sang "Lonelyville") seems incongruous today, but illustrates the problems Reese had in the area of career direction. RCA didn't know whether to sell her records to teenagers or their parents, and the lack of clear promotional focus eventually hampered her as a singles artist. By the time the company figured out the possibilities of her sound and style, her career momentum had changed. Reese spent less time in recording studios after that, but television has bolstered her fame quite nicely. She has been a guest on practically every major variety program of the last 30 years, hosted her own talk show, and maintained a viable career as a character actress. In 1997, she summed it all up with the title of her autobiography: *Angels Along the Way: My Life with Help from Above.*

what to buy: Reese's run of classy late '50s and early '60s hits, including "Don't You Know," "And Now," and "Someday (You'll Want Me to Want You)," are on *Voice of an Angel* 🎝🎝🎝🎝 (RCA, 1996, prod. various).

what to buy next: *The Angel Sings* 🎝🎝🎝 (Amherst, 1997, compilation prod. Leonard Silver, Chris Beilor), a collection of her '60s sides for the Avco-Embassy label, is full of pleasingly gritty soul music, including Reese's last chart hit, "If It Feels Good Do It," as well as four previously unreleased tracks.

the rest:
Della 🎝🎝🎝 (RCA 1959/1996)

Della Reese **(AP/Wide World Photos)**

Della Della Cha Cha Cha ✍✍✍ (RCA 1961/1993)

(With Duke Ellington) *1962 Live Guard Session & at Basin St. East* ✍✍✍ (Jazz Band, 1994)

Best Thing for You ✍✍✍ (Jasmine, 1997)

Story of the Blues ✍✍✍ (Westside, 1998)

Jubilee Years ✍✍✍ (Westside, 1998)

worth searching for: Reese's jazz and gospel roots are joyously displayed on *And That Reminds Me: The Jubilee Years* ✍✍✍ (Collector's Choice, 1996), a 24-track disc containing everything she recorded for Jubilee.

influences:

◀◀ Clara Ward, Mahalia Jackson, Dinah Washington, Sarah Vaughan

▶▶ Leslie Uggams, Dionne Warwick, Martha Reeves

Ken Burke

Henri Rene
Born Harold Grant, in Germany.

"Toolie-Oolie-Doolie (The Yodel Polka)" was this classically trained composer's biggest hit, in 1948, and his music tended to be just as goofy as that title, with playful rhythms and bizarre boinging noises. Despite a prolific solo career, though, he was most famous for backing singers Perry Como, April Stevens, and Eartha Kitt. As a German youth, Rene began studying at Berlin's Royal Academy of Music; he did orchestra work in the U.S. for a few years in the 1920s, but returned to his native country to arrange for a record company. After emigrating to the U.S. in 1936, he earned a music director job with RCA Victor, formed a small orchestra, then joined the U.S. Army. Throughout the 1950s, in addition to backing the more-prominent singers, he put out several albums of bouncy, playful music that perfectly fit the "space-age bachelor-pad" label—"Hansel and Pretzel" and "Manhattan Idyl" were among his most weird and fun instrumental compositions.

what's available: As is the case with many prominent lounge artists of the 1950s, Rene's archives have so far escaped the CD era. One of his classics, *Riot in Rhythm* ✍✍✍ (RCA Victor, 1959, prod. Herman Diaz), includes "Hansel and Pretzel," but you'll save much time and aggravation by picking up the song on *Cocktail Mix, Vol. 1: Bachelor's Guide to the Galaxy* ✍✍✍ (Rhino, 1995, compilation prod. Irwin Chusid).

influences:

◀◀ Ray Noble, Nelson Riddle, Enoch Light, Paul Weston, Raymond Scott

▶▶ Juan Garcia Esquivel, Martin Denny, Stereolab, Combustible Edison

Steve Knopper

Alvino Rey
Born Alvin McBurney, July 1, 1911, in Oakland, CA.

A historically important musician, Rey worked diligently with the Gibson company to develop the console or pedal steel guitar, and popularized its use in orchestras led by Phil Spitalney, Russ Morgan, Freddy Martin, and Horace Heidt. Rey's jazzy work on this early version of the amplified guitar produced a vibrant, Theremin-like sound which became the basis for the "exotica" genre. Though an immensely popular session man and featured attraction with other bands, Rey had trouble keeping his own groups going during the war years of the '40s. His most popular "sweet" band featured the King Sisters (Rey was married to Louise King) and recorded for the Bluebird and Victor labels before being decimated by military service inductions (including his own). A later, more jazzy incarnation of his orchestra appeared in such films as *Follow the Band* and *Larceny with Music,* but their popularity was stymied by a musicians' union recording ban. After the war, Rey formed another outfit and recorded for Capitol Records with modest success until the end of the big-band era. After several years with smaller combos and tons of studio work, his resurgence came in 1964 via TV's *The King Family Show,* a *Lawrence Welk* knock-off with Rey astonishing audiences by actually seeming to make his steel guitar talk. During the program's five-year run, Rey produced and played on many LPs by the King Sisters and the show's other regulars, though no hint of his jazz background seeped through. Not content to let such a whitebread show be the final word on his career, Rey has stayed active, playing with various small combos and amazing the faithful with his unique steel-guitar style.

what's available: Rey's unusual guitar leads fill up *By Request* ✍✍✍ (Hindsight, 1993, prod. Thomas Gramuglia, Wally Heider), a collection of live radio performances from 1946 with his popular themes "Nighty Night," "Blue Rey," and several jazzy takes on such standards as "April in Paris," "Sheik of Araby," and many others. It's a nice disc, but it's a shame such little material exists from such a groundbreaking artist.

influences:

◀◀ Horace Heidt, Freddy Martin, Russ Morgan

▶▶ Ray Conniff, Juan Garcia Esquivel, George Cates, Martin Denny

Ken Burke

Debbie Reynolds

Born Mary Frances Reynolds, April, 1, 1932, in El Paso, TX.

When Debbie Reynolds wasn't starring in classic motion picture musicals—ranging from 1952's *Singin' in the Rain* to 1966's *The Singing Nun*—she had a nice part-time job as a top recording artist.

Her 1950 duet with Carlton Carpenter on "Abba Dabba Honeymoon" ("Abba dabba-dabba-dabba-dabba-dabba-dabba, said the monkey to the chimp. . . ") from the film *Two Weeks in Love* was a million-seller, but Reynolds was just too busy with her budding movie career to follow up. The 1957 film *Tammy and the Bachelor* (the least moronic entry in the Tammy series) supplied her next major hit. Reynolds's "Tammy" went all the way to #1, fighting off competition from top male stars of the rock 'n' roll era such as Jerry Lee Lewis, Paul Anka, and Buddy Holly. After one subsequent hit, though, she didn't return to the charts until after her messy divorce from pop singer Eddie Fisher. At that point, her version of "Am I That Easy to Forget"—viewed by fans as a pointed jibe at her ex-husband—showed she had the chops to be a compelling country-crossover artist. Still, her focus remained acting, such as her Oscar-nominated turn in *The Unsinkable Molly Brown* and her '70s Broadway smash *Irene*. These were peak Reynolds performances, but outside of soundtrack LPs, no more pop or country discs were forthcoming. In a career wracked by misfortune and heartache, Reynolds has made and lost several fortunes, but through sheer will and enormous talent has always persevered. In the late '80s and early '90s, two highly succesful exercise videos allowed her to cash in on the fitness fad. In 1993, she opened the Debbie Reynolds Hotel. Four years later, the hotel filed for bankruptcy, but Reynolds quickly rebounded with a critically acclaimed role in the Albert Brooks comedy, *Mother*.

what to buy: *Greatest Hits* ♪♪♪♪ (Curb, 1991) is a nice budget-priced collection of Reynolds's big hits, from the children's favorite "Abba Dabba Honeymoon" to the countrypolitan "City Lights."

what to buy next: Two of Reynolds's original LPs are contained on one disc, *Debbie/Am I That Easy to Forget* ♪♪♪♪ (Jasmine Records, 1996, prod. various), with big hits and some surprisingly effective country-crossover sounds.

what to avoid: Unlike the video version of *Do It Debbie's Way* ♪♪ (Baker & Taylor, 1990), it's apparent that Reynolds is not actually exercising on the audiotape. Nice big-band music in the background, though.

Cocktail Classics

Swinging on a Star

18-Karat **Bing Crosby**
Bing's Gold Records
(Decca/MCA)

Bombsville! **The Four Freshmen**
Capitol Sings Kids'
Songs for Grown-Ups
(Capitol)

worth searching for: No one tells her story of great success and monumental disappointments better than Reynolds herself on *Debbie: My Life* ♪♪♪ (Dove Audio Books, 1991), a charmingly frank biography.

influences:

◀◀ Doris Day, Judy Garland

▶▶ Shirley Jones, Julie Andrews

Ken Burke

Tim Rice

See: Andrew Lloyd Webber

Charlie Rich

Born December 14, 1932, in Forest City, AR. Died July 25, 1995, in Hammond, LA.

Rich was the last great singer-songwriter to come out of Sun Records in the late 1950s. A Stan Kenton fan and aspiring jazz performer, Rich's audition for the pioneering Memphis rockabilly label went awry when he voiced the opinion that Sun's biggest selling artist, Jerry Lee Lewis, was a terrible pianist. Producer/arranger Bill Justis pointed out Lewis had just sold 21 million records in less than 18 months and Rich should "come back when you're that bad."

When Rich returned, he worked extensively as a house producer, session pianist, and writer. Rich conjured such melancholy country-jazz gems as "Don't Put No Headstone on My Grave," "Who Will the Next Fool Be," and label chief Sam Phillips's favorite song, "Stay." His fusion of blues, gospel, country, rock, and jazz took the label's sound to a higher, more technically proficient level, while never abandoning the roots music feel Phillips demanded. In 1959, Rich's "Lonely Weekends" hit #22 on the pop charts, but nothing else sold as well. Later, on the RCA label, his work with big-name country producer Chet Atkins produced many wonderful jazz-influenced sides that were either ignored by the public or remained in the can. Then he signed with Smash/Mercury, where he recorded the jivey "Mohair Sam," a Top 30 hit. Finally, in 1967, producer Billy Sherrill (another Sun Records veteran) brought Rich to Epic Records, where the producer-artist duo slowly established a slicker, more countrypolitan (which is to say, lounge-worthy) style. "I Take It on Home," one of the bluesiest why-I-don't-cheat songs ever, was a Top 10 country hit, and its similarly themed follow-up "Behind Closed Doors," became one of the biggest country-crossover smashes of all time. In 1974, Rich won the Country Music Association's Entertainer of the Year award, and his Epic hit string continued with "My Elusive Dreams," "Every Time You Touch Me (I Get High)," and "All Over Me." Always a reticent personality, after the first flush of his great success, Rich withdrew—drinking and behaving erratically, on stage and off. As a presenter at the 1975 CMA Awards, an inebriated Rich jokingly set fire to the envelope holding the name of the new Entertainer of the Year (John Denver). The big hits, despite one final #1 country single, "Rollin' with the Flow," slowed down after that. In the '80s, Rich recorded for Elektra, took the reins of his own management, and appeared in a Dr. Pepper commercial just before he seemed to disappear from the entertainment world. He resurfaced in 1992 to make his last LP, the jazzy, critically acclaimed

Pictures & Paintings, recorded in a studio owned by Sam Phillips in Memphis, Tennessee.

what to buy: A great introduction to the "Silver Fox," *Feel Like Going Home: The Essential Charlie Rich* ♫♫♫♫ (Columbia/Legacy, 1997, prod. Sam Phillips, Chet Atkins, Billy Sherrill, Scott Billington) culls Rich's most interesting tracks from his eras with Sun, RCA-Groove, Mercury, and Epic. Rich's best early recordings and a few poignant song demos are featured on *Lonely Weekends: Best of the Sun Years* ♫♫♫♫ (AVI, 1996, prod. Sam Phillips), where he demonstrated he could rock with the best.

what to buy next: Rich's years as a sometimes bluesy, mostly countrypolitan chart-topper are chronicled on *American Originals* ♫♫♫♫ (Columbia, 1989, prod. Billy Sherrill), *Greatest Hits* ♫♫♫♫ (Epic, 1996, prod. Billy Sherrill), and *Super Hits* ♫♫♫♪ (Epic, 1995, prod. Billy Sherrill), all available at budget prices. However, his best start-to-finish LP was his last, *Pictures & Paintings* ♫♫♫♫ (Sire, 1992, prod. Scott Billington), which includes a wonderful, melancholy version of "Feel Like Going Home." *Complete Smash Sessions* ♫♫♫♫ (Mercury, 1992, prod. Jerry Kennedy) features the bluesy hit "Mohair Sam" and many unjustly neglected mid-1960s tracks. Rich's days with another famous Memphis label, Hi Records, are cohesively packaged on *Sings Hank Williams Plus . . .* ♫♫♫ (Diablo Records, 1994, prod. various).

the rest:
That's Rich ♫♫♫ (RCA, 1965/Charly, 1996)
Set Me Free ♫♫♪ (Epic, 1968/Koch International, 1995)
The Fabulous Charlie Rich ♫♫♫♪ (Epic, 1969/Koch International, 1994)
Boss Man ♫♫♫ (Epic, 1970/Koch International 1994)
Behind Closed Doors ♫♫♫♫ (Epic, 1973)
Midnight Blues ♫♫♫ (Quicksilver, 1993)
The Sun Sessions ♫♫♫♫ (Varese Vintage, 1996)

worth searching for: Rich was intensely prolific at the beginning of his career, as *Original Hits & Midnight Demos* ♫♫♫♫ (Charly, 1990, prod. Sam Phillips) attests. His demo sessions, with just voice and piano, are strikingly intimate, and the material runs from the sublime ("Stay," "Sittin' & Thinkin'") to the ridiculous ("Popcorn Polly").

influences:

◄◄ Elvis Presley, Ray Charles, Stan Kenton, Jerry Lee Lewis

►► Ray Smith, Bobby "Blue" Bland, Ronnie Milsap

Ken Burke

Cliff Richard

Born Harry Roger Webb, October 14, 1940, in Lucknow, India.

Richard was mostly missing in action during the '60s British Invasion, yet it couldn't have taken place without him. Richard's early work with his band, the Shadows, helped establish England's rock industry, and inspired the dozens of acts (both pro- and anti-Richard) who would eventually change the course of pop-music history.

Richard began his career with Dick Teague's Skiffle Group in 1957, but left to form his first rock 'n' roll band, Harry Webb and the Drifters, when musical trends changed. Promotion men eventually changed the lead singer's name to Cliff Richard (the band didn't become the Shadows until 1960). Richard's initial recordings on EMI were fairly respectable Elvis Presley–style pop-rock, and with regular exposure on Jack Good's television program *Oh Boy!,* songs such as "Move It Over," "Living Doll," and "Traveling Light" became massive British hits. The Shadows, led by England's first guitar hero, Hank Marvin, compounded their success by releasing hit instrumentals such as "Apache," "Man of Mystery," and "Wonderful Land"—the Shadows became the model for all British rock 'n' roll bands, and Marvin was the guy that kids like Pete Townsend, Jimmy Page, and Mark Knopfler wanted to be when they grew up. Richard's boy-next-door good looks made him a natural for movies, and, like Presley, he appeared in a few fine films, such as *Espresso Bongo* and *Serious Charge,* before sinking into a morass of lightweight (though highly profitable) drive-in fare. As the '60s progressed, Richard widened his U.K. appeal with more easy-listening pop ballads, but alienated many of the hardcore British rockers for whom he opened the doors. Though Richard made a strong appearance on *The Ed Sullivan Show* a full two years before the Beatles, he never quite caught on with American audiences. Cover versions of Tommy Edwards's "It's All in the Game" and Ruth Brown's "Lucky Lips" were his strongest-charting U.S. singles during the Fab Four–era, though he remained a powerhouse at home well into the '70s. Richard retooled his look for the glam-pop crowd and finally broke into the American Top 10 with "Devil Woman" in 1978 (a record seemingly at odds with his image as a born-again Christian). "We Don't Talk Anymore," "Dreamin'," "Suddenly" (with Olivia Newton-John), and several others peppered the U.S. charts well into the '80s. Whether recording solo or dueting with the likes of Elton John, Van Morrison, or Phil Everly, Richard is still cutting hit records on a fairly regular basis in England. More than 100 of his records have reached the U.K. charts. Does that make him the British King of Rock 'n' Roll? Maybe not, but he is bona fide royalty, having been knighted Sir Cliff Richard.

what to buy: A strong compilation of Richard's later work, *The Cliff Richard Collection (1976–1994)* 🎵🎵🎵 (Razor & Tie, 1994, compilation prod. Mike Ragogna) features his big glitz and glam-pop hits "Devil Woman," "We Don't Talk Any More," "Dreamin'," and hit duets with Elton John and Olivia Newton-John. Two other collections can be found in some import racks and catalog services: Richard's days as an influential British teen-idol are well-documented on *40 Golden Greats* 🎵🎵🎵 (Virgin, 1993, prod. various), which includes his best rocking sides with the Shadows as well as gushier '60s pop numbers; *Hit List* 🎵🎵🎵 (EMI, 1995, prod. various) is more concise, mixing his biggest-charting records from all phases of his career.

what to avoid: Unless you wish to hear Richard's many European hits sung in phonetic German, French, Italian, or Spanish, steer clear of *On the Continent* 🎵🎵 (Bear Family, 1998, reissue prod. Richard Weize), a five-disc, 102-song set that beats dead horses in all the aforementioned languages.

influences:

⏮ Lonnie Donegan, Elvis Presley, Tommy Steele, Terry Dene

⏭ Adam Faith, Vince Taylor, Billy Fury

Ken Burke

Jonathan Richman

Born May 16, 1951, in Boston, MA.

It took Richman a few decades to find the lounge. He started out as a clean-cut boy from a middle-class suburb during, curiously enough, the glorious heyday of cock-rock, when Led Zeppelin and Emerson, Lake and Palmer made amazing guitar licks and sexy, masculine singers requisites for rock radio. He was no Robert Plant. He had short hair, looked half his age (still does), and didn't do drugs. Mesmerized by the underground art-punk group Velvet Underground, Richman, then 18, moved to New York City, then returned to Boston to form the Modern Lovers with keyboardist Jerry Harrison (later in Talking Heads), drummer David Robinson (later in the Cars), and bassist Ernie Brooks. Warner Bros. was interested and brought in ex–Velvet Underground violist John Cale to produce a handful of demos, including "Roadrunner" and "Pablo Picasso," with its opening, "Some people try to pick up girls and get called asshole/This never happened to Pablo Picasso." The tapes inexplicably sat untouched for three years. When finally released, the demo collection *The Modern Lovers* made Richman a punk hero, his songs covered by Alex Chilton, the Sex Pistols, and Joan Jett.

By then, Richman had sworn off loud music, dissolved the original Modern Lovers, and pledged to play only high schools and hospitals. Richman's new Modern Lovers hit the streets at the same time as the Warner Bros. material. The music was stripped-down 1950s rock, the lyrics over-the-top, including titles like "Abominable Snowman in the Market" and "Hey There Little Insect." For a time, this childlike persona bugged just about everyone, especially those aching to hear the Cale demos played live. But Richman pressed on and, slowly, his lounge persona emerged, especially in his charmingly cheesy covers—"The Wheels on the Bus," "Blue Moon," "The Rose," and "The Heart of Saturday Night." A series of spots on the Conan O'Brien show solidified Richman's camp status. After more than two decades of doing the same thing, Richman has developed a loyal following for what he is: quick-witted, innocent, nostalgic, sometimes cloying, and always ready to play.

what to buy: Most of the songs on *Jonathan, Te Vas a Emocionar* ♫♫♫ (Rounder, 1994, prod. Brennan Totten) have been previously recorded, but there's a fresh spirit of schmaltz here, from the Latin-tinged piano on "No Te Oye" to the slashing acoustic guitar on the instrumental, "Melodia Traditional Ecuadoriana." It's some of Richman's strongest singing yet—with one catch: it's all in Spanish. For a trusty survey of Richman's 1970s work, go for *The Beserkley Years* ♫♫♫♫ (Rhino, 1986, prod. Bill Inglot), which starts with a few of the Cale demos (including "Roadrunner") and spins through 1979's "Back in Your Life."

what to buy next: Recorded after a four-year silence, *Jonathan Sings!* ♫♫♫ (Sire, 1983, prod. Peter Bernstein) features a full backing band and our fearless leader with a really bad cold on at least one song. The rhythm and bop of "Somebody to Hold Me" and "Stop This Car" are well worth the price of admission. For a good dose of late period Richman, try *Having a Party with Jonathan Richman* ♫♫♫♫ (Rounder, 1991, prod. Brennan Totten). For something truly different, there's *Jonathan Goes Country* ♫♫♫ (Rounder, 1990, prod. Lou Whitney, D. Clinton Thompson), which generated a smattering of sneers from the country intellegencia who considered it insulting (despite the presence of the Skeletons and Richman's contribution to the country canon, "Reno").

the rest:
Modern Lovers ♫♫♫♫ (Beserkley, 1976/Rhino, 1989)
Jonathan Richman and the Modern Lovers ♫♫♫ (Beserkley, 1976)

Rock 'N' Roll With ♫♫♫ (Beserkley, 1976)
Live ♫♫♫♫ (Beserkley, 1977)
Back in Your Life ♫♫♫ (Beserkley, 1979)
The Original Modern Lovers ♫♫♫ (Bomp!, 1981)
Rockin & Romance ♫♫♫♫ (Twin/Tone, 1985)
It's Time for Jonathan Richman ♫♫♫ (Upside, 1986)
Modern Lovers '88 ♫♫♫ (Rounder, 1987)
Jonathan Richman ♫♫♫♫ (Rounder, 1989)
23 Great Recordings by Jonathan Richman and the Modern Lovers ♫♫♫ (Castle Comm., 1990)
I, Jonathan ♫♫♫♫ (Rounder, 1992)
Precise Modern Lovers Order ♫♫♫ (Rounder, 1994)
You Must Ask the Heart ♫♫♫♫ (Rounder, 1995)
Surrender to Jonathan ♫♫♫ (Vapor, 1996)

influences:

◀◀ The Velvet Underground, Chuck Berry

▶▶ The Violent Femmes, Papas Fritas

Geoff Edgers

Nelson Riddle

Born June 1, 1921, in Oradell, NJ. Died October 6, 1985, in Los Angeles, CA.

His long and profitable associations as an arranger for performers like Judy Garland, Nat King Cole, Frank Sinatra, Johnny Mathis, Ella Fitzgerald, and others has ensured that Riddle's name is rarely the first one mentioned in his capsule biographies. He started as a trombonist for Tommy Dorsey and other bandleaders in the mid-'40s and quickly moved on to arranging, working first with Garland, then with Cole, and finally with Sinatra on a trio of landmark mid-'50s albums, *In the Wee Small Hours*, *Songs for Young Lovers/Swing Easy*, and *Songs for Swingin' Lovers!* That these are Sinatra's finest albums is due in large part to Riddle's superbly nuanced arrangements and orchestration. His sense of timing, especially, is faultless, and his control of his orchestra masterful. After the release of these albums Riddle was in high demand as an arranger. As a solo artist, he also recorded several easy-listening and orchestral versions of pop songs, including the Beatles' "I Want to Hold Your Hand," and worked as a television and film composer, creating the theme for *The Untouchables* and *Route 66* and scoring films like *The Pajama Game*. Illness sidelined Riddle in the late '70s, but he returned to arrange a trio of albums for Linda Ronstadt, including the Grammy-winning *What's New* in 1983, as well as a project for opera singer Kiri Te Kanawa.

what to buy: *Songs for Swingin' Lovers!* ♫♫♫♫♫ (Capitol, 1956, prod. Voyle Gilmore) is Sinatra's outright masterpiece, with classics like "You Make Me Feel So Young," "I Thought About You," "It Happened in Monterey," and many more. It's Sinatra's album, of course, but it's Riddle's too—his overall vision as arranger makes this a true collaboration.

what to buy next: *The Best of Nelson Riddle* &&&& (Curb, 1997, prod. Don Ovens) is a budget collection of Riddle's best performances as an artist, including "Lisbon Antigua," "Ramblin' Rose," "Walkin' My Baby Back Home," "I Want to Hold Your Hand," and the *Route 66* theme.

worth searching for: Get a sense of Riddle's later work with Linda Ronstadt's *What's New* &&& (Asylum, 1983, prod. Peter Asher) and Kiri Te Kanawa's *Blue Skies* &&& (London, 1985, prod. Don Lewzey).

influences:

◄◄ Gordon Jenkins, Axel Stordahl, George Siravo

►► Billy May, Johnny Mandel, Neal Hefti, Quincy Jones

Ben Greenman

Minnie Riperton

See: Rotary Connection

Howard Roberts

Born October 2, 1929, in Phoenix, AZ. Died June, 1992.

You've probably heard Howard Roberts's guitar hundreds, possibly thousands, of times without even knowing it. In addition to his own career as an eclectic instrumental jazz artist throughout the 1950s, 1960s, and 1970s, Roberts was a ubiquitous session guitarist, playing on literally thousands of dates. A small sampling: he recorded for the TV programs *I Dream of Jeannie* and *The Twilight Zone*; played on the soundtracks of *The Pink Panther* and *West Side Story*; appeared on hit records by the Beach Boys, Pat Boone, Dean Martin, Lou Rawls, Elvis Presley, and the Monkees; and recorded with jazzmen Art Pepper, Jimmy Smith, Shorty Rogers, Bobby Troup, and Buddy Rich. Roberts played in a fluid jazz style that was at once subtle and awe-inspiring. Also a guitar educator, he co-founded the Guitar Institute of Technology in Los Angeles and created the Playback Publishing Co., which produced guitar instructional materials.

what to buy: *The Real Howard Roberts* &&&& (Concord Jazz, 1978/1994, prod. Carl E. Jefferson) showcases Roberts's warm, clean tone as he embraces the work of Herbie Hancock, Miles Davis, and Jimmy Van Heusen to name a few.

what to buy next: *The Magic Band, Live at Donte's* &&& (VSOP, 1995, engineer George Jerman) was recorded in July 1968 at Donte's in Los Angeles and features Tom Scott on alto and soprano saxophones. It's a wide-open, improvisational set, with five songs totaling more than 70 minutes, and the shortest track clocking in at more than 12 minutes. The cover of Miles Davis's "All Blues" is worth the purchase price alone. Roberts's play is more boistrous and aggressive than his work on the Concord set, which is more structured. The contrast makes the two releases excellent complements to one another. Buy them both.

worth searching for: Despite Roberts's active recording career, virtually all of his albums are out of print. For starters, find *H.R. Is a Dirty Guitar Player* &&& (Capitol, 1963), *Color Him Funky* &&& (Capitol, 1963), or *Mr. Roberts Plays Guitar* &&& (Verve 1957/1981). Good luck.

influences:

◄◄ Andres Segovia, Barney Kessel, Charlie Parker, Igor Stravinsky, Bela Bartok

►► Steve Morse, Pat Metheny

Bryan Powell

Paul Robeson

Born April 9, 1898, in Princeton, NJ. Died January 23, 1976, in Philadelphia, PA.

Robeson's basso profundo served him well in acting, both on stage (in 1921's *Simon the Cyrenian* and 1924's *All God's Chillun Got Wings*) and on screen (such as 1936's *Show Boat* and 1938's *Jericho*). It also made any Robeson recording an experience. His biggest hit, of course, was his 1928 version of Jerome Kern's "Ol' Man River," later covered by Ray Charles. Robeson's career was finally derailed by official government harrassment throughout the 1940s and 1950s over his political views—he was a socialist, visited the Soviet Union, and was outspoken in his condemnation of racism. He died in 1976 after a long illness.

what to buy: *Ballad for Americans* &&&&& (Vanguard, 1965) doesn't have "Ol' Man River," but it has almost everything else—spirituals, folk songs, and traditional ballads, such as "Scandalize My Name," "Go Down Moses," "Joshua Fit the Battle of Jericho," "Sometimes I Feel Like a Motherless Child," and Cole Porter's "All Through the Night."

what to buy next: *The Power & the Glory* &&&&& (Columbia/ Legacy, 1991) is almost as good, with a stronger emphasis on spirituals and work songs ("John Henry," "Water Boy," and a wonderful "No More Auction Block"). *The Essential Paul Robe-*

Son 𝄟𝄟𝄟 (Vanguard, 1987) is a little diffuse, but it does have "Ol' Man River," along with "Volga Boat Song," "John Brown's Body," "Joe Hill," and others.

what to avoid: *Voice of the Mississippi* 𝄟𝄟𝄟 (Prism, 1997) is a quickie package, a set of Robeson songs slapped together without any apparent rhyme or reason. If you buy this, you'll still get majestic vocals, but the frustration with the shoddy product may be too much to take.

worth searching for: *Big Fella* 𝄟𝄟𝄟𝄟 (Conifer, 1994) collects several early performances recorded while Robeson was in England making movies, and doesn't have any songs recorded later than 1941. As a result, the album finds the singer in peak form, performing traditionals, cabaret songs, and American standards.

influences:

◀◀ Al Jolson

▶▶ Ray Charles, the Weavers, Harry Belafonte, Josh White, Odetta

Ben Greenman

Richard Rodgers /Rodgers & Hammerstein /Rodgers & Hart

Born June 28, 1902, in New York City, NY. Died December 30, 1979, in New York City, NY.

Rodgers wasn't the first to write popular Broadway musicals, but the musician and his lyric-writing partners—first Lorenz Hart (born May 2, 1895, in New York City, NY; died November 22, 1943, in New York City, NY), then Oscar Hammerstein II (born July 12, 1895, in New York City, NY; died August 23, 1960, in Doylestown, PA)—created *A Connecticut Yankee, The King and I, The Sound of Music, Carousel, South Pacific,* and *Oklahoma!* to name a few of the most enduring shows in history. In the process they created the blueprint for today's Broadway, from Andrew Lloyd Webber's *Cats* to Pete Townshend's rock opera *The Who's Tommy.*

Some of this century's greatest singers based their entire careers on signature versions of Rodgers's songs—crooner Gordon MacRae will forever be remembered as the ambitious hick who sang about the tall corn in *Oklahoma!*'s "Oh, What a Beautiful Mornin'," and singer Mary Martin, for all her other accomplishments, will always be the hair-washing Navy nurse Nellie Forbush in *South Pacific.* No less than the most popular singers

of this century—Judy Garland, Nancy Wilson, Al Martino, Peggy Lee, Nelson Eddy, Julie Andrews—performed the songwriting teams' material. Until Elvis Presley, Bob Dylan, and the Beatles came along to rewrite the rules, most songwriters followed the formula set by Irving Berlin and Cole Porter in an earlier era. Rodgers and his two partners wrote shows, and hoped popular singer-actors would turn them into hits.

Rodgers, son of a doctor father and pianist mother, began copyrighting songs and writing for amateur shows at age 15. As a Columbia University student, he met the older Lorenz Hart, a witty lyric writer who emulated W.S. Gilbert of Gillbert and Sullivan, and the two began a prolific partnership. At first, publishers adamantly rejected their stabs at musical comedy, and Rodgers was ready to begin selling children's underwear. But they hooked up with the Junior Section of the Theatre Guild, penned the surprisingly popular 1925 musical *The Garric Gaieties,* and success followed quickly. The pair penned almost 30 shows, including *A Connecticut Yankee* and *Babes in Arms,* but after several years, Hart, an alcoholic, became erratic and unreliable and Rodgers had to look elsewhere for the right lyrical fit. He found Hammerstein, son of a theater manager and a writer who preferred big sentimental shows (as compared to Hart's more upscale, almost snobby, style), and the two immediately collaborated on a play, *Green Grow the Lilacs.* No less than the most popular musicals in American history followed—1943's *Oklahoma!,* 1945's *Carousel,* 1949's *South Pacific,* 1951's *The King and I,* and 1959's *The Sound of Music*—almost all of which subsequently reproduced their stage success on film. Just as the shows both teams wrote are regularly revived on Broadway, and many of the film versions have become classics, the individual songs have endured as well. "My Funny Valentine" (from Rodgers and Hart's *Babes in Arms*) became a classic Miles Davis album, and the kids' classic "My Favorite Things" (from *The Sound of Music*) went through a 17-minute live workout by pioneering jazz saxophonist John Coltrane. When Hammerstein died in 1960, Rodgers maintained a decent writing career, collaborating occasionally with younger names such as Stephen Sondheim. He died in 1979, when his musicals' straightforward moral messages had lost just about all their relevance to contemporary theater goers—two years later, his innocent young *Sound of Music* actress, Julie Andrews, bared her breasts in the film *S.O.B.*

what to buy: Every time a new cast revives an old Rodgers & Hart or Rodgers & Hammerstein musical, a soundtrack album shows up someplace. So don't look simply for the Rodgers name when buying a CD, go for the best cast. *Capitol Sings Rodgers & Hammerstein* 𝄟𝄟𝄟𝄟 (Capitol, 1994, compilation prod. Brad Benedict) contains some of the better-sung versions of the team's work—standouts are Gordon MacRae and Ray Anthony with their *Oklahoma!* film hit "The Surrey with the Fringe on Top," Peggy Lee making like a jazz chanteuse on "Something Wonderful," Judy Garland doing "You'll Never Walk Alone," and Tennessee Ernie Ford adding a touch of country on "My Favorite Things." The original cast album for *Oklahoma!* 𝄢𝄢𝄢𝄢 (Sony Broadway, 1951/1993, prod. Goddard Lieberson) features Nelson Eddy in a key role; *The King and I* 𝄢𝄢𝄢𝄢 (Sony Broadway, 1964/1993) has Barbara Cook; and *The Best of Rodgers and Hammerstein* 𝄢𝄢𝄢𝄢 (Laserlight, 1994, prod. various) includes classic snippets from *The Sound of Music, Carousel, The King and I,* and others.

what to buy next: Rodgers & Hart material hasn't endured quite as well as Rodgers & Hammerstein, which explains the lack of recorded material available on CD. However, singers Lena Horne and Bing Crosby are among the stars on *With a Song in Their Hearts* 𝄢𝄢𝄢𝄢 (Avid, 1996).

what to avoid: Unless you're fanatical about today's theater productions, or the names Victoria Clark, Jason Graae, and Alyson Reed give you goosebumps, there's no real reason to buy *A Grand Night for Singing* 𝄢𝄢 (Varese Sarabande, 1994) above the better-known original cast soundtrack CDs. Still, there are nice selections from *Cinderella, Carousel,* and others.

best of the rest:

Show Boat 𝄢𝄢𝄢𝄢 (Sony Broadway, 1946/1993)
Mary Martin Sings Richard Rodgers 𝄢𝄢𝄢𝄢 (RCA Victor, 1990)
Victory at Sea 𝄢𝄢𝄢 (RCA Victor, 1992)
More Victory at Sea 𝄢𝄢𝄢 (RCA Victor, 1992)
The Boys from Syracuse 𝄢𝄢𝄢 (Sony Broadway, 1993)
Rodgers and Hammerstein Song Book 𝄢𝄢𝄢 (Sony, 1993)
South Pacific 𝄢𝄢𝄢𝄢 (Sony Broadway, 1993)
Carousel 𝄢𝄢 (Angel, 1994)
Broadway—10 Show Stoppers 𝄢𝄢𝄢 (Michele, 1994)
Bravissimo/Richard Rodgers 𝄢𝄢𝄢 (Centaur, 1996)

worth searching for: Just as Charlie Parker rearranged popular showtune melodies of his day (usually written by the Gershwins), bebop pioneers Miles Davis and John Coltrane took on the work of Richard Rodgers. Davis's *The Complete Concert 1964/My Funny Valentine + Four & More* 𝄢𝄢𝄢𝄢𝄢 (Columbia/Legacy, 1992, prod. Teo Macero) includes a wonderful 15-minute version of the Rodgers & Hart classic "My Funny Valentine." The great trumpeter improvises frenetically, almost to the point where the original melody is unrecognizable, but always keeps the romantic tone of the original song. It's an amazing performance. *The John Coltrane Anthology* 𝄢𝄢𝄢𝄢𝄢

Cocktail Classics

That Old Black Magic

18-Karat Louis Prima & Keely Smith
Louis Prima: Capitol Collector's Series
(Capitol)

Bombsville! Kevin Spacey
Midnight in the Garden of Good and Evil (Soundtrack)
(Malpaso/Warner Bros.)

(Rhino/Atlantic Jazz, 1993, compilation prod. Joel Dorn) includes both studio and 17-minute live versions of Rodgers & Hammerstein's *Sound of Music* classic, "My Favorite Things," stretching the song into a series of brilliant and occasionally squawky solos. If you listen carefully, as members of the Doors undoubtedly did, you can hear the blueprint for the band's rock classic "Light My Fire." So indirectly, Julie Andrews was an inspiration for Jim Morrison, and there you have it.

influences:

◀◀ Gilbert & Sullivan, Cole Porter, Irving Berlin, Jerome Kern, Hoagy Carmichael, Al Jolson

Richard Rodgers (l) and Oscar Hammerstein **(AP/Wide World Photos)**

▶▶ Julie Andrews, Gordon MacRae, Stephen Sondheim, Andrew Lloyd Webber, John Coltrane, Miles Davis, Paul McCartney, Jo Stafford

Steve Knopper

Ginger Rogers
See: Fred Astaire

Kenny Rogers
Born Kenneth Donald Rogers, August 21, 1938, in Houston, TX.

Rogers is fabulously wealthy now, having attained the kind of stardom in country music during the 1970s that only Garth Brooks has managed to surpass since. Though his idiom is country, his entire persona—from the soothing beard to middle-of-the-road signature songs like "The Gambler"—screams "easy listening." He's a mainstay at casino theaters and adult-contemporary radio stations all over the country.

He came from a poor family in Houston, where he played in a high school rockabilly band and eventually released a couple of singles, including the 1956 national hit "Crazy Feeling," that were popular enough to get him on *American Bandstand*. Several members of his early bands formed First Edition, a folk-rock group that Rogers fronted. Though the group's first taste of success was a quasi-psychedelic reading of Mickey Newbury's "Just Dropped In (To See What Condition My Condition Was In," it wasn't until a few years later, as Kenny Rogers and the First Edition, that they cracked the Top 10 with "Ruby, Don't Take Your Love to Town," a heartbreaking account of a wheelchair-bound Vietnam vet whose lover is unfaithful. Rogers went solo in 1973 with the help of producer Larry Butler, who had a knack for finding easy, light country songs that suited Rogers's pleasant but thin wisp of a voice. He had several hits, including "Lucille" and "Daytime Friends," but his popularity reached unprecedented heights after the story-song "The Gambler" paid huge dividends as both a country and pop hit in 1978. Rogers would rule those charts for nearly 10 years after that, teaming with duet partners like Dottie West and Sheena Easton while collaborating with such pop heavyweights as Lionel Richie, who wrote and produced Rogers's smash version of the ballad "Lady." By the time Rogers's *Greatest Hits* came out, retailers couldn't keep his records in the stores and his concerts typically sold out. Rogers, wary of fickle audience tastes, took measures to ensure his continued stardom, turning "The Gambler" into a series of TV movies (five in all) while branching out into such other areas as clothing lines. His career cooled considerably during the mid-1980s: his duet with Dolly Parton on the Barry Gibb-penned schlock ballad "Islands in the Stream" was one of his last big hits and his concert audiences dwindled. He keeps plugging away with popular Christmas tours, a chain of fast-food chicken restaurants, and, most recently, a Christmas album, *The Gift*, which topped the contemporary Christian charts late in 1996.

what to buy: Rogers's career was at its zenith in 1980 when the singer with the peppery black and grey hair and raspy, woodsy voice could do no wrong. His *20 Greatest Hits* 🎵🎵🎵 (Liberty, 1983, prod. Larry Butler, Lionel Richie, David Foster, David Malloy, Kenny Rogers) is a pretty complete snapshot of that period, spanning the best of the First Edition with his biggest hits up to that point, from "Just Dropped In . . ." and "Ruby" to "Don't Fall in Love with a Dreamer," a duet with Kim Carnes.

what to buy next: *Kenny Rogers' Greatest Hits* 🎵🎵🎵 (Liberty, 1980, prod. Larry Butler, Lionel Richie, Kenny Rogers) isn't as extensive, but this multi-platinum collection captures most of that period with fewer songs, while *Ten Years of Gold* 🎵🎵🎵 (EMI America, 1977, prod. Larry Butler, Kenny Rogers) nicely sums up his First Edition and early country years.

what to avoid: *Timepiece: Orchestral Sessions with David Foster* 🎵 (Atlantic, 1994, prod. David Foster) was an unabashed attempt to jump on Natalie Cole's career-rejuvenating *Unforgettable* bandwagon. It sounds just like what you'd expect at this point in his career: a desperate singer teamed up with a schmaltzy producer to tackle treacle like "You Are So Beautiful" and such classy standards as Rodgers & Hart's "My Funny Valentine."

the rest:
Kenny 🎵🎵 (Razor & Tie, 1979)
Gideon 🎵🎵 (Razor & Tie, 1980)
Share Your Love 🎵🎵 (Liberty, 1982)
We've Got Tonight 🎵🎵🎵 (Liberty, 1983)
Greatest Hits 🎵🎵🎵 (RCA, 1983)
Eyes that See in the Dark 🎵🎵🎵 (RCA, 1983)
What about Me 🎵🎵 (RCA, 1984)

Duets 🎵🎵 (EMI America, 1984)
Once upon a Christmas 🎵🎵🎵 (RCA, 1984)
The Heart of the Matter 🎵🎵 (RCA, 1985)
They Don't Make Them Like They Used To 🎵🎵 (RCA, 1986)
I Prefer the Moonlight 🎵🎵🎵 (RCA, 1987)
25 Greatest Hits 🎵🎵🎵 (EMI America, 1987)
A Kenny Rogers Christmas 🎵🎵 (Capitol, 1987)
(With the First Edition) *The Best of Kenny Rogers and First Edition* 🎵🎵🎵 (K-Tel, 1987)
(With the First Edition) *Greatest Hits* 🎵🎵🎵 (MCA, 1987)
20 Great Years 🎵🎵🎵 (Reprise, 1988)
Something Inside So Strong 🎵🎵 (Reprise, 1989)
Christmas in America 🎵🎵🎵 (Reprise, 1989)
Love Is Strange 🎵🎵 (Reprise, 1990)
Back Home Again 🎵🎵 (Reprise, 1991)
(With the First Edition) *Lucille and Other Classics* 🎵🎵🎵 (CEMA Special Product, 1992)
The Best of Kenny Rogers 🎵🎵 (CEMA Special Products, 1992)
Heart to Heart 🎵🎵 (RCA Special Products, 1992)
The Ultimate Kenny Rogers 🎵🎵🎵 (Bransounds, 1994)
The Gift 🎵🎵🎵 (Magnatone, 1996)
(With the First Edition) *Greatest Hits* 🎵🎵🎵 (Hip-O, 1996)

worth searching for: One of the first production jobs Rogers ever took was for a little-known band called Shiloh in 1970. He produced their debut album, *Shiloh* 🎵🎵🎵🎵 (Amos, 1970), which has been out of print in the United States for years. The group had two noteworthy members, a pianist and guitarist named Jim Ed Norman, who would become Rogers's producer and the head of Warner Bros. Nashville, and drummer Don Henley of Eagles fame.

influences:

◀◀ The Kingston Trio, Merle Haggard

▶▶ Dolly Parton, Neil Diamond, Bob Seger

Doug Pullen

Rolley Polley
Formed 1960s.

Bobby Black, arranger; other members unknown.

This '60s space-age Latin-tinged lounge group has only one single in print, "Blue Rhumba," a Bobby Black–arranged romp available on two modern-day lounge-music CD collections. According to Rhino Records liner notes, "Blue Rhumba" originally appeared on *Mad Drums: Swinging Percussion Sounds featuring Bongos, Congas, Tom-Toms, and Traps*, a 1960 Capitol release, and was reissued a year later on Capitol's *!Wild! Stereo Drums*. On the latter, "Blue Rhumba" is credited to Latin per-

cussionist Pepe Dominguin, so apparently Rolley Polley was a pseudonym. The career of the band should be further explored in an upcoming episode of *The X-Files*.

what's available: "Blue Rhumba" is on the excellent mood-enhancing *Cocktail Mix, Vol. 1: Bachelor's Guide to the Galaxy* ♪♪♪♪ (Rhino, 1996, prod. Bill Inglot) and *Ultra-Lounge, Vol. 9: Cha Cha De Amor* ♪♪♪♪ (Capitol, 1996, compilation prod. Brad Benedict), a CD that dares you to not dance.

influences:

◄◄ The Three Suns, Juan Garcia Esquivel, Martin Denny

►► Combustible Edison

Alex Gordon

Linda Ronstadt

Born July 15, 1946, in Tucson, AZ.

Rarely hitting with songs that weren't already popularized or recorded by other artists, Linda Ronstadt grew into one of the top female solo performers of the 1970s, thanks to smart choices and tough performances. When she shifted away from Top 40, people noticed. Her 1980s trilogy of albums with bandleader Nelson Riddle began a mainstream revitalization of pop standards that continues today. Ronstadt's career began with California's Stone Poneys, a folk trio spawned in the late 1960s. The hit single, "Different Drum," served as her launching pad to a solo career; she left in 1968. Her early 1970s country-rock albums featured backing musicians who later banded together as the Eagles. That band, along with Fleetwood Mac and Ronstadt, defined the laid-back Southern California rock sound synonymous with the 1970s. By the end of the decade, Ronstadt had drawn on folk, country, rock, and new wave in building her platinum catalog. As her chart potency dipped in the early 1980s, she turned to pop standards, partnering with legendary arranger-conductor Riddle, who famously backed Frank Sinatra and many others. Since the mid-1980s, Ronstadt has dabbled in traditional country, Mexican and Spanish folk songs, and middle-of-the-road pop fare.

what to buy: *What's New* ♪♪♪♪ (Asylum, 1983, prod. Peter Asher) is the first and best of her three Riddle-arranged albums of standards, including charming performances of the title track, "What'll I Do," and "I Don't Stand a Ghost of a Chance."

Greatest Hits, Vol. 1 ♪♪♪♪ (Asylum, 1976, prod. Peter Asher) collects her essential singles and key album tracks up to 1975, while *Greatest Hits, Vol. 2* ♪♪♪♪ (Asylum, 1980, prod. Peter Asher) does the same for her 1976–80 output. *Heart Like a Wheel* ♪♪♪♪ (Capitol, 1974, prod. Peter Asher) began Ronstadt's long association with producer Asher, with whom she worked up some unforgettable arrangements and performances ("When Will I Be Loved," "You're No Good").

what to buy next: *Different Drum* ♪♪♪ (Capitol, 1974, prod. Chip Douglas, Elliott Mazer, John Boylan) includes the Mike Nesmith–penned title track and other stand-outs from Ronstadt's first three solo albums. The bluest of her lounge trilogy, *Sentimental Reasons* ♪♪♪ (Asylum, 1986, prod. Peter Asher) is most noteworthy for its haunting version of the jazz classic "Round Midnight." *Trio* ♪♪♪♪ (Warner Bros., 1987, prod. George Massenburg) has Dolly Parton and Emmylou Harris joining Ronstadt for a sweetly sung collection of country that enlivened the new traditionalist movement in that genre.

what to avoid: *Get Closer* ♪♪ (Asylum, 1982, prod. Peter Asher) was Ronstadt's last roll of the dice in Top 40 rock 'n' roll, and the lackluster performances and material suggest her heart wasn't in it.

the rest:

Hand Sown Home Grown ♪♪ (Capitol, 1969)
Silk Purse ♪♪♪ (Capitol, 1970)
Linda Ronstadt ♪♪♪ (Capitol, 1971)
Don't Cry Now ♪♪♪ (Asylum, 1973)
Prisoner in Disguise ♪♪♪♪ (Asylum, 1975)
The Stone Poneys featuring Linda Ronstadt ♪♪ (Capitol, 1975)
Hasten Down the Wind ♪♪♪ (Asylum, 1976)
Simple Dreams ♪♪♪♪ (Asylum, 1977)
Living in the U.S.A. ♪♪♪ (Asylum, 1978)
Mad Love ♪♪♪ (Asylum, 1980)
The Pirates of Penzance—Original Cast Album ♪♪♪ (Elektra, 1980)
Lush Life ♪♪♪ (Asylum, 1984)
Canciones de Mi Padre ♪♪♪ (Asylum, 1987)
Cry Like a Rainstorm—Howl Like the Wind ♪♪♪ (Asylum, 1989)
Mas Canciones ♪♪♪ (Asylum, 1990)
Frenesi ♪♪♪ (Asylum, 1992)
Winter Light ♪♪ (Asylum, 1994)
Feels Like Home ♪♪ (Asylum, 1995)
Dedicated to the One I Love ♪♪♪ (Asylum, 1996)

worth searching for: *'Round Midnight* ♪♪♪ (Asylum, 1986, prod. Peter Asher) is a nicely packaged set that fits the three Nelson Riddle collaborations onto two compact discs.

Kenny Rogers (© Ken Settle)

4
1
0   *david rose*

influences:

◄◄ Kitty Wells, Patsy Cline, Rosemary Clooney, Gilbert & Sullivan, the Beatles, the Rolling Stones, Buddy Holly, the Everly Brothers, Gram Parsons

►► Trisha Yearwood, Jennifer Warnes, Carly Simon, Sheryl Crow, Stevie Nicks, the Eagles

Jay Dedrick

David Rose

Born June 15, 1910, in London, England. Died August 23, 1990, in Burbank, CA.

"The Stripper" is the unfortunate legacy of this well-respected and hitmaking light-orchestra composer ("Holiday for Strings" was a smash in 1943 and went on to widespread use in films, commercials, cartoons, and *The Red Skelton Show*). He wrote his first wave of best-known hits, all incredibly catchy in that easy-listening netherworld between classical and pop, in just one week—"One More Time" and "Manhattan Square Dance," among them. Because of his movie work and memorable scores for TV shows such as *Bonanza,* he won several Emmys and Grammys, plus an Oscar nomination. After his family moved from England to Chicago, when he was four, Rose studied at the Chicago College of Music and started a respectable radio career. He was a performer in radio bands, then became music director of a Hollywood radio network in the 1930s; after a stint in the U.S. Air Force (he directed the show *Winged Victory*), he became a prolific score-writer for films, including 1964's *Never Too Late* and 1944's *The Princess and the Pirate.* But his best-known work remains his leering, curvy, twisty, horn-heavy instrumentals, from "Dance of the Spanish Onion" in 1942 to, of course, "The Stripper." Today's gentlemen's clubs have long since stopped playing Rose's material, but his music continues to invoke all sorts of untoward images.

what's available: Poor Rose: for all his respectable work, the only thing you can buy without much trouble is an English import, *Stripper and Other Favourites* ♪♪♪ (Reper, 1997, prod. various), which contains "The Stripper," as you'd expect, plus his carnival-sounding solo hits from the '40s, '50s, and '60s. That track opens *Take It Off! Striptease Classics* ♪♪♪ (Rhino, 1997, compilation prod. Andrea Kinloch, Jill Ruzich, James Austin), a campy but musically excellent ba-ba-ba-BOOM soundtrack for, well, you know. The mysterious Sonny Lester (creator of the inimitable *How to Strip for Your Husband* LPs) dominates the album, but Rose's track, in addition to the goofy naked women photos amid the hilarious liner notes, is the reason for buying.

influences:

◄◄ Al Jolson

►► John Barry, Raymond Scott, Mötley Crüe

see also: *Sonny Lester*

Steve Knopper

Nino Rota

Born December 3, 1911, in Milan, Italy. Died April 10, 1979, in Rome, Italy.

A reviewer once said, "If I could have a set of background melodies playing in my head as the soundtrack for my life, it would be Nino Rota." As popular and prolific as his American counterpart, Henry Mancini, Rota wrote the scores for more than 100 films, eight operas, and four symphonies. In addition to his work with Fellini, Rota scored such classics as Francis Ford Coppola's first two *Godfather* films and had a Top 10 hit with the theme from Franco Zeffirelli's *Romeo and Juliet*. After writing an oratorio at age 11 and an opera two years later, Rota began working in the Italian film industry in Rome in the 1940s. The prolific one-time literature student composed in many different musical styles, but his major career-changing connection came in 1951, when he began a lifelong collaboration with filmmaker Federico Fellini. For almost 30 years, Rota's melodies, in such films as 1959's *La Dolce Vita* and 1971's *The Clowns*, became yet another character in Fellini's delightfully eccentric cinematic universe.

what to buy: Two compilations provide an excellent overview of Rota's career: *Nino Rota Movies* ♪♪♪♪ (Polydor, 1973, prod. Carlo Savina) and the double-CD *Tutto Fellini* ♪♪♪♪♪ (CAM, 1993, prod. Carlo Savina), which includes the title track from every Rota/Fellini effort. *Amarcord Nino Rota* ♪♪♪♪ (Hannibal, 1981, prod. Hal Willner) is an excellent tribute played by jazzers such as Wynton Marsalis and Jaki Byard, with punkers Deborah Harry and Chris Stein.

what to buy next: *Concerta Per Archi* ♪♪♪ (Philips, 1986, prod. Gianluigi Gelmetti), written in 1964–65, displays Rota's "serious" musical side. Katyna Ranieri interprets the major Rota/Fellini scores in an operaesque-style on *Chansons pour Fellini* ♪♪♪ (Milan, 1992). Fellini's *Intervista* ♪♪♪ (Virgin, 1987, prod. Pietro Notarianni) was composed by Nicola Piovani as "Hommage a Nino Rota."

the rest:
Romeo and Juliet ♪♪♪♪ (Capitol, 1968)
The Godfather ♪♪♪ (Paramount, 1972/1974)

Hurricane ♫♫♫ (Elektra, 1979)
La Strada, Le Notti di Cabiria ♫♫♫♫ (Legend, 1992)
Nino Rota: Film Music ♫♫♫ (EMI, 1992)
Il Maestro di Vigevao, La Grande Guerra, Fortunella ♫♫♫ (Legend, 1996)

worth searching for: Rota's last Fellini score, before his death, was *Prova d'Orchestra* ♫♫♫♫ (CAM, 1992, prod. Carlo Savina). It's one of 11 original Rota titles, released by CAM in the early 1990s. These Italian releases, packaged with excellent movie stills and liner notes written in French, Italian, German, and English, have long been out of print and command $50-100 on the collector's market. Also, *Boccaccio '70* ♫♫♫ (RCA, 1962, prod. Franco Ferrara), *Fellini Satyricon* ♫♫♫ (United Artists, 1970, prod. Carlo Savina), and *Fellini Roma* ♫♫♫ (United Artists, 1972, prod. Carlo Savina) are available only on out-of-print LPs.

influences:

◄◄ Cole Porter, Duke Ellington, Nelson Riddle, Henry Mancini

►► Ennio Morricone, Lalo Schifrin, John Barry, Deborah Harry, Wynton Marsalis, Phil Spector

Jay Reeg

Rotary Connection

Formed 1967, in Chicago, IL.

Minnie Riperton (born November 8, 1947, in Chicago, IL; died 1979), vocals; Bobby Simms, guitar (1967–69); Mitch Aliotta, bass (1967–70); Tommy Vincent Donlinger, drums (1967–70); Sidney Barnes, vocals; Judy Hauff, vocals (1967–68); Jimmy Nyeholt, keyboards (1967–68); Kenny Venegas, drums (1969–71); Jon Stocklin, guitar (1969–71); John Jeremiah, keyboards (1969–71); Charles Stepney, arrangements, keyboards; Syd Simms, bass (1971); Donny Simmons, drums (1971); Phil Upchurch, guitar (1971); Pat Ferreri, guitar (1971).

Rotary Connection began with a really bad idea: Marshall Chess, owner of Chicago's prestigious blues-and-soul label Chess Records, heard a few Cream records and decided to mix psychedelic rock with soul music. The lounge aspect arrived with Minnie Riperton, a singer with three-octave range who had been frequently compared to the great torch-crooner Yma Sumac. (Riperton, who was classically trained at the Lincoln Center in a poor Chicago neighborhood, sang in high school choirs before joining the Gems, a Chess group that linked—get this—opera and soul. She sang under the pseudonym Andrea Davis before Rotary Connection surfaced in 1967.) Together, the unmixable styles of the band members somehow, well, mixed—into a smooth, swirling, romantic sound. Guitars jam like Santana, strings shimmer like Mantovani, triangles ting like tiki music,

and Riperton's slinky voice goes up and down seamlessly with the music. The band put out a handful of records through the early 1970s, and despite a spacey version of Cream's "We're Doing Wrong," an unrecognizable take on the Otis Redding-Aretha Franklin classic, "Respect," and a pretty weird Christmas album, its main claim to fame was fashion. The surviving Rotary Connection photos show the '70s at their most extreme: the members wear elaborate fur shawls and hair, lots of hair. After failing to hit the pop charts, the group broke up, and Riperton continued to sing solo until she died of cancer in 1979.

what to buy: Two CD sets comprise the highlights of the out-of-print Rotary Connection albums. *Rotary Connection* ♫♫♫ (MCA, 1996, prod. Marshall Chess) has most of the best stuff, including bizarre versions of the Rolling Stones' "Lady Jane" and "Ruby Tuesday," and a song called "Pink Noise," which actually manages to capture the image of its title. (Why anybody would want to do that, we couldn't say.) Though *Minnie Riperton: Her Best* ♫♫ (Chess/MCA, 1997, prod. various) is billed as a solo collection, it contains 13 RC songs, including Cream's "We're Going Wrong," Jimi Hendrix's "Burning of the Midnight Lamp," and two bouncy Christmas standards.

what to buy next: Chess's Riperton collection is mistitled, which means the only place you can really find her solo material on CD is *Capitol Gold: The Best of Minnie Riperton* ♫♫ (Capitol, 1993, prod. Wayne Watkins), which closes with a version of the Doors' "Light My Fire."

worth searching for: The cover of *Perfect Angel* ♫♫ (Capitol, 1974, prod. Stevie Wonder) shows a smiling Riperton, in sexy overalls, with a vanilla ice cream cone dripping all over her hand. Despite Stevie Wonder's presence in the studio and on keyboards and guitars, the album is a mish-mosh of unfocused funk, from the aptly titled "Take a Little Trip" to the more straightforward but just as trippy "Reasons."

influences:

◄◄ Stevie Wonder, Yma Sumac, Cream, the Doors, Billie Holiday, Jimi Hendrix, Otis Redding

►► Bela Fleck and the Flecktones, Blues Traveler, Phish, Whitney Houston, Vanessa Williams

Steve Knopper

David Lee Roth

Born October 10, 1955, in Bloomington, IN.

David Lee Roth's celebrated tenure as frontman for power-pop-metal mavens Van Halen was rife with the spirit of vaudeville. Suburban metalheads thought they were responding to Diamond Dave's larger-than-life persona and its "sex, drugs, rock 'n' roll" credo—little did they know that Al Jolson lurked just beneath the surface. The highly entertaining *Crazy from the Heat* EP was recorded before he officially parted company with Van Halen and is probably the most concentrated, essential dose of solo Roth. His vampy version of "Just a Gigolo" (meshed with "I Ain't Got Nobody") not only updates the classics, but shows off Roth's stagey showmanship—the accompanying video, a hilarious spoof of MTV, features Roth as host of "Dave TV," conducting a parade of celebrity impersonators (Prince, Boy George, Billy Idol, and Michael Jackson). And who would have guessed that the Beach Boys' "California Girls" would work as a fantastically overblown showgirl revue? Unfortunately, after *Eat 'Em and Smile* Roth's solo career tapered off with several unremarkable albums. In October 1995, Roth boldly went where few rock performers have wisely gone before: Vegas. For a week Roth's revue of his own material ran at the MGM Grand Showroom. He was backed by a 14-piece ensemble (including fellow rock dinosaur Edgar Winter) and two showgirls.

what to buy: The *Crazy from the Heat* ♫♫♫ (Warner Bros., 1985, prod. Ted Templeman) EP is a perfect dose of solo Roth that finds him in fine form, exposing his musical roots as he struts his way through "California Girls," "Easy Street," "Coconut Grove," and a medley of "Just a Gigolo" and "I Ain't Got Nobody" (the last of which plays with all the grandiose irony of Mick Jagger's 1965 declaration, "(I Can't Get No) Satisfaction").

what to buy next: In addition to the excellent single "Yankee Rose," *Eat 'Em and Smile* ♫♫♫ (Warner Bros., 1986, prod. Ted Templeman) features some fantastic playing from a lineup that includes axe-meister Steve Vai and bassist extraordinaire Billy Sheehan; *Skyscraper* ♫♫♫ (Warner Bros., 1987, prod. David Lee Roth, Steve Vai) features the same lineup and yielded the hit "Just Like Paradise." *David Lee Roth: The Best* ♫♫♫ (Rhino, 1997, prod. various) neatly compiles all of Roth's integral singles on one disc and features a new single, "Don't Piss Me Off."

influences:

◀◀ Al Jolson, Louis Armstrong, Jim Morrison, Tom Jones, the Rolling Stones, Kiss

▶▶ Ugly Kid Joe, Poison, Mötley Crüe, Green Day, Offspring

Sandy Masuo

Royal Crown Revue

Formed 1989, in Los Angeles, CA.

Eddie Nichols, vocals; Mando Dorame, tenor sax; James Achor, guitar; Bill Ungerman, baritone sax; Scott Steen, trumpet; Veikko Lepisto, bass; Daniel Glass, drums.

Swinging ahead of the rest of the swing-music revivalists, Royal Crown Revue helped rescue swing from the past, giving the music a rock-infused shot in the arm in the late '80s. Singer Eddie Nichols and Co. remain one of the swing-revival's most popular and talented bands, in part because of their considerable chops and keen collective sense of style. Of course, an appearance in the Jim Carrey smash, *The Mask,* didn't hurt: in the pre-*Swingers* film, the then-unsigned septet performed its original song "Hey Pachuco!" as Carrey and Cameron Diaz do their, um, swing. RCR was one of the first modern swing bands to land a major-label recording contract (with Warner Bros. in the spring of 1995). And confirming its coolness quotient, the band—which consistently packs rooms up and down the West Coast, including the Derby in Los Angeles—secured a nine-week stint at the end of 1997 headlining at the Desert Inn, the newly renovated Las Vegas lounge made famous by Louis Prima, Sam Butera, and, of course, Frank Sinatra and the Rat Pack. No slaves to nostalgia, though, Royal Crown Revue—whose members have experienced playing everything from jazz and soul to skiffle, rockabilly, and even punk—give the music a decidedly contemporary spin, playing with the edge and intensity of a rock band. No wonder, then, the band landed an gig opening for KISS, as well as a spot on the thrash-metal-oriented Warped Tour.

what to buy: The major-label debut, *Mugzy's Move* ♫♫♫ (Warner Bros., 1996, prod. Ted Templeman), is a mix of brazen originals (the big-band-style "Park's Place," the zippy "Zip Gun Bop," the manic "Hey Pachuco!") and smart covers, including Bobby Darin's somewhat obvious "Beyond the Sea" and Willie Dixon's not-so-obvious "I Love the Life I Live." Veteran rock producer Ted Templeman (Doobie Brothers, Van Halen) does a fine job at capturing, in the studio, the same sort of energy and excitement the band delivers on stage.

the rest:
Caught in the Act ♫♫♫ (Surfdog, 1997)

influences:

◀◀ Frank Sinatra, Bobby Darin, Bad Religion

▶▶ Big Bad Voodoo Daddy, Dutch Falconi & His Twisted Orchestra, Indigo Swing, *Swingers*

Josh Freedom du Lac

Todd Rundgren
/Utopia

Born June 22, 1948, in Upper Darby, PA.

Utopia: Todd Rundgren, guitars, vocals; John Siegler, bass, cello (1974–76); Kasim Sulton, bass, vocals (1977–85); Mark "Moogy" Klingman, keyboards (1974–76); Ralph Shuckett, keyboards (1974–76); M. Frog Labat, synthesizers (1974); Roger Powell, keyboards, vocals (1975–85); Kevin Ellman, drums (1974); John Wilcox, drums, vocals (1975–85).

As pretentious as it sounds, Renaissance Man may be the most accurate description befitting Rundgren. A musician, songwriter, producer, and techno-dabbler, Rundgren is the da Vinci of rock 'n' roll, having left no corner of the music industry untouched. From his early work with the Nazz (1968–70), Rundgren showed a tremendous melodic gift and an ability to craft a sophisticated sound fused from various genres. While his music ranges from Beatles-influenced pop to Hendrix-inspired rock and Philadelphia soul—with an appropriately trendy side trip into loungey bossa nova with 1997's *With a Twist*—he retains a gift for honest sentiment, inspiring lyrics, and laconic wit throughout his ample body of work. Proficient on an almost shameful number of instruments, Rundgren has frequently displayed his ample chops by performing all vocals and instruments on some of his albums (well before digital sampling was possible). His adventurous use of synthesizers during the early '70s helped to usher that instrument into widespread use in popular music, and while at times he could use it to the point of distraction, he also showed what was possible. If his musical dexterity has at times bordered on grandstanding, it has also clearly inspired many artists, most notably Prince, to follow suit. As a producer, Rundgren can be most likened to Phil Spector: brilliant, innovative, and at times wildly erratic. Despite his self-indulgent tendencies with such acts as the Patti Smith Group, Hall & Oates, Grand Funk Railroad, and XTC, he has more often than not helped musicians score chart hits (most notably Meat Loaf's mega-hit *Bat out of Hell*). With the advent of digital recording techniques in the late '70s, Rundgren began breaking new ground in music technology, producing some of the most advanced rock videos and exploring new possibilities in digital technology with interactive CD-ROMs (such as his 1993 release, *No World Order*). Beginning in 1975, Rundgren began releasing a number of albums in the progressive-rock mode with his band Utopia; despite his best efforts to blend in, Rundgren's character permeates the band's catalog, making it at times indistinguishable from his solo work.

Cocktail Classics

Theme from Shaft

18-Karat Isaac Hayes
Shaft (Soundtrack)
(Enterprise)

Bombsville! The Hollyridge Strings
*Ultra-Lounge:
On the Rocks, Pt. 1*
(Capitol)

what to buy: Rundgren's lounge entry, *With a Twist* ♫♫♫ (Guardian, 1997, prod. Todd Rundgren), recasts several of his biggest hits in bossa-nova styles. It's a restrained and tasteful affair, but only in rare cases—"Fidelity," for instance—do the new versions hold a swizzle stick to the originals. Rundgren is better experienced via the double-CD extravaganza *Something/Anything?* ♫♫♫♫ (Bearsville/Rhino, 1972, prod. Todd Rundgren), a landmark work filled with lovely pop confection, pristine production, and a lighthearted sense of humor. Rundgren performs and sings the first three-quarters of the album, a nervy feat that's still breathtaking to behold. Those looking for the hits will find them here ("I Saw the Light," "It Wouldn't Have Made Any Difference," "Hello, It's Me") along with a host of stellar though lesser-known treasures ("Torch Song" and "Breathless"). Rundgren's followup effort, *A Wizard, a True Star* 𝄫𝄫𝄫𝄫 (Bearsville/Rhino, 1973, prod. Todd Rundgren), is a fascinating sonic collage that skews his pop-star image 180 degrees. Opening with a dizzying 30-minute medley of short songs and musical skits, the album catches its breath midway, relaxing into the Philly soul number "Sometimes I Don't Know What to Feel," a clever medley of '60s tunes and the hit anthem "Just One Victory." Rundgren never hit the mark so solidly again until *Nearly Human* 𝄫𝄫𝄫𝄫 (Warner Bros., 1989, prod. Todd Rundgren). Sliding into the soul groove he knows so well, Rundgren turns in an emotional and inspiring effort. Although none of the songs here are as well known as his earlier hits, a few of them—"The Want of a Nail," "The Waiting Game," and "Parallel Lines"—are among his best work.

what to buy next: The double CD *Anthology (1968–1985)* 𝄫𝄫𝄫𝄫 (Rhino, 1989, prod. various) is a tidy retrospective of Rundgren's career dating back to his days with the Nazz. Rhino does a first-class job here, compiling and remastering all the essential Rundgren tunes from a nearly 20-year period, among them "A Dream Goes on Forever," "Love of the Common Man," "Can We Still Be Friends?," and "Bang the Drum All Day."

what to avoid: The interactive CD (CD-I) *No World Order* 𝄽 (Forward/Rhino, 1993, prod. Todd Rundgren) is an intriguing idea that never quite takes off. Rundgren offers some four hours of musical snippets for listeners to manufacture into new songs via their CD-I. For those without the required hardware, the disk includes 10 lackluster dance tracks on which Rundgren ventures unsuccessfully into rap. *No World Order Lite* **woof!** (Forward/Rhino, 1994) excludes the interactive element and, with it, what little enjoyment it offered.

the rest:
Todd Rundgren:
Runt 𝄫𝄫𝄽 (Bearsville/Rhino, 1970)
The Ballad of Todd Rundgren 𝄫𝄫𝄽 (Bearsville/Rhino, 1971)
Todd 𝄫𝄫𝄽 (Bearsville/Rhino, 1974)
Initiation 𝄫𝄫 (Bearsville/Rhino, 1975)
Faithful 𝄫𝄫𝄫𝄽 (Bearsville/Rhino, 1976)
Hermit of Mink Hollow 𝄫𝄫 (Bearsville/Rhino, 1978)
Back to the Bars 𝄫𝄫𝄽 (Bearsville/Rhino, 1978)
Healing 𝄫𝄫 (Bearsville/Rhino, 1981)
The Ever Popular Tortured Artist Effect 𝄫𝄫𝄽 (Bearsville/Rhino, 1983)
A Cappella 𝄫𝄫𝄽 (Warner Bros./Rhino, 1985)
2nd Wind 𝄽 (Bearsville/Rhino, 1991)
The Best of Todd Rundgren 𝄫𝄫𝄫𝄫 (Rhino, 1994)
Individualist 𝄫𝄫 (Digital Entertainment Enhanced CD, 1995)

Utopia:
Todd Rundgren's Utopia 𝄫𝄽 (Bearsville/Rhino, 1974)
Another Live 𝄫𝄽 (Bearsville/Rhino, 1975)
RA 𝄫 (Bearsville/Rhino, 1977)
Oops! Wrong Planet 𝄫𝄫 (Bearsville/Rhino, 1977)
Deface the Music 𝄫𝄫𝄫 (Bearsville/Rhino, 1980)
Adventures in Utopia 𝄫 (Bearsville/Rhino, 1980)
Utopia 𝄫𝄫 (Network/Rhino, 1982)
Swing to the Right 𝄫𝄫 (Bearsville/Rhino, 1982)
Oblivion, P.O.V. & Some Trivia 𝄫𝄫𝄫 (Rhino, 1986)
Anthology 1974–1985 𝄫𝄫𝄫 (Rhino, 1989)

worth searching for: If there is a Holy Grail for Rundgren fans, it is the alternate release of his solo debut, *Runt* 𝄫𝄫𝄫 (Ampex, 1970, prod. Todd Rundgren). Although the covers and track listing are identical to the more commonly found release, the rare *Runt* features numerous differences, including a complete version of "Baby Let's Swing," an unlisted and haunting track called "Say No More," and an early recording of "Hope I'm Around," a later version of which appeared on *The Ballad of Todd Rundgren*.

influences:

◀◀ The Beach Boys, the Beatles, Jimi Hendrix, Stevie Wonder, the Move

▶▶ Electric Light Orchestra, Meat Loaf, Hall & Oates, the Tubes, Queen, XTC, Prince, Madonna

Christopher Scapelliti and Gary Graff

RuPaul

Born RuPaul Andre Charles, November 17, 1960, in San Diego, CA.

One of the central tenets of the "lounge" aesthetic is a fascination with artifice. "Posing" has earned a nasty reputation in the world of rock where legitimacy and credibility are at a premium, but in the lounge realm, posing is truly an art in and of itself. Of course, it's important that performers convey genuine feeling, but the poses they use to communicate it are no less important than the emotion itself. Cross-dressing and cabaret have had a long relationship, but RuPaul is probably the first female impersonator to enjoy substantial mainstream success. Though he works his way through two albums of dance music with competent singing, his success is really based on the surfeit of personality that suffuses his music, and for that reason it's much more effective to watch him perform. Whether he's on stage voguing or on magazine pages modelling what's in vogue (he is a bona fide supermodel, complete with a Mac Cosmetics contract), the glamour and the guise fit him/her like a glove.

what to buy: RuPaul's debut album, *Supermodel of the World* ♫♫♫ (Tommy Boy, 1993, prod. Eric Kupper), is a lively mixture of ebullient dance floor energy and RuPaul's sassy personality. It features the hit "Supermodel (You Better Work)."

what to buy next: *Foxy Lady* ♫♫♫ (Rhino, 1997, prod. Pete Lorimer, Richard "Humpty" Vission, Welcome & Carrano, Eric Kupper, Jimmy Harry, Nick Martinelli, Bruce Weeden) revisits the same terrain as *Supermodel.*

the rest:
Go-Go Box Classics N/A (Rhino, 1998)

worth searching for: *VH1 Presents: RuPaul Ho Ho Ho* ♫♫♫ (Rhino, 1997, prod. Welcome & Carrano) is the soundtrack to RuPaul's holiday special and features holiday tunes as only Ru-Paul can do them, including "I Saw Daddy Kissing Santa Claus" and "You're a Mean One, Mr. Grinch."

influences:

 Diana Ross, Patti LaBelle, Liza Minnelli, Judy Garland, Tim Curry, Donna Summer, David Bowie

Sandy Masuo

Tommy Ryan
See: Sammy Kaye

S

Sade
Formed 1982, in London, England.

Helen Folasade Adu (born January 16, 1959, in Ibadan, Nigeria), vocals; Stewart Matthewman, guitar and saxophone; Andrew Hale, keyboards; Paul Denman, bass.

Sade is an it, not a she. Helen Folasade Adu, the Nigerian-born, London-raised chanteuse with the striking looks and impressive voice, has become synonymous with the name Sade, but in fact the moniker refers to the whole of her band. (Though that support, including Matthewman and Hale, now also records as an R&B/acid-jazz collective called Sweetback.) Regardless, much of the world sees only the cover girl with the Jagger-like lips and mysterious eyes when the word Sade is uttered. As easy listening goes, Sade is a weird one to figure. Is she R&B, lounge, adult contemporary, or smooth-jazz? Or all of

Cocktail Classics

(There's) Always Something There to Remind Me

18-Karat Burt Bacharach
Burt Bacharach Plays His Hits
(MCA)

Bombsville! Naked Eyes
Promises, Promises: The Very Best of Naked Eyes
(EMI America)

them? It's never been an easy call. Her first Top 10 hits—"Your Love Is King," "Diamond Life," and "Hang on to Your Love"—suggested all those qualities, and she hasn't been content to rest in one category since. Adu and her band are meticulous, however, taking several years between releases. (It has been six years since her last.) The delays are also based on Adu's need for a private life, but such gaps only add to Sade's mystique, helping to bring out fans in droves whenever they decide to tour.

what to buy: As greatest-hits packages go, *The Best of Sade* ♫♫♫♫ (Epic, 1994, prod. various) is a reasonable entry point into the band's brief but varied output. It's got the hits, including the marvelously silky "The Sweetest Taboo" and the grinding "No Ordinary Love," and that's what matters to most people, but it lacks the spiciness and solemnity that mark Sade's other releases. For its establishment of Adu as an exotic diva alone, *Diamond Life* ✍✍✍ (Epic, 1984, prod. Robin Millar) is essential. It is heavy with contemporary slickness and high-fashion presentation, but you can still feel the mood and the conviction of attitude under it all. Far superior is *Promise* ✍✍✍✍ (Epic, 1985, prod. Robin Millar, Ben Rogan, Sade), a langorous, rich, and focused work with Adu perfectly straddling the barrier between Billie Holiday and Marvin Gaye. Some find its updated torch atmosphere sterile, and, true, there is a touch of rainy-day ho-hum to its pacing. Still, it's an hourlong showcase of one of the strongest voices around.

what to buy next: *Stronger Than Pride* ✍✍✍ (Epic, 1988, prod. Sade) contains two of Sade's most arresting songs, the title track and the hushed, aching "Haunt Me." But the backing band puts down its often-leaded foot on lumbering cuts like "Never As Good As the First Time," which predicts the complete shift in tone of *Love Deluxe* ✍✍✍✍ (Epic, 1992, prod. Sade, Mike Pela). In many ways, this last disc is a culmination of the previous three, combining the polish of the first, the lushness of the second, and the thumping wiggle of the third. The hits "No Ordinary Love" and "Kiss of Life" are the blueprint for the whole.

worth searching for: For hardcore fans and electronic wizards only, there is *Remix Deluxe* ✍✍✍ (Sony Japan, 1993, prod. various), a pricey but interesting Japanese import that features retoolings of key Sade tunes by the likes of Nellee Hooper and Mad Professor. Also, one of Sade's most swinging tracks, the ultra-smoky "Killer Blow," can be found on the soundtrack to *Absolute Beginners* ✍✍✍ (Virgin, 1986, prod. various), a glossy, failed British musical about '50s cool cats. David Bowie, the Style Council, and Ray Davies also appear on the disc.

influences:

◀◀ Nina Simone, Eartha Kitt, Natalie Cole, Aretha Franklin

▶▶ Everything but the Girl, Basia, Swing out Sister

Ben Wener

Santo & Johnny

Formed 1959, in Brooklyn, NY.

Santo Farina (born October 24, 1937), steel guitar; Johnny Farina (born April 30, 1941), rhythm guitar.

Brothers from Brooklyn, Santo & Johnny hit #1 with their very

first recording in 1959. One of the best of many slow-dancing instrumentals of the period, "Sleep Walk" has become a ubiquitous hit, represented in films, commercials, and television for nearly 40s years and still a favorite of guitarists around the world. (On his website, the Smashing Pumpkins' Billy Corgan lists "Sleep Walk" as one of his favorite singles, and even metal behemoth Iron Butterfly recorded a version of it.) The Farinas wrote it with their sister, Ann, and recorded it in Manhattan. Licensed by a North Dakota label called Canadian-American Records, it hit the top single spot within eight weeks of its release. They followed "Sleep Walk" with five lesser entries on the charts between 1959 to 1964, the most successful of which was "Tear Drop," which hit #23 on the heels of "Sleep Walk." Later records never reached the heights of that original single.

what's available: "Sleep Walk" is available on any number of collections. One of the best is *Rock Instrumental Classics: The Fifties* ✍✍✍✍ (Rhino, 1994), where it resides alongside other period hits like Dave Baby Cortez's "The Happy Organ," Link Wray's "Raw-Hide," and the Viscounts' "Harlem Nocturne," among others.

worth searching for: Any of their vinyl albums would be highly collectible items, including *Santo & Johnny* ✍✍✍✍ (Canadian-American, 1960), *Encore* ✍✍✍ (Canadian-American, 1960), and *Brilliant Guitar Sounds* ✍✍✍ (Imperial, 1967), all in pure monophonic sound.

influences:

◀◀ Link Wray, Duane Eddy, the Ventures, Lonnie Mack, Jimmy Bryant

▶▶ Jorgen Ingmann, Billy Corgan, Midge Ure

Leland Rucker

Erik Satie

Born Erik Alfred Leslie Satie, May 17, 1866, in Honfleur, France. Died July 1, 1925.

One of the great-grandfathers of modern lounge music, Satie was a sort of rock star in his day, complete with the trademark personal eccentricities and ego. He believed it was important for a musician not to compromise his art, but he was known to vociferously challenge his critics while giving his own pieces titles such as "Drivelling Preludes for a Dog" and "Unappetizing

Sade (© Ken Settle)

Chorale." He lived in Arceuil for the last 27 years of his life, and he was alternately described as incredibly irritating and irresistibly charming. With influences ranging from medieval music to the French composers who preceded him, he created a melodic and inventive body of work that started to be "rediscovered" in the '60s. He was a pioneer in inventing his own melodic systems, instruments, and primitive recording devices, and his concept of making music for the background of social events was a very modern one indeed.

what to buy: The classical salon is a much different place than the lounge: Satie didn't record his own compositions, of course, and there are literally hundreds of albums featuring various orchestras interpreting his work. If you're looking to experience his music, his most famous compositions (and the titles to look for) include the serene and beautiful "Gymnopédies," three similar piano pieces from 1888; the mystical "Vexations," a short piano piece repeated 840 times, from 1893; the popular piano suite, "Trois Morceaux en forme de Poire," for two pianos, from 1903; the ballet "Parade," scored for his odd, homemade instruments, from 1917; and the ballet "Relâche" (set to early film sequences, from 1924).

influences:

▶▶ Claude Debussy, Brian Eno, Francis Poulenc, Maurice Ravel

Jim DeRogatis

Leo Sayer

Born Gerard Sayer May 21, 1948, in Shoreham-on-Sea, Sussex, England.

British-born solo singer-songwriter Sayer—nicknamed Leo for his much-discussed mane of curly hair—began his search for musical notoriety in the late 1960s as frontman for the London-based Terraplane Blues Band, followed by formation of the duo Patches in 1971. During that band's short stint, Sayer answered an ad placed by David Courtney (former drummer with Adam Faith, an early 1960s British pop star), who was looking for local talent to help establish a talent agency. Courtney gave the band a thumbs down, but was intrigued with Sayer's songwriting and vocal talents, and the two formed a partnership. Sayer began recording with Courtney at studios owned by the Who's lead singer Roger Daltrey, who himself recorded a few of the songs he was hearing, including "Giving It All Away," which became a U.K. hit in 1973. Sayer's first solo hit came later that year with the #2 U.K. smash "The Show Must Go On." The song failed to launch him in the U.S., where Three Dog Night had quickly covered the song and turned it into a Top Five single.

Many more hits followed, including the #1 "You Make Me Feel Like Dancing," which not only was his signature song but a pop summation of the entire 1970s, and the entrancing #1 "When I Need You." Though his career stalled in the U.S., in the U.K., the hits didn't stop until 1983, with the melancholy "Orchard Road." For the rest of the decade, Sayer laid low, then attempted an ill-fated comeback in 1990. In more recent times, continued interest in Sayer's fine work has kept his name alive this decade. In addition, at the end of 1997, Celine Dion chose to cover "When I Need You" on her album *Let's Talk about Love*.

what to buy: Two stellar retrospectives have been assembled on CD, *All the Best* ⏴⏴⏴⏴ (Chrysalis, 1993, prod. various) and, for fans, the more exhaustive *Show Must Go On: Anthology* ⏴⏴⏴⏴ (Rhino, 1996, prod. various). Also, the original smash album, *Endless Flight* ⏴⏴⏴⏴ (Chrysalis, 1976/Rhino, 1996, prod. Richard Perry), later reissued, spawned the novel "You Make Me Feel Like Dancing" and "When I Need You."

what to buy next: Sayer's first album, *Silverbird* ⏴⏴⏴ (Chrysalis, 1974, prod. Adam Faith, David Courtney), was hailed by the British press as the beginning of something big. *Another Year* ⏴⏴⏴⏴ (Warner Bros., 1975) served up two more hit singles, "One Man Band" and "Long Tall Glasses (I Can Dance)." The latter at last broke him on the U.S. charts, reaching the Top 10 in 1975.

what to avoid: Sayer's hastily released second effort, *Just a Boy* ⏴⏴ (Warner Bros., 1974, prod. Adam Faith, David Courtney) briefly stalled his commercial momentum in the mid-1970s.

the rest:
Leo Sayer ⏴⏴⏴ (Warner Bros., 1978)
Here ⏴⏴⏴⏴ (Warner Bros., 1979)
World Radio ⏴⏴⏴ (Chrysalis, 1982)
Have You Ever Been in Love ⏴⏴⏴ (Warner Bros., 1984)
Collection ⏴⏴⏴⏴ (Castle, 1992)

worth searching for: *Thunder in My Heart* ⏴⏴⏴⏴ (Warner Bros., 1977, prod. Richard Perry) continued the development of a more Americanized sound under producer Perry, featuring the title track, a disco nugget complete with telltale sweeping strings and Chic-like guitars. *Living in a Fantasy* ⏴⏴⏴⏴ (Warner Bros., 1980, prod. Alan Tarney) included the #2 hit "More Than I Can Say," which, along with the Cliff Richard-esque title track, became Sayer's final hits in the U.S.

influences:

◀◀ The Carpenters, Elton John, Roger Daltrey, Barry Manilow, Chic

⏭ Michael Bolton, Celine Dion

Chuck Taylor

Lalo Schifrin

Born June 21, 1932, in Buenos Aires, Argentina.

Whatever else this jazz-loving composer and pianist does—whether it's an exhaustive tribute to bebop saxophonist Charlie Parker or becoming the first man to walk on Mars—Schifrin will always be remembered for the "Theme from *Mission: Impossible.*" More people can recognize that sinister-sounding instrumental than can recall what happened in any given episode of the old television spy show (or even the recent unmemorable Tom Cruise movie). It was a huge hit in 1967, then resurged in 1996, when U2 bassist Adam Clayton and drummer Larry Mullen recorded a buzzing new hit version. Schifrin, who studied music and film history while growing up, became a fan of the American bebop jazz masters when he was 16. He formed his own Buenos Aires jazz group, then became Latin-jazz bandleader Xavier Cugat's primary arranger in 1958; he wound up pianist and arranger for jazz trumpeter Dizzy Gillespie. His reputation thus established, Schifrin moved to Hollywood in 1964 and started to work on film scores. He did dozens of them, including 1965's *The Cincinnati Kid,* 1967's *Cool Hand Luke,* and 1971's *Dirty Harry,* occasionally branching out to write quirky, organ-and-flute-heavy themes for syndicated television shows. After he produced his big-time serious project, *The Rise and Fall of the Third Reich* oratorio, in 1968, he eased into a jazz-classical career that included a recent stint with the London Philharmonic Orchestra.

what to buy: Yes, Schifrin is a serious composer, but let's be real: what you really want is *Music from Mission: Impossible* 🎵🎵🎵🎵 (Hip-O/MCA, 1996, prod. Tom Mack), which opens, of course, with the main theme, but also includes psychedelic jazz themes and the tinkly piano "Barney Does It All." There are lots of packages and repackages of Schifrin's *Mission: Impossible* music, but this CD is the most thorough.

what to buy next: Oh yes, jazz. Schifrin rarely gets his own entry in the snooty jazz guides, but he did some nice work—usually characterized by clear-sounding piano and horn solos above a bebop rhythm—on *Firebird* 🎵🎵🎵 (Four Winds, 1996, prod. Lalo Schifrin), which includes fun stuff like "Around the Day in Eighty Worlds" and several Charlie Parker homages.

what to avoid: The hefty *Jazz Meets the Symphony* 🎵🎵 (Atlantic, 1993, prod. Lalo Schifrin) is a not-too-successful 1992 marriage of Schifrin's straightforward, sometimes playful jazzy instrumentals and overkill from the London Philharmonic Orchestra. Don't bother, either, with the sequel: *More Jazz Meets the Symphony* 🎵🎵 (Atlantic, 1994, prod. Lalo Schifrin).

worth searching for: Schifrin has yet to be revisited with the same loving care as, say, Ennio Morricone, the longtime soundtrack composer who keeps putting out giant multi-CD retrospectives. So you have to dig for Schifrin's soundtracks in the bargain LP bins—begin with his first, *The Cincinnati Kid* 🎵🎵🎵 (MGM/MCA, 1965), then work your way through 1969's *Eye of the Cat,* 1967's *The Venetian Affair,* and 1970's *Kelly's Heroes.* As with James Bond soundtrack master John Barry, Schifrin's

Diane Schuur (© Jack Vartoogian)

out-of-print LPs, such as *Enter the Dragon*, command up to $100 at some record conventions and collectible stores.

influences:

⏪ Ennio Morricone, Charlie Parker, Dizzy Gillespie, Xavier Cugat, Thelonious Monk

⏩ Michael Kamen, Randy Newman, Henry Mancini, Laika and the Cosmonauts, Los Straightjackets

Steve Knopper

Diane Schuur

Born 1953, in Seattle, WA.

A skilled pianist and interpreter of standards, Schuur always wanted to be more than just a hip lounge singer. Blinded after birth in a hospital accident, she got her big break in 1979 when she was invited to sing with Dizzy Gillespie at the Monterey Jazz Festival. She became one of the first acts signed to Dave Grusin and Larry Rosen's GRP label in 1984 after they spotted her singing with Stan Getz on a PBS-televised White House concert. Her Grammy-winning 1987 collaboration with the Count Basie Orchestra showcased the roof-raising power of her voice and endeared her to the burgeoning audience of new jazz listeners enticed by the sonic clout of the then-fledgling compact disc. But conquering the contemporary jazz market so early in her career left Schuur searching for material to challenge her formidable vocal skills. A self-professed disciple of R&B-jazz singer Dinah Washington, she has spent the past decade veering from Brazilian to adult-contemporary pop to blues in hopes of escaping the daunting "next Ella" pigeonhole. GRP has steered her toward numerous conceptual jazz-vocal projects but perhaps she'd be better suited to rekindling the gospel and R&B roots she celebrated on 1988's underrated *Talkin' 'bout You*.

what to buy: The live *Diane Schuur and the Count Basie Orchestra* ♫♫♫ (GRP, 1987, prod. Morgan Ames, Jeffrey Weber) cap-

Jimmy Scott (© Jack Vartoogian)

tures Schuur on a sassy, scat-laden big-band summit on such standards as "I Loves You Porgy," her signature rendition of "Travelin' Light," and a thrilling horn-driven romp through Aretha Franklin's "Climbing Higher Mountains." On the other end of the vocal spectrum, *In Tribute* 🎵🎵🎵 (GRP, 1992, prod. Andre Fischer), an homage to such heroines as Ella Fitzgerald, Sarah Vaughan, Billie Holiday, and Dinah Washington, marks her transition from bluesy belter to soulful stylist. Her versions of "Guess I'll Hang My Tears Out to Dry" and "God Bless the Child" are marked by hushed authority rather than pyrotechnic flourishes.

what to buy next: On *Talkin' 'bout You* 🎵🎵🎵 (GRP, 1988, prod. Steven Miller), Schuur taps into her gospel and R&B roots on a repertoire-stretching set that boasts three Ray Charles covers and Helen Humes's "Hard Drivin' Mama II."

what to avoid: Her anemic debut album, *Deedles* 🎵 (GRP, 1984, prod. Dave Grusin, Larry Rosen), is dragged down by tepid versions of Billy Joel's "New York State of Mind" and Jackson

Browne's "Rock Me on the Water," not to mention the annoying omnipresence of the dated Yamaha DX-7 keyboard.

the rest:
Schuur Thing 🎵🎵🎵 (GRP, 1985)
Timeless 🎵🎵🎵🎵 (GRP, 1986)
Collection 🎵🎵🎵🎵 (GRP, 1989)
Pure Schuur 🎵🎵🎵 (GRP, 1991)
Love Songs 🎵🎵🎵 (GRP, 1993)
(With B.B. King) *Heart to Heart* 🎵🎵🎵 (GRP, 1994)
Love Walked In 🎵🎵🎵 (GRP, 1996)
Blues for Schuur 🎵🎵🎵 (GRP, 1997)
The Very Best of Diane Schuur 🎵🎵🎵🎵 (GRP, 1997)

worth searching for: Schuur sings a lovely version of "The Christmas Song" on the first volume of *A GRP Christmas Collection* 🎵🎵🎵 (GRP, 1988, prod. Michael Abene).

influences:
⏪ Dinah Washington, Ella Fitzgerald, Sarah Vaughan

▶▶ Dianne Reeves, Anita Baker

David Okamoto

Jimmy Scott

Born July 17, 1925, in Cleveland, OH.

One of the most evocative vocalists on the planet, Scott has endured a life marked by tragedy and weathered a career that has culminated in triumph. Raised in a foster home after his father was killed in an automobile accident, Scott suffered a childhood disease that stunted his growth and kept his voice from lowering. He toured in tent-show reviews, where his unusual voice and appearance caused a sensation. He joined Lionel Hampton's band, and later started a solo career, but was seldom paid or credited properly for his work. Finally, an album he was to release on Ray Charles's Tangerine label was blocked by threats of a lawsuit by Savoy, which claimed it still had Scott under contract. Disgusted, Scott quit the business shortly thereafter, and faded into obscurity. His reemergence with Warner Bros. in the '90s is a tribute to his persistence and his lasting gift, for the years seem only to have improved his voice, making his lovelorn anthems even more heart rending. Scott is truly a unique presence in music.

what to buy: Few comeback albums are as impressive as *All the Way* 🎜🎜🎜🎜 (Sire/Warner Bros./Blue Horizon, 1992, prod. Tommy LiPuma) because few performers have had to come back from such a distance. But Scott emerged from years outside the music business with this stunner, a collection of standards such as "All the Way," "Embraceable You," and "Someone to Watch Over Me," his voice soaring over simple, understated arrangements.

what to buy next: Considering Scott's otherworldly voice, an album of material themed around the concept of *Heaven* 🎜🎜🎜 (Warner Bros., 1996, prod. Craig Street) seems a natural, and it is. David Byrne's title track envisions heaven as a "place where nothing ever happens." But there's plenty happening on Scott's gorgeous readings of Julie Miller's "All My Tears," Curtis Mayfield's "People Get Ready," and the traditional tunes "Wayfarin' Stranger," "Just As I Am," and "There's No Disappointment in Heaven."

the rest:
Regal Records: Live in New Orleans 🎜🎜🎜 (1951/Specialty, 1991)
Lost and Found 🎜🎜🎜 (Rhino, 1993)
Dream 🎜🎜🎜 (Sire/Warner Bros./Blue Horizon, 1994)
All Over Again 🎜🎜🎜 (Savoy, 1995)

worth searching for: Scott's is the perfect voice for the eerie "Under the Sycamore Trees," a tune penned by filmmaker David Lynch for the soundtrack of *Twin Peaks: Fire Walk with Me* 🎜🎜🎜 (Warner Bros., 1992).

influences:
◀◀ Billie Holiday, the Mills Brothers

▶▶ Marvin Gaye, Nancy Wilson, Stevie Wonder, David Lynch

Daniel Durchholz

Raymond Scott

Born Harry Warnow, September 10, 1908, in New York City, NY. Died February 8, 1994.

"Dinner Music for a Pack of Hungry Cannibals" was one of the many brilliant song titles devised by Scott, an obsessive tinkerer and perfectionist bandleader who created some of this century's most playful swing instrumentals. Many listeners already have a thorough knowledge of Scott's music, even if they've never heard of him, because percussion-heavy pieces like "Powerhouse" were the soundtracks for Porky Pig and Bugs Bunny on *Looney Tunes* cartoons.

A serious classical music student schooled at Juilliard, Scott joined his brother Mark's CBS orchestra in the early 1930s, then headed his own highly experimental quintet through decade's end. His compositions, such as "Confusion Among a Fleet of Taxicabs upon Meeting with a Fare," were filled with quirky Dixieland horns, playful percussion, and dizzying mood changes. Though he developed a prominent reputation as an arranger, many viewed his songs as novelty music, which explains their later appeal to Warner Bros., which licensed them for *Looney Tunes.*

Scott formed a more traditional big band in the early 1940s, working with Frank Sinatra, Cozy Cole, and Ben Webster, among others, then ran a record label and performed with his wife, singer Dorothy Collins. He was also a prolific inventor, creating one of the first known synthesizers in 1949, and devising contraptions called the electronium and the clavivox. He retired in 1977, but recorded with MIDI computer techniques through 1987, when he suffered his first debilitating stroke.

what to buy: On *Reckless Nights and Turkish Twilights: The Music of Raymond Scott* 🎜🎜🎜🎜 (Columbia, 1992, prod. Irwin Chusid) the producer quotes a commentator saying, "Scott's music is very seldom revived nowadays," then responds, "I decided to make that statement untrue." There's novelty appeal here, of course, as the opening song "Powerhouse" evokes any number of Bugs Bunny episodes; but the real surprise is just how inventive, complex, and plain fun Scott's music remains.

what to buy next: *The Uncollected Raymond Scott* 🎵🎵🎵 (Hindsight, 1983) is a live recording from a 1940 Chicago ballroom show; its sequel, *The Uncollected Raymond Scott, Vol. 2* 🎵🎵🎵 (Hindsight, 1985), comes from 1944.

what to avoid: Every Scott collection includes "Powerhouse," because it's the most recognizable of his cartoon theme music—the Columbia set dwarfs past projects such as *The Raymond Scott Project, Powerhouse, Vol. 1* 🎵🎵 (Stash, 1991).

worth searching for: Unsurprisingly, Scott's ready-for-the-cartoons style downshifted easily into kids' music, and he put out several volumes of it—*Soothing Sounds for Baby, Vols. I-III* 🎵🎵🎵 (Epic, 1963/Basta, 1997) is certainly as much as you'll need.

influences:

⏮ Benny Goodman, Duke Ellington, Frank Sinatra, Nelson Riddle

⏭ Juan Garcia Esquivel, Frank Zappa, They Might Be Giants, Devo, Combustible Edison

Steve Knopper

Neil Sedaka

Born March 13, 1939, in Brooklyn, NY.

A child prodigy at age 9, worldwide star at 20, has-been at 25, and defiant Comeback Kid a decade after that, Sedaka's story is full of typical showbiz ups and downs. But despite what you might think of his music, you have to give Sedaka credit for not only persevering whenever all seemed lost, but for carrying on fearlessly to this day, serenading all who'll listen with his own eunuch style of Tin Pan Alley rock.

Fresh into Lincoln High School, Sedaka was already singing in local vocal groups such as the Tokens (later of "Lion Sleeps Tonight" fame) when Arthur Rubinstein chose him as New York City's outstanding classical pianist, which led to a scholarship at the prestigious Juilliard School of Music. Still, Sedaka continued to dabble with the popular music of the day, and in 1957 released his first single, "Fly, Don't Fly on Me." The following year, he and Howard Greenfield were brought to the attention of song hucksters Don Kirshner and Al Nevins, who quickly signed them; the duo immediately began to place songs with such reputable artists as Clyde McPhatter and LaVern Baker, though Connie Francis first hit with their "Stupid Cupid" in

1958. Shortly afterwards, Nevins played a demo of "The Diary" to RCA Victor, who were impressed enough with Sedaka's voice to sign him as a recording artist in his own right. Thus was launched a four-year run of worldwide smashes beginning in December of 1959 with "Oh! Carol," written in honor of Neil's childhood crush Carole Klein (who later composed "Oh! Neil," using her new songwriting alias Carole King). Sedaka eventually relocated to London, where he recorded with a Manchester group who would soon become better known as 10CC. Several successful U.K.-only releases, culminating in 1974 with "Laughter in the Rain," brought an offer from long-time fan Elton John to release these recordings in the U.S. on his new Rocket label, and within a year Sedaka was back atop the American charts with a remake of his 1962 classic "Breaking Up Is Hard to Do," a hit duet with John ("Bad Blood"), and a Grammy-winning cover of "Love Will Keep Us Together" as sung by the Captain and Tennille. Although Sedaka last visited the charts in 1980 with "Should've Never Let You Go," sung alongside his daughter Dara, he remains active to this day recording and performing, and penned a surprisingly candid autobiography, *Laughter in the Rain*.

what to buy: Both *All-Time Greatest Hits* ♫♫ (RCA, 1991, prod. Don Wardell) and *All-Time Greatest Hits, Vol. 2* ♫♫♫ (RCA, 1991, compilation prod. John Snyder, Ron Furmanek, Steve Kolanjian) house the best of his early-1960s work, while *Laughter in the Rain: The Best of Neil Sedaka, 1974–1980* ♫♫♫ (Varese Vintage, 1994, prod. Cary E. Mansfield) ably covers the highlights of his 1970s renaissance.

what to avoid: Caveat emptor: The invitingly titled *Tuneweaver* ♫♫ (Varese Vintage, 1995 comp. prod. Cary E. Mansfield, Leba Sedaka) actually contains 10 re-recordings of old Sedaka/Greenfield chestnuts mixed with 10 lackluster new compositions.

the rest:
Neil Sedaka Sings His Greatest Hits ♫♫ (RCA, 1962)
My Friend ♫♫ (Polydor, 1986)
Oh! Carol and Other Big Hits ♫♫ (RCA, 1989)
Greatest Hits Live ♫♫♫ (K-Tel, 1992)
The Collection ♫♫ (Royal Collection, 1993)

influences:
◀◀ Cole Porter, the Penguins, Hotlegs

▶▶ Frankie Valli, Barry Manilow, George Michael

Gary Pig Gold

The Senders

Formed 1988, in Minneapolis, MN.

Charmine Michelle, vocals; David Brown, guitar and vocals; Bill Black, upright bass; Marty Bryduck, drums; Bruce Pendalty, keyboards; Scott Johnson, tenor sax; Bob Byers, baritone and alto sax; Pete Masters, trombone.

If life were fair, the terrific swing-dancing scene at the heart of the movie *Swingers* would have brought back the big bands the way *Urban Cowboy* once rescued the entire country music industry. But the Squirrel Nut Zippers' popularity notwithstanding, the mid-1990s swing revival's days are probably numbered. Remember, the reason Benny Goodman and his contem-

poraries eventually died out was because it got too expensive to drag all those people, buses, and equipment around the country. The Senders, whose singer, Charmin Michelle, has a funny Betty Boop-like pitch, have the right spirit. They know how to swing, and they have enough connections to lure guest pianist-legend Charles Brown into the studio to perform energetic covers of B.B. King's "Everything I Do Is Wrong" and Wynonie Harris's "Wasn't That Good." With luck, they, and the Zippers and the Royal Crown Revue, will stick around long enough for every American to learn (or re-learn) the jitterbug and the foxtrot.

what to buy: *Jumpin' Uptown* ♫♫♫ (Blue Loon, 1996, prod. Pete Masters) has a lot of great energy, and nice sax and guitar solos—plus Michelle is a fun, charismatic singer—but this is a bar band that hasn't fully captured its live sound in the studio.

what to buy next: The band's debut, *Bar Room Blues* ♫♫♫ (Blue Loon, 1994, prod. Duke Robillard, the Senders), is interesting enough to make listeners pay a cover charge.

influences:
◀◀ Benny Goodman, Charles Brown, Glenn Miller, Billie Holiday, Doris Day, B.B. King

Steve Knopper

The Sentinels

Formed 1961, in San Luis Obispo, CA.

Tommy Nunes, lead guitar; Johnny Barbata, drums; Peter Graham, rhythm guitar; Gary Winburne, bass; Kenny Hinkle, keyboards; Bobby Holmquist, saxophone.

The Sentinels came to surf instrumentals more deeply rooted than many of the roughhouse ragers of 1960–63's pre-Beatles surf-music craze. They were managed (and later joined on saxophone) by Norman Knowles, who had unwittingly pioneered the genre with the Revels, who had hits with "Church Key" and "Comanche." Though the Sentinels were a surf band, and never created lounge music to any extent, today the instrumentals sound surprisingly cohesive on a tape or jukebox with Martin Denny's Hawaiian exotica or Juan Garcia Esquivel's Mexican space-age bachelor pad music.

Because central California was the area where most of the state's crops were produced, and migrant farmworkers and their families populated the area, the Sentinels absorbed Latin overtones and soul beats. To meet audience demand, the Revels, the Sentinels, and other bands from the San Luis Obispo area had the "Latin soul" groove far more entrenched than the groups from the greater Los Angeles area. "Latin'ia" (pronounced la-'teen-ya), one of the most beautiful instrumentals in surf, became their biggest hit during the surf craze (surfers loved taking oceanside trips to Mexico), and "Tor-Chula," with its cross-up of the Champs' "Tequila," the Fireballs' "Torquay," and pachuko-party atmosphere, is a favorite cut of even casual surf listeners.

what to buy: The Sentinels' first Del Fi album, *Big Surf* ✍✍✍✍ (Del Fi, 1963, prod. Bob Keane), is one of the best surf LPs ever recorded, crossing heavy surf throbbers such as the title track (with howl by Johnny Barbata), serene mood music ("Sunset Beach"), Latin soul ("Latin Soul"), and a Freddy King blues instrumental ("Hideaway") for good measure.

what to buy next: Their second LP, *Surfer Girl* ✍✍✍ (Del Fi, 1964, prod. Bob Keane), comes off more like a surfing movie soundtrack, with the horn section coming into play for a jazzier R&B surf sound. If the cheapo contract stuff can be sorted out, this is a band worthy of a box set.

worth searching for: The missing link is the wide variety of amazing 45s that were never committed to LP or CD to this date—including "Roughshod" b/w "Copycat Walk" (Admiral, 1961), "Infinity" b/w "Encinada" (Era, 1963), "The Bee" b/w "Over You" (Point, 1962)—yet feature crucial moments such as the Latin soul/surf "Telstar" take off "Infinity," the subdued beauty of "Christmas Eve," the bongo beatin' madness of "Roughshod," and some wild-as-hell frat-party stompers. *KFWB's Battle of the Surfing Bands* ✍✍✍✍ (Del Fi, 1963, Bob Keene) features one previously unreleased Sentinels track, the old Revels song "Vesuvius."

influences:

◄◄ The Revels, Tito Puente, Cal Tjader, Xavier Cugat

►► Dick Dale, the Beach Boys, Jan & Dean, Man or Astro-Man?, the Ventures, the Mermen, the Aqua Velvets

Domenic Priore

Doc Severinsen

Born Carl H. Severinsen, July 7, 1927, in Arlington, OR.

One of the most visible trumpet players of the last 40 years, Severinsen is a consummate professional who can execute a wide variety of musical genres with equal skill. Whether a bandleader, guest star, or hired hand, Severinsen has never allowed his legendary sartorial style or immense fame to intrude upon the character of his music.

The son of an Oregon dentist, he was nicknamed "Little Doc," and began playing trumpet at age seven. As a teenager, Severinsen won the Music Educator's National Contest, and was good enough to tour with the Ted Fiorito Orchestra. After World War II, he played trumpet and flugelhorn with bands led by Charlie Barnet, Tommy Dorsey, and Benny Goodman, before joining NBC as a staff musician in 1949. When he wasn't playing on the big network variety shows of the 1950s and early 1960s (the *Steve Allen* show among them), Severinsen recorded solid jazz with the likes of Stan Getz, Tito Puente, Gene Krupa, Milt Jackson, and softer, more commercial sounds with Dinah Washington and Ray Conniff. When Johnny Carson took over *The Tonight Show* from Jack Paar in 1963, Severinsen was the assistant bandleader behind Skitch Henderson. Carson discovered he had better comedic chemistry with the affable trumpet player than the dour Henderson, and by 1967 made Severinsen the bandleader of his nightly program. Always a colorful dresser, Severinsen began wearing increasingly wilder outfits to accommodate the jokes in Carson's monologues, and crystallized his TV persona as the goofy hipster. TV fame led to a series of well-received jazz and pop LPs, as well as being voted the Top Brass Player in more than a dozen *Playboy* music polls. When Carson left *The Tonight Show* in 1992, so did Severinsen, who has since led successful tours with his TV band and been named the principal pops conductor for orchestras in Phoenix, Minnesota, Milwaukee, and Buffalo. Though Severinsen is past 70 years old, he still has a pretty good lip.

what to buy: Severinsen's best recording with his fabled *Tonight Show* band is *Once More . . . with Feeling!* ✍✍✍✍ (Amherst, 1991, prod. Jeff Tyzik). In addition to the band's fine regular soloists, 14 popular jazz standards, and refreshing, colorful charts (written mostly by top arrangers Bill Holman and Tommy Newsom), this CD features guest appearances by Wynton Marsalis and Tony Bennett on one tune each. It includes classic gems such as "St. Louis Blues," "I Can't Get Started" (featuring Bennett), "Avalon" (with Marsalis), "What Is This Thing Called Love," and "Body and Soul."

what to buy next: Almost as good are *Doc Severinsen & the Tonight Show Orchestra* ✍✍✍ (Amherst, 1990, prod. Jeff Tyzik) and *Tonight Show Band, Vol. 2* ✍✍✍ (Amherst, 1990, prod. Jeff Tyzik), where the group alternates between playing big-band standards and fusion workouts in their inimitable, polished style.

what to avoid: There's too much Cincinnati Pops and not enough Severinsen on *Erich Kunzel/Cincinnati Pops* ✍✍ (Telarc, 1991, prod. Robert Woods, Elaine Martone).

4
2
6

paul shaffer

Doc Severinsen **(AP/Wide World Photos)**

best of the rest:
Facets 🎵🎵 (Amherst, 1988)
Doc Severinsen & Xebron 🎵🎵 (Passport Records, 1989)
Ja-Da 🎵🎵 (MCA, 1992)
Lullabies and Goodnight 🎵🎵 (Critique, 1992)
Good Medicine 🎵🎵 (RCA Bluebird, 1992)
Doc Severinsen & Friends 🎵🎵 (MCA Special Products, 1992)
Merry Christmas from Doc Severinsen & the Tonight Show Orchestra 🎵🎵🎵 (Amherst, 1992)
Two Sides of Doc Severinsen 🎵🎵🎵 (The Right Stuff, 1993)

worth searching for: The out-of-print *Tonight Show Band, Vol. 1* 🎵🎵🎵🎵 (Amherst, 1986, prod. Jeff Tyzik) won a Grammy for Best Jazz Instrumental—Big Band in 1987. If you're a real completist, you'll definitely want *Big Band Hit Parade* 🎵🎵🎵🎵 (Telarc, 1988, prod. Robert Woods), *Erich Kunzel/Cincinnati Pops Orchestra: Fiesta* 🎵🎵 (Telarc, 1990, prod. Robert Woods), *Unforgettably Doc* 🎵🎵🎵 (Telarc, 1992, prod. Robert Woods, Elaine Martone), and *Christmas with the Pops* 🎵🎵🎵🎵 (Telarc, 1993, prod. Robert Woods).

influences:
⏪ Harry James, Ray Anthony
⏩ Herb Alpert, Chuck Mangione

Ken Burke

Paul Shaffer

Born November 28, 1949, in Thunder Bay, Ontario, Canada.

The most unlikely candidate for leader of the *hipoisie,* Shaffer proves that being short, Canadian, and bald are no hindrances to fame in America. But that's only if you have a genuine reverence for show-biz schmaltz, a sense of ironic distance that matches the times, a true passion for rock 'n' roll, and a platform as appropriate as *Late Night with David Letterman* (and now *The Late Show*) to let your freaky flag fly, baby. Like that prototype of talk-show bandleaders, Doc Severinsen, Shaffer's peacock suits are undercut by his knowing asides, reminding us how the only stars who aren't phonies are the ones who know they are.

A one-time member of the *Saturday Night Live* band and a supporting Not Ready for Prime Time Player, Shaffer parlayed his *Late Night* fame into some impressive gigs: he produced, arranged, and played on a number of notable releases, served as musical director for each of the Rock and Roll Hall of Fame's induction ceremonies and the closing Atlanta Olympics ceremonies. As a recording artist, though, Shaffer has floundered, and neither of his two albums reveal much of his personality or his true musical ability. It just may be that television is his medium and he should stick to it.

what to buy: The concept for *Coast to Coast* 𝅘𝅥𝅮𝅘𝅥𝅮 (SBK, 1989, prod. Paul Shaffer, Tim Carr, others) was to fly Shaffer to the musical hot spots of America—Miami, Detroit, Minneapolis, New Orleans, Chicago—that shaped his musical world as a boy growing up in Canada and have him record songs old and new with the various cities' resident geniuses. It's an intriguing idea that meets with mixed results. Because he's not much of a vocalist, Shaffer's personality never really surfaces, so it's up to his guests—George Clinton, Brian Wilson, Don Covay, Alan Toussaint, and many others—to deliver. The album earned two Grammy nominations, but produced little of lasting value, save the doo-wop-meets-hip-hop opener, "When the Radio Is On," featuring Dion and then-Fresh Prince Will Smith.

what to avoid: With the Party Boys of Rock 'n' Roll, *The World's Most Dangerous Party* **woof!** (SBK, 1993, prod. Todd Rundgren) finds Shaffer and the *Late Night* band doing what they do on television—make like a modern Booker T. and the MG's and groove on instrumental versions of Talking Heads' "Burning Down the House," the Band's "Chest Fever," and assorted others, which is fine. But the two-disc affair is overlong and spoiled by inane "party" chatter —"Jon Lovitz, geez, it's nice of you to come!"—and forcing Tony Bennett to shower-sing a chorus of James Brown's "Doing It to Death."

worth searching for: Shaffer co-wrote the camp classic "It's Raining Men," which was recorded by the Weather Girls, and is available on their brief but snappy six-song release, *Success* 𝅘𝅥𝅮𝅘𝅥𝅮𝅘𝅥𝅮 (Columbia, 1983, prod. Paul Jabara). Despite his broad musical experience, Shaffer's most memorable performances have been on film: his turns as oily record promotion man Artie Fufkin in *This Is Spinal Tap* and Don Kirschner in the Gilda Radner-filmed stage play, *Gilda Live,* are definitive Shaffer moments. And if his years of ironic commentary on *Letterman* haven't made him a cartoon character, Disney did in *Hercules,* where Shaffer voiced the role of sidekick Hermes, whose impish visage also bore an uncanny resemblance to Shaffer's.

influences:
◄◄ Booker T. & the MG's, Doc Severinsen, Phil Spector
►► Young TV bandleaders and game-show hosts everywhere

Daniel Durchholz

Bud Shank
Born May 27, 1926, in OH.

Bud Shank reinvented himself as a hard bopper in the 1980s, but for decades, he was one of the alto sax's finest representatives of "cool jazz"—a softer, more subtle approach to bebop. Originally from Ohio, Shank moved to Los Angeles in the 1940s and became a fixture in West Coast jazz circles. Shank, who was known for a light style comparable to Lee Konitz, played with Charlie Barnet in the late 1940s and Stan Kenton in 1950–51, and he soon became a member of the Lighthouse All-Stars. This '50s band was so named because Shank, trumpeter Shorty Rogers, tenor saxman Bob Cooper, and other members played together regularly at the Lighthouse, a legendary jazz club in the Hermosa Beach suburb. During the '50s, Shank (who played the flute as a second instrument) also teamed up with Brazilian guitarist Laurindo Almeida for the groundbreaking *Brazilliance* sessions. The 1960s found Shank doing his share of film scores and soundtracks without giving up jazz, and in the 1970s he formed the L.A. Four with Almeida, Ray Brown, and Chuck Flores. Shank gave listeners some major surprises in the 1980s, when he gave up the flute for good, toughened his alto considerably, and went for a more aggressive hard bop approach. In the early '90s, he co-led a Lighthouse All Stars Reunion with Rogers.

what to buy: Recorded in 1953 and 1958, the superb Shank/Almeida collaborations reissued on *Brazilliance, Vol. 1* 𝅘𝅥𝅮𝅘𝅥𝅮𝅘𝅥𝅮𝅘𝅥𝅮𝅘𝅥𝅮 (Capitol, 1991, prod. Richard Bock) and *Brazilliance, Vol. 2* 𝅘𝅥𝅮𝅘𝅥𝅮𝅘𝅥𝅮𝅘𝅥𝅮𝅘𝅥𝅮 (Capitol, 1991, prod. Richard Bock) boast a landmark fusion of cool jazz and Brazilian music that predicted the bossa nova explosion of the early 1960s. While the *Brazilliance* sessions favor softness and restraint, Shank offered a tougher approach to Brazilian jazz on *Tomorrow's Rainbow* 𝅘𝅥𝅮𝅘𝅥𝅮𝅘𝅥𝅮𝅘𝅥𝅮 (Contemporary, 1989, prod. Bud Shank, David Keller). Keyboardist Marcos Silva, guitarist Richard Piexoto, and other Brazilian players clearly bring out the best in Shank, who is at his most soulful on treasures ranging from the rueful "The Colors of Despair" to the optimistic "The Railroad." Shank plays the flute exclusively on *Crystal Comments* 𝅘𝅥𝅮𝅘𝅥𝅮𝅘𝅥𝅮 (Concord, 1980, prod. Bud Shank), an intimate trio date featuring Bill Mays primarily on electric piano and Alan Broadbent mostly on acoustic piano.

As much warmth as he brings to the flute on "I'll Take Romance" and "On Green Dolphin Street," one can't help but wish Shank hadn't given it up entirely several years later.

what to buy next: Recorded when Shank was only 29, in January 1956, *Live at the Haig* 🎵🎵🎵 (Bainbridge, 1956) illustrates the richness of "cool jazz" and features the lyrical pianist Claude Williamson. Reborn as a hard bopper, Shank spares no passion on *I Told You So!* 🎵🎵🎵 (Candid, 1993, prod. Alan Bates, Mark Morganelli), recorded live at New York's Birdland and unites him with pianist Kenny Barron, bassist Lonnie Plaxico, and drummer Victor Lewis. On "Limehouse Blues" and George Cables's "I Told You So!" Shank is much more Phil Woods-ish than he was in his youth, and he leaves no doubt that he was enjoying the change immensely.

best of the rest:
Sunshine Express 🎵🎵🎵 (Concord, 1976)
That Old Feeling 🎵🎵🎵 (Contemporary, 1986)
Live at Jazz Alley 🎵🎵🎵 (Contemporary, 1986)
(With the Roumanis String Quartet) *Drifting Timelessly* 🎵🎵🎵 (Capri, 1991)

worth searching for: Led by Shank and Shorty Rogers and featuring Conte Candoli and Bob Cooper, the Lighthouse All Stars were reunited with exciting results on *America the Beautiful* 🎵🎵🎵 (Candid, 1991, prod. Bud Shank, Shorty Rogers, David Keller). From Bud Powell's "Un Poco Loco" to Rogers's "Lotus Bud," the group goes for a harder sound than it was known for in the 1950s.

influences:
◀◀ Lee Konitz

▶▶ Laurindo Almeida, João Gilberto

Alex Henderson

William Shatner

Born March 22, 1931, in Montreal, Quebec.

If you think William Shatner's hairpieces are funny, wait until you hear him sing. Captain Kirk's all-too-brief recording career consists of one album, 1968's *The Transformed Man*, and although Shatner wasn't the only actor to delude himself into thinking he could record contemporary hits in the late '60s, his album transcends kitsch and ventures into a territory no man had ever boldly gone before.

what to buy: *The Transformed Man* 🎵🎵🎵 or **woof!**, depending on your attitude (Varese Vintage, 1994) contains a pastiche of

Shakespeare soliloquies, dramatic readings, and pop covers, which Shatner reworks in his distinctive style by investing too much or too little emotion in every syllable and accentuating words seemingly at random. Easily the twin highlights of the CD are his interpretations of the Beatles' "Lucy in the Sky with Diamonds" and Bob Dylan's "Mr. Tambourine Man," the latter of which is capped off by a series of plaintive cries that has been likened to a kid running after an ice-cream truck.

what to buy next: *Golden Throats 1: The Great Celebrity Sing-Off!* 🎵🎵🎵 (Rhino, 1988, prod. various), which features Mae West, *Dragnet* star Jack Webb, and Jim Nabors, is filled with disastrous star attempts to vocalize, and Shatner's "Lucy in the Sky with Diamonds" and "Mr. Tambourine Man" are the centerpieces of this theater of the grotesque.

influences:
◀◀ William Shakespeare, Robert Goulet, John Lennon, Bob Dylan

▶▶ Thankfully no one

see also: *Leonard Nimoy*

Alex Gordon

Sandie Shaw

Born Sandra Goodrich, February 26, 1947, in Dagenham, Essex, England.

While neither a particularly distinctive vocalist nor an artist whose goals seemed at all challenging or even well thought out, Shaw remained nothing less than a colorful character, both on stage and off, throughout her long and varied career.

After toiling away as a teen-aged IBM machine operator, Sandra Goodrich made good on her dreams of stardom by sneaking backstage at an Adam Faith concert, cornering his manager, and bursting into an impromptu vocal audition in an unused dressing room. The manager was impressed more with the girl's nerve than with her ability, but nevertheless signed the 17-year-old to a contract, renamed her Sandie Shaw, and quickly put her into the studio alongside then red-hot producer Tony Hatch. By year's end, the song she'd sung on a special Beatles episode of ABC Television's *Shindig*, "(There's) Always Something There to Remind Me," became her first U.K. chart-topper, and she was a sensation on the British concert stage thanks to her alluring, barefoot persona. But for every hit she recorded over the next several years, she seemed to let an equal number slip through her fingers (including "It's Not Unusual" and "Alfie," both of which she declined to record before they became huge hits for Tom Jones and Cilla Black, respectively). She prematurely moved onto the career-killing European cabaret circuit as well, an ill-advised turn towards the middle of the road that was at odds with her somewhat controversial private life. (She was branded as the dastardly "other woman" in a highly publicized British divorce case.) Shaw then hosted her own BBC television series and recorded a string of increasingly anemic singles before retiring to theatrical work and, ultimately, domestic life. However, her career improved dramatically a decade later as she began collaborating on recordings with everyone from Heaven 17 to Chrissie Hynde, even scoring a comeback hit in 1984 alongside the Smiths.

what to buy: The definitive collection of her work remains *64/67 Complete Sandie Shaw Set* ♫♫♫ (Sequel, 1994, prod. various), an exhaustive two-disc, 55-track overview of her best 1960s recordings. Meanwhile, *Long Live Love* ♫♫♫ (Sequel, 1996, prod. various) offers a more abridged sampling.

what to buy next: Check the import bins for *Sandie/Me* ♫♫♫ (See For Miles, 1996, prod. Chris Andrews), *Love Me, Please Love Me* ♫♫♫ (RPM, 1996, prod. various), *The Sandie Shaw Supplement* ♫♫♫ (RPM, 1996, prod. various), and especially *Reviewing the Situation* ♫♫♫ (RPM, 1996, prod. various), all original British LP releases lovingly repackaged with Shaw's assistance and featuring, on the RPM discs, a multitude of intriguing single sides from her golden era as bonus tracks.

worth searching for: The 1980s recordings, in which Shaw tackled the work of Morrissey and the Jesus and Mary Chain to varying degrees of excess, are best assembled on *Collection* ♫♫♫ (Castle, 1991, prod. various) along with a selection of earlier cuts as well.

influences:

◀◀ Dusty Springfield, Petula Clark

▶▶ Marianne Faithfull, Nico, Anne Murray

Gary Pig Gold

George Shearing

Born August 13, 1919, in London, England.

Though this blind-at-birth pianist has always played straightforward jazz, his "block chord" style gives his improvisations a light, sunny air. Many of his albums, especially his Capitol Records material from the 1950s to the 1970s, have more in common with the melodic exotica music of Martin Denny and Arthur Lyman than the more-serious jazzmen who continue to cover his classic composition "Lullaby of Birdland." He also col-

laborated on countless recordings with Nat King Cole, Nancy Wilson, Dakota Staton, and Mel Tormé.

After studying music at the Linden Lodge School for the Blind, Shearing made a few recordings and toured with a band of blind musicians. The great jazz critic Leonard Feather helped him move from England to New York City in the 1940s, and he absorbed bebop into his already-developed swing style. The combination, especially given Shearing's natural melodic sense, became incredibly popular, and he scored lots of hit solo records in the late '40s before moving to Capitol. (Even Miles Davis recorded one of his songs, albeit renamed from "Conception" to "Deception.") Since switching from Capitol to the Concord Jazz label in the late '70s, Shearing has returned to pure jazz, and while the romantic lilt has never disappeared from his music, he's hardly a space-age bachelor pad cat anymore.

what to buy: Jazz fans may want a more thorough tour of Shearing's later material, but his instrumentals from the '50s and '60s are frequently playful and bouncy, with superb piano playing throughout. *Best of George Shearing (1955–1960)* ♫♫♫♫ (Blue Note, 1994, prod. various) begins with 18 tracks, including walking-barefoot-on-the-beach ballads like "Midnight in the Air," "Cheek to Cheek," and "Sand in My Shoes." *Best of George Shearing, Vol. 2 (1960–1969)* ♫♫♫♫ (Blue Note, 1997, prod. various) is just as strong as the first volume, only it adds Shearing's classic "Lullaby of Birdland."

what to buy next: Before Shearing discovered Miles Davis and Charlie Parker, he was a swing fanatic, having learned from Art Tatum and Earl Hines. The sides on *The London years 1939–1943* ♫♫♫♫ (Hep, 1995, prod. various) are mostly piano instrumentals (although Shearing plays the accordion on one) and they're even more straightforward and bouncy than his slightly more difficult bebop phase. One of his best original albums, *Jazz Moments* ♫♫♫ (Blue Note, 1962/1995), includes "Blues in 9/4," a jaunty "Makin' Whoopee," and "Gone with the Wind."

what to avoid: *Best of George Shearing* ♫♫ (Curb, 1993, prod. various) collects just 10 tracks, mostly standards like "Stardust" and "A Foggy Day," but it isn't nearly as comprehensive or interesting as the other *Best of* sets.

best of the rest:
My Ship ♫♫ (Verve, 1974)
On a Clear Day ♫♫♫ (Concord Jazz, 1980/1993)
Grand Piano ♫♫♫ (Concord Jazz, 1985)
Dexterity ♫♫♫ (Concord Jazz, 1987)
Compact Jazz ♫♫♫ (Verve, 1987)
Blues Alley and Jazz ♫♫♫ (Concord Jazz, 1989)
Piano ♫♫♫ (Concord Jazz, 1990)
I Hear a Rhapsody: Live at the Blue Note ♫♫♫♫ (Telarc, 1992)
I'll Take Romance ♫♫♫ (Capitol Special Products, 1992)
How Beautiful Is Night ♫♫♫ (Telarc, 1993)
That Shearing Sound ♫♫♫ (Telarc, 1994)
George Shearing and Friends ♫♫ (Pair, 1995)
Walkin' ♫♫♫ (Telarc, 1995)
Paper Moon ♫♫♫ (Telarc, 1996)

worth searching for: One of Shearing's original LPs, *The Swingin's Mutual* ♫♫♫♫ (Capitol, 1961), includes vocals by an early-career Nancy Wilson and, in addition to a revamped in-

strumental "Lullaby of Birdland," is a nice document of Shearing's prolonged melodic, swinging-exotica career phase.

influences:

◄◄ Art Tatum, Teddy Wilson, Earl Hines, Erroll Garner, Miles Davis, Thelonious Monk

►► Cal Tjader, Israel Crosby, Mel Tormé, Paul Weston, Morton Gould

Steve Knopper

Dinah Shore

Born Frances Rose Shore, March 1, 1917, in Winchester, TN. Died February 24, 1994, in Beverly Hills, CA.

After naming herself after her own hit song—1939's "Dinah"—this actress and singer achieved massive media stardom in three different decades. First, thanks to timely connections with bandleader Xavier Cugat and singer-TV personality Eddie Cantor, she was a hit singer; in 1941, she earned her own radio show; and for almost 20 years, beginning in the 1950s, she hosted *The Dinah Shore Show,* one of the most popular programs on television. Though Shore's family moved to Nashville when she was six, the pop songs she sang were almost the anthesis of country-western twang. She struggled, initially, failing auditions to sing for the Dorsey Brothers and Benny Goodman big bands, then got a job singing at a Long Island, New York, nightclub (which was later canceled). A chance connection with Cugat, then a big-time bandleader, became her first major break, and she used it to sing for radio networks and a well-known chamber music group. By the time Eddie Cantor hired her to sing on his popular radio program, she was ready to sing big, vibrato-filled pop standards like "Baby, It's Cold Outside" and "Buttons and Bows." Her charm was a natural for another medium, television, where she reigned as hostess, mistress of ceremonies, interviewer, and personality through the 1970s.

what to buy: Shore's recorded material comes mostly from the 1940s; the complementary collections *16 Most Requested Songs* ♫♫♫ (Sony, 1991, prod. various) and *16 Most Requested Songs: Encore* ♫♫♫ (Sony, 1995, prod. Didier C. Deutsch) show off Shore's clear-voiced, straightforward talent for standards, such as "Willow Weep for Me" and "Mad about the Boy."

what to buy next: "Buttons and Bows," a campy 1940s hit, shows up on several other hits sets, including *Best of* ♫♫♫ (Curb, 1991) and *More of the Best* ♫♫♫ (Laserlight, 1996, prod. Rod McKuen).

what to avoid: *Greatest Hits* ♫♫ (Laserlight, 1994) merely duplicates the other sets on the market.

worth searching for: Shore played comedian-singer-radio-host Eddie Cantor's singing straightwoman for several years, and her material comes across nicely on Cantor's hard-to-find comedy-variety album *The Show That Never Aired* ♫♫♫ (Original Cast, 1993).

influences:

◀◀ Judy Garland, Billie Holiday, Bing Crosby, Eddie Cantor, Xavier Cugat

▶▶ Jo Stafford, Rosemary Clooney, Gordon MacRae, Rosie O'Donnell, Eddie Fisher

Steve Knopper

Bobby Short

Born Robert Waltrip, September 15, 1926, in Danville, IL.

One of the best, if not *the* best, cabaret performers alive, Short has made the Cafe Carlyle—where he has performed eight months out of the year since 1968—a New York institution. His playful renderings of just about every jazz standard, from Gershwin to Porter to Rodgers and Hart, are made even better by his ebullient personality. His collection of even the most obscure Gershwin tunes is practically mind-boggling. Short left home at age 11 when, with his mother's permission, he went to Chicago to perform. His boyish smile and crisp delivery made him a favorite of the 1940s, when he met influences Art Tatum and Nat King Cole. Fans of jazz standards are likely to be pulled in by his boundless enthusiasm for the music.

what to buy: *Bobby Short Is K-RA-ZY for Gershwin* ♫♫♫♫ (Atlantic, 1990, prod. Lewis Hahn, Nesuhi Ertegun, Bob Porter) is a beautiful, two-disc set of Short's best Gershwin tunes—from the familiar to the completely foreign. Short is able to show off his catalog-like repertoire of Gershwin's songs, and the bubbly mood of the album is infectious. *Bobby, Noel & Cole* ♫♫♫ (Atlantic, 1989, prod. Lewis Hahn) is a combination set of two albums: *Bobby Short Loves Cole Porter* and *Bobby Short Is Mad about Cole Porter*. Both give Short the chance to show off his encyclopedic knowledge of jazz songs.

what to buy next: *50 by Bobby Short* ♫♫♫ (Atlantic, 1986, prod. various) is a fun collection of tunes, boosted by Short's already buoyant personality. The best tracks: "Manhattan" and a song originally made famous by Groucho Marx, then sung again by Robin Williams in *The Fisher King:* "Lydia, the Tattooed Lady."

best of the rest:

Celebrates Rodgers & Hart ♫♫♫♫ (Atlantic, 1975)

worth searching for: With *Songs of New York* ♫♫♫♫ (Telarc, 1995), which includes tunes from "Autumn in New York" to "She's a Latin from Manhattan," Short finds an eclectic mix of songs that say something about the Big Apple. Short is joined by two fine musicians: Warren Vache, a top-notch cornet player, and the terrifically named Bucky Pizzarelli on guitar.

influences:

◀◀ Nat "King" Cole, Art Tatum

▶▶ Michael Feinstein, Harry Connick Jr.

Carl Quintanilla

Jane Siberry

Born October 12, 1955, in Toronto, Ontario, Canada.

A Canadian musician who brings song, poetry, film, and technology together, Siberry sings in a style that makes her nearly impossible to fit into any format—"electrified modern folk" is as close a description as you can probably get. She began humbly, financing her first record, *No Borders Here*, with tips earned waitressing as she studied microbiology at the University of Guelph. Since then, she has tackled rock and jazz in styles reminiscent of Laurie Anderson—only more melodic. Her most recent works are fodder for easy-listeners who like something a little sexy and blue with their love songs. Siberry's concert performances wow audiences with self-produced videos, stream-of-consciousness rambles, and even question-and-answer sessions. "How do you do your hair?" is one question that seems to pop up frequently to this multi-coiffed musician.

what to buy: *When I Was a Boy* ♫♫♫♫ (Reprise, 1993, prod. Jane Siberry, Brian Eno, Michael Brook) is a dark, beautiful masterpiece. It's a wash of vocal and keyboard textures, and some of the songs resemble short movies, complete with a cast of singing angels and medieval-style sinners, such as the electronic "Temple" or "An Angel Stepped Down," both heavy on Old Testament imagery.

what to buy next: *Bound by the Beauty* ♫♫♫♫ (Reprise, 1989, prod. Jane Siberry, John Switzer) has the excellent title track and "Something about Trains," two k.d. lang–like country-folk-rock songs anchored by Siberry's powerful, angelic voice. *No Borders Here* ♫♫♫ (Duke Street Records, 1984, prod. Jon Goldsmith, Kerry Crawford, Jane Siberry, John Switzer) was Siberry's first release and is worth getting for "Mimi on the Beach," an underground hit in Canada.

what to avoid: Siberry recorded 13 songs she wrote as a teenager on the appropriately titled *Teenager* &&& (Sheeba, 1996). Clean and sparse, the songs charm in their innocent way—but they're recommended for die-hard fans interested in a historical point of view.

the rest:
The Walking &&& (Reprise, 1988)

worth searching for: Siberry's brooding "She's Like the Swallow" on Hector Zazou's Arctic-song collection *Songs from the Cold Seas* &&& (Sony, 1995, prod. Hector Zazou) is a gem following in the same style as *When I Was a Boy.*

influences:

◀◀ Laurie Anderson, Joni Mitchell, Kate Bush, Emmylou Harris, Peter Gabriel, Brian Eno, Daniel Lanois

▶▶ Suzanne Vega, Sinéad O'Connor, k.d. lang, Enya, Björk

Jack Jackson

Carly Simon

Born June 25, 1945, in New York, NY.

Strength, honesty, independence, and a mellow mood were what the top female singer-songwriters strove to deliver in the early 1970s, and Simon fit the bill. Her work obviously influenced 1990s stars known for confessional songwriting—Jewel, Tori Amos, Shawn Colvin, and so forth—but she also was among the first rock-era artists to look back into pop standards and torch songs for contemporary album fodder.

Simon and her sister, Lucy, formed a duo in the mid-1960s, but it wasn't until Simon went solo in the early 1970s that she found national success, namely with "That's the Way I've Always Heard It Should Be." She had several pop hits throughout the 1970s, a decade when she was married to fellow mellow popster James Taylor (they married in 1972 and divorced 11 years later). Her commercial appeal began slipping in the late 1970s, and she rarely toured due to stage fright. But Simon continues to land the occasional chart hit.

what to buy: Two years before Linda Ronstadt scored with her first of three albums of standards, Simon released *Torch* &&& (Warner Bros., 1981, prod. Mike Mainieri), a steamy set of traditional pop by the likes of Hoagy Carmichael and Stephen

Sondheim. Simon's best-known early 1970s hits comprise *The Best of Carly Simon* &&&& (Elektra, 1975, prod. Richard Perry, Paul Samwell-Smith, Eddie Kramer). Simon's pen strokes romantic disillusionment ("That's the Way I've Always Heard It Should Be"), wicked gossip ("You're So Vain"), and vulnerable confession ("Haven't Got Time for the Pain") in a mostly mellow musical setting. *No Secrets* &&&& (Elektra, 1972, prod. Richard Perry) is Simon's strongest studio set, living up to the title with lyrical honesty and boasting in "You're So Vain" and "The Right Thing to Do."

what to buy next: The first disc of three included with *Clouds in My Coffee: 1965–1995* &&&& (Arista, 1995, exec. prod. Carly Simon, Frank Filipetti) rounds up Simon's 18 biggest hits from various labels; it includes the hard-to-find "Nobody Does It Better," the Carole Bayer Sager/Marvin Hamlisch–written theme for *The Spy Who Loved Me.* Rarities and key album tracks round out the box set.

what to avoid: "Carly Simon" and "operetta" rarely occur in the same sentence; the overly ambitious *Carly Simon's Romulus Hunt: A Family Opera* && (Angel, 1993, prod. various) demonstrates why. Simon sings only one track here. *Spoiled Girl* && (Epic, 1985, prod. various) found Simon teetering, trying to gain footing on the day's slick and slippery pop landscape.

the rest:
Carly Simon &&& (Elektra, 1971)
Anticipation &&& (Elektra, 1971)
Hotcakes &&& (Elektra, 1974)
Playing Possum &&& (Elektra, 1975)
Another Passenger &&& (Elektra, 1976)
Boys in the Trees &&& (Elektra, 1978)
Spy &&& (Elektra, 1979)
Come Upstairs &&& (Warner Bros., 1980)
Hello Big Man &&& (Warner Bros., 1983)
Coming Around Again &&& (Arista, 1987)
Greatest Hits Live &&& (Arista, 1988)
My Romance &&& (Arista, 1990)
Have You Seen Me Lately? &&& (Arista, 1990)
This Is My Life && (Qwest, 1992)
Letters Never Sent &&& (Arista, 1994)
Film Noir &&& (Arista, 1997)

influences:

◀◀ Barbra Streisand, Peggy Lee, Ella Fitzgerald, Frank Sinatra, Carole King, Elton John, the Beatles, the Rolling Stones

▶▶ Tori Amos, Jewel, Suzanne Vega

Jay Dedrick

Bobby Short (© Jack Vartoogian)

Nina Simone (© Jack Vartoogian)

Nina Simone

Born Eunice Waymon, February 21, 1933, in Tryon, NC.

Since she started recording in the late '50s, Simone has proven herself a master of most modern genres—R&B, pop, jazz-pop, gospel, and blues. Her mastery comes from the absolute originality of her vocals, idiosyncratic phrasing, and stark coloration. And Simone's success as an African American woman paralleled some of the century's most important gains in the social status of both African Americans and women.

Simone came to New York from North Carolina to study classical piano at the Juilliard School, and she went to work as a nightclub singer for the money in the late '50s. Soon, she was singing for more than money, and she was singing more material than the traditional nightclub singer—an early Simone album on the Bethlehem or Candix label might include a show tune, a jazz standard, a traditional gospel composition, and a French ballad. Through the '60s, the social upheaval occurring around Simone affected her music deeply. Simone wrote her

own songs occasionally ("Old Jim Crow," "Mississippi Goddam," "I Want a Little Sugar in My Bowl") but usually worked as an interpreter, and her versions of "Don't Let Me Be Misunderstood," "I Put a Spell on You," "Here Comes the Sun," and "I Shall Be Released" are all career high points. And in the late '60s she co-wrote "Young, Gifted, and Black," which would become a hit for Aretha Franklin. But to think of Simone as a balladeer with a social agenda is to ignore the almost willful eclecticism that has characterized her work from the start. Who else has recorded songs by Anthony Newley, George Gershwin, Jimmy Webb, and Chuck Berry? In the early '70s, Simone divorced her husband and manager Andy Stroud and virtually stopped recording until 1993, when the high visibility of her songs in the film *Point of No Return* and a new album, *Single Woman*, returned her to the public eye.

what to buy: *The Blues* 🎵🎵🎵🎵 (1964/BMG/Jive/Novus, 1991) is one of her towering achievements, with sinuous, chilling, beautiful music, including versions of "Day and Night," "Since

I Fell for You," "Gin House Blues," and Bob Dylan's "I Shall Be Released."

what to buy next: *Little Girl Blue* ℣℣℣℣ (Bethlehem, 1959) is early Simone, but it's still wonderful, especially "My Baby Just Cares for Me," "I Loves You Porgy," and "Mood Indigo." *Nina Simone at the Village Gate* ℣℣℣℣ (Collectables, 1993, prod. Cal Lampley) is a live 1961 performance that has definitive versions of "The House of Rising Sun" and the gospel staple "Children Go Where I Send You."

what to avoid: *Single Woman* ℣℣ (Asylum, 1993) was hailed at the time as return to form, and it was in some sense, since it marked Simone's return to major-label recording after almost two decades. But the arrangements here are weak, the selection of material is perplexing (three compositions by Rod McKuen?), and while the vocals are as elegant and bewitching as ever, the whole project has a sense of defeat. Not an embarrassment, but nothing to write home about, either.

best of the rest:
Broadway, Blues, Ballads ℣℣℣ (Verve, 1964)
Pastel Blues/Let It All Hang Out ℣℣℣ (Verve, 1965)

worth searching for: *Baltimore* ℣℣℣ (Sony, 1993) was a 1978 comeback album, and it's noteworthy for the Randy Newman title track and an odd cover of the Hall and Oates hit "Rich Girl."

influences:
◀◀ Marian Anderson, Billie Holiday, Sarah Vaughan, Kitty White

▶▶ Harry Belafonte, Aretha Franklin, Dusty Springfield, Diamanda Galas, Cassandra Wilson

Ben Greenman

Frank Sinatra

Born December 12, 1915, in Hoboken, NJ. Died May 14, 1998, in Los Angeles, CA.

The Rat Pack–era Frank Sinatra was the model of all things lounge—he had the swagger, the hat perched at a jaunty angle on his head, the loosened tie, the cigarette, and the babes lined up from Las Vegas to Los Angeles. Countless performers have imitated the 1950s and 1960s Sinatra, from crooner Vic Damone's testing goofy turns of phrase to comedian Bill Murray pulling off a hilarious *Saturday Night Live* parody decades later. But for all the emphasis on image, there's no imitating Sinatra's talent and command: he picked his phrases carefully and told each song's story as though his way were the only way it could be told.

Cocktail Classics

Unchained Melody

18-Karat **The Righteous Brothers**
*Unchained Melody:
The Very Best Of*
(PolyGram)

Bombsville! **Andy Williams**
Best of Andy Williams
(Curb)

An only child of Italian immigrant parents, the teen-aged Sinatra began singing professionally against their wishes. He stubbornly clung to his ambitions, so his mother caved in and found him a breakthrough gig at the Rustic Cabin in Englewood, New Jersey, in the late '30s. By 1939, he had signed on with Harry James's orchestra, then moved to Tommy Dorsey's big band. Sinatra's voice jumped out of the speakers on "I'll Never Smile Again," the first vocal he recorded with Dorsey. When they played New York's famous Paramount Theater in 1942, Sinatra's effect on the crowd was electric, and the bobby-soxers swooned in their seats. Dorsey was miffed that his singer was getting a better reaction than the band. Sinatra soon left to start a solo career that changed the course of the music business, from big bands to individual star singers.

The young Sinatra sang ballads in a deceptively breathless near-whisper, holding notes with the slightest of quavers, sounding sincere and more vulnerable and sensuous than any mainstream pop singer before him. (Billie Holiday's singing was a major influence.) When his career as a crooner went bust toward the end of the '40s, he methodically reinvented himself as a mature singer (and movie actor). At age 37, he signed with Capitol Records and began to refocus his image as a swinging, rambunctious bon vivant, who sometimes got very low in the wee, small hours of the morning—and developed a confident, huskier sound to match. This was the era of the Rat Pack, the gang of entertainers that included Dean Martin, Sammy Davis Jr., Peter Lawford, and Joey Bishop. The group defined the lounge ethos with their swaggering, cocktail-in-hand, doll-on-each-arm, hipper-than-thou attitude; see the films *Ocean's Eleven* and *Robin and the Seven Hoods* to witness this species of lizard in its natural habitat.

Despite the swagger of his approach, Sinatra maintained an interesting humility in concert, dutifully crediting the songwriters and arrangers who provided him with crucial springboard material. In the '60s, he continued to swing, but also ventured into folk-influenced contemporary pop and even soft rock. He "retired" in 1971, only to come back in 1973 and continuing to release records through 1985. Although his voice was deteriorating (his upper register became raw and his pitch sometimes wavered), his interpretive skills diminished only slightly, and he remained a major concert draw until his 1995 retirement. On the 1993 *Duets* album, in which a collaboration with rock singer Bono slammed against a more conventional one with Bette Midler, the duets reportedly were overdubbed at separate sessions—suggesting that Sinatra needed studio tweaking to make coherent recordings. You can hear technology clamp down the sound as he loses his breath at the end of phrases. Still, these records were big events that extended Sinatra's hitmaking punch into the '90s.

what to buy: *The Capitol Years* 🎵🎵🎵🎵 (Capitol, 1990, executive prod. Ron McCarrell, Wayne Watkins, prod. Ron Furmanek) is a succinct overview of Sinatra's classic period in three CDs; his best work during this time was in collaboration with Nelson Riddle, whose arrangements on such tunes as "I've Got the World on a String" nailed the optimistic, prime-of-life feeling Sinatra brought to his singing. (Sinatra was also successful working with Gordon Jenkins, whose arrangements had a more stately, reflective feeling, and Billy May, whose arrangements swung more forcefully than Riddle's.) If the price tag for the

four-CD set is too high, *Best of "The Capitol Years"* 🎵🎵🎵🎵 (Capitol, 1992, compilation prod. Wayne Watkins) and *Frank Sinatra: Capitol Collector's Series* 🎵🎵🎵🎵 (Capitol, 1989, compilation prod. Ron Furmanek) offer excellent single-CD overviews. Capitol released 23 Sinatra albums from 1953 to 1961; 16 of them were cohesive units (ushering in the era of the concept album), all collected in a box called *Concepts* 🎵🎵🎵🎵 (Capitol, 1992, prod. Voyle Gilmore, David Cavanaugh). You can buy them separately—all 16 are must-buys—but in CD form some questionable bonus tracks have been added. *The Complete Capitol Singles Collection* 🎵🎵🎵🎵 (Capitol, 1996, compilation prod. Brad Benedict, executive prod. Wayne Watkins) is a four-CD set that lives up to its title with A-sides and B-sides, many of which had not been available on CD before. *The Columbia Years (1943–1952): The Complete Recordings* 🎵🎵🎵🎵 (Columbia, 1993, compilation prod. Didier C. Deutsch) collects on 12 CDs the Sinatra sides that defined a new role for pop singers. They were revolutionary then and enjoyable now; a four-disc distillation called *The Best of the Columbia Years: 1943–1952* 🎵🎵🎵🎵 (Columbia, 1995, compilation prod. Didier C. Deutsch) came out later, for the budget-conscious.

what to buy next: *The Song Is You* 🎵🎵🎵🎵 (RCA, 1993, prod. Paul Williams) is the definitive collection of Sinatra's work with Tommy Dorsey, on five CDs; another version is distilled to one CD: *I'll Be Seeing You* 🎵🎵🎵🎵 (RCA, 1993, prod. Paul Williams). Then, there's *The Reprise Collection* 🎵🎵🎵🎵 (Reprise, 1990, compilation prod. Mo Ostin, Joe McEwen, James Isaacs), which isn't as satisfying as the collections of earlier work, but presents a picture of adventurous maturity. The four-CD set is overlong, yet it covers a much longer time period than the Capitol collection—from a 1960 recording of "Let's Fall in Love" to a 1986 recording of "Mack the Knife." In 1991, Reprise released the condensed, single-CD *Sinatra Reprise: The Very Good Years* 🎵🎵🎵🎵 (Reprise, 1991, compilation prod. Mo Ostin, Joe McEwen, James Isaacs), then went the other way, with *The Complete Reprise Studio Recordings* 🎵🎵🎵🎵 (Reprise, 1995, compilation prod. Mo Ostin, Joe McEwen, James Isaacs) on 20 discs. Yikes!

what to avoid: *Duets* 🎵 (Capitol, 1993, prod. Phil Ramone) and *Duets II* 🎵 (Capitol, 1994, prod. Phil Ramone) may have revived Sinatra's recording career, but they consist of mostly meaningless (and chemistry-less) re-recordings. This is said with infinite sadness. For the first time in his career, Sinatra had to depend on others to carry him. For two-thirds of the over-ambitious *Trilogy* 🎵🎵 (Reprise, 1980, prod. Sonny Burke), Sinatra summed up where he was in the late '70s. The gorgeous Nelson Riddle arrangement of George Harrison's "Something" and the swaggering "Theme from

Frank Sinatra **(AP/Wide World Photos)**

New York, New York" became virtual signature tunes of the early autumn of Sinatra's career. Conceived as a three-LP look at the past, present, and the future, Sinatra could have skipped the future part, which is goofy at best, ponderous at worst. A boiled-down, single album from these sessions could have been dynamite. Also, *All-Time Greatest Hits, Vols. 1–4* 🎵🎵 (RCA, late 1980s) is a badly done collection of Sinatra's work with Dorsey.

best of the rest:

Songs for Swingin' Lovers! 🎵🎵🎵🎵 (Capitol, 1956/1997)
A Swingin' Affair! 🎵🎵🎵🎵 (Capitol, 1957/1991)
Come Fly with Me 🎵🎵🎵🎵 (Capitol, 1957/1987)
Where Are You? 🎵🎵🎵🎵 (Capitol, 1957/1991)
(Frank Sinatra Sings for) Only the Lonely 🎵🎵🎵🎵 (Capitol, 1958/1996)
Come Dance with Me! 🎵🎵🎵🎵 (Capitol, 1958/1987)
No One Cares 🎵🎵🎵🎵 (Capitol, 1959/1991)
Nice 'N' Easy 🎵🎵🎵🎵 (Capitol, 1960/1991)
Sinatra's Swingin' Session!!! 🎵🎵🎵🎵 (Capitol, 1960/1987)
Sinatra/Basie 🎵🎵🎵🎵 (Reprise, 1963/1988)
September of My Years 🎵🎵🎵🎵 (Reprise, 1965/1988)

Francis Albert Sinatra and Antonio Carlos Jobim 🎵🎵🎵🎵 (Reprise, 1967/1988)
Francis A. Sinatra & Edward K. Ellington 🎵🎵🎵🎵 (Reprise, 1968/1988)
V-Discs 🎵🎵🎵🎵 (Columbia, 1994)
Sinatra and Sextet: Live in Paris 🎵🎵🎵🎵 (Reprise, 1994)
Portrait of Sinatra 🎵🎵🎵🎵 (Columbia, 1997)
Frank Sinatra with the Red Norvo Quartet: Live in Australia 1959 🎵🎵🎵🎵 (Blue Note, 1997)

worth searching for: There's a wealth of radio, TV, and concert performances available on small labels that aren't often easy to find at your local CD store. The place to start is with such '40s material as *The Unheard Frank Sinatra, Vols. 1–4* 🎵🎵🎵 (VJC, 1990), and then such '50s material as *Perfectly Frank* 🎵🎵🎵 (BCD, 1990). The Sinatra-searcher's grail is *From the Vaults*, a 750-copy pressing that's almost impossible to track down.

influences:

⏪ Billie Holiday, Bing Crosby, Russ Columbo, Louis Armstrong, Nelson Riddle, Duke Ellington, Cole Porter, Al Jolson

▶▶ Tony Bennett, Harry Connick Jr., Vic Damone, Rosemary Clooney, Jo Stafford, Bono, Billy Joel, Bruce Springsteen, Eddie Fisher, Rudy Vallee, Nancy Sinatra, Frank Sinatra Jr.

Salvatore Caputo

Frank Sinatra Jr.

Born 1943.

Best known as a kidnapping victim, the son of Frank Sinatra has been a celebrity all his life. But as a singer, he has been something of a joke, a limited imitator of his father blessed with similar mannerisms, the all-important Sinatra name, and none of his father's talent, voice, or preternatural sense of phrasing. At the end of 1963, when he was only 19, Sinatra Jr. was snatched from a Lake Tahoe motel and held in the San Fernando Valley. The kidnappers demanded a ransom of $240,000 from his father. Lawmen like Robert Kennedy and J. Edgar Hoover, as well as outlaws like Sam Giancana, offered to help. The kidnappers were quickly apprehended, tried, convicted, and sentenced. One of them, Barry Keenan, is now a successful Los Angeles–area businessman. Meanwhile, for the past several years, Frank Jr. has been leader of several touring big bands that play almost exclusively standards, including standards Frank Sr. made famous. Still, Frank Jr. would not even merit a footnote without his father's legacy. With it, and with his father's generosity—Ol' Blue Eyes invited his son to sing with him on the 1991 *Duets* album—he is still only a footnote, albeit an interesting one.

what to buy: *As I Remember It* ♫♫♫ (Angel, 1996) finds Frank covering Frank, with Sinatra *fils* offering his versions of Sinatra *pere*'s "Night and Day," "I've Got the World on a String," "Three Coins in a Fountain," and "In the Wee Small Hours of the Morning." Not essential by any means, but given the crushing weight of history, not too shabby.

what to buy next: Young Blue Eyes is the centerpiece of Pat Longo's Super Big Band's record *Billy May for President* ♫♫♫ (Townhall Records, 1983, prod. Lincoln Mayorga), a tribute to the venerable jazz arranger and Sinatra collaborator. Here, son takes on a set of mostly originals, and even contributes a song of his own, "Missy."

worth searching for: After cooking up dream projects for vocalists like Iggy Pop and Ozzy Osbourne, Detroit avant-funksters Was (Not Was) assembled an incredibly weird group of musicians for *What Up Dog?* ♫♫♫♫ (Chrysalis, 1988, prod. Don Was, David Was, Paul Staveley O'Duffy). Guitar shredder Stevie Salas is here, along with organ legend Al Kooper, jazz bassist Marcus Miller, horn star Mark Isham—and Frank Sinatra Jr., warbling his way through the Sinatra parody "Wedding Vows in Vegas."

influences:

◀◀ Frank Sinatra

Ben Greenman

Nancy Sinatra

Born June 8, 1940, in Jersey City, NJ.

Nancy Sinatra may not have inherited her famous father's pipes or skill (and truth be told, brother Frank Jr. had greater vocal range and better technique), but she could channel her old man's attitude to great effect. In the early '60s she had been recording trite teen pop singles such as "Cuff Links and a Tie Clip" and the Paris Sisters' "Tonight You Belong to Me" for her father's Reprise Records with little success. In 1965, veteran producer Lee Hazelwood toughened her vocal manner, added a slab of rockabilly echo, jangly acoustic guitar, tambourine, and some punchy Billy Strange horn arrangements. Their first collaboration, "So Long, Babe" was a modest chart entry, but "These Boots Are Made for Walkin'," with its catchy descending bass line, became an international #1 hit and recast Sinatra's public persona from prim pop singer to world weary go-go dancer (the perfect correlation to her dad's image as a sexually aggressive hipster). She sang soft and sweet on her idealistic 1967 hit, "Sugar Town," and the chart-topping duet with her father, "Somethin' Stupid" (on which daddy Frank is clearly carrying Nancy). With the go-go craze played out and the face of pop music becoming more eclectic, Sinatra teamed up with her gravel-voiced producer to create a sort of country version of Sonny and Cher. Sinatra's appearance as a sexy, with-it IRS agent in the 1968 assembly-line turkey film *Speedway* not only gave Elvis Presley his first important co-star in years, but allowed her to strut her stuff on "Your Groovy Self." By 1969, the hits stopped coming and Sinatra moved on to make two fine LPs for RCA; her final chart entry was a double-entendre country reunion with Lee Hazelwood, "Did You Ever (All the Time)." Sinatra wouldn't record again until a heavily hyped 1995 comeback, and these days, she mostly works as her father's official biographer—though she still looks pretty good in a mini-skirt and go-go boots.

Nancy Sinatra (Archive Photos)

what to buy: Sinatra's big run of sexy and sweet '60s hits and some interesting LP tracks, with and without Hazelwood, are included on *The Hit Years* 𝄞𝄞𝄞𝄞 (Rhino, 1986, prod. Lee Hazelwood) and *Lightning's Girl* 𝄞𝄞𝄞𝄞 (Raven, 1994, prod. various), which has more tracks, but is harder to find.

what to buy next: Sundazed has reissued all of the distaff Sinatra's Reprise LPs, and has added several bonus tracks to each one. The best of these are *Boots* 𝄞𝄞𝄞 (Reprise, 1966/Sundazed 1995, reissue prod. Bob Irwin) and *How Does That Grab You?* 𝄞𝄞𝄞 (Reprise, 1966/Sundazed, 1995 reissue prod. Bob Irwin), both featuring all the slap and sass you'd expect. Also, the addition of movie theme songs "Tony Rome" and "You Only Live Twice" considerably enliven the reissue of *Nancy in London* 𝄞𝄞𝄞 (Reprise, 1966/Sundazed, 1996, reissue prod. Bob Irwin), which includes her duet with Frank Sinatra on the seriously weird "Life's a Trippy Thing."

what to avoid: The novelty of Hazelwood's craggy-voiced collaborations with Nancy Sinatra on *Fairy Tales & Fantasies: Best of Nancy Sinatra & Lee Hazelwood* 𝄞𝄞 (Rhino, 1989, prod. Lee Hazelwood) wears thin awfully fast.

the rest:
Country My Way 𝄞𝄞𝄞 (Reprise, 1967/Sundazed, 1996)
Sugar 𝄞𝄞 (Reprise, 1967/Sundazed, 1995)
Movin' with Nancy 𝄞𝄞𝄞 (Reprise, 1968/Sundazed, 1996)
Nancy 𝄞𝄞𝄞 (Reprise, 1969/Sundazed, 1996)
One More Time 𝄞𝄞𝄞 (Cougar, 1995)
Sheet Music: Her Favorite Love Songs N/A (DCC, 1998)

worth searching for: Sinatra does right by her dad on *Frank Sinatra, My Father* 𝄞𝄞𝄞 (Dove Books on Tape, 1995, prod. Nancy Sinatra), and it's pretty cool to hear her tell what she knows about his life.

influences:
◀◀ Frank Sinatra, Wanda Jackson, Gogi Grant
▶▶ k.d. lang, Patty Loveless, Lisa Germano, the Spice Girls

Ken Burke

Singers Unlimited
See: The Hi-Lo's

Sir Julian
Born Julian Gould, date and place unknown.

This peppy Hammond organist put out several instrumental albums in the 1950s and 1960s, but he's a mysterious character today, winding up on loungey organ collections and that's

about it. His grooves were ominous, almost soulful, but he managed to wrench every possible cheesy tone out of his Hammond solos. As far as we know, he wasn't a real knight.

what's available: Sir Julian's organ-heavy instrumentals "Movin' at Midnight" and "A Man and a Woman" are some of the best tracks on the novelty-heavy *Ultra-Lounge, Vol. 11: Organs in Orbit* 𝄞𝄞𝄞 (Capitol, 1996, compilation prod. Brad Benedict); other artists include Martin Denny, Walter Wanderley, and Jackie Davis. Julian's handful of original solo LPs, which are far out of print, include the terrific *The Thirteen Fingers of Sir Julian* 𝄞𝄞𝄞 (RCA Victor, 1962, prod. Hugo and Luigi).

influences:
◀◀ Walter Wanderley, Lenny Dee, Antonio Carlos Jobim
▶▶ Denny McLain

Steve Knopper

Keely Smith
See: Louis Prima & Keely Smith

Stephen Sondheim
Born March 22, 1930, in New York City, NY.

Sondheim has written some of the more memorable musicals of the last several decades, and many critics say he's one of this century's best theatrical composers and lyricists, although Irving Berlin, Cole Porter, and Rodgers and Hammerstein are tough acts to follow. Because of his consistently strong writing (he did the lyrics to *West Side Story* and scored *Reds,* among many others) and continued popularity, Broadway productions never went out of style, even though rock 'n' roll took over the pop-music industry from theatrical showtunes. Sondheim's supporters scoff at comparisons to the overwrought Andrew Lloyd Webber, but the lyricist and composer's influential work certainly paved the way for Lloyd Webber's massive popularity in the '80s and '90s.

The son of wealthy parents, Sondheim attended private schools and wrote his first musical when he was 15. He attended Princeton University, winning all sorts of awards and eventually landing a job at CBS. After he collaborated with Leonard Bernstein on *West Side Story,* which became one of the most popular musicals and films of this century, his reputation was established. Sondheim's first major successful play was 1962's *A Funny Thing Happened on the Way to the Forum,* and while he continued to write prolifically, other composers started paying high-profile tribute—Ned Sherrin compiled the popular 1975 London show *Side by Side by Sondheim,* for example. Sondheim hasn't written many old-school theatrical productions in recent years, but he wrote several songs for Madonna in 1990's movie *Dick Tracy* and penned a short, critically acclaimed 1991 play called *Assassins*.

what to buy: The three-CD set *A Collector's Sondheim* 𝄞𝄞𝄞 (RCA Victor, 1987, prod. Thomas Z. Shepard) is a massive examination of Sondheim's career. The set combines the best of his out-of-print LPs—including a sampling of the London cast version of *Side by Side by Sondheim*, the composer himself on piano for *A Stephen Sondheim Evening*, and his score *Marry Me a Little*. His songs, from "Ah, Paree" to "Love Is in the Air," are just as good, if not as wholly influential, as classics by Berlin, Porter, and Rodgers and Hammerstein.

what to buy next: Some of the best cast recordings of Sondheim musicals (and films) are still available on CD: *A Funny Thing Happened on the Way to the Forum* 𝄞𝄞𝄞 (Angel, 1996, prod. Phil Ramone) includes actor Nathan Lane; *West Side Story* 𝄞𝄞𝄞𝄞 (Sony, 1961), the famous film featuring Natalie Wood; and *Marry Me a Little* 𝄞𝄞𝄞 (RCA, 1990, prod. Thomas Z. Shepard) are among the best. Also, pianist Terry Trotter continues the tradition of jazz artists transforming popular showtunes into instrumental improvisations on *Stephen Sondheim's A Little Night Music* 𝄞𝄞𝄞 (Varese Sarabande, 1997) and, with a trio, *Sweeney Todd* 𝄞𝄞𝄞 (Varese Sarabande, 1995).

best of the rest:
Sondheim: A Musical Tribute 𝄞𝄞𝄞𝄞 (RCA, 1973)
Sondheim: A Celebration at Carnegie Hall 𝄞𝄞𝄞 (RCA Victor, 1993)

worth searching for: Madonna does "Sooner or Later (I Always Get My Man)" and a few other Sondheim tracks, thus proving for the first time she's a standards-singing chanteuse in the tradition of Dinah Washington and Judy Garland, on the soundtrack for *Dick Tracy* 𝄞𝄞𝄞 (Sire, 1990, prod. various).

influences:

◀◀ Rodgers & Hammerstein, Cole Porter, Irving Berlin

▶▶ Andrew Lloyd Webber, Michael Kamen, Hans Zimmer

Steve Knopper

Sonny & Cher /Cher

Formed 1964, in Los Angeles, CA.

Salvatore "Sonny" Bono (born February 16, 1935, in Detroit, MI; died January 5, 1998, in South Lake Tahoe, NV), vocals; and Cherilyn Sarkasian La Pier (born May 20, 1946, in El Centro, CA), vocals.

Sonny and Cher began as the Ozzie and Harriet of the Flower

Power set, invariably garbed in mod rags throughout the 1960s. But their minutes of fame never fully ran out, even when they became so annoying listeners practically ran them off the pop charts. At that point, naturally, they gravitated to their inevitable destination: Las Vegas, which led to high-profile television variety-show appearances and the production of monstrosities called *The Sonny and Cher Comedy Hour* and *The Sonny and Cher Show*.

They met while working for producer Phil Spector. She was a 19-year-old backup singer; he was a glorified gofer with a variety of dubious accomplishments. They recorded a couple of singles under the name Caesar and Cleo but only started to click when, as Sonny and Cher, they scored a modest regional hit with "Baby Don't Go." After a switch to Atco Records and the #1 hit "I Got You Babe," they began a bubblegum career that favored style well over substance. Bono cut Spectorian duo records for one label and even tossed off one immortal protest record of his own, *Laugh at Me*, after being asked to leave a restaurant because he wasn't wearing a tie. Cher did solo records for Liberty (notably *Bang Bang*). Their decline from Top 40 popularity may have been inevitable, but their '70s resurrection as a kind of Louis Prima–Keely Smith comedic pop vocal team could hardly have been predicted. With a top-rated weekly TV program and a series of hit records produced by the sage veteran Snuff Garrett (Bobby Vee, Gary Lewis and the Playboys), Sonny and Cher were back entertaining the parents of the people who only a few years before were buying their records. In the wake of their divorce, personal and professional, Cher established herself as one of Hollywood's leading ladies. Music dropped to little more than a sideline for her; in fact, her albums became more noteworthy for fleshy covers (which is perhaps what attracted Beavis and Butt-head, the vulgar TV cartoons, to arrange for a Cher cameo) than the music inside.

Bono, meanwhile, opened a restaurant and entered politics in sleepy Palm Springs, which he represented as a Republican congressman before dying in a freak ski accident in early 1998. Bono's funeral service, attended by Cher, Tony Orlando, U.S. senator Newt Gingrich, and other luminaries, recalled the fun, sincerity, and self-deprecating sense of humor that characterized the singer-congressman's rich life. Said Cher in a eulogy: "He was smart enough to turn an introverted 16-year-old girl and a scrawny Italian guy with a bad voice into the most beloved television couple of this generation."

what to buy: Because of the number of different labels involved, no single set comprehensively covers the career of Sonny and Cher, but *The Beat Goes On: The Best of Sonny & Cher* 🎧🎧🎧 (Rhino, 1991, prod. Sonny Bono) covers their most fruitful period.

what to buy next: The double-CD set, *All I Ever Need Is You: The Kapp/MCA Anthology* 🎧🎧 (MCA, 1995, prod. various) may be rather more Sonny and Cher from their TV years than anyone truly needs.

what to avoid: On the other hand, there is an abundance of mediocre recordings in their *oeuvre*. Take your pick: *Allman and Woman* 🎧 (Capricorn, 1976), a bizarre collaboration between Cher and her second husband, Gregg Allman (of *those* Allmans); any of the Kapp/Uni albums with one of the hit songs

in the title—*Gypsies, Tramps and Thieves* 🎧 (MCA, 1971), *All I Ever Need Is You* 🎧 (MCA, 1972), *Half Breed* 🎧 (MCA, 1973); or her disco-era excesses, currently collected on one convenient set, *The Casablanca Years* **woof!** (Polydor, 1996, prod. various).

the rest:
Look at Us 🎧🎧 (Atco, 1965/Sundazed, 1998)
The Wondrous World of Sonny & Cher 🎧🎧 (Atco, 1966/Sundazed, 1998)
In Case You're in Love 🎧🎧 (Atco, 1967/Sundazed, 1998)
All I Really Want to Do/The Sonny Side of Cher 🎧🎧 (EMI, 1992)
Greatest Hits 🎧🎧🎧 (MCA, 1998)

worth searching for: Two bona fide Phil Spector–produced singles productions, both collector's items, feature Cher as lead vocalist: "Ringo I Love You," by Bobbie Jo Mason (Annette, 1964), her first record, and "A Love Like Yours" (Warner Spector, 1975), a duet with Harry Nilsson.

solo outings:
Cher:
Cher 🎧🎧 (Geffen, 1987)
Heart of Stone 🎧🎧 (Geffen, 1989)
Bang Bang and Other Hits 🎧🎧 (Capitol Special Products, 1992)
It's a Man's Man's World 🎧🎧 (Geffen, 1996)

influences:
◀◀ Louis Prima & Keely Smith, Phil Spector
▶▶ ABBA, the Captain & Tennille, Madonna

Joel Selvin

David Soul

Born David Solberg, August 28, 1943, in Chicago, IL.

When he wasn't busting street hoods as Detective Ken "Hutch" Hutchinson on the '70s detective series *Starsky and Hutch*, B-actor David Soul was fostering a brief singing career, recording two albums, *David Soul* and the eerily prophetic *Playing to an Audience of One*, in the mid-'70s and scoring one major hit with 1976's "Don't Give Up on Us Baby." Soul actually first dabbled in music before becoming a full-time actor in the late '60s, appearing as a hooded mystery singer several times on the *Merv Griffith Show* and opening up concerts for the Byrds and Frank Zappa. In the days since *Starsky and Hutch,* Soul has tried to revitalize his singing career, releasing two little-known albums in the '80s in between made-for-TV movies. At press time, Soul was threatening to unleash another CD titled *Leave the Light On* upon an unsuspecting public as soon as he could find a label.

what's available: Since all of his albums are out of print in the United States, your best chance to get a little bit of Soul (with his one hit "Don't Give Up on Us Baby") is on *Heart Beats: Behind Closed Doors, '70s Swingers* 🎵🎵🎵 (Rhino, 1997, prod. various), a collection of songs all the swinging yet sensitive bachelors had on their hi-fis back in the mid-'70s. It also features Leo Sayer, John Travolta, B.J. Thomas, and other male crooners.

worth searching for: Look for the out-of-print LPs *David Soul* 🎵🎵 (Private Stock, 1976, prod. Elliott Mazer) and *Playing to an Audience of One* 🎵🎵 (Private Stock, 1977) at that next rummage sale or church bazaar. And if you're so inclined, Soul released two albums abroad in the early '80s, *Band of Friends* and *Best Days of My Life*, both on the Energy label.

influences:

◀◀ Leo Sayer, Gino Vannelli

Alex Gordon

Space

Formed 1995, in Liverpool, England.

Tommy Scott, vocals, bass; Franny Griffiths, keyboards, samples; Jamie Murphy, vocals, guitar; Andy Parle, drums.

With one great radio hit, the bouncy, glockenspiel-driven "Female of the Species," this British band earned a spot on the Burt Bacharach–worshiping *Austin Powers* movie soundtrack. Before that, for almost six years, Space played fast, guitar-heavy British pop music, like Oasis, the La's, or the Beatles; but when Griffiths joined in 1995, his samples and sound effects shifted the style towards playful, dreamy lounge music. Though "Female of the Species" isn't totally representative of Space's overall sound—the debut, *Spiders*, also includes straightforward pop-rock and harder electronic anthems—it immediately hit #13 on the British pop charts and dominated American alternative radio stations briefly in 1997.

what's available: "Female of the Species" is at least a three-bone song, but *Spiders* 🎵🎵 (Universal, 1997, prod. Steve Lironi) is comparatively mediocre, with a not-scary-enough song about a serial killer and bland attempts to link hard rock and techno. If Space continues in the lounge vein, the band could easily wind up a more commercially acceptable version of neo-lounge bands like Combustible Edison or Love Jones.

influences:

◀◀ The La's, the Beatles, Burt Bacharach, Combustible Edison, Frank Sinatra

Steve Knopper

Dusty Springfield

Born Mary O'Brien, April 16, 1939, in London, England.

A beehived British balladeer, Springfield transformed herself from a folk musician to the preeminent blue-eyed soulstress of the '60s, an evolution that climaxed with her triumphant 1969 album, *Dusty in Memphis*.

Springfield began her singing career as the female third of the British folk trio the Springfields (think Peter, Paul, and Mary from the other side of the Atlantic), which also included her brother Tom. The trio's "Silver Thread and Golden Needles" was a Top 20 hit in 1963, but the bandmates soon parted ways, allowing Springfield to embark upon a solo career. Her first charting single, the Motownesque "I Only Want to Be with You," led to a string of stirring hits like "Wishin' and Hopin'" and "24 Hours to Tulsa," which were marked by Springfield's increasing vocal confidence and a keen eye for quality material penned by some of the era's preeminent songwriters. In 1969, Springfield traveled to Memphis's famous Stax studios and teamed with primary producer Jerry Wexler for the remarkable *Dusty in Memphis*. The album and its soaring single "Son of a Preacher Man" (a rendition so soulful that Aretha Franklin refused to record the song after hearing Springfield's version) would prove to be Springfield's career pinnacle. After recording a few more albums in the early '70s, including the underrated *Brand New Me*, she moved to America and semi-retired. In 1978, she mounted a comeback with the feeble *It Begins Again*, but it wasn't until her guest lead on the 1987 Pet Shop Boys' mesmerizing hit single, "What Have I Done to Deserve This," that she would make an impact again. In recent years Springfield has produced a couple of new CDs, but it's her classic work that still wins her fans. Recent hit films like *Pulp Fiction* ("Son of a Preacher Man") and *My Best Friend's Wedding* (a dead-on cover of "Wishin' and Hopin'" by punk folkie Ani DiFranco) have exposed her talents and charms to a new generation.

what to buy: *Dusty in Memphis* 🎵🎵🎵 (Rhino, 1981, prod. Jerry Wexler, Tom Dowd, Arif Mardin) is a must for any CD collection. The Rhino re-release features three bonus tracks including the wistful "What Do You Do When Love Dies." Granted, it's a lot of Dusty, but listening to *Anthology* 🎵🎵🎵 (Mercury, 1997, prod. various) over three CDs and 77 tracks, a portrait of her whole fine career, from her folk days with the Springfields to her collaboration with the Pet Shop Boys, joyously emerges.

what to buy next: If you have less than $40 for a Springfield set, there's no excuse for not picking up *Golden Hits* 🎵🎵🎵 (Mercury, 1966, prod. various), a cassette-only collection of her early pop hits. As a follow-up to *Memphis*, *Brand New Me* 🎵🎵🎵 (Rhino, 1992, prod. various) predictably pales, but judged on its own merit it warrants respect. The Rhino re-release offers nine bonus tracks.

what to avoid: Springfield goes disco on *White Heat* 🎵 (Casablanca, 1982) with disastrous results.

the rest:
A Very Fine Love 🎵🎵 (Columbia, 1995)
Stay Awhile/I Only Want to Be with You/Dusty 🎵🎵🎵 (Tarragon, 1997)
The Very Best of Dusty Springfield N/A (Mercury/Chronicles, 1998)

worth searching for: Having already captured a piece of Americana on *Memphis*, Springfield lends a hand with background vocals on fellow Brit Elton John's concept album about the American West, *Tumbleweed Connection* 🎵🎵🎵 (PolyGram, 1970, prod. Gus Dudgeon).

influences:
◀◀ Aretha Franklin, Martha Reeves
▶▶ Lulu, Hall & Oates, Annie Lennox

Alex Gordon

The Squadronaires

See: Ronnie Aldrich

Squirrel Nut Zippers

Formed 1993, in Chapel Hill, NC.

Tom Maxwell, guitar, horns, vocals; James Mathus, guitar, piano, vocals; Katherine Whalen, banjo, vocals; Chris Phillips, drums; Ken Mosher, horns, guitar, vocals; Stacy Guess, trumpet (1993–95); Je Widenhouse, trumpet (1996–present); Don Raleigh, bass (1993–96); Stu Cole, bass (1996–present).

The Squirrel Nut Zippers originally came together as a lark—people from a wide variety of alternative rock bands playing prohibition-vintage "hot jazz." Certainly, it's a shtick with a lot of inherent commercial appeal, although you'd figure it would only get them as far as NPR, not MTV. Yet MTV was precisely where the Zippers found themselves in 1997, with a hit single in the calypso shout-along "Hell" (which was omnipresent enough that a sample of it showed up as the hook to a rap single before the end of the year, Funkdoobiest's "Papi Chulo"). That resulted in one of the unlikeliest platinum albums in recent memory. One can only hope that the Zippers' spirit and ragged-but-right chemistry will withstand the skewed expectations that inevitably accompany success.

what to buy: *Hot* 🎵🎵🎵 (Mammoth, 1996, prod. Brian Paulson, Mike Napolitano) is the album that benefitted from the hit status of the aforementioned single, "Hell," and it's a wonderful record. Recorded in New Orleans for that Crescent City feel, the album also works in a bit of Memphis and Las Vegas—and swings with a vengeance. The Bessie Smith–styled "Put a Lid on It" stands as Katherine Whalen's finest on-record vocal moment.

what to buy next: While not as solid as *Hot*, the debut, *The Inevitable Squirrel Nut Zippers* 🎵🎵🎵 (Mammoth, 1995, prod. Brian Paulson), is still tremendous fun. The group's chemistry was evident even then, a balance between Whalen's Betty Boop, James Mathus's soul man, and Tom Maxwell's Fred Schneider. *Sold Out* 🎵🎵🎵 (Mammoth, 1997, prod. various) is a stopgap live record. Rough but nevertheless charming, it includes a recording that dates back to the group's second-ever rehearsal. Among the unlisted bonus tracks are the hilarious "Santa Claus Is Smoking Reefer" and some vintage radio spots for Squirrel Nut Zippers candy, from whence came the group's name. Also charmingly rough is *Roasted Right* 🎵🎵🎵 (Merge EP, 1993), the Zippers' debut four-song single. As a measure of how quickly the Zippers progressed, compare the *Roasted Right* rendition of "Anything but Love" with the more polished version of the song that appears on *Inevitable* (the latter version is the one that plays over the opening credits of the 1995 Ben Stiller film *Flirting with Disaster*, by the way).

worth searching for: Prior to forming the Zippers, Mathus played in the twangy rockabilly band Metal Flake Mother, which left behind the album *Beyond the Java Sea* 🎵🎵🎵 (Moist 1991/Hep-Cat 1997, prod. Lou Giordano). Maxwell played drums in the art rock band What Peggy Wants, whose lone album, *Death of a Sailor* 🎵🎵 (Moist, 1992, prod. Tim Harper), will probably have you scratching your head wondering how he got from there to the Zippers. Drummer Chris Phillips can also be heard on the $2 Pistols' *On Down the Track* 🎵🎵🎵🎵 (Scrimshaw, 1997, prod. John Plymale), a fabulous album of straight honky tonk à la Lefty Frizzell. Go figure. Mathus comes by his bluesier leanings honestly, having grown up in Clarksdale, Mississippi, where Rosetta Patton (daughter of the legendary bluesman Charlie Patton) was his nanny. Her ailing health was the impetus behind the benefit record *Jas. Mathus and His Knock-Down Society Play Songs for Rosetta* 🎵🎵🎵 (Mammoth, 1997, prod. James Mathus). Recorded in Mathus's hometown with a large crew of friends and associates, *Songs for Rosetta* has a free-wheeling house-party vibe similar to those old sides from the *Anthology of American Folk Music*.

The Squirrel Nut Zippers **(AP/Wide World Photos)**

influences:

 The B-52's, Red Clay Ramblers, Fats Waller, Louis Prima, Bessie Smith, Billie Holiday, Django Reinhardt

Asylum Street Spankers, the Senders, Royal Crown Revue, Blue Rags

David Menconi

Jo Stafford
/Jonathan & Darlene Edwards

Born November 12, 1919, in Coalinga, CA.

Though Stafford's smooth, no-vibrato crooning tone occasionally sounds as serious as Frank Sinatra on "Angel Eyes," she always maintained a terrific underlying sense of humor and camp. In addition to her specialty—solemn romantic ballads—Stafford sang under aliases, such as Darlene Edwards or Cinderella G. Stump. (Stump's first novelty hit, "Timtayshun," a parody of the earlier standard "Temptation," was so convincing that even diehard Stafford fans didn't recognize—or believe—that their heroine was singing. Edwards, the wife of pianist Paul "Jonathan Edwards" Weston, had a blast missing notes and cutting up on record.) After a stint as a teen singer in the Pied Pipers, Stafford hooked up with Tommy Dorsey's big band and developed her straightforward, no-frills singing tone to go with the bandleader's trombone. Before long, she became one of the country's most beloved female crooners, singing such hits as "You Belong to Me" and "I'll Be Seeing You," and competing with Dinah Shore as a radio and television star. She got to work with Benny Goodman, Harry James, Lionel Hampton, Buddy Rich, and Duke Ellington, to name just a few jazz heroes, and sing smash-hit duets with the hunky Gordon MacRae before she retired in the 1960s.

what to buy: The massive three-disc box, *The Portrait Edition* 🎵🎵🎵🎵 (Sony Special Products, 1994, prod. various), has absolutely everything, but non-obsessives may opt for *16 Most*

Requested Songs ♪♪♪ (Columbia/Legacy, 1995, prod. various), which includes crucial hits like "Jambalaya," "Shrimp Boats," and "If."

what to buy next: *Capitol Collector's Series* ♪♪♪ (Alliance, 1991/1996, prod. Ron Furmanek, Bob Furmanek) focuses more on Stafford's serious stuff, including "I Love You" and "It Could Happen to You," and it's a nice supplement to the more prominent greatest-hits collections. Among Stafford's best original releases are *Jo + Jazz* ♪♪♪ (Corinthian, 1987) and *The "Big Band" Sound* ♪♪♪ (Corinthian).

best of the rest:
Drifting and Dreaming with Jo Stafford ♪♪♪ (Jazz Classics, 1950/1996)
Broadway Revisited ♪♪♪ (Corinthian, 1991)
G.I. Jo (Sings Songs of World War II) ♪♪♪ (Corinthian)
Spotlight on . . . Jo Stafford ♪♪ (Alliance, 1996)

worth searching for: Compared to, say, the kitschy contemporary band Love Jones, or even mid-'50s cats like Juan Garcia Esquivel, the camp-happy Jonathan and Darlene Edwards were downright serious. But their sense of fun is infectious, and rare when you're listening to mid-century pop crooners, so *Jonathan and Darlene's Greatest Hits* ♪♪♪ (Corinthian, prod. various) and *Jonathan and Darlene's Greatest Hits, Vol. 2* ♪♪♪ (Corinthian, prod. various) are still valuable lighthearted collections.

influences:

◄◄ Dinah Shore, Frank Sinatra, Judy Garland, Benny Goodman, Tommy Dorsey

►► Rosemary Clooney, Patsy Cline, k.d. lang, Sinéad O'Connor, Doris Day, Ann-Margret

see also: *The Pied Pipers*

Steve Knopper

Carl Stalling

Born 1888, in Lexington, MO. Died 1974.

You may not know the name, but you know the music. Stalling started his long career in music and animation when he scored a couple of animated shorts for Walt Disney in Kansas City, where he also added his organ music to silent flicks. Moving to Hollywood, he worked for Disney through 1930 before joining Warner Bros. in 1936, where he would score 600 *Merrie Melodies* and *Looney Tunes* cartoons over the next 22 years before he retired in 1958. With orchestrator Milt Franklyn, voice master Mel Blanc, and sound-effects whiz Treg Brown, Stalling created some of the most outrageous, sophisticated, and avant-garde music of the period. Stalling used music from other sources—among his favorites were classical melodies and the songs of bandleader and composer Raymond Scott—and created numerous compositions of his own for the cartoons, using bassoons, trombone slides, violin glissandos, and viola effects to create those sounds we all remember. Because cartoons were considered lowbrow entertainment, Stalling's musical gifts were overlooked; today he is considered a great composer and skilled arranger of some of the most familiar and lovable music known to anybody who grew up after the 1940s.

what's available: Even the director cracks up as he announces the title of "Puddy Tat Trouble" in the recording studio, but Carl Stalling's intricacies and skills are in full bloom on *Music from Warner Bros. Cartoons, 1936–1958* ♪♪♪♪ (Warner Bros., 1990, prod. Hal Willner). You'll recognize more than you might think, from slapstick to serious, including his reworking of Raymond Scott's "Dinner Music for a Pack of Hungry Cannibals," "Porky in Wackyland," some illuminating recording-session discussions, several complete scores of cartoons, and all the famous intros and codas from Warner Bros. cartoons. If that isn't enough to satiate you, try *Vol. 2*, released four years later.

influences:

◄◄ Raymond Scott, Mendelssohn, Brahms

►► John Zorn

Leland Rucker

Kay Starr

Born Katherine LaVerne Starks, July 21, 1922, in Dougherty, OK.

Had Starr not been a pop crooner who emulated Jo Stafford and Margaret Whiting, she might have made it as a clear-voiced blues belter. Though her songs were mostly pop standards, including Cole Porter's "Allez-Vous-En" and Hoagy Carmichael's "Lazy River," she sang them deep and warm, like a more debutante-ish Patsy Cline or a less-salacious Bessie Smith.

Born to Native American parents—though not on a reservation, as some 1940s publicists suggested—Katherine Starks began singing as a child to chickens in a family-owned henhouse. A supportive aunt entered her in a radio station's talent contest, which she won, then moved with her parents to Memphis (which may account for the country and blues influences). Inevitably, her singing talent drifted to the right people's ears, and by the late 1930s she was working with bandleaders Joe Venuti, Bob Crosby, Wingy Manone, and even Glenn Miller. After replacing Lena Horne in Charlie Barnet's band, and then taking a year-long hiatus to battle pneumonia, she went solo in 1946 and quickly signed a deal with Capitol Records. Singing older jazz material, Starr started reeling off hits, including 1948's "So Tired" and Pee Wee King's country song, "Bonaparte's Retreat," which led to a collaboration with singer Tennessee Ernie Ford. Unafraid to try any pop-music trend, the versatile-voiced Starr had big country, waltz, rock 'n' roll, jazz, and even polka hits through the 1950s.

what to buy: _Capitol Collector's Series_ 🎱🎱🎱🎱 (Capitol, 1991, compilation prod. Bob Furmanek, Ron Furmanek) generously tours Starr's 1940s material, and you can hear her growing slowly more confident as she shifts from straightforward pop ("You Were Only Fooling (While I Was Falling in Love)") to country ("I'll Never Be Free," with her frequent duet partner Ford) to a superb amalgamation of both (her masterful hit "Wheel of Fortune").

what to buy next: _Greatest Hits_ 🎱🎱🎱 (Curb, 1991, prod. various) includes "Wheel of Fortune," of course, and tours material from Starr's hitmaking 1950s years with RCA, so it's more diverse but less thorough than the Capitol set.

what to avoid: _Spotlight on Kay Starr_ 🎱🎱🎯 (Capitol/EMI, 1995, prod. various) is a less-impressive synthesis of the same Capitol material.

best of the rest:
The Uncollected Kay Starr: In the 1940s 🎱🎱🎯 (Hindsight, 1990)
The Uncollected Kay Starr: Vol. 2 🎱🎱🎱 (Hindsight, 1992)
Movin'! 🎱🎱🎱 (Jasmine, 1994)
Rising Starr 🎱🎱🎯 (Jasmine, 1994)
Them There Eyes 🎱🎱🎯 (Pickwick, 1997)

worth searching for: Starr's early material, which leaned on old, old songs even by 1940s pop standards, are documented on _Back to the Roots_ (GNP/Crescendo, 1996, prod. various), including "Exactly Like You" and "When a Woman Loves a Man."

influences:
◀◀ Margaret Whiting, Jo Stafford, Tennessee Ernie Ford, Roy Acuff, Bessie Smith, Judy Garland

▶▶ Rosemary Clooney, Vic Damone, Jack Jones, Liza Minnelli

Steve Knopper

Dakota Staton
Born Aliyah Rabia, June 3, 1931, in Pittsburgh, PA.

Though she frequently sang jazz and blues material, Staton's clear, charismatic voice made her a crooner worthy of Rose-

Cocktail Classics

Volare

18-Karat **Dean Martin**
Capitol Collector's Series
(Capitol)

Bombsville! **Alex Chilton**
19 Years:
A Collection of
Alex Chilton
(Rhino)

mary Clooney, Margaret Whiting, or any of the other female vocal stars of the '50s. She's best known for her version of Stan Getz's "Misty" and a superb collaboration with pianist George Shearing in 1958, but she was an excellent pop standards singer—her takes on the Gershwins' "Someone to Watch Over Me" and "I Can't Get Started" are some of the songs' definitive readings. As Staton aged, her voice grew deeper and more commanding and she tended to record more soulful, jazz-oriented albums.

what to buy: Staton's best two original albums, _Dakota Staton at Storyville_ 🎱🎱🎱🎱 (Capitol, 1962/Collectables, 1994) and _The Late, Late Show_ 🎱🎱🎱🎱 (Capitol, 1957/Collectables, 1994), have happily made it to CD stores. Staton is still in showtune mode, despite the jazzy piano backing, belting "Broadway" (not to be confused with the more-famous "On Broadway") with clarity and command.

best of the rest:

More Than the Most 🎵🎵🎵 (Collectables, 1994)

Spotlight on . . . Dakota Staton 🎵🎵🎵 (Gold Rush, 1996/1997)

worth searching for: Staton's two tracks on *Sweet and Lovely: Capitol's Great Ladies of Song* 🎵🎵🎵🎵 (Capitol, 1992, prod. Brad Benedict) place her among some of the most famous crooners of her era, including Betty Hutton, Jo Stafford, Dinah Washington, Dinah Shore, and Judy Garland. She handles the Gershwins' "Someone to Watch Over Me" and "I Can't Get Started" nicely, distinguishing them with a natural swing the other singers lack.

influences:

◀◀ Billie Holiday, Etta James, Jo Stafford, Nancy Wilson

▶▶ Rosemary Clooney, Blossom Dearie, Cleo Laine

Steve Knopper

Stereolab

Formed 1990, in London, England.

Tim Gane, guitar, keyboards (1991–present); Laetitia Sadier, vocals, keyboards (1991–present); Mary Hansen, guitar, keyboards, vocals (1992–present); Morgane Lhote, organ (1995–present); Andrew Ramsay, drums, percussion, vocals (1992–present); Duncan Brown, bass (1993–96); Richard Harrison, bass (1996–present); Joe Dilworth, drums (1991–92); Katharine Gifford, keyboards, vocals (1993–95); Martin Kean, bass (1991–93); Sean O'Hagan, keyboards, string arrangements (1993).

The pioneer himself might not approve, but in fusing Juan Garcia Esquivel's disciplined space-age inventiveness with the haunting, moody aspects of the Velvet Underground, Nico, and Astrud Gilberto, the Franco-English pop collective Stereolab has placed itself at the forefront of progressive music today. But such artistry comes with a caveat: Stereolab is not always for the faint of heart, or for those looking for mood over meaning.

Formed out of the ashes of post-punk unknowns McCarthy, Stereolab's core remains multi-instrumentalist Tim Gane and vocalist Laetitia Sadier, with the latter's aloof, placid style often compared to Gilberto's. Still, the modus operandi of the group is avant-garde experimentation—the common catchphrase for its sound is "John Cage Bubblegum," which is also the title of one of its best songs—and its lyrical intent is often subversive;

Sadier sings in both English and French, but she conveys an obvious social humanist (if not out-and-out Marxist) underlying attitude. The 'Lab's world is one where '60s French film soundtracks, Ennio Morricone, Lou Reed, and Brian Wilson form an otherworldly collage, but the band's restless spirit makes its output ever-changing. Recently it has relied heavily upon High Llamas leader Sean O'Hagen to bolster its sound with *Pet Sounds*–era strings and horn arrangements—a bold step toward accessibility.

what to buy: Though its title is slightly misleading, the EP *The Groop Played "Space Age Batchelor Pad Music"* 🎵🎵🎵 (Too Pure/American, 1993/Beggars Banquet, 1998, prod. Stereolab, Andy Ramsay) is nevertheless as good a place to start with Stereolab as any, offering both the streamlined and harsh aspects of its sound. Don't come looking for Esquivel's patented "pows" and "zu-zu-zus"—in fact, the second half, labeled "New Wave," is closer to rock than anything else—but cuts such as "Avant Garde M.O.R." and "Space Age Bachelor Pad Music (Mellow)" set the stage for what to expect on later efforts. Fast-forward to *Emperor Tomato Ketchup* 🎵🎵🎵🎵 (Elektra, 1996, prod. Stereolab) and *Dots and Loops* 🎵🎵🎵🎵 (Elektra, 1997, prod. Stereolab, John McIntire) and you find the group at its most genre-bending satisfying. *Emperor* may be more challenging to those who are put off by Dada-ist musical forms, but *Dots* is a marvel of modern warmth and layering—a supreme trance-like quality accomplished almost completely through computers. Flowery tracks such as "Miss Modular" and "Rainbo Conversation" are probably the most immediate things Stereolab has offered, though even a 17-minute-plus epic like "Refractions in the Plastic Pulse" is as hypnotic and beguiling as the most detailed easy listening.

what to buy next: Here it gets more complicated. If you like the 'Lab's odd mix of dreamy and drony, then step up to its groundbreaking works, *Transient Random-Noise Bursts with Announcements* 🎵🎵🎵🎵 (Elektra, 1993, prod. Phil Wright) and *Mars Audiac Quintet* 🎵🎵🎵🎵 (Elektra, 1994, prod. Stereolab). The latter is more jangle-pop than space-age quirkiness, but still contains some of the band's strongest works. The former is a landmark in minimalist pop, packaged like a high-frequency system tester, and features the grandiose 18-minute epic "Jenny Ondioline," whose title stems somewhat from the now-antiquated electronic keyboard.

Morgane Lhote of Stereolab (© Jack Vartoogian)

what to avoid: Stereolab is nothing if not prolific—it has issued nine full-length albums in six years and a multitude of rare and hard-to-find singles and vinyl-only releases. But, as the compilations *Switched On* 𝄞𝄞𝄞 (Slumberland, 1992, prod. various) and *Refried Ectoplasm (Switched On, Vol. 2)* 𝄞𝄞𝄞𝄞 (Duophonic, 1995, prod. various) make clear, sometimes the band's desire to record should be reigned in. Though they each feature memorable work, these are for die-hard followers and collectors only.

the rest:
Peng! 𝄞𝄞𝄞 (Too Pure/American Recordings, 1992)

worth searching for: Recorded for a modern-art exhibit, in which sounds are linked to furniture displays and architectural designs, *Music for the Amorphous Body Centre* 𝄞𝄞𝄞 (Duophonic, 1995, prod. Stereolab) is mood music of a bizarre sort—which says quite a lot, considering what band we're dealing with. Obviously it would work better within the context of the gallery show, but even in the home the textures can create imaginative realms of both relaxation and unease.

influences:

◀◀ Juan Garcia Esquivel, Nico, Astrud Gilberto

▶▶ Combustible Edison, the High Llamas, Mouse on Mars, Tortoise

Ben Wener

Steve & Eydie
See: Steve Lawrence & Eydie Gorme

April Stevens
Born Carol Lo Tempio, April 29, 1936, in Niagara Falls, NY.

Carol Lo Tempio and her older brother, Nino, sang their way out of the cradle. The kids' mom, frustrated out of a show-biz career by a traditionally strict Italian dad, acted as her talented offspring's chief advocate. She put seven-year-old Nino up to fibbing to Benny Goodman that he had made a $5 bet that he could sing with the band. Goodman bought it, and Nino brought the house down. Goodman had him come back to do the same bit six more nights. The family moved to California because mom wanted her kids to be in an entertainment mecca. Eventually, they changed the family name to Tempo because people had trouble saying loh-TEM-pyoh. A record executive walked up to teenager Carol at Wallichs' Music City in Hollywood and told her, "You look like a singer." She brushed that off as a wolfish come-on, but gave him her phone number anyway. It turned out he was legitimate and had a sexy tune called "No No No Not That," which she duly recorded. When she realized the record would be banned from airplay because of its "suggestiveness," she decided to take on an alias to protect any future career. "April" came from her birth month, and "Stevens" just sounded all-American to her. For the love of a jealous Houston oil man, she walked away from a career that produced the 1951 Top 10 hit, "I'm in Love Again." In 1959, she returned to the scene with the campy, heavy-breathing "Teach Me Tiger." (The crew of space shuttle *Challenger* asked for that tune as their wake-up call on April 6, 1983.) In 1963, Ahmet Ertegun met Nino, who was a session saxophone player with Bobby Darin at the time. Tempo told Ertegun he was thinking of forming an act with his sister, and Ertegun, who'd been a Stevens fan, signed them up. They released "Deep Purple," a #1 hit and a Grammy winner, in October. The Beatles showed up early the next year and almost immediately rendered L.A. teen-scene players obsolete. The pair continued to record, but without much success. Stevens pretty much retired from music in 1979, despite some demos and solo albums with Tempo in the 1980s and 1990s. They have done small-scale reunion gigs since. Tempo remained in demand as a session player well after their hitmaking days and recorded some jazz albums on his own.

what's available: *Sweet and Lovely: The Best of Nino Tempo & April Stevens* 𝄞𝄞𝄞𝄞 (Varese Sarabande, 1996, compilation prod. Cary E. Mansfield) contains all four of their Top 40 hits, as well as Stevens's breathless "Teach Me Tiger." Stevens's bluesy style hints that she could be dynamite on old standards. She sounds pretty earthy on their back-beat version of "Sweet and Lovely" and her self-penned number, "(We'll Always Be) Together." The album, a cheerful hodgepodge of tunes fairly typical of the Phil Spector era of Los Angeles hitmaking, offers two mysteries: how could "Deep Purple," amateurishly recorded in 14 minutes, became a #1 hit despite its obvious flaws? Why didn't more of the material—such as "The Coldest Night of the Year" and "I Can't Go on Livin' Baby without You"—become hits? Also included are "I'm Fallin' for You," a country tune recorded in 1985, and "Why Don't You Do Right?," a lightly funky piece of jacuzzi jazz, recorded in 1996. *Carousel Dreams* 𝄞𝄞𝄞 (USA Music Group, 1990, prod. Nino Tempo), a solo comeback bid, is an OK piece of journeyman work but feels a bit flat without the nostalgia element of the compilation.

worth searching for: *Teach Me Tiger* 𝄞𝄞𝄞 (Imperial, 1959, prod. Henri Rene) fits the best into the mondo-wacko world of Martin Denny and Les Baxter. Stevens's playful goof on her recurring sex-kitten role as a vocalist may not play to her strengths, but as a period piece it has kitschy charms to soothe the savage beast.

influences:
◀◀ Dinah Shore, Marilyn Monroe

▶▶ Karen Carpenter, Nancy Sinatra

Salvatore Caputo

Barbra Streisand
Born April 24, 1942, in Brooklyn, NY.

Had she only been an actress or filmmaker, Streisand still would have been one of the most successful entertainers of the past four decades. But it is her singing, her voice, that is most unique and influential. She has recorded everything from classical to show tunes and torch songs to rock and disco, and is the top-selling female recording artist in the world. After graduating early from high school, she won a singing contest at a Manhattan club and soon developed her own nightclub act. Her Broadway career began with 1962's "I Can Get It for You Wholesale"; a year later, she landed a recording contract with Columbia. She eschewed frequent touring in favor of more work on Broadway (including 1964's "Funny Girl," the 1967 movie adaptation of which earned her an Oscar) and television specials (which in turn spawned albums). Continuing to act in musicals, comedies, and dramas throughout the 1960s and 1970s, her film work eventually included producing (starting with 1977's *A Star Is Born*) and directing (1983's *Yentl* marked her debut). Some 35 years after catching the world's attention with The Voice, and despite frequent accounts of prima donna behavior, Streisand continues to mine success in concert, on record, and on film.

what to buy: The Grammy-winning *The Barbra Streisand Album* 🎵🎵🎵🎵🎵 (Columbia, 1963, prod. Mike Berniker), her solo debut, includes her trademark melancholy rendition of "Happy Days Are Here Again," but just about every song here is a revelation. *The Broadway Album* 🎵🎵🎵🎵 (Columbia, 1985, exec. prod. Barbra Streisand, Peter Matz), a big seller and also a Grammy winner, marked Streisand's return to show tunes, wrapped up in a pretty-sounding pop package. Her David Foster–produced "Somewhere" is stunning. *Barbra Streisand's Greatest Hits* 🎵🎵🎵🎵 (Columbia, 1969, prod. Mike Berniker, Robert Mersey, Ettore Stratta, Jack Gold, Warren Vincent) isn't truly a "hits" album—she only had two Top 40 hits in the '60s, both of which are here—but these 11 tracks demonstrate why her singing made such an immediate impact. *Barbra Streisand's Greatest Hits, Vol. 2* 🎵🎵🎵🎵🎵 (Columbia, 1978, prod. Barbra Streisand, Phil Ramone, Gary Klein, Charlie Calello, Marty Paich, Bob Gaudio, Tommy LiPuma, Richard Perry) includes her most potent chart hits (three of the 10 tracks hit #1) and most confident singing.

what to buy next: *Stoney End* 🎵🎵🎵🎵 (Columbia, 1971, prod. Richard Perry) set the stage for Streisand's arrival on the contemporary pop-rock scene, and included contributions from Laura Nyro, Gordon Lightfoot, and Randy Newman. *Guilty* 🎵🎵🎵🎵 (Columbia, 1980, prod. Barry Gibb, Albhy Galuten, Karl Richardson) grew into Streisand's biggest-selling album, thanks to a trio of great singles ("Woman in Love," "Guilty," and "What Kind of Fool"). From a jazzified "My Favorite Things" to an achingly reverent "Ave Maria," *A Christmas Album* 🎵🎵🎵🎵 (Columbia, 1967, prod. Jack Gold, Ettore Stratta) is a holiday must.

what to avoid: *What about Today?* 🎵 (Columbia, 1969, prod. Wally Gold) features three Beatles songs, including a truly dreadful, vaudevillian arrangement of "Honey Pie" (which, to begin with, is a pretty dreadful Beatles song). A real mess. *The Owl and the Pussycat* 🎵 (Columbia, 1970, prod. Thomas Z. Shepard) is filled with dialogue from the Buck Henry–penned comedy, and no Streisand songs.

the rest:
I Can Get It for You Wholesale—Original Broadway Cast Recording 🎵🎵🎵 (Columbia, 1962)

Pins and Needles 🎵🎵🎵 (Columbia, 1962)

The Second Barbra Streisand Album 🎵🎵🎵 (Columbia, 1963)

The Third Album 🎵🎵🎵🎵 (Columbia, 1964)

Funny Girl—Original Broadway Cast Recording 🎵🎵🎵 (Angel, 1964)

People 🎵🎵🎵🎵 (Columbia, 1964)

My Name Is Barbra 🎵🎵🎵 (Columbia, 1965)

My Name Is Barbra, Two 🎵🎵🎵 (Columbia, 1965)

Color Me Barbra 🎵🎵🎵 (Columbia, 1966)

Je M'Appelle Barbra 🎵🎵🎵 (Columbia, 1966)

Simply Streisand 🎵🎵🎵 (Columbia, 1967)

Funny Girl—Original Soundtrack Recording 🎵🎵🎵🎵 (Columbia, 1968)

A Happening in Central Park 🎵🎵🎵 (Columbia, 1968)

Hello, Dolly!—Original Motion Picture Soundtrack Album 🎵🎵🎵 (Philips, 1969)

On a Clear Day You Can See Forever—Original Soundtrack Recording 🎵🎵🎵 (Columbia, 1970)

Barbra Joan Streisand 🎵🎵🎵🎵 (Columbia, 1971)

Live Concert at the Forum 🎵🎵🎵 (Columbia, 1972)

Barbra Streisand . . . and Other Musical Instruments 🎵🎵🎵 (Columbia, 1973)

The Way We Were 🎵🎵🎵 (Columbia, 1974)

The Way We Were—Original Soundtrack Recording 🎵🎵🎵 (Columbia, 1974)

Butterfly 🎵🎵🎵 (Columbia, 1974)

Funny Lady—Original Soundtrack Recording 🎵🎵 (Arista, 1975)

Lazy Afternoon 🎵🎵🎵 (Columbia, 1975)

Classical Barbra 🎵🎵🎵 (Columbia, 1976)

A Star Is Born 🎵🎵🎵 (Columbia, 1976)

Streisand Superman 🎵🎵🎵🎵 (Columbia, 1977)

Songbird ♫♫ (Columbia, 1978)
The Main Event—Music from the Original Motion Picture Soundtrack ♫♫ (Columbia, 1979)
Wet ♫♫♫ (Columbia, 1979)
Memories ♫♫♫ (Columbia, 1981)
Yentl—Original Motion Picture Soundtrack ♫♫♫ (Columbia, 1983)
Emotion ♫♫♫♥ (Columbia, 1984)
One Voice ♫♫♫♫ (Columbia, 1987)
Till I Loved You ♫♫♥ (Columbia, 1988)
A Collection: Greatest Hits . . . and More ♫♫♫ (Columbia)
Just for the Record ♫♫♫♫ (Columbia, 1991)
The Prince of Tides—Original Motion Picture Soundtrack ♫♫♫ (Columbia, 1991)
Highlights from Just for the Record ♫♫♫ (Columbia, 1992)
Back to Broadway ♫♫♫♫ (Columbia, 1993)
The Concert ♫♫ (Columbia, 1994)
The Concert—Highlights ♫♫♫♫ (Columbia, 1995)
The Mirror Has Two Faces—Music from the Motion Picture ♫♫ (Columbia, 1996)
Higher Ground ♫♫♫ (Columbia, 1997)

worth searching for: *The Event of the Decade* ♫♫♫♫ (Columbia, 1994, prod. various) is the closest thing to an all-time greatest-hits album. But this double-disc set was strictly a promotional piece released in Great Britain to promote her London concerts.

influences:

◀◀ Judy Garland, Fanny Brice

▶▶ Bette Midler, Melissa Manchester, Barry Manilow, Carly Simon, Donna Summer, Sheena Easton, Laura Branigan, Madonna, Michael Bolton, Celine Dion, Linda Eder

Jay Dedrick

Cinderella G. Stump

See: Jo Stafford

The Style Council

Formed 1983, in London, England. Disbanded 1990.

Paul Weller (born John William Weller, May 25, 1958, in Woking, England), guitar, bass, keyboards, vocals; Mick Talbot, keyboards, vocals; Dee C. Lee, vocals (1985–90).

Looking to explore more eclectic styles of music, Paul Weller broke up his seminal British new wave band, the Jam, and teamed with former Dexy's Midnight Runners keyboardist Mick Talbot to form the Style Council. Casting the band as urbane sophisticates, the Style Council's U.S. debut album, *My Ever Changing Moods* (released earlier with a different song sequence in the U.K. as *Cafe Bleu*), was an intoxicating but uneven mix of jazz, lounge, soul, and R&B influences teemed with acutely left-leaning political lyrics. While the Jam never made much of a commercial impact stateside, *Moods* reached #56 on the album charts and spawned a Top 30 song with the title track. On subsequent Style Council albums the lyrics grew more politically pretentious while the duo tweaked the band's eclectic musical mix, adding soulful vocalist Dee C. Lee, whom Weller would later marry. Critics and consumers soon grew tired of Weller's self-important approach, which reached an zenith with 1988's bloated *Confessions of a Pop Group.* The following year the group's label, Polydor, refused to issue the band's newest acid-house influenced album and dropped the Style Council from its roster, prompting Talbot and Weller to call it quits in 1990. Weller embarked upon a solo career in 1991 (occasionally playing with Talbot) and has slowly regained his fans' and the critics' favor with a series of improving CDs.

what to buy: Separating the wheat from the chaff, *Confessions of a Pop Group* ♫♫♫♫ (Polydor, 1989, prod. various) culls the band's finest moments, like "You're the Best Thing," "Walls Come Tumbling Down," and "My Ever Changing Moods," while sparing us from the group's frequent indulgences.

what to buy next: Only ardent fans need explore the B-sides, demos, and unreleased tracks collected on *Here's Some That Got Away* ♫♫♫ (Polydor, 1994, prod. various). Ranging from the wonderful "Party Chambers" and "Call Me" to Weller's ill-advised stab at "Who Will Buy" from the musical *Oliver,* it's the record label's version of a rummage sale.

what to avoid: Weller defines pompous on the universally panned *Confessions of a Pop Group* ♥ (Polydor, 1988, prod. Michael Talbot, Paul Weller), the worst offense being the 10-minute "Gardener of Eden."

worth searching for: Beyond the aforementioned compilations, the band's entire catalog is out of print in the United States. But there are plenty of used discs out there, the best of which is *Our Favourite Shop* ♫♫♫♫ (Polydor, 1985, prod. Peter Wilson, Paul Weller), a remarkably cohesive album for such a spasmodic band.

influences:

◀◀ Curtis Mayfield, Dave Brubeck, the Who, Jimmy Ruffin

▶▶ Everything but the Girl, the Beautiful South, Tears for Fears

Alex Gordon

Barbra Streisand **(UPI/Corbis-Bettmann)**

Yma Sumac

Born Zoila Emperatriz Charrari del Castillo, c. 1921–28, in Ichocan, Peru.

The woman North America came to know as Yma Sumac developed a phenomenal voice with what is often reported to have been a five-octave range. (Granted, this sounds unlikely, but objective observers documented that she could indeed span four and a half octaves.) She was discovered at an early age and performed on radio and in movies throughout South America. In the '40s, she came to the U.S., and in 1950, she was signed to Capitol Records, where she was paired with the incomparable Les Baxter. Sumac made a career singing Americanized versions of Incan and South American folk songs, until leaving Capitol in 1959. She continued performing regularly and recording whenever there was interest—just as she does today. She lives in Los Angeles.

what to buy: *Voice of the Xtabay* ♪♪♪♪ (1950/The Right Stuff, 1996, prod. Les Baxter) is a reissue compiling Sumac's original *Voice of the Xtabay* and *Inca Taqui* albums, her most popular releases; the former includes some great work by Baxter. *Mambo! Yma Sumac* ♪♪♪ (1955/The Right Stuff, 1996, reissue prod. Tom Cartwright) is exactly what the title advertises, with tracks such as "Bo Mambo," "Goomba Boomba," "Malambo No. 1," and "Five Bottle Mambo."

the rest:
Legend of the Sun Virgin ♪♪♪ (1956/The Right Stuff, 1996)
Legend of the Jivaro ♪♪♪ (1957/The Right Stuff, 1996)
Fuego Del Ande ♪♪♪ (1959/The Right Stuff, 1996)

worth searching for: *Miracles* ♪♪♪ (London, 1972) is a rock "tour de force"; Sumac also cut a track for *Stay Awake: Interpretations of Vintage Disney Films* ♪♪♪ (A&M, 1988), a recording of Disney songs interpreted by various modern artists.

influences:
◀◀ Les Baxter, Perez Prado, Xavier Cugat, Martin Denny, Juan Garcia Esquivel, Rosemary Clooney

▶▶ Combustible Edison, Love Jones

Jim DeRogatis

Swing out Sister

Formed 1985, in Manchester, England.

Corrine Dewery, vocals; Andy Connell, keyboards; Martin Jackson, drums (1985–87).

Led by the sultry and sunny vocals of lead singer and former fashion designer Corrine Dewery, Swing out Sister emerged in the mid-'80s in the wake of the British light jazz-pop tide headed by groups like Sade and Everything but the Girl. The group's U.S. debut, 1987's *It's Better to Travel*, is best remembered for the MTV-friendly breakout single "Breakout." After that album, drummer and founding member Martin Jackson left, but the band hardly missed a beat, enduring now for more than a decade by revisiting the same material. The result is a pleasant but not terribly innovative or challenging body of work. Still, Dewery's emotive vocals occasionally transcend the material, hinting at the duo's overall potential.

what to buy: The band's debut, *It's Better to Travel* ♪♪♪♪ (Mercury, 1987, prod. Paul Staveley O'Duffy), smartly features not one but two versions of the irresistible effervescent single "Breakout." Beyond that, the lush "Surrender" is the album's strongest track.

what to buy next: *Shapes and Patterns* ♪♪♪ (PolyGram, 1997) finds the band returning once more to the jazzy synthesizer-heavy pop of their debut, with nice, but not striking, results.

the rest:
Kaleidoscope World ♪♪♪ (PolyGram, 1989)
Get in Touch with Yourself ♪♪♪ (PolyGram, 1991)
Living Return ♪♪♪ (PolyGram, 1994)

worth searching for: Among the light love songs collected on the soundtrack for *Four Weddings and a Funeral* ♪♪♪ (PolyGram, 1994) is Swing out Sister's bouncy cover of the Motown classic "La La La (Means I Love You)."

influences:
◀◀ Basia, Sade, Everything but the Girl, the Style Council

▶▶ Wet, Wet, Wet, Ace of Base, Rick Astley

Alex Gordon

The Swingle Singers

Formed 1963, in Paris, France.

Ward Swingle, vocals; Sarah Eyden, first soprano; Macaela Haslam, second soprano; Rachel Weston, first alto; Heather Cairncross, second alto; Gavin Cuthbertson, first tenor; Jonathan Rathbone, second tenor; Mark Williams, first bass; David Porter Thomas, second bass.

The Swingle Singers enjoyed a brief spell of popularity in the '60s with their jazzy vocal adaptations of classical works—which is to say, they vocally mimicked the melody lines of compositions by the great classical artists. When the original lineup disbanded in the early '70s, Swingle relocated to London and formed a new version of the group, this time using vocalists with classical, as opposed to jazz, backgrounds. Although Swingle retired in 1984, the Singers continue to record and tour concert halls all over the world.

what to buy: *Anyone for Mozart, Bach, Handel, or Vivaldi?* 𝄞𝄞𝄞𝄞 (Verve, 1989) puts a jazz-pop spin on some of the most well-known compositions in the classical canon.

the rest:
Jazz Sebastian Bach 𝄞𝄞 (Verve, 1987)
Place Vendome 𝄞𝄞𝄞 (Verve, 1989)
Bach Hits Back 𝄞𝄞𝄞 (Virgin Classics, 1995)

influences:
 Leroy Anderson, 101 Strings, Living Strings, Paul Weston, Mystic Moods Orchestra, Hollyridge Strings, Arthur Fiedler, the Four Freshmen

▶▶ Peter Allen

Marc Weingarten

Dellareese Taliaferro

See: Della Reese

Jimi Tenor

Born Lassi Lehto, March 27, 1965, in Finland.

Tenor is Finland's first techno cabaret star. Actually, he is Finland's only techno cabaret star. While most of his labelmates name Juan Atkins, Kraftwerk, Carl Craig, and other electronic-music pioneers as influences, Tenor draws his inspiration from soul men Barry White and Isaac Hayes, and '70s B-movies—definitely a different well. A lo-fi descendant of the cheesy lounge performers who proliferated in Vegas throughout the '60s, Tenor owns more sunglasses than Elton John. After training for 12 years as a classical musician, he formed a band, Jimi Tenor and the Shamens, and released a series of albums in the late '80s on obscure record labels. Later, he settled in New York as a photographer, then returned to Finland in 1995, where he made connections with dance-oriented record labels and his career began to take hold. Tenor is working on Tenor-Ware, a line of reversibly shiny zippable clothing.

what's available: *Intervisions* 𝄞𝄞𝄞𝄞 (Warp/Sire, 1997, prod. Jimi Tenor) is easy to find compared to his various quirky Fin-

Cocktail Classics

We've Only Just Begun

18-Karat The Carpenters
The Singles, 1969–1973
(A&M)

Bombsville! Richard Clayderman
Carpenters Collection
(Quality)

land and Germany releases; it's very possibly the tape Barry Manilow and Barry White groove to in their hot tubs. Funky, cheesy, and fun, "Can't Stay with You Baby" provides the best geeky soul since Beck.

influences:
 Isaac Hayes, Beck, Barry White

Sam Wick

John Tesh

Born July 9, 1952, in Long Island, NY.

What began as a moonlighting gig for this former co-host of *En-*

tertainment Tonight has evolved into a full-time job. On his own record label, GTSP (each letter stands for the name of a family member, including "S" for his wife, actress Connie Selleca, and "P" for his newly born daughter), the keyboardist has produced and released more than a dozen discs, three of which have gone gold. Tesh's musical career is completely the product of television. His entry occurred when he took advantage of his job as a sports commentator for CBS to incorporate his own compositions as backdrops to his reporting assignments. Television gave him a built-in audience. His first release, a cassette called *Tour de France*, from his coverage of the bicycle race, sold more than 30,000 copies by mail-order alone.

Tesh, who began hawking relationship videos made with Selleca while the two were still newlyweds, is like easy listening—but with a furrowed brow that comes from his high school days playing Jethro Tull and Yes covers in prog-rock bands. In concert (he tours frequently, hopping a plane on weekends to surburban symphony halls across America) as well as on disc, he delivers the notes with swashbuckling flourishes and an over-the-top bravado that are best viewed with tongue in cheek. The man is nothing if not prolific; most of what he writes has a meandering, tuneless, faux-classical quality, with no real beginning or end.

what to buy: *Live at Red Rocks* 𝄞𝄞𝄾 (GTS, 1995, prod. John Tesh) accompanies a concert filmed for a PBS fund-raiser and shows Tesh at his full-blown peak, backed by an 80-piece orchestra. *Victory: The Sport Collection* 𝄞𝄞𝄾 (GTS, 1997, prod. John Tesh) combines the music he wrote for the televised broadcast of the 1992 Olympic Games in Barcelona with music he wrote for the 1996 Olympics in Atlanta. Somehow, the subtext of athletics makes his music seem a little less insipid.

what to buy next: *Sax by the Fire* 𝄞𝄞𝄾 (GTS, 1994, prod. John Tesh) is the best of three all-saxophone projects recorded as the John Tesh Project.

what to avoid: *Sax All Night* **woof!** (GTS, 1997, prod. John Tesh)—enough already with the "sax" puns.

the rest:
A Romantic Christmas 𝄞𝄞𝄾 (GTS, 1992)
Monterey Nights 𝄞𝄞 (GTS, 1993)
A Family Christmas 𝄞𝄞 (GTS, 1994)
Winter Song 𝄞𝄞 (GTS, 1994)
Sax on the Beach 𝄞𝄞 (GTS, 1995)
The Choirs of Christmas 𝄞𝄞𝄾 (GTS, 1996)
Avalon 𝄞𝄞𝄾 (GTS, 1997)

influences:
◀◀ Emerson, Lake & Palmer, Yes, Electric Light Orchestra, Mike Oldfield

▶▶ Yanni, Kenny G

Teresa Gubbins

Roger Thorpe
See: Sammy Kaye

The Three Suns
Formed 1939, in Washington, DC. Disbanded 1965.

Al Nevins (born 1916, in Washington, DC; died January 25, 1965, in New York, NY), guitar; Morty Nevins (born May 26, 1917, in Washington, DC; died July 23, 1990, in Beverly Hills, CA), accordion; Artie Dunn (born in Dorchester, MA), accordion; Johnny Buck, guitar (1954); Joe Negri, guitar (1954–57); Tony Lovello, accordion (1957–65); Johnny Romano, guitar (1957–65).

Beginning with the 1944 hit "Twilight Time," which sold more than three million copies and later became a soul standard for the Platters, the Three Suns were one of the most popular instrumental acts before Dick Dale and Booker T. and the MG's took over the genre. They were also big players in the music industry: Allan Nevins's late '50s publishing house, which he founded with Don Kirshner across the street from the famed Brill Building, was responsible for pop classics like "Will You Still Love Me Tomorrow" and "Up on the Roof." Nevins kept his hand in the Suns, however, experimenting vigorously in the early 1960s with clinky-clanky exotica versions of hit songs, such as "Fever"—complete with wind bells, harpsichords, and shoes tapping.

The Nevins brothers, with their cousin, Dunn, began performing in the late 1930s as a bluegrassy trio before Al Nevins switched from violin to guitar for a smoother, more pop sound. After establishing themselves via hotel-lounge performances in Philadelphia, they won a short booking at New York City's Circus Lounge of the Hotel Picadilly, then parlayed that into a seven-year gig. Their first hits, "Twilight Time" and a version of Jerry Murad and the Harmonicats' "Peg O' My Heart," began an unexpectedly durable career, which had its second peak with RCA Victor's "Living Stereo" album series in the early '60s. Al Nevins suffered a series of heart attacks in the early 1960s, and gave up touring and much album production work for the Suns.

what's available: Sadly, the Suns' wonderful early '60s LPs, which rival surf-rockers' more familiar instrumental albums, have been reduced to thin inventory for the CD era. Two terrific tracks, "Fever" and the goofy "Danny's Inferno," show up on *Cocktail Mix, Vol. 1: Bachelor's Guide to the Galaxy* ♫♫♫♪ (Rhino, 1995, compilation prod. Irwin Chusid). But the original albums, *Fever & Smoke* ♫♫♫ (RCA Victor, 1960, prod. Al Nevins, Don Kirshner) and *Movin' 'n' Groovin'* ♫♫♫ (RCA Victor, 1962, prod. Al Nevins, Don Kirshner), are out of print and considerably collectible. Only the band's classic *Twilight Memories* ♫♫♫♫ (RCA Victor/BMG, 1996), reissued as a German import, can be found on CD in the big record stores.

influences:

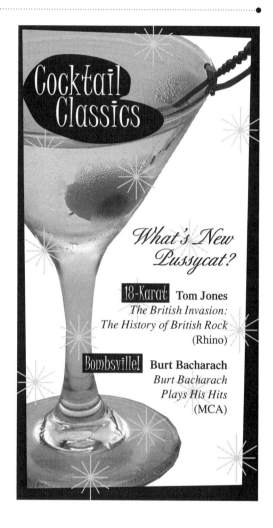

◀◀ Les Paul, Jerry Murad's Harmonicats, Martin Denny, Juan Garcia Esquivel

▶▶ The Platters, Dick Dale, Duane Eddy, Combustible Edison, Shadowy Men on a Shadowy Planet, Southern Culture on the Skids

Steve Knopper

Tindersticks

Formed 1992, in Nottingham and Kilburn, England.

Neil Fraser; Dickon Hinchcliffe; Dave Boulter; Mark Colwill; Al Macaulay, all various instruments; Stuart Staples, vocals.

The solitudinous, morning-after yang to Nick Cave's demonic, shot-through-with-heroin yin, England's Tindersticks are one of today's most intriguing pop curios. Rivaled only by Scotland's Belle and Sebastian in their fragile but buoyant arrangements and intoxicating, supple etherealness—a jazzier sort, though, not so much like the Cocteau Twins'—this publicity-shy sextet creates mysterious, moody music that in its tone harkens as much to the acidic humor of the Velvet Underground as to the instrumental panache of Ennio Morricone or Angelo Badalamenti.

The band's first two efforts (both self-titled) rely equally on macabre drama and soothing shading—a tough mix—and vocalist Stuart Staples's rumbling mumble remains the source of much consternation for casual fans. Push past that exterior, however, and what's uncovered is an intricate web of tear-stained emotions that counterbalance the supposed spookiness. Smart, highbrow, self-sufficient, exquisitely outfitted (by London's Timothy Everest, as the band routinely mentions) but never stuffy, Tindersticks were formed from the ashes of the short-lived Asphalt Ribbons. By the start of 1993 they were issuing now-rare singles and EPs on the independent British label Tippy Toe. Critical accolades for the group's striking sound and live performances quickly elevated it to cult status,

where it has remained. Its fourth proper album (discounting the soundtrack to *Nenette et Boni*) is due out in 1998.

what to buy: The adventurous will want to start at the beginning, but the strictly easy-listening fan should jump ahead to *Nenette et Boni* ♫♫♫ (Bar/None, 1997, prod. Tindersticks), the soundtrack to a mostly unknown Claire Denis film from 1996. Though too fragmented for pure pop classicists, it nevertheless serves as a fine sampler for someone just beginning to get into darkly textured instrumental work. Staples's unique baritone, for many the element that makes Tindersticks great, is largely absent, but the atmospheric slowness (think *Twin Peaks*) still intrigues.

what to buy next: *Tindersticks* ✍✍✍ (London, 1993, prod. Tindersticks), the debut, is the blueprint for the whole. Conceived as a musical evening in four parts, it's the soundtrack to a dinner party at which most would become extremely antsy. The second self-titled work, *Tindersticks* ✍✍✍✍ (London, 1995, prod. Tindersticks), introduces elements of Spanish guitar and lush orchestration to a decidedly far-reaching proceeding. The standout is Boulter's tragic, sardonic "My Sister," an eight-minute yarn of childhood trauma, but cuts such as "She's Gone" and "A Night In," with their assured sense of melody, constitute bolder steps forward for the band. *Curtains* ✍✍✍ (London, 1997, prod. Tindersticks), finds the 'Sticks beginning to tread water with their formula, though a newfound crispness to the songwriting and arranging offers hope of a progressive breakthrough.

worth searching for: They're hard to find in stores, but two live imports are worth tracking down. *Amsterdam* ✍✍✍ (Tindersticks, 1994, prod. Tindersticks) was available initially only by mail, so it's likely only to be found in used-CD bins now. Still, it has several shining moments. *The Bloomsbury Theater 12.3.95* ✍✍✍ (Tindersticks, 1995, prod. Tindersticks) benefits greatly from the addition of a 24-piece orchestra. There are several vinyl-only singles as well—notably Sub Pop's amusing "The Smooth Sounds of Tindersticks"—but they're exceedingly difficult to acquire.

influences:

◀◀ Nick Cave & the Bad Seeds, Birthday Party, the Velvet Underground, Nico, Angelo Badalamenti

▶▶ Julee Cruise, Friends of Dean Martinez, Belle & Sebastian

Ben Wener

Tiny Tim

Born Herbert Khaury, April 12, 1930, in New York, NY. Died November 30, 1996, in Minneapolis, MN.

It was hard to shock the Woodstock generation in the late '60s, but Tiny Tim, with his long clump of disheveled curly hair, otherworldly quavering voice, and ever-present ukelele, managed it. To fans of the Grateful Dead, Jimi Hendrix, and the Who, to whom Tim performed at the Isle of Wight and other significant social happenings, he was the ultimate square. But in truth, though he was unique by any standard, he actually was a vaudeville-style performer throwing back to an earlier era.

Tim loved publicity, and he earned plenty of it with his ultra-weird 1968 hit, the #17 "Tip-Toe thru' the Tulips with Me"; his marriage to "Miss Vicky," Victoria May Budinger, on a hugely popular 1969 episode of Johnny Carson's *The Tonight Show*; frequent appearances on *Laugh-In,* and, more recently, MTV; and late-career collaborations with the rock bands Brave Combo and New Duncan Imperials. Tiny Tim, a fan of Rudy Vallee and other campy pop singers of the 1920s and 1930s, set out to become a novelty singer in serious-folk-music–obsessed Greenwich Village in the early '60s. Somehow, he became famous, with *Tonight Show* appearances and a bizarre connection with hippie audiences. Though nobody would ever rate him in the same league with, say, Bob Dylan or Frank Sinatra, it's important to remember that he had true talent in his own strange idiom. He died during a major comeback, shortly after leaving a Minneapolis stage with health problems while performing "Tip-Toe thru' the Tulips."

what to buy: Tim's "classic" albums are out of print, but almost as good are his '90s collaborations with the wacky polka-rock group Brave Combo. *Girl* ✍✍✍✍ (Rounder, 1996, prod. Brave Combo, Bucks Burnett) fueled Tim's comeback, and it includes the singer's prototypical approach to standards, such as the gurgling "Stardust." More interestingly, he and the Combo swing mightily on a tinkly version of the Beatles' "Hey Jude," and they throw in "Stairway to Heaven" for good measure.

what to buy next: Tim's pairing with the equally goofy rock band New Duncan Imperials didn't get quite as much attention, but *Live in Chicago* ✍✍✍ (Bug House, 1995) is notable for its high-speed version of "Tip-Toe thru' the Tulips," plus—and this is not a factual error—AC/DC's "Highway to Hell." The joke is starting to get old, though.

the rest:
I Love Me ✍✍✍ (Seeland, 1995)
Tiny Tim Christmas Album ✍✍✍ (Rounder, 1996)

worth searching for: In the fish out of water category, Tim jumps wholeheartedly into peace, love, and rock 'n' roll on *Message to Love: The Isle of Wight Festival 1970* ✍✍✍✍ (Sony, 1996, prod. Jon Astley, Andy MacPherson), with a version of the forgotten standard, "There'll Always Be an England." In the context of Tim's solo career, it's a nice unearthed gem for collectors (not to mention comic relief). In the context of the CD's other tracks, by rockers Jimi Hendrix, the Who, Emerson, Lake, and Palmer and serious jazzman Miles Davis, it's strange and jarring. Also, Tim's original LPs, including the so-weird-it's-a-classic *God Bless Tiny Tim* ✍✍✍✍ (Reprise, 1968), are hard to find but contain the original, definitive versions of his hits.

influences:

◀◀ Rudy Vallee, Lawrence Welk

▶▶ "Weird Al" Yankovic, Brave Combo, the New Duncan Imperials, Johnny Carson

Steve Knopper

Cal Tjader

Born Callen Radcliffe Tjader Jr., July 16, 1925, in St. Louis, MO. Died May 5, 1982, in Manila, Philippines.

With mambo rhythms and an improvisational jazz spirit, this talented vibraphonist's career touched down halfway between Tito Puente and Perez Prado. He wasn't quite as concerned about commercial success as Prado, the mambo master, but he was willing to create soothing, easy-listening melodies that probably were beneath Puente's artistic purity. Tjader, who wasn't Latin but mastered the sound perfectly enough to lead Latin orchestras and combos, is still best known for his bouncy, lighthearted nonsense instrumental "Soul Sauce (Guacha Guaro)."

The percussionist and occasional pianist studied music at San Francisco State University before hooking up with jazz star Dave Brubeck in the late 1940s. After working with Alvino Rey and George Shearing—who encouraged Tjader to switch to vibes—he started indulging his interest in Afro-Latin rhythms. Throughout his career, which lasted lucratively into the 1970s, Tjader kept his bottom-line musical ideas the same. His influence, however, stretched into many different areas, including Latin, jazz, soul, and—evidenced on the *Talkin' Verve: Roots of Acid Jazz* collection—acid jazz.

what to buy: Tjader's classic was *Soul Sauce* 𝄞𝄞𝄞𝄞 (Verve, 1965/1994), which includes the irresistible chantalong "Soul Sauce (Guacha Guaro)" and other wonderful vibes solos set to irresistible Latin rhythms. But he also released dozens of albums, so it's more cost effective to get *Greatest Hits* 𝄞𝄞𝄞𝄞 (Fantasy, 1997, prod. various), a reissue of two previous greatest-hits volumes that includes the excellent "Cubano Chant," plus a few mambo-instrumental interpretations of *West Side Story* standards.

what to buy next: Tjader recorded for the jazz label Verve for much of his late career, and he frequently indulged his dark, smoky side, even though he never lost the Latin rhythm. His best jazz material includes *Heat Wave* 𝄞𝄞𝄞 (Concord Jazz, 1982/1987), a collaboration with singer Carmen McRae; *Amazonas* 𝄞𝄞𝄞 (Original Jazz Classics, 1975/1995, prod. Airto Mor-

eira); *Cal Tjader Plays, Marty Stallings Sings* 𝄞𝄞𝄞 (Original Jazz Classics, 1987); *Latino* 𝄞𝄞𝄞 (Fantasy, 1960); and *Black Orchid* 𝄞𝄞𝄞𝄞 (Fantasy, 1993, prod. various), a collection of the previously released albums *Cal Tjader Goes Latin* and *Cal Tjader Quintet*.

best of the rest:

Latin Kick 𝄞𝄞𝄞 (Original Jazz Classics, 1956/1991)
Jazz at the Blackhawk 𝄞𝄞𝄞 (Original Jazz Classics, 1957/1991)
Latin Concert 𝄞𝄞𝄞 (Original Jazz Classics, 1958/1991)
Monterey Concerts 𝄞𝄞𝄞 (Prestige, 1959/1989)
Latino 𝄞𝄞𝄞 (Fantasy, 1960/1996)
Concert on the Campus 𝄞𝄞𝄞 (Original Jazz Classics, 1960/1987)
Latin & Jazz 𝄞𝄞𝄞 (DCC, 1968/1990)
Descarga 𝄞𝄞 (Fantasy, 1972/1997)
Here & There 𝄞𝄞 (Fantasy, 1977/1996)
The Shining Sea 𝄞𝄞𝄞 (Concord Picante, 1981)
A Fuego Vivo 𝄞𝄞 (Concord Picante, 1988)

worth searching for: It's a bit of a stretch, but *Talkin' Verve: Roots of Acid Jazz* 𝄞𝄞 (Verve, 1996, prod. Creed Taylor) adequately reinterprets Tjader's exotic rhythms as an avatar for the recent slow, electronic acid jazz trend. Obviously, it's all re-released music.

influences:

◀◀ Perez Prado, Tito Puente, Dizzy Gillespie, Dave Brubeck, Alvino Rey, Xavier Cugat

▶▶ Kenny Burrell, Stan Getz, Rosemary Clooney, Julio Iglesias

Steve Knopper

Mel Tormé

Born September 13, 1925, in Chicago, IL.

With the exception of Frank Sinatra, Tormé may be the most enduring and influential male jazz vocalist of his generation. Graced with an almost absurdly lyrical voice (he hated the nickname critics gave him, "The Velvet Fog"), the cherubic singer is as comfortable scatting with a big band as he is milking ballads with a trio. His pipes have improved with age—his honey-dipped 1940s tenor has lowered to a commanding baritone. More than that, Tormé has been blessed by the fact that his voice is instantly recognizable; there's simply no one who sounds like him.

Tormé has been in show business since he was four, when he began singing professionally on Chicago's South Shore. After getting some radio airplay with a local band in the 1930s, he joined Chico Marx's band as a boy singer and eventually formed his own vocal group, the Mel-Tones, with singers like

Les Baxter and Henry Mancini's future wife, Ginny O'Connor. The Mel-Tones had plenty of hits, such as the swinging "Truckin'," and recorded other songs with Artie Shaw's band. They also laid the groundwork for other jazz vocal groups like the Manhattan Transfer. Tormé came out of a generation of singers in the 1940s who could do it all—Sammy Davis Jr. and Mickey Rooney, for instance. Like those entertainers, Tormé could sing, dance, act, and tell a joke. It wasn't long before he embarked on what became a respectable movie career, debuting in 1943's *Higher and Higher* for R.K.O. Pictures. Unlike Sinatra, Tormé's talent runs beyond vocals: he played drums for Count Basie's band on occasion, he arranges, and he even accompanies many of his own charts. Since the 1980s, he has written novels (his best one is a book called *Wynner*), biographies of Judy Garland and Buddy Rich, and an autobiography titled *It Wasn't All Velvet*. Every Christmas, the nation swoons to his most famous composition, "The Christmas Song," which he co-wrote on an extremely hot day in 1940 while trying to think of something cool. By the time Nat King Cole recorded it in 1947, the song was set in the exclusive club of successful twentieth-century Christmas carols.

Maligned by some as a cheesy lounge singer, Tormé has probably been underrated for his entire career. But in the 1980s and 1990s, he experienced a professional rebirth—building a string of accomplished albums (including some terrific live recordings), becoming a spokesman for Mountain Dew, and doing a series of guest spots on NBC's sitcom *Night Court*. The reason for the latter: the show's star, Harry Anderson, idolized him. *Night Court* turned Tormé into something of a curiosity—the legendary jazz singer reborn as retro pitch-man. But that renaissance was cut short in 1996 when he was hit with a massive stroke. Tormé hasn't resumed touring yet, but is reportedly enjoying his enormous video collection and model railroad setup.

what to buy: *Fujistu-Concord Jazz Festival in Japan* 🎵🎵🎵🎵 (Concord, 1990, prod. Carl E. Jefferson, George Otaki), one of Tormé's finest performances, shows off a charm so infectious even an audience full of non-English speakers gets into the mood. Frank Wess, one of Count Basie's favorite sax players, brings his own orchestra to back up the singer. Tormé even shows off his drumming skills on Basie's "Swingin' the Blues." There are also terrific renditions of "Wave" and "Tokyo State of Mind"—a takeoff on Billy Joel's "New York State of Mind." The

live album *A Vintage Year* 🎵🎵🎵🎵 (Concord, 1988, prod. Carl E. Jefferson) puts Tormé in the middle of a Paul Masson vineyard with George Shearing on piano, and the results are fabulous. Shearing and Tormé share a terrific wit, as seen on a hilarious medley of "New York" songs. Shearing's impressionistic style works well with Tormé's laid-back sound.

what to buy next: For *That's All* 🎵🎵🎵🎵 (Columbia, 1997, prod. Robert Mersey) the liner notes simply say, "A lush, romantic album." That's a fair enough assessment. Some of the tracks border on mushiness, but Tormé's voice is in its prime, and tracks like "Ho-Ba-La-La" and "Haven't We Met?" will be with you long after the CD player has been turned off. *A Tribute to Bing Crosby* 🎵🎵🎵🎵 (Concord, 1994, prod. Carl E. Jefferson), a very quiet and tasteful album, celebrates one of the few who came close to out-crooning Tormé. An orchestra of violins sometimes gets in the way of Tormé's interpretations, but others will make you want to dance on a moonlit balcony.

what to avoid: Tormé and Marty Paich had a strong partnership prior to *Reunion: Mel Tormé and the Marty Paich Dek-tette* 🎵🎵🎵 (Concord, 1988, prod. Mel Tormé, Marty Paich), but the sparks never materialize. The album also falls victim to one of Tormé's few shortcomings: an inexplicable affinity for song medleys in which each song gets little more than three seconds of airtime.

best of the rest:

It's a Blue World 🎵🎵🎵🎵 (Bethlehem, 1955)
Mel Tormé Swings Shubert Alley 🎵🎵🎵🎵 (Verve, 1960)
Encore at Marty's 🎵🎵🎵🎵 (DCC Jazz, 1982)
Mel Tormé with Rob McConnell and the Boss Brass 🎵🎵🎵🎵 (Concord, 1986)
Night at the Concord Pavilion 🎵🎵🎵🎵 (Concord, 1990)
Mel & George "Do" World War II 🎵🎵🎵 (Concord, 1991)
Sing, Sing, Sing 🎵🎵🎵🎵 (Concord, 1993)
Velvet and Brass 🎵🎵🎵🎵 (Concord, 1995)
A&E: An Evening with Mel Tormé 🎵🎵🎵🎵 (Concord, 1996)
The Mel Tormé Collection: 1942–1985 🎵🎵🎵🎵 (Rhino, 1996)

worth searching for: *Smooth as Velvet* 🎵🎵🎵 (Laserlight, 1991) is a nice reissue of some of Tormé's earlier, smooth ballads—including a great rendition of "Prelude to a Kiss." Tormé's voice here is so smooth it almost cries out for a shriek. But it's still a terrific moodsetter.

influences:

◀◀ Mickey Rooney, Bing Crosby, Sammy Davis Jr., Nat "King" Cole

▶▶ Harry Connick Jr., Mandy Patinkin, Johnny Hartman

Mel Tormé and Peggy Lee (Archive Photos)

Carl Quintanilla

Tuck & Patti (© Jack Vartoogian)

Jackie Trent

See: Tony Hatch & Jackie Trent

Tuck & Patti

Tuck Andress (born October 25, 1952, in Tulsa, OK), guitar; Patti Cathcart (born October 4, 1950, in San Francisco, CA), vocals.

Husband-wife duo Tuck Andress and Patti Cathcart have been making beautiful music together for more than a decade, blending the thick, soulful licks of his Gibson L-5 electric guitar with her husky, gospel-trained singing to create an unapologetically hopeful celebration of both divine and romantic love. Their lounge credentials are impeccable: in the early 1980s, they became a fixture at the Fairmont Hotel's Venetian Room in San Francisco, where they mixed Ella Fitzgerald and Joe Pass tunes with covers of Steely Dan's "Peg" and the theme from *Grease.* Signed to New Age kingpin Windham Hill's jazz subsidiary record label in 1987, they quickly established an intimate, spellbinding sound by recording live without overdubs in their Menlo Park, California, home studio. Their repertoire still leans heavily on originals, standards, and contemporary covers, ranging from Jimi Hendrix to Cyndi Lauper. But since graduating to Epic Records in 1995, Tuck & Patti have started experimenting with percussion, processing techniques, and the occasional saxophone. The heart of their sound, however, remains the nuances—the audible breaths, the squeaks of fingers on guitar strings, the purposeful silences—that speak volumes.

what to buy: *Dream* 🎸🎸🎸🎸 (Windham Hill Jazz, 1991, prod. Patti Cathcart) is Tuck & Patti's musical manifesto, a passionate plea for racial unity, world peace, and true love. "We can change this world, but first you're gonna have to dream," Cathcart sings. The cover choices are typically eclectic—"One Hand, One Heart" from *West Side Story,* Jimmy Cliff's "Sitting in Limbo," Horace Silver's "Togetherness," Stevie Wonder's "I Wish"—but their vision has crystallized.

what to buy next: *Love Warriors* ♪♪♪ (Windham Hill Jazz, 1989, prod. Patti Cathcart) is equally hopeful but a little more playful than *Dream*, thanks to a swinging romp through the Beatles' "Honey Pie," Hendrix's "Castles Made of Sand/Little Wing," and their own "Hold Out, Hold Up and Hold On."

what to avoid: The contract-fulfilling *The Best of Tuck & Patti* ♪♪♪ (Windham Hill Jazz, 1994) draws highlights from their three Windham Hill albums but loses the thematic thread that neatly ties their messages together.

the rest:
Tears of Joy ♪♪♪ (Windham Hill Jazz, 1988)
Learning How to Fly ♪♪♪♪ (Epic, 1995)

worth searching for: The lovely holiday ballad, "Christmas Wish," can be found on the compilation *Winter, Fire & Snow: Songs for the Holiday Season* ♪♪♪ (Atlantic, 1995, prod. various).

solo outings:
Tuck Andress:
Reckless Precision ♪♪♪♪ (Windham Hill Jazz, 1990)
Hymns, Carols and Songs about Snow ♪♪♪ (Windham Hill Jazz, 1991)

influences:
 Wes Montgomery, Sarah Vaughan, Ella Fitzgerald
▶▶ Dianne Reeves

David Okamoto

Cocktail Classics

When You Wish upon a Star

18-Karat **Barbara Cook**
The Disney Album
(MCA)

Bombsville! **Mantovani**
Mantovani Film Encores, Vol. 2
(Decca/London)

Up with People
Formed 1965, in Tucson, AZ.

At least 16,500.

In the '60s, everyone was asking, "Are you down?" A foggy-eyed youth culture deadened its senses with drugs. Political anarchists took to the streets with cries of "down with the establishment." What the world needed was something cheery and positive, something bright and bubbly—the world needed to get "up." A young, enthusiastic answer to America's explosive violence, Up with People came to fruition more as a concept than a band: it's a revolving entourage of cheery-faced international youths singing songs with positive messages. With a goal of building understanding and cooperation among people from different countries and cultures, Up with People is still operating today. Granted, 16,500 sunny alumni, ages 17 to 25, from more than 90 countries, is likely to give almost any red-blooded American shivers and nighttime visions of Rev. Sun Myung Moon or Rajhneshi. (It has not been proven, however, that "a unique global experience" and "a commitment to serving one's communities" can be considered a cult, even under the loosest of definitions.) By the late '60s, Up with People was so popular the group had spawned international touring versions, as well as copycat entourages (such as Impact). Up with People's extensive catalog is effectively a series of cast recordings to the group's ever-popular and annually updated stage spectacular. With songs like "New Dimension" and "Man's

Gotta Go Somewhere," Up with People are a saccharine-coated white-bread suburban view of a utopian future.

what to buy: *Up with People* 𝄞𝄞𝄞 (Pace, 1969), the first Up with People album, is still the greatest (not that this is saying much). The album that "will propel people in the '70s" is the first chance to experience Up with People staples "Up with People," "What Color Is God's Skin," "A New Dimension," and "Man's Gotta Go Somewhere." This is one of the few Up with People albums not plagued by poor production.

what to buy next: The bicentennial release *The '76/'77 Show Album* 𝄞𝄞 (Up with People Records, 1975) shows UWP attempting to capitalize on the recent rise of folk rock, disco, and southern rock (sometimes on the same song). C'mon, let's get that backbone going, y'all.

what to avoid: *The Festival* 𝄞 (Up with People Records, 1996) will give you an idea of what Up with People is "up to" today. Featuring tracks penned by Marvin Hamlisch (*A Chorus Line*), *The Festival* follows a young couple through a two-day world festival, giving a chance for youths of every nationality to sing a little ditty. One can admire the politically correct ambitions of UWP, yet the quality of songs and folksy harmonies that made its early material so much squeaky fun is sorely lacking.

best of the rest:
Up with People 3 𝄞𝄞 (Pace, 1971)

influences:
◀◀ White soulless church and choir groups, the Lettermen
▶▶ Gentle People, the Fifth Dimension, the Undisputed Truth

Sam Wick

Jerry Vale

Born Gernaro Louis Vitaliano, July 8, 1932, in the Bronx, NY.

All right, so he's no Al Martino. But Vale was camp before there was camp, and before he was camp, he was a popular paesan with a heart and a voice that oozed romance. Vale, who made his bones as a ballad singer in the '50s and '60s, had a classic poor-boy-makes-good upbringing, working as a shoeshine boy and a factory worker before he was enlisted by Guy Mitchell, who saw him performing in a New York nightclub and came away im-

pressed. At Columbia Records, A&R legend Mitch Miller paired the young Vale with Percy Faith's orchestra, and the results were successful, if predictable. "Al Di La" was Vale's signature song; on that tune, as on many of his other chart hits ("You Don't Know Me," "Have You Looked into Your Heart"), Vale made up in sincerity what he lacked in range. It was terrific make-out music, even if you couldn't dance to most of it. David Letterman was the latest in a long line to get a laugh (several laughs) at Vale's expense, kidding on the air about the singer's patented, corny lounge act. Vale apparently took it all in good humor, appearing himself several times on *The Late Show,* waving to the nation from the audience as Letterman introduced him.

what to buy: Because Vale recorded for much of his career with music-industry powerhouse Columbia Records, many of his hits have been reissued on several different compilation CDs. It's confusing to determine which is the best, but begin with *17 Most Requested Songs* 𝄞𝄞𝄞 (Columbia/Legacy, 1987, prod. Tim Geelan, Mike Berniker), a sure-thing collection of "Have You Looked into Your Heart," "Al Di La" (of course), "Mama," "Two Purple Shadows," and even his stab at Italian pop-opera, "O Sole Mio."

what to buy next: Beyond that, three sets complement each other reasonably well: *Standing Ovation! Jerry Vale at Carnegie Hall* 𝄞𝄞𝄞 (Columbia, 1989, prod. Ernie Altschuler) is a nice mix of his crowd-pleasing banter, trademark hits, and Italian pop-opera songs like "O Sole Mio"; *The Jerry Vale Italiana Album* 𝄞𝄞𝄞 (Columbia, 1988, prod. various) explores his heritage, with "Oh Marie," "Amore," "Vieni Su," and other romantic hits from the old country; and *The Essence of Jerry Vale* 𝄞𝄞𝄞 (Columbia/Legacy, 1994, prod. Didier C. Deutsch), which, like all CDs in *The Essence of* series, focuses on his slightly more obscure material, including versions of other people's standards like "My Way," "What a Wonderful World," "Sunrise, Sunset," and "Stardust." Those three CDs are available on a one-stop set, *Standing Ovation!/The Jerry Vale Italian Album/The Essence of Jerry Vale* 𝄞𝄞𝄞 (Epic, 1997, prod. various).

what to avoid: Many of Vale's greatest-hits collections are redundant, including the cassette-only *All-Time Greatest Hits* 𝄞𝄞𝄞 (Columbia, 1987), *Sings the Greatest Italian Hits* 𝄞𝄞𝄞 (Columbia, 1987), and *Greatest Hits* 𝄞𝄞𝄞 (Columbia, 1987). Why Columbia keeps scooping itself with Vale's catalog is unclear.

best of the rest:
Love Me the Way I Love You 𝄞𝄞𝄞 (Columbia/Legacy, 1995)
Best of 𝄞𝄞𝄞 (Curb, 1996)
On Broadway 𝄞𝄞𝄞 (Sony Special Products, 1996)

influences:

◀◀ Frank Sinatra, Al Martino, Tony Bennett, Rudy Vallee, Bing Crosby, Perry Como, Vic Damone

▶▶ Jack Jones, Ann Hampton Callaway, Buddy Greco, Wayne Newton

Stephen Williams and Steve Knopper

Rudy Vallee

Born Hubert Prior Vallee, July 28, 1901, in Island Pond, VT. Died July 3, 1986, in Hollywood, CA.

"I've never had much of a voice," Vallee once said. He didn't sing, he crooned. He didn't emote, he said, "Heigh-ho, everybody!" and used his personality, good looks, and charisma to endear himself to huge audiences. He even used a megaphone—which became his famous concert prop—so people could hear his soft, gentle voice. It all worked; he was a major singing star in the 1920s and 1930s until the more-talented Bing Crosby took over the mass market.

Nicknamed "The Vagabond Lover" after an early song and a 1929 film, Vallee was a self-taught saxophonist who served in the U.S. Coast Guard and later enrolled at Yale University. His talented first band, the Yale Collegians, was quickly booked to a long run at the Heigh-Ho Club in New York City; by coincidence, WABC Radio chose the club as a site for broadcasts, which was Vallee's first step to the big time. Vallee proved a major radio talent, with the ability to charm countless female listeners who had never even seen his face. But Crosby usurped his popularity, and beginning in the early 1940s, Vallee's still-young career was relegated to a series of character roles in bad movies. He eventually hit the nostalgia circuit, did cameos on TV's *Batman,* and maintained a decent nightclub career until his death in 1986.

what to buy: *Heigh-Ho Everybody, This Is Rudy Vallee* ♫♫♫ (Living Era, 1992/Pearl Flapper, 1995), a collection of Vallee's 1928–30 radio broadcasts with the Connecticut Yankees and Yale Collegians, leans heavily on college rah-rah crooning, such as "Betty Co-Ed" and "Let's Do It."

what to buy next: Moving on into the 1930s, *Rudy Vallee, Sing for Your Supper* ♫♫♫ (Conifer) includes "The Whiffenpoof Song," "This Can't Be Love," and 16 other tracks.

worth searching for: *How to Succeed in Business without Really Trying* ♫♫♫ (RCA, 1962) documents Vallee's successful comeback stint in the 1961 Broadway musical, and it includes several excellent Vallee croons.

influences:

◀◀ Al Jolson

▶▶ Bing Crosby, Fabian, Elvis Presley, Frank Sinatra, Tony Bennett, Vic Damone

Steve Knopper

Frankie Valli /Four Seasons

Formed 1956, as the Four Lovers. Became the Four Seasons in 1959.

Frankie Valli (born Francis Castelluccio, May 3, 1937, in Newark, NJ), vocals; Nick Massi (born Nicholas Macicoci, September 19, 1935, in Newark, NJ), vocals; Charlie Callelo, vocals; Joe Long, vocals; Tommy DeVito (born June 19, 1936, in Belleville, NJ), vocals; Bob Gaudio (born December 17, 1942, in the Bronx, NY), vocals.

The Four Seasons' satirical approach to '50s doo-wop gave their teen symphonies an edgy feel that allowed them to compete successfully in the eras of both Phil Spector and the Beatles. Valli had been around since doo-wop's golden age in the mid-'50s, working as a studio backup singer and cutting unsuccessful discs with various bands. With the Four Lovers in 1956, Valli scored a small national hit, "You're the Apple of My Eye." Unable to capitalize on this success, he joined yet another band, and a failed audition at a New Jersey bowling alley inspired the group to adopt its name: the Four Seasons. The addition of ex–Royal Teen Bob Gaudio and the attentions of producer Bob Crewe gelled the group's sound and creative approach—they burst onto the charts with a series of teen-pop classics, including "Sherry," "Big Girls Don't Cry," and "Candy Girl." Valli's freakishly high falsetto was a surprisingly novel and expressive instrument, and Gaudio's songwriting tapped into teen angst and romance with a fresh, sometimes mocking approach. Nick Massi's ability to arrange group harmonies successfully modernized doo-wop and heightened both the humor and tragedy of the songs, and Bob Crewe effortlessly imitated and improved upon Phil Spector's production techniques. After switching record labels and billing themselves "The Four Seasons Featuring the Sound of Frankie Valli," the group battled the wildly successful wave of British Invasion groups with the hits "Dawn (Go Away)," "Rag Doll," and "Working My Way Back to You," among many others.

Valli dropped the shrieking falsetto for his first solo hit, 1967's "Can't Take My Eyes off of You," a record geared more towards Las Vegas lounge habitues than teen dreamers. But neither the Four Seasons nor Valli adjusted well to pop music's Age of Relevance and the hits tapered off around 1969. A stint at Motown sans Bob Crewe produced some good music, but no sales. In 1975, Valli took an emotive ballad from his final Motown session, "My Eyes Adored You," and leased it to the Private Stock label, where it became a #1 smash. Valli's career was reborn and he quickly followed up with the disco-flavored "Swearin' to God" and "Our Day Will Come." The disco beat also drove major hits "Who Loves You" and "December 1963 (Oh What a Night)" for Valli and a radically changed Four Seasons. Valli's final #1 hit was the title song from the movie *Grease*, a Barry Gibb–penned paean to the '50s. The disco era mercifully died, and a series of ear operations took Valli out of the picture in the early '80s. Since then he has toured with various new line-ups of the Four Seasons, recorded an undeservedly overlooked single with the Beach Boys, "East Meets West," and has licensed his group and solo hits for dozens of reissue packages. Frankie Valli and the Four Seasons were inducted into the Rock 'n' Roll Hall of Fame in 1990.

what to buy: The groups' big hits from Vee-Jay and Philips as well as a sprinkling of Valli's solo hits from the disco era are spread across *Greatest Hits, Vol. 1* ���� (Rhino, 1991, compilation prod. Richard Foos, Gary Stewart) and *Greatest Hits, Vol. 2* ���� (Rhino, 1991, prod. Bob Crewe, Barry Gibb, Bob Gaudio, Karl Richardson), which feature several CD-only bonus tracks. Also, *Anthology* ���� (Rhino, 1988, compilation prod. Bill Inglot), a 26-song single disc with all their hits, is still available in Rhino's catalog.

what to buy next: With all their chart hits and best LP cuts, *25th Anniversary Collection* ���� (Rhino, 1987, prod. various), a three-disc, 54-track set, is all the Four Seasons most people will ever need.

what to avoid: The spiritless rehash of hits on *20 Greatest Hits Live* �� (Curb, 1990) is made redundant by abundant superior studio versions. An item for completists only. Also, unless you dig dance remixes of the group's big hits, stay away from *Dance Album* � (Curb, 1993/EMI, 1997). Stuff like this cheapens both the artist and the listener.

the rest:
Christmas Album �� (Philips, 1967/Rhino, 1980)
Genuine Imitation Life Gazette �� (Philips, 1969/Rhino, 1990)
Working My Way Back to You and More ���� (Rhino, 1988)
Rarities, Vol. 1 ��� (Rhino, 1990)
Rarities, Vol. 2 ��� (Rhino, 1990)
The Four Seasons—Hits ��� (Curb, 1991)
Sings for You ��� (Warner Bros., 1994)
Oh What a Night ��� (Curb, 1995)

Original Classics Collection, Vol. 1: Sherry & 11 Other Hits ��� (Curb, 1995)
Original Classics Collection, Vol. 2: Big Girls Don't Cry & 12 Other Hits ��� (Curb, 1995)
Original Classics Collection, Vol. 3: Ain't That a Shame & 11 Other Hits ��� (Curb, 1995)
Original Classics Collection, Vol. 4: Dawn (Go Away) & 11 Other Hits ��� (Curb, 1995)
Original Classics Collection, Vol. 5: Rag Doll & 10 Other Hits ��� (Curb, 1995)
Original Classics Collection, Vol. 6: Let's Hang On & 11 Other Hits ��� (Curb, 1995)
Original Classics Collection, Vol. 7: New Gold Hits �� (Curb, 1995)
Original Classics Collection, Vol. 8: Who Loves You �� (Curb, 1995)
Gold Vault of Hits ��� (Curb, 1997)
2nd Vault of Hits ��� (Curb, 1997)
The Very Best of Frankie Valli & the Four Seasons ��� (Laserlight, 1997)

worth searching for: One of the few collections that doesn't feature a substantial hit, *The Four Seasons Sing Big Hits by Burt Bacharach, Hal David & Bob Dylan* ���� (Philips 1965/Rhino 1988, prod. Bob Crewe) shows just how good these guys could be on material that isn't exactly teen-oriented.

solo outings:
Frankie Valli:
Best of Frankie Valli: Girl Crazy ��� (Essex, 1997)
Very Best of Frankie Valli ���� (PolyGram TV, 1996)

influences:

◀◀ The Royal Teens, Danny & the Juniors, Maurice Williams & the Zodiacs, the Four Freshmen, the Dovells

▶▶ The Beach Boys, the Beatles, the Cryan' Shames, the Bee Gees, Billy Joel

Ken Burke

The Randy Van Horne Singers
See: Juan Garcia Esquivel, Martin Denny

Sarah Vaughan
Born March 27, 1924, in Newark, NJ. Died April 3, 1990.

Sarah Vaughan earned the nickname "Sassy" for her feistiness, but as a vocal performer she was nothing short of divine. Ella Fitzgerald once called Vaughan "the greatest singing talent in the world today." And Frank Sinatra thought her one of the finest vocalists in the history of pop music. She was considered bop's greatest diva, the queen of jazz vocals, who wielded her voice like a brass horn. She could improvise, quickly change a song's mood, and embellish it with rhythms and melodies that made any music to which she contributed unique and inspired.

The daughter of a carpenter father and laundress mother, Vaughan began her singing career in church choir, notably Mt. Zion Baptist Church, and by age 12 was the church's organist. In 1942, she launched her professional singing career after winning a Harlem talent contest. After working with Earl Hines and Billy Eckstine, she went solo in 1945. She continued to collaborate with Eckstine, though one of her breakthrough songs was the jazz tune "Lover Man," which she recorded with Dizzy Gillespie and Charlie Parker in 1945. Though her roots were in jazz, she recorded many early-career albums simply backed by an orchestra. When Vaughan hopped to Mercury in 1954, she began working in jazz again and collaborated with some of the greats of her time, including Count Basie, Clifford Brown, and Cannonball Adderley; she made some of her best music during this period, especially her big hit "Broken-Hearted Melody." By the 1950s, she was an international star, touring the world and drawing huge crowds for her concerts in the United States. She continued this success through the 1960s—recording the finger-snapping classic "One Mint Julep" at the height of the space-age bachelor-pad music trend—but eventually took a five-year break from recording. She returned in 1971, and while many of her 1970s ventures were disappointing, her Duke Ellington songbook project with Count Basie and Oscar Peterson was a career standout. Vaughan's health declined during the 1980s, forcing her to cut back on her performances. In 1989, she won a Grammy for her Lifetime Achievement in music. That same year, she was diagnosed with cancer, and she died in 1990. Her albums have since been reissued by the dozens, though many Vaughan fans are still not satisfied and wait for more of her work to be reissued and collected.

what to buy: Though you can get *In the Land of Hi-Fi* ♫♫♫♫♫ (Verve/Emarcy, 1955) if you buy the massive (and pricey) *The Complete Sarah Vaughan on Mercury, Vol. 1*, the individual album is a good place to start. One of Vaughan's best efforts, this album offers up some solid jazz with an Ernie Wilkins orchestra that features a young Cannonball Adderley. (Besides, as all Esquivel fans know, any album with "Hi-Fi" in the title is usually high quality.) *Sarah Sings Soulfully* ♫♫♫♫ (EMD/Capitol, 1963/1993) was Vaughan's final Roulette session before returning to Mercury, and features some of the best vocals of her career on "A Taste of Honey," "What Kind of Fool Am I," "'Round Midnight," and "Moanin'." *1960s, Vol. 4* ♫♫♫♫♫ (PGD/Verve, 1963, prod. various) and *Columbia Years 1949–1953* ♫♫♫♫♫

(Deuce/Sony, 1949, prod. various) feature a wider selection of some of Vaughan's best work.

what to buy next: If you get *1960s, Vol. 4*, you'll have a lot of the material on *Sassy Swings the Tivoli* ♫♫♫♫ (Verve, 1963/1987, prod. Quincy Jones), but this individual release shows how Vaughan does the songs live with great accompaniment on "I Cried for You," "Misty," and "Tenderly." Likewise, if you're looking for hip Sassy that busts loose and hits the stratosphere in that best-of-career way, then *With Clifford Brown* ♫♫♫♫ (Verve/Emarcy, 1954) is a choice pick. Vaughan didn't record as much with Brown as she should have, but the light that burns half as long burns twice as bright, and this one's blinding. *Crazy and Mixed Up* ♫♫♫♫♫ (Fantasy, 1982/Pablo, 1987, prod. Sarah Vaughan) is Vaughan in total control and at her best. This is not a reissue; in 1982, she had been singing and recording for almost 50 years.

what to avoid: Vaughan actually has some weak collections, including *Rodgers & Hart Songbook* ♫♫ (Verve, 1954) and the unfortunate *Send in the Clowns* ♫ (Sony, 1981, prod. Norman Granz). The songbook does not feature Vaughan at her best; Rodgers & Hart is not the kind of music that made her famous. And "Send in the Clowns" is considered cruel and unusual torture in some countries.

the rest:
It's You or No One ♫♫♫♫ (Pair, 1946/1992)
Duke Ellington Songbook #1 ♫♫♫♫♫ (Fantasy, 1953)
Swingin' Easy ♫♫♫♫ (Verve, 1954)
Great Jazz Years '54–'56, Vol. 1 ♫♫♫♫ (PGD/Verve, 1954)
Gershwin Songbook #1 ♫♫♫♫ (Verve, 1955)
At Mister Kelly's ♫♫♫♫ (PGD/Verve, 1957)
Great Show on Stage '54–'56 ♫♫♫♫ (PGD/Verve, 1957)
Live: Compact Jazz ♫♫♫♫ (PGD/Verve, 1957)
Misty ♫♫♫♫ (PGD/Verve, 1958/1964)
Gershwin Songbook #2 ♫♫♫♫ (Verve, 1958)
Golden Hits ♫♫♫♫ (Verve, 1958)
Roulette Years ♫♫♫♫ (EMD/Capitol, 1960)
After Hours ♫♫♫♫ (EMD/Capitol, 1961)
Best Of ♫♫♫♫ (Fantasy, 1961)
1963 Live Guard Sessions ♫♫♫♫ (Jazz Band, 1963)
Sassy Swings Again ♫♫♫♫ (Verve, 1967)
Jazz Fest Masters ♫♫♫♫ (WEA, 1969/1992)
I Love Brazil! ♫♫♫ (Fantasy, 1977)
Copacabana ♫♫♫ (Fantasy, 1979)
Duke Ellington Songbook #2 ♫♫♫♫ (Fantasy, 1979)
Gershwin Live! ♫♫♫♫ (Sony, 1982)
Mystery of Man ♫♫ (Kokopelli, 1984)
The Complete Sarah Vaughan on Mercury, Vol. 1 ♫♫♫♫ (Mercury, 1986)
The Complete Sarah Vaughan on Mercury, Vol. 2 ♫♫♫♫ (Mercury, 1986)

The Complete Sarah Vaughan on Mercury, Vol. 3 🎵🎵🎵🎵 (Mercury, 1986)
The Complete Sarah Vaughan on Mercury, Vol. 4 🎵🎵🎵🎵 (Mercury, 1986)
Compact Jazz 🎵🎵🎵 (Verve, 1987/Emarcy, 1990)
Song of the Beatles 🎵🎵🎵 (WEA/Atlantic, 1990)
The Essential Sarah Vaughan: The Great Songs 🎵🎵🎵 (PGD/PolyGram, 1992)
Jazz 'Round Midnight 🎵🎵🎵 (PGD/Verve, 1992)
Sassy Sings & Swings 🎵🎵🎵 (Capitol, 1992)
16 Most Requested Songs 🎵🎵🎵 (Sony, 1993)
Benny Carter Sessions 🎵🎵🎵🎵 (EMD, 1994)
Essence of Sarah Vaughan 🎵🎵🎵 (Sony, 1994)
Verve Jazz Masters: Vol. 18 🎵🎵🎵🎵 (Verve, 1994)
Verve Jazz Masters: Vol. 42 🎵🎵🎵🎵 (Verve, 1995)
Memories 🎵🎵🎵🎵 (Black Label)
Sings Broadway 🎵🎵🎵🎵 (PGD/Verve, 1995)
Sings Great American Songs, Vol. 2, '56-'57 🎵🎵🎵🎵 (Verve)
This Is Jazz #20 🎵🎵🎵 (Sony, 1996)
You're Mine You 🎵🎵🎵🎵 (Member's Edition, 1997)
Ultimate Sarah Vaughan 🎵🎵🎵🎵 (Verve, 1997)

worth searching for: When Fantasy reissued *How Long Has This Been Going On* 🎵🎵🎵🎵 (Fantasy, 1978/Pablo, 1987), Vaughan fans wept with delight. This disc collects 10 best-of selections that will disappoint neither the newcomer nor the veteran Vaughan lover. Likewise, if you need a good Vaughan fix, *No Count Sarah* 🎵🎵🎵🎵 (PGD/Verve, 1958) offers her collaboration with the Count Basie Orchestra, which is ultimate Vaughanism.

influences:

◀◀ Billie Holiday, Bessie Smith, Ella Fitzgerald

▶▶ Carmen McRae, Shirley Horn, Lena Horne, Maxine Sullivan, Diana Ross, Whitney Houston, Gladys Knight, Bette Midler, Barbra Streisand

Chris Tower

Billy Vaughn

Born Richard Smith Vaughn, April 12, 1931, in Glasgow, KY. Died September 26, 1991, in Escondido, CA.

Vaughn was part of the armada of orchestra leaders who heard cash registers ringing every time a catchy song came on the radio. He could set anything, from R&B to rock 'n' roll, to a smooth easy-listening arrangement and notch dozens of smash hits in the process—in this spirit, he was the first to sire singer Pat Boone, who got rich off vanilla versions of hard-rock-

ing hits, while musical director at Dot Records. (Other notable smash Vaughn rewrites included Gale Storm's schmaltzy version of Smiley Lewis's R&B classic "I Hear You Knockin'" and the Fontaine Sisters' take on the Charms' "Hearts of Stone.") Vaughn, a composer, arranger, orchestra leader, and songwriter, began his own string of hits with 1954's "Melody of Love," and 36 of his records hit the pop charts from 1958 to 1970. He began as a singer, forming a hitmaking quartet called the Hilltoppers; he quit the band in 1955 to become Dot's musical director, and his formula led to quick, prolonged success. Though Vaughn was supposedly the most successful orchestra leader during the rock era, his career dwindled in the mid-'70s along with beautiful-music radio stations.

what to buy: It's hard for a rock fan not to sniff at Vaughn's handiwork, especially when he created schmaltzy versions of hits that outsold their superior originals. But he was talented and created nice pop music. *Greatest Hits* 🎵🎵🎵 (Curb, 1990, prod. various) collects his standards-oriented material, including romantic instrumental interpretations of "Mack the Knife," "Blue Hawaii," "Melody of Love," and "Wheels." *Melody of Love—Best of Billy Vaughn* 🎵🎵🎵 (Varese Sarabande, 1994), with "Sail Along Sil'very Moon" and "La Paloma," makes an excellent complementary set.

what to buy next: In the late '50s, Latin music was the ultimate romantic soundtrack, and Vaughn met demand with *La Paloma* 🎵🎵🎵 (Dot, 1958/Varese Sarabande, 1997), which includes "Mexicali Rose," "Say Si Si," "Brazil," and other instrumentals for people not hyper enough for Tito Puente's sprightly Latin jazz.

what to avoid: *Plays 22 of His Greatest Hits* 🎵🎵 (Ranwood, 1988, prod. various) is a redundant compilation of hits you can get more easily on better CDs.

the rest:
Billy Vaughn Plays the Music You Remember 🎵🎵🎵 (Pair, 1991)
Red Roses for a Blue Lady 🎵🎵🎵 (MCA Special Products, 1996)

worth searching for: For novelty purposes, the Swiss import *Best Of* 🎵🎵🎵 (Drive, 1991/1993, prod. various) is a decent collection of Vaughn's rock revisions, including the Eagles' "Hotel California" and Simon and Garfunkel's "Bridge over Troubled Water." But kitsch-hunters are steered instead towards Capitol Records' *On the Rocks* sets of easy-listening rock versions, and standards-lovers will prefer Vaughn's *Greatest Hits* or *Melody of Love* sets.

influences:

◀◀ Paul Weston, Mantovani, 101 Strings, Living Strings, Morton Gould, Les Baxter

Sarah Vaughan **(AP/Wide World Photos)**

▶▶ Hollyridge Strings, Ray Conniff, Percy Faith

Steve Knopper

The Ventures

Formed 1959, in Seattle, WA.

Don Wilson, guitar; Bob Bogle, guitar, bass; Noel "Nokie" Edwards, guitar, bass (1960–67, 1970–85); Howie Johnson, drums (1959–61); Mel Taylor, drums (1961–96); Gerry McGee, guitar (1968–72, 1985–present); Johnny Durrill, keyboards (1969–80); Leon Taylor, drums (1996–present).

The Ventures have released more than 250 albums during their undisputed three-decade-plus reign as Kings of Instrumental Rock, influencing scores of musicians around the world to pick up electric guitars and strum along to the nearest TV theme or dance craze. They're the most popular and influential band of their kind in history, with more than 90 million records sold (40 million in Japan alone!), and in retrospect some of their staccato, jumpy surf music surprisingly resembles the less-rocking lounge sounds of Juan Garcia Esquivel, Martin Denny, and even Walter Wanderley.

Their story began on a construction site in Seattle when Don Wilson and Bob Bogle met and decided to perform together at local sock hops. They soon added a rhythm section and, as the Versatones, recorded two songs, which Don's mother Josie released on her Blue Horizon label. Their second single, a cover of Johnny Smith's "Walk, Don't Run," was the first released under the Ventures name. After a DJ friend began using it as background music behind the hourly news bulletins, the song eventually soared to #2 nationwide. The band relocated to Los Angeles to record a quickie follow-up instrumental album of contemporary hits, and by early 1961 this too was lodged firmly in the Top 20. Throughout the 1960s, the Ventures' dance, surf, pops, on-stage, and TV-theme albums sold millions of copies worldwide, influencing future Who drummer Keith Moon, among others, and cementing their lifelong popularity in Japan. But perhaps most influential of all was their "Play Guitar with the Ventures" series of instructional LPs, upon which an entire generation of would-be axe-wielders cut their teeth using, if they were lucky, brand-new Venture-model Mosrite guitars.

what to buy: There's not a single style of music the Ventures haven't tried to bend to their own twangy designs at least once, and the cream of this crop can be found on the exemplary *Walk, Don't Run: The Best of the Ventures* 𝄢𝄢𝄢𝄢 (EMI America, 1990, compilation prod. Steve Kolanijan, Ron Furmanek). Also essen-

tial is *Live in Japan '65* 𝄢𝄢𝄢𝄢 (Capitol, 1995, prod. Bruce Harris), a long-overdue domestic release of a blistering double-LP concert—and it includes a version of Duke Ellington's "Caravan."

what to buy next: Dick Dale may have done it first, and probably better, but *Surfing* 𝄢𝄢𝄢 (GNP Crescendo, 1995, prod. various) shows that the Ventures could hang at least ten whenever they put their minds to it. *Play Guitar with the Ventures* 𝄢𝄢𝄢 (One Way, 1997, prod. various) is a wonderful three-disc reissue of the entire instructional-record series, while *Tele-Ventures: The Ventures Perform the Great TV Themes* 𝄢𝄢𝄢 (EMI, 1996, compilation prod. Steve Kolanijan, Ron Furmanek), though somewhat marred by kitschy-at-best renditions of "Charlie's Angels"–caliber material from 1976, contains sleek versions of "Batman," "The Man from U.N.C.L.E.," and other small-screen classics. Similarly, *The Ventures' Christmas Album* 𝄢𝄢𝄢𝄢 (Razor & Tie, 1996, prod. Joe Saraceno) is a fine repackage of the band's clever 1965 weave of holiday standards and non-Yule hits.

the rest:
Another Smash!!/The Ventures 𝄢𝄢𝄢 (One Way, 1996)
Twist with the Ventures/Twist Party, Vol. 2 𝄢𝄢 (One Way, 1996)
Go with the Ventures!/Batman Theme 𝄢𝄢𝄢 (One Way, 1996)
Super Psychedelics/$1,000,000 Weekend 𝄢𝄢𝄢 (One Way, 1996)
Walk, Don't Run/Walk, Don't Run, Vol. 2 𝄢𝄢 (One Way, 1996)
Where the Action Is!/The Ventures Knock Me Out! 𝄢𝄢𝄢♭ (One Way, 1996)
Flights of Fantasy/Underground Fire 𝄢𝄢𝄢♭ (One Way, 1996)
Hawaii Five-O/Swamp Rock 𝄢𝄢𝄢 (One Way, 1996)
Surfing/The Colorful Ventures 𝄢𝄢𝄢♭ (One Way, 1996)
Mashed Potatoes & Gravy/Going to the Ventures Dance Party! 𝄢𝄢𝄢 (One Way, 1996)
Rock & Roll Forever/Now Playing 𝄢𝄢 (One Way, 1997)
TV Themes/Bobby Vee Meets the Ventures 𝄢𝄢𝄢 (One Way, 1997)
The Fabulous Ventures/Ventures A Go-Go 𝄢𝄢♭ (One Way, 1997)
Guitar Freakout/Wild Things! 𝄢𝄢𝄢♭ (One Way, 1997)
Let's Go!/Ventures Play the Country Classics 𝄢𝄢𝄢 (One Way, 1997)

influences:
◀◀ Duane Eddy, Chet Atkins, Johnny & the Hurricanes
▶▶ The Who, Teisco Del Rey, Shadowy Men on a Shadowy Planet, the Mermen

Gary Pig Gold

Joyce Vincent-Wilson
See: Tony Orlando

Bobby Vinton
Born April 16, 1941, in Canonsburg, PA.

Vinton has had a long career with several peaks, and he dominated the charts through the early '60s. The king of overwrought emotional vocals and lush, string-dense instrumentation, Vinton is best remembered for the song "Blue Velvet," an eerie piece of romantic melodrama that rose out of America's collective unconsciousness thanks to the David Lynch film of the same name. But "Blue Velvet" was by no means his only achievement. Vinton notched more than two dozen Top 40 hits between "Roses Are Red (My Love)" in 1962 and "Melody of Love" in 1974, including "Take Good Care of My Baby," "Please Love Me Forever," and the epochal 1964 #1 hit "Mr. Lonely." Vinton also serves as an important footnote in music history—his 1963 number one single, "There! I've Said It Again," surrendered the top pop spot to the Beatles' "I Want to Hold Your Hand." After his chart-topping days ended, Vinton hosted a television variety series, then moved to the cabaret and nightclub circuit, where he remains a popular draw. Many of his recent releases have been Christmas albums; all show that Vinton is still a smooth balladeer capable of great moments.

what to buy: Most of Vinton's early albums are no longer in print, but you can get all the great early singles on *Greatest Hits* 𝄢𝄢𝄢𝄢 (Sony, 1993), including "Mr. Lonely," "Roses Are Red (My Love)," "Tell Me Why," "Rain Rain Go Away," "There! I've Said It Again," and "Blue Velvet."

what to buy next: *Greatest Polka Hits of All Time* 𝄢𝄢𝄢 (WEA/Atlantic, 1991) lets Vinton show off his Polish heritage, much as he did in the hit single "Melody of Love." The polkas here aren't anything different from what you'd hear in a Frankie Yankovic record—there's "Beer Barrel Polka," "Polka Doll," and "Pennsylvania Polka"—but it's nice to hear a balladeer like Vinton take a crack at party music.

what to avoid: *Hits Of—Volume 1* 𝄢𝄢 (Sound Choice, 1993) doesn't have anything you can't find elsewhere, and the cheap packaging is somewhat off-putting.

the rest:
Mr. Lonely—His Greatest Hits Today 𝄢𝄢𝄢 (Sony, 1991)
Kissin' Christmas: The Bobby Vinton Christmas Album 𝄢𝄢𝄢 (Sony, 1997)

worth searching for: *As Time Goes By* 𝄢𝄢𝄢 (WEA/Atlantic, 1992, prod. Michael Lloyd) is a one-off collaboration between Vinton and comedian George Burns that includes the song "I Know What It Is to Be Young (But You Don't Know What It Is to Be Young)" and the poignant "Gracie."

influences:
◀◀ Frankie Yankovic, Fred Astaire, Vic Damone, Jimmy Scott

Cocktail Classics

White Christmas

18-Karat **Bing Crosby**
Bing's Gold Records
(Decca/MCA)

Bombsville! **Arthur Lyman**
With a Christmas Vibe
(Rykodisc)

▶▶ Vic Dana, Bobby Goldsboro, Wayne Newton

Ben Greenman

Roseanna Vitro

Born February 28, 1954, in Hot Springs, AR.

A talented and soulful jazz singer with an impressive range, Vitro deserves to be much better known. She lived in Texarkana, Arkansas, and later moved to Houston, where she sang blues and rock during the early to mid-1970s before becoming jazz-oriented and singing with Arnette Cobb. Vitro moved to New York in 1980 and soon found herself working with vibesman Lionel Hampton.

what to buy: Joined by talents such as tenor player George Coleman and pianist Fred Hersch, Vitro is especially inspired on the impressive *Softly* 𝄞𝄞𝄞𝄞 (Concord, 1993, prod. Paul Wickliffe, Roseanna Vitro). The title is either misleading or ironic because a very passionate and soaring Vitro doesn't hesitate to let loose on versions of "Softly, As in a Morning Sunrise," "Falling in Love with Love," and "I'm through with Love." She's equally uninhibited on *Passion Dance* 𝄞𝄞𝄞𝄞 (Telarc, 1996, prod. Paul Wickliffe), which contains some emotional alto sax solos by Gary Bartz and finds Vitro excelling on jazz standards such as Benny Golson's "Whisper Not" and Eddie Harris's "Freedom Jazz Dance."

what to buy next: Vitro salutes one of her idols with thrilling results on *Catchin' Some Rays: The Music of Ray Charles* 𝄞𝄞𝄞𝄞 (Telarc, 1997, prod. Paul Wickliffe). With her versions of "One Mint Julep," "Lonely Avenue," and others, she never allows her love of the soul man to obscure her own identity.

the rest:
Listen Here 𝄞𝄞𝄞 (Texas Rose, 1984)
A Quiet Place 𝄞𝄞𝄞 (Skyline, 1987)

worth searching for: Though not quite as strong as *Softly* or *Passion Dance*, *Reaching for the Moon* 𝄞𝄞𝄞 (Chase, 1993, prod. Paul Wickliffe) is an enjoyable and heartfelt date that offers noteworthy interpretations of "Yesterdays," "In a Sentimental Mood," and Brazilian composer Ivan Lins's "The Island."

influences:
◀◀ Sarah Vaughan, Carmen McRae, Ella Fitzgerald, Ray Charles, Billie Holiday

▶▶ Nancy LaMott, Ann Hampton Callaway

Alex Henderson

Tom Waits

Born December 7, 1949, in Pomona, CA.

Billy Joel may claim he's the Piano Man, but if you picture the piano being in a smoke-filled bar in some cheap motel by the bus station where grizzled has-beens guzzle bargain-brand whiskey, then *Waits* is your piano man. Waits's persona is genuine; he was born in the backseat of a Yellow Cab, grew up worshipping the Beats, learned to play music on cheap Mexican guitars, and dropped out of high school. Waits was living out of his car and working as a bouncer at a small club when he realized he should be inside the club performing his own songs. He drew inspiration for his early material from the burnouts and lowlifes hanging on to their vague impossible dreams that populated the underbelly of Los Angeles.

He had built up a substantial local following by the time he recorded his first album, *Closing Time*, in 1973. With its songs of raw emotion, lonely longing, and barstool beatnik banter sung in a voice that could generously be described as raspy, and sparsely backed by acoustic instruments, the album was hailed within the industry but largely ignored by the public. With subsequent albums in the '70s, Waits consistently revisited the same themes and characters, while his music grew more diverse and esoteric and his voice grew more weary and guttural. By the time he switched labels in the early '80s, going from Asylum to Island, Waits had outgrown the confines of his early image. Through the '80s he recorded landmark avant-garde albums like *Swordfishtrombones* and *Rain Dogs* while also branching out into acting, playwriting, and soundtrack composing. In the '90s his work has grown even more recondite. For instance, in 1993 he worked with Beat author William Burroughs and opera director Robert Wilson on *The Black Rider,* a satirical take on an early nineteenth-century opera that melded conventional showtune melodies into a bizarre cacophony. Still, for all his critical acclaim and cultural trailblazing, he's never forgotten his roots; one of his most recognizable film roles was that of a booze-soaked limo driver living in a trailer with his coffee shop waitress wife (a perfectly cast Lily Tomlin) in Robert Altman's *Short Cuts,* exactly the type of character that Waits himself would have sung about on his early albums.

what to buy: *Closing Time* 𝄞𝄞𝄞𝄞 (Asylum, 1973, prod. Jerry Yester) is a stunning debut populated with barroom misfits longing for past loves (the heart-wrenching "Martha") and looking for new ones ("I Hope That I Don't Fall in Love with You"). The album also finds Waits's "singing" at his clearest and most melodic. Marking his maturation as an artist, *Rain Dogs* 𝄞𝄞𝄞𝄞 (Island, 1985, prod. Tom Waits) ups the ante from the equally ambitious *Swordfishtrombones*, the result being a

sprawling 19-track musical collage combining elements from his earlier work like beatnik scat and the occasional straightforward tune ("Downtown Train," which Rod Stewart would later make a hit) with all-new textures, beats, and instrumentations.

what to buy next: A bitter album that reflects Waits's growing impatience with the tepid audience response to his work, *Small Change* &&&& (Asylum, 1976, prod. Bones Howe) also marks a point in Waits's career where he's both embracing and recoiling from his past persona, as illustrated in songs like "The Piano Has Been Drinking (Not Me)" and "Tom Traubert's Blues." From the first track on *Swordfishtrombones* &&&&& (Island, 1983, prod. Tom Waits), the surreal "Underground," you can tell Waits has made a radical and ultimately rewarding departure from his early period. Though by no means definitive, *Anthology of Tom Waits* &&&& (Asylum, 1985, prod. Bones Howe, Jerry Yester) serves as a good introduction to Waits's Asylum era with 13 great tracks, including a duet with Bette Midler on "I Never Talk to Strangers," and "Jersey Girl," which Bruce Springsteen would later make famous. Unfortunately, it's only available on cassette.

what to avoid: Depending on your level of fandom, you could say that *The Early Years* && (Bizarre/Straight, 1991, prod. Bob Duffey) and *The Early Years, Vol. 2* && (Bizarre/Straight, 1992, prod. Bob Duffey) offer a fascinating insight into Waits's, well, early years. More than likely, you'll find both volumes filled with unpolished and redundant material.

the rest:
Heart of Saturday Night &&&& (Asylum, 1974)
Nighthawks at the Diner &&& (Asylum, 1975)
Foreign Affairs &&& (Asylum, 1977)
Blue Valentine &&& (Asylum, 1978)
Heartattack and Vine &&&& (Asylum, 1980)
Franks Wild Years &&&& (Island, 1987)
Big Time &&& (Island, 1988)
Bone Machine &&&& (Island, 1992)
Night on Earth &&& (Island, 1992)
Black Rider &&& (Island, 1993)

worth searching for: Waits has done so many fascinating side projects that this category could merit its own page. He's shown up everywhere from the soundtrack of *Bill & Ted's Bogus Journey* to a tribute to German composer Kurt Weill. One album especially worth combing the bins for is the soundtrack to the Francis Ford Coppola film *One from the Heart* &&& (Columbia, 1982, prod. Bones Howe), which found Waits teamed with an unlikely partner in country star Crystal Gayle. The

album even earned Waits an Academy Award nomination for best score.

influences:
◀◀ Ray Charles, George Gershwin, Frank Sinatra, Ken Nordine, Randy Newman, Spike Jones

▶▶ Buster Poindexter, Rod Stewart, Bruce Springsteen, Beck, Bonnie Raitt

Alex Gordon

Scott Walker
Born Noel Scott Engel, January 9, 1943, in Hamilton, Ontario, Canada.

His was a strange career, and the facts are sometimes hazy, but one thing is for sure: those who've heard Scott Walker have been unable to forget that rich baritone. The singer spent most of his childhood in Los Angeles, singing in talent shows and eventually becoming a session player working with pros like Sandy Nelson. In 1964, he met guitarist John Maus and drummer Gary Leeds, and the three rechristened themselves as Walkers, perhaps taking a cue from the Righteous Brothers. Leeds had toured England with P.J. Proby, and he convinced his bandmates that it would be easier to "make it" in swinging London. He was right, and the Walker Brothers scored a string of lounge-flavored hits starting in 1962. These included Burt Bacharach and Hal David's "Make It Easy on Yourself" and the fabulous, Phil Spector–styled "The Sun Ain't Gonna Shine Anymore." The Brothers disbanded in 1967, and Walker released four influential and similarly titled solo albums, becoming a major teen idol before the fickle tides of passing fashion abandoned him. The Walker Brothers tried a reunion at one point in the '70s, but it didn't last, and Scott (who had always battled severe stage fright) lived up to his promise to disappear from public view. He has returned to the spotlight only occasionally and very briefly, issuing wonderfully idiosyncratic solo albums that continue to assure him a devoted cult following.

what's available: Walker's first two solo albums, 1967's *Scott* and 1968's *Scott 2*, consist primarily of covers, including songs by Jacques Brel, while 1969's *Scott 3* and dark and moody *Scott 4* add more and more originals to the mix. *It's Raining Today: The Scott Walker Story (1967–70)* &&&& (Razor & Tie, 1996, prod. various) compiles the finest moments from those albums, including "Big Louise," "Joanna," "Through a Long and Sleepless Night," and "The Seventh Seal."

worth searching for: The best compilation of Walker Brothers material is a German disc: *The Walker Brothers: Gala* &&&

(Philips, 1986), originally released in 1986 and still available as an import. There's also a fine English solo Walker best-of called *Scott Walker: Boy Child, The Best of 1967–1970* ♫♫♫ (Fontana, 1990). Hard to find in the U.S. are later Walker releases such as *Climate of Hunter* (Virgin, 1984), which has been compared to Roxy Music post-*Avalon*, and *Tilt* ♫♫♫ (Drag City, 1995), the sort of wonderful dark-night-of-the-soul recording that Nick Cave wishes he could make. Also, Walker's "I Threw It All Away" winds up on the low-key, classical-gloom Nick Cave/Mick Harvey soundtrack project *To Have and to Hold* ♫♫♫ (Mute, 1997, prod. Gareth Jones, Blixa Bargeld, Nick Cave, Mick Harvey).

influences:

◀◀ Burt Bacharach & Hal David, Tony Bennett, Frank Sinatra

▶▶ Marc Almond, Nick Cave, Julian Cope, Richard Davies, Eric Matthews

Jim DeRogatis

Walter Wanderley

Born 1931, in Sao Paulo, Brazil. Died September 4, 1986, in San Francisco, CA.

Without Wanderley, Americans would know far less about the Brazilian-derived bossa-nova beat and the Hammond organ. After becoming a popular instrumentalist in his home country, Wanderley did his best to export the samba, an amalgam of various Latin American musical styles, to the U.S. His fingers had a feathery touch, and instead of playing heavy chords, he flitted through notes in a bouncy, staccato style—irresistible enough to make 1966's "Summer Samba" a Top 40 hit. Before shifting to less-commercial jazz fusion in the early 1970s, Wanderley led a trio that backed "The Girl from Ipanema" chanteuse Astrud Gilberto for several years in the 1960s. After martini-loving hipsters revived Juan Garcia Esquivel's space-age bachelor pad music in the early 1990s, they turned attention towards Wanderley's career, which resulted in excellent reissue CDs of his best-known material.

what to buy: Thanks to lounge-loving producer Irwin Chusid, who also oversaw the great quirky big-band re-releases of maverick Raymond Scott, *Samba Swing!* ♫♫♫♫ (Scamp, 1996, prod. Irwin Chusid) complemented the recent Esquivel CDs as important and hilarious documents of the cocktail era. It includes "Call Me," "Taste of Sadness," and several tracks with Astrud Gilberto.

what to buy next: *Brazil's Greatest Hits* ♫♫♫ (Crescendo, 1990, prod. various) has more essential songs than *Samba Swing!*, but it's not quite as lovingly packaged; Wanderley does the de-

finitive version of Antonio Carlos Jobim's elevator-ready "The Girl from Ipanema," since copied by many lounge organists, including ex–Detroit Tigers pitcher Denny McLain.

worth searching for: *Boss of the Bossa Nova* ♫♫♫ (1996), with 45 songs on two CDs, is as much Wanderley as any bachelor pad could possibly need.

influences:

◀◀ Antonio Carlos Jobim, Astrud Gilberto, Perez Prado, Xavier Cugat, Tito Puente

▶▶ Denny McLain, Sir Julian, Ernie Freeman

Steve Knopper

Dionne Warwick

Born December 12, 1940, in East Orange, NJ.

Dionne Warwick's gospel beginnings, if nothing else, prepared her for belting out the intricate pop songs that have marked her solo career. When budding songwriter Burt Bacharach spotted Warwick singing backup on the Drifters' "Mexican Divorce" session in 1961, he immediately seized the opportunity to align himself—along with his Brill Building partner, lyricist Hal David—with the relatively unknown singer. It was a shrewd move indeed, for their association garnered a virtual non-stop run of hits (all but one bearing Bacharach/David songwriting credits) and an armful of Grammys for Warwick. The whole of the Warwick/Bacharach/David union (1962–75) was significantly out of kilter with the pop mainstream in Bacharach's shifting time signatures, complex arrangements, and maddeningly melodic sensibility. Warwick herself brought a crystallized ringing vitality that could be tool-like in its precision and also capable of a near-operatic sweeping intensity. When Bacharach and David split unexpectedly in 1974, Warwick basically floundered for the remainder of the decade. She bounced back, commercially speaking, with a slew of pallid easy-listening duets in the 1980s, earning her fifth Grammy alongside Elton John, Gladys Knight, and Stevie Wonder with the saccharine do-gooder "That's What Friends Are For" in 1985. In a flatline epilogue, Warwick, apparently under a spell, was hawking the Psychic Friends Network in gurgling late night infomercials until the organization went belly-up in 1998.

what to buy: A walloping 24 singles comprise *The Dionne Warwick Collection: Her All-Time Greatest Hits* ♫♫♫♫ (Rhino, 1989, compilation prod. Bill Inglot), and you'll be hard-pressed to find a clunker in the bunch. The best tracks—"Walk on By," "Always Something There to Remind Me," "Do You Know the Way to San

Jose?" and "Trains and Boats and Planes"—unfold like lessons in melody. And when Warwick pines for unrequited love, she mesmerizes.

what to buy next: *Hidden Gems* 𝄢𝄢𝄢 (Rhino, 1992) is a more subdued but solid collection of B-sides and overlooked album tracks, some of which are as sprightly and challenging ("I Smiled Yesterday") or as lilting ("Wishin' and Hopin'") as her more celebrated work.

what to avoid: Hooking up with niece Whitney Houston ups the bland quotient on *Friends Can Be Lovers* 𝄢𝄢 (Arista, 1993, prod. Burt Bacharach). Lisa Stansfield, Luther Vandross, and Darlene Love jump aboard as well. Even Bacharach can't save it.

the rest:

The Sensitive Sound of Dionne Warwick 𝄢𝄢𝄢𝄢 (Scepter, 1965/MSI, 1997)
Here Where There Is Love 𝄢𝄢𝄢 (Scepter, 1967/MSI, 1997)
Valley of the Dolls 𝄢𝄢𝄢𝄢 (Scepter, 1968/MSI, 1997)
The Windows of the World 𝄢𝄢𝄢𝄢 (Scepter, 1968/MSI, 1997)
Soulful 𝄢𝄢 (Scepter, 1969/MSI, 1997)
Friends 𝄢𝄢𝄢 (Arista, 1985)
At Her Very Best 𝄢𝄢𝄢𝄢 (Pair, 1989)
Greatest Hits: 1979–1990 𝄢𝄢𝄢 (Arista, 1989)
Sings Cole Porter 𝄢𝄢𝄢 (Arista, 1990)
Aquarela Do Brasil 𝄢𝄢𝄢 (Arista, 1994)
Love Songs 𝄢𝄢𝄢 (Warner Special Products, 1994)
From the Vaults 𝄢𝄢𝄢 (Ichiban, 1995)
Her Greatest Hits 𝄢𝄢 (Special Music Company, 1996)
Her Classic Songs 𝄢𝄢𝄢𝄢 (Curb, 1997)

worth searching for: "Then Came You," her hit 1974 duet with the Spinners, is best found on that group's *One of a Kind Love Affair: The Anthology* 𝄢𝄢𝄢𝄢 (Rhino, 1991, prod. various).

influences:

⏮ Dusty Springfield, Aretha Franklin, Dee Dee Warwick, Herb Alpert, Engelbert Humperdinck

⏭ Whitney Houston, Luther Vandross, Gladys Knight, Elton John

Allan Orski

Dinah Washington

Born Ruth Lee Jones, August 29, 1924, in Tuscaloosa, AL. Died December 14, 1963, in Chicago, IL.

Unquestionably, Washington is one of the greatest, most versatile voices in the entire canon of American song. A consummate master of jazz, blues, R&B, and pop, Washington spent most of her career imprisoned in the ghetto divadom constructed for

the likes of Ella Fitzgerald, Billie Holiday, and Sarah Vaughan (she didn't escape until 1959's "What a Diff'rence a Day Makes"). Washington's ascent to that point was long and arduous, yet fruitful. She started as a piano prodigy in her mother's church at the age of 10. In 1939, a 15-year-old Ruth won an amateur contest at Chicago's famous Regal Theater, singing "I Can't Face the Music." From that point on, the sinful call of the secular world was ringing in her ears. The gospel circuit beckoned, but by the early 1940s, Dinah Washington quit that and plunged into the jazz underworld. After a brief stint with trumpeter Henry Red Allen, Washington hooked up with Lionel Hampton's big band. Her work with him earned a contract with Keynote Records, and her first single, 1943's "Evil Gal Blues," heralded the promise of a new voice to jukeboxes throughout African America. By the 1950s, Washington became a quiet people's favorite, triumphing with excellent and pedestrian material alike. More prolific than most (she would cut almost 500 sides for the Emarcy, Keynote, Mercury, and Wing labels between 1943 and 1961), when she finally hit her stride she was unbeatable. Her crossover successes ("Unforgettable," "This Bitter Earth," and "Baby, You've Got What It Takes"), plus 1960 duets with Brook Benton on "A Rockin' Good Way to Mess Around" and "Fall in Love," made her the toast of pop and the darling of *Jet* magazine. Washington would leave Mercury in 1961 for a more lucrative deal with Roulette Records, but she never had the same impact again. She died from an accidental overdose of diet pills in 1963. Since her prominence as the musical leitmotif of Clint Eastwood's film *The Bridges of Madison County*, Washington's legacy has undergone a renaissance. For an artist of her caliber, it's long overdue.

what to buy: *First Issue: The Dinah Washington Story* 𝄢𝄢𝄢𝄢𝄢 (Verve, 1993, prod. various) is the definitive collection. Buy it. Her classic *What a Diff'rence a Day Makes* 𝄢𝄢𝄢𝄢𝄢 (Mercury, 1959/1987) is also available in a nicely polished Mobile Fidelity audiophile issue released in 1997.

what to buy next: *Mellow Mama* 𝄢𝄢𝄢𝄢 (Delmark, 1945/1993, prod. Robert Koester, Steve Wagner) and *Dinah Jams* 𝄢𝄢𝄢𝄢 (PSM, 1954/Verve, 1997) are tremendous early works that set the tone for her future magic. *The Bessie Smith Songbook* 𝄢𝄢𝄢𝄢 (Emarcy, 1957/1986) is one of the finest interpretive efforts of our time. *The Best of Dinah Washington: The Roulette Years* 𝄢𝄢𝄢𝄢 (Roulette, 1993) is a fine chronicling of her later work.

Dinah Washington **(AP/Wide World Photos)**

what to avoid: *Golden Classics* 🎜🎜 (Collectables, 1990) is a hodgepodge affair that doesn't serve Washington's memory well, though she sounds fine throughout.

the rest:
For Those in Love 🎜🎜🎜🎜 (Emarcy, 1955/1992)
In the Land of Hi-Fi 🎜🎜🎜🎜 (Emarcy, 1956/1987)
Dinah 🎜🎜🎜 (Emarcy, 1956/1991)
The Fats Waller Songbook 🎜🎜🎜🎜 (Emarcy, 1957/1987)
Unforgettable 🎜🎜🎜 (Mercury, 1959/1991)
(With Brook Benton) *The Two of Us* 🎜🎜🎜🎜 (Verve, 1960/1995)
Dinah '63 🎜🎜 (Roulette, 1963/1990)
Compact Jazz 🎜🎜🎜🎜 (Verve, 1987)
Compact Jazz: Dinah Washington Sings the Blues 🎜🎜🎜🎜 (Verve, 1987/1990)
The Complete Dinah Washington on Mercury, Vol. 1–7 🎜🎜🎜🎜 (Mercury, 1989)
In Love 🎜🎜🎜 (Roulette, 1991)
The Essential Dinah Washington: The Great Songs 🎜🎜🎜🎜 (Verve, 1992)
Jazz 'Round Midnight 🎜🎜🎜 (Verve, 1993)
Verve Jazz Masters #19 🎜🎜🎜 (Verve, 1994)
Sings Standards 🎜🎜🎜 (Verve, 1994)
Blue Gardenia: Songs of Love 🎜🎜🎜🎜 (Emarcy, 1995)
Jazz Profile 🎜🎜🎜🎜 (Blue Note, 1997)
Back to the Blues 🎜🎜🎜🎜 (Blue Note, 1997)

worth searching for: The 1992 video *The Swingin' Years: Vintage Jazz Classics* features performances by Washington, Stan Kenton, Louis Jordan, and others on a 1960 telecast hosted by Ronald Reagan.

influences:
◀◀ Maxine Sullivan, Sarah Vaughan, Mildred Bailey
▶▶ Patti LaBelle, Patti Austin, Aretha Franklin, Erykah Badu

Tom Terrell and Gary Graff

Eunice Waymon
See: Nina Simone

Harry Roger Webb
See: Cliff Richard

Jimmy Webb
Born August 15, 1946, in Elk City, OK.

Webb's accomplishments as a songwriter span the worlds of rock, country, and pop music, and his songs have been recorded by a diverse lot, ranging from Glen Campbell, Art Garfunkel, and Frank Sinatra to Barbra Streisand and R.E.M. But he'll always be a hero to lounge lizards for penning the bizarre and grandiose epic "MacArthur Park," a '60s chart hit for actor Richard Harris, and a '70s dance-floor triumph for disco diva Donna Summer. As a recording artist, Webb's accomplishments are far more modest. His voice is warm and intimate, but very limited, which has no doubt contributed to the commercial failure of nearly all of his albums, most of which are out of print. Generally, he has given his best material to others, and the work that appears on his own albums is perhaps more personal, but maddeningly erratic. Webb's place in history is assured, yet some enterprising record company needs to drive the point home with a collection of his best songs done by the original artists.

what to buy: Webb had to be dragged to the project, but he finally agreed to record an album of his songs with which others had massive hits. *Ten Easy Pieces* 🎜🎜🎜🎜 (Guardian, 1996, prod. Jay Landers) features simple, heartfelt arrangements of "Galveston," "Wichita Lineman," "All I Know," and "MacArthur Park," among others. Webb's singing is not up to that of the original artists, but the overall effect is that of studio-quality demos, or a private recital at an intimate gathering.

the rest:
Angel Heart 🎜🎜 (Columbia, 1982)
Suspending Disbelief 🎜🎜🎜 (Elektra, 1993)

worth searching for: Richard Harris's *A Tramp Shining* 🎜🎜🎜 (MCA, 1993, prod. Jimmy Webb) is a re-release of the oddball classic from 1968, featuring the original version of MacArthur Park and other songs written by Webb.

influences:
◀◀ Elvis Presley, the Beatles, George & Ira Gershwin
▶▶ Glen Campbell, the Fifth Dimension, Linda Ronstadt

Daniel Durchholz

Andrew Lloyd Webber
See: Lloyd Webber, Andrew

Ben Webster
Born March 27, 1909, in Kansas City, MO. Died September 20, 1973, in Amsterdam, Holland.

Known as "the Brute" for his barely-sheathed violent temper, tenor sax giant Ben Webster could never hide his romantic core. A master of gruff blues when he played as a sideman in Duke Ellington's band in the 1940s, Webster developed a gorgeous, breathy sax tone that he honed as a studio nomad in the 1950s, issuing a series of classic ballad albums. When Webster picked up on Charlie Parker's cue and played with string sections in the early 1950s, the results were often as sublime as Bird's. Where Parker soared around the violins, Webster practically played through them, his lonely foghorn sound almost enveloping the thinnish wall of violins. Verve marketed "the Brute" as if he were a mood maestro, issuing his classic *Music for Loving* with a sketch of a negligee-clad society dame on the cover. But the contents were jazz landmarks—from the stately wisps of Duke Ellington's "Chelsea Bridge" to the hymnal "There Is No Greater Love." Webster's string sessions were such an immediate triumph that he tried to repeat himself in early 1960, teaming up with arranger Johnny Richards. But he had lesser songs to work with—"The Sweetheart of Sigma Chi" was not exactly vintage Ellington—and the lushness of the earlier charts was gone. After Webster exiled himself to Holland and Sweden in the 1960s and 1970s, he attempted a few string sessions with European musicians. Again, compared to his magisterial work of the 1950s, the later tryouts just didn't cut it.

what to buy: *Music for Loving: Ben Webster with Strings* 𝄞𝄞𝄞𝄞 (Verve, 1995, prod. Norman Granz) is an ample two-disc collection of all of Webster's Verve string workouts, including a brace of unissued alternate takes along with the 25 original tracks. And to top it off, there is even one more helping of heaven—a rich strings confection boasting the booming baritone sax of veteran Ellington sideman Harry Carney.

what to buy next: *The Soul of Ben Webster* 𝄞𝄞𝄞𝄞 (Verve, 1994) is another two discs crammed with classic Webster ballads, only without strings. Added to these early 1950s sessions is a third album—just as stunning—pairing Webster with Ellington bandstand-mate Johnny Hodges.

best of the rest:
Stormy Weather 𝄞𝄞𝄞𝄞 (Black Lion, 1988)
Soulville 𝄞𝄞𝄞𝄞 (Verve, 1989)
At the Renaissance 𝄞𝄞𝄞𝄞 (Original Jazz Classics, 1989)
On Emarcy—Master Takes 𝄞𝄞𝄞𝄞 (Emarcy Japan, 1992)
Gerry Mulligan Meets Ben Webster 𝄞𝄞𝄞𝄞 (Verve, 1997)

worth searching for: As much as gentle Ben loved rifing against violins, he must have stared a few daggers when he was handed such exercises in tripe as "The Sweetheart of Sigma Chi" and "The Whiffenpoof Song," which make up the nonetheless intense and excellent *The Warm Moods* 𝄞𝄞𝄞 (Discovery, 1989). Still, it was probably the occasional Ellington and Rodgers and Hart classics that must have kept the Brute from wrecking some expensive violin wood.

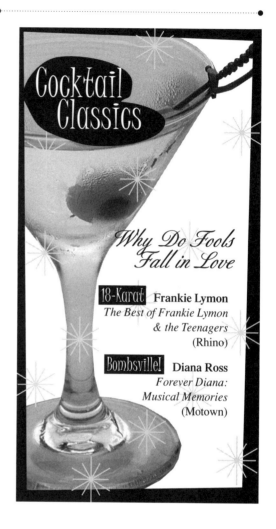

Cocktail Classics

Why Do Fools Fall in Love

18-Karat **Frankie Lymon**
*The Best of Frankie Lymon
& the Teenagers*
(Rhino)

Bombsville! **Diana Ross**
*Forever Diana:
Musical Memories*
(Motown)

influences:
◀◀ Coleman Hawkins, Budd Johnson, Duke Ellington, Fletcher Henderson
▶▶ Sonny Rollins, Charlie Rouse, Archie Shepp

Steve Braun

Kurt Weill

Born March 2, 1900, in Dessau, Germany. Died April 3, 1950, in New York, NY.

Along with Bertolt Brecht, Weill revolutionized the American theater when he introduced elements of German expressionism to the Broadway musical. A successful (though controversial) composer in his homeland, Weill's paeans to murderers, prostitutes, and thieves skirted the fine line between satire and decadence.

His work with Brecht on such new-wave operas as *The Threepenny Opera* and *The Rise and Fall of the City of Mahoganny* were so politically and socially provocative, they caused riots in the streets. The Nazis in particular took offense to the liberal bent of their work, and eventually forced the composers and Weill's wife, singer Lotte Lenya, from the country. In America, Weill's rich orchestral style and memorable melodies made him a favorite of theater-going sophisticates worldwide, and it didn't hurt that he worked with some of the leading lights of the Broadway stage. Weill collaborated with Maxwell Anderson on the hit *Knickerbocker Holiday,* which spawned the melancholy standard "September Song" (since covered by everyone from Frank Sinatra to Jimmy Durante). His work on Moss Hart's *Lady in the Dark* helped introduce Danny Kaye to Broadway audiences, and Weill's collaboration with Ira Gershwin and Ogden Nash for *One Touch of Venus* provided the Mary Martin hits "Speak Low" and "That's Him." Weill innovatively adapted the lyrics of noted black poet Langston Hughes for the award-winning folk opera *Street Scene* and brought fresh romantic strains to his collaboration with Alan Jay Lerner for *Love Life.* It wasn't until after his death that Weill's *The Threepenny Opera* became a success in the United States, and its breakout tune "Mack the Knife" became a mainstream hit for jazz great Louis Armstrong and finger-snapping teen idol Bobby Darin (not to mention Frank Sinatra). Decades after his death, Weill's music still has impact. Late at night, in posh cabarets and upscale piano bars, whenever performers want to evoke world-weary emotion (and more than a little snob appeal), they darken the stage, step into a baby blue spotlight, and croon something moody and melodious by Weill.

what's available: Kurt Weill was not a performer, but he can be heard rehearsing songs ("Speak Low" among them) with Ira Gershwin for the shows *One Touch of Venus* and *Where Do We Go from Here* on *Tryout* ᎂᎂᎂ (DRG, 1953/1979), a fascinating glimpse into the creative process of these two legends of the musical theater.

worth searching for: Many of Weill's finest compositions can be heard in their proper context on such original cast LPs as *Kurt Weill on Broadway* ᎂᎂᎂ (Angel, 1996, prod. Simon Woods), *The Threepenny Opera* ᎂᎂᎂ (TER, 1989, prod. John Yap), and *American Songbook Series: Kurt Weill* ᎂᎂᎂ (Smith-

sonian, 1995). Possibly the finest solo interpreter of Weill's material was his wife, the incomparable Lotte Lenya, whose *The Lotte Lenya Album: Lotte Lenya Sings Theater Songs of Kurt Weill* ᎂᎂᎂ (Columbia, 1979, prod. various) is a pleasing mixed-language anthology of Weill's best work (though an acquired taste). Also, for an example of how far the influence of Kurt Weill's material reaches, check out the Psychedelic Furs' two-disc set, *Should God Forget: A Retrospective* ᎂᎂᎂ (Legacy, 1997, compilation prod. Bruce Dickinson, Tim Butler), which features a previously unreleased, appropriately decadent version of "Mack the Knife."

influences:

◄◄ Bertolt Brecht, Engelbert Humperdinck, Ferriccio Busoni

►► Arnold Schoenberg, Hans Eisler, Lotte Lenya, Scott Walker, Nick Cave

Ken Burke

Lawrence Welk

Born March 11, 1903, in Strasburg, ND. Died May 17, 1992, in Santa Monica, CA.

Born in a sod farmhouse, Welk rose from his humble Great Plains beginnings to become one of the world's best-known entertainers, especially after July 2, 1955, when *The Lawrence Welk Show* was first telecast as a summer replacement program on the ABC television network. Critics panned it as mechanical and out of date and his distinctive "uh one and uh two" countdowns and "wunnaful, wunnaful" critiques alienated an entire population of nascent rock 'n' rollers, but Welk's trademark "champagne music" and perspicuous performance style has endured.

Welk recreated the music of his times—mostly big-band, country swing, and polka—by emphasizing songs and melodies over solos and improvisation. Welk ran his operation like a big family, and his musicians, whom he chose as much for their Christian morality as the heftiness of their chops, performed without hyperbole behind their stiff yet charismatic chief. His generous revue style, from which he never wavered, allowed nearly everyone, and certainly the cream of the crop—"da lovely Lennon Sisters" singing group, piano-pounding Jo Ann Castle, the mustachioed violinist Aladdin, booming bass man Larry Hooper—to take center stage at one time or another.

Lawrence Welk (Archive Photos)

Though he didn't consider himself anything more than an average musician, Welk was a keen businessman and a perfectionist, a rigorous taskmaster who demanded the same from his musicians. (He fired the popular Champagne Lady, Alice Lon, in 1959 for showing too much skin after she sat on a desk and crossed her legs on camera, a hugely unpopular move for the fan-conscious Welk at the time.)

It was a long road for the German/Russian boy from North Dakota who left home at age 21 to fulfill a childhood dream of being a musician. After frustration as a soloist, the accordionist soon formed his own band and endlessly roamed the prairie dance halls and ballrooms. By 1938 Welk had a 13-piece orchestra, but it took more than another decade of perseverance before a local television crew broadcast one of his Los Angeles–area dances in 1951. The ensuing four-year local stint eventually ended 28 years of hard touring when ABC gave Welk and Company an open Saturday night invitation to reach a place their travels never took them—into practically every American home, most of them filled with a nostalgic, post–World War II generation of adults aware that rock and R&B were attracting their children. At 52 years of age, Welk was the ultimate late bloomer, and a symbol of adult, Wonder-Bread America. When ABC cancelled the program in 1971, on the grounds that it was too old-fashioned and out of touch, Welk signed a syndication deal that made him richer and even more popular and practically guaranteed his immortality. He also built an enviable real estate, publishing, and recording empire. Today, more than 17 years after the last program was taped and seven years after Welk's death, *The Lawrence Welk Show* is still one of PBS's top-rated and requested programs; on Saturday nights the machine is still blowing bubbles and champagne music flows into America's living rooms. Videos have proliferated, "new" records continue to be released every year in his name, and Welk Entertainment operates the Welk Resort Center & Champagne Theatre in Branson, Missouri. All are dedicated to keeping the Welk legacy alive and well into the next century.

what to buy: Very little of Welk's original work has made the transition to CD, which makes the best buy the budget-priced *Musical Anthology* 𝄢𝄢𝄢 (Ranwood, 1992), a three-disc mix of full-tilt champagne music in all its guises: big-band classics ("Begin the Beguine"), novelties ("Winchester Cathedral"), Americana ("Scarlet Ribbons," "Old Man River"), country ("San Antonio Rose"), religious/inspirational ("How Great Thou Art," "Climb Every Mountain"), contemporary covers ("Raindrops Keep Falling on My Head," "Tie a Yellow Ribbon 'round the Old

Oak Tree"), actual Welk charters ("Calcutta," "Baby Elephant Walk"), and numerous other polkas and waltzes. It even opens with the familiar bubble-popping "Champagne Time" opening segment from the show.

what to buy next: Many Welk titles are available only on cassette tape, a reflection of the strength of his elderly audience. Of the many recent releases on his own label, *22 All-Time Big Band Favorites* 𝄢𝄢𝄢 (Ranwood, 1989) includes "Woodchopper's Ball," "Take the 'A' Train," and "String of Pearls," although *16 Most Requested Songs* 𝄢𝄢𝄢 (Sony, 1989) and *22 All-Time Favorite Waltzes* 𝄢𝄢𝄢 (Ranwood, 1988) are equally proficient in more specific categories.

best of the rest:
22 Great Waltzes 𝄢𝄢 (Ranwood, 1987)
Best of Lawrence Welk 𝄢𝄢𝄢 (MCA, 1987)
22 Great Songs for Dancing 𝄢𝄢𝄢 (Ranwood, 1988)
Blowing Bubbles 𝄢𝄢 (Ranwood, 1988)
Champagne and Romance 𝄢𝄢 (Hamilton, 1992)
22 Great Songs for Easy Listening 𝄢𝄢𝄢 (Ranwood, 1993)
The Champagne Music of Lawrence Welk 𝄢𝄢𝄢 (MCA Special Products, 1993)
Best of Lawrence Welk 𝄢𝄢 (Ranwood, 1993)
Celebrates 25 Years on Television 𝄢𝄢𝄢 (Ranwood, 1993)
22 Country Music Hits 𝄢𝄢 (Ranwood, 1994)
American Favorites 𝄢𝄢 (Ranwood, 1996)
Hallelujah 𝄢𝄢 (Ranwood, 1997)

worth searching for: The North Dakota State University Welk Archive includes 352 albums in its collection, and Welk's best recordings can only be found on his early Coral and Dot sides. Although highly collectible, the good stuff is hard to find. Two vinyl-only platters to begin with should include *Calcutta* 𝄢𝄢𝄢 (Dot, 1961), which includes the harpsichord-drenched title track (and Welk's only #1 hit), or *Baby Elephant Walk* 𝄢𝄢𝄢 (Dot, 1962).

influences:
◄◄ Benny Goodman, Glenn Miller, Tommy Dorsey, Jimmy Dorsey, Guy Lombardo, Paul Whiteman, Artie Shaw, Woody Herman, Red Nichols & His Five Pennies, Cab Calloway, Louis Armstrong

►► Myron Floren, Pete Fountain, Jo Ann Castle, the Lennon Sisters, Lynn Anderson, k.d. lang

see also: *Pat Boone, Billy May, Kay Kyser, Les Brown, Mantovani, Liberace, Ray Anthony, Myron Floren*

Leland Rucker

Mae West

Born Mary Jane West, August 17, 1892, in Brooklyn, NY. Died November 22, 1980, in Los Angeles, CA.

When West was born, there were no motion pictures and Brooklyn was still an independent city. By the time she died, she had created one of the dominant personas of Depression-era cinema, a brazen sexpot who could match wits with W.C. Fields (in *My Little Chickadee*) or Cary Grant (in *I'm No Angel* and *She Done Him Wrong*). More than a movie star, West was a singing star, a mannered, limited vocalist who still brought personality to such sultry compositions as "A Guy What Takes His Time," "Easy Rider," and "Nobody Loves Me Like That Dallas Man." Late in life, she also covered a set of rock songs, including compositions by the Beatles and Bob Dylan, with predictably hilarious results.

what's available: *Way Out West* ♪♪♪ (Tower, 1966) is difficult to find, but worthwhile, if only to hear West mangle rock tunes. The import *I'm No Angel* ♪♪♪ (Jasmine, 1996) collects some of West's movie hits, including the title track, which is drawn from the 1933 comedy that paired West with Cary Grant. Easier to find is *Golden Throats* ♪♪♪♪ (Rhino, 1988), a legendary compilation of has-beens and no-talents taking on the songs of the early rock era. It's full of shining examples of absolute awfulness, including Jack Webb's "Try a Little Tenderness" and William Shatner's "Lucy in the Sky with Diamonds." West is on the collection, too, with a truly horrible version of "Twist and Shout." Is there anything more embarrassing than a hip-swiveling rock song performed irony-free by an aging sixtysomething jezebel? Probably not. *This Is Art Deco* ♪♪♪ (Columbia, 1982) is a largely useless, somewhat confusing collection of songs from actors/singers, including Al Jolson, Jack Lemmon, Bert Williams, and Alberta Hunter. West is represented by "A Guy What Takes His Time."

influences:

▶▶ Marilyn Monroe, RuPaul

Ben Greenman

Paul Weston

Born March 12, 1912, in Springfield, MA. Died September 20, 1996, in Santa Monica, CA.

A wicked sense of humor separated this composer, arranger, and conductor from his more stodgy counterparts, but for every *Laugh In* television episode he oversaw, Weston also wrote a solemn standard like "Autumn in Rome" or "Day by Day." After graduating from Dartmouth University in 1933,

Weston was attending graduate school when singer Rudy Vallee heard his previously sold arrangements and hired him to work on the radio show "Fleischman Hour." The connection led to work with Bing Crosby, Fred Astaire, Tommy Dorsey, and Weston's eventual wife, Jo Stafford. He nailed lucrative management gigs at both Capitol and Columbia Records, then slowly started shifting his emphasis from swing jazz to "mood music." His 1945 album, *Music for Dreaming*, was an archetype for the entire easy-listening genre. In addition to mood music, Weston spent his later career arranging for Sarah Vaughan, Dinah Shore, Doris Day, and many others; working on *Laugh In*; directing music for *The Bob Newhart Show* and *Disney on Parade*; and recording tongue-in-cheek lounge albums with his wife, Stafford, under the pseudonym Jonathan and Darlene Edwards.

what to buy: Weston's first "mood-music" album, *Music for Dreaming* ♫♫♫ (Capitol, 1945/1992), which is packaged on CD with *Music for Memories*, was the exact point where big-band swing music gave way to lush, heavily orchestrated easy-listening ballads. With gentle, unobtrusive instrumentals like "I'm in the Mood for Love" and "I Only Have Eyes for You," it was a precursor—although Weston later criticized elevator-music purveyors for stamping out the swing-jazz elements entirely—for such successors as Ray Conniff, Percy Faith, and Mantovani.

best of the rest:
Easy Jazz ♫♫ (Corinthian)
The Original Music for Easy Listening ♫♫ (Corinthian)
Columbia Album of Jerome Kern ♫♫♫ (Columbia)
Crescent City—Music of New Orleans ♫♫♫ (Corinthian, 1957)

worth searching for: Weston's deliberate missed notes and campy conversation make *Jonathan and Darlene's Greatest Hits* ♫♫♫ (Corinthian, prod. various) and *Jonathan and Darlene's Greatest Hits, Vol. 2* ♫♫♫ (Corinthian, prod. various) valuable lighthearted collections.

influences:

◀◀ Rudy Vallee, Benny Goodman, Glenn Miller, Bing Crosby, Al Jolson

▶▶ Jackie Gleason, the Captain & Tennille, Ray Conniff, Percy Faith, Mantovani

see also: *The Pied Pipers*

Steve Knopper

Ian Whitcomb

Born July 10, 1941, in Woking, Surrey, England.

Proving that with the right accent (British) and the right hairstyle (over the ears) at the right time (summer of 1965) *anything* was possible on the U.S. charts, Whitcomb—while still ostensibly studying political science at Trinity College in Dublin—had a Top 10 hit with an innocuous little song full of barrelhouse piano and heavy breathing called "You Turn Me On." He was duly summoned to Hollywood to appear on all the pop shows of the day and to tour with all the other pop stars of the moment. He never again visited the Top 40, but Whitcomb remained in Southern California, carving out a career for himself as a record producer, television producer (several documentaries for PBS and the BBC), radio host (currently on NPR),

and all-around musicologist (his 1983 book *Rock Odyssey* remains a definitive study of popular music in the 1960s, and his best-selling *After the Ball* covers every aspect of pop from rock to his beloved ragtime). He has continued making records of his own since 1965, if of a decidedly non-rock nature, and continues to sell his wares through a post office box high in the California hills. "His frivolity knows no bounds," spoke Ian's old headmaster in 1959; "You're the Evelyn Waugh lavender type and I'm pure Rough Trade," declared no less than Jim Morrison a decade later. But Eric Clapton said it best: "He was a bit of a character back in the '60s, and do you know what? He's *still* a bit of a character. Carry on!"

what to buy: While *The Very Best of Ian Whitcomb: The Rock 'n' Roll Years* ♫♫♫♫ (Varese Vintage, 1998, compilation prod. Cary E. Mansfield, Ian Whitcomb) wonderfully covers his brief career as a teen sensation, *You Turn Me On!/Ian Whitcomb's Mod, Mod Music Hall!* ♫♫♫♫ (Tower, 1965, 1966/Sundazed, 1997, compilation prod. Bob Irwin) demonstrates just how quickly—and entertainingly—Whitcomb metamorphosed from the self-proclaimed Father of Irish Rock to the lovable if eccentric savior of British musical traditions. The best of his full-fledged explorations into the world of ragtime and Tin Pan Alley have been compiled as *The Golden Age of Lounge* ♫♫♫ (Varese Vintage, 1997, compilation prod. Ian Whitcomb, Cary E. Mansfield). On it, Whitcomb makes a good case that the roots of easy-listening creep far, far back into the salons and drawing rooms of the Edwardian and even Victorian ages. "The songs sport the kind of rolling melodies and candy chords that I have always loved," writes Whitcomb in the accompanying booklet. "We are not trying to recreate here; we are not nostalgiacs or camp followers. We are, in fact, creating new recipes from old and trusted ingredients." Mission accomplished.

what to buy next: Speaking of timely reissues, at the height of the *Titanic* movie hoopla Ian and his newly re-christened White Star Orchestra recorded *Titanic: Music as Heard on the Fateful Voyage* ♫♫♫ (Rhino, 1997, prod. Ian Whitcomb), providing a modern, if chilling, recreation of the actual songs played by the mighty vessel's band before they too went down with the ship.

the rest:
Happy Days Are Here Again ♫♫♫ (Audiophile, 1989)
Ragtime America ♫♫♫ (ITW Industries, 1992/Audiophile, 1995)
Comedy Songs ♫♫♫ (ITW Industries, 1992/Dove Music, 1996)
Lotus Land ♫♫♫♫ (ITW Industries, 1992/Audiophile, 1995)
Spread a Little Happiness ♫♫♫ (ITW Industries, 1993)

Margaret Whiting (© Jack Vartoogian)

influences:

◀◀ Jerry Lee Lewis, Irving Berlin, Rudy Vallee, Dick Zimmerman
▶▶ Tiny Tim, the Kinks, David Bowie

Gary Pig Gold

Margaret Whiting

After Perry Como and Frank Sinatra shifted pop music's focus from the big dance band to the charismatic singer, the well-connected and well-voiced Whiting stepped in to become one of World War II–era America's most beloved female singers. She crooned the definitive versions of "Moonlight in Vermont" (which sold more than two million copies) and "It Might As Well Be Spring," scored 13 gold records, and while she doesn't quite have the name recognition of her pop-singer forebears, her nightclub gigs continue to draw huge crowds all over the country.

Thanks to her father, songwriter Richard Whiting, Margaret was born with an impeccable musical pedigree and, more important, great connections. Johnny Mercer became an important mentor when her father died, setting her up with a microphone for the first time (on an NBC tribute to her father), collaborating on a duet, and feeding her terrific material. Whiting was a smart, confident teen singer, and talent took her the rest of the way. After the war, like her contemporary Jo Stafford, she affected a smooth, clear style, which fit perfectly with the big easy-listening arrangements developing from mood-music pioneers Paul Weston and Percy Faith. But her sidestep into television didn't have much impact—she and her singing sister Barbara starred briefly in a forgotten *I Love Lucy* summer replacement called *Those Whiting Girls*—and her career quickly lost momentum to rock 'n' roll. In one of the most interesting examples of strange pop-music bedfellows this side of Michael Jackson and Lisa Marie Presley, the high-society Whiting married a 20-years-younger adult-film star, Jack Wrangler, in the early 1980s. She continues to sing at countless charity benefits.

what's available: *Then and Now* 🎵🎵🎵 (DRG, 1990, prod. various) is far from definitive—the ultimate Whiting collection has yet to be compiled on CD—but it contains her signature first hit "Moonlight in Vermont," plus excellent versions of "That Old Black Magic," "What Is a Man," and "My Best Friend," and guest help from jazzman Gerry Mulligan. *Come a Little Closer* 🎵🎵🎵 (Audiophile, 1994) and *Too Marvelous for Words* 🎵🎵🎵 (Audiophile, 1995) focus on more recent material.

influences:

◀◀ Art Tatum, Frank Sinatra, Perry Como, Jo Stafford, Peggy Lee, Al Jolson, Judy Garland

▶▶ Rosemary Clooney, Jack Jones, Andy Williams

see also: *Johnny Mercer*

Steve Knopper

Roger Whittaker

Born March 22, 1936, in Nairobi, Kenya.

One of the most aggressively TV-marketed performers of our time, Whittaker has managed to parlay a modest string of British and Canadian hits into international stardom. Fortunately, Whittaker does have something to sell. His cordial, urbane manner and pleasing "mixed baritone" brings an authentic, dramatically precise feel to the romantic folk ballads he sings. Also, he is a pretty fair songwriter, co-writing much of his best-known material, and taking justifiable pride in his ability as a whistler.

Whittaker, born of English parents, spent his early years in Africa before moving to Wales to study marine biology. Part-time gigs in folk clubs proved so satisfying that Whittaker funded his own independent label release, which led to a contract with Fontana Records and the end of a potential teaching career. Under the name "Rog" Whittaker, he scaled the lower regions of the U.K. charts in 1961 with "Steel Man," and became a popular figure on TV shows in Northern Ireland. Whittaker scored his first big European hit with "The Mexican Whistler," his prize-winning number at Belgium's 1967 Knokke music festival. Subsequent British hits, such as "Durham Town," "I Don't Believe in If Anymore," "New World in the Morning," and "Why," earned Whittaker his own popular series on BBC-TV (later rebroadcast in Canada). "The Last Farewell" was Whittaker's sole American hit, reaching the Top 20 in 1975. His last British Top Ten record was his duet with music hall performer Des O'Connor on "The Skye Boat Song." Whittaker's phenomenal popularity through TV advertising (which allows him to bypass finicky radio programmers) has created a continual demand for fresh product. As a result, though he writes very little these days, he has recorded dozens of country, folk, and pop LPs of other people's songs in his warm, easy-listening style. A keen judge of material, Whittaker released a sterling version of "Wind Beneath My Wings" many years before Bette Midler did, but for the most part he has followed trends rather than created them. To accommodate his vast European audience, Whittaker has recorded in several different languages, ensuring that somewhere in the world, at any given moment, someone is reaching for the phone to order the latest TV repackaging of his greatest hits.

what to buy: Whittaker's trademark songs "The Last Farewell," "The Mexican Whistler," "Durham Town," and many others are collected on *Greatest Hits* 🎵🎵🎵🎵 (RCA, 1994, prod. Chet Atkins, Nick Munro, Ian Summer, Roger Whittaker), an easy-to-find mid-priced disc.

what to buy next: Possibly his best non-hit collection, *Celebration* 🎵🎵🎵🎵 (RCA, 1993, prod. various), boasts Whittaker in top vocal form on such ditties as "If My Life Is Worth a Dime," "Do You Remember," and "The Best I Can." It's a strong LP from start to finish.

what to avoid: Be forewarned that the misleadingly titled *Best of Roger Whittaker* 🎵🎵 (Curb, 1994) showcases not a single song associated with Whittaker. Instead, it features him singing fairly straightforward versions of other people's hits, such as "Gentle on My Mind," "Honey," and "Leaving on a Jet Plane."

the rest:
The Roger Whittaker Christmas Album 🎵🎵🎵 (RCA, 1978/1994)
The World of Roger Whittaker 🎵🎵 (Pair, 1989)
Fire & Rain 🎵🎵 (Pair, 1989)
Love Will Be Our Home 🎵🎵 (Word/Epic, 1991)
Roger Whittaker Live 🎵🎵🎵 (Drive Entertainment)
I Will Always Love You 🎵🎵🎵🎵 (RCA, 1994)
What a Wonderful World 🎵🎵🎵 (RCA, 1994)
Annie's Song 🎵🎵 (RCA, 1994)
Live! 🎵🎵🎵 (RCA, 1994)
Wind Beneath My Wings 🎵🎵 (RCA, 1994)
Feelings 🎵🎵🎵 (RCA, 1994)
Danny Boy & Other Irish Favorites 🎵🎵🎵 (RCA, 1994)
The Christmas Song 🎵🎵 (RCA, 1995)
On Broadway 🎵🎵🎵 (RCA, 1995)
A Perfect Day: His Greatest Hits & More 🎵🎵🎵🎵 (RCA, 1996)
Star Gold 🎵🎵🎵 (Polydor, 1997)
Happy Holidays 🎵🎵🎵 (BMG Special, 1997)

Andy Williams and actress Ann Sothern learn the bossa nova (**AP/Wide World Photos**)

worth searching for: The out-of-print *Best Loved Ballads, Vol. 1* 🎵🎵🎵 (Liberty, 1990, prod. Peter Moss) is a strong match of artist and material. Whittaker brings his inimitable personal touch to every song.

influences:

◀◀ Lonnie Donegan, Glen Yarborough, Ed Ames

▶▶ Gordon Lightfoot, Harry Chapin, Des O'Connor

Ken Burke

Andy Williams

Born December 3, 1930, in Wall Lake, IA.

If Elvis Presley made young 1950s couples want to do the bump and grind, Williams's safe, comfortable, milquetoast brand of crooning made them want to hold hands while their parents drove them to the movies. His vanilla versions of "Moon River" and "Love Story (Where Do I Begin?)" were hits, but he was most famous for television's *Andy Williams Show* throughout the 1960s.

Son of an amateur musician, Williams and his three older brothers started out singing in their church, then earned radio work and a movie contract. When two of his brothers were drafted, Williams became a freelance backup singer, helping out Bing Crosby and actress Lauren Bacall, among others. In 1953, after the Williams Brothers tried the group thing one more time but gave up, Williams snagged a record contract and regular work on *The Tonight Show* with Steve Allen. This was his stepping-stone to prime-time stardom, although the show's ratings sagged and NBC pulled the plug in 1971. Today, he's more of an all-purpose celebrity than a singer, painting and appearing at golf events to spice up his mostly quiet life. He continues to do a yearly Christmas show, too, and even winked at his own reputation on a recent installment of Comedy Central's sarcastic *The Daily Show*—in an interview, Williams saluted his "homies," Snoop Doggy Dogg and Puff Daddy, in a perfect poker face.

what to buy: A ton of Williams's greatest-hits collections glut the market; *16 Most Requested Songs* 𝄞𝄞𝄞 (Sony, 1986, compilation prod. Tim Geelan, Mike Berniker) contains all of his most familiar croons, including "Moon River" and "Days of Wine and Roses"; *16 Most Requested Songs: Encore!* 𝄞𝄞𝄞 (Sony, 1995, compilation prod. Didier C. Deutsch) adds lesser-known versions of "Michelle" and "Lonely Street."

what to buy next: Williams had a voice tailored for holiday music, and his versions of "Silent Night" and "O! Come All Ye Faithful" make Bing Crosby sound like Mick Jagger. Best of the many available Christmas collections include *Personal Christmas Collection* 𝄞𝄞𝄞 (Sony, 1994, compilation prod. Didier C. Deutsch) and *Christmas Album* 𝄞𝄞𝄞 (Laserlight, 1994). The most comprehensive collection of Williams's vintage material, recorded from 1956 to 1962, before he hit the television airwaves, is *I Like Your Kind of Love: The Best of the Cadence Years* 𝄞𝄞𝄞 (Varese Sarabande, 1996, prod. various).

what to avoid: Of all Williams's *Greatest Hits* titles on the market, pass on the misleadingly labeled *Greatest Hits* 𝄞𝄞 (Laserlight, 1994), which is actually live songs recorded in Branson, Missouri, the capitol of mush and schmaltz.

best of the rest:

Love Story 𝄞𝄞 (Sony, 1988)
Greatest Hits, Vol. 2 𝄞𝄞𝄞 (Sony, 1989)
Unchained Melody: Greatest Songs 𝄞𝄞𝄞 (Curb, 1990)
Blue Hawaii: Greatest Songs of the Island 𝄞𝄞𝄞 (Curb, 1992)
Songs of Faith 𝄞𝄞 (Sony, 1993)
Greatest Hits/Greatest Hits, Vol. 2/Love Story 𝄞𝄞𝄞 (Sony, 1997)

worth searching for: Though Williams never had anything close to a reputation as a jazz singer, he does a decent job with jazzier material—thanks to the help of guest Dave Grusin and producer Quincy Jones—on the recently reissued *Under Paris Skies* 𝄞𝄞𝄞 (Varese Sarabonde, 1960/1997, prod. Quincy Jones).

influences:

◀◀ Bing Crosby, Frank Sinatra, Vic Damone, Rosemary Clooney, Jo Stafford, Steve Allen

▶▶ Mariah Carey, Celine Dion, Michael Bolton, Kenny G

Steve Knopper

John Williams

See: Arthur Fiedler

Mason Williams

Born August 24, 1938, in Abilene, TX.

Something of a modern-day renaissance man, Williams is an entertainment triple threat. Best known as a recording artist and composer, his most popular work is the enduring "Classical Gas," a piece which combines intricate guitar picking with sweeping orchestral accompaniment. But he's also a comedy writer who won an Emmy for his work on the groundbreaking '60s TV show *The Smothers Brothers Comedy Hour* (it was Williams who conceived the satirical "Pat Paulsen for President" gag). Finally, he has written many books of prose and poetry, and is also a conceptual artist whose work includes a short film in which a biplane draws a stem and leaves beneath the sun, turning it into the "world's largest sunflower."

what to buy: A compilation of tracks from his five Warner Bros. records, *Music 1968–1971* 𝄞𝄞𝄞 (Vanguard, 1992) shows the range of Williams's work, from "Classical Gas" and "Greensleeves" to more whimsical material such as "The Smothers Brothers Theme" and the wonderfully titled "I've Heard That Tear Stained Monologue You Do There by the Door Before You Go."

what to avoid: Proving there's no accounting for taste, *Classical Gas* 𝄞𝄞 (American Grammaphone, 1987)—recorded with New Age techno weenies Mannheim Steamroller and including a synthesized version of the title track—has proven to be one of Williams's most popular releases.

the rest:

The Mason Williams Phonograph Record 𝄞𝄞𝄞 (Warner Bros., 1968)
A Gift of Song 𝄞𝄞𝄞 (Real Music, 1992)

worth searching for: Williams has recorded a dozen or so albums, most of which are out of print. You're welcome to dig them up, but you might also want to stop by New York's Museum of Modern Art, where Williams's "Bus," a life-sized photographic poster of a Greyhound bus, is in the permanent collection.

influences:

◀◀ Andres Segovia, Flatt & Scruggs

▶▶ Mannheim Steamroller, Ottmar Liebert

Daniel Durchholz

Roger Williams

Born Louis Weertz, 1925, in Omaha, NE.

Williams brought the snob appeal of classical music to the middle of the road. His cool (sometimes jazzy) touch on schmaltzy standards, refitted classical pieces, and movie themes emphasized melody but also asserted his musical personality and masterful technique.

The son of a music teacher and a preacher, Williams attended Juilliard and trained under such cool-school jazz masters as Teddy Wilson and Lenny Tristano. Set to accompany a fellow student on the *Arthur Godfrey Talent Scouts* program, Williams performed solo (to great acclaim) when the singer did not show up. Subsequent appearances proved popular and led to his 1951 signing with Kapp Records. According to Joseph Lanza's book *Elevator Music,* label chief Dave Kapp deterred Williams from playing abstract jazz by dragging into the studio a cigar-store Indian with a sign on its head reading, "Where's the melody?" Forced to concentrate on melody, Williams began blending disparate forms of popular song into a base of classical music, but without abandoning the expressionism of jazz. This approach eventually resulted in Williams's 1955 #1 hit "Autumn Leaves." Mistakenly believing the tune to be titled "The Falling Leaves," Williams added descriptive descending arpeggios that soon became the trademark of his newfound style. Williams's big string of instrumental hits included "Wanting You," "Beyond the Sea," "Tumbling Tumbleweeds," "Lara's Theme," and the movie theme "Born Free." Comparisons between Williams and Liberace are inevitable. Certainly the sequined showman opened the door for Williams's style, but while Liberace was clearly the greater in-person attraction, he never even approached Williams's chart power. Also, Williams was simply the better musician, and though both played in a somewhat florid style, Liberace simply could not build a song to its inspirational peak the way Williams did. The hits kept coming for Williams all through the '60s, but easy-listening eventually faded as a commercially viable market. Still active, Williams's name has been kept alive by countless TV record offers. In a career that virtually defined "beautiful music," Williams has had nearly two dozen hit singles and 38 chart LPs. He is the most commercially successful popular music pianist of our time.

what to buy: If you just want a small helping of Williams's talent, *Greatest Hits* 𝄢𝄢𝄢𝄢 (MCA, 1971/1989, prod. Stan Farber, Hy Grill) is a 14-track budget disc featuring the hits "Autumn Leaves," "September Song," and "Piano Concerto #1," and will leave you wanting more. The main course is on *The Greatest Popular Pianist: The Artist's Choice* 𝄢𝄢𝄢𝄢 (MCA, 1992, compilation prod. Roger Williams, James McKaie), a two-disc, 22-song collection featuring his best work on a variety of popular tunes, from "Those Were the Days" to "Bess You Is My Woman," plus all the hits.

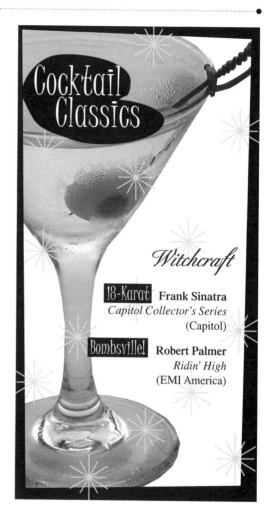

Cocktail Classics

Witchcraft

18-Karat **Frank Sinatra**
Capitol Collector's Series
(Capitol)

Bombsville! **Robert Palmer**
Ridin' High
(EMI America)

what to buy next: Williams turns "Lara's Theme," "Love Is a Many Splendored Thing," "Come Saturday Morning," and "Call Me Irresponsible" into gratifying mini piano concertos on *Greatest Movie Themes* 𝄢𝄢𝄢 (Hip-O, 1996, compilation prod. Roger Williams, James Austin).

what to avoid: It's not a bad disc, but be forewarned: *Greatest Hits* 𝄢𝄢 (Curb, 1990) features re-recordings of Williams's big instrumental hits. The original sides are still the best.

the rest:
Somewhere in Time 𝄢𝄢𝄢 (Bainbridge, 1986)
Best of the Beautiful 𝄢𝄢𝄢 (MCA, 1988)

Phantom of the Opera 🎵🎵🎵 (Curb, 1990)
Nadia's Theme and Some of the Most Beautiful Girls in the World 🎵🎵
    (MCA Special Products, 1990)
Golden Christmas 🎵🎵🎵 (Special Music Company, 1992)
Golden Hits 🎵🎵🎵🎵 (MCA Special Products, 1993)
Moments to Remember 🎵🎵 (MCA Special Products, 1993)
Plays the Songs of Love 🎵🎵🎵 (MCA Special Products, 1994)
The Great Piano Hits 🎵🎵🎵 (Pair, 1995)
Classic Praise 🎵🎵 (Sonrise, 1995)
Plays More Golden Songs of Love 🎵🎵🎵 (MCA Special Products, 1995)
Christmas Time 🎵🎵🎵 (MCA Special Products, 1995)
Roger Williams 🎵🎵 (MCA Special Products, 1995)
Autumn Leaves 🎵🎵🎵 (MCA Special Products, 1995)

worth searching for: Williams is quite amusing on *Roger Williams Live* 🎵🎵🎵🎵 (MCA, 1987), wherein the pianist makes entertaining medleys out of the many disparate styles and songs in his vast repertoire. (Sort of like that other big pianist from the '50s did—you know . . . the guy who wore a lot of sequins.)

influences:

◀◀ Lenny Tristano, Teddy Wilson, Liberace

▶▶ Floyd Cramer, Peter Nero, Carlos Avalon

Ken Burke

Brian Wilson

See: The Beach Boys

Cassandra Wilson

Born 1960, in Jackson, MI.

Wilson's smoky, sensuous reinterpretations of standards by Sarah Vaughan, Betty Carter, Dinah Washington, and Billie Holiday have prompted near-unanimous raves from critics, including the *New York Times* ("the most important singer to come along in jazz in the last 10 years") and *Time* ("the most accomplished jazz vocalist of her generation"). Her luscious contralto oozes through dusky, slowed-down moods, usually set by lulling guitar, bass, percussion, and horns. But along with her increasingly accomplished original compositions and the older standards, Wilson has also reinterpreted contemporary rock and popular songs. She wrings all possible emotion from "Last Train to Clarksville," which the Monkees played for fun, and gives the same dripping treatment to pieces by U2, Joni Mitchell, Neil Young, and Van Morrison.

Born to an elementary-school-teacher mother who favored Motown music, and a jazz-musician father who was a dreamy in-ventor, Wilson quickly discovered folk singer Mitchell as a primary inspiration. Jazz became her passion while singing with the Black Arts Music Society in Jackson. After a brief tutoring period in New Orleans, she moved to New York, where Wilson became established on the local jazz club scene in the late 1980s, before gaining international attention with 1993's *Blue Light 'Til Dawn* and 1995's even more exquisite *New Moon Daughter*.

what to buy: Start with *New Moon Daughter* 🎵🎵🎵🎵 (Blue Note, 1995, prod. Craig Street), where Wilson breathes moody depth into contemporary rock (U2's "Love Is Blindness," the Monkees' "Last Train to Clarksville," and Neil Young's "Harvest Moon"); brooding versions of Hank Williams's "I'm So Lonesome I Could Cry," Hoagy Carmichael's "Skylark," and the Billie Holiday classic "Strange Fruit" contrast nicely with her more stirringly performed original songs, "Solomon Sang," "A Little Warm Death," and "Until." *Blue Light 'Til Dawn* 🎵🎵🎵 (Blue Note, 1993, prod. Craig Street) has a more bluesy feel, with songs by Robert Johnson, Joni Mitchell, and Van Morrison; the *a cappella* "Sankofa," which she composed, is haunting and redemptive.

what to buy next: *Cassandra Wilson Songbook* 🎵🎵🎵 (Jazz Music Today, 1995, prod. various) samples from Wilson's eight lesser-known releases prior to *Blue Light 'Til Dawn*, with common jazz standards rather than the contemporary turns she has taken since. *Live* 🎵🎵🎵 (Jazz Music Today, 1992, prod. various) has more of a spontaneous, intimate nightclub feel.

the rest:
Point of View 🎵🎵🎵 (Verve, 1985)
Days Aweigh 🎵🎵🎵 (Verve, 1987)
Blue Skies 🎵🎵🎵 (Verve, 1988)
Jumpworld 🎵🎵🎵 (Verve, 1989)
She Who Weeps 🎵🎵🎵 (Verve, 1990)
After the Beginning Again 🎵🎵🎵 (Verve, 1992)
Dance to the Drums Again 🎵🎵🎵 (DIW/Columbia, 1993)

worth searching for: On the soundtrack to *Midnight in the Garden of Good and Evil* 🎵🎵🎵🎵 (Warner Bros., 1997, prod. Matt Pierson, Clint Eastwood), Wilson makes "The Days of Wine and Roses" even more haunting than it was originally intended.

influences:

◀◀ Sarah Vaughan, Billie Holiday, Betty Carter, Dinah Washington, Joni Mitchell, Earl Turbinton

Roger Matuz

Murry Wilson

Born Murry Gage Wilson, July 2, 1917, in Hutchinson, KS. Died June 4, 1973, in Whittier, CA.

Remembered today, if at all, as the father of three actual Beach Boys, the tempestuous, overbearing, larger-than-life Murry Wilson was at heart a music lover. He wasn't a musician, mind you, but a man for whom only a gentle tune could truly tame the savage beast.

"I've been writing songs for as long as I can remember," boasted Murry on the back cover of his one and only album. "My family has always had a great appreciation for the value of music." True enough, despite his meager income as owner of a small machinery company, he always found enough money when his sons needed musical instruments, or to convert the garage of the nondescript Wilson homestead in Hawthorne, California, into a rehearsal studio for eldest son Brian to hone his craft. When Brian's remarkable gift for melody and arrangement became obvious, Murry quickly became the youngster's champion—a fierce, demanding musical drill sergeant. Evidence of child abuse notwithstanding, it's hard to deny that without his father's tireless support, Brian's beautiful music would never have made it far out of that Hawthorne garage. Naturally, once the Beach Boys became a growing concern of their own, Murry immediately appointed himself their manager and record producer, and it was not until the height of their initial mid-1960s success that the band was finally able to banish the man forever from their midst. Unperturbed, he simply hacked together another Beach Boys–type band, the Sunrays, and helped them actually enter the Top 40 with a couple of Brian Wilson retreads. Murry even managed to talk Capitol Records into releasing his own album in 1967, and it flopped. Wilson remained Brian's music publisher until he ruthlessly sold the copyrights to A&M Records in the late 1960s, convinced his eldest son's compositions would never live beyond the 1970s. (It took more than two decades of legal wrangling for Brian to retrieve the rights to this now-priceless catalog.) Murry Wilson didn't live beyond the 1970s, either, finally succumbing to a heart attack in his wife's arms.

what to buy: Until some tongue-in-cheek record label gets around to reissuing Wilson's own LP, the only easy way to experience him is on the Sunrays' box set *For Collectors Only: Vintage Rays* ♫♫♫ (Collectables, 1996, prod. Richard Henn). This was the nondescript California band Murry commandeered following his dismissal from the Beach Boys' operation, and is probably the only album on earth where one can find Murry Wilson compositions sitting alongside the bizarre rock producer Kim Fowley's.

what to buy next: An utterly chilling "Help Me, Rhonda" session tape, on which a drunken Murry accosted his sons in the recording studio, is preserved for, uh, posterity on the Beach Boys' *Time to Get Alone* ♫♫♫ (Silver Shadow, 1993, prod. Brian Wilson). This terrifying encounter supposedly inspired Brian to write the hilariously wicked "I'm Bugged at My Ol' Man."

worth searching for: Good luck in finding Murry's one and only uneasy-listening masterpiece *The Many Moods of Murry Wilson* ♫♫♫ (Capitol, 1967, prod. Murry Wilson), but be assured the jacket alone is well worth the hunt.

influences:

◄◄ Jimmy Haskell, Lawrence Welk, Eck Kynor

►► Brian Wilson, Rick Henn, Dr. Eugene E. Landy

see also: *The Beach Boys*

Gary Pig Gold

Nancy Wilson

Born February 20, 1937, in Chillicothe, OH.

Wilson doesn't refer to herself as a jazz or pop singer, or even a chanteuse. She considers herself a song stylist: "I just like to sing good music and good lyrics," she once said, "and I've never cared what anybody else calls it. My job is to take good material and deliver it."

Compared to blues singer Joe Williams for her ability to blend pop, jazz, and blues so seamlessly, Wilson, who grew up in Columbus, Ohio, began her professional career with Rusty Bryant's band in 1956 after singing in church choirs, winning talent contests, and attending one semester at Ohio College. After touring the continent, she went solo in 1958 and headed to the Big Apple in 1959, only to wind up behind a desk. As fate would have it, though, she got a chance to fill in for Irene Reid at the Blue Morocco, a Bronx club, where jazzman Cannonball Adderley heard her. He set up her connection with Capitol Records, and his agent, John Levy, became her manager. Wilson's first album, one of dozens she would record for Capitol and other labels, was *Like in Love*.

Though her early work with Adderley and George Shearing was considered jazz, Wilson turned pop and remained so for a good portion of her career. She returned to jazz in the early '80s with Hank Jones's Great Jazz Trio and the Griffith Park Band, a batch of all-stars including Joe Henderson and Chick Corea. During her career, she has sung tunes by all the great composers, from Johnny Mercer and Billy Strayhorn to Marvin Gaye, Rodgers and Hart,

and Jule Styne. Virtually none of Wilson's earliest work is in print, but enough of it is available on compilations and reissues that any Wilson fan can get more than a small taste of her style.

what to buy: The songs of Johnny Mercer make for beautiful music, just like the old radio format. But *With My Lover Beside Me* 𝄞𝄞𝄞𝄞 (Columbia, 1991, prod. Barry Manilow, Eddie Arkin) was special in that the music was set posthumously to lyrics discovered by Mercer's widow, who rang up Barry Manilow and asked him if he'd like to compose around them. He did a terrific job, and chose Wilson to debut what he called "the best of the lot." Unlike Manilow's own schlock, there's nothing syrupy about these tunes—or maybe that's just Wilson's masterful handling of them. "Heart of Mine, Cry On" drips emotion without schmaltz. That doesn't come until the last cut, when Manilow and Wilson do an apparently unavoidable vocal duet. There's lots of big-band production work on *The Best of Nancy Wilson: The Jazz and Blues Sessions* 𝄞𝄞𝄞𝄞 (Capitol, 1996, compilation prod. Will Friedwald), but Wilson also beautifully handles the spare arrangements, such as "In a Sentimental Mood"—which is much more affecting than her Broadway covers.

what to buy next: Wilson delivers much bluesier jazz on *Love, Nancy* 𝄞𝄞𝄞 (Columbia, 1994, prod. Andre Fischer). "Day Dream" is an excellent treatment of the Ellington/Strayhorn/La-Touche composition. This is slow, contemplative, cry-in-your-martini lounge music. *A Lady with a Song* 𝄞𝄞𝄞 (Epic/Sony, 1989, prod. Kiyoshi Itoh) is a very poppy outing, sounding like an attempt to be commercial—though Wilson's voice is as fine and nuanced as ever.

what to avoid: *The Swingin's Mutual!* 𝄞𝄞 (Capitol, 1961/1992, prod. Michael Cuscuna, Pete Welding), rereleased with five previously unreleased tracks, was recorded as the George Shearing Quintet with Nancy Wilson. The disc, featuring Shearing's piano work and Wilson's vocals, is schmaltzy, with Wilson's voice going shrill at times; the instrumental tunes (that is, without Wilson) are better. *Forbidden Lover* 𝄞𝄞 (Columbia, 1987, prod. Kiyoshi Itoh) features Leon Russell's "A Song for You" and is funkier, but inconsistent. On *Ramsey & Nancy—The Two of Us* 𝄞𝄞𝄞 (Columbia, 1984, prod. Stanley Clarke), Nancy goes techno with the help of Stanley Clarke (on the opening cut, "Ram," by Ramsey Lewis and Stanley Clarke); eventually, the disc slips into straight-ahead jazz, without much to offer in the way of lounge-ness.

Nancy Wilson (© Jack Vartoogian)

best of the rest:

Lush Life 𝄞𝄞𝄞 (Blue Note, 1967)
But Beautiful 𝄞𝄞𝄞𝄟 (Capitol, 1969)
Keep You Satisfied 𝄞𝄞𝄞 (Columbia, 1985)
Spotlight On 𝄞𝄞𝄞𝄞 (Capitol, 1995)
Ballads, Blues & Big Bands: The Best of Nancy Wilson 𝄞𝄞𝄞𝄞 (Capitol, 1996)
If I Had My Way 𝄞𝄞𝄞 (Sony, 1997)

influences:

◀◀ Billie Holiday, Sarah Vaughan, Jimmy Scott, Dinah Washington

▶▶ Diana Ross, Anita Baker, Oleta Adams, Dionne Warwick

Lynne Margolis

George Winston

Born 1949, in MI.

Establishing his own "rural folk piano" style and clad in a rumpled flannel shirt and stocking feet, George Winston could well be termed the "Henry David Thoreau of New Age music." His solo works find Mother Nature right there inside his instrument, with moonlight, seasonal winds, mountain brooks, and snow falling out from under a Steinway piano lid. With crystal clarity, Winston tinkers around rich chord themes much like Keith Jarrett does in his free-form jazz solo piano concerts, but Winston is more precise in his meaning and his music is easier on the nerves. Inspired by the "stride" piano work of Fats Waller and the booze-soaked boogies of Professor Longhair and James Booker, Winston treats the keys with a more reserved energy than these two New Orleans legends. While it may be difficult to hear their influence in Winston's delicate, seasonal recordings—which recall theme music to Charles Kuralt's peaceful nature images on Sunday-morning television— they show when he gives one of his rare concert appearances. There, he usually pays homage to one of his heroes, Vince Guaraldi, the jazzman behind the piano music to the "Peanuts" TV specials. Winston inspired a slew of other New Age musicians for the Windham Hill label, but they have sounded like poor imitations, lacking the mysterious sparkle that holds Winston's records together. Recently, Winston has recorded a similar style of calm music on the Hawaiian "slack-key" guitar.

what to buy: *December* 𝄞𝄞𝄞𝄞 (Windham Hill, 1982, prod. William Ackerman, George Winston) and *Autumn* 𝄞𝄞𝄞𝄞 (Windham Hill, 1980, prod. William Ackerman) are Winston's best, with pieces like "Thanksgiving" and "Moon" that capture the feeling of crisp breaths of icy air while walking on leaf-covered dirt roads. *Sedako and the Thousand Paper Cranes* 🎵🎵🎵🎵 (Dancing Cat/Windham Hill, 1995) is Winston's refreshing foray into the slack key guitar. On the first part of the disc, he plays behind Liv Ullmann's narration of the children's story; on part two, he plays alone—a quiet, calming soundtrack.

what to buy next: *Linus & Lucy: The Music of Vince Guaraldi* 🎵🎵🎵🎵 (Windham Hill, 1996, prod. George Winston) gives Winston the elbow room to romp around on the keys in honor of his hero. He doesn't quite let loose like Dr. John or Professor Longhair would, but on the gritty "Treat Street," you can almost hear James Booker whooping. If you must have it all, look for the seven-CD box set *Complete Solo Recordings 1972–1996* 🎵🎵🎵🎵 (Windham Hill, 1996).

what to avoid: On *The Velveteen Rabbit* 🎵🎵 (Dancing Cat/Windham Hill, 1982), Winston accompanies Meryl Streep's narration of this children's story; it's a good listen, but not the best listening music.

the rest:
Winter into Spring 🎵🎵🎵 (Windham Hill, 1982)
Summer 🎵🎵🎵 (Windham Hill, 1991)
Forest 🎵🎵🎵 (Windham Hill, 1994)
All the Seasons Of 🎵🎵🎵🎵 (Windham Hill, 1998)

worth searching for: *Ballads and Blues* 🎵🎵🎵 (Dancing Cat/Windham Hill, 1972, prod. John Fahey, Doug Decker, George Winston) is Winston's hard-to-find first recording, with numbers like "Highway Hymn Blues" and "Miles City Train" foreshadowing the energy and styles apparent in Winston's later work.

influences:
◄◄ Vince Guaraldi, Professor Longhair, Fats Waller, James Booker, Teddy Wilson, Mannheim Steamroller, Steve Reich, Keith Jarrett, Abdullah Ibrahim

►► Andreas Vollenweider, Peter Kater, Philip Aaberg, Martha Stewart

Jack Jackson

Hugo Winterhalter

Born August 15, 1909, in Wilkes-Barre, PA. Died September 17, 1973, in Greenwich, CT.

With love as his bottom line, this well-respected arranger—he conducted symphony orchestras, then worked with Tommy Dorsey, the Ames Brothers, Kay Starr, and Perry Como before going solo in 1950—became one of the world's top easy-listening stars in the '50s. Many of his lush instrumental singles, filled with strings and French horn, plus catchy melodies and upbeat rhythms, were Top 40 hits, including 1956's piano-driven "Canadian Sunset," which went to #2.

After studying at the New England Conservatory of Music, Winterhalter worked briefly as a schoolteacher, then wrote for prominent big-band stars, such as Raymond Scott and Count Basie. Later, as music director for Columbia and other big record labels, he handled the arrangements for star singers Como, Eddy Arnold, and Eddie Fisher. As a solo artist, Winterhalter took the kitchen-sink approach, channeling dozens of seemingly incongrous instruments, from trumpets to tambourines, into the same unobtrusive song. This formula, on pure-love albums filled with titles like "I Only Have Eyes for You" and "I See Your Face Before Me," made him a pioneer, along with Mantovani and Percy Faith, of the massively popular easy-listening style. After his fame subsided, he worked for television networks and Broadway shows, and recorded a solo album every now and then.

what's available: Though almost every hippie's parents had a huge cachet of Winterhalter vinyl albums in the '50s and '60s, no CD manufacturer has bothered to revisit his extensive catalog. Just one in-print collection, *16 Beautiful Hits* 🎵🎵 (Deluxe, 1994, prod. various), gathers his material, mostly ignoring his lucrative 1950–56 hitmaking period and focusing on late '60s dredge such as "MacArthur Park" and "Feelings."

worth searching for: The German import *Two Sides of Hugo Winterhalter* 🎵🎵🎵 (RCA, 1996) is slightly more fun, with "A Chap from Chappaqua," "Gigi," "Laura," and other songs perfect for 1950s hand-holding but slightly outdated today. Best you should dig in the used-record bins to add yet another cornball cover picture to your vinyl collection.

influences:
◄◄ Mantovani, Benny Goodman, Percy Faith, Morton Gould, Paul Weston

►► Ray Conniff, Living Strings, 101 Strings, Kay Starr, Eddy Arnold

Steve Knopper

Jimmy Witherspoon

Born August 8, 1923, in Gurdon, AR. Died September 18, 1997, in Los Angeles, CA.

Instead of following the exodus of southern bluesmen to Chicago, Jimmy "Spoon" Witherspoon turned in the opposite direction, both geographically and musically: Los Angeles. So instead of discovering the raw, dirty, electric blues that later influenced so many British rock 'n' rollers, Witherspoon downshifted into a slick, jazzy cocktail style that recalled Duke Ellington and T-Bone Walker as much as it did Muddy Waters and Charley Patton.

Witherspoon started out singing in his church but didn't get his first real professional opportunity until Walker asked Witherspoon, who had been washing dishes at a drugstore, to sing with him during a Little Harlem nightclub show in Watts. After that, Spoon became a cook in the Merchant Marine and earned opportunities to sing on Armed Forces Radio; in 1945, after his discharge, he hooked up with band leader Jay McShann, and the two recorded the classic "Confessin' the Blues" and spent four years together.

When 'Spoon left the band he was primed for a solo career, which began lucratively with the hits "Ain't Nobody's Business, Parts 1 & 2," and later "No Rollin' Blues" and "Wind Is Blowing." After several more hits, rock 'n' roll destroyed his R&B career, but the irrepressible Witherspoon re-emerged as a jazz singer, playing festivals, touring the world, appearing on the Steve Allen and Johnny Carson shows, recording for many influential labels, and even notching the minor 1975 hit "Love Is a Five Letter Word." Though throat cancer threatened to end his career in the early 1980s, Witherspoon overcame it with radiation treatments and returned to singing. Where his friend Muddy Waters transformed Delta juke-joint blues into rocking electric Chicago blues, Witherspoon's slicker direction continues to remind people where jazz came from. His 1993 version of "Kansas City" opens with pure jazz, then detours into Waters's trademark "Got My Mojo Workin'." Very few musicians have combined blues and jazz with as much musical success.

what to buy: Witherspoon has had an amazingly consistent, prolific career, so it's tough to pick a starting point: *Blowin' in from Kansas City* 𝄞𝄞𝄞𝄞 (Flair/Virgin, 1991, prod. various) not only is an essential historic document of the singer's jazzy jump blues, but it swings wonderfully, with a horn section and the presence of arrangers Jay McShann and Tiny Webb; *'Spoon and Groove* 𝄞𝄞𝄞𝄞 (Tradition/Rykodisc, 1996, prod. various) tours his 1960s material with organist Richard Arnold "Groove" Holmes; *Call My Baby* 𝄞𝄞𝄞𝄞 (Night Train, 1991, prod. Dan Nooger) reissues his 1940s classics for Supreme and Swing Time, including both versions of "Ain't Nobody's Business" and "Hey Mr. Landlord."

what to buy next: *Evenin' Blues* 𝄞𝄞𝄞𝄞 (Original Blues Classics, 1964/Fantasy, 1993) operates in that gray zone between rock 'n' roll (a version of "Good Rockin' Tonight"), jazz ("Kansas City"),

and pure blues ("How Long Blues"). The compilation *Ain't Nobody's Business* 𝄞𝄞𝄞 (Polydor, 1967/Drive, 1994) is somewhat mysterious because the liner notes don't refer specifically to the performances on this disc; they're from 1948, 1949, and 1950, and these versions of "Ain't Nobody's Business" and "New Orleans Woman" are among the best Witherspoon recorded.

what to avoid: Even 'Spoon made missteps, including *Midnight Lady Called the Blues* 𝄞𝄞 (Muse, 1986, prod. Doc Pomus, Mac Rebbenack), in which Witherspoon sings bland, uninspired versions of songs written by Pomus and Dr. John. (Note ridiculous cover photo of babe in blue sequins.)

the rest:
Jay's Blues 𝄞𝄞𝄞 (Charly)
Mean Old Frisco 𝄞𝄞𝄞 (Prestige)
Jimmy Witherspoon and Jay McShann 𝄞𝄞𝄞 (DA, 1949)
Goin' to Kansas City Blues 𝄞𝄞𝄞 (RCA, 1958)
The 'Spoon Concerts 𝄞𝄞𝄞 (Fantasy, 1959)
Roots 𝄞𝄞 (Reprise, 1962)
Baby Baby Baby 𝄞𝄞 (Original Blues Classics, 1963/Fantasy, 1993)
Blues around the Clock 𝄞𝄞𝄞 (Original Blues Classics, 1963/Fantasy, 1995)
Some of My Best Friends Are the Blues 𝄞𝄞𝄞 (Original Blues Classics, 1964/Fantasy, 1994)
Hey Mr. Landlord 𝄞𝄞𝄞 (Route 66, 1965)
Blues for Easy Livers 𝄞𝄞𝄞 (Original Blues Classics, 1966/Fantasy, 1996)
The Spoon Concerts 𝄞𝄞𝄞 (Fantasy, 1972)
Spoonful 𝄞𝄞𝄞 (Avenue Jazz, 1975/Rhino, 1994)
Live 𝄞𝄞𝄞 (Avenue Jazz/Rhino, 1976)
Rockin' L.A. 𝄞𝄞 (Fantasy, 1988)
Spoon Go East 𝄞𝄞𝄞 (Chess/MCA, 1990)
Spoon So Easy: The Chess Years 𝄞𝄞𝄞 (Chess/MCA, 1990)
Call Me Baby 𝄞𝄞𝄞 (Night Train, 1991)
Ain't Nothin' New about the Blues 𝄞𝄞 (Aim, 1994)
Spoon's Life 𝄞𝄞𝄞 (Evidence, 1994)
Spoon's Blues 𝄞𝄞𝄞 (Stony Plain, 1995)
(With Robben Ford) *Live at the Mint* 𝄞𝄞𝄞 (On the Spot/Private, 1996)

worth searching for: *Jimmy Witherspoon Sings the Blues* 𝄞𝄞𝄞 (Aim, 1993, prod. Peter Noble) comes from 1980 studio sessions with a Melbourne, Australia, band. Witherspoon is in powerful, happy voice in relaxed versions of "C.C. Rider," "Kansas City," and his hero Joe Turner's song, "Roll 'Em Pete."

influences:

◄◄ Louis Jordan, T-Bone Walker, Jay McShann, Muddy Waters, Big Joe Turner, Charles Brown

►► Robben Ford, the Animals, B.B. King, Roy Eldridge, Phil Alvin

Steve Knopper

Erica Wright

See: Erykah Badu

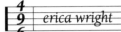

Frankie Yankovic

Born July 28, 1915, in Davies, WV.

Long before polka was a joke, the Bohemian party music (a hop-step-close-step dance, usually accompanied by double-time accordion-driven folk music) was a legitimate genre, and no one polkaed with as much verve as Yankovic. No relation to pop parodist "Weird Al" Yankovic, Frankie was one of the nation's premier bandleaders in the late '40s and early '50s, and the country's most important polka popularizer. His band's kinetic take on the Czechoslovakian folk song "Blue Skirt Waltz" hit the charts in the late '40s, and Yankovic has been with us ever since. A generous showman, he has continued to perform well into the '90s.

what to buy: When you think of Christmas, you probably think of Santa Claus, trees, and mangers. You probably don't think of polka. Well, all that will change the minute you buy the delightful *Christmas Memories* 𝄞𝄞𝄞 (PolyGram, 1984), Yankovic's strongest album of recent years and one of his best ever. Along with the traditional "Silent Night," there are nine Yule-themed polkas.

what to buy next: *Songs of the Polka King, Vol. 1* 𝄞𝄞𝄞𝄞 (Cleveland International, 1996) is more like a variety show than a simple polka record—surprise guests include comedian Drew Carey and polka star wannabe "Weird Al" Yankovic. This carnival approach sometimes eclipses the music, but this record is a fine starting point for polka standards, including "Blue Skirt Waltz," "Beer Barrel Polka," and "Who Stole the Kiska?"

what to avoid: *48 Polka and Waltz Medley* 𝄞𝄞𝄞 (Ross, 1995) isn't an embarassment, but there's nothing here that you couldn't find elsewhere.

the rest:
Frankie Yankovic Plays in Person the All-Time Great Polkas 𝄞𝄞𝄞 (CBS, 1990)
Dance Little Bird 𝄞𝄞𝄞 (Ross, 1997)

worth searching for: Yankovic's version of "Pennsylvania Polka" spices up the soundtrack to the movie *Groundhog Day* 𝄞𝄞𝄞 (Epic Soundtrax, 1993, prod. George Fenton), which also includes a George Fenton score and the late Sonny Bono's towering achievement, "I Got You, Babe."

influences:
▶▶ Stan Wolowic, the Polka Kings, the Andrews Sisters, Bobby Vinton, "Weird Al" Yankovic

Ben Greenman

Asa Yoelson

See: Al Jolson

Pia Zadora

Born May 4, 1956, in New York, NY.

Because there is no distinction between fame and notoriety in America anymore, Zadora is a star. A child actress who appeared in the patently awful 1964 film *Santa Claus Conquers the Martians,* Zadora grew into a woman-child with no discernable talent but just the right connections. Her husband, millionaire Meshulam Riklis, bought her way into starring roles beginning with the tawdry 1982 incest tale *Butterfly.* For that film, Zadora won a Golden Globe Award as Best New Star of the Year, a distinction that besmirched the Awards more than it ever helped her. She followed it up with *The Lonely Lady,* a soft-porn bomb widely regarded as one of the worst films ever. Having failed spectacularly on film, Zadora also began a singing career, producing one minor hit, "The Clapping Song," in 1983 and a duet with Jermaine Jackson, "When the Rain Begins to Fall," which flopped in 1984. Several years later, though, she transformed herself into a big-band thrush, and actually seemed to have a knack for it. Her albums have all gone out of print, but she toured with Sinatra and played Vegas (her husband owned the hotel). Her silver screen career remains dubious, however, and with the exception of John Waters's *Hairspray,* nearly all of her film appearances are as herself, a woman famous for being famous. When she has fun with that fact, as in *Naked Gun 33 1/3,* she can be surprisingly appealing.

Pia Zadora **(AP/Wide World Photos)**

what's available: With all of Pia's platters out of print, the only product that's currently available on her is *Pia Zadora's American Songbook* ♫♫♫ (20th Century-Fox Home Entertainment, 1987) a brief but breezy video featuring lavish sets and digital sound. A surprisingly classy affair, the song selection leans heavily on American standards such as "Maybe This Time," "It Had to Be You," "The Man That Got Away," "All of Me," and "I Am What I Am."

worth searching for: A copy of "The Clapping Song" single (Elektra, 1983) would make a campy addition to nearly any party. For those wishing to explore Zadora's torch-song period, check out *Pia and Phil* ♫♫♫ (Epic Associated, 1985), the "Phil" of the title being the London Philharmonic. Other efforts include *I Am What I Am* ♫♫ (Epic Associated, 1986), and more pop-oriented *Pia Z.* ♫♫ (Epic Associated, 1989).

influences:

◀◀ Madonna, Rosemary Clooney

Daniel Durchholz

Zamfir

Born 1941, in Romania.

Panpipe and flute master Zamfir, star of constant late-night television commercials hawking his pre–New Age albums, has a first name—it's Gheorghe. He has a nationality—he's Romanian. He even has a long history as a recording artist, first charting in Britain with the 1976 hit "Doina De Jale," the melody of which was lifted from a traditional Eastern funeral piece. Most important, Zamfir has a following as one of the world's premier easy-listening recording artists, integrating folk melodies and classical compositions into his soothing soundscapes. He has also recorded a significant amount of film music, most notably the compositions of soundtrack innovator Ennio Morricone (*The Good, the Bad, and the Ugly*).

what to buy: On *Lonely Shepherd* ♫♫♫♫ (Mercury, 1984, prod. Jean-Pierre Hebrard, Will Hoebee, James Last), Zamfir turns his flute magic on a collection of pop standards new and old, including the Bee Gees' "Run to Me," Charles Chaplin's "Theme from Limelight," and Andrew Lloyd Webber's "Don't Cry for Me, Argentina."

what to buy next: Zamfir is still plying his panpipe trade on *Gypsy Passion* ♫♫♫ (Special Music, 1995), which is something of a departure from his romantic standards into a more focused folk-music setting.

what to avoid: *Romance of the Pan Flute* ♫♫♫ (Philips, 1982) isn't abysmal, but you can get better quality Zamfir elsewhere. And who really needs to hear pan-flute covers of the Beatles' "Yesterday," Elton John's "Your Song," or Billy Joel's "Just the Way You Are"?

the rest:

Fantasy: Romantic Favorites for Pan Flute ♫♫♫ (Laserlight, 1985)

worth searching for: *The Ennio Morricone Anthology: A Fistful of Film Music* ♫♫♫♫ (Rhino/BMG, 1995, prod. David McLees) features Zamfir's magic flute in the context of the film composer's work, along with other Morricone themes and songs performed by artists such as Joan Baez, Baldo Maestri, and Alessandro Allessandroni.

influences:

◀◀ Gandalf, Paul Winter

▶▶ Vangelis, Yanni, John Tesh

Ben Greenman

musicHound *Lounge*

Resources and Other Information

Compilation Albums

Books and Magazines

Web Sites

Record Labels

Radio Stations

Movies

If you're looking for some lounge or easy-listening music by a variety of performers, these compilation albums would be a good place to start.

Ballroom Dancing and Weddings

Bride's Guide to Wedding Music ♫♫ (Angel, 1993)

The Fabulous Ballroom Collection ♫♫ (RCA Victor, 1998)

Let's Dance! Best of Ballroom: Fox Trots & Waltzes ♫♫♫ (Rhino, 1997)

Let's Dance! Best of Ballroom: Swing, Lindy, Jitterbug & Jive ♫♫♫ (Rhino, 1997)

Christmas

Christmas Cocktails, Pt. 1 ♫♫♫♫ (Capitol, 1996)

Christmas Cocktails, Pt. 2 ♫♫♫♫ (Capitol, 1997)

Pop Vocal Christmas Classics ♫♫♫ (Rhino, 1995)

Crooners

A Cappella Party: Best of the Ivy League Singing Groups ♫♫♫ (Rhino, 1996)

Art Deco: The Crooners ♫♫♫♫ (Columbia/Legacy, 1993)

Capitol Sings Around the World ♫♫♫ (Capitol, 1994)

Capitol Sings Coast to Coast ♫♫♫ (Capitol, 1994)

Capitol Sings Kids' Songs ♫♫♫ (Capitol, 1992)

Cigar Classics, Vol. 1: The Standards ♫♫♫ (Hip-O/MCA, 1997)

The Crooners ♫♫♫ (BMG)

Eh, Paisano! Italian-American Classics ♫♫♫ (Rhino, 1997)

Great Ladies of Song, Vol. 2 ♫♫♫ (Capitol, 1992)

Jackpot! The Las Vegas Story ♫♫♫♫♫ (Rhino, 1996)

Jazz Vocalists: Greatest Hits ♫♫♫ (RCA Victor, 1997)

Lounge Legends ♫♫♫ (K-Tel, 1996)

Sirens of Song: Classic Torch Singers ♫♫♫ (Rhino, 1997)

Songs That Got Us Through World War II, Vols. 1 and 2 ♫♫♫ (Rhino, 1994)

Sweet and Lovely: Capitol's Great Ladies of Song ♫♫♫ (Capitol, 1992/1996)

Vocal Classics ♫♫♫ (Atlantic, 1998)

Easy Listening/ Beautiful Music

Bachelor in Paradise ♫♫♫ (Laserlight, 1996)

Cocktail Mix, Vol. 1: Bachelor's Guide to the Galaxy ♫♫♫ (Rhino, 1996)

Instrumental Moods ♫♫ (Virgin, 1998)

Instrumental Themes for Young Lovers ♫♫♫ (Columbia/Legacy, 1997)

Music for a Bachelor's Den, Vol. 4: Easy Rhythms for Your Cocktail Hour ♫♫♫ (DCC, 1995)

The Sound Gallery, Vol. 1 ♫♫♫ (Scamp/Caroline, 1996)

The Sound Gallery, Vol. 2 ♫♫♫ (Scamp/Caroline, 1996)

Titanic: Music As Heard on the Fateful Voyage ♫♫♫ (Rhino, 1997)

Ultra-Lounge: On the Rocks, Pt. 1 ♫♫♫ (Capitol, 1997)

Ultra-Lounge: On the Rocks, Pt. 2 ♫♫♫ (Capitol, 1997)

Electronic

Synth Me Up: 14 Classic Electronic Hits ♫♫ (Hip-O/MCA, 1997)

Latin

Instrumental Favorites: Latin Rhythms ♫♫♫♫ (Rhino)

Lounge Music Goes Latin ♫♫♫ (Chronicles/PolyGram, 1996)

Mambo Mania: The Kings & Queens of Mambo ♫♫♫ (Rhino, 1995)

Music for a Bachelor's Den, Vol. 3: Latin Rhythms in Hi-Fi ♫♫♫♫ (DCC, 1995)

Nova Bossa: Red Hot on Verve ♫♫♫♫ (Verve, 1996)

Red Hot + Rio ♫♫♫♫ (Antilles/Verve, 1996)

A Twist of Jobim ♫♫♫ (i.e. Music/Verve, 1997)

Ultra-Lounge, Vol. 2: Mambo Fever ♫♫♫ (Capitol, 1996)

Ultra-Lounge, Vol. 14: Bossa Novaville ♫♫♫ (Capitol, 1997)

Lounge Revival

Livin' Lounge: The Fabulous Sounds of Now! (Continuum, 1995)
Lounge-A-Palooza (Hollywood, 1997)
20 Loungecore Favorites (Sequel)

Movie Music

Bachelor in Paradise: Cocktail Classics from MGM Films (Rhino, 1996)
Cocktail Mix, Vol. 4: Soundtracks with a Twist! (Rhino, 1996)

Pop Hits

Billboard Pop Memories: The 1920s (Rhino, 1994)
Billboard Pop Memories: The 1930s (Rhino, 1994)
Billboard Pop Memories: 1940–44 (Rhino, 1994)
Billboard Pop Memories: 1945–49 (Rhino, 1994)
Billboard Pop Memories: 1950–54 (Rhino, 1994)
Billboard Pop Memories: 1955–59 (Rhino, 1994)
Hits of '31 (Living Era, 1997)
Hits of '32 (Living Era, 1997)
Hits of '33 (Living Era, 1996)
Hits of '34 (Living Era, 1996)
Hits of '35 (Living Era, 1996)
Hits of '36 (Living Era, 1996)
Hits of '38 (Living Era, 1993)
Hits of '39 (Living Era, 1993)
Hits of '40 (Living Era, 1992)
Hits of '41 (Living Era, 1993)
Hits of '42 (Living Era, 1993)
Hits of '44 (Living Era, 1995)
Hits of '45 (Living Era, 1996)
Hits of '46 (Living Era, 1997)
Hits of '47 (Living Era, 1998)
Sentimental Journey: Pop Vocal Classics, Vol. 1 (1942–1946) (Rhino, 1993)
Sentimental Journey: Pop Vocal Classics, Vol. 2 (1947–1950) (Rhino, 1993)
Sentimental Journey: Pop Vocal Classics, Vol. 3 (1950–1954) (Rhino, 1993)
Sentimental Journey: Pop Vocal Classics, Vol. 4 (1954–1959) (Rhino, 1993)
16 Most Requested Songs: The 1950s, Vol. 1 (Columbia, 1989)

Show Tunes

Capitol Sings Broadway: Makin' Whoopee! (Capitol, 1995)
Charming Gents of Stage & Screen (Columbia/Legacy, 1994)
Leading Men, Vol. 1 (Hammer & Lace, 1996)
Leading Men, Vol. 2 (Hammer & Lace, 1996)
Lovely Ladies of Stage and Screen (Columbia/Legacy, 1994)
Take It Off! Striptease Classics (Rhino, 1997)

Soundtracks

Austin Powers: International Man of Mystery (Hollywood, 1997)
Big Night (TVT, 1996)
The Bridges of Madison County (Warner Bros., 1995)
Carousel (Angel, 1956/1993)
The Glenn Miller Story (MCA, 1992)
The Godfather (MCA, 1991)
The Good, the Bad, and the Ugly (United Artists, 1967)
The Mambo Kings (Elektra, 1992)
Oklahoma! (Angel, 1955/1993)
Swingers (Hollywood, 1996)
Trees Lounge (MCA, 1996)
Vampyros Lesbos (Bar/None, 1996)
The Winner (Rykodisc, 1997)
The Wizard of Oz (Rhino, 1995)

Space-Age Bachelor Pad/Exotica

Another Crazy Cocktail Party (RCA, 1997)
Bachelor Pad Pleasures (Chronicles/PolyGram, 1996)
Cigar Classics, Vol. 3: Cool Smokes (Hip-O/MCA, 1997)
Cigar Classics, Vol. 4: Smokin' Lounge (Hip-O/MCA, 1997)
Cocktail Mix, Vol. 2: Martini Madness (Rhino, 1996)
Cocktail Mix, Vol. 3: Swingin' Singles (Rhino, 1996)
Hi-Fi Daze/Cocktail Nights (includes *In a Cocktail Mood* and *Music for the Jet Set*) (Tradition/Rykodisc, 1997)
The History of Space Age Pop, Vol. 1: Melodies and Mischief (RCA, 1995)
The History of Space Age Pop, Vol. 2: Mallets in Wonderland (RCA, 1995)
The History of Space Age Pop, Vol. 3: The Stereo Action Dimension (RCA, 1995)
In a Cocktail Mood (Tradition/Rykodisc, 1997)
Instrumental Favorites: Exotic Moods (Rhino)
Martinis and a Broken Heart to Go (Columbia/Legacy, 1997)
Music for a Bachelor's Den, Vol. 1: Music for a Bachelor's Den in Hi-Fi (DCC, 1995)
Music for a Bachelor's Den, Vol. 2: Exotica (DCC, 1995)
Music for a Bachelor's Den, Vol. 7: Sex Kittens in Hi-Fi—The Blondes (DCC, 1995)
Music for a Bachelor's Den, Vol. 8: Sex Kittens in Hi-Fi—The Brunettes (DCC, 1995)
Music for the Jet Set (Tradition/Rykodisc, 1997)
Musical Meals: Cocktail Hour (Sony, 1994)
RE/Search: Incredibly Strange Music, Vol. 1 (Caroline, 1993)
RE/Search: Incredibly Strange Music, Vol. 2 (Asphodel)
The Sound Spectrum (Sequel)
Stirring with Soul (Rykodisc, 1997)
Ultra-Lounge, Vol. 1: Mondo Exotica (Capitol, 1996)
Ultra-Lounge, Vol. 3: Space Capades (Capitol, 1996)
Ultra-Lounge, Vol. 4: Bachelor Pad Royale (Capitol, 1996)
Ultra-Lounge, Vol. 5: Wild, Cool & Swingin' (Capitol, 1996)
Ultra-Lounge, Vol. 6: Rhapsodesia (Capitol, 1996)
Ultra-Lounge, Vol. 8: Cocktail Capers (Capitol, 1996)
Ultra-Lounge, Vol. 9: Cha-Cha de Amor (Capitol, 1996)
Ultra-Lounge, Vol. 10: A Bachelor in Paris (Capitol, 1996)
Ultra-Lounge, Vol. 11: Organs in Orbit (Capitol, 1996)
Ultra-Lounge, Vol. 12: Saxophobia (Capitol, 1996)
Ultra-Lounge, Vol. 16: Mondo Hollywood (Capitol, 1997)
Ultra-Lounge, Vol. 17: Bongoland (Capitol, 1997)
Ultra-Lounge, Vol. 18: Bottoms Up! (Capitol, 1997)

Spy/Crime

The Best of James Bond: 30th Anniversary Collection 🎵🎵🎵 (EMI, 1992)

Crime Jazz: Music in the First Degree 🎵🎵🎵🎵 (Rhino, 1998)

Crime Jazz: Music in the Second Degree 🎵🎵🎵 (Rhino, 1998)

Ultra-Lounge, Vol. 7: The Crime Scene 🎵🎵🎵 (Capitol, 1996)

Surf

Cocktail Companion 🎵🎵🎵 (Estrus, 1996)

Cowabunga! The Surf Box 🎵🎵🎵🎵 (Rhino, 1996)

Monster Summer Hits: Drag City 🎵🎵🎵 (Capitol, 1991)

Monster Summer Hits: Wild Surf 🎵🎵🎵 (Capitol, 1991)

Pebbles, Vol. 4: Surf'n Tunes! 🎵🎵🎵 (Archive International, 1992)

Swing and Big Band

An Anthology of Big Band Swing (1930–1955) 🎵🎵🎵 (GRP, 1993)

Best of the Big Bands: The 1940s 🎵🎵 (Ranwood, 1996)

Big Bands: Greatest Hits 🎵🎵🎵 (RCA Victor, 1996)

Big Bands of the Swinging Years 🎵🎵🎵 (Tradition, 1996)

The Essential Big Bands 🎵🎵🎵🎵 (Verve, 1992)

Great Singers, Great Bands 🎵🎵🎵 (RCA, 1992)

Jazz of the 1940s: Greatest Hits 🎵🎵🎵 (RCA Victor, 1997)

16 Most Requested Songs: Big Band Instrumentals 🎵🎵🎵 (Columbia/Legacy, 1992)

Swing! Greatest Hits 🎵🎵🎵 (RCA Victor, 1996)

Swing: The Best of the Big Bands 🎵🎵🎵 (MCA, 1988)

Swing Time! The Fabulous Big Band Era, 1925–1955 🎵🎵🎵🎵 (Columbia/Legacy, 1993)

Ultra-Lounge, Vol. 15: Wild, Cool & Swingin' Too 🎵🎵🎵 (Capitol, 1997)

Television

Batmania! Songs Inspired by the TV Series 🎵🎵🎵 (Varese Sarabande, 1997)

Music for TV Dinners 🎵🎵🎵 (Scamp/Caroline, 1997)

Music for TV Dinners: The '60s 🎵🎵🎵 (Scamp/Caroline, 1997)

Ultra-Lounge, Vol. 13: TV Town 🎵🎵🎵🎵 (Capitol, 1997)

Can't get enough lounge music? Here are some books, magazines, and newspapers you can check out for further information. Happy reading!

Books

BIOGRAPHIES

ABBA: The Name of the Game
Andrew Oldham (Music Book Services, 1996)

All or Nothing at All: A Life of Frank Sinatra
Donald Clarke (Fromm International, 1997)

All the Way: A Biography of Frank Sinatra
Michael Freedland (St. Martin's, 1998)

And the Beat Goes On
Sonny Bono (Pocket Books, 1992)

Andrew Lloyd Webber: His Life and Works—A Critical Biography
Michael Walsh (Harry N. Abrams, 1997)

Angels Along the Way: My Life with Help from Above
Della Reese, with Franklin Lett and Mim Eichler (Thorndike Press, 1998)

Barbra: An Actress Who Sings—An Unauthorized Biography
James Kimbrell (Branden Publishing, 1989)

Barbra: An Actress Who Sings—An Unauthorized Biography, Vol. 2
James Kimbrell and Cheri Kimbrell (Branden Publishing, 1992)

Barbra Streisand: The Untold Story
Nellie Bly (Pinnacle Books, 1994)

Bette: An Intimate Biography of Bette Midler
George Mair (Citadel Press, 1996)

Billie Holiday
Stuart Nicholson (Northeastern University Press, 1995)

Billie's Blues: The Billie Holiday Story, 1933–1959
John Chilton (Da Capo Press, 1989)

Bobby Short: The Life and Times of a Saloon Singer
Bobby Short, with Robert G. MacKintosh and Betty A. Prashker (Clarkston Potter, 1995)

Brian Eno: His Music and the Vertical Color of Sound
Eric Tamm (Faber & Faber, 1989)

Brother Ray: Ray Charles' Own Story
Ray Charles, with David Ritz (Da Capo Press, 1992)

Call Me Lucky
Bing Crosby, with Pete Martin (Da Capo Press, 1993)

Cleo
Cleo Laine (Simon & Schuster, 1997)

Confessions of a Sex Kitten
Eartha Kitt (Publishers' Group West, 1991)

Dino: Living High in the Dirty Business of Dreams
Nick Tosches (Dell Books, 1993)

Diva: Barbara Streisand and the Making of a Superstar
Ethlie Ann Vare, ed. (Boulevard, 1996)

Divided Soul: The Life of Marvin Gaye
David Ritz (Da Capo Press, 1991)

Ella Fitzgerald: A Biography of the First Lady of Jazz
Stuart Nicholson (Da Capo Press, 1995)

Elvis
Albert Goldman (McGraw-Hill, 1981)

Elvis
Dave Marsh (Times Books, 1982)

Elvis and Me
Priscilla Beaulieu Presley and Sandra Harmon (G.P. Putnam's Sons, 1985)

The Elvis Encyclopedia
David E. Stanley and Frank Coffey (General Publishing Group, 1994)

First Lady of Song: Ella Fitzgerald for the Record
Geoffrey Mark Fidelman (Citadel Press, 1996)

Frank Sinatra: A Celebration
Stan Britt (Macmillan, 1995)

Frank Sinatra: A Personal Portrait
John Frayn Turner (Hippocrene Books, 1983)

Frank Sinatra: An American Legend
Nancy Sinatra (General Publishing Group, 1995)

Frank Sinatra: My Father
Nancy Sinatra (Pocket Books, 1986)

The Frank Sinatra Reader
Steven Petkov and Leonard Mustazza, ed.
(Oxford University Press, 1997)

The Great One: The Life and Legend of Jackie Gleason
William A. Henry III (Doubleday, 1992)

Her Name Is Barbra: An Intimate Portrait of the Real Barbra Streisand
Randall Riese (Birch Lane Press, 1993)

High Times, Hard Times
Anita O'Day (Limelight Editions, 1989)

His Way: The Unauthorized Biography of Frank Sinatra
Kitty Kelley (Bantam Books, 1987)

I Put a Spell on You: The Autobiography of Nina Simone
Nina Simone, with Stephen Cleary (Da Capo Press, 1993)

Jackie Gleason: An Intimate Biography of the Great One
W.J. Weatherby (Pharos Books, 1992)

Jolson: The Story of Al Jolson
Michael Freedland (Virgin, 1995)

Julie Andrews: A Life on Stage and Screen
Robert Windeler (Birch Lane Press, 1997)

Julio: The Unsung Story
Daphne Lockyer (Birch Lane Press, 1997)

Last Train to Memphis: The Rise of Elvis Presley
Peter Guralnick (Little, Brown & Co., 1994)

Legend: Frank Sinatra and the American Dream
Ethlie Ann Vare, ed. (Boulevard, 1995)

Let the Good Times Roll: The Story of Louis Jordan and His Music
John Chilton (University of Michigan Press, 1997)

Madonna: Bawdy and Soul
Karlene Faith (University of Toronto Press, 1997)

Madonna: The Rolling Stone Files—The Ultimate Compendium of Interviews, Articles, Facts, and Opinions from the Files of Rolling Stone
Editors of *Rolling Stone* magazine, ed.
(Hyperion, 1997)

Mike Douglas: When the Going Gets Tough
Mel White (Word Books, 1983)

My Life with Barbra: A Love Story
Barry Dennen (Prometheus Books, 1997)

My Vagabond Lover: An Intimate Biography of Rudy Vallee
Eleanor Vallee, with Jill Amadio (Taylor Publishing, 1996)

Neil Diamond
Diana Karanikas Harvey and Jackson Harvey (Metro Books, 1996)

Nice Work If You Can Get It: My Life in Rhythm and Rhyme
Michael Feinstein, with David Cashion (Hyperion, 1996)

Ol' Blue Eyes: A Frank Sinatra Encyclopedia
Leonard Mustazza (Greenwood Publishing Group, 1998)

Piaf
Margaret Crosland (Fromm International, 1987)

Rage to Survive: The Etta James Story
Etta James, with David Ritz (Da Capo Press, 1998)

Rat Pack Confidential: Frank, Dean, Sammy, Peter, Joey, and the Last Great Showbiz Party
Shawn Levy (Doubleday, 1998)

Sinatra: Behind the Legend
J. Randy Taraborrelli (Birch Lane Press, 1997)

Sinatra 101: The 101 Best Recordings and the Stories Behind Them
Ed O'Brien and Robert Wilson (Boulevard, 1996)

The Sinatra Scrapbook
Gary L. Doctor (Citadel Press, 1991)

Sinatra: The Artist and the Man
John Lahr (Random House, 1998)

Sinatra! The Song Is You: A Singer's Art
Will Friedwald (Da Capo Press, 1997)

Snowbird: The Story of Anne Murray
Barry Grills (Quarry Press, 1996)

Streisand: A Biography
Anne Edwards (Little, Brown & Co., 1997)

Streisand: Her Life
James Spada (Ivy Books, 1996)

Swing, Swing, Swing: The Life and Times of Benny Goodman
Ross Firestone (W.W. Norton, 1993)

Take Me Home: An Autobiography
John Denver, with Arthur Tobier (Harmony Books, 1994)

Tony Bennett: The Best Is Yet to Come
Matthew Hoffman (Metro Books, 1997)

Under the Rainbow: The Real Liza Minnelli
George Mair (Birch Lane Press, 1996)

The Way You Wear Your Hat: Frank Sinatra and the Lost Art of Livin'
Bill Zehme (HarperCollins, 1997)

Wunnerful, Wunnerful! The Autobiography of Lawrence Welk
Lawrence Welk, with Bernice McGeehan (Prentice-Hall, 1971)

GENERAL INTEREST

All Music Guide: The Experts' Guide to the Best CDs, Albums & Tapes
Michael Erlewine, Vladimir Bogdanov, Chris Woodstra, and Stephen Thomas Erlewine, ed. (Miller Freeman, 1997)

The American Popular Ballad of the Golden Era, 1924–1950
Allen Forte (Princeton University Press, 1995)

American Popular Song: The Great Innovators, 1900–1950
Alec Wilder (Oxford University Press, 1990)

Discovering Great Singers of Classic Pop: A New Listener's Guide to the Sounds and Lives of the Top Performers and Their Recordings, Movies, and Videos
Roy Hemming and David Hajdu (Newmarket Press, 1992)

Elevator Music: A Surreal History of Muzak, Easy-Listening, and Other Moodsong
Joseph Lanza (Picador, 1994)

Enchanted Evenings: The Broadway Musical from Show Boat to Sondheim
Geoffrey Block (Oxford University Press, 1997)

The Encyclopedia of Pop, Rock, and Soul
Irwin Stambler (St. Martin's, 1989)

Encyclopedia of Rock Stars
Dafydd Rees and Luke Crampton (Dorling Kindersley, 1996)

Incredibly Strange Music, Volume 1
V. Vale and Andrea Juno, ed. (RE/Search Publications, 1993)

Incredibly Strange Music, Volume 2
V. Vale and Andrea Juno, ed. (Juno Books, 1994)

The Melody Lingers On: The Great Songwriters and Their Movie Musicals
Roy Hemming (Newmarket Press, 1988)

MusicHound Blues: The Essential Album Guide
Leland Rucker, ed. (Visible Ink Press, 1998)

MusicHound Country: The Essential Album Guide
Brian Mansfield and Gary Graff, ed. (Visible Ink Press, 1997)

MusicHound Folk: The Essential Album Guide
Neal Walters and Brian Mansfield, ed. (Visible Ink Press, 1998)

MusicHound Jazz: The Essential Album Guide
Steve Holtje and Nancy Ann Lee, ed. (Visible Ink Press, 1998)

MusicHound R&B: The Essential Album Guide
Gary Graff, Josh Freedom du Lac, and Jim McFarlin, ed. (Visible Ink Press, 1998)

The New Rolling Stone Encyclopedia of Rock & Roll
Patricia Romanowski and Holly George-Warren, ed. (Rolling Stone Press, 1995)

The Oxford Companion to Popular Music
Peter Gammond (Oxford University Press, 1991)

The Penguin Encyclopedia of Popular Music
Donald Clarke, ed. (Penguin Books, 1990)

The Poets of Tin Pan Alley: A History of America's Great Lyricists
Philip Furia (Oxford University Press, 1992)

Rolling Stone Album Guide
Anthony DeCurtis and James Henke, ed., with Holly George-Warren (Random House, 1992)

The Song Is Ended: Songwriters and American Music, 1900–1950
William G. Hyland (Oxford University Press, 1995)

Swing! The New Retro Renaissance
V. Vale, ed. (V/Search, 1998)

They're Playing Our Song: Conversations with America's Classic Songwriters
Max Wilk (Da Capo Press, 1997)

Ultra Lounge: The Lexicon of Easy Listening
Dylan Jones (Universe Publishing, 1997)

VideoHound's Soundtracks: Music from the Movies, Broadway, and Television
Didier C. Deutsch (Visible Ink Press, 1998)

Magazines

Billboard
1515 Broadway
New York, NY 10036
(212) 764-7300

Cannot Become Obsolete
PO Box 1232
Lorton, VA 22199
E-mail: itsvern@ibm.net

Cigar Aficionado
387 Park Ave. South
New York, NY 10016
(212) 481-1540

CMJ New Music Monthly
11 Middleneck Rd., Ste. 400
Great Neck, NY 11021
(516) 466-6000

Cool and Strange Music! Magazine
1101 Colby Ave.
Everett, WA 98201
Fax: (425) 303-3404
E-mail: coolstrge@aol.com

Details
632 Broadway
New York, NY 10012
(212) 598-3710

Down Beat
102 N. Haven Rd.
Elmhurst, IL 60126
(800) 535-7496

Esquire
250 W. 55th St.
New York, NY 10019
(212) 694-4020

Goldmine
700 E. State St.
Jola, WI 54990
(715) 445-4612

ICE
PO Box 3043
Santa Monica, CA 90408
(800) 647-4ICE

Jazziz
3620 NW 43rd St.
Gainesville, FL 32606
(352) 375-3705

JazzTimes
8737 Colesville Rd., 5th Fl.
Silver Spring, MD 20910
(301) 588-4114

Lounge
3010 Wilshire Blvd., Bungalow #92
Los Angeles, CA 90010
(310) 470-7674

Musician
1515 Broadway
New York, NY 10036
(212) 536-5208

The New Yorker
20 W. 43rd St.
New York, NY 10036
(212) 536-5400

Playboy
680 N. Lake Shore Dr.
Chicago, IL 60611
(312) 751-8000

Spin
6 W. 18th St., 8th Fl.
New York, NY 10011-4608
(212) 633-8200

Rolling Stone
1290 Avenue of the Americas, 2nd Fl.
New York, NY 10104
(212) 484-1616

Tiki News
2215-R #177 Market St.
San Francisco, CA 94114
E-mail: Ottotemp@aol.com

Lounge and easy listening are every-where, even out in cyberspace. Point your Web browser to these sites for more information on your favorite artists or the music in general.

Artists

ABBA
http://www.danbbs.dk/~janbach/musik.htm
http://www.dur.ac.uk/~d5owwy/abbafaq.html
http://home.cdsnet.net/~brians/abba.htm

Barry Adamson
http://www.mutelibtech.com/mute/adamson/adamson.htm

Mose Allison
http://www.bluenote.com/allison.html
http://www.mcs.net/~modika/mose.html

Herb Alpert
http://www.geffen.com/almo/herbalpert/
http://www.rudyscorner.com/

Leroy Anderson
http://www.leroy-anderson.com/index.html
http://home.earthlink.net/~spaceagepop/anderson.htm

Julie Andrews
http://www.geocities.com/College Park/Union/8176/julie.html

http://www.angelfire.com/wa/Julie Andrews/

The Andrews Sisters
http://holly.colostate.edu/~carleen/andrews/

Maya Angelou
http://www.cwrl.utexas.edu/~mmaynard/Maya/maya5.html
http://www.geocities.com/Athens/1523/maya.html
http://members.aol.com/bonvibre/mangelou.html

Paul Anka
http://www.canoe.ca/JamMusicPop EncycloPages/anka.html

Ann-Margret
http://www.ann-margret.com/index.html
http://home6.swipnet.se/~w-60241/Ann-Margret/index.html
http://members.iquest.net/~sabrina/

Louis Armstrong
http://www.foppejohnson.com/armstrong/

Desi Arnaz
http://desi.simplenet.com/Desi.htm
http://www.geocities.com/Hollywood/Lot/7100/home.html
http://members.aol.com/CHICKA2/desi.html

The Art of Noise
http://rtt.colorado.edu/~baur/aon/aon.html
http://darkwing.uoregon.edu/~wbwolf/AON.html

Patti Austin
http://www.mca.com/grp/grp/artists/austin.rel.html

Burt Bacharach/Hal David
http://studentweb.tulane.edu/~mark/bacharach.html
http://dekalb.dc.peachnet.edu/~jdelacru/burt.htm

Angelo Badalamenti
http://www.mindspring.com/~stewarts/bad.htm

Erykah Badu
http://www.kedar.com/kedar20a.htm
http://www.wsu.edu:8080/~dstrolis/badu1.html

Pearl Bailey
http://www.gateway-va.com/pages/bhistory/bailey.htm

The Baja Marimba Band
http://www.rudyscorner.com/

Chet Baker
http://home.ica.net/~blooms/bakerhome.html
http://hotel.prosa.dk/~jes/chet.htm
http://www.book.uci.edu/Jazz/CDLists/ChetBaker_CDL.html

Josephine Baker
http://www.classicalmus.com/artists/baker.html

Basia
http://www.epiccenter.com/EpicCenter/docs/artistupdate.qry?artistid=12

http://www.ddm-international.com/
savage/basia.htm

http://skew2.kellogg.nwu.edu/
~zzbiegie/BASIA/basia.html

Shirley Bassey
http://home.wxs.nl/~doorno3o/

Les Baxter
http://home.earthlink.net/~spaceage
pop/baxter.htm

The Beach Boys/Brian Wilson
http://www.mindspring.com/~sfrazier/
bbfc.htm
http://www.geocities.com/SunsetStrip/
Stage/1476/beachboys.html
http://www.cabinessence.com/brian/

The Beautiful South
http://www.beautiful-south.co.uk/
http://hsfstud.hisf.no/~964289/bs.
htm
http://www-public.tu-bs.de:8080/
~yooo3231/b_south/b_south.
html

Harry Belafonte
http://www.classicalmus.com/artists/
belafont.html

Tony Bennett
http://www.music.sony.com/Music/
ArtistInfo/TonyBennett/

Big Bad Voodoo Daddy
http://www.coolsvillerecords.com/
bbvd/index.htm

Björk
http://members.aol.com/glitterbog/
bjork/bjork.htm
http://userwww.sfsu.edu/~jfuzz/
http://nic2.hawaii.edu/~kiriu/bjork.
html

Björn Again
http://www.demon.co.uk/bjornagain/

Pat Boone
http://www.mcarecords.com/amp14/
reverb/boone.html
http://www.rossetta.com/patboone.
htm

Brave Combo
http://www.brave.com/bo/

Charles Brown
http://www.rosebudus.com/brown/
http://www.wco.com/%7Eckthom/
charlesbrown.html

Clifford Brown
http://www.brownradio.com/cbjf.htm

Dave Brubeck
http://www.schirmer.com/composers/
brubeck_bio.html

Harold Budd
http://www.matson.it/Artists/Budd/
BuddHome.html
http://www.sleepbot.com/ambience/
page/budd.html

Al Caiola
http://home.earthlink.net/~spaceage
pop/caiola.htm

Ann Hampton Callaway
http://www.annhamptoncallaway.com/

Glen Campbell
http://www.glencampbellshow.com/

Eddie Cantor
http://members.aol.com/ecantor/
index.html

The Captain & Tennille
http://www.vcnet.com/moonlight/

The Cardigans
http://www.gryphon.com/cardigans/
http://www.mhv.net/~kev/cardig/
index.html
http://www.geocities.com/College
Park/Quad/2567/

The Carpenters
http://www.ftech.net/~miller/cath_
html/carpnter/index.html
http://www.geocities.com/Sunset
Strip/Palladium/6328/
http://home.earthlink.net/~eeyore/

Nick Cave
http://www.RepriseRec.com/Reprise
_HTML_Pages/NickCaveFolder/
NickCave.html
gopher://wiretap.spies.com/oo/
Library/Music/Disc/nickcave.dis
http://www.zephyr.net/users/cave/

Ray Charles
http://www.raycharles.com/

Don Cherry
http://www.ecmrecords.com/ecm/
artists/380.html
http://www.nwu.edu/WNUR/jazz/
artists/cherry.don/
http://www.harmolodic.com/related/
doncherry.html

Cherry Poppin' Daddies
http://www.bitech.com/daddies/index.
html

Alex Chilton
http://www.ardentrecords.com/
AlexPage1.html

June Christy
http://www.ibmpcug.co.uk/~jws/jim/
misty.htm

Petula Clark
http://www.geocities.com/
~petulaclark/

Richard Clayderman
http://www.pe.net/~james/

Rosemary Clooney
http://www.clooney.com/

Holly Cole
http://www.hollycole.com/
http://www.altech.ab.ca/kdever/holly.
htm

Nat "King" Cole
http://www.tip.net.au/~bnoble/
natkcole/nat_cole.htm

Natalie Cole
http://www.elektra.com/randb_club/
cole/cole.html

Edwyn Collins
http://www.bar-none.com/bios/
Edwynbio.html

Judy Collins
http://digink.com/home/jcollins/

Combustible Edison
http://www.subpop.com/bands/
combustible/comed/index.html
http://www.mindspring.com/
~jpmckay/comed.html

Perry Como
http://www.geocities.com/Broadway/
9109/

Harry Connick Jr.
http://www.hconnickjr.com/
http://www.connick.com/connick.html
http://weber.u.washington.edu/
~no1husky/harry/connick.html

Ray Conniff
http://home.earthlink.net/~spaceage
pop/conniff.htm

Jack Costanzo
http://home.earthlink.net/~spaceage
pop/costanzo.htm

Elvis Costello
http://www.wbr.com/elvis/
http://east.isx.com/~schnitzi/ec/
information/ecinfo.html
http://www.angelfire.com/ok/
ecostello/index.html

Jim Croce
http://ccs.compubell.com/~awtom/
index.html
http://www.jim-croce.com/
http://www.geocities.com/Colosseum/
Field/2273/jimcroce.html

Bing Crosby
http://www.kcmetro.cc.mo.us/
pennvalley/biology/lewis/crosby/
bing.htm
http://www.geocities.com/Bourbon
Street/3754/bing.html
http://www.tir.com/~rtw/bing.htm

Bob Crosby
http://members.aol.com/famemgt/
fame/crosby.htm

Christopher Cross
http://www.christophercross.com/

Julee Cruise
http://www.mindspring.com/
~stewarts/julee.htm

Xavier Cugat
http://home.earthlink.net/~space
agepop/cugat.htm

Tim Curry
http://www.geocities.com/Hollywood/
Set/9100/
http://members.aol.com/gzach75206/
mainpage/index.html
http://www.geocities.com/Broadway/
Stage/2192/tim.html

Miles Davis
http://www.music.sony.com/Music/
ArtistInfo/MilesDavis/
http://users.cybercity.dk/~ccc6517/
http://www.nettally.com/dbird/
milesm.htm

Sammy Davis Jr.
http://www.geocities.com/College
Park/8182/samtro.htm
http://www.interlog.com/~wad/
sambio.html
http://www.skypoint.com/members/
happyjac/sampage.html

Doris Day
http://www.netlink.co.uk/users/
funkin/dorisday/dorisday.html

http://www.ozemail.com.au/
~bywaters/main.htm
http://laurie.dreamhost.com/doris.
html

Blossom Dearie
http://www.angelfire.com/ny/blossom
dearie/

Lenny Dee
http://home.earthlink.net/~space
agepop/dee.htm

Martin Denny
http://sparky.cis.smu.edu/brad/
music/mdenny/mdenny.html

John Denver
http://members.aol.com/mumze/
newhome.html
http://www.jdenver.net/gabry/
http://www.geocities.com/Sunset
Strip/Palms/2916/INDEX.HTML

Devo
http://www.mutato.com/lowband/
mmwww5.html
http://www.alaska.net/~lerxst/Devo/
defram.htm
http://www.astro.ucla.edu/~sammy/
dpa.htm

Neil Diamond
http://www.diamondville.com/
http://www.worldaccess.nl/
~hogensti/
http://www.music.sony.com/Music/
ArtistInfo/NeilDiamond/

Marlene Dietrich
http://www.marlene.com/
http://www.ivnet.co.at/streif/
http://www.pcs.sk.ca/sjk/dietrich/

Dimitri from Paris
http://www.geocities.com/Paris/
Rue/2894/

Divine Comedy
http://members.aol.com/tormentile/
divine.htm
http://venus.va.com.au/indulgence/
http://users.aol.com/catharton/
divinecomedy/intro.htm

Tommy Dorsey/The Dorsey Brothers
http://www.teleport.com/~rfrederi/
wtommy01.htm

Robert Drasnin
http://home.earthlink.net/~space
agepop/drasnin.htm

Sheena Easton
http://www.sheenaeaston.com/
http://www.sheenaweb.com/
http://www.planet.eon.net/~jim/
sheena.html

Clint Eastwood
http://www.man-with-no-name.com/
http://www.cadvision.com/eastwood/
http://localsonly.wilmington.net/
~solomon/clinteastwood.html

Billy Eckstine
http://www.servtech.com/~pnm/
stardust/billy.htm

Nelson Eddy
http://home.earthlink.net/~maceddy/

Danny Elfman
http://www.rit.edu/~elnppr/faqs/
defaq.html
http://elfman.vendetta.com/
http://www.geocities.com/Hollywood/
2595/

Duke Ellington
http://duke.fuse.net/
http://www.dnsmith.com/ellington/
http://www.ilinks.net/~holmesr/duke.
htm

Cass Elliot
http://members.aol.com/Rbcsoup/
index.html

Brian Eno
http://www.spies.com/Eno/EnoFAQ.
html
http://www.hyperreal.org/music/
artists/brian_eno/
http://www.dream.com/Oblique.html

Erasure
http://www.elektra.com/ambient_
club/erasure/erasure.html
http://www.taynet.co.uk/users/
bennett/music/erasure-faq.html
http://www.free.cts.com/crash/z/
zamfir/erasure.html

Juan Garcia Esquivel
http://home.earthlink.net/~space
agepop/esquivel.htm

Everything but the Girl
http://www.ebtg.com/
http://www.terabit.net/icho/ebtg1.
htm
http://www.indigocat.com/ebtg.html

Donald Fagen
http://www.andrew.cmu.edu/~paw/
music/steelydan.htm

Percy Faith
http://home.earthlink.net/~space
agepop/faith.htm

Marianne Faithfull
http://www.planete.net/~smironne/

Michael Feinstein
http://feature.atlantic-records.com/
Michael_Feinstein/

Jose Feliciano
http://www.areacom.it/html/arte_
cultura/feliciano/index.htm

Bryan Ferry
http://www.cco.caltech.edu/~bryan/
roxy/
http://www.dlc.fi/~hope/

Ella Fitzgerald
http://www.enviromedia.com/ella/
http://www.public.iastate.edu/
~vwindsor/Ella.html
http://www.seas.columbia.edu/~tts6/
ella.html

Stan Freberg
http://www.access.avernus.com/
~rogue/stan.html
http://atlantic.evsc.virginia.edu/julia/
Freberg.html
http://www.southern.edu/people/
eahullqu/freberg/

Friends of Dean Martinez
http://shiva.subpop.com/bands/
fodm/website/retrofrm.html

Serge Gainsbourg
http://www2.ec-lille.fr/~viguier/
Gainsbourg.html
http://home.dti.net/enoklite/serge/

The Galaxy Trio
http://www.aracnet.com/~jcrabbe/

Judy Garland
http://www.zianet.com/jjohnson/
index.html
http://users.aol.com/robotb9/private/
garland.htm
http://users.delta.com/rainbowz/

Marvin Gaye
http://www.calvin.edu/~cdykho15/
marvin/
http://www.sedgsoftware.com/marvin/

The Gentle People
http://www.gentleworld.com/

George & Ira Gershwin
http://www.sju.edu/~bs065903/
gershwin/homepage.htm
http://www.missouri.edu/~c642474/
gershwin.html
http://www.northernnet.com/
pdehnert/gershwin/

Stan Getz
http://www.book.uci.edu/Jazz/
CDLists/StanGetz_CDL.html

Astrud Gilberto
http://www.gregmar.com/astrud.htm

João Gilberto
http://www.nic.com/~silkpurs/

Jackie Gleason
http://home.earthlink.net/~space
agepop/gleason.htm

Benny Goodman
http://www.flash.net/~rdreagan/
index.shtml
http://qlink.queensu.ca/~3pje2/bg.
html

Lesley Gore
http://members.tripod.com/~Lesley_
Gore/index.html

Robert Goulet
http://www.robertgoulet.com/

Buddy Greco
http://www.buddy-greco.com/index.
htm

Dave Grusin
http://www.mca.com/grp/grp/artists/
grusin_dave.rel.html
http://www.geocities.com/Hollywood/
Academy/1201/

Vince Guaraldi
http://g2303m.unileoben.ac.at/
guaraldi/vince_guaraldi.html

Herbie Hancock
http://www.mercuryrecords.com/
mercury/artists/hancock_herbie/
hancock_herbie.html
http://www.netspace.org/~was/
music_11/hjh.html

Neal Hefti
http://home.earthlink.net/~space
agepop/hefti.htm

Mel Henke
http://home.earthlink.net/~space
agepop/henke.htm

The Hi-Lo's
http://www.singers.com/hi-los.html

The High Llamas
http://www.cabinessence.com/
high-llamas/

Don Ho
http://www.hohouse.com/

Billie Holiday
http://www.enmu.edu/~daym/
mus103/billie.htm
http://users.bart.nl/~ecduzit/billy/
index.html

Lena Horne
http://www.bluenote.com/horne.html

Engelbert Humperdinck
http://www.engelbert.com/

Betty Hutton
http://web.starlinx.com/fwsiegle/
index.htm-ssi

Phyllis Hyman
http://www.geocities.com/Heartland/
Meadows/2318/

Julio Iglesias
http://www.music.sony.com/Music/
ArtistInfo/JulioIglesias/

Joe Jackson
http://www.joejackson.com/

Horst Jankowski
http://home.earthlink.net/~space
agepop/jankowsk.htm

Antonio Carlos Jobim
http://nortemag.com/tom/e.index.
html
http://www.winet.com.br/tomjobim/
http://www.geocities.com/Bourbon
Street/Delta/7824/

Billy Joel
http://www.music.sony.com/Music/
ArtistInfo/BillyJoel/
http://www.cs.wisc.edu/~msteele/
bjoel/
http://www.idcnet.com/~ecnal/
winubj.htm

Al Jolson
http://www2.ari.net/ajr/recs/
http://www.btinternet.com/~jolson/
main.htm

Quincy Jones
http://www.wbr.com/quincyjones/

Spike Jones
http://www.geocities.com/Sunset
Strip/4020/spike.html

Tom Jones
http://kspace.com/KM/spot.sys/
Jones/pages/bio.html
http://www.kensai.com/tomjones/
http://www.catch.com/snack/
tomjones/

Bert Kaempfert
http://home.earthlink.net/~space
agepop/kaempfer.htm

Gene Kelly
http://members.aol.com/humorone/
gene.htm
http://mgmua.com/gkelly.html

Stan Kenton
http://www.geocities.com/Bourbon
Street/5046/
http://hiwaay.net/~crispen/kenton/

Eartha Kitt
http://www.chaoskitty.com/b_kitty/
html/kitt.html

Diana Krall
http://www.mca.com/grp/grp/artists/
krall.rel.html

Gene Krupa
http://www.geocities.com/Bourbon
Street/Delta/3898/
http://www.concentric.net/~thompjr/
gene_krupa/index.shtml

Cleo Laine
http://quarternotes.com/cleohome.
htm

Nancy LaMott
http://www.nancylamott.com/
http://www.geocities.com/Broadway/
4206/jk.nancy.html

k.d. lang
http://www.kdlang.com/
http://www.geocities.com/West
Hollywood/Heights/2615/
http://www.geocities.com/Hollywood/
Hills/6880/

Brenda Lee
http://www.geocities.com/Nashville/
4481/

Peggy Lee
http://www.geocities.com/Broadway/
Stage/2481/home.html

Tom Lehrer
http://www.wiw.org/~drz/tom.lehrer/
index.html
http://www.keaveny.demon.co.uk/
lehrer/lehrer.htm

Annie Lennox
http://www.well.com/user/sunspot/
annielennox.htm
http://www.geocities.com/Sunset
Strip/Palladium/2935/annie.html

The Lettermen
http://www.thelettermen.com/

Jerry Lewis
http://www.jerry-lewis-comedy.com/
http://users.aol.com/norky1995/
index.html

Liberace
http://www.liberace.org/museum.
html
http://www.birdhouse.org/words/
scot/liberace/liberace.html

Enoch Light
http://easyweb.easynet.co.uk/~rcb/
light/

Gordon Lightfoot
http://www.mmlc.nwu.edu/~mfifer/
lightfoot/index.html

Andrew Lloyd Webber
http://www.serve.com/dougmac/
http://www.westegg.com/alw/

Guy Lombardo
http://members.aol.com/famemgt/
fame/lombardo.htm

Julie London
http://www.chaoskitty.com/b_kitty/
html/jlond.html

Claudine Longet
http://users.deltanet.com/~gondola/
longet/longet.html

John Lurie/The Lounge Lizards
http://www.inch.com/~lagarto/

Arthur Lyman
http://home.earthlink.net/~space
agepop/lyman.htm
http://www.tikipub.com/lyman/index.
html

Madonna
http://www.users.globalnet.co.uk/
~ultiog/webhome1.htm
http://www.mit.edu:8001/people/
jwb/Madonna.html
http://www-scf.usc.edu/~caulfiel/
madonna.html

Man or Astro-Man?
http://www.astroman.com
http://hubcap.clemson.edu/
~bpmccal/moam.html
http://www.ipinc.net/~kepler/asr3k.
html

Chuck Mangione
http://www.calicchio.com/players/
mangione/home.htm

The Manhattan Transfer
http://www.west.net/~jrpprod/tmt/
tmt.html
http://www.singers.com/manhattan
transfer.html

Barry Manilow
http://www.aristarec.com/aristaweb/
BarryManilow/index.html
http://www.manilow.com/
http://www.netfusion.com/maniweb/

Mannheim Steamroller
http://www.amgram.com/

Dean Martin
http://www.primenet.com/~drbmbay/
memor.html

Al Martino
http://www.almartino.com/

Johnny Mathis
http://www.music.sony.com/Music/
ArtistInfo/JohnnyMathis/

Eric Matthews
http://www.subpop.com/bands/
ericmatthews/matthews.html

Joe Meek
http://www.concentric.net/~meek
web/telstar.htm

Johnny Mercer
http://johnnymercer.com/

Ethel Merman
http://www.ethelmerman.com/

Bette Midler
http://members.aol.com/DvaLasVgas/
betteonline.html
http://www.geocities.com/Hollywood/
4863/

Glenn Miller
http://jagor.srce.hr/~bbarisic/
glenn1.htm

The Mills Brothers
http://www.cumberlink.com/mills/

Liza Minnelli
http://pages.prodigy.com/liza.
minnelli/
http://www.oberlin.edu/~dfortune/
lizaonline.html

Carmen Miranda
http://www.geocities.com/Hollywood/
2148/index.html

Robert Mitchum
http://tcm.turner.com/TCMWeb96/
Nov96/Mitchum.htm

Marilyn Monroe
http://www.cmgww.com/marilyn/
marilyn.html
http://www.geocities.com/Hollywood/
Studio/7073/
http://mozart.lib.uchicago.edu/
Marilyn/

Hugo Montenegro
http://home.earthlink.net/~space
agepop/monteneg.htm

The Moog Cookbook
http://www.restless.com/moog.html

Ennio Morricone
http://www.londontheatre.co.uk/
ennio-morricone/index.html

Morrissey
http://www.Morrissey-solo.com/
http://www.geocities.com/Sunset
Strip/Towers/1503/
http://www.lionheart.net/rachael/
media/music/morrissey/

Nana Mouskouri
http://alexander.cc.ece.ntua.gr/
~agaret/nana/mouskouri.html

Peter Nero
http://www.peternero.com

Wayne Newton
http://www.angelfire.com/mo/wayne
newton/
http://www.outofthenight.com/
newton.html
http://members.aol.com/alomes/
homepage.htm

Olivia Newton-John
http://www.netlink.co.uk/users/
ermine/olivia/
http://www.geocities.com/Sunset
Strip/Palladium/4212/olivia
newtonjohn.html
http://www.netlink.co.uk/users/
ermine/onj/index.html

Leonard Nimoy
http://www.calweb.com/~ejr/spock_
sings.html
http://members.aol.com/nimoyclub/
index.htm

Ken Nordine
http://www.ellipsis.com/meltdown/
nordine/maybe/normay2.html

The Nylons
http://www.thenylons.com/
http://www.singers.com/nylons.html

Sinéad O'Connor
http://www.telebyte.nl/~bobbink/
sinead/sinead.htm
http://members.tripod.com/~yoav/
sinead.html
http://uts.cc.utexas.edu/~erick/
sinead/sinead.html

The 101 Strings
http://www.101strings.com/

Charlie Parker
http://www.wam.umd.edu/~losinp/
music/bird.html

Mandy Patinkin
http://www2.ari.net/aater/patinkin.
html
http://members.aol.com/caresseb/
mpmain.htm

Pet Shop Boys
http://www.unimaas.nl/~mathysen/
psb/
http://members.aol.com/somespec/
index.html
http://home.sol.no/~wattne/PET1.
htm

Bernadette Peters
http://home.earthlink.net/~cosmocat/

Edith Piaf
http://pantheon.cis.yale.edu/
~bodoin/edith_piaf.html

Pizzicato Five
http://www.matador.recs.com/bios/
bio_p5.html

http://www.clark.net/pub/fan/pizz.
html
http://www2.hawaii.edu/~evaldez/
pizzicato5/pizzicato5.htm

Cole Porter
http://www.doitall.com/cole/index.
html

Portishead
http://www.polygram-us.com/
portishead/
http://www.cls.dk/~jqj/portishead/
http://www.geocities.com/Sunset
Strip/Studio/8424/

Perez Prado
http://home.earthlink.net/~space
agepop/prado.htm

Elvis Presley
http://www.elvis-presley.com/
http://www.robyn.on.net/elvis/
http://www.elvispresleyonline.com/

Louis Prima/Keely Smith
http://home.earthlink.net/~space
agepop/prima.htm

Cliff Richard
http://www.starnet.com.au/sheppard/
2cliff.html

Jonathan Richman
http://www.base.com/jonathan/
jonathan.html
http://members.aol.com/gustoeater/
jojo/jojohome.htm
http://www.finlayson-design.co.uk/
simes/jojo/

Kenny Rogers
http://www.kennyrogers.net/
http://www.zeebyrd.com/kenny.html
http://members.aol.com/Mixer5000/
index.html

Linda Ronstadt
http://www.ais-gwd.com/~tpartridge/
http://people.delphi.com/slanoue/
ronstadt.htm
http://www.reno.quik.com/stanpren/
linda.htm

David Lee Roth
http://shrike.depaul.edu/~bgrabner/
index.html
http://www2.cybernex.net/~gambito/
dave.html
http://mflwp.bhcom1.com/

Royal Crown Revue
http://www.rcr.com/

Todd Rundgren
http://www.tr-i.com/
http://www.roadkill.com/todd/trconn
http://www.wu-wei.com/eutopia/
trffhb.html

RuPaul
http://members.aol.com/gcen76/

Sade
http://www.epiccenter.com/Epic
Center/docs/artistupdate.qry?
artistid=147
http://www.epix.net/~akwarner/sade/
http://www.flash.net/~titan1/sade.
html

Erik Satie
http://www.af.lu.se/~fogwall/satie.
html

Leo Sayer
http://www.wesjen.simplenet.com/
sayer/leomenu.htm

Lalo Schifrin
http://siteworks.com/szabo/ls_list.
htm

Diane Schuur
http://www.mca.com/grp/grp/artists/
schuur.rel.html

Raymond Scott
http://users.aol.com/DevilDrums/
RS.html

Neil Sedaka
http://members.aol.com/sedaka1/
index.html

Doc Severinsen
http://scribers.midwest.net/pnotuner/
doc.htm
http://home.earthlink.net/~space
agepop/severins.htm

William Shatner
http://www.loskene.com/singalong/
kirk.html
http://www.shatner.com/
http://comp.uark.edu/~breed/shatner.
html

Sandie Shaw
http://www.creativepitch.com/amajor/
sandiesh.html

Jane Siberry
http://www.RepriseRec.com/reprise_
html_pages/janesiberry
http://www.sheeba.ca/

Carly Simon
http://www.ziva.com/carly/

Nina Simone
http://www.adapta.it/nina/
http://seercom.com/nina/

Frank Sinatra
http://www.blue-eyes.com/
http://www.vex.net/~buff/sinatra/
http://www.asylum.com/sinatra/
index.html
http://www.sinatraclub.com/
http://www.pscentral.com/frank/
http://www.clever.net/rich2000/

Stephen Sondheim
http://www.sondheim.com/
http://www.geocities.com/Broadway/
9432/

Sonny & Cher
http://www.inch.com/~harbur/cher/
index.html
http://www.mase.net/sonnybono/

Dusty Springfield
http://www.isd.net/mbayly/
http://www.rainbow.net.au/~dusty/

Squirrel Nut Zippers
http://www.mammoth.com/mammoth/
bands/snz/
http://www.squirrelnutzippers.com/

Stereolab
http://www.elektra.com/alternative_
club/stereolab/stereolab.html
http://www.maths.monash.edu.au/
~rjh/stereolab/

Barbra Streisand
http://www.music.sony.com/Music/
ArtistInfo/BarbraStreisand/
http://members.aol.com/barbramusc/
index.html
http://members.aol.com/markjayeye/
bjsfaq/

Yma Sumac
http://www.accesscom.com/~pc/
sumac
http://www.chaoskitty.com/b_kitty/
html/ymas.html

Swing out Sister
http://www.rit.edu/~kbk4834/swing
out/swing.html

John Tesh
http://www.tesh.com/
http://www.well.com/user/vanya/
tesh.html

Tindersticks
http://huizen.dds.nl/~totos/tinder.htm

Tiny Tim
http://www.tinytim.org/

Up with People
http://www.upwithpeople.org/

Frankie Valli
http://www.srv.net/~roxtar/valli_
frankie.html

Sarah Vaughan
http://www.geocities.com/Vienna/
8244/

Billy Vaughn
http://home.earthlink.net/~spaceage
pop/vaughn.htm

The Ventures
http://www.theventures.com/
http://www.geocities.com/Cape
Canaveral/3098/venture.htm

Roseanna Vitro
http://members.aol.com/rvitrojazz/
index.html

Tom Waits
http://weber.ucg.ie/waits
http://www.gameverse.com/music/
waits/
http://www.geocities.com/SoHo/
7587/

Kurt Weill
http://www.kwf.org/

Lawrence Welk
http://welk.buffnet.net/
http://www.zeldman.com/welk.html

Mae West
http://www.sirius.com/~kims/
maewest.html
http://www.slip.net/~hsstern/
maewest/

Roger Williams
http://home.earthlink.net/~space
agepop/williams.htm

Cassandra Wilson
http://www.geocities.com/Bourbon
Street/4587/

Nancy Wilson
http://www.missnancywilson.com/

Hugo Winterhalter
http://home.earthlink.net/~space
agepop/winterha.htm

Other Lounge and Music-Related Sites

The American Gallery of Exotic Album Covers
http://www.users.interport.net/
~joholmes/index.html

Billboard Magazine
http://www.billboard.com/

BMG Music Service
http://www.bmgmusicservice.com/

CD Universe
http://www.cduniverse.com/

CDnow
http://www.cdnow.com/

Cigar Aficionado Magazine
http://www.cigaraficionado.com/

Club Velvet
http://www.tamboo.com/

Cocktail at HotWired
http://www.hotwired.com/cocktail/

Columbia House Music Club
http://www.columbiahouse.com/

The Dead Lounge
http://www.pacificnet.net/~polar
beast/deadlounge/

Easy Tune Home Page
http://people.zeelandnet.nl/poulus/
easytune.htm

ICE Magazine
http://www.icemagazine.com/

Las Vegas.com
http://www.lasvegas.com/

Mainly Big Bands
http://www.btinternet.com/~j.r.killoch/
home.htm

Music Boulevard
http://www.musicblvd.com/

Music Newswire
http://www.musicnewswire.com/

New Jack Web: Lounge Nation
http://www.polaris.net/~merlin/
lounge.html

Primarily A Cappella
http://www.singers.com/

Rat Pack Home Page
http://www.primenet.com/~drbmbay/

RockOnTV
http://www.rockontv.com/

Space Age Bachelor Pad Music
http://www.chaoskitty.com/sabpm/

Space Age Pop Music Standards Page
http://home.earthlink.net/~space
agepop/index.htm

Swank-O-Rama
http://www.mindspring.com/
~jpmckay/

Tiki News
http://www.indieweb.com/indieweb/
tiki/

Ultra-Lounge
http://www.ultralounge.com/

USA Today (Music Index)
http://www.usatoday.com/life/enter/
music/lem99.htm

Vik's Lounge and Radio Vik
http://www.chaoskitty.com/t_chaos/
lounge.html

Wall of Sound
http://www.wallofsound.com/

Women of Exotica
http://www.chaoskitty.com/b_kitty/
exotica.html

X-RE/Specs (formerly RE/Search)
http://www.postfun.com/xre/welcome.
html

The following record labels are just some of the labels that have substantial lounge or easy-listening catalogs. You may want to contact them if you have questions regarding specific releases.

A&M Records
1416 N. La Brea Ave.
Hollywood, CA 90028
(213) 469-2411
Fax: (213) 856-2600

Almo Sounds
360 N. La Cienega Blvd.
Los Angeles, CA 90048
(310) 289-3080
Fax: (310) 289-8662

Arista Records
6 W. 57th St.
New York, NY 10019
(212) 489-7400
Fax: (212) 830-2238

Atlantic Recording Corp.
1290 Avenue of the Americas
New York, NY 10104
(212) 707-2000
Fax: (212) 405-5507

Bear Family Records
PO Box 1154
27727 Hambergen, Germany
(49) 04794-93000
Fax: (49) 04794-930020

E-mail: bear@bear-family.de

Bellmark Records/Life Records
7060 Hollywood Blvd., 10th Fl.
Hollywood, CA 90028
(213) 464-8492
Fax: (213) 464-0785

Blue Note Records
304 Park Ave. S., 3rd Fl.
  New York, NY 10010
(212) 253-2000
Fax: (212) 253-3150

Capricorn Records
1100 Spring St. NW, Ste. 103.
Atlanta, GA 30309-2823
(404) 873-3918
Fax: (404) 873-1807

Collectables Records
2320 Haverford Rd.
Ardmore, PA 19003
(800) 446-8426
(610) 649-7650
Fax: (610) 649-0315

Collectors Choice Music
PO Box 838
Itasca, IL 60143-0838
(800) 923-1122

Columbia Records
550 Madison Ave.
New York, NY 10022-3211
(212) 833-8000
Fax: (212) 833-7731

Concord Records
2450-A Stanwell Dr.

Concord, CA 94520
(510) 682-6770
Fax: (510) 682-3508

Corinthian Records
PO Box 6296
Beverly Hills, CA 90212
Fax: (310) 455-2649

The Curb Group
47 Music Sq. E.
Nashville, TN 37203
(615) 321-5080
Fax: (615) 255-2855

Decca Records
60 Music Sq. E.
Nashville, TN 37203
(615) 244-8944
Fax: (615) 880-7475

EastWest Records
75 Rockefeller Plz.
New York, NY 10019
(212) 275-2500
Fax: (212) 974-9314

Elektra Entertainment Group
75 Rockefeller Plz.
New York, NY 10019-6907
(212) 275-4000
Fax: (212) 974-9314

EMI-Capitol Records
1750 N. Vine St.
Hollywood, CA 90028
(213) 462-6252
Fax: (213) 467-6550

Epic Records
550 Madison Ave.
New York, NY 10022-3211

(212) 833-8000
Fax: (212) 833-5134

Evidence Music
1100 E. Hector St., Ste. 392
Conshohocken, PA 19428
(610) 832-0844
Fax: (610) 832-0807

Geffen/DGC Records
9130 Sunset Blvd.
Los Angeles, CA 90069-6197
(310) 278-9010
Fax: (310) 273-9389

Giant Records
1514 South St.
Nashville, TN 37212
(615) 256-3110
Fax: (615) 742-1560

GNP Crescendo Records
8480-A Sunset Blvd.
West Hollywood, CA 90069
(213) 656-2614
Fax: (213) 656-0693

GRP Recording Co.
555 W. 57th St., 10th Fl.
New York, NY 10019
(212) 424-1000
Fax: (212) 424-1007

Hollywood Records
500 S. Buena Vista St.
Burbank, CA 91521
(818) 560-5670
Fax: (818) 841-5140

Ichiban Records
PO Box 724677
Atlanta, GA 31139-1677

(770) 419-1414
Fax: (770) 419-1230

Impulse! Records
555 W. 57th St., 10th Fl.
New York, NY 10019
(212) 424-1000
Fax: (212) 424-1007

Island Records
825 Eighth Ave., 24th Fl.
New York, NY 10019
(212) 333-8000
Fax: (212) 603-3965

Laserlight Digital
Delta Music Company
1663 Sawtelle Blvd.
Los Angeles, CA 90025
(310) 268-1205
Fax: (310) 268-1279

London Records
825 Eighth Ave., 23rd Fl.
New York, NY 10019
(212) 333-8000
Fax: (212) 333-8030

Maverick Records
8000 Beverly Blvd.
Los Angeles, CA 90048
(213) 852-1177
Fax: (213) 852-1505

MCA Records
70 Universal City Plz.
Universal City, CA 91608
(818) 777-4000
Fax: (818) 733-1407

MCG/Curb
3907 W. Alameda Ave., Ste.
101
Burbank, CA 91505
(818) 843-1616
Fax: (818) 843-5429

Mercury Records
World Wide Plz.
825 Eighth Ave.
New York, NY 10019
(212) 333-8000
Fax: (212) 333-1093

Metropolitan Recording Corp.
900 Passaic Ave.
East Newark, NJ 07029

(201) 483-8080
Fax: (201) 483-0031

N2K Encoded Music
55 Broad St., 18th Fl.
New York, NY 10004
(212) 378-6100
Fax: (212) 742-1775

Polydor Records
1416 N. La Brea Ave.
Hollywood, CA 90028
(213) 856-6600
Fax: (213) 856-6610

Private Music
8750 Wilshire Blvd.
Beverly Hills, CA 90211
(310) 358-4500
Fax: (310) 358-4520

Qwest Records
3800 Barham Blvd., Ste. 503
Los Angeles, CA 90068
(213) 874-7770
Fax: (213) 874-5049

Ranwood Records
Welk Music Group
1299 Ocean Avenue
Santa Monica, CA 90401
(310) 451-5727

Razor & Tie Records
214 Sullivan St., #4A
New York, NY 10012
(212) 473-9173
Fax: (212) 473-9174

RCA Records
1540 Broadway
New York, NY 10036
(212) 930-4000
Fax: (212) 930-4468

Reader's Digest Music
261 Madison Ave.
New York, NY 10016
(212) 907-6968
Fax: (212) 986-2507

Relativity Records
79 Fifth Ave., 16th Fl.
New York, NY 10003
(212) 337-5300

Reprise Records
3300 Warner Blvd.

Burbank, CA 91505-4694
(818) 846-9090
(818) 953-3223
Fax: (818) 953-3211

Restless Records
1616 Vista Del Mar Ave.
Hollywood, CA 90028
(213) 957-4357
(800) 573-7853
Fax: (213) 957-4355

Rhino Records
10635 Santa Monica Blvd.
Los Angeles, CA 90025-4900
(310) 474-4778
Fax: (310) 441-6575

The Right Stuff
1750 N. Vine St.
Hollywood, CA 90028
(213) 960-4634
Fax: (213) 960-4666

Rounder Records
One Camp St.
Cambridge, MA 02140
(617) 354-0700
Fax: (617) 491-1970

Rykodisc
27 Congress St.
Salem, MA 01970
(508) 744-7678
Fax: (508) 741-4506

Scamp/Caroline Records
104 West 29th St.
New York, NY 10001
(212) 886-7500

Sire Records
75 Rockefeller Plz., 17th Fl.
New York, NY 10019
(212) 275-2500
Fax: (212) 275-3562

Sony 550 Music
550 Madison Ave.
New York, NY 1022
(212) 833-8000
Fax: (212) 833-7120

Tag Recordings
14 E. 60th St., 8th Fl.
New York, NY 10022
(212) 508-5450

Fax: (212) 593-7663

TVT Records
23 E. Fourth St., 3rd Fl.
New York, NY 10003
(212) 979-6410
Fax: (212) 979-6489

Universal Records
1755 Broadway, 7th Fl.
New York, NY 10019
(212) 373-0600
Fax: (212) 247-3954

Varese Sarabande Records
11846 Ventura Blvd., Ste. 130
Studio City, CA 91604
(818) 753-4143

Verve Records
825 Eighth Ave., 26th Fl.
New York, NY 10019
(212) 333-8000
Fax: (212) 333-8194

Virgin Records
338 N. Foothill Rd.
Beverly Hills, CA 90210
(310) 278-1181
Fax: (310) 278-6231

Warner Bros. Records
3300 Warner Blvd.
Burbank, CA 91510
(818) 846-9090
(818) 953-3223
Fax: (818) 846-8474

Windham Hill Records
8750 Wilshire Blvd.
Beverly Hills, CA 90211-2713
(310) 358-4800
Fax: (310) 358-4805

The Work Group
2100 Colorado Ave.
Santa Monica, CA 90404
(310) 449-2666
Fax: (310) 449-2095

These are just some of the U.S. radio stations that play easy listening, beautiful music, soft adult-contemporary, or a combination of all three. Please be advised that radio station formats often change like the weather. Your best bet would be to check the local radio listings in the cities below. (Radio station listings courtesy of BIA Publishing.)

Alabama

Birmingham
WYSF (94.5 FM)

Centre
WRHY (105.9 FM)

Decatur
WRSA (96.9 FM)

Geneva
WRJM (93.7 FM)

Jackson
WHOD (94.5 FM)

Ozark
WOZK (900 AM)

Alaska

Houston
KQEZ (92.1 FM)

North Pole
KJNP (100.3 FM)

Arizona

Phoenix
KESZ (99.9 FM)

Prescott
KAHM (102.1 FM)

Quartzsite
KBUX (94.3 FM)

Arkansas

Cherokee Village
KFCM (100.9 FM)

El Dorado
KDMS (1290 AM)

Fayetteville
KEZA (107.9 FM)

Pocahontas
KPOC (104.1 FM/1420 AM)

Sheridan
KVLO (102.9 FM)

California

Carpinteria
KSBL (101.7 FM)

Cathedral City
KWXY (98.5 FM/1340 AM)

Dinuba
KSOF (98.9 FM)

Los Angeles
KOST (103.5 FM)

Modesto
KJSN (102.3 FM)

Palm Desert
KEZN (103.1 FM)

Ridgecrest
KZIQ (1360 AM)

San Diego
KJQY (102.9 FM)

San Francisco
KOIT (96.5 FM/1260 AM)

San Jacinto
KWRP (96.1 FM)

Colorado

Brush
KSIR (107.1 FM/1010 AM)

Denver
KIUP (930 AM)

Grand Junction
KJYE (92.3 FM)

Widefield
KKLI (106.3 FM)

Connecticut

New Britain
WRCH (100.5 FM)

New London
WTYD (100.9 FM)

Delaware

Seaford
WSUX (98.5 FM)

District of Columbia

Washington
WGAY (99.5 FM)

Florida

Arcadia
WWRZ (98.3 FM)

Bradenton
WDUV (103.5 FM)

Cocoa
WRFB (860 AM)

Crawfordville
WAKU (94.1 FM)

Holmes Beach
WISP (98.7 FM)

Jacksonville
WEJZ (96.1 FM)

Marco
WAVV (101.1 FM)

Miami
WAVV (101.1 FM)

Mt. Dora
WLYF (101.5 FM)
WMGF (107.7 FM)

Niceville
WNCV (100.3 FM)

Ocala
WMFQ (92.9 FM)

Pensacola
WMEZ (94.1 FM)

St. Petersburg
WSUN (620 AM)

Solana
WCVU (104.9 FM)

Tampa
WWRM (94.9 FM)

West Palm Beach
WEAT (104.3 FM)
WRLX (92.1 FM)

Georgia

Adel
WDDQ (92.1 FM)

Atlanta
WPCH (94.9 FM)
WSB (98.5 FM)

Dublin
WMLT (1330 AM)

Fitzgerald
WBHB (1240 AM)
WRDO (96.9 FM)

Hawkinsville
WCEH (610 AM)
WQSY (103.9 FM)

Nashville
WJYF (95.3 FM)

Tennille
WJFL (101.9 FM)

Hawaii

Honolulu
KUMU (94.7 FM)

Kahului
KNUI (99.9 FM)

Idaho

Eagle
KXLT (107.9 FM)

Rexburg
KADQ (94.3 FM)

Illinois

Christopher
WUEZ (103.5 FM)

Clinton
WHOW (95.9 FM)

Nashville
WNSV (104.7 FM)

Pontiac
WJEZ (93.7 FM)

Robinson
WTAY (1570 AM)
WTYE (101.7 FM)

Indiana

Brookston
WEZV (95.3 FM)

Rochester
WROI (92.1 FM)

Seymour
WZZB (1390 AM)

Terre Haute
WLEZ (102.7 FM)

Iowa

Ames
KLTI (104.1 FM)

Ankeny
KMXD (106.3 FM)

Dubuque
KATF (92.9 FM)

Mason City
KCMR (97.9 FM)

Waverly
KWAY (99.3 FM)

Kansas

Beloit
KVSV (105.5 FM)

Goodland
KKCI (102.5 FM)

Hugoton
KFXX (106.7 FM)

Kansas City
KUDL (98.1 FM)

Newton
KOEZ (92.3 FM)

Kentucky

Calvert City
WCCK (95.7 FM)

Lawrenceburg
WKYL (102.1 FM)

Maysville
WFTM (95.9 FM/1240 AM)

Louisiana

Natchitoches
KDBH (97.7 FM)

New Orleans
WLMG (101.9 FM)

Reserve
WADU (94.9 FM)

Maine

Bangor
WEZQ (92.9 FM)

Bath
WJTO (730 AM)

Boothbay Harbor
WCME (96.7 FM)

Fairfield
WCTB (93.5 FM)

Kennebunkport
WQEZ (104.7 FM)

Rockland
WRKD (1450 AM)

Maryland

Baltimore
WLIF (101.9 FM)

Hagerstown
WWMD (104.7 FM)

Prince Federick
WMJS (92.7 FM)

Salisbury
WSBY (98.9)

Massachussetts

Cambridge
WJIB (740 AM)

North Adams
WMNB (100.1 FM)

Quincy
WJDA (1300 AM)

Worcester
WNEB (1230 AM)

Michigan

Hart
WCXT (105.3 FM)

Houghton
WAAH (102.3 FM)

Ishpeming
WIAN (1240 AM)

Marquette
WDMJ (1320 AM)

Menominee
WAGN (1340 AM)

Mt. Pleasant
WCZY (104.3 FM)

Petoskey
WLXT (96.3 FM)

Three Rivers
WLKM (95.9 FM)

Walker
WQFN (100.5 FM)

Minnesota

East Grand Forks
KZLT (104.3 FM)

Minneapolis
WLTE (102.9 FM)

Montevideo
KMGM (105.5 FM)

Mora
KBEK (95.5 FM)

St. Peter
KRBI (105.5 FM/1310 AM)

Sauk Centre
KMSR (94.3 FM)

Stewartville
KYBA (105.3 FM)

Winona
KHME (101.1 FM)

Mississippi

Greenville
WBAQ (97.9 FM)

Gulfport
WROA (1390 AM)

Kosciusko
WLIN (1340 AM)

Petal
WMFM (106.3 FM)

Vicksburg
WJKK (98.7 FM)

Missouri

Carthage
KMXL (95.1 FM)

Eldon
KBMX (101.9 FM)

St. Louis
KEZK (102.5 FM)

Sikeston
KRHW (1520 AM)

Springfield
KTXR (101.3 FM)

Montana

Libby
KTNY (101.7 FM)

Nebraska

Lincoln
KEZG (107.3 FM)

Nebraska City
KESY (97.7 FM)

Nevada

Las Vegas
KSNE (94.9 FM)

New Hampshire

Laconia
WEZS (1350 AM)

Mt. Washington
WHOM (94.9 FM)

Somersworth
WBYY (98.7 FM)

New Jersey

Paterson
WPAT (93.1 FM)

New Mexico

Lovington
KLEA (630 AM)

Roswell
KBIM (94.9 FM)

New York

Albany
WYJB (95.5 FM)

Center Moriches
WLVG (96.1 FM)

Deposit
WIYN (94.7 FM)

Elmira
WENY (92.7 FM)

New York
WLTW (106.7 FM)

Norwich
WCHN (970 AM)

Remsen
WRFM (93.5 FM)

Rochester
WRMM (101.3 FM)

Southold
WBAZ (101.7 FM)

Syracuse
WLTI (105.9 FM)

North Carolina

Albemarle
WZKY (1580 AM)

Beech Mountain
WECR (102.3 FM)

Hickory
WLYT (102.9 FM)

Highlands
WHLC (104.5 FM)

Pinehurst
WIOZ (550 AM)

Shallotte
WLTT (103.7 FM)

Ohio

Ashland
WNCO (1340 AM)

Barnesville
WBNV (93.5 FM)

Canton
WCER (900 AM)

Cleveland
WDOK (102.1 FM)

Greenfield
WVNU (97.5 FM)

Marietta
WMOA (1490 AM)

McConnelsville
WJAW (100.9 FM)

New Boston
WIOI (1010 AM)

Oklahoma

Lawton
KBZQ (99.5 FM)

Oklahoma City
KQSR (94.7 FM)

Roseburg
KQEN (1240 AM)

Oregon

Waldport
KORC (820 AM)

Pennsylvania

Altoona
WFBG (1290 AM)

Central City
WSRA (101.7 FM)

Chambersburg
WCBG (1590 AM)

Greenville
WGRP (940 AM)

Honesdale
WWCC (1590 AM)

Huntingdon
WQHG (106.3 FM)

Lancaster
WROZ (101.3 FM)

Mercer
WLLF (96.7 FM)

Millersburg
WQLV (98.9 FM)

Mt. Carmel
WSPI (99.7 FM)

Nanticoke
WNAK (730 AM)

Palmyra
WNCE (92.1 FM)

Pittsburgh
WSHH (99.7 FM)

Pittston
WWSH (102.3 FM)

Port Allegany
WHKS (94.9 FM)

St. Marys
WKBI (1400 AM)

Scranton
WICK (1400 AM)

Sharpsville
WWSY (95.9 FM)

Warren
WRRN (92.3 FM)

Wilkes-Barre
WYCK (1340 AM)

Williamsport
WSFT (107.9 FM)

South Carolina

Clearwater
WSLT (98.3 FM)

Greenville
WMUU (94.5 FM)

Hilton Head
WIJY (106.9 FM)

Myrtle Beach
WJYR (92.1 FM)

Spartanburg
WSPA (98.9 FM)

Sumter
WDXY (1240 AM)

South Dakota

Custer
KFCR (1490 AM)

Sioux Falls
KELO (92.5 FM)

Tennessee

Alamo
WCTA (810 AM)

Chattanooga
WDEF (92.3 FM)

Germantown
WPLX (1170 AM)

Jefferson City
WEZG (99.3 FM)

Memphis
WRVR (104.5 FM)

Morristown
WCRK (1150 AM)

Nashville
WJXA (92.9 FM)

Waynesboro
WFRQ (94.9 FM)

Texas

Austin
KKMJ (95.5 FM)

Crockett
KBHT (93.5 FM)

El Paso
KTSM (99.9 FM)

Jacksonville
KOOI (106.5 FM)

Lamesa
KIOL (104.7 FM)

Livingston
KETX (1440 AM)

Navasota
KMBV (92.5 FM)

Pampa
KGRO (1230 AM)

Pharr
KVJY (840 AM)

Utah

Brian Head
KREC (98.1 FM)

Manti
KMXU (105.1 FM)

North Salt Lake
KFAM (700 AM)

Provo
KSRR (1400 AM)

Salt Lake City
KSFI (100.3 FM)

Vermont

Bellows Falls
WZSH (107.1 FM)

Marlboro
WSSH (101.5 FM)

White River Junction
WKXE (95.3 FM)

Virginia

Charlottesville
WKAV (1400 AM)

Crozet
WCYK (810 AM)

Lynchburg
WRVX (97.9 FM)

New Market
WBHB (103.3 FM)

Spotsylvania
WYSK (99.3 FM)

Suffolk
WFOG (92.9 FM)

Yorktown
WXEZ (94.1 FM)

Washington

Bremerton
KRWM (106.9 FM)

Kennewick
KONA (105.3 FM)

Olympia
KXXO (96.1 FM)

Raymond
KSWW (97.7 FM)

Spokane
KXLY (99.9 FM)

West Virginia

Bridgeport
WDCI (104.1 FM)

Dunbar
WBES (94.5 FM)

Huntington
WKEE (800 AM)

Wisconsin

Baraboo
WRPQ (740 AM)

Chippewa Falls
WCFW (105.7 FM)

Ft. Atkinson
WSJY (107.3 FM)

Marshfield
WLJY (106.5 FM)

Milwaukee
WLTQ (97.3 FM)

Neenah-Menasha
WROE (94.3 FM)

Platteville
WPVL (1590 AM)

Racine
WEZY (92.1 FM)

River Falls
WEVR (1550 AM)

Sauk City
WMLI (96.3 FM)

Sheboygan
WWJR (106.5 FM)

Sturgeon Bay
WLTM (99.7 FM)

Wauwatosa
WAMG (103.7 FM)

Looking for a movie that features some great lounge music or one of your favorite crooners? The following films—rated on a scale of 1–4 bones—are available on video, so you can enjoy them at home. (For more information on these and other movies, consult MusicHound's big brother, VideoHound's Golden Movie Retriever.)

After the Fox ♫♫
(1966)
Cast: Peter Sellers, Victor Mature, Martin Balsam, Britt Ekland. *Director:* Vittorio De-Sica. *Music:* Burt Bacharach. Sellers is a con artist posing as a film director to carry out a bizarre plan to steal gold from Rome. Features occasional backhand slaps at Hollywood, with Mature turning in a memorable performance as the has-been actor starring in Sellers's movie. Though the screenplay was co-written by Neil Simon, the laughs are marginal.

Alexander's Ragtime Band ♫♫♫
(1938)
Cast: Tyrone Power, Alice Faye, Don Ameche, Ethel Merman, Jack Haley, Jean Hersholt, Helen Westley, John Carradine, Paul Hurst, Joe King, Ruth Terry. *Director:* Henry King. *Music:* Irving Berlin. Energetic musical that spans 1915 to 1938 and has Power and Ameche battling for Faye's affections. Power is a society nabob who takes up ragtime. He puts together a band, naming the group after a piece of music (hence the title), and finds a singer (Faye). Ameche is a struggling composer who brings a Broadway producer to listen to their performance. Faye gets an offer to star in a show and becomes an overnight success. Over the years the trio win and lose success, marry and divorce, and finally end up happy. Corny but charming.

The Ambushers woof!
(1967)
Cast: Dean Martin, Janice Rule, James Gregory, Albert Salmi, Senta Berger. *Director:* Henry Levin. *Music:* Hugo Montenegro. Martin's third Matt Helm farce finds him handling a puz-zling case involving the first United States spacecraft. When the craft is hijacked with Rule on board, it's Matt to the rescue, regaining control before unfriendly forces can take it back to earth. Tired formula seems to have worn Martin out while the remainder of the cast goes to camp. Followed by *The Wrecking Crew.*

An American in Paris ♫♫♫♫
(1951)
Cast: Gene Kelly, Leslie Caron, Oscar Levant, Nina Foch, Georges Guetary. *Director:* Vincente Minnelli. *Music:* George Gershwin, Ira Gershwin. Lavish, imaginative musical features a sweeping score and knockout choreography by Kelly. Ex-G.I. Kelly stays on in Paris after the war to study painting, supported in his efforts by rich American Foch, who hopes to acquire a little extra attention. But Kelly loves the lovely Caron, unfortunately engaged to an older gent. Highlight is an astonishing 17-minute ballet which holds the record for longest movie dance number—and one of the most expensive, pegged at over half-a-million dollars for a month of filming. For his efforts, the dance king won a special Oscar citation. While it sure looks like Paris, most of it was filmed in MGM studios.

Anatomy of a Murder ♫♫♫♫
(1959)
Cast: James Stewart, George C. Scott, Arthur O'Connell, Ben Gazzara, Lee Remick, Eve Arden, Orson Bean, Kathryn Grant, Murray Hamilton, Joseph Welch. *Director:* Otto Preminger. *Music:* Duke Ellington. Considered by many to be the best courtroom drama ever made. Small-town lawyer in northern Michigan faces an explosive case as he defends an army officer who has killed a man he suspects was his philandering wife's rapist. Realistic, cynical portrayal of the court system isn't especially concerned with guilt or innocence, focusing instead on the interplay between the various courtroom characters. Classic performance by Stewart as the down-home but brilliant defense lawyer who matches wits with Scott, the sophisticated prosecutor; terse and clever direction by Preminger. Though tame by today's standards, the language used in the courtroom was controversial. Filmed in upper Michi-

gan; based on the best-seller by judge Robert Traver.

Anchors Aweigh 🎜🎜🎜
(1945)
Cast: Frank Sinatra, Gene Kelly, Kathryn Grayson, Jose Iturbi, Sharon McManus, Dean Stockwell, Carlos Ramirez, Pamela Britton. *Director:* George Sidney. *Music:* Jule Styne, Sammy Cahn. Snappy big-budget (for then) musical about two horny sailors, one a girl-happy dancer and the other a shy singer. While on leave in Hollywood they return a lost urchin to his sister. The four of them try to infiltrate a movie studio to win an audition for the girl from maestro Iturbi. Kelly's famous dance with Jerry the cartoon Mouse (of *Tom and Jerry* fame) is the second instance of combining live action and animation. The young and handsome Sinatra's easy crooning and Grayson's near operatic soprano are blessed with music and lyrics by Styne and Cahn. Lots of fun, with conductor-pianist Iturbi contributing and Hollywood-style Little Mexico also in the brew.

Austin Powers: International Man of Mystery 🎜🎜🎜
(1997; PG-13)
Cast: Mike Myers, Elizabeth Hurley, Michael York, Seth Green, Mimi Rogers, Tom Arnold, Carrie Fisher, Robert Wagner, Fabiana Udenio, Paul Dillon, Charles Napier. *Director:* George Roach. *Music:* George Clinton. Hilarious spoof of '60s spy and babe movies. Groovy '60s spy Austin Powers (Myers) discovers that his arch-enemy, Dr. Evil (Myers again), has frozen himself in order to elude capture, so the swingin' dentally challenged Brit decides to do the same. They awaken 30 years later in the same state: woefully out of touch. Dr. Evil

is attempting to blackmail the British government and deal with his Gen-X son, Scott Evil (Green), who wants more quality time and less world conquest. Austin, on the other hand, is trying to "shag" every "groovy bird" he sees. He is teamed with Vanessa (Hurley), the daughter of his former partner, and they try to stop the evil machinations of . . . well . . . Evil. A festival of crushed velvet, political incorrectness, and female robots with lethal breasts. Myers revels in playing the fool, and he may step over the line every once in a while, but he gets plenty of mileage out of the one-joke premise.

Bathing Beauty 🎜🎜🎜
(1944)
Cast: Red Skelton, Esther Williams, Basil Rathbone, Bill Goodwin, Jean Porter, Carlos Ramirez, Donald Meek, Ethel Smith, Helen Forrest. *Director:* George Sidney. *Music:* Xavier Cugat. This musical stars Skelton as a pop music composer with the hots for college swim teacher Williams. Rathbone is a music executive who sees the romance as a threat to Skelton's career and to his own profit margin. Full of aquatic ballet, Skelton's shtick, and wonderful original melodies. The first film in which Williams received star billing.

Beat Girl 🎜🎜
(1960)
Cast: Gillian Hills, David Farrar, Noelle Adam, Christopher Lee, Shirley Anne Field, Oliver Reed. *Director:* Edmond T. Greville. *Music:* John Barry. Pouty, rebellious teen Jennifer (Hills) spends her days in art school and her nights at a London beat hangout. She's jealous when daddy (Farrar) marries sexy French Nichole (Adam) and plots to break them up. When Jennifer dis-

covers Nichole's sordid past she winds up in a burlesque club, attracting the unsavory attentions of owner Kenny (Lee). Then Kenny winds up dead. Singer Adam Faith performs and Reed has a bit as a youthful tough.

Big Night 🎜🎜🎜
(1995; R)
Cast: Tony Shalhoub, Stanley Tucci, Ian Holm, Minnie Driver, Campbell Scott, Isabella Rossellini, Mark Anthony, Allison Janney. *Director:* Stanley Tucci, Campbell Scott. *Music:* Gary DeMichele. Set in '50s New Jersey, film provides an Old World/New World look at Italian brothers Primo (Shalhoub) and Secondo (Tucci) Pilaggi and their elegant but failing restaurant. Primo is the perfectionist chef who hates compromise while Secondo wants to Americanize the place in an effort to make it a success. (He knows the customer is always right even if they can't appreciate Primo's exquisitely authentic Italian dishes). In order to get attention, Secondo arranges a special night in honor of jazz great Louis Prima, with Primo out to cook the feast of a lifetime—if they can pull it off. Another food film guaranteed to make you hungry.

Bird 🎜🎜🎜
(1988; R)
Cast: Forest Whitaker, Diane Venora, Michael Zelniker, Samuel E. Wright, Keith David, Michael McGuire, James Handy, Damon Whitaker, Morgan Nagler, Peter Crook. *Director:* Clint Eastwood. *Music:* Lennie Niehaus. The richly textured, sadly one-sided biography of jazz sax great Charlie Parker, from his rise to stardom to his premature death via extended heroin use. A remarkably assured, deeply imagined film from Eastwood

that never really shows the Bird's genius of creation. The soundtrack features Parker's own solos re-mastered from original recordings.

Black Orpheus 🎜🎜🎜🎜
(1958)
Cast: Breno Mello, Marpessa Dawn, Lea Garcia, Fausto Guerzoni, Lourdes DeOliveira. *Director:* Marcel Camus. *Music:* Antonio Carlos Jobim, Luis Bonfa. The legend of Orpheus and Eurydice unfolds against the colorful background of the carnival in Rio de Janeiro. In the black section of the city, Orpheus is a street-car conductor and Eurydice a country girl fleeing from a man sworn to kill her. Dancing, incredible music, and black magic add to the beauty of this film. Based on the play *Orfeu da Conceica*. In Portuguese with English subtitles or dubbed.

Blue Velvet 🎜🎜🎜
(1986; R)
Cast: Kyle MacLachlan, Isabella Rossellini, Dennis Hopper, Laura Dern, Hope Lange, Jack Nance, Dean Stockwell, George Dickerson, Brad Dourif. *Director:* David Lynch. *Music:* Angelo Badalamenti. Disturbing, unique exploration of the dark side of American suburbia, involving an innocent college youth who discovers a severed ear in an empty lot and is thrust into a turmoil of depravity, murder, and sexual deviance. Brutal, grotesque, and unmistakably Lynch; an immaculately made, fiercely imagined film that is unlike any other. Mood is enhanced by the Badalamenti soundtrack. Graced by splashes of Lynchian humor, most notably the movie's lumber theme. Hopper is riveting as the chief sadistic nutcase and *Twin Peaks'* MacLachlan is a study in loss of innocence.

Born Free 🎵🎵🎵
(1966)
Cast: Virginia McKenna, Bill Travers. *Director:* James Hill. *Music:* John Barry. The touching story of a game warden in Kenya and his wife raising Elsa the orphaned lion cub. When the cub reaches maturity, they work to return her to life in the wild. Great family entertainment based on Joy Adamson's book. Theme song became a hit.

Born to Dance 🎵🎵🎵
(1936)
Cast: Eleanor Powell, James Stewart, Virginia Bruce, Una Merkel, Frances Langford, Sid Silvers, Raymond Walburn, Reginald Gardiner, Buddy Ebsen. *Director:* Roy Del Ruth. *Music:* Cole Porter. A quintessential MGM 1930s dance musical, wherein a beautiful dancer gets a sailor and a big break in a show. Great songs by Cole Porter sung in a less than great manner by a gangly Stewart. Powell's first starring vehicle.

Brazil 🎵🎵🎵🎵
(1985; R)
Cast: Jonathan Pryce, Robert DeNiro, Michael Palin, Katherine Helmond, Kim Greist, Bob Hoskins, Ian Holm, Peter Vaughan, Ian Richardson. *Director:* Terry Gilliam. *Music:* Michael Kamen. The acclaimed nightmare comedy about an everyman trying to survive in a surreal paper-choked bureaucratic society. There are copious references to *1984* and *The Trial,* fantastic mergings of glorious fantasy and stark reality, and astounding visual design. Central to Michael Kamen's score is the 1930 Ary Borroso tune "Brazil," which refers both to the character of revolutionary Jill Brazil and to a place better than the dismal bureaucratic world in which Sam Lowry lives.

Breakfast at Tiffany's 🎵🎵🎵🎵
(1961)
Cast: Audrey Hepburn, George Peppard, Patricia Neal, Buddy Ebsen, Mickey Rooney, Martin Balsam, John McGiver. *Director:* Blake Edwards. *Music:* Henry Mancini. Truman Capote's amusing story of an endearingly eccentric New York City playgirl and her shaky romance with a young writer. Hepburn lends Holly Golightly just the right combination of naivete and worldly wisdom with a dash of melancholy. A wonderfully offbeat romance.

Butch Cassidy and the Sundance Kid 🎵🎵🎵🎵
(1969; PG)
Cast: Paul Newman, Robert Redford, Katharine Ross, Jeff Corey, Strother Martin, Cloris Leachman, Kenneth Mars, Ted Cassidy, Henry Jones, George Furth, Sam Elliott. *Director:* George Roy Hill. *Music:* Burt Bacharach. Two legendary outlaws at the turn of the century take it on the lam with a beautiful, willing ex-school teacher. With a clever script, humanly fallible characters, and warm, witty dialogue, this film was destined to become a box office classic. Featured the hit song "Raindrops Keep Falling on My Head" and renewed the buddy film industry, as Newman and Redford trade insult for insult. Look for the great scene where Newman takes on giant Ted Cassidy in a fist fight.

Cabaret 🎵🎵🎵🎵
(1972; PG)
Cast: Liza Minnelli, Joel Grey, Michael York, Marisa Berenson. *Director:* Bob Fosse. *Music:* Ralph Burns. Hitler is rising to power, racism and anti-Semitism are growing, and the best place to hide from it all is the cabaret. With dancing girls, androgynous master of ceremonies Grey, and American expatriate and singer Minnelli, you can laugh and drink and pretend tomorrow will never come. Minnelli does just that. Face to face with the increasing horrors of Nazism, she persists in the belief that the "show must go on." Based on John Kander's hit Broadway musical (taken from the Christopher Isherwood stories), the film is impressive, with excellent direction and cinematography.

Camelot 🎵🎵
(1967)
Cast: Richard Harris, Vanessa Redgrave, David Hemmings, Franco Nero, Lionel Jeffries. *Director:* Joshua Logan. *Music:* Frederick Loewe, Alan Jay Lerner. The long-running Lerner and Loewe Broadway musical about King Arthur, Guinevere, and Lancelot was adapted from T.H. White's book, *The Once and Future King.* Redgrave and Nero have chemistry as the illicit lovers, Harris is strong as the king struggling to hold together his dream, but muddled direction undermines the effort. Laserdisc edition contains 28 minutes of previously edited footage, trailers, and backstage info.

Can-Can 🎵🎵
(1960)
Cast: Frank Sinatra, Shirley MacLaine, Maurice Chevalier, Louis Jourdan, Juliet Prowse, Marcel Dalio, Leon Belasco. *Director:* Walter Lang. *Music:* Cole Porter, Nelson Riddle. Lackluster screen adaptation of the Cole Porter musical bears little resemblance to the stage version. MacLaine is a cafe owner who goes to court to try and get the "Can-Can," a dance considered risque in gay Paree at the end of the 19th century, made legal. Love interest Sinatra happens to be a lawyer.

Carmen Jones 🎵🎵🎵
(1954)
Cast: Dorothy Dandridge, Harry Belafonte, Pearl Bailey, Roy Glenn, Diahann Carroll, Brock Peters. *Director:* Otto Preminger. *Music:* George Bizet, Herschel Burke Gilbert. Bizet's tale of fickle femme fatale Carmen heads South with an all black cast and new lyrics by Oscar Hammerstein II. Soldier Belafonte falls big time for factory working belle Dandridge during the war, and runs off with miss thang after he kills his C.O. and quits the army. Tired of prettyboy Belafonte, Dandridge's eye wanders upon prize pugilist Escamillo, inspiring ex-soldier beau to wring her throaty little neck. Film debuts of Carroll and Peters. More than a little racist undertone to the direction. Actors' singing is dubbed.

Carnal Knowledge 🎵🎵🎵
(1971; R)
Cast: Jack Nicholson, Candice Bergen, Art Garfunkel, Ann-Margret, Rita Moreno, Carol Kane. *Director:* Mike Nichols. Carnal knowledge of the me generation. Three decades in the sex-saturated lives of college buddies Nicholson and Garfunkel, chronicled through girlfriends, affairs, and marriages. Controversial upon release, it's not a flattering anatomy of Y-chromosome carriers. Originally written as a play. Kane's debut.

Carousel 🎵🎵🎵
(1956)
Cast: Gordon MacRae, Shirley Jones, Cameron Mitchell, Gene Lockhart, Barbara Ruick, Robert Rounseville, Richard Deacon, Tor Johnson. *Director:* Henry King. *Music:* Richard Rodgers, Oscar Hammerstein. Much-loved Rodgers & Hammerstein musical based on Ferenc Molnar's play *Liliom* (filmed by Fritz Lang in 1935)

about a swaggering carnival barker (MacRae) who tries to change his life after he falls in love with a good woman. Killed while attempting to foil a robbery he was supposed to help commit, he begs his heavenly hosts for the chance to return to the mortal realm just long enough to set things straight with his teenage daughter. Now indisputably a classic, the film lost $2 million when it was released.

Charade 🎬🎬🎬🎬
(1963)
Cast: Cary Grant, Audrey Hepburn, Walter Matthau, James Coburn, George Kennedy. *Director:* Stanley Donen. *Music:* Henry Mancini. After her husband is murdered, a young woman finds herself on the run from crooks and double agents who want the $250,000 her husband stole during WWII. Hepburn and Grant are charming and sophisticated, as usual, in this stylish intrigue filmed in Paris. Based on the story *The Unsuspecting Wife* by Marc Behm and Peter Stone.

Days of Wine and Roses 🎬🎬🎬🎬
(1962)
Cast: Jack Lemmon, Lee Remick, Charles Bickford, Jack Klugman, Jack Albertson. *Director:* Blake Edwards. *Music:* Henry Mancini, Johnny Mercer. A harrowing tale of an alcoholic advertising man who gradually drags his wife down with him into a life of booze. Part of the "A Night at the Movies" series, this tape simulates a 1962 movie evening with a Bugs Bunny cartoon ("Martian Through Georgia"), a newsreel, and coming attractions for *Gypsy* and *Rome Adventure.* Big screen adaptation of the play originally shown on television.

Diamonds Are Forever 🎬🎬🎬
(1971; PG)
Cast: Sean Connery, Jill St. John, Charles Gray, Bruce Cabot, Jimmy Dean, Lana Wood, Bruce Glover, Putter Smith, Norman Burton, Joseph Furst, Bernard Lee, Desmond Llewelyn, Laurence Naismith, Leonard Barr, Lois Maxwell, Margaret Lacey, Joe Robinson, Donna Garrat, Trina Parks. *Director:* Guy Hamilton. *Music:* John Barry. 007 once again battles his nemesis Blofeld, this time in Las Vegas. Bond must prevent the implementation of a plot to destroy Washington through the use of a space-orbiting laser. Fabulous stunts include Bond's wild drive through the streets of Vegas in a '71 Mach 1. Connery returned to play Bond in this film after being offered the then record-setting salary of one million dollars.

Dirty Harry 🎬🎬🎬🎬
(1971; R)
Cast: Clint Eastwood, Harry Guardino, John Larch, Andrew (Andy) Robinson, Reni Santoni, John Vernon. *Director:* Donald Siegel. *Music:* Lalo Schifrin. Rock-hard cop Harry Callahan attempts to track down a psychopathic rooftop killer before a kidnapped girl dies. Harry abuses the murderer's civil rights, however, forcing the police to return the criminal to the streets, where he hijacks a school bus and Harry is called on once again. The only answer to stop this vicious killer seems to be death in cold blood, and Harry is just the man to do it. Taut, suspenseful direction by Siegel, who thoroughly understands Eastwood's on-screen character. Features Callahan's famous "Do you feel lucky?" line, the precursor to his "Go ahead, make my day."

Doctor Dolittle 🎬🎬
(1967)
Cast: Rex Harrison, Samantha Eggar, Anthony Newley, Richard Attenborough, Geoffrey Holder, Peter Bull. *Director:* Richard Fleischer. *Music:* Leslie Bricusse. An adventure about a 19th-century English doctor who dreams of teaching animals to speak to him. Realistic premise suffers from poor script. Based on Hugh Lofting's acclaimed stories.

Dr. Goldfoot and the Bikini Machine 🎬🎬
(1966)
Cast: Vincent Price, Frankie Avalon, Dwayne Hickman, Annette Funicello, Susan Hart, Kay Elkhardt, Fred Clark, Deanna Lund, Deborah Walley. *Director:* Norman Taurog. *Music:* Les Baxter. A mad scientist employs gorgeous female robots to seduce the wealthy and powerful, thereby allowing him to take over the world. Title song by the Supremes.

Dr. No 🎬🎬🎬
(1962; PG)
Cast: Sean Connery, Ursula Andress, Joseph Wiseman, Jack Lord, Zena Marshall, Eunice Gayson, Margaret LeWars, John Kitzmiller, Lois Maxwell, Bernard Lee, Anthony Dawson. *Director:* Terence Young. *Music:* John Barry. The world is introduced to British secret agent 007, James Bond, when it is discovered that a mad scientist is sabotaging rocket launchings from his hideout in Jamaica. The first 007 film is far less glitzy than any of its successors, but boasts the sexiest "Bond girl" of them all in Andress, and promptly made stars of her and Connery. On laserdisc, the film is in widescreen transfer and includes movie bills, publicity photos, location pictures, and the British and American trail-

ers. The sound effects and musical score can be separated from the dialogue. Audio interviews with the director, writer, and editor are included as part of the disc.

Doctor Zhivago 🎬🎬🎬
(1965; PG-13)
Cast: Omar Sharif, Julie Christie, Geraldine Chaplin, Rod Steiger, Alec Guinness, Klaus Kinski, Ralph Richardson, Rita Tushingham, Siobhan McKenna, Tom Courtenay. *Director:* David Lean. *Music:* Maurice Jarre. Sweeping adaptation of the Nobel Prize–winning Boris Pasternak novel. An innocent Russian poet-intellectual is caught in the furor and chaos of the Bolshevik Revolution. Essentially a poignant love story filmed as a historical epic. Panoramic film popularized the song "Lara's Theme." Overlong, with often disappointing performances, but gorgeous scenery. Lean was more successful with *Lawrence of Arabia,* where there was less need for ensemble acting.

Easter Parade 🎬🎬🎬🎬
(1948)
Cast: Fred Astaire, Judy Garland, Peter Lawford, Ann Miller, Jules Munshin, Joi Lansing. *Director:* Charles Walters. *Music:* Irving Berlin. A big musical star (Astaire) splits with his partner (Miller), claiming that he could mold any girl to replace her in the act. He tries and finally succeeds after much difficulty. Astaire and Garland in peak form, aided by a classic Irving Berlin score.

Evita 🎬🎬🎬
(1996; PG)
Cast: Madonna, Antonio Banderas, Jonathan Pryce, Jimmy Nail, Victoria Sus, Julian Littman, Olga Meediz, Laura Pallas, Julia Worsley. *Director:* Alan Parker. *Music:* Andrew

Lloyd Webber, Tim Rice. Webber/Rice rock opera about the life and death of Eva Peron finally comes to the big screen with all its extravaganza intact. Madonna's in the title role (in fine voice, lavishly costumed but unflatteringly lit) about an ambitious poor girl willing to do anything to make her mark—in this version by sleeping her way up the ladder of power to Argentine strongman Juan Peron (Pryce as wax dummy). Evita becomes a would-be champion of the people, even as the government ruthlessly suppresses their freedoms. The surprisingly strong-voiced Banderas (perhaps his emphatic enunciation is to make his English as clear as possible) is everyman narrator Che (changed from the stage version's revolutionary Che Guevera). The highlight is still Madonna's balcony scene, singing "Don't Cry for Me, Argentina," but some of the other songs are drowned by loud orchestration. Director Parker has a cameo as a frustrated film director trying to work with Evita.

A Fistful of Dollars 🎵🎵🎵
(1964; R)
Cast: Clint Eastwood, Gian Marie Volonte, Marianne Koch. *Director:* Sergio Leone. *Music:* Ennio Morricone. The epitome of the "spaghetti Western" pits Eastwood as "the man with no name" against two families who are feuding over land. A remake of Akira Kurosawa's *Yojimbo*, and followed by Leone's *For a Few Dollars More* and *The Good, the Bad, and the Ugly.*

Follow the Boys 🎵🎵🎵
(1944)
Cast: George Raft, Vera Zorina, Grace McDonald, Charles Butterworth, Martha O'Driscoll, Charley Grapewin, Elizabeth

Patterson. *Director:* Edward Sutherland. *Music:* Jule Styne. Vaudeville performer Tony West (Raft) heads out to California to try his luck and gets a double break when he's noticed by leading lady Gloria Vance (Zorina). Not only does he become a star but he marries Gloria as well. When WWII breaks out Tony's turned down for military service, so he organizes camp shows for the soldiers. They're a big success, but misunderstandings have put his marriage in jeopardy. Plot's merely an excuse to have haute Hollywood (including Marlene Dietrich, Orson Welles, Jeanette MacDonald, and W.C. Fields) sing, dance, and tell jokes.

From Russia with Love 🎵🎵🎵🎵
(1963; PG)
Cast: Sean Connery, Daniela Bianchi, Pedro Armendariz Sr., Lotte Lenya, Robert Shaw, Eunice Gayson, Walter Gotell, Lois Maxwell, Bernard Lee, Desmond Llewelyn, Nadja Regin, Alizia Gur, Martine Beswick, Leila. *Director:* Terence Young. *Music:* John Barry. Bond is back and on the loose in exotic Istanbul looking for a super-secret coding machine. He's involved with a beautiful Russian spy and has the SPECTRE organization after him, including villainess Rosa Klebb (she of the killer shoe). Lots of exciting escapes, but not an over-reliance on the gadgetry of the later films. The second Bond feature, thought by many to be the best. The laserdisc edition includes interviews with director Terence Young and others on the creative staff. The musical score and special effects can be separated from the actors' dialogue. Also features publicity shots, American and British trailers, on-location photos, and movie posters.

Funny Face 🎵🎵🎵
(1957)
Cast: Fred Astaire, Audrey Hepburn, Kay Thompson, Suzy Parker. *Director:* Stanley Donen. *Music:* George Gershwin, Ira Gershwin. A musical satire on beatniks and the fashion scene also features the May–December romance between Astaire and the ever-lovely Hepburn. He is a high-fashion photographer (based on Richard Avedon); she is a Greenwich Village bookseller fond of shapeless, drab clothing. He decides to take her to Paris and show her what modeling's all about. The elegant musical score features classic Gershwin. The laserdisc includes the original theatrical trailer and is available in widescreen.

Funny Girl 🎵🎵🎵
(1968; G)
Cast: Barbra Streisand, Omar Sharif, Walter Pidgeon, Kay Medford, Anne Francis. *Director:* William Wyler. *Music:* Walter Scharf, Jule Styne. Follows the early career of comedian Fanny Brice, her rise to stardom with the Ziegfeld Follies, and her stormy romance with gambler Nick Arnstein in a fun and funny look at backstage music hall life in the early 1900s. Streisand's film debut followed her auspicious performance of the role on Broadway. Score was augmented by several tunes sung by Brice during her performances. Excellent performances from everyone, captured beautifully by Wyler in his musical film debut. Followed by *Funny Lady.*

Girl Crazy 🎵🎵🎵
(1943)
Cast: Mickey Rooney, Judy Garland, Nancy Walker, June Allyson. *Director:* Norman Taurog. *Music:* George Gershwin, Ira Gershwin. A wealthy young playboy is sent to an all-boys

school in Arizona to get his mind off girls. Once there, he still manages to fall for a local girl who can't stand the sight of him. The eighth film pairing for Rooney and Garland.

The Glenn Miller Story 🎵🎵🎵
(1954; G)
Cast: James Stewart, June Allyson, Harry (Henry) Morgan, Gene Krupa, Louis Armstrong, Ben Pollack. *Director:* Anthony Mann. *Music:* Henry Mancini. The music of the Big Band Era lives again in this warm biography of the legendary Glenn Miller, following his life from the late '20s to his untimely death in a WWII plane crash. Stewart's likeably convincing and even fakes the trombone playing well.

The Godfather 🎵🎵🎵🎵
(1972; R)
Cast: Marlon Brando, Al Pacino, Robert Duvall, James Caan, Diane Keaton, John Cazale, Talia Shire, Richard Conte, Richard Castellano, Abe Vigoda, Alex Rocco, Sterling Hayden, John Marley, Al Lettieri, Sofia Coppola, Al Martino, Morgana King. *Director:* Francis Ford Coppola. *Music:* Nino Rota. Coppola's award-winning adaptation of Mario Puzo's novel about a fictional Mafia family in the late 1940s. Revenge, envy, and parent-child conflict mix with the rituals of Italian mob life in America. Minutely detailed, with excellent performances by Pacino, Brando, and Caan as the violence-prone Sonny. Film debut of Coppola's daughter Sofia, the infant in the baptism scene, who returns in *Godfather III.* The horrific horse scene is an instant chiller. Indisputably an instant piece of American culture. Followed by two sequels.

Goldfinger 🎬🎬🎬
(1964; PG)

Cast: Sean Connery, Honor Blackman, Gert Frobe, Shirley Eaton, Tania Mallet, Harold Sakata, Cec Linder, Bernard Lee, Lois Maxwell, Desmond Llewelyn, Nadja Regin. *Director:* Guy Hamilton. *Music:* John Barry. Ian Fleming's James Bond, Agent 007, attempts to prevent international gold smuggler Goldfinger and his pilot Pussy Galore from robbing Fort Knox. Features villainous assistant Oddjob and his deadly bowler hat. The third in the series is perhaps the most popular. Shirley Bassey sings the theme song. The laserdisc edition includes audio interviews with the director, the writer, the editor, and the production designer; music and sound effects/dialogue separation; publicity stills, movie posters, trailers, and on-location photos. A treat for Bond fans.

Good Neighbor Sam 🎬🎬🎬
(1964)

Cast: Jack Lemmon, Romy Schneider, Dorothy Provine, Mike Connors, Edward G. Robinson, Joyce Jameson. *Director:* David Swift. *Music:* Frank DeVol. A married advertising executive (Lemmon) agrees to pose as a friend's husband in order for her to collect a multimillion-dollar inheritance. Complications ensue when his biggest client mistakes the friend for his actual wife and decides they're the perfect couple to promote his wholesome product—milk.

The Good, the Bad, and the Ugly 🎬🎬🎬🎬
(1967)

Cast: Clint Eastwood, Eli Wallach, Lee Van Cleef, Chelo Alonso, Luigi Pistilli. *Director:* Sergio Leone. *Music:* Ennio Morricone. Leone's grandiloquent, shambling tribute to the American Western. Set during the Civil War, it follows the seemingly endless adventures of three dirtbags in search of a cache of Confederate gold buried in a nameless grave. Violent, exaggerated, beautifully crafted, it is the final and finest installment of the *Dollars* trilogy: a spaghetti Western chef d'oeuvre.

Guys and Dolls 🎬🎬🎬
(1955)

Cast: Marlon Brando, Jean Simmons, Frank Sinatra, Vivian Blaine, Stubby Kaye, Sheldon Leonard, Veda Ann Borg. *Director:* Joseph L. Mankiewicz. *Music:* Frank Loesser. New York gambler Sky Masterson takes a bet that he can romance a Salvation Army lady. Based on the stories of Damon Runyon with Blaine, Kaye, Pully, and Silver recreating their roles from the Broadway hit. Brando's not-always-convincing musical debut.

The Harvey Girls 🎬🎬🎬
(1946)

Cast: Judy Garland, Ray Bolger, John Hodiak, Preston Foster, Angela Lansbury, Virginia O'Brien, Marjorie Main, Chill Wills, Kenny L. Baker, Selena Royle, Cyd Charisse. *Director:* George Sidney. *Music:* Johnny Mercer, Harry Warren. Lightweight musical about a restaurant chain that sends its waitresses to work in the Old West.

Hello, Dolly! 🎬🎬
(1969; G)

Cast: Barbra Streisand, Walter Matthau, Michael Crawford, Louis Armstrong, E.J. Peaker, Marianne McAndrew, Tommy Tune. *Director:* Gene Kelly. *Music:* Jerry Herman. Widow Dolly Levi, while matchmaking for her friends, finds a match for herself. Based on the hugely successful Broadway musical adapted from Thornton Wilder's play *Matchmaker*. Lightweight story needs better actors with stronger characterizations. Original Broadway score helps.

High Society 🎬🎬🎬
(1956)

Cast: Frank Sinatra, Bing Crosby, Grace Kelly, Louis Armstrong, Celeste Holm, Sidney Blackmer, Louis Calhern. *Director:* Charles Walters. *Music:* Cole Porter. A wealthy man attempts to win back his ex-wife, who's about to be remarried, in this enjoyable remake of *The Philadelphia Story*. Letterboxed laserdisc format also includes the original movie trailer.

Higher and Higher 🎬🎬
(1944)

Cast: Frank Sinatra, Leon Errol, Michele Morgan, Jack Haley, Mary McGuire. *Director:* Tim Whelan. *Music:* C. Bakaleinikoff, Jimmy McHugh. Bankrupt aristocrat conspires with servants to regain his fortune, and tries to marry his daughter into money. Sinatra's first big-screen role.

Holiday Inn 🎬🎬🎬
(1942)

Cast: Bing Crosby, Fred Astaire, Marjorie Reynolds, Walter Abel, Virginia Dale. *Director:* Mark Sandrich. *Music:* Irving Berlin. Fred Astaire and Bing Crosby are rival song-and-dance men who decide to work together to turn a Connecticut farm into an inn, open only on holidays. Remade in 1954 as *White Christmas*.

How to Stuff a Wild Bikini 🎬🎬
(1965)

Cast: Annette Funicello, Dwayne Hickman, Frankie Avalon, Beverly Adams, Buster Keaton, Harvey Lembeck, Mickey Rooney, Brian Donlevy, Jody McCrea, John Ashley, Marianne Gaba, Len Lesser, Irene Tsu, Bobbi Shaw, Luree Holmes. *Director:* William Asher. *Music:* Les Baxter. Tired next-to-last feature in the overlong tradition of Frankie and Annette doing the beach thing, featuring a pregnant Funicello (though this is hidden and not part of the plot). Avalon actually has only a small role as the jealous boyfriend trying to see if Annette will remain faithful while he's away on military duty. Keaton is the witch doctor who helps Frankie keep Annette true. *Playboy* playmates wander about in small swimsuits, garage band extraordinare "The Kingsmen" play themselves, and Brian Wilson of the Beach Boys drops by. Followed by *Ghost in the Invisible Bikini*, the only movie in the series that isn't on video.

The Jazz Singer woof!
(1980; PG)

Cast: Neil Diamond, Laurence Olivier, Lucie Arnaz, Catlin Adams, Franklin Ajaye. *Director:* Richard Fleischer. *Music:* Leonard Rosenman. Flat and uninteresting (if not unintentionally funny) remake of the 1927 classic about a Jewish boy who rebels against his father and family tradition to become a popular entertainer. Stick with the original; this is little more than a vehicle for Diamond to sing.

The Jungle Book 🎬🎬🎬
(1967)

Voices: Phil Harris, Sebastian Cabot, Louis Prima, George Sanders, Sterling Holloway, J. Pat O'Malley, Verna Felton, Darlene Carr. *Director:* Wolfgang Reitherman. *Music:* George Bruns. Based on Kipling's classic, a young boy raised by wolves must choose between his jungle friends and human "civilization." Along the way he meets a variety of jungle characters, including zany King Louie, kind-hearted Baloo, wise Bagherra, and the evil Shere Khan. Great classic songs, including "Trust in Me," "I Wanna Be Like You," and the Oscar-nominated "Bare Necessities." Last Disney feature overseen by Uncle Walt himself and a must for kids of all ages.

Klondike Annie 🎵🎵🎵
(1936)
Cast: Mae West, Victor McLaglen, Philip Reed, Helen Jerome Eddy, Harold Huber, Conway Tearle, Esther Howard, Harry Beresford. *Director:* Raoul Walsh. West stars as a woman on the lam for a murder (self-defense) who heads out for the Yukon aboard McLaglen's ship. He falls for her, finds out about her problems, and helps her with a scam to pass herself off as a missionary, only she begins to take her saving souls seriously (although in her own risque style).

La Dolce Vita 🎵🎵🎵🎵
(1960)
Cast: Marcello Mastroianni, Anita Ekberg, Anouk Aimee, Alain Cuny, Lex Barker, Yvonne Furneaux, Barbara Steele, Nadia Gray, Magali Noel, Walter Santesso, Jacques Sernas, Annibale Ninchi. *Director:* Federico Fellini. *Music:* Nino Rota. In this influential and popular work a successful, sensationalistic Italian journalist covers the showbiz life in Rome, and alternately covets and disdains its glitzy shallowness. The film follows his dealings with the "sweet life" over a pivotal week. A surreal, comic tableaux with award-winning costuming; one of Fellini's most acclaimed films. In this film Fellini called his celebrity-hungry photographers the Paparazzo—and it is the "paparazzi" they have been ever

since. In Italian with English subtitles.

Love Story 🎵🎵🎵
(1970; PG)
Cast: Ryan O'Neal, Ali MacGraw, Ray Milland, John Marley, Tommy Lee Jones. *Director:* Arthur Hiller. *Music:* Francis Lai. Melodrama had enormous popular appeal. O'Neal is the son of Boston's upper crust at Harvard; MacGraw's the daughter of a poor Italian on scholarship to study music at Radcliffe. They find happiness, but only for a brief period. Timeless story, simply told, with artful direction from Hiller pulling exceptional performances from the young duo (who have never done as well since). The end result is perhaps better than Erich Segal's simplistic novel, which was produced after he sold the screenplay and became a best-seller before the picture's release—great publicity for any film. Remember: "Love means never having to say you're sorry."

The Magnificent Seven 🎵🎵🎵🎵
(1960)
Cast: Yul Brynner, Steve McQueen, Robert Vaughn, James Coburn, Charles Bronson, Horst Buchholz, Eli Wallach, Brad Dexter. *Director:* John Sturges. *Music:* Elmer Bernstein. Western remake of Akira Kurosawa's classic *The Seven Samurai*. Mexican villagers hire gunmen to protect them from the bandits who are destroying their town. Most of the actors were relative unknowns, though not for long. Sequelled by *Return of the Seven* in 1966, *Guns of the Magnificent Seven* in 1969, and *The Magnificent Seven Ride* in 1972. Excellent score. Uncredited writing by Walter Newman and Walter Bernstein.

A Man and a Woman 🎵🎵🎵
(1966)
Cast: Anouk Aimee, Jean-Louis Trintignant, Pierre Barouh, Valerie Lagrange. *Director:* Claude Lelouch. *Music:* Francis Lai. A man and a woman, both widowed, meet and become interested in one another but experience difficulties in putting their past loves behind them. Intelligently handled emotional conflicts within a well-acted romantic drama, acclaimed for excellent visual detail. Remade in 1977 as *Another Man, Another Chance*. Followed in 1986 with *A Man and a Woman: 20 Years Later*.

The Man with the Golden Arm 🎵🎵🎵
(1955)
Cast: Frank Sinatra, Kim Novak, Eleanor Parker, Arnold Stang, Darren McGavin, Robert Strauss, George Mathews, John Conte, Doro Merande. *Director:* Otto Preminger. *Music:* Elmer Bernstein. A gripping film version of the Nelson Algren junkie melodrama, about an ex-addict who returns to town only to get mixed up with drugs again. Considered controversial in its depiction of addiction when released. Sinatra's performance as Frankie Machine is a stand-out.

Meet Me in St. Louis 🎵🎵🎵🎵
(1944)
Cast: Judy Garland, Margaret O'Brien, Mary Astor, Lucille Bremer, Tom Drake, June Lockhart, Harry Davenport. *Director:* Vincente Minnelli. *Music:* Ralph Blane, Hugh Martin, George E. Stoll. Wonderful music in this charming tale of a St. Louis family during the 1903 World's Fair. One of Garland's better musical performances.

Morocco 🎵🎵🎵🎵
(1930)
Cast: Marlene Dietrich, Gary Cooper, Adolphe Menjou, Ullrich Haupt, Francis McDonald, Eve Southern, Paul Porcasi. *Director:* Josef von Sternberg. *Music:* Karl Hajos. A foreign legion soldier falls for a world-weary chanteuse along the desert sands. Cooper has never been more earnest, and Dietrich has never been more blase and exotic. In her American film debut, Dietrich sings "What Am I Bid?" A must for anyone drawn to improbable, gloriously well-done kitsch. Based on Benno Vigny's novel, *Amy Jolly*.

Murderers' Row 🎵🎵
(1966)
Cast: Dean Martin, Ann-Margret, Karl Malden, Beverly Adams, James Gregory. *Director:* Henry Levin. *Music:* Lalo Schifrin. Daredevil bachelor and former counter-espionage agent Matt Helm is summoned from his life of leisure to ensure the safety of an important scientist. Martin's attempt as a super-spy doesn't wash, and Margret is implausible as the kidnapped scientist's daughter. Unless you want to hear Martin sing "I'm Not the Marrying Kind," don't bother. Second in the *Matt Helm* series.

Muriel's Wedding 🎵🎵🎵
(1994; R)
Cast: Toni Collette, Bill Hunter, Rachel Griffiths, Jeanie Drynan, Gennie Nevinson Brice, Matt Day, Daniel Lapaine. *Director:* P.J. Hogan. *Music:* Peter Best. Muriel (Collette) can catch a bridal bouquet, but can she catch a husband? Her blonde, bitch-goddess friends don't think so. But dowdy, pathetic, overweight Muriel dreams of a fairy tale wedding anyway. How she fulfills her obsessive fantasy is

the basis for this quirky, hilarious, and often touchingly poignant ugly duckling tale with the occasional over-the-top satiric moment. Strong cast is led by sympathetic and engaging performances from Collette (who gained 40-plus pounds for the role) and Griffiths as her best friend, Rhonda. '70s pop supergroup ABBA lends its kitschy but catchy tunes to the plot and soundtrack. Not released in the U.S. until 1995.

The Nat "King" Cole Story ♫♫♫

(1955)
Cast: Nat "King" Cole, Nipsey Russell, Mantan Moreland. *Director:* Will Cowan. Nat "King" Cole stars in this short documentary about his life, from saloon pianist to recording artist. Songs include "Sweet Lorraine," "Pretend," and "Straighten Up and Fly Right."

The Nightmare Before Christmas ♫♫♫

(1993; PG)
Voices: Danny Elfman, Chris Sarandon, Catherine O'Hara, William Hickey, Ken Page, Ed Ivory, Paul (Pee-wee Herman) Reubens, Glenn Shadix. *Director:* Henry Selick. *Music:* Danny Elfman. Back when he was a animator trainee at Disney, Burton came up with this adventurous idea but couldn't get it made; subsequent directorial success brought more clout. Relies on a painstaking stop-motion technique that took more than two years to film and is justifiably amazing. The story revolves around Jack Skellington, the Pumpkin King of the dangerously weird Halloweentown. Suffering from ennui, he accidentally discovers the wonders of Christmastown and decides to kidnap Santa and rule over this peaceable holiday. Fast pace is maintained

by the equally breathless score. Not cuddly, best appreciated by those with a feel for the macabre.

The Nutty Professor ♫♫♫

(1963)
Cast: Jerry Lewis, Stella Stevens, Howard Morris, Kathleen Freeman. *Director:* Jerry Lewis. *Music:* Walter Scharf. A mild-mannered chemistry professor creates a potion that turns him into a suave, debonair, playboy type with an irresistible attraction to women. Lewis has repeatedly denied the slick character is a Dean Martin parody, but the evidence is quite strong. Easily Lewis's best film.

Ocean's Eleven ♫♫♫

(1960)
Cast: Frank Sinatra, Dean Martin, Sammy Davis Jr., Angie Dickinson, Peter Lawford. *Director:* Lewis Milestone. *Music:* Nelson Riddle, James Van Heusen. A gang of friends plans to rob five Las Vegas casinos simultaneously. Part of the "A Night at the Movies" series, this tape simulates a 1960 movie evening, with a Bugs Bunny cartoon ("Person to Bunny"), a newsreel, and coming attractions for *The Sundowners* and *Sunrise at Campobello.*

Oklahoma! ♫♫♫♫

(1955; G)
Cast: Gordon MacRae, Shirley Jones, Rod Steiger, Gloria Grahame, Eddie Albert, Charlotte Greenwood, James Whitmore, Gene Nelson, Barbara Lawrence, Jay C. Flippen. *Director:* Fred Zinnemann. *Music:* Richard Rodgers, Oscar Hammerstein. Jones's film debut; a must-see for musical fans. A cowboy and country girl fall in love, but she is tormented by another unwelcomed suitor. At over two hours, cuteness wears thin for

some. Actually filmed in Arizona. Adapted from Rodgers and Hammerstein's broadway hit with original score; choreography by Agnes de Mille.

Oliver! ♫♫♫♫

(1968; G)
Cast: Mark Lester, Jack Wild, Ron Moody, Shani Wallis, Oliver Reed, Hugh Griffith. *Director:* Carol Reed. *Music:* Lionel Bart, Johnny Green. Splendid big-budget musical adaptation of Dickens's *Oliver Twist.* An innocent orphan is dragged into a life of crime when he is befriended by a gang of pickpockets.

Orchestra Wives ♫♫♫

(1942)
Cast: George Montgomery, Glenn Miller, Lynn Bari, Carole Landis, Jackie Gleason, Cesar Romero, Ann Rutherford, Virginia Gilmore, Mary Beth Hughes, Harry (Henry) Morgan. *Director:* Archie Mayo. *Music:* Mack Gordon, Alfred Newman, Harry Warren. A drama bursting with wonderful Glenn Miller music. A woman marries a musician and goes on the road with the band and the other wives. Trouble springs up with the sultry singer who desperately wants the woman's new husband. The commotion spreads throughout the group.

Pee-wee's Big Adventure ♫♫♫♫

(1985; PG)
Cast: Paul (Pee-wee Herman) Reubens, Elizabeth Daily, Mark Holton, Diane Salinger, Judd Omen, Cassandra Peterson, James Brolin, Morgan Fairchild, Tony Bill, Jan Hooks. *Director:* Tim Burton. *Music:* Danny Elfman. Zany, endearing comedy about an adult nerd's many adventures while attempting to recover his stolen bicycle. Chock full of classic sequences, including a

barroom encounter between Pee-wee and several ornery bikers and a tour through the Alamo. A colorful, exhilarating experience.

Pete Kelly's Blues ♫♫

(1955)
Cast: Jack Webb, Janet Leigh, Edmond O'Brien, Lee Marvin, Martin Milner, Peggy Lee, Ella Fitzgerald, Jayne Mansfield. *Director:* Jack Webb. *Music:* Arthur Hamilton, Ray Heindorf. A jazz musician in a Kansas City speakeasy is forced to stand up against a brutal racketeer. The melodramatic plot is brightened by a nonstop flow of jazz tunes sung by Lee and Fitzgerald and played by an all-star lineup that includes Dick Cathcart, Matty Matlock, Eddie Miller, and George Van Eps.

The Pink Panther ♫♫♫

(1964)
Cast: Peter Sellers, David Niven, Robert Wagner, Claudia Cardinale, Capucine, Brenda de Banzie. *Director:* Blake Edwards. *Music:* Henry Mancini. Bumbling, disaster-prone inspector invades a Swiss ski resort and becomes obsessed with capturing a jewel thief hoping to lift the legendary "Pink Panther" diamond. Said thief is also the inspector's wife's lover, though the inspector doesn't know it. Slick slapstick succeeds on strength of Sellers's classic portrayal of Clouseau, who accidentally destroys everything in his path while speaking in a funny French accent. Followed by *A Shot in the Dark, Inspector Clouseau* (without Sellers), *The Return of the Pink Panther, The Pink Panther Strikes Again, Revenge of the Pink Panther, Trail of the Pink Panther,* and *Curse of the Pink Panther.* Memorable theme supplied by Mancini.

Red Garters 🎤🎤🎤
(1954)
Cast: Guy Mitchell, Rosemary Clooney, Jack Carson, Gene Barry, Pat Crowley, Joanne Gilbert, Frank Faylen, Reginald Owen, Buddy Ebsen. *Director:* George Marshall. *Music:* Jay Livingston, Ray Evans. A musical parody of old-time Westerns which doesn't quite come off. Mitchell plays the cowpoke who comes to town to avenge the death of his brother, with Clooney as the saloon singer who uses him to make boyfriend Carson jealous. The adequate songs include "Red Garters," "Man and Woman," "A Dime and a Dollar," and "Vaquero."

Robin and the Seven Hoods 🎤🎤🎤
(1964)
Cast: Frank Sinatra, Bing Crosby, Dean Martin, Sammy Davis Jr., Peter Falk, Barbara Rush, Allen Jenkins. *Director:* Gordon Douglas. *Music:* Nelson Riddle, James Van Heusen. Runyon-esque Rat Pack version of 1920s Chicago, with Frank and the boys as do-good gangsters in their last go-round. Fun if not unforgettable.

The Rose 🎤🎤🎤
(1979; R)
Cast: Bette Midler, Alan Bates, Frederic Forrest, Harry Dean Stanton, David Keith. *Director:* Mark Rydell. *Music:* Amanda McBroom. Modeled after the life of Janis Joplin, Midler plays a young, talented, and self-destructive blues/rock singer. Professional triumphs don't stop her lonely restlessness and confused love affairs. The best exhibition of the rock and roll world outside of documentaries. Electrifying film debut for Midler features an incredible collection of songs.

Shaft 🎤🎤🎤
(1971; R)
Cast: Richard Roundtree, Moses Gunn, Charles Cioffi. *Director:* Gordon Parks. *Music:* Isaac Hayes. A black private eye is hired to find a Harlem gangster's kidnapped daughter. Lots of sex and violence; suspenseful and well directed. Great ending. Academy Award–winning theme song by Isaac Hayes, the first music award from the Academy to an African American. Adapted from the novel by Ernest Tidyman. Followed by *Shaft's Big Score* and *Shaft in Africa*.

Silk Stockings 🎤🎤🎤
(1957)
Cast: Fred Astaire, Cyd Charisse, Janis Paige, Peter Lorre, George Tobias. *Director:* Rouben Mamoulian. *Music:* Cole Porter. Splendid musical comedy adaptation of *Ninotchka*, with Astaire as a charming American movie man, and Charisse as the cold Soviet official whose commie heart he melts. Music and lyrics by Cole Porter highlight this film adapted from George S. Kaufman's hit Broadway play. Director Mamoulian's last film.

Singin' in the Rain 🎤🎤🎤🎤
(1952)
Cast: Gene Kelly, Donald O'Connor, Jean Hagen, Debbie Reynolds, Rita Moreno, King Donovan, Millard Mitchell, Cyd Charisse, Douglas Fowley, Madge Blake, Joi Lansing. *Director:* Stanley Donen. *Music:* Nacio Herb Brown, Arthur Freed, Lennie Hayton. One of the all-time great movie musicals—an affectionate spoof of the turmoil that afflicted the motion picture industry in the late 1920s during the change-over from silent films to sound. Co-director Kelly and Hagen lead a glorious cast. Served as basis of story by Betty Comden and Adolph Green. Also available on laserdisc with the original trailer, outtakes, behind the scenes footage, and commentary by film historian Ronald Haver. Later a Broadway musical.

The Sound of Music 🎤🎤🎤🎤
(1965)
Cast: Julie Andrews, Christopher Plummer, Eleanor Parker, Peggy Wood, Charmian Carr, Heather Menzies, Marni Nixon, Richard Haydn, Anna Lee, Norma Varden, Nicholas Hammond, Angela Cartwright, Portia Nelson, Duane Chase, Debbie Turner, Kym Karath. *Director:* Robert Wise. *Music:* Richard Rodgers, Oscar Hammerstein. The classic film version of the Rodgers and Hammerstein musical based on the true story of the singing von Trapp family of Austria and their escape from the Nazis just before WWII. Beautiful Salzburg, Austria, location photography and an excellent cast. Andrews, fresh from her Oscar for *Mary Poppins,* is effervescent, in beautiful voice, but occasionally too good to be true. Not Rodgers and Hammerstein's most innovative score, but lovely to hear and see. Plummer's singing was dubbed by Bill Lee. Marni Nixon, behind-the-scenes songstress for *West Side Story* and *My Fair Lady,* makes her on-screen debut as one of the nuns.

South Pacific 🎤🎤🎤🎤
(1958)
Cast: Mitzi Gaynor, Rossano Brazzi, Ray Walston, France Nuyen, John Kerr, Juanita Hall, Tom Laughlin. *Director:* Joshua Logan. *Music:* Richard Rodgers, Oscar Hammerstein. A young American Navy nurse and a Frenchman fall in love during WWII. Expensive production included much location shooting in Hawaii. Based on Rodgers and Hammerstein's musical; not as good as the play, but pretty darned good still. The play in turn was based on James Michener's novel *Tales of the South Pacific.*

Speedway 🎤🎤
(1968; G)
Cast: Elvis Presley, Nancy Sinatra, Bill Bixby, Gale Gordon, William Schallert, Carl Ballantine, Ross Hagen, Richard Petty, Cale Yarborough, Teri Garr. *Director:* Norman Taurog. *Music:* Jeff Alexander. Elvis the stock car driver finds himself being chased by Nancy the IRS agent during an important race. Will Sinatra keep to the business at hand? Or will the King melt her heart? Some cameos by real-life auto racers. Watch for a young Garr. Movie number 27 for Elvis.

A Star Is Born 🎤🎤🎤🎤
(1954; PG)
Cast: Judy Garland, James Mason, Jack Carson, Tommy Noonan, Charles Bickford, Emerson Treacy, Charles Halton. *Director:* George Cukor. *Music:* Harold Arlen, Ira Gershwin, Ray Heindorf. Aging actor helps a young actress to fame. She becomes his wife, but alcoholism and failure are too much for him. She honors his memory. Remake of the 1937 classic was Garland's triumph, a superb and varied performance. Newly restored version reinstates over 20 minutes of long-missing footage, including three Garland musical numbers.

A Star Is Born 🎤🎤
(1976; R)
Cast: Barbra Streisand, Kris Kristofferson, Paul Mazursky, Gary Busey, Sally Kirkland, Oliver Clark, Marta Heflin, Robert Englund. *Director:* Frank Pierson. *Music:* Paul Williams, Barbra Streisand, Kenny Ascher, Roger Kellaway. Miserable

update of the 1937 and 1954 classics permitting Ms. Streisand to showcase her hit song "Evergreen." The tragic story of one rock star (the relentlessly un-hip Streisand) on her way to the top and another (good old boy Kristofferson) whose career is in decline. Kristofferson is miscast, Streisand eventually numbing, but the film may interest those looking into big-budget, big-star misfires.

Stormy Weather 🎵🎵🎵

(1943)
Cast: Lena Horne, Bill Robinson, Fats Waller, Dooley Wilson, Cab Calloway, Nicholas Brothers. *Director:* Andrew L. Stone. In this cavalcade of black entertainment, the plot takes a backseat to the nearly non-stop array of musical numbers, showcasing this stellar cast at their performing peak.

Sun Valley Serenade 🎵🎵🎵

(1941)
Cast: Sonja Henie, John Payne, Glenn Miller, Milton Berle, Lynn Bari, Joan Davis, Dorothy Dandridge. *Director:* H. Bruce Humberstone. *Music:* Mack Gordon, Emil Newman, Harry Warren. Wartime musical fluff about a band that adopts a Norwegian refugee waif as a publicity stunt. She turns out to be a full-grown man-chaser who stirs up things at a ski resort. Fun, but it ends abruptly—because, they say, Henie fell during the huge skating finale, and Darryl Zanuck wouldn't greenlight a reshoot. One of only two feature appearances by Glenn Miller and his Orchestra (the other was *Orchestra Wives*), on video with a soundtrack restored from original dual-track recordings.

Swingers 🎵🎵🎵

(1996; R)
Cast: Jon Favreau, Vince Vaughn, Ron Livingston, Patrick Van Horn, Alex Desert, Brooke Langton, Heather Graham, Deena Martin, Katherine Kendall, Blake Lindsley. *Director:* Doug Liman. *Music:* Justin Reinhardt. Hip, hilarious, and highly entertaining low-budget comedy features five young showbiz wannabes on the prowl for career breaks and beautiful "babies" in the Hollywood retro club scene. Mike (screenwriter Favreau) is a struggling actor/comedian from New York who's having trouble getting over his ex. His slick, handsome friend Trent (Vaughn, in a star-making turn) and the rest of his neo-Rat Pack buddies try to get him back in the game with nightly parties and lounge-hopping. Witty script and clever camera work make this one "money, baby, money!"

10 🎵🎵🎵

(1979; R)
Cast: Dudley Moore, Julie Andrews, Bo Derek, Dee Wallace Stone, Brian Dennehy, Robert Webber. *Director:* Blake Edwards. *Music:* Henry Mancini. A successful songwriter who has everything finds his life is incomplete without the woman of his dreams, the 10 on his girl-watching scale. His pursuit brings surprising results. Also popularizes Ravel's "Bolero."

Thoroughly Modern Millie 🎵🎵🎵

(1967; G)
Cast: Julie Andrews, Carol Channing, Mary Tyler Moore, John Gavin, Beatrice Lillie, James Fox, Noriyuki "Pat" Morita. *Director:* George Roy Hill. *Music:* Elmer Bernstein. Andrews is a young woman who comes to New York in the early 1920s and meets an-

other newcomer, the innocent Moore. Andrews decides to upgrade her image to that of a "modern" woman, a flapper, and sets out to realize her ambition, to become a stenographer and marry the boss. Meanwhile, Moore has become an object of interest to Lillie, who just happens to run a white-slavery ring. Lots of frantic moments and big production numbers in this campy film. Channing and Lillie are exceptional fun.

Too Many Girls 🎵🎵🎵

(1940)
Cast: Lucille Ball, Richard Carlson, Eddie Bracken, Ann Miller, Desi Arnaz Sr., Hal LeRoy, Libby Bennett, Frances Langford, Van Johnson. *Director:* George Abbott. *Music:* Richard Rodgers, Lorenz Hart, George Bassman. Beautiful heiress goes to a small New Mexico college to escape from a cadre of gold-digging suitors. Passable adaptation of the successful Rodgers and Hart Broadway show, with many original cast members and the original stage director. Lucy and Desi met while making this film, and married shortly after.

Touch of Evil 🎵🎵🎵🎵

(1958)
Cast: Charlton Heston, Janet Leigh, Joseph Calleia, Akim Tamiroff, Marlene Dietrich, Valentin de Vargas, Dennis Weaver, Zsa Zsa Gabor, Mort Mills, Victor Milian, Joanna Moore, Joi Lansing, Ray Collins, Mercedes McCambridge, Joseph Cotten. *Director:* Orson Welles. *Music:* Henry Mancini. Stark, perverse story of murder, kidnapping, and police corruption in Mexican border town. Welles portrays a police chief who invents evidence to convict the guilty. Filled with innovative photography reminiscent of

Citizen Kane, as filmed by Russell Metty.

Twin Peaks: Fire Walk with Me 🎵🎵

(1992; R)
Cast: Sheryl Lee, Moira Kelly, David Bowie, Chris Isaak, Harry Dean Stanton, Kyle MacLachlan, Ray Wise, Dana Ashbrook, Kiefer Sutherland, Peggy Lipton, James Marshall. *Director:* David Lynch. *Music:* Angelo Badalamenti. Prequel to the cult TV series is weird and frustrating, chronicling the week before Laura Palmer's death. Suspense is lacking since we know the outcome, but Lynch manages to intrigue with dream-like sequences and interestingly offbeat characters. On the other hand, it's exploitative and violent enough to alienate series fans. Includes extremely brief and baffling cameos by Bowie as an FBI agent and Stanton as the manager of a trailer park. Several of the show's regulars are missing, and others appear and disappear very quickly. On the plus side are the strains of Badalamenti's famous theme music and Isaak as an FBI agent with amazingly acute powers of observation.

Two Weeks with Love 🎵🎵

(1950)
Cast: Debbie Reynolds, Jane Powell, Ricardo Montalban, Louis Calhern, Ann Harding, Phyllis Kirk, Carleton Carpenter, Clinton Sundberg, Gary Gray. *Director:* Roy Rowland. Reynolds and family wear funny bathing suits in the Catskills in the early 1900s while the Debster sings songs and blushes into young adulthood.

The Unsinkable Molly Brown 🎵🎵🎵

(1964)
Cast: Debbie Reynolds, Harve Presnell, Ed Begley Sr., Mar-

tita Hunt, Hermione Baddeley. *Director:* Charles Walters. *Music:* Meredith Willson. A spunky backwoods girl is determined to break into the upper crust of Denver's high society and along the way survives the sinking of the Titanic. This energetic version of the Broadway musical contains many Meredith Willson (*Music Man*) songs and lots of hokey, good-natured fun.

Victor/Victoria 🎵🎵🎵
(1982; PG)

Cast: Julie Andrews, James Garner, Robert Preston, Lesley Ann Warren, Alex Karras, John Rhys-Davies. *Director:* Blake Edwards. *Music:* Henry Mancini. An unsuccessful actress in Depression-era Paris impersonates a man impersonating a woman and becomes a star. Luscious music and sets. Warren as femme fatale and Preston as Andrews's gay mentor are right on target; Garner is charming as the gangster who falls for the woman he thinks she is.

Viva Las Vegas 🎵🎵🎵
(1963)

Cast: Elvis Presley, Ann-Margret, William Demarest, Jack Carter, Cesare Danova, Nicky Blair, Larry Kent. *Director:* George Sidney. *Music:* George E. Stoll. Race car driver Elvis needs money to compete against rival Danova in the upcoming Las Vegas Grand Prix. He takes a job in a casino and romances fellow employee Ann-Margret, who turns out to be his rival for the grand prize in the local talent competition. Good pairing between the two leads, and the King does particularly well with the title song.

The Way We Were 🎵🎵🎵
(1973; PG)

Cast: Barbra Streisand, Robert Redford, Bradford Dillman,

Viveca Lindfors, Herb Edelman, Murray Hamilton, Patrick O'Neal, James Woods, Sally Kirkland. *Director:* Sydney Pollack. *Music:* Marvin Hamlisch. Big box-office hit follows a love story between opposites from the 1930s to the 1950s. Streisand is a Jewish political radical who meets the handsome WASP Redford at college. They're immediately attracted to one another, but it takes years before they act on it and eventually marry. They move to Hollywood where Redford is a screenwriter and left-wing Streisand becomes involved in the Red scare and the blacklist, much to Redford's dismay. Though always in love, their differences are too great to keep them together. An old-fashioned and sweet romance, with much gloss. Hit title song sung by Streisand. Adapted by Arthur Laurents from his novel.

What's New Pussycat? 🎵🎵🎵
(1965)

Cast: Peter Sellers, Peter O'Toole, Romy Schneider, Paula Prentiss, Woody Allen, Ursula Andress, Capucine. *Director:* Clive Donner. *Music:* Burt Bacharach, Hal David. A young engaged man, reluctant to give up the girls who love him, seeks the aid of a married psychiatrist who turns out to have problems of his own. Allen's first feature as both actor and screenwriter. Oscar-nominated title song sung by Tom Jones.

When Harry Met Sally . . . 🎵🎵🎵
(1989; R)

Cast: Billy Crystal, Meg Ryan, Carrie Fisher, Bruno Kirby, Steven Ford, Lisa Jane Persky, Michelle Nicastro, Harley Jane Kozak. *Director:* Rob Reiner. *Music:* Harry Connick Jr., Marc Shaiman. Romantic comedy follows the long relationship

between two adults who try throughout the changes in their lives (and their mates) to remain platonic friends — and what happens when they don't. Wry and enjoyable script is enhanced by wonderful performances. Another directorial direct hit for "Meathead" Reiner, and a tour de force of comic screenwriting for Nora Ephron, with improvisational help from Crystal. Great songs by Sinatra wannabe Connick.

Where the Boys Are 🎵🎵🎵
(1960)

Cast: George Hamilton, Jim Hutton, Yvette Mimieux, Connie Francis, Paula Prentiss, Dolores Hart. *Director:* Henry Levin. *Music:* George E. Stoll. Four college girls go to Fort Lauderdale to have fun and meet boys during their Easter vacation. Features the film debuts of Francis, who had a hit single with the film's title song, and Prentiss. Head and shoulders above the ludicrous '84 remake.

White Christmas 🎵🎵🎵
(1954)

Cast: Bing Crosby, Danny Kaye, Rosemary Clooney, Vera-Ellen, Dean Jagger. *Director:* Michael Curtiz. *Music:* Irving Berlin. Two ex-army buddies become a popular comedy team and play at a financially unstable Vermont inn at Christmas for charity's sake. Many swell Irving Berlin songs rendered with zest. Paramount's first Vista Vision film. Presented in widescreen on laserdisc.

Willy Wonka and the Chocolate Factory 🎵🎵🎵
(1971; G)

Cast: Gene Wilder, Jack Albertson, Denise Nickerson, Peter Ostrum, Roy Kinnear, Aubrey Woods, Michael Bollner, Ursula Reit, Leonard Stone,

Dodo Denney. *Director:* Mel Stuart. *Music:* Leslie Bricusse. When the last of five coveted "golden tickets" falls into the hands of sweet but very poor Charlie, he and his Grandpa Joe get a tour of the most wonderfully strange chocolate factory in the world. The owner is the most curious hermit ever to hit the big screen. He leads the five young "winners" on a thrilling and often dangerous tour of his fabulous factory. Adapted from Roald Dahl's *Charlie and the Chocolate Factory*. Without a doubt one of the best "kid's" movies ever made; a family classic worth watching again and again.

The Wizard of Oz 🎵🎵🎵🎵
(1939)

Cast: Judy Garland, Margaret Hamilton, Ray Bolger, Jack Haley, Bert Lahr, Frank Morgan, Charley Grapewin, Clara Blandick, Mitchell Lewis, Billie Burke. *Director:* Victor Fleming. *Music:* Herbert Stothart. From the book by L. Frank Baum. Fantasy about a Kansas farm girl (Garland, in her immortal role) who rides a tornado to a brightly colored world over the rainbow, full of talking scarecrows, munchkins, and a wizard who bears a strange resemblance to a Kansas fortune-teller. She must outwit the Wicked Witch if she is ever to go home. Delightful performances from Lahr, Bolger, and Hamilton; King Vidor is uncredited as co-director. Director Fleming originally wanted Deanna Durbin or Shirley Temple for the role of Dorothy, but settled for Garland who made the song "Over the Rainbow" her own. She received a special Academy Award for her performance. For the 50th anniversary of its release, *The Wizard of Oz* was restored and includes rare film clips of Bolger's "Scarecrow

Dance" and the cut "Jitterbug" number, and shots of Buddy Ebsen as the Tin Man before he became ill and left the production. Laserdisc edition includes digital sound, commentary by film historian Ronald Haver, test footage, trailers, and stills, as well as Jerry Maren talking about his experiences as a Munchkin. Yet another special

release of the film, "The Ultimate Oz," contains a documentary on the making of the film, a reproduction of the original script, still photos, and liner notes.

You Only Live Twice ♫♫♫
(1967; PG)
Cast: Sean Connery, Mie Hama, Akiko Wakabayashi, Tetsuro

Tamba, Karin Dor, Charles Gray, Donald Pleasence, Tsai Chin, Bernard Lee, Lois Maxwell, Desmond Llewelyn. *Director:* Lewis Gilbert. *Music:* John Barry. 007 travels to Japan to take on arch-nemesis Blofeld, who has been capturing Russian and American spacecraft in an attempt to start WWIII. Great location photography;

theme sung by Nancy Sinatra. Implausible plot, however, is a handicap, even though this is Bond.

musicHound *Lounge*

Indexes

Five-Bone Album Index

Band Member Index

Producer Index

Roots Index

Category Index

musicHound *Five-Bone Album Index*

The following albums achieved the highest rating possible—5 bones—from our discriminating MusicHound Lounge writers. You can't miss with any of these recordings. (Note: Albums are listed under the name of the entry (or entries) in which they appear and are not necessarily albums by that individual artist or group. The album could be a compilation album, a film soundtrack, an album on which the artist or group appears as a guest, etc. Consult the artist or group's entry for specific information.)

ABBA
Gold: Greatest Hits (Polydor, 1993)

Eden Ahbez
Eden's Island (Del Fi, 1960/1995)

Mose Allison
Allison Wonderland: The Mose Allison Anthology (Rhino, 1994)

The Ames Brothers
The Best of the Ames Brothers (Varese Vintage, 1995)

Louis Armstrong
The Complete Studio Recordings of Louis Armstrong and the All Stars (Mosaic, 1993)
Ella Fitzgerald and Louis Armstrong (Verve, 1957)
Hot Fives and Hot Sevens—Vol. 2 (CBS, 1926/Columbia, 1988)

Louis Armstrong and Earl Hines (CBS, 1927/Columbia Jazz Masterpieces, 1989)
Portrait of the Artist as a Young Man, 1923–1934 (Columbia/Legacy, 1994)

Fred Astaire
The Astaire Story (Verve, 1988)

Chet Baker
The Best of the Gerry Mulligan Quartet with Chet Baker (Pacific Jazz, 1991)
Complete Pacific Jazz Live Recordings (Mosaic, 1954)
Complete Pacific Jazz Studio Recordings of the Chet Baker Quartet with Russ Freeman (Mosaic, 1953–56)
Quartet: Russ Freeman and Chet Baker (Pacific Jazz, 1956)

Charlie Barnet
Complete Charlie Barnet, Vols. 1–6 (Bluebird, 1935–42)

Mario Bauza
My Time Is Now (Messidor, 1993)
Tanga (Messidor, 1992)

The Beach Boys
Good Vibrations (Capitol, 1993)
Pet Sounds (Capitol, 1966/1990)

Harry Belafonte
All-Time Greatest Hits, Vols. 1–3 (RCA, 1987)
Belafonte at Carnegie Hall (RCA, 1959)
Calypso (RCA, 1956)

Tony Bennett
Forty Years: The Artistry of Tony Bennett (Columbia, 1991)

Tony's Greatest Hits, Vol. III (Columbia, 1965)

Bunny Berigan
Bunny Berigan and His Boys: 1935–36 (Classics, 1993)
Mound City Blues Blowers (Timeless, 1994)
Portrait of Bunny Berigan (ASV Living Era, 1992)
Swingin' High (Topaz, 1993)

Charles Brown
The Complete Aladdin Recordings of Charles Brown (Mosaic, 1994)

Clifford Brown
At Basin Street (Emarcy, 1956)
Clifford Brown with Strings (Emarcy, 1997)
Study in Brown (Emarcy, 1955)

Dave Brubeck
Time Further Out (Columbia/Legacy, 1961/1996)
Time Out (Columbia/Legacy, 1959/1997)
Time Signatures: A Career Retrospective (Columbia/Legacy, 1992)

Cab Calloway
Are You Hep to the Jive? (Columbia/Legacy, 1994)

Hoagy Carmichael
The Classic Hoagy Carmichael (Smithsonian, 1994)

Ray Charles
Anthology (Rhino, 1988)
The Best of Ray Charles: The Atlantic Years (Rhino, 1994)

Tom Waits
Closing Time (Asylum, 1973)
Rain Dogs (Island, 1985)

Dinah Washington
First Issue: The Dinah Washington Story
(Verve, 1993)
What a Diff'rence a Day Makes (Mercury,
1959/1987)

Ben Webster
Music for Loving: Ben Webster with
Strings (Verve, 1995)
The Soul of Ben Webster (Verve, 1994)
Stormy Weather (Black Lion, 1988)

Roger Williams
The Greatest Popular Pianist: The Artist's
Choice (MCA, 1992)

Cassandra Wilson
New Moon Daughter (Blue Note, 1995)

Jimmy Witherspoon
Blowin' in from Kansas City (Flair/Virgin,
1991)

musicHound *Band Member Index*

Can't remember what band a certain musician or vocalist is in? Wondering if a person has been in more than one band? The Band Member Index will guide you to the appropriate entry (or entries).

The *Producer Index* lists the albums in MusicHound Lounge *that have a producer noted for them. Under each producer's name is the name of the artist or group in whose entry the album can be found, followed by the album title. If an album is produced by more than one individual/group, the album name will be listed separately under the names of each of the producers. (Note: The entry in which the album can be found is not necessarily that of the artist or group whose album it is. The album could be a compilation album, a film soundtrack, an album on which the artist or group appears as a guest, etc. Consult the artist or group's entry for specific information.)*

Michael Abene

Diane Schuur, *A GRP Christmas Collection*

Herb Abramson

Billy Eckstine, *Mister B and the Band*

Mark Abramson
Judy Collins, *In My Life*
Judy Collins, *Judy Collins #3*
Judy Collins, *Wildflowers*

William Ackerman
George Winston, *Autumn*
George Winston, *December*

Joe Adams
Ray Charles, *Anthology*
Ray Charles, *Modern Sounds in Country and Western Music*

Barry Adamson
Barry Adamson, *The Negro Inside Me*
Barry Adamson, *Soul Murder*

Lou Adler
Tim Curry, *The Rocky Horror Show Original Roxy Cast Recording*

Peter Afterman
Bryan Ferry, *Honeymoon in Vegas*
Elvis Presley, *Honeymoon in Vegas*

Brian Ahern
Anne Murray, *The Best . . . So Far*

Larry Alexander
Phyllis Hyman, *Under Her Spell: Phyllis Hyman's Greatest Hits*

Jean-Philippe Allard
Stan Getz, *People Time*

John Allen
The Association, *Association 95: A Little Bit More*

Steve Allen
Steve Allen, *On the Air! The Classic Comedy of Steve Allen*
Jerry Lewis, *On the Air! The Classic Comedy of Steve Allen*

Darren Allison
Divine Comedy, *Cassanova*

Herb Alpert
Herb Alpert, *Foursider*
Herb Alpert, *Whipped Cream and Other Delights*
The Baja Marimba Band, *Baja Marimba Band*
Sergio Mendes, *Greatest Hits of Brasil '66*
Chris Montez, *The More I See You*

Joe Altruda
Joey Altruda with the Cocktail Crew/Jump with Joey, *Ska-Ba*

Ernest Altschuler
Tony Bennett, *At Carnegie Hall: The Complete Concert*
Tony Bennett, *I Left My Heart in San Francisco*

Ray Conniff, *Christmas Album*
Ray Conniff, *Somewhere My Love*
Jerry Vale, *Standing Ovation! Jerry Vale at Carnegie Hall*

Morgan Ames
Diane Schuur, *Diane Schuur and the Count Basie Orchestra*

Benny Andersson
ABBA, *Gold: Greatest Hits*
ABBA, *More ABBA Gold: More ABBA Hits*
ABBA, *Oro*
ABBA, *Ring Ring*
ABBA, *Super Trouper*
ABBA, *Thank You for the Music*

Chris Andrews
Sandie Shaw, *Sandie/Me*

Ray Anthony
Ray Anthony, *I Remember Glenn Miller*
Ray Anthony, *Macarena Dance Party*
Ray Anthony, *Swing Back to the '40s*

Dave Appell
Tony Orlando, *The Casablanca Years*

Ramon Arcusa
Julio Iglesias, *1100 Bel Air Place*
Julio Iglesias, *Julio*

Eddie Arkin

Barbara Cook, *Showstoppers*
Barry Manilow, *2:00 A.M. Paradise Cafe*
Barry Manilow, *Because It's Christmas*
Barry Manilow, *Greatest Hits, Vol. III*
Barry Manilow, *Swing Street*
John Raitt, *Broadway Legend*
Nancy Wilson, *With My Lover Beside Me*

Gerry Arling

Easy Tunes, *All-In*
Easy Tunes, *Best of Easy Tunes*

The Art of Noise

The Art of Noise, *The Ambient Collection*
The Art of Noise, *The Best of the Art of Noise*
The Art of Noise, *Daft*
The Art of Noise, *The Drum and Bass Collection*
The Art of Noise, *The FON Mixes*
The Art of Noise, *In Visible Silence*
The Art of Noise, *Who's Afraid Of? (The Art of Noise!)*

Peter Asher

Neil Diamond, *Christmas Album*
Neil Diamond, *Christmas Album, Vol. 2*
Nelson Riddle, *What's New*
Linda Ronstadt, *Get Closer*
Linda Ronstadt, *Greatest Hits, Vol. 1*
Linda Ronstadt, *Greatest Hits, Vol. 2*
Linda Ronstadt, *Heart Like a Wheel*
Linda Ronstadt, *'Round Midnight*
Linda Ronstadt, *Sentimental Reasons*
Linda Ronstadt, *What's New*

Jon Astley

Tiny Tim, *Message to Love: The Isle of Wight Festival 1970*

Chet Atkins

Floyd Cramer, *The Best of Floyd Cramer*
Floyd Cramer, *The Essential Series: Floyd Cramer*
Floyd Cramer, *Hello Blues*
Charlie Rich, *Feel Like Going Home: The Essential Charlie Rich*
Roger Whittaker, *Greatest Hits*

James Austin

Mose Allison, *Allison Wonderland: The Mose Allison Anthology*
Buddy Greco, *Jackpot! The Las Vegas Story*
Sonny Lester, *Take It Off! Striptease Classics*
David Rose, *Take It Off! Striptease Classics*
Roger Williams, *Greatest Movie Themes*

George Avakian

Victor Borge, *Live*
Miles Davis, *Miles Ahead*
Les Elgart, *Best of the Big Bands: Sophisticated Swing*
Duke Ellington, *Ellington at Newport*

John Avila

Danny Elfman, *Boingo*

David Axelrod

Cannonball Adderley, *Mercy, Mercy, Mercy! Live at "The Club"*

Burt Bacharach

Dionne Warwick, *Friends Can Be Lovers*

Steve Backer

Bunny Berigan, *Bunny Berigan: Pied Piper*
Glenn Miller, *Glenn Miller: A Memorial*

The Bad Seeds

Nick Cave & the Bad Seeds, *The Firstborn Is Dead*
Nick Cave & the Bad Seeds, *The Good Son*
Nick Cave & the Bad Seeds, *Let Love In*

Angelo Badalamenti

Angelo Badalamenti, *Floating into the Night*
Angelo Badalamenti, *Secret Life*
Angelo Badalamenti, *Twin Peaks: Fire Walk with Me, Original Soundtrack*
Angelo Badalamenti, *Twin Peaks: Original TV Soundtrack*
Angelo Badalamenti, *The Voice of Love*
Julee Cruise, *Floating into the Night*
Julee Cruise, *The Voice of Love*
Marianne Faithfull, *A Secret Life*

Bob Badami

Danny Elfman, *Music for a Darkened Theatre: Film and Television Music, Vol. 1*

Erykah Badu

Erykah Badu, *Live*

Mayrton Bahia

João Gilberto, *João*

John Bahler

The Lennon Sisters, *22 Songs of Faith and Inspiration*

Carol Sue Baker

Joey Altruda with the Cocktail Crew/Jump with Joey, *The Winner Original Soundtrack*

Roy Thomas Baker

Devo, *Oh, No! It's Devo*

Russ Ballard

Christopher Cross, *View from the Ground*

Gordon Banks

Marvin Gaye, *Dream of a Lifetime*

Chris Barber

Bunny Berigan, *Mound City Blues Blowers*

Blixa Bargeld

Scott Walker, *To Have and to Hold*

Ron Barron

Maureen McGovern, *Another Woman in Love*
Maureen McGovern, *Naughty Baby*

John Barry

John Barry, *Moviola*
John Barry, *Moviola II: Action and Adventure*
John Barry, *Octopussy*

Steve Bartek

Danny Elfman, *Boingo*

David Bascome

Erasure, *Abba-Esque*

Basia

Basia, *Basia on Broadway*
Basia, *London Warsaw New York*
Basia, *The Sweetest Illusion*

Alan Bates

Andre Previn, *Previn at Sunset*
Bud Shank, *I Told You So!*

Mike Batt

Andrew Lloyd Webber, *Premiere Collection Encore*

Mario Bauza

Mario Bauza, *My Time Is Now*
Mario Bauza, *944 Columbus*
Mario Bauza, *Tanga*

Les Baxter

Les Baxter, *Colors of Brazil African Blue*
Les Baxter, *The Lost Episode*
Les Baxter, *Que Mango*
Les Baxter, *Voice of the Xtabay*
Yma Sumac, *Voice of the Xtabay*

The Beach Boys

The Beach Boys, *15 Big Ones*
The Beach Boys, *L.A. (Light Album)*
The Beach Boys, *M.I.U.*
The Beach Boys, *Surf's Up*

Yves Beauvais

Madeleine Peyroux, *Dreamland*

Walter Becker

Donald Fagen, *Kamakiriad*

Chris Beilor
Della Reese, *The Angel Sings*

Al Bell
Isaac Hayes, *Hot Buttered Soul*

Brad Benedict
Elmer Bernstein, *Ultra-Lounge, Vol. 7: Crime Scene*
Sammy Cahn, *It's Magic: Capitol Sings Sammy Cahn, Vol. 14*
Al Caiola, *Ultra-Lounge, Vol. 18: Bottoms Up!*
Al Caiola, *Ultra-Lounge, Vol. 8: Cocktail Capers*
Jack Costanzo, *Ultra-Lounge, Vol. 17: Bongoland*
Martin Denny, *The Exotic Sounds of Martin Denny*
The Four Freshmen, *Spotlight on . . . The Four Freshmen*
Jackie Gleason, *The Romantic Moods of Jackie Gleason*
The Hollyridge Strings, *Ultra-Lounge: On the Rocks, Part One*
The Hollyridge Strings, *Ultra-Lounge: On the Rocks, Part Two*
Betty Hutton, *Spotlight on Great Ladies of Song—Betty Hutton*
Denny McLain, *Ultra-Lounge, Vol. 11: Organs in Orbit*
Denny McLain, *Ultra-Lounge, Vol. 18: Bottoms Up!*
Matt Monro, *Spotlight on Matt Monro*
The Out-Islanders, *Ultra-Lounge: Mondo Exotica*
Dave Pell, *Ultra-Lounge, Vol. 4: Bachelor Pad Royale*
Richard Rodgers/Rodgers & Hammerstein/Rodgers & Hart, *Capitol Sings Rodgers & Hammerstein*
Rolley Polley, *Ultra-Lounge, Vol. 9: Cha Cha De Amor*
Frank Sinatra, *The Complete Capitol Singles Collection*
Sir Julian, *Ultra-Lounge, Vol. 11: Organs in Orbit*
Dakota Staton, *Sweet and Lovely: Capitol's Great Ladies of Song*

Danny Bennett
Tony Bennett, *The Art of Excellence*

Jeff Berger
James Galway, *Greatest Hits, Vol. 2*

Mike Berniker
Jack Jones, *The Gershwin Album*
Andre Kostelanetz, *16 Most Requested Songs*
Cleo Laine, *A Beautiful Thing*
Barbra Streisand, *The Barbra Streisand Album*
Barbra Streisand, *Barbra Streisand's Greatest Hits*
Jerry Vale, *17 Most Requested Songs*
Andy Williams, *16 Most Requested Songs*

Howie Bernstein
Björk, *Post*

Peter Bernstein
Jonathan Richman, *Jonathan Sings!*

Andre Betts
Madonna, *Erotica*

Big Bad Voodoo Daddy
Big Bad Voodoo Daddy, *Big Bad Voodoo Daddy*
Big Bad Voodoo Daddy, *Whatchu' Want for Christmas?*

Jules Bihari
Hadda Brooks, *Femme Fatale*

Janet Billig
Bob Dorough, *Schoolhouse Rock! Rocks*
Man or Astro-Man?, *Schoolhouse Rock! Rocks*

Scott Billington
Charlie Rich, *Feel Like Going Home: The Essential Charlie Rich*
Charlie Rich, *Pictures & Paintings*

Björk
Björk, *Debut*
Björk, *Post*

Leigh Blake
Cole Porter, *Red Hot + Blue*

Kevin Blanq
Harry Connick Jr., *20*

Adam Block
Charles Brown, *Driftin' Blues: The Best of Charles Brown*

Gert-Jan Blom
The Beau Hunks, *The Beau Hunks Play the Original Little Rascals Music*
The Beau Hunks, *The Beau Hunks Sextette Celebration on the Planet Mars: A Tribute to Raymond Scott*
The Beau Hunks, *The Beau Hunks Sextette Manhattan Minuet*
The Beau Hunks, *On to the Show: The Beau Hunks Play More Little Rascals Music*

Richard Bock
Laurindo Almeida/Laurindo Almeida & the Bossa Nova All-Stars, *Brazilliance, Vol. 2*
Chet Baker, *The Best of the Gerry Mulligan Quartet with Chet Baker*
Chet Baker, *Quartet: Russ Freeman and Chet Baker*
Chet Baker, *The Route*
Chet Baker, *Songs for Lovers*
Red Norvo, *The Red Norvo Trio with Tal Farlow and Charles Mingus*
Bud Shank, *Brazilliance, Vol. 1*
Bud Shank, *Brazilliance, Vol. 2*

Dieter Bohley
Engelbert Humperdinck, *Feelings*

Bob Bollard
Harry Belafonte, *Belafonte at Carnegie Hall*
Harry Belafonte, *Jump Up Calypso*

Sonny Bono
Sonny & Cher/Cher, *The Beat Goes On: The Best of Sonny & Cher*

Dennis Bovell
Edwyn Collins/Orange Juice, *The Orange Juice*
Edwyn Collins/Orange Juice, *Texas Fever*

Jimmy Bowen
Bing Crosby, *Hey Jude/Hey Bing!*
Sammy Davis Jr., *The Sounds of '66: Sammy Davis Jr./Buddy Rich*
Frankie Laine, *The Very Best of Frankie Laine*
Dean Martin, *The Best of Dean Martin 1962–1968*

Jim Boyer
Rupert Holmes, *Partners in Crime*
Billy Joel, *Kohuept (In Concert)*

John Boylan
Linda Ronstadt, *Different Drum*

Marilee Bradford
Lena Horne, *Lena Horne at MGM*

Owen Bradley
k.d. lang, *Shadowland*
Brenda Lee, *The Brenda Lee Story*

Brave Combo
Brave Combo, *Girl*
Brave Combo, *The Hokey Pokey*
Brave Combo, *It's Christmas, Man!*
Brave Combo, *Musical Varieties*
Brave Combo, *No, No, No, Cha Cha Cha*
Brave Combo, *Polkas for a Gloomy World*
Tiny Tim, *Girl*

Buddy Bregman
Anita O'Day, *Rules of the Road*

David Briggs
Nick Cave & the Bad Seeds, *Henry's Dream*

Michael Brook
Jane Siberry, *When I Was a Boy*

David Cavanaugh

The Lettermen, *All-Time Greatest Hits*

Frank Sinatra, *Concepts*

Nick Cave

Nick Cave & the Bad Seeds, *Henry's Dream*

Scott Walker, *To Have and to Hold*

Nick Cave & the Bad Seeds

Nick Cave & the Bad Seeds, *The Boatman's Call*

Nick Cave & the Bad Seeds, *From Her to Eternity*

Nick Cave & the Bad Seeds, *Kicking Against the Pricks*

Nick Cave & the Bad Seeds, *Murder Ballads*

Nick Cave & the Bad Seeds, *Tender Prey*

Nick Cave & the Bad Seeds, *Your Funeral, My Trial*

André Chapelle

Nana Mouskouri, *Concierto En Aranjuez*

Nana Mouskouri, *Falling in Love Again—Great Songs from the Movies*

Nana Mouskouri, *Nuestras Canciones, Vol. 1 & 2*

Nana Mouskouri, *Oh Happy Day*

Nana Mouskouri, *Passport*

Nana Mouskouri, *Song for Liberty*

Nana Mouskouri, *Vieilles Chansons de France*

Nana Mouskouri, *Why Worry?*

Don Charles

Connie Francis, *Souvenirs*

Marshall Chess

Rotary Connection, *Rotary Connection*

Alex Chilton

Alex Chilton, *Bach's Bottom*

Alex Chilton, *Clichés*

Alex Chilton, *Feudalist Tarts/No Sex*

Alex Chilton, *High Priest/Black List*

Irwin Chusid

Lenny Dee, *Cocktail Mix, Vol. 1: Bachelor's Guide to the Galaxy*

Juan Garcia Esquivel, *Music from a Sparkling Planet*

Juan Garcia Esquivel, *Space-Age Bachelor Pad Music*

Henri Rene, *Cocktail Mix, Vol. 1: Bachelor's Guide to the Galaxy*

Raymond Scott, *Reckless Nights and Turkish Twilights: The Music of Raymond Scott*

The Three Suns, *Cocktail Mix, Vol. 1: Bachelor's Guide to the Galaxy*

Walter Wanderley, *Samba Swing!*

Hank Cialo

Michael Feinstein, *Nice Work If You Can Get It: Songs by the Gershwins*

Ciccone Youth

Madonna, *The Whitey Album*

Stanley Clarke

Nancy Wilson, *Ramsey & Nancy—The Two of Us*

Greg Cohen

Madeleine Peyroux, *Dreamland*

Tony Cohen

Nick Cave & the Bad Seeds, *Intoxicated Man*

Nick Cave & the Bad Seeds, *Let Love In*

Nick Cave & the Bad Seeds, *Murder Ballads*

Nick Cave & the Bad Seeds, *Pink Elephants*

Nick Cave & the Bad Seeds, *Your Funeral, My Trial*

Richie Cole

Boots Randolph, *Yakety Madness*

Edwyn Collins

Edwyn Collins/Orange Juice, *Gorgeous George*

Edwyn Collins/Orange Juice, *I'm Not Following You*

Judy Collins

Judy Collins, *Come Rejoice! A Judy Collins Christmas*

Tom Collins

James Galway, *The Wayward Wind*

Combustible Edison

Combustible Edison, *Schizophonic! The Progressive Sound of Combustible Edison*

Harry Connick Jr.

Harry Connick Jr., *When Harry Met Sally*

Ray Conniff

Ray Conniff, *'S Always Conniff*

Don Costa

Trini Lopez, *The Best of Trini Lopez*

David Courtney

Leo Sayer, *Just a Boy*

Leo Sayer, *Silverbird*

Kerry Crawford

Jane Siberry, *No Borders Here*

Bob Crewe

Frankie Valli/The Four Seasons, *The Four Seasons Sing Big Hits by Burt Bacharach, Hal David & Bob Dylan*

Frankie Valli/The Four Seasons, *Greatest Hits, Vol. 2*

Criswell

The Galaxy Trio, *In the Harem*

Jim Croce

Jim Croce, *Faces I've Been*

Bill Crowley

Tom Jones, *Back to Back: Tom Jones/Engelbert Humperdinck*

Chick Crumpacker

Tommy Dorsey/The Dorsey Brothers, *Tommy Dorsey/Frank Sinatra: Greatest Hits*

Eddie Fisher, *All-Time Greatest Hits, Vol. 1*

Alfredo Cruz

Tito Puente, *Live at the Village Gate*

James Cunningham

Ken Nordine, *Colors*

Michael Cuscuna

Louis Armstrong, *The Complete Studio Recordings of Louis Armstrong and the All Stars*

Charles Brown, *The Complete Aladdin Recordings of Charles Brown*

Nat "King" Cole, *Jazz Encounters*

Benny Goodman, *Benny Goodman: Complete Capitol Small Group Recordings*

Johnny Hartman, *For Trane*

Johnny Hartman, *The Voice That Is*

Woody Herman, *Keeper of the Flame: Complete Capitol Recordings of the Four Brothers Band*

Lena Horne, *An Evening with Lena Horne (Live at the Supper Club)*

Nancy Wilson, *The Swingin' Mutual!*

John Dankworth

Cleo Laine, *A Beautiful Thing*

Cleo Laine, *Blue & Sentimental*

Ron Dante

Barry Manilow, *Barry Live*

Barry Manilow, *Barry Manilow II*

Barry Manilow, *Even Now*

Barry Manilow, *Greatest Hits*

Barry Manilow, *Greatest Hits, Vol. I*

Barry Manilow, *Greatest Hits, Vol. II*

Barry Manilow, *Greatest Hits, Vol. III*

Bobby Darin

Bobby Darin, *Born: Walden Robert Cosotto*

Jason Darrow

Jane Olivor, *Best Side of Goodbye*

Jane Olivor, *First Night*

Jack Daugherty

The Carpenters, *The Singles, 1969–1973*

John R.T. Davies

Bunny Berigan, *Harlem Lullaby*

Richard Davies

Richard Davies, *Instinct*
Richard Davies, *There's Never Been a Crowd Like This*

Chip Davis

Mannheim Steamroller, *A Fresh Aire Christmas*
Mannheim Steamroller, *Fresh Aire—Interludes*
Mannheim Steamroller, *Fresh Aire III*
Mannheim Steamroller, *Fresh Aire V*

Don Davis

The Fifth Dimension, *I Hope We Get to Love in Time*

Rhett Davis

Bryan Ferry, *Boys and Girls*

Sammy Davis Jr.

Sammy Davis Jr., *His Greatest Hits, Vols. 1 & 2*

Frank Day

Helen Reddy, *Greatest Hits (And More)*

Lex de Azevedo

Mrs. Elva Miller, *Mrs. Miller's Greatest Hits*

Phil De Lancie

Etta Jones, *Don't Go to Strangers*
Etta Jones, *Something Nice*
Red Norvo, *The Red Norvo Trios with Jimmy Raney or Tal Farlow and Red Mitchell*

Aloysio de Oliviera

Astrud Gilberto, *The Girl from Ipanema: The Antonio Carlos Jobim Songbook*

Paul de Senneville

Richard Clayderman, *Love Songs of Andrew Lloyd Webber*

Nick DeCaro

Claudine Longet, *We've Only Just Begun*

Doug Decker

George Winston, *Ballads and Blues*

Gary Delorme

k.d. lang, *a truly western experience*

Al DeLory

Glen Campbell, *By the Time I Get to Phoenix*
Glen Campbell, *Gentle on My Mind*
Glen Campbell, *Wichita Lineman*

Didier C. Deutsch

Fred Astaire, *Top Hat: Hits from Hollywood*
Tony Bennett, *Forty Years: The Artistry of Tony Bennett*
The Boswell Sisters, *That's How Rhythm Was Born*
Les Brown, *Best of the Big Bands: His Great Vocalists*
Eddie Cantor, *Charming Gents of Stage & Screen*
Buddy Clark, *16 Most Requested Songs*
Vic Damone, *16 Most Requested Songs*
Doris Day, *16 Most Requested Songs*
Doris Day, *16 Most Requested Songs: Encore!*
Buddy Greco, *16 Most Requested Songs*
Al Jolson, *You Ain't Heard Nothin' Yet: Jolie's Finest Columbia Recordings*
Johnny Mathis, *The Music of Johnny Mathis: A Personal Collection*
Ennio Morricone, *The Legendary Italian Westerns*
Alex North, *Music from Hollywood*
Dinah Shore, *16 Most Requested Songs: Encore*

Frank Sinatra, *The Best of the Columbia Years: 1943–1952*
Frank Sinatra, *The Columbia Years (1943–1952): The Complete Recordings*
Jerry Vale, *The Essence of Jerry Vale*
Andy Williams, *Personal Christmas Collection*
Andy Williams, *16 Most Requested Songs: Encore!*

Devo

Devo, *Devo E-Z Listening Disk*
Devo, *Total Devo*

Dave Dexter Jr.

Rosemary Clooney, *The Uncollected Rosemary Clooney, 1951–1952*
Denny McLain, *Denny McLain at the Organ*

Herman Diaz Jr.

Desi Arnaz, *The Best of Desi Arnaz: The Mambo King*
Harry Belafonte, *Calypso*
Henri Rene, *Riot in Rhythm*

Bruce Dickinson

Kurt Weill, *Should God Forget: A Retrospective*

Willie Dixon

Charles Brown, *Southern Blues 1957–63*

Stephen Hartley Dorff

Jim Nabors, *Sincerely/Town & Country*

Joel Dorn

Mose Allison, *Allison Wonderland: The Mose Allison Anthology*
Bette Midler, *The Divine Miss M*
Richard Rodgers/Rodgers & Hammerstein/Rodgers & Hart, *The John Coltrane Anthology*

Chip Douglas

Linda Ronstadt, *Different Drum*

Steve Douglas

Regis Philbin, *It's Time for Regis!*

Tom Dowd

Dusty Springfield, *Dusty in Memphis*

Daryl Dragon

The Captain & Tennille, *Captain & Tennille's Greatest Hits*
The Captain & Tennille, *Come in from the Rain*
The Captain & Tennille, *Love Will Keep Us Together*
The Captain & Tennille, *Song of Joy*

Gus Dudgeon

Dusty Springfield, *Tumbleweed Connection*

Anne Dudley

The Art of Noise, *Below the Waste*
The Art of Noise, *In No Sense? Nonsense!*

Bob Duffey

Tom Waits, *The Early Years*
Tom Waits, *The Early Years, Vol. 2*

Paul duGre

Love Jones, *Powerful Pain Relief*

Mallory Earl

Chuck Mangione, *Live at the Village Gate*

Barry J. Eastman

Phyllis Hyman, *I Refuse to Be Lonely*

Clint Eastwood

Clint Eastwood, *Bird*
Clint Eastwood, *Honkytonk Man*
Clint Eastwood, *Midnight in the Garden of Good and Evil*
Johnny Hartman, *Bridges of Madison County*
Johnny Mercer, *Midnight in the Garden of Good and Evil*
Cassandra Wilson, *Midnight in the Garden of Good and Evil*

Bob Keane

Eden Ahbez, *Eden's Island*
The Sentinels, *Big Surf*
The Sentinels, *Surfer Girl*

Helen Keane

João Gilberto, *Amoroso/Brasil*

Danny Kee

Kathie Lee Gifford, *It's Christmas Time*
Kathie Lee Gifford, *Sentimental*
Regis Philbin, *It's Christmas Time*

Orrin Keepnews

Cannonball Adderley, *Know What I Mean?*
Chet Baker, *Chet Baker in New York*
Chet Baker, *Chet Baker with 50 Italian Strings*
Hoagy Carmichael, *Stardust & Much More*
Jimmy Dorsey, *Contrasts*
Ella Fitzgerald, *75th Birthday Celebration*
Benny Goodman, *Benny Goodman/The Birth of Swing*
Benny Goodman, *The Complete RCA Victor Small Group Recordings*
Carmen McRae, *Sings Great American Songwriters*
Glenn Miller, *The Spirit Is Willing (1939–42)*

Brian Kehew

The Moog Cookbook, *The Moog Cookbook*
The Moog Cookbook, *Plays the Classic Rock Hits*

David Keller

Bud Shank, *America the Beautiful*
Bud Shank, *Tomorrow's Rainbow*

Keith Keller

Alex Chilton, *Clichés*

Jon Kelly

The Beautiful South, *0898*

Rob Kemp

Joe Meek, *It's Hard to Believe It: The Amazing World of Joe Meek*

Elliot Kendall

The Hi-Lo's, *The Best of the Hi-Lo's: Nice Work If You Can Get It*

Jerry Kennedy

Charlie Rich, *Complete Smash Sessions*

David Kershenbaum

Joe Jackson, *Body and Soul*
Joe Jackson, *Look Sharp!*
Joe Jackson, *Night and Day*
Joe Jackson, *This Is It: The A&M Years, 1979–1989*

Jamie Kidd

k.d. lang, *a truly western experience*

Adam Kidron

Edwyn Collins/Orange Juice, *You Can't Hide Your Love Forever*

Peter King

Carmen McRae, *Live in Robbie Scott's*

Gershon Kingsley

Perrey & Kingsley, *The In Sound from Way Out!*

Andrea Kinloch

Sonny Lester, *Take It Off! Striptease Classics*
David Rose, *Take It Off! Striptease Classics*

Dennis Kirk

Bette Midler, *Divine Madness*

Don Kirshner

The Three Suns, *Fever & Smoke*
The Three Suns, *Movin' 'n' Groovin'*

Gary Klein

Judy Collins, *Hard Times for Lovers*
Barbra Streisand, *Barbra Streisand's Greatest Hits, Vol. 2*

Larry Klein

Holly Cole, *Dark Dear Heart*

Pete Kline

Harry James, *Bandstand Memories*

Lester Koenig

Chet Baker, *Witch Doctor*
Andre Previn, *Andre Previn/Russ Freeman: Double Play!*
Andre Previn, *King Size*
Andre Previn, *Plays Songs by Jerome Kern*

Robert Koester

Dinah Washington, *Mellow Mama*

Steve Kolanijan

Neil Sedaka, *All-Time Greatest Hits, Vol. 2*
The Ventures, *Tele-Ventures: The Ventures Perform the Great TV Themes*
The Ventures, *Walk, Don't Run: The Best of the Ventures*

Brian Koonin

Buster Poindexter, *Buster's Spanish Rocket Ship*

Dan Kortchmar

Billy Joel, *River of Dreams*

Kiyoshi Koyama

Billy Eckstine, *Billy Eckstine Sings with Benny Carter*

Richard Kraft

Angelo Badalamenti, *Blue Velvet*
Danny Elfman, *Music for a Darkened Theatre: Film and Television Music, Vol. 1*

Robert Kraft

Tito Puente, *The Mambo Kings*

Eddie Kramer

Carly Simon, *The Best of Carly Simon*

Eric Kupper

RuPaul, *Foxy Lady*
RuPaul, *Supermodel of the World*

Joe Lambert

Black Velvet Flag, *Come Recline with Black Velvet Flag*

Cal Lampley

Dave Brubeck, *The Great Concerts*
Miles Davis, *Porgy and Bess*
Nina Simone, *Nina Simone at the Village Gate*

Jay Landers

Bernadette Peters, *Sondheim, Etc.: Live—At Carnegie Hall*
John Raitt, *Broadway Legend*
Jimmy Webb, *Ten Easy Pieces*

Richard Landis

Neil Diamond, *Tennessee Moon*

k.d. lang

k.d. lang, *Absolute Torch and Twang*
k.d. lang, *Drag*
k.d. lang, *Ingenue*
k.d. lang, *a truly western experience*

Clive Langer

Morrissey, *Bona Drag*
Morrissey, *Kill Uncle*

Joseph F. Laredo

Eddy Howard, *The Best of Eddy Howard: The Mercury Years*

Tony Lash

Richard Davies, *Cardinal*

John Steven Lasher

Alex North, *At the Movies*

Steven Lasker

Bing Crosby, *Bing Crosby: His Legendary Years, 1931–1957*
Les Paul, *Les Paul: The Complete Decca Trios–Plus (1936–47)*

James Last

James Last, *Romantic Dreams*
Zamfir, *Lonely Shepherd*

Bill Laswell/Material

Herbie Hancock, *Sound System*

Andrew Leary
Bob Dorough, *Schoolhouse Rock! Rocks*
Man or Astro-Man?, *Schoolhouse Rock! Rocks*

Jim Lee
Chris Montez, *Let's Dance: The Monogram Sides*

Kyle Lehning
Clint Eastwood, *Heroes & Friends*

Tom Lehrer
Tom Lehrer, *Songs & More Songs by Tom Lehrer*

Rod Leissle
Björn Again, *Flashback*
Björn Again, *Live Album*

Jeffrey Lesser
Rupert Holmes, *Rupert Holmes*
Rupert Holmes, *Singles*
Rupert Holmes, *Widescreen*

Sonny Lester
Sonny Lester, *Ann Corio Presents: How to Strip for Your Husband/Music to Make Marriage Merrier*
Sonny Lester, *Ann Corio Presents: More How to Strip for Your Husband, Vol. 2/Music to Make Marriage Merrier*

Bill Levenson
Connie Francis, *Souvenirs*

Maurice Levine
Sammy Cahn, *An Evening with Sammy Cahn*

Ron Levy
Charles Brown, *All My Life*
Charles Brown, *Just a Lucky So and So*
Charles Brown, *Someone to Love*

Jack Lewis
Duke Ellington, *The 1952 Seattle Concert*

Don Lewzey
Nelson Riddle, *Blue Skies*

Goddard Lieberson
Richard Rodgers/Rodgers & Hammerstein/Rodgers & Hart, *Oklahoma!*

Enoch Light
The Ray Charles Singers, *Love Me with All Your Heart*
Enoch Light, *Persuasive Percussion*
Enoch Light, *Provocative Percussion*

Gordon Lightfoot
Gordon Lightfoot, *Endless Wire*
Gordon Lightfoot, *Summertime Dream*

Steve Lillywhite
Morrissey, *Southpaw Grammar*

Alfred Lion
Cannonball Adderley, *Somethin' Else*
Herbie Hancock, *Empyrean Isles*
Herbie Hancock, *Maiden Voyage*
Herbie Hancock, *Takin' Off*

Stephen Lipson
Annie Lennox, *Diva*
Annie Lennox, *Medusa*

Tommy LiPuma
Burt Bacharach, *What the World Needs Now: The Music of Burt Bacharach*
Natalie Cole, *Take a Look*
Natalie Cole, *Unforgettable*
Michael Franks, *The Art of Tea*
Michael Franks, *Burchfield Nines*
João Gilberto, *Amoroso/Brasil*
Diana Krall, *All for You: A Dedication to the Nat King Cole Trio*
Diana Krall, *Love Scenes*
Diana Krall, *Only Trust Your Heart*
Claudine Longet, *Claudine*
Claudine Longet, *Love Is Blue*
Jimmy Scott, *All the Way*
Barbra Streisand, *Barbra Streisand's Greatest Hits, Vol. 2*

Steve Lironi
Space, *Spiders*

Michael Lloyd
Pat Boone, *In a Metal Mood: No More Mr. Nice Guy*
Barry Manilow, *Barry Manilow*
Maureen McGovern, *Greatest Hits*
Bobby Vinton, *As Time Goes By*

Andrew Lloyd Webber
Andrew Lloyd Webber, *Evita*
Andrew Lloyd Webber, *Highlights from Jesus Christ Superstar*
Andrew Lloyd Webber, *Premiere Collection Encore*

Siegfried Loch
Dave Brubeck, *We're All Together Again for the First Time*

Nancy Lombardo
The Baja Marimba Band, *Bachelor Pad Pleasures*
The Baja Marimba Band, *Lounge Music Goes Latin*

Jim Long
Jack Jones, *New Jack Swing*

Michael Lorant
Andrew Lloyd Webber, *Jesus Christ Superstar—A Resurrection*

Jeff Lorber
Michael Franks, *Dragonfly Summer*

Pete Lorimer
RuPaul, *Foxy Lady*

Love Jones
Love Jones, *Here's to the Losers*

Nick Lowe
Elvis Costello, *Armed Forces*
Elvis Costello, *Blood and Chocolate*
Elvis Costello, *Get Happy!!*
Elvis Costello, *My Aim Is True*
Elvis Costello, *This Year's Model*

John Lurie
John Lurie/The Lounge Lizards, *No Pain for Cakes*

David Lynch
Angelo Badalamenti, *Floating into the Night*
Angelo Badalamenti, *Twin Peaks: Fire Walk with Me, Original Soundtrack*
Angelo Badalamenti, *Twin Peaks: Original TV Soundtrack*
Angelo Badalamenti, *The Voice of Love*
Angelo Badalamenti, *Wild At Heart, Original Soundtrack*
Julee Cruise, *Floating into the Night*
Julee Cruise, *The Voice of Love*

Ralph Mace
James Galway, *Beauty and the Beast: Galway at the Movies*
James Galway, *The Enchanted Forest—Melodies of Japan*
James Galway, *In Ireland*
James Galway, *In the Pink*
James Galway, *The Lark in the Clear Air*
James Galway, *Over the Sea to Skye*
James Galway, *The Wind Beneath My Wings*
James Galway, *Wind of Change*

Teo Macero
Dave Brubeck, *The Great Concerts*
Dave Brubeck, *Time Further Out*
Dave Brubeck, *Time Out*
Cab Calloway, *Hi De Ho Man: Classics*
Miles Davis, *In a Silent Way*
Miles Davis, *Kind of Blue*
Miles Davis, *Quiet Nights*
Miles Davis, *Sketches of Spain*
Woody Herman, *Woody's Winners*
John Lurie/The Lounge Lizards, *The Lounge Lizards*

Richard Rodgers/Rodgers &
  Hammerstein/Rodgers &
  Hart, *The Complete Concert 1964/My Funny Valentine + Four & More*

Tom Mack
Leonard Nimoy, *Leonard
  Nimoy Presents Mr.
  Spock's Music from Outer
  Space*
Ken Nordine, *Best of Word
  Jazz, Vol. 1*
Lalo Schifrin, *Music from Mis-
  sion: Impossible*

Andy MacPherson
Tiny Tim, *Message to Love:
  The Isle of Wight Festival
  1970*

Madonna
Madonna, *Erotica*

Mike Mainieri
Carly Simon, *Torch*

David Malloy
Kenny Rogers, *20 Greatest
  Hits*

Paddy Maloney
James Galway, *In Ireland*
James Galway, *Over the Sea to
  Skye*

Leslie Mandoki
Engelbert Humperdinck, *Feel-
  ings*
Engelbert Humperdinck, *You
  Are So Beautiful*

Chuck Mangione
Chuck Mangione, *Bellavia*
Chuck Mangione, *Greatest
  Hits*
Chuck Mangione, *Live at the
  Village Gate*
Chuck Mangione, *Love Notes*

Barry Manilow
Barbara Cook, *Showstoppers*
Barry Manilow, *2:00 A.M. Par-
  adise Cafe*
Barry Manilow, *Barry Live*
Barry Manilow, *Barry Mani-
  low II*
Barry Manilow, *Because It's
  Christmas*
Barry Manilow, *Even Now*

Barry Manilow, *Greatest Hits*
Barry Manilow, *Greatest Hits,
  Vol. I*
Barry Manilow, *Greatest Hits,
  Vol. II*
Barry Manilow, *Greatest Hits,
  Vol. III*
Barry Manilow, *Swing Street*
Bette Midler, *The Divine
  Miss M*
Nancy Wilson, *With My Lover
  Beside Me*

Earle Mankey
Helen Reddy, *Greatest Hits
  (And More)*

Herbie Mann
Maya Angelou, *Evolution of
  Mann*

Peter Mann
The Nylons, *Run for Cover*

Roger Manning
The Moog Cookbook, *The
  Moog Cookbook*
The Moog Cookbook, *Plays
  the Classic Rock Hits*

Terry Manning
Alex Chilton, *1970*

Cary E. Mansfield
The Ames Brothers/Ed Ames,
  *The Best of the Ames
  Brothers*
Teresa Brewer, *Music! Music!
  Music! The Best of Teresa
  Brewer*
Fabian, *The Best of Fabian*
Ferrante & Teicher, *Blast Off!*
The Hi-Lo's, *The Best of the Hi-
  Lo's: Nice Work If You Can
  Get It*
The Hollyridge Strings, *The
  Best of the Beatles Song
  Book*
Jerry Murad's Harmonicats,
  *Harmonicats: Original
  RKO/Unique Masters*
Helen Reddy, *When I Dream:
  The Eighties Collection*
Neil Sedaka, *Laughter in the
  Rain: The Best of Neil
  Sedaka, 1974–1980*
Neil Sedaka, *Tuneweaver*

April Stevens, *Sweet and
  Lovely: The Best of Nino
  Tempo & April Stevens*
Ian Whitcomb, *The Golden
  Age of Lounge*
Ian Whitcomb, *The Very Best
  of Ian Whitcomb: The
  Rock 'n' Roll Years*

Bob Marcucci
Fabian, *This Is Fabian*

Arif Mardin
Judy Collins, *Judith*
The Manhattan Transfer,
  Tonin'
Bette Midler, *Experience the
  Divine: Greatest Hits*
Dusty Springfield, *Dusty in
  Memphis*

George R. Marek
Pearl Bailey, *Hello, Dolly!*

Larry Marks
Liza Minnelli, *At Carnegie Hall*
Helen Reddy, *Greatest Hits
  (And More)*

George Martin
Bert Kaempfert, *Anthology 1*
Matt Monro, *Matt Monro
  Sings Hoagy Carmichael*
Matt Monro, *My Kind of Girl*

Nick Martinelli
Phyllis Hyman, *I Refuse to Be
  Lonely*
RuPaul, *Foxy Lady*

Elaine Martone
Doc Severinsen, *Erich Kun-
  zel/Cincinnati Pops*
Doc Severinsen, *Unforgettably Doc*

George Massenburg
Linda Ronstadt, *Trio*

Michael Masser
Jane Olivor, *Best Side of
  Goodbye*

Graham Massey
Björk, *Post*

Pete Masters
The Senders, *Jumpin' Uptown*

Material
Herbie Hancock, *Future Shock*

Greg Mathieson
Sheena Easton, *A Private
  Heaven*
Sheena Easton, *Todo Me Re-
  cuerda a Ti*

James Mathus
Squirrel Nut Zippers, *Jas.
  Mathus and His Knock-
  Down Society Play Songs
  for Rosetta*

Eric Matthews
Eric Matthews, *It's Heavy in
  Here*
Eric Matthews, *The Lateness
  of the Hour*

Peter Matz
Rosemary Clooney, *White
  Christmas*
Nancy LaMott, *Listen to My
  Heart*
Barbra Streisand, *The Broad-
  way Album*

Lincoln Mayorga
Frank Sinatra Jr., *Billy May for
  President*

Elliott Mazer
Linda Ronstadt, *Different
  Drum*
David Soul, *David Soul*

Robin McBride
Tony Bennett, *At Carnegie
  Hall: The Complete Con-
  cert*

Ron McCarrell
Frank Sinatra, *The Capitol
  Years*

John McClure
Henry Mancini, *Cinema Italiano*

Joe McEwen
Frank Sinatra, *The Complete
  Reprise Studio Record-
  ings*
Frank Sinatra, *The Reprise
  Collection*
Frank Sinatra, *Sinatra Reprise:
  The Very Good Years*

Bob McGinnis
The Mystic Moods Orchestra,
  Erogenous

PRODUCER INDEX

Jane Siberry
Jane Siberry, *Bound by the Beauty*
Jane Siberry, *No Borders Here*
Jane Siberry, *When I Was a Boy*

Ben Sidran
Mose Allison, *Tell Me Something*
Georgie Fame, *The Blues and Me*
Georgie Fame, *Cool Cat Blues*
Georgie Fame, *The Go Jazz All-Stars*
Michael Franks, *Dragonfly Summer*

Davitt Sigerson
Olivia Newton-John, *The Rumour*

Joel Sill
Dave Grusin, *The Fabulous Baker Boys*

Leonard Silver
Della Reese, *The Angel Sings*

Alan Silverman
Judy Collins, *Come Rejoice! A Judy Collins Christmas*

Carly Simon
Carly Simon, *Clouds in My Coffee: 1965–1995*

John Simon
Neil Diamond, *The Last Waltz*

Nancy Sinatra
Nancy Sinatra, *Frank Sinatra, My Father*

Shelby S. Singleton
Patti Page, *Greatest Hits—Finest Performances*
Patti Page, *16 Best of Patti Page*
Patti Page, *16 Greatest Hits*

Howard Smiley
The Baja Marimba Band, *Bachelor Pad Pleasures*
The Baja Marimba Band, *Lounge Music Goes Latin*
Tom Jones, *Back to Back: Tom Jones/Engelbert Humperdinck*

Robin Smith
Nana Mouskouri, *Nana*

Nana Mouskouri, *Why Worry?*

Sherman Sneed
Lena Horne, *An Evening with Lena Horne (Live at the Supper Club)*
Lena Horne, *We'll Be Together Again*

John Snyder
Charles Brown, *Honey Dripper*
Charles Brown, *These Blues*
Dave Brubeck, *Night Shift: Live at the Blue Note*
Don Cherry, *Art Deco*
Tommy Dorsey/The Dorsey Brothers, *Best of Tommy Dorsey*
Coleman Hawkins, *The Hawk in Paris*
Louis Jordan, *Rock 'n' Roll Call*
Andre Previn, *A Touch of Elegance*
Neil Sedaka, *All-Time Greatest Hits, Vol. 2*

Frank Socolow
Maya Angelou, *Evolution of Mann*

Ray Stanley
Jack Costanzo, *Latin Fever*

Allan Steckler
Martin Denny, *Bachelor in Paradise: The Best of Martin Denny*

Jim Steinman
Barry Manilow, *Greatest Hits, Vol. III*

Stereolab
Stereolab, *Dots and Loops*
Stereolab, *Emperor Tomato Ketchup*
Stereolab, *The Groop Played "Space Age Batchelor Pad Music"*
Stereolab, *Mars Audiac Quintet*
Stereolab, *Music for the Amorphous Body Centre*

Art Stewart
Marvin Gaye, *Vulnerable*

Dave Stewart
Annie Lennox, *Revenge*

Annie Lennox, *Sweet Dreams (Are Made of This)*

Gary Stewart
Tony Orlando, *Best of Tony Orlando & Dawn*
Frankie Valli/The Four Seasons, *Greatest Hits, Vol. 1*

Michael Stewart
Billy Joel, *Piano Man*

Radford Stone
Blossom Dearie, *Schoolhouse Rock!*
Bob Dorough, *Schoolhouse Rock!*

Ettore Stratta
Tony Bennett, *The Art of Excellence*
Barbra Streisand, *Barbra Streisand's Greatest Hits*
Barbra Streisand, *A Christmas Album*

Craig Street
Holly Cole, *Temptation*
k.d. lang, *Drag*
Jimmy Scott, *Heaven*
Cassandra Wilson, *Blue Light 'Til Dawn*
Cassandra Wilson, *New Moon Daughter*

Stephen Street
Morrissey, *Bona Drag*
Morrissey, *Viva Hate*

Barbra Streisand
Barbra Streisand, *Barbra Streisand's Greatest Hits, Vol. 2*
Barbra Streisand, *The Broadway Album*

Ian Summer
Roger Whittaker, *Greatest Hits*

Bill Summers
Herbie Hancock, *Dis Is da Drum*

John Switzer
Jane Siberry, *Bound by the Beauty*
Jane Siberry, *No Borders Here*

Michael Talbot
The Style Council, *Confessions of a Pop Group*

Greg Talenfeld
Richard Davies, *Instinct*

Alan Tarney
Leo Sayer, *Living in a Fantasy*

Creed Taylor
Patti Austin, *Live at the Bottom Line*
Stan Getz, *The Artistry of Stan Getz: The Best of the Verve Years, Vol. 1*
Stan Getz, *Stan Getz and Bill Evans*
Astrud Gilberto, *Compact Jazz: Astrud Gilberto*
Astrud Gilberto, *Getz/Gilberto*
Astrud Gilberto, *Getz/Gilberto, Vol. 2*
Astrud Gilberto, *The Girl from Ipanema: The Antonio Carlos Jobim Songbook*
Astrud Gilberto, *Verve Jazz Masters 9*
João Gilberto, *Getz/Gilberto*
Dizzy Gillespie, *Perceptions*
Cal Tjader, *Talkin' Verve: Roots of Acid Jazz*

Gerry Teekens
Chet Baker, *Chet's Choice*

Rod Temperton
Patti Austin, *Every Home Should Have One*

Ted Templeman
David Lee Roth, *Crazy from the Heat*
David Lee Roth, *Eat 'Em and Smile*
Royal Crown Revue, *Mugzy's Move*

Nino Tempo
April Stevens, *Carousel Dreams*

Toni Tennille
The Captain & Tennille, *Captain & Tennille's Greatest Hits*
The Captain & Tennille, *Come in from the Rain*
The Captain & Tennille, *Love Will Keep Us Together*
The Captain & Tennille, *Song of Joy*

Murry Wilson, *Time to Get Alone*

Murry Wilson
Murry Wilson, *The Many Moods of Murry Wilson*

Peter Wilson
The Style Council, *Our Favourite Shop*

Steve Wilson
Tony Orlando, *The Brill Building Sound: Singers & Songwriters Who Rocked the '60s*

Matthias Winckelmann
Chet Baker, *The Legacy, Vol. 1*

Hal Winn
The Mystic Moods Orchestra, *Erogenous*

George Winston
George Winston, *Ballads and Blues*
George Winston, *December*
George Winston, *Linus & Lucy: The Music of Vince Guaraldi*

Nils Winther
Dexter Gordon, *More Than You Know*

Joseph Wissert
Gordon Lightfoot, *If You Could Read My Mind*
Helen Reddy, *Greatest Hits (And More)*

Andy Wiswell
Pearl Bailey, *Hello, Dolly!*
Al Martino, *The Exciting Voice of Al Martino*

David L. Wolper
Anthony Newley, *Willy Wonka and the Chocolate Factory: Special 25th Anniversary Edition Soundtrack*

Stevie Wonder
Rotary Connection, *Perfect Angel*

Robert Woods
Liza Minnelli, *At Carnegie Hall*
Doc Severinsen, *Big Band Hit Parade*

Doc Severinsen, *Christmas with the Pops*
Doc Severinsen, *Erich Kunzel/Cincinnati Pops Orchestra: Fiesta*
Doc Severinsen, *Erich Kunzel/Cincinnati Pops*
Doc Severinsen, *Unforgettably Doc*

Simon Woods
Kurt Weill, *Kurt Weill on Broadway*

John Wooler
Hadda Brooks, *Time Was When*

Nigel Wright
Andrew Lloyd Webber, *Evita*
Andrew Lloyd Webber, *Highlights from Jesus Christ Superstar*
Andrew Lloyd Webber, *Premiere Collection Encore*

Phil Wright
Stereolab, *Transient Random-Noise Bursts with Announcements*

"Weird" Al Yankovic
Desi Arnaz, *Babalu Music: I Love Lucy's Greatest Hits*

John Yap
Kurt Weill, *The Threepenny Opera*

The Yellowjackets
Michael Franks, *Dragonfly Summer*

Jerry Yester
Tom Waits, *Anthology of Tom Waits*
Tom Waits, *Closing Time*

Oscar A. Young
Tommy Edwards, *The Sullivan Years: Rock 'n' Roll Pioneers*

Hector Zazou
Jane Siberry, *Songs from the Cold Seas*

Walter Zwiefel
Jaymz Bee, *Cocktail: Shakin' and Stirred*

Which artists or groups have had the most influence on the acts included in MusicHound Lounge? The Roots Index will help you find out. Under each artist or group's name— not necessarily a lounge or easy-listening act—are listed the acts found in MusicHound Lounge that were influenced by that artist or group. By the way, Frank Sinatra (of course) is the influence champ: he appears in the ◀◀ section of a whopping 46 artists or groups.

ABBA

Björn Again
The Cardigans
Richard Clayderman
Erasure

Roy Acuff
Kay Starr

Jack Albin
Freddy Martin

Fred Allen
Stan Freberg

Steve Allen
Steve Lawrence & Eydie Gorme
Andy Williams

Mose Allison
Steve Allen
Georgie Fame
Michael Franks

Laurindo Almeida
Richard Clayderman
Jose Feliciano

Herb Alpert
Sergio Mendes
Dionne Warwick

Herb Alpert & the Tijuana Brass
The Baja Marimba Band

Ed Ames
Roger Whittaker

The Ames Brothers
The Four Lads

Laurie Anderson
Jane Siberry

Leroy Anderson
Lenny Dee
Arthur Fiedler
Mitch Miller
Peter Nero
The Swingle Singers

Marian Anderson
Nina Simone

Julie Andrews
Petula Clark
Pizzicato Five

The Andrews Sisters
The Four Freshmen
Bette Midler

Paul Anka
Tony Orlando

Ann-Margret
Francoise Hardy
Olivia Newton-John
Bernadette Peters

Ray Anthony
Doc Severinsen

Don Apiazo
Mario Bauza

Harold Arlen
Judy Garland
The Pied Pipers

Louis Armstrong
Steve Allen
John Barry
Bunny Berigan
Sam Butera
Cab Calloway
Eddie Cantor
Hoagy Carmichael
Nat "King" Cole
Bing Crosby
Bob Crosby
Billy Eckstine
Slim Gaillard
Dizzy Gillespie

Coleman Hawkins
Dick Haymes
Billie Holiday
Harry James
Al Jarreau
Louis Jordan
Frankie Laine
Guy Lombardo
The Manhattan Transfer
Louis Prima & Keely Smith
David Lee Roth
Frank Sinatra
Lawrence Welk

Eddy Arnold
Elvis Presley

Carlos Arruza
Herb Alpert

Fred Astaire
Eddie Cantor
Russ Columbo
Nelson Eddy
Eddie Fisher
Gene Kelly
Dick Powell
Bobby Vinton

Chet Atkins
Al Caiola
Floyd Cramer
The Ventures

Gene Autry
Les Paul

Frankie Avalon
Fabian

Human League
Pet Shop Boys

Engelbert Humperdinck
Richard Harris
Steve Lawrence & Eydie
    Gorme
Barry Manilow
Dionne Warwick
Kurt Weill

Ivory Joe Hunter
Tommy Edwards

Betty Hutton
Björk
Doris Day

Dick Hyman
The Moog Cookbook
Tony Mottola
Perrey & Kingsley

Abdullah Ibrahim
George Winston

Julio Iglesias
Richard Clayderman

The Impalas
The Fleetwoods

The Ink Spots
The Ames Brothers
The Mills Brothers
Elvis Presley

Burl Ives
Jaymz Bee

Mahalia Jackson
Maya Angelou
Brenda Lee
Della Reese

Michael Jackson
Madonna

Wanda Jackson
Nancy Sinatra

Dick Jacobs
Ron Goodwin

Mick Jagger
Tim Curry

Ahmad Jamal
Herbie Hancock

Etta James
Annie Lennox

Dakota Staton

Harry James
Ray Anthony
Ray Conniff
Dick Haymes
Al Hirt
Doc Severinsen

Maurice Jarre
Michael Kamen

Keith Jarrett
George Winston

Bobby Jaspar
Blossom Dearie

Florence Foster Jenkins
Mrs. Elva Miller

Gordon Jenkins
Nelson Riddle

Claude Jeter
Ray Charles

Antonio Carlos Jobim
Michael Franks
Astrud Gilberto
Sergio Mendes
Sir Julian
Walter Wanderley

David Johansen
Tim Curry

Elton John
ABBA
Billy Joel
Leo Sayer
Carly Simon

Little Willie John
Marvin Gaye

Johnny & the Hurricanes
The Ventures

Arnold Johnson
Freddy Martin

Budd Johnson
Charlie Parker
Ben Webster

Eric Johnson
Christopher Cross

James Johnson
Dick Hyman

James P. Johnson
Duke Ellington

Robert Johnson
Nick Cave & the Bad Seeds

Al Jolson
Peter Allen
Gene Austin
Pat Boone
Eddie Cantor
Russ Columbo
Bing Crosby
Jimmy Durante
Slim Gaillard
Dick Haymes
Spike Jones
Mickey Katz
Frankie Laine
Jerry Lewis
Dean Martin
Ethel Merman
Carmen Miranda
Mandy Patinkin
Regis Philbin
Louis Prima & Keely Smith
Paul Robeson
Richard Rodgers
David Rose
David Lee Roth
Frank Sinatra
Rudy Vallee
Paul Weston
Margaret Whiting

Jon & the Nightriders
The Galaxy Trio

Allan Jones
Jack Jones

Isham Jones
Les Brown
Eddy Howard
Gordon Jenkins
Sammy Kaye
Kay Kyser
Guy Lombardo

Jack Jones
Engelbert Humperdinck

Quincy Jones
Dave Grusin

Spike Jones
Stan Freberg
Mel Henke
Mickey Katz
Tom Waits

Tom Jones
Richard Harris
Engelbert Humperdinck
David Lee Roth

Tommy Jones
Les Baxter

Janis Joplin
Bette Midler

Scott Joplin
Harold Arlen
Charles Brown
Don Byron
Dick Hyman
Frank Mills
Red Norvo

Louis Jordan
Big Bad Voodoo Daddy
Sam Butera
Ray Charles
Cherry Poppin' Daddies
Nat "King" Cole
Tommy Edwards
Joe Jackson
The Mighty Blue Kings
Louis Prima & Keely Smith
Jimmy Witherspoon

Joy Division
Björk

Dick Jurgens
Eddy Howard

Bert Kaempfert
Horst Jankowski

Kitty Kallen
Helen Forrest

Helen Kane
Bernadette Peters

The Karminsky Brothers
The Gentle People

Mickey Katz
Don Byron

Danny Kaye
Victor Borge
Tom Lehrer

Howard Keel
John Raitt

Hal Kemp
Kay Kyser

Stan Kenton
Laurindo Almeida
June Christy
Jack Costanzo
João Gilberto
Charlie Rich

Jerome Kern
George & Ira Gershwin
Richard Rodgers

Jack Kerouac
Ken Nordine

Barney Kessel
Glen Campbell
Antonio Carlos Jobim
Howard Roberts

Chaka Khan
Erykah Badu

B.B. King
The Senders

Carole King
Tony Orlando
Helen Reddy
Carly Simon

Charles King
Paul Page

King Curtis
Boots Randolph

The Kingston Trio
The Four Preps
The Limeliters
Robert Mitchum
Kenny Rogers

The Kinks
Alex Chilton
Morrissey

George Kirby
Sammy Davis Jr.

Kiss
David Lee Roth

Eartha Kitt
Julie London
Sade

Roy C. Knapp
Gene Krupa

Lee Konitz
Bud Shank

Andre Kostelanetz
Arthur Fiedler
Morton Gould
Gordon Jenkins
Mitch Miller
The 101 Strings

Kraftwerk
The Art of Noise
Devo
Erasure
The Moog Cookbook
Pet Shop Boys

Dagmar Krause
Ute Lemper

Fritz Kreisler
Mantovani

Gene Krupa
Tito Puente

Billy Kyle
Dave Brubeck
Nat "King" Cole

Eck Kynor
Murry Wilson

Kay Kyser
Sammy Kaye

Patti LaBelle
Natalie Cole
RuPaul

Francis Lai
Ronnie Aldrich
Michel Legrand

Laika & the Cosmonauts
The Galaxy Trio

Cleo Laine
Nancy LaMott

Frankie Laine
Sammy Davis Jr.
Guy Mitchell
Anita O'Day
Johnnie Ray

Eddie Lang
Les Paul

Daniel Lanois
Jane Siberry

Mario Lanza
Al Martino
Jim Nabors

The La's
Space

Carol Lawrence
Vikki Carr

Leadbelly
Harry Belafonte
Lonnie Donegan

Brenda Lee
Lesley Gore
Anne Murray

Peggy Lee
The Cardigans
Holly Cole
Julie London
Marilyn Monroe
Carly Simon
Margaret Whiting

Raymond Legrand
Michel Legrand

Claude Lelouch
Francis Lai

John Lennon
William Shatner

Lotte Lenya
Ute Lemper

Eddie Leonard
Al Jolson

The Lettermen
The Beach Boys
Up with People

Oscar Levant
Victor Borge
Michael Feinstein

Barbara Lewis
Patti Austin

Danny Lewis
Jerry Lewis

Jerry Lee Lewis
Tom Jones
Charlie Rich
Ian Whitcomb

Liberace
Ferrante & Teicher
Roger Williams

Jimmy Liggins
The Mighty Blue Kings

Enoch Light
Al Caiola
The Ray Charles Singers
Combustible Edison
Ray Conniff
Arthur Lyman
Tony Mottola
Perrey & Kingsley
Henri Rene

Gordon Lightfoot
Jim Croce

The Limeliters
The Four Preps

Little Rascals
The Beau Hunks

Little Richard
Pat Boone
Doug Clark & the Hot Nuts
Elvis Costello
Tom Jones
Elvis Presley

Living Colour
Don Byron

Living Strings
Richard Clayderman
Norman Luboff Choir
The Swingle Singers
Billy Vaughn

Carol Lofner
Phil Harris

Casa Loma
Benny Goodman

Guy Lombardo
Sammy Kaye
Freddy Martin
Lawrence Welk

Julie London
Marilyn Monroe
Olivia Newton-John
Sinéad O'Connor

Orestes Lopez
Perez Prado

Trini Lopez
Don Ho
Chris Montez

Lord Melody
Robert Mitchum

Louis Jordan
Ethel Merman
Ella Mae Morse
Madeleine Peyroux
Squirrel Nut Zippers
Kay Starr
Sarah Vaughan

Clara Smith
Josephine Baker

Willie "The Lion" Smith
Duke Ellington

The Smiths
The Beautiful South
The Cardigans
Pet Shop Boys

Hank Snow
Elvis Presley

Stephen Sondheim
Rupert Holmes

Sonny & Cher
The Captain & Tennille
Tony Orlando

Soul II Soul
Björk

Soundgarden
Steve Lawrence & Eydie Gorme

Spandau Ballet
Everything but the Girl

Otis Spann
Mose Allison

Sparks
The Moog Cookbook

The Specials
Joey Altruda with the Cocktail
   Crew
Cherry Poppin' Daddies

Phil Spector
The Beach Boys
Lesley Gore
Tony Hatch & Jackie Trent
Joe Meek
Paul Shaffer
Sonny & Cher

Ronnie Spector
Madonna

Victoria Spivey
Hadda Brooks

Dusty Springfield
Sandie Shaw
Dionne Warwick

Squirrel Nut Zippers
The Mighty Blue Kings
The Senders

Jo Stafford
Teresa Brewer
Ann Hampton Callaway
Doris Day
Connie Francis
Betty Hutton
Peggy Lee
Patti Page
Kay Starr
Dakota Staton
Margaret Whiting
Andy Williams

Carl Stalling
The Beau Hunks
Danny Elfman
Mel Henke

Kay Starr
Teresa Brewer
Connie Francis
Patti Page

Dakota Staton
Patti Austin

Tommy Steele
Cliff Richard

Steely Dan
Donald Fagen

Gertrude Stein
k.d. lang

Stereolab
The Cardigans

Cat Stevens
Jim Croce

Karlheinz Stockhausen
Brian Eno

Axel Stordahl
Nelson Riddle

Edward B. Straight
Gene Krupa

Teresa Stratas
Ute Lemper

Igor Stravinsky
Howard Roberts

Billy Strayhorn
Lena Horne

Barbra Streisand
Sheena Easton
Kathie Lee Gifford
Steve Lawrence & Eydie
   Gorme
Barry Manilow
Bette Midler
Jane Olivor
Helen Reddy
Carly Simon

The Style Council
The Beautiful South
Everything but the Girl
Swing out Sister

Maxine Sullivan
Ella Fitzgerald
Dinah Washington

Yma Sumac
The Out-Islanders
Rotary Connection

Donna Summer
RuPaul

The Sundays
The Cardigans

The Supremes
The Manhattan Transfer

Tangerine Dream
The Art of Noise

Art Tatum
Mose Allison
Harold Arlen
Tony Bennett
Hadda Brooks
Charles Brown
Dave Brubeck
Lenny Dee
Bent Fabric
Erroll Garner
Michel Legrand
Andre Previn
George Shearing
Bobby Short
Margaret Whiting

James Taylor
Jim Croce
John Denver

Johnnie Taylor
Alex Chilton

Tchaikovsky
Don Byron
Arthur Fiedler
Andre Kostelanetz

Jack Teagarden
The Four Freshmen

Telex
The Moog Cookbook

Clark Terry
Miles Davis
Quincy Jones

Sonny Terry
Les Paul

Sister Rosetta Tharpe
Pearl Bailey

Rufus Thomas
Isaac Hayes

Big Mama Thornton
Elvis Presley

The Three Suns
Combustible Edison
Rolley Polley

Dmitri Tiomkin
Ennio Morricone

Cal Tjader
Laurindo Almeida
The Baja Marimba Band
The Sentinels

Ernst Toch
Alex North

Mel Tormé
Tony Bennett
Harry Connick Jr.
Michael Feinstein
Johnny Hartman

Merle Travis
Al Caiola

The Treniers
The Mighty Blue Kings

Lenny Tristano
Roger Williams

The Tubes
Man or Astro-Man?

The Category Index represents an array of categories put together to suggest some of the many groupings under which lounge music and lounge acts can be classified. The Hound welcomes your additions to the existing categories in this index and also invites you to send in your own funny, sarcastic, prolific, poignant, or exciting ideas for brand new categories.

Aloha
Martin Denny
Don Ho
Arthur Lyman

At the Pet Shop
Bunny Berigan
The High Llamas
The Lounge Lizards
Jerry Murad's Harmonicats
Pet Shop Boys
Squirrel Nut Zippers

Bandleaders
Leroy Anderson
Elmer Bernstein
Cab Calloway
Martin Denny
Duke Ellington

Juan Garcia Esquivel
Arthur Fiedler
Benny Goodman
Neal Hefti
Woody Herman
Gordon Jenkins
Quincy Jones
Stan Kenton
Gene Krupa
Kay Kyser
Lester Lanin
Sonny Lester
Guy Lombardo
Henry Mancini
Billy May
Glenn Miller
Mitch Miller
Nelson Riddle
David Rose
Raymond Scott
Billy Vaughn
Hugo Winterhalter

Bossa Nova, Baby (plus Mambo, Mariachi, Cha Cha Cha & Latin Jazz)
Laurindo Almeida
Herb Alpert
The Baja Marimba Band
Stan Getz
Astrud Gilberto
João Gilberto
Dizzy Gillespie
Sergio Mendes
Tito Puente
Perez Prado
Cal Tjader

Cartoon Kings
Danny Elfman
Raymond Scott
Carl Stalling

Classic Crooners
Ray Anthony
Gene Austin
Pearl Bailey
Harry Belafonte
Tony Bennett
Eddie Cantor
Buddy Clark
Rosemary Clooney
Nat "King" Cole
Russ Columbo
Perry Como
Bing Crosby
Vic Damone
Billy Eckstine
Eddie Fisher
Helen Forrest
John Gary
Johnny Hartman
Dick Haymes
Al Hirt
Eddy Howard
Betty Hutton
Jack Jones
James Last
Tom Lehrer
Dean Martin
Freddy Martin
Tony Martin
Al Martino
Guy Mitchell
Matt Monro
Vaughn Monroe

Chris Montez
Alex North
Paul Page
Dick Powell
Johnny Ray
Alvino Rey
Jimmy Scott
Sandie Shaw
Dinah Shore
Bobby Short
Frank Sinatra
Jo Stafford
Kay Starr
Dakota Staton
Mel Tormé
Jerry Vale
Rudy Vallee
Margaret Whiting
Roger Whittaker
Andy Williams

Country Crooners
Glen Campbell
Floyd Cramer
Jim Croce
Mac Davis
John Denver
Frankie Laine
k.d. lang
Anne Murray
Minnie Pearl
Boots Randolph
Charlie Rich
Kenny Rogers
Linda Ronstadt

Divas
Erykah Badu

Pearl Bailey
Josephine Baker
Basia
Ann Hampton Callaway
Carol Channing
June Christy
Cass Elliot
Ella Fitzgerald
Connie Francis
Lesley Gore
Billie Holiday
Lena Horne
Phyllis Hyman
Eartha Kitt
Cleo Laine
Nancy LaMott
Brenda Lee
Annie Lennox
Madonna
Carmen McRae
Ethel Merman
Bette Midler
Liza Minnelli
Patti Page
Della Reese
RuPaul
Sade
Nina Simone
April Stevens
Barbra Streisand
Sarah Vaughan
Dinah Washington

Don't Quit Your Day Job
Maya Angelou
Clint Eastwood
Kathie Lee Gifford
Denny McLain
Robert Mitchum
Leonard Nimoy
Regis Philbin
William Shatner
John Tesh
Mae West
Pia Zadora

007 Digs Them
John Barry
Shirley Bassey
Sheena Easton
Tom Jones
Carly Simon

Electronic Innovators
Brian Eno
Dick Hyman
Perrey & Kingsley

Elevator Music
Ronnie Aldrich
Herb Alpert & the Tijuana
    Brass
Leroy Anderson
The Baja Marimba Band
The Ray Charles Singers
Richard Clayderman
Ray Conniff
Christopher Cross
Brian Eno
Percy Faith
Michael Feinstein
Ferrante & Teicher
Ron Goodwin
Morton Gould
The Hollyridge Strings
Horst Jankowski
Andre Kostelanetz
Francis Lai
Raymond Lefevre
Living Strings
Norman Luboff Choir
Mantovani
George Melachrino
The Mystic Moods Orchestra
The 101 Strings
Paul Weston
Roger Williams
Gheorghe Zamfir

From the Space-Age Bachelor Pad
Eden Ahbez
Les Baxter
Al Caiola
Jack Costanzo
Martin Denny
Robert Drasnin
Juan Garcia Esquivel
Enoch Light
Joe Meek
Tony Mottola
Jerry Murad's Harmonicats
The Out-Islanders
Korla Pandit
Perrey & Kingsley
Henri Rene
Rolley Polley
Raymond Scott
Sir Julian
Yma Sumac
The Three Suns
Walter Wanderley

Getting Folksy
Judy Collins
Jose Feliciano

Gordon Lightfoot
The Limeliters
Maureen McGovern
Dusty Springfield

Hepster Cats
Cab Calloway
Sammy Davis Jr.
Slim Gaillard
Louis Jordan
Dean Martin
Frank Sinatra

Husbands & Wives
Jonathan & Darlene Edwards
Tony Hatch & Jackie Trent
Steve Lawrence & Eydie
    Gorme
Louis Prima & Keely Smith
Sonny & Cher
Tuck & Patti

I Got Rhythm (& Blues)
Teresa Brewer
Charles Brown
Nat "King" Cole
Natalie Cole
Marvin Gaye
Isaac Hayes
Al Hibbler
The Ink Spots
Quincy Jones
Louis Jordan
Eartha Kitt
Gladys Knight
The Mills Brothers
Ella Mae Morse
Helen Reddy
Rotary Connection
Sarah Vaughan
Dionne Warwick
Dinah Washington
Cassandra Wilson
Jimmy Witherspoon

Ivory Ticklers
Ronnie Aldrich
Steve Allen
Victor Borge
Hadda Brooks
Charles Brown
Ray Charles
Holly Cole
Nat "King" Cole
Harry Connick Jr.
Duke Ellington
Bent Fabric
Michael Feinstein

Ferrante & Teicher
Joe Jackson
Billy Joel
Diana Krall
Liberace
George Shearing
John Tesh

Jazzin' It Up
Cannonball Adderley
Mose Allison
Patti Austin
Chet Baker
Josephine Baker
Clifford Brown
Dave Brubeck
Don Byron
Don Cherry
Cy Coleman
Miles Davis
Blossom Dearie
Bob Dorough
Georgie Fame
Erroll Garner
Dexter Gordon
Dave Grusin
Vince Guaraldi
Herbie Hancock
Johnny Hartman
Coleman Hawkins
Billie Holiday
Dick Hyman
Al Jarreau
Etta Jones
Stan Kenton
Diana Krall
Chuck Mangione
The Manhattan Transfer
Mannheim Steamroller
Red Norvo
Jane Olivor
Charlie Parker
Diane Schuur
Doc Severinsen
Dinah Shore
Roseanna Vitro
Ben Webster
George Winston

Kitschy '70s pop
ABBA
Peter Allen
Björn Again
The Captain & Tennille
The Carpenters
Neil Diamond
Barry Manilow
Olivia Newton-John

Live and in Color
Black Velvet Flag
Charles Brown
Clifford Brown
The Mighty Blue Kings
Red Norvo
Orange Juice

Lounge Revival
Joey Altruda with the Cocktail
    Crew
Jaymz Bee
Björn Again
Black Velvet Flag
The Cardigans
Combustible Edison
Devo
Dimitri from Paris
Divine Comedy
Easy Tunes
Friends of Dean Martinez
The Gentle People
Rupert Holmes
The Lounge Lizards
Love Jones
The Moog Cookbook
Pet Shop Boys
Pizzicato Five
Buster Poindexter
Portishead
Space
Stereolab
Jimi Tenor
Tindersticks

Neo-Swing
The Beau Hunks
Big Bad Voodoo Daddy
Cherry Poppin' Daddies
Harry Connick Jr.
The Mighty Blue Kings
Royal Crown Revue
The Senders
Squirrel Nut Zippers

On the Dark Side
Barry Adamson
Angelo Badalamenti
Harold Budd
Nick Cave & the Bad Seeds
Julee Cruise
Marianne Faithfull
Bryan Ferry
Serge Gainsbourg
Ute Lemper
Scott Walker

One-Hit Wonders
Rupert Holmes
Julie London
Trini Lopez
Frank Mills
Nancy Sinatra

Polka People
Brave Combo
Myron Floren
Frankie Yankovic

Rat Pack Royalty
Sammy Davis Jr.
Dean Martin
Frank Sinatra

Rockers with a Twist
The Art of Noise
The Beach Boys
The Beautiful South
Björk
Brave Combo
The Cardigans
Alex Chilton
Edwyn Collins
Elvis Costello
Richard Davies
Cass Elliot
Brian Eno
Erasure
Everything but the Girl
Donald Fagen
Bryan Ferry
The High Llamas
Joe Jackson
Peggy Lee
Eric Matthews
Morrissey
Sinéad O'Connor
Madonna
Les Paul
Elvis Presley
Jonathan Richman
David Lee Roth
Todd Rundgren
Jane Siberry
Carly Simon
The Style Council
Swing out Sister
Tom Waits

Score One for Movies
Angelo Badalamenti
Burt Bacharach
John Barry
Les Baxter
Elmer Bernstein

Danny Elfman
Maurice Jarre
Michael Kamen
Francis Lai
Michel Legrand
Henry Mancini
Hugo Montenegro
Ennio Morricone
Anthony Newley
Nino Rota
Lalo Schifrin

Send in the Clowns
Victor Borge
Frank Fontaine
Stan Freberg
Jackie Gleason
Mel Henke
Al Jolson
Spike Jones
Mickey Katz
Jerry Lewis
Ethel Merman
Mrs. Elva Miller
Tiny Tim

Sibling Rivalry
The Ames Brothers
The Andrews Sisters
The Boswell Sisters
The Lennon Sisters
The Mills Brothers
Frank Sinatra Jr.–Nancy Sina-
    tra

Someone's in the Kitchen
Chet Baker
Josephine Baker
Don Cherry
Cherry Poppin' Daddies
Doug Clark & His Hot Nuts
Michael Franks
The Moog Cookbook
Orange Juice

Spanning the Globe
Charles Aznavour
Holly Cole
Marlene Dietrich
Francois Hardy
Julio Iglesias
James Galway
João Gilberto
Horst Jankowski
Antonio Carlos Jobim
Ute Lemper
Claudine Longet
Carmen Miranda

Nana Mouskouri
Peter Nero
Madeleine Peyroux
Edith Piaf
Diane Schuur

Stars of the Silver Screen
Julie Andrews
Ann-Margret
Louis Armstrong
Fred Astaire
Nat"King" Cole
Tim Curry
Doris Day
John Denver
Marlene Dietrich
Jimmy Durante
Clint Eastwood
Judy Garland
Robert Goulet
Al Jolson
Gene Kelly
Jerry Lewis
Gordon MacRae
Dean Martin
Bette Midler
Liza Minnelli
Robert Mitchum
Marilyn Monroe
Elvis Presley
Debbie Reynolds
Paul Robeson
Frank Sinatra
Barbra Streisand
Pia Zadora

Surf's Up!
The Beach Boys
The Galaxy Trio
Man or Astro-Man?
Santo & Johnny
The Sentinels
The Ventures

Swingers
Louis Armstrong
Charlie Barnet
Bunny Berigan
Les Brown
Bob Crosby
Jimmy Dorsey
Tommy Dorsey
The Dorsey Brothers
Duke Ellington
Benny Goodman
Buddy Greco
Woody Herman
Harry James